S0-BDS-631

Personal Financial Planning

Fifth Edition

Lawrence J. Gitman
San Diego State University

Michael D. Joehnk
Arizona State University

The Dryden Press
Chicago   Fort Worth   San Francisco
Philadelphia   Montreal   Toronto
London   Sydney   Tokyo

Acquisitions Editor: Ann Heath
Developmental Editor: Millicent Treloar
Project Editor: Karen Steib
Design Director: Alan Wendt
Production Manager: Barb Bahnsen
Permissions Editor: Doris Milligan
Director of Editing, Design, and Production: Jane Perkins

Text and Cover Designer: Jeanne Wolfgeher
Copy Editor and Indexer: Maggie Jarpey
Compositor: Weimer Typesetting Co., Inc.
Text Type: 10/12 ITC Garamond Light

Library of Congress Cataloging-in-Publication Data

Gitman, Lawrence J.
  Personal financial planning.

  Includes index.
  1. Finance, Personal.   I. Joehnk, Michael D.
  II. Title.
  HG179.G54   1990   332.024   89-11981
  ISBN 0-03-030142-4

Printed in the United States of America
901-032-987654321
Copyright © 1990, 1987, 1984, 1981, 1978 by The Dryden Press, a
division of Holt, Rinehart and Winston, Inc.

All rights reserved. No part of this publication may be
reproduced or transmitted in any form or by any means, electronic
or mechanical, including photocopy, recording, or any information
storage and retrieval system, without permission in writing from
the publisher.

Requests for permission to make copies of any part of the work
should be mailed to: Copyrights and Permissions Department,
Holt, Rinehart and Winston, Inc., Orlando, FL 32887.

Address orders:
The Dryden Press
Orlando, FL 32887

Address editorial correspondence:
The Dryden Press
908 N. Elm St.
Hinsdale, IL 60521

The Dryden Press
Holt, Rinehart and Winston
Saunders College Publishing

Cover Source: Courtesy of Ford Motor Company

The Dryden Press Series in Finance

Berry and Young
Managing Investments: A Case Approach

Boyet
**Security Analysis for Investment
Decisions: Text and Software**

Brigham
Fundamentals of Financial Management
Fifth Edition

Brigham, Aberwald, and Ball
**Finance with Lotus 1-2-3®:
Text, Cases, and Models**

Brigham and Gapenski
Cases in Financial Management

Brigham and Gapenski
Financial Management: Theory and Practice
Fifth Edition

Brigham and Gapenski
Intermediate Financial Management
Third Edition

Campsey and Brigham
Introduction to Financial Management
Second Edition

Chance
An Introduction to Options and Futures

Clayton and Spivey
The Time Value of Money

Cooley
**Advances in Business Financial Management:
A Collection of Readings**

Cooley and Roden
Business Financial Management

Crum and Brigham
Cases in Managerial Finance
Sixth Edition with 1986 Tax Law Changes

Fama and Miller
The Theory of Finance

Gardner and Mills
**Managing Financial Institutions:
An Asset/Liability Approach**

Gitman and Joehnk
Personal Financial Planning
Fifth Edition

Goldstein Software, Inc.
Joe Spreadsheet

Harrington
Case Studies in Financial Decision Making
Second Edition

Johnson
Issues and Readings in Managerial Finance
Third Edition

Johnson and Johnson
Commercial Bank Management

Kidwell and Peterson
Financial Institutions, Markets, and Money
Fourth Edition

Koch
Bank Management

Martin, Cox, and MacMinn
**The Theory of Finance:
Evidence and Applications**

Mayo
Finance: An Introduction
Third Edition

v

ABOUT THE AUTHORS

Lawrence J. Gitman is a professor of finance at San Diego State University. He received his bachelor's degree from Purdue University, his M.B.A. from the University of Dayton, and his Ph.D. from the University of Cincinnati. Professor Gitman is a prolific author of ten textbooks and over thirty articles appearing in *Financial Management,* the *Financial Review,* the *Journal of the Institute of Certified Financial Planners,* the *Journal of Risk and Insurance,* the *Journal of Financial Research,* the *Journal of Cost Analysis and Planning,* the *Journal of Financial Education,* and other publications. His textbooks include *Principles of Managerial Finance,* fifth edition, *Basic Managerial Finance,* second edition, *Business World,* second edition, *Fundamentals of Investing,* fourth edition, and *Managerial Finance,* the last two of which were co-authored with Michael Joehnk. Gitman and Joehnk also wrote *Investment Fundamentals: A Guide to Becoming a Knowledgeable Investor,* which was selected as one of 1988's ten best personal finance books by *Money* magazine.

An active member of numerous professional organizations, Professor Gitman is president-elect of both the Academy of Financial Services and the Midwest Finance Association. In addition, he is a Certified Financial Planner (CFP). He lives with his wife and two children in La Jolla, California, where he is an avid bicyclist.

Michael D. Joehnk is a professor of finance at Arizona State University. He received his bachelor's and Ph.D. degrees from the University of Arizona and his M.B.A. from Arizona State University. He is also a Chartered Financial Analyst (CFA). Professor Joehnk is active in research and consulting and has been widely published. His articles have appeared in *Financial Management,* the *Journal of Finance,* the *Journal of Bank Research,* the *Journal of Portfolio Management,* the *Journal of Consumer Affairs,* the *Journal of Financial and Quantitative Analysis,* and other publications. In addition to co-authoring two textbooks with Lawrence Gitman, Professor Joehnk is the author of a highly successful paperback trade book, *Investing for Safety's Sake* and is a contributor to the *Handbook of Fixed Income Securities.* A past vice-president of the Financial Management Association, he continues to serve as the secretary-treasurer of the Western Finance Association and is actively involved in numerous other professional organizations, including the Institute of Chartered Financial Analysts; in addition, he is currently the Executive Editor of the *Journal of Financial Research.* He and his wife live in Scottsdale, Arizona, where they enjoy collecting native Indian art.

PREFACE

The financial services revolution that began nearly two decades ago continues to usher in exciting changes in the institutions, instruments, and techniques of personal financial planning. The widespread use of personal computers, along with tax reforms, major changes in financial institutions, new methods of borrowing, expanded insurance products, and new investment vehicles have dramatically changed the field of personal finance. It has evolved into a well-structured, fully integrated discipline that we now call *personal financial planning*.

The fifth edition of this book reflects feedback from past users as well as nonusers, practicing financial planners, students, and our own research. It provides helpful new approaches, expanded coverage in selected areas, and special pedagogical features while retaining the basic organizational structure, topical coverage, superior readability, and useful instructional aids that marked the success of the first four editions. As with the preceding edition, this one continues to emphasize comprehensive personal financial planning. The most notable addition in this regard has been the introduction of a continuous case that gives students hands-on experience in personal financial planning decision making.

MAJOR CHANGES IN THE FIFTH EDITION

The fifth edition has been thoroughly updated to reflect the cutting edge of contemporary personal financial planning. The most notable changes will be described first as general changes and then as specific chapter-by-chapter changes.

General Changes

- A greater emphasis is given throughout the text to *real-life* financial planning and decision making.

- By taking an action-oriented perspective, the text continues to emphasize and illustrate personal financial decision-making *procedures*. This emphasis has been further enhanced by the inclusion of the *Mark and Ana Williams continuous case,* which provides personal and financial information about a real-life family in order to allow students to develop a specific comprehensive financial plan.

- To facilitate the decision-making process, the book's *worksheets* have been greatly expanded as well as refined. Each provides a step-by-step framework for making a particular financial decision.

- The *computer-based problem-solver disk,* described inside the back cover of this book, has been completely rewritten and refined by Professor James B. Pettijohn, a recognized expert in the development of financial software. "FP/PC: Financial Planning on the Personal Computer" is a fully interactive teaching device that affords students a practical look at the role of the computer in the personal financial planning process.

Specific Chapter-by-Chapter Changes

- A psychological discussion of the behavioral side of personal financial planning was added to Chapter 1. In addition, the *Mark and Ana Williams continuous case* is introduced at this point, along with relevant personal and financial data.

- In Chapter 2, the discussion of tracking financial progress (through the use of personal financial statements) has been greatly streamlined, and now includes coverage of the debt service ratio.

- The discussion of the financial planning process and the role of the personal financial planner in Chapter 3 has been altered to reflect recent changes in the market environment.

- Chapter 4 contains a complete up-to-date discussion of the Tax Reform Act of 1986, including recent interpretations and technical refinements contained in the *Technical and Miscellaneous Revenue Act of 1988.*

- The descriptions of savings and short-term investment vehicles in Chapter 5 have been revised to reflect the types of financial products—like *brokered CDs*—currently available in the marketplace.
- Mortgage affordability analysis is now covered in Chapter 6, along with *convertible ARMs* and *mortgage refinancing*; in addition, the *automobile lease-versus-purchase* decision is addressed in detail.
- Chapter 7 now includes a discussion of what it takes to build a strong credit history; in addition, material on credit bureaus has been enhanced and coverage of *Optima, Discover,* and *affinity cards* added.
- Chapter 8 contains a new section—including a worksheet—on the question of whether it's better to buy on time or pay cash for big-ticket items; also addressed is the gradual elimination of consumer interest expense as a legitimate tax deduction.
- Chapter 9 on life insurance now begins with an in-depth discussion of *employee benefits and cafeteria-style programs;* in addition, the life insurance needs worksheet has been modified to cover various stages of the life cycle, and material on the *Personal Earnings and Benefit Estimate Statement* now available from the Social Security Administration has been added. Also, the discussion of single-premium life, universal, and variable life insurance policies has been greatly expanded, with particular emphasis on their insurance and investment merits.
- Chapter 10 now contains discussion of *long-term care insurance, second surgical opinions,* and *employee rights* to continued health care coverage upon their voluntary or involuntary termination of employment.
- The discussion of renters insurance has been revised considerably in Chapter 11, and material has been added on ways to lower the cost of auto insurance including raising policy deductibles.
- The material on investment planning in Chapter 12 has been enhanced by the addition of a discussion (and a worksheet) on finding the amount of investment capital needed to meet a given financial goal; in addition, material on *event risk*, the importance of *interest-on-interest* to investor returns, *dividend reinvestment plans,* and *junk bonds* has been added. Equally important, considerable coverage is now given to the market crash of October 1987.
- In Chapter 13, the coverage of the various securities markets and market indexes has been greatly expanded, and new material has been added on binding arbitration and the role of asset allocation in portfolio management.
- The coverage of *mutual fund fees and expenses* has been revised considerably in Chapter 14, as has the coverage of mutual fund performance measures and the mutual fund selection process.
- The discussion of retirement planning, in Chapter 15, now includes additional information on *social security benefits* and the new *Personal Earnings and Benefit Estimate Statement;* moreover, the discussion of various types of *annuity contracts* has been substantially revised and updated to include the tax considerations and investment merits of single- and installment-premium annuities and fixed versus variable annuities. Also addressed in this chapter are the new vesting requirements for company-sponsored pension plans, the most recent funding requirements for self-directed pension plans, and steps to take in evaluating employer-sponsored pension plans.
- The impact of recent tax legislation on estate planning and the effects of the latest legislative developments on trusts and estates are covered in Chapter 16.

ORGANIZATION OF THE BOOK

Personal Financial Planning addresses all of the major personal financial planning problems that individuals and families encounter. It presents a model of the major elements of effective money management. All of the latest financial planning tools and techniques are discussed. Most of the widely used examples involve young people so that the student reader may more easily identify with each situation.

This comprehensive text is written in a low-key, personal style and uses state-of-the-art pedagogy to present the key concepts and procedures used in sound financial planning and effective money management. The roles of various financial decisions in the overall personal financial planning process are clearly delineated.

The book is divided into six parts. Part One presents the basic principles of personal financial planning and then covers personal financial statements, cash budgets, and taxes. Part Two concerns the management of assets, including cash and savings instruments, housing, and other major assets. Part Three covers debt management, including the various types of open account borrowing and consumer loans. Part Four deals with insurance planning and considers life insurance, health care plans, and property and liability insurance. Part Five concerns investments, including stocks, bonds, mutual funds, real estate, and other investment vehicles, and how to make transactions in securities markets. Part Six is devoted to retirement and estate planning. All these parts are tied together via the *Mark and Ana Williams continuous case,* which begins at the end of Chapter 1 with an extensive inventory of personal and financial data. Additional elements of the Williamses financial plans are then introduced at the ends of Parts One through Five, and Chapters 15 and 16 so that the students can deal with the unfolding elements of a complete financial plan.

PEDAGOGY

Each chapter opens with an element called *Financial Facts or Fantasies,* a series of six true-false questions concerning the material covered, for which answers and brief explanations are appropriately placed throughout the chapter. In addition, each major section of the chapter begins with a question designed to stimulate interest in the material that follows by challenging the student to relate it to his or her personal life. Each chapter contains two boxes set off from the text material and containing brief discussions of relevant personal financial planning material that serve to enrich the topical coverage. Numerous exhibits, each containing descriptive captions, are used throughout to more fully illustrate key points in the text.

Many chapters contain discussions and illustrations of how the personal computer can be used in various phases of financial planning and, where appropriate, brief descriptions of some of the more popular computer software are included. A running glossary provides brief definitions of key terms.

End-of-chapter material includes roughly 20 review questions and problems that students can use to test their grasp of the material. Two case problems highlighting the important analytical topics and concepts are also supplied.

The final item in each chapter is a listing of ten information sources, including general information articles from popular personal finance publications such as *Changing Times, Money,* and *Consumers Digest,* and a separate listing of relevant government documents and other publications. And, of course, as noted before, each part of the book ends with the Williamses continuous case.

ANCILLARY MATERIALS

Recognizing the importance of outstanding support materials to the instructor and the student, we have significantly improved and expanded our ancillary package.

Worksheets

A pad of *blank worksheets* is included free of charge with each new copy of the book. This pad includes copies of the worksheets developed and introduced in the text.

Instructor's Manual and Test Bank

A comprehensive *Instructor's Manual and Test Bank* has been prepared to assist the teacher. For each chapter, the manual includes

- An outline
- Discussion of major topics
- A list of key concepts
- Solutions to all end-of-chapter questions, problems, and cases
- *Outside projects* that can be assigned to students so that they can apply major concepts and techniques presented in the chapter (instructions for outside projects are printed on separate sheets to make duplication for classroom distribution a simple task)
- Solutions to all questions on the text continuous case
- A second continuous case, with solutions, that the instructor can use if he or she desires

▪ A complete test bank that has been revised, updated, and expanded, including true-false and multiple-choice questions, as well as four to six short problems for nearly every chapter.

Transparency Masters

A set of 150 transparency masters is provided. The set includes lecture outlines, significant text exhibits, and blank worksheets.

Workbook

Elizabeth Hennigar of the University of San Diego has updated the *Workbook* to assist students in mastering the information and techniques presented in the text and to serve as a resource manual as they develop personal financial plans. Specific components for each chapter include

▪ A thorough outline of concepts discussed
▪ Completion exercises that stress vocabulary
▪ Matching exercises to test mastery of new terms
▪ Problem-solving exercises with solutions
▪ A comprehensive case (with solutions) that demonstrates the application of chapter concepts

Personal Financial Planning Disk

A new computer-based problem solver—*FP/PC: Financial Planning on the Personal Computer*—was prepared specifically for this edition of the book by Professor James B. Pettijohn of Southwest Missouri State University. The disk performs like any of the widely used commercially available software packages and is completely interactive; best of all, being very user-friendly, it streamlines the recordkeeping and problem-solving activities presented in the text. A computer logo is used in the margin to identify sections of the book to which the disk is applicable. End-of-chapter problems and cases that can be solved with the disk are keyed with the same logo. Some worksheets used in the text are formatted on the disk to provide assistance in applying some of the more complex procedures, ranging from financial statements and budget preparation to tax estimation, investment management, and retirement planning. The software has been extensively tested in classes at the University of Texas at Austin to ensure its accuracy and ease of use.

ACKNOWLEDGMENTS

In addition to the many individuals who made significant contributions to this book by their expertise, classroom experience, guidance, general advice, and reassurance, we also appreciate the students and faculty who used the book and provided valuable feedback on it, confirming our conviction that a truly teachable personal financial planning text could be developed.

Of course, we are indebted to all the academicians and practitioners who have created the body of knowledge contained in this text. We particularly wish to thank several people who gave the most significant help in developing and revising it. The first is Vickie Hampton of the University of Texas at Austin for her work on the continuous case. In addition, we want to thank Jim Pettijohn for developing the state-of-the-art software; Murray Rosen, CLU, ChFC, of the College of Insurance (in New York) for his work on the life insurance chapter; Henry Young, also of the College of Insurance, for his help on the health insurance chapter; Richard Holliday, CPCU, of the College of Insurance for assistance with the property and casualty insurance chapter; John Talbott, professor of taxation at Wright State University, for his assistance in the chapter on taxes; and Stephan R. Leimberg, chairman of the Department of Estate Planning at American College, for his contribution to the estate planning chapter.

The Dryden Press, which shared our objective of producing a truly teachable text, relied on the experience and advice of numerous excellent reviewers. We appreciate their many suggestions that have had a significant impact on the various editions of this book. Our thanks go to the following: Linda Afdahl, Michael J. Ahern III, Robert J. Angell, H. Kent Baker, Catherine L. Bertelson, P. R. Chandy, Maurice L. Crawford, Ronald Ehresman, Sharon Hatten Garrison, Carol Zirnheld Green, John L. Grimm, Forrest Harlow, Kendall P. Hill, Darrell D. Hilliker, Frank Inciardi, Xymena S. Kulsrud, Carole J. Makela, Charles E. Maxwell, Robert Nash, Albert Pender, Franklin Potts, Arnold M. Rieger, Gayle M. Ross, Gary Watts, Grant J. Wells, Betty Wright, and R. R. Zilkowski.

In addition, we offer special thanks to the following reviewers of the fifth edition for their outstanding contributions to the manuscript: Steve Blank, University of California at Davis; Dan Casey, Coastline Community College; Carlene Creviston, Ball State University; David Durst, University of Akron; Mary Ellen Edmundson, University of Kentucky; Arlene Holyoak, Oregon State University; Kenneth Jacques, Ball State University; Dixie Porter Johnson, Purdue University; Peggy Keck, Western Kentucky University; Karol Kitt, University of Texas at Austin; George Klander, Anne Arundel Community College; George Muscal, SUNY—Morrisville; Vivian Rippentrop, Central University of Iowa; and Rosemary Walker, Michigan State University.

Because of the wide variety of topics covered in this book, we called upon many experts for whose insight on recent developments we are deeply grateful. We would like to thank them and their firms for allowing us to draw on their knowledge and resources, particularly Pat Rupp, CFP, IDS, Inc.; Marty Henne, Acacia Financial Services Center (Phoenix); Jack Landis, Landis and Associates Insurance; Jeff Middleton, Boettcher & Company; Mark D. Militano, Security Pacific Bank of Arizona; Bob Moore, Paine Webber; Ed Morrow, Confidential Planning Services, Inc.; R. Daniel Sadlier, Bank One; Fred Weaver, Great Western Bank; Linda Tauffen, Northern Trust Bank; and Flora Weston, Coldwell Banker Realtors.

A number of colleagues have also provided expertise as well as encouragement and support. We particularly wish to thank Khurshid Ahmad, Peter W. Bacon, and Daniel J. Kaufman, Jr., of Wright State University, and Paul Troeh and Glenn Wilt of Arizona State University for their help. Also, we want to thank Mary Beth Kaminski, managing editor of the *Journal of Financial Research* (at Arizona State)

for her research assistance and editorial help. We would also like to express our appreciation to Elizabeth Hennigar of the University of San Diego for her assistance in revising the *Instructor's Manual, Test Bank,* and *Workbook,* and William J. Kane of Wright State University for developing the lecture-outline transparency masters. Special mention is due to Tammy Johns and Hope Klassen for their outstanding efforts in typing the manuscript, running numerous errands, and generally keeping things in order.

The editorial staff of The Dryden Press has been most cooperative. We wish to thank Maggie Jarpey, copy editor and indexer, and Doris Milligan, permissions editor. Special thanks go to Ann Heath, acquisitions editor, and Millicent Treloar, developmental editor, without whose support this revision would not have been as lively and contemporary in approach as we believe it is and whose expert management of the writing and reviewing of the text proved invaluable. We are also grateful to Karen Steib, project editor, who ably assured the book's timely and accurate production.

Finally, our wives, Robin and Charlene, have provided needed support and understanding during the writing of this book. We are forever grateful to them.

Lawrence J. Gitman
La Jolla, California

Michael D. Joehnk
Scottsdale, Arizona

October 1989

CONTENTS

PART I

Foundations of Financial Planning

C H A P T E R 1

Understanding the Financial Planning Process

Financial Facts or Fantasies

Are the following statements financial facts (true) or fantasies (false)?

- An improved standard of living is one of the payoffs of sound money management.
- A savings account is an example of a real asset, as it represents something on deposit at a bank or S&L.
- Personal financial planning involves the restatement of personal financial goals into specific plans and, ultimately, into financial arrangements that put those plans into action.
- Over the long run, gaining an extra percent or two on an investment makes little difference in the amount of earnings generated.
- Generally speaking, inflation has little effect on personal financial planning.
- Your income level is a function of your age, education, and career.

Would you believe that as a college graduate you can expect to earn, on average, about $1.7 *million* over your lifetime? And if your spouse is also a college graduate with his or her own career, you can just about double that number! Two-career/two-income families are becoming a fact of life today, especially among the young. Take, for example, Matt and Jennifer Fredricks. Both are college educated and in their late twenties. Together they earn $54,000 a year—he is a senior credit analyst for a large commercial bank, and she is a data processing manager for a major manufacturing firm. While the Fredricks have the money to enjoy a comfortable lifestyle, they also recognize the importance of gaining control over their finances, so they are denying themselves some luxuries in order to do so. Matt and Jennifer are smart: They're doing something about their financial future. Unfortunately, many people treat personal financial decisions like a series of unorganized/uncoordinated events. Consequently, their quest for some form of financial security is probably doomed. The attainment of financial security usually requires organized plans and coordinated actions.

THE REWARDS OF SOUND FINANCIAL PLANNING

A person's standard of living and patterns of consumption are related and can profoundly affect the accumulation of wealth. If your primary financial goal is to achieve maximum wealth accumulation, what kind of standard of living and consumption patterns would you exhibit? Before reading on, take a few moments to consider the tradeoffs among standard of living, consumption, and wealth accumulation.

We all need goals of one sort or another to give direction to our lives. This is just as true in personal money management as it is in any other area, perhaps even more so. Most of us would like to be able to afford a nice automobile, live in a well-furnished home, take expensive vacations, and generally enjoy some of the finer things in life. Basically, this is what personal financial planning has to offer, since it helps individuals and families achieve their personal financial goals more easily. Personal financial planning cannot guarantee success, but if effectively plied, it can have a profound impact on one's standard of living, consumption patterns, and, ultimately, the amount of accumulated wealth.

Standard of Living

One of the major benefits of planning is that it helps us to more effectively marshal and control our financial resources. In essence, it allows us to gain a greater level of enjoyment from our income and thus improve our **standard of living.** The quality of our lives is, for most of us, closely tied to our standard of living. The presence or absence of certain material items, such as a home, cars, and jewelry, are commonly associated with quality of life. Large, expensive, or "fancy" items, for example, are viewed as components of a high standard of living. The availability of money for entertainment, health, education, art, music, and travel also con-

tributes to the quality of life. Although many other factors—geographical location, public facilities, local cost of living, pollution, traffic, and population density—also affect the quality of an individual's life, wealth is commonly viewed as its primary determinant. Of course, many so-called wealthy people live "plain" lives, choosing to save or invest their money rather than spend it on luxuries and frills. Even so, their quality of life is probably no lower than that of the flamboyant consumer.

One trend that has had a profound effect on our standard of living is the *two-income family.* What was relatively rare in the early sixties has become commonplace today, and, in the process, the incomes of millions of families have risen sharply. Granted, two incomes increase the things we can afford to buy, but they also carry with them greater responsibilities for managing money wisely. This is where personal financial planning comes in: By carefully planning future purchases and financial activities, people can set goals consistent with their desired quality of life.

An improved standard of living is one of the payoffs of sound money management. **Fact:** The very heart of sound financial planning and effective money management is the ability to gain a greater level of enjoyment from the money one makes and thus improve one's standard of living.

Consumption Patterns

Spending money more wisely is another payoff of financial planning; basically, such planning gives you a better idea of what you should do with the money you make. Given a certain level of income, you can either consume it currently or save a portion of it for future consumption. The determination of both your current and future **consumption** patterns is an important aspect of the personal money management process. Defining your consumption involves planning how you will spend your money—the goal, of course, is to get the most from your income dollar.

Current Consumption. Your current level of consumption is based on the necessities of life and your average propensity to consume. A minimum level of consumption is that which allows you to obtain only the **necessities of life:** food, clothing, and shelter. Although the quantity and types of food, clothing, and shelter purchased may differ among individuals depending on their wealth, some amount of these items is essential for survival. **Average propensity to consume** refers to the percentage of each dollar of income that is spent, on average, for current consumption rather than saved. People exhibiting high average propensities to consume may do so because their income is low and they must spend a large portion of it just for basic necessities. On the other hand, as the *Issues in Money Management* box indicates, the middle class now includes many "ultra consumers" who splurge on a few items and scrimp elsewhere. Clearly these people exhibit high average propensities to consume. Conversely, individuals earning large amounts quite often have low 'average propensities to consume, since the cost of necessities represents only a small proportion of their income. Still, it is not unusual to find two people with significantly different incomes but the same average propensity to consume due to differences in standard of living. The person making more money may believe it is essential to buy better-quality and/or more items and thus on average spend the same percentage of each dollar of income as the person making far less.

Future Consumption. In any carefully developed financial plan, a portion of current income will be set aside for deferred, or future, consumption. For example, we may want to put money aside to build up a retirement fund so that we can maintain a desirable standard of living in our later years. In this case, we fully intend to spend the money put aside, but not until we retire; thus, we are deferring actual consumption to some time in the future. Other examples of deferred consumption include putting money away for a child's education, a primary residence or vacation home, a major acquisition (like a car or home entertainment center), or even a vacation. The money put aside for such deferred consumption is placed in various savings and/or investment vehicles so as to generate a return over the time it is held. The portion of our current income committed to future consumption will be a function of the amount of money we earn on the one hand and our level of current spending

on the other. The more we earn and/or the less we devote to current consumption, the more we can commit to meeting future consumption needs. In any case, *some* portion of current income should be set aside *regularly* for future consumption purposes—this creates good saving habits.

Accumulation of Wealth

A certain portion of current income is used to meet the everyday *expenses* of living: food, clothing, insurance, utilities, entertainment, and so on; another part is used to acquire *assets,* such as cars, a home, or stocks and bonds. For the most part, it is our assets that determine how wealthy we are. Personal financial planning plays a critical role in the accumulation of wealth, as it helps us direct our financial resources to the most productive areas. As a rule, a person's **wealth** at any point in time is a function of the total value of all the items he or she owns. Wealth, then, is made up of financial and real assets. **Financial assets** are intangible, paper as-

---

standard of living
The necessities, comforts, and luxuries enjoyed or aspired to by an individual or group.

consumption
The using up of goods or services in the satisfaction of wants.

necessities of life
Items that are needed for survival—food, clothing, and shelter.

average propensity to consume
The percentage of each dollar of income that a person spends, on average, for current consumption.

wealth
The total value of all items owned by an individual, such as bank accounts, stocks, bonds, home, and automobiles.

financial assets
Intangible assets, such as savings accounts and securities, that are acquired for some promised future return.

ISSUES IN MONEY MANAGEMENT

The Middle-Class Ultra Consumers

Some 3.3 million American households have incomes that enable them to live affluent lives. But far more—26 million—partake of the good life only some of time, treating themselves to Godiva chocolates, Giorgio Armani cologne, and long weekends in St. Thomas and Jamaica on incomes of less than $40,000. These are the Joneses of the eighties.

Market researchers at Grey Advertising, a New York agency with billings of $2 billion a year, discovered this new mass of "ultra consumers" while trying to figure out who has been buying so many $380 Burberry raincoats, $250 Louis Vuitton purses, and $200 Mont Blanc fountain pens. There simply aren't enough affluent or near-affluent Americans to account for all the spending on luxury goods.

The ad agency interviewed people across the country between the ages of 21 and 50 with household incomes of more than $25,000 a year, a slice representing about a quarter of the adult population. Of those surveyed, just over half said they bought the top of the line whenever they could afford it. Yet only 5 percent of these ultra consumers had incomes above $75,000, *Fortune*'s minimum for an affluent lifestyle.

The vast majority of these folks obviously aren't in the market for Rolls-Royces or complete designer wardrobes. But they do rent limos from time to time and are devotees of designer-label accessories like Hermes scarves and Gucci loafers. "This is more an attitude of the mind than the pocketbook," says Barbara Feigin, an executive vice-president at Grey.

Wanting it all has long been a hallmark of the middle class. Ultra consumers also want the best. Buying the best is a way to set themselves apart and bolster their self-image. Madison Avenue strives to reinforce that desire. Ads for premium-priced products as varied as Ultress hair coloring and Mitsubishi cars have a cloying sameness: sensual, provocative, and elegant, no matter what's for sale.

Since they cannot afford across-the-board extravagance, most ultra consumers splurge on a few items and scrimp elsewhere. They get by with fewer clothes to afford the Toshiba DX-7 digital VCR with hi-fi sound and do without the new bed so they can sleep between all-cotton sheets. "They don't have all that many wonderful things at once," says Feigin. Small doses of opulence must suffice.

Source: Adapted from Jaclyn Fierman, "The High-Living Middle Class," *Fortune,* April 13, 1987, p. 27. Copyright © *Time Inc.* All rights reserved.

---

sets, such as savings accounts and securities (stocks, bonds, mutual funds, and so forth); they are earning assets that are held for the returns they promise. **Real assets,** in contrast, are tangible, physical assets, such as real estate, that can be held for either consumption (like the home you live in) or investment purposes (like the duplex you bought for rental purposes). In general, the goal of most people is to accumulate as much wealth as possible while maintaining current consumption at a level that provides a desired standard of living.

A savings account is an example of a real asset, as it represents something on deposit at a bank or S&L. **Fantasy:** A savings account, like stocks, bonds, and mutual funds, is an example of a *financial asset*—an intangible, "paper" asset. Real assets, in contrast, refer to *tangibles*—long-lived, physical items like houses, cars, and appliances.

PERSONAL FINANCIAL PLANNING

> Assume that you have decided to take charge of your financial future through personal financial planning. Once you establish your financial goals, in what specific areas will you need to develop plans? Try to answer this question before reading on.

Personal financial planning is the key to achieving financial goals. No one is exempt from the need to develop personal financial plans—not the growing number of single, mobile, urban professionals, nor recently divorced women with children and mid-career, married breadwinners. Knowing what you hope to accomplish financially and how you intend to do it clearly gives you an edge over someone who merely reacts to financial events as they unfold. For example, purchasing a new car immediately after graduation may be important to you, but evaluating and possibly arranging financing before your shopping trip—as opposed to simply accepting the financing arrangement offered by an auto dealer—might save you a considerable amount of money. Moreover, since some dealers advertise low-interest loans but then charge higher prices for their cars, knowing all your costs in advance can help you identify the best deal. For most people, buying a car represents a major expenditure that warrants careful consideration and planning. It not only involves a substantial outflow of cash up front but also usually results in an increased level of consumer debt that must be repaid over time.

Defining Your Financial Goals

What are your **financial goals?** Have you spelled them out, at least over the short run? The fact is, without financial goals it is difficult, if not impossible, to effectively manage your financial resources. We all need to know where we are going, in a financial sense, in order to direct the major financial events in our lives. Perhaps achieving financial independence at a relatively early age is important to you; if so, then things like saving, investing, and retirement planning will become an important part of your life. Whatever your financial goals or preferences, they must be stated in monetary terms, since money, and the *utility* (defined later) it buys, is an integral part of financial planning.

The Role of Money. **Money** is the common denominator by which all financial transactions are gauged. It is the medium of exchange used as a measure of value in our economy. Without the standard unit of exchange provided by the dollar, it would be difficult to set specific personal financial goals and to measure progress in achieving them. Money, as we know it today, is therefore the key consideration in establishing *financial* goals. Yet it

---

real assets
Tangible physical assets, such as real estate and automobiles, that can be held for either consumption or investment purposes.

personal financial planning
Planning that covers the key elements of an individual's financial affairs and is aimed at achievement of his or her financial goals.

financial goals
Short- and long-range results that an individual wants to attain, such as controlling living expenses, managing one's tax burden, establishing savings and investment programs, and meeting retirement needs.

money
The medium of exchange used as a measure of value in financial transactions.

is not money as such that most people want; rather, it is the utility that money makes possible. **Utility** refers to the amount of satisfaction a person receives from purchasing certain types or quantities of goods and services. Often the utility, or satisfaction provided, rather than the cost, is the overriding factor in the choice between two items of differing price. A special feature may provide additional utility in one item, causing it to be the preferred one. This added utility may result from the actual usefulness of the special feature or from the "status" it is expected to provide. Regardless, different people receive varying levels of satisfaction from similar items that are not necessarily related to the items' cost. In evaluating alternative qualities of life, consumption patterns, and forms of wealth accumulation, it is clear, therefore, that utility should be considered along with cost.

Psychology and Money. Money and its utility are not only economic concepts, but are also closely linked to the psychological concepts of emotion and personality. Depending upon timing and circumstances, emotional responses to money may be positive, such as love, happiness, and security, or negative, such as fear, greed, and insecurity. Some people, upon receipt of a paycheck, feel satisfaction in their work. Others feel relief in knowing they can pay past-due bills. Still others experience anxiety over what to do with the money. Also, for some people saving and accumulating money to provide financial security is a high priority, while others place greater emphasis on spending money on material goods in order to reduce anxiety and enhance feelings of self worth.

Each individual's unique personality and emotional makeup determines the importance and role of money in his or her life. Consequently, some introspection is advisable for you to assess the role of money in your life. Such an understanding is prerequisite to the development of realistic and effective financial goals and plans. For example, if you are a person who prefers immediate satisfaction, you will find it more difficult to achieve long-term net worth or savings goals than if you are highly disciplined and primarily concerned with achieving a comfortable retirement at an early age.

Clearly, tradeoffs between current and future benefits are strongly affected by emotion and personality.

While this book emphasizes a rational, unemotional approach to personal financial planning, it is important to recognize that universally applicable financial plans do not exist. Every financial plan must not only consider the individual's wants, needs, and financial resources, but must also *realistically reflect* his or her personality and emotional reactions to money. Conflicts between personality and goals must be resolved early in the planning process. Obviously, plans requiring high levels of annual savings to achieve future consumption goals will be inconsistent with a highly indulgent personality that is fueled by a need to consume. In such a case, goals will have to be moderated in order to achieve an acceptable balance between current and future consumption. In all cases, a key to effective personal financial planning is a *realistic* understanding of the role of money and its utility in the individual's life. Effective financial plans are both economically and psychologically sound.

Types of Financial Goals. Financial goals should be set in terms of the *results we want to attain*. Equally important, as just mentioned, the goals should be *realistically attainable,* since they form the basis on which the financial plans are established. Clearly, if the goals are little more than "pipe dreams," the integrity of the financial plans may be suspect as well (not to mention a possible source of frustration). Finally, the financial goals should be ranked in order of priority and set with a definite time frame in mind—are they short-range goals, to be attained within the next year or so or long-range goals, not to be realized for many more years?

Exhibit 1.1 provides a worksheet that lists different types of financial goals. This list includes a wide variety of financial desires—from controlling living expenses to meeting retirement needs and from setting up a savings and investment program to minimizing your tax burden. Even so, it is not intended to be an exhaustive inventory of each and every kind of personal financial objective; rather, it is meant to be representative of some of the more common and important types of financial goals. Some individuals certainly could have other, more personal or more detailed goals in addition to some of those listed; also, it is highly unlikely that anyone at any given point in time would be pursuing all of the listed goals at once. Instead, as we go through life, we'll find that some financial goals become more important than others.

A Lifetime of Planning

How will you achieve the financial goals you set for yourself? The answer, of course, lies in the financial plans that you establish. Financial plans provide the direction necessary for achieving your financial objectives. Once in place, they can be put into action through various types of financial strategies. There are a variety of different types of financial plans, which can perhaps best be categorized as follows:

- Liability and insurance plans
- Savings and investment plans
- Tax plans
- Retirement and estate plans

Together these plans cover most of the important financial dimensions of our lives—from the amount of debt we incur to how effectively we dispose of our assets. In addition, personal financial planning involves financial budgeting (examined in detail in Chapter 3) and evaluating/planning home and other major acquisitions (addressed in Chapter 6). Activities such as these deal with the more immediate aspects of financial planning and focus on how to manage money. In essence, meeting expenses and making purchases both involve *spending patterns,* the control of which is essential to sound financial planning.

Personal financial planning involves the restatement of personal financial goals into specific plans and, ultimately, into financial arrangements that put those plans into action. **Fact:** Personal financial plans are based on the various financial goals that individuals set for themselves. Once in place, the plans are put into action through various types of financial strategies.

The Life Cycle of Financial Plans. As we move from childhood to retirement age, we go through different life stages. Exhibit 1.2 illustrates the various components of a typical *financial planning life cycle* as it compares to these different life stages. It shows that as we pass from one state of maturation to the next, our patterns of income change simultaneously. From our early childhood days, when we relied on our parents for support, to our early adulthood, when we started our families and, very likely, held our first "real" jobs, we can see a noticeable change in income pattern. First, the negative income—in the form of reliance on our parents for money—is eventually replaced with a rapidly increasing positive stream of earnings as we embark on our chosen careers. Then, as we move from career development to preretirement years, our income becomes more stable. Finally, our income begins to trail off (ideally, only a bit) as we enter our retirement years. Thus, as our emphasis in life changes, so do the kinds of financial plans we pursue—that is, at various points in our lives, different types of financial goals and plans become more important than others.

Exhibit 1.3 summarizes data drawn from 1,200 responses to a 1986 survey of its readers by *Consumer Reports* that clearly demonstrate life cycle differences in the finances of various groups (singles, young couples, traditionals, moderns, empty-nesters, and retirees). It can be seen that income tends to increase, then decline over one's life cycle. In addition, home ownership, the equity in one's home, and other investments tend to increase, debts tend to increase and then decline, and savings as a percent of income tend to decline and then increase over the life cycle. Clearly those in mid-life (ages 35 to 55) tend to have more income and debts than those persons below age 35 and above age 55.

> **utility**
> The amount of satisfaction an individual receives from purchasing certain types or quantities of goods and services.

EXHIBIT 1.1

A Summary of Personal Financial Goals

It is important to set financial objectives carefully. They must be realistically attainable, since they are the basis for financial planning.

PERSONAL FINANCIAL GOALS

Name(s) _____ Date _____

Type of Financial Goal	Brief Description	Degree of Priority (High, Medium, or Low)	Time Frame (Short- or Long- Range)	Target Date
Increase Income				
Gain control over living expenses				
Have more money left over for discretionary/ entertainment purchases				
Set up an education fund for yourself, your spouse, and/or your children				
Establish an emergency fund to meet unexpected expenses				
Implement procedures to keep your tax burden to a minimum				
Put money aside for a home, car, and/or other major expenditures				
Pay off/reduce personal debt; bring monthly debt service requirements down to a more manageable level				
Provide adequate protection against personal risks—life, disability, health, property, and liability insurance				
Start a general savings and investment program to accumulate capital and achieve financial security				
Start your own business				
Set up a retirement fund to supplement social security and employer-sponsored retirement programs				
Maximize the disposition/transfer of estate to heirs				
Other personal financial objectives and goals				

EXHIBIT 1.2

The Personal Financial Planning Life Cycle

As people go through different stages in their lives, their income patterns change as well as the types of financial plans they pursue.

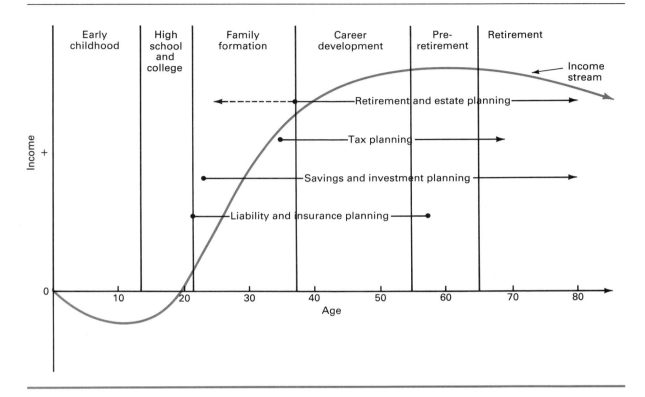

Liability and Insurance Planning. A *liability* is something we owe and is represented by the amount of debt we have incurred. We create liabilities by borrowing money. Most people at some point borrow money to make major purchases, such as a home, car, or major appliance. Effectively, we also borrow money when we "buy on credit," through use of a credit card. Regardless of the source of credit, such transactions have one thing in common: *The debt must be repaid at some future time.* Using credit effectively requires careful planning and is the topic of Chapters 7 and 8. As we will see, how we manage our debt burden is just as important as how we manage our assets.

Obtaining adequate *insurance coverage* is also essential. Like borrowing money, it is generally something that is introduced at a relatively early point in our life cycle (usually early in the family

foundation stage). Insurance provides a means of protecting both our income (life and health insurance) and our assets (property and liability insurance). Most consumers regard insurance as absolutely essential—and for good reason. One serious illness or accident can wipe out everything that one has accumulated over years of hard work. However, overinsuring or misinsuring can be costly too. The appropriate types and amounts of insurance coverage are examined in Chapters 9, 10, and 11.

Planning Your Savings and Investment Programs. As your income begins to increase, so does the importance of savings and investment planning. People *save* initially in order to establish an emergency fund for meeting unexpected expenses. Eventually, however, they devote greater at-

EXHIBIT 1.3
Life Cycle Financial Data

The finances of those in different stages of the life cycle vary. Income tends to increase, then decline over the life cycle, while home ownership, the equity in one's home, and other investments tend to increase, debts tend to increase and then decline, and savings as a percent of income tend to decline and then increase over the life cycle.

Group	Household Income	Percent Who Own Home	Equity in Home	Investments Besides Home	Debts	Percent of Income Saved
Singles (one in household; average age: 35)	$34,000	57%	$44,000	$38,000	$27,000	8%
Young Couples (two in household, both working; average age: 39)	$50,000	79%	$62,000	$52,000	$42,000	8%
Traditionals (married, one income, two kids; average age: 39)	$47,000	88%	$63,000	$46,000	$46,000	6%
Moderns (married, two incomes, two kids; average age: 39)	$50,000	89%	$54,000	$43,000	$45,000	5%
Empty-nesters (two in household, one working; average age: 56)	$49,000	90%	$90,000	$87,000	$32,000	8%
Retirees (two in household, at least one retired; average age: over 65)	$36,000	95%	$87,000	$100,000	$7,000	7%

Source: "Where Does All The Money Go?", *Consumer Reports,* September 1986, pp. 581–592.

tention to *investing* excess income as a means of accumulating wealth, either for retirement or for major expenditures such as a child's college education. Wealth may be acquired through savings and subsequent investing of funds in various investment media—common or preferred stocks, government or corporate bonds, real estate, and so on. Success is determined by how profitably excess funds are invested.

The impact of alternative rates of return on accumulated wealth is illustrated in Exhibit 1.4. It shows that if you had $1,000 today and could keep it invested at 10 percent, you would accumulate a considerable sum of money over time; for example, at the end of 40 years you would have $45,259 from your original $1,000. Earning a higher rate of return has even greater rewards. Some might assume that earning, say, two percentage points more—that is, 12 rather than 10 percent—would not matter a great deal. But it certainly would! Note that if you could earn 12 percent over the 40 years, you would accumulate $93,051, or *more than twice as much*

as what you would accumulate at 10 percent. Note also that *how long you invest* is just as important as *how much you earn* on your investments. As shown in Exhibit 1.4, with either rate of return, investing for 40 rather than 30 years results in about three times as much accumulated capital! This is the magic of compound interest, which explains why it's so important to start creating strong savings and investment habits early in life. We will more fully examine savings in Chapter 5 and investments in Chapters 12, 13, and 14.

Over the long run, gaining an extra percent or two on an investment makes little difference in the amount of earnings generated. **Fantasy:** Gaining an extra percent or two on an investment can make a *tremendous* difference—often thousands of dollars— that increases the longer the investment is held.

Tax Planning. In spite of all the talk about tax reform, and even after the sweeping tax revision of 1986, the fact is that our tax code continues to be

EXHIBIT 1.4

How a $1,000 Investment Can Grow over Time

Differences in the rates of return earned on investments can have a dramatic impact on the amount of money you make from your investments, especially as the length of the investment period increases.

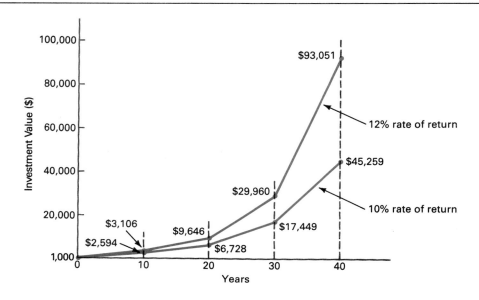

highly complex. Some income is taxed as ordinary income; some is treated as investment income; some is treated as passive income; some is tax free; and some is tax deferred. Then there are tax shelters, which use various aspects of the tax code (such as depreciation expenses) to legitimately reduce an investor's tax liability. *Tax planning* considers all these dimensions and more; basically, it involves looking at an individual's current and projected earnings and developing strategies that will *defer* and/or *minimize taxes.* Tax plans should reflect the desired form in which returns are to be received—earned income, investment income, passive income, capital gains, or tax-sheltered income. These plans are closely tied to investment plans and will often specify certain investment strategies. Although the use of tax planning is most common among individuals with high incomes, sizable savings can also result for people with lower levels of income. We will examine taxes and tax planning in Chapter 4.

Retirement and Estate Planning. While you are still working, you should be managing your finances to attain those goals you feel are important in old age. These might include extensive travel, plans for visiting children, dining out frequently at better restaurants, and perhaps a vacation home or boat. It is important to see that *retirement planning* begins long before you actually retire. As a rule, most people do not start thinking about retirement until well into their forties or fifties. This is unfortunate, since it usually results in a *substantially reduced* level of retirement income. The sooner you start, the better off you will be. Take, for example, the IRA (individual retirement account), in which certain wage earners are allowed to invest up to $2,000 per year. If you can earn 12 percent and put $2,000 per year in an IRA for 25 years (that is, start investing for retirement at age 40), your account will grow to $267,000. However, if you start your retirement program 10 years earlier (at age 30), your IRA will grow to a whopping $865,000—even

S·M·A·R·T   M·O·N·E·Y

Using the PC in Financial Planning

Make no mistake about it: personal financial planning is made a lot easier through the use of a personal computer. Within a matter of minutes, a PC can compute and analyze enormous amounts of data and then project the results on a screen in the form of charts, tables, or graphs. A well-programmed personal computer can readily accomplish all of the following tasks and more:

- Prepare detailed financial budgets, complete with month-by-month recaps of how actual figures compare to budgeted ones
- Evaluate the financial benefits and costs of major purchases
- Analyze the investment merits of all sorts of securities and investment vehicles
- Monitor the risk-and-return performance of a fully diversified investment portfolio
- Keep a full inventory of all types of insurance coverage
- Prepare tax returns and perform complicated tax planning
- Evaluate alternative retirement plans and identify actions necessary to achieve a desired level of income at retirement

Of course, the computer won't do all the work by itself—*you* have to provide the necessary data and operate the unit (which generally involves nothing more than responding to questions or sets of instructions). What it will do is dramatically reduce the amount of time and effort necessary to set up your financial plans and effectively manage your money.

A minimum knowledge of how to operate a computer is essential to effectively apply the PC to financial planning. Fortunately, such expertise can usually be obtained from one or two short courses in computers, which are readily available from most computer stores, community colleges, and universities. (Learning how to *program* a computer is another matter altogether and takes considerably more time.) A complete computer system is made up of both hardware and software. A criti-

---

though you are investing a total of only $20,000 more ($2,000 per year for an extra 10 years), your IRA will *triple* in size. We will look at IRAs and other aspects of retirement planning in Chapter 15.

Accumulating assets to enjoy in retirement is only part of the long-run planning process. As people grow older, they eventually must start considering how they can most effectively pass on their wealth to heirs—an activity called *estate planning*. We will examine this complex subject, which deals with such topics as wills, trusts, and the effects of gift, estate, and inheritance taxes, in Chapter 16.

The Personal Computer in Financial Planning

As it has in so many other aspects of our lives, the personal computer (PC) has found its way into financial planning. Indeed, financial planning is a natural application of the PC—what better way to handle all the number crunching? Consider the different elements of personal financial planning—the preparation and monitoring of budgets, the management of investment portfolios, the evaluation and control of exposure to taxes, and the systematic evaluation of major purchases, insurance coverage, and credit decisions. Many of these elements include a good deal of time-consuming, analytical work and mathematical computations, all of which can be aided considerably by the personal computer.

Rapidly changing PC technology has made available very sophisticated **hardware** (the physical parts of a computer system, such as the processor, disk drive, monitor, and printer) and **software** (the programs that tell the computer which functions to

cal question about hardware is the amount of memory the unit has—clearly, it must be enough to permit the financial planning applications you have in mind. Perhaps most important, *before* buying any PC, be sure you have a good idea of how it will be used, both immediately and in the more distant future.

The following figures represent what it cost in early 1989 to buy a reasonably sophisticated PC system:

Hardware	Cost
Computer unit (processor, keyboard, monitor, hard disk, 640K of internal memory)	$1,800
Printer (with graphics capabilities)	400
Modem (allows connection to a phone line)	200
Total	$2,400

With the right software, such a system will enable you to do just about anything you want in the way of computer-based financial planning. (Note: The modem is essential in the area of investment management, as it allows access to data bases of historical and current information covering such things as earnings, prices, and dividends on literally thousands of companies.)

The other part of a PC system is the software—the programs that tell the computer which functions to perform. Without software, the computer is useless. There are virtually hundreds of different programs available in the area of personal financial planning and money

management, and the list grows almost daily. The cost of most of the consumer-oriented programs (as opposed to those tailored for professional money managers) runs from as low as $50 to $500 or more. Since it usually takes at least two or three programs to effectively implement a complete computer-based financial planning/money management system, you can expect to spend around $500 or more just for the software. Clearly, computer systems—even for home use—aren't cheap; but if properly used, they can be worth the money.

perform). While PCs have been getting more powerful and sophisticated, their prices have plunged over the past several years. Today their cost is very reasonable; for the serious financial planner who wants to do a lot of his or her own work, they can well be worth an investment of about $2,500. At the same time, there has been a proliferation of reasonably priced, "user-friendly" software on the market; countless programs are now available for doing taxes, monitoring investments, evaluating securities, devising retirement plans, constructing budgets and financial plans, and even writing your checks at bill-paying time. The accompanying *Smart Money* box reviews the benefits and costs of computer-based financial planning.

We feel that just as the PC is widely used in the everyday world of financial planning, it should be used in the teaching of personal finance. Accord-

ingly, we will introduce the personal computer repeatedly throughout this book. In addition, a simple, menu-driven computer program has been developed for use with many of the analytical and computational procedures addressed in the text. Known as the *Personal Financial Planning Disk,* this program is written for IBM and IBM-compatible computers and is keyed to various sections of

hardware
The physical parts of a computer system, such as processor, disk drives, monitor, and printer.

software
Programs that tell a computer which functions to perform.

the book for use in performing many of the routine financial calculations and procedures presented. To help you recognize these sections throughout the text, we have keyed the major text headings and selected end-of-chapter problems with the following symbol: ∎

THE PLANNING ENVIRONMENT

> The financial planning environment is made up of a number of players and is affected by economic conditions and consumer prices. What effect do you think government, business, consumers, economic conditions, and consumer prices will have on your financial plans? Spend a few moments answering this question before reading on.

Financial planning is not carried out in isolation but in an economic environment created by the actions of government, business, and consumers. Thus, personal financial planning must be able to respond to various economic conditions.

For example, a strong economy can lead to big profits in the stock market, which can positively affect your investment and/or retirement programs. The economy can also affect the interest rates you pay on your mortgage and credit cards. Periods of high inflation can lead to price increases that come so fast it is hard to make ends meet. It is important, therefore, to understand the environment in which you will carry out your financial plans and strategies. This section briefly looks at three key aspects of the planning environment: the major players in the environment, the economy, and the behavior of consumer prices.

The Players

The financial planning environment contains various groups of players, each attempting to fulfill certain goals (see Exhibit 1.5). Although their objectives are not necessarily incompatible, they do impose some constraints on one another. There are three vital groups: the government, business, and consumers.

Government. The federal, state, and local governments provide us with many essential services, such as police and fire protection, national defense, highways, and health care. In doing so, however, they also constrain businesses and consumers, as indicated in Exhibit 1.5. The two principal constraints from the perspective of financial planning are taxes and government regulations.

Taxation. The federal government levies taxes on income, state governments on sales and income, and local governments primarily on real estate and personal property. The largest tax bite for consumers is the federal one, which may take as much as 33 percent of earnings. These taxes are somewhat progressive since (up to a point) the greater the taxable income, the higher the rate at which taxes are paid. Careful consideration should be given to the effects of taxes on personal money management activities. Due to the constraints of the tax structure and the potential magnitude of taxes, *financial decisions should be evaluated on an "after-tax" basis.*

Regulation. Federal, state, and local governments place many regulations on consumer- and citizen-related activities. Aimed at protecting the consumer from fraudulent and undesirable actions by sellers and lenders, these regulations require certain types of businesses to have licenses, maintain certain hygienic standards, adequately disclose financial charges, and warrant their goods and services. Other laws protect sellers from adverse activities by consumers, for example, shoplifting and nonpayment of services rendered. Certainly, any decisions relating to achieving personal financial goals should take into consideration both the legal requirements that protect consumers and those that constrain their activities.

Business. As shown in Exhibit 1.5, business provides consumers with goods and services and in return receives payment in the form of money. In order to produce these goods and services, firms must hire labor and use land and capital (what economists refer to as *factors of production*); in return, firms pay out wages, rents, interest, and profits to the various factors of production. Thus, businesses are a key part of the circular flow of income that sustains our free enterprise system. In general, their presence creates a competitive environment in which consumers may select from an array of

EXHIBIT 1.5
The Financial Planning Environment

Business, government, and consumers are the major participants in our economic system. They all interact with one another to produce the environment in which we carry out our financial plans.

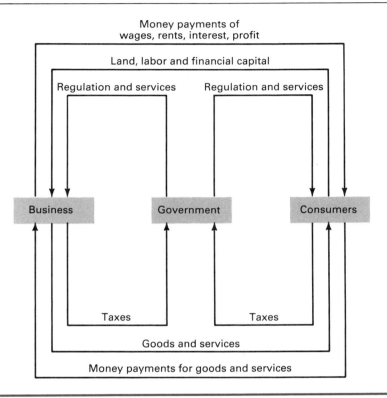

goods and services. There are, of course, certain industries, such as public utilities, in which the degree of competition or choice offered the consumer is limited, for economic reasons, by various regulatory bodies. As indicated in the preceding section, all businesses are limited in some way by federal, state, and/or local laws. An understanding of various business activities should permit consumers to make better purchases and help them determine with which firms to deal.

Consumers. The consumer is the party around whom the financial planning environment centers. Consumer choices are what ultimately determine the kinds of goods and services businesses will provide. In addition, the consumer's choice of whether to spend or save has a direct impact on the present and future circular flows of income. A cutback in spending is usually associated with a decline in economic activity, while an increase helps the economy recover. Although consumers are often thought to have free choices in the marketplace, they must operate within an environment that interacts with government and business. While they can affect these parties through their elected officials and by their purchase actions, lobbyists and consumer groups are necessary for any real impact; the individual consumer should not expect to change government or business independently. As an *individual* consumer, you are best off accepting the existing environment and planning your transactions within it.

EXHIBIT 1.6

The Economic Cycle

The economy goes through various stages over time, though real depressions are extremely rare. These stages tend to be cyclical and directly affect the levels of employment and production.

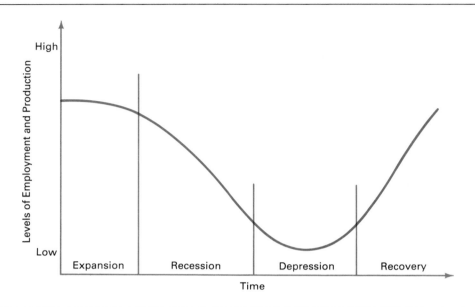

The Economy

Our economy is the result of interaction among government, business, and consumers, as well as the economic conditions in other nations. Although the government's goal is to regulate the economy and provide economic stability and high levels of employment, swings in economic activity do occur. An economic cycle can contain four stages: **expansion, recession, depression,** and **recovery.** Each of these stages as it relates to employment and industrial production is depicted in Exhibit 1.6. As can be seen, the stronger the economy, the higher the levels of employment and production. For more than 45 years, the government has been reasonably successful in keeping the economy out of a depression, although we have experienced periods of rapid expansion and high inflation followed by periods of deep recession.

The swings in unemployment from one phase of the cycle to the next can be substantial. For example, during the Great Depression of the 1930s, U.S. unemployment reached a staggering 25 percent of the work force; in contrast, during the expansion

in 1968, unemployment dropped to slightly less than 4 percent. More recently, the 1981–1982 recession—in which unemployment rose to over 10 percent—was the worst experienced in this country since the Great Depression. Unemployment, inflation, interest rates, bank failures, corporate profits, taxes, and government deficits are all examples of economic conditions that can have a direct and profound impact on our financial well-being, since they affect the very heart of our financial plans: our level of income, investment returns, interest earned and paid, taxes paid, and, in general, prices paid for goods and services consumed.

Consumer Price Behavior

As we just saw, our economy is based on the exchange of goods and services between businesses and consumers for a medium of exchange called money. The mechanism that facilitates this exchange is a system of *prices*. Technically speaking, the price of something is *the amount of money the seller is willing to accept in exchange for a given quantity of some good or service*—for example, $3 for a pound of meat or $8 for an hour of work. When the general level of prices *increases* over time, the economy is said to be experiencing a period of **inflation**. The United States has experienced a general rise in the level of prices for the past 35 years or so. And at times the rate of inflation has been fairly substantial—in 1980, for instance, prices went up by 15 percent. While a 15 percent rise in prices is very high for this country, it is nothing in comparison to what has happened in some others: in 1987, for example, prices went up 86 percent in Peru, 130 percent in Mexico, nearly 230 percent in Brazil, 240 percent in Uganda, and an incredible 900 percent in Nicaragua. Fortunately, inflation has dropped dramatically in this country and the annual rate of inflation in 1985, 1986, and 1987 has remained below 4 percent; indeed, there is considerable hope that inflation is finally under control and will remain in the 3 to 5 percent range for the foreseeable future.

Inflation is of vital concern to financial planning. It affects not only what we pay for the various goods and services we consume but also what we earn in our jobs. Inflation also directly affects interest rates; high rates of inflation drive up the cost of money, ultimately leading to higher mortgage payments, higher monthly car payments, and so on. High inflation rates also have a detrimental effect on stock prices, causing investment returns to go down. Finally, sustained high rates of inflation can have devastating effects on retirement plans and other long-run financial goals—indeed, for many people it can put such goals out of reach. Worst of all, inflation tends to give an illusion of something that does not exist; that is, while we seem to be making more money, we really aren't, since each dollar we earn has less purchasing power. All of which explains why the low inflation rates of the mid-1980s were embraced so enthusiastically; clearly, low inflation is good for the economy, for interest rates and investment returns, and in general, for financial planning.

Generally speaking, inflation has little effect on personal financial planning. **Fantasy:** Inflation is a vital concern to financial planning, as it affects not only the prices we pay for the goods and services we consume, but also the amount of money we make; clearly, if ignored, inflation can wreak havoc on our budgets and financial plans.

WHAT DETERMINES YOUR PERSONAL INCOME?

The amount of money you make is a function of your age, your level of education, and your career. What combination of age, educational level, and career do you think will provide you with the best opportunity to make a lot of money? Take a moment to answer this question before reading on.

An obvious and important factor in determining how well we live is the amount of income we earn. In the absence of any inheritance or similar financial windfall, your income will depend in large part on your age, education, and career. Making a lot of money is not easy. But it can be done! A high level of income—whether derived from your job, your own business, or your investments—is within your reach if you are willing to provide the necessary

expansion
The phase of the economic cycle during which the levels of employment and economic activity/growth are both high; generally accompanied by rising prices for goods and services.

recession
The phase of the economic cycle during which the levels of employment and economic activity/growth are both slowing down.

depression
The phase of the economic cycle during which the employment level is low and economic activity and growth are at a virtual standstill.

recovery
The phase of the economic cycle during which the employment level is improving and the economy is experiencing increased activity and growth.

inflation
A state of the economy in which the general price level is rising due to excessive demand or rapidly rising production costs; usually occurs during the recovery and expansion phases of the economic cycle.

EXHIBIT 1.7

How Age, Education, and Career Are Related to Annual Income (1986 Data)

The amount of money you earn is closely tied to your age, education, and career. Generally, the closer you are to middle age (35 to 55), the more education you have, and the more professionally or managerially oriented your career, the greater your income will be.

	Annual Income (Head of Household)				
	Under $20,000	$20,000 –$34,999	$35,000 –$49,999	Over $50,000	Median Income
Age	**Percent in Each Income Bracket by Age**				
15–24	62.9%	26.6%	7.6%	3.0%	$15,310
25–34	36.2	32.4	18.8	12.7	25,898
35–44	25.7	27.9	22.2	24.4	32,787
45–54	25.0	23.9	21.3	29.8	35,660
55–64	37.3	26.1	16.6	20.1	26,778
65 and over	66.9	19.3	7.4	6.3	13,845
Education (highest level)	**Percent in Each Income Bracket by Education**				
Elementary					
Less than 8 years	76.7%	16.0%	5.2%	2.1%	$10,413
8 years	67.7	20.6	8.0	3.8	13,231
High School					
1–3 years	60.8	23.2	10.2	5.9	15,524
4 years	40.3	30.5	17.6	11.7	24,271
College					
1–3 years	32.2	29.5	19.7	18.6	28,644
4 or more years	15.9	23.2	22.1	39.0	41,677

	Median Income by Sex		
Career (full-time)	**Women**	**Men**	**Total**
Executive, administrators, and managerial	$21,432	$34,962	$30,227
Professional specialty	23,076	35,143	29,954
Technical and related support	19,236	27,880	23,990
Sales	12,956	26,803	22,233
Admin. support (incl. clerical)	15,509	22,718	17,095
Precision production, craft and repair	16,810	24,281	23,683
Machine operators, assemblers and inspectors	12,324	20,551	17,589
Transportation and material moving	14,310	21,770	21,472
Handlers, equipment cleaners, helpers, and laborers	12,198	17,694	16,980
Service workers	10,367	17,332	13,919
Farming, forestry, and fishing	8,032	10,748	10,504

Source: U.S. Bureau of the Census, *Statistical Abstract of the United States: 1988* (108th edition) Washington, D.C., 1987, Tables No. 653 (page 395) and No. 692 (page 423).

dedication and hard work, along with a well-thought-out set of financial plans. Exhibit 1.7 presents data relative to the effect of age, education, and career on annual income. Looking at the median income shown in the far right column it can be seen that, as a rule, the closer you are to middle age, the more education you have, and the more professionally or managerially oriented your career, the greater your income will be.

Your Age

Although age is a variable over which you have no control, it is interesting to look at its relationship to income. Typically, people with low incomes fall into the very young or very old age groups, while the period of highest earnings generally occurs between the ages of 35 and 55. This distribution results because those below age 35 are just developing their trades or beginning to move up in their jobs, while many over 55 are working only part-time or are completely retired. In the under-35 age group, the median income of the heads of household is about $24,000; this jumps to just over $34,000 for those in the 35-to-55 age group and then falls sharply in the 55-and-over group to about $19,000. It is very likely that your own income will vary over time; thus, when setting financial goals and making financial plans, you should consider expected changes in earnings.

Your Education

Your level of formal education is a controllable factor that has a considerable effect on your income. This is not to say that all people with equivalent formal educations will earn similar incomes; rather, formal education is simply a tool that, when properly applied, can help carve out an improved level of earnings. As can be seen in Exhibit 1.7, heads of household who have more formal education earn higher annual incomes than those with lesser degrees. Although this is not strictly a cause-and-effect relationship, it strongly suggests that in order to enhance your earnings opportunities, you should obtain a good formal education—certainly, your chances of earning a high income will be improved.

Your Career

Your choice of a *field* of study is closely related to your *level* of education and is likely to determine the type of career you choose. Of course, formal education is not a prerequisite for many types of careers, such as sales, service, and certain types of clerical work. But generally, as can be seen in Exhibit 1.7, the more responsibilities for decision making associated with a given career, the greater the annual income that career can be expected to provide. For example, the highest earnings tend to occur among professional and managerial workers, whose formal education is likely to include a college degree. Exhibit 1.8 presents an alphabetical list of the estimated annual incomes (including bonuses and commissions) for rookies, veterans, and winners in various occupations as compiled in 1986 by *Money*. The list clearly indicates that those careers requiring greater formal education or specialized skills typically offer higher incomes. Thus, only when you have set your educational and career goals can you establish your personal financial goals with a view toward your expected lifetime earnings.

Your income level is a function of your age, education, and career. **Fact:** All three variables are important influences in determining your level of income, particularly if accompanied by adequate ambition and good work habits.

AN OVERVIEW OF THE TEXT

This text is divided into six parts, each devoted to the explanation of a different aspect of personal financial planning:

Part One: Foundations of Financial Planning
Part Two: Managing Basic Assets
Part Three: Managing Credit
Part Four: Managing Insurance Needs
Part Five: Managing Investments
Part Six: Retirement and Estate Planning

The book is developed around the organizational model shown in Exhibit 1.9.

Our organizational scheme revolves around financial decision making that is firmly established on an operational set of financial plans. We believe that through sound financial plans, individuals can make financial decisions that will lead to desired financial results. Therefore, starting with Part One, where we look at personal accounting, budgeting and financial planning, and taxes, we move successively through the various types of decisions that individuals make in implementing their financial plans.

In order to allow you to gain some hands-on financial planning experience, a continuous case is developed and presented at the end of various chapters and parts of the text. The case begins at the end of this chapter with an inventory of per-

EXHIBIT 1.8

Incomes of Rookies, Veterans, and Winners in Various Occupations (1986)

Professional and managerial workers tend to have higher earnings than those with occupations requiring less formal education. Clearly, careers requiring more formal education or specialized skills earn higher annual incomes.

Occupation	Rookies	Veterans	Winners
Accountant	$23,900	$31,700	Partner, Deloitte Haskins & Sells, San Diego: $90,000
Actor	$11,800	$11,800	Sylvester Stallone for Over the Top: $12 million
Advertising executive	$13,500	$54,700	JWT Group CEO Don Johnston, New York City: $742,300
Airline pilot	$55,000	$110,000	Senior 747 pilot United Airlines: $161,000
Chef	$18,000	$45,500	Larger luxury hotel, San Francisco: $105,000
Chemist	$39,600	$56,900	Nobel Prize winner Yual T. Lee, University of California at Berkeley: $84,700
Commercial banker	$28,550	$54,600	Citicorp chairman John Reed: $575,000
Computer programmer	$20,800	$32,900	Senior software engineer, SRI International: $50,000
Dentist	$55,000	$90,600	Private practitioner, New York City: $300,000
Diplomat	$24,900	$60,100	U.S. ambassador to Greece Robert Keeley: $75,100
Electrician, unionized	$14,800	$40,100	Foreman: $43,600
Elementary school teacher	$16,900	$31,300	Ph.D., Denver Public School District 1: $41,600
Executive recruiter	$70,000	$150,000	Senior VP, Boyden International, New York City: $300,000
Geologist	$27,000	$80,700	Head of exploration team, major oil company: $148,000
Investment banker	$97,500	$250,000	Morgan Stanley chairman S. Parker Gilbert: $1.5 million
Lawyer	$48,000	$225,000	Senior partner, Cahill Gordon & Reindel, New York City: $1.2 million
Librarian	$18,300	$31,300	City librarian, Phoenix Public Library: $57,800
Life insurance agent	$15,900	$52,600	Top producer, Northwestern Mutual Life: $300,000
Mail carrier	$20,100	$27,100	Postmaster, Philadelphia: $68,000
Model, major agency	$60,000	$175,000	Isabella Rossellini, under contract with Lancome cosmetics: $400,000
Mutual fund manager	$50,000	$250,000	T. Rowe Price CEO George Collins: $692,000
Newspaper reporter	$19,100	$29,800	New York Times: $46,800 minimum
Paralegal	$16,000	$35,000	Supervisor, large New York City law firm: $50,000
Photographer	$16,600	$28,950	Contract photographer, National Geographic: $52,500 max
Physician	$78,900	$129,200	Private practitioner who specializes in high-risk pregnancies: $350,000
Professor	$26,700	$44,600	Full professor, Harvard University: $66,000
Registered nurse	$20,300	$24,500	Head nurse, UCLA Medical Center: $44,250
Social worker	$18,000	$24,000	Texas Department of Human Services: $26,100
Stockbroker	$35,600	$79,600	Fred Berens, Prudential-Bache Securities, Miami: $2 million

Source: "Other People's Paychecks", *Money,* December 1986, page 63. Used with permission.

sonal and financial data for the Mark and Ana Williams family. Using this data, opportunities to develop various components of the Williamses' financial plan appear at the end of Parts One through Five, Chapter Fifteen, and Chapter Sixteen. At each of these points, any additional data is presented, if needed, along with statements and questions aimed at directing the development of the aspect of the Williamses' financial plan related to the material presented in that part or chapter of the text. Completion of all of these components will result in a comprehensive financial plan for the Williamses. Of course, depending on course objectives and time constraints, the preparation of the Williamses' financial plan may or may not be required by your instructor.

EXHIBIT 1.9

Organizational Model

This text emphasizes making financial decisions relative to assets, credit, insurance, investments, and retirement and estates in a fashion consistent with financial plans developed to achieve desired financial results.

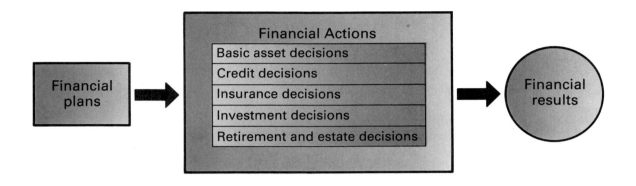

SUMMARY

- One of the major benefits of personal financial planning is that it helps you to more effectively marshal and control your financial resources and thus gain an improved standard of living.
- In order to effectively manage your financial resources, you must *realistically* spell out your financial goals. Such objectives are essential to sound financial planning and should be set in terms of the desired results.
- A fully integrated set of financial plans includes financial budgets (covering living expenses and major acquisitions), liability and insurance planning, savings and investment planning, tax planning, and retirement and estate planning. Though these plans change over time, they provide the direction necessary for achieving our financial goals.

- The practice of financial planning is ideally suited to the personal computer because of all the number crunching involved.
- Financial planning is conducted in an environment in which the government, business, and consumers are all influential participants, and financial decisions are affected by economic conditions and the behavior of consumer prices.
- Your age, education, and chosen career are all important factors in defining your level of income. As a rule, people in the 35-to-55 age group tend to earn more than others, as do those in the more professional or managerial positions. Equally important, statistics show a strong, direct relationship between level of education and amount of income.

QUESTIONS AND PROBLEMS

1. What is a standard of living? What are the factors that affect quality of life?
2. Are consumption patterns related to quality of life? Explain.
3. What is average propensity to consume? Is it possible for two people with very different incomes to have the same average propensity to consume?

4. Discuss the various forms in which wealth can be accumulated.

5. What is the role of money in setting financial plans? What is the relationship of money to utility? Explain why financial plans must be psychologically as well as economically sound.

6. Identify at least five financial goals that are important to you. Use a worksheet like the one in Exhibit 1.1 to describe your goals. Generally speaking, why is it important to set realistically attainable financial goals?

7. Mark Peters' investments over the past several years have not lived up to his full expectations. He is not really concerned, though, since the difference is only about two percentage points. Do you have any advice for Mark?

8. "There's no sense in worrying about retirement until you reach middle age." Discuss this point of view.

9. Describe tax planning. How does it fit into the financial planning framework?

10. What are the various components normally found in a complete set of financial plans?

11. What role can a personal computer play in personal financial planning?

12. Discuss the following statement: "It is the interaction among government, business, and consumers that determines the environment in which personal financial plans must be made."

13. What are the stages of an economic cycle? Explain their significance for one's personal finances.

14. What is inflation, and why should it be a concern in financial planning?

15. "All people having equivalent formal education earn similar incomes." Do you agree or disagree with this statement? Explain your position.

CASE PROBLEMS

1.1 Neil's Need to Know: Personal Finance or Tennis?

During the Christmas break of his final year at Mountain View College, Neil Stone planned to put together his résumé in preparation for his actively seeking full-time employment as a medical technician during the spring semester. To help Neil prepare for the job interview process, his older brother arranged for him to meet with a friend, Marilyn Nave, who has been a practicing medical technician since her graduation from Mountain View two years earlier. Neil and Marilyn met for lunch, and Marilyn provided him with numerous pointers on résumé preparation, the interview process, job opportunities, and so on.

After answering Neil's many questions, Marilyn asked Neil to bring her up to date on a variety of topics related to Mountain View College. Of special interest to Marilyn were the many changes that had taken place in the faculty and curriculum of the medical technology department since her graduation. As they discussed courses, Marilyn indicated that of all the electives she had taken, she had found the course in personal finance most useful. Neil

said that he still had one elective to take and had been giving some thought to personal finance, although he was currently leaning toward a beginning tennis course. Neil felt that since a number of his friends would be taking tennis, it would be a lot of fun. He pointed out that since he never expected to get rich and already knew how to balance his checkbook, the personal finance course did not seem well suited to his needs. Marilyn said that there is certainly much more to personal finance than balancing one's checkbook and that the course was highly relevant regardless of one's income level. She strongly believed that the personal finance course would be more beneficial to Neil than beginning tennis—a course that she herself had taken while at Mountain View College.

Questions

1. Describe to Neil the goals and rewards of the personal financial planning process.

2. Explain to Neil what is meant by financial planning and why it is important regardless of one's income.

3. Describe the financial planning environment to Neil. Explain the role of the consumer in, and the impact of economic conditions on, this environment.

4. What arguments would you present in order to convince Neil that the personal finance course would be more beneficial for him than beginning tennis?

1.2 Patty Ponders Her Career Options

Patty Kaufman will soon receive her bachelor's degree in accounting and finance from a large midwestern university. Because Patty has maintained a high grade-point average, she has been swamped with job offers. After considerable deliberation, she has narrowed her choices down to two firms and is presently trying to make a decision between the following two opportunities:

1. One of the Big Eight accounting firms has offered her employment as an audit staff assistant at an annual salary of $23,500. Her job will be to audit the books of its large corporate clients. During the first two years of her tenure with the firm, she will be spending a lot of time traveling to various cities and thus will be away from her home, family, and new husband. Further, every summer the company will send her to its training school in Virginia. If she qualifies as a CPA after joining the firm, she is assured of a big raise and a very bright future. She could be made a manager within five years and a partner three to five years after that. This would increase her earnings fourfold or more.

2. A large manufacturing company has offered her the position of management trainee in its managerial planning and finance division. Besides a monthly salary of $2,140, other benefits offered Patty include a two-week vacation every year and liberal retirement, health, and insurance benefits. This division is headed by a vice-president and includes a number of managerial positions. However, in terms of seniority, there will be at least 25 people ahead of her; thus, she will not reach the manager level for 10 to 15 years. The job will require no traveling.

The atmosphere and location of both firms are unusually good.

Questions

1. What are the advantages and disadvantages that Patty must consider in evaluating the two job offers?

2. Having considered the pros and cons of both jobs, which would you recommend she accept? Why?

3. List and discuss, in order of importance, five factors that *you* feel must be present in order for a job opportunity to be acceptable.

4. How would consideration of each position align with *your* long-range career plans? Explain.

FOR MORE INFORMATION

General Information Articles

Fierman, Jaclyn, "What it Takes to Be Rich in America," *Fortune,* April 13, 1987, pp. 22–28.

Goode, Erica E., "On the Delicate Subject of Money," *U.S. News & World Report,* March 7, 1988, pp. 68–69.

McGrath, Anne, "Financing the Single Way of Life," *U.S. News & World Report,* August 3, 1987, pp. 56–57.

Reid, Jeanne L., "Twelve Steps to Financial Security," *Money,* January 1988, pp. 66–74.

"10 Steps to Financial Freedom," *Changing Times,* September 1988, pp. 23–37.

"Your Finances," *Money Extra,* 1988, pp. 95–115.

Government Documents and Other Publications

Financial Planning Bibliography (Denver, CO: College for Financial Planning); 9725 E. Hampden Avenue; Denver, CO 80231: 303–755–7101.

The Jobs Rated Almanac by Les Krantz (Chicago: World Almanac, 1988).

Kiplinger's Changing Times Financial Services Directory; Editors Park; Hyattsville, MD 20782; 202–887–6400.

Your Money Personality: What It Is and How You Can Profit From It by Kathleen Gurney (New York: R.L. Doubleday & Co., 1988).

Mark and Ana Williams are a young couple in their mid-twenties. They are married and both working at jobs they enjoy. Not only do they like their employment, but they are earning good salaries for recent college graduates. Together they make over $50,000 a year. Mark comes from an affluent family and is accustomed to having this kind of money, but Ana's family is not as well off financially. Because of her father's temporary job loss while she was growing up and then his death when she was 16, Ana is much more concerned about financial security than is Mark.

Mark and Ana have always been very open with each other when it comes to money. They had many discussions on how they felt about money and what they wanted to accomplish financially even before they were married; however, in the past few months both of them have started to realize that if they really want to accomplish their financial goals they need to establish a financial plan. While watching one of the many New Year's Day college football games, they saw an advertisement for a financial planning firm. Later that evening Mark and Ana decided to get some professional financial planning advice.

After talking with several financial planners, Mark and Ana selected a professional, Jack Andrews, to work with. During their first conference with Mr. Andrews, they discussed many things that would influence their financial plan. It was reaffirmed that Ana is more security oriented and less willing to take risk than is Mark. Mark, on the other hand, really enjoys spending more than saving. Both of them agreed, however, that they would like to purchase a condominium just as soon as they can.

Mr. Andrews made a point to emphasis the sizable income they have for such a young couple. He also noted the fact that Ana currently earns more than Mark. Mark was clear that this disparity in their incomes was not a problem in their relationship for either him or Ana. Ana agreed, adding that, as with most pharmacists, she started out at a relatively high income but her income would peak by the time she was in her thirties unless she wanted to go into business for herself. At this time she does not plan on starting her own business. She is more interested in having a family and being able to spend time with Mark and the children (after they arrive).

Mark feels that his income will continue to increase more than Ana's. He is quite ambitious and is considering returning to college for his MBA after working a few years. If Mark is still with his current employer, First Federal Savings will pay for his continuing education.

In their conversation, Mark and Ana brought up the concern that they had not been able to save as much money since their marriage as they would have liked. Most of their current assets are from gifts given to Mark before they were married and to both of them as wedding presents. They are concerned that they will not be able to build up an adequate emergency fund and meet their other goals if they don't find some way to start saving more regularly. Ana also noted that they had started using credit more than she would like. Mark agreed, but he isn't as concerned about this as is Ana.

Mark wants to be sure that Ana would be able to live comfortably in case of his premature death. Ana feels she can get by on her salary, but Mr. Andrews assured both of them that life insurance evaluation would be included in their financial plan. He also pointed out that all types of personal insurance and their employer benefit plans would be evaluated.

At the end of their first conference, Mr. Andrews gave Mark and Ana some forms to fill out and mail to him before their next meeting. These forms are presented on the following pages. Read over the information Mark and Ana provided so that you can "get acquainted" with them. As you first read the case, you will probably not understand all the vocabulary or why certain information is even included on the forms. But remember, this is just Chapter One of the text. By the time you reach Chapter Sixteen, Mark and Ana, as well as their financial data, will be old friends, and you will feel very comfortable with what all of this means!

WILLIAMS

Background

PERSONAL FINANCIAL INFORMATION

CLIENT INFORMATION		SPOUSE INFORMATION	
Name	Mark Allen Williams	Name	Ana Marie Williams
Birth Date	6/7/65	Birth Date	7/28/66
Social Security No.	263-55-4312	Social Security No.	103-76-8667
Business Phone	512/555-2842	Business Phone	512/555-6287
Residence Address	12608 Hallow Trail		
City, State & Zip	Milford, USA 61703		
Residence Phone	512/555-8163		
Wedding Date	10/28/88		

CHILDREN

Name	Birth Date	Grade
None		

EDUCATION

	School	Degree	Year Received
Mark	State University	B.S. Economics	5/87
Ana	State University	B.S. Pharmacy	5/88

OCCUPATION

	Employer	Position	Years From	To
Mark	First Federal Savings	Loan Officer	6/87 — present	
Ana	Consumers' Drug Emporium	Staff Pharmacist	9/88 — present	

CONSULTANTS FOR FINANCIAL PLANNING

	Name	Address	Phone
Attorney	Stanley Madison	112 Park Tower Road Milford, USA 61703	555-4168
Accountant	None		
Bank Officer	Sandra Ortega	First Federal Savings Milford, USA 61704	555-2842
Insurance Agent	William Brown	3562 Main Street Milford, USA 61704	555-5221
Securities Broker	Robert McDonald	Riverview Towers, Suite 805 Milford, USA 61704	555-1151

LOCATION OF DOCUMENTS	
Wills/Trusts	None
Insurance: Life	Group policies through 1st Federal Savings & Consumer' Drug Emporium Information booklets on file at apartment
Health	Group policy through 1st Federal Savings & Consumers' Drug Emporium Information booklets on file at apartment
Disability	Group policy through Consumers' Drug Emporium Information booklet on file at apartment
Auto	File at apartment
Deeds: Title to cars	File at apartment
Birth/**Marriage**/Other Cert.	File at apartment

ASSETS - January 1, 1990

	Location	Balance	Rate of Interest	Maturity
Checking:	First Federal Savings (opened 10/15/88)	$1,500	4.5%	N/A
Money Market Accounts/Funds:	Milford National Bank (opened 6/5/85)	$3,050	6.0%	N/A
CDs	First Federal Savings	$1,000	7.0%	6/13/90
	First Federal Savings	$ 500	6.5%	6/5/90
Cash on Hand		$ 150		

Security Investments:

Number of Shares	Security	Cost or Basis			Current Value	
		Date Acquired	Per Share	Total	Per Share	Total
100	Apple Computer stock (Mark's property)	3/5/83	45-1/2	$4,550	38-3/4	$3,875
50	General Motors stock (wedding present)	10/28/88	80-1/2	$4,025	86-3/8	$4,319
192.75	Fidelity Puritan Fund	12/13/88	$12.97	$2,500	$12.71	$2,450

	Year	Make	Model	Cost	Current Value
Current Automobiles:	1986	Mazda	626	$10,300	$ 6,500
	1988	Ford	Bronco	$14,800	$11,000

		Market Value
Personal Property:	Clothing	$3,600
	Furniture and appliances	$2,050
	Stereo & T.V.	$2,400
	Jewelry	$1,500
	(Other) computer equipment	$4,000

LIABILITIES - January 1, 1990

To Whom Owed	Original Amount of Account	Property or Service Purchased	Interest Rate	Current Balance
First Federal Savings	$10,800	Ford Bronco	10.5%	$7,055
First Federal Savings	$ 4,500	Computer Equipment	13.0%	$1,698
Milford National Bank	$ 3,000	Education (Mark)	5.0%	$1,840
Milford National Bank	$ 6,500	Education (Ana)	5.0%	$5,226

	Payment Amount	How Often Paid	Total Number of Payments	Date of First Payment
First Federal Savings	$276.52	monthly	48	7/10/88
First Federal Savings	$151.62	monthly	36	2/07/88
Milford National Bank	$ 56.61	monthly	60	1/20/88
Milford National Bank	$122.66	monthly	60	1/20/89

CREDIT CARDS - all joint accounts

Company	Number	Annual Fee	Interest Rate	Maximum Line of Credit	Outstanding Balance
Texaco	33 231 17718 61991	$ 0	18%	—	$ 0
Visa	4310 4516 3100 3259	$ 0	21%	$2,500	$1,362
MasterCard	3529 0317 2432 0917	$35	16%	$3,000	$2,505
American Express	2782 163539 62005	$45	—	—	$ 0
Neiman-Marcus	1626 5512 7	$ 0	18%	—	$ 250
Sears	0 50186 96182 0	$ 0	18%	$1,500	$ 685
Dominique's Boutique	361 05891	$ 0	18%	—	$ 516

Company	Minimum Monthly Payment	Grace Period	Calculation Method
Texaco	10% of balance or $20, whichever is greater	yes	Av. Daily Bal.
Visa	5% of balance or $25, whichever is greater	no	Av. Daily Bal.
MasterCard	5% of balance or $20, whichever is greater	yes	Adjusted Bal.
American Express	Total balance	—	—
Neiman-Marcus	10% of balance or $50, whichever is greater	yes	Av. Daily Bal.
Sears	3% of balance or $15, whichever is greater	yes	Av. Daily Bal.
Dominique's Boutique	10% of balance or $50, whichever is greater	yes	Past Due Bal.

1989 INCOME

	Current Year
Salary (Mark's)	$24,500
Bonuses	
Salary (Ana's)	28,000
Bonuses (received in September)	1,500
Interest[1]	488
Dividends[2]	388
Capital gains distributions[3]	104
Sale of Securities	
Lexington Global Mutual Funds	900
(Capital loss of $265)	

[1]Checking ($68 paid monthly), money market accounts/funds ($317 paid monthly),
  CDs ($103 paid in June)

[2]Apple Computer ($40), General Motors ($250), Fidelity Puritan Fund ($98)
  All dividends paid quarterly in March, June, September, and December

[3]All distributions paid quarterly in March, June, September, and December

Income after tax deductions (take-home pay):

Mark	$1,515 per month
Ana	$1,733 per month

Background

WILLIAMS

1989 EXPENSES

	Cash Flow Monthly[1]	Cash Flow Annually
Medical/Dental Expenses (not covered by insurance)	$	$ 500
Rent	450	5,400
Charitable contributions	50	600
Food/Groceries, etc.	315	3,780
Food away from home	200	2,400
Clothing	200	2,400
Utilities	145	1,740
Telephone	35	420
Appliance and furniture purchases		1,200
Auto maintenance - gas, tires, etc.	175	2,100
Auto loan payments	277	3,324
Entertainment	150	1,800
Vacation (taken in August)		2,500
Gifts, birthdays, etc. ($325 in December, $25/month for all other months)		600
Disability insurance	20	240
Life insurance	10	120
Auto insurance (paid semiannually in June and January		985
Health and hygiene	65	780
Income taxes withheld	798	9,576
Social Security taxes withheld	345	4,055
Education loan payments	179	2,148
Computer loan payments	152	1,824
Revolving credit minimum payments	316	3,792

[1]Regular monthly expenditures

INSURANCE INFORMATION

LIFE INSURANCE

Insured:	Mark	Ana
Type of L.I.	Group Term	Group Term
Face Amount	$24,500 (1 times salary)	$50,000
Beneficiary	Ana	Mark
Owner	Mark	Ana
Annual Premium	Employer paid	$10/month (payroll deduction)

DISABILITY INSURANCE

Insured:		Ana
Policy number		Employer group policy
Definition of Disability		Own job for 2 years, any job educationally suited for after 2 years
Mo. Benefit		65% of gross monthly salary
Waiting Period	Sick	90 days
	Acc.	90 days
Benefit Period	Sick	to age 65
	Acc.	to age 65
Premiums		$20/month (payroll deduction)

WILLIAMS   *Background*

MEDICAL INSURANCE

INSURED

	Mark	Ana
Company	American Health & Life	US Health (HMO)
Policy Number	Group #063-111	Group #168521 AGC

HOSPITALIZATION

Room Rate	80% of semiprivate rate	100% of semiprivate rate
Number of Days	unlimited	unlimited

MAJOR MEDICAL

Maximum	$100,000/year	unlimited
Deductible	$500/person/year	$10 copayment per doctor's visit $ 5 copayment per perscription
% Participation	80/20	—
Cap on Participation	$1,500/year	—
Maternity	covered	covered
Dental	no	no
Annual Premiums	employer paid for employee	employer paid for employee

COMMENTS

Mark's Policy:	Spouse could be covered for $80/month. Coordination of benefits provision is included in policy.
Ana's Policy:	Must use HMO facilities and selected hospitals. Spouse could be covered for $100/month. Coordination of benefits provision is included in policy.

AUTO INSURANCE

	(1) 1986 Mazda 626	(2) 1988 Ford Bronco
Auto Covered	(1) 1986 Mazda 626	(2) 1988 Ford Bronco
Company	U.S. Casualty	U.S. Casualty
Policy Number	156-88876-A0B6	same
Liability	40,000 or 20/40/15	40,000 or 20/40/15
Medical Payments	$2,500/person	$2,500/person
Uninsured Motorists	40,000 or 20/40/15	40,000 or 20/40/15
Collision	(Actual Cash Value)	(Actual Cash Value)
Deductible	$200	$200
Comprehensive	(Actual Cash Value)	(Actual Cash Value)
Deductible	$ 50	$ 50
Annual Premium	$450	$535
Comments	Paid semiannually in June and January	same

RETIREMENT INFORMATION

Person Covered	Mark	Ana
Type of Pension Plan	Qualified, noncontributory, defined benefits	No pension plan offered
Vesting	5-year vesting, nothing currently vested	—
Beneficiary	Ana	—
Other Plans Available	401(k)—no employer contribution. 12% average return over the past 4 years	401(k)—employer contributes 50¢ for each $1.00 of employee contribution. 10% average return over the past 3 years
Vesting	Immediate	Immediate
Current Value	$0	$0

ESTATE PLANNING INFORMATION

Mark and Ana would each like to leave all of their assets to each other in case of death. They would also like to reduce estate transfer costs as much as possible.

Mark would like his secondary beneficiaries to be his mother and his father. Ana would like her mother to be her secondary beneficiary.

FINANCIAL GOALS

Short range (1 year):

> To start a regular savings plan, to have an adequate emergency fund, to buy a condominium.

Intermediate range (1–5 years):

> To pay off all revolving credit debt, to buy a house, to have a child. They plan to keep the condo as rental property.

Long term (over 5 years):

> To have a second child, to be able to retire when Mark is 60 and live at least as well as they are now.

What is your single most important financial objective at this time:

> To buy a condominium

FINANCIAL PRIORITIES

		Mark	Ana
a.	LIVING: paying monthly bills	1	1
b.	PLEASURE: spending money	2	5
c.	RETIREMENT: invest in future	8	6
d.	DISABILITY: protect against	7	3
e.	DEATH: take care of family	3	8
f.	REDUCE TAXES: spend to save	4	7
g.	INVESTING: accumulate assets	5	2
h.	CHILDREN: future needs	6	4

Prioritized with 1 being most important and 8 being least important

OTHER INFORMATION

1. Are you able to save regularly?   No

2. How much are you able to save annually? $500   Where?   Money market account

3. Do you invest regularly?   No   Current assets were gifts from parents

4. Do you feel that you are financially organized?   Yes — somewhat

5. Do you budget your money?   No written budget

6. If you were to die, could your spouse handle the finances?

    Mark: yes
    Ana: yes

7. How do you feel about saving for retirement?   It's important, but have other goals that are more important right now

8. If you had an extra $5,000 what would you do with it?

    Mark: buy a condominium
    Ana: pay off the revolving credit debt

9. How do you feel about taking investment risks?

    Mark: moderate risk taker
    Ana: risk adverse.

10. How is your health?

    Mark: Excellent
    Ana: Excellent

CHAPTER 2

Measuring Your Financial Standing

Financial Facts or Fantasies

Are the following statements financial facts (true) or fantasies (false)?

- Since financial statements are used to record actual results, they're really not that important in personal financial planning.
- You would list a leased car as an asset on your personal balance sheet.
- Only the principal portion of a loan should be recorded on the liability side of a balance sheet.
- Whereas the balance sheet summarizes your financial condition at a given point in time, the income and expenditures statement reports on your financial performance over time.
- Generating a cash surplus is desirable, since it adds to your net worth.
- When evaluating your income and expenditures statement, primary attention should be given to the top line: income received.

In order to develop sound financial plans and effectively manage your money, you must be able to keep track of your current financial condition and periodically assess the progress you're making toward your financial goals. Such are the functions of personal financial statements. There are two types of personal financial statements, the balance sheet and the income and expenditures statement, both of which are essential to developing and monitoring personal financial plans. In fact, trying to manage money without the aid of personal financial statements is a lot like being left aboard a drifting ship. Not knowing where you are within the ocean's vast expanse, you would first need to determine your location; then, with the assistance of certain navigational aids, you could plot your course to safety. Think of financial statements as navigational aids: You use them to gauge your financial position at various points in time and to judge the progress you're making toward your financial goals. Understanding how to prepare and interpret personal financial statements is one of the cornerstones of personal financial planning. Without some standards by which to measure your financial condition, establishing financial goals and evaluating your progress toward those goals is difficult, if not impossible.

THE ROLE OF FINANCIAL STATEMENTS IN FINANCIAL PLANNING

Personal financial statements contain important information used in the financial planning process. What kind of personal financial information would you need in order to assess your financial position at various points in time and monitor the progress you're making toward your financial goals? Try to answer this question before reading on.

As we saw in Chapter 1, personal financial planning involves the establishment of an integrated set of financial plans and the development of corresponding financial strategies for putting them into action. Clearly, in order to set realistic plans and strategies, we must know where we stand financially; then, once the plans and strategies are in place, we need a system for monitoring our progress. Personal financial statements can help in both stages by defining your current financial condition and enabling you to track changes in your financial position over time.

To begin with, the *balance sheet* provides a statement of your financial condition by describing the assets you hold, debts you owe, and your net worth at a given point in time. Then it helps you keep track of the progress you're making toward your goals, in building up your assets and/or reducing your debt. Thus, it is indispensable in setting, monitoring, and revising financial plans. Also, by revealing the kinds of changes that are taking place in your financial position, it helps you know when it is time to alter your financial plans.

In contrast, the *income and expenditures statement* provides a measure of financial performance over time; it keeps track of income earned, as well as expenditures made, over a given period of time (usually a year). A key ingredient in financial planning is gaining budgetary control over expenses and purchases. Without such control, you could well find yourself without the funds necessary for carrying out your financial plans. A statement of income and expenditures is helpful in this regard as it provides a way to check actual expenses and purchases against the amounts budgeted. Corrective action is typically taken when discrepancies exist between the actual and budgeted amounts.

In essence, the primary function of financial statements is to summarize your financial position as it *actually* exists and report on various financial transactions that have *really* occurred. Financial plans, in contrast, deal with mapping out the *future* and, at first glance, may appear to be incompatible with financial statements because of their different time references. Yet the whole planning system would indeed collapse without statements to provide feedback on your financial progress. Somewhere along the line, you must look at how actual results are stacking up against your plans. It is appropriate, therefore, to think of financial statements as *planning tools* that provide an up-to-date evaluation of your financial well-being, help you identify potential financial problems, and in general to make better-informed financial decisions. The following sections take a detailed look at the basic personal financial statements, starting with the balance sheet.

Since financial statements are used to record actual results, they're really not that important in personal financial planning. **Fantasy:** Personal financial statements let you know where you stand financially. As such, they not only help you to set up realistic financial plans and strategies but also provide a system for monitoring the amount of progress you're making toward the financial goals you've set.

THE BALANCE SHEET: A STATEMENT OF YOUR FINANCIAL CONDITION

A balance sheet reports the things you own on the one hand relative to the money you owe and your financial worth on the other. What do you currently own and owe? List and evaluate all items you own and owe, noting their current dollar value, before reading on.

The **balance sheet**—or *statement of financial position*—summarizes a person's (or family's) financial condition at a certain point in time. Think of a

EXHIBIT 2.1

Commonly Held Personal Assets

The specific types and amounts of personal assets held will vary from one person or family to another. Most households will likely hold some liquid assets as well as real and personal property and possibly even some investments.

Liquid Assets	**Investments**
Cash:	Stocks and bonds:
On hand	Common stock
In checking accounts	Preferred stock
Savings accounts:	Corporate bonds
At banks, S&L, etc.	Government and municipal bonds
At other thrift institutions	Certificates of deposit
Money market funds and deposits	Investment companies:
	Closed-end funds
Real Property	Mutual funds
	Real estate
Housing	Business ownership
Automobiles	Cash value of life insurance
Recreational equipment	Cash value of pensions
	Other investment vehicles:
Personal Property	Commodities and financial futures
	Options
Furniture	Precious minerals
Stereos, TVs, and appliances	Collectibles
Clothing	Annuities and limited partnerships
Jewelry	
Artworks	

balance sheet as a snapshot taken of a person's financial position on one day out of the year; technically, you could have a (slightly) different balance sheet each day of the year. A balance sheet can be viewed as a summary of one's assets balanced against one's debt and net worth positions. Every balance sheet must "balance" such that total assets equal total liabilities and net worth.

Assets: The Things You Own

Assets are the items you own. They are mostly tangible, although in certain instances they may also be intangible. An item is classified as an asset regardless of whether it was purchased for cash or financed with debt. In other words, even if an asset has not been fully paid for, it is considered owned by the individual and should be listed on the balance sheet. An item that is leased, in contrast, is not shown as an asset, since it is actually owned by someone else.

Assets can be grouped in a variety of ways. One useful procedure is to group them on the basis of their underlying characteristics and uses, as shown in Exhibit 2.1. This results in four broad categories: liquid assets, real property, personal property, and investments. **Liquid assets** are the cash and near-cash holdings of individuals that are used to meet living expenses, make purchases, and pay bills and loans. **Real property** is represented by tangible assets that generally have fairly long life spans and are held to provide basic shelter, transportation, and recreation; these assets also carry relatively

balance sheet
A key financial statement that summarizes a person's assets, liabilities, and net worth as measured at a specified point in time.

assets
Items that one owns.

liquid assets
Assets that are held in the form of cash or can be readily converted to cash with minimal or no loss in value; used to meet everyday living expenses.

real property
Tangible assets that are held to fill basic shelter, transportation, and recreation needs; usually have relatively long lives and high costs.

high price tags. **Personal property** is also tangible but generally is less costly than real property; such assets provide the general creature comforts of life. Finally, **investments** include those (mostly intangible) assets that are acquired in order to earn a return. These assets may consist of either real property or financial assets; they are usually held for future rather than current consumption.

Regardless of their type, all assets are recorded on the balance sheet at their current **fair market value,** which may differ considerably from their original purchase price. Fair market value is either the actual value of the asset (such as money in a checking account) or the price that the asset can reasonably be expected to sell for in the open market (like a used car or home).

You would list a leased car as an asset on your personal balance sheet. **Fantasy:** You are only "using" the leased car; you do not own it. Accordingly, it should not be included as an asset on the balance sheet.

Liquid Assets.   Liquid assets are those financial assets that are held in the form of cash or can readily be converted to cash with little or no loss in value. These assets are held to meet the everyday needs of life. Cash can be held either in the form of cash on hand or in a *demand deposit* (checking account). Savings are also part of one's liquid assets and can be held in such financial instruments as *time deposits* (savings accounts), money market deposit accounts, or money market mutual funds.

Real and Personal Property.   Real and personal property are tangible assets that can be lived in, sat on, driven, or worn. They are held for use in our everyday lives and, in essence, provide support for our daily activities. Examples of real and personal property include homes, cars, recreational vehicles, second homes (mountain cabins or lakeside cottages), tractors, lawn mowers and other yard equipment, tools, furniture and appliances, VCRs and home entertainment centers, clothing and jewelry, and artworks. Some families spend a lot of money on such things; others get by with far less. Except for real estate, some kinds of (older) cars, and perhaps jewelry and artworks, most types of real and personal property rapidly decline in value shortly after being put into use; in fact, the resale value of some of these assets, such as clothing and furniture,

may quickly drop to only a small fraction of their original cost.

Investments.   Investments are assets that are acquired in order to earn a return rather than provide a service. These assets, which typically consist largely of intangible *financial assets* (stocks, bonds, and other types of securities), tend to be held for the anticipated future benefit they offer. Popular investment assets include common and preferred stocks and corporate, government, and municipal bonds. Shares in investment companies—especially mutual funds—and real estate are also popular. Business ownership, the cash values of life insurance and pensions, and other investment vehicles, such as commodities and financial futures, and options, represent still other forms of investment assets. Investment assets tend to be acquired in order to achieve long-run personal financial goals. They vary in liquidity from high (stocks and bonds) to low (real estate and business ownership investments).

Liabilities: The Money You Owe

Liabilities represent an individual's or family's debts. They could result from department store charges, bank credit card charges, installment loans, or mortgages on housing and other real estate. A given liability, regardless of its source, is something that is owed and must be repaid in the future. Some liabilities are due immediately—as soon as you receive the statement or bill—while others are more long term and may be paid off over a period of months or years. Exhibit 2.2 presents a listing of some common types of liabilities that may appear on a personal balance sheet. The level and status of an individual's liabilities are given careful consideration by potential lenders; very high levels of debt and overdue debts are both viewed with a great deal of disfavor.

Unpaid bills include all items that must be paid in full upon receipt of the bill or statement. In practice, most people do not pay these bills immediately but wait until about one to three weeks after receipt. Unpaid bills normally represent short-term obligations resulting from charges for the purchase of consumable goods and services. Utility bills, rent, insurance premiums, taxes, medical bills, repair bills, and all similar debts fall into this category.

EXHIBIT 2.2
Common Types of Personal Liabilities

The type of debt you have can include everything from unpaid utility bills and credit card charges to consumer loans and mortgages. Regardless of the type, they all have one thing in common: They are obligations that must be paid off in the future.

Unpaid Bills	**Consumer Installment Loans**
Utility bills	Automobiles
Rent	Appliances and furniture
Insurance premiums	Home improvements
Taxes	Other
Medical/dental bills	
Repair bills	**Mortgage Loans**
Other bills	Home (primary residence)
	Other residences (e.g., second
Revolving Credit	home)
Bank credit cards	Real estate investments
Department store credit cards	
Travel and entertainment cards	**Other loans**
Gas and other credit cards	Single-payment bank loans
Bank lines of credit	Educational loans
	Margin loans (on securities)
	Other

You must show all outstanding charges—even if you have not received the bill—as unpaid bills on the balance sheet. In other words, a charge incurred prior to the balance sheet statement date that *remains unpaid* should be included as a liability regardless of whether a bill for it has been received.

Another source of debt that is similar in some respects to unpaid bills is revolving credit. Basically **revolving credit** involves the use of preestablished credit lines to make purchases of various types of goods and services. For most people, such credit means the use of "plastic"—that is, a credit card. The balances on some credit cards (like bank and department store credit cards) can be paid off over time with small "minimum payments"; others, like gas or most travel and entertainment cards (American Express, for example), require payment in full upon receipt of the monthly statement. Another type of revolving credit is the line of credit offered by most banks and S&Ls. A *line of credit* lets you do anything a credit card does, except that you write a check rather than use your card. Depending on the type of line you have, you can write your check against either your regular checking account or a special credit line set up at your bank or financial institution.

Consumer installment loans include all debts (other than mortgages) for which a series of pay-

personal property
Tangible assets that are held to provide the general comforts of life; includes things like clothing, house furnishings, and jewelry.

investments
Assets like stocks, bonds, and mutual funds that are acquired for the purpose of earning a return rather than providing a service.

fair market value
The price that an asset can reasonably be expected to sell for in the open market.

liabilities
Debts, such as credit card charges, installment loan balances, and real estate mortgages.

unpaid bills
Items that must be paid in full upon receipt of the bill or statement.

revolving credit
A preestablished credit line against which a person may borrow to purchase various types of goods and services.

consumer installment loan
A loan that is repaid in a series of fixed, scheduled payments.

EXHIBIT 2.3

The Weavers' Balance Sheet

A balance sheet is set up to show what you own on one side (your assets) and how you paid for them on the other (debt or equity).

<table>
<tr>
<td colspan="8" align="center">**BALANCE SHEET**</td>
</tr>
<tr>
<td colspan="4">Name(s) *Fred & Denise Weaver*</td>
<td colspan="4">Dated *December 31, 1989*</td>
</tr>
<tr>
<td colspan="4" align="center">**ASSETS**</td>
<td colspan="4" align="center">**LIABILITIES AND NET WORTH**</td>
</tr>
<tr>
<td rowspan="4">Liquid Assets</td>
<td>Cash on hand</td>
<td>$</td>
<td>40</td>
<td rowspan="7">Unpaid Bills</td>
<td>Utilities</td>
<td>$</td>
<td>60</td>
</tr>
<tr>
<td>In checking</td>
<td></td>
<td>220</td>
<td>Rent</td>
<td></td>
<td></td>
</tr>
<tr>
<td>Savings accounts</td>
<td></td>
<td>650</td>
<td>Insurance premiums</td>
<td></td>
<td></td>
</tr>
<tr>
<td>Money market</td>
<td></td>
<td>800</td>
<td>Taxes</td>
<td></td>
<td>80</td>
</tr>
<tr>
<td rowspan="5">Real Property</td>
<td>funds and deposits</td>
<td></td>
<td></td>
<td>Medical/dental bills</td>
<td></td>
<td></td>
</tr>
<tr>
<td>Primary residence</td>
<td></td>
<td>60,000</td>
<td>Repair bills</td>
<td></td>
<td>30</td>
</tr>
<tr>
<td>Second home</td>
<td></td>
<td></td>
<td>Other bills</td>
<td></td>
<td></td>
</tr>
<tr>
<td>Car(s): '84 *Cutlass*</td>
<td></td>
<td>4,000</td>
<td rowspan="5">Revolving Credit</td>
<td>Bank credit cards</td>
<td></td>
<td>40</td>
</tr>
<tr>
<td>Car(s): '80 VW</td>
<td></td>
<td>1,300</td>
<td>Dept. store credit cards</td>
<td></td>
<td>90</td>
</tr>
<tr>
<td>Recreation Equipment</td>
<td></td>
<td>400</td>
<td>Travel & entertnmnt. cards</td>
<td></td>
<td></td>
</tr>
<tr>
<td>Other</td>
<td></td>
<td></td>
<td>Gas and other credit cards</td>
<td></td>
<td></td>
</tr>
<tr>
<td rowspan="5">Personal Property</td>
<td>Furniture and appliances</td>
<td></td>
<td>1,400</td>
<td>Bank lines of credit</td>
<td></td>
<td></td>
</tr>
<tr>
<td>Stereos, TVs, etc.</td>
<td></td>
<td>600</td>
<td rowspan="4">Consumer Installment Loans</td>
<td>Auto loans</td>
<td></td>
<td>1,500</td>
</tr>
<tr>
<td>Clothing</td>
<td></td>
<td>800</td>
<td>Appliance/furniture</td>
<td></td>
<td>400</td>
</tr>
<tr>
<td>Jewelry</td>
<td></td>
<td>1,000</td>
<td>Home improvements</td>
<td></td>
<td></td>
</tr>
<tr>
<td>Other</td>
<td></td>
<td></td>
<td>Others</td>
<td></td>
<td></td>
</tr>
<tr>
<td rowspan="10">Investments</td>
<td>Stocks</td>
<td></td>
<td>840</td>
<td rowspan="4">Mortgage Loans</td>
<td>Primary residence</td>
<td></td>
<td>55,200</td>
</tr>
<tr>
<td rowspan="2">Bonds *Corp.*</td>
<td></td>
<td rowspan="2">1,000</td>
<td>Second home</td>
<td></td>
<td></td>
</tr>
<tr>
<td>Real estate investments</td>
<td></td>
<td></td>
</tr>
<tr>
<td>*Gov.*</td>
<td></td>
<td>450</td>
<td>Others</td>
<td></td>
<td></td>
</tr>
<tr>
<td>Certificates of Deposit</td>
<td></td>
<td></td>
<td rowspan="3">Other Loans</td>
<td>Single-payment loans</td>
<td></td>
<td></td>
</tr>
<tr>
<td>Mutual funds</td>
<td></td>
<td></td>
<td>Education loans</td>
<td></td>
<td></td>
</tr>
<tr>
<td>Real estate</td>
<td></td>
<td></td>
<td>Other: from parents</td>
<td></td>
<td>3,600</td>
</tr>
<tr>
<td>Other *Stamps*</td>
<td></td>
<td>2,500</td>
<td>**(II) Total Liabilities**</td>
<td>$</td>
<td>61,000</td>
</tr>
<tr>
<td></td>
<td></td>
<td></td>
<td>**Net Worth [(I) – (II)]**</td>
<td>$</td>
<td>15,000</td>
</tr>
<tr>
<td></td>
<td></td>
<td></td>
<td></td>
<td></td>
<td></td>
</tr>
<tr>
<td colspan="2" align="right">**(I) Total Assets**</td>
<td>$</td>
<td>76,000</td>
<td colspan="2" align="right">**Total Liabilities and Net Worth**</td>
<td>$</td>
<td>76,000</td>
</tr>
</table>

ments are required over a specified period of time—usually six months to five years or more. Installment loans are generally used to finance such purchases as automobiles, appliances, furniture, and boats. *Mortgage loans* are associated with housing or other real estate purchases and normally have lives of 15 years or more. They most commonly result from the purchase of a home but sometimes from real estate investments such as apartments or office buildings. Mortgage loans are normally paid on an installment basis.

Other types of loans must be shown on the balance sheet as well. These may be bank loans requiring single payments, educational loans, margin loans (to purchase stocks or bonds), or other specialized loans. Regardless of the type of loan, *only the latest outstanding loan balance should be shown as a liability on the balance sheet,* since at any given point in time it is the *latest* balance still due—not the initial loan balance—that matters. Another important and closely related point is that *only the principal portion of a loan or mortgage* should be listed as a liability on the balance sheet; in other words, you should not include the interest portion of your payments as part of your balance sheet debt. The principal actually defines the amount of debt you owe at a given point in time and does not include any future interest payments.

Only the principal portion of a loan should be recorded on the liability side of a balance sheet. **Fact:** The principal portion of a loan represents the unpaid balance and is the amount of money you owe; interest, in contrast, is a charge that will be levied over time for the use of the money.

Net Worth: A Measure of Your Financial Worth

Net worth is the amount of actual wealth or **equity** an individual or family has in owned assets. It can be viewed as the amount of money that would remain after selling all owned assets at their estimated fair market values and paying off all liabilities. The accounting relationship between assets, liabilities, and net worth is called the *balance sheet equation:*

Total assets − Total Liabilities = Net worth.

Once the fair market value of assets and the level of liabilities have been established, net worth is easily calculated by subtracting total liabilities from total assets. If net worth is less than zero, the family is technically insolvent. While this form of **insolvency** does not mean that the family will end up in bankruptcy proceedings, it does reflect the absence of adequate financial planning. In the long-run financial planning process, the level of net worth is important. Once a family has established a goal of accumulating a certain level or type of wealth, progress toward that goal is best analyzed by monitoring net worth. The *Money in Action* box explains how achieving your net worth and other financial goals is likely to enhance your happiness as well as your wealth.

Balance Sheet Format

The balance sheet is prepared on the date that the various asset, liability, and net worth figures are measured. As we'll see in Exhibit 2.3 (on facing-page), assets are listed on the left side of the balance sheet and liabilities on the right. The net worth entry is shown on the right side of the statement just below the liabilities. The subheadings included in Exhibits 2.1 and 2.2 may be used to break the statement into various categories. Often the totals for these categories are shown as subtotals in the statement. Regardless of how the various assets and liabilities are categorized, the statement should *balance:* Total assets should equal the sum of total liabilities and net worth, as shown in the balance sheet equation.

---

net worth
An individual's or family's actual wealth; determined by subtracting total liabilities from total assets.

equity
The actual ownership interest in a specific asset or group of assets.

insolvency
The financial state in which net worth is less than zero.

MONEY IN ACTION

Can Money Really Make You Happy?

How happy would you say you are these days? Your answer is likely to depend in part on your income. A recent study supported by *Everybody's Money* (EM) and its publisher, the Credit Union National Association, shows greater happiness is related to higher income.

HAPPINESS IN GENERAL

Since World War II several studies have shown that the "distribution of happiness" has remained stable. The results of the EM study back up earlier ones—22 percent say they are very happy, 65 percent say they are pretty happy, and 13 percent say they are not too happy.

If reported happiness remains stable in spite of considerable political, social, and economic change, then what does affect happiness? People most often cite economic, family, and health concerns. These everyday, personal matters figure much more prominently than do social and political issues.

Briefly, these findings emerge:

- There is an increase in unhappiness with age.
- Higher levels of education are associated with greater happiness.
- The relationship between income and happiness is especially strong; greater happiness is related to higher income.

This last point is a potentially provocative one. Some may think it means money does buy happiness. Others interpret it to mean that having money reduces a potential source of worry. But not all rich people are happy, nor are the less affluent all unhappy.

HAPPINESS AND MONEY

The EM study tried to shed some light on this issue with this summary.

1. Results clearly support the relationship between higher income and greater personal happiness. Happiness varied significantly by household income.
2. Respondents' answers provided the basis for assessing what stress they experience managing money. This stress is connected less with major economic problems than with everyday hassles. The relationship between happiness and financial stress is even stronger than that between happiness and income.
3. Just as important as an individual's income is the subjective assessment that he or she makes of that in-

A Balance Sheet for Fred and Denise Weaver

The relationship between assets, liabilities, and net worth, and the general format of the balance sheet, are perhaps best illustrated with an example. Toward that end, we will now examine the financial statements of Fred and Denise Weaver, a young couple whose balance sheet as of December 31, 1989, appears in Exhibit 2.3.

Fred and Denise were married three years ago and currently have no children. Fred is 26 years old and has just completed his third year as a marketing representative for a large soap manufacturer. He is quite satisfied with his job and expects to continue his career in the sales and marketing area. Fred's boss recently assured him that the company is quite pleased with his performance and has "big plans" for him. Denise is 24 and holds a bachelor's degree in primary education. After teaching for one year,

come. One standard is the income of friends and associates. The second is past income levels. This year's $25,000 will likely seem adequate if you made $20,000 last year, less adequate if you made $30,000.

4. Regardless of income, most people experience financial pressures and strains. Yet not all experience high or unmanageable levels of stress. And some people are better at coping than others.

BECOME HAPPIER

The study identifies the coping strategies people develop in managing their money, and include:

▪ *Economizing.* Though most of us resolve to do a better job of "cutting back," economizing is more preached than practiced. Many people don't believe substantial sums can be saved by scaling down buying plans, replacing them with cheaper alternatives, or postponing until more pressing needs are met. But others raise budget trimming to an art form.

▪ *Expanding income.* Some people are adept at finding and exploiting opportunities to make extra money, which can augment discretionary income and be an asset when faced with unanticipated expenses. But those extra funds can trap people into becoming dependent upon them to meet fixed expenses.

▪ *Increasing household production.* A prudent decision to substitute your own time for money can bring impressive returns both materially and psychologically. That means "do it yourself" whenever you have the time and ability.

▪ *Managing money efficiently.* When spending, investing, and borrowing, some people get "more for their money." These people both seek out lower prices and rates and also learn about quality and value; they don't blindly seek the lowest price in all choices. Many people pursue several coping strategies. An observation to be made is that while money influences our happiness, what we do with it is also important.

In conclusion, those who manage their money are usually happier than those who let their money manage them.

Source: Adapted from Jim Fisher, "Can Money Really Make You Happy?" *Financial Focus,* November 1988, page 8.

---

she realized that a career in education was not for her, so she went back to school full-time and got a master's degree in business administration (M.B.A.). She currently works as a graduate assistant at the university and has a job lined up with a local advertising firm after she graduates this spring. The Weavers live in their own condominium, which they purchased in October 1988. Fred and Denise love to travel; snow skiing is one of their favorite pastimes. They plan to have children in a few years but for now want to devote their efforts toward developing some degree of financial stability and independence.

The Weavers' Assets. Given their ages, the Weavers' asset position looks quite good. Their dominant asset is their condo, which they purchased a year ago. Another item that strengthens their asset position is a stamp collection, which was a wedding gift from Fred's grandparents. In addition, they have a total of $2,290 spread among investments in common stock, corporate bonds, and government securities. The Weavers' cash on hand of $260 and savings of $1,450 are liquid assets that should allow them to meet their bill payments and cover small, unexpected expenditures. But the real strength of their financial position cannot be evaluated without examining their debts, since these may be high as a result of their borrowing to purchase certain of their assets, especially their home.

The Weavers' Liabilities. Looking at the Weavers' liabilities, we can see that their primary liability is the $55,200 mortgage on their condo. As might be expected, since they purchased their condo just over a year ago, the mortgage is still quite large relative to the condo's market value of $60,000. The Weavers' *equity,* or actual ownership interest in the condo, is approximately $4,800 ($60,000 market value minus the $55,200 outstanding mortgage loan). Their outstanding bills total only $300. It is likely that these bills must be paid, at least partially, within the next month, since monthly billing cycles are most common. Other debts shown on the balance sheet include a $1,500 balance on an installment loan used to purchase one of their cars, a $400 balance on an installment loan used to purchase furniture, and a $3,600 balance on a personal loan from their parents that was used to partly finance the down payment on their house. Contrasting the Weavers' total liabilities of $61,000 to their total assets of $76,000 provides a more realistic view of their present wealth position.

The Weavers' Net Worth. The Weavers' balance sheet in Exhibit 2.3 shows their net worth as $15,000. Actually, considering their ages, Fred and Denise are not doing too badly! Their net worth can be explained in large part by the $7,500 inheritance they received some 18 months ago. The $15,000 net worth figure is the amount Fred and Denise would have if they sold their assets for the $76,000 (at which they are valued on the balance sheet) and used the proceeds to repay their debts of $61,000. Of course, they are not expected to take such actions, but by calculating their net worth at specified points in time, they can measure the results of their financial plans and decision on their

wealth position. As you might expect, a large or increasing wealth position is preferred to a low or declining one.

THE INCOME AND EXPENDITURES STATEMENT: A MEASURE OF YOUR FINANCIAL PERFORMANCE ⬛

> An income and expenditures statement provides a summary of the income you received and the money you spent over a given period of time, usually one year. Do you know how much you received and spent during the last year? Before reading on, make a list of each item and amount of your income and expenditures during the most recent year.

While the balance sheet describes a person's or family's financial position at a given point in time, the **income and expenditures statement** captures the various financial activities that have occurred over time—normally over the course of a year, although it technically can cover any time period (monthly, quarterly, and so on). Think of this statement as a motion picture that not only shows actual results over time but allows for their comparison to budgeted financial goals as well. Equally important, the statement evaluates the amount of saving and investing that has taken place during the time period covered.

The income and expenditures statement is made up of three major parts: *income, expenditures,* and *cash surpluses (or deficits);* as we will see a bit later, a cash surplus (or deficit) is merely the difference between income and expenditures. The statement is prepared on a **cash basis,** which means that *the only transactions recorded are those involving actual cash receipts or actual cash outlays.* In effect, the statement describes a person's or family's financial activities in terms of the cash flow involved. (As a point of clarification, the term *cash* is used in this case to include not only coin and currency but also checks drawn against demand deposits and certain types of savings accounts.)

EXHIBIT 2.4

Sources of Income

For most gainfully employed people, the vast majority of total income is made up of wages and salaries.

Wages and salaries
Bonuses and commissions
Pensions and annuities
Investment income:
    Interest received
    Dividends received
    Proceeds from sale of securities
    Rents received from leased assets
Other income:
    Proceeds from sale of assets
    Tax refunds
    Miscellaneous

Whereas the balance sheet summarizes your financial condition at a given point in time, the income and expenditures statement reports on your financial performance over time. **Fact:** A balance sheet is like a photograph of your financial condition (covering just one day out of the year), while an income and expenditures statement is like a motion picture (covering the full year or some other time period).

Income: The Amount of Cash In

Items shown as **income** on the income and expenditures statement include earnings received as wages, salaries, bonuses, and commissions; interest and dividends received from savings and investments; and proceeds from the sale of assets, such as stocks and bonds or a car. Other income items include rent received from leased assets, tax refunds, pension or annuity income, and other miscellaneous types of income. As noted above, only income that has actually been received should be shown. This approach forces an honest representation of the way things were during the year, not the way they were expected to be. Note also that the proper figure to use is *gross* wages, salaries, and commissions, which constitute the amount of income you receive from your employer *before* taxes and other payroll deductions are taken out; you should not use *take-home* pay, since that will understate your income by the amount of these deductions. Common sources of income, which should be shown on the income and expenditures statement, are listed in Exhibit 2.4.

Expenditures: The Amount of Cash Out

Items shown as **expenditures** on the income and expenditures statement represent money used for outlays. Due to the many different kinds of expenditures, it is perhaps easiest to categorize them by the types of benefits they provide, as shown in Exhibit 2.5. A quick review of the exhibit reveals that expenditures consist of several different types of transactions: (1) *living expenses* (such as food, medical expenses, repairs, insurance, and utilities), (2) *purchases of various kinds of assets* (like cars, stereos, furniture, appliances, and clothing), (3) *tax payments,* and (4) *debt payments* (on mort-

income and expenditures statement
A key financial statement that presents one's income, expenditures, and cash surpluses or deficits over a designated time period.

cash basis
A method of preparing financial statements in which only cash income and cash expenditure items are recorded.

income
Earnings received as wages, salaries, bonuses, and commissions, interest and dividends received from savings and investments, and proceeds from the sale of assets.

expenditures
Money spent on living expenses, to purchase assets, pay taxes, and/or repay debt.

EXHIBIT 2.5

Common Types of Household Expenditures

The percentages shown represent the approximate proportion of *before-tax* income spent by the average American family on each major category.

Housing (18%)
Mortgage payments
Rent
Repairs and additions
Household services

Utilities (7%)
Gas and electric
Garbage service
Telephone
Water
Cable TV

Food (19%)
Groceries
Dining out

Automobile (10%)
Purchase or loan payments
Gas and oil
License fees
Repairs
Lease payments

Medical (5%)
Doctor bills
Dental bills
Hospital bills
Drugs and medicine

Clothing and Shoes (6%)

Insurance (2%)
Life
Health
Homeowner's
Auto

Taxes (9%)
Income
Property

Appliances, Furniture, or Other Assets (5%)
Purchases
Installment payments
Repairs and maintenance
Home accessories

Health and Hygiene (1%)
Laundry and dry cleaning
Cosmetics
Hairdresser

Recreation, Entertainment, and Vacation (5%)
Admissions
Alcoholic beverages
Hobby supplies
Film and developing
Cigarettes and tobacco
Sports equipment
Records and tapes
Vacation and travel

Other Items (13%)
Postage and stationery
Personal allowance
Books and magazines
Tuition
Legal fees
Interest expenses
Dues and club memberships
Gifts
Church and charity
Pets
Child care
Miscellaneous unclassified
    expenditures

Source: U.S. Bureau of the Census, *Statistical Abstract of the United States: 1988* (108th edition) Washington, D.C., 1987, Table No. 688, p. 421.

gages, installment loans, credit cards, and so on). Thus, expenditures involve the outflow of cash for living expenses, to purchase or acquire assets, pay taxes, and/or reduce debt. Some are **fixed expenditures** to the extent that they involve equal payments each period (typically each month)—examples include mortgage and installment loan payments, insurance premiums, professional or union dues, and possibly religious or charitable contributions. Others (such as on food, clothing, and en-

tertainment) are **variable expenditures**, since their amounts are always changing.

Just as only the amounts of cash actually received are shown as income, only the amounts of money actually paid out in cash are listed as expenditures. If an item—particularly an asset—is acquired through borrowing, only the net or actual dollar amount of money paid out (that is, purchase price minus amount borrowed) is included as an expenditure. In effect, the financed portion of such an outlay is not viewed as an expenditure until debt payments are actually made. Instead, credit purchases of this type are shown as an asset and corresponding liability *on the balance sheet.* Payments against these loans are shown on the income and expenditures statement in the year they are actually made; in other words, included as part of the cash expenditures are actual *payments* against loans obtained during the period but not the amounts of the loans themselves. Finally, when developing your list of expenditures for the year, remember to include the amount of income and social security taxes withheld from your paycheck as well as any other payroll deductions taken out, such as for health and life insurance, savings plans, retirement and pension contributions, and professional/union dues. These represent personal expenditures even if they do not involve the *direct* payment of cash.

Working Up the Figures. Working up the figures for an income and expenditures statement is really not as difficult as it may appear. If you are like most people, you probably have a very good idea of how much you make at work; but if you are unsure, you can always look at your check stubs for the amount of your *gross* pay. Regardless of the procedure you use, you should not overlook bonuses, commission checks, and overtime pay. You can look to bank statements for interest earned on savings accounts and statements from brokerage houses, mutual funds, and so on for information on securities bought and sold, dividends received, and other investment matters. You should also keep a running list of other income sources such as rents, tax refunds, and sales of assets.

On the expenditures side, it is probably best to break out the fixed and variable expenses. Information on monthly house (or rent) payments, loan payments, and other fixed payments (such as for insurance premiums and cable TV) is readily available from either the payment book often provided or your checkbook (or, in the case of payroll deductions, your check stubs). (Note: Be careful with so-called *adjustable-rate loans,* since the amount of monthly loan payments will change along with changes in the interest rates.) Variable expenses are undoubtedly the toughest things to keep track of! Since trying to keep receipts for each and every transaction usually does not work too well, most people tend to rely on their check registers for

information on these items. In many cases, the figures that show up on the income and expenditures statement amount to little more than educated "guesstimates" of the amount of money spent on the various categories of expenses, purchases, credit card payments, and the like. While some of this is obviously necessary and appropriate, too much guesswork can lead to unreliable numbers that will greatly reduce the usefulness of these statements. Fortunately, there are a number of good computer software packages available that take much of the work out of financial reporting. Such programs are designed specifically for personal computers and will print out not only personalized income and expenditure statements but also up-to-date balance sheets.

Cash Surplus (or Deficit)

The third component of the income and expenditures statement captures the net result of the period's financial activities. The cash surplus (or deficit) for the period is obtained by subtracting total expenditures from total income and allows you to determine at a glance how you did financially over the period. The figure can be zero, positive, or negative. A value of zero indicates that expenditures were exactly equal to income for the period. A positive figure indicates that the expenditures were less than income and therefore a **cash surplus** resulted. A negative value indicates that the period's expenditures exceeded income, thereby resulting in a **cash deficit.**

---

fixed expenditures
Expenditures involving equal payments each period (typically each month).

variable expenditures
Expenditures that involve payments of varying amounts from one time period to the next.

cash surplus
An excess amount of income over expenditures, resulting in increased net worth.

cash deficit
An excess amount of expenditures over income, resulting in insufficient funds that must be made up either by reducing savings or investments or through borrowing.

EXHIBIT 2.6

Impact of a Cash Surplus on the Balance Sheet

A cash surplus on the income and expenditures statement will lead to an increase in net worth on the balance sheet and can be used to either acquire assets or reduce debts.

Balance Sheet A

December 31, 1988

Assets		Liabilities and Net Worth	
Total assets	$30,000	Total liabilities	$22,000
Total	$30,000	Net worth	8,000
		Total	$30,000

Balance Sheet B

December 31, 1989 ($1,500 Surplus Used to Increase Assets)

Assets		Liabilities and Net Worth	
Total assets	$31,500	Total liabilities	$22,000
Total	$31,500	Net worth	9,500
		Total	$31,500

Balance Sheet C

December 31, 1989 ($1,500 Surplus Used to Repay Debts [Decrease Liabilities])

Assets		Liabilities and Net Worth	
Total assets	$30,000	Total liabilities	$20,500
Total	$30,000	Net worth	9,500
		Total	$30,000

When a cash surplus exists, it can be used for savings or investment purposes, to acquire assets, or reduce (that is, make payments on) debt. Additions to savings or investments (it is hoped) will result in increased future income; likewise, payments on debt will have a favorable effect on cash flow by reducing future expenditures. In contrast, when a cash deficit occurs, the shortfall must be covered by either drawing your savings or investments down or borrowing. Either strategy will have undesirable effects on your financial future. One final point: The cash surplus (or deficit) figure does not necessarily indicate that funds are simply lying around waiting to be used. Because the income and expenditures statement reflects what has actually occurred, the disposition of the surplus (or deficit) is reflected in the asset, liability, and net worth accounts on the balance sheet. For example, if the surplus were used to make investments, it would be represented by an increase in the asset account; if it were used to pay off a loan, it would be repre-sented by a reduction in that liability account. Of course, if the surplus were used to increase cash balances, the funds would be available for use.

Balance Sheet Effects of a Cash Surplus. The effect of a cash surplus on the income and expend-itures statement is to *increase* the net worth ac-count on the balance sheet. This increase results because an asset account increases without a cor-responding increase in any liability; note that this could be *any* asset, from an investment or savings account to a new car or room addition. In order for the balance sheet equation to balance, an in-crease in assets without any increase in liabilities must result in an increase in net worth. Even if the cash surplus is used to reduce a liability, *an in-crease in net worth will still result.* To illustrate, assume that Balance Sheet A in Exhibit 2.6 repre-sents a family's balance sheet at December 31, 1988. If the family's income and expenditures statement for the *following* year, 1989, showed a cash surplus

EXHIBIT 2.7

Impact of a Cash Deficit on the Balance Sheet

A cash deficit on the income and expenditures statement is undesirable, since it leads to a decrease in the balance sheet's net worth; this shortfall has to be covered by either reducing assets (selling some investments) or taking on more debt.

Balance Sheet A

December 31, 1988

Assets		Liabilities and Net Worth	
Total assets	$30,000	Total liabilities	$22,000
Total	$30,000	Net worth	8,000
		Total	$30,000

Balance Sheet B

December 31, 1989 ($1,500 Deficit Financed by a Reduction in Assets)

Assets		Liabilities and Net Worth	
Total assets	$28,500	Total liabilities	$22,000
Total	$28,500	Net worth	6,500
		Total	$28,500

Balance Sheet C

December 31, 1989 ($1,500 Deficit Financed by Borrowing [Increase Liabilities])

Assets		Liabilities and Net Worth	
Total assets	$30,000	Total liabilities	$23,500
Total	$30,000	Net worth	6,500
		Total	$30,000

of $1,500 and these funds were used to *increase assets,* Balance Sheet B would represent the family's financial position at December 31, 1989. If the $1,500 surplus were used instead to repay a debt, Balance Sheet C would reflect the family's financial position at December 31, 1989. Regardless of what is done with the surplus, the family's net worth increases by the amount of the surplus ($1,500) from its level of $8,000 at the end of 1988 to $9,500 at the end of 1989.

Generating a cash surplus is desirable, since it adds to your net worth. **Fact:** A cash surplus on the income and expenditures statement will increase your net worth on the balance sheet.

Balance Sheet Effects of a Cash Deficit. While surpluses add to net worth, deficits *reduce* it. Again, in order for the balance sheet equation to balance, this has to be the case. If the shortfall (deficit) is

financed by reducing an asset (for example, by drawing down a savings account), a reduction in net worth will result. If it is financed by borrowing, the net worth will still be reduced, as the example in Exhibit 2.7 indicates. Again, Balance Sheet A represents a family's financial position at December 31, 1988. Assume that the family's income and expenditures statement for the *following* year, 1989, shows a cash deficit of $1,500. Balance sheets B and C show the two alternatives for meeting the deficit: in B by reducing assets and in C by borrowing. Regardless of the method used, the family's net worth decreased by $1,500 in 1989.

In summary, cash surpluses, regardless of how used, result in increases in net worth and cash deficits, regardless of how covered, result in decreases. Since increases in net worth are associated with *growing* financial strength, they are clearly preferred to cash deficits, which indicate *declining* financial strength.

EXHIBIT 2.8

The Weavers' Income and Expenditures Statement

The income and expenditures statement essentially shows what you earned, how
you spent your money, and how much you were left with (or, if you spent more than
you took in, how much you went "in the hole").

INCOME AND EXPENDITURES STATEMENT		
Name(s) *Fred & Denise Weaver*		
For the *Year*	Ending *December 31, 1989*	
INCOME		
Wages and salaries	Name: *Fred Weaver*	$ 28,941
	Name: *Denise Weaver*	3,176
	Name:	
Bonuses and commissions		
Pensions and annuities		
Investment income	Interest received	178
	Dividends received	50
	Rents received	
	Sale of securities	
	Other	
Other income		
	(I) Total Income $	32,345
EXPENDITURES		
Housing	Rent/mortgage payment (include insurance and taxes, if applicable)	8,280
	Repairs, maintenance, improvements	1,700
Utilities	Gas, electric, water	1,600
	Phone	240
	Cable TV and other	
Food	Groceries and eating out	3,800
Autos	Loan payments	960
	License plates, fees, etc.	200
	Gas, oil, repairs, tires, maintenance	1,700
Medical	Health, major medical, disability insurance (not provided by employer)	
	Doctor, dentist, hospital, drugs	240
Clothing	Clothes, uniforms, shoes, etc.	1,100
Insurance	Homeowner's (if not covered by mortgage payment)	365
	Life (not provided by employer)	290
	Auto	270
Taxes	Income and social security	4,890
	Property (if not included in mortgage)	
Appliances, furniture, and others	Loan payments	400
	Purchases and repairs	
Health and hygiene	Laundry, cosmetics, hair care	340
Recreation and entertainment	Vacations	1,800
	Other Recreation and entertainment	980
Other items	*Tuition and books: Denise*	1,890
	Gifts	150
	Loan Payments: parents	300
	(II) Total Expenditures $	31,495
	CASH SURPLUS (OR DEFICIT) [(I) − (II)] $	850

A Format for the Income and Expenditures Statement

The income and expenditures statement is dated to define the period covered. The first set of entries includes all income items and a total income figure. Next, the expenditures are listed and totaled. Although not essential, the statement's readability is greatly enhanced by including various income and expenditure category headings. These not only permit a better understanding of the general nature of the income and expenditure items but also greatly simplify the budget control process (described in Chapter 3). The final entry, representing the cash surplus (or deficit), is shown as the result obtained by subtracting total expenditures from total income. This entry constitutes the *bottom line* of the statement and basically is a summary of the *net cash flow* that resulted from the financial activities during the designated period.

An Income and Expenditures Statement for Fred and Denise Weaver

Fred and Denise Weaver's income and expenditures statement for the year ended December 31, 1989, is provided in Exhibit 2.8 (on facing page), and serves to illustrate the relationship among total income, total expenditures, and cash surplus (or deficit). This statement, which was prepared using the background material presented earlier, along with the Weavers' balance sheet (Exhibit 2.3), is best evaluated by separately analyzing their income, expenditures, and cash surplus (or deficit).

The Weavers' Income. Fred's wages clearly represent the family's chief source of income, though the $3,176 earned by Denise as a graduate assistant is definitely a nice supplement. Other sources of income include $178 in interest received on their savings accounts and bond investments and $50 in dividends received on their common stock holdings. The Weavers' total income for the year ended December 31, 1989, amounts to a respectable $32,345.

The Weavers' Expenditures. The Weavers' major expenditures, as shown in Exhibit 2.8, can be traced to their home mortgage, food, and income taxes. Other sizable expenditures during the year included home repairs and additions, gas and electricity, auto loan payments, gas and oil for the cars, clothing and shoes, insurance, furniture loan payments, health and hygiene, recreation, and tuition and books. Total expenditures for the year amounted to $31,495. Note that the expenditure categories in the Weavers' income and expenditures statement are similar to those given in Exhibit 2.5. Ideally these categories should be set up in a manner most suitable to the individual's—or family's—data requirements. Note too that the expenditure items represent actual cash outlays made by the Weavers during the year ended December 31, 1989.

The Weavers' Cash Surplus. The Weavers' cash surplus of $850 for the year is found by subtracting the total expenditures of $31,495 from the total income of $32,345. They end up with a cash surplus, since they took in more money than they spent. This surplus could be used to increase savings; invest in stocks, bonds, or other vehicles; or make payments on some outstanding debts. The correct strategy depends on their financial goals. If a cash deficit had resulted, the Weavers would have had to withdraw savings, liquidate investments, or borrow an amount equal to the deficit in order to meet their financial commitments (that is, "make ends meet"). With their *surplus* of $850, the Weavers have made a positive contribution to their net worth.

USING YOUR PERSONAL FINANCIAL STATEMENTS ▪

Personal financial statements can be used to assess your progress toward achievement of long-term financial goals. How would you use your personal financial statements to do this? Take a few moments to answer this question before reading on.

Your financial statements—the balance sheet and the income and expenditures statement—should provide the information you need to examine your

ISSUES IN MONEY MANAGEMENT

Keeping Good Records of Your Financial Affairs

An up-to-date file of your financial records should contain not only assets, liabilities, sources of income, and expenditure items, but also other records that are important for tax purposes or would be relevant in the event of disability or death. Most of these records can be kept at home. A shoebox may be sufficient for some people, but you are probably better off paying about $50 for a sturdy, fireproof box that can typically hold at least six years' worth of documents. Hard-to-replace records such as stock certificates, a divorce decree, or a power of attorney should be stored in a safe-deposit box. Banks charge about $25 to $50 a year for a box 3″ × 5″ × 24 ″, sufficient for most families.

The records you must safeguard at home or at your bank can be divided into the following two groups, depending on how long you must keep them (see the accompanying table for suggestions):

For six or more years. If the IRS hasn't begun an audit of your tax return six years after you file it, you can reward yourself by tossing out copies of the return and of the records that prove your income, deductions, and other entries for the year. (Only if you are suspected of filing a fraudulent return is there no statute of limitations on an IRS audit.)

Similarly, investment records such as annual mutual fund accountings and partnership

K–1 statements must be kept until six years after you have sold the asset. That same holding period applies to receipts and canceled checks for improvements to your home and to documents identifying nondeductible contributions to an individual retirement account. Without verification of the amount and date of the nondeductible contribution, you could be hit with a stiff tax bill when you make withdrawals from your IRA.

For life. A copy of your will can be stored in a safe-deposit box, but keep the original at home or with your lawyer. In many states your safe-deposit box will be sealed when you die, thus making it hard for relatives to take from

---

financial position, monitor your financial activities, and track the progress you're making toward your financial goals. Very likely, your financial statements are like those of most other people: not a lot of substance at present perhaps, but certainly no shortage of potential. Regardless of the particulars surrounding your case, it should be clear that a thorough understanding of your current financial status will enable you to better direct your financial plans and activities toward your personal financial goals.

The Need for Adequate Records

Financial statements should be prepared at least once each year, ideally in conjunction with budget

preparation. In order to simplify the preparation process, a **ledger**, or financial record book, should be set up. The ledger should contain a separate section for assets, liabilities, sources of income, and expenditure items. Separate accounts can be established for each item within each section. Whenever a transaction or change in any of these accounts occurs, an appropriate entry should be made in the ledger. For example, if you make a $300 cash purchase of a VCR, the item should be recorded both as an asset and an expenditure of $300. When you later prepare your financial statements, the VCR would be shown as an asset valued at its fair market value on the balance sheet and as a $300 expenditure on the income and expenditures statement. Of course, had you borrowed to pay for the VCR, the

it your will and funeral instructions. Moreover, planners generally suggest you keep up-to-date photos and fingerprints of your children in case of emergency.

Finally, make a list of all your records, as well as of the names, addresses and phone numbers of advisers such as your accountant, broker, financial planner, insurance agents and lawyer. Copies of the lists should be kept in the safe-deposit box and with your lawyer or planner.

Above all, don't lose control of your paper trail. "Once you get a handle on your records, don't let go," says financial planner Victoria Ross. "It's important to be organized—for you and your relatives."

How Long and Where to Keep Your Records

RECORDS TO KEEP SIX OR MORE YEARS

At home:

Accident reports
Brokerage and fund transactions
Insurance policies
Keogh statements
Loan records
Major purchase receipts
Stock-option agreements
Tax records, including alimony payments, charitable contributions, copies of tax returns, medical bills, partnership agreements, property tax records, 1099s

In your safe-deposit box:

Certificates of deposit
House records, including deed, title insurance policy, receipts, and canceled checks for capital improvements
Nondeductible IRA records
Partnership statements (K–1s)

RECORDS TO KEEP ALL YOUR LIFE

At home:

Birth certificates
Death certificates
List of bank accounts
List of financial assets
List of financial advisers
Medical records
Powers of attorney
Trust agreements
Wills
W–2 statements

In your safe-deposit box:

Alimony agreement
Custody agreement
Divorce decree
Military papers
Naturalization papers
Prenuptial agreement
Videotape or photos of valuables

Source: Carla A. Fried, "Records: Most of Us Squirrel More Paper Than Is Necessary," *Money*, September 1988, pp. 157–158. Used with permission.

---

amount borrowed would be recorded and shown as a liability on the balance sheet rather than as an expenditure on the income and expenditures statement. Similar records must be maintained for asset sales, loan repayment, sources of income, and so on.

Clearly, a good recordkeeping system that provides up-to-date data for use in preparing financial statements is a cornerstone of effective financial planning. Without current data, the likelihood of omitting some of these items from the financial statements or the planning process is much greater. Of course, if your finances are not very complicated, you may be able to maintain accurate records using some other, less sophisticated arrangement.

Regardless of the system used, some type of records should be maintained to provide accurate information for use in preparing the balance sheet and the income and expenditures statement. Good records will make the preparation of financial statements a lot easier; toward that end, the *Issues in Money Management* box provides helpful advice for keeping good records of your financial affairs.

ledger

A financial record book containing sections for assets, liabilities, sources of income, and expenditure items.

Tracking Financial Progress

Each time you prepare your financial statements, you should analyze them in order to assess how well you are doing in light of your financial goals. For example, with an income and expenditures statement, you can compare actual financial results to budgeted figures to make sure you have your spending under control. Likewise, comparing a set of financial plans to a balance sheet will reveal how you are doing in meeting your savings and investment goals, reducing your debt, or building up a retirement reserve. In addition to assessing your future, financial statements help you track your progress over time—that is, you can compare current to historical performance.

In effect, you want to find out if things are improving or getting worse. You can usually do this by examining certain financial ratios. These ratios can be compared over time to evaluate your financial performance. Moreover, if you need to apply for a loan, there is a good chance that the lending agency will also look at these ratios to judge your ability to carry additional debt. Four of the most important money management ratios are (1) solvency ratio, (2) liquidity ratio, (3) savings ratio, and (4) debt service ratio. The first two are associated primarily with the balance sheet, while the last two relate primarily to the income and expenditures statement.

Balance Sheet

When evaluating your balance sheet, you should be most concerned with the net worth figure, since it indicates your financial worth at a given point in time. As explained earlier in this chapter, you are technically insolvent when your total liabilities exceed your total assets—that is, when you have a negative net worth. The **solvency ratio** shows, in percentages, just how solvent you are; put another way, it shows the extent to which you are exposed to insolvency. It is calculated as follows:

$$\text{Solvency ratio} = \frac{\text{Total net worth}}{\text{Total assets}}.$$

The Weavers' solvency ratio in 1989 is

$$\frac{\$15,000}{\$76,000} = 0.20, \text{ or } 20 \text{ percent}$$

This tells us that Fred and Denise could withstand only about a 20 percent decline in the market value of their assets before they would be insolvent. The low value for this ratio suggests they should consider improving it in the future.

While the solvency ratio gives an indication of potential financial problems, it does not deal directly with the ability to pay current debts. This issue is addressed more appropriately with the **liquidity ratio**, which is found by dividing liquid assets by total current debts; "current" in this case means any bills or charges that must be paid within one year. It is computed in the following manner:

$$\text{Liquidity ratio} = \frac{\text{Liquid assets}}{\text{Total current debts}}.$$

The Weavers' liquid assets (see Exhibit 2.3) are made up of cash on hand and in their checking account, savings, and the money market mutual fund balance; these total $1,710 ($40 + $220 + $650 + $800). Their total current debts are the sum of unpaid bills and revolving credit balances, which total $300 ($60 + $80 + $30 + $40 + $90) plus that portion of their mortgage, installment, and personal loans that are due within one year. These total $9,940 ($8,280 in mortgage payments + $960 in auto loan payments + $400 in furniture loan payments + $300 in loan payment to parents—all found on the income and expenditures statement in Exhibit 2.8). Adding their total unpaid bills and revolving credit balance ($300) to the current portion of their loans ($9,940) yields a grand total of $10,240. Thus, the Weavers have a liquidity ratio of

$$\frac{\$1,710}{\$10,240} = 0.17, \text{ or } 17 \text{ percent}$$

This ratio indicates that the Weavers can cover only about 17 percent of their existing one-year debt obligations with their current liquid assets; in other words, they have about two months (one month is $\frac{1}{12}$, or 8 percent) of coverage. If an unexpected event occurred that curtailed their income, their liquid reserves would be exhausted very quickly. While there is no hard and fast rule as to what this ratio should be, it seems low for the Weavers; they should consider strengthening it along with their effort to improve their solvency ratio. They could do this by holding any added cash surpluses in the form of liquid assets, ideally through additions to their money market fund.

Income and Expenditures Statement. When evaluating your income and expenditures statement, you should be concerned with the *bottom line,* which shows the amount of the cash surplus (or deficit) resulting from the period's activities. This figure indicates how well you have done during the period. You can relate it to income by calculating a **savings ratio**, which is done most effectively with after-tax income, as follows:

$$\text{Savings ratio} = \frac{\text{Cash surplus}}{\text{Income after taxes}}.$$

For the Weavers, the savings ratio is

$$\frac{\$850}{\$32,345 - \$4,890} = \frac{\$850}{\$27,455} = 0.03, \text{ or } 3 \text{ percent}$$

Fred and Denise saved about 3 percent of their after-tax income, which is a bit on the low side (American families, on average, normally save about 5 to 8 percent). How much to save is a personal choice; some families would plan much higher levels, particularly if they are saving to achieve an important goal, such as buying a home.

While maintaining an adequate level of savings is obviously important to personal financial planning, so is the ability to pay debts promptly. In fact, debt payments have a higher priority. The **debt service ratio** allows you to make sure you're carrying a reasonable debt load. It is calculated as follows:

$$\begin{array}{l}\text{Debt}\\\text{service} =\\\text{ratio}\end{array} \frac{\text{Total monthly loan payments}}{\text{Monthly gross (before-tax) income}}$$

This ratio excludes unpaid bills and revolving credit balances and therefore considers only mortgage, installment, and personal loan obligations. Reviewing the Weavers' income and expenditure statement in Exhibit 2.8, it can be seen that on an *annual* basis, these obligations total $9,940 ($8,280 in mortgage payments plus $960 in auto loan payments plus $400 in furniture loan payments plus $300 in loan payments to parents). Dividing this total by 12 results in an estimate of the Weavers' total *monthly* loan payments of $828. The Weavers' *annual* gross income, also found in Exhibit 2.8, totals $32,345, which equals $2,695 monthly

($32,345/12). Substituting the Weavers' $828 total monthly loan payment and their monthly gross income of $2,695 into the formula yields a debt service ratio of

$$\frac{\$828}{\$2,695} = .31 = 31 \text{ percent}$$

Monthly loan payments account for about 31 percent of Fred and Denise's gross income. A debt service ratio of around 30 percent means that the Weavers should have little, if any, difficulty in meeting their monthly loan payments. From a financial planning perspective, you should try to keep your debt service margin to somewhere under 35 percent or so, since that's generally viewed as a manageable level of debt—and, of course, the lower the debt service ratio, the easier it is to meet loan payments as they come due.

When evaluating your income and expenditures statement, primary attention should be given to the top line: income received. **Fantasy:** You should give most of your attention to the *bottom* line (the amount of the cash surplus or deficit), since it indicates how well you have controlled your expenditures relative to the amount of income available and, in turn, how you contributed to your net worth position.

Getting a Window on the Future

So far, we have looked at financial statements in terms of helping us evaluate what has happened in the past. However, they can also be used to assist us in achieving future financial goals; they serve best in that capacity when they are tied to the an-

---

solvency ratio
Total net worth divided by total assets.

liquidity ratio
Liquid assets divided by total current debts.

savings ratio
Cash surplus divided by after-tax income.

debt service ratio
Total monthly loan payments divided by monthly gross (before-tax) income; provides a measure of ability to service monthly loan payments in a prompt and timely fashion.

EXHIBIT 2.9

Forecasted Changes in the Weaver Net Worth Position (as of December 31, 1990)

Increases in net worth do not have to happen by chance; rather, they can be planned out in advance.

A. Increases in Net Worth Planned with the 1990 Budget:

(1) Make $8,280 in monthly payments on home mortgage; $7,728 is interest, leaving payments to reduce the loan by	$ 552
(2) Make payments on auto loan of $960 and furniture loan of $400; combined interest on both is $260, leaving payments to reduce the loan by	1,100
(3) Reduce loan to parents	800
(4) Increase savings (and invest in money market fund)	1,000
(a) Budgeted increase in net worth	$3,452

B. Expected Increases (Decreases) in Market Value of Assets:

(1) House (3% increase)	$1,800
(2) Automobiles (10% decrease)	(530)
(3) Recreational equipment (50% decrease)	(200)
(4) Personal property (jewelry will increase, but furniture and clothing will decrease; assume they offset)	0
(5) Stocks and bonds (5% increase)	115
(6) Cash value of life insurance (from policy)	50
(7) Stamp collection (2% increase)	50
(b) Expected net increase in market value of assets	$1,285
Total expected increase in net worth in 1990 = (a) + (b)	$4,737

nual budgeting process, described in detail in the next chapter. For the moment, let us suppose that Fred and Denise have set a goal to increase their net worth by at least $4,000 in 1990. Such an increase can take place in two different ways. On one hand, the Weavers can prepare a 1990 cash budget (using procedures described in the next chapter) that will specifically provide for an increase in net worth by controlling their income and expenditures. Alternatively, they can rely on increases in the market value of some of their assets—particularly their stocks and bonds and, possibly, their house and stamp collection. They must be concerned, though, that some of their assets could also *decline* in market value, causing their net worth to decrease. Clearly, this is a virtual certainty with their automobiles, recreational equipment, and personal property items.

Exhibit 2.9 details how the Weavers expect their net worth to increase in 1990. Part A shows a budgeted increase of $3,452, and part B shows the Weavers' estimates of increases and decreases in their assets' market values (the net increase from this source in 1990 is expected to be $1,285). Line B is only an estimate, of course, and Fred and Denise certainly are not relying on it alone to achieve their net worth goal. They expect that in the long run many of their assets will increase in value—that is one of the reasons they purchased them—but they are less sure of these increases on a year-to-year basis. If everything does work out as planned, the Weavers' net worth at December 31, 1990, will be almost $20,000—or $19,737, to be exact—which is found by adding the total expected increase to their net worth of $4,737 (found in Exhibit 2.9) to their latest net worth of $15,000 (from Exhibit 2.3).

SUMMARY

▪ The preparation and use of personal financial statements is important to financial planning, since they enable you not only to keep track of your current financial position but also to moni-

tor the amount of progress being made toward your financial goals.
▪ A balance sheet reports on your financial condition at a given point in time by providing a sum-

mary of the things you own (assets), the money you owe (liabilities), and your financial worth (net worth).

▪ The asset side (left side) of the balance sheet reflects the things you own and is made up of liquid assets, real and personal property, and investments. The other side (right side) of the balance sheet shows how you used debt and net worth to finance your assets and is made up of unpaid bills, revolving credit, various kinds of loans and mortgages, and net worth.

▪ The income and expenditures statement provides a summary of the income you received and the money you spent over a given period of time; it is prepared on a cash basis and, as such, reflects the actual cash flow. Expenditures consist of the outflow of cash to (1) meet living expenses, (2) purchase various kinds of assets, (3) pay taxes, and (4) reduce debt.

▪ An important element of the income and expenditures statement is the size of the cash surplus (or deficit). A cash surplus can be used to increase assets and/or reduce debts and will have a direct positive effect on the net worth account in the balance sheet. A cash deficit, in contrast, reduces assets and/or increases debts and acts as a drain on net worth.

▪ In addition to tracking your progress toward your financial goals, personal financial statements are also useful in assessing how well you are doing relative to your past performance (that is, are things getting better or worse?). Such insight can usually be obtained through the use of financial ratios like the solvency, liquidity, savings, and debt service ratios.

QUESTIONS AND PROBLEMS

1. Match each lettered item below with the most appropriate description:
   a. Balance sheet
   b. Time deposits
   c. Liquid assets
   d. Cash surplus/deficit
   e. Income and expenditures statement
   f. Liabilities
   g. Demand deposits
   h. Expenditures greater than income
   i. Income
   j. Assets
   ___ Money owned
   ___ Checking account
   ___ Earnings
   ___ Financial position
   ___ Items owned
   ___ Savings or money market account
   ___ Demand and time deposits
   ___ Financial performance
   ___ Increase/decrease in assets or investments
   ___ Deficit

2. Distinguish real and personal property from investments. Categorize the following as real property, personal property, or investments:
   a. Clothing and shoes
   b. Promissory notes
   c. Gold bars
   d. Priceless paintings
   e. Automobiles

3. Chris Jones is preparing his balance sheet as of June 30, 1989. He is having difficulty classifying three items and asks for your help. Which, if any, of the following transactions are assets or liabilities?
   a. He rents a house for $400 a month.
   b. On June 21, 1989, he bought a diamond ring for his wife and charged it to his VISA card. The ring cost $600, but he has not yet received the bill.
   c. He makes monthly payments of $120 on an installment loan, about half of which is interest and the balance repayment of principal; he has 20 payments left totaling $2,400.

4. What is the balance sheet equation? Explain when a family may be viewed as technically insolvent.

5. Put yourself ten years into the future. Construct a fairly detailed and realistic balance sheet and income and expenditures statement reflecting what you would like to achieve by that time.

6. Deborah Lee bought a new house with a fair market value of $65,000. She has an outstanding mortgage loan of $58,700. How much is her equity in the house?

7. What is an income and expenditures statement? What role does it serve in personal financial planning? What are its three components?

8. Name some of the major sources of income. What are the four basic types of expenditures?

9. Chris Jones is preparing his income and expenditures statement for the year ending June 30, 1989. He is having difficulty classifying some items and asks for your help. Which, if any, of the following transactions are income or expenditure items?
   a. He borrowed $2,000 from his parents last fall but so far has made no payments.
   b. He paid $1,200 in taxes last year but is due a tax refund of $450, which he has not yet received.
   c. He invested $1,800 in some common stock.

10. Explain what *cash basis* means in the following statement: "An income and expenditures statement should be prepared on a cash basis." How and where are credit purchases shown when statements are prepared on a cash basis?

11. Is it possible to have a cash deficit on an income and expenditures statement?

12. Describe some of the areas or items you would consider when evaluating your balance sheet. Cite several ratios that could help in this effort.

13. Explain why primary emphasis in the evaluation of an income and expenditures statement is placed on the "bottom line." Discuss how you might go about analyzing your own income and expenditures statement. What ratio would be useful here?

14. Jessica Wright has monthly gross income of $1,750 and total monthly loan payments of $780. How would you characterize Jessica's ability to meet her loan payments? What if her monthly gross income were the same, but her monthly loan payments were only $500?

■ 15. Bill and Nancy Ballinger are about to construct their balance sheet and income and ex-

penditures statement for the year ending December 31, 1989. They have put together the following information:

Rent received on mountain cabin	$ 1,250
Other debts	23,000
Bill from State Farm Insurance	120
Amount spent on groceries	3,800
Income tax paid in 1989	18,190
Other expenses incurred in 1989	9,200
Certificates of deposit	20,000
Cash	60
Car loan	2,900
Bill's salary	55,200
Balance due on J. C. Penney credit card	450
Phone bills paid in 1989	640
Gas and electric bills paid in 1989	1,990
Principal amount of home loan	121,000
Property taxes paid in 1989	3,180
Estimated value of home	149,500
1984 Datsun	2,700
Other assets	15,000
Amount invested in mutual funds	58,000
Principal amount of cabin loan	30,000
Nancy's pay	28,750
1988 tax refund received	1,560
Doctor bill	60
Gas, oil, and car repairs	1,800
Mortgage payments on house	15,000
Life insurance premiums paid	850
Laundry and hair care expenses	1,230
Checking account	1,520
Savings accounts	7,250
Bill from gas and electric companies	140
Income received from interest, dividends, etc.	7,000
Balance due on Visa card	1,550
Market value of mountain cabin	47,000
Home entertainment center	1,800
Amount outstanding on MasterCard	900
Loan payments made on car	2,150
Shoes, clothing, etc. purchased in 1989	2,600
Money spent on Arizona vacation	7,400
1987 Chevrolet	7,500
Estimated value of clothes and other personal effects	6,500
Value of home furnishings	15,200
Loan payments made on cabin	6,250
Doctor and dentist bills paid in 1989	980

Based on this information, construct the Ballingers' December 31, 1989, balance sheet *and* income and expenditures statement for the year ending December 31, 1989; use forms like the ones in Exhibits 2.3 and 2.8.

16. Why might you be interested in forecasting a balance sheet, an income and expenditures statement, or a segment of either one, such as net worth?

17. Explain two ways in which net worth could increase (or decrease) from one period to the next. Which way would make the change in net worth more likely to occur? Why?

CASE PROBLEMS

⊡ 2.1 The Walkers Prepare a Balance Sheet for Their Banker

Richard and Elizabeth Walker have been asked by their banker to submit their personal balance sheet as of June 30, 1989, in support of an application for a $3,000 home improvement loan. They have come to you for help in preparing it. So far, they have prepared a list of their assets and liabilities as follows:

Cash on hand		$ 70
Balance in checking account		180
Balance in money market deposit account with Mid-America Savings		650
Bills outstanding:		
Telephone	$ 20	
Electricity	70	
Charge account balance	190	
Visa	180	
MasterCard	220	
Taxes	400	
Insurance	220	1,300
Home and property		68,000
Home mortgage loan		52,000
Automobiles:		
1983 Dodge Aires	$3,000	
1987 Ford LTD	4,800	7,800
Installment loan balances:		
Auto loans	$4,500	
Furniture loan	500	5,000
Personal property:		
Furniture	$1,050	
Clothing	900	1,950
Investments:		
U.S. government savings bonds	$ 500	
Stock of WIMCO Corporation	3,000	3,500

Questions

1. From the data given, prepare Richard and Elizabeth Walker's balance sheet, dated June 30, 1989 (follow the balance sheet form shown in Exhibit 2.3).
2. Evaluate their balance sheet relative to the following factors: (a) solvency, (b) equity in their dominant asset, (c) liquidity, and (d) debt serviceability.
3. If you were their banker, how would you feel about giving the Walkers the loan if you had to base your decision solely on their balance sheet? Explain.

⊡ 2.2 Chuck Takes a Look at the Schwartz Finances

Chuck and Judy Schwartz recently have become a bit concerned about their finances. Judy is an engineer for a large petroleum company while Chuck is a full-time student majoring in industrial design at Generic State University. Chuck also tends to the housekeeping chores and maintains the financial records. In order to find out how well he managed their finances last year, Chuck has amassed the following data for the year ending December 31, 1989:

Judy's salary	$26,000
Reimbursement for travel expenditures	1,950
Interest on:	
Savings account	110
Bonds of Alpha Corporation	70
Groceries	3,800
Rent	6,000
Utilities	960
Cash and auto expenditures	650
Chuck's tuition, books, and supplies	3,300
Books, magazines, and periodicals	280
Clothing and other miscellaneous expenditures	2,700
Cost of photographic equipment purchased with charge card	2,200
Amount paid to date	1,600
Judy's travel expenditures	1,950
Purchase of a new car (cost)	7,500
Outstanding loan balance on car	4,200
Purchase of bonds in Alpha Corporation	4,900

Questions

1. Using the information provided, prepare an income and expenditures statement for the Schwartzes for the year ending December 31, 1989 (follow the form shown in Exhibit 2.8).
2. Based on the statement you prepared, assess the Schwartzes' financial performance last year, commenting on the following: (a) their total income, (b) their total expenditures, (c) their cash surplus (or deficit), and (d) the resulting increase or decrease in their net worth.
3. Forecast their net worth a year form now (at December 31, 1990) assuming their total income increases by 10 percent, their total expenses increase by 7 percent, and the market value of their total assets increases by 8 percent. (Their December 31, 1989, total assets were $18,000 and net worth was $2,000.) Discuss your findings.

FOR MORE INFORMATION

General Information Articles

Egan, Jack, "Sizing Up Your Finances," *U.S. News & World Report,* June 8, 1987, pp. 52–55.

Harris, Diane, "Who Owns the Most—and Why," *Money,* December 1986, pp. 74–76.

Henderson, Nancy, "Get Organized," *Changing Times,* January 1987, pp. 63–65.

Lewin, Elizabeth, "Where Does all the Money Go?" *Sylvia Porter's Personal Finance,* May 1987, pp. 74–75.

Miller, Theodore J., "Are You Better Off Than You Think?" *Changing Times,* January 1988, pp. 50–53.

Paulson, Morton C., "Keeping the Right Records," *Changing Times,* June 1988, pp. 47–51.

Schiffres, Manuel, "Do You Really Want to be Rich?" *Changing Times,* October 1987, pp. 73–79.

Sivy, Michael, "Fifteen Trends That Will Shape Your Financial Future," *Money,* Fall 1987, pp. 26–30.

Stauffer, Brooke, "Getting a Grip on Your Spending," *Changing Times,* January 1988, pp. 45–48.

Topolnicki, Denise M. "Who Earns the Most—and Why," *Money,* December 1986, pp. 62–66.

Planning Your Financial Future

Financial Facts or Fantasies

Are the following statements financial facts (true) or fantasies (false)?

- Financial plans are set up after the annual budget is prepared.
- Most professional financial planners earn their income from the commissions they receive on the financial products they sell.
- Defining financial goals is the first step in the personal financial planning process.
- A cash budget is a report that shows the amount of money you will be spending from month to month.
- If a budget shows a cash deficit for the year, then you have no choice but to borrow enough money to make up the shortfall.
- One of the final steps in the cash budgeting process is to compare actual results to budgeted amounts.

Go ahead, fantasize for a moment. Picture yourself a few years from now—out of school (at last!), married, and with a good-paying job that holds promise for the future. Then one day, you receive a registered letter informing you that a great-uncle you didn't even know has passed away, leaving you part of his estate. Attached to the letter is a cashier's check payable to you in the amount of $100,000. Clearly , your financial future has just taken a big turn for the better. Of course, sooner or later, you are going to have to decide what to do with all that money; you will need to do some financial planning. Your financial future depends on it. The point is, whether you have a lot of money or a little money, personal financial planning is still necessary. If the fantasy of a big monetary windfall never materializes in your life, if indeed your income seems inadequate, you can nevertheless take steps to improve your financial situation. And taking the right steps is basically what personal financial planning is all about: a conscientious and systematic climb toward achievement of preset financial goals. In order to reap the full benefits of personal financial planning, though, you need a well-defined set of financial goals, a fully developed set of financial plans, and a carefully prepared series of cash budgets.

FINANCIAL PLANNING AND BUDGETING: MAPPING OUT YOUR FINANCIAL FUTURE

Budgeting provides not only direction for future financial activities but also a way of keeping financial transactions on track. How might a budget prove useful in helping you achieve your financial goals? Take a few moments to answer this question before reading on.

Financial planning and budgeting enable families to achieve greater wealth and financial security by means of well-defined plans and carefully developed and implemented strategies and controls. On the one hand, they provide *direction* by helping us work toward specific financial goals; on the other, they provide *control* by bringing the various dimensions of our personal financial affairs into focus. Financial planning and budgeting are a lot like road maps: Once we know where we want to go, they show us how to reach our destination. Both are essential to sound personal money management and to the attainment of personal financial goals.

Which Comes First— the Budget or the Plan?

Taking a closer look at financial planning, it is a process by which personal financial goals are translated first into specific financial plans and then into financial strategies through which the plans can be implemented. In contrast, a **budget** is a detailed short-term financial forecast that is used to monitor and control expenditures and purchases. *Budgets exist as a way to help us achieve the financial goals we set in our financial plans.* They provide the mechanism through which the financial plans are carried out. Developed in line with established financial plans, budgets provide a detailed statement of estimated income versus estimated expenditures, purchases, and investments.

Exhibit 3.1 gives a schematic overview of various financial statements and reports, and their relationship to one another. Note that whereas financial plans provide direction to annual budgets, the success (or lack thereof) in carrying out the budget will directly affect our balance sheet and income and expenditures statement. As we move from plans to budgets to actuals, we see the critical role that financial statements play in providing *feedback* to the financial plans and budgets—that is, they let us know what kind of progress we are making toward our financial goals and whether or not we are staying within our budget.

Financial plans are set up after the annual budget is prepared. **Fantasy:** The financial plans come first, then the budget. The budget is part of our financial plans and exists as a way to help us carry them out.

The Financial Planning Process

The financial planning process generally involves the following steps:

1. Define financial goals.
2. Develop financial plans and strategies for achieving goals.
3. Implement financial plans and strategies.
4. Periodically develop and implement budgets for use in monitoring and controlling progress toward goal achievement.
5. Periodically evaluate results relative to plans and budgets and, when necessary, take corrective action.
6. Revise and replace goals as warranted.

The first step in financial planning is to define your financial goals. The next step is to develop financial plans and strategies that will be compatible with your goals. Once these have been defined, it is time to put them to work, that is, to implement them. But you cannot just turn the switch on and walk away. Rather, you must periodically develop and implement budgets for monitoring and controlling outcomes, and, when necessary, you must alter your financial objectives. In effect, the financial planning process runs full circle as you come back to defining revised goals and making corresponding revisions in your financial plans.

A Comprehensive Financial Plan. To get an idea of what is involved in a **comprehensive personal financial plan**, let us use a professionally prepared plan as a basis. Essentially, what a comprehensive plan should do is provide an individual

EXHIBIT 3.1

The Interlocking Network of Financial Plans and Statements

Personal financial planning involves a whole network of financial reports that link future goals and plans with actual results. Such a network provides direction, control, and feedback.

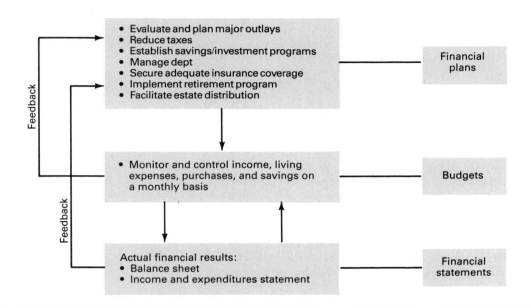

or family with a whole set of detailed plans and recommendations to follow in order to achieve a variety of specific financial goals. A well-defined financial plan is based on a complete inventory of a family's personal and financial circumstances. This includes a family profile (health status, number and ages of children, education status, and any special considerations); information on current income, expenses, and financial condition (assets, investments, and debts); tax returns; insurance coverages; retirement programs; and estate plans. In addition, information about personal and family expectations, motivations, risk tolerances, and objectives must be obtained. A professional financial planner would gather such information using an extensive, multipage questionnaire and personal interviews.

Once this inventory is complete, the first step in the financial planning process can be taken: to define and prioritize personal financial goals. These goals would pertain to such general activities as (1) capital accumulation for specific needs and

goals (like the purchase of a house or vacation home, children's education, or retirement); (2) reduction of income taxes; (3) investment and property management; (4) protection against personal risk (insurance coverage); and/or (5) maximizing the distribution of an estate to the heirs. A written plan would then be prepared that included all of

budget
A detailed financial forecast used to monitor and control expenditures and purchases; it provides a mechanism for carrying out financial plans to achieve short-run financial goals.

comprehensive personal financial plan
A set of detailed plans and recommendations for achieving specific financial goals, as compiled from a family profile; information on current income, expenses, and financial condition; tax returns; insurance coverages; retirement programs; and estate plans.

EXHIBIT 3.2

Summary of the Recommendations from a Comprehensive, Professionally Prepared Financial Plan

Professionally prepared, comprehensive financial plans are custom-tailored to provide detailed recommendations aimed at the achievement of specific personal financial goals. However, to be effective, the financial plans and recommendations must be implemented—they should be viewed as a launching pad, not a landing strip!

Education of Children

- Recommendation: Engage in a systematic program of prefunding the children's education by putting $60,000 in a custodial account or by setting aside $9,500 annually for the next nine years.
- Desired result: Savings of $39,000 and $13,500, respectively, as opposed to paying these costs out of annual cash flow.

Income for Disability

- Recommendation: Make no change to present disability program.
- Desired result: Adequate income provided in the event of long-term disability.

Medical Insurance

- Recommendation: Increase major medical insurance to at least $500,000.
- Desired result: Adequate insurance coverage in the event of serious illness.

Property and Casualty Insurance

- Recommendation 1:   Reduce liability coverage under present insurance to the suggested minimum and purchase an excess liability policy in the amount of $2 million.
- Recommendation 2:   Confirm that the dwelling coverage is at least 80 percent of its replacement value.
- Desired result: Adequate overall insurance protection.

Proper Disposition of Estate

- Recommendation 1:   Purchase $250,000 of universal life insurance on husband's life at an annual cost of approximately $3,000 to provide both insurance and tax-free accumulation.
- Desired result: Provide capital for projected survivor income shortages.
- Recommendation 2:   New wills should first place the unified credit amount in trust for the surviving spouse; the balance of each spouse's estate should qualify for the unlimited marital deduction.
- Desired result: Estate tax savings of $80,000 and $45,000, respectively.
- Recommendation 3:   Consider the use of a testamentary trust in their wills for the benefit of their children.
- Desired result: Protection and management of assets until minor children have completed school.

Retirement Income

- Recommendation: Follow systematic investment program (described in detail).
- Desired result: Monthly income in first year of retirement will be $10,500.
- Investment Program
- Recommendation: Over a period of time to be determined by tax advice, couple should:
  - Place $20,000 in commercial real estate
  - Place $12,000 in a cash reserve account
  - Place $16,000 in a tax-deferred annuity
  - Place $10,000 in municipal bonds
  - Place $15,000 in growth stock
  - Place $12,500 in an exploratory oil and gas partnership
  - Invest excess cash flow annually
- Desired results: Write-offs will save $10,500 in income taxes; capital at retirement will be $725,000.

the family's major financial goals, along with detailed strategies and recommendations for each. Such a professionally prepared plan could well be a 25-to-50 page (or longer) document that explained, summarized, and recorded the recommendations as well as the results expected from their implementation.

A summary of the recommendations from a real-life comprehensive, professionally prepared financial plan is shown in Exhibit 3.2 (on facing page). This particular financial plan covered 77 pages, plus an appendix, and cost $1,500. It was prepared for a couple in their early forties with two children; the husband is a bank executive earning nearly $70,000 a year, and the wife earns $35,000 a year as an accountant for a regional department store chain. Note the recommendations covering children's education, insurance planning, estate planning, retirement plans, and investment programs. This couple is now at the point where they can implement the recommendations and begin working toward their established goals. They now have something specific to shoot for and can set up their annual budget accordingly.

Professional Financial Planners

The number of people turning to financial planning as a way of gaining control over their financial affairs is increasing almost as rapidly as the variety and complexity of the financial products being offered to them. This environment, not surprisingly, has led to one of the fastest-growing fields in finance: that of **professional financial planners**. These are the people to whom others turn for professional help in setting up and carrying out fully developed financial plans. In 1979 there were about 25,000 financial planners plying their trade; it is estimated that in 1988 their ranks had grown to about 250,000 nationwide.

Types of Planners. All financial planners work for some sort of fee; most are compensated from the commissions they earn on the financial products they sell, while others charge only a fee based on the complexity of the plan they prepare. Some financial planners are simply converted insurance salespeople or securities dealers who do little more than continue to sell the same financial prod-

ucts they always have (life insurance, stocks, bonds, mutual funds, and annuities), except now they do it under the guise of being a "financial planner." On the other hand, many large, established financial institutions, recognizing the enormous potential, are getting into this field in a big way and stand ready to compete with the best financial planners. There are also a number of independent financial planners who offer nothing but sound, high-quality service. Regardless of whether they are independent or affiliated operations, full-service financial planners help their clients to articulate their long- and short-run financial goals and alert them to the importance of systematically planning for their financial needs.

In addition to this type of personal financial planning service, there is a growing list of institutions offering **computerized financial plans**. For $0 to $500, these computerized services—which include Paine Webber, Merrill Lynch, Prudential-Bache, E.F. Hutton, and IDS/American Express—offer simple advice on how to keep up with current bills, save for college or retirement, reduce taxes, or restructure investment portfolios. These professional planners may be the most appropriate course of action for those who have neither the time, inclination, nor expertise to do the planning on their own. The costs may well be worth the benefits, especially when you consider that for some people the alternative is to not plan at all.

Most professional financial planners earn their income from the commissions they receive on the financial products they sell. **Fact:** The vast majority of professional financial planners make their living by selling financial products (life insurance, mutual funds, annuities, and so on) to you—in fact, some merely use the "financial plan" as a tool for selling these products.

---

professional financial planner
An individual or firm that assists clients in establishing long- and short-run financial goals and in developing and implementing financial plans aimed at their achievement.

computerized financial plans
Computer-generated financial plans that offer simple advice on major areas of personal money management; while they are relatively inexpensive, they are also somewhat impersonal.

Choosing a Financial Planner. Planners who have completed the required course of study and earned the Certified Financial Planner (CFP) or Chartered Financial Consultant (ChFC) designation are often a better choice than the many self-proclaimed financial planners. Of course, CPAs, attorneys, and other professionals without such certifications in many instances do provide sound financial planning advice. Unfortunately, though, planners aren't currently regulated by either government or self-regulatory groups, and some fraudulent acts have occurred. Tips for choosing a competent planner are given in Exhibit 3.3. Clearly, you should do your homework before engaging the services of a professional financial planner.

DEFINING YOUR FINANCIAL GOALS

> The financial planning process begins with the definition of both long-run and short-run financial goals, which in turn provide direction for financial plans and budgets. Do you have long-run and short-run financial goals? Before reading on, spend a few moments formulating and listing them.

As noted earlier, setting financial goals is the first step in the personal financial planning process. Once set, these goals provide direction for your financial plans. But just as you cannot prepare plans for attaining goals that are not yet formulated, you cannot begin the financial planning process without a knowledge of your current financial position. (Methods for evaluating current financial position via personal financial statements were described in Chapter Two.)

After your current financial position has been evaluated, both long-run and short-run financial goals can be established. It is important to involve your immediate family in the goal-setting process in order to eliminate potential future conflicts. By having each family member effectively "buy into" these plans, a cooperative team effort should result, thereby improving the family's chances of achieving its goals. Once your goals have been defined

and approved, appropriate cash budgets can be prepared. Normally, long-run financial goals are set first, followed by a series of corresponding short-run goals.

Defining financial goals is the first step in the personal financial planning process. **Fact:** Once we've specified our financial goals, we can develop financial plans, strategies, and budgets consistent with achieving them.

Setting Long-Run Financial Goals

Long-run financial goals should indicate the individual's or family's wants and desires for the next 2 to 5 years on out to the next 30 to 40 years. Of course, many people find it difficult to pinpoint exactly what they will want 30 or so years from now; however, if they at least give some thought to the matter, they should be able to establish some tentative long-run financial goals. Recognize, though, that many long-run goals will change over time. For example, an individual might set a goal of retiring at age 55 with a net worth of $400,000. At age 50, this same person might decide to purchase a condominium in Florida and retire at age 62 with a net worth of $500,000. Although this individual's long-run goal is changed, note that his short-run goals will remain pretty much the same: to make substantial, regular contributions to savings or investments in order to accumulate the desired net worth.

Putting a Dollar Value on Financial Goals. Some financial goals can be defined in rather general terms. Others should be defined more precisely, perhaps even to the extent of assigning fairly specific dollar values. Consider, for example, the goal of buying your first home in six years. The first question you must answer is how much to spend. Let's say that you have done some "window shopping" and feel that, *taking future inflation into consideration,* you will have to spend about $90,000 to get the kind of house you like. Of course, you will not need the full amount, but given a 20 percent down payment ($90,000 × .20 = $18,000) plus closing costs, you estimate that you will need around $20,000. You now have a fairly well-defined long-run financial goal: *to accumulate $20,000 in 6 years in order to buy a home that will cost about $90,000.*

EXHIBIT 3.3

Tips for Picking a Competent Financial Planner

The following tips offered by Price Waterhouse's Consumer Financial Institute and others should prove useful in choosing a competent personal financial planner.

1. Shop around. Get recommendations and interview several candidates.
2. Scrutinize backgrounds. Look for degrees in economics, accounting, business, or finance. Are their previous occupations (bookkeeper, tollbooth operator) germane to planning? How long have they been in business?
3. Check for participation in continuing education programs. Someone whose last class was five years ago may be poorly informed today.
4. Insist on proof of registration or certification. Firms that offer securities advice must register with the Securities and Exchange Commission or the National Association of Securities Dealers. CFPs must be registered with the International Board of Certified Financial Planners (Denver, CO; (303) 850–0333) and ChFCs must be registered with the American Society (Bryn Mawr, PA; (215) 526–2500).
5. Ask to see plans your candidates prepared for other clients. Make sure the plans are thorough and individualized.
6. Get client references, and check them.
7. Find out to whom the planners consult to prepare their plans. Who are their lawyers and accountants? If they have no reputable backup, beware.
8. If a planner is affiliated with a larger firm, check its reputation with state regulators, the SEC, and industry associates.
9. Perhaps most important, find out how your candidates are compensated. Are they paid through fees, commissions, or both? Many believe that fee-based financial planners are generally more objective, since their income is not tied directly to selling financial products.

Source: Excerpted from David Morrow, "A Checklist for Picking a Planner," *FORTUNE 1989 Investors' Guide*, page 202. Copyright © 1989 *Time Inc.* All rights reserved.

The next question is how to get all that money. If you are like many people, you will probably accumulate it by saving or investing a set amount each month or year. You can easily figure what you will have to save or invest each year if you know what your goal is and how much you think you can earn on your savings or investments. In this case, if you have to start from scratch (that is, have nothing saved today) and if you estimate that you can earn about 10 percent on your money, you will have to save or invest about $2,600 per year for each of the next 6 years to accumulate $20,000 over that time period. Now you have another vital piece of information: *You know what you must do over the next six years in order to reach your financial goal.* The accompanying "Smart Money" box offers more information on how to find **future values** and describes the basic computation procedures used in this example.

Putting Target Dates on Financial Goals. Financial goals are most effective when set in reference to certain goal dates. *Goal dates* are target points in the future at which time certain financial activities are expected to be concluded; they may serve as checkpoints in the progress toward some financial goals or as deadlines for the achievement

of others. For example, one goal may be to purchase a boat in 1991 (the goal date) and another to accumulate a net worth of $200,000 by 2011, with goal dates of 1994 and 2003 set as checkpoints for the attainment of net worth of $75,000 and $140,000, respectively. It is usually helpful to set goal dates at intervals of two to five years for the first ten years or so and at five to ten-year intervals thereafter. As time passes, adjustments to the financial plans may have to be made; or, as desired financial outcomes are realized, goals may also have to be changed. In other words, the person or family may recognize that the goals were set either too high or too low. If the goals appear to be too high, they must be revised and made more realistic. If

long-run financial goals
Goals that are set well into the future, typically to retirement and sometimes beyond.

future value
The amount to which a dollar will grow over time when it earns a given rate of return. This concept can also be used to estimate the yearly savings needed to accumulate a given future amount of money.

S·M·A·R·T   M·O·N·E·Y

The Arithmetic of Financial Planning: Finding Future Value

Frequently in financial planning you will need to attach specific dollar values to your long-run financial goals. For example, you may want to buy your first home in six years or build a pool of money for your children's college education. It really makes no difference what you want to do—so long as it involves a long-run monetary goal, you can lay out a path for getting there. The only requirement is that you have a good idea of how much you will need in the future.

For instance, suppose you will need $20,000 to buy a new home in 6 years. Given such a goal, you can address the basic problem of how to accumulate such a sum of money. You might be tempted to solve this problem by simply dividing the $20,000 goal by the 6-year period: $20,000/6 = $3,333. Unfortunately, this procedure would be incorrect, since it would fail to take into account the *time value of money,* or the

idea that money can earn a positive rate of return over time. The correct way to approach this problem is to use the future value concept. Basically, *future value* is the amount to which a dollar will grow over time when it earns a given rate of return. For example, if you can invest $100 today at 10 percent, you will have $110 in a year: You will earn $10 on your investment ($100 × .10 = $10), plus get your original $100 back. Once you know the length of time *and* rate of return involved, you can find the future value of any investment by using the following simple formula:

Future value =
          Amount invested ×
          Future value factor.

Tables of future value factors are available to facilitate and simplify the computations in this formula (see Appendix A). The table is very easy to use: Simply find the factor that

corresponds to a given year *and* interest rate. Referring to Appendix A, you will find the future value factor for a 6-year investment earning 10 percent to be 1.772 (the factor that lies at the intersection of 6 years and 10 percent).

Returning to the problem at hand, let us say you already have accumulated $5,000 toward the purchase of a new home. To find the future value of that investment in 6 years earning 10 percent, you can use the above formula as follows:

Future value = $5,000 × 1.772
            = $8,860.

The $8,860 is how much you will have in 6 years if you invest the $5,000 at 10 percent. Because you feel you are going to need $20,000, you are still $11,140 short of your goal. How are you going to accumulate an additional $11,140.

Again you can utilize the future value concept, but this

they are too low, they should be evaluated and set at a level that will force the individual or family to make financially responsible decisions rather than squandering surplus funds.

Goals for the Short-Run

Short-run financial goals are set each year; they cover a 12-month period and should be consistent

with established long-run goals. These short-run goals become the key input for the *cash budget*—a tool used to plan for short-run income and expenditures. The individual's or family's immediate goals, expected income for the year, and long-run financial goals must all be taken into account when defining short-run goals. In addition, consideration must be given to the latest financial position, as reflected by the current balance sheet, and spend-time you will employ an annuity factor. An *annuity* is an equal cash flow that occurs annually—for example, $1,000 per year for each of the next 5 years, with payment to be made at the end of each year. You can find out how much you will have to save each year to accumulate a given amount by using the following equation:

$$\text{Yearly savings} = \frac{\text{Amount of money desired}}{\text{Annuity factor}}.$$

When dealing with an annuity you will have to use a different table of factors, such as that in Appendix B. Note that it is very much like the table of future value factors and, in fact, is used in exactly the same way: The proper annuity factor is the one that corresponds to a given year *and* interest rate. As an example, you'll find in Appendix B that the annuity factor for 6 years and 10 percent is 7.716. Using this factor in the above equation, you can find out how much to save each year to accumulate $11,140 in 6 years given a 10 percent rate of return, as follows:

$$\text{Yearly savings} = \frac{\$11,140}{7.716}$$
$$= \underline{\$1,443.75}.$$

You will have to save about $1,445 a year to reach your goal. Note in the example that you must add $1,445 a year to the $5,000 you already have in order to build up a pool of $20,000 in 6 years. At a 10 percent rate of return, the $1,445 per year will grow to $11,140 and the $5,000 will grow to $8,860 so that in 6 years you will have $11,140 + $8,860 = $20,000.

How much, you may ask, would you have to save each year if you did not have the $5,000 to start with? In this case, your goal would still be the same (to accumulate $20,000 in 6 years), but, since you would be starting from scratch, the full $20,000 would have to come from yearly savings. Assuming you can still earn 10 percent over the 6-year period, you can use the same annuity factor (7.716) and compute the amount of yearly savings as follows:

$$\text{Yearly savings} = \frac{\$20,000}{7.716}$$
$$= \underline{\$2,592.02},$$

or approximately $2,600.

Note that this amount corresponds to the $2,600 figure cited in the text illustration.

Using the future value concept, you can readily find either the future value to which an investment will grow over time or the amount that you must save each year to accumulate a given amount of money by a specified future date. In either case, the procedures will enable you to put monetary values on long-run financial goals.

---

ing in the year immediately preceding, as reflected in the income and expenditures statement for that period. Short-run planning should also include the establishment of an emergency fund containing three to six months' worth of income. This special savings account serves as a safety valve that can be used in case of financial emergencies—for example, a temporary loss of income.

The degree of effectiveness in reaching short-run goals significantly affects the ability to achieve long-

short-run financial goals
Goals that are set for a period of one year or less and are consistent with established long-run goals.

EXHIBIT 3.4
The Weaver's Summary of Long-Run and Short-Run Personal Financial Goals

It is important to establish long-run financial goals in order to lend a general sense of direction to the financial decisions and activities we undertake. Short-run financial goals support the long-run goals by specifying what we hope to achieve in the next year or so; they specify the dollar outlay required for their achievement as well as relative priority.

PERSONAL FINANCIAL GOALS

Name(s) *Fred & Denise Weaver*   Date *December 26, 1989*

LONG-RUN GOALS

Goal Date	Goal Description
1992	Pay off all loans other than mortgage
	Save money for new home
	Begin to build an investment portfolio
	Start family
	Buy new car (replace Volkswagen, trade every three years)
1996	Build investment portfolio
	Save money for new home
	Buy station wagon (replace Cutlass, trade every three years)
2000	Buy new $150,000 home
	Purchase new furniture
	Start saving for children's college education
2004	Buy sailboat
	Purchase summer home
	Accumulate net worth of $65,000
2011	Send children to college
	Buy third car for children
	Accumulate net worth of $90,000
	Travel to Europe
	Remodel home
2018	Children finish education
	Buy larger sailboat
	Travel to Australia
	Accumulate net worth of $150,000
2023	Sell home and buy condominium
	Retire from job
	Accumulate net worth of $250,000

SHORT-RUN GOALS (for the coming year)

Priority	Goal Description	Dollar Outlay
1	Denise finish school	$ 1,670
2	Purchase new tires for Cutlass	300
3	Purchase career clothes for Denise	1,750
4	Buy new suit for Fred	800
5	Accumulate net worth of $18,000	—
6	Take two-week vacation to Canada	4,000
7	Buy workshop equipment	1,500
8	Take ski trip to Colorado	4,800
9	Purchase electric garage door opener	350
10		

run goals. If short-run goals are not attained, the likelihood of achieving long-run goals is greatly reduced. In setting short-run goals, current desires must not be allowed to override the requirements for achieving long-run goals. The general tendency to prefer current consumption over consumption in the distant future may be the greatest challenge in setting short-run goals. Short-run sacrifices may be necessary in order to provide for a comfortable future; realizing this fact 10 or 20 years too late may make some important financial goals unattainable.

The Financial Goals of Fred and Denise Weaver

In Chapter 2, we were introduced to Fred and Denise Weaver, whose financial data were used to develop their financial statements. We will use the Weavers' financial data throughout this chapter to illustrate various aspects of financial planning and budgeting. The Weavers' long- and short-run financial goals, which they set in December of 1989, are described in the following sections.

The Weavers' Long-Run Financial Goals. Since Fred and Denise are 26 and 24 years old, respectively, they have set their most distant long-run financial goal 34 years from now—a point in time at which they would like to retire. The top portion of Exhibit 3.3 presents a summary of the Weavers' long-run financial goals. They have set their goal dates arbitrarily at 1992, 1996, 2000, 2004, 2011, 2018, and 2023. As time passes, they will probably adjust both the goals and the dates. Although most of their goals do not have dollar amounts attached, Fred and Denise can still use them to lend general direction to their short-run financial plans. In the planning process, the Weavers have made estimates of the costs of achieving their various long-run goals and then set the short-run goals necessary for attaining them.

The Weavers' Short-Run Financial Goals. In the final week of December 1989, Fred and Denise set their short-run financial goals for the coming year. They considered three factors: (1) their current financial condition as reflected in their balance sheet (Exhibit 2.3); (2) their latest income and expenditures statement (Exhibit 2.8), from which they were able to evaluate their past spending patterns in order to estimate their spending requirements

for 1990; and (3) their *long-run* financial goals (top of Exhibit 3.4), (on facing page) which provided the framework for the Weavers' short-run goals. The Weavers' short-run financial goals for the coming year, along with the dollar outlay required to achieve each of them, are given in the bottom portion of Exhibit 3.4.

In order to simplify the process of eliminating expenditures in the event that sufficient funds are not available, the Weavers have assigned priorities to their short-run goals. The first four items are considered necessities, and the fifth is associated with their long-run net worth goal. (Note that because of the many interactions affecting it, the dollar outlay required to achieve the net worth goal cannot be clearly specified.) The remaining items are extras, or luxuries, that the Weavers would like to acquire during the year but probably can do without. Once they have prepared their budget, the Weavers will be able to determine which of their short-run goals they can afford during the coming year.

SETTING UP A CASH BUDGET ◼

Cash budgets are prepared from schedules of estimated income and expenditures for the coming year and provide a system of disciplined spending. How would you go about estimating your income and expenditures for the coming year? Before reading on, spend a few moments answering this question.

Once you have established your short-run financial goals, you can prepare a cash budget for the coming year. Recall that a budget is a short-term financial planning device designed to allow you to achieve your short-run financial goals. As such, it also makes a positive contribution toward the achievement of your *long-run* financial goals. If carefully followed, a budget will enable you to accomplish two very important objectives. First, it will help you implement a system of *disciplined spending* as opposed to just existing from one paycheck to the next. Second, it will assist you in reducing the amount of money wasted on *needless spending*

EXHIBIT 3.5

The Weavers' Schedule of Estimated Income for 1990

While Fred's take-home pay will be the dominant source of income, their combined earnings will increase in July, when Denise has her M.B.A. and the Weavers join the ranks of two-career, two-income families.

CASH BUDGET: ESTIMATED INCOME

Name(s) *Fred & Denise Weaver*

For the *Year* Ending *December 31, 1990*

SOURCES OF INCOME		Jan.	Feb.	Mar.	Apr.	May	June	July	Aug.	Sep.	Oct.	Nov.	Dec.	Total for the Year
Take-home pay	Name: *Fred*	$2,050	$2,050	$2,050	$2,050	$2,050	$2,050	$2,360	$2,360	$2,360	$2,360	$2,360	$2,360	$26,460
	Name: *Denise*	310	310	310	310	310	310	1,450	1,450	1,450	1,450	1,450	1,450	10,560
	Name:													
Bonuses and commissions													1,000	1,000
Pensions and annuities														
Investment income	Interest			45			45			45			45	180
	Dividends			12			12			12			12	48
	Rents													
	Sale of securities													
	Other													
Other income														
	TOTAL INCOME	$2,360	$2,360	$2,417	$2,360	$2,360	$2,417	$3,810	$3,810	$3,867	$3,810	$3,810	$4,867	$38,248

and, in so doing, increase the amount of funds allocated to savings and investments.

Like the income and expenditures statement, *a budget should be prepared on a cash basis;* thus, we refer to this document as a **cash budget**. In essence, a cash budget deals with cash receipts and cash expenditures that are expected to occur in the coming year. For budgeting purposes, it makes no difference whether money is being spent on living expenses or on loan payments; in either case, an outflow of cash is involved, and therefore the amounts would be included in the cash budget. On the other hand, an asset purchased on credit would not be included, at least not until payments were made on the loan. Basically, a cash budget contains estimates of income and expenditures, including savings and investments, that are expected to occur in the coming year. It is usually divided into monthly intervals, although in some cases other time intervals may be more convenient.

The cash budget preparation process has three stages: estimating income, estimating expenditures, and finalizing the budget. When estimating income and expenditures, you should take into account any anticipated changes in the cost of living and their impact on your budget components. If your income is fixed—not expected to change over the budgetary period—increases in various items of expenditure will probably cause the purchasing power of your income to deteriorate.

A cash budget is a report that shows the amount of money you will be spending from month to month. **Fantasy:** A cash budget is a projection of *both* income and expenditures and is usually prepared on a monthly basis.

Estimating Income

The first step in the cash budget preparation process is to prepare a **schedule of estimated income** for the coming year. Since bills are most commonly rendered and paid monthly, it is best to estimate income as well as expenditures using monthly intervals. The income forecast takes into consideration all income expected for the year—for example, the take-home pay of both spouses, expected bonuses or commissions, pension or annuity income, and interest, dividend, rental and security sale income. Many families find it useful to use a schedule like the one in Exhibit 3.5 (on facing page) to project their income.

When estimating income, keep in mind that *any item expected to be received for which repayment is required is not considered income.* For example, a loan is treated not as a source of income but as a *liability* for which scheduled repayments are required. Note also that unlike the income and expenditures statement, it is *take-home pay* that should be used on the cash budget rather than gross income before deductions and withholdings. This makes sense, since in a cash budget you want to direct your attention to those areas over which you have some control—and most people certainly have little, if any, control over things like taxes withheld, contributions to company insurance and pension plans, and the like. In effect, take-home pay represents the amount of *disposable income* you receive from your employer.

Estimating Expenditures

The second step in the cash budgeting process is by far the most difficult: It involves preparing a **schedule of estimated expenditures** for the coming year. This is usually done by using the actual expenditures from previous years (as found on income and expenditures statements for those periods), along with predetermined short-run financial goals. Families without past expenditure data must use a "needs approach" to develop spending forecasts; that is, needs are projected and dollar values attached to them in order to make estimates of future expenditures. Careful attention should be given to expenditures associated with medical dis-

---

cash budget
A budget that takes into account estimated monthly cash receipts and expenditures for the coming year.

schedule of estimated income
A part of the cash budget that shows an item-by-item breakdown of the estimated income for each month of the coming year.

schedule of estimated expenditures
A part of the cash budget that shows an item-by-item breakdown of the estimated expenditures for the coming year.

EXHIBIT 3.6

The Weavers' Initial Schedule of Estimated Annual Expenditures for 1990

The initial schedule of estimated expenditures is usually prepared on an annual basis, since some of the numbers are probably going to have to be changed anyway; preparing the schedule this way saves a lot of time if the budget does not balance. (Note: the parenthetical numbers provide suggested guidelines of how much to spend in each major category.)

CASH BUDGET: ESTIMATED EXPENDITURES

Name(s) _Fred & Denise Weaver_

For the _Year_ Ending _December 31, 1990_

EXPENDITURE CATEGORIES		Annual Amounts
Housing (12–30%)	Rent/mortgage payment (include insurance and taxes, if applicable)	$ 8,280
	Repairs, maint., improvements _Gar. Door Opener_	350
Utilities (4–8%)	Gas, electric, water	1,820
	Phone	300
	Cable TV and other	
Food (15–25%)	Groceries	2,280
	Eating out	1,920
Autos (5–18%)	Loan payments	960
	License plates, fees, etc.	200
	Gas, oil, repairs, tires, maintenance	1,500
Medical (2–10%)	Health, major medical, disability insurance (not provided by employer)	
	Doctor, dentist, hospital, drugs	240
Clothing (3–8%)	Clothes, uniforms, shoes, etc.	3,200
Insurance (4–8%)	Homeowner's (if not covered by mortgage payment)	370
	Life (not provided by employer)	290
	Auto — _liability only_	300
Taxes (N/A)	Income and social security	
	Property (if not included in mortgage)	
Appliances, furniture, and other (2–8%)	Loan payments	400
	Purchases and repairs _—workshop equipment_	1,500
Health and hygiene (1–3%)	Laundry, cosmetics, hair care	960
Recreation and entertainment (2–8%)	Vacations — _Canada & Colo._	5,800
	Other recreation and entertainment	1,440
Savings and investments (3–10%)	Savings, stocks, bonds, etc.	2,000
Other expenditures (1–10%)	Charitable contributions	160
	Gifts	300
	Education expenses — _Denise_	1,670
	Subscriptions, magazines, books	
	Other: _Loan payments to parents_	800
	Other: _misc._	600
Fun money (1–5%)		2,520
	TOTAL EXPENDITURES	$ 40,160

abilities, divorce and child support, and similar special circumstances.

Regardless of whether or not historical information is available, it is important that you *become aware of your expenditure patterns and how your money is being spent.* Carefully study your spending habits to see if you are doing things that should be eliminated (like writing too many small, frivolous checks or using your credit cards too freely). In addition, you will probably find it easier to budget expenditures if you group them into several general categories, rather than trying to estimate each and every item. An example of one such grouping scheme—patterned after the categories used with the income and expenditures statement in Chapter Two—is provided in Exhibit 3.6 (on facing page).

Initially, achievement of all short-run goals should be built into your expenditure estimates. To do this effectively, the cost of achieving the goals as well as the timing of the expenditures should be estimated. Any current or short-run contributions toward achievement of long-run goals should also be quantified and appropriately scheduled into the budget. Equally important are scheduled additions to savings and investments, since *planned savings* should be high on everyone's list of goals. If the inclusion of all these items will not allow the budget to balance, some of them may have to be removed from the final budget. Estimates of expenditures should be based on current price levels and then increased by a percentage that reflects the anticipated rate of inflation. For example, if the monthly food bill is estimated at $300 and 8 percent inflation is expected in food prices, the estimated monthly food expenditure should be budgeted at $324—or $300 + $24 ($300 × 8 percent). An expenditure category of **fun money** should also be included. This money, which family members use as they wish without reporting how they spent it, gives each one some degree of financial independence and thus helps provide for a healthy family budget relationship.

Finalizing and Preparing the Cash Budget

Once income and expenditures estimates have been made, the budget can be *finalized.* This involves comparing projected income and expenditures on month-to-month and annual bases. A **balanced budget** results when the total income for the year *equals or exceeds* total expenditures.

The Budget Format. The **budget summary** basically summarizes and combines projections from the schedules of estimated income and expenditures. It is broken into three sections: income, expenditures, and the difference between them, which may be either a surplus or a deficit. Within the first two sections, the individual items of income and expenditure are shown separately. Usually the budget shows monthly figures as well as an annual total for each income and expenditure item. In many situations, the number of budget entries dictates whether it is better to break the budget into separate schedules, as we have illustrated— one for estimated income, one for estimated expenditures (including savings and investments), and one summarizing the total monthly cash budget. The income and expenditures schedules can be prepared separately and the budget summary then used to bring these components together to determine the amount of any surpluses or deficits. Admittedly, there is a lot of "number crunching" in personal cash budgeting. Accordingly, as the accompanying "Money in Action" box reveals, personal finance software for use with a personal computer has been made available.

What to Do with Monthly Deficits. Even though the budget for the year may balance, expenditures in certain months may exceed income, causing a monthly **budget deficit**; likewise, in-

---

fun money
Money that is allocated to family members to use as they wish without regard to how they spend it.

balanced budget
A budget in which total income for the year equals or exceeds total expenditures.

budget summary
A statement that summarizes and combines projections of estimated income, estimated expenditures, and the difference between them, which may be either a surplus or a deficit.

budget deficit
A situation that occurs when the expenditures exceed the income in a cash budget.

MONEY IN ACTION

Using Personal Finance Software

You can buy personal finance software packages in colorful shrink-wrapped packages at prices ranging from about $50 to as much as $250. (A brief description of each of the five most popular personal finance programs is given in the accompanying table.) These packages are designed for tasks like check writing, budgeting, figuring your net worth and balancing your checkbook. They have been widely heralded as a natural—even destined—step in the evolution of the personal computer, the idea being to let the machine do the tedious work in keeping track of one's money. But destiny be damned—after six years on the market, personal finance software is still struggling to find a solid constituency.

Some programs, notably *Andrew Tobias' Managing Your Money (MYM),* have established loyal cadres. *MYM*'s publisher reports selling more than 250,000 copies since the pro-

gram was issued in 1984. But it's unclear how many of these users are cultists who would cut their toenails by computer if they had the right peripheral device and how many are ordinary folk with limited tolerance for making backup disks and spending hours entering data.

Managing Your Money is widely regarded as the class act in the field. In an October 1988 *PC World* magazine poll, 55 percent of the respondents rated Tobias' program as the best. (*Dollars and Sense,* by Monogram, got the silver medal with 16 percent.) Recent upgrades have added a card file and a word processor, making *MYM* an all-purpose desktop tool for most of the business—financial and nonfinancial—that goes on at home or in a one-person office. And the program is justifiably acclaimed for the wit and elegance of its users' manual, written by Tobias.

Once inside, you begin by setting up a budget and elec-

tronic checkbook. Most personal finance software offers at least these two stalwarts (Intuit's *Quicken,* the cheapest and best-selling of the batch, offers nothing more). A computerized budget is very much like a paper budget and just as hard to honor. The only easy part is that it is electronically connected to the checkbook, so that every check you write automatically gets credited to one of your budget categories. The program tallies your balance with bug-busting accuracy and prints checks and envelopes. (If you insist on carrying one of those old-fashioned checkbooks, remember to enter your transactions into the computer too.)

MYM also has a built-in tax estimator that scans your budget, then prints up hypothetical tax forms reflecting the latest changes in tax law—and perhaps ruining an otherwise blissful August. It will do the 1040 form, Schedules A, B, C, D, E, F, W, SE, 2106 and the one for

come in some months may exceed expenditures, causing a monthly **budget surplus**. Two remedies exist: (1) Expenditures might be transferred from months in which budget deficits occur to months in which budget surpluses exist or, conversely, income might be transferred from months with surpluses to months with deficits. (2) Savings, investments, or borrowing may be used to cover temporary deficits. Since the budget for the year is balanced, the need for funds to cover these short-

ages is only temporary. Once a month having a budget surplus is reached, funds used to cover deficits can be returned to savings and investments, or loans can be repaid. Either of the preceding remedies for a monthly budget deficit in a balanced annual budget is possible, but the second is probably more practical.

What to Do If You End the Year in the Red. Situations in which the budget for the year is not

the alternative minimum tax. The program's Help screens suggest ways you can save taxes; elsewhere in the program they offer basic financial planning advice (the section on insurance is excellent). A built-in financial calculator in the program can be used to do all the figuring needed in refinancing a mortgage, planning for retirement and college costs, or making rent/buy decisions.

According to MECA, the company that produced *MYM,* most of the users are male professionals whose household incomes of more than $75,000 a year may explain the popularity of the program's last important feature, the portfolio manager. This lets you store and update 300 stocks or other investments. It's not not exclusive to *MYM. Sylvia Porter's Personal Finance* series can juggle investments this way, as can *Dollars and Sense.* But *MYM* adds an extra: a data retrieval package, *Managing the Market* ($149.95),

that lets you get financial data over the telephone using a modem.

The time these programs consume is their main drawback. Even with *MYM,* you should count on spending two hours every week entertaining financial bric-a-brac—statements, bills, changes in stock values, and the like—that come by mail. This is the real price of admission. Are you prepared to commit the effort needed to feed your program's thirst for data? If not, I suggest that you save yourself both time and money and get by with your old checkbook—bugs and all.

Popular Personal Finance Software

Here's a rundown on personal finance software for IBM-PC-compatible computers (IBM) or Macintosh (Mac).
Andrew Tobias' Managing Your Money (MECA $219.98)
The reigning champ, *MYM* is powerful, well documented and

easy to . . . well, no personal finance software is truly easy to use, but this comes close (IBM, Mac).
Dollars and Sense (Monogram, $179.95).
This one is particularly strong in connecting to electronic banking services (IBM, Mac).
Sylvia Porter's Personal Financial Planner (Timeworks, $99)
Made to work with other Timeworks software, this program provides worksheets for various financial scenarios (IBM).
Quicken (Intuit, $49.95)
This planner does only checkwriting and budgeting but outsells the rest (IBM, Mac).
MacMoney (Survivor, $119.95)
Use the mouse to create line graphs, bar graphs, and pie charts for every budget category, from checking accounts to tax deductions (Mac).

Source: Augustin Hedberg, "Pestered by an Unbalanced Budget? Personal-Finance Software Can Help," *Money,* November, 1988, pp. 47–48. Used with permission.

in balance are more difficult to cope with. Three approaches exist. One is either *liquidate enough savings and investments* or *borrow enough* to meet the total budget shortfall for the year. This action is not recommended, because it violates the objective of budgeting: to set expenditures at a level that will provide for a reasonable standard of living while allowing positive contributions toward the achievement of long-run goals. Drawing down savings and investments or borrowing in order to make

the budget balance tends to reduce net worth. People who use this approach are not living within their means.

budget surplus
A situation that occurs when the income exceeds the expenditures in a cash budget.

A second—and preferred—approach is to *cut low priority expenditure items* out of the budget in order to bring the total budget into balance. This approach forces the budget to balance without using external sources of funds. Low-priority expenditures are those items associated with the short-run financial goals believed to be least important. Some people who use this technique to bring their budgets into balance divide their expenditures into two groups—inflexible and flexible. *Inflexible expenditures* are those that must be made on the basis of either contracts or necessity; mortgage payments, loan payments, and utility bills are examples. *Flexible expenditures* are for noncontractual, nonnecessity items, such as recreation, entertainment, and certain clothing purchases. These flexible expenditures can be cut from the budget in order to bring it into balance.

A third approach is to *increase income* by assuming a second, perhaps part-time job or finding an alternative job that pays more. This is probably the most difficult approach, for it is likely to result in a significant change in leisure activities and lifestyle. Individuals who have no savings or investments to liquidate and are unable to meet expenditures for necessity items may find that taking a second job or changing jobs provides the only feasible course of action for balancing their budgets.

The budget is complete once all monthly deficits have been considered, and the total annual budget is balanced. As a result, the income for the year should equal or exceed the year's expenditures, and no monthly deficits should exist.

If a budget shows a cash deficit for the year, then you have no choice but to borrow enough money to make up the shortfall. **Fantasy:** While borrowing is one way to cover a budget shortfall, there are other alternatives: reducing your spending or liquidating some of your savings or investments are two of them.

A Cash Budget for Fred and Denise Weaver

Using their short-run financial goals (bottom of Exhibit 3.4) and their past financial statements (Exhibits 2.3 and 2.8), Fred and Denise Weaver have prepared their cash budget for the 1990 calendar year. They have done this by using separate schedules of estimated income and expenditures along with a budget summary.

Schedule of Estimated Income. The Weavers' schedule of estimated income for the year ended December 31, 1990, is shown in Exhibit 3.5 and provides an item-by-item breakdown for each month in that year. Their total annual income, which is derived primarily from Fred's wages, is expected to be $38,248. Using the amount of take-home pay, as the Weavers did, eliminates the need to show taxes, social security payments, and other payroll deductions in the expenditure portion of the budget. Note also that a projected salary increase for both Fred and Denise has been incorporated in the estimated income figures beginning in July, when Denise starts a new job (after graduating with her M.B.A. in June).

Schedule of Estimated Expenditures. The Weavers' initial schedule of estimated *annual* expenditures, for the year ended December 31, 1990, is presented in Exhibit 3.6. Note that Fred and Denise have built $2,250 (or $210 a month) into their budget as fun money. They will divide the fun money equally between them and will not report on its disposition. Another significant aspect of their schedule of estimated expenditures is the $2,000 included under savings and investments. In light of scheduled debt repayment, Fred and Denise estimate that putting that amount aside will enable them to easily exceed their net worth goal of $18,000 (as discussed at length in Chapter 2). Note also that the Weavers are anticipating only a slight amount of inflation and have considered the effects on their budget by adjusting certain expenditures upward for anticipated price increases. Aside from this, the schedule of estimated expenditures shown in Exhibit 3.6 is self-explanatory. Of course, it represents only the Weavers' first estimate of their expenditures, aimed at the achievement of *all* of the short-run goals listed in the bottom portion of Exhibit 3.4.

Finalizing the Weavers' Cash Budget. Reviewing the Weavers' initial schedule of expenditures (Exhibit 3.6), we can see that the initial estimate results in total expenditures of $40,160. Given their estimated income of $38,248 (Exhibit 3.5), it is clear that their budget is not balanced; a budget deficit of approximately $1,900 exists. In order to bring the budget into balance, Fred and Denise are going to have to cut certain low-priority goals from their budget, reschedule some of their loan payments, and/or reduce their fun money allocation. After some deliberation, they decide to make the following adjustments:

1. Eliminate purchase of electric garage-door opener costing $350.
2. Shorten trips to Canada and Colorado, saving $600.
3. Reduce purchase of workshop equipment by $600.
4. Reschedule $200 of loan repayment to parents.
5. Reduce allocation of fun money by $240 for the year ($20 per month).

These expenditure reductions of $1,990 have lowered the total scheduled expenditures for the year to $38,170, which now falls within the total income estimate of $38,248. Since expenditures are now at desired levels, the schedule of estimated expenditures can now be prepared on a monthly basis, as is done in Exhibit 3.7. The expenditure totals, as adjusted, are given in the final column of the schedule. Once these adjustments are made, estimated annual expenditures no longer exceed estimated annual income, and the budget is now balanced.

The Weavers' final step in the budgeting process is to analyze monthly surpluses and deficits in order to estimate whether or not savings, investments, or borrowing should be used to meet any monthly deficits. To do this, they have prepared the budget summary that appears in Exhibit 3.8. Estimated income figures are derived from Exhibit 3.5 and estimated expenditures from Exhibit 3.7. The summary shows monthly cash surpluses and deficits that total $78 in the black for the year. This surplus can be used to add to the Weavers' savings and investments or to repay a portion of one of their loans. The bottom line of the budget summary lists the cumulative, or running, totals of the cash surpluses and deficits.

Note that although monthly deficits occur on and off from January through August, their magnitude and timing result in a cumulative deficit for the months of January through October. In order to cover these deficits, Fred and Denise have arranged an interest-free loan from their parents. Had they been required to use their savings to finance these temporary deficits, they would have had to forgo some of their interest earnings, included as part of their estimated income. Were the Weavers completely unable to obtain funds to cover these deficits, they would have had to reschedule their planned expenditures or income.

Comparing Actual Results to Budgeted Figures

In the final analysis, a cash budget will have value only if (1) it is put into use and (2) careful records are kept of actual income and expenditures. Keeping such records tells you whether you are staying within budget limits. Record income and expenditures often enough to ensure that nothing of any significance is overlooked, yet not so often that it becomes a nuisance. You can then use this information each month to compare actual income and spending to budgeted figures. This way it will be easy to identify the major budget categories in which income is falling far short (by 5 to 10 percent or more) or where spending is far exceeding desired results (that is, actuals 5 to 10 percent or more above budget). Once you have identified these areas, you can take corrective action to ensure that the budget will stay on course.

A **budget record book** facilitates such recordkeeping. Looseleaf binders with separate pages for each of the various income and expenditure categories serve this purpose quite well. At the beginning of each month, the amount budgeted for each category should be recorded. Then, as income is received and money spent, entries should be made in the appropriate categories. Instead of making these entries each day in the book, many people prefer to record them first on a **master income and expenditure sheet**, from which the appropriate entries are posted to the record book at specified intervals, such as every five to seven days. In either case, entries are rounded to the nearest dol-

---

budget record book
A document, usually a looseleaf binder, that has separate pages for each of the various income and expenditure categories.

master income and expenditure sheet
A record of income and expenditure items from which appropriate entries are posted to the record book at specified intervals.

EXHIBIT 3.7

The Weavers' Final Schedule of Estimated Monthly Expenditures for 1990

When put on a monthly basis, the schedule of estimated expenditures shows in detail projected month-by-month spending patterns; you can tell at a glance where most of your money is going each month.

CASH BUDGET: ESTIMATED EXPENDITURES

Name(s): *Fred & Denise Weaver*

For the *Year*   Ending *December 31, 1990*

Category	Expenditure	Jan.	Feb.	Mar.	Apr.	May	June	July	Aug.	Sep.	Oct.	Nov.	Dec.	Total for the Year
Housing	Rent/mortgage payment (include insurance and taxes, if applicable)	$690	$690	$690	$690	$690	$690	$690	$690	$690	$690	$690	$690	$8,280
	Repairs, maint., improvements													0
Utilities	Gas, electric, water	175	175	175	100	100	145	145	185	175	135	135	175	1,820
	Phone	25	25	25	25	25	25	25	25	25	25	25	25	300
	Cable TV and other													
Food	Groceries	190	190	190	190	190	190	190	190	190	190	190	190	2,280
	Eating out	160	160	160	160	160	160	160	160	160	160	160	160	1,920
Autos	Loan payments	80	80	80	80	80	80	80	80	80	80	80	80	960
	License plates, fees, etc.		200											200
	Gas, oil, repairs, tires, maintenance	200	200	200	100	100	100	100	100	100	100	100	100	1,500
Medical	Health, major medical, disability insurance (not provided by employer)	*Paid by Fred's Employer...*												
	Doctor, dentist, hospital, drugs	20	20	20	20	20	20	20	20	20	20	20	20	240
Clothing	Clothes, uniforms, shoes, etc.	150	150	250	250	600	800	200	150	100	200	200	250	3,200
Insurance	Homeowners (if not covered by mortgage payment)						185						185	370
	Life (not provided by employer)													
	Auto – *liability only*											290		290
Taxes	Income and social security		150						150					300
	Property (if not included in mortgage)	*Included in Mortgage Payment...*												
Appliances, furniture and other	Loan payments	33	33	33	33	33	33	33	33	33	33	33	37	400
	Purchases and repairs								300	300	300			900
Health and hygiene	Laundry, cosmetics, hair care	80	80	80	80	80	80	80	80	80	80	80	80	960
Recreation and entertainment	Vacations – *Canada & Colo.*								3,600				1,600	5,200
	Other recreation and entertainment	120	120	120	120	120	120	120	120	120	120	120	120	1,440
Savings and investments	Savings, stocks, bonds, etc.	100	100	100	100	100	100	100	100	100	100		1,000	2,000
Other expenditures	Charitable contributions	100					30			30				160
	Gifts				20	40			40				200	300
	Education expenses – *Denise*		1,500			100	70							1,670
	Subscriptions, magazines, books													
	Other: *Loan payments to parents*									200	200	200		600
	Other: *Misc.*	50	50	50	50	50	50	50	50	50	50	50	50	600
Fun money		190	190	190	190	190	190	190	190	190	190	190	190	2,280
TOTAL EXPENDITURES		$2,363	$4,113	$2,323	$2,208	$2,678	$3,068	$2,183	$6,263	$2,643	$2,573	$2,563	$5,152	$38,710

Taxes — Income and social security: Assumed Equal to Amounts Withheld From Paychecks...

EXHIBIT 3.8

The Weavers' Monthly Cash Budget Summary

The Weavers' cash budget summary shows several months in which substantial cash deficits are expected to occur; they can use this information to develop plans for covering these monthly shortfalls.

CASH BUDGET: MONTHLY SUMMARY

Name(s) Fred & Denise Weaver

For the Year   Ending December 31, 1990

	Jan.	Feb.	Mar.	Apr.	May	June	July	Aug.	Sep.	Oct.	Nov.	Dec.	Total for the Year
INCOME													
Take-home pay	$2,360	$2,360	$2,360	$2,360	$2,360	$2,360	$3,810	$3,810	$3,810	$3,810	$3,810	$3,810	$37,020
Bonuses and commissions												1,000	1,000
Pensions and annuities													
Investment income			57			57			57			57	228
Other income													
(I) Total Income	$2,360	$2,360	$2,417	$2,360	$2,360	$2,417	$3,810	$3,810	$3,867	$3,810	$3,810	$4,867	$58,248
EXPENDITURES													
Housing	$690	$690	$690	$690	$690	$690	$690	$690	$690	$690	$690	$690	$8,280
Utilities	200	200	200	125	125	170	170	210	200	160	160	200	2,120
Food	350	350	350	350	350	350	350	350	350	350	350	350	4,200
Autos	280	480	280	180	180	180	180	180	180	180	180	180	2,660
Medical	20	20	20	20	20	20	20	20	20	20	20	20	240
Clothing	150	150	250	250	600	800	200	150	100	100	200	250	3,200
Insurance		150				185		150			290	185	960
Taxes													
Appliances, furniture, and other	33	33	33	33	33	33	33	333	333	333	33	37	1,300
Health and hygiene	80	80	80	80	80	80	80	80	80	80	80	80	960
Recreation and entertainment	120	120	120	120	120	120	120	3720	120	120	120	1,720	6,640
Savings and investments	100	100	100	100	100	100	100	100	100	100		1000	2,000
Other expenditures	150	1550	50	70	190	150	50	90	280	250	250	250	3,330
Fun money	190	190	190	190	190	190	190	190	190	190	190	190	2,280
(II) Total Expenditures	$2,363	$4,113	$2,363	$2,208	$2,678	$3,068	$2,183	$6,263	$2,643	$2,573	$2,563	$5,152	$38,170
CASH SURPLUS (OR DEFICIT) [(I) − (II)]	($3)	($1,753)	$54	$152	($318)	($651)	$1,627	($2,453)	$1,224	$1,237	$1,247	($285)	$78
CUMULATIVE CASH SURPLUS (OR DEFICIT)	($3)	($1,756)	($1,702)	($1,550)	($1,868)	($2,519)	($892)	($3,345)	($2,121)	($884)	$363	$78	$78

EXHIBIT 3.9

The Weavers' Budget Control Schedule for January, February, and March 1990

The budget control schedule provides important feedback on how the actual cash flow is stacking up to the forecasted cash budget.
If the variances are significant enough and/or continue month after month, that is perhaps a signal that either spending habits or the cash budget should be altered.

BUDGET CONTROL SCHEDULE

Name(s) _Fred & Denise Weaver_

For the __3__ Months Ending _March 31, 1990_

INCOME	January Budgeted Amount (1)	January Actual (2)	January Monthly Variance (3)	January Year-to-Date Variance (4)	February Budgeted Amount (5)	February Actual (6)	February Monthly Variance (7)	February Year-to-Date Variance (8)	March Budgeted Amount (9)	March Actual (10)	March Monthly Variance (11)	March Year-to-Date Variance (12)
Take-home pay	$2,360	$2,348	($ 12)	($ 12)	$2,360	$2,352	($ 8)	($ 20)	$2,360	$2,352	($ 8)	($ 28)
Bonuses and commissions												
Pensions and annuities												
Investment income												
Other income									57	64	7	7
(I) Total Income	$2,360	$2,348	($ 12)	($ 12)	$2,360	$2,352	($ 8)	($ 20)	$2,417	$2,416	($ 1)	($ 21)
EXPENDITURES												
Housing	$ 690	$ 690	$ 0	$ 0	$ 690	$ 690	$ 0	$ 0	$ 690	$ 690	$ 0	$ 0
Utilities	200	224	24	24	200	194	(6)	18	200	175	(25)	(7)
Food	350	340	(10)	(10)	350	378	28	18	350	348	(2)	16
Autos	280	305	25	25	480	505	25	50	280	266	(14)	36
Medical	20	0	(20)	(20)	20	34	14	(6)	20	0	(20)	(26)
Clothing	150	187	37	37	150	122	(28)	9	250	212	(38)	(29)
Insurance					150	150	0	0				0
Taxes												
Appliances, furniture, and other	33	33	0	0	33	33	0	0	33	64	31	31
Health and hygiene	80	89	9	9	80	71	(9)	0	80	86	6	(6)
Recreation and entertainment	120	104	(16)	(16)	120	142	22	6	120	108	(12)	(6)
Savings and investments	100	100	0	0	100	100	0	0	100	100	0	0
Other expenditures	150	88	(62)	(62)	1,550	1,605	55	(7)	50	0	(50)	(57)
Fun money	190	190	0	0	190	190	0	0	190	230	40	40
(II) Total Expenditures	$2,363	$2,350	($ 13)	($ 13)	$4,113	$4,214	$ 101	$ 88	$2,363	$2,279	($ 84)	$ 4
CASH SURPLUS (OR DEFICIT)(I) – (II)	($ 3)	($ 2)	$ 1	$ 1	($1,753)	($1,862)	($ 109)	($ 108)	$ 54	$ 137	$ 83	($ 25)
CUMULATIVE CASH SURPLUS (OR DEFICIT)	($ 3)	($ 2)	$	$	($1,756)	($1,844)	$	$	($1,702)	($1,727)	$	$

Key: Col. (3) = Col. (2) – Col. (1); Col. (7) = Col. (6) – Col. (5); Col. (11) = Col. (10) – Col. (9)
Col. (4) = Col. (3); Col. (8) = Col. (4) + Col. (7); Col. (12) = Col. (8) + Col. (11)

lar—that is accurate enough for budget purposes, and it makes the arithmetic a lot easier.

At the end of each month, the income and expenditure category accounts in the budget record book should be totaled; each of these monthly totals should then be compared to the amounts budgeted for the month and any surplus or deficit determined. In theory, there should be zero variances in each budget category, but this normally occurs only for income accounts, like take-home pay, or for single, fixed-payment accounts, like mortgages, loan payments, and insurance premiums. More often than not, the other categories will end each month with positive or negative variances, indicating that a cash surplus or shortfall has occurred. It is not enough to simply determine the size of the monthly variances; they should be subjected to some analysis, particularly the larger ones. The presence of a surplus, of course, is no cause for concern; however, a deficit—which indicates either that the income did not materialize as expected or spending exceeded projections—does require attention.

An account deficit that occurs in only one period is less of a problem than one that occurs in a series of periods. If recurring deficits indicate that an account may have been underbudgeted, the budget may need to be adjusted to a level sufficient to cover the outlays. Budget adjustments of this type are usually accomplished by reducing the amount budgeted for accounts that may be either over-budgeted or nonessential. Only in exceptional situations should budget adjustments be financed by drawing down savings and investments, or by borrowing.

Control is important not only in individual categories or accounts but also in the total budget for the month. By examining end-of-month totals for all accounts, it is possible to determine whether a net budget surplus or deficit exists. Based on this finding, you can take appropriate action to maintain a balanced budget for the remainder of the year. The existence of total budget surpluses is advantageous, since the excess funds can be used for savings, investments, or debt repayment. Total period deficits, however, signal the need for corrective action, which normally consists of adjusting spending in subsequent months in order to end the year with a balanced budget.

An example of a budget control schedule for the Weaver budget is shown in Exhibit 3.9 (on facing page). The **budget control schedule** provides a summary of how actual income and expenditures compare to the various budget categories and where budget variances exist. Surpluses and deficits are recorded for each account category as well as for the total budget for the month. This kind of periodic feedback is essential for budgetary control and to make sure that actual income and expenditures are staying within the amounts budgeted. A budget control schedule enables the user to identify problem areas and take the actions necessary to bring individual accounts and/or the whole budget into balance. As far as the Weavers' budget is concerned, we can see that the actual income and expenditure levels are very close to their targets. The Weavers, in fact, were almost right on the button in January and while they were off by about $100 in February and March, there was no single income or expenditure item that stood out. The biggest variances occurred in *auto expenses* and *other expenditures,* but neither was far off the mark. Thus, through the first three months of the year, the Weavers seem to be doing a very good job of controlling their income and expenditures and, generally, in sticking to their budget. If, in contrast, there had been substantial variances in one (or more) of the accounts, they would have been able to look more closely at that account (or accounts) to learn the cause of any variances and then initiate corrective action.

One of the final steps in the cash budgeting process is to compare actual results to budgeted amounts. **Fact:** Comparing actual results to budgeted figures is essential to sound budgetary control, and provides a mechanism for isolating areas in need of corrective actions.

---

budget control schedule
A summary that shows how actual income and expenditures compare to the various budget categories and where surpluses or deficits exist.

SUMMARY

- Personal financial planning provides a logical framework for making financial decisions that are consistent with your long- and short-run financial goals; that is, sound financial planning involves not only defining financial goals and objectives, but developing, implementing, and controlling plans and strategies for putting goals into action.

- Long-run financial goals should provide general direction for the long haul, while short-run goals should be more specific in nature. Of course, short-run goals should be consistent with established long-run goals.

- When putting a dollar value on your financial goals, be sure to consider the *time value of money* and if appropriate, use the notion of *future value* when preparing your estimates.

- One of the major benefits of a cash budget is that it will help you to implement a system of disci-

plined spending; in addition, by curbing the amount of money wasted on needless spending, it can increase the amount of funds allocated to savings and investments.

- Household budgets should be set up on a cash basis and should identify the planned monthly cash receipts and cash expenditures for the coming year; the objective is to take in more money than you spend, so that you'll be able to save money and thereby add to your net worth over time.

- The final step in the cash budgeting process is to compare actual receipts and expenditures to budgeted figures to learn if, in fact, you are living within your budget and if not, to initiate appropriate corrective actions.

QUESTIONS AND PROBLEMS

1. What is the difference between a budget and a financial plan? Does a budget play any role in a financial plan?

2. Identify the six key steps involved in the financial planning process.

3. Describe a comprehensive financial plan. How are such plans constructed, and what kind of information do they contain?

4. What is a professional financial planner? Does it make any difference whether the financial planner earns money from commissions made on products sold, or on the fees he or she charges?

5. Distinguish between long-run and short-run financial goals. Be sure to mention:
   a. flexibility
   b. inflation considerations
   c. goal dates
   d. the key input to the cash budget

6. Over the past several years, Helen Daley has been able to put aside money on a regular basis; as a result, today she has $14,188 in savings and investments. She wants to establish her own business in 5 years and feels she will need $50,000 to do so.

   a. If she can earn 12 percent on her money, how much will her $14,188 savings/investments be worth in 5 years?

   b. Given your answer to part a, will Helen have the $50,000 she needs? If not, how much more money will she need?

   c. Given your answer to part b, how much will Helen have to save each year over the next 5 years to accumulate the additional money assuming she can earn interest at a rate of 12 percent?

   d. If Helen feels she can afford to save only $2,000 a year, given your answer to part a, will she have the $50,000 she needs to start her own business in 5 years?

7. Use future value techniques to solve the following problems:

   a. Starting with $10,000, how much will you have in 10 years if you can earn 15 percent on your money? If you can earn only 8 percent?

   b. If you inherited $25,000 today and invested all of it in a security that paid a 10 percent rate of return, how much would you have in 25 years?

c. If the average new home costs $75,000 today, how much will it cost in 10 years if the price increases by 6 percent each year?

d. You feel that in 15 years it will cost $30,000 to give your child a college education. Will you have enough if you take $10,000 *today* and invest it for the next 15 years at 8 percent? If you must start *from scratch,* how much will you have to save each year to have $30,000 in 15 years if you can earn an 8 percent rate of return on your investments?

e. Given you can earn 12 percent, how much will you have to save each year if you want to retire in 35 years with $1 million?

8. What is a budget deficit? How does it differ from a budget surplus?

9. The Smith family has prepared their annual budget for 1990. They have divided it into 12 monthly budgets. Although only one monthly budget balances, they have managed to balance the overall budget for the year. What remedies are available to the Smith family for meeting the monthly budget deficits?

10. Following is a portion of the Cook family's budget record for April 1990. Fill in the blanks in columns 6 and 7.

11. Why is it important to analyze actual budget surpluses or deficits at the end of each month?

12. How can accurate records and control procedures be utilized to ensure effectiveness in the financial planning process?

13. Dave and Betty Williamson are preparing their budget for 1990. Help the Williamsons reconcile the following differences, giving reasons to support your answers:

a. Their only source of income is Dave's salary, which amounts to $2,000 a month before taxes. Betty wants to show the $2,000 as their monthly income, whereas Dave argues that his take-home pay of $1,650 is the correct value to show.

b. Betty wants to make a provision for fun money, an idea that Dave cannot understand. He asks, "Why do we need fun money when everything is provided for in the budget?"

▪ 14. Prepare a record of your income and expenditures for the last 30 days; then prepare a personal budget for the next month (using a schedule of estimated expenditures like the one in Exhibit 3.5). Use the budget to control and regulate your expenditures during the month. Discuss the impact of the budget on your spending behavior as well as any differences between your expected and actual spending patterns.

15. Explain the role that the personal computer can play in the budgeting process; briefly discuss some of the software programs that are available for home budgeting purposes.

Item Number (1)	Item (2)	Amount Budgeted (3)	Amount Expended (4)	Beginning Balance (5)	Monthly Surplus (Deficit) (6)	Cumulative Surplus (Deficit) (7)
1	Rent	$350	$360	$20	$_____	$_____
2	Groceries	310	275	−15	_____	_____
3	Telephone	25	38	−5	_____	_____
4	Utilities	150	145	15	_____	_____
5	Recreation and entertainment	50	60	−50	_____	_____

CASE PROBLEMS

3.1 The Sullivans' Version of Financial Planning

John and Irene Sullivan are a married couple in their mid-twenties. John is a computer analyst and earns $20,000 per year after taxes. Irene works as a sales rep and takes home $16,500 per year. Since their marriage four years ago, John and Irene have been living comfortably. Their income has exceeded their expenditures, and they have accumulated a net worth of nearly $25,000—$15,000 represents equity in their home, cars, furniture, and other personal belongings, and the other $10,000 is held in the form of savings accounts and common stock investments. Because their income has always been more than adequate to allow them to live in the fashion they desire, the Sullivans have done no financial planning.

Irene has just learned that she is two months pregnant and is concerned about how they will make ends meet once she quits work and their child is born. Each time she and John discuss the matter, John tells her not to worry since "we have always managed to pay our bills on time." Irene cannot understand this, as her income will be completely eliminated. In order to convince Irene that there is no need for concern, John has prepared the following income statement for the past year.

Income Statement for John and Irene Sullivan (Past Year)

Income

John's take-home pay	$20,000
Irene's take-home pay	16,500
Total income	$36,500

Expenditures

Necessities:

Food	$3,800	
Clothing	1,800	
Housing	8,000	
Utilities and telephone	2,900	
Medical (nonreimbursed)	500	
Insurance	800	
Transportation	2,700	
Total necessities		$20,500

Luxuries and investments:

Trip to Europe	$5,500	
Recreation and entertainment	4,500	
Purchase of common stock	5,500	
Addition to money market account	500	
Total luxuries		16,000
Total expenditures		$36,500

He points out that their expenditures for necessities last year were $20,500, which just about equaled his take-home pay, and with an anticipated 10 percent pay raise, his income next year should exceed this amount. John also points out that they can always draw down their savings or sell some of their stock if they get in a bind. When asked about the long-run implications of their finances, John

replies that there will be "no problems" since his boss has assured him of a bright future with the company. John also emphasizes that in a few years Irene can go back to work if necessary. If spite of John's somewhat convincing arguments, Irene still feels uncomfortable with their rather matter-of-fact approach to financial planning—she knows there has to be a better way.

Questions

1. If the Sullivans continue to manage their finances as described, what do you expect the long-run consequences to be? Discuss.
2. Critically evaluate the Sullivans' approach to financial planning. Point out any fallacies in John's arguments, and be sure to mention (a) implications for the long run, (b) the potential impact of inflation, and (c) the impact on their net worth.
3. Describe to John and Irene the procedures they should use to get their financial house in order. Be sure to discuss the role that long- and short-run financial plans and budgets might play.

■ 3.2 **The Baker Budget Begins to Take Shape**
Evelyn and Harold Baker are a young couple with a 7-year-old daughter. Harold is a foreman in a shipping and packing department and earns $20,160 a year after taxes and health insurance payments. Concerned about their living from paycheck to paycheck, Evelyn decides to set up a budget that she hopes will help them bring their expenditures under control and live within their means. The Bakers' expenditures for 1989 were as follows:

Gas and electricity	$2,080
Water	192
Groceries	3,500
Dining out	1,000
Telephone	450
Dentist	330
Donations	250
Home repairs	400
Health and hygiene	360
Home mortgage (including property taxes)	6,240
Auto loan and insurance	2,300
Life insurance	325
Laundry	180
Recreation and entertainment	378
Miscellaneous	360
Gas, oil, and car repair	960
Clothing	400

All expenditures are expected to remain unchanged in 1990, with the following exceptions:

1. Gas and electricity rates will rise by 5 percent.
2. Grocery prices are expected to rise by 9 percent.
3. Telephone charges are expected to rise by $5 a month.
4. The entire family goes for dental checkups in March and October.
5. Harold pays life insurance premiums in February and August. He has bought an additional life insurance policy of $10,000, which is expected to increase his total premiums by $225 a year to a total of $550 a year.

Questions

1. Assuming all expenditures except dental and life insurance are budgeted in equal monthly amounts, prepare the Bakers' monthly budget for the calendar year 1990. Do so by preparing first a monthly expenditures schedule (like Exhibit 3.6) and then a monthly cash budget summary (like Exhibit 3.7)
2. Analyze the budget, and advise the Bakers on their finances as reflected there.
3. Would you recommend that the Bakers continue to prepare their own budgets? Explain.

FOR MORE INFORMATION

General Information Articles

Bayless, Pamela J., "Financial Planning for Newly Weds (or Newly Re-Weds)," *Sylvia Porter's Personal Finance,* June 1987, pp. 67–73.

Morrow, David J., "The Financial Planning Jungle," *FORTUNE 1989 Investor's Guide,* pp. 197–201.

Reid, Jeanne L., "How to Reach Your Goals," *Money,* April 1988, pp. 76–77.

Schurenberg, Eric, "Canned Plans Get Panned," *Money,* September 1987, pp. 117–128.

Walbert, Laura R., "Shopping for Advice," *Forbes,* June 27, 1988, pp. 260–262.

Wilder, Susan, "Do You Need a Financial Planner?" *The Independent Investor,* August 10, 1988, pp. 115–116.

Government Documents and Other Publications

Consumer Guide to Financial Independence (Atlanta, GA: Foundation for Financial Planning); Two Concourse Parkway, Suite 800; Atlanta, GA 30328: (404) 395–1605.

Financial Planning as a Career (Atlanta, GA: International Association for Financial Planning); Two Concourse Parkway, Suite 800; Atlanta, GA 30328: (404) 395–1605.

Lifetime Financial Planner by William E. Donoghue (New York: Harper & Row Publishers, 1987).

Personal Financial Planning, 4th ed. by G. Victor Hallman and Jerry S. Rosenbloom (New York: McGraw-Hill, 1987).

CHAPTER 4

Coping with Taxes

Financial Facts or Fantasies

Are the following statements financial facts (true) or fantasies (false)?

- Every individual or married couple is required to file a federal income tax return regardless of the amount of income earned.
- The amount of federal income tax withheld depends on both your level of earnings and the number of withholding allowances claimed.
- Federal income taxes are levied against the *total* amount of money earned.
- A tax credit is like a deduction or exemption in that it reduces your taxable income.
- Gains on the sale of investments such as stocks, bonds, and real estate are taxed at the lower capital gains tax rate.
- An easy way to earn tax-deferred income is to invest in Series EE savings bonds.

The average American family currently pays federal income and social security taxes of about $6,000 on an income of about $30,000. In addition, it must pay state income taxes, state and local sales taxes, and state and local property taxes. It is estimated that, when all these taxes are totaled, *the average American family pays about a third of its income in taxes.* It is not surprising, therefore, that tax planning is viewed as such an important element in personal financial planning. The overriding objective of tax planning is very simple: to *maximize* the amount of money you keep by *minimizing* the amount of taxes you pay. So long as it is done honestly and within the tax codes, there is nothing immoral, illegal, or unethical about trying to minimize your tax bite. Most tax planning centers on ways to minimize income and estate taxes. Chapter 16 considers estate taxes. This chapter concentrates on income taxes, particularly on the federal income tax, which is the largest and most important tax for the individual or family. In addition, it is concerned only with those provisions that apply to us as individual taxpayers (there's another whole body of tax laws and tax rates that apply to corporations and businesses—which we do not consider in this book).

PRINCIPLES OF FEDERAL INCOME TAXES

The amount of income you report for tax purposes and the way you file your returns both have significant bearing on the amount of taxes you must pay. Why must we pay federal income taxes, and what procedures must we follow in preparing and filing federal income tax returns? Before reading on, spend a few moments answering these questions.

The federal income tax law was outlined in the *Internal Revenue Code of 1939.* In 1954 this code was revised to further clarify and more precisely state its provisions. Since then, a number of amendments have been added to the code that have attempted to simplify it, eliminate infrequently used provisions, and repeal and modify other provisions. The code's various sections and amendments deal with the tax effects of practically all personal and business transactions. The *Tax Reform Act of 1976* was an extensive tax reform measure aimed at curbing abuses and simplifying taxes. It was followed by the *Tax Reduction and Simplification Act of 1977* and the *Revenue Act of 1978,* both of which further modified and simplified tax laws and procedures.

Other major tax legislation has included the *Economic Recovery Tax Act (ERTA) of 1981,* the *Tax Equity and Fiscal Responsibility Act (TEFRA) of 1982,* and the *Tax Reform Act of 1984.* ERTA was designed to stimulate a sluggish economy by lessening the tax burden on savings and investments. However, prospects of huge federal deficits for 1983 and beyond brought forth TEFRA, which was intended to raise over $100 billion primarily by increasing excise taxes and eliminating abuses and unintended benefits (the so-called loopholes) of the existing tax code. The Tax Refund Act of 1984 was passed as part of the Deficit Reduction Act of that same year; it was designed to raise another $50 billion in revenues by delaying or repealing certain provisions passed in recent years, closing various loopholes, and enforcing compliance through additional reporting measures.

Without a doubt, the biggest and perhaps most controversial piece of tax legislation to come out of Congress in the last 50 years was the *Tax Reform Act of 1986.* (The *Technical and Miscellaneous Revenue Act of 1988* later refined and clarified a number of the 1986 act's provisions.) The purpose of this act was threefold: (1) to simplify the tax code for individual taxpayers; (2) to reduce taxpayer abuses by closing many existing loopholes; and (3) to shift a significant amount of the tax burden from individuals to corporations. The net result of this legislation was far-reaching, as it removed millions of low-income families from the tax rolls, reduced the number of tax brackets from fifteen down to just three, eliminated some popular tax deductions, did away with the preferential treatment of capital gains, and sharply curbed the ability of individual taxpayers to generate tax-sheltered income. Unfortunately, in spite of all the political rhetoric to the contrary, for taxpayers who itemize their deductions, the U.S. tax code remains so complex that is often requires costly professional help just to file a return.

The Economics of Income Taxes

It should come as little surprise to learn that most people simply do not like to pay taxes! Some of this feeling undoubtedly stems from the widely held perception that a lot of government spending amounts to little more than bureaucratic waste. But a good deal of it is probably also due to the fact that the taxpayer really gets nothing tangible in return for his or her money. After all, paying taxes is not like spending $6,000 on a car, boat, or European vacation. The fact is, we too often tend to overlook or take for granted the many services that are provided by the taxes we pay—public schools and state colleges, roads and highways, and parks and recreational facilities, not to mention police and fire protection, retirement benefits, and many other health and social services.

Income taxes provide the major source of revenue for the federal government. Personal income taxes are scaled on progressive rates. To illustrate how this **progressive tax structure** works, we will use the following data for single taxpayers filing 1988 returns:

Taxable Income	Tax Rate
$0 to $17,850	15%
$17,851 to $43,150	28%
$43,151 to $89,560	33%

Now consider three possible taxable incomes: (1) $15,000, (2) $30,000, and (3) $60,000. The tax liability on these incomes would be:

(1) $2,250—i.e., $15,000 × .15
(2) $6,080—i.e., [($30,000 − $17,850) × .28]
            + [$17,850 × .15]
(3) $15,322—i.e., [($60,000 − $43,150) × .33]
              + [($43,150 − $17,850) × .28]
              + [$17,850 × .15]

Notice that as income moves from a lower to a higher bracket, the higher rate applies *only to the additional income in that bracket* and not to the entire income. For example, you pay the 28 percent rate only on that portion of the $30,000 in income that exceeds $17,850. As a result of this kind of progressive scale, the more money you make, the progressively more you pay in taxes. Note also that the progressive tax structure actually results in total taxes that are lower than implied by the stated tax rates; when you relate the amount of taxes paid to the level of income earned, the tax rate drops considerably.

Returning to the three income levels illustrated above, we can see what happens to the **average tax rate:**

Taxable Income	Tax Liability	Stated Tax Rate	Average Tax Rate
(1) $15,000	$2,250	15%	15%($2,250/$15,000)
(2) $30,000	$6,080	28%	20.3%($6,080/$30,000)
(3) $60,000	$15,322	33%	25.5%($15,322/$60,000)

Clearly, taxes are still progressive, but the size of the bite is not as bad as the stated tax rate might suggest.

An important part of ERTA was its attempt to mitigate the impact of inflation on our income taxes, often referred to as **bracket creep**. Here, even when the rate of increase in your income matches the rate of inflation, you may still wind up losing to inflation if your additional income is taxed at higher rates; if this occurs, the growth in your after-tax income will fall short of the inflation rate. The progressive nature of taxes is at the core of bracket creep and, when combined with inflation, can have a cruel effect on family income. Inflation leads to a higher level of income, which pushes you into a higher tax bracket and causes you to pay even more taxes, resulting in your take-home pay going up at a slower rate than inflation. In an attempt to keep bracket creep in check, one of the provisions of ERTA was to *index* the tax rates, standard deduc-

tions, and personal exemptions to the consumer price index. In this way, as inflation increased, so, too, would both the income-level steps in each tax bracket and the personal exemption amounts. The Tax Reform Act of 1986 further curtailed the effects of bracket creep by sharply *reducing* the number of tax brackets and *widening* the income levels within each bracket. Thus, a jump to a higher tax bracket occurs far less often today than it did in the past, and it takes a much larger increase in income to trigger a jump to a new bracket.

Every individual or married couple who earns a specified level of income is required to file a tax return. Exhibit 4.1 provides a list of some of the more common filing requirements that existed in 1988. Like the personal tax rates, these minimums are adjusted annually in keeping with the annual rate of inflation. Note that if your income falls below the prevailing minimum levels, you are not required to file a tax return. However, if you had any tax withheld during the year, you must file a tax return—even if your income falls *below* minimum filing amounts—in order to receive a refund of these taxes. The administration and enforcement of federal tax laws is the responsibility of the *Internal Revenue Service (IRS),* which is part of the U.S. Department of the Treasury. The IRS is responsible for making sure that people pay their taxes as required by the various tax codes.

income taxes
A type of tax levied on taxable income by the federal government as well as many state and local governments.

progressive tax structure
A tax structure in which the larger the amount of taxable income, the higher the rate at which it is taxed.

average tax rate
The rate at which each dollar of taxable income is taxed on average; calculated by dividing tax liability by taxable income.

bracket creep
A situation in which increases in income are taxed at higher rates, causing the growth in after-tax income to fall short of the inflation rate.

EXHIBIT 4.1

Income Tax Filing Requirements (1988)

Individuals and married couples are required to file tax returns only if their incomes meet or exceed minimum levels.

Filling Status	Minimum Income
Single individual, under 65	$ 4,950
Single individual, 65 or older	5,700
Married couple, joint return, both under 65	8,900
Married couple, joint return, one spouse 65 or older	9,500
Married couple, joint return, both 65 or older	10,100

Every individual or married couple is required to file a federal income tax return regardless of the amount of income earned. **Fantasy:** Only those individuals or married couples who earn a specified minimum level of income or wish to receive a refund of withheld taxes are required to file a tax return.

Your Take-Home Pay

Income taxes are usually collected on a **pay-as-you-go** basis, under which your employer withholds (deducts) a portion of your income every pay period and periodically sends it to the Internal Revenue Service on a scheduled basis. Self-employed persons must likewise deduct and forward a portion of their income to the Internal Revenue Service each quarter. After the close of the taxable year, you calculate the taxes you owe and file your tax return. At the time of filing, you receive full credit for the amount of taxes withheld from your income during the year. Depending on whether the amount of taxes withheld is larger or smaller than the actual taxes you incurred, you will either (1) receive a refund from the Internal Revenue Service (if too much tax was withheld from your paycheck) or (2) have to pay additional taxes (when the amount withheld was not enough to cover your tax liability). Witholdings are normally made not only for federal income taxes, but also for FICA (or social security) taxes and if applicable, state and local income taxes. In addition to taxes, you may have other deductions for items such as life and health insurance, savings plans, retirement programs, professional or union dues, and/or charitable contributions—all of which lower your take-home pay. You *take-home pay* is what you are left with after subtracting the amount withheld from your *gross earnings.*

Federal Withholding Taxes. The amount of **federal witholding taxes** deducted from your gross earnings each pay period depends on both the level of your earnings and the number of withholding allowances you have claimed on a form, called a W-4, that you must complete for your employer(s). Obviously, given the progressive nature of federal income taxes, the more you make, the more you can expect to have withheld from your paycheck. Withholding allowances are based, for the most part, on the number of people your income supports; they act to reduce the amount of taxes withheld from your income. A taxpayer is entitled to one for himself or herself, one for the spouse (if filing jointly), and one for each dependent claimed; in addition, a *special allowance* can be taken by those (1) who are single and have one job; (2) who are married, have only one job, and have a nonworking spouse; or (3) whose wages from a second job or whose spouse's wages are less than $2,500. *Additional witholding allowances* can be claimed by (1) heads of households; (2) those with at least $1,500 of child or dependent-care expenses for which they plan to claim to credit; and (3) those with an unusually large amount of deductions. Of course, you can elect to have your employer withhold amounts greater than those prescribed by the withholding tables.

FICA (or Social Security Taxes). All employed workers (except certain federal employees) have to pay a combined old-age, survivor's, disability, and hospital insurance tax under provisions of the **Federal Insurance Contributions Act (FICA)**. Known more commonly as the **social security tax**, it is applied to a stipulated amount of every employee's wages as mandated by Congress. For example, in 1988 social security taxes were levied at the rate of 7.51 percent against the first $45,000 of an employee's income (7.51 percent of the first $48,000 in 1989). The tax rate changes (that is, rises) over time, as does the tax base, which is linked to the cost of living. As with income taxes, your employer is required by law to withhold social security taxes from your paycheck. However, unlike income taxes, you have to pay social security only up to a stipulated maximum amount. In 1988, for example, once your salary went over $45,000, you stopped paying social security taxes for the balance of that year. Finally, while the number of withholding allowances you claim has a bearing on the amount of income taxes withheld, it has absolutely no effect on the amount of social security taxes you pay. Everybody pays the same rate on the same amount of earnings, regardless of the number of dependents claimed.

The amount of federal income tax withheld depends on both your level of earnings and the number of withholding allowances claimed. **Fact:** The more you make and the fewer withholding allowances you claim, the more will be withheld from your paycheck.

State and Local Income Taxes.

Unlike federal income taxes, state and local income taxes differ from state to state. If levied, these taxes are generally tied to the individual's level of earnings. While state and local income taxes that have been withheld (or paid) are deductible on federal returns, federal taxes may or may not be deductible on the state or local return, depending on state and local laws. Especially in large cities, local income taxes can amount to as much as 2 percent of income—and in some states, the state income tax can be 15 percent or more.

It's Taxable Income That Matters

Various sections of the Internal Revenue Code define the key components of **taxable income**. Unfortunately, because of the numerous conditions and exceptions surrounding the tax treatment and/or deductibility of certain income and expense items, the actual amount of taxable income is often difficult to determine. In its simplest form, taxable income can be found according to the following procedure:

	Gross income
Less:	Adjustments to (Gross) Income
Equals:	Adjusted gross income
Less:	Larger of standard deduction or itemized deductions
Less:	Exemptions
Equals:	Taxable income

The above looks simple enough—just subtract certain adjustments, deductions, and exemptions from your gross income, and you will get taxable income. As we will see, however, there are a number of problems that arise in defining what is included in these items.

Gross Income. Basically, **gross income** includes any and all income that is subject to federal taxes. Some of the more common forms of gross income include:

- Wages and salaries
- Bonuses, commissions, and tips
- Interest and dividends received

pay-as-you-go basis
A method of paying income taxes in which the employer (or self-employed person) deducts a portion of income every pay period (or quarter) and sends it to the IRS.

federal withholding taxes
Taxes–based on the number of withholding allowances claimed—that are deducted by an employer from the employee's gross earnings each pay period.

Federal Insurance Contributions Act (FICA); social security tax
The law establishing the combined old-age, survivor's, disability, and health insurance tax levied on both employer and employee; also called the *social security tax.*

taxable income
The amount of income that is subject to taxes; calculated by subtracting adjustments, the larger of standard or itemized deductions, and exemptions from gross income.

gross income
The total of all income (before any adjustments, deductions, and/or exemptions) generated by a taxpayer; it includes active, portfolio, and passive income.

EXHIBIT 4.2

Common Types of Tax-Exempt Income

On some forms of income, you do not have to pay any taxes at all, since they can be totally or partially excluded from gross income.

Child-support payments
Compensation from accident, health, and life insurance policies
Disbability payments (limited in some cases)
Employee fringe benefits (limited to certain items)
Federal income tax refunds
Gifts
Inheritances
Interest on state or local government obligations
Military allowances
Return of original investment capital
Scholarships and fellowships (limited as to amount and time)
Social security benefits (amount exempted depends on total income)
Stock rights and stock dividends
Veterans' benefits

- Alimony received
- Business and farm income
- Gains from the sale of assets
- Income from pensions and annuities
- Income from rents and partnerships
- Prizes, lottery, and gambling winnings

In addition to these sources of income, there are other types that are considered to be *tax exempt* and as such are excluded—totally or partially—from gross income. Tax-exempt income does not even have to be listed on the tax return. A partial list of different types of tax-exempt income is shown in Exhibit 4.2.

Federal income taxes are levied against the total amount of money earned. **Fantasy:** Federal income taxes are levied against your *taxable income,* which is the amount remaining after adjustments, deductions, and exemptions have been subtracted from gross income.

Three Kinds of Income.

One of the major provisions of the 1986 Tax Reform Act was the creation of three basic categories of income, devised as a way to limit write-offs from tax-sheltered investments: (1) active (ordinary "earned") income, (2) portfolio (investment) income, and (3) passive income. *Active income* is the broadest category and consists of everything from wages and salaries to bonuses, tips, pension income, and alimony. It is made up of income earned on the job, as well as most other forms of *noninvestment* income. *Portfolio income,* in contrast, is comprised of the earnings generated from various types of investment holdings—in fact, this category of income covers most (but not all) types of investments, from stocks, bonds, savings accounts, and mutual funds to stock options and commodities. For the most part, portfolio income consists of interest, dividends, and capital gains (i.e., the profit on the sale of an investment). Finally, there is *passive income,* a special category of income that is comprised chiefly of income derived from real estate, limited partnerships, and other forms of tax shelters.

The key feature of these categories is that they limit the amount of deductions and write-offs that can be taken, particularly with regard to portfolio and passive income. Specifically, the amount of allowable, deductible expenses associated with portfolio and passive income *is limited to the amount of income derived from these two sources.* For example, if you had a total of $380 in portfolio income for the year, you could write off no more than $380 in portfolio-related interest expense. Note, however, that if you have more portfolio expenses than income, you can "accumulate" the difference and write it off in later years (when you have sufficient portfolio income) or when you finally sell the investment. Likewise, the same rules generally apply to passive income and related expenses (with a few notable exceptions. which will be discussed later in this chapter). Thus, if you own limited partnerships that generate no income, you cannot write off the losses from those partnerships (at least not in the year in which they occur—as with investment expenses, you can "accumulate" these losses and write them off later).

It is important to understand that for deduction purposes, the portfolio and passive income categories cannot be mixed and/or combined with each other or with active income! *Investment-related expenses can be used only with portfolio income,* and with a few exceptions, *passive investment expenses can be used only to offset the income from passive investments.* As it turns out, therefore, all the other allowances and deductions (as described below) are written off against the total amount of *active* income generated by the taxpayer. In essence, the taxpayer's income from wages, salaries, bonuses, tips, pensions, alimony, etc. is all added up, and it is against this amount that the various deductions are subtracted to arrive at adjusted gross income and, ultimately, the amount of taxable income. [*NOTE:* Since such limitations did not exist prior to the 1986 Tax Reform Act, a five-year phase-in was established for the portfolio and passive income provisions to ease the transition to the new standards. Thus, regardless of the level of portfolio and passive income, up to 40 percent of the write-offs from these investments could be deducted from other (active) income in 1988, with the amount dropping to 20 percent in 1989, and finally to 10 percent in 1990, making the law fully operational by 1991. For our purposes here, however, we ignore the phase-in provisions and discuss the tax implications as if the law were fully implemented.]

Adjustments to (Gross) Income. Adjustments to income are allowable deductions from gross income that include certain types of employee and personal retirement, insurance, and support expenses. Most of these deductions are nonbusiness in nature. The following list, though not exhaustive, includes items that can be treated as adjustments to income:

- Reimbursed employee business expenses
- IRA deductions
- Self-employed health insurance deduction
- Keogh retirement plan and self-employed SEP deduction

- Penalty on early withdrawal of savings
- Alimony paid

There are some important restrictions that were placed on IRA deductions by the 1986 Tax Reform Act that taxpayers should be aware of. In particular, contributions to IRA accounts (of up to $2,000 for a wage earner and $250 for a nonworking spouse) are tax deductible only if the taxpayer is not covered by a qualified company-sponsored retirement program, or if the taxpayer's annual income is below a specified minimum: *$40,000 for married couples, $25,000 for single individuals.* (Note that if one spouse is covered by an employer plan, then both individuals' IRA contributions are restricted as a tax deduction depending on their income.) In essence, a taxpayer can be covered by an employer pension plan and also contribute to his/her own IRA account so long as the income constraints are met. Note that allowable tax deductible IRA contributions are phased out between $40,000 and $50,000 for married couples (and $25,000–$35,000 for individuals) so that a married worker making, say $45,000 a year would be able to deduct an IRA contribution of only $1,000 (plus $125 for a nonworking spouse); workers earning more than $50,000 (or $35,000 if single) who are covered by a company pension plan would not be allowed any deduction. (The income limitations apply only to workers who are covered by employer-provided retirement plans; there is no income limitation on workers who are not covered by company programs.) When the total of any IRA contributions and any other allowable adjustments to income are subtracted from gross income, you are left with **adjusted gross income (AGI)**, which in itself is an important calculation, since certain itemized deductions are limited by its amount.

---

adjustments to (gross) income
Allowable deductions from gross income that include certain types of employee and personal retirement, insurance, and support expenses.

adjusted gross income (AGI)
The amount of income remaining after subtracting adjustments to income from gross income.

Itemized Deductions. Deducting **itemized expenses** allows taxpayers to reduce their AGI by the amount of their allowable personal expenditures. The Internal Revenue Code defines the types of nonbusiness items that can be deducted from adjusted gross income. Some of the more common ones are as follows:

- Medical and dental expenses (in excess of 7.5 percent of AGI)
- State, local, and foreign income and property taxes; and state and local personal property taxes
- Residential mortgage interest and investment interest (limited)
- Charitable contributions (limited to 50 percent of AGI)
- Casualty and theft losses (in excess of 10 percent of AGI)
- Moving expenses (some limits)
- Job and other expenses (in excess of 2 percent of AGI)

A deduction is allowed for medical and dental expenses paid during the taxable year; however, it is limited to the amount by which such expenditures *exceed,* not equal, 7.5 percent of adjusted gross income. Any expenses incurred in the diagnosis, cure, mitigation, and treatment of disease and injury or in the prevention of disease may be counted as medical and dental expenses. Specifically, they include costs related to doctors, dentists, hospitals, corrective devices such as eyeglasses, transportation, medicine and drugs, education for the physically or mentally handicapped, and the cost of medical insurance. Of course, you cannot deduct any item for which you are reimbursed by medical insurance. The Internal Revenue Code also allows taxpayers to deduct certain taxes from AGI, including state, local, and foreign income taxes; state, local, and foreign real property taxes; and state and local personal property taxes.

Another deduction is permitted for interest paid or incurred on first and second mortgages; the only limitations are (1) that the mortgages must be on the principal residence and a second home (such as a summer cabin or vacation condo) and (2) that the amount borrowed must be no more than the price originally paid for the home(s) plus the costs of any home improvements. Thus, a taxpayer may have both a first and second mortgage on both the principal residence and a vacation home, and the interest on all the mortgages will be fully tax deductible as long as the total amount of the mortgages does not exceed the total amount paid for the two houses plus home improvements. Any amount in excess of that is tax deductible only if it is used for educational or medical purposes. A homeowner can, of course, take out a second mortgage on his home (such as the *home equity credit lines* we'll discuss in Chapter 7) and use the proceeds for anything he likes; the interest would be deductible subject to the limitations just noted. Exhibit 4.3 employs a simple illustration to summarize and clarify the treatment of interest expense on home equity loans.

As explained in preceding material on *gross income,* interest may also be deductible when incurred for investment purposes as long as such interest expense does not exceed the amount of *portfolio income* reported by the taxpayer. You'll notice that interest on consumer loans, tax deductible for decades, no longer is, due to the Tax Reform Act of 1986. To help ease the transition from full deductibility (of the interest paid on credit cards, car loans, personal loans, and other types of consumer loans) to no deductibility, a five-year phase-in period was included in the tax bill, making 40 percent of such interest deductible in 1988, only 20 percent in 1989, 10 percent in 1990, and then nothing from 1991 on. (For purposes of our discussions/illustrations, we'll ignore this phase-in provision.)

To encourage charitable giving, a deduction is allowed for the amount of such contributions up to a maximum of 50 percent of adjusted gross income. Contributions must be made to qualified organizations outlined by the IRS. Another deduction that can be taken is for any personal casualty losses, such as those suffered from fire, storms, vandalism, or theft; they are limited to the amount of each loss of above $100 and then only to that portion in excess of 10 percent of adjusted gross income. Moving expenses are also treated as itemized deductions; in essence, as long as the move meets certain IRS restrictions, some or all of the expenses associated with the move can be written off against income.

The final category of allowable deductions is for job and other expenses. This catchall category includes everything from unreimbursed employee expenses such as job travel, union dues, and job

EXHIBIT 4.3

Some Interest Is Deductible, Some Is Not

Because interest paid on first and second mortgages on a principal residence and a second home is the only form of noninvestment interest that can be deducted for tax purposes, borrowing against home equity has become popular in recent years. To be deductible, these loans must conform to rather rigid ground rules, which are illustrated in the following example.

Here's a hypothetical example of how the new rules on deductibility of *mortgage interest expense* would affect the tax return of a married couple who want to borrow against the value of their home, which is now worth $160,000:

Price the couple originally paid for home	$100,000
Cost of improvements they made	+$10,000
Total invested	$110,000
Amount owed on present mortgage	−$80,000
Remaining unrestricted borrowing power for tax purposes	$30,000

The couple *can deduct* interest on a home equity loan of—

- Up to $30,000 for any purpose
- Up to $80,000 for tuition ($160,000 value − $80,000 mortgage)
- Up to $80,000 for medical expenses ($160,000 value − $80,000 mortgage)
- Whatever it costs to add a room to the house

They *cannot deduct* interest on loans of—

- More than $30,000 to buy cars or boats
- More than $30,000 for vacations, furniture, and other major consumer expenses
- More than $30,000 for cash for living costs

education to safe deposit box rental and tax preparation fees (the amount of allowable deductions for business-related meals and entertainment is limited to 80 percent of the amount actually spent on them). The total of all these job and other expenses is deductible *only to the extent that it exceeds 2 percent of adjusted gross income.* Thus, if you have an AGI of $25,000, your total job and other expense deductions would have to exceed $500 (which is 2 percent of the AGI, or .02 × $25,000 = $500); if expenses amounted to $800, for instance, you would write off $300 in these deductions: $800 − $500 = $300. The accompanying *Smart Money* box provides useful suggestions for documenting not only your itemized expenses and deductions, but your income as well. Records like those suggested are important both for preparing your return and justifying your return under audit.

Standard Deductions. Instead of itemizing personal deductions, a taxpayer can take the **standard deduction**, which is a type of blanket deduction that is meant to capture the various deductible expenses that taxpayers normally incur. People who don't want to itemize their deductions take the stipulated standard deduction, which varies depending on the taxpayer's filing status (single, married filing jointly, etc.), age (65 or older), and vision (blind). In 1988 the standard deduction varied from $2,500 to $7,400. Exhibit 4.4 includes the 1988 standard deduction table that can be used to calculate your standard deduction. After 1988 the standard deduction amounts will be indexed to the cost of living.

itemized expenses
Personal expenditures that can be deducted from adjusted gross income in determining taxable income.

standard deduction
A blanket deduction that depends on the taxpayer's filing status, age, and vision and can be taken by a taxpayer instead of itemizing deductions.

S·M·A·R·T M·O·N·E·Y

Documenting Your Income, Deductions, and Expenses

It's not enough that you have to pay taxes. In figuring out how much, you may practically suffocate under a blanket of paper, especially if you itemize (as a third of all taxpayers do). In this case, each deduction, from babysitting expenses to gambling losses, must be substantiated with standard forms, receipts, statements, diaries and canceled checks. And, of course, all taxpayers must document earnings, from wages to tips to dividends.

The job must be done not only to figure out what you owe—or, glory be, what Uncle Sam owes you—but also to justify the return in case of an audit.

Even if you plan to hire a preparer to do your return, you should identify your deductions yourself. Otherwise, one might be overlooked. After all, only you can know what each chit of paper represents. Furthermore, if you hand the paper pile to your accountant, he will bill you perhaps hundreds of dollars to do the sorting.

Once the papers are organized by income and deduction category, you are ready to add up your totals. These lump sums are all your tax preparer wants to see; leave the receipts at home. "I'm not your auditor," says Alan Westheimer, a tax partner with Pannell Kerr Forster in Houston. "What I need is numbers you can back up if you have to." If you do give papers to your tax preparer, be sure to make copies for your own files.

Here is what you will generally need to assemble, depending on your sources of income, deductions and expenses:

INCOME AND LOSSES

The W-2 form (showing salary, wages and taxes withheld) and the W-2P (for monthly distribution from a pension) must be attached to your return. Most other income, such as self-employment income, interest, royalty income, dividends, lump-sum payments from pensions and annuities, state and local tax refunds, and mutual fund earnings and gains, is documented on 1099 forms. Capital gains and losses are also reported on 1099s: one form is mailed to you, one to the Internal Revenue Service. The IRS uses a computer matching system that spots discrepancies be-

tween income statements on your return and the 1099s they have received. A 1099 needs to be attached to the return only in the event that tax has been withheld.

Income from tips should be backed up with Forms 4070-A, 4070 and 4137. Income (and losses) from partnerships, estates and trusts, and S corporations is documented on Schedule K-1.

The IRS requires that both W-2 forms and 1099s be sent to taxpayers by January 31. The law does not require, however, that K-1 schedules be available by April 15. If the party responsible—such as a brokerage, bank or even the company you work for—does not mail your schedules on time, you should call them. If you do not receive the schedules by the April 15 deadline, tax experts recommend that you file for an automatic extension and complete your return when you have the required information.

EXPENSES

- **Mortgage interest**. Form 1098, which the lender sends you, covers this.

- **Consumer interest**. You will need statements from creditors showing interest paid in 1988; normally it is printed on the first page of your December or January statement. Only 40 percent of consumer interest is deductible for 1988.
- **Dependent-care payments**. Canceled checks and statements from caretakers, baby-sitters or child-care organizations will document your expenses.
- **Charitable contributions**. Any charitable deduction for items worth $500 or more must be supported by statements from receiving organizations verifying the fair market value of the property. For items over $5,000, you need a professional appraisal. Old clothes should be valued at what a buyer might reasonably pay in a thrift shop or secondhand outlet. You should have a log for out-of-pocket costs on service done for a charity, such as the use of your car.
- **Medical expenses not reimbursed by insurance**. To be deductible, expenses must exceed 7½ percent of your adjusted gross income.

One exception is the cost of premiums paid by self-employed taxpayers for medical- and dental-care coverage. Twenty-five percent of those expenses are deductible from your self-employment income. The 75 percent balance is subject to the 7½ percent floor. Pull together receipts for prescription medicine or special health equipment authorized by your doctor and bills from doctors, clinics and the like for treatment. If travel was necessary for medical treatment, you will want lodging (up to $50 a night) and meal receipts.

- **Miscellaneous expenses**. Document these with receipts for expenditures such as union dues, safe-deposit box rental, investment advice, membership dues for a professional organization, and business publications. A comprehensive listing is included in the 1040 instruction booklet. Generally, they must be more than 2 percent of your adjusted gross income.
- **Employee business expenses that are not reimbursed are treated as miscellaneous expenses**.

You may deduct 80 percent of entertainment bills. Collect receipts showing the date, cost, place of entertainment, name of those entertained, and purpose of the event. Travel expenses are fully deductible if substantiated by receipts. A log will document business car trips and mileage, on which you may deduct 24¢ a mile up to 15,000 miles and 11¢ for each additional mile.

- **Rental-property expenses**. Collect your real estate tax bill and itemized receipts for repairs and maintenance. Back up the depreciation deduction with the closing statement from your purchase of the property. If you plan to deduct expenses connected with a vacation house that you rent out for a minimum of 14 days, you must have a log showing the number of days you rented the property and how many days you used it yourself.

Source: Holly Wheelright, "Checklist: What You Need to Collect," *Money,* January 1989, pp. 75–78. Used with permission.

EXHIBIT 4.4

Calculating Standard Deduction Amounts Under Various Filing Alternatives (1988)

The standard deduction for taxpayers depends on filing status, age, and vision. The following IRS forms can be used to estimate your allowable standard deduction.

STEP 1. Check the correct number of boxes below.

You	65 or older___	Blind___
Your Spouse	65 or older___	Blind___

Total number of boxes you checked . . . . ___

STEP 2. Find your standard deduction.

If your filing status is:	and number of boxes you checked in Step 1 above are:	your standard deduction is:
Single	0	$3,000
	1	3,750
	2	4,500
Married filing jointly	0	$5,000
	1	5,600
	2	6,200
	3	6,800
	4	7,400
Married filing separately[a]	0	$2,500
	1	3,100
	2	3,700
	3	4,300
	4	4,900
Head of household	0	$4,400
	1	5,150
	2	5,900
Qualifying widow(er)	0	$5,000
	1	5,600
	2	6,200

[a]If your spouse itemizes deductions on a separate return, your standard deduction is zero.

The decision to itemize deductions or take the standard deduction may be changed from year to year, or even in the same year: taxpayers who find they have chosen the wrong option and paid too much may recompute their tax using the other method and claim a refund for the difference. For example, suppose you computed and paid your taxes, which amounted to $2,450, using the standard deduction. A few months later you find that had you itemized your deductions, your taxes would have been only $1,950. Using the appropriate forms, you can file an *amended return (Form 1040X)* showing a $500 refund ($2,450 − $1,950). In order to avoid having to file an amended return as a result of using the wrong deduction technique, you should estimate your deductions using both the itemized and standard deduction amounts and then choose the alternative that results in lower taxes. As a matter of interest, most taxpayers use the standard deduction; generally homeowners who pay home mortgage interest and property taxes itemize, however, since those expenses alone typically exceed the allowable standard deduction.

Exemptions. Deductions based on the number of persons supported by the taxpayer's income are called **exemptions**. A taxpayer can claim an exemption for himself or herself, his or her spouse, and any *dependents*—which include children or other relatives earning less than a stipulated minimum level of income ($1,950 in 1988) and for whom the taxpayer provides at least 50 percent of the dependent's support. In 1988 each exemption claimed is worth $1,950; this amount rises to $2,000 in 1989, after which the amount deductible for personal exemptions will be tied to the cost of living and, as such, will be increased from year to year in line with the prevailing rates of inflation.

These exemptions are phased out and eliminated altogether for taxpayers in the very high income brackets—that is, single filers with *taxable income* (discussed further later on) above $89,560 and married couples with taxable income of $149,250 or more. Moreover, a personal exemption can be claimed only once. Thus, children or full-time students who earn more than the stipulated minimum amount and claim themselves as an exemption can no longer be claimed on their parent's returns (even if the parents provide more than half the support). In other words, an exemption can be taken on one return or the other, but not both. Note that if a child is *eligible* to be claimed as an exemption by his/her parents, then the child does not have the choice of using a personal exemption on his/her own tax return regardless of whether or not the parents use the child's exemption.

In 1988 a family of four could take total exemptions of $7,800—that is 4 × $1,950. Subtracting the amount claimed for itemized deductions (or the standard deduction) and exemptions from AGI results in the amount of your *taxable income,* which is the basis on which your taxes are figured. A taxpayer who makes $40,000 a year may have only, say, $25,000 in taxable income after deductions and exemptions. It is the *lower,* taxable income figure that determines how much tax an individual must pay.

Tax Credits. Once taxable income has been determined, the *tax liability,* or amount of taxes owed, must be calculated. This is done either with the help of a table or by applying certain specified formulas. Taxpayers, however, are allowed to make certain deductions, known as **tax credits**, directly from their tax liability.

A tax credit is much more valuable than a deduction or an exemption, since it directly reduces, dollar for dollar, the amount of *taxes due,* whereas a deduction or an exemption merely reduces the amount of *taxable income.* For example, assume that a taxpayer in the 28 percent tax bracket has

$1,000 in deductions and another in the same bracket has a $1,000 tax credit. Look at what happens to the amount of taxes paid.

		$1,000 Deduction	$1,000 Tax Credit
	Gross income	$38,000	$38,000
Less:	Other deductions/ exemptions	6,000	6,000
Less:	$1,000 deduction	1,000	—
	Taxable income	$31,000	$32,000
	Tax liability*	4,813	5,093
Less:	$1,000 tax credit	—	1,000
	Taxes paid	$4,813	$4,093

*Note: tax liability figured as follows: the first $29,750 of taxable income taxed at 15%, the balance at 28%.

In effect, the tax credit in this example has reduced taxes (and therefore *increased* after-tax income) by over $700!

A frequently used tax credit is for child- and dependent-care expenses. Other common tax credits include

- Alcohol fuel credit
- Credit for the elderly and permanently disabled
- Foreign tax credit
- Minimum tax credit
- Mortgage interest credit

In order to receive one of these credits, the taxpayer usually must file along with his or her tax return a separate schedule in support of the tax credit claimed.

A tax credit is like a deduction or exemption in that it reduces your taxable income. **Fantasy:** A tax credit is far more valuable than a deduction or exemption, since it directly reduces, dollar for dollar, the amount of taxes due.

---

exemptions
Deductions from adjusted gross income based on the number of persons being supported by the taxpayer's income.

tax credits
Deductions from a taxpayer's tax liability that directly reduce his or her taxes due rather than taxable income.

There's Nothing out of the Ordinary about Capital Gains

Prior to the Tax Reform Act of 1986, capital gains were taxed at highly preferential rates—i.e., such gains were taxed at much lower rates than active earned income. Technically, a capital gain occurs whenever an asset (such as a stock, bond, or real estate) is sold for more than its original cost. Thus, if you purchased stock for $50 per share and sold it for $60, you'd have a capital gain of $10 per share. Today, capital gains are taxed at the same rate as any other form of income; as such, if you're in, say, the 28 percent tax bracket, any capital gains you generate will be taxed at the same 28 percent rate. There is no longer any preferential treatment given to capital gains.

As a rule, most capital gains will probably be included as part of the taxpayer's *portfolio income;* any capital gains (actually realized) are simply added to the amount of dividends, interest, and rents generated by the taxpayer to arrive at total investment income. While there are no limits on the amount of capital gains one can generate, there are some IRS-imposed restrictions on the amount of *capital losses* that can be taken in a given year. (In contrast to a capital gain, a *capital loss* occurs when an asset is sold for less than its original cost.) Specifically, a taxpayer can write off capital losses, dollar-for-dollar, against any capital gains. For example, if a taxpayer has $10,000 in capital gains, he can write off up to $10,000 in capital losses. After that, no more than $3,000 in additional capital losses can be written off against other (active, earned) income. Thus, in our example, if the taxpayer had $18,000 in capital losses, he could only write off $13,000 of it in the current year: $10,000 against the capital gains he generated in that year and another $3,000 against his active income. Anything left ($5,000 in this case) would have to be written off in later years in the same order as indicated above: first against any capital gains and then up to $3,000 against active income. (Note: to qualify as a deductible item, the capital loss *must result from the sale of some income-producing asset,* such as stocks and bonds. The capital loss on a nonincome-producing asset, such as a car or TV set, does *not* quality for tax relief.)

Gains on the sale of investments, such as stocks, bonds, and real estate are taxed at the lower capital gains tax rate. **Fantasy:** One of the major provisions of the Tax Reform Act of 1986 was to eliminate the preferential treatment of capital gains. Today, capital gains are taxed at the same rate as any other source of income.

The Special Case of Selling Your Home. Homeowners, for a variety of reasons, are given special treatment in the tax codes, and the way capital gains are taxed on the sale of a home is no exception. Essentially, the tax on any gain you make from the sale of your home can be *deferred* almost indefinitely so long as you buy another home of equal or greater value within a stipulated time period. Note that this provision applies only to your *principal residence* and not to any other homes or real estate you may own. Here is how it works: If you sell your home and purchase and use a new one within 24 months, any gain made on the sale of the old home will not be taxable so long as the amount paid for the new home is equal to or greater than the sale proceeds from the old home. (Note that the home you purchase need not be a new home in order to qualify for this special tax treatment; it only need be "new" to you and, as such, can be a previously occupied, older house.) If a new home is not purchased within 24 months from the date of the sale of the old home, taxes must be paid on all capital gains realized from the sale of this *and any previous homes.*

If the price of the new home is lower than the sale price of the old home, the amount by which the price of the old residence exceeds that of the new one is subject to tax. For example, assume that you sell your first home, which you purchased for $70,000 three years ago, for $83,000. In this case, you will have a capital gain of $13,000 ($83,000 − $70,000). Further, suppose that within 24 months of the sale of your old home you purchase and use a new one costing $80,000. As a result, you have to pay taxes on the $3,000 in profits that you pocketed. In contrast, if the new home cost $90,000, no taxes will be due in the current year, since the $90,000 purchase price exceeds the $83,000 for which the old home was sold.

While you can sell and buy homes over and over again and defer the taxes on all profits literally to the day you die, there is a provision in the tax code that allows people 55 or older to take a one-time exclusion of $125,000 in capital gains earned from the sale of principal residences. For married couples filing joint returns, it requires merely that one of the spouses be 55 or older and that the couple have owned and lived in the house as their principal residence for three years out of the five-year period ending on the date of sale. This feature provides a real break for homeowners, since it allows them a one-time chance to earn up to $125,000 of tax-free income.

To illustrate, consider the case of Homer and Lucile Greenman, who are both 58 years old and have decided to retire in sunny Arizona. They purchased their first house 30 years ago for $25,000 and have since owned three other homes, each higher priced than the last. They have been offered $250,000 for their present home, for which they paid $100,000 in the mid 1970s. Their records show that they realized $40,000 in profits from their first three houses. When this is added to the $150,000 gain they will realize on their present home, they will have to declare $190,000 in capital gains if they decide to retire into a rental unit. However, because of their ages, they are eligible for the $125,000 tax-free exclusion; thus, they will have to pay taxes on only $65,000 of their gain (i.e., $190,000 − $125,000). On the other hand, if the Greenmans decide to buy another home when they retire, all they have to do is buy one for $125,000 (the $250,000 sale price of their current home less the one-time exclusion of $125,000) and they can keep $125,000—*tax free*—and avoid any taxes altogether.

Filing Your Return

There are several ways of filing your tax returns. Your choice will depend on your marital status and on the amount of income you earn. The two basic types of return are the individual return and the joint return. The individual return is for a single person (with no dependents) or for a *head of household,* which is defined by the IRS as a single person who has dependents (for example, a divorced person with dependent children living in the household). The joint return is for married couples, though they can file separate returns if they wish (sometimes the amount and composition of a couple's income is such that they can actually save taxes by filing separately). In addition to these standard filing procedures, taxpayers can file a declaration of their *estimated taxes,* file an *amended return,* or seek an *extension* of the filing deadline.

Joint and Individual Returns. A husband and wife may file a **joint return** if they are married as of the last day of the year. In the joint return, the gross income and deductions of both the husband and wife are totaled together so that despite two taxpayers being represented, there is only one adjusted gross income amount and only one taxable income. A couple generally benefits by filing a joint return rather than separate returns, but in some instances, separate returns may be more advantageous. For example, if one spouse has substantial medical expenditures and a moderate income while the other has no medical expenses and a low income, filing separately may provide a tax saving.

A taxpayer may also file an **individual return** as either a single person or if the taxpayer is a single person with dependents to support, as a head of household. When married persons file separately from their spouses, they do so as if they were single individuals. Of course, the total exemptions claimed by married individuals filing separately cannot exceed those for which they are eligible as a married couple. Because there is a difference in the tax rates for individual filers and joint filers, single persons, married persons filing separately, and heads of household all have their incomes taxed at rates that differ considerably from those levied on joint returns.

Estimated Taxes. Because federal withholding taxes are taken only from income earned on a reg-

---

joint return
A method of filing a tax return available to married couples in which the income and deductions of both the husband and wife are totaled and their taxes calculated on the basis of their combined taxable income.

individual return
A method of filing a tax return as either a single individual or a head of household.

ular basis, such as that paid in the form of wages, the Internal Revenue Service requires certain people to pay **estimated taxes** on income earned from other sources. This requirement allows the principle of "pay as you go" to be applied not only to wages subject to withholding but also to other sources of income. The payment of estimated taxes is most commonly required of investors, consultants, lawyers, business owners, and various other professionals who are likely to receive income in a form that is not subject to withholding. Generally, if all of your income is subject to withholding, you probably do not need to make estimated tax payments. Suppose, however, you figure that your estimated tax in the coming year will be $500 or more, while the total amount of income withheld and your credits will be less than the smaller of (1) 90 percent of the tax to be shown on your coming year's income tax return or (2) 100 percent of the tax shown on your prior year's tax return (assuming it covered all 12 months of that year). In this case you should file a declaration of estimated taxes (Form 1040-ES) and make estimated tax payments.

The declaration of estimated taxes is normally filed with the tax return. The amount of estimated taxes must be paid in four quarterly installments: April 15, June 15, and September 15 of the coming year, and January 15 of the following year. Failure to estimate and pay these taxes can result in a penalty levied by the IRS if the total taxes paid through withholding and estimated payments is less than both 90 percent of your actual tax liability and 100 percent of the tax shown on your prior year's return.

April 15: Filing Deadline. At the end of each tax year, those taxpayers who are required to file a return must determine the amount of their *tax liability*—the amount of taxes that they owe as a result of the past year's activities. The tax year corresponds to the calendar year and covers the period January 1 through December 31. Taxpayers are asked to file their returns as soon after the end of the tax year as possible and *must* do so by no later than April 15 of the year immediately following the tax year (or by the first business day after that date if it falls on a weekend or federal holiday). Depending on whether the total of taxes withheld and any estimated tax payments is greater or less than the computed tax liability, the taxpayer will either re-

ceive a refund or have to pay additional taxes. For example, assume that you had $2,000 withheld and paid estimated taxes of $1,200 during the year. After filling out the appropriate tax forms, you find your tax liability amounts to only $2,800. In this case, you have overpaid your taxes by $400 ($2,000 + $1,200 − $2,800) and will receive a $400 refund from the IRS. On the other hand, if your tax liability had amounted to $4,000, you would have a balance due the IRS of $800 ($4,000 − $2,000 − $1,200).

Filing Extensions and Amended Returns. It is possible to receive an extension of time for filing your federal tax return. An automatic four-month **filing extension**, which makes the due date August 15, can be applied for simply by submitting the appropriate form (Form 4868). In filing for an extension, however, the taxpayer must estimate the taxes due and remit that amount with the application. Beyond the four-month automatic extension other extensions can be requested, but before granting them the IRS must be convinced that they are justified.

After filing a return, you may discover that you overlooked some income or a major deduction and as a result paid too little or too much in taxes. You can easily correct this simply by filing an **amended return** (Form 1040X), which will show the corrected amount of income or deductions and the amount of taxes that should have been paid along with any tax refund or additional taxes due. If a mistake or oversight has been made, then file an amended return. If your amended return is properly prepared and filed and reflects nothing out of the ordinary, it generally will not trigger an audit. By all means, do not "correct" an oversight in one year by "adjusting" next year's tax return—the IRS frowns on that!

Audited Returns. Since taxpayers themselves provide the key information and fill out the necessary tax forms, the IRS has no proof that taxes have been correctly calculated. Therefore, it more or less randomly selects some returns for **tax audit**. The odds of being audited are actually quite low: About 1.0 to 1.5 percent of all returns are audited annually. However, higher-income earners tend to have a greater chance of audit. For example, those with income over $50,000 have about a 3 percent chance.

IRS audits attempt to confirm the validity of filed returns by carefully examining the data reported in them. In the course of an audit, the IRS may deem it necessary to arrange a meeting in which the taxpayer is asked to explain and document some of the deductions taken. Even when the documentation is provided, the IRS examiner may still question the legitimacy of the deductions. If the taxpayer and the IRS examiner cannot informally agree on the disputed items, the taxpayer can meet with the examiner's supervisor to discuss the case further. If there is still disagreement, the taxpayer can appeal through the IRS Appeals Office. Finally, if satisfaction is not obtained from the hearing before the Appeals Office, the case can be brought before the U.S. Tax Court, the U.S. Claims Court, or a U.S. District Court.

It is important to keep satisfactory tax records, because some day you may be audited by the IRS. Although the IRS does not specify any type of recordkeeping system, you should keep track of the source or use of all cash receipts and cash payments. Notations with respect to the purpose of the expenditures are important, as well as proof that you actually made the expenditures for which you have claimed deductions. Typically, audits question both (1) whether all income received has been properly reported and (2) the amounts and legitimacy of deductions taken. Since the IRS can take as many as three years from the date of filing to audit your return—and in some cases an unlimited period of time—records and receipts used in preparing returns are best kept on hand for several years. Severe financial penalties—even prison sentences—can result from violating tax laws.

In sum, while you should take advantage of all legitimate deductions in order to minimize your tax liability, you must also be sure to properly report all items of income and expenditure as required by the Internal Revenue Code. Should the auditor call, it is helpful to know your rights. The accompanying *Money in Action* box summarizes some highlights of the "taxpayer bill of rights" passed by Congress in October 1988.

Tax Preparation Services: Getting Help on Your Returns

Many people prepare their own tax returns. These "do-it-yourselfers" typically have fairly simple returns that can be prepared without a great deal of difficulty. Of course, some taxpayers with quite complicated financial affairs may also invest their time in preparing their own returns. The Tax Reduction and Simplification Act of 1977 and the Tax Reform Act of 1986 were both aimed, among other things, at simplifying the process of filing a tax return. Each year, additional simplifications are incorporated into the system. There are numerous IRS informational publications to aid persons who prepare their own returns. You can call the IRS's toll-free number (1–800–424–3676) to request forms or publications. An excellent (and free) reference source is IRS Publication 17, *Your Federal Income Tax*.

Help from the IRS. The Internal Revenue Service, in addition to issuing various publications for use in preparing tax returns, also provides direct assistance to taxpayers. The IRS will compute taxes for those whose adjusted gross income is $50,000 or less and who do not itemize deductions. Persons who use this IRS service are required to fill in certain data, sign and date the return, and send it to the IRS on or before April 15 of the year immediately following the tax year. The IRS attempts to calculate taxes so as to result in the "smallest" tax bite. Taxpayers are then sent a refund, if their withholding exceeds their tax liability, or a bill, if their tax liability is greater than the amount of withholding. People who either fail to qualify for or do not want to use this total tax preparation service can still obtain IRS assistance in preparing their returns.

---

estimated taxes
Quarterly tax payments required on income not subject to withholding.

filing extension
A period of time following the April 15 deadline during which taxpayers may file their returns without incurring penalties.

amended return
A tax return filed to correct errors or adjust for information received after the filing date of the taxpayer's original return.

tax audit
The procedure used by the IRS to validate the accuracy of a given tax return.

MONEY IN ACTION

If the Auditor Calls . . .

Some 200 years after granting Americans a basic bill of rights, Congress has finally done the same for taxpayers. The taxpayer's bill of rights, approved as part of the tax measure that cleared Congress in October 1988, is designed to give taxpayers more leverage in disputes with the Internal Revenue Service. While a few of the provisions will mean changes in IRS procedures, many others simply put into law guidelines the agency is already trying to follow.

Here are some of the main new weapons in the taxpayer's arsenal:

Liens and levies: The IRS must now wait 30 days, rather than 10, after giving a series of notices before it begins collecting taxes by levy. The types of property and amount of wages exempt from levy also have been expanded. For example, property exemption of $1,000 for books, tools, machinery or equipment necessary for the taxpayer's trade or business is raised to $1,050 for 1989 and to $1,100 for 1990 and later years. The amount of exempt wages is increased by basing it on a new formula tied to the taxpayer's standard deduction and per-

sonal exemptions. The measure also specifies how a taxpayer can appeal for the release of erroneous liens.

Statement of rights: When the IRS contacts a taxpayer over uncollected taxes, it must now send a statement of taxpayer rights and IRS obligations covering the audit, appeals, refund and collections processes. The IRS last week [November 1988] began distributing "Publication 1, Your Rights as a Taxpayer" and will update the statement to conform with the new law.

Right to sue: Taxpayers gained a right to sue for dam-

The IRS provides a toll-free service through which taxpayers can have questions answered. Consult your telephone directory for the toll-free number of the IRS office closest to you.

Private Tax Preparers. Many taxpayers prefer to use private *tax preparation services* because (1) they are concerned about accuracy and minimizing their tax liability as much as possible and (2) they believe the complexity of the tax forms makes preparation too difficult and/or time consuming. Taxpayers who do not wish to prepare their returns and have relatively common types of income and expenditures might consider using a *national tax service,* like H&R Block. Many *local tax preparation services* are also available. Caution is recommended in selecting a tax preparation service, however, since differing levels of competence exist.

Taxpayers with more complex finances often employ an enrolled agent, an attorney with tax training, or a *certified public accountant (CPA)*. These

professionals know the various technical points and are able to advise the taxpayer on how to defer income, qualify for deductions, and generally minimize tax liability. *Enrolled agents (EAs)* are individual tax practitioners who have demonstrated their competence in the area of taxation through a grueling, two-day, IRS-administered exam; they are fully qualified to handle tax preparation at various levels of complexity. *Tax attorneys* generally devote most of their attention to counseling taxpayers in the area of tax planning, while CPAs not only provide tax counseling but also are heavily involved with the actual preparation of returns. Since the services provided by EAs, tax attorneys, and CPAs can be expensive, they are usually best used only by those taxpayers whose financial situations are relatively complicated. Taxpayers should check completed returns carefully before signing them, since *the taxpayers themselves must accept primary responsibility for the accuracy of their returns*. The IRS requires professional tax preparers to sign each

ages over reckless or intentional disregard of the tax code by an agency employee who collects taxes. The bill doesn't allow suits for damages against other IRS employees.

Installment agreements: The IRS frequently enters into agreements allowing taxpayers to pay their debt to the agency over time. The new law provides guidelines for when the IRS can cancel these agreements for such reasons as taxpayer failure to make payments. It also requires the agency to provide notice before ending accords with taxpayers whose finances have improved.

Quotas: This provision prohibits the use of production quotas or goals to evaluate IRS employees involved in collection. It essentially codifies IRS policy that agency critics contend is widely ignored in the field.

Taxpayer interviews: The IRS must issue regulations setting standards for selecting reasonable times and places for taxpayer interviews. The measure also specifies that taxpayers may bring attorneys or other representatives to the sessions. Formerly, IRS guidelines on interviews were vague and

weren't always followed, critics say.

Erroneous advice: This provision requires the IRS to withdraw penalties caused by erroneous written advice the agency provides. It doesn't require the IRS to give written advice or require the withdrawal of penalties caused by information received orally.

Source: Adapted from Rose Gutfeld, "Taxpayers Get Bill of Rights to Ease Disputes with IRS," *The Wall Street Journal,* November 10, 1988, p. B1.

---

return as the preparers, enter their own social security numbers and addresses, and provide the taxpayer with a copy of the return being filed. In 1988 the IRS began allowing designated tax preparers with the necessary hardware to electronically file their clients' tax returns, thereby permitting eligible taxpayers to more quickly receive refunds.

Computer-Based Tax Returns. More and more people are turning to their personal computers for help in preparing their tax returns and doing tax planning. A number of tax software packages are available to save hours of figuring and refiguring all the forms and schedules involved in filing tax returns. These computer programs are not for everyone, however. Very simple returns do not require them; and for very complex returns, there is no substitute for the skill and expertise of an attorney or tax accountant. Those who itemize deductions but do not need tax advice are the ones most likely to find the computer helpful.

Basically there are two kinds of software: tax planning and tax preparation. Programs are available to help you in your tax planning by letting you experiment with different stategies to see their effects on the amount of taxes you must pay. Typical of the tax planning software is *Taxmode,* which runs through a number of "what-if" situations to show you the tax impact of all sorts of investment and financial decisions. In addition, it computes taxes under a variety of assumptions, including the alternative minimum tax, variations in deductions and exemptions, and so on. Other programs aimed primarily at tax planning include *EZ Tax-Plan, Tax Command Planner,* and *The Tax Strategist.* In contrast to these programs, some software is designed mainly to help you complete your returns and print them out. Examples of such programs include *PC/ TaxCut, EZ-Prep, Turbo Tax, Mac In Tax, AM-Tax,* and *Tax Preparer.* These programs all perform pretty much the same functions in that they enable you to input income, expenses, and other infor-

EXHIBIT 4.5

Tax Rate Schedules for Individual and Joint Returns (1988 and later years)

Tax rates levied on personal income vary with the amount of reported taxable income and the taxpayer's filing status.

INDIVIDUAL (SINGLE) RETURNS:

Taxable Income	Tax Rates	Taxes Due
$0 to 17,850	15%	15% of reported taxable income
$17,851 to 43,150	28%	$2,678 *plus* 28% of the portion of your income that *exceeds* $17,850
$43,151 to $89,560[a]	33%	$9,762 *plus* 33% of the portion of your income that *exceeds* $43,150
over $89,560[a]	28%	$25,077 *plus* 28% of the portion of your income that *exceeds* $89,560

JOINT RETURNS:

Taxable Income	Tax Rates	Taxes Due
$0 to 29,750	15%	15% of reported taxable income
$29,751 to 71,900	28%	$4,463 *plus* 28% of the portion of your income that *exceeds* $29,750
$71,901 to 149,250[a]	33%	$16,265 *plus* 33% of the portion of your income that *exceeds* $71,900
over $149,250[a]	28%	$41,790 *plus* 28% of the portion of your income that *exceeds* $149,250

[a]*Note:* In order to phase out exemptions, an additional amount equal to the lesser of (1) 5% of income in *excess of* $89,560 (for individual returns) or $149,250 (for joint returns) or (2) $546 multiplied by the number of exemptions claimed must be included in taxes due.

mation pertinent to most or all of the major forms and schedules; then they made all the necessary entries, cross-entries, and calculations. Most of these programs print completed forms that are formatted in a fashion that is acceptable to the IRS, thereby eliminating the need to fill-in the forms provided by the IRS. This software, like the tax-planning programs, usually applies only to federal tax returns, not state, and has to be revised annually to incorporate changes in the tax laws.

DETERMINING YOUR TAXES ■

> The amount of taxes you pay depends on the rate at which your income is taxed and the amount of taxable income you have. On average, what percent of every dollar of your income do you pay out in taxes? Try to estimate this percentage before reading on.

Now that we have reviewed the general principles of federal income taxes, we can direct our attention to calculating taxable income and the amount

of income taxes due. To do this, we will need to address several key aspects of measuring taxable income and taxes: (1) the tax rates applicable to various types of personal income, (2) the basic tax forms and schedules, and (3) the procedures for determining one's tax liability.

Tax Rates

As we saw earlier in this chapter, the amount of *taxable income* is found by subtracting itemized deductions (or the standard deduction for non-itemizers) *and* personal exemptions from adjusted gross income. This procedure is used for *both itemizers and nonitemizers* and is a key calculation in determining your tax liability because the amount of income subject to federal income taxes is specified by the amount of taxable income you report. Once the amount of your taxable income is known, you can refer to *tax rate tables* to find the amount of taxes you owe.

Tax rates are such that they vary not only with the amount of reported taxable income but also with filing status. Thus, there is one structure of tax rates for taxpayers filing *individual* returns and another for those filing *joint* returns. Exhibit 4.5 provides the *basic* tax rates for individual and joint returns;

EXHIBIT 4.6

Taxable Income and the Amount of Income Taxes Due (1988)

Given the progressive tax structure that exists in this country, it follows that the larger your income, the more you can expect to pay in taxes.

	Taxes Due	
Taxable Income	**Individual Returns**	**Joint Returns**
$ 500	$ 75*	$ 75*
1,000	150	150
1,500	225	225
2,000	300	300
2,500	375	375
5,000	750	750
7,500	1,125	1,125
10,000	1,500	1,500
12,500	1,875	1,875
15,000	2,250	2,250
20,000	3,280**	3,000
25,000	4,680	3,750
30,000	6,080	4,533**
35,000	7,480	5,933
40,000	8,880	7,333
50,000	12,022***	10,133
60,000	15,322	12,933
75,000	20,272	17,133***

*Income is taxed at 15%.
**28% tax rate now applies.
***33% tax rate now applies.

they are the rates specified in the 1986 Tax Reform Act and applicable in 1988 and later tax years. The vast majority of taxpayers—perhaps 90 percent or more—fall into the first two brackets and are subject to tax rates of either 15 or 28 percent.

To see how the tax rates in Exhibit 4.5 work, consider two single taxpayers: one has taxable income of $12,500, the other has $29,600 in taxable income. We would calculate their respective tax liabilities as follows:

▪ for taxable income of $12,500—

$$\$12,500 \times .15 = \$1,875$$

▪ for taxble income of $29,600—

$$\$2,678 + [(\$29,500 - \$17,850) \times .28]$$
$$= \$2,678 + \$3,290 = \$5,968$$

As we can see, the income of $12,500 is taxed at the 15 percent tax rate, and the $29,600 is taxed first at 15 percent and then at 28 percent. Keep in mind that the same procedures would be used whether the taxpayer itemizes or not. In order to show how the amount of tax liability will vary with the level of taxable income, Exhibit 4.6 lists the taxes due on a range of taxable incomes from $500 to $75,000 for both single and married taxpayers.

Recall from our earlier discussions that the *average tax rate* is found by dividing your tax liability by the amount of reported taxable income. Returning to our example involving the taxpayer with an income of $29,600, we see that this individual had an average tax rate of $5,968 ÷ $29,600 = 20.2%, which is considerably *less* than the stated tax rate of 28%. Actually, the 28% represents the taxpayer's **marginal tax rate**—it is the rate at which the next dollar of income is taxed. Notice in our calculations that the 28% tax rate applies only to that portion of the income that exceeds $17,850. Thus, the first $17,850 in income is taxed at 15%—only the balance ($29,600 − $17,850 = $11,750) is subject to the marginal tax rate of 28%.

---

marginal tax rate
The rate at which the next dollar of taxable income is taxed.

EXHIBIT 4.7

Commonly Used Tax Forms

If a standard 1040 is used, a tax return could contain one or more of the following forms, depending on the amount and types of deductions claimed.

1040	Standard tax return, used with itemized deductions
1040A	Short-form tax return
1040EZ	Short-form tax return for single persons with no dependents
1040-ES	Estimated tax payments
1040X	Amended tax return
2106	Employee business expenses
2119	Sale or exchange of principal residence
2441	Credit for child and dependent care expenses
3903	Moving expenses
4562	Depreciation and amortization expenses
4684	Casualties and Thefts
4868	Application for automatic filing extension

The 5% Tax Surcharges. The current tax structure has three marginal tax rates: 15 percent, 28 percent, and 33 percent. The 33 percent tax rate, however, actually represents a 5 percent surcharge that is levied against taxpayers with high incomes. It is done as a way to phase out the initial 15 percent tax rate; that is why in Exhibit 4.5 the 33 percent tax rate exists only for a specified range of incomes and then drops back to 28 percent. In essence, *after* the specified maximum income levels ($89,560 on individual returns and $149,250 on joint returns), both the marginal and average tax rates equal 28 percent. For example, consider a single taxpayer with $100,000 in taxable income. She would have to pay taxes of $28,000 (from Exhibit 4.5: $25,077 + 28% of $10,440 = $25,077 + $2,923). Such a tax liability would result in an average tax rate of 28 percent ($28,000 ÷ $100,000), the same as the stated 28 percent (marginal) tax rate that exists for this income level (see the tax rates in Exhibit 4.5).

In addition, there's another 5 percent surcharge that is assessed at $89,560 on individual returns (and $149,250 on joint returns), which is intended to phase out the personal exemptions for wealthy taxpayers. The net result is that the maximum 33% tax rate will stay in effect a bit longer—the precise amount determined by the number of exemptions claimed by the taxpayer. Thus, a married couple claiming three exemptions would be subject to the maximum 33 percent tax rate for taxable income up to $182,010. Neither of these surcharges would be of concern to most people because the sur-

charges affect only a very small percentage of taxpayers. For example, the personal exemption phase out affects less than one percent of all taxpayers.

Tax Forms and Schedules

The Internal Revenue Service requires taxpayers to file their returns using certain specified tax forms. As noted earlier, these forms and a variety of instruction booklets on how to prepare them are available to taxpayers free of charge (1–800–424–3676). Generally, all persons who filed tax returns in the previous year are automatically sent a booklet containing tax forms and instructions for preparation of returns for the current year. Inside the booklet is a form that can be used to obtain additional tax forms for filing various tax-related returns and information. Exhibit 4.7 provides a list of some of the more commonly used tax forms.

Variations of Form 1040. All individuals use Form 1040 in one variation or another to file their tax returns. If you do not itemize deductions, you can use *Form 1040A,* which is known as the *short form.* If you are single, have no more than one exemption, have an income of less than $50,000, have interest income of less than $400, and do not itemize (characteristic of many students), you may be able to use *Form 1040EZ,* a simple, one-page form that is almost mistake-proof. If you itemize your deductions, you must use the standard *Form 1040* along with the appropriate schedules, briefly described as follows:

Schedule	Description
A	For itemized deductions
B	For interest and dividend income of more than $400 each
C	For profit (or loss) from a personally owned business
D	For capital gains and losses
E	For supplemental income from rents, royalties, partnerships, estates, trusts, etc.
F	For income and expense from farming
R	For credit for the elderly or disabled
SE	For reporting social security self-employment tax

The use of these schedules, which provide detailed guidelines for calculating certain entries on the first two pages of Form 1040, varies among taxpayers depending on the relevance of these entries to their situations. Pages 1 and 2 of Form 1040 summarize all items of income and deduction detailed on the accompanying schedules and note the taxable income and associated tax liability.

The 1988 Tax Return of Terry and Evelyn Becker

Terry and Evelyn Becker are both 33 years old. They have been married for 11 years and have three children—Tom (age 9), Dick (age 7), and Harriet (age 3). Terry is a staff accountant for a major oil company headquartered in the Beckers' hometown of Anywhere, Ohio. Evelyn Becker, who has one-and-a-half years of college, works part-time as a sales clerk in a major department store. During 1988, Terry's salary totaled $27,115 while Evelyn earned $4,900. Terry's employer withheld taxes of $3,800 and Evelyn's $543. During the year, the Beckers earned $1,700 interest on their joint savings account, received $1,800 in dividends from stock they owned jointly, and realized $800 in capital gains on the sale of securities. In addition, Terry kept the books for his brother's car dealership, from which he netted $3,600 during the year. Since no taxes were withheld from any of their outside income, during the year they made estimated tax payments totaling $500. The Beckers' records indicate that they had $8,614 of itemized deductions during the year. Finally, Terry Becker plans to contribute $2,000 to his IRA account, something he's been doing for the past six years. He does this each year without fail, not only to reap immediate tax

benefits but also because he strongly feels that such investments are an important part of sound retirement planning.

Finding the Beckers' Tax Liability: Form 1040. An examination of the Beckers' 1988 tax return will show the basic calculations required in preparing Form 1040. Although the supporting schedules are not included here, the basic calculations they require are illustrated. The Beckers have kept detailed records of their income and expenditures, which they use not only for tax purposes but also as an important input into their budgeting process. Using this information, the Beckers intend to prepare their 1988 tax return in a fashion that will allow them to reduce their tax liability as much as possible. A hypothetical 1988 tax return for the Beckers is given in Exhibit 4.8, like most married couples, the Beckers file a *joint return.*

Gross Income. The Beckers' gross income in 1988 amounted to $39,915; this is the amount shown as "Total Income" on line 23 of their tax return. Their income is composed of both *active income* and *portfolio income,* as follows:

Active Income

Terry's earnings	$27,115	
Evelyn's earnings	4,900	
Terry's business income (net)	3,600	
Total Active Income		$35,615

Portfolio Income

Interest from savings account	$1,700	
Stock dividends	1,800	
Capital gains realized	800	
Total Portfolio Income		4,300
Total Income		$39,915

They have no investment expenses to offset their portfolio income, so they'll be liable for taxes on the full amount of portfolio income. Because they have portfolio income, the Beckers will have to file Schedule B (for their interest and dividend income) with the 1040 Form. In addition, Terry will have to file Schedule C, detailing the income earned and expenses incurred in his bookkeeping business.

Adjustments to (Gross) Income. The Beckers have only one adjustment to income: Terry's IRA contribution. Because the Beckers fall below the income ceiling (just barely), they can put the max-

EXHIBIT 4.8

1988 Tax Return (Form 1040) for the Beckers

Because they itemize deductions, the Beckers use standard Form 1040 to file their tax returns. When filed with the IRS, their return will include not only Form 1040 but also other schedules and forms that provide details on many of the expenses and deductions claimed by the Beckers. *Note:* The 1040 form depicted here is the one used in 1988; it is expected that there will be slight modifications in this form in subsequent years.

Form **1040** Department of the Treasury—Internal Revenue Service **1988** (0)
U.S. Individual Income Tax Return
For the year Jan.–Dec. 31, 1988, or other tax year beginning , 1988, ending , 19 OMB No. 1545-0074

Label
Use IRS label. Otherwise, please print or type.

Your first name and initial (if joint return, also give spouse's name and initial) Last name
Terry B. & Evelyn H. Becker
Your social security number *123 45 6789*

Present home address (number, street, and apt. no. or rural route). (If a P.O. Box, see page 6 of Instructions.)
123 Dreamy Draw Pass
Spouse's social security number *987 65 4321*

City, town or post office, state, and ZIP code
Anywhere, Ohio 45400
For Privacy Act and Paperwork Reduction Act Notice, see Instructions.

Presidential Election Campaign ▶
Do you want $1 to go to this fund? . . . . Yes ✓ No
If joint return, does your spouse want $1 to go to this fund? . . Yes ✓ No
Note: *Checking "Yes" will not change your tax or reduce your refund.*

Filing Status
Check only one box.

1 ☐ Single
2 ✓ Married filing joint return (even if only one had income)
3 ☐ Married filing separate return. Enter spouse's social security no. above and full name here. _____
4 ☐ Head of household (with qualifying person). (See page 7 of Instructions.) If the qualifying person is your child but not your dependent, enter child's name here. _____
5 ☐ Qualifying widow(er) with dependent child (year spouse died ▶ 19). (See page 7 of Instructions.)

Exemptions
(See Instructions on page 8.)

6a ✓ Yourself If someone (such as your parent) can claim you as a dependent, do not check box 6a. But be sure to check the box on line 33b on page 2. . . . .
b ✓ Spouse . . . .
No. of boxes checked on 6a and 6b *2*

c Dependents:

(1) Name (first, initial, and last name)	(2) Check if under age 5	(3) If age 5 or older, dependent's social security number	(4) Relationship	(5) No. of months lived in your home in 1988
Tom T. Becker		456 78 9123	*Son*	12
Dick L. Becker		123 98 7654	*Son*	12
Harriet Z. Becker	✓	912 34 6578	*Daughter*	12

No. of your children on 6c who:
● lived with you *3*
● didn't live with you due to divorce or separation
No. of other dependents listed on 6c

If more than 6 dependents, see Instructions on page 8.

d If your child didn't live with you but is claimed as your dependent under a pre-1985 agreement, check here ▶ ☐
e Total number of exemptions claimed . . . .
Add numbers entered on lines above ▶ *5*

Income
Please attach Copy B of your Forms W-2, W-2G, and W-2P here.

If you do not have a W-2, see page 6 of Instructions.

7 Wages, salaries, tips, etc. (attach Form(s) W-2) . . . . | 7 | *32,015*
8a Taxable interest income (also attach Schedule B if over $400) . . . . | 8a | *1,700*
b Tax-exempt interest income (see page 11). DON'T include on line 8a | 8b |
9 Dividend income (also attach Schedule B if over $400) . . . . . | 9 | *1,800*
10 Taxable refunds of state and local income taxes, if any, from worksheet on page 11 of Instructions . | 10 |
11 Alimony received . . . . | 11 |
12 Business income or (loss) (attach Schedule C) . . . . | 12 | *3,600*
13 Capital gain or (loss) (attach Schedule D) . . . . | 13 | *800*
14 Capital gain distributions not reported on line 13 (see page 11) . . . | 14 |
15 Other gains or (losses) (attach Form 4797) . . . . | 15 |
16a Total IRA distributions | 16a | 16b Taxable amount (see page 11) | 16b |
17a Total pensions and annuities | 17a | 17b Taxable amount (see page 12) | 17b |
18 Rents, royalties, partnerships, estates, trusts, etc. (attach Schedule E) . . | 18 |
19 Farm income or (loss) (attach Schedule F) . . . . | 19 |
20 Unemployment compensation (insurance) (see page 13) . . . . . | 20 |
21a Social security benefits (see page 13) . . . . . | 21a |
b Taxable amount, if any, from the worksheet on page 13 . . . . | 21b |

Please attach check or money order here.

22 Other income (list type and amount—see page 13) _____ | 22 |
23 Add the amounts in the far right column for lines 7 through 22. This is your **total income** ▶ | 23 | *39,915*

Adjustments to Income
(See Instructions on page 13.)

24 Reimbursed employee business expenses from Form 2106, line 13 . | 24 |
25a Your IRA deduction, from applicable worksheet on page 14 or 15 | 25a | *2000*
b Spouse's IRA deduction, from applicable worksheet on page 14 or 15 | 25b |
26 Self-employed health insurance deduction, from worksheet on page 15 | 26 |
27 Keogh retirement plan and self-employed SEP deduction . . . | 27 |
28 Penalty on early withdrawal of savings . . . . | 28 |
29 Alimony paid (recipient's last name _____ and social security no. _____ | 29 |
30 Add lines 24 through 29. These are your **total adjustments** . . . . . ▶ | 30 | *2,000*

Adjusted Gross Income

31 Subtract line 30 from line 23. This is your **adjusted gross income.** *If this line is less than $18,576 and a child lived with you, see "Earned Income Credit" (line 56) on page 19 of the Instructions. If you want IRS to figure your tax, see page 16 of the Instructions* . . ▶ | 31 | *37,915*

Form 1040 (1988)   Page **2**

Tax Compu-tation	32	Amount from line 31 (adjusted gross income)	32	*37,915*	
	33a	Check if: ☐ **You** were 65 or older ☐ Blind; ☐ **Spouse** was 65 or older ☐ Blind.			
		Add the number of boxes checked and enter the total here . . . . . ▶	33a ☐		
	b	If someone (such as your parent) can claim you as a dependent, check here . . ▶	33b ☐		
	c	If you are married filing a separate return and your spouse itemizes deductions, or you are a dual-status alien, see page 16 and check here . . . . ▶	33c ☐		
	34	Enter the { • Your **standard deduction** (from page 17 of the Instructions), **OR** **larger** { • Your **itemized deductions** (from Schedule A, line 26). of: { If you itemize, attach Schedule A and check here ▶ ☑ }	34	*7,133*	
	35	Subtract line 34 from line 32. Enter the result here	35	*30,782*	
	36	Multiply $1,950 by the total number of exemptions claimed on line 6e	36	*9,750*	
	37	**Taxable income.** Subtract line 36 from line 35. Enter the result (if less than zero, enter zero)	37	*21,032*	
		Caution: If under age 14 and you have more than $1,000 of investment income, check here ▶ ☐ and see page 17 to see if you have to use Form 8615 to figure your tax.			
	38	Enter tax. Check if from: ☐ Tax Table, ☑ Tax Rate Schedules, or ☐ Form 8615	38	*3,155*	
	39	Additional taxes (see page 17). Check if from: ☐ Form 4970 ☐ Form 4972	39		
	40	Add lines 38 and 39. Enter the total . . . . ▶	40	*3,155*	

Credits (See Instructions on page 18.)	41	Credit for child and dependent care expenses (attach Form 2441)	41		
	42	Credit for the elderly or the disabled (attach Schedule R) . . .	42		
	43	Foreign tax credit (attach Form 1116)	43		
	44	General business credit. Check if from: ☐ Form 3800 or ☐ Form (specify) _____	44		
	45	Credit for prior year minimum tax (attach Form 8801)	45		
	46	Add lines 41 through 45. Enter the total	46		
	47	Subtract line 46 from line 40. Enter the result (if less than zero, enter zero) . . . ▶	47	*3,155*	

Other Taxes (Including Advance EIC Payments)	48	Self-employment tax (attach Schedule SE)	48		
	49	Alternative minimum tax (attach Form 6251)	49		
	50	Recapture taxes (see page 18). Check if from: ☐ Form 4255 ☐ Form 8611 . . .	50		
	51	Social security tax on tip income not reported to employer (attach Form 4137)	51		
	52	Tax on an IRA or a qualified retirement plan (attach Form 5329)	52		
	53	Add lines 47 through 52. This is your **total tax** . . . . ▶	53	*3,155*	

Payments Attach Forms W-2, W-2G, and W-2P to front.	54	Federal income tax withheld (If any is from Form(s) 1099, check ▶ ☐)	54	*4,343*	
	55	1988 estimated tax payments and amount applied from 1987 return .	55	*500*	
	56	Earned income credit (see page 19)	56		
	57	Amount paid with Form 4868 (extension request)	57		
	58	Excess social security tax and RRTA tax withheld (see page 20) .	58		
	59	Credit for Federal tax on fuels (attach Form 4136).	59		
	60	Regulated investment company credit (attach Form 2439) . . .	60		
	61	Add lines 54 through 60. These are your **total payments** . . . . ▶	61	*4,843*	

Refund or Amount You Owe	62	If line 61 is larger than line 53, enter amount **OVERPAID** . . . . ▶	62	*1,688*	
	63	Amount of line 62 to be **REFUNDED TO YOU** . . . . ▶	63	*1,688*	
	64	Amount of line 62 to be applied to your 1989 estimated tax . ▶	64		
	65	If line 53 is larger than line 61, enter **AMOUNT YOU OWE.** Attach check or money order for full amount payable to "Internal Revenue Service." Write your social security number, daytime phone number, and "1988 Form 1040" on it	65		
		Check ▶ ☐ if Form 2210 (2210F) is attached. See page 21. **Penalty: $**			

Please Sign Here

Under penalties of perjury, I declare that I have examined this return and accompanying schedules and statements, and to the best of my knowledge and belief, they are true, correct, and complete. Declaration of preparer (other than taxpayer) is based on all information of which preparer has any knowledge.

Your signature	Date	Your occupation
Terry B. Becker	*4-1-89*	*Accountant*
Spouse's signature (if joint return, BOTH must sign)	Date	Spouse's occupation
Evelyn Becker	*4-1-89*	*Sales Clerk*

Paid Preparer's Use Only

Preparer's signature	Date	Check if self-employed ☐	Preparer's social security no.
Firm's name (or yours if self-employed) and address ▶		E.I. No.	
		ZIP code	

✿U.S. GOVERNMENT PRINTING OFFICE: 1988-205-102 E.I. 43-0787287

imum amount into an IRA account even if Terry and/or Evelyn are already covered by a company-approved retirement program. Even though they could put more money into the IRA, they have chosen to stick with Terry's $2,000 contribution (see line 25a).

Adjusted Gross Income. After deducting the $2,000 IRA contribution from their gross income, the Beckers are left with an adjusted gross income of $37,915, as reported on lines 31 and 32.

Itemized Deductions or Standard Deduction? The Beckers are filing a joint return and neither is over age 65 or blind, so according to Table 4.4 (married filing jointly with zero boxes checked), they are entitled to a standard deduction of $5,000. However, they want to evaluate their itemized deductions before deciding which type of deduction to take—obviously they'll take the highest deduction, because it will result in the lowest amount of taxable income and keep their tax liability to a minimum. Their preliminary paperwork resulted in the following deductions:

Medical and dental expenses	$723
State income and property taxes paid	960
Mortgage interest	5,193
Charitable contributions	475
Job and other expenses	1,263
Total	$8,614

The taxes, mortgage interest, and charitable contributions are deductible in full; so at the minimum, the Beckers will have itemized deductions that amount to $6,628 ($960 + $5,193 + $475). However, to be deductible, the medical and dental expenses and job and other expenses must exceed stipulated minimum levels of adjusted gross income (AGI)—only that portion which exceeds the specified minimum levels of AGI can be included as part of their itemized deductions. For medical and dental expenses, the minimum is 7½ percent of AGI and for job and other expenses it is 2 percent of AGI. Since 7½ percent of the Beckers' AGI is $2,844 (.075 × $37,915), they cannot deduct any medical or dental expense—they fall short of the minimum. In contrast, because 2 percent of the Beckers' AGI is $758 (.02 × $37,915), they can deduct any job and other expenses that exceed that amount, or $1,263 − $758 = $505. Adding the amount of their allowable job and other expenses ($505) to their other allowable deductions ($6,628)

results in total itemized deductions of $7,133. Since this amount exceeds the standard deduction by a comfortable margin, the Beckers itemize their deductions. The details of these deductions would be provided on Schedule A and attached to the Beckers' 1040 Form. (The total amount of itemized deductions is listed on line 34 of the 1040 Form.)

Personal Exemptions. The Beckers are entitled to claim two exemptions for themselves and another three exemptions for their three dependent children; thus, they can claim a total of five exemptions. Since each exemption is worth $1,950, they receive a total personal exemption of $9,750 (5 × $1950), which is the amount listed on line 36.

The Beckers' Taxable Income and Their Tax Liability. Taxable income is found by subtracting itemized deductions *and* personal exemptions from adjusted gross income. Thus, in the Beckers' case, taxable income amounts to $37,915 − $7,133 − $9,750 = $21,032. This is the amount shown on line 37. Given this information, the Beckers can now refer to the tax rate schedule (like the one in Exhibit 4.5) to find their appropriate tax rate and, ultimately, the amount of taxes they'll have to pay. (Note: Since the Beckers' taxable income is less than $50,000, they should use the *tax tables* (not shown) to find their tax. For clarity and convenience, the schedules are used here.) As can be seen, the Beckers' $21,032 in taxable income places them in the lowest (15 percent) tax bracket. Note in the tax rate schedule that joint returns with taxable incomes of up to $29,750 fall into the 15 percent tax bracket. At this point, all the Beckers have to do is multiply their taxable income by 15 percent to find their tax liability; it amounts to $21,032 × .15 = $3,155; this amount is entered on line 38. (Note: Had the tax table been used, the tax would have been $3,154.) Since they have no tax credits and do not owe any other taxes, they also enter this tax liability on lines 47 and 53.

Do They Get a Tax Refund? Because the total amount of taxes withheld of $4,343 ($3,800 from Terry's salary and $543 from Evelyn's wages) shown on line 54 plus estimated tax payments of $500 shown on line 55 amount of $4,843, the Beckers' total tax payments exceed their tax liability and as a result, they are entitled to a refund. The amount of the refund is found by subtracting the tax liability (on line 53) from total tax payments (on line 61):

$4,843 − $3,155 = a tax refund of $1,688 shown on lines 62 and 63. Instead of paying the IRS, they'll be getting money back. (Generally it takes one to two months after a tax return has been filed to receive a refund check.) All the Beckers have to do now is sign their completed 1040 and send it, along with any supporting forms and schedules, to the nearest IRS district office on or before April 15, 1989. As a final point here, because the Beckers are going to receive such a large tax refund, they might want to stop making estimated tax payments because their combined withholdings more than cover the amount of taxes they owe. Note that if total tax payments had been less than the Beckers' tax liability, they would have owed the IRS money—the amount due is found by subtracting the tax liability from total tax payments made. A check in this amount would then be included with Form 1040 when they filed their tax return.

OTHER FORMS OF PERSONAL TAXES

> In addition to federal income taxes, individuals must pay other types of taxes at the federal, state, and local levels. What other taxes might an employed homeowner have to pay? Spend a few moments answering this question before reading on.

Although the largest tax a person will normally pay is federal income taxes, there are other forms of taxes to contend with. For example, additional federal taxes may be levied on income as well as on specific types of transactions. At the state and local levels, sales transactions, income, property ownership, and licenses may be taxed. Because most individuals have to pay many of these other types of taxes, their impact on one's financial condition must be understood. Thus, a person saving to purchase a new automobile costing $12,000 should realize that the state and local sales taxes, as well as the cost of license plates and registration, may add another $1,000 or so to the total cost of the car.

Other Federal Taxes

While income taxes are the single most important source of revenue, the federal government also raises funds through social security, excise, and gift and estate taxes. Next to income taxes, the most common form of tax is social security, which is paid by just about every gainfully employed individual except certain federal employees and some state and local governmental employees. None of the federal taxes described in the following sections, including social security, can be claimed as a deduction for federal income tax purposes.

Social Security Taxes. People probably pay more in social security taxes than in any other form of federal tax except income taxes. In fact, many families (especially those with incomes of less than $15,000 to $20,000 a year) actually pay more in social security taxes than they do in federal income taxes. As noted earlier in this chapter, social security taxes are paid at a uniform, stipulated rate on a specified maximum amount of income earned from sources such as wages, salaries, bonuses, and commissions. The basis for determining the amount of social security taxes due is the total amount of gross earnings before any adjustments, deductions, or exemptions. In essence, *social security taxes are taken out of the first dollar you earn* and continue to be withdrawn up to a specified maximum amount of taxable income. Once you hit that maximum, your social security taxes stop for the year and start up again on January 1.

In 1988, with a tax rate of 7.51 percent and maximum taxable earnings of $45,000, the maximum tax was $3,380 (7.51% × $45,000); note that this same amount is also paid by the taxpayer's employer, so that the total amount of social security taxes paid for every wage earner amounts to twice the amount the employee pays (employers are subject to the same tax rates and taxable maximums as employees). Of course, if you earn less than the maximum taxable income, your social security benefits will also be less than the maximum; the social security tax rate, however, remains the same no matter how much or how little you make. For example, if you made only $20,000 in 1988, you would have paid social security taxes of only $1,502 (7.51% × $20,000). Keep in mind that the full amount of social security taxes is paid by each wage earner, regardless of what the spouse or any other household member pays. Thus, if both the husband and wife have maximum taxable incomes, both will pay the maximum in social security taxes (in 1988, that couple would have paid $3,380 \times 2 = \$6,760$ in social security taxes).

On the other hand, if an individual works for more than one employer during the year and pays more than the maximum amount of social security taxes, he or she is entitled to a tax credit for the amount of overpayment. For example, if you changed jobs during 1988 such that the total withheld for social security (by both employers) amounted to $4,000, you could apply the overpayment of $620 ($4,000 − $3,380) to your federal income tax return and, in effect, receive a tax refund for the full amount of the overpayment.

Excise Taxes. Taxes levied by the federal government on the purchase of certain luxury items and services—such as jewelry, automobiles, gasoline, telephone services, tobacco products, and liquor—are called **excise taxes**. These taxes are added to the purchase price of the products and services and paid at the time of purchase. In recent years many of these excise taxes have been substantially increased in order to increase government revenues and reduce budget deficits.

Gift and Estate Taxes The federal and state governments both tax gifts and estates. *Gift taxes* are levied on a gift; they must be paid by the *giver* and are based on the value of the gift. *Estate taxes* are levied on the value of an estate left upon the death of its owner. These taxes reduce the amount of the inheritance passed on to the heirs. A detailed discussion of these taxes is included in Chapter 16 on estate planning.

Other Taxes. Duties on imports, entrance fees to federal facilities such as parks and museums, and taxes on special types of transactions are still other types of federal taxation.

State Taxes

In order to raise revenue needed to finance their operations, state governments levy a variety of taxes. Probably the largest source of state revenue is the sales tax, levied on sales transactions. Other sources are income taxes, property taxes, and licensing fees.

State Sales Tax. All states except for a few apply statewide **sales taxes** to most consumer purchases, though some may exempt food, drugs, and/or services. While sales tax rates vary from state to state, most are in the 3 to 6 percent range.

Sales taxes are applied to the amount of the purchases and are levied by the merchant at the point of sale. The merchant is then responsible for remitting their tax receipts to the appropriate state authorities. Most states allow the merchant to retain a small portion of the receipts as payment for performing the collection function. Because sales taxes are tied to purchases, there is really no practical way to avoid them. When making or budgeting for large purchases, you should recognize that sales taxes will add to their cost.

State Income Taxes Most states currently have personal income taxes, which may range above 15 percent of reported taxable income. Although numerous states have graduated tax rates that increase with taxable income, many have fixed rates that apply to all levels of income. Nearly all states follow the federal law in defining taxable income, though many provide for varying exclusions and adjustments. As a result, the calculation of state taxes is generally similar to that for federal income taxes, which makes filing of state tax returns relatively easy. Like the federal government, most states operate on a pay-as-you-go basis by withholding a portion of income from each paycheck. Many allow taxpayers to deduct federal taxes from taxable income prior to calculating their state tax liability. (Persons who itemize can deduct state income taxes paid for federal tax purposes.) Nearly all states have personal income taxes, although some states tax only certain types of income, such as interest, dividends, and capital gains.

State Property Taxes, Licensing Fees, and Other Taxes. Although most states obtain the vast majority of their revenues from sales and income taxes, some also tax various forms of property, particularly automobiles and other types of motor vehicles. However, as a principal source of revenue, property taxes are levied primarily by *lo-*

cal governments. State governments also obtain revenues from the sale of automobile licenses and by licensing certain professions. In addition, the vast majority of states have excise taxes on gasoline, tobacco, liquor, and other luxuries. Most also have gift and estate taxes similar to those levied by the federal government (see chapter 16). Of these miscellaneous types of state taxes, only property taxes are considered deductible for federal income tax purposes.

Local Taxes

Local governments, which include everything from cities and counties to school districts and stadium authorities, levy taxes in order to obtain the revenues needed to provide a variety of public services. Although the majority of local revenues come from property taxes, local governments often use income taxes, sales taxes, and licensing fees to add to their coffers.

Local Property Taxes. The primary source of revenues to cities, counties, school districts, and other municipalities is the taxation of real estate and other personal property, such as automobiles and boats. Since the largest source of property ownership for most people is their home, the dominant form of **property taxes** is the *real estate tax.* Property taxes are typically collected by the county and then distributed among other governmental units—the city and school district, for example. The value of the property on which taxes are levied is determined by the governmental unit to which taxes are paid. In general, the more expensive the home, the higher the real estate taxes, and vice versa. If deductions are itemized, these taxes can be deducted in calculating federal income taxes. Further discussion of these taxes is included in Chapter 6 on housing.

Local Income Taxes. Local governments—typically larger cities in the eastern part of the United States—sometimes levy taxes on the incomes of all those employed within their boundaries. These taxes are similar to federal and state income taxes, but the rates are lower—usually about 1 to 2 percent but sometimes as high as 4 to 5 percent of taxable income (an exception is the District of Columbia, which has an income tax rate that rises

above 10 percent). Most city income taxes are withheld and therefore charged on a pay-as-you-go basis, with final settlement made at the end of the year. These taxes are also a deductible itemized expense for federal income tax purposes.

Local Sales Taxes and Licensing Fees. A large number of cities also have sales taxes, which are collected and remitted to the state government by merchants as part of the *total* sales tax on purchased items. The state government, whose levy makes up the major portion of the tax, then returns to the cities their portion of the collections. *Licensing fees,* such as building permits, also provide local governments with added revenue. In some states, a portion of the fees collected for automobile and other licenses represents a local licensing fee or property tax.

EFFECTIVE TAX PLANNING

> Comprehensive tax planning is aimed at reducing taxes immediately as well as in the long run; it involves several activities that are closely tied to other areas of financial planning. How might you go about preparing your immediate and long-run tax plans? Try to answer this question before reading on.

excise taxes
Taxes levied at the point of sale on the purchase of certain luxury items and services, such as jewelry, automobiles, gasoline, and tobacco products.

sales taxes
Taxes levied at the point of sale by state and local governments on most consumer purchases, though food, drugs, and/or services may be exempt.

property taxes
Taxes typically levied by local and state governments on the value of real estate and certain other personal property in order to raise revenue needed to finance their operations.

A key ingredient of personal financial planning is *tax planning*. The overriding objective of effective tax planning is to maximize total after-tax income by reducing, shifting, or deferring taxes to as low a level as is legally possible.

Keep in mind that *avoiding* taxes is one thing, but *evading* them is another matter altogether! By all means, don't confuse tax avoidance with **Tax evasion**, which includes illegal activities such as omitting income or overstating deductions. Tax evasion, in effect, involves a failure to fairly and accurately report income and/or expenses and, in extreme cases, a failure to pay taxes altogether. Persons found guilty of tax evasion are subject to severe financial penalties and even prison terms. **Tax avoidance**, in contrast, is concerned with reducing taxes in ways that are legal and compatible with the intent of Congress.

Fundamental Objectives of Tax Planning

Tax planning basically involves the use of various investment vehicles, retirement programs, and estate distribution procedures that have the effect of (1) reducing, (2) shifting, or (3) deferring taxes. You can *reduce* taxes, for example, by using techniques that create tax deductions or credits, or that receive preferential tax treatment; included here would be investments that produce depreciation (like real estate) or that generate tax-free income (like municipal bonds). You can *shift* taxes by using gifts or trusts to shift some of your income to other family members who are in lower tax brackets and to whom you intend to provide some level of support anyway, such as a retired, elderly parent.

The idea behind *deferring* taxes is to reduce or eliminate your taxes today by postponing them to some time in the future when you may be a lower tax bracket. Perhaps more important, *deferring taxes gives you use of the money that would otherwise go to taxes*—which you can invest to make even more money. Deferring taxes is usually done through various types of retirement plans, such as individual retirement accounts, by investing in certain types of annuities, variable life insurance policies, or even Series EE savings bonds.

The fundamentals of tax planning include making sure you take all the deductions to which you are entitled and taking full advantage of the various tax provisions that will minimize your tax liability.

Thus, comprehensive tax planning is an ongoing activity with both an immediate and a long-term perspective. *Its plays a key role in personal financial planning*—in fact, one of the major components of a comprehensive financial plan is a summary of the potential tax impacts of various recommended financial strategies. Tax planning is closely interrelated with many financial planning activities, including investment, retirement, and estate planning.

Some Popular Tax Strategies

Tax planning can become very complex at times and involves rather sophisticated investment strategies; in such cases, especially those involving large amounts of money, you are well advised to seek professional help. Many tax strategies, however, are fairly simple and straightforward and can be used by the average middle-income taxpayer. You certainly don't have to be in the top income bracket to enjoy the benefits of many (and perhaps most) of these tax-saving ideas and procedures. For example, the interest income on Series EE (U.S. savings) bonds is free from state income tax, and the holder can elect to delay payment of taxes on the federal level until the earlier of the year the bonds are redeemed for cash or the year in which they finally mature. This feature makes Series EE bonds an excellent vehicle for earning tax-deferred income. Some other popular (and fairly simple) tax strategies follow.

Income Shifting.   One way of reducing income taxes is to use a technique known as **income shifting**. Here the taxpayer shifts a portion of his or her income—and thus taxes—to relatives in lower tax brackets. This can be done by creating trusts or custodial accounts or by making outright gifts of income-producing property to family members. For example, parents with $125,000 of taxable income and $18,000 in corporate bonds paying $2,000 in annual interest might give the bonds to their 15-year-old child—with the understanding that such income is to be used ultimately for the child's college education. The $2,000 would then belong to the child, who would probably have to pay little or no tax on this income, and at the same time the parents' taxable income would be reduced by $2,000 (along with a reduction in their taxes of nearly $700). Unfortunately, this strategy is not as simple as it might at first appear. The Tax Reform Act of 1986 specifies that the income of a minor (under the age of 14) is taxed at the same rate as the parents *to the extent that it exceeds $1,000*. For example, if a 5-year-old child received $2,400 from a trust set up for her by her parents, the first $1,000 of that income (subject to a minimum $500 standard deduction) would be taxed at the child's rate, and the remaining $1,400 would be subject to the parents' (higher) tax rate. These restrictions do not apply to children over the age of 14, so it is possible to employ such techniques with older children (and presumably, with other older relatives, like elderly parents).

The reason income shifting is allowed in the first place is because there is a positive side to the practice. It is presumed that income shifting is done not only to reduce taxes, but also to buildup a pool of savings for the purpose of meeting some specific future outlay such as a child's college education. According to what is known as the "fruit-of-the-tree" doctrine, individuals cannot give away or place in trust income (fruit) alone; instead, they must also give away the income-producing property (fruit-bearing tree) as well. Additional tax implications of gifts to dependents are discussed in Chapter 16.

Tax Shelters. **Tax shelters** are forms of investments that take advantage of certain *tax write-offs*. Some real estate (income-generating property) and natural-resource (oil and gas drilling) investments provide these desirable deductions.

The favorable write-offs come from deductions from gross income that are permitted by the IRS but do not involve an actual outlay of cash by the investor. In accounting terminology, these write-offs are called *depreciation, amortization,* or *depletion*. The presence of these noncash expenditures can lower the amount of taxes paid by taxpayers in certain income brackets. Tax-shelter investments are generally considered to be *passive* investments; the amount of write-offs that can be taken is limited to the amount of income generated. There are a few exceptions, however. For example, this rule does not apply to income-property investments of taxpayers with adjusted gross income under $100,000 and to certain oil and gas investments. Thus, if your income is under $100,000 a year and

you own some rental property, or you invest in an oil or gas drilling partnership, you may be able to benefit from all or most of the associated tax write-offs. Specifically, if your write-offs from these investments exceed the income they generate, you can use the excess write-offs *to shelter your other income*—the net result will be to reduce your taxable income and, therefore, the amount of taxes you have to pay. For example, you could invest in an apartment project that provided both an actual cash return of $5,000 and a depreciation deduction (from gross income) of $9,000. The net result of this investment would be to completely shelter the $5,000 cash income from taxes; even better, given the fact that you met the income limitations, you would have an additional $4,000 write-off ($9,000 − $5,000) that would reduce both your taxable income and tax liability.

An easy way to earn tax-deferred income is to invest in Series EE savings bonds. **Fact:** The interest income from a Series EE savings bond can be tax deferred, since the holder can elect to delay payment of taxes until the earlier of the year the bonds are redeemed for cash or the year in which they finally mature.

With the exceptions noted above, the 1986 Tax Reform Act has pretty much eliminated tax-shelter investments that rely heavily on tax write-offs as the major (or only) source of income. Indeed, many

tax evasion
The failure to accurately report income and/or expenses and, in extreme cases, a failure to pay taxes altogether.

tax avoidance
The process of reducing taxes in ways that are legal and compatible with the intent of Congress.

income shifting
A technique used to reduce taxes in which a taxpayer shifts a portion of income to family members in lower tax brackets.

tax shelters
Certain types of investments, such as real estate and natural resources, that provide tax write-offs in the form of depreciation, amortization, or depletion.

tax-shelter limited partnerships in the past were structured so that all or more of the return from these investments was derived from nothing more than the tax write-offs (and, therefore, the tax savings) they provided. No longer is this true. Today, these investments, too, have to stand on their investment merits. To ease the transition, the tax-shelter provision was set up so that it would be phased in over a period of five years. For example, in 1988 only 40 percent of the "excess" write-offs from passive investments could be used against other types of income, with this amount dropping to 10 percent by 1990. Another noteworthy provision written into the law provides that as much as $25,000 in write-offs from *rental real estate* could be used each year (to offset income from other sources) by people who "actively participate in the rental activity" and whose adjusted gross income is less than $100,000. This provision is phased out completely for adjusted gross incomes of $150,000 or more.

Tax-Free Income, or Tax Deferred? There are some investments that provide tax-free income; in most cases, however, the tax on the income is only deferred (or delayed) to a later date. Although there aren't many forms of tax-free investments left today, probably the best example would be the *interest* income earned on *municipal bonds*. Such income is free from federal income tax: no matter how much interest income you make, you don't have to pay any taxes on it. (Tax-exempt municipal bonds are discussed in Chapter 12.) Income that is **tax deferred**, in contrast, does not cause taxes to be paid now, but delays their payment to a future date. Until that time occurs, however, the advantage of these vehicles is that they allow you to *accumulate earnings* in a tax-free fashion. A good example of tax-deferred income would be income earned in an *individual retirement account* (IRA). See Chapter 15 for a detailed discussion of this vehicle.

Basically, any wage earner can open an IRA account and contribute up to $2,000 a year to the account. Of course, as noted earlier in this chapter, although any employed person can contribute to an IRA, only those people meeting certain pension and/or income constraints can deduct the annual

contributions from their tax returns. If you fail to meet these restrictions, you can still have an IRA but you can't deduct the $2,000 annual contribution from your income. So why have an IRA? *Because all the income you earn in your IRA accumulates tax free!* Since this is a *tax-deferred* form of investment, you'll eventually have to pay taxes on these earnings, but not until you start drawing down your account, which cannot occur until you're over age 59½. Thus, if you were in, say, the 33 percent tax bracket and could not write off your annual IRA deduction, you'd still be well advised to put $2,000 a year into an IRA to obtain the tax-deferred income feature. That is, if you could earn 12 percent before taxes on your investments, you could put $2,000 a year into fully taxable investments and end up with about $146,000 in 25 years. Or you could put the $2,000 each year into a tax-deferred IRA account and (given the same 12 percent rate of return) end up with approximately *$267,000* at the end of 25 years. You'll eventually have to pay taxes on your earnings when you start drawing down your IRA account, but you can't overlook the fact that the tax-deferred IRA investment results in fully *80 percent more income* (that is, $267,000 with the IRA versus $146,000 without). In addition to IRAs, tax-deferred income can also be obtained from certain types of annuities and pension and retirement plans. See Chapter 15 for more information on these financial products and strategies.

---

tax deferred
Income that is not subject to taxes immediately but which will be subject to taxes at a later date.

SUMMARY

- Because taxes have an impact on most individuals and families, a basic understanding of them is essential for effective financial planning and intelligent money management.

- The dominant tax in our country today is the federal income tax—a levy that provides the government with most of the funds it needs to cover its operating costs. The administration and enforcement of federal tax laws is the responsibility of the Internal Revenue Service (IRS), a branch of the U.S. Treasury Department. Because the government operates on a pay-as-you-go basis, employers are required to withhold taxes from their employees' paychecks.

- The amount of taxes you owe depends on the amount of *taxable income* you report. To find taxable income, start with your *gross* income (which could be made up of active income, portfolio income, and/or passive income), make allowable adjustments to get adjusted gross income (AGI), and subtract from it the amount of deductions and personal exemptions claimed.

- Personal tax returns can be filed as *joint returns* (by a husband and wife filing together as a married couple) or as *individual (single) returns* (by a single person, head of household, or married person filing separately). Regardless of the type of return, they are filed (on or before April 15) by using one of the following tax forms: 1040, 1040A, or 1040EZ.

- In addition to federal income taxes, there are sometimes state and/or local income taxes. Other forms of personal taxes that individuals have to pay at the federal, state, or local level include: social security taxes, excise taxes, gift and estate taxes, sales taxes, property taxes, and a few other taxes and fees that may not be obvious.

- Effective tax planning is closely tied to other areas of financial planning. The objectives of tax planning are to reduce, shift, and/or defer taxes in such a way that the taxpayer is able to get maximum use/benefits from the money he/she earns. Some of the more popular tax strategies include shifting income to relatives in lower tax brackets, investing in real estate and other types of tax shelters, investing in tax-exempt municipal bonds, setting up individual retirement accounts, and using annuities and pension and retirement plans to generate tax-deferred income.

QUESTIONS AND PROBLEMS

1. Discuss the following items, and explain their significance with respect to personal taxes: (a) Internal Revenue code of 1939, (b) the IRS, (c) withholding allowances, and (d) FICA. What were the purposes of the Economic Recovery Tax Act of 1981 and the Tax Reform Act of 1986?

2. What does *progressive taxation* mean? What is the economic rationale underlying the notion of progressive income taxes?

3. Mo Huang has an opportunity to earn $2,000 working overtime during the Christmas season. He thinks he will turn it down, however, since the extra income would put him in a higher tax bracket and the government would probably get most of it. Discuss Mo's reasoning.

4. Distinguish between gross earnings and take-home pay. What does the employer do with the difference?

5. What two factors determine the amount of federal withholding taxes that will be deducted from gross earnings each pay period? Explain.

◨ 6. Mary Parker is 24 years old, single, lives in an apartment, and has no dependents. Last year she earned $19,600 as a sales representative for Texas Instruments; $1,800 of her wages were withheld for federal income taxes; in addition, she had interest income of $142. Estimate her taxable income, tax liability, and refund or tax due.

7. Tina Marcelle received the following items and amounts of income during 1989. Help her calculate (a) her gross income and (b) that portion (dollar amount) of her income that is tax exempt.

Salary	$9,500
Dividends	800
Gift from mother	500
Child support from ex-husband	2,400
Interest on savings account	250
Rent	900
Loan from bank	2,000
Interest on state government bonds	300

8. Define and differentiate between gross income and adjusted gross income.

9. If you itemize your deductions, certain taxes may be included as part of your itemized deductions. Discuss two of these taxes, and indicate their source.

10. Larry Tolle was married on January 15, 1989. His wife, Rebecca, is a full-time student at the university and earns $125 a month working in the library. How many personal exemptions will Larry and Rebecca be able to claim on their joint return? Would it make any difference if Rebecca's parents paid for more than 50 percent of her support? Explain.

11. How does a tax credit differ from an itemized deduction? Demonstrate the differences resulting from a $1,000 tax credit versus a $1,000 deduction for a taxpayer in the 28 percent tax bracket with $10,000 of pre-tax income.

12. Define what is meant by capital gains and capital losses. If Jenny Perez is in the 33 percent tax bracket, calculate the tax associated with each of the following transactions:
    a. She sold stock for $1,200 that she purchased for $1,000 five months earlier.
    b. She sold bonds for $4,000 that she purchased for $3,000 three years earlier.
    c. She sold stock for $1,000 that she purchased for $1,500 eighteen months earlier.

13. Describe the two most common methods for filing a tax return.
    Also explain the different filing requirements.

14. Define estimated taxes, and explain under what conditions such tax payments are required.

15. Briefly discuss the tax preparation services available from (1) the IRS, (b) national or local tax preparation services, (c) an enrolled agent, (d) tax attorneys and CPAs, and (e) tax preparation computer software. When is each of these preferred? Discuss the relative costs.

16. Explain how the following are used in filing a tax return: (a) Form 1040, (b) various schedules that accompany Form 1040, and (c) tax rate schedules.

17. Briefly describe several forms of personal taxes other than federal income taxes.

18. Explain each of the following strategies for reducing current taxes: (a) income shifting, (b) tax shelters, and (c) tax deferral.

19. Identify and briefly discuss at least six specific tax strategies that can be used by individuals to reduce their current taxes.

20. Milo Whitehead is married and has one child. He is currently in the process of putting together some figures so he can prepare their joint 1989 tax return. So far, he's been able to determine the following:

- He can claim 3 personal exemptions (including himself)
- Total unreimbursed medical expenses incurred: $1,155
- Gross wages and commissions earned: $38,470
- IRA contribution: $2,250
- Mortgage interest paid: $5,200
- Capital gains realized: $1,450
- Income from limited partnership: $200
- Job expenses and other allowable deductions: $875
- Interest paid on credit cards: $380
- Dividend and interest income earned: $610
- Sales taxes paid: $2,470
- Charitable contributions made: $1,200
- Capital losses incurred: $3,475
- Interest paid on a car loan: $570
- Alimony paid by Milo to first wife: $6,000
- Social Security taxes paid: $2,750
- Property taxes paid: $700
- State income taxes paid: $1,700

Given the above information, how much taxable income will the Whiteheads have in 1989? (*Note:* Assume Milo is covered by a pension plan where he works, the standard deduction amounts in Exhibit 4.4 are applicable, and each exemption claimed is worth $1,950.)

CASE PROBLEMS

◪ 4.1 The Aggarwals Tackle Their Tax Return

Sabash and Sue Aggarwal are a married couple in their early twenties living in Dallas. Sabash earned $30,000 in 1989 from his job as a sales manager with Carson Corporation. During the year, his employer withheld $2,900 for income tax purposes. In addition, the Aggarwals received interest of $200 on a joint savings account, $750 interest on tax-exempt municipal bonds, and a dividend of $400 on jointly owned stocks. At the end of 1989, the Aggarwals sold two stocks, A and B. Stock A was sold for $700 and had been purchased four months earlier for $800. Stock B was sold for $1,500 and had been purchased three years earlier for $1,100. Their only child, Rohn, age 2, received (as his sole source of income) dividends of $200 on stock of Kraft, Inc.

In spite of the fact that Sabash was covered by his Carson Corporation's pension plan, he planned to contribute $2,000 to an IRA for 1989. Following are the amounts of money paid out during the year by the Aggarwals:

Medical and dental expenses (unreimbursed)	$200
State and local property taxes	831
Interest paid on home mortgage	4,148
Charitable contributions	1,360
Total	$6,539

In addition, Sabash incurred some travel costs (not reimbursed) for an out-of-town business trip as follows:

Airline ticket	$250
Taxis	20
Lodging	60
Meals (as adjusted to 80% of cost)	36
Total	$366

Questions

1. Using the above information, prepare a joint tax return for Sabash and Sue Aggarwal for the year ended December 31, 1989, in a manner that will result in the smallest tax liability—that is, either itemize their deductions or take the standard deduction. (Note: Use form 1040 and the tax schedule in Exhibit 4.5 to determine the Aggarwals' taxes. Assume the standard deduction amounts in Exhibit 4.4 are applicable and each exemption claimed is worth $1,950.)

2. How much have you saved the Aggarwals as a result of your treatment of their deductions?

3. Discuss whether the Aggarwals need to file a tax return for their son.

◪ 4.2 Joan Cavander: Bartender or Tax Expert?

Joan Cavander, who is single, is a bartender at the Twin Towers Supper Club in Atlanta. During the past year (1989), her gross income was $16,700 made up of wages and tips. She has decided to prepare her own tax return, since she cannot afford the services of a tax expert. After preparing her return, she has come to you for advice. The following is a summary of the figures she has prepared thus far:

Gross income:	Wages	$9,500
	Tips	7,200
Adjusted gross income		$16,700
Less: Itemized deductions		1,900
		$14,800
Less: Standard deduction		3,000
Taxable income		$11,800

Joan believes that if an individual's income falls below $17,850, the federal government considers him or her "poor" and allows both itemized deductions and a standard deduction.

Questions

1. Calculate Joan Cavander's taxable income, being sure to consider her exemption. (Assume the standard deduction amounts in Exhibit 4.4 are applicable and each exemption claimed is worth $1,950.)

2. Explain to her the difference between itemized deductions and the standard deduction.

3. Joan has been dating Sam Haley for nearly four years; they are seriously thinking about getting married. Sam has income and itemized deductions identical to Joan's. How much taxes would they pay as a married couple (filing a joint return) versus the total amount the two paid as single persons (filing separate individual returns). Strictly from a tax perspective, does it make any difference whether Joan and Sam stay single or get married? Explain.

FOR MORE INFORMATION

General Information Articles

Anrig, Greg Jr., "Keys to the Forms," *Money*, January 1989, pp. 90–99.

Hedberg, Augustin, "Your Guide to the 1989 Tax Guides," *Money*, January 1989, pp. 101–105.

McCormally, Kevin, "50 Ways to Save Time & Money on Your Taxes," *Changing Times*, February 1989, pp. 26–33.

_____ "How to Survive a Tax Audit," *Changing Times*, September 1988, pp. 39–43.

Towle, Lisa H., "Lining Up a First-Rate Preparer," *Money*, January 1989, pp. 64–65.

Weinman, Sidney, "Filing an Amended Return," *Sylvia Porter's Personal Finance*, May 1987, pp. 22–24.

Government Documents and Other Publications

Federal Taxation, Annual Edition by James W. Pratt, Jane O. Burns, and William N. Kulsrud (Homewood, IL: Irwin, annual).

HBJ Federal Tax Course, Annual by John O. Everett, Richard Boley, William A. Duncan, and Robert W. Jamison (Orlando, FL: Harcourt Brace Jovanovich, Publishers, annual).

Prentice Hall's Federal Taxation, Annual: Individuals by Lawrence C. Phillips and John L. Kramer (Englewood Cliffs: N.J.: Prentice Hall, annual)

Your Federal Income Taxes, Annual, Internal Revenue Service, Publication 17 (Washington, D.C.: U.S. Government Printing Office, annual).

Mark and Ana Williams, who were introduced to you at the end of Chapter 1, would like your help in starting their financial plan. Review the Williams' financial and personal information on pages 28–42 before answering the following questions.

1. Using the January, 1990 asset and liability information, develop a balance sheet for Mark and Ana Williams.

2. Using the income and expenditure information for 1989, complete an income and expenditure statement for Mark and Ana.

3. Based on their financial statements, calculate the following ratios:

    - Savings ratio
    - Liquidity ratio
    - Solvency ratio
    - Debt service ratio

4. Based on the information in the original case and in their financial statements, state at least two positive and two negative aspects of Mark and Ana's current financial position.

After reading Chapter 3, you probably realize that Mark and Ana's financial goals are not defined well enough in the original case to serve as the basis for their financial plan and cash budget. Upon further discussion they have restated their financial goal as follows:

- To buy a $90,000 condominium as soon as possible. Mark's grandmother has promised a $25,000 gift to help with the down payment. They are willing to sell their shares of stock and/or mutual fund to pay for the rest of the down payment and closing costs.
- To have a total of $5,000 accumulated in money market accounts/funds in two years to be used as their emergency fund.
- To pay off all of their revolving credit debt within the next year.
- To save $3,000 as a buffer account for the birth of their first child in three years.
- To save $15,000 for a down payment and closing costs on a new house in four years. They plan to keep their condo as a rental real estate investment.
- To each contribute $1,000 a year to their respective 401(k) retirement accounts.
- To establish a regular savings program in an amount that will accomplish their stated goals.

5. How much would Mark and Ana have to save this year to be on track in meeting their goals for:

    - Their emergency fund
    - The buffer account for their first child's birth
    - A new house
    - Each of their 401(k) retirement accounts?

Use future value calculations for goals that will be achieved over two or more years. Assume Mark and Ana can earn 5 percent after taxes on their savings.

6. Prepare a cash budget for Mark and Ana using the income and expenditure data from the original case as well as the figures from Question 5 needed to meet their goals. In addition, Mark and Ana would need to make monthly payments totaling approximately $490 in order to pay off their revolving

WILLIAMS   *Current Position*

credit debt within the next year. (It is greater than the $443 a month you get when you divide their revolving debt of $5,318 by 12 because interest would continue to accrue until the debts were paid off.) Assume that income and other expenditures for the upcoming year will be the same as the current year except that there will be no sale of securities.

7. Can Mark and Ana achieve all of their stated goals considering their current income and expenditure patterns? If not, what recommendations would you make to help them achieve their goals? If they have trouble agreeing on how their money should be spent, what could they do that might make both of them feel better about their budget?

8. Prepare a 1989 tax return (form 1040) for Mark and Ana using the financial data in the original case. Do they owe more taxes, or will they receive a refund? If the answer is a refund, how much?

9. Assuming that 1990 will be similar to 1989, should they make any adjustments to their withholding allowances? If the answer is yes, should they increase or decrease the number of withholding allowances claimed?

10. What is Mark and Ana's average tax rate? What is their marginal tax rate?

11. Approximately how much would they save in taxes next year if they did invest $2,000 in their 401(k) retirement accounts? (This move would reduce their taxable income by $2,000.)

12. What tax strategies would you recommend to help Mark and Ana reduce their tax liability.

WILLIAMS *Current Position*

PART II

Managing Basic Assets

CHAPTER 5

Managing Your Savings and Other Liquid Assets

Financial Facts or Fantasies

Are the following statements financial facts (true) or fantasies (false)?

- An asset is considered liquid only if it is held in the form of cash.
- The financial supermarkets of today offer consumers a full range of financial products and services, all under one roof.
- Unlike money market mutual funds, money market deposit accounts are federally insured.
- In all but a few cases, the nominal (stated) interest rate on a savings account is the same as its effective rate of interest.
- U.S. savings bonds are not a very good way to save.
- At most banks and other depository institutions, you will be hit with a hefty service charge if your checking account balance falls just $1 below the stipulated minimum amount for just one day out of the month.

How would you like to receive $3,000 a month? Wouldn't be bad, would it? Think of what you could buy and do if you knew you would have $3,000 flowing in month after month. If this sounds farfetched, then stop for a moment and consider the fact that this could very well happen to you in just a few short years. Actually an individual earning $50,000 per year takes home (after taxes) about $3,000 a month. While it's true that most college graduates do not initially earn $50,000 a year, many young, two-income couples do. Unfortunately, those who realize that level of income often spend it away on relatively meaningless purchases (which is all too easy to do). Handling it wisely requires establishing financial goals and cash budgets as discussed in Chapter 3. This is how you control the way you spend your money. And such control is necessary to ensure that you are getting the most from it.

THE ROLE OF CASH MANAGEMENT IN PERSONAL FINANCIAL PLANNING

Cash management involves making sure that you have funds available for planned and unplanned expenditures and that your spending patterns are within budgetary limits. What methods do you currently employ in order to make sure that you pay bills promptly and have funds available for unexpected expenditures? Before reading on, spend a few moments answering this question.

This chapter is concerned with **cash management**—an activity that deals with the routine, day-to-day administration of cash and near-cash resources. We identified these resources in Chapter 2 as *liquid, or financial assets*. They are considered liquid because they are either held in cash or can be readily converted to cash with little or no loss in value. In addition to cash, there are several other kinds of liquid assets, including checking accounts, savings accounts, money market accounts and funds, and other short-term investment vehicles. Exhibit 5.1 provides a list and brief description of the more popular types of liquid assets and the representative rates of return they earned in early 1989. As a rule, near-term needs are met using cash on hand, and unplanned or future needs are met using some type of savings or short-term investment vehicle.

In personal financial planning, cash management is the way you make sure that funds are available for making household outlays as well as establishing an effective savings program. The success of your financial plans depends on your faithfulness to established cash budgets. An effective way of keeping your spending in line is to make all household transactions (even the allocation of fun money or weekly cash allowances) using a tightly controlled *checking account*. In effect, you should write checks only at certain times of the week or month and, more important, you should avoid carrying your checkbook with you when you might be tempted to write checks for unplanned purchases. If you are going shopping, establish a maximum spending limit beforehand—ideally, an amount consistent with your cash budget. Such a system will not only help you avoid frivolous, impulsive expenditures, but it will also provide valuable documentation on how and where you are spending your money. Then, if your financial outcomes are not consistent with your plans, you can better identify causes and initiate appropriate corrective actions.

Another aspect of cash management, establishing an ongoing savings program, is an important part of personal financial planning. Savings are not only a cushion against financial emergencies but also a vehicle for accumulating funds for meeting future financial goals. You may want to put money aside so you can go back to school in a few years to earn a graduate degree, or to buy a new home, or perhaps to take a luxury vacation—these are all examples of specific financial objectives that can be met through savings. There are many different ways to save, some are better suited to accumulating emergency funds, and others are more appropriate for building reserves for future expenditures. Clearly specifying the objectives of your savings program is a prerequisite to selecting appropriate savings vehicles.

An asset is considered liquid only if it is held in the form of cash. **Fantasy:** A liquid asset is one that is held in cash or can be readily converted to cash with little or no loss in value; thus, liquid assets include checking accounts, savings accounts, money market accounts and funds, and other short-term investment vehicles.

THE NEW FINANCIAL MARKETPLACE

Because of deregulation, the financial markets and institutions of today are vastly different (and greatly improved) from what they were five to ten years ago; today's financial supermarkets provide a full menu of financial products and services. What are some of the financial products and services available from major financial institutions in your area? Spend a few moments listing them before reading on.

EXHIBIT 5.1

Popular Liquid Assets

The wide variety of savings vehicles available makes it possible to meet just about any savings or short-term investment need.

Type	Representative Rates of Return (Early 1989)	Description
Cash	0%	Pocket money—the coin and currency in one's possession.
Checking Account		A substitute for cash. Offered by commercial banks as well as other financial institutions such as savings and loans and credit unions.
Minimum Balance Maintained		
$ 0 to $ 999	4.0	
$ 1,000 to $ 9,999	4.7	
$10,000 to $24,999	5.0	
Greater than $25,000	5.1	
Savings Account		Money is available at any time but cannot be withdrawn by check. Offered by banks and other financial institutions.
Minimum Balance Maintained		
$ 0 to $ 999	4.0	
$ 1,000 to $ 9,999	5.8	
$10,000 to $24,999	6.0	
Greater than $25,000	6.1	
Money market deposit account (MMDA)	6.3	Primarily a savings vehicle that pays market rates of interest. Offers limited check-writing privileges and requires a fairly large (typically $1,000 or more) minimum deposit.
Money market mutual fund (MMMF)	8.5	Savings vehicle that is actually a mutual fund (not offered by banks, S&Ls, and other depository institutions). Like an MMDA, it also offers check-writing privileges.
Certificate of deposit (CD)	8.4	A savings instrument where funds are left on deposit for a stipulated period of time (one week to one year or more); imposes a penalty for withdrawing funds early. Market yields vary by size and maturity; no check-writing privileges.
U.S. Treasury bill (T-bill)	8.5	Short-term, highly marketable security issued by the U.S. Treasury (originally issued with maturities of 13, 26, and 52 weeks); smallest denomination is $10,000.
U.S. savings bond (EE)	7.8	Issued by U.S. Treasury; rate of interest is tied to U.S. Treasury securities. Long a popular savings vehicle (widely used with payroll reduction plans). Maturities are approximately five years; sold in denominations of $50 and more.

From the viewpoint of the individual consumer, today's financial marketplace is far superior to that of just ten years ago. Most noticeable are the wider array of financial products and services, and the more competitive rates of return. The price of these benefits appears to be today's generally higher costs of financial services.

The major reason for this "new look" in the financial marketplace was the *Depository Institutions Deregulation and Monetary Control Act of 1980.* Prior to passage of this act, the distinctions between various kinds of financial institutions were clear. A bank, for example, was for maintaining a checking account or obtaining a loan, while a brokerage firm was for buying or selling stocks and bonds. Since deregulation, however, bankers are initiating stock and bond transactions, and brokers are offering check-writing services and making loans. Today it is difficult to distinguish between the numerous providers of financial products and services.

cash management

The routine, day-to-day administration of cash and near-cash liquid resources by an individual or family.

The Birth of One-Stop Financial Supermarkets

The current trend is clearly toward the giant **financial supermarket** that provides "one-stop shopping" for all financial needs. These financial (and nonfinancial) institutions offer consumers a full range of financial products and services under one roof. It is no longer necessary to go one place to do your banking, a second to buy insurance, and a third to trade securities. You can now go to the store and, while shopping, look into that renter's insurance policy you've been thinking about or make a deposit into your money market mutual fund.

The development of financial supermarkets has been a natural outcome of the growing list of institutional participants who, thanks to deregulation, are widening their range of financial products and services. In addition to the traditional banking and savings outlets (commercial banks, S&Ls, savings banks, and credit unions), adopters of the financial supermarket approach include many of the major insurance companies, most of the major national and regional brokerage firms, a number of mutual funds, and other financial companies such as American Express and Household Finance. Also becoming a growing force are the nonfinancial firms such as Sears, Kroger, J.C. Penney, General Motors, and General Electric.

As a result, specialization within the financial institutions industry has begun to disappear. Today it is difficult to tell a savings and loan from a commercial bank, since both offer so many of the same financial products and services; in fact, S&Ls as well as credit unions are now commonly referred to as "banks," much to the chagrin of commercial bankers. And in response to competition from nonfinancial institutions, many banks and S&Ls have begun to offer help with personal financial planning, to take deposits across state lines, sell insurance, and offer discount brokerage services.

Thus, the *financial services* industry as we know it today embraces all institutions that market various kinds of *financial products,* such as checking and savings accounts, credit cards, loans and mortgages, insurance, and mutual funds, and *financial services,* such as financial planning, taxes, real estate, trusts, retirement, and estate planning. In effect, what used to be several distinct (though somewhat related) industries is now, in essence, one industry.

The financial supermarkets of today offer consumers a full range of financial products and services, all under one roof. **Fact:** A financial supermarket offers financial products such as checking and savings accounts, credit cards, loans and mortgages, insurance, and mutual funds, and financial services concerned with financial planning, taxes, real estate, trusts, retirement, and estate planning. Such products and services are offered by banks and savings outlets, insurance companies, brokerage firms, mutual funds, and even nonfinancial companies like Sears, Kroger, and General Motors.

Traditional Financial Institutions: "Banks"

In spite of the presence of financial supermarkets and the growing number of firms entering the financial services field, individuals and families continue to make the vast majority of their financial transactions at traditional financial institutions: commercial banks, savings and loan associations, savings banks, and credit unions. Although these are organized and regulated by different agencies, they are frequently referred to as "banks" due to the similarity of their product and service offerings. Compared to their nonbanking counterparts, probably the two biggest advantages these institutions have over their competition is that they are familiar and convenient. Further, while most people have checking and savings accounts, a much smaller number own stocks, bonds, or mutual funds. As a result, most people are not accustomed to dealing with brokerage firms and other types of financial service companies.

Commercial Banks. To millions of Americans, banking means doing business with a **commercial bank**. Of the four types of traditional financial institutions, commercial banks are by far the largest. In addition to checking accounts, commercial banks offer a full array of financial services, including a variety of savings vehicles, credit cards, several kinds of loans, trust services, and such items as safe-deposit boxes, traveler's checks, and check-cashing privileges. It is little wonder that they are commonly called *full-service banks.*

Commercial banks are the only financial institutions that can offer *noninterest-paying checking accounts* (demand deposits)—a feature that in today's deregulated financial market provides little competitive advantage. Therefore, commercial banks also offer a variety of checking accounts that combine check-writing privileges with features of savings accounts. In addition, they offer several types of pure savings accounts. Most prevalent among these is the *passbook account,* which is a regular savings account on which interest is paid. There is no limit on how much interest a bank can pay on its passbook accounts, so it clearly pays to shop around. However, most passbook accounts still pay low (4 to 5 percent) interest rates. Whereas to many savers, passbook accounts are simply a convenient way of accumulating money, for many others, they represent the only savings or investment vehicle used. Rather than giving each account holder a passbook in which to record all transactions, most banks today issue separate deposit/withdrawal receipts and at the end of the quarter send each depositor a statement itemizing all account transactions during the period.

Commercial banks typically differentiate between their *special savings accounts* on the basis of deposit minimums. For higher minimums they offer a slightly higher rate of interest (¼ to ½ percent) than on accounts requiring lower or no minimum balance. If the account holder does not maintain the required minimum balance, the interest is usually paid on the account as if it were an account requiring no minimum balance. The savings account data in Exhibit 5.1 show minimum account balances and associated interest rates prevailing in early 1989.

In addition to offering a variety of special savings accounts, many banks offer *club accounts.* These accounts are established for a special purpose, such as saving money for Christmas shopping. They act as a budgeting device for the customer by requiring specified weekly or monthly deposits toward the particular savings goal—for example, $500 for Christmas shopping. To assist club members in keeping track of scheduled deposits, banks often issue some type of coupon book showing the date and amount of each transaction. Club accounts generally pay less interest than passbook accounts, since the bank must perform additional clerical chores in order to establish and maintain them.

With the variety of products and services and range of fees offered by commercial banks, choosing a bank is no simple matter. Many variables have to be considered.

Savings and Loan Associations. Savings and loan associations (S&Ls) are found in most parts of the country. One type of S&L is a *mutual association,* in which the depositors actually own the institution and the returns they receive technically are called *dividends* rather than *interest* (Note: In finance, the word *mutual* indicates a type of cooperative ownership arrangement.) Although these payments are called dividends, they are treated as interest for all practical purposes. The other type of S&L is *stockholder owned;* depositors in this case actually do receive interest on their deposits instead of dividends.

Regardless of their organizational structure, savings and loans are important because they channel people's savings into mortgage loans for purchasing and improving homes. Since deregulation, S&Ls have greatly expanded their product and service offerings. Although they still cannot offer noninterest-paying checking accounts (demand deposits), they do offer many of the same checking, savings, and lending products and services as commercial banks—in fact, it is difficult to differentiate between the two institutions. Typically savings deposits at S&Ls earn about ¼ to ½ percent more

financial supermarket
A financial or nonfinancial institution that offers consumers a full range of financial products and services under one roof.

commercial bank
A financial institution that offers checking and savings accounts and a full range of financial products and services, including various types of consumer loans. It's the only institution that can offer noninterest-paying checking accounts (demand deposits).

savings and loan association (S&L)
A financial institution that channels the savings of its depositors primarily into mortgage loans for purchasing and improving homes; due to deregulation, however, S&Ls now offer a competitive range of financial products and services.

than those at commercial banks. The availability of products and services at numerous branch offices and their attractive rates of interest contribute to the popularity of savings and loan associations.

Savings Banks. **Savings banks** are a special type of savings institution, similar to savings and loan associations and found primarily in the New England states. In addition to offering a number of different interest-paying checking accounts, they accept a variety of savings deposits on which they pay interest at a rate on par with that paid by savings and loans. Because most savings banks are *mutuals,* depositors are their actual owners. The savings bank accepts deposits and, after deducting the expenses of doing business, distributes the profits to the owners in the form of dividend payments, which are technically equivalent to interest payments. However, instead of distributing all profits, the mutual savings bank typically distributes only enough to provide depositors with a stated return of, say, 5.5 percent. It then reinvests any remaining profits in order to provide greater protection for depositors.

Credit Unions. A **credit union** is a special type of mutual association that provides financial products and services to specific groups of people who belong to a common occupation, religious or fraternal order, or residential area. Credit unions are owned (and, in some cases, operated) by their members. Although credit unions are used by over 50 million people, they are quite small when compared to commercial banks or S&Ls. A person who qualifies for membership in a credit union may buy a share by making a minimum deposit—often $5 or less. One *must* be a member—that is, have money on deposit—in order to borrow from a credit union. Because the credit union is run to benefit the members, the rate of interest it pays on savings is normally ½ to 1½ percent above that paid by other savings institutions. Being a mutual association in which the savers own shares, credit unions technically pay dividends rather than interest on savings.

Most credit unions, in addition to offering different types of interest-paying checking accounts—called **share draft accounts**—offer a variety of savings accounts to their members. Savers often do not know the dividend rate until the end of the savings period, since the dividends paid in each period depend on the credit union's earnings for that period. Since credit unions not only yield a favorable return on members' savings but also allow them to borrow money at advantageous rates, they are attractive to many people. Most also provide free life insurance (up to a maximum amount) for each dollar deposited.

The Growing Menu of Checking and Savings Products

People basically hold cash and other forms of liquid assets, like checking and savings accounts, for the convenience they offer in (1) making purchases; (2) meeting normal, recurring living expense and purchase requirements; and (3) providing a safety valve (or cushion) for meeting unexpected expenses or taking advantage of unanticipated opportunities. As mentioned before, the competition caused by deregulation has resulted in financial institutions today providing a wide array of products with which to meet every liquid asset need. Let us now take a brief look at the various types of checking and savings accounts. We will look at other short-term investment vehicles later in this chapter.

Checking Accounts. A checking account held at a financial institution is basically a **demand deposit**, meaning that the withdrawal of these funds must be permitted whenever demanded by the account holder. You put money into your checking account by *depositing* funds; you withdraw it by *writing checks.* As long as you have sufficient funds in your account, the bank, when presented with a valid check, must immediately pay the amount indicated. This is done by charging your account for the amount of the check. Money held in checking accounts is liquid and therefore can easily be used to pay bills and make purchases.

Regular checking is the most common type of checking account; it pays no interest, and any service charges that exist can be waived if you maintain a minimum balance (usually about $500). Technically, noninterest-paying regular checking accounts can be offered only by commercial banks; S&Ls, savings banks, and credit unions also offer checking accounts, but these must pay interest and, as such, are known as *NOW accounts* or, in the case of credit unions, *share draft accounts*. Because checks are generally accepted in paying bills and purchasing goods and services, demand deposit balances are considered a common and important type of cash balance. One of the primary advantages of demand deposits is that the use of checks to pay bills provides a convenient record of payment.

Savings Accounts. A savings account is another type of liquid asset that may be kept in commercial banks, savings and loan associations, credit unions, and many other types of financial institutions. Since a passbook is sometimes used to record transactions in these accounts, they are called **passbook accounts**, and their rate of interest is called the *passbook rate*. Savings deposits are referred to as **time deposits**, since they are expected to remain on deposit for a longer period of time than demand deposits. Because generally higher interest rates apply to savings deposits, savings accounts are generally preferable to checking accounts when the depositor's purpose is to accumulate money for a future expenditure or maintain balances for meeting unexpected expenditures.

While financial institutions generally retain the right to require a savings account holder to wait a certain number of days before receiving payment of a withdrawal, most are willing to pay withdrawals immediately. In addition to withdrawal policies and deposit insurance, the rate and method of calculating interest paid on savings accounts are important considerations in choosing the financial institution in which to place savings.

Interest-Paying Checking Accounts. As a result of changes that took place in the late 1970s and early 1980s, depositors now have far greater flexibility in choosing how to satisfy their checking and cash balance needs. Beginning with the highly successful money market mutual funds (MMMFs), a variety of new financial products were introduced, including money market deposit accounts (MMDAs) and NOW accounts. These last two are available at virtually every deposit-taking financial institution in the United States and are marketed under various names (Checkmatic Accounts, PrimeChecking, PreferredChecking, Premium Accounts, and so on).

Money market mutual funds. Starting from zero in the mid-1970s, money market mutual funds grew to over $300 billion in deposits in early 1989, making them the most successful type of mutual fund ever offered. (Mutual funds are discussed in greater detail in Chapter 14.) A **money market mutual fund (MMMF)** pools the funds of many small investors and purchases high-yielding short-term marketable securities offered by the U.S. Treasury, major corporations, large commercial banks, and various government organizations. The portfolio of a typical MMMF contains specialized short-term securities that mature in as little as one day to as long as one year. The securities are all highly liquid and marketable forms of debt that are sold

saving bank
A type of savings institution, similar to an S&L and found mainly in the New England states, that is most often a mutual association owned by its depositors.

credit union
A depositor-owned mutual association that offers different types of interest-paying checking (share draft) accounts, savings accounts, and loans to its members.

share draft account
An account offered by credit unions that is similar to interest-paying checking accounts offered by other financial institutions.

demand deposit
An account held at a financial institution from which funds can be withdrawn (in check or cash) upon demand by the account holder; same as a *checking account*.

passbook account
A savings account in which transactions are sometimes recorded in a passbook; it pays the going passbook rate of interest.

time deposit
A savings deposit at a financial institution; so called because it is expected to remain on deposit for a longer period of time than a demand deposit.

money market mutual fund (MMMF)
A mutual fund that pools the funds of many small investors and purchases high-yielding short-term marketable securities offered by the U.S. Treasury, major corporations, large commercial banks, and various government organizations.

in denominations of at least $10,000 and often as much as $250,000 or more. Because of their lofty minimum denominations, few people are able to buy these securities directly. However, they can do so indirectly through the purchase of MMMFs, many of which have minimum deposits of as little as $500 to $1,000. The interest rate earned on an MMMF depends on returns earned on its investments, which fluctuate with overall credit conditions. At their peak, most MMMFs earned annual rates in excess of 15 percent, which is considerably better than the rate paid on typical savings deposits. Moreover, investors have instant access to their funds through check-writing privileges, although the checks often must be written for a stipulated minimum amount (usually $500). These checks look and are treated like any other check drawn on a demand deposit account except that, as with any other interest-bearing checking account, *you continue to earn interest on your money while the checks make their way through the banking system.*

Money market deposit accounts. **Money market deposit accounts (MMDAs)** were introduced in December 1982 and were extremely popular with depositors almost at once. They were created as a way of giving banks and other depository institutions a vehicle to compete for deposits with money market mutual funds. MMDAs are popular with some savers and investors due to their convenience and safety; the deposits, unlike those in money funds, are *federally insured.* Depositors have convenient access to their MMDAs through check-writing privileges or automated teller machines. A total of six transfers (only three by check) are allowed each month, after which a penalty is charged for additional withdrawals. Although this feature obviously reduces the flexibility of these accounts, most depositors, who apparently look upon MMDAs as savings rather than convenience accounts, do not consider it a serious obstacle. Moreover, MMDAs pay the highest rate of any bank account on which checks can be written.

Unlike money market mutual funds, money market deposit accounts are federally insured. **Fact:** Money market deposit accounts are funds deposited in special, high-paying savings accounts at banks, S&Ls, and other depository institutions and thus are covered by the same federal deposit insurance as any other checking or savings account, which is something money funds don't have.

NOW accounts. **Negotiable order of withdrawal (NOW) accounts** are checking accounts on which the financial institution can pay whatever rate of interest it deems appropriate. They were first made available on a limited basis in 1972 and were made available to all depository financial institutions beginning in 1980. Since the deregulation of interest rates beginning in January 1986, the NOW account has become widely accepted as an "interest-paying checking account." Today there is no legal minimum balance for a NOW, but many institutions impose their own requirement, often between $500 and $1,000. Some have no minimum, paying interest on any balance in the account. Many institutions pay interest at a higher rate for all balances over a specified amount, such as $2,500. The seemingly high rates of interest, however, can be misleading; as we will see later in this chapter, one of the major problems in the growth of these interest-paying checking accounts has been a rise in monthly bank *charges* that often has virtually wiped out any interest earned on all but the highest account balances. NOW accounts should be viewed primarily as *checking accounts* that can also serve as potentially attractive savings vehicles. In this capacity, they allow individuals and families to earn interest on balances that must be kept for transaction purposes anyway and would otherwise lie idle.

How Safe Is Your Money?

With the growing publicity about "problem" banks and S&Ls—and, even worse, the increasing number of financial institutions that have had to close their doors—depositors are justifiably concerned about the safety of their money. The vast majority of commercial banks, S&Ls, savings banks, and credit unions are in fact *federally insured* by U.S. government agencies. Those that are not usually provide insurance through either a state-chartered or private insurance agency. Most experts feel that these so-called *privately insured* institutions provide less protection against loss than do the federally insured ones. Fortunately, privately insured institutions are in the minority; it is estimated that over 95 percent of commercial banks are federally insured as are nearly 90 percent of the S&Ls, 70 percent of the savings banks, and 80 percent of the credit unions. Exhibit 5.2 lists the insuring agencies and maximum insurance amounts provided under

EXHIBIT 5.2

Federal Deposit Insurance Programs

If you have your checking and savings accounts at a federally insured institution, you are covered by at least $100,000 of insurance as provided by one of the following federal insurance agencies.

Savings Institution	Insuring Agency	Amount of Insurance
Commercial bank	Federal Deposit Insurance Corporation (FDIC)	$100,000/depositor
Savings and loan association	Federal Savings and Loan Insurance Corporation (FSLIC) or FDIC	$100,000/depositor
Savings bank	Federal Deposit Insurance Corporation (FDIC)	$100,000/depositor
Credit union	National Credit Union Share Insurance Fund (NCUSIF)	$100,000/depositor

the various federal deposit insurance programs. As a result of the large number of S&L failures that threatened the survival of the FSLIC during the "S&L crisis" of the late 1980s, the Bush administration's bailout plan now makes FDIC insurance available to certain S&Ls. Although the roles of the FDIC and FSLIC are currently in transition, S&L deposits remain insured by a federal agency.

Deposit insurance protects the funds you have on deposit at banks and other depository institutions against institutional failure. In effect, the insuring agency stands behind the financial institution and guarantees the safety of your deposits up to a specified maximum amount ($100,000 per depositor in the case of federal insurance). Actually, the deposit insurance is provided to each depositor and *not* on the deposit account. Thus, both the checking and the savings accounts of each depositor are insured and, *as long as the maximum insurable amount is not exceeded,* the depositor can have any number of accounts and still be fully protected. Each account in the financial institution, or any of its branches, will be fully covered regardless of number or type. This is an important feature to keep in mind, since many people mistakenly believe that the maximum insurance applies to each of their accounts. Not so! For instance, an individual with three accounts in one commercial bank totaling $125,000—e.g., a passbook savings account balance of $5,000, MMDA with a $70,000 balance at a branch office, and a NOW account with a $50,000 balance at the home office—is covered by

only $100,000 of insurance. Of course, if either the MMDA or the NOW account were transferred to another bank or financial institution, it would be insured for up to $100,000 and the total amount in all the accounts would then be fully protected.

While $100,000 in deposit insurance is, to say the least, quite a bit, it is possible to increase the amount of coverage if the need arise. Specifically, depositors who carefully follow federal guidelines can increase their coverage by opening accounts in multiple depositor names at the same institution. A married couple, for example, can obtain $500,000

---

money market deposit account (MMDA)

A savings account that is meant to be competitive with a MMMF, offered by banks and other depository institutions.

negotiable order of withdrawal (NOW) account

A checking account on which the financial institution can pay whatever rate of interest it deems appropriate.

deposit insurance

A type of insurance that protects funds on deposit against failure of the institution. Insuring agencies include the *Federal Deposit Insurance Corporation (FDIC),* the *Federal Savings and Loan Insurance Corporation (FSLIC),* and the *National Credit Union Share Insurance Fund (NCUSIF).*

in coverage by setting up *individual* accounts in the name of each spouse (good for $200,000 in coverage), *joint* accounts in both names (good for another $100,000), and *separate trust or IRA* accounts in the name of each spouse (good for an additional $200,000). Note that in this case each depositor is treated as a separate legal entity and as such receives full insurance coverage—the husband alone is considered one legal entity, the wife another, and the man and wife as a couple a third. In addition, the trust and IRA accounts are also viewed as legal entities.

ESTABLISHING A SAVINGS PROGRAM ▪

> To get the most from your savings program, it is important to develop sound savings habits and understand your savings options. Before reading on, spend a few moments describing your savings program, the available savings options, and those that you've chosen to include in your program.

It is estimated that more than 75 percent of American households have some money put away in savings. Surveys have shown that while age and income have a lot to do with the amount saved, over half of the people who do save have *more than $10,000* socked away! Clearly, saving money is considered an important activity by many individuals and families, a deliberate, well-thought-out activity designed to preserve the value of their money, insure liquidity, and earn a high rate of return. Almost by definition, *smart savers are smart investors;* they regard saving as more than putting loose change into a piggybank; rather, they recognize the importance of savings and know that savings must be managed as astutely as any security. After all, what we normally think of as "savings" is really a form of investment—a short-term, highly liquid, fixed-dollar investment that is subject to minimum

risk. Establishing and maintaining an ongoing savings program is a vital element of personal financial planning. To get the most from your savings, however, you must understand your savings options and how different savings vehicles pay interest.

Choices Involved in Establishing a Savings Program

Careful financial planning dictates that a portion of your assets be held for the purposes of meeting liquidity needs and as a way of accumulating wealth. While opinions differ as to how much should be held as liquid reserves, the general consensus is that an amount equal to three to six months' after-tax income is best for most families. This means that if you take home $1,500 a month, you should have between $4,500 and $9,000 in liquid reserves. If your employer has a strong salary continuation program during extended periods of illness and/or you have a sizable line of credit available, the lower figure is probably suitable; if you lack one or both of these, however, the larger amount is probably more appropriate.

A specific savings plan is needed with which to accumulate funds. In this regard, saving should be considered as important as any other budget activity rather than an event that occurs only when income happens to exceed expenditures. Some people do this by arranging savings withholding directly from their paychecks. This has been a common practice for many years with U.S. savings bonds purchase plans and credit union deposits; today it is also possible to have funds regularly transferred to other financial institutions such as commercial banks, savings and loans, savings banks, and even money market mutual funds. Not only do direct deposit arrangements help your savings effort, they also enable your funds to earn interest sooner. The key to success is to establish a *regular* pattern of savings. You should make it a practice to set aside an amount that you can comfortably afford *each month,* even if it is only $50 to $100. (Keep in mind that earning 10 percent interest, a series of $100 monthly deposits will grow to over $75,000 in 20 years!) The *Smart Money* box suggests several ways you can discipline yourself to achieve your savings goals.

Many financial planning experts recommend keeping a minimum of 10 to 25 percent of your investment portfolio in savings-type instruments in addition to the three to six months' holding of liquid reserves noted above. Thus, someone with, say, $50,000 in investments should probably have a minimum of $5,000 to $10,000—and possibly even more—in such short-term vehicles as MMDAs, U.S. savings bonds, or CDs. Also, at times the amount invested in short-term securities could well exceed the recommended minimum and approach 50 percent or more of the portfolio. The amount held in savings accounts and short-term securities—both for the purpose of maintaining liquid reserves and as a part of an investment portfolio—can therefore be substantial.

Finding Interest Earned on Your Money

Interest earned is the reward for putting your money in a savings account or short-term investment vehicle. Because with such accounts or securities there really is no other source of return, it is important for you to understand how interest is earned. Unfortunately, even in the relatively simple world of savings, you will quickly discover that all interest rates are not created equal.

The Matter of Compounding. Basically, interest can be earned in one of two ways. First, some short-term investments are sold on a *discount basis*. This means that the security is sold for a price that is lower than its redemption value, the difference being the amount of interest earned. Treasury bills, for instance, are issued on a discount basis. Another way to earn interest on short-term investments is by *direct payment,* such as what occurs when interest is applied to a passbook savings account. Although this is a simple process, determining the actual rate of return can involve several complications.

The first of these relates to the method used to arrive at the amount and rate of **compound interest** earned annually. You have probably read or seen advertisements by banks or other depository institutions touting the fact that they pay daily, rather than simple, interest. To understand what this means, consider the following example. As-

sume you invest $1,000 in a savings account advertised as having an annual interest rate of 10 percent **simple**. This means that if the $1,000 is left on deposit for one year, you will earn $100 in interest, and the account balance will total $1,100 at the end of the year. Note that in this case the **nominal (stated) rate of interest** is the same as the effective rate. In contrast, the **effective rate of interest** is the annual rate of return *actually earned* on the transaction. It is found in the following manner:

$$\frac{\text{Effective rate}}{\text{of interest}} = \frac{\text{Amount of interest earned during the year}}{\text{Amount of money invested or deposited}}$$

In our example, since $100 was earned during the year on an investment of $1,000, the effective rate is $100/$1,000 = 10%, which is the same as the nominal rate of interest. (Note that in the above formula it is interest earned during the *year* that matters; thus, if you wanted to find the effective return on an account that you had for six months, you would have to double the amount of interest earned.)

But suppose you can invest your funds elsewhere at a 10 percent rate, *compounded semiannually.* Since interest is applied to your account at midyear, this means you will earn *interest on interest* for the

---

compound interest
When interest earned in each subsequent period is determined by applying the nominal (stated) interest rate to the sum of the initial deposit and the interest earned in each prior period.

simple interest
Interest that is paid on only the initial amount of the deposit.

nominal (stated) rate of interest
The promised rate of interest paid on a savings deposit or charged on a loan.

effective rate of interest
The rate of interest that is actually earned (charged) over the period of time funds are held (borrowed).

EXHIBIT 5.3

Nominal and Effective Interest Rates with Different Compounding Periods

The amount of interest that you actually earn from a savings account will exceed the stated nominal rate if interest is compounded more than once a year (as are most savings and interest-paying accounts).

Nominal Rate	Effective Rate				
	Annually	**Semiannually**	**Quarterly**	**Monthly**	**Daily**
4%	4.00%	4.04%	4.06%	4.07%	4.08%
5	5.00	5.06	5.09	5.12	5.13
6	6.00	6.09	6.14	6.17	6.18
7	7.00	7.12	7.19	7.23	7.25
8	8.00	8.16	8.24	8.30	8.33
9	9.00	9.20	9.31	9.38	9.42
10	10.00	10.25	10.38	10.47	10.52
11	11.00	11.30	11.46	11.57	11.62
12	12.00	12.36	12.55	12.68	12.74

last six months of the year, thereby increasing the total interest for the year. The actual dollar earnings are determined as follows:

First
6 months' = $1,000 × 0.10 × 6/12 = $ 50.00
interest
Second
6 months' = $1,050 × 0.10 × 6/12 = 52.50
interest

Total interest = $102.50

Interest is being generated on a larger investment in the second half of the year, since the amount of money on deposit has increased by the amount of interest earned in the first half year ($50). Although the nominal rate on this account is still 10 percent, the effective rate is 10.25 percent ($102.50/$1,000). As you may have guessed, the more frequently interest is compounded, the greater the effective rate for any given nominal rate. These relationships are shown for a sample of interest rates and the compounding periods in Exhibit 5.3. Notice that with a 10 percent nominal rate, daily compounding adds more than half a percent to the size of the total return—not a trivial amount.

Compound Interest Equals Future Value. Compound interest is the same as the *future value* concept introduced in the *Smart Money* box in Chapter 3. You can use the procedures described

there to find out how much an investment or deposit will grow to equal over time at a compound rate of return. For example, using the future value formula and the future value factor table from Appendix A, you can determine how much $1,000 will be worth in 4 years if it is deposited into a savings account that earns 10 percent per year, compounded annually:

$$\frac{\text{Future}}{\text{value}} = \frac{\text{Amount}}{\text{deposited}} \times \frac{\text{Future value}}{\text{factor}}$$
$$= \$1,000 \times 1.464$$
$$= \underline{\$1,464}.$$

You can use the same basic procedure to find the future value of a *series* of deposits, except that you would use the annuity factor table from Appendix B. For instance, if you put $1,000 a year into a savings account that pays 10 percent per year, compounded annually, in four years you will have

$$\frac{\text{Future}}{\text{value}} = \frac{\text{Amount}}{\text{deposited}} \times \frac{\text{Annuity}}{\text{factor}}$$
$$= \$1,000 \times 4.641$$
$$= \underline{\$4,641}.$$

Measuring the Account Balance Qualified to Earn Interest. Not only are there differences among financial institutions in the way interest is compounded; there may also be differences with

EXHIBIT 5.4

Four Methods of Determining Interest (Nominal Rate = 10%)

In addition to the compounding procedures used, the amount of interest you earn
will depend on how the financial institution measures the size of your account
balance.

A. Quarterly Activity

Day	Transaction	Account Balance
1	Opening balance	$10,000
30	Deposit $2,000	12,000
60	Withdrawal $6,000	6,000
90	Ending balance	6,000

B. Interest Calculations

1. *Minimum balance method:*
$$\$\,6{,}000 \times 0.10 \times 90/360 = \underline{\underline{\$150.00}}$$

2. *FIFO method:*
$$\$\,4{,}000 \times 0.10 \times 90/360 = \$100.00$$
$$2{,}000 \times 0.10 \times 60/360 = \underline{\quad 33.33}$$
$$\text{Total} = \underline{\underline{\$133.33}}$$

3. *LIFO method:*
$$\$\,6{,}000 \times 0.10 \times 90/360 = \underline{\underline{\$150.00}}$$

4. *Actual balance method:*
$$\$10{,}000 \times 0.10 \times 30/360 = \$\,83.33$$
$$12{,}000 \times 0.10 \times 30/360 = 100.00$$
$$6{,}000 \times 0.10 \times 30/360 = \underline{\quad 50.00}$$
$$\text{Total} = \underline{\underline{\$233.33}}$$

respect to how account balances qualify to earn interest—that is, how the size of the account balance is measured. There are four methods in wide use: (1) the minimum balance method, (2) the FIFO method, (3) the LIFO method, and (4) the actual balance method. The minimum balance and actual balance methods are by far the most widely used procedures, but we will look at all four.

The differences in these methods are best illustrated with an example such as the one given in Exhibit 5.4. The depositor here has $10,000 at the beginning of the quarter and adds $2,000 to this balance 30 days later; then, on day 60, the depositor withdraws $6,000, leaving an ending balance of $6,000. While either simple or compound interest could be used, we will assume that the account pays simple interest of 10 percent. In all illustrations, interest earned is computed in the following manner:

$$\frac{\text{Interest}}{\text{earned}} = \frac{\text{Amount}}{\text{invested}} \times \frac{\text{Annual}}{\text{interest}} \times \frac{n}{360},$$
$$\text{(or on deposit)} \quad \text{rate}$$

where n equals the number of days funds are on deposit. Notice that a 360-day year is assumed, which is common for many financial calculations. To see how this equation works, consider the sum of $1,000 left on deposit for 30 days at an annual rate of 7½ percent; the depositor in this case would earn interest of

$$\$1{,}000 \times .075 \times 30/360 = \$6.25$$

In all but a few cases, the nominal (stated) interest rate on a savings account is the same as its effective rate of interest. **Fantasy:** In only a few cases are the two rates the same. Because the nominal (stated) interest rate paid by a bank or other depository institution typically compounds during the year, the effective rate is greater than the nominal rate.

S·M·A·R·T M·O·N·E·Y

Tips for Becoming a Disciplined Saver

To improve your financial health, the obvious thing to do is to save more money—but Americans have a notoriously hard time doing that. Here are 12 tips for mustering financial willpower:

1. **Pay yourself first.** Take your savings out of each paycheck immediately, before paying bills and making purchases. Otherwise, you may have nothing left to save at the end of the month.

2. **Set a realistic goal.** You're more likely to become a successful saver if you establish an objective in league with your budget. Though many financial planners suggest setting aside 10 percent, there's nothing wrong with setting a lesser goal of 5 or even 3 percent. "The basic rule is to save whatever you can, but save something," says Paul Strassels, a Burke, Va., financial consultant.

3. **Remember that savings beget savings.** Leave your nest egg alone and spend only the interest or dividends. If you pump $2,000 a year into a money-market mutual fund for five years but spend the interest, you'll still wind up with $10,000. Better yet, let the earnings ride at an average annual yield of, say, 7 percent, and you'll amass $2,300 in interest to go with your $10,000.

4. **Keep it simple.** Stick to just a few basic instruments, such as certificates of deposit (CDs), mutual funds or perhaps U.S. savings bonds. Stocks, bonds, and more exotic fare such as real-estate investment trusts require brokerage fees, research effort—and considerable attention. When picking a mutual fund, remember that the no-load variety does not charge sales commissions and historically has done as well as funds that do.

5. **Hold cash reserves to a minimum.** Your checking-account balance should be just big enough to cover monthly expenses. It is recommended that you also keep an amount equal to twice your monthly take-home pay in investments that can be quickly turned to cash—for example, a money-market mutual fund or short-term CDs—to help you cope with any emergencies. The rest of your savings can go to higher-yielding investments, such as long-term CDs or mutual funds that emphasize growth-oriented stocks.

6. **Be yield-conscious.** Banks calculate interest in various ways, so true yields can vary widely on CDs with the same maturity and interest rate. For instance, the annual return on a five-year, 9 percent CD with quarterly compounding is 9.31 percent, but the same CD with daily compounding could yield as much as 9.55 percent. Over five years, the difference would

---

Minimum balance method. With this method, interest is paid on the *lowest* balance in the account during the quarter. Since the minimum is $6,000 in our illustration (see Exhibit 5.4), the interest earned amounts to only $150. Since this method places a heavy penalty on withdrawals made late in the period, it is not recommended if substantial withdrawals are anticipated.

FIFO method. FIFO means *first-in, first-out*. It is an assumption that the financial institution makes

amount to $175 on a $10,000 CD. It's not a lot, but why walk away from it?

7. **Don't confuse tax savings with real savings.** People often justify credit card interest and certain big expenses by the fact that they are tax deductible. But the new tax law has seriously cramped Uncle Sam's generosity. This year, the maximum tax rate on federal returns is 33 percent. Thus, every dollar you deduct from your income will net no more than 33 cents in tax savings. Moreover, Uncle Sam is phasing out the interest deductions for car loans, credit cards, and other consumer debts. You'll save more by trimming all your expenses, even the deductible ones.

8. **Enlist a "savings enforcer."** If you lack the discipline to write a check to yourself each month, get somebody else to do it. For example, your bank can regularly transfer a specified sum from your checking account to a savings plan. Better yet, you can arrange for payroll deductions that go to a company credit union or employer-sponsored thrift plan. These can be very sweet deals. Credit unions often pay higher yields on basic savings accounts than commercial banks or savings associations, while many employers will match all or part of your contributions to a thrift plan.

9. **Swap debt for equity.** After you retire an auto loan or another consumer debt, continue to write the same monthly installment checks, but send them to your savings account.

10. **Reward yourself occasionally.** Saving for retirement or your toddler's college education can be hard, since the payoff won't be realized for a long time. So establish a rule that if you exceed your savings goal for a year, you're entitled to spend the extra bucks on something you covet— maybe a new stereo or a trip to the beach.

11. **Try a few gimmicks.** Some people need a little push to put themselves into the savings habit. For example, assess yourself $10 penalty every time you break your diet, and put the money into a savings account. If you're not sure you'll play fair, ask your spouse to be a referee. Some families augment their savings by making a ritual of collecting all the loose change in their pockets, wallets, and drawers once a week or so.

12. **Don't rob the piggy bank.** Diehard spendthrifts should say "No" to mutual funds or savings accounts with check-writing privileges. The temptation is just too great.

Source: Patricia M. Scherschel, "A Dozen Painless Ways to Help a Nest Egg Grow," *U.S. News & World Report,* June 8, 1987, pp. 58–60. Copyright, June 8, 1987, U.S. News & World Report.

---

with respect to when withdrawals are charged; specifically, it assumes withdrawals are charged against the earlier or opening balances of an account. Thus, the $6,000 withdrawal on day 60 is assumed to reduce the *opening* balance of $10,000, leaving a balance of $4,000. Exhibit 5.4 shows how the interest income of $133.33 is determined. Note that because the $6,000 withdrawal is charged against the opening balance, it is only the remaining amount ($4,000) that earns interest over the full quarter

(90 days), whereas the deposit ($2,000) earns interest only over the 60 days it was on deposit. For the data given in this illustration, the depositor earns even less with this method than with the minimum balance method, although this is not always the case.

LIFO method. LIFO means *last-in, first out*. With this method, the bank assumes withdrawals are charged to the most recent deposits or balances. This is to the depositor's advantage, since it means earlier deposits are left untouched and thereby earn interest for the entire period. Thus, the $6,000 withdrawal on day 60 is assumed to first reduce the $2,000 deposit made on day 30, with the remaining $4,000 carried back as an offset against the opening balance of $10,000. This leaves $6,000 ($10,000 − $4,000) against which interest is earned. As it works out in the illustration in Exhibit 5.4, the $150 of interest earned is the same as under the minimum balance method. Although this method is somewhat fairer to the depositor than the FIFO method, it still does not provide interest for the full period over which the money is on deposit.

Actual balance method. This method is the most accurate and gives depositors the highest interest earnings on their money; it is also considered the fairest procedure, as it gives depositors full credit for all funds on deposit. This procedure is sometimes called *daily interest,* but it should not be confused with the daily *compounding* of interest, which is an entirely different concept. Daily interest does not necessarily mean daily compounding, although competition among financial institutions is moving most of them in that direction. Before opening a deposit account, a depositor should ask two questions: (1) How often does compounding take place, and (2) what method is used to determine which balances earn interest? (It is the second question we have been addressing here; the first was discussed earlier.) Exhibit 5.4 indicates how the interest of $233.33 is calculated for our example using the actual balance method; as can be seen, more is earned under this method than with any of the others.

A Variety of Ways to Save

Over the past decade or so, there has been a tremendous proliferation of savings and short-term investment vehicles, particularly for the individual of modest means. Saving and investing in short-term securities is no longer the easy task it once was, when the decision for most people boiled down to whether funds should be placed in a passbook savings account or in Series E bonds. Today, investors can choose from savings accounts, NOW accounts, money market mutual funds and deposit accounts, certificates of deposit, Treasury bills, Series EE bonds, and central asset accounts. We examined several of these savings vehicles earlier in this chapter, including savings accounts, NOW accounts, MMMFs and MMDAs; accordingly, our attention here will center on the four remaining types of deposits and securities.

Certificates of deposit. Certificates of deposit (CDs) differ from the savings instruments discussed earlier in this chapter in that CD funds must remain on deposit for a specified period of time, which can range from seven days to one year or more. Although it is possible to withdraw funds prior to maturity, an interest penalty usually makes withdrawal somewhat costly. While the bank or other depository institution is free to charge whatever penalty it likes, most result in a severely reduced rate of interest—typically a rate no greater than that paid on its most basic passbook savings account. Since October of 1983, banks, S&Ls, and other depository institutions have been free to offer any rate and maturity CD they wish. As a result, today a wide variety of CDs are offered by most banks and depository institutions, though as a rule, most pay higher rates for larger deposits and longer periods of time. CDs are convenient to buy and hold; they offer attractive and highly competitive yields plus federal deposit insurance protection.

In addition to purchasing CDs directly from the issuer, they can be purchased from stockbrokers. **Brokered CDs** are simply certificates of deposit sold by stockbrokers. The brokerage house searches for the best deal (highest yield) it can get, and then sells these CDs to its customers. In essence, a bank or S&L issues the CDs, and the brokerage house merely sells (or places) them with the investing public. The minimum denomination is usually only $1,000, so they are affordable, and there's no commission to pay since the broker earns its commission from the issuing bank or S&L. Brokered CDs are attractive for two reasons: First, you can sell them prior to maturity without incurring a penalty, since the brokerage firms maintain active secondary markets; therefore, you can improve your liquidity. But remember, there are no guarantees here; the market prevails, so if rates go up, the relative value of your CD falls and you don't end up earning the rate you started out with. Second, you may be able to get higher yields from brokered CDs than from your local bank or other depository institution. Frequently, you can gain ¼ to ¾ of a percent by dealing with a broker. But be careful. The broker can always get higher yields by selling CDs issued by troubled financial institutions. Therefore, *buy a brokered CD only from a federally insured institution*—ask your broker, just to be sure.

U.S. Treasury Bills. The **U.S. Treasury bill (T-bill)** is considered the ultimate safe haven for saving and investments. T-bills are obligations of the U.S. Treasury issued as part of its ongoing process of funding the national debt. They are sold on a discount basis in minimum denominations of $10,000 followed by increments of $5,000 and are issued with 3-month (13-week), 6-month (26-week), and 1-year maturities. The 3- and 6-month bills are auctioned off every Monday and 1-year bills roughly every 4 weeks. They are backed by the full faith and credit of the U.S. government and pay an attractive and safe yield that is free from state and local income taxes.

T-bills are almost as liquid as cash, since they can be sold at any time (in a very active secondary market) without any interest penalty. However, should you have to sell before maturity, you may lose some money on your investment if interest rates have risen, and you will have to pay a broker's fee as well. Treasury bills pay interest on a *discount basis* and as such are different from other savings or short-term investment vehicles—that is, their interest is equal to the difference between the purchase price paid and its worth at maturity. For example, if you paid $9,800 for a bill that will be worth $10,000 at maturity, you will earn $200 in interest ($10,000 − $9,800).

An individual investor may purchase T-bills directly through participation in the weekly Treasury auctions or indirectly through a commercial bank or a security dealer who buys bills for investors on a commission basis. Outstanding Treasury bills can also be purchased in the secondary market through banks or dealers. The biggest advantage to this approach is that the investor has a much wider selection of maturities from which to choose, ranging from less than a week to as long as a year.

It is actually relatively simple to buy T-bills directly: To participate in the weekly auction, all you need do is submit a "tender" to the nearest Federal Reserve Bank or branch specifying both the amount and maturity desired (tender forms are easy to fill out and readily available from commercial banks). The Treasury tries to accommodate individual investors through its *noncompetitive* bidding system, which most individual investors use because of its simplicity. In essence, all noncompetitive tender offers are awarded T-bills at a price equal to the average of all the accepted competitive bids. Thus, the investor is assured of being able to buy bills in the quantity desired while obtaining the benefit of an open auction system—and without going through the hassle of a competitive bid.

Series EE Bonds. **Series EE bonds** are the well-known savings bonds that have been around

---

certificate of deposit (CD)
A type of savings certificate that is issued by certain financial institutions in exchange for a deposit; typically requires a minimum deposit and has a maturity ranging from seven days to one year or more.

brokered CD
A certificate of deposit, typically with a $1,000 minimum denomination, that can be purchased with no commission from a stockbroker and can be sold without penalty prior to maturity.

U.S. Treasury bill (T-bill)
A short-term (three-month to one-year maturity) debt instrument issued by the federal government in the ongoing process of funding the national debt.

Series EE bond
A savings bond issued in various denominations by the U.S. Treasury.

for decades; they were first issued in 1941 and used to be called Series E bonds. They are often purchased through payroll deduction plans. Though issued by the U.S. Treasury, they are quite different from T-bills; in fact, perhaps their only similarity is that they are sold on a discount basis and are also free of state and local income taxes. These bonds are *accrual-type securities,* which means that interest is paid when they are cashed, on or before maturity, rather than periodically over their lives. (The government does make Series HH bonds available through the exchange of Series E or Series EE bonds; they have a ten-year maturity and come in denominations of $500 to $10,000. (Unlike EE bonds, HH bonds are issued at their full face value and pay interest semiannually at the current fixed rate of 6 percent.)

Series EE bonds are backed by the full faith and credit of the U.S. government and can be replaced without charge in case of loss, theft, or destruction. They can be purchased at banks or other depository institutions, or through payroll deduction plans. Issued in denominations from $50 through $10,000, their purchase price is a uniform 50 percent of the face amount (thus, a $100 bond will cost $50 and be worth $100 at maturity).

The actual maturity date on EE bonds is unspecified, since the issues pay a variable rate of interest. The higher the rate of interest being earned, the shorter the period of time it takes for the bond to accrue from its discounted purchase price to its maturity value. In an effort to make these securities more attractive to investors, all EE bonds held five years or longer receive interest at the higher of 6 percent or 85 percent of the average return on five-year Treasury securities, as calculated every six months in May and November. The yield, therefore, changes every six months in accordance with prevailing Treasury security yields, although it can never drop below a guaranteed minimum rate of 6 percent. Current rates on Series EE bonds can be obtained from your bank or simply by calling 1–800–872–6637. (Note: The rate being quoted in May 1989 was 7.81 percent.) EEs held for less than five years (they can be redeemed any time after the first six months) earn interest according to a fixed, graduated scale beginning at 4.16 percent for bonds held six months and rising gradually to not less than the 6 percent guaranteed minimum rate at five years.

In addition to being exempt from state and local taxes, Series EE bonds provide their holders with an appealing tax twist: *Savers need not report interest earned on federal tax returns until the bonds are redeemed.* Although interest can be reported annually (for example, when the bonds are held in the name of a child who has limited interest income), most investors choose to defer it. In effect, this means the funds are being reinvested at an after-tax rate of no less than the guaranteed minimum rate of 6 percent.

A second attractive tax feature allows complete tax avoidance of EE bond earnings when proceeds are used to pay educational expenses, such as college tuition, by married couples with less than $60,000 of adjusted gross income ($40,000 or less for single filers).

U.S. savings bonds are not a very good way to save. **Fantasy:** Investing in Series EE savings bonds is an excellent way to save, because they offer highly competitive rates of return and several attractive tax features.

Central Asset Accounts. With the advent of the new financial marketplace has come a greatly increased number of providers of banking services. No longer are banks and S&Ls the only ones that can provide traditional banking services. Perhaps the best example of this is the **central asset account.** This type of account was first introduced as its *cash management account,* or *CMA,* by the Wall Street brokerage firm of Merrill Lynch in 1977. It is not a separate investment vehicle, but rather a comprehensive deposit account that combines checking, investing, and borrowing activities. Such accounts are offered by banks, other depository institutions, brokerage houses, mutual funds, and insurance companies. Their distinguishing feature is that they automatically "sweep" excess balances into short-term investments. For example, a bank central asset account might be set up to combine a NOW and a MMDA. At the end of each day, if the NOW account balance exceeds $500, the excess is automatically swept into the higher-yielding MMDA. Thus, Merrill Lynch's CMA automatically sweeps the account holder's funds into its MMMF, and if securities are purchased for an amount greater than the current balance, the needed funds are supplied automatically through a loan. Along

EXHIBIT 5.5

Some Central Asset Accounts

Most central asset accounts have large minimum investment requirements. If you can meet the minimum, you will find such accounts available at banks, mutual funds, brokerage houses, and even Sears (through its Dean Witter brokerage subsidiary).

Company/Account	Minimum Investment[a]	Annual Fee	Frequency of Sweep
A.G. Edwards & Sons (Total Asset Account)	$20,000	$ 50	Over $500—daily Under $500—weekly
Charles Schwab (Schwab One Account)	$ 5,000	$ 0	All amounts—daily
Citibank (FOCUS Account)	$ 5,000 cash	$100	All amounts—daily
Dean Witter (Active Assets Account)	$10,000	$ 80	All amounts—daily
E.F. Hutton (Asset Management Account)	$10,000	$ 80	Over $1,000—daily Under $1,000—monthly
Fidelity Brokerage Services (Fidelity USA)	$ 5,000 cash or $10,000 securities	$ 36	Over $1,000—daily Under $1,000—weekly
Kidder Peabody (Premium Account)	$25,000	$ 90	All amounts—daily
Merrill Lynch (Cash Management Account)	$20,000	$ 65	Over $1,000—daily Under $1,000—weekly
Paine Webber (Resource Management Account)	$15,000	$ 60	Over $500—daily Under $500—weekly
Prudential Bache (Command Account)	$10,000	$ 50	Over $1,000—daily Under $1,000—weekly
Shearson Lehman Bros. (Financial Management Account)	$15,000	$ 50	Over $1,000—daily Under $1,000—weekly
Smith Barney (Vantage Account)	$20,000	$ 40	Over $1,000—daily Under $1,000—weekly
Thomson McKinnon Securities (Asset Director)	$10,000	$ 30	Over $100—daily Under $100—no sweep

[a]Unless otherwise indicated, minimum investment can be in the form of either cash or securities.

with one-stop financial supermarkets, central asset accounts are exceptionally popular with investors. However, stipulated minimum balance requirements ranging from $5,000 to $20,000—the CMA, for example, requires an initial balance of $20,000 in cash or securities—limit the availability of central asset accounts to those with greater savings. Exhibit 5.5 provides a representative list of some of the institutions offering these accounts, along with recent data on their minimum investment requirements, annual fees, and frequency of sweeps.

central asset account

A comprehensive deposit account, offered by major financial institutions, that combines checking, investing, and borrowing activities and automatically sweeps excess funds into short-term investments and provides loans when shortages exist.

MAINTAINING A CHECKING ACCOUNT ▪

> Maintaining a checking account is both a safe way to hold money and a convenient way to pay for the goods and services consumed in everyday life. How frequently and for what purposes can you use a checking account? Spend a few moments answering this question before reading on.

Checking account balances are an important component of the money supply. They are a near-perfect substitute for cash and today are viewed by most people as absolutely essential. Checking accounts not only provide a safe and convenient way to hold money but also streamline point-of-sale purchases, debt payments, and other basic transactions. In one form or another (regular or interest-paying checking accounts), they can be maintained at commercial banks, S&Ls, savings banks, credit unions, and even at brokerage houses through central asset accounts. For convenience, we will focus our attention on commercial bank checking accounts, although our discussion applies to checking accounts maintained at other types of financial institutions as well.

Opening a Checking Account

The factors that typically influence the choice of where to maintain a checking account are convenience, services provided, and cost. Many people choose a bank solely on the basis of such convenience factors as business hours, location, number of drive-in windows, and/or number and location of branch offices and automatic teller machines (ATMs). Some states permit branch banking throughout communities, while others prohibit branches altogether. Ease of access is obviously an important consideration; most people prefer to bank near their homes or places of employment. Services provided differ from bank to bank. Depending on their size, banks may rent safe-deposit boxes, provide for direct deposits and withdrawals, make loans, offer financial planning, and provide

various types of bank card and check-cashing services.

The Cost of a Checking Account. Free checking used to be fairly common but is not so today. One of the by-products of deregulation and the growth of interest-paying checking accounts has been a sharp increase in bank service charges. Today it is estimated that fewer than 5 percent of the banks and other depository institutions let you write as many checks as you like free of charge; the rest levy monthly and/or per-check fees when your balance drops below a stipulated minimum, and some charge you for checking no matter how large a balance you carry in your account.

Usually you must maintain a minimum balance of $500 to $1,000 or more in order to avoid a service charge. While some banks use the *average* monthly balance in an account to determine whether to charge, the vast majority use the *daily* balance procedure. This means that if your account should happen to fall below the minimum balance just once during the month, you will be hit with the full service charge even if you keep an average balance that is three times the stipulated minimum. Let your balance fall $1 below the minimum on just one day out of the month, and you'll pay! Further, the amount of service charge you will pay will be quite substantial. If the daily balance falls below the minimum, you can expect to get hit in two ways: (1) with a base service charge of, say, $5.00 a month, and (2) with an additional charge of, say, 30 cents for each check you write. Using these fees as an illustration and assuming you write 20 checks in a given month, if your balance should fall below the minimum, you will have to pay a service charge of $5.00 + (20 × $.30) = $11.00.

In addition to the service charges levied on checking accounts, banks have pushed up most of their other check-related charges. The charge on a returned check can now amount to $20 or more. The amount of minimum balance required and the fee structure vary from bank to bank. Further, the service charges on regular checking accounts are usually much less than on NOW accounts; thus, if you intend to keep only a small amount in your checking account, you may be better off with a no-frills, regular checking account. All too often individuals find that the service charges they pay on their NOW accounts far exceed any interest they earn and that the net result is a very costly form of checking. It is not surprising, therefore, that many smart consumers today are using cost as the single most important variable in choosing where to set up a checking account.

At most banks and other depository institutions, you will be hit with a hefty service charge if your checking account balance falls just $1 below the stipulated minimum amount for just one day out of the month. **Fact:** Most banks and other depository institutions use the *daily* balance in your account, rather than the *average* monthly balance, to determine whether you must pay a service charge; thus, letting it fall below the minimum even once can have a significant cost.

Single or Joint Account. Two people wishing to open a checking account may do so in one of three ways: (1) They can each open individual checking accounts (on which the other cannot write checks); (2) they can open a joint account that requires both signatures on all checks; or (3) they can open a joint account that allows either one to write checks (the most common type of joint account). One advantage of the joint account over two single accounts is that it lowers the service charges. In addition, the account has rights of survivorship, which, in the case of a married couple, means that if one spouse dies, the surviving spouse, after fulfilling a specified legal time requirement, can draw checks on the account. (If account owners are treated as tenants in common rather than having rights of survivorship, the survivor gets only his or her share of the account. Thus, when opening a joint account it is important to specify the rights preferred.)

Checking Account Procedures

A check should always be written in ink. It should include the name of the person to whom it is made out (the payee), the amount, and the date. The amount of the check should be written both in numerals and in script in order to insure accuracy; if these amounts do not agree, the *written* amount is considered legally correct. The check should be signed the same way as on the signature card, which was completed when the account was initially opened; otherwise, it may not be accepted by the bank. It is also a good idea to note its purpose directly on the check itself—usually on the line provided in the lower left-hand corner. For example, on the personal check written by Mary Morrison shown in Exhibit 5.6, Mary has noted that the $65.17 made out to Gulf Oil Company is payment due on their Gulf credit card. This information can be used for both budgeting and tax purposes at some future date.

The Checkbook Ledger. Whenever a check is written or a deposit made, a corresponding entry must be made in the **checkbook ledger**, which is provided with the checkbook for purposes of maintaining records of all transactions in the account (see Exhibit 5.6). By subtracting the amount of each check written and adding the amount of each deposit made to the previous balance, the account balance can be kept up to date. Good records of transactions and an accurate balance help avoid overdrawing the account.

Making Deposits. Deposit slips are normally included in your checkbook and are also readily obtainable from your bank. Filling out a deposit slip is the first step in making a deposit. Separate entries for currency, coins, and checks are typically included on deposit slips (see Exhibit 5.6). Each check deposited is listed separately by its so-called *transit I.D. number,* which is usually printed just to the right of the date. For example, the Morrisons' check in Exhibit 5.6 contains the numbers 70–196/711; this is the transit I.D. number for their bank, the National Bank and Trust Company of Tulsa, Oklahoma. You should use the top group of numbers (here 70–196) to identify the checks you are depositing—that is, for each check you deposit, you should list the appropriate transit I.D. number and the amount of the check. If you were depositing

---

checkbook ledger
A ledger provided with a checkbook for maintaining accurate records of all transactions in a checking account.

EXHIBIT 5.6

Checking Account Transactions

Three important parts of a checking account are the checks written, the deposits made, and the checkbook ledger, in which checks written, deposits made, and the latest account balance are recorded.

CHECK

CHECKBOOK LEDGER

DEPOSIT SLIP

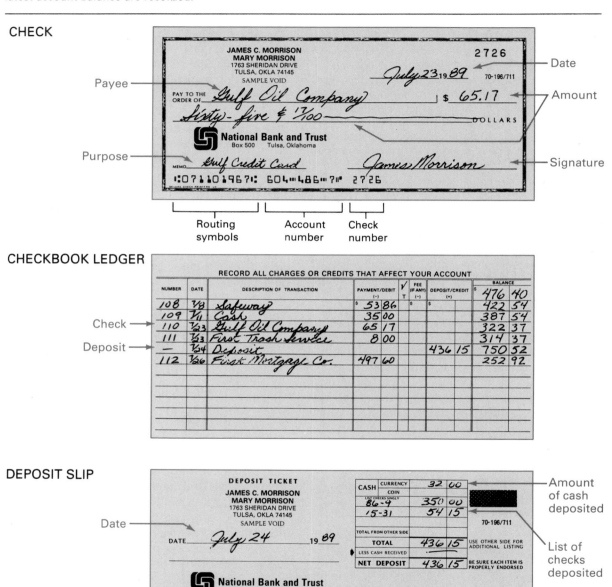

Source: Courtesy of National Bank and Trust Company, Tulsa, Oklahoma.

Mary's check in Exhibit 5.6, you would enter the following on your deposit slip: 70–196 $65.17.

You should also be sure to properly endorse all checks. Federal regulations require your endorsement to be made in black or blue ink and to be within 1½ inches of the check's trailing edge (left end of check when viewed from the front) so as not to interfere with endorsements from the bank at which the check is deposited. (If you don't comply, you'll still get your money, but it may take longer.)

To protect against possible loss of endorsed checks, it is common practice to use a special endorsement, such as "Pay to the order of XYZ Bank," or a restrictive endorsement, such as "For deposit only." If the way your name is written on the check differs from the way you signed the signature card, you should sign your correct signature below your endorsement. In order to further ensure that the deposit is properly entered into your account, write your account number below your endorsement.

You can submit your deposit to your bank in several ways: at the bank during normal banking hours; at a remote banking facility, such as a drive-in window; at an **automatic teller machine (ATM)**, a type of remote computer terminal at which transactions can be made 24 hours a day, 7 days a week; in the bank's **night depository**, a protected type of mail slot on the exterior of the bank, in the special envelopes banks usually provide for after-hours deposits; or by mail in the self-addressed, sometimes postage-paid deposit envelopes often provided for this purpose. The use of ATMs, night depositories, and banking by mail is not advised when cash is being deposited because of the risk of an unaccountable loss. Of course, when checks are deposited, a delay in the availability of the funds may result due to the time required for them to clear.

Endorsing Checks. When you receive a check from someone, you can either cash, deposit, or make a payment to someone else (a third party). Regardless of how you use the check, you will have to endorse it on the back in exactly the same way it has been made out on the front. The common forms of endorsement—*blank, special, restrictive,* and *conditional*—are illustrated in Exhibit 5.7. It is important to make sure that all endorsements conform with the federal regulations cited earlier.

Overdrafts. When a check is written for an amount greater than the current account balance, the result is an **overdraft**. Poor bookkeeping on the part of the account or a delay in the bank's receipt of a deposit can be the cause. If the overdraft is proven to have been intentional, the bank can initiate legal proceedings against the account holder. The action taken by a bank on an overdraft depends on the amount involved and the strength of its relationship with the account holder. In many cases, the bank stamps the overdrawn check with the words "insufficient balance (or funds)" and returns it to the party to whom it was written. The account holder is notified of this action, and a penalty fee of $7 to $20 or more is deducted from his or her checking account. In addition, the depositor of a "bad check" may be charged as much as $10 to $15 by its bank, which explains why merchants typically charge customers who given them bad checks $10 to $20 or more and often refuse to accept future checks from them.

In instances in which a strong relationship has been established between the account holder and the bank or in which arrangements have been made for **overdraft protection**, the bank will go ahead and pay a check that overdraws the account. In cases where overdraft protection has not been prearranged but the bank pays the check, the account holder is usually notified by the bank and charged a penalty fee for the in-

---

automatic teller machine (ATM)
A type of remote computer terminal at which customers of a bank or other depository institution can perform basic transactions 24 hours a day, 7 days a week.

night depository
A protected type of mail slot on the exterior of a financial institution that its customers can use to make after-hours deposits.

overdraft
The result of writing a check for an amount greater than the current account balance.

overdraft protection
An arrangement between the depository institution and account holder wherein the institution automatically advances money to cover an overdrawn check.

EXHIBIT 5.7

Types of Check Endorsement

There are a variety of ways to endorse a check, from a blank endorsement to a highly restrictive one. Regardless of which endorsement is used, technically, it must be made in black or blue ink and be within 1½ inches of the check's trailing edge.

Blank

> *Mary Morrison*

This is the most common form of endorsement. One merely endorses the check by signing his or her name. Once endorsed, the check becomes payable to whoever possesses it.

Special

> *Pay to the order of John Smith*
> *Mary Morrison*

This endorsement includes a notation specifically indicating to whom the check is to be paid. Such an endorsement does not preclude that person from endorsing the check over to yet another person (fourth party).

Restrictive

(1)

> *Pay to the order of John Smith only*
> *Mary Morrison*

(2)

> *For deposit only*
> *Mary Morrison*

By adding the word "only" after the third party's name, the check cannot be endorsed over to a fourth party. The third party in this case could be either an individual or a bank.

Conditional

> *Pay to the order of John Smith only upon completion of landscaping*
> *Mary Morrison*

This endorsement, although not legally binding, specifies some condition. Its use restricts further negotiation of the check and makes the third party (John Smith) liable to the second party (Mary Morrison) if he or she violates the condition.

convenience. However, the check does not bounce, and the check writer's creditworthiness is not damaged.

Stopping Payment. Occasionally it is necessary to **stop payment** on a check that has been issued. This may be due to any of several possible reasons: (1) Checks or a checkbook are either lost or stolen; (2) a good or service paid for by check is found to be faulty (Note: Some states prohibit you from stopping payment on faulty goods or services.); or (3) a check is issued as part of a contract that is not carried out. Payment on a check is stopped by notifying the bank. Normally the account holder must fill out a form indicating the check number and date, amount, and the name of the person to whom it was written. Sometimes stop-payment orders can be initiated over the telephone, in which case a written follow-up is normally required. Telephone-initiated stop payments generally remain in effect for 14 days and written ones for 6 months.

Once a stop-payment order has been issued, the bank tellers are told to refuse payment on the affected check. At the same time, the stop-payment information is placed in the bank's data processing system so that the check will be rejected if it is presented by another bank in the check-clearing process. Most banks require account holders who wish to stop payment to sign a statement relieving the bank of any liability if payment is erroneously made on the check in question. A fee ranging from $10 to $15 is usually charged for stopping payment on a check.

Monthly Statements

Once each month, your bank will provide a statement that contains an itemized listing of all transactions (checks written and deposits made) within your checking account; also included are any service charges levied and interest earned. (See the Morrisons' August 1989 bank statement shown in Exhibit 5.8) Many banks include canceled checks and deposit slips with the bank statement, although they are slowly (but surely) moving away from this practice. You can use the monthly statements to verify the accuracy of your account records and to reconcile differences between the statement balance and the balance shown in your checkbook

ledger. The monthly statement is also an important source of information for your tax records.

Account Reconciliation. It is advisable to reconcile your bank account as soon as possible after you receive your monthly statement. The **account reconciliation** process (or *balancing the checkbook,* as the process is also known) can uncover errors in recording checks or deposits, in addition or subtraction, and, occasionally, in the bank's processing of the checks. It can also help you avoid overdrafts, since it forces you to periodically verify your account balance. Discrepancies between the account balance reflected in your checkbook ledger and that shown in the bank statement can be attributed to one of four basic factors, assuming neither you nor the bank has made any errors:

1. Certain checks that you have written and deducted from your checkbook balance have not yet been received by your bank and therefore remain outstanding.
2. Certain deposits that you have made and added to your checkbook balance have not yet been credited to your account. The recent regulations referred to in the *Issues in Money Management* box should help to reduce both the delay in crediting deposits and the amount of checks outstanding (noted in factor 1 in this list).
3. Certain service (activity) charges levied on your account by the bank have not yet been deducted from your checkbook balance.
4. Interest earned on your account (if it is a MMDA or NOW account) has not yet been added to your checkbook balance.

---

stop payment
An order made by an account holder asking the depository institution to refuse payment on an already issued check.

account reconciliation
The process of verifying the accuracy of your checking account records in light of the bank's records reflected in the monthly statement, which shows checks written, deposits made, service charges levied, and interest earned during the month.

EXHIBIT 5.8

A Checking Account Statement

Each month you receive a statement from your bank or depository financial institution that summarizes the transactions you have made over the month and shows your latest account balance. Similar statements are also sent out for certain kinds of savings accounts, like NOWs and MMDAs.

STATEMENT OF CHECKING ACCOUNT

National Bank & Trust
Box 500   Tulsa, Oklahoma

1
PAGE

JAMES C. OR MARY MORRISON
1765 SHERIDAN DRIVE
TULSA, OK 74145

1-234-567-8
ACCOUNT NUMBER

08/31/89
STATEMENT DATE

TRANSACTIONS POSTED SINCE LAST STATEMENT

NUMBER	DATE	AMOUNT	ID	NUMBER	DATE	AMOUNT	ID	NUMBER	DATE	AMOUNT	ID	NUMBER	DATE	AMOUNT	ID
	08/03	715.33	CR												
	08/04	200.00	CR												
	08/10	6.75	CR												
	08/31	250.00	CR												
0080	08/03	3.50													
0092	08/03	12.44													
0110	08/04	65.17													
0113	08/03	14.75													
0115	08/10	15.50													
0116	08/07	50.00													
0117	08/06	10.00													
0118	08/07	16.80													
0119	08/10	21.37													
0120	08/05	4.18													
0122	08/11	8.00													
0123	08/11	7.27													
0124	08/14	30.00													
0125	08/17	45.80													
0126	08/20	24.83													
0127	08/20	25.00													
0128	08/19	132.00													
0129	08/27	159.07													
0131	08/31	497.60													
	08/31	2.85	DR												

PLEASE EXAMINE THIS STATEMENT PROMPTLY, REPORT ANY DIFFERENCE TO THE AUDITING DEPARTMENT.

DATE LAST STATEMENT			DATE THIS STATEMENT		
07	31	89	08	31	89

BALANCE LAST STATEMENT		NUMBER Checks-Debits	AMOUNT CHECKS-DEBITS		NUMBER Deposits-Credits	AMOUNT DEPOSITS-CREDITS		BALANCE THIS STATEMENT
65.10	LESS	20	1146.13	PLUS	4	1172.08	EQUAL	91.05

Source: Courtesy of National Bank and Trust Company, Tulsa, Oklahoma.

ISSUES IN MONEY MANAGEMENT

Checks Clear More Quickly . . . Bankers Worry

Fraudulent checks and check-kiting schemes have always plagued banks. But many bankers fear that new federal laws will increase check fraud and possibly change the entire checking relationship banks have with customers.

To the dismay of bankers, regulations implementing the Expedited Funds Availability Act of 1988 became effective September 1 [1988]. Bankers fear that the regulations, designed to reduce the amount of time a bank can hold deposited funds, will cause security risks and large losses.

Generally, the new law requires a bank to make cash and certain check deposits available for withdrawal the next business day. These include certified, teller's, cashier's, and certain government checks, and any check drawn on a local bank.

In the past, a bank could hold checks for several days until they cleared. Critics had claimed banks held these checks too long and invested the money on their own behalf.

"The new law is a license for people to rip off banks," said a president of a Northeast savings and loan association, who declined to be named. "It's going to be a nightmare," said a security executive at a money center bank, who also requested anonymity.

Check-related fraud losses—now running about $10 billion a year—may double or even triple as banks reluctantly comply with the new law, said Royce D. Brown, senior vice president of J. D. Carreker and Associates, Inc., a Dallas consulting firm.

Security officers fear that dishonest customers can deposit a stolen or forged check into a new account and withdraw money the next day, before the funds actually clear. The depository bank bears the loss. Joseph R. Alexander, a senior attorney at the Federal Reserve System,

said: "We see the potential for danger."

Banks will be particularly vulnerable to check-kiting schemes, security officers say. In a typical kiting scheme, a malefactor deposits a bad check from Bank A in his account in Bank B to cover the check he wrote drawn on Bank A. Knowledge of the bank's clearing schedule, and the shorter holding period, gives the crook "a much greater opportunity to con money," Brown said.

In the long term, however, the new law is likely to make it more difficult to open a checking account. Banks are likely to require more extensive applications, and even credit checks, on potential customers. This, along with the anticipated losses from fraud, is expected to drive up the cost of checking to the consumer.

Source: "Cashing Checks—Just a Little Too Fast," *The New York Times,* December 11, 1988, p. F–11.

Take the following steps to reconcile your account:

1. Upon receipt of your bank statement, arrange all canceled checks in descending numerical order based on their sequence numbers or issuance dates.
2. Compare each check with the corresponding entry in your checkbook ledger to make sure no recording errors exist. Place a checkmark in your ledger alongside each entry compared.

Also, check off any other withdrawals, such as from ATMs, or automatic payments.

3. List the checks and other deductions (ATM withdrawals) still *outstanding*—that is, those deducted in your checkbook but not returned with your bank statement (see step 2). Total their amount.
4. Compare the deposit slips returned with the statement to deposits shown in your check-

EXHIBIT 5.9

An Account Reconciliation Form—The Morrisons' August 1989 Statement

The Morrisons used this form to reconcile their checking account for the month of August 1989. Because line A equals line B, they have fully reconciled the difference between the $91.05 bank statement balance and their $310.47 checkbook balance. Accounts should be reconciled each month—as soon as possible after receipt of the bank statement.

CHECKING ACCOUNT RECONCILIATION

For the Month of *August*, 19 *89*

Accountholder Name(s) *James C. or Mary Morrison*

Type of Account *Joint Regular Checking*

1. Ending balance shown on bank statement — **$ 91.05**

Add up checks and withdrawals still outstanding:

Check Number or Date	Amount	Check Number or Date	Amount
121	$ 81.55		$
130	196.50		
131	22.23		
132	100.00		
133	76.31		
	TOTAL $ 476.59		

2. *Deduct* total checks/withdrawals still outstanding from bank balance — **− $476.59**

Add up deposits still outstanding:

Date	Amount	Date	Amount
8/28	$ 595.00		
8/30	98.16		
	TOTAL $ 693.16		

3. *Add* total deposits still outstanding to bank balance — **+ $ 693.16**

A **Adjusted Bank Balance** (1 − 2 + 3) — **$ 307.62**

4. Ending balance shown in checkbook — **$ 310.47**

5. *Deduct* any bank service charges for the period — **− $ 2.85**

6. *Add* interest earned for the period — **+ $ 0.00**

B **New Checkbook Balance** (4 − 5 + 6) — **$ 307.62**

Note: Your account is reconciled when line A equals line B.

book. Total the amount of deposits still *outstanding*—that is, those shown in your checkbook ledger but not yet received by the bank. Be sure to include all automatic deposits and deposits made at ATMs in your calculations.

5. *Subtract* the total amount of checks outstanding (from step 3) from your bank statement balance, and *add* to this balance the amount of outstanding deposits (from step 4). The resulting amount is your *adjusted bank balance*.

6. Deduct the amount of any service charges levied by the bank from, and add any interest earned to, your checkbook ledger balance. Make sure you include all service charges for the period, including those for returned checks, stop payments, and/or new checks ordered. The resulting amount is your *new checkbook balance*. This amount should equal, your *adjusted bank balance* (from step 5). If it is not, you should check all addition and subtraction in your checkbook ledger, since you have probably made an error.

Tax Records. Your monthly bank statement is an important tax record. It can be reviewed along with the checkbook ledger to evaluate past income and expenditures. Although you may maintain accurate records of these items as part of your budgeting process, the statement can be used to provide proof of payment, which you might need if the Internal Revenue Service decides to audit your tax return. At the time a check is written, it is advisable to indicate its purpose both in the checkbook ledger and on the front of the check. Bank statements should be retained for a period of at least five years, since an audit can still be conducted several years after a tax return has been filed.

Special Types of Checks

Because there is no way to be absolutely sure that a check is good, some type of verification is often necessary. This is common for large purchases or when the buyer is not located in the area in which the purchase is being made. The most common instruments used to guarantee payment are *cashier's checks, traveler's checks,* and *certified checks*.

The reverse side of your bank statement usually provides a form for reconciling your account along with step-by-step instructions. Although a number of different approaches to reconciliation exist, the one described here is the most straightforward. Exhibit 5.9 (on facing page) includes an account reconciliation form, following these procedures, that was completed by the Morrisons for the month of August 1989. The form can be used to reconcile regular checking accounts or any type of interest-paying checking account (like NOW accounts or MMDAs).

Cashier's Check. Anyone can buy a **cashier's check** from a bank. These checks are often used by people who do not have checking accounts. They can be purchased for about $5 and are occasionally issued at no charge to bank customers. In exchange for an appropriate amount of money—the amount of the check plus a service charge—the bank issues a check drawn on itself. In this way, the *bank* is now writing the check, *not* you—which is about the best assurance you can give that the check is good.

Traveler's Check. A number of large financial organizations—such as First National City Bank, American Express, VISA, and Bank of America—issue **traveler's checks**, which can be purchased at commercial banks and most other financial institutions in denominations ranging from $20 to $100. A fee of about 1.5 percent is charged on their purchase. If properly endorsed, traveler's checks are accepted by most U.S. businesses and can be exchanged for local currencies in most parts of the world. Since these checks are not valid unless prop-

---

cashier's check
A check payable to a third party that is drawn by a bank on itself in exchange for the amount specified plus, in most cases, a service fee (of about $5).

traveler's check
A check sold (for a fee of about 1.5 percent) by many large financial institutions, in denominations ranging from $20 to $100, that can be used for making purchases and exchanged for local currencies.

erly countersigned by the purchaser, and since they are insured against loss or theft by the issuing agency, they provide a safe, convenient, and popular form of money for travel.

Certified Check. A **certified check** is made out to whomever is to be paid. The bank immediately deducts the amount of the check from your account and then stamps the check to indicate its certification. There is normally a charge of $10 to $15 or more for this service. In effect, the bank has guaranteed that the funds are there to cover the check—i.e., that the check is good. Since the bank has become the guarantor, it usually will not return the canceled check to you but will keep it for its own records.

Other Bank Services

Banks and other depository institutions offer a number of other conveniences, such as safe-deposit boxes, automatic teller machines (ATMs), pre-authorized payments, bank-by-phone accounts, and now even computer-based banking-at-home.

Safe-Deposit Boxes. A safe-deposit box is nothing more than a rented drawer in a bank's vault. The annual rental fee depends on the box size; small boxes can be rented for about $25 per year, while large ones may cost hundreds of dollars per year. When you rent a box, you receive one key to it, and the bank retains another key. The box can be opened only when both keys are used. This arrangement protects items in the box from theft and makes it an excellent storage place for jewelry, contracts, stock certificates, titles, and other special documents.

Automatic Teller Machines. Recent advances in computer technology have resulted in the development and use of *automatic teller machines (ATMs)* by many of the nation's banks. A type of remote computer terminal at which bank customers can make deposits, withdrawals, and other types of basic transactions, the ATM is a completely mechanical device and can operate 24 hours a day, 7 days a week. Banks and other depository institu-

tions locate these terminals in shopping centers, office buildings, colleges and universities, airline terminals, and other places suited to enhance and protect their competitive position. Some banks charge 25 to 50 cents per ATM transaction.

Pre-authorized Payments. Another area of growth in bank conveniences is the *pre-authorized payment*. This mechanism allows the bank to make payments from customers' accounts at their directions. This service is typically initiated over the telephone with the customer directing payments in specified amounts to various vendors. Banks typically require the customer to maintain a minimum deposit balance and charge a fee of about 25 cents per item paid. Not only does this system allow the customer to earn interest on money held in order to pay bills, it is also a convenient payment mechanism that provides savings in postage.

Bank-by-Phone Accounts. Prompted by competition from other financial institutions and coupled with recent advances in computer and communications technology, some banks offer *bank-by-phone accounts*. These accounts are similar to pre-authorized payments except that they allow the bank customer to initiate a variety of transactions using a pushbutton telephone. Persons with such accounts are given a secret code number that allows them access to their account over the telephone. By pushing a series of numbered codes, the customer can perform a variety of transactions, such as determining his or her account balance, transferring money to other accounts, and paying bills to participating merchants. All transactions are made via phone to the bank's computer—no human intervention is involved in making the transactions. A number of checks are built into these systems in order to allow the customers to confirm the accuracy of their transactions. The cost of participation in bank-by-phone accounts varies depending upon minimum (or average) account balances. The service is generally free to those with both high checking and savings balances—for example, a $500 checking minimum and a $1,500 savings minimum. At the maximum, a bank-by-phone account will probably add about $3 per month to the monthly account charge and cost about 25 cents per transaction.

Computer-Based Banking-at-Home. The latest innovation in banking, and one that holds tremendous growth potential, is *computer-based banking-at-home,* which allows you to handle nearly all your account transactions from your personal computer at any time of the day or night and on any day of the week. Basically, a home banking setup lets you instruct your bank to pay bills by taking money from your account and electronically transmitting it to the electric company, credit card concern, mortgage holder, or other payee. The bank provides you with a list of hundreds of merchants, banks, insurance companies, and the like. You merely type in the payee's code number and the dollar amount of the transaction, then press a computer key, and the bill will be paid instantly. You can also specify additional personal payees into whose accounts you occasionally might need to transfer money—perhaps your dentist or a child in college. And you can order the bank to switch funds among your accounts 24 hours a day. Because the bank usually lets your computer "talk" to its computer toll-free or for the cost of a local call, the service is feasible even for customers who live far away.

You can call up a current "statement" on your computer screen at any time. It will show your balance and recent transactions, including any checks written the traditional way. Because most systems let you instruct the bank to make automatic payments on a regular basis, you no longer need to remember to send off the monthly mortgage payment or the quarterly insurance premium. A home system is no help if you have forgotten to draw cash from an ATM, but it can save you that special trip to get postage stamps.

The cost of most electronic home banking systems is small—usually $10 to $15 a month. The system can pay for itself if it spares you from inadvertently dropping below a minimum balance or being charged for an overdraft. However, since banking-at-home requires a computer costing hundreds of dollars or more, your first consideration should be whether paying bills electronically and having up-to-the-minute account statements is of major importance. On the other hand, if you already have a personal computer, home banking can make it more useful by giving you easy access to the figures you need for budgeting and tax planning.

---

certified check

A personal check that (for a fee of $10 to $15 or more) is certified by the bank on which it is drawn that the maker's signature is genuine and that the funds are available for payment.

SUMMARY

- Cash management plays a vital role in personal financial planning, as it involves the administration and control of liquid financial assets, i.e., cash, checking accounts, savings, and other short-term investment vehicles.
- Financial deregulation has had an enormous impact on the financial institutions and markets of this country, including the creation of financial supermarkets and an increase in the number of financial services and financial services providers; in a relatively short period of time, the traditional way of doing things has undergone tremendous change.
- In spite of all the change, individuals and families continue to rely heavily on the traditional depository financial institutions for most of their financial services needs—that is, the commercial banks, S&Ls, savings banks, and credit unions, all of which provide a full range of checking accounts, savings accounts, and other financial products and services.
- The variety of checking, savings, and other liquid financial assets that the consumer can choose from has never been greater; included in this growing menu are not only regular checking and passbook savings accounts, but also money market mutual funds, money market deposit accounts, NOW accounts, certificates of deposit, Treasury bills, Series EE bonds, and central asset accounts.
- Finding earnings on an interest-paying deposit is often easier said than done, as you have to deal

not only with different compounding periods, but also with a confusing array of different ways of measuring qualifying account balances.

▪ Given the sharp increase in bank service charges that has occurred with deregulation, it's more important than ever to effectively manage your checking account—toward that end, you should become familiar with checking account procedures and the account reconciliation process; in addition, you should be aware of special types of checks and other bank services.

QUESTIONS AND PROBLEMS

1. What is cash management? What are its major functions?
2. Give two broad reasons for holding liquid assets. Identify and briefly describe the popular types of liquid assets.
3. Discuss the effect that deregulation has had on financial markets and institutions. What is a financial supermarket?
4. Distinguish among a passbook account, special savings accounts, and a club account.
5. Briefly describe the basic operations and services provided by each of the following traditional banking institutions: (a) commercial bank; (b) savings and loan association; (c) savings bank; and (d) credit union.
6. Define and discuss (a) demand deposits; (b) savings accounts; and (c) interest-paying checking accounts.
7. Briefly describe the key characteristics of each of the following forms of interest-paying checking accounts: (a) money market mutual funds (MMMFs); (b) money market deposit accounts (MMDAs); and (c) NOW accounts.
8. What does "Member FDIC," a sign that is commonly displayed in a bank, mean to a depositor? Do other depository financial institutions provide similar protection? Explain.
9. Would it be possible for an *individual* to have, say, six or seven checking and savings accounts at the same bank and still be fully protected under federal deposit insurance? Explain. Describe how it would be possible for a *married couple* to obtain as much as $500,000 in federal deposit insurance coverage without going to several banks.
10. Bill and Betty Jacobs together earn approximately $36,000 a year after taxes. Through an inheritance and some wise investing, they also have an investment portfolio with a value of almost $75,000.

a. How much of their annual income do you recommend they hold in some form of savings as liquid reserves? Explain.
b. How much of their investment portfolio do you recommend they hold in savings and other short-term investment vehicles? Explain.
c. How much, in total, should they hold in short-term liquid assets?

11. Define and distinguish between the nominal rate of interest and the effective rate of interest. Explain why a savings and loan association that pays 5.5 percent interest, compounded daily, on its savings accounts actually pays an effective rate of 5.65 percent.
12. If you put $5,000 in a savings account that pays interest at the rate of 8 percent, compounded annually, how much will you have in five years? (Hint: Use the *future value* formula.) How much will you earn in interest over the five years? If you put $5,000 a year into a savings account that pays interest at the rate of 8 percent a year, how much would you have after five years?
13. Briefly describe the four methods used to measure the savings balances that qualify to earn interest. Which approach would you prefer your savings institution to adopt?
14. Briefly describe the basic features of each of the following savings vehicles: (a) certificates of deposit; (b) U.S. Treasury bills, (c) Series EE bonds; and (d) central asset accounts.
15. Describe and differentiate between each of the following forms of check endorsement: (a) blank; (b) special; (c) restrictive; and (d) conditional.
16. Is it possible to bounce a check due to insufficient funds when the checkbook ledger shows a balance available to cover it? Explain what happens when a check bounces.

Is it possible to obtain protection against overdrafts?

17. Describe the procedure used to stop payment on a check. Why might one wish to initiate this process?

18. What type of information is found in the monthly bank statement, and how is it used? Explain the basic steps involved in the account-reconciliation process.

19. Briefly describe (a) banking at ATMs and (b) computer-based banking-at-home.

◼ **20.** Hun Park has a NOW account at the Third State Bank. His checkbook ledger lists the following checks:

Check Number	Amount
654	$206.05
658	55.22
662	103.00
668	99.00
670	6.10
671	50.25
672	24.90
673	32.45
674	44.50
675	30.00
676	30.00
677	111.23
678	38.04
679	97.99
680	486.70
681	43.50
682	75.00
683	98.50

In addition, he made the following withdrawals and deposits at an ATM near his home:

Date	Amount
11/1	$ 50.00 (withdrawal)
11/2	525.60 (deposit)
11/6	100.00 (deposit)
11/14	75.00 (withdrawal)
11/21	525.60 (deposit)
11/24	150.00 (withdrawal)
11/27	225.00 (withdrawal)
11/30	400.00 (deposit)

Hun's checkbook ledger shows an ending balance of $286.54. He has just received his bank statement for the month of November. It shows an ending balance of $622.44; it also shows that he had interest earned for November of $3.28, had a check service charge of $8 for the month, and had another $12 charge for a returned check. His bank statement indicates the following checks have cleared: 654, 662, 672, 674, 675, 676, 677, 678, 679, and 681. ATM withdrawals on 11/1 and 11/14 and deposits on 11/2 and 11/6 have cleared; no other checks or ATM activities are listed on his statement, so anything remaining should be treated as outstanding. Use a checking account reconciliation form like the one in Exhibit 5.9 to reconcile Hun's checkbook.

CASE PROBLEMS

5.1 The Theisens Want to Maximize Their Interest

Anne and Dave Theisen wish to open a savings account and are currently in the process of selecting a savings institution. Having taken courses in personal finance, they know they should inquire with respect to (1) the effective rate of interest paid on the account and (2) the methods used to determine the balance on which interest will be paid.

Questions

1. Discuss the four basic methods used to measure the size of an account, that is, the amount of money on deposit that is eligible to receive interest for the period.

2. Assume Anne and Dave opened a checking account on Sept. 1; use the account transaction data on the next page to determine *the balances* on which the Theisens will be eligible to receive interest for the month of September 1989 under each of the four methods. (Assume that there are twelve 30-day months in the year.)

3. Assuming the effective rate of interest is 6 percent and using the balance data given, calculate the amount of *interest earned* under each of the four methods for the month ended September 30, 1989.

4. Based on your analysis, which of the four methods would allow the Theisens to maximize their interest earnings? Explain.

Account Transactions for Month of September 1989	Date	Transaction	Amount	Account Balance
	1 (initial balance)	—	—	$1,000
	3	Deposit	$2,000	3,000
	14	Deposit	1,000	4,000
	17	Withdrawal	2,500	1,500
	24	Withdrawal	1,000	500
	25	Deposit	4,000	4,500
	30 (ending balance)	—	—	$4,500

■ **5.2 Reconciling the Pattersons' Checkbook**

Nick and Rosalyn Patterson opened their first checking account at The Barclays Bank on September 14, 1989. They have just received their first bank statement for the period ending October 5, 1989. The statement and checkbook ledger are as follows:

Bank Statement

	NICK & ROSALYN PATTERSON 2128 E. 51ST ST. DETROIT, MICHIGAN			THE BARCLAYS BANK 800–231–4567 STATEMENT PERIOD SEPT. 6 to OCT. 5, 1989
	Opening Balance	Total Deposits for Period	Total Checks/Withdrawals for Period	Ending Balance
	$0	$569.25	$473.86	$ 95.39

Date	Withdrawals (Debits)			Deposits (Credits)	Balance
Sept. 14				$360.00	$360.00
Sept. 23				97.00	457.00
Sept. 25	$ 45.20			9.25	421.05
Oct. 1				103.00	524.05
Oct. 1	3.00 BC				521.05
Oct. 2	65.90	$49.76	$45.00		360.39
Oct. 5	265.00				95.39

RT = Returned Checks   DM = Debit Memo   BC = Bank Charges
FC = Finance Charges   CM = Credit Memo

Checkbook Ledger

Check Number	Date 1989	Details	Check Amount	Deposit Amount	Account Balance
—	Sept. 14	Cash—gift from wedding		$360.00	$360.00
—	" 24	Nick's wages from library		97.00	457.00
101	" 24	Kroger—groceries	$ 45.20		411.80
102	" 27	Michigan Bell Telephone bill	28.40		383.40
—	Oct. 1	Nick's wages for library work		103.00	486.40
103	" 1	Univ. book store—college books	65.90		420.50
104	" 1	K mart—sewing material	16.75		403.75
105	" 1	G. Heller—apartment rent	265.00		138.75
106	" 2	Blue Cross—health insurance	17.25		121.50
107	" 3	Kroger—groceries	49.76		71.74
108	" 4	Cash, gas, entertainment, laundry	45.00		26.74
—	" 5	Rosalyn's salary—Universal Corp.		450.00	476.74

Questions

1. From this information, prepare a bank reconciliation for the Pattersons as of October 5, 1989, using a checking account reconciliation form like the one in Exhibit 5.9.

2. Given your answer to Question 1, what, if any, adjustments will the Pattersons need to make in their checkbook ledger? Comment on the procedures used to reconcile their checkbook as well as on your findings.

3. If the Pattersons earned interest on their idle balances as a result of the account being a NOW account, what impact would this have on the reconciliation process? Explain.

FOR MORE INFORMATION

General Information Articles

"Banking," *Consumer Reports;* Part One: July 1988, pp. 455–463; Part Two: August 1988, pp. 495–503; and Part Three: September 1988, pp. 556–563.

Boroson, Warren, "The Myths and Facts About Money Market Funds," *Sylvia Porter's Personal Finance,* March 1988, pp. 68–75.

Edgerton, Jerry, "How Much Are You Saving? Is It Enough?" *Money,* March 1988, pp. 58–60.

Hedberg, Augustin, "Ways to Get the Most from Your Bank," *Money,* March 1988, pp. 96–115.

Kosnett, Jeff, and Morton C. Paulson, "Safe Places to Keep Your Money," *Changing Times,* January 1988, pp. 28–34.

Miller, Theodore J., "Where to Take Your Financial Business," *Changing Times,* November 1988, pp. 88–92.

Williams, Linda, "Let Your Fingers Do the Banking," *Sylvia Porter's Personal Finance,* September 1988, pp. 80–81.

Government Documents and Other Publications

Buying Treasury Securities at Federal Reserve Banks (Richmond, VA: Federal Reserve Bank of Richmond); Public Services Department; Box 27622; Richmond, VA 23261.

Financial Institutions, Markets, and Money, 4th edition by David S. Kidwell and Richard L. Peterson (Hinsdale, IL: The Dryden Press, 1990).

Make Your Money Grow by Theodore J. Miller (Washington, D.C.: Kiplinger Books, 1988).

CHAPTER 6

Making Housing and Other Major Acquisitions

Financial Facts or Fantasies

Are the following statements financial facts (true) or fantasies (false)?

- The most popular form of single-family housing is the condominium.
- Mortgage insurance guarantees the lender that the loan will be paid off in the event of the borrower's death.
- As a rule, the closing costs on a home are rather insignificant and seldom amount to more than a few hundred dollars.
- The amount of money you earn has a lot to do with the amount of money you can borrow.
- In an adjustable-rate mortgage, the size of the monthly mortgage payment will change periodically, along with prevailing mortgage interest rates.
- For most people, an automobile will be their second largest purchase.

Phillipe and Caron Dominguez just bought their first home after three years of saving money regularly toward that end. The Dominguezes are typical of many young families; they have two incomes, are around 30 years old, and paid about $90,000 for their home, making a down payment of 15 percent ($13,500). Home ownership is an important part of the American way of life. Your home very likely will be the largest purchase you will ever make—spending $90,000 or more for a single item is not an everyday event for most people. To prepare for purchasing a home, you will need to carefully itemize your housing needs and then assess your ability to afford them. Home buying is not all facts and figures, however; it nearly always involves a strong emotional undercurrent. Be aware of this, and try to temper your emotion with rational analysis. Automobiles, furniture, and appliances are other big-ticket acquisitions that, while less costly than a home, can have a substantial effect on the family budget.

MEETING HOUSING NEEDS

> A family's housing needs depend on such factors as age, income level, and number of children; these can be met in a variety of ways—from single-family homes to condos and apartments. What are your current as well as planned future housing needs, and what are the key factors shaping each of them? Before reading on spend a few moments answering these questions.

Everybody's housing needs differ. Some people prefer quiet and privacy; other like the hustle and bustle of big-city life. Some demand to live within walking distance of work, shopping, and restaurants; others do not mind a 45-minute commute. Because you will have your own unique set of likes and dislikes, the best way to start your search for housing is to list your needs and then classify them according to whether their satisfaction is essential, desirable, or merely a "plus." Such a classification is important for three reasons. First, it serves to screen out housing that will not meet your minimum requirements. Second, it helps you recognize that you may have to make trade-offs, since you will seldom find any single home that meets all of your needs. Third, it can help you focus on those needs for which you are willing and able to pay.

Alternative Forms of Housing

Because there are so many different types of residences, it is difficult to describe a "typical" home. We do know a few things, however, about what the "average" American home is like. First, it is getting smaller: Today's new home typically has only about 1,500 square feet. In that space, you'll usually find at least three bedrooms and probably more than one bathroom; in addition, it will have at least a one-car garage or carport, a fireplace, and central heating and air conditioning. We also know something about home prices. For example, in early 1989 the average price for existing homes was about $90,000. However, as shown in Exhibit 6.1, prices varied widely from one part of the country to another. The stock of housing in America is nearly as diverse as its prices, consisting of not only single-family homes but also manufactured homes, condominiums, cooperative apartments, and numerous types of rental apartments and houses.

The most popular form of single-family housing is the condominium. **Fantasy:** The most popular form of single-family housing is the *single-family home*—a detached residence that sits on its own legally defined lot. Condos, in contrast, are built in large, multiunit developments on grounds that are common to all residents.

Single-Family Homes. The single-family, detached home remains the first choice in housing. Basically, such homes stand alone on their own legally defined lots. Sometimes homes are built side by side so that they share common side walls; these are known as *row houses* and are especially prevalent east of the Mississippi. As a rule, single-family homes offer their buyers privacy, prestige, pride of ownership, and maximum property control. In recent years, however, the cost of single-family residences—and especially residential lots—has increased dramatically. At the same time, the size of the average U.S. household has drastically decreased. These factors have led to much smaller homes; to compensate for their smaller size, other amenities and features have been introduced. For example, so-called *patio homes* are fairly small in size, yet have many luxurious appointments such as cathedral ceilings and jacuzzis; they are built on very small lots, and may even have common walls. Higher costs and changing lifestyles also have led to alternative types of housing; thus, while the single-family, detached home is still the most popular type of residence, its dominant position is declining.

Manufactured Homes. **Manufactured homes** are factory-produced housing units that can be transported to a desired location, placed on either a permanent or temporary foundation, and then connected to utilities and used as residences. Because these homes used to be more mobile than they are today, they were at one time called *mobile homes.* Depending on whether they are single or double-wide units (that is, two units placed side by side to make one larger home), they can provide anywhere from 400 to 1,400 square feet of living

EXHIBIT 6.1

Housing Prices around the United States (January 1989)

The price of housing varies widely from one location to another. For example, the average price is $190,600 in San Diego, while similar housing has an average price of $84,700 in Columbus, Ohio.

Location	Average Home Price*	Location	Average Home Price*
Akron, OH	$ 72,700	Miami, FL	$109,300
Albuquerque, NM	106,700	Milwaukee, WI	91,600
Anaheim-Santa Ana-Garden Grove, CA	268,400	Minneapolis-St. Paul, MN	96,400
Atlanta, GA	127,800	Mobile, AL	135,500
Austin, TX	129,200	Nashville-Davidson, TN	100,400
Baltimore, MD	105,400	New Orleans, LA	141,600
Baton Rouge, LA	83,300	New York City (NJ suburbs)	247,000
Birmingham, AL	95,800	Newark, NJ	266,100
Boston, MA	223,900	Oklahoma City, OK	71,700
Buffalo, NY	92,100	Orlando, FL	103,100
Charlotte-Gastonia, NC	103,200	Philadelphia, PA	138,000
Chicago, IL	121,600	Phoenix, AZ	100,700
Cincinnati, OH	80,200	Pittsburgh, PA	163,200
Cleveland, OH	81,000	Portland, OR	111,400
Columbia, SC	124,100	Providence-Warwick-Pawtucket, RI	179,200
Columbus, OH	84,700	Raleigh-Durham, NC	135,500
Dallas, TX	112,400	Sacramento, CA	171,900
Denver, CO	113,400	Salt Lake City-Ogden, UT	87,100
Detroit, MI	82,300	San Antonio, TX	86,000
El Paso, TX	78,300	Saint Louis, MO	94,600
Fresno, CA	120,200	San Diego, CA	190,600
Hartford-New Britain-Bristol, CT	232,400	San Francisco-Oakland, CA	240,900
Honolulu, HI	264,300	San Jose, CA	216,300
Houston, TX	83,600	Seattle-Everett, WA	163,000
Indianapolis, IN	74,800	Syracuse, NY	108,500
Jacksonville, FL	92,700	Tampa-St. Petersburg, FL	86,000
Kansas City, KS + MO	84,800	Tucson, AZ	135,000
Las Vegas, NV	123,100	Tulsa, OK	82,700
Los Angeles, CA	226,900	Washington, D.C. (MD, VA suburbs)	161,500
Memphis, TN	97,100	West Palm Beach-Boca Raton, FL	127,000

Source: "What Your Home Will be Worth by City," *Changing Times*, January 1989, p. 56. Adapted with permission from *Changing Times* Magazine, © 1989 Kiplinger Washington Editors, Inc. This reprint is not to be altered in any way, except with permission from *Changing Times*.

space. They range in cost from $10,000 to $70,000 depending on size and features. Although occasionally used as temporary housing, manufactured homes provide *permanent* residences for many families, especially retired couples. Their prices are low, and as long as it qualifies as a "permanent" structure, loans with low down payments and 10- to 15-year maturities are available. Their low maintenance costs are another attractive feature. Nevertheless, in most parts of the country the market price of manufactured homes is likely to decline over time; thus, they are not considered good investments.

Condominiums. The buyer of a **condominium** receives title to an individual unit and a joint ownership of any common areas and facilities, such as lobbies, swimming pools, lakes, and tennis courts. Since buyers own their units, they arrange

manufactured home

A factory-produced housing unit that can be transported to a desired location, placed on either a permanent or temporary foundation, and then connected to utilities and used as a residence.

condominium

A system of direct ownership of an individual unit in a multiunit project in which lobbies, swimming pools, and other common areas and facilities are jointly owned by all property owners in the project.

EXHIBIT 6.2

Things to Do before Buying a Condo

In the long run, it pays to carefully check out the various operating and occupancy features of a condo before you buy.

- Thoroughly investigate the reputation of the developer—through local real estate brokers, banks, or the Better Business Bureau—whether the building is brand new, under construction, or being converted.
- Read the rules of the organization.
- Investigate the condo government association, the restrictions on condo owners, and the quality of the property management.
- Check the construction of the building and its physical condition. If the building is being converted to condos, ask to see an independent inspection firm's report on the building's condition.
- Insist that any future changes in the building be put in writing.
- Query the occupants to see if they are satisfied with the living conditions.
- Determine how many units are rented; generally, owner-occupied units are better maintained.
- Determine if there is sufficient parking space.
- Watch for unusually low maintenance fees that will probably have to be increased soon.
- Consider the resale value (this was especially important in the mid-1980s when many condo units were impossible to sell without sharp price reductions).
- Compare the projected monthly assessment fees with those on similar buildings already in operation.

Source: Adapted from *Your Housing Dollar* (Prospect Heights, Ill.: Money Management Institute of Household Finance Corporation, 1987), p. 13.

their own mortgages, pay their own taxes, and pay for maintenance and building services. They are typically assessed, on a monthly basis, an amount deemed sufficient to cover their proportionate share of the cost of maintaining common facilities. The owners of condominium units elect a board of managers to supervise their building and grounds. The cost of condominiums is generally lower than that of single-family, detached homes, since they tend to be built in a fashion that results in more efficient land use and lower construction costs.

Due to the phenomenal growth in the cost of new homes over the past decade or so, many existing apartment projects have gone through *condo conversions*. In effect, the apartments have been converted from rental to occupant-owned units. The pace of condo conversion began to slow down considerably by the late 1980s as the market became saturated with new units.

Although condominiums traditionally have appealed primarily to retired persons who do not want the responsibilities of maintaining and caring for their property, many younger people now have begun to buy them for similar reasons. Exhibit 6.2 lists some of the key points that should be considered before buying a condominium.

Cooperative Apartments. An apartment in a building in which each tenant owns a share of the corporation that owns the building is known as a **cooperative apartment** or co-op. Residents lease their units from the corporation and are assessed monthly in proportion to their ownership shares, which are based on the amount of space they occupy. The assessments cover the cost of service, maintenance, taxes, and the mortgage on the entire building. These are subject to change depending on the actual costs of operating the building and the actions of the board of directors, which determine the corporation's policies. Owners of cooperatives may find that the value of their ownership interest increases over time as a result of increased market values and a reduction in the outstanding loan balance. Because cooperative apartments are not profit-motivated, monthly assessments are likely to be lower than the rent on similar accommodations in a rental unit. Also, the cooperative owner receives the tax benefits resulting from interest and property taxes attributable to his or her proportionate ownership interest.

Rental Apartments and Houses. All of the forms of housing discussed above represent different ways of achieving home ownership. However, for one reason or another, a large number of individuals and families choose to *rent* or *lease* their place of residence rather than own it. They live in apartments and other types of rental units ranging from duplexes, four-plexes, and even single-family homes to large, high-rise apartment complexes containing several hundred units. *Garden apartments* are usually built in groups of four to six units that may be either one or two stories and are separated by landscaped areas. *Efficiency apartments* are generally one-room apartments suitable for single people. *Townhouses* are two- or three-story apartments that usually have the bedrooms upstairs. All of these types of housing are popular and widely available.

The cost and availability of rental units vary from one geographic area to another. Unfurnished units, of course, rent for less than furnished ones. The U.S. Department of Housing and Urban Development (HUD) administers various programs that provide low-rent housing opportunities for people in lower income brackets. Because such a wide variety of rental units are available, people who wish to rent can usually find units that conform to their location, physical, and financial requirements.

HOW MUCH HOUSING CAN YOU AFFORD? ▱

> People buy homes for the emotional and financial payoffs they provide; accompanying these benefits are the costs of buying homes, such as down payments, closing costs, monthly mortgage payments, and homeowner's insurance. What are the typical motives for buying a home, and what purchase and ownership costs must be considered when assessing its affordability? Spend a few moments answering this question before reading on.

Spending thousands of dollars to buy a home obviously involves a good deal of careful planning and analysis. Not only must you spend time deciding on

the kind of home you want (its location, number of bedrooms, and so on), you must also consider its cost, what kind of mortgage to get, how large a monthly payment you can afford, what kind of homeowner's insurance coverage to have, and so forth. It should be clear that buying a home (or any other major, big-ticket item) touches on many of the elements in personal financial planning: The money you use for a down payment will likely be drawn from your *savings program;* the homeowner's policy you choose is a part of your *insurance planning;* and your monthly mortgage payments undoubtedly will have an enormous impact on your *cash budget.* Sound financial planning dictates caution in buying a home or any other major item. Spending too much for a home or car can have a detrimental effect not only on your budget and lifestyle, but also on your savings and investment plans, and possibly even your retirement plans. Knowing how much housing you can afford will go a long way toward helping you achieve your financial goals.

Motives for Owning a Home

Whether it is a detached home, a patio home, a manufactured home, or a condominium, home ownership is important to most people. It is preferred over renting for several reasons, the most important of which is probably the basic security and peace of mind derived from living in one's own home—pride of ownership, a feeling of permanence, and sense of stability. This so-called "psychic reward" is the only reason that many people need to own a home. In addition to the emotional payoff, there's also a financial pay-off from home ownership.

The Home as a Tax Shelter. Perhaps the biggest financial payoff from owning a home is the tax shelter it offers. You get a tax break from owning a

cooperative apartment (co-op)
An apartment in a building in which each tenant owns a share of the corporation that owns the building.

home because you can deduct the interest you pay on your mortgage and property taxes from your federal and state income taxes. As explained in Chapter 4, mortgage interest (on loans up to a maximum amount, equal to the amount the homeowner originally paid for the house plus the cost of any home improvements) and property taxes can be treated as a tax deduction for both a primary residence and a second home such as a vacation home. Such write-offs reduce your taxable income and thus the amount of taxes you pay. The only requirement is that you itemize your deductions. This tax break is so good that people who have never itemized usually begin doing so after they buy their first house. Also, keep in mind that for the first 15 to 20 years of ownership (assuming a 30-year mortgage) most of your monthly mortgage payment is made up of interest and property taxes—in fact, during the first 5 to 10 years or so, these could well account for *85 to 90 percent of your total payment*. This means you are allowed to write off nearly all of your monthly mortgage payment.

Here is how it works. Suppose you make mortgage payments of $1,000 a month of which $850 is interest and property taxes. That is about $10,000 a year in tax deductions; put another way, when treated as a tax deduction the net result will be to lower your taxable income by $10,000. If you are in the 28 percent tax bracket, such a tax deduction will reduce the amount of taxes you pay by $10,000 × .28 = $2,800!

The Home as an Inflation Hedge. Another financial payoff is the **inflation hedge** allegedly provided by home ownership. An inflation hedge is an investment or asset that appreciates in value at a rate equal to or greater than the rate of inflation. During the 1970s there were few inflation hedges that could match the performance of home ownership; in fact, a home became one of the best investments you could make, since it generated a far better return than stocks, bonds, mutual funds, and so on. Many people were buying homes simply for their investment value, and in many parts of the country, the local real estate markets became so speculative they took on an almost feverish pitch. Even though the 1970s was a time of unprecedented inflation, owning a home remained an excellent hedge.

All that came to an abrupt halt in the early 1980s, as the rate of appreciation in home prices slowed dramatically and not only fell below the rate of inflation but, in many areas, changed to a decline in housing prices! Today, housing prices in most parts of the country are moving at a rate about equal to or slightly above the rate of inflation. As a result of this, and the fact that the inflation rate has dropped dramatically, housing prices in most areas (except for the East and West Coasts) are rising at a much slower pace than during the 1970s. Most experts agree that it will probably be a long time before we experience another housing market like that. While today most people can make some money on their homes, they certainly do not serve as the inflation hedge (or the investment) that they might have been during that decade.

The Cost of Home Ownership

While there definitely are some strong emotional and financial reasons for owning a home, there's still the question of whether or not you can afford to own one. Affordability is a two-edged sword: There is the matter not only of coming up with the down payment and other closing costs but also of meeting the recurring cash flow requirements associated with monthly mortgage payments and other home maintenance expenses. In particular, there are five items you should consider when evaluating the cost of home ownership and determining how much home you can afford: (1) the down payment, (2) points and closing costs, (3) mortgage payments, (4) property taxes and insurance, and (5) maintenance and operating expenses.

The Down Payment. The first hurdle is the **down payment**. Most buyers finance a major part of the purchase price of the home, but they are also required by lenders to invest money of their own, called *equity*. The actual amount of down payment required varies among lenders, mortgage types, and properties. To determine the amount of down payment that will be required in specific instances, lenders use the **loan-to-value ratio**, which specifies the maximum percentage of the value of a property that the lender is willing to loan. For example, if the loan-to-value ratio is 80 percent, the buyer will have to come up with a down payment equal to the remaining 20 percent. The loan-to-value ratio is normally based on the *greater of the market or appraised value*.

A property that is financed with a high loan-to-value ratio involves only a small percentage of borrower equity. For example, a mortgage that equals 90 to 95 percent of a property's purchase price is a high-ratio loan. It involves only 5 to 10 percent equity dollars; thus, if you buy a $100,000 home with a 95 percent loan-to-value ration, you will need to put down only $5,000 and can finance the other $95,000 through a mortgage.

Generally first-time home buyers must spend a number of years accumulating enough money to afford the down payment and other costs associated with the home purchase transaction. You can best accumulate these funds on a planned basis, using future value techniques (presented in Chapters 3 and 5) to determine the monthly or annual savings (at a given rate of interest) necessary in order to have a stated amount by a specified future date. While detailed demonstration of this process is included in Chapter 12, for now suffice it to say that a disciplined savings program is the best way to obtain the funds needed to purchase a home or any other big-ticket item requiring a sizable down payment or purchase outlay.

As a rule, when the down payment is less than 20 percent, the lender will require that the loan be made with **mortgage insurance**, which protects the lender from loss in event the borrower defaults on the loan. Usually the mortgage insurance covers the lenders risk above 80 percent of the price of the house. Thus, with a 10 percent down payment, the mortgage will result in a 90 percent loan, and the mortgage insurance would cover 10 percent of the home's price. You will be charged a one-time fee of about ¾ of 1 percent of the amount of the loan (paid at closing) plus an annual premium of about ¼ of 1 percent (which is included in your monthly payments), until the loan balance is less than 75 percent of the appraised value of your home.

Mortgage insurance guarantees the lender that the loan will be paid off in the event of the borrower's death. **Fantasy:** Mortgage insurance protects the lender from loss in the event the borrower defaults on the loan.

Points and Closing Costs.

A second hurdle to home ownership relates to mortgage points and closing costs. **Mortgage points** are fees charged by lenders at the time they grant a mortgage loan. In appearance, points are like interest in that they are a charge for borrowing money. They are related to the lender's supply of loanable funds and the demand for mortgages; the greater the demand relative to supply, the more points you can expect to pay. One point equals 1 percent of the amount borrowed. If you borrow $70,000, and loan fees equal 3 points, the amount of money you will pay in points will be $70,000 × .03 = $2,100.

Lenders typically use points as a way of charging interest on their loans. They can vary the interest rate along with the number of points they charge to create loans with comparable effective rates. For example, a lender might be willing to give you a 10 percent mortgage rather than an 11 percent one if you are willing to pay more points; that is, you take your pick: an 11 percent mortgage with 2 points or a 10 percent mortgage with 6½ points. If you choose the 10 percent loan, you will end up paying a lot more *at closing* (though the amount of interest paid *over the life of the mortgage* may be less). According to recent IRS rulings, the points paid on a mortgage at the time a home is originally purchased are usually considered to be tax deductible,

---

inflation hedge
An investment or asset that appreciates in value at a rate equal to or greater than the rate of inflation.

down payment
A portion of the full purchase price provided by the purchaser at the time of purchase of a house or other major asset; often called *equity.*

loan-to-value ratio
The maximum percentage of the value of a property that the lender is willing to loan.

mortgage insurance
A type of insurance policy that protects the mortgage lender from loss in the event the borrower defaults on the loan.

mortgage points
Fees (each point equals 1 percent of the amount borrowed) charged by lenders at the time they grant a mortgage loan; they are related to the lender's supply of loanable funds and the demand for mortgages.

EXHIBIT 6.3

The Hidden Costs of Buying a Home: Closing Costs

The closing costs on a home mortgage loan can be substantial—as much as 5 to 7 percent of the price of the home. Except for the real estate commission (which is generally paid by the seller), the biggest share of the closing costs is charged to the buyer and must be paid—in addition to the down payment—at the time the loan is closed and title to the property is conveyed.

Item	Size of Down Payment	
	20%	10%
Loan application fee	$ 200	$ 200
Loan origination fee	800	900
Points	1,600	2,700
Mortgage insurance	—	675
Title search and insurance	500	550
Attorneys' fees	400	400
Appraisal fees	150	150
Home inspection	250	250
Mortgage tax	575	650
Filing fees	25	25
Credit reports	25	25
Miscellaneous	100	100
Total closing costs	**$4,625**	**$6,625**

Note: Typical closing costs for a $100,000 home—2 points charged with 20 percent, 3 points with 10 percent down. Actual amounts will vary by lender and location.

though the same points are not considered tax deductible if they are incurred when *refinancing* a mortgage (unless they are paid in connection with the purchase or improvement of a home)—rather, the amount paid in points must be written off (*amortized*) over the life of the new mortgage loan.

Closing costs are all other expenses (including mortgage points) that borrowers ordinarily pay at the time a mortgage loan is closed and title to the purchased property is conveyed to them. Closing costs are like down payments: They represent money you must come up with *at the time you buy the house.* Closing costs are made up of such items as (1) loan application fees, (2) loan origination fees, (3) points (if any), (4) title search and insurance, (5) attorneys' fees, (6) appraisal fees, and (7) other miscellaneous fees for things like mortgage taxes, filing fees, inspections, credit reports, and so on.

The loan application and origination fees are charges the lender makes for doing all the paperwork; the other charges are associated primarily with fulfilling the legal and credit requirements necessary to complete the home-purchase transaction. As Exhibit 6.3 shows, these costs can total an amount equal to 50 percent or more of the down payment. For example, with a 10 percent down payment on a $100,000 home, the closing costs, as shown in Exhibit 6.3 can amount to nearly 70 percent of the down payment, or $6,625. A little simple arithmetic also indicates that this buyer will need nearly $17,000 to buy the house (the $10,000 down payment plus another $6,625 in closing costs).

Many first-time home buyers are shocked to find out how much they must pay in closing costs. In many instances, *sellers,* by custom or contract, will assume the responsibility for some of a buyer's mortgage points and closing costs. Seldom, however, can a buyer escape all—or even most— of the expenses. At best, the seller will probably pick up just a small percentage (perhaps 10 to 15 percent) of the total amount of the closing costs, leaving the buyer to pay the rest. The accompanying *Money in Action* box suggests a few strategies for raising the funds needed to cover the required down payment and closing costs.

As a rule, the closing costs on a home seldom amount to more than a few hundred dollars. **Fantasy:** Closing costs—most of which must be paid by the *buyer*—on most home purchases can amount to several thousand dollars and often total an amount equal to 50 percent or more of the down payment.

EXHIBIT 6.4

Typical Principal and Interest Payment Patterns on a Mortgage Loan

For most of the life of a mortgage loan, the vast majority of each monthly payment goes to interest and only a small portion goes toward repayment of principal. Over the 30-year life of the 12 percent, $75,000 mortgage illustrated here, the homeowner will pay more than $200,000 in interest.

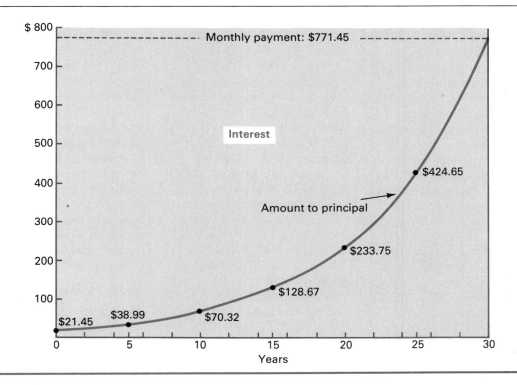

Mortgage Payments. The monthly mortgage payment is determined through a fairly complex formula. Each monthly mortgage payment is made up partly of principal repayment on the loan and partly of interest charges. However, as Exhibit 6.4 shows, for most of the life of the mortgage the vast majority of each monthly payment goes to *interest.* The loan illustrated in the exhibit is a $75,000, 30-year, 12 percent mortgage with monthly payments of $771.45. Note that it is not until after the 24th year of this 30-year mortgage that the principal portion of the loan payment exceeds the amount that goes to interest.

In practice, mortgage lenders and realtors use *comprehensive mortgage payment tables* to find monthly payments. These tables contain monthly payments for virtually every combination of loan

size, interest rate, and maturity. Exhibit 6.5 provides an excerpt from one such comprehensive mortgage payment table; it lists the *monthly payments* that would be associated with a $10,000 fixed-rate loan for maturities of 10 to 30 years and interest rates of 7½ to 15 percent. It can be used to find the monthly payment for any size loan.

---

closing costs

All expenses (including mortgage points) that borrowers ordinarily pay at the time a mortgage loan is closed and title to the purchased property is conveyed to them.

MONEY IN ACTION

Raising Funds for the Down Payment and Closing Costs

The first time you buy a house, you're faced with raising, on average, enough cash up front to equal 11 percent of the purchase price, according to a national survey by Chicago Title Insurance Co. That comes to $9,900, for example, on a $90,000 house (the cost of an average-priced home in 1989). Mortgage fees, points, and other closing costs might add $4,000, bringing your cash needs to $13,900.

Unless you have saved long and diligently or can use the proceeds from a previous house, you may have a problem paying these costs. Consider the following solutions.

RETIREMENT FUNDS

People whose fringe benefits include a profit-sharing or thrift

plan may be able to withdraw contributions that were deducted from their paychecks and borrow from company contributions. In a typical plan, you may be able to tap as much as $50,000. At recent rates, this sort of loan would average 11½ percent interest.

Or turn to your IRA. Untouchable though you vowed it would be, this retirement fund is a reasonable way to contribute to the purchase of as solid a long-term investment as a house. You'll pay a 10 percent penalty on the withdrawal and pay taxes on it, too. Even so, the economics can be persuasive. Here's how a $10,000 withdrawal might work out on the purchase of a $100,000 house if you were in the 28 percent tax bracket: A year after you buy the

house, you'll pay an extra $2,800 in federal income tax, which you would have paid anyway if you hadn't put the money in your IRA. You'll also pay a $1,000 penalty and forego income on the withdrawal—let's say another $1,000. Total cost: $4,800. As an offset, your house would generate tax deductions. A year's interest on the mortgage, plus property taxes, might net you $3,000 in tax savings a year after you bought the house. Break-even point: sometime in the second year.

EQUITY SHARING

If your parents want to bestow on you the money for a down payment, fine. Their generosity's bounds can be as large as $40,000. Eileen Hollowell accepted such

Suppose you wish to find the monthly loan payment on a $75,000, 12 percent, 30-year mortgage. To do this, simply divide the amount of the loan ($75,000) by $10,000 and then multiply this factor (7.5) by the payment amount shown in Exhibit 6.5 for a 12 percent, 30-year loan ($102.86):

$$\$75,000/\$10,000 = 7.5 \times \$102.86 = \underline{\$771.45}$$

The resulting monthly mortgage payment would be $771.45.

Obviously, the key issue with respect to mortgage payments is *affordability*. To ensure that the purchase of a home stays within your budget, you must

determine the size of monthly mortgage payment you can afford. This, in turn, will determine how much you can borrow to finance the purchase of a home.

Affordability ratios. In order to obtain a mortgage, a potential borrower must be "qualified"—that is, must demonstrate that he or she has adequate income with which to comfortably make scheduled loan payments. Various federal and private mortgage insurers, as well as institutional mortgage investors, have certain standards they expect borrowers to meet in order to reduce as much as possible the risk of default. Because of the influence these insurers/investors have on the

a gift toward her first house in Tucson, but when she and her husband split up in 1982, the gift money added to her anguish. Says her father, William White, dean of the College of Business and Economics at the University of Nevada, Las Vegas: "We didn't mind, but Eileen felt guilty."

Early in 1986 Eileen made a deal she felt more comfortable with. The divorce had left her low on cash with which to buy a house for herself and her two children. This time her parents became joint owners with her. They extended her half of the down payment in return for rent of $325 a month—enough to satisfy an Internal Revenue Service requirement that such rentals reflect fair market value. As part owners, they get tax write-offs for depreciation

and their half of the mortgage interest and taxes.

You may be able to set up a similar joint ownership through a commercial expediter. The best-known arranger of equity-sharing deals between parents and children is the Family Backed Mortgage Association of Oakland, Calif., with its Daddy Mac loan package (800–323–3262; in California 800–232–3262). For a $750 fee this firm will work out the specifics.

GOVERNMENT BACKING

Former members of the armed forces are eligible for no-down-payment Veterans Administration–guaranteed financing from commercial mortgage lenders. Closing costs may be included in such loans.

Institutions participating in the FHA mortgage insurance

program can accept down payments as low as 5 percent. Qualifying, however, has become more difficult. With FHA loans, as with conventional ones, lenders increasingly insist that your mortgage payments and all other fixed debts not exceed 33 percent of your gross income and that mortgage payments alone be within 25 percent of that income. These guidelines used to be 36 percent and 28 percent. FHA loans have never had income requirements, although such proposals have in the past been discussed by Congress.

Source: Excerpted from Robert Runde, "Digging up the Down Payment," *Money,* April 1986, p. 95. Reprinted with permission.

mortgage market, their guidelines tend to be widely followed.

Probably the most important affordability guideline is the one that relates *borrower income to monthly payments.* This is done by relating monthly income to (1) the size of the monthly mortgage payment and (2) the borrower's total monthly installment loan payments (which would include payments not only on the mortgage, but also on automobile loans, furniture loans and any other type of consumer installment loan). In this regard, the most widely followed ratios stipulate that (1) monthly mortgage payments cannot exceed 25 to 30 percent of the borrower's monthly *gross* (before-tax) income and (2) the borrower's total

monthly installment loan payments cannot exceed 33 to 38 percent of monthly gross income. Since both conditions stipulate a range, the lender has some leeway in deciding on the most appropriate ratio for a particular loan applicant.

Here is how these affordability ratios work. Assume you have a monthly income of $3,000. Using the lower end of the ranges (that is, 25 percent and 33 percent) for illustrative purposes, we see that such an income level could support mortgage payments of $750 a month *so long as total monthly installment obligations do not exceed $1,000.* (These values were found as follows: $3,000 × .25 = $750 and $3,000 × .33 = $1,000.) Note that if your other monthly installment loan payments ex-

EXHIBIT 6.5

A Table of Monthly Mortgage Payments
(Monthly payments necessary to repay a $10,000 loan)

The monthly loan payments on a mortgage vary not only by the amount of the loan, but also by the rate of interest and loan maturity.

Rate of Interest	Loan Maturity				
	10 years	15 years	20 years	25 years	30 years
7½%	$118.71	$ 92.71	$ 80.56	$ 73.90	$ 69.93
8%	121.33	95.57	83.65	77.19	73.38
8½%	123.99	98.48	86.79	80.53	76.90
9%	126.68	101.43	89.98	83.92	80.47
9½%	129.40	104.43	93.22	87.37	84.09
10%	132.16	107.47	96.51	90.88	87.76
10½%	134.94	110.54	99.84	94.42	91.48
11%	137.76	113.66	103.22	98.02	95.24
11½%	140.60	116.82	106.65	101.65	99.03
12%	143.48	120.02	110.11	105.33	102.86
12½%	146.38	123.26	113.62	109.04	106.73
13%	149.32	126.53	117.16	112.79	110.62
13½%	152.28	129.84	120.74	116.57	114.55
14%	155.27	133.18	124.36	120.38	118.49
14½%	158.29	136.56	128.00	124.22	122.46
15%	161.34	139.96	131.68	128.09	126.45

Note: *To use:* (1) Divide amount of loan by $10,000; (2) Find loan payment amount in table for specific interest rate and maturity; (3) multiply the amount from step 1 by the amount from step 2.

To illustrate: The monthly payment for a $98,000, 11½%, 15 year loan would be: (1) $98,000/ $10,000 = 9.8; (2) payment associated with a 15 year, 11½%, loan, from table, is *$116.82;* (3) monthly payment required to repay a $98,000, 11½%, 15 year mortgage is: 9.8 × $116.82 = $1,144.84.

ceeded $250 (The difference between $1,000 and $750), your mortgage payment would have to be reduced accordingly; for instance, if you had $350 in other installment payments, your maximum monthly mortgage payment would be $1,000 − $350 = $650.

The amount of money you earn has a lot to do with the amount of money you can borrow. **Fact:** Your monthly income is a key factor in determining how large a mortgage loan you can afford. Also important are your credit record and the level of your total monthly installment loan payments.

Property Taxes and Insurance. Aside from loan costs, mortgage payments often include property tax and insurance payments. When this occurs, the monthly mortgage payment is made up of four parts: (1) part of the loan payment goes to reduce the *principal* amount of the loan; (2) part goes to pay the *interest* on the loan; (3) some of it goes to property *taxes;* and (4) some goes to homeowner's *insurance.* Thus, together, the loan payment con-

sists of *p*rincipal, *i*nterest, *t*axes, and *i*nsurance (or **PITI** for short). Actually, that portion of the loan payment that goes for taxes and insurance is paid into an *escrow account,* where it accumulates over time. Then, once or twice a year, the lending institution draws funds from this account to pay required property taxes and homeowner's insurance premiums. Increases in tax rates and/or insurance premiums are passed on to the home buyer in the form of higher monthly loan payments.

Interestingly, some but not all lenders pay interest—typically at no higher than the passbook rate—on escrow account balances. Generally, though, it is advisable for disciplined borrowers to negotiate with the lender in order to avoid having to pay into an escrow account. Such a strategy, if successful, gives you greater flexibility and an opportunity to earn a higher return on the funds that would otherwise have been held in an escrow account.

Because they are local taxes levied to support schools, law enforcement, and other local services, the level of **property taxes** differs from one community to another. And within a given community, individual property taxes will vary with the *assessed value* of the property—generally the more expensive the home, the higher the property taxes, and vice versa. As a rule, annual property taxes vary from less than one-half of 1 percent to more than 2 percent of a home's approximate market value. Thus, the property taxes on a $1,000 home could vary from about $500 to more than $2,000 a year, depending on location and geographic area.

The other component of the monthly mortgage payment is **homeowner's insurance**. Its cost varies with such factors as the age of the house, location, materials used in construction, and geographic area. Homeowner's insurance is carried only on the replacement value of the home and its contents and not on the land. Annual insurance costs usually amount to approximately one-fourth to one-half of 1 percent of the home's market value. Thus, the annual cost of insurance for a $100,000 house should range between $250 and $500. The types, characteristics, and features of homeowner's insurance policies are discussed in Chapter 11.

Maintenance and Operating Expenses. In addition to the monthly mortgage payments, home buyers incur maintenance and operating expenses. Maintenance costs should be anticipated even on new homes. Painting, mechanical repairs, leak repairs, and lawn maintenance, for example, are inescapable facts of homeownership. Such costs are likely to be greater, though, for older, larger homes. Thus, while a large, established home may have an attractive purchase price, a new, smaller home may be the better buy in view of its lower maintenance and operating costs.

Another point to consider in the selection process is the cost of operating the home, specifically the cost of utilities, such as electricity, gas, water, and sewage. These costs have skyrocketed in the past 10 to 15 years and today represent a sizable component of homeownership costs. Because they are unavoidable and vary with geographic location, type of heating and air conditioning, size of home, amount of insulation, and other factors, operating cost estimates should be obtained when evaluating a particular home purchase candidate.

Performing Home Affordability Analysis. An estimate of the amount you can afford to spend on a home can be made using the form given in Ex-

hibit 6.6. This analysis determines the maximum home-purchase price using both your monthly income and the amount you have available for a down payment after meeting estimated closing costs. In our example, the Rene and Pierre Goulet family had combined annual income of $48,400 and had $22,500 available for making a down payment and paying closing costs. They estimated monthly taxes and homeowner's insurance of $150 and expected the mortgage lender to use a 28 percent monthly mortgage-payment affordability ratio, to lend at an average interest rate of 12 percent on a 30-year mortgage, and to require a 10 percent down payment. The Goulets' analysis showed that they can afford to purchase a home costing about $110,000. Their available monthly income (Item 13) rather than the amount available for down payment (Item 15) was the key determinant of the maximum affordable home-purchase price.

The Option of Renting

Many people either cannot afford to buy or choose not to buy their own home. For example, young adults usually rent for one or more of the following reasons: (1) They do not have the funds for a down payment and closing costs; (2) they are unsettled in their job and family status; (3) they do not want the additional responsibilities associated with homeownership. Monthly rent payments serve only to pay for the use of the property and are in no part tax deductible. Those who choose to rent should be familiar with rental contracts and know how to compare the costs of renting versus purchasing.

PITI
Notation used to refer to a mortgage payment that includes stipulated portions of *p*rincipal, *i*nterest, property *t*axes, and homeowner's *i*nsurance.

property taxes
Taxes levied by local governments on the assessed value of real estate for the purpose of funding schools, law enforcement, and other local services.

homeowner's insurance
Insurance required by mortgage lenders that typically covers the replacement value of a home and its contents.

EXHIBIT 6.6

Home Affordability Analysis for the Rene and Pierre Goulet Family

By using the following variables in the home affordability analysis form, the Goulets estimate a maximum home purchase price of about $110,000: their combined annual income of $48,000; the $22,500 available for a down payment; closing costs along with estimated monthly taxes and homeowner's insurance of $150; the lender's 28 percent monthly affordability ratio; an average interest rate of 12 percent and expected loan maturity of 30 years; and a minimum down payment of 10 percent.

HOME AFFORDABILITY ANALYSIS*

Name *Rene and Peter Goulet*   Date *December 12, 1989*

Item	Description	Amount
1	Amount of annual income	$ *48,400*
2	Monthly income (Item 1 ÷ 12)	$ *4,033*
3	Lender's affordability ratio (in decimal form)	*.28*
4	Maximum monthly mortgage payment (PITI) (Item 2 × Item 3)	$ *1,130*
5	Estimated monthly tax and homeowner's insurance payment	$ *150*
6	Maximum monthly loan payment	$ *980*
7	Approximate average interest rate on loan	*12%*
8	Planned loan maturity (years)	*30*
9	Mortgage payment per $10,000 (using Item 7 and Item 8 and Monthly Mortgage Payment Table in Exhibit 6.5)	*102.86*
10	Maximum loan based on monthly income ($10,000 × Item 6 ÷ Item 9)	$ *95,275*
11	Funds available for making a down payment and paying closing costs	$ *22,500*
12	Funds available for making a down payment (Item 11 × 2 ÷ 3)	$ *15,000*
13	Maximum purchase price based on available monthly income (Item 10 + Item 12)	$ *110,275*
14	Minimum acceptable down payment (in decimal form)	*.10*
15	Maximum purchase price based on down payment (Item 12 ÷ Item 14)	$ *150,000*
16	Maximum home purchase price (lower of Item 13 and Item 15)	$ *110,275*

***Note:** This analysis assumes that ⅓ of the funds available for making the down payment and paying closing costs are used to meet closing costs while the remaining ⅔ are available for a down payment. This assumption means that closing costs will represent an amount equal to 50 percent of the down payment.

Rental Contract. When you rent an apartment, duplex, house, or any other type of unit, you normally will be required to sign a **rental contract**, or **lease agreement**. Although oral agreements are generally binding, a written contract is a legal instrument that better protects both the *lessor* (the person who owns the property) and the *lessee* (the person who leases the property). Because the rental contract binds you—the lessee—to various actions, you should make certain that you fully understand it before signing it. As a rule, the contract specifies the *amount* of the monthly payment, the payment *date, penalties* for late payment, the *length* of the lease agreement, *deposit* requirements, the distribution of *expenses, renewal* options, and any *restrictions,* for example, on children, pets, or the use of facilities.

Most leases have a minimum term of either six months or one year, and require payments at the beginning of each month and either a deposit or the last month's payment as security against damages and infringement of the lease agreement. In the absence of any serious damage, most of the deposit should be refunded to the lessee shortly after the lease expires; a portion of the deposit is sometimes retained by the lessor to cover the cost of cleaning and minor repairs, regardless of how clean and well-kept the unit is left. Because the landlord has control over the deposit, a written statement describing any damage in evidence *prior* to occupancy may help the lessee avoid losing the entire deposit. Renters should also clarify who bears expenses such as utilities and trash collection and exactly what, if any, restrictions are placed on use of the property. It's also a good idea for renters to check the various renter-landlord laws in their states in order to fully understand their *rights,* as well as responsibilities.

The Rent-or-Buy Decision. During the 1970s, renting a place to live generally was more expensive than buying. This was due, in large party, to three factors: (1) relatively low housing prices and mortgage interest rates; (2) generous tax write-offs for homeowners; and (3) rapid appreciation in home values. However, by 1980 things began to change. Housing prices became out of reach for many families, and interest rates skyrocketed; in addition, housing prices stopped appreciating and even began to decline in many areas. Although in-

terest rates later declined and home prices began to recover in the mid-1980s, the percentage of families living in their own homes had dropped from 65.6 percent in 1980 to 63.7 percent by the middle of 1988. Clearly a decline in homeownership occurred during the decade of the 1980s.

Some people are forced to rent rather than buy: They either do not have the money needed to make a down payment and pay closing costs or they do not have adequate income to safely make monthly mortgage payments. Others, however, rent because they prefer to: They have more mobility, they do not have to worry about maintenance and upkeep, or, for them, renting makes more economic sense than buying.

In such a situation, a simple rent-or-buy analysis can be used to choose the least-cost alternative, as illustrated in Exhibit 6.7, which compares the cost of renting with the cost of buying. Note that the procedure assumes that if the residence is purchased, the homeowner will itemize deductions on his or her tax return. If instead the homeowner elects to take the standard deduction, the value of the two tax-shelter entries in Exhibit 6.7—marked with an asterisk—should be set equal to zero—and in that case, the attractiveness of buying will be greatly diminished.

Assume that you must decide between renting an apartment for $700 a month or buying a $95,000 patio home. Purchasing the home would involve a $15,000 down payment, an $80,000, 12 percent, 30-year mortgage (from Exhibit 6.5, we find monthly mortgage payments would be $822.88), and $4,000 in closing costs, as well as property taxes, insurance, and maintenance. With renting, the only costs would be the $700 monthly rental payment and an annual renter's insurance premium of $300. Assume that you will itemize deductions if you pur-

---

rental contract (lease agreement)
A legal instrument that protects both the lessor and the lessee from an adverse action by the other party; it specifies the amount of the monthly payment, the payment date, the length of the lease agreement, deposit requirements, the distribution of expenses, renewal options, and restrictions, for example, on children, pets, or the use of facilities.

EXHIBIT 6.7

Rent-or-Buy Cost Comparison

Using this procedure to make the rent-or-buy decision, you should *rent* if the total cost of renting is less than the total cost of buying, and *buy* if the total cost of renting is more than the total cost of buying. In this illustration, the rental option requires monthly payments of $700. The purchase option is a $95,000 home, financed with a $15,000 down payment and an $80,000, 12-percent, 30-year mortgage, with additional closing costs of $4,000.

RENT-OR-BUY ANALYSIS			
A. COST OF RENTING			
1. Annual rental costs			
(12 × monthly rental rate of $ _700_)		$8,400	
2. Renter's insurance		300	
Total cost of renting			$8,700
3. COST OF BUYING			
1. Annual mortgage payments			
(12 × monthly mortgage payment of $ _823_)	$9,876		
2. Property taxes			
(_2_ % of price of home)	1,900		
3. Homeowner's insurance			
(_.5_ % of price of home)	475		
4. Maintenance			
(_.8_ % of price of home)	760		
5. After-tax cost of interest lost on down payment and closing costs			
($ _19,000_ × _6_ % after-tax rate of return)	1,140		
6. Total costs		$14,151	
Less:			
7. Principal reduction in loan balance (see note below)	$276		
8. Tax savings due to interest deductions* (Interest portion of mortgage payments $ _9,600_ × tax rate of _28_ %)	2,688		
9. Tax savings due to property tax deductions* (line B. 2 × tax rate of _28_ %)	532		
10. Total deductions		$3,496	
11. Annual after-tax cost of home ownership (line B.6. − line B.10.)		$10,655	
12. Less: Estimated annual appreciation in value of home (_3½_ % of price of home)		$3,325	
Total cost of buying (line B.11. − line B.12.)			$7,330

Note: Find monthly mortgage payments from Exhibit 6.5. An easy way to approximate the portion of the *annual* loan payment that goes to interest (line B.8.) is to multiply the interest rate by the size of the loan (in this case, $80,000 × .12 = $9,600). To find the principal reduction in the loan balance (line B.7.), simply subtract the amount that goes to interest from total annual mortgage payments ($9,876 − $9,600 = $276).

*Tax-shelter items.

chase the home and that you are in the 28 percent tax bracket. Substituting the appropriate values into Exhibit 6.7 (on facing page) and making the required calculations results in the total cost of each alternative. *Buying* is preferred over renting, since the total cost of renting is nearly $1,600 a year more than the total cost of buying. Alternatively, of course, you could look for a less expensive apartment. If you could lower the rent by $150 a month —that is, $1,600/12—renting would be preferred. Renting would also be the preferred course of action if you plan to take the standard deduction (do not plan to itemize) on your tax return, since the values of the entries on lines B.8. and B.9. would then equal zero, thus raising the cost of homeownership by slightly more than $3,200 a year.

BUYING A HOME

Finding the right house at the right price is only part of the home-buying process; other important activities include financing the transaction with the right kind of mortgage and closing the deal. Assuming you are interested in buying a home, how would you identify the "right" house, finance its purchase, and close the deal? Before reading ahead, spend a few moments responding to this question.

Buying a home usually requires a good deal of time, effort, and money. Learning of the available properties and their prices requires a systematic search and careful property analysis. Also, a buyer should have a basic understanding of mortgages, real estate sales contracts, and other documents required to close a deal.

Shop the Market First

Most people who shop the housing market rely on real estate agents for information, access to properties, and advice. Other sources of information, such as newspaper ads, are also widely used to identify available properties. Occasionally a person

seeking to buy or rent property will advertise his or her needs and wait for sellers to initiate contact.

Using an Agent. Most home buyers rely on real estate agents because they are in daily contact with the housing market. Once you describe your needs to an agent he or she can begin to search for appropriate properties. The agent also will help you negotiate with the seller, assist you in obtaining satisfactory financing, and, although not empowered to give explicit legal advice, help you prepare a real estate sales contract.

Most real estate firms belong to the local **Multiple Listing Service (MLS)**. Basically, MLS compiles a list of properties for sale from information provided by the member firms in a given community or metropolitan area. A brief description of each property and its asking price are included, and the list is updated weekly. As a rule, it is best to deal with a realtor that works for a MLS member firm; otherwise, you might lack access to a large part of the market.

Buyers should remember that, *agents typically are employed by sellers.* Unless you have agreed to pay a fee to the sales agent you are working with, that agent's primary responsibility, by law, is to sell listed properties at the highest possible prices. Further, because agents are paid only if they make a sale, some might pressure you to "sign now or miss the chance of a lifetime." You should avoid that type of agent. Select someone who will listen to your wants and then work to match you with the right property under terms that will benefit both the seller and you. Good agents recognize that their best interests are served when all parties to a transaction are satisfied. Depending on the geographic location, real estate commissions range from 5 to 6 percent for new homes and 6 to 7 percent for previously occupied homes. However, such commissions are paid only by the seller; the buyer pays the

Multiple Listing Service (MLS)
An organization of real estate companies that compiles and updates weekly a list and brief description, including asking price, of all properties for sale by the member firms in a given community or metropolitan area.

real estate agent nothing. Of course, since the price of a home is likely to be affected by the size of the real estate commission—indeed, many builders are believed to factor commission costs into the prices of their new homes—the buyer probably absorbs some or even all of the commission paid by the seller.

The Real Estate Sales Contract

State laws generally specify that in order to be enforceable in court, real estate buy-sell agreements must be in writing and contain certain information, including (1) names of buyer(s) and seller(s), (2) a description of the property sufficient to provide positive identification, (3) specific price and other terms, and (4) usually the signatures of the buyer(s) and seller(s). Real estate sales transactions often take weeks and sometimes months to complete. They involve a fair amount of legal work and therefore require expert assistance in preparation. Contract requirements help keep the facts straight and reduce the chance for misunderstanding, misrepresentation, or fraud.

Although these requirements fulfill the minimums necessary for court enforcement, in practice real estate sales contracts usually contain several other contractual clauses. Among these are provisions relating to earnest money deposits, contingencies, personal property, and closing costs. An **earnest money deposit** is the money you are asked to pledge at the time you make an offer in order to show good faith. If, after you sign a sales contract, you withdraw from the transaction without a valid reason, you forfeit this deposit. A valid reason for withdrawal would be one stated in the contract as a contingency clause. With a **contingency clause**, you can condition your agreement to buy on such factors as the availability of financing, a termite or other physical inspection of the property, or the advice of a lawyer or real estate expert. Generally speaking, your lawyer should review and approve all agreements before you sign them.

Financing the Transaction

Often the success of a real estate transaction hinges on obtaining a mortgage with favorable terms. Earlier in the chapter, we saw that the mortgage terms can have a dramatic effect on the amount you can afford to spend on a home. A **mortgage loan** is secured by the property in which the lender obtains the legal right to liquidate the property to recover their funds in the event of borrower default. To obtain such a loan, you must be familiar with the available sources of mortgage loans and the types of mortgage contracts.

Sources of Mortgage Loans. The primary source of home mortgages is *savings and loan associations,* which either use customers' deposits to make loans or originate and sell loans to private investors. S&Ls concentrate in first mortgage on one- to four-family houses, though some actively participate in the commercial real estate market as well. While their lending policies are dictated by regulators and mortgage market conditions, their terms are generally more attractive than those of other mortgage lenders.

The second most important source of mortgage money is *commercial banks*. Although traditionally viewed as short-term lenders, today they are a growing force in the mortgage market. Commercial banks are an especially important source of **interim construction loans** made to those who are building a home. Such loans provide short-term financing while the home is being constructed. After the home is completed, *permanent financing* (in the form of a standard long-term first-mortgage loan) is obtained and used to pay off the construction loan.

Next in order of importance come *savings banks,* 90 percent of which are located in the northeastern states. These institutions direct a lot of their mortgage-lending activity toward their depositors; because they are most often *mutual* organizations, and therefore depositor-owned, terms of their mortgage loans are generally slightly more favorable than those made by S&Ls and commercial banks. Additionally, although not a major source of mortgage loans, some *credit unions* make mortgage loans available to their members.

Another way to obtain a mortgage loan is through a **mortgage banker** or **mortgage broker**. Both solicit borrowers, originate loans, and place them with mortgage lenders such as life insurance companies and pension funds. While *mortgage bankers* frequently use their own money to initially fund mortgages that they later resell, *mort-*

gage brokers merely take loan applications and then find lenders willing to grant the mortgage loans under the desired terms. Another difference between them is that mortgage bankers deal primarily in government-insured and -guaranteed loans, whereas mortgage brokers concentrate on finding conventional loans for consumers willing to pay their fee. While most mortgage bankers and mortgage brokers are legitimate, some of them—especially mortgage brokers—in recent years have been found guilty of accepting front-end fees and then skipping town or of steering consumers to high-priced lenders. In view of this possibility, it is generally best for you to shop for a mortgage loan on your own, or possibly with the assistance of your realtor, who under current law is prohibited from collecting fees or kickbacks for helping a home-buyer obtain financing.

Seller Financing

One other increasingly important source of mortgage money is the seller of the property. Known as **seller financing**, this type of loan has long been in use, although it is most popular during periods of generally high interest rates. Seller financing can take one of two forms: balloon payments or buy-downs.

Balloon Payments.   If provided by the seller of an older home, seller financing will usually involve a **balloon payment**, which is a single, very large principal payment due at a specified future date. In this case, the seller of the home is a private party—the current occupant, whose primary motivation is to sell the house. The balloon payment will be included in the transaction if the buyer does not have the money required for the down payment and/or does not want to commit to as large a mortgage loan as would otherwise be required. Under such circumstances, the buyer will look to the seller for financing.

Here is how it works. Suppose a potential buyer wants to purchase a $100,000 home that you have offered for sale; she has $15,000 available for a down payment but, because of high interest rates, does not wish to commit to a mortgage of more than $75,000. In order to sell the house, you agree to take a *note,* secured by a second mortgage, in the amount of $10,000. The note is set up so that it

will mature (in full) in, say, five years; in addition, it will usually carry an interest rate that is at least a point or two below the market and will require monthly payments of *interest only* over the five-year term of the loan. In this case, the loan has only one, principal (balloon) payment of $10,000, due at maturity. The buyer, of course, is hoping that interest rates drop within five years so that the balloon payment note can be refinanced at a considerably lower rate.

---

earnest money deposit
Money pledged by a buyer to show good faith when making an offer to buy a home.

contingency clause
A clause in a real estate sales contract that makes the agreement conditional on such factors as the availability of financing, property inspections, and obtaining expert advice.

mortgage loan
A loan secured by real property in which the lender obtains the legal right to liquidate the property to recover its funds in the event of borrower default.

interim construction loan
A loan that provides short-term financing while a home is being constructed.

mortgage banker
A firm that solicits borrowers, originates primarily government-insured and -guaranteed loans, and places them with mortgage lenders; frequently uses its own money to initially fund mortgages it later resells.

mortgage broker
A firm that solicits borrowers, originates primarily conventional loans, and places them with mortgage lenders; merely takes loan applications and then finds lenders willing to grant the mortgage loans under the desired terms.

seller financing
A type of loan provided either as a balloon payment by the seller of an older home or as a buy-down by a builder-developer of a new home in order to assist the buyer in purchasing their property; these incentives are commonly offered during periods of generally high interest rates.

balloon payment
A single, very large mortgage principal payment due at a specified future date.

A word of caution: Such forms of *creative financing* can cause serious problems for both the buyer and seller when interest rates fail to drop as expected or the buyer is simply unable to obtain alternative financing. The net result often is that the seller is left with a balloon-payment note that the buyer is unable to repay at its maturity.

Buy-Downs. The other type of seller financing involves new homes and usually takes the form of a **buy-down**. In this case, a builder-developer will arrange with a financial institution (like an S&L) for mortgage financing at interest rates that are will below the market—say, 10 percent financing on his homes at a time when the market of interest is around $11\frac{1}{2}$ or 12 percent. This obviously looks like a good deal, but how is it accomplished? Typically the builder/seller puts his money up front; in effect, he buys a reduced rate of interest by paying a specified number of points. In our example, the builder might have to pay 6 to 10 points to buy down the mortgage. Of course, such an arrangement can be costly and involve thousands of dollars. While the builder is trying to give the buyer the impression that he or she can finance a home bought from him at a special low interest rate, the fact is that the buyer will pay for the reduced interest in the form of a higher home-purchase price.

The intent behind buy-downs is to reduce the monthly mortgage payment—which can be accomplished even with a higher home price. Probably the most popular form of buy-down is the so-called "3–2–1 buy-down," meaning that the builder arranges a discount of 3 percentage points the first year, 2 percentage points the second year, and 1 point the third year. If the prevailing rate of interest is 12 percent, in a 3–2–1 buy-down on a 30-year mortgage the builder will arrange financing at 9 percent for year 1, 10 percent for year 2, 11 percent for year 3, and 12 percent for the years 4 through 30. Thus, the monthly mortgage payments will start out low but will build up each year until the fourth year, when they will level off. For example, on a $70,000, 30-year mortgage loan, first-year payments would amount to around $565 a month; in the second year, they would jump to $615; in the third, they would go up to $665; and in the fourth and following years they would be up to about $720.

Buy-downs have come under a lot of criticism because they tend to encourage homebuyers to overextend themselves and accept a larger mortgage loan than they can afford, especially under 3–2–1 type arrangements. In addition, the homeowner is often in for a big surprise when he has to sell his home after only three or four years. This occurs when the homeowner finds that the market value of his house is actually less than the amount he still owes on the mortgage! The reason, of course, is that the cost of the buy-down not only increased the price of the home, but it also added to the amount of the mortgage. Thus, a home buyer, should exercise caution when considering a buy-down arrangement, or any other form of creative financing.

Types of Mortgage Loans

Knowing where to look for mortgage money is just the start. You also must choose the type of mortgage that is right for you. The mortgage market today is quite different from before. In 1970, for example, just a few basic types of mortgages were available. Today there is a full menu of mortgages; many S&Ls offer more than ten different kinds. Selecting the right mortgage obviously is an important aspect of buying a home.

Fortunately, personal computers can be used to help in this task. Programs are available for analyzing different loan terms in order to find those that best fit your budget. In addition, when hooked up to a network of mortgage lenders, a computer can digest your loan application data and, for a fee, identify lenders that will provide you with the best loans.

The cost differentials among different types of mortgages can be substantial. It is not unusual to find differences of two full percentage points or more; for example, in early 1989 in a major market the quoted rate on one popular form of mortgage ranged from 10 to 12 percent, depending on the lender. Mortgage interest rates have always been a concern to homebuyers—a high interest rate can seriously affect your limits of affordability.

There is no single way to classify mortgages. For our purposes here, we will look at them in two ways: (1) terms of payment and (2) whether they are conventional, insured, or guaranteed. As far as terms of payment are concerned, there are literally dozens of different types of home mortgages from which to choose. For example, there are *graduated payment* and *growing equity* mortgages, in which the amount of the monthly mortgage payment gets progressively larger over time; or there is the *bi-weekly* mortgage, where payments (equal to half of a regular monthly payment) are made every two weeks, rather than once a month. Yet, in spite of all these different types of mortgages, the vast majority of mortgage loans made today fall into just two basic categories: fixed-rate mortgages and adjustable-rate mortgages. These two types of mortgages alone account for 90 percent, or more, of all loans made today; because of their enormous popularity, we now take a closer look at both of them.

Fixed-Rate Mortgage. In spite of the fact that since mid-1975 a number of other types of mortgages have been developed, marketed, and popularized, the **fixed-rate mortgage** today still accounts for a major chunk of all home mortgages written. It is characterized by the fact that both the rate of interest and the monthly mortgage payment are fixed over the full term of the loan. The most common type by far is the *30-year fixed-rate* loan. Because of the risks that the lender assumes in this type of mortgage, it is usually the most expensive form of home financing.

A variation of this standard fixed-rate loan that is rapidly gaining in popularity is the *15-year fixed-rate* mortgage. Its chief appeal is that it is paid twice as fast (15 years versus 30) and yet, the monthly payments don't increase significantly. Obviously, to pay off a loan in less time, the homeowner's going to have to pay more each month. But the big (pleasant) surprise comes from the fact that it does not take twice as large a monthly payment to pay off the loan in half the time; rather, the monthly payment on a 15-year loan is generally only about 10 percent larger than the payment on a 30-year loan. (Monthly mortgage payments on fixed-rate loans vary according to interest rates and loan terms, and these can be found by using the mortgage payment table in Exhibit 6.5.)

The basic features of 30- and 15-year fixed-rate mortgages are compared in the following table. In both cases, it is assumed that the purchaser borrows $80,000 at a 12 percent fixed rate of interest:

Type of Loan	Regular Payment	Term of Loan	Total Interest Paid Over Life of Loan
Standard 30-year fixed rate	$822.88 per month	30 years	$216,237
15-year fixed rate	$960.16 per month	15 years	$ 92,829

Perhaps the most startling feature is the substantial difference in the total amount of interest paid. In effect, you can save *nearly $125,000* just by financing your home with a 15-year mortgage rather than a traditional 30-year one—not bad, considering it is only an $80,000 loan. Note that this amount of savings is possible even though monthly payments differ by just less than $140. In practice this difference would be even less, since 15-year mortgages are usually available at interest rates that are about half a percentage point below comparable 30-year loans. Thus, if the 30-year mortgage carried a 12 percent rate, you would expect the 15-year loan to be priced at, say, 11½ percent. The monthly payments would then amount to only $935 rather than $960—a more realistic difference in monthly payments of *less than $115* ($935 − $823 = $112)!

Adjustable-Rate Mortgages. Another popular form of home loan is the **adjustable-rate mortgage (ARM)**. Unlike the fixed-rate mortgage, the rate of interest, and therefore the size of the monthly payment, on an ARM is adjusted up and

---

buy-down
A type of mortgage financing made available by a builder-developer to a potential new-home buyer at below-market interest rates, often only for the first few years of the mortgage.

fixed-rate mortgage
The traditional type of mortgage, in which both the rate of interest and the monthly mortgage payment are fixed over the full term of the loan.

adjustable-rate mortgage (ARM)
A mortgage on which the rate of interest, and therefore the size of the monthly payment, is adjusted up and down in line with movements in interest rates.

down in line with movements in interest rates. In essence, the rate of interest on the mortgage is linked to a specific *interest rate index* and adjusted at specific intervals (usually once a year) in accordance with changes in the index. When the index moves up, so does the rate of interest on the mortgage and, in turn, the size of the monthly mortgage payment. The new interest rate and monthly mortgage payment will then remain fixed until the next adjustment date, when the adjustment process will repeat itself.

The term of an ARM is set (usually at 30 years but sometimes at 15), while its interest rate and monthly payments are not. Since the size of the monthly payments will vary with interest rates, there is no way for you to tell what your future payments will be. However, because the borrower/home buyer assumes most or all of the interest rate risk in these mortgages, the *initial* rate of interest on an adjustable-rate mortgage is normally well below—2 to 3 percentage points—the rate on a standard 30-year fixed-rate loan. Of course, whether or not the borrower actually will end up paying less interest depends on the behavior of market interest rates over the term of the loan.

Basic features. There are several basic features of an ARM that a homebuyer should understand. One is the **adjustment period**, which is the period of time between one rate/payment change and the next. Most ARMs have adjustment periods of one year (these are known as *one-year ARMs*), though some have adjustment periods as short as six months and others as long as five years. Another feature is the **index rate**, which is meant to capture the movement in interest rates. Many lenders use an index rate that is based on the behavior of *one-year U.S. Treasury securities.* Another common index is the average interest paid to depositors in savings institutions, which is commonly measured by the *11th Federal Home Loan Bank District's monthly cost of funds.* One other index occasionally used is the *national mortgage contract rate,* which is the average rate on all new mortgages issued to buyers of previously occupied homes.

To determine the rate of interest on an ARM, lenders will add to the index a few percentage points called the **margin**, which is usually a fixed amount over the life of the loan. Thus, the rate of interest on an ARM equals the index rate plus the margin. This procedure is used in most cases not only to initially set up the loan but also to periodically adjust interest rates and monthly payments.

Consider a lender who uses an index rate that at inception of the loan equals 10 percent; if it charges a 2 percent margin, the loan will be set up initially as a 12 percent mortgage (since 10 percent + 2 percent = 12 percent). Because most ARMs are 30-year loans, the initial monthly payment is found like any other 12 percent, 30-year mortgage. For example, for a $65,000 loan, we can use Exhibit 6.5 to find its first-year monthly payments of $668.59. Assuming a one-year adjustment period, if the index rate rises to, say, 11½ percent, the interest rate for the second year will be 13½ percent; that is, since the margin is fixed at 2 percent, we have 11½ percent + 2 percent = 13½ percent. The size of the monthly payment for the next 12 months will then be adjusted upward and the process repeated each year thereafter until the loan matures.

To protect the borrower from extreme increases in interest rates and monthly payments, many adjustable-rate mortgages have **interest rate caps**, which place a limit on the amount the interest rate can increase over a given period. There are two kinds: (1) *periodic caps,* which limit the interest rate increase from one adjustment to the next, and (2) *overall caps,* which limit the interest rate increase over the life of the loan. Many ARMs have both a periodic and an overall interest rate cap. Typically lenders cap annual rate adjustments at two percentage points and set lifetime interest rate caps at five to six percentage points. Some ARMs may include *payment caps,* which act to limit the monthly payment increase at the time of each adjustment to a certain amount—usually defined as a percentage of the previous payment. In other words, if your ARM has a 5 percent payment cap, that is the most your monthly payment can increase from one year to the next regardless of what happens to interest rates.

Beware of negative amortization. It is important to recognize that some ARMs are subject to **negative amortization**—an increasing principal balance resulting from the fact that the monthly loan payments are lower than the amount of monthly interest being charged. In other words, with some of these loans you can wind up with a larger mortgage balance on the next anniversary of the loan than on the last. This occurs either when the initial payment is intentionally set below the interest charge or when the ARM has interest rates that adjust monthly, although the actual monthly payment can be adjusted only annually. In this latter case, when rates are rising on these loans the current monthly payment can be less than the interest being charged, and the difference is added to the principal, thereby increasing the size of the loan. For example, assume the monthly payment on an $80,000 loan is currently $750 and the loan's next annual adjustment date is in ten months. If, as a result of rising interest rates, the applicable interest rate increases to 12 percent (i.e., 1 percent per month), the monthly interest owed would be $800 (i.e., 1 percent $\times$ $80,000). Thus, negative amortization would occur in the amount of $50 per month ($800 interest—$750 monthly payment). If no other interest rate changes were to occur over the ten months remaining until the next annual adjustment, at that time the mortgage balance would be $80,500—the increase of $500 is attributable to the $50 per month negative amortization over the ten months. When considering an ARM, it is important to learn whether or not negative amortization can occur. Generally loans without the potential for negative amortization are available, although they tend to have slightly higher initial rates and interest rate caps.

Convertible ARMs. Since 1987 a majority of large lenders have begun to offer **convertible ARMs**, loans that allow borrowers to convert from an adjustable-rate to a fixed-rate loan, usually at any time from the 13th to the 60th month. While these loans seldom provide the lowest initial rate, they allow the borrower, for a fee, to convert to a fixed-rate loan if interest rates decline. A conversion fee of around $500 is typical, and the fixed rate is normally set at one-fourth to one-half percent above the going rate on fixed-rate loans at the time you convert. Borrowers who like the generally low initial ARM rates and feel that interest rates will decline during the first 60 months or so of the loan may find the convertible ARM an attractive compromise between a fixed-rate and an adjustable-rate loan.

Adjustable-rate mortgages are relatively complex and place the borrower or homebuyer at the mercy of the market. Their popularity is due not to their simplicity but to their low initial cost. Before buying a home with an adjustable-rate mortgage, you should take the time to become acquainted with all the terms and conditions of the loan. As noted in the accompanying *Issues in Money Management* box, it is important to understand the index used as a base rate when considering an ARM, since the index significantly affects the magnitude and stability of the mortgage payments over the term of the loan. If you do not know what is going on, *ask*— that is the best way to avoid payment shock!

In an adjustable-rate mortgage, the size of the monthly mortgage payment will change periodically in accordance with prevailing mortgage interest rates. **Fact:** In this popular form of home mortgage loan, the term of the loan is fixed (usually at 30 years), but the rate of interest, and therefore the size of the monthly mortgage payment, is adjusted up and down in line with movements in interest rates.

adjustment period
In an adjustable-rate mortgage, the period of time between one rate/payment change and the next.

index rate
An interest rate index that is meant to capture the movement of interest rates; used by mortgage lenders as a base rate for determining the rate of interest to charge on ARMs.

margin
An interest rate surcharge of up to a few percentage points that is added to the basic index rate on an adjustable-rate mortgage loan to determine its prevailing rate of interest; it is usually fixed over the life of the loan.

interest rate cap
A feature of an adjustable-rate mortgage loan that places a ceiling on the amount by which the interest rate can be raised each adjustment period (*periodic cap*) as well as over the life of the loan (*overall cap*).

negative amortization
When the principal balance on a mortgage loan increases due to the fact that the monthly loan payment is lower than the amount of monthly interest being charged; some ARMs are subject to this undesirable situation.

convertible ARM
An adjustable-rate mortgage that allows the borrower to convert from an adjustable-rate to a fixed-rate loan, usually at any time from the 13th to the 60th month.

ISSUES IN MONEY MANAGEMENT

A Primer for Picking the Right ARM Index

Does it matter what index you get when you sign up for an adjustable-rate mortgage? In this mercurial money market environment, you bet it does. Here's a primer on how to pick the right index for your objective and pocketbook.

The index is the base rate for any adjustable-rate mortgage. On top of the index the lender tacks a "margin," which can be anywhere from two to three extra percentage points, to arrive at your fully indexed rate. If your index is at 7.5, for example, and your margin is 2.5, your mortgage interest rate is 10 percent. If your index rises to 8.5 on the first anniversary of the loan, your revised rate will be 11 percent (8.5 plus 2.5).

The fundamental choice faced by most borrowers is whether to go with a Treasury bill index or its cost-of-funds competitor. One-year Treasuries traditionally have been the dominant index in the eastern half of the country. On the West Coast, by contrast, the 11th Federal Home Loan Bank District's monthly cost of funds index is more common.

Treasury rates rose steadily through most of 1988 and early 1989, and as a consequence the cost-of-funds index began to gain popularity in Eastern, Southern, and Midwestern markets. It's likely that at least a handful of lenders in your area are offering it.

What's the critical difference between Treasury indexes and the cost-of-funds index? Volatility.

U.S. Treasury bill rates reflect the roller-coaster movements of the international capital markets as sharply and rapidly as they occur. In the early summer of 1980, for instance, one-year Treasuries were hovering just over 8 percent. By December of the same year, they stood at 14.8 percent, a breathtaking seven-point jump in as many months. By May of 1981, the one-year Treasury index topped 16 percent and spurted to 16.7 percent by August.

In effect, the baseline Treasury index governing thousands of adjustable-rate mortgages more than doubled in the span of one wild year. Many of these loans—unlike virtually all of 1989's adjustables—came with no rate or payment caps to protect consumers against the inherent instability of the Treasury bill index. Picture yourself sitting with one of those explosive

---

Conventional, Insured, and Guaranteed Loans. A **conventional mortgage** is a mortgage offered by a lender who assumes all the risk of loss. To protect themselves on this type of mortgage, lenders usually require a down payment of at least 20 percent of the value of the mortgaged property. Of course, the down payment can be far less than this (sometimes 5 percent or less), but when this happens, the lender usually requires some form of mortgage insurance. Experience has shown that high borrower equity greatly lessens the chance of a mortgage default and a subsequent loss to the lender. However, such a high down payment

requirement makes home buying more difficult for many families and individuals.

To promote homeownership, the federal government, through its Federal Housing Administration (FHA), offers lenders mortgage insurance on high loan-to-value ratio loans. The **FHA mortgage insurance** program helps people buy homes even when they have very little money available for a down payment and closing costs. In exchange for an insurance premium of one-half of 1 percent of the average mortgage balance outstanding for the year (which is paid by the borrower at the time of closing), the FHA agrees to reimburse lenders for

loans on your first rate-change anniversary.

Of course, borrowers whose mortgages were pegged to Treasury bill indexes rode the roller coaster downward, too. By January of 1983, one-year T-bills were back to about 8.6 percent. In 1985, they dropped below 8 percent and bottomed out at 5.7 percent in October of 1986.

What was the 11th District cost-of-funds index doing while Treasuries were rocketing up and down the charts? Very different things. For starters, cost-of-funds borrowers never really saw the scary heights of Treasury bill-indexed loans. The top rate they experienced was 12.6 percent in mid-1983.

Nor did borrowers tied to the cost-of-funds index see the nightmarish month-to-month

changes that bedeviled Treasury-indexed consumers in 1980 and 1981. Their index rose steadily but undramatically throughout the 1980–1982 period.

Conversely, cost-of-funds borrowers never enjoyed the steep rate decline that their Treasury-indexed colleagues did. Their base rate eased downward from 1983 to 1986, but was a full two points higher (7.7 vs. 5.7) when Treasuries bottomed out in 1986.

The upshot of all this for shoppers in the adjustable-rate mortgage bazaar?

- If you want an index that's guaranteed to give you a soft ride, both up and down, the cost-of-funds option may be right for you. Bear in mind, though, that it won't necessar-

ily give you the lowest index rate when you covet it most. It lags Treasuries on the way down and lags them on the way up.

- If your loan comes with tight annual rate caps (one or two percentage points) and you believe rates could trend downward if the economy cools next year, go with a one-year T-bill index.

Or, better yet, take out a three-year adjustable and forget about rates until the mid-1990s.

Source: Adapted from Kenneth R. Harney, "Which Index is Used is a Matter of Interest in Mortgage Markets," © 1988, Washington Post Writers Group. Reprinted with permission.

their losses up to a specified maximum amount in the event of buyer default. The maximum mortgage amount that the FHA can insure traditionally has just about kept pace with the national median sale price of homes. Although the ordinary FHA mortgage ceiling on single-family homes is $67,500, many areas of the country qualify for higher ceilings—now up to $101,250 where housing costs are especially high. As a result, the FHA program offers little benefit for people buying expensive homes. For those who plan to buy homes equal to or less than the median price, however, an FHA loan might be worth pursuing. In addition to the FHA, a

conventional mortgage

A mortgage offered by a lender who assumes all the risk of loss; typically requires a down payment of at least 20 percent of the value of the mortgage property.

FHA mortgage insurance

A program under which the Federal Housing Administration offers lenders mortgage insurance on loans having a high loan-to-value ratio; its intent is to encourage loans to homebuyers who have very little money available for a down payment and closing costs.

number of private companies insure low-down-payment mortgage loans for lenders. These plans, called **private mortgage insurance (PMI)** programs, work in a way similar to the FHA program, but their credit standards, insurable loan amounts, and insurance premiums are somewhat different. Their cost depends on the size of your down payment: put down 10 percent on an $80,000 loan and you'll pay about one-half percent of the amount of the mortgage ($400) at closing and then about $20 per month; put down 5 percent on the same loan and you'll pay 1¼ percent ($1,000) at closing and about $30 per month; generally the monthly payment is made only during the first 7 to 9 years of a 30-year mortgage.

If you would like to buy a house, cooperative, or condominium but have only, say, 5 percent for a down payment, you should ask your real estate agent or mortgage lender whether you might qualify for either an FHA or PMI program. Both types of plans have helped millions of home buyers.

Guaranteed loans are like insured loans, only better—if you qualify. **VA loan guarantees** are provided by the U.S. Veterans Administration to lenders who make qualified mortgage loans to eligible veterans of the U.S. Armed Forces and their unmarried surviving spouses. This program, however, does not require lenders or veterans to pay a premium for the guarantee. In many instances, an eligible veteran must pay only closing costs; in effect, under such a program, a veteran can buy a home with no down payment. (By the way, this can be done *only once* with a VA loan.) The mortgage loan—subject to a maximum amount—can go up to 100 percent of a purchased property's appraised value. The maximum VA guarantee is currently $36,000; since lenders will usually loan an amount equal to four times the guarantee, the maximum loan obtainable with a VA guarantee is currently about $144,000. The VA loan guarantee is a great "fringe benefit" for those who have served in the armed forces.

Closing the Deal

After your loan has been approved, the closing process begins. There are three important parts to a closing: (1) the RESPA statement, (2) the title check, and (3) the closing statement.

RESPA. Since 1974, closings on owner-occupied houses, condominiums, and apartment buildings of four units or fewer have been governed by the **Real Estate Settlement Procedures Act (RESPA)**. The purpose of this act (and its 1975 amended version) was to spur closing cost reductions primarily by prohibiting kickbacks made in conjunction with closing services and by requiring advance disclosure of costs to buyers. Prior to the act, real estate closing costs were believed to be higher than necessary because in many areas real estate agents, attorneys, and others received kickbacks from lenders or title insurance companies in return for steering business to them. Furthermore, because buyers often learned the total amount of closing costs late in the closing process, they did not have time to shop for competing providers of services.

The specific requirements of RESPA are given in a U.S. Department of Housing and Urban Development booklet entitled *Settlement Costs and You: A HUD Guide for Homebuyers*. The law requires lenders to give a copy of this guide to potential borrowers. It can take much of the mystery out of the closing process. Although closing expenses still may climb into the thousands of dollars, homebuyers often can save significant amounts if they shop for financing, insurance coverages, and other closing items rather than merely accepting the costs quoted by any one lender or other provider of closing services.

Title Check. Numerous legal interests can exist in real estate simultaneously, for example, those of the owner(s), lender(s), lienholders (such as an unpaid roofing contractor), and easement holders. Before you take title to a property, therefore, you should make sure that the title is free of all liens and encumbrances (except those that are specifically referred to in the sales contract) and that the owners who are conveying title to you actually have the legal interest they claim.

Although it is up to you to question the quality of the title to the property you are buying, in most cases an attorney or title insurance company performs a **title check**, which consists of the necessary research of legal documents and courthouse records. The customary practices and procedures and the costs involved vary widely throughout the country. Regardless of the specific custom in your area, you should make some form of title check an essential part of your closing process.

Closing Statement. A **closing statement**, provided to both buyer and seller at closing, accounts for the monies that change hands during that procedure. The statement reconciles the borrower's and the seller's costs and shows how much the borrower owes and the seller receives from the transaction. Exhibit 6.8 shows a simplified closing statement for both the borrower (buyer) and seller in a transaction involving sale of a home for $100,000. It can be seen that, in addition to the $100,000 purchase price, the borrower must pay 3 points on the $90,000 mortgage loan with a number of other charges, advance payments, reserve deposits with the lender, title charges, and recording fees—resulting in a gross amount due of $105,273.69. After subtracting the $3,000 earnest money deposit, the $90,000 of loan proceeds, and the county tax credit of $103.68, it can be seen that the borrower will have to pay $12,377.37 at closing. After charges are subtracted, including a $7,000 real estate commission, the seller's mortgage payoff of $65,867.50, and the unpaid county taxes of $103.68 (to be paid by the seller), from the $100,000 sale price, the amount the seller will receive at closing is $26,048.32. Note that frequently the RESPA form developed by the U.S. Department of Housing and Urban Development is used. Before closing a home purchase transaction, you should be given an opportunity to review the closing statement and have your questions answered. Be sure to carefully and critically review the statement in order to make sure that it is accurate and consistent with the contractual terms of the transaction; if not, have the statement corrected before closing the deal.

Refinancing Your Mortgage

It sometimes occurs that after you've purchased a home and closed the transaction, interest rates on similar loans will drop. If rates drop by 1 to 2 or more percent, you should consider the economics of refinancing. In the years between 1985 and 1988 many people who obtained mortgage loans in the period of 1979–1985 found refinancing attractive;

loans with fixed rates as high as 12 percent could be refinanced for fixed rates as low as 9 percent. The decision to refinance should be made after carefully considering the terms of the old and new mortgage, the anticipated number of years you expect to remain in the home, any prepayment penalty on the old mortgage, and the closing costs associated with the new mortgage.

Exhibit 6.9 presents a form that can be used to analyze a potential refinancing. The data for the Philipatos family's analysis is shown. Their current 5-year-old, 12 percent mortgage with a balance of $80,000 requires monthly payments of $825 per month for 25 more years. If refinanced at the prevailing rate of 10 percent over the remaining 25-year life of the current mortgage, the monthly payment would drop to $725. The Philipatos are very happy with their house and plan to live there for at least five more years. They will not have to pay any penalty for prepaying their current mortgage, and closing and other costs associated with

private mortgage insurance (PMI)

An insurance plan offered by a private company that insures low-down-payment mortgage loans for lenders.

VA loan guarantee

A guarantee offered by the U.S. Veterans Administration to lenders who make qualified mortgage loans to eligible veterans of the U.S. Armed Forces and their unmarried surviving spouses.

Real Estate Settlement Procedures Act (RESPA)

A law passed in 1974 that requires mortgage lenders to provide clear, advance disclosure of closing costs to home buyers.

title check

The research of legal documents and records to verify that the title is free of all liens and encumbrances and that the seller conveying title to property actually has the legal interest he or she claims.

closing statement

A statement provided to both buyer and seller at closing that accounts for the monies that change hands during that procedure.

EXHIBIT 6.8

A Simple Closing Statement

At the top in the borrower's (buyer's) statement, his charges, advance payments, reserve deposits with the lender, title charges, and recording fees are added to the $100,000 purchase price, and then the earnest money deposit, principal amount of the loan, and county tax credit are subtracted from the total to find the amount due from the borrower of $12,377.37. In the seller's statement, the total charges, mortgage payoff, and county tax credit to borrower are subtracted from the $100,000 sale price to find the $26,048.32 cash to be paid the seller.

A. Borrower's Statement

Contract Purchase Price		$100,000.00
Plus: Charges		
Points (3% × $90,000)	$ 2,700.00	
Appraisal Fee	175.00	
Credit Report	84.00	
Tax Service	32.00	
Total		2,991.00
Plus: Advance Payments		
Interest to End of Month	547.09	
Mortgage Insurance Premium	855.00	
Homeowners Insurance Premium	347.00	
Total		1,749.09
Plus: Reserves Deposited with Lender		
Homeowner's Insurance (2 mos.)	$ 57.84	
Mortgage Insurance (2 mos.)	56.26	
County Property Taxes (2 mos.)	59.00	
Total		173.10
Plus: Title Charges		
Closing Fee	$ 103.50	
Title Insurance	245.00	
Total		348.50
Plus: Government Recording and Transfer Charges		
Recording Fees		12.00
GROSS DUE FROM BORROWER		$105,273.69
Less: Amounts Paid By or on Behalf of Borrower		
Earnest Money Deposit	$ 3,000.00	
Principal Amount of Loan	90,000.00	
County Tax Credit	(103.68)	
Total		(92,896.32)
AMOUNT DUE FROM BORROWER		$ 12,377.37

B. Seller's Statement

Contract Sales Price		$100,000.00
Less: Charges		
Real Estate Commission	$ 7,000.00	
Closing Fee	103.50	
Title Insurance	535.00	
Affidavit of Value	2.00	
Termite Inspection	25.00	
1 year Home Warranty	315.00	
Total		(7,980.50)
Less: Payoff of Mortgage		(65,867.50)
Less: Credit to Borrower for County Taxes Owed		(103.68)
CASH TO SELLER		$ 26,048.32

EXHIBIT 6.9

Mortgage Refinancing Analysis for the Philipatos

Using the form below, the Philipatos find that by refinancing their 5-year-old, $80,000, 12-percent, 30-year mortgage (which has no prepayment penalty and requires payments of $825 per month) with an $80,000, 10-percent, 25-year mortgage requiring $725 monthly payments and $2,000 in closing costs, it will take 20 months to break even. Since the Philipatos plan to stay in their home for at least 60 more months, the refinancing is easily justified.

MORTGAGE REFINANCING ANALYSIS*

Name _Demi and Nicholas Philipatos_   Date _January 6, 1990_

Item	Description	Amount
1	Current monthly payment	$ 825
2	Anticipated additional years in house	5
3	Additional months in house (Item 2 × 12)	60
4	Total payment (Item 1 × Item 3)	$ 49,500
5	New mortgage payment	$ 725
6	New total payment (Item 3 × Item 5)	$ 43,500
7	Potential savings (Item 4 − Item 6)	$ 6,000
8	Prepayment penalty on current mortgage	$ 0
9	Closing costs on new mortgage	$ 2,000
10	Refinancing cost (Item 8 + Item 9)	$ 2,000
11	Total savings (Item 7 − Item 10)	$ 4,000
12	Monthly savings (Item 1 − Item 5)	$ 100
13	Months to break even (Item 10 ÷ Item 12)	20

*Form adapted from Jane Bryant Quinn, "Your Refinancing Worksheet," *Woman's Day*, July 29, 1986.

---

the new mortgage are $2,000. Substituting these values into the form in Exhibit 6.9 reveals (in Item 13) that it will take the Philipatos 20 months to break even with the new mortgage. Since 20 months is considerably less than their anticipated 60 months (Item 3) in the home, the economics easily support refinancing their mortgage under the specified terms.

OTHER BIG-TICKET ITEMS ⬛

Though less expensive than housing, automobiles, furniture, and appliances are all examples of costly, big-ticket purchases that require careful consideration and deliberation. How would you go about carefully considering, analyzing, and financing the purchase of a big-ticket item such as an automobile? Take a few moments to answer this question before reading on.

As a rule, a car is probably the first major expenditure that most people make. (While pickup trucks, four-wheel drives, and similar vehicles are popular forms of transportation in many parts of the country, in the material that follows we will use the terms "automobile" or "car" to describe these and all other types of passenger vehicles.) An individual typically purchases an automobile every two to five years and pays anywhere from $1,000 to $20,000 (or more) for it, depending on its make, model, and age. The automobile purchase is second only to housing in terms of amount of money spent by the typical consumer. Because you will probably make an automobile-purchase decision many times during your life, a systematic approach to selection and financing can help you realize significant savings. Furniture and appliances are also big-ticket items and, although less costly and less frequently purchased than automobiles, they represent major budget items whose purchase requires careful analysis.

Automobiles

The automobile plays a major role in our society. It is an important factor in the economy, since the automobile industry provides hundreds of thousands of jobs and is a major consumer of raw materials produced by the steel and other vital industries. Although the primary motivation for automobile ownership is to provide transportation, automobiles are sometimes viewed as status symbols or purchased as part of a hobby or as an investment. There are a wide variety of models, styles, sizes, and colors. In addition to domestically produced automobiles, imported cars today account for a large share of the American automobile market.

An automobile is the second largest purchase for most people. **Fact:** A car ranks second only to housing with respect to amount of money spent.

Affordability. Before you shop for a car, you should determine how much you can afford to spend. This estimate should be stated on a monthly basis in order to be consistent with your budget. The amount you arrive at should result from a careful analysis of your available resources in view of other necessary expenses (including housing) and your transportation requirements. Once you have estimated the monthly amount available, you should evaluate the costs of owning (or leasing) various types of automobiles in order to select the one most suitable for you.

Operating Costs. The monthly out-of-pocket cost of operating an automobile consists of not only car payments, but also insurance, licenses, fuel, oil, tires, and other operating and maintenance outlays. Certain of these costs are *fixed* and remain so regardless of how much you drive; others are *variable* with the number of miles you drive. The biggest fixed cost is likely to be the *installment payments* associated with the loan used to buy the car; the biggest variable cost will probably be fuel. Another cost is **depreciation**, which is the loss in value that occurs from driving the vehicle. In effect, depreciation is the difference between the price you paid for the car and what you can get for it when you sell it. If you paid $12,000 for an automobile that can be sold three years later for $6,000, the car will cost you $6,000 in depreciation. While depreciation costs may not be a recurring out-of-pocket cost, it is nonetheless an important operating expense that should not be overlooked.

Exhibit 6.10 provides an example of what it might cost to operate a motor vehicle. Since the cost of operating an automobile varies with the year and make of the car, its mechanical condition, and even where you live, the figures in the exhibit should be viewed as only *representative* of the kinds of costs you can expect to incur. Note that the biggest cost component is the fixed out-of-pocket costs, followed by depreciation, and finally the var-

EXHIBIT 6.10

Automobile Operating Costs

This car costs nearly $7,000 a year to operate. If it is driven about 12,000 miles a year, the car costs about 57 cents for every mile driven.

	Annual Costs[a]	Monthly Costs[a]	Costs per Mile	
			12,000 Miles/Year	25,000 Miles/Year
(1) Fixed Costs				
Installment loan payments	$3,180	$ 265	$ .265	$ .128
Auto insurance	360	30	.030	.014
License plates and taxes	180	15	.015	.007
Total fixed costs	$3,720	$ 310	$ .310	$ .149
(2) Variable Costs				
Fuel	$ 720	$ 60	$ .060	$ .060
Oil and tires	96	8	.008	.008
Repairs and maintenance	264	22	.022	.022
Total variable costs	$1,080	$ 90	$ .090	$ .090
Total out-of-pocket costs [(1) + (2)]	$4,800	$ 400	$ .400	$ .239
(3) Depreciation	$2,000	$ 167	$ .167	$ .080
Total operating costs [(1) + (2) + (3)]	$6,800	$ 567	$ .567	$ .319

[a]Annual and monthly *variable* costs are based on mileage of 12,000 a year.

iable costs. In total, this particular vehicle costs about $7,000 a year to operate, nearly $5,000 of which is annual out-of-pocket expenses. The figures are shown on an annual, monthly, and cost-per-mile basis. Clearly the more miles you drive each year, the lower the cost per mile. This is due to the fact that the *annual* fixed costs and depreciation do not change; thus, on a cost-per-mile basis these expenses go down with increased mileage. You should, of course, make sure that the expected (or actual) out-of-pocket operating costs of owning an automobile remain within budgeted amounts. (Note that for budgetary purposes depreciation can be ignored, since it does not represent an out-of-pocket expense in the normal sense.)

The Purchase Transaction. Once you have selected one car that meets your requirements, the purchase process begins with your making an offer. If a dealer is involved in the transaction, the offer will consist of a written **sales contract**. To show good faith, you may be required to include a deposit of $100 or more with your offer. Since such a contract becomes binding when accepted by the dealer, you should make certain that your offer is not too high. Always offer less than the asking or

sticker price (on a new car); all the seller can do is say no. The seller will likely counter with a price somewhere between your offer and the asking price.

New cars typically can be purchased for around 15 percent below the sticker price for American cars and about 10 percent below the sticker price for imported cars. Once your offer has been accepted by the seller, you will have to pay him or her and take possession of the car. At the time you pay, you should also receive the title to the car. If you are not paying cash for the car, you will need to arrange financing through the dealer or some

---

depreciation
The loss in the value of an asset such as an automobile that occurs over its period of use.

sales contract
A formal, contractually binding agreement to purchase a home, automobile, or other big-ticket item that states the offering price and all conditions—such as repairs, closing date, and inspections—required by buyer and seller.

EXHIBIT 6.11

Comparing Mary Dixon's Automobile Lease versus Purchase Costs

The form that follows demonstrates Mary Dixon's analysis of whether it is better to lease or purchase a new car costing $13,000. Under the lease, a down payment of $250 and monthly payments of $250 are required over the four-year term of the closed-end lease, while if purchased a $2600 down payment, sales tax of 5 percent ($650) on the purchase price, and monthly payments of $270 over the four-year term of the loan are required. A 6 percent interest rate on savings and an estimated value for the car at the end of four years of $6,000 is assumed. Because the total cost of leasing is $12,060 which is greater than the $10,834 total cost of purchasing, the purchase is preferred.

AUTOMOBILE LEASE VERSUS PURCHASE ANALYSIS

Name *Mary Dixon*   Date *March 3, 1990*

LEASE

Item	Description	Amount
1	Security deposit required	$ 250
2	Term of lease and loan (years)*	4
3	Term of lease and loan (months) (Item 2 × 12)	48
4	Monthly lease payment	$ 250
5	Total payments over term of lease (Item 3 × Item 4)	$ 12,000
6	Interest rate earned on savings (in decimal form)	.06
7	Opportunity cost of down payment (Item 1 × Item 2 × Item 6)	$ 60
8	Payment/refund for market value adjustment at end of lease ($0 for closed-end leases)	$ 0
9	Total cost of leasing (Item 5 + Item 7 + Item 8)	$ 12,060

PURCHASE

Item	Description	Amount
10	Purchase price	$ 13,000
11	Down payment	$ 2,600
12	Sales tax rate (in decimal form)	.05
13	Sales tax (Item 10 × Item 12)	$ 650
14	Monthly loan payment	$ 270
15	Total payments over term of loan (Item 3 × Item 14)	$ 12,960
16	Opportunity cost of down payment (Item 2 × Item 6 × Item 11)	$ 624
17	Estimated value of car at end of loan	$ 6,000
18	Total cost of purchase (Item 11 + Item 13 + Item 15 + Item 16 − Item 17)	$ 10,834

DECISION

If the value of Item 9 is less than the value of Item 18 leasing is preferred; otherwise the purchase alternative is preferred (as is the case above).

---

*This form is based upon assumed equal terms for the lease and the installment loan, which is assumed to be used to finance the purchase.

other financial institution. (The key aspects of an automobile loan, which is an installment loan that can be quickly negotiated with good credit, are included in Chapter 8.)

Maintaining Your Automobile. Like any tangible asset, the automobile must be properly maintained and repaired in order to preserve its function as well as to enhance its resale value. Maintenance and repairs should be performed by a dealership or independent garage that will stand behind its work and not do unneeded repairs. Performing *preventive maintenance,* which typically involves regularly scheduled changes and checks of various fluids, filters, and other key components, should reduce the frequency, seriousness, and cost of repairs.

Leasing an Automobile. An alternative to purchasing a car is *leasing,* which typically involves receiving the use of a car in exchange for contractually agreeing to make monthly lease payments over a specified period of time, usually two to four years. The size of the lease payments depends on the car's cost, the term of the lease, the number of miles the car is expected to be driven, other financial factors, and the type of lease—closed-end or open-end. Nearly 80 percent of all consumers choose the **closed-end lease**, which is often called the *walk-away lease* because at the end of its term you simply turn in the car, assuming you have neither exceeded the mileage limits nor abused the car. Under the less popular **open-end lease**, the estimated *residual value* of the car at the end of the lease is used to determine lease payments; if the car is actually worth less at the end of the lease, you have to make up the difference.

Leasing has experienced significant growth over the last ten years; in 1988 leased automobiles accounted for 10 percent of all automobile sales. The appeal of leasing is attributed to its ability to allow a person to obtain use of a car for a smaller down payment and monthly payment than would be required if it were purchased. Of course, the lessee (person who leases) gives up the right to the residual value of the car at the end of the lease. To decide whether it is less costly to lease rather than purchase a car, **lease versus purchase analysis** can be used to estimate the total cost of each alternative over equal periods. Generally in such an

analysis the purchase is assumed to be financed with an installment loan with a maturity just equal to the term of the lease. For example, assume that Mary Dixon is considering either leasing or purchasing a new car costing $13,000. If she leases, a $250 down payment and monthly payments of $250 would be required over the four-year term of the closed-end lease she is considering. If she purchases the car, she will make a $2,600 down payment and finance the balance with a four-year loan requiring monthly payments of $270; in addition, she will have to pay a 5 percent sales tax ($650) on the purchase, and she expects the car to have a residual value of $6,000 at the end of the four years. Mary can earn 6 percent interest on her savings. After filling in the worksheet shown in Exhibit 6.11 (on facing page), Mary concludes that purchase is best, since its total cost of $10,834 is more than $1,200 less than the $12,060 total leasing cost. Clearly, all else being equal, the least costly alternative is preferred.

Furniture and Appliances

Another group of tangible assets that you will purchase during your lifetime consists of furniture and appliances. Although these assets can be leased, most people purchase them. Since the cost of furniture and appliances can be great, a few comments about purchase and financing are in order here.

---

closed-end lease
The most popular form of automobile lease, often called a *walk-away lease* because at the end of its term the lessee simply turns in the car, assuming the preset mileage limit has not been exceeded and the car hasn't been abused.

open-end lease
An automobile lease under which the estimated residual value of the car is used to determine lease payments; if the car is actually worth less at the end of the lease, the lessee must pay the difference.

lease versus purchase analysis
A procedure used to determine the total cost of leasing and the total cost of purchasing (using an installment loan) a car over equal terms in order to choose the least costly alternative.

Purchase Considerations. When buying furniture or appliances, attention should be given to the purchase cost, function, operating and repair expenses, and appearance. By shopping around, you should be able to find pieces that will perform the desired function at the best price. Often, by paying an extra $50 to $100 you can purchase an asset that will provide significantly greater satisfaction. In order to get an indication of the quality and general reliability of a given item of furniture or appliance, it is helpful to consult some type of consumer *buying guide,* such as the monthly magazines *Consumer Reports* (which publishes its *Annual Buying Guide* in December), *Changing Times,* and *Consumers Digest.* These are valuable sources of ratings and comparative statistics on furniture, appliances, and many other consumer goods. The operating—including energy—costs and repair costs of items requiring power and/or having moving parts or fabric components should also be considered. In spite of a low purchase price, an item of furniture or an appliance often will have a high total ownership cost if its operating, energy, and repair costs are excessive. Information on these costs can be obtained from consumer publications and friends who have purchased similar items. Many appliances come with an "Energy Guide" rating attached. A final consideration that might enter into your purchase decision is appearance, which may offer a degree of personal satisfaction.

The Purchase Transaction. Once you have selected the basic brands and models that interest you, you should check several stores for the best deal. Many furniture and appliance dealers will negotiate prices. You may be able to pay less than the amount shown on the price tag if you simply ask. You may be able to learn from friends and business associates which dealers have the best prices. Considering the purchase of a floor model or a second-hand item is sometimes worthwhile. Because furniture and appliances have fairly long lives, you may find that the savings resulting from the purchase of used items more than compensates for their slight wear. However, you should know which model you are buying—the preceding year's model or the floor model. Before finalizing your purchase, you should find out who pays for delivery, whether taxes are included in the quoted price, and whether there are any installation costs. If you are able to plan the timing of your purchases, you can often take advantage of sales on furniture in January and August and on appliances in October and November.

Financing the Purchase. Because of the relatively high cost of furniture and appliances, borrowing money may be necessary. Of course, before you begin to shop, you should have some idea about whether or not you need financing. Some furniture and appliance dealers offer "90 days same as cash" or "30–60–90 day" financing arrangements, which allow you to pay for the merchandise in three monthly installments without interest. A number of the installment payment plans used to purchase these types of assets are discussed in detail in Chapter 8. If you will need financing on a purchase, you should analyze and compare the costs of financing plans offered by various dealers.

SUMMARY

- A family's housing needs can be met in many different ways—in addition to single family homes, there are manufactured homes, condominiums, cooperative apartments, and numerous types of rental apartments and houses.
- In addition to the emotional rewards, other benefits of homeownership are the tax shelter and inflation hedge it provides.
- Homeownership costs include the down payment, points and closing costs, monthly mortgage payments, property taxes and insurance, and normal home maintenance and operating expenses. Any of these can amount to a considerable sum of money, and all of them should be carefully considered when estimating how much you can afford to spend on a home.
- Many people rent because they cannot afford to buy a home; others choose to rent because renting is less costly and more convenient for their lifestyle and economic situation.
- Normally, people shopping for a home seek the help of a real estate agent to obtain needed infor-

mation, access to properties, and advice; the agent earns a 5 to 7 percent commission, paid by the seller, when the transaction is closed. A real estate sales contract is used to confirm in writing all terms of the transaction between the buyer and seller.

▪ Mortgage loans can be obtained from S&Ls, commercial banks, savings banks, and through a mortgage banker or mortgage broker; in addition, seller-financing has become an important source of mortgage money. While there are many types of mortgage loans available, the two most widely used are the 15- and 30-year fixed-rate mortgage and the adjustable-rate mortgage.

▪ After a mortgage loan is approved, the loan is closed; this involves certain disclosures required by RESPA, a title check, and preparation of a closing statement that shows how much the borrower owes and the seller receives from the transaction. Sometimes interest rates will drop a number of years after closing, and mortgage refinancing will become attractive.

▪ In addition to your home, other big-ticket expenditures that you'll likely make include the purchase of automobiles, furniture, and appliances—all of which are costly budget items that require careful financial consideration and deliberation. In the case of automobiles one should consider the economics of leasing rather than purchasing by means of using an installment loan.

QUESTIONS AND PROBLEMS

1. In addition to single-family homes, what other forms of housing are available in the United States? Differentiate between a condominium and a cooperative apartment.

2. Briefly describe the various motives for owning a home. Which one do you think is most important? Which is least important?

3. What does the *loan-to-value ratio* on a home represent? Is the down payment on a home related to its loan-to-value ratio? Explain. How much would you have to put down on a house costing $80,000 if the home had an appraised value of $85,000 and the lender required an 80 percent loan-to-value ratio?

4. What are points? How much would a home buyer have to pay if the lender wanted to charge 2½ points on a $75,000 mortgage? When would this amount have to be paid? What effect do points have on the mortgage's rate of interest?

5. What are closing costs? Who pays these costs, and when? Are points part of closing costs? What items are included in closing costs? How much might a home buyer expect to pay in closing costs on a $75,000 house with a 10 percent down payment? How much *in total* would the home buyer have to pay at the time of closing in the above transaction, taking into account closing costs, down payment, and a loan fee of 3 points?

6. Find the monthly mortgage payments on the following mortgage loans:
   a. $60,000/10 percent/30 years
   b. $50,000/13½ percent/20 years
   c. $85,000/10½ percent/15 years

7. What are the most common guidelines used to determine the amount of monthly mortgage payments one can afford? Using the maximum ratios, how big a monthly payment could the Bacon family afford if their income amounted to $4,000 a month? Would it make any difference if they were already making monthly installment loan payments of $750 on two car loans?

8. Why is it advisable for the prospective home buyer to investigate property taxes, insurance, maintenance, and operating costs when shopping for a home? Explain.

9. Selma and Rodney Jackson wish to estimate the amount they can afford to spend to purchase their first home. They have a combined annual income of $37,500 and have $21,000 available to make a down payment and pay closing costs. The Jacksons estimate that homeowners insurance and property taxes will be $125 per month. They expect the mortgage lender to use a 30 percent monthly mortgage payment affordability ratio, to lend at an average interest rate of 11½ percent on a 30-year mortgage, and to require a 15 per-

cent down payment. Based on this information, use the home affordability analysis form given in Exhibit 6.6 to determine the maximum-priced home the Jacksons can afford.

10. Discuss the relative advantages and disadvantages of renting a home. Does a homeowner have any advantage over a renter with respect to taxes? Explain.

11. What role does a real estate agent play in the purchase of a house? How is the real estate agent compensated, and by whom?

12. What clauses are normally included in a real estate sales contract? What is an earnest money deposit? Explain the purchase negotiation process.

13. Describe the various sources of mortgage financing. What is seller-financing? Give two examples of seller-financing.

14. Briefly describe the two basic types of mortgage loans. Which has the lowest initial rate of interest? What is *negative amortization,* and which type of mortgage can experience it?

■ **15.** What would the monthly payments be on a $75,000 loan if the mortgage were set up as
   a. A 15-year, 10 percent fixed-rate loan?
   b. A 30-year adjustable-rate mortgage in which the lender added a margin of 2½ points to the index rate (which presently stands at 6 percent)? Find the monthly mortgage payments for the first year only.

16. Latha Yang purchased a condominium four years ago for $70,000. She has been paying $675 per month on her $60,000, 13 percent, 25-year mortgage. Recently interest rates have dropped sharply, causing Latha to consider refinancing the condo at the prevailing 11 percent rate. She expects to remain in the condo for at least four more years and has found a lender that will make an 11 percent, 21-year loan requiring $610 monthly payments. Although there is no prepayment penalty on her current mortgage, Latha will have to pay $1,500 in closing costs on the new mortgage. Based on this information, use the mortgage refinancing analysis form given in Exhibit 6.9 to determine whether Latha should refinance her mortgage under the specified terms.

17. Jack Williamson purchased a new car on January 1, 1990, for $11,000 and plans to keep it for five years. At the end of five years, the car is expected to be worth 25 percent of the original purchase price. How much will the car be forth after five years? Define *depreciation,* and calculate the depreciation cost per year and per month on Jack's new car. What are some of the nonfinancial decisions Jack had to make when selecting his car?

■ **18.** Janet Wilhite has an established budget in which she has allotted $500 a month to the out-of-pocket operating costs of a car. She is presently looking at a sporty model with monthly payments of $275; plates and taxes would amount to $360 a year and car insurance $750 annually. Fuel is expected to cost about $75 for every 1,000 miles driven; because the car is under warranty, repairs, maintenance, tires, and oil are expected to amount to only $20 for each 1,000 miles. The car is expected to depreciate at the rate of about $2,500 a year. Given that Janet drives about 15,000 miles a year, find the total operating costs of this car on both an annual and a cost-per-mile basis (break the cost out by fixed, variable, and depreciation). Will she be able to stay within her budget with this car?

19. Chris Svenson is trying to decide whether to lease or purchase a new car costing $12,000. If he leases, he will have to make a $400 down payment and agree to make monthly payments of $285 over the 36-month term of the closed-end lease. If, on the other hand, he purchases the car, he will have to make an $1,800 down payment and will finance the balance with a 36-month loan requiring monthly payments of $340; in addition, he will have to pay a 6 percent sales tax ($720) on the purchase price, and he expects the car to have a residual value of $4,300 at the end of three years. Chris can earn 5 percent interest on his savings. Use the automobile lease versus purchase analysis form in Exhibit 6.11 to find the total cost of both the lease and the purchase, and recommend the best strategy to Chris.

20. Briefly describe the most important factors to consider when shopping for and financing the purchase of furniture and appliances.

CASE PROBLEMS

◲ 6.1 Evaluating a Mortgage Loan for the Newtons

Farrah and Sam Newton, both in their early thirties, have been married for five years. Sam has an accounting degree and is presently employed as a senior cost accountant at an annual salary of $39,000. The Newtons have two children, ages 2 and 4. At present, they are renting a duplex but wish to buy a home in the suburbs of their rapidly developing city. They have decided that they can afford a $90,000 house and hope to find one with the features they desire in a good neighborhood.

The insurance costs on such a home are expected to be $500 per year, taxes are expected to be $1,000 per year, and annual utility bills are estimated at $1,200—an increase of $500 over those they pay in the duplex. The Newtons are considering financing their home with a fixed-rate, 30-year, 11½ percent mortgage; also, the lender charges 2 points on mortgages with 20 percent down and 3 points if less than 20 percent is put down (the S&L with which the Newtons will deal requires a minimum of 10 percent down). Other closing costs are estimated at 5 percent on the purchase price of the home. Because of their excellent credit record, the lender will probably be willing to let the Newton's monthly mortgage payments equal as much as 28 percent of their monthly gross income. Over the last four years, the Newtons have been saving for the purchase of a home and how have $18,000 in their savings account.

Questions

1. How much would the Newtons have to put down if the lender required a minimum 20 percent down payment? Could they afford it?
2. Given the Newtons want to put only $10,000 down, how much would closing costs be? Considering only principal and interest, how much would their monthly mortgage payments be? Would they qualify for a loan using a 28 percent affordability ratio?
3. Using a $10,000 down payment on a $90,000 home, what would the Newtons' loan-to-value ratio be? Calculate the monthly mortgage payments on a PITI basis.
4. What recommendations would you make to the Newtons? Explain.

◲ 6.2 Julie's Rent-or-Buy Decision

Julie Brown is a single career woman in her late twenties. She currently rents an apartment in the fashionable part of town for $920 a month. After considerable deliberation, she is seriously considering the purchase of a luxury condominium for $125,000. She intends to put 20 percent down and expects that closing costs will amount to another $5,000; an S&L has agreed to lend her money at the fixed rate of 10 percent on a 15-year mortgage. Julie would have to pay an annual condominium owner's insurance premium of $600 and property taxes of $1,200 a year (she is presently paying renter's insurance of $550 per year). In addition, she estimates that annual maintenance and upkeep expenses will be about .5 percent of the price of her condo (which includes a $30 monthly fee to the property owners' association). Julie's income puts her in the 28 percent tax bracket (she itemizes her deductions on her tax returns), and she earns an after-tax rate of return on her investments of around 6 percent.

Questions

1. Given the information provided above, evaluate and compare Julie's alternatives of remaining in the apartment or purchasing the condo.
2. Working with a friend who is a realtor, Julie has learned that luxury condos like the one she is thinking of buying are appreciating in value at the rate of 5 percent a year and are expected to continue doing so. Would such information affect the rent-or-buy decision made in Question 1: Explain.
3. Rework your calculations assuming that Julie does not itemize her deductions on her tax return but instead takes the standard deduction. Would that affect the rent-or-buy decision made in Question 1? Explain.
4. Discuss any nonquantitative factors that should be considered when making a rent-or-buy decision.
5. Which alternative would you recommend for Julie in light of your analysis?

FOR MORE INFORMATION

General Information Articles

Eisenberg, Richard, "Starter Home: Your First Step Is the Biggest," *Money,* June 1987, pp. 72–82.

Giese, William, "How to Buy the House You Want," *Changing Times,* May 1988, pp. 38–46.

McCormally, Kevin, "Best Ways to Pay for Your New Car," *Changing Times,* October 1988, pp. 93–96.

McGrath, Ann, and Rachel Wilder, "Affording the Unaffordable," *U.S. News & World Report,* September 19, 1988, pp. 62–71.

"Should You Lease Your Next Car?" *Consumer Reports,* April 1988, pp. 115–119.

Tai, Pauline, "Getting Past Today's Monster Mortgage Choices," *Money,* April 1988, pp. 115–119.

Government Documents and Other Publications

The Car Book by Jack Gillis (New York: Harper & Row Publishers, Inc., annual).

Real Estate Principles and Practices, 11th edition by Alfred A. Ring and Jerome Dasso (Englewood Cliffs, NJ: Prentice-Hall, Inc., 1989).

Top Dollar for Your Property by James Lumley (New York: John Wiley & Sons, Inc., 1988).

Your Housing Dollar (Prospect Heights, IL: Money Management Institute of Household Financial Services, 1987); 2700 Sanders Road; Prospect Heights, IL 60070.

1. Evaluate the amount of Mark and Ana's liquid assets. According to the general consensus of financial experts, do they currently have enough assets in a highly liquid form? If not, how much should be added to their liquid assets in order to meet the minimum requirements?

Mark and Ana have just received their July bank statement for their NOW account. It contains the following information:

—ending balance	$1,476.39
—service charge	5.00
—interest earned	4.88

Their checkbook ledger shows a final balance of $1,245.12 and lists the following checks and ATM transactions for the period:

Check #	Amount	Check #	Amount	ATM Transaction	Amount
789	$450.00	806	$ 38.72	Deposit	$1,515.00
790	276.52	807	147.85	Withdrawal	50.00
791	46.13	808	165.99	Deposit	1,703.00
793	151.62	809	34.16	Withdrawal	75.00
794	56.61	810	67.33	Withdrawal	50.00
795	122.66	811	168.88	Withdrawal	125.00
796	68.00			Withdrawal	50.00
798	125.00			Withdrawal	100.00
799	50.00			Withdrawal	75.00
800	21.00			Deposit	214.66
801	52.00				
802	50.00				
803	73.98				

The bank statement does not list check numbers 802, 808, and 811, nor does it include the $214.66 ATM deposit; therefore, you should consider them outstanding.

2. Reconcile Mark and Ana's July bank statement. What adjustments, if any, do Mark and Ana need to make in their checkbook ledger?

Mark and Ana currently maintain their checking account at Mark's place of employment, First Federal Savings. However, Mark would feel more comfortable if the account were at a different financial institution. Mark and Ana are investigating the following two NOW accounts. Both are at institutions that are convenient and are covered by federal deposit insurance.

United Savings and Loan
▪ no service charge for accounts maintaining a minimum daily balance of $800
▪ monthly service charge of $7 plus $.15 a check if minimum daily balance falls below $800
▪ 6.5 percent (annual percentage rate) interest is paid monthly on the minimum daily balance
▪ ATM fee of $.50 per deposit and withdrawal
▪ stop payment fee of $15.00
▪ insufficient fund fee of $15.00

Milford National Bank
▪ no service charge for accounts maintaining a minimum daily balance of $1,000
▪ monthly service charge of $10 plus $.10 a check if minimum daily balance falls below $1,000
▪ 5 percent (annual percentage rate) interest is paid monthly on the average daily balance

- ATM fee of $.25 per deposit and withdrawal
- stop payment fee of $10.00
- insufficient fund fee of $15.00

Mark and Ana report that in an average month they write 20 checks and make 10 ATM transactions. They maintain an average daily balance in their checking account of $1,500, but the minimum daily balance often falls to $1,100. They have never used the stop-payment service, nor have they bounced a check.

3. Using the preceding information, compare the positive and the negative aspects of these two accounts. How much interest would they earn in a month with each account? Which one would you recommend for Mark and Ana?

4. Mark and Ana are wanting to start a regular savings program to help them achieve several goals. Assuming they want to make monthly contributions, what type of account would you recommend for:

   - their emergency fund
   - the buffer account for their first child's birth

5. If Mark and Ana can afford to contribute a total of $2,000 each year to a 401(k) retirement account earning 8 percent compounded annually, how much will they have accumulated in 35 years when they want to retire? How much more would they have if they can earn 10 percent rather than 8 percent?

One of Mark and Ana's short-term goals is to buy a condominium as soon as possible. They have been condo hunting for several months and have found a home they like that costs $90,000. They plan to make a down payment of $28,250 with Mark's grandmother contributing $25,000 of the $28,250.. They have also shopped for home mortgages and narrowed their choices to the following:

30-year fixed-rate mortgage	**30-year adjustable-rate mortgage**
10.5% interest with 2 points other closing costs of $3,000 monthly payments	8.0% interest with 1.5 points other closing costs of $3,250 1.5% annual interest rate cap 5.0% overall interest rate cap monthly payments

Mark and Anna expect to have the following costs associated with the purchase and maintenance of the condo:

- Property taxes of 1.0% of the value
- Homeowners insurance of $200 for personal property and liability coverage
- Maintenance of 1.5% of the value (on a condo this will include insurance on the structure)

They expect that the condo will appreciate in value 5 percent a year, and that the after-tax cost of interest lost on the front-end costs (down payment, points, and other closing costs) is 6 percent.

6. Compare and evaluate the two mortgages for Mark and Ana. What would be the front-end costs and the monthly payments for principal and interest on each of these mortgages? How much could the monthly payments for principal and interest go up on the adjustable-rate mortgage? Keeping in mind their financial situation and risk tolerances, which mortgage would you recommend for Mark and Ana? Why?

7. Complete a rent-or-buy analysis for Mark and Ana assuming they would buy his condo using the fixed-rate mortgage. Use the rental information from the

original case and their marginal tax rate calculated in Part One, Question 10. Compare the total cost of renting versus buying.

8. Will Mark and Ana be able to qualify for the fixed rate mortgage if the lender applies the following two affordability ratios:

- Monthly mortgage payment cannot exceed 30 percent of the borrower's monthly before-tax income.
- Total monthly installment-loan payments cannot exceed 36 percent of monthly before-tax income?

In figuring if Mark and Ana will qualify, consider all of their income except the sale of securities. Also consider the minimum required payments for the revolving credit ($316) rather than the higher amount needed to pay off this debt within a year. The amount of their monthly payment will be the sum of the following:

- Monthly payment for principal and interest
- One-twelfth of their annual property taxes
- One-twelfth of their homeowners insurance premium

9. Assume that Mark and Ana buy the condo March 1, 1990, using the fixed-rate mortgage. They sell their Apple Computer stock for $37.75 a share and their General Motors stock for $85.50 to pay the front-end costs not covered by Mark's grandmother's $25,000 gift. The broker's commissions on the sale are $205, and the remaining funds are added to their money market account. Revise the Williams' balance sheet to reflect the changes in their assets and liabilities. Why did their net worth change?

10. Revise Mark and Ana's budget to reflect any changes in income and expenditures caused/required by the condo purchase. Don't forget maintenance costs as well as property taxes and homeowners insurance.

P A R T III

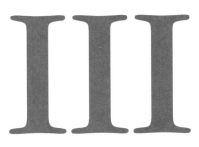

Managing Credit

can negotiate
- documentation fee (not required by law to pay)   [1425 passes
      pure profit to the car dealer   requires doc fee

  buyer protection, rust proofing - warranties

  credit life ins.   accident/health ins - must be off   ) expensive
     35% profit   45% profit   14-30 days

     beneficiary is the bank - not spouse
     don't have to buy the ins. to get a loan

Contracts
don't sign altered contract

only required to sign once - extra signatures mean extra things

loans - dealer reserve
  shop yourself   finance co. - highest rate
    credit

  pre-computed Rule 18   pay $\checkmark$ up front (74%)
\# simple interest - only pay $\checkmark$ for time you use the loan

rebate usually wins - unless use it as trade in

no balloon fee

Credit Cards   no 900# cards
    other states can be higher $\checkmark$ rate
  how they calculate the $\checkmark$ rate:
      average daily balance
    - adjusted rate
      previous month balance   make major purchase 1st day after
have a grace period   closing date

CHAPTER 7

Borrowing on Open Account

Financial Facts or Fantasies

Are the following statements financial facts (true) or fantasies (false)?

- One of the benefits of using credit is that it allows you to purchase expensive goods and services while spreading the payment for them over time.
- It's a good idea to consult your creditors immediately if, for some reason, you can't make payments as agreed.
- Excluding mortgage payments, most families will have little or no credit problems so long as they limit their monthly credit payments to 25 to 30 percent of their monthly take-home pay.
- When you make application for credit, most big lenders will contact the local credit bureau and let them decide whether or not you should receive the credit.
- Credit card issuers are required by truth-in-lending laws to use the average daily balance in your account when computing the amount of finance charges you'll have to pay.
- You use a check rather than a credit card to obtain funds from an unsecured personal line of credit.

Just say "Charge it." And with those two words, and a little piece of plastic, you can buy gas for your car, have a gourmet meal at an expensive restaurant, or furnish an apartment. Credit, in fact, has become a common part of our everyday life and we, as consumers, use it in one form or another to purchase just about every type of good or service imaginable. Consider Dave Roberts, a young construction foreman and father of two; he recently used a revolving line of credit that he has at his bank to buy a new car. Or Sara Thomas, who although only a junior in college, has a bank credit card with a $500 line of credit that she uses on those occasions when she's short of cash. Indeed, because of the ready availability and widespread use of credit, our economy is often called a "credit economy." And for good reason: by year-end 1988, individuals in this country had amassed over $650 billion in consumer debt—and that *excludes* home mortgages. There's no doubt that credit is a convenient way to make transactions; but when misused, the "buy now—pay later" attitude can lead to some real problems—even bankruptcy! *Managing credit wisely is a vital part of personal financial planning.*

THE BASIC CONCEPTS OF CREDIT

> Consumer credit is a convenient and effective way to purchase a variety of goods and services; results can be disastrous, however, if the use of credit is not kept to a manageable level. Stop for a moment to think of the ways you would use consumer credit. What steps would you take to make sure your use of credit doesn't get out of hand?

Consumer credit is important in the personal financial planning process because of the impact that it can have on (1) the attainment of financial goals, and (2) cash budgets. For one thing, various forms of consumer credit can help you reach your objectives by enabling you to acquire some of the more expensive items in a systematic fashion, and without throwing your whole budget into disarray. But there's another side to consumer credit: It has to be paid back! And unless it's used intelligently, debt repayment loads can quickly turn an otherwise orderly budget into a budgetary nightmare. So, really, the issue is one of moderation and affordability.

The fact is in our economy today, consumers, businesses, and governments alike rely on the widespread use of credit to make transactions. Without credit, businesses could not supply the goods and services needed to satisfy consumer demand. The availability of credit to businesses also provides for higher levels of employment and helps raise our overall standard of living. Local, state, and federal governments use borrowing to implement various projects and programs that result not only in an increased standard of living but in additional employment opportunities as well. Clearly, borrowing helps fuel our economy and enhance the overall quality of our lives. Consequently, consumers in a credit economy need to know how to establish credit and how to avoid the dangers of using it improperly.

Why Borrow?

People typically use credit as a way to pay for goods and services that cost more than their current re-

sources can cover. This is particularly true for people in the 25-to-44 age group, who in many cases have not had time to accumulate the liquid assets required to pay cash outright for major purchases and expenditures. As people begin to approach their mid-forties, their savings and investments start to build up, and their debt loads, in turn, tend to decline.

The Principal Reasons for Borrowing. Most people do not pay cash for *large outlays,* such as for the purchase of houses and cars; rather, they borrow a portion of the purchase price and then repay the loan on some scheduled basis. In this way, people can obtain the immediate use of an expensive asset without having to fully pay for it for many years. By spreading the payments for them over time, big-ticket transactions are made more affordable. Another reason people sometimes borrow is to meet a *financial emergency*—for example, to cover living expenses and make payments on loans during a period of unemployment, or to purchase plane tickets in order to visit a sick relative. As indicated in Chapter 5, however, use of savings (not credit) is the ideal way to provide for financial emergencies.

An increasingly common motive for borrowing is *convenience.* Merchants as well as banks have made available a variety of charge accounts and credit cards that allow consumers to charge the purchase of all sorts of goods and services. Today just about anything can be charged to a credit card—from gas and oil or clothes and stereos to doctor and dental bills and even college tuition. Further, in a lot of places, it is far easier to use a credit card than to write a check (in restaurants, for instance). And by purchasing with a credit card, the consumer receives a permanent, itemized record of the transaction that can be used for budgetary purposes (to keep track of actual versus budgeted expenditures). Although in many cases no interest is levied on such transactions (at least initially), these credit card purchases are still a form of borrowing, since payment is not made at the time of the transaction.

Finally, borrowing is also done for *investment* purposes. As we'll see in Chapters 13 and 14, it's relatively easy for an investor to partially finance the purchase of many different kinds of securities and investment vehicles with borrowed funds.

EXHIBIT 7.1

Some Credit Danger Signs

If one or more of these signs exist, you should take them as an indication that it is time to proceed with caution in your credit spending. Revise and update your spending patterns, cut back on the use of credit, and be alert for other signs of overspending.

You may be headed for serious trouble if:

- You are borrowing just to meet normal living expenses.
- You can barely make the minimum required payments on bills.
- You are using one form of credit, such as a line of credit or a debt-consolidation loan, to make payments on other debt.
- You are using more than 20 percent of your take-home income to pay credit card bills and personal loans (excluding mortgage payments).
- Your revolving cards are charged to the limit.
- Your checks are bouncing.
- You have no cash reserve.
- You are so far behind on credit payments that collection agencies are after you.

One of the benefits of using credit is that it allows you to purchase expensive goods and services while spreading the payment for them over time. **Fact:** One of the major benefits of buying on credit is that expensive purchases are made more affordable because the consumer is able to pay for them systematically over time.

Improper Uses of Credit

Many people use consumer credit to live beyond their means. Overspending is the biggest danger in borrowing, especially because it is so easy to do. Once hooked on "plastic," people may use their credit cards to make even routine purchases and often do not realize they have overextended themselves until it is too late. To avoid the possibility of future repayment shock, you should keep in mind the types of transactions for which it would be improper to (routinely, at least) use credit: (1) to meet basic living expenses; (2) to make impulse purchases, especially expensive ones; and (3) to purchase nondurable (short-lived) goods and services. Except in those situations where credit cards are used only occasionally for the sake of convenience (such as for gasoline and entertainment) and/or payments on recurring credit purchases are built into the monthly budget, a good rule to remember when considering the use of credit is that *the product purchased on credit should outlive the payments*.

Unfortunately, people who overspend eventually arrive at the point where they must choose to either become delinquent in their payments or sacrifice necessities, such as food and clothing. If payment obligations are not met, the consequences are likely to be a damaged credit rating, lawsuits, or even personal bankruptcy. Exhibit 7.1 lists some common signals that indicate it may be time to stop buying on credit. Ignoring such clear signs that you are overspending can only lead to more serious problems.

Establishing Credit

The willingness of lenders to extend credit depends on their assessment of your creditworthiness—your ability to repay the debt on a timely basis. They look at a number of factors in making this decision, such as your present earnings and net worth. Equally important, they look at your current debt position and your credit history. Thus, it's worth your while to do what you can to build a strong credit rating.

First Steps in Establishing Credit. First, open checking and savings accounts. These signal stability to lenders and also indicate that you handle your financial affairs in a businesslike fashion. Second, use credit—open one or two charge accounts and use them periodically, even if you prefer paying cash. For example, get a credit card from a major oil company, and charge your gas and oil. You might pay slightly higher prices for these products, but you will partially offset them by having the use of your money for a longer period of time. In the process, you will become identified as a reliable credit customer. Third, obtain a small loan, even if you don't need one. If you don't actually need the money, put it in a liquid investment, such as a money market account or certificate of deposit. The interest you earn should offset most of the interest expense on the loan; you can view the difference as a cost of building good credit. (It goes without saying that you should repay the loan promptly, perhaps even ahead of schedule, to minimize the difference in interest rates.) Keep in mind, your ability to obtain a large loan in the future will depend in part on how you managed smaller loans in the past.

Build a Strong Credit History.   From a financial perspective, maintaining a strong credit history is just as important as developing a solid employment record! Don't take credit lightly, and don't assume that once you get the loan or receive the credit card the toughest part is over. It's not. Getting the credit is just the first step; servicing it (i.e., making payments) in a prompt and timely fashion—month in and month out—is the really tough part of the consumer credit process. And in many respects, it's the most important element of consumer credit, as it determines you creditworthiness. By using credit wisely and repaying it on time, you're establishing a *credit history* that tells lenders you're a dependable, reliable, and responsible borrower.

The consumer credit industry keeps very close tabs on your credit and your past payment performance (more on this when we discuss *credit bureaus* later in the chapter). So the better job you do in being a responsible borrower, the easier it's going to be for you to get credit when and where you want it. The best way to build up a strong credit history and maintain your creditworthiness is to make payments *on time,* and to do so *consistently,* month after month. Being late occasionally—say, two or three times a year—might label you a "late payer." When you take on credit, you have an *obligation* to live up to the terms of the loan, including how and when the credit will be repaid.

If you foresee difficulty in meeting a monthly payment, let the lender know and usually some sort of arrangements can be made to help you through the situation. This is especially true with installment loans that require fixed monthly payments. If you

have one or two of these loans and, for one reason or another, you encounter a month that's going to be really tight, the first thing you should try to do is get an extension on your loan. Don't just skip a payment, because that's going to put your account into a *late status until you make up the missed payment*—in other words, until you make a *double* payment, your account/loan will remain in a late status, subject to a monthly late penalty. The alternative of trying to work out an extension with your lender obviously makes a lot more sense. Here's what you do: explain the situation to the loan officer and ask for an extension of one (or two) months on your loan. In most cases, so long as this hasn't occurred too often, the extension is almost automatically granted. The maturity of the loan is formally extended for a month (or two) and the extra interest of carrying the loan for another month (or two) is either added to the loan balance or, more commonly, paid at the time the extension is granted (such an extension fee generally amounts to a small fraction of the normal monthly payment). Then, in a month (or two), you pick up where you left off and resume your normal monthly payments on the loan. This is the most sensible way of making it through those rough times since it doesn't harm your credit record. Just don't do it too often.

To summarize, here are some ways to build a strong credit history:

- Use credit only when you can afford it and only when the repayment schedule fits comfortably into the family budget—in short, don't overextend yourself.
- Fulfill all the terms of the credit.
- Be *consistent* in making payments *promptly.*
- Consult creditors immediately if you cannot meet payments as agreed.
- Be truthful when applying for credit. Lies are not likely to go undetected.

It's a good idea to consult your creditors immediately if, for some reason, you can't make payments as agreed. **Fact:** Let the lenders know and they'll often try to help you out by giving you a credit extension. This is one of the smartest things you can do to build a sound credit history; however, except for those occasional tight spots, it's important to try to make credit payments consistently and on time!

The Special Credit Problems of Women. Credit limitations for women are diminishing rapidly. Nevertheless, some—especially those who are divorced or widowed—still have difficulty getting credit because they do not have a *credit history of their own*. The following steps can help overcome this problem.

First, use your own name when filing a credit application. Do not use a social title, such as Mrs. Thomas Watkins; instead, use your legal name. In marriage, you have your choice of several legal names; for example, if your maiden name is Joan Brown and you take your husband's name of Watkins, you can choose Joan Watkins or Joan Brown Watkins. By selecting a legal name and *using it consistently,* you build your own credit history.

Second, make sure that information reported to the credit bureau is in your name as well as your husband's. This will have been done automatically since June 1977, but account activity prior to then may be in your husband's name only.

Third, when you marry you may wish to retain a credit file separate from your husband's, particularly if you have already established a good credit rating. You should then notify creditors of your name change and of your intention to maintain your own file.

How Much Credit Can You Stand? Sound financial planning dictates that if you are going to use credit, you should have a good idea of how much you can comfortably tolerate. The easiest way to avoid repayment problems and ensure that your borrowing will not place an undue strain on your monthly budget is to *limit the use of credit to your ability to repay the debt!* In this regard, a useful *credit guideline* (and one that is widely used by lenders) is to make sure your monthly repayment burden does not exceed 20 percent of your monthly *take-home pay.* Most experts regard the 20 percent figure as the *maximum* debt burden and strongly recommend debt ratios closer to 10 to 15 percent. Note that the monthly repayment burden here is *exclusive* of your monthly mortgage obligation.

To illustrate, consider an individual who takes home $1,500 a month. Using a 20 percent ratio, she should have monthly consumer credit payments of no more than $300—that is, $1,500 × .20 = $300. This is the maximum amount of her monthly dis-

posable income that she should use to pay off both personal loans and other forms of consumer credit (such as credit cards and revolving lines of credit). This, of course, is not the maximum amount of consumer credit this person can have outstanding—in fact, her total consumer indebtedness can, and likely would, be considerably larger. The key factor is that with her income level, *her payments on this type of debt* should not exceed $300 a month. (Caution: This is not to say that credit terms should be lengthened just to accommodate this guideline; rather, in all cases, it is assumed that standard credit terms apply.)

Exhibit 7.2 provides a summary of low (10 percent), manageable (15 percent), and maximum (20 percent) monthly credit payments for a number of income levels. Obviously, the closer your total monthly payments are to your desired debt safety ratio, the less future borrowing you can undertake. Conversely, *the lower the debt safety ratio, the better shape you're in, creditwise, and the easier it will be for you to service your outstanding consumer debt.* To find your **debt safety ratio**, simply use the following formula:

$$\text{Debt safety ratio} = \frac{\text{Total monthly consumer credit payments}}{\text{Monthly take-home pay}}$$

Thus, if you take home $1,360 a month and make total payments of $180 a month on outstanding consumer credit, you will have a debt safety ratio of $180/$1,360 = 13 percent, which is well within the manageable range.

Excluding mortgage payments, most families will have little or no credit problems so long as they limit their monthly credit payments to 25 to 30 percent of their monthly take home pay. **Fantasy:** Most experts suggest that you keep your monthly debt repayment burden, excluding mortgage payments, to 20 percent or less of your take-home pay. Letting it get as high as 25 to 30 percent can lead to serious credit problems.

debt safety ratio
The proportion of total monthly consumer credit obligations to monthly take-home pay.

EXHIBIT 7.2

Alternative Consumer Credit Guidelines Based on Ability to Repay

Using this credit guideline, the amount of consumer credit you should have outstanding depends on the monthly payment you can afford to make.

Monthly Take-Home Pay	Monthly Consumer Credit Payments		
	Low Debt Safety Ratio (10%)	Manageable Debt Safety Ratio (15%)	Maximum Debt Safety Ratio (20%)
$ 500	$ 50	$ 75	$100
750	75	112	150
1,000	100	150	200
1,250	125	188	250
1,500	150	225	300
2,000	200	300	400
2,500	250	375	500
3,000	300	450	600

OBTAINING CREDIT THROUGH AN OPEN ACCOUNT

In open account credit, the consumer obtains a revolving line of credit—which may or may not involve the use of a credit card. What types of open account credit would be most appealing to you? Take a minute to think about this question before reading on.

Open account credit is a form of credit extended to a consumer in advance of any transactions. Typically, a retail outlet or bank agrees to allow the consumer to buy or borrow up to a specified amount on open account. Credit is extended as long as the consumer does not exceed the established **credit limit**, and makes payments in accordance with the specified terms. Open account credit issued by a retail outlet, such as a department store or oil firm, is usually applicable only in that establishment or one of its locations. In contrast, open account credit issued by banks, such as *MasterCard* and *Visa* accounts, can be used to make purchases at a wide variety of businesses. In the remainder of this chapter, we will direct our attention to various characteristics and types of open account credit; in Chapter 8, we will look at various forms of single-payment and installment loans.

An Illustration of Open Account Credit

Having open account credit is a lot like having your own personal line of credit—it's there when you need it. But unlike most other forms of debt, consumers who use open account credit can generally avoid paying interest charges *if they promptly pay the full amount of the account balance.* For example, assume that in a given month you charge $75.58 worth of purchases on an open account at a department store. Sometime within the next month or so, you will receive a **credit statement** from the store that summarizes recent transactions on your account. In particular, the statement will show any unpaid balances (which is the amount of credit that was outstanding at the beginning of the month and should not be confused with past-due, or late, payments) along with a list of new charges made during the past month, any finance charges (interest) on the unpaid balance, the preceding period's payment, any other credits (such as those for returns), and the new balance.

A typical consumer credit statement is shown in Exhibit 7.3. Notice that in addition to the list of transactions (there was one payment, followed by four purchases), the *previous balance* (of $182) is shown toward the bottom of the statement. This represents the *unpaid* account balance at the end of the previous billing period; as such, it also represents the credit balance in the account at the start of the current billing period. The charges made during the current month are then added to this unpaid balance: thus, a total of $75.58 in charges incurred during the current period is added to the $182 previous account balance. Also added to the previous balance are any interest charges applicable to the account; in this case, there was a finance charge of $2.49. (A detailed discussion of how finance charges are determined is presented later in this chapter.) Finally, any payments received and other credits are subtracted from the balance to arrive at the new account balance. The $25 payment is the only deduction shown in Exhibit 7.3. Apparently, no other credits were received during the month. The resulting new balance on the account is $235.07.

Making Minimum Monthly Payments. Most open accounts do not require payment of the entire new balance, but they generally do impose some type of **minimum monthly payment**, usually a specified percentage of the new balance. For example, the statement in Exhibit 7.3 indicates that a minimum payment of $25 is required. The back side of the statement (shown as the bottom half of Exhibit 7.3) explains the method of calculating this minimum payment; here it is figured as 10 percent of the new balance ($235.07) adjusted to the next highest increment of $5 ($25). Of course, any past-due payment will be added to this amount. In our example, as long as the $25 minimum payment is made before next month's billing date (December 10, 1989), the customer's credit privileges will not be jeopardized.

Types of Open Account Credit

Open account credit generally is available from two broadly defined sources: (1) financial institutions and (2) retail stores/merchants. *Financial institutions* issue general-purpose credit cards as well as secured and unsecured revolving lines of credit and overdraft protection lines. Commercial banks have long been a major provider of consumer credit; and since deregulation, so have S&Ls and, to a lesser extent, credit unions, savings banks, and consumer finance companies. Deregulation has also brought other financial institutions into this market—most notably, the major stockbrokerage firms and a growing list of commercial banks that have gone *interstate* to market their credit cards and other consumer credit products across the country. *Retail stores and merchants* make up the other major source of open account credit. They provide credit chiefly as a way of financing the sales of their products. Their principal forms of credit include open charge accounts and credit cards.

Of the various *types* of open account credit, the two biggest are retail charge cards and bank credit cards; together, there are several hundred million of these cards outstanding today. **Retail charge cards** are issued by department stores, oil companies, drug and specialty store chains, hotels, airlines, car rental agencies, and so on. They allow consumers to use prearranged lines of credit to purchase the goods and services sold by the issuing

---

open account credit
A form of credit extended to a consumer in advance of any transaction; type of credit that accompanies charge accounts and credit cards.

credit limit
A specified amount beyond which a customer may not borrow or purchase on credit.

credit statement
A monthly statement that summarizes the transactions in a consumer credit account; includes a record of new charges, credits and payments, any interest charged, and the minimum monthly payment required on the account.

minimum monthly payment
In open account credit, a minimum specified percentage of the new account balance that must be paid in order to remain current.

retail charge card
A type of credit card issued by retailers, airlines, and so on, that allows customers to charge goods and services up to a preestablished amount.

EXHIBIT 7.3

An Open Account Credit Statement

The monthly credit statement provides a summary of the various transactions in an account, including purchases, finance charges (if any), payments, and other credits.

DEPARTMENT NUMBER	DATES MONTH	DATES DAY	TRANSACTION DESCRIPTION	CHARGES	CREDITS
99	10	22	PAYMENT		25.00
265	10	25	GLOVES	4.98	
64	10	25	SKIRTLINER PT	10.00	
111	11	09	MEN'S SHOES	45.20	
184	11	09	TOILETRIES	15.40	

TO YOUR PREVIOUS BALANCE	WE ADDED YOUR CHARGES	WE ADDED YOUR FINANCE CHARGES	WE DEDUCTED PAYMENTS	WE DEDUCTED OTHER CREDITS	THIS IS YOUR NEW BALANCE
$ 182.00	$ 75.58	$ 2.49	$ 25.00	$	$ 235.07

Account Number	Billing Dates This Month	Next Month	Finance Charge 1½% (Annual Percentage Rate 18%) Computed On Avg. Daily Balance Of	Minimum Amount To Send
	11-10-89	12-10-89	$ 165.87	$ 25.00

*To Avoid Additional Finance Charges, Pay New Balance Before Billing Date Next Month. See Reverse Side For Explanation Of Finance Charges.

EXPLANATION OF FINANCE CHARGES

If the "NEW BALANCE" is received by the "BILLING DATE NEXT MONTH", no additional FINANCE CHARGE is imposed.

If a FINANCE CHARGE is shown, it is computed as follows:
1½% of the AVERAGE DAILY BALANCE as shown on the front hereof; this being an ANNUAL PERCENTAGE RATE of 18%. When the AVERAGE DAILY BALANCE for a monthly billing period is $33.33, or less, the FINANCE CHARGE for that monthly billing period will be 50¢.

The AVERAGE DAILY BALANCE is determined by dividing the sum of the balances outstanding for each day of the monthly billing period by the number of days in the monthly billing period. The balance outstanding each day of the monthly billing period is determined by subtracting all payments and credits (excepting credits for merchandise purchased and returned within the same monthly billing period) from the previous day's balance, excluding any purchases added to the account during the monthly billing period and excluding any unpaid finance charges.

MINIMUM PAYMENT

A minimum payment of one-tenth (1/10) of the unpaid balance (adjusted to the next highest increment of $5.00) appearing on each monthly billing statement (but not less than $10.00 monthly) PLUS any amount which is past due from previous months must be paid by the "BILLING DATE NEXT MONTH" as shown on the front hereof.

Source: Typical major department store.

firm. **Bank credit cards**, in contrast, are issued by commercial banks and other financial institutions—Visa and MasterCard are the two dominant types. These cards allow their holders to charge purchases at thousands of stores, restaurants, gas stations, and other establishments. In addition, bank credit cards can be used to obtain **cash advances** (loans of money on which interest begins to accrue immediately) without having to make any formal application. While these are the two major types of open account credit—both of which will be examined in more detail later in the chapter—there are several other kinds of credit that you should be aware of, including 30-day charge accounts, travel and entertainment cards, prestige cards, affinity cards, and revolving lines of credit.

30-Day Charge Account. Commonly offered by certain types of businesses for the general convenience of their customers, the **30-day**, or **regular, charge account** requires the customer to pay the full amount billed within 10 to 20 days after the billing date. If payment is made within the specified period, no interest is charged; if received after the due date, however, an interest penalty is usually tacked on to the account balance. These accounts generally do not involve the use of a charge card. They are typically offered by gas and electric companies, telephone companies, doctors and dentists, drugstores, and repair services.

Travel and Entertainment Cards. **Travel and entertainment (T&E) cards** are similar to bank credit cards in that they enable holders to charge purchases at a variety of locations. Businesses willing to accept these cards typically are travel- and entertainment-related—hotels, motels, airlines, and restaurants. However, such cards are being increasingly accepted at other locations, such as upscale department, clothing, and jewelry stores. In order to obtain one, the applicant must pay an annual fee of up to $300 just for the privilege of using it. In sharp contrast to retail and bank credit cards, however, most T&E cards do *not* carry an extended line of credit; instead, the outstanding balances must be *paid in full* each month for the account to remain current. *American Express* is the biggest issuer of this type of card (over 20 million cardholders), followed by *Diners Club* (5 million) and *Carte Blanche* (around half a million). However, these

numbers are minute compared to the number of bank credit cards outstanding: there are over 125 million Visa cards and another 100 million or so MasterCards in circulation.

American Express has recently added a new twist to this segment of the market by introducing the *Optima* card. Like the regular American Express card, the Optima is aimed at affluent cardholders who want not only convenience, but also a regular revolving charge account. Since the Optima card's outstanding balance need not be paid in full each month, it is, for all practical purposes, just another type of *bank credit card!*

Prestige Cards. Not all credit cards are created alike! Some offer more advantages and features than others. **Prestige cards** offer higher credit limits (up to $100,000 or more), worldwide travel services, and other features meant to attract the upscale cardholder. Such cards impose higher credit standards for qualification, along with higher

---

bank credit card
A credit card issued by a bank or other financial institution that allows the holder to charge purchases at any establishment that accepts it; can also be used to obtain cash advances.

cash advance
A loan that can be obtained by a bank credit cardholder at any participating bank or financial institution; begins to accrue interest immediately and requires no formal application.

30-day (regular) charge account
A charge account that requires customers to pay the full amount billed within 10 to 20 days after the billing date.

travel and entertainment (T&E) card
A credit card, such as American Express, Diners Club, Carte Blanche, and Optima, that typically is accepted by travel- and entertainment-related establishments and upscale department and specialty stores; all these cards except Optima require the holder to pay current balances *in full*.

prestige card
A type of bank or T&E card that offers higher credit limits, has stricter requirements for qualification, and generally offers more features than its "regular" counterpart.

EXHIBIT 7.4

Major Credit Card Features

There are some important differences among the major credit cards, including the annual fee, maximum amount of credit available, required minimum monthly payment, and number of outlets that accept the card.

	Bank Cards					
	MasterCard[a]	Gold MasterCard[a]	VISA[a]	Premier VISA[2]	Discover Card	American Express Optima
Annual fee	$0–$75, as set by issuing bank	$0–$75, as set by issuing bank	$0–$75, as set by issuing bank	$0–$75, as set by issuing bank	$0–$15[b]	$15
Criteria	Set by issuing bank	Set by issuing bank	Set by issuing bank	Set by issuing bank	Varies by state	Existing holders of AMEX Green, Gold, or Platinum for at least one year
Minimum credit	None	$5,000	None	$5,000	$1,000	None
Maximum credit	$10,000	$50,000	$10,000	$50,000	None	None
Minimum payment	Bank sets according to state regulations; expressed as a percentage of amount owed				Percentage of amount owed	Set by state law; expressed as percentage of amount owed
Individual receipts returned	No	No	No	No	No	Yes
Cash machine link	Yes	Yes	Yes	Yes	Yes	Yes
Cash advances available	Yes	Yes	Yes	Yes	Yes	Yes
Number of outlets that accept card	4,300,000 (worldwide)		4,400,000 (worldwide)		800,000	2,500,000 worldwide

	T&E Cards				
	American Express (Green)	American Express (Gold)	American Express (Platinum)	Citicorp Diner's Club	Citicorp Carte Blanche
Annual fee	$55	$75	$300	$55	$40
Criteria	Minimum income of $15,000	Minimum income of $20,000	Minimum charged by holder must be $10,000 annually	Minimum income of at least $25,000	Minimum income of at least $18,000
Minimum credit	None	$10,000	$10,000	None	None
Maximum credit	None	None	None	None	None
Minimum payment	Balance	Balance	Balance	Balance	Balance
Individual receipts returned	Yes	Yes	Yes	Only upon request	Only upon request
Cash machine link	Yes (bank checking)	Yes	Yes	Yes	No
Cash advances available	No	Yes	Yes	Only in foreign countries	No
Number of outlets that accept card	2,500,000 worldwide			N/A	N/A

[a]Data for MasterCard and VISA are meant to reflect the features that are typically found on the vast majority of these cards; unfortunately, more exact information is not available, as the cards are issued by thousands of financial institutions worldwide, and these institutions are pretty much free to set their own standards.

[b]North Carolina and Wisconsin, in 1988, were the only states to charge a $15 annual fee on Discover Card users.

annual fees. MasterCard, Visa, American Express, and Optima all offer prestige cards: MasterCard has its *Gold* MasterCard, Visa its *Premiere* card, and American Express and American Express Optima each have two prestige cards—the *Gold* card and, the "ultimate" in credit cards, the *Platinum* card, which is available by invitation only.

Exhibit 7.4 (on facing page) compares some of the major features of different bank and T&E cards. Clearly, many of these cards are almost fully interchangeable, since they perform many of the same functions. Together these cards account for about 70 percent of all credit card activity, the balance of transactions being made with retail charge cards.

Affinity Cards. Credit cards with a cause. That's the way to describe **affinity cards**. Issued as Visas or MasterCards, an affinity card is nothing more than a standard bank credit card that has been issued in conjunction with some charitable, political, or other sponsoring group. So named because of the bond between the sponsoring group and its members, affinity cards are sponsored by such nonprofit organizations as the American Heart Association, CARE, MADD, Easter Seals, the Sierra Club, and Special Olympics; in addition, they're issued by college and university alumni groups, labor organizations, religious and fraternal groups, professional societies, even airline frequent flyer programs. In many cases, all you have to do is support the cause in order to obtain one of these cards (as in the case of MADD or CARE); in other cases, you'll have to belong to a certain group in order to get one of their cards (for example, you may have to be a graduate of the school, or a member of a particular frequent flyer program to qualify).

Why even bother to carry one of these cards? Because, unlike traditional bank cards, affinity cards make money for the group backing the card, as well as for the bank. In short, the sponsoring groups share in the profits. For example, a certain percentage (usually one-half to 1 percent) of retail purchases made with the card go to the sponsoring organization. So, for the credit cardholder, it's a form of "painless philanthropy." But be careful. For while these cards may pull at your heartstrings, they can also tug at your purse strings. Someone has to cover the money that's going to the sponsoring

organization, and that someone is usually the cardholder—in the form of higher fees and/or higher interest costs. In spite of this, for some, it may be viewed as a great way to contribute to a worthy cause; others, however, may feel it makes more sense to use a traditional credit card and then write a check to their favorite charity.

Revolving Lines of Credit. The last type of open account credit is the **revolving line of credit** offered by banks, S&Ls, brokerage houses, and other financial institutions. These credit lines do not involve the use of credit cards; rather, they are accessed by simply writing checks on common checking accounts or specially designed credit line accounts. There are basically three types of revolving lines of credit: (1) overdraft protection lines, (2) unsecured personal credit lines, and (3) home equity revolving lines of credit. *Overdraft protection* is a revolving line of credit that is added to a regular checking or NOW account and provides protection against overdrawing the account. An *unsecured personal line of credit* lets individuals tap their credit lines whenever the need arises, usually by just writing checks. The *home equity revolving line of credit* is a form of credit that is secured by a second mortgage on one's home and operates much like a personal line of credit: Whenever individuals want to draw money from their home equity lines of credit, they simply write checks against their credit accounts. These types of open credit lines are discussed in detail later in this chapter under "Other Kinds of Credit Lines."

affinity cards
A standard bank credit card issued in conjunction with some charitable, political, or other sponsoring nonprofit organization; these cards are a source of revenue to the sponsoring group since they normally earn a small percentage of all retail transactions.

revolving line of credit
A type of open account credit offered by banks, S&Ls, and other financial institutions that can be accessed by writing checks against demand deposit or specially designated credit line accounts.

EXHIBIT 7.5

A Bank Credit Card Application

This credit application, like most, seeks information about the applicant's place of employment, monthly income, place of residence, credit history, and other financial matters that are intended to help the lender decide whether or not to extend credit.

Application For The Arizona Bank's Visa Classic Credit Card.

This application contains information required for your protection as a consumer. Please read it carefully and answer each question as completely and accurately as possible.

Important Notice:

Under Arizona Law, property (including salary or wages) acquired by either husband or wife during marriage is the community property of both; property acquired before marriage or acquired after marriage by gift or inheritance and the income therefrom is the separate property of the spouse who acquired it.

Community Obligation:

"This application, UNLESS OTHERWISE MARKED BELOW, is an application for credit extended as a debt of the marital community, based on the credit-worthiness of that community." Supply all information requested on the application.

☐ Sole and separate obligation: This is an application for individual credit as a SOLE AND SEPARATE DEBT which will be evaluated without regard to the assets, income or creditworthiness of the applicant's spouse or the applicant's marital community (if any). (The applicant should list only marital status, and no other information should be given regarding the spouse (if any) except name and address. Applicant should also list all debts for which he/she is obligated by signing a promise to pay and should also list all sole and separate assets and income.)

Credit Card Requirements:

"Please approve this application for The Arizona Bank's VISA Classic Credit Card and related Personal Indentification Number (required for use of the 24HR Teller) with the highest credit line for which I/we qualify." Cards are requested for each person signing the application and also for the following names:

PERSONAL						
APPLICANT NAME LAST FIRST MIDDLE		BIRTHDATE	SOCIAL SECURITY NO.			HOME PHONE
PRESENT ADDRESS		CITY	STATE		ZIP	HOW LONG
FORMER ADDRESS		CITY	STATE		ZIP	HOW LONG
PRESENT EMPLOYER		POSITION	GROSS INCOME $ ___ MONTHLY		BUSINESS PHONE	HOW LONG
PREVIOUS EMPLOYER		POSITION	GROSS INCOME $ ___ MONTHLY		HOW LONG	NO. YRS. LIVED IN ARIZONA
☐ UNMARRIED ☐ MARRIED ☐ SEPARATED					NUMBER OF DEPENDENTS	

Income from alimony, child support or maintenance payments need not be revealed if you wish not to disclose such income in applying for credit. As a creditor, we may inquire whether any income stated in an application is derived from such a source.

SOURCE OF OTHER INCOME	NAME OF NEAREST RELATIVE OR FRIEND NOT LIVING WITH YOU
AMOUNT OF OTHER INCOME PER MONTH	ADDRESS

SPOUSE OR CO-APPLICANT					
SPOUSE OR CO-APPLICANT'S NAME	BIRTHDATE	SOCIAL SECURITY NO.			HOME PHONE
ADDRESS	CITY	STATE		ZIP	HOW LONG
EMPLOYER	POSITION	GROSS INCOME $ ___ MONTHLY		BUSINESS PHONE	HOW LONG

FINANCIAL					
BANK OR SAVINGS AND LOAN ASSOCIATION OR CREDIT UNION (NAME & BRANCH)			CHECKING ACCOUNT NO.		SAVINGS ACCOUNT NO.
☐ RENT ☐ OWN HOME	MORTGAGEHOLDER OR LANDLORD	PURCHASE PRICE $	AMOUNT OWING $		MONTHLY PAYMENT OR RENT $
YEAR & MAKE OF AUTO	AUTO FINANCED THROUGH	DRIVER'S LICENSE NO.	AMOUNT OWING $		MONTHLY PAYMENT $
NAME AND ADDRESS OF CREDITOR		ACCOUNT NUMBER	ORIGINAL AMOUNT/ CREDIT LINE	BALANCE OWING	MONTHLY PAYMENT
			$	$	$
			$	$	$
			$	$	$
			$	$	$
			$	$	$
HAVE YOU EVER HAD A REPOSSESSION ☐ YES ☐ NO		HAVE YOU EVER FILED BANKRUPTCY ☐ YES ☐ NO	IF YES, WHERE		YEAR

In submitting the foregoing application, I guarantee its accuracy with the intent that it be relied upon by the Bank in extending credit or service to me. I warrant that I have no known obligations, direct or contingent, which have not been set forth hereon and that I have not knowingly withheld any material information of an adverse nature. I hereby authorize you to obtain such credit information and verification as you may require. I understand that if my VISA Classic Credit Card application is approved, I will be billed for, and promise to pay you, the $15.00 annual fee. VISA Classic Credit Cards issued to me will be used only upon the terms and conditions set forth in the Cardholder's Agreement contained as a separate enclosure accompanying the cards.

X_____
APPLICANT'S SIGNATURE   DATE

X_____
SPOUSE OR CO-APPLICANT'S SIGNATURE   DATE

Source: The Arizona Bank.

Opening an Account

For the sake of convenience, people often maintain a variety of open accounts. Obviously, all households use 30-day charge accounts to pay their utility bills, phone bills, and so on. In addition, most families have one or more retail charge cards, a couple of bank cards, and possibly a T&E card; some people, in fact, may have as many as 15 to 20 cards, or more! And that's not all—families can also have one or more revolving credit lines in the form of an overdraft protection, unsecured personal, and/or home equity line. When all these cards and lines are totaled together, a family conceivably can have tens of thousands of dollars of readily available credit. Thus, it is easy to see why consumer credit has become such a popular way of making relatively routine purchases. Although open account credit can increase the risk of budget overload, these accounts can also serve as a useful way of keeping track of expenditures.

Unlike many 30-day charge accounts, retail charge cards, bank credit cards, T&E cards, and revolving lines of credit all require *formal application procedures*. Let's look now at how you'd go about obtaining open account credit, including the normal credit application, investigation, and decision process. We'll couch our discussion in terms of credit cards, but please understand that similar procedures apply to revolving lines of credit, as well.

The Credit Application. With several hundred million credit cards in the hands of American consumers, one would think that consumer credit is readily available. And it is—but you have to apply for it. Applications are usually available at the store or bank involved. Sometimes they can be found at the businesses that accept these cards or obtained on request from the issuing companies. Exhibit 7.5 (on facing page) provides an example of a bank credit card application. In this case, it is for a Visa card. The information requested concerns personal/family matters, housing, employment and income, assets and liabilities, existing charge accounts, and credit references. This information is intended to provide the lender with insight about the applicant's creditworthiness. In essence, the lender is trying to determine whether the applicant has the *character* and *capacity* to handle the debt in a prompt and timely manner. When applying for credit, you should provide the information requested as accurately and thoroughly as possible, since it will be verified during the credit investigation process.

The Credit Investigation. Once the credit application has been completed and returned to the establishment issuing the card, it is subject to a **credit investigation**. The purpose is to evaluate what kind of credit risk you pose to the lender (the party issuing the credit or charge card). So be sure to fill out your credit application in a careful manner. Believe it or not, they really do look at those things. The key items lenders look at are how much money you make, how much debt you presently have outstanding and how well you handle it, and how stable you are (e.g., your age, employment history, whether you own or rent a home, etc). Obviously, the higher your income and the better your credit history, the greater the chances of having your credit application approved. As a part of the investigation process, the lender will attempt to verify much of the information provided by you on the credit application—for obvious reasons, false or misleading information will almost certainly result in outright rejection of your application. For example, the lender will verify your place of employment, level of income, current debt load and debt service history, and so forth. Often, this can be done through one or two quick phone calls; if you've lived in the area for a number of years and have established relations with a local bank, a call to your banker may be all it takes to confirm your creditworthiness. If you haven't established such strong banker relations—and most young people have not—then the lender is likely to turn to the local credit bureau for a *credit report* on you.

---

credit investigation

An investigation that involves contacting credit references or corresponding with a credit bureau in order to verify information on a credit application.

S·M·A·R·T   M·O·N·E·Y

What's Your Credit Bureau Saying About You?

No matter how unsullied you think your credit history is, you'd be wise to review your credit bureau report at least once every two years. That way you can ensure that the information on file is accurate and pertains only to you—not to someone with the same name in another part of the country. To find out who's been keeping credit tabs on you, ask your bank or a retailer with whom you have an account for the name of the credit bureau it uses. Local credit bureaus collect information about your bill-paying habits, yet they use the computer facilities of national firms to store your history. If you move, your file will be transmitted to a bureau in your new town the first time you apply for credit there.

Credit bureaus are obliged by law to give you either a copy of your record or a summary of its contents. If you call and ask to see your report, you'll likely pay up to $10. But if you've been turned down for credit within the past 30 days because of your report, you can review your record for free.

Your credit report will list your payment history with all creditors that feed information to the bureau. If you hold an account jointly with your spouse, the payment record should be listed on your report as well as your partner's. Don't be surprised to find some of your accounts omitted. For example, American Express doesn't supply credit bureaus with any information on its cardholders' accounts, asserting that to do so would violate its customers' privacy. Many oil companies that issue gasoline credit cards report only on delinquent accounts. And while house payments may represent the biggest chunk of your debt load, mortgage lenders seldom supply information to credit bureaus, because creditors assume that you'll meet those obligations even if you're behind on others.

Most of the information in your report has a much briefer life span than you might expect. Says Walter Kurth, president of Associated Credit Bureaus, a national trade group: "Generally, credit granters want information about your payment history over only the past 12 to 24 months. So, many bureaus purge from their files any older data." Even if your report does contain outdated information, you can assume that most black-marks will be ignored by lenders as long as you've been in good standing for two years or so. Some credit scars, however, linger much longer. Bankruptcy can stay on your record for ten years, and debts written off by the lender as uncollectible can haunt you for seven.

By law, the bureau must investigate any errors you discover in your report. Then it must delete any information that turns out to be mistaken and notify any lender who received your report within the past six months that erroneous material has been removed from your file. If there is a dispute that the credit bureau's investigation doesn't settle, you're entitled to add to your file a short (100-word) statement giving your side of the story. Future reports to prospective lenders must include your explanation.

Source: Adapted from "Your Credit Bureau Report," *Money,* September 1984, 124. Reprinted from the September 1984 issue of *Money* Magazine, by special permission; © 1984, Time Inc. All rights reserved.

The Credit Bureau. Basically, a **credit bureau** is a type of reporting agency that gathers and sells information about individual borrowers. If, as is most often the case, the lender does not know you personally, it must rely on a cost-effective way of verifying your employment and credit history. It would be far too expensive and time-consuming for individual creditors to confirm your credit application on their own, so they turn to credit bureaus that maintain fairly detailed credit files about you. Information in your file comes from one of three sources: creditors who subscribe to the bureau, other creditors who supply information at your request, and publicly recorded court documents (such as tax liens or bankruptcy records). Contrary to popular opinion, your credit file does not contain everything anyone would want to know about you—there's nothing on your lifestyle, friends, habits, religious or political affiliations. Instead, all of the information is pretty dull stuff, and covers such things as:

- Your name, social security number, age, number of dependents, and current and previous addresses.
- Your employment record, including current and past employers, and salary data, if available.
- Your credit history, including the number of loans and credit lines you have, number of credit cards issued in your name, your payment record, and account balances.
- Public records data involving bankruptcies, tax liens, foreclosures, civil suits and criminal convictions, etc.
- Finally, the names of firms and financial institutions that recently requested copies of your file is also recorded.

Local credit bureaus are typically established and mutually owned by local merchants and banks. They collect and store credit information on people living within the community and make it available, for a fee, to members who request it. If the information requested can be transmitted over the phone, the cost of the inquiry is typically about $5. On the other hand, if the credit bureau must obtain, either through its own investigation or from another credit bureau, additional information in order to update the applicant's file, the cost of the report will be much higher. Local bureaus are linked together nationally through one of the "big

five" national bureaus—Trans-Union, Chilton, CBI, Associated Credit Services, and TRW Credit Data, Inc.—each of which provides the mechanism for obtaining credit information from almost any place in the United States. It's important to understand that credit bureaus merely collect and provide credit information; they do not analyze it, they do not rate it, and they certainly do not make the final credit decision. Because a credit report can have an important bearing on whether or not you get credit, you should make sure that the information in your credit file is correct! Take some time to read the accompanying *Smart Money* box about *credit bureau reports;* note that it recommends that you review your credit file at least once every two years.

When you make application for credit, most big lenders will contact the local credit bureau and let them decide whether or not you should receive the credit. **Fantasy:** Credit bureaus collect information and maintain credit files about individual borrowers, but they do not make the credit decision; that's done by the merchant or financial institution extending the credit.

The Credit Decision Using the data provided by the credit applicant along with any information obtained from the credit bureau, the store or bank must decide whether or not to grant credit. Very likely, some type of **credit scoring** scheme is used to make the credit decision. By assigning values to such factors as income, number of years on your present job, whether you rent or own your home and how long you have lived there, age of your car(s), number and type of credit cards you hold, level of your existing debts, and general credit references, an overall credit score for you can be de-

---

credit bureau
An organization, typically established by local banks and merchants, that collects and stores credit information about individual borrowers and, for a specified fee, supplies it to financial institutions that request it.

credit scoring
A method of evaluating an applicant's creditworthiness by assigning values to factors such as income, existing debts, and credit references.

veloped. Generally, the higher the credit score, the better. Thus, if your score equals or exceeds a predetermined minimum, you will be given credit; if not, credit will be refused. Sometimes borderline cases are granted credit on a limited basis. For example, a large department store that normally limits the outstanding balance on its revolving charge accounts to $500 might give a customer with a marginal credit score a revolving charge account with a $100 credit limit. Even when a formal credit scoring scheme is used, the credit manager or loan officer is normally empowered to offer credit if such action seems appropriate. Applicants who are granted credit are notified and sent a charge card and/or checks, along with material describing the credit terms and procedures.

Important Consumer Credit Legislation

When you apply for consumer credit of any kind, you should be aware of the legal obligations of the issuing establishment. There is always a possibility that your rights will be violated. Over the past decade or so, several important pieces of consumer legislation have been passed affecting the extension of credit. The major concerns of this legislation have been credit discrimination; disclosure of the credit information; errors and complaints; disclosure of finance charges (or so-called *truth in lending*); loss of credit card; recourse on unsatisfactory purchases; and protection against collector harassment.

Credit Discrimination. As of October 1975, the *Equal Credit Opportunity Act (ECOA)* makes it illegal for a creditor to discriminate on the basis of sex or marital status when considering a credit application. The act was passed in order to extend to women the credit rights already held by men. Questions about an applicant's sex, marital status, and childbearing plans are therefore prohibited. Lenders are required to view the income of women in exactly the same fashion as they do that of men. In addition, they must consider alimony and child support as part of a woman's income. Severe penalties exist for the violation of this law.

On March 23, 1977, ECOA was expanded to prohibit credit discrimination based on race, national origin, religion, age, or the receipt of public assistance. A subsequent extension of the act—effective

June 1, 1977—requires that if a husband and wife open a joint account or cosign a loan, the credit grantor must report the information to the credit bureau in the name of both parties. This change was intended to allow a wife to establish a credit history, which would make it easier for her to obtain credit in the event of her husband's death or a divorce. Prior to this modification of the Equal Credit Opportunity Act, credit files were maintained in the name of the husband only.

Disclosure of Credit Information. On April 25, 1971, the *Fair Credit Reporting Act* went into effect. It includes numerous provisions, among which are the following. First, credit bureau reports must contain accurate, relevant, and recent information about the personal and financial situation of credit applicants. Second, only bona fide users of financial information may review credit files. Third, consumers who are refused credit or who find their borrowing costs increased as the result of a credit investigation must be informed of the reasons for such actions as well as the name and address of the reporting credit agency. Perhaps most important, as explained in the preceding *Smart Money* box, credit reporting agencies must let individuals review their credit files personally and correct any inaccurate information.

Mailing, Error Complaints, and Cash Discounts on Bills. Because of errors and abuses in credit billing and the poor handling of credit complaints that resulted primarily from the use of computer-generated bills, the *Fair Credit Billing Act* was passed in October 1975. One provision of the act requires creditors to mail bills at least 14 days prior to the payment-due date and to include all credits and refunds on the bill for the period in which they occurred. Another provision requires customers to notify the creditor (in writing), within 60 days of the date they receive the statement, regarding any billing errors. The creditor is required to respond within 30 days to customer inquiries concerning a billing error complaint and to resolve the complaint within 90 days of its receipt. During the period in which the complaint is being resolved, the creditor is prohibited from collecting the bill or issuing an unfavorable credit report as a result of the disputed charge. A third provision of the act allows merchants to give cash discounts of any size to customers who pay cash instead of using credit. Since the merchants have to pay credit card companies, such as MasterCard, Visa, and American Express, for the privilege of accepting customers' cards, this act allows them to pass the savings on to those who choose not to use credit cards. The Fair Credit Billing Act also includes a provision concerned with the credit purchaser's recourse to the creditor; this provision is discussed in greater detail a bit later.

Truth in Lending: Full Disclosure of Finance Charges. Another major piece of consumer legislation is the *Consumer Credit Protection Act.* Commonly referred to as the **Truth in Lending Act**, it initially went into effect July 1, 1969, and has been amended several times since then. The directives for complying with the act are outlined in *Regulation Z*, which was issued by the Federal Reserve Board. Its most significant provision is the requirement that prior to extending credit, all lenders must disclose both the dollar amount of finance charges and the annual percentage rate charged (accurate to the nearest 0.25 percent). This enables credit applicants to make valid comparisons of alternate sources of credit. Such disclosure is included on the reverse side of monthly credit card statements, an example of which was shown earlier in Exhibit 7.3 (see "Explanation of Finance Charges").

The *dollar amount* of finance charges referred to above includes all interest and fees that must be paid in order to receive the loan. The **annual percentage rate (APR)** is the true rate of interest paid over the life of the loan and must be calculated in the manner outlined by the law. Note that on open account credit, creditors cannot specify in advance the dollar amount of interest since they do not know how much will be purchased on the account. The annual percentage rate on these accounts can be stated, however, since there are no fees charged other than interest. Remember: It is your right as a consumer to be told the dollar amount of charges and APR on any financing you consider.

Loss or Theft of Credit Card. The Consumer Credit Protection Act requires every credit card to contain some form of user identification—generally a picture or signature—and limits the liability of the credit card owner in the event the card is lost or stolen to a maximum of $50 per card. Credit card issuers are also required to send to their account holders a self-addressed form for notification of lost or stolen cards and an explanation of their rights at the time of issue. Some issuers also have toll-free numbers that can be used to report lost or stolen credit cards. In addition, companies are prohibited from sending unrequested credit cards to potential users. Credit cards can be sent only in response to a request or application for them.

Recourse on Unsatisfactory Purchases. One of the provisions in the Fair Credit Billing Act concerns the right of credit cardholders to obtain recourse on unsatisfactory goods or services charged to their accounts. This provision applies mostly to situations in which the credit used to make a purchase was provided by someone other than the seller—through the use of a bank credit card or a travel and entertainment credit card, for example. This feature protects people who have used credit to purchase goods or services that are subsequently found to be defective or do not perform satisfactorily. If, after good-faith attempts, they cannot satisfactorily work out their disagreement with the seller, they have the right to stop paying the creditor.

By placing some of the burden of guaranteeing the value of the purchase on the creditor, this provision has caused creditors to be more concerned with the reputation of the providers of the goods or services being financed. The transaction, however, must be made within 100 miles of the cardholder's current mailing address or the state of residence and the amount contested must exceed $50.

Protection against Collector Harassment. Beginning March 20, 1978, the *Fair Debt Collection*

Truth in Lending Act
A law passed in 1969 that, among other provisions, requires creditors to give customers advance, full disclosure of dollar amounts of finance charges and annual percentage rates.

annual percentage rate (APR)
The actual or true rate of interest paid over the life of a loan.

Practices Act gave consumers protection against unreasonable collection practices. To begin with, the law requires that within five days of first being contacted by a debt collector, the credit customer must be informed *in writing* as to (1) how much money is owed, (2) to whom, and (3) steps that can be taken if the debt is disputed. If the customer disagrees with the claim, he or she has 30 days in which to send the collector written notification of the dispute; then, the collector cannot continue collection efforts until the customer has been provided with written verification of the debt. Further, the customer can prevent a collector from communicating with him or her by notifying the collector in writing. Finally, if the collector presses suit for payment, it must be filed in the judicial district in which the customer lives or the contract was signed.

You may have heard stories of unsavory credit collectors gaining access to people's homes by posing as ministers or policemen and, once inside, grabbing a television set or other item on which credit payments were overdue. Frequently violence was threatened, and sometimes used, to collect unpaid bills. All these tactics are now illegal. The act specifically makes it a federal offense for collectors to (1) use abusive language, threaten the customer, or call at inconvenient times or at the place of work; (2) misrepresent themselves; (3) use unfair tactics in an effort to collect the debt; (4) contact anyone else about the customer's debt unless they are trying to locate him or her; and (5) collect an amount greater than the debt or apply payments to another disputed debt.

Credit Card Insurance

Before the passage of the Consumer Credit Protection Act, the liability of credit cardholders for charges made on lost or stolen cards was virtually unlimited. The cardholder was held liable for all charges made prior to the time the issuer received written notice of the card's loss or theft. In order to protect themselves against the consequences of possible loss or theft of their credit cards, many people would purchase **credit card insurance**. Such insurance really isn't necessary anymore, since the *cardholder's liability in case of loss or theft*

of the card is limited to $50 under provisions of the Consumer Credit Protection Act anyway. In fact, liability is the *lesser* of two amounts: that charged on the card prior to notification of the issuer, or $50. Clearly, prompt notification of the issuer of a lost or stolen card is important. In order to afford yourself maximum protection, it is a good idea to keep a list of credit card numbers along with the addresses and phone numbers provided by the issuers for use if cards are lost or stolen. Also, you should destroy credit cards that you no longer use.

Bankruptcy: Paying the Ultimate Price for Credit Abuse

As pointed out earlier, open account credit is a great convenience. Some people, however, abuse it by incurring more debt than they can afford to repay. When that happens, their credit rating is the first to go; and unless some corrective steps are taken, this is followed by repossession of property and eventually even bankruptcy. Every year, hundreds of thousands of people in this country file for **personal bankruptcy**. These people have reached the end of a long line of deteriorating financial affairs. Filing a petition for bankruptcy is a serious act and should be taken only as a last resort. Insolvency does not happen overnight; it usually reflects continually increasing use of credit until the total monthly payments can no longer be met. The family may have been pursuing a lifestyle beyond its means, or an unfortunate event, such as an illness or loss of a job, may have taken place. People who cannot resolve the insolvency situation on their own need protection from the courts. Two legal remedies are available: (1) a Wage Earner Plan and (2) straight bankruptcy.

Wage Earner Plan. The **Wage Earner Plan** is a workout procedure that schedules debt repayment over future years. It may be a viable alternative to straight bankruptcy for a person who has a steady source of income and a reasonable chance of being able to repay the debts in three to five years. The majority of creditors must agree to the plan, and interest charges, along with late-payment penalties, are waived for the repayment period. Creditors usually will go along with this plan because they stand to lose more in a straight bankruptcy. After the plan is approved, the individual makes periodic payments to the court that in turn are used to pay off the creditors. Throughout the process, the individual retains the use of, and keeps title to, all of his or her assets.

Straight Bankruptcy. Straight bankruptcy can be viewed as a legal procedure that results in "wiping the slate clean and starting anew." However, straight bankruptcy does not eliminate all of the debtor's obligations, nor does the debtor necessarily lose all of his or her assets. For example, the debtor must keep up alimony and child-support payments but is allowed to retain certain payments from social security, retirement, veterans', and disability benefits. In addition, the debtor may retain equity in a home (up to $7,500), a car (up to $1,200), and other personal assets, such as clothing, books and tools of his or her trade.

Obtaining Professional Advice. The bankruptcy laws have undergone important changes in recent years. Professional legal advice is obviously needed if a formal petition is filed. Agencies that assist—usually without charge—in credit counseling include the National Foundation for Consumer Credit, which provides counseling services in over 200 locations throughout the country. Another good place to look for help is the local Better Business Bureau or Chamber of Commerce. Such organizations are very concerned that consumer credit be widely available and properly used. In most instances, a debtor can work with a **credit counselor** who will help prepare a budget and may even negotiate with creditors to establish workable schedules for repaying outstanding debts. The counseling service will often go so far as to collect money from the debtor and distribute it to creditors.

There are also private firms that, for a fee, will act as intermediaries between borrowers and creditors and provide counseling services. These counselors generally attempt to reduce the size of payments, the size of the outstanding debt, or both. Because of their high fees, such profit-driven credit counseling services are not highly recommended.

RETAIL CHARGE CARDS

While retail charge cards, like those issued by department stores and oil companies, can be fairly costly, they do offer a number of advantages if effectively used. What do you perceive as the major advantages of using retail charge cards? What do you feel are the major disadvantages? Before reading on, spend a few moments to answer these questions.

"Will that be cash or charge?" At many retail establishments, those are the first words you'll hear from the clerk. That's indicative of the widespread pervasiveness of the retail charge card. These cards

credit card insurance
A type of insurance that covers charges made on a lost or stolen credit card; no longer necessary because of the Consumer Credit Protection Act's provision limiting cardholder's liability in such instances.

personal bankruptcy
A form of legal recourse open to insolvent debtors in which they may petition a court for protection from creditors and arrange for the orderly liquidation and distribution of their assets.

Wage Earner Plan
An arrangement for scheduled debt repayment over future years that is an alternative to straight bankruptcy; used when a person has a steady source of income and there is a reasonable chance of repayment within three to five years.

straight bankruptcy
A legal proceeding that results in "wiping the slate clean and starting anew"; where most of a debtor's obligations are eliminated in an attempt to put the debtor's financial affairs in order.

credit counselor
A professional financial advisor who assists overextended consumers in repairing budgets for both spending and debt repayment.

are popular with merchants because they build consumer loyalty and enhance sales; and, of course, consumers like them because they are a convenient way to shop. As explained earlier in this chapter, retail charge cards are a form of open account credit; they are *credit cards* issued by retail firms and intended for use by their customers while shopping at one of the firm's outlets. These cards carry a pre-set credit limit—a **line of credit**—that varies with the creditworthiness of the cardholder.

This form of credit is most common in department and clothing stores and other high-volume outlets, where customers are likely to make a number of purchases each month. Most large oil companies also offer charge cards, but unlike, say, department store credit cards, customers can use their credit to buy gas and oil products, but they're expected to pay for such purchases *in full* upon receipt of the monthly bill. To promote the sale of their more expensive products, oil companies frequently offer revolving credit for use in purchasing items such as tires, batteries, and accessories. Many families have—and regularly use—five or six different retail charge cards. And because you too are likely to use this form of credit, you should understand the methods used to compute finance charges, as well as the attending advantages and disadvantages of using this kind of credit.

Computing Finance Charges

Since merchants do not know in advance how much you will charge on your account, they cannot specify the dollar amount of interest you will be charged. But they can—and must, according to the Truth in Lending Act—disclose the rate of interest that they change and their method of computing finance charges. (See an example of such a disclosure in the bottom half of Exhibit 7.3.) The four basic techniques for computing finance charges are (1) the previous balance method, (2) the average daily balance method, (3) the adjusted balance method, and (4) the past-due balance method. The transactions in the following examples are taken from the statement presented in Exhibit 7.3. The monthly interest rate used is 1.5 percent, which represents an annual rate of 18 percent. As is customary, any credit purchases made during the current month are not subject to a finance charge if paid before the specified billing date; instead, finance charges are computed *only on the unpaid balance from previous months' purchases.* Also, in computing finance charges, our calculations *ignore* all credit purchases made during the current month; this practice, which was fairly common in the past, is still followed by a number of lenders, though not by all.

Previous Balance Method. A commonly used method of computing finance charges, the **previous balance method** is the most expensive for the consumer, since interest is charged on the outstanding balance at the beginning of the billing period. In Exhibit 7.3, $182 is the balance at the beginning of the period—*this is the balance on which interest would be calculated.* The resulting finance charge for the period using this method would be 1.5 percent of $182, or .015 × $182 = $2.73.

Average Daily Balance Method. In the **average daily balance method**—the procedure used in Exhibit 7.3—the interest is applied to the average daily balance of the account over the billing period. The calculations used to compute this balance do not reflect purchases or returns of purchases made *during the billing period,* though they do reflect payments made on account. Keep in mind, however, that some companies routinely include any new purchases in the average daily balance.

The billing period in Exhibit 7.3 extended from October 10, 1989, through November 10, 1989—a total of 31 days. The outstanding balance for the first 11 days of the period (October 11 through 21) was the beginning balance of $182; for the remaining 20 days (October 22 through November 10) the outstanding balance was $157.00—$182 less the $25 payment. (Recall that with this method the purchases made in the period are *not* included in the average daily balance figure; thus, we can ignore the four purchases made during the month.) Using the appropriate figures, the average daily balance is computed according to the procedure shown in Exhibit 7.6—that is, the outstanding balances are weighted by the number of days that the balance existed and then averaged (divided) by the number of days in the billing period. By multiplying the average daily balance of $165.87 by the 1.5 percent interest rate, the result is a finance charge of $2.49.

EXHIBIT 7.6

Finding the Average Daily Balance

The average daily balance method is the procedure most widely used by credit card issuers to determine the monthly finance charge on an account.

Number of Days (1)	Balance (2)	Weighted Balance [(1) × (2)] (3)
11	$182	$2,002
20	157	3,140
Total 31		Total $5,140

$$\text{Average daily balance} = \frac{\$5,142}{31 \text{ days}} = \$165.87$$

The average daily balance method is less expensive than the previous balance method (which yielded a finance charge of $2.73) and therefore preferable for the consumer. It, too, is widely used by stores that offer retail charge cards.

Adjusted Balance Method. In the **adjusted balance method,** the interest charge is applied to the *balance remaining at the end of the billing period* (ignoring purchases or returns made during that time). This procedure results in lower finance charges than those under either of the above two methods. In Exhibit 7.3, the account balance at the end of the billing period would have been $157 ($182 − $25 payment) and, when the 1.5 percent interest rate is applied to this balance, the resulting charge would amount to $2.36.

Past-Due Balance Method Merchants occasionally use the **past-due balance method** in order to motivate customers to fully repay their accounts. Under this method, customers who pay their accounts in full within a specified period of time, such as 30 days from the billing date, are relieved of the finance charge that otherwise would be imposed under one of the three preceding methods. If this method were used with the statement in Exhibit 7.3, the customer would have $2.49 in finance charges waived if payment for the full amount of $232.58 ($235.07 − $2.49) were made prior to a specified date, say, December 10, 1989. A comparison of the interest charges resulting from

each of these four methods is given in Exhibit 7.7. Because the finance charge varies with the method used to determine the account balance, the wise consumer determines which procedure is used prior to buying on credit.

line of credit
The maximum amount of credit that a customer is allowed to have outstanding at any point in time.

previous balance method
A method of computing finance charges by calculating interest on the outstanding balance at the beginning of the billing period.

average daily balance method
A method of computing finance charges by applying interest charges to the average daily balance of the account over the billing period, excluding purchases or returns made during that period.

adjusted balance method
A method of computing finance charges by applying interest charges to the balance remaining at the end of the billing period, excluding purchases or returns made during that period.

past-due balance method
A method of computing finance charges in which interest is charged on any account balance that is not paid in full in the current period.

EXHIBIT 7.7

Finance Charges under Alternative Methods of Determining Account Balances

The amount of finance charges that a cardholder pays depends not only on the rate of interest being charged but also on the method used to determine the account balance.

Method of Determining Balance	Balance (1)	Monthly Interest Rate (2)	Finance Charge [(1) × (2)] (3)
Previous balance	$182.00	1.5%	$2.73
Average daily balance	165.87	1.5	2.49
Adjusted balance	157.00	1.5	2.36
Past due balance	—[a]	1.5	0.0

[a]The finance charge, which does *not* have to be paid if full payment is remitted by a specified date, would be calculated using one of the other three methods.

Credit card issuers are required by truth-in-lending laws to use the average daily balance in your account when computing the amount of finance charges you'll have to pay. **Fantasy:** Truth in lending requires that lenders fully disclose the effective rate of interest being charged and the method used to compute finance charges, but they can use any one of four different methods: the average daily balance method (which is the most widely used), previous balance method, adjusted balance method, or past-due balance method.

Advantages of Retail Charge Cards

The most significant advantage of retail charge cards is that by charging purchases, customers can delay payment until the end of the billing period. Note, however, that because of the high finance charges levied on balances carried from period to period, there is no real advantage to delaying payment beyond this point. Some of the advantages of using retail charge cards include the following.

Interest-Free Loans. Carrying charge account costs merchants money. Since this is one of their business expenses, it is reflected in the price you pay for their goods or services. Therefore, you might as well maximize the benefits you receive from them. By delaying payment to the end of the billing period during which you made your purchases, you in effect receive an interest-free loan for up to 30 days. Thus you can, without penalty, keep your money in some interest-earning form—

such as MMDAs or NOW accounts—until the payment is due.

Recordkeeping, Unsatisfactory Purchases, and Credits. Store charges provide detailed records of transactions in the form of monthly statements. Because there may be errors in these statements, you should save your receipts and check them against the statement entries before paying. It is also easier to resolve any disagreement over goods or services purchased if you have not yet paid for them. If you charge your purchases, you have approximately 30 days in which to insure that they are satisfactory; if they are not, you can refuse to pay that amount. In addition, when you purchase an item on credit and later wish to return it, you need only have the store credit your account. Some stores credit your account for returns whether the purchase was charged on the store or a bank charge. In this way, the purchase price can be written off the books and no cash need change hands. Some stores use *due bills* to compensate customers who return items purchased for cash. Due bills can be used only to make purchases within the store and thus are less advantageous than a simple crediting of the account.

Preferred Customer Status. Customers who have charge accounts in good standing normally receive preferred customer status, which provides such benefits as notification of forthcoming sales, invitations to special shopping events, and check-cashing privileges. Although these benefits may be rather limited, many people do find them appealing.

Convenience. Some people find the use of retail charge cards convenient because they eliminate the need to write a check each time a purchase is made. By charging all transactions during the month, the customer need write only one check to pay each monthly bill. This convenience is a particularly important consideration for people who make a large number of transactions at a given store during the month.

Use in Emergencies. A final advantage of retail charge cards is that they provide a means for purchasing needed items when sufficient cash is not available. With proper planning and budgeting, the consumer should be able to avoid running short of cash; however, charging a needed item because of a cash shortage may be justifiable in some situations. A tendency to run short of cash on a regular basis, however, signals the need to reevaluate one's budget.

Disadvantages of Retail Charge Cards

The use of retail charge cards has two major disadvantages: (1) They offer the temptation to overspend, and (2) their high interest costs add to the price of purchases.

Tendency to Overspend. People who do not use budgets tend to forget that what they charge eventually must be paid for. The credit card gives them a sense of buying power that may not be supported by actual income. One of the consequences of this type of overspending is a tendency not to pay the full amount of the bill; since consumers who overspend typically don't have enough funds to cover their ever-increasing bills, they make only the minimum payment and thus incur finance charges. If their overspending is not curtailed, the size of the unpaid balance carried from period to period may become so large that it cannot be paid off without curtailing the purchase of necessity items. A realistic budget, as well as good budget control, should help you to avoid this type of overspending.

High Interest Costs on Unpaid Balances. The rate of interest charged on unpaid balances is usually quite high. The typical 1.5 percent per month represents an 18 percent annual rate; in a number of states, the APR can go as high as 21 percent (1.75 percent per month), or more. Compared to other consumer rates, this is very high! Since most consumer loans can be obtained at annual rates of between 10 and 15 percent, people who need to borrow money should not do so through their credit cards; rather, they should pay off their credit cards in full each period and then look to some other, lower-cost form of borrowing, such as a consumer loan. It's easy to use a credit card to make purchases you can't afford. But when you do that, it's just like borrowing money from a bank—except you're very likely paying a much higher rate of interest. To make matters even worse, only a small portion of these interest charges (20 percent in 1989) are tax deductible, and in a couple of years, *none* of it will be! Thanks to the Tax Reform Act of 1986 (see Chapter 4), the deductability of interest charges on most forms of consumer loans (including all types of credit cards) is being gradually phased out—it'll be totally gone in 1991. The net result is that the after-tax cost of this type of credit is growing progressively higher, and when such expenses can no longer be written off against your taxes, *you'll be carrying the full load of this very expensive form of financing, which if nothing else, should discourage the use of this kind of credit!*

BANK CREDIT CARDS AND OPEN LINES OF CREDIT

> Bank and other financial institutions offer several different types of open account credit, including bank credit cards, overdraft protection, unsecured personal lines, and home equity credit lines. Before reading on, give some thought to these forms of credit, and how you might be able to use each of them.

Probably the most popular type of open account credit is the *bank credit card*. These cards are accepted at retail stores and banks worldwide, as well as by state and municipal governments, colleges and universities, medical groups, and mail-order houses, among many others. They can be used to pay for just about anything, from college tuition and income taxes to football tickets, airline tickets, and car rentals. *Visa* and *MasterCard* are the leaders in this field. There are literally thousands of banks, S&Ls, credit unions, brokerage houses, and other financial services institutions that issue Visa and MasterCard, and each issuer, within reasonable limits, can set its own credit terms and conditions. And in the past four years, two more big-league players have entered the field. Sears has introduced its *Discover* card and American Express now has its *Optima* card (mentioned earlier). These two are meant to compete head-on with, and in time be as widely accepted as, Visa and MasterCard. The remainder of this chapter considers the features and basic uses of bank credit cards. In addition, it looks at *debit cards* as well as several other kinds of *revolving lines of credit,* including overdraft protection, unsecured lines of credit, and home equity credit lines—all of which are available from banks and other financial services institutions.

Features of the Bank Credit Cards

Bank credit cards are similar to retail charge cards except that they are issued by a third party and can be used to borrow money as well as buy on credit. Because of their potential for use in thousands of businesses and banks, they can be of great convenience and value to consumers. Individuals who use them, however, should be thoroughly familiar with their basic features.

Line of Credit. The line of credit provided to the holder of a bank credit card is set by the issuer for each card. It is the maximum amount that the cardholder can owe the issuer at any point in time. The size of the credit line depends on both the applicant's request and the results of the issuer's investigation of the applicant's credit and financial status. Lines of credit offered by issuers of bank cards can reach $5,000 or more, but for the most part they range from about $500 to $2,500. While the card issuers fully expect you to keep your credit within the specified limits, most won't take any real action unless you extend your account balance a certain percentage beyond the account's stated

maximum amount. For example, if you had a $500 credit limit, you probably wouldn't hear a thing from the card issuer until your outstanding account balance exceeded $600; that is, 20 percent above the $500 line of credit. On the other hand, don't count on getting off scot-free, for an increasing number of card issuers are beginning to assess so-called *over-the-limit* fees whenever you go over your credit limit (more on this later).

Merchandise Purchases. Merchants who participate in a given bank credit card program can generally be recognized by the card insignia that they affix near the entries to their businesses and display in their advertisements. Merchants who accept these cards must pay a fee amounting to as much as 5 percent of the transaction. Although this may seem a high price to pay, the opportunity to make purchases on credit appeals to consumers, so many merchants expect that the cost will be more than off-set by an added volume of business.

When you purchase goods or services with bank credit cards, the key information—account number, name, and expiration date—is imprinted from the card onto the sales slip, the amount of the purchase is filled in, and you are asked to sign it. You should be sure to check the accuracy of the purchase prices recorded before you sign the sales slip. Merchants can determine whether you are the legitimate user of the card by comparing your signature with that on the card, checking the card's number against a printed list of invalid card numbers, requiring additional identification (such as a driver's license), or verifying over the telephone that you are an account holder in good standing and that your card has not been reported lost or stolen. (Merchants must also verify by telephone the validity of a credit card for all purchases in excess of a specified amount—typically $50.) Merchants make these checks because bank credit card issuers hold them responsible for losses incurred as a result of accepting a lost or stolen card.

Cash Advances. The holder of a bank credit card can also obtain a *cash advance* from any bank participating in the given credit card program. Cash advances are transacted in the same fashion as merchandise purchases except that they take place at a commercial bank or some other financial institution and involve the receipt of cash (or a check) instead of goods and services. Of course, the bank, like a participating merchant, checks to insure that the card user is legitimate and the line of credit will not be exceeded as a result of the advance. Some banks will not make cash advances for amounts of less than $50.

Interest Rates on Bank Card Charges. With very few exceptions, the *annual* rate of interest charged on bank credit cards ranges from about 16 to 21 percent, irrespective of whether the transaction was a purchase or a cash advance; in fact, in late 1988, the national average was over 18 percent on such transactions. However, in some states these rates may be limited by **usury laws** to something more like 12 to 15 percent, and in some areas the interest rate on merchandise purchases may differ from that on cash advances. Generally speaking, *the interest rates on credit cards are among the highest* as far as interest rates on consumer credit are concerned. Indeed, given the gradual elimination of the tax deductability of credit card interest charges, this form of credit is going to become even more expensive than it already is.

The legal requirements with respect to disclosure of interest costs and related information are no different for bank credit cards than for other forms of consumer credit. In the case of purchases of merchandise and services, the specified interest rate is comparable to rates on store charges and, as with store charges, normally applied only to the unpaid balances carried from previous periods. Interest on cash advances, however, begins the day the advance is taken out, and is charged on a daily basis for the actual number of days the advance remains unpaid.

Other Fees. In addition to the interest charged on bank credit cards, there are a few other fees you should be aware of. To begin with, many bank cards today levy what are known as annual fees just for the "privilege" of being able to use the card. In most cases, the fee is around $15 to $25, though it can amount to much more for some of the prestige cards. As a rule, the larger the bank or S&L, the more likely it is to charge an annual fee for one of its credit cards. What's more, many issuers also charge a *transaction fee* for each cash advance; this fee usually amounts to about $2 per cash advance *or* 2 percent of the amount obtained in the trans-

action, whichever is more. And now, more and more card issuers are coming up with new ways to sock it to you. The newest twists: late-payment fees and over-the-limit charges. If you're a bit late in making your payment, at some banks you'll be hit with a late-payment fee—which is really a redundant charge since you're already paying interest on the unpaid balance anyway. In a similar fashion, if you happen to go over your credit limit, you'll get hit with a charge for that, too (again, this is on top of the interest you're already paying). Critics really dislike this fee because they maintain it's very difficult for cardholders to know when they've hit their credit ceilings. Regardless of when or why any of these fees are levied, the net effect is that *they add to the true cost of using bank credit cards.*

The Statement. If you use a bank credit card, you will receive monthly statements showing all transactions, payments, account balances, finance charges, available credit, and the minimum payment. A sample bank card statement is given in Exhibit 7.8; as can be seen, it is similar in many respects to the monthly statements you would receive with retail charge cards. Although merchandise and cash advance transactions are separated on this statement, the finance charge in each case is calculated at the rate of 1.75 percent per month (21 percent annually). And note that the average daily balance method is used to compute the finance charge in this statement. The minimum payment required on this account, as noted on the bottom of the statement, is $27, which is equal to 5 percent of the new balance, rounded to the nearest full dollar: $534.81 $\times$ .05 = $26.74 = $27.00. If the new balance had been less than $250, the bank would have required a payment of $10 (which is the absolute minimum *dollar* payment), or of the total new balance, if less than $10.

Payments. Users of bank credit cards can avoid *future* finance charges by paying the total new balance shown on their statement each month. For

usury laws

State laws governing interest rates on consumer and other types of credit.

EXHIBIT 7.8

A Bank Credit Card Monthly Statement

Each month, a bank credit cardholder receives a statement that provides an itemized list of charges and credits as well as a summary of previous activity and finance charges.

Please detach the above portion and return it with your payment to insure proper credit.

Bank Card Statement   MasterCard   VISA

Retain this statement for your records.

Account Number	Name(s)		8-24-89	09-21-89
			Statement Date	Payment Due Date

Account Activity

					Finance Charge Calculation		

Previous Balance	203.64	**Credit Status**		**Amounts Subject to Finance Charge**		**This Month's Charge**	
Payments −	119.89	Your Credit Limit is:		A. *Average Daily Balance	293.25 =	5.13	ENTIRE BAL. 1.75% 21.00%
Credits −	.00						
Subtotal	83.75		2000.00	B. *Cash Advance	.00 =	.00	Monthly Nominal Periodic Annual Rate Rate
New Transaction +	445.93			C. *Loan Advance	.00 =	.00	
Finance Charge +	5.13	Your Available Credit is:				5.13	21.00%
Late Charge +	.00						
NEW BALANCE	534.81		1465.19	*Finance Charges explained on reverse side		Finance Charge	Annual Percentage Rate

Mail Billing Inquiries to: Post Office Box 7760, Van Nuys, California, 91409, or call   800/000-0000
For inquiries on Past Due Accounts, Overlimits or Credit Line Increase, call   800/000-0000

Posted Mo./Day	Transaction Description or Merchant Name and Location		Purchase Mo./Day	Bank Reference Number	Purchases/ Advances/Debits	Payments Credits
8-08	AIR WEST	LOS ANGELES	07-25	850000008823395192	42.00	
8-13	HACIENDA MOTOR	COSTA MESA	08-05	015400018537022316	166.86	
8-15	RICOS RESTAURANT	PALM SPRG	08-10	114500018856161722	132.47	
8-12	PAYMENT - THANK YOU		08-11	4501000182MD02139		119.89
8-24	RENEES RESTAURANT	NEWPORT	08-13	114500068201632483	104.60	

Notice   See reverse side for important information.

			Total Debits	Total Credits
MIN. PAYMENT: 27.00	**NEW BALANCE:** 534.81		445.93	119.89

Source: Courtesy of United California Bank. Revised for fourth edition.

Source: Typical bank credit card monthly statement.

example, if the $534.81 total new balance shown in Figure 7.8 is paid by the due date of September 21, 1989, no additional finance charges will be incurred (the cardholder, however, will still be liable for the $5.13 in finance charges incurred to date). If cardholders cannot pay the total new balance, they can pay any amount that is equal to or greater than the minimum payment specified on the statement. They will, however, incur additional finance charges in the following month. Cardholders who fail to make the minimum payment are considered in default on their account, and the bank issuing the card can take whatever action it deems necessary.

Returning Merchandise.   When you return merchandise purchased with your bank credit card, the merchant will issue a *credit* to your bank account, as opposed to a charge. The credit is transacted in the same fashion as a purchase and will appear on your statement as a *deduction* from the balance. If you purchase an item and have problems with it, you may not have to pay the bank credit card company for it if you have attempted in good faith and failed to resolve the problem with the merchant. This protection is provided by the Fair Credit Billing Act. Of course, if the problem is resolved in the merchant's favor, you will ultimately have to pay.

The Effective Use of Bank Credit Cards

Much like charge cards, bank credit cards can be helpful tools if used properly. They have the same basic advantages and disadvantages as do retail charge cards.

Interest-Free Loans.   Like retail charge cards, many bank credit cards provide short-term, interest-free loans on the purchase of goods or services. Known as **grace periods**, they generally cover a 25- to 30-day period of time during which you can pay your bill in full and not incur any interest charges (note that such grace periods do not apply to cash advances). Unfortunately, while most banks still offer grace periods, there's a rapidly growing trend to shorten or eliminate such provisions. In addition, a growing number of card issuers are including purchases made during the current period when computing average daily balances. As a rule,

bank credit cards should be used primarily to charge merchandise and services, and then monthly statements should be paid in full to avoid any finance charges. If the card issuer does not offer a grace period, or includes current purchases in the average daily balance, the card should be used only in financial emergencies, since interest would be charged beginning at the time of the transaction. Use of the card for any other purpose (such as for cash advances) signals poor personal financial management.

Consolidated Statement of Expenses.   While bank credit cards offer their users obvious conveniences, probably the most valid reason for using them is to consolidate records of purchases. No matter how many and varied the stores at which bank credit card transactions occur, the consumer receives only one statement that records them all. This greatly simplifies the recordkeeping process. And it makes bill paying a lot easier, since only one check needs to be written to pay for all the different transactions.

A Word of Caution.   One of the real dangers of bank credit cards results from their ease of use. Many people tend to overlook the fact that they must eventually pay for the merchandise charged with their bank cards—but each time they make a transaction this way, they are incurring a liability to the issuer. Indeed, as the accompanying *Money in Action* box illustrates, a growing number of college students are learning this lesson the hard way!

As a rule, bank card charges should be limited to those items or transactions that have been budgeted. Only in financial emergencies should cardholders use their credit to make nonbudgeted transactions, leave a portion of the balance unpaid, or receive cash advances on account. If these cards are used properly, their convenience and widespread acceptance make them worthwhile vehicles for the efficient management of personal finances.

---

grace period
A short period of time, usually 25 to 30 days, during which you can pay your credit card bill in full and not incur any interest charges.

MONEY IN ACTION

"College Students and Credit Cards: Easy Come—Easy Go"

When it comes to credit cards, a lot of college students fail the subject. Bombarded with seductive invitations from banks, department stores and oil companies, many students succumb to the "buy now, pay later" hook—only to find themselves deep in debt when they're barely out of their teens.

Much of the problem stems from the ubiquitous nature of credit cards and their perceived clout, prestige and convenience. But credit-card issuers, trying to build a loyal following among future big spenders, also have made it easier for students to get cards than it is for many other adults.

While most college-enrolled holders handle their credit cards responsibly, the 4% that card issuers say default create a nightmare for themselves and their families, sometimes derailing college careers as they whittle down a mountain of personal debt built by prodigal spending.

Robert Rodriguez, for example, applied for and got a MasterCard in 1984 when he was a junior at the University of Houston. Then he added two Visa cards and two department-store cards, as well as some oil-company cards. His credit-card spending was "definitely frivolous," Mr. Rodriguez says. He ate out often, bought clothes and went to concerts. He even got cash advances from one card to make payments on others. Within a couple of years he was $7,000 in debt.

As he fell behind on his payments, Mr. Rodriguez began working double shifts at a parcel-delivery company from 8 p.m. to 5 a.m. Soon he was too exhausted to keep up in school. "I couldn't make my 8 o'clock class," says the 25-year-old. "And I couldn't concentrate because I was worrying whether I was working enough hours to make enough money." After his grades slipped, he was suspended. Now the former economics major is working full time to pay his debts—and trying to save enough money to return to college next year.

Credit counselors and parents say card issuers have made it far too easy for young, financially inexperienced students to qualify for the cards. "The sooner (the card issuers) can get them hooked on spending so much a month, the more money they can make," says Joseph Yura, a professor at the University of Texas, Austin, and a member of the school's financial-aid advisory committee. Others say the card issuers lure students because they know parents are likely to pick up the tab if anything goes wrong.

Getting a credit card *is* simple for many of the nation's 12 million college students. Unsolicited cards and pre-approved applications arrive by mail; ads

A Debit Card Is *Not* a Form of Credit

It looks like a credit card, it spends like a credit card, and it even has the familiar MasterCard and Visa credit card markings. However, it is not a *credit* card—rather it is a *debit* card! Simply put, a **debit card** provides direct access to your checking account and, as such, *works like writing a check.* For example, when you use a debit card to make a purchase, the amount of the transaction is charged directly to your checking account. Thus, using a debit card is not the same thing as buying on credit; it may appear that you are charging, but actually you are paying with cash. Accordingly, there are no finance charges with debit cards and normally, there are no annual fees to pay.

Debit cards are as convenient as credit cards (they are accepted at any establishment displaying the Visa or MasterCard logo), but they function as an alternative to writing checks. If you use a debit card to make a purchase at a department store or

and applications plaster school bulletin boards. Often the process is about as tough as filling in a magazine subscription form. Filene's department store in Boston, for instance, asks for little more than a student's name, Social Security number and a personal reference. Rarely is a student application denied, says Lori Schlager-Herscott, Filene's credit marketing manager.

On many campuses, American Express uses this siren call to students: "It may never be this easy again." American Express and most other card issuers allow students to get around income and employment requirements by counting other sources of money, such as financial aid and allowances. The card issuers usually don't impose any additional restrictions—such as lower spending limits—on cards issued to students. The Visa and MasterCard applications that often are dis-

tributed in shopping bags at campus bookstores even emphasize the wisdom of building credit history now for financing later to buy that first car or condominium. The companies say they are eager to sign up students in hopes of latching onto longtime customers.

Card issuers say that students default at about the same rate as other card holders, and some say students are even more responsible than other customer groups. "I think they view (credit cards) as a symbol of adulthood and are reluctant to shirk that responsibility," says Betsy Ludlow, vice president for new accounts at American Express. Such praise, though, is no solace to students faced with runaway debt. Raed Kolaghassi, a 21-year-old architecture major at the University of Houston, has run up a bill of $4,000 on his Visa card in the six months he's had it. Mr. Kolaghassi says

he manages to make the minimum monthly payments, but the bills add up faster than what he's able to pay.

Students who use their credit cards improperly can end up ruining their credit ratings—or jeopardizing their college degrees if they have to cut back on school to pay the bills. A huge debt may also limit the careers that students feel they can choose from, requiring them to put big paychecks ahead of other considerations when picking a first job. In the end, many students learn the hard way—as did Mr. Rodriguez, who has since taken a pair of scissors to all but one of his credit cards. Now, he says, besides cash, "the only things in my wallet are photos."

Source: Adapted from Susan Ayala, "Students Find Credit Cards Easy to Get." *The Wall Street Journal,* Aug. 16, 1988, p. 25. Reprinted by permission of *The Wall Street Journal,* © Dow Jones & Company, Inc. 1988. All Rights Reserved Worldwide.

restaurant, the transaction will show up on your next monthly *checking account* statement. Needless to say, to keep your records straight, you should enter debit card transactions directly into your checkbook ledger as they occur and treat them as withdrawals, or checks, by subtracting them from your checking account balance. Debit cards can also be used at most banks and S&Ls to gain access to your account through 24-hour teller machines or ATMs—which is the closest thing to a cash advance that these cards have to offer.

The big disadvantage of a debit card, of course, is that it does not provide a line of credit. In addition, it can cause overdraft problems in your check-

---

debit card

A card used to make transactions for *cash* rather than credit; replaces the need for cash or checks by initiating charges against one's *checking* account.

ing account if you fail to make the proper entries to your account or inadvertently use it (pay cash) when you think you are using a credit card (charging). On the plus side, a debit card does not carry with it the potential credit problems and high costs that credit cards do. Further, it is every bit as convenient to use as a credit card—in fact, if convenience is the major reason you use a credit card, you might want to consider switching to a debit card for at least some transactions, especially at outlets such as gas stations that give discounts for cash purchases and consider a debit card to be as good as cash.

Other Kinds of Credit Lines

While the use of "plastic" is widespread throughout our economy, there are other forms of revolving credit available to consumers. These alternatives are often a far better deal, not only because they offer more credit but also because they can be a lot less expensive; and, according to the latest tax laws, there may even be a tax advantage to using one of these other kinds of credit! None of these alternatives involves the use of credit cards and thus cannot be used to charge goods and services in the normal sense of the word. Instead, these credit lines provide their users with ready access to borrowed money (that is, cash advances) through revolving lines of credit. They are every bit as convenient as credit cards, since access is gained by simply writing a check. The three major forms of open (non-credit-card) credit are: overdraft protection lines, unsecured personal lines of credit, and home equity credit lines.

Overdraft Protection. An **overdraft protection line** is simply a line of credit linked to a checking account that enables a depositor to overdraw his or her checking account up to a predetermined limit. These lines are usually set up with credit limits of $500 to $1,000, but they can be for as much as $5,000 or more. The consumer taps this line of credit by simply writing a check. If this check happens to overdraw the account, the overdraft protection line will automatically advance funds in an amount necessary to put the account back in the black. The bank or S&L often stipulates a minimum amount for each advance (say, $50), and some lenders may even have a policy of making advances only

in *minimum multiples* (of, for example, $25 or $50). Of course, this does not mean that you must overdraw that amount before the line kicks in—on the contrary, as soon as your checking account balance falls below zero, funds will be advanced to cover the overdraft.

Unfortunately, you never know for sure just how much a given check will overdraw your account (if in fact it does). The reason is that unless you write very few checks, the balance shown on your checkbook ledger will seldom be the same as the amount shown by the bank. The way to handle this is to simply record the check in your checkbook ledger as you normally would, including the new balance after the check is written. If this overdraws your account—at least as far as your checkbook ledger is concerned—this will not be a problem, since you have an overdraft protection line to cover it. If it does in fact overdraw your account, the bank will notify you of this in a matter of days and inform you that it has advanced funds to your checking account. The amount of the advance will be shown on the notice and should immediately be entered into your checkbook ledger as a *deposit*.

The funds from an overdraft protection line are usually advanced at the rate of 12 to 15 percent, though rates as high as 18 percent are not uncommon. Once an advance is made, a monthly repayment schedule is set up for systematically repaying the loan, along with all interest charges—generally with monthly payments being set up so that the amount of funds advanced will be repaid over a period of 18 to 36 months. A statement is sent out each month, along with the monthly check statement, summarizing any activity in the overdraft protection line (new advances, repayments, new balance, and amount of credit still available) and indicating the required monthly payment. Note that since there ordinarily is no limit on the number of times you can overdraw your account, the amount of the monthly payment will change every time the bank advances money to your account.

It should be clear that if you are not careful, you can quickly exhaust this line of credit by writing a lot of overdraft checks. As with any line of credit, there is a limit to how much you can obtain. You should be extremely careful with such a credit line and under no circumstances take it as a license to routinely overdraw your account! If you are doing so on a regular basis, you should take this as a signal that you are probably mismanaging your cash and/or living beyond your budget. It is best to view an overdraft protection line strictly as an *emergency* source of credit—and any funds advanced should be repaid as quickly as possible.

Unsecured Personal Lines. Another form of revolving credit that is becoming increasingly popular is the **unsecured personal credit line**, which basically makes a line of credit available to an individual on an as-needed basis. In essence, it is a way of borrowing money from a bank, S&L, credit union, savings bank, or brokerage firm any time you wish, without going through all the hassle of setting up a new loan. Here is how it works. Suppose you apply for a personal line of credit at your bank. Of course, you will have to submit a loan application to obtain the credit line, but once you have been approved and the credit line established, you will be issued *checks* that you can write against it. Thus, if you need a cash advance, all you need do is write a check (against your credit line account) and deposit it into your checking account. Alternatively, if you need the money to buy some high-ticket item—say, an expensive stereo system— you can just make the credit line check out to the dealer and, when it clears, it will be charged against your credit line as an advance. (These credit line checks look and behave just like regular checks and as such do not have to be channeled through your normal checking account.)

Personal lines of credit are usually set up for minimums of $2,000 to $5,000 and often amount to $10,000 or more. As with an overdraft protection line, once an advance is made, repayment is set up on a monthly installment basis. Depending on the amount outstanding, repayment is normally structured over a two-to-five-year period; to keep the monthly loan payments low, larger amounts of debt are usually given longer repayment periods. As a rule, these credit lines are set up with adjustable rates of interest so that the interest charged on advances varies with the prime or some other benchmark rate—normally, floating 2 to 4 percent above the prime/benchmark rate. Monthly statements are sent out that summarize the activity in the credit line and stipulate the required minimum monthly payment.

While these credit lines do offer attractive terms to the consumer, they do not come without their share of problems, perhaps the biggest of which is the ease with which they can be obtained. In addition, these lines normally involve *substantial* credit limits and are about as easy to use as credit cards. This combination can have devastating effects on a family's budget if it leads to overspending or excessive reliance on the credit. To be safe, these lines should be used only for emergency purposes or to make *planned credit expenditures.* In addition, systematic repayment on the debt should be built into the budget and every effort made—*before* making the expenditure—to insure that it will not place undue strain on the family finances.

You use a check rather than a credit card to obtain funds from an unsecured personal line of credit. **Fact:** Credit cards are not issued with unsecured personal credit lines; instead, if you want to borrow money through such a line, you do it by simply writing a check directly against it.

Home Equity Credit Lines. Here is a familiar situation. A couple buys a home for $75,000; some 15 years later, it is worth twice that much. The couple now has an asset worth $150,000 on which all they owe is the original mortgage, which may now have a balance of, say $50,000. The couple clearly has built up a substantial amount of equity in their home—$150,000 − $50,000 = $100,000! The problem is how can they tap that equity without having to sell their home? The answer is to obtain a **home equity credit line**. Such lines are much like unsecured personal credit lines except that they are *secured* with a second mortgage on the home. Offered by most S&Ls, banks, major brokerage firms, and a growing number of credit unions,

---

overdraft protection line
A line of credit linked to a checking account that allows a depositor to overdraw the account up to a specified amount.

unsecured personal credit line
A line of credit that is made available to an individual on an as-needed basis in the form of check-writing privileges against it.

home equity credit line
A line of credit issued against the existing equity in a home.

EXHIBIT 7.9

Comparative Home Equity Credit Line Terms

Home equity credit lines are offered by a number of different types of financial services institutions, involve relatively large credit limits, and normally have rather generous repayment terms.

Equity Credit Line Product	Minimum/ Maximum Credit Line	Maximum Percent of Equity Lent	Interest Rate Formula	Minimum Advances	Repayment Terms	Minimum Monthly Payments
Beneficial Home Equity Credit Line	$10,000/ $200,000	75%	Prime + 4%	None	Amortized over 10 to 15 years	Recalculated on balance
Chemical Bank Home Equity Credit Line	$15,000/ none	80% of market value, less first mortgage	Prime + 2.25% for noncustomers; prime + 2% for regular customers; prime + 1.75% for preferred customers	$ 500	Up to 15 years	Interest only
Citicorp Equity Source Account	$7,500/ none	75% of first $200,000; 50% of amount above that	Prime + 1.25% or prime + 1.75%, depending on origination fee	$ 500	10 years interest only, then becomes 15-year amortized loan	Interest only for first 10 years
Dean Witter Homeowner's Resource	Varies by state/none	70%	Prime + 2%; adjusts monthly	Varies by state	In full in 5 years	Interest only
Merrill Lynch Equity Access	$15,000/ $2 million	80%	Up to $50,000 prime + 2%; $50,000–$100,000, prime + 1.75%; more than $100,000, prime + 1.5%	None	In full in 10 years	Interest only
Pathway Financial Equity Line of Credit	$10,000/ $250,000	75% of value, less first mortgage	Up to $25,000, prime + 1%; more than $25,000, prime	$ 500	In full in 5 years	Interest only
Shearson/Lehman, Hutton Home Equity Credit Line	$25,000/ none	80% of value, less existing mortgage	Prime + 2% for noncustomers; prime + 1.5% for brokerage customers	$1,000	10 years interest only, 20-year amortization	Interest only
Talman Home Federal S&L Equity Line of Credit	$10,000/ $100,000	80% of balance under $25,000; 70% of balance over $25,000	Up to $25,000, prime + 2%; $25,000–$50,000, prime + 1%; $50,000–$100,000, prime + .5%	$ 500	In full in 5 years	Interest only
Wells Fargo Equity Line	$10,000/ $500,000	80%	One-month CD rates + 3.5%	$ 300	Open-ended	Interest only

these lines of credit allow you to tap up to 75 percent of the equity in your home by merely writing a check.

Here is how it works. The above couple has built up an equity of $100,000 in their home—equity against which they can borrow through a home equity credit line. Assuming they have a good credit record and using a 75 percent loan-to-market-value ratio (which is the most common ratio employed with this kind of credit), an S&L would be willing

to lend up to $112,500; that is, 75 percent of the value of the house is .75 × $150,000 = $112,500. Subtracting the $50,000 still due on the first mortgage, we see that our couple could qualify for a home equity credit line of a whopping $62,500.

Home equity lines also have an interesting tax feature that you should be aware of: the annual interest charges on such lines may be fully tax deductible for those who itemize. This is the only type of consumer loan that still qualifies for such a tax treatment. In particular, according to the latest (1988) provisions of the tax code, a homeowner is allowed to *fully deduct the interest charges on home-equity loans of up to $100,000,* regardless of the original cost of the house or use of the proceeds. Indeed, the only restriction is that the amount of total indebtedness on the house cannot exceed its fair market value—which is highly unlikely, since you usually cannot borrow more than 75 to 80 percent of the market value of the house anyway. Thus, in our preceding example, the homeowner could take out the full amount of his credit line ($62,500), and every dime that he paid in interest would be tax deductible. If he paid, say, $7,500 in interest, and if he were in the 28 percent tax bracket, this feature would reduce his tax liability by some $2,100— ($7,500 × .28)—given, of course, that he itemizes his deductions.

A home equity credit line usually involves a fairly extensive credit application process, including an appraisal of the property. In addition, there'll probably be *closing costs* to pay when the line of credit is set up, even if the borrower does not use the line right away (such closing costs are usually lower than those on first mortgages, but they still can easily amount to $1,500 or more). When the credit line is set up, the homeowner receives a book of checks that can be used to obtain funds just like the checks used with unsecured personal lines. Repayment terms are flexible, with most lenders charging adjustable rates of interest and giving the borrower 10 to 15 years to repay. Monthly statements are sent out that recap the activity in the account and indicate the size of the monthly payment.

Exhibit 7.9 (on facing page) provides a sample of various home equity credit lines offered by a variety of financial institutions. What is perhaps most star-

tling is the maximum amount of credit available under these lines. Note that $100,000 figures are not at all unusual; one lender—the brokerage firm of Merrill Lynch—offers a maximum credit line of $2 million! With this kind of credit available, it is not surprising that home equity lines are the fastest-growing form of consumer credit. And its precisely because of the enormous amount of money available that this form of credit should be used with caution. The fact that you have the equity in your home does not mean that you have the cash flow necessary to service the debt that such a credit line imposes. At the minimum, major expenditures should be made only after you have determined that you can afford the purchase and that the required monthly payments will fit comfortably within your budget. Also, because of the closing costs involved, a home equity credit line should be set up only after you have decided to actually use it—otherwise, it is too expensive to have just as a form of emergency credit.

Perhaps the biggest problem with this type of credit is the temptation to use the long-term repayment schedule that this type of credit offers to keep payments *artificially* low and, in so doing, purchase items whose lives will be nowhere near as long as that of the associated debt. For example, to use a 15-year second mortgage to buy a car with a 5-year life makes absolutely no sense! You will still be paying for the car 10 years after you have sold it. The fact is that if the only way you can afford the car is to buy it with 15 years of payments, you cannot afford it in the first place. Home equity credit lines can be an effective way of tapping the built-up equity in a home, but you should avoid using them to buy items you could not otherwise afford.

SUMMARY

▪ Families and individuals use credit as a way to pay for relatively expensive purchases and occasionally, to deal with a financial emergency; in addition, consumer credit is being used increasingly simply because it is so convenient. Finally, it is also used to partially finance the purchase of various types of investments.

▪ Unfortunately, while there are some definite positive aspects to the use of consumer credit, there

is also the negative side—it can be misused to the point where people live beyond their means by purchasing goods and services they simply can't afford, which is all too easy to do with readily available credit. Such overspending can get so bad that it eventually leads to bankruptcy.

▪ Open account credit is one of the most popular forms of consumer credit; it is available from various types of financial institutions, as well as all sorts of retail stores and merchants. The major types of open account credit include 30-day charge accounts, retail charge cards, bank credit cards, travel and entertainment cards, affinity and prestige cards, and various forms of revolving lines of credit.

■ Most types of open account credit require formal application, which generally involves an extensive investigation of your credit background and an evaluation of your creditworthiness. You, as a borrower, have certain rights when you apply for and obtain consumer credit; such consumer credit protection is mandated by legislation and covers such things as credit discrimination, full disclosure (truth-in-lending), loss of credit cards, and your recourse on unsatisfactory purchases.

■ The amount of finance charges, if any, due on consumer credit depends in large part on the technique used to compute the account balance, of which there are four in use today: the previous balance method, the average daily balance method, the adjusted balance method, and the past due balance method.

■ Although credit cards account for a significant portion of consumer transactions, the most rapidly growing segment of consumer credit is the personal revolving line of credit; while you can use credit cards for merchandise transactions and/or cash advances, revolving lines of credit provide their users with ready access to borrowed money (by simply writing checks). Basically, there are three types of revolving credit lines; they include: overdraft protection lines, unsecured personal lines of credit, and home equity credit lines.

QUESTIONS AND PROBLEMS

1. Why do people borrow? What are some of the improper uses of credit? Are there any dangers associated with borrowing? Explain.

2. What steps can you take to establish a good credit rating? What extra steps might be necessary for a woman?

3. Josh Schwartz has a monthly take-home pay of $1,200; he makes payments of $250 a month on his outstanding consumer credit (excluding the mortgage on his home). How would you characterize Josh's debt burden? What if his take-home pay were $850 a month and his monthly credit payments $90?

4. What is open account credit? Explain the workings of (a) a 30-day charge account and (b) a retail charge card account.

5. Distinguish between bank credit cards and travel and entertainment cards. Give examples of each.

6. Briefly describe the steps involved in opening a charge account; provide your answer from the customer's point of view.

7. Describe the basic operations and functions of a credit bureau. What kind of information do they gather about you? Is there anything you can do if the information they have on file is wrong?

8. How does recent consumer credit legislation relate to (a) credit discrimination, (b) disclosure of credit information, (c) disclosure of finance charges, (d) loss of credit card, (e) recourse on unsatisfactory purchases, and (f) protection against collector harassment?

9. What are the provisions of the Fair Credit Billing Act of 1975 with respect to mailing, error complaints, and cash discounts on bills?

10. Explain the conditions that might make bankruptcy necessary. Distinguish between a Wage Earner Plan and straight bankruptcy.

11. Describe the four methods used to compute finance charges. Assume that Karen Rivers has a balance of $380 on her retail charge card; if the store levies a finance charge of 21 percent per annum, how much monthly interest will be added to Karen's account?

12. What are the advantages of using retail charge cards.

13. What is a line of credit? Explain. Does a line of credit come with all types of credit cards?

14. How does a person make a purchase using a retail or bank credit card? What are the benefits of making this type of transaction? Explain.

15. What's the typical rate of interest charged on bank credit cards, and how are interest charges usually computed? What, if any, are the legal requirements with respect to disclosure of interest rates?

16. In addition to interest rates, many bank credit card issuers also impose different types of fees; briefly describe three of these fees. Do these fees have any impact on the true (effective) cost of using credit cards? Explain.

17. Briefly discuss the federal tax provisions as they apply to interest charges paid on various types of credit cards; note especially how recent changes in the tax law are going to affect the cost of borrowing.

18. One of the key features of bank credit cards is the monthly statement. What does this statement disclose? Why are merchandise and cash-advance transactions often separated?

19. Comment on the following statement: "If used intelligently, bank credit cards can be quite useful."

20. What is a debit card? How is it similar to a credit card? How does it differ?

21. Mary Maffeo has an overdraft protection line. Explain how she would obtain an advance from this line of credit. Assume that her October 1989 statement showed a latest (new) balance of $862. If the line had a minimum monthly payment requirement of 5 percent of the latest balance (rounded to the nearest $5 figure), what would be the minimum amount she would have to pay on her overdraft protection line?

22. Describe the basic features of a home equity credit line. Don and Judy Summers have a home with an appraised value of $180,000 and a mortgage balance of only $90,000. Given that an S&L is willing to lend money at a loan-to-value ratio of 75 percent, how big a home equity credit line can Don and Judy obtain? How much, if any, of this line would qualify as tax deductible interest if their house originally cost $100,000?

CASE PROBLEMS

7.1 The Carpenters Seek Some Credit Card Information

Ellwood and Angela Carpenter are a newly married couple in their mid-twenties. Ellwood is a senior at a state university and will graduate in the summer of 1990. Angela recently started working as a sales representative for the Alhambra Corporation. She supports both of them on her monthly salary of $1,500 after taxes. At present, the Carpenters pay all of their expenses by cash or check. They would, however, like to use a bank credit card for some of their transactions. Because neither Ellwood nor Angela is familiar with the procedure for opening a credit card account, they approach you for help.

Questions

1. Advise the Carpenters on how they should go about filling out a credit application.

2. Explain to them the procedure that the bank will probably follow in processing their application.

3. Explain how the bank will arrive at a credit decision.

4. What kind of advice would you offer the Carpenters on the "correct" use of their card? What would you tell them about building a strong credit record?

7.2 The Andersons Find Out What "Charge It" Means

Sean and Amy Anderson, a couple in their late twenties, reside in a suburb of Boston. Sean is employed by Norton International, and Amy is a schoolteacher. Six months ago, they established credit at a fashionable department store where they often make purchases. They used to pay the full amount on all their bills before the due date. Of late, however, they have not been able to budget their expenses as well. Their most recent bill from the department store (on next page) showed a previous balance of $215, on which the store had levied a finance charge of 18 percent per annum (APR). The Anderson's statement from the department store is on the next page. It covers all account activity for the 31-day period beginning August 15, 1989, and ending September 14, 1989.

Department Number	Dates		Transaction Description	Charges	Credits
	Month	Day			
100	8	30	Payment		$45.00
105	9	01	Fashion Wear	$18.26	
335	9	01	Hosiery	22.54	
271	9	01	Footwear	17.10	

To Your Previous Balance	We Added Your Charges	We Added Your Finance Charges	We Deducted Payments	We Deducted Other Credits	This Is Your New Balance
$215.00	$57.90	$?	$45.00	$0	$?

Account Number	Billing Dates		Average Daily Balance	Finance Charge (1½%) Computed on Average Daily Balance	Minimum Amount to Send
	This Month	Next Month			
070652981	9/14/89	10/14/89	$?	$?	$20.00

Note: If a finance charge is shown, it is calculated by taking 1½ percent of the average daily balance. Purchases made during the current billing period are *not* included in the calculation of the average daily balance. This calculation results in an annual percentage rate of 18%.

Questions

1. ·Calculate the average daily balance that the department store would use to determine the applicable finance charges.
2. How large a finance charge will be levied on that balance?
3. Compute the new balance that would be shown on the statement.
4. Using the information presented, calculate the finance charges by the (a) previous balance method, (b) adjusted balance method, and (c) past due balance method assuming full payment is rendered within the time allotted.
5. Which method of computing finance charges would be preferable for the Andersons? Explain.

FOR MORE INFORMATION

General Information Articles

Boronson, Warren, "The Truth About Home-Equity Loans," *Sylvia Porter's Personal Finance,* June 1987, pp. 46–54.

Brooks, Patricia, "Forging a Debt-Free Future," *Sylvia Porter's Personal Finance,* May 1986, pp. 87–95.

Dunnan, Nancy, "Your Credit Report—Is It Really You?" *Sylvia Porter's Personal Finance,* June 1988, pp. 72–78.

Klein, Robert J., "How to Borrow Like a Pro," *Money,* April 1987, pp. 133–141.

Updegrave, Walter L., "How Lenders Size You Up," *Money,* April 1987, pp. 145–154.

Government Documents and Other Publications

Consumer Handbook to Credit Protection Laws. Publication Services, MS138; Board of Governors; Federal Reserve System; Washington, D.C. 20551.

Home Equity Credit Lines. FTC Publications; Federal Trade Commission; Sixth St. and Pennsylvania Ave., N.W.; Washington, D.C. 20580.

Some General Information About Bankruptcy. Administrative Office of the U.S. Courts; Bankruptcy Division; Washington, D.C. 20544.

Understanding Credit Bureaus. Bankcard Holders of America; 460 Spring Park Place, Suite 1000; Herndon, VA 22070.

What Truth in Lending Means to You. FTC Publications; Federal Trade Commission; Sixth St. and Pennsylvania Ave., N.W.; Washington, D.C. 20580.

CHAPTER 8

Using Consumer Loans

Financial Facts or Fantasies

Are the following statements financial facts (true) or fantasies (false)?

- Buying a new car is the major reason that people borrow money through consumer loans.
- Consumer loans can be set up with fixed rates of interest or with variable loan rates.
- An S&L is the only type of financial institution that is prohibited from making consumer loans.
- Most single-payment loans are secured with some type of collateral and are usually relatively short term in duration (maturities of one year or less).
- Using the discount method to figure interest is one way of lowering the effective cost of a consumer loan.
- The Rule of 78s is a regulation that grew out of the Consumer Credit Enhancement Act of 1978 and mandates how installment loans will be set up.

Several months after his graduation from college, Chris Jenkins decided it was time to buy a new car. After a few weeks of careful comparison shopping, he settled on a new Ford Probe GT; with some options added, the car had a sticker price of $16,000. Chris, of course, could not afford to pay cash for the car, so using his old car as a trade-in and some money he had received as a graduation gift, he put $4,000 down and financed the rest with a $12,000, 48-month loan. Fortunately, he held a good-paying job as a film editor for a major West Coast advertising agency and easily qualified for the loan.

At one time or another, most people find themselves in a situation just like the one Chris Jenkins faced: They need to borrow money in order to finance the purchase of a car or some other expensive item. This is where *consumer loans* come into play, for they provide families and individuals with the financial wherewithal for making expensive purchases. Unlike open account credit, discussed in Chapter 7, these are individually negotiated loans that are made for specific purposes and terminate when they are paid off.

BASIC FEATURES OF CONSUMER LOANS

In addition to open account credit, consumers can also *borrow money* from banks and other financial institutions; these loans can be set up as either single-payment or installment loans, and they can be used to pay for just about any type of big-ticket item. Can you list some reasons why you might want to borrow money through a consumer loan? How important do you think it is that the loan-repayment schedule fit into your monthly budget? Take a few minutes before reading on to think about these questions.

At several points in this book, we have discussed the different types of financial goals that individuals and families can set for themselves. These goals often involve substantial sums of money and may include such things as the purchase of a new car or perhaps a once-in-a-lifetime vacation. One way to reach these goals is to systematically save the necessary money. Another is to use a consumer loan to partially finance the transaction. Consumer loans are important to the personal financial planning process because of the help they provide in reaching certain types of financial goals. Working a major expenditure or purchase into a financial plan can be done just as easily with a consumer loan as it can by saving. The key, of course, is to successfully manage the credit by keeping the amount of debt used and the debt-repayment burden *well within the budget!*

Using Consumer Loans

As we saw in Chapter 7, the use of open account credit can prove helpful to those who plan and live within their personal financial budgets. More important to the long-run achievement of personal financial goals, however, are single-payment and installment consumer loans. These long-term liabilities are used most commonly to finance durable goods that are too expensive to purchase out of current funds, or, occasionally, for certain types of nondurable items, such as a college education or vacations. Of course, the extent to which this type of borrowing is used must be dictated by personal financial plans and budgets.

These loans differ from open account credit in the formality of their lending arrangements. While open account credit results from a rather informal process, consumer loans are formal, negotiated contracts that specify both the terms for borrowing and the repayment schedule. In addition, whereas an open account credit line can be used over and over again, consumer loans are one-shot transactions that are made for specific purposes. Because there is no revolving credit with a consumer loan, there is no more credit available (from that particular loan) once it is paid off. Further, there are no credit cards or checks issued with this form of credit. Finally, while open account credit is used chiefly to make repeated purchases of relatively low-cost *goods and services,* consumer loans are used mainly as a way to *borrow money* (that is, obtain cash) to pay for big-ticket items.

Reasons for Borrowing. While they can be used for just about any legitimate purpose, most consumer loans fall into one of the following categories:

■ Auto loans
■ Loans for other durable goods
■ Education loans
■ Personal loans
■ Consolidation loans

The most common reason for borrowing money through a consumer loan is to buy a new car (or truck or van)—in fact, *auto loans* account for nearly half of all consumer loans. As a rule, about 80 percent of the cost of a new vehicle (somewhat less with used cars) can be financed with credit; the buyer must come up with the rest through a *down payment.* The loan is *secured* with the auto— that is, the vehicle serves as **collateral** for the loan and can be repossessed by the lender in the event the buyer fails to make payments. These loans generally have maturities of from 36 to 60 months, and perhaps longer.

Buying a new car is the major reason that people borrow money through consumer loans. **Fact:** Buying a new car accounts for nearly half of all consumer loans outstanding.

Consumer loans can also be taken out on other kinds of costly *durable goods,* such as furniture, TVs and home appliances, camper trailers, snowmobiles and other recreational equipment, home computers, and even small airplanes and mobile homes. These loans are also secured, with the item(s) purchased serving as collateral. Some down payment is almost always required with these loans, and their maturities vary with the type of asset purchased: 9- to 12-month loans are common with less costly items, such as TVs and stereos, whereas 7- to 10-year loans are the rule with mobile homes.

Another reason for taking out a consumer loan is to pay for an *education.* Available for both undergraduate and graduate education, these loans often carry low (subsidized) interest rates and have loan-repayment schedules that do not start until the student is out of school.

Still another form of consumer loan is the **personal loan**. This type of credit typically is used to make expenditures for nondurables, such as an expensive European vacation, or to cover temporary cash shortfalls. Many personal loans are made on an *unsecured* basis—that is, there is no collateral in the loan other than the borrower's good name.

Finally, there are **consolidation loans**, which are used in an attempt to straighten out an unhealthy credit situation. For various reasons, consumers sometimes use credit cards, credit lines, and/or consumer loans to the point where they simply cannot service the debt according to the terms of agreement. When this happens, a consolidation loan can help them to systematically bring their credit situation under control. By borrowing money from one source to pay off other forms of credit, they can replace, say, five or six monthly payments that total $400 with one payment amounting to $250. People who use consolidation loans must be careful to abstain from using credit cards and other forms of credit until the loans have been fully paid off; otherwise, they may end up right back where they started.

Single Payment or Installment Payments. Consumer loans can also be broken into categories based on the type of repayment arrangement—single-payment or installment. **Single-payment loans** are made for a specified period of time at the end of which payment in full (principal plus interest) is due. They are generally used to finance purchases that are expected to be repaid within a year and usually have maturities ranging from 30 days to one year; rarely do these loans run for two years or more. Sometimes single-payment loans are made to finance purchases or pay bills when the cash to be used for repayment is known to be forthcoming in the near future; in this case, they serve as a form of **interim financing**. In other situations, single-payment loans are used by consumers who want to avoid being strapped with monthly installment payments and choose instead to make one large payment at the end of the loan. Often these loans are negotiated on short notice in order to meet some unexpected need.

Installment loans are repaid in a series of fixed, scheduled payments rather than a lump sum. The payments are almost always set up on a monthly basis, with each installment being made up partly of principal and partly of interest; for example, out of a $75 monthly payment, $60 might be credited to principal and the balance to interest. These loans are typically made to finance the pur-

---

collateral
An item of value that is used to secure the principal portion of a loan.

personal loan
A type of consumer loan typically used for the purchase of nondurable items or for covering a temporary cash shortfall.

consolidation loan
A loan made from one source to pay off other, existing debts; used to reduce monthly debt-repayment burden.

single-payment loan
A loan made for a specified period of time at the end of which payment in full is due.

interim financing
The use of a single-payment loan to finance a purchase or pay bills in situations where either the funds to be used for repayment are known to be forthcoming in the near future or permanent financing is to be arranged.

installment loan
A loan that is repaid in a series of fixed, scheduled payments rather than a lump sum.

chase of a good or service for which current resources are inadequate. The repayment period can run from six months to six years, or more.

Installment loans have become a way of life for many consumers; they are popular because they provide a convenient way in which to "buy now and pay later" in fixed monthly installments that can be readily incorporated into a family budget. The process of using installment loans to finance purchases is often referred to as "buying on time."

Fixed or Variable Rate. The majority of consumer loans are made at fixed rates of interest—that is, the interest rate charged (as well as the monthly payment) remains the same over the life of the obligation. However, variable-rate loans are also being made with increasing frequency, especially on longer-term installment loans; for example, they are becoming more and more common with 7- to 10-year mobile-home loans and 36- to 60-month auto loans. As with a variable-rate home mortgage, the rate of interest charged on such credit changes every 6 to 12 months in keeping with prevailing market conditions. If market interest rates go up, the rate of interest on the loan goes up accordingly, as does the monthly loan payment. These loans have periodic adjustment dates (6 to 12 months apart), at which time the interest rate and monthly payment are adjusted as necessary. Once an adjustment is made, the new rate remains in effect until the next adjustment date (sometimes the amount of the payments remains the same, but the number of payments changes).

Variable rates can also be used with single-payment loans, but the mechanics are a bit different. That is, the rate charged is usually pegged to the prime rate. For example, the rate might be prime plus 3 points; if prime is 12 percent, the borrower starts with a rate of interest of 12 + 3 = 15 percent. When the prime rate changes, the rate of interest on the loan changes automatically, except that in this case the adjustment is made *immediately* (there are usually no adjustment dates with single-payment, variable-rate loans). The loan will then carry a new rate of interest that will remain in effect until the next change. At maturity, interest charges at the different rates will be totaled and added to the principal to determine the size of the (single) loan payment. Variable-rate loans are desirable *if*

interest rates are expected to fall over the course of the loan; in contrast, fixed-rate loans are preferable *if interest rates are expected to rise*.

Consumer loans can be set up with fixed rates of interest or with variable loan rates. **Fact:** While fixed-rate loans still dominate the consumer loan market, variable-rate loans are becoming more common, particularly with longer-term debt.

The Rising Cost of Borrowing. Regardless of whether consumer loans are fixed or variable, their cost tends to vary over time with market conditions. Inevitably, there are times when the cost of credit simply becomes too high to justify borrowing as a way of making major purchases. So when market rates start climbing, you should ask yourself whether the cost is really worth it; financially, you may be better off delaying the purchase until rates come down. This is especially true today, since the effective cost of borrowing has gone way up with recent changes in the tax laws. In particular, one of the things that the Tax Reform Act of 1986 began to eliminate was the tax deduction of consumer loan interest. The way it stands now, only 20 percent of such interest expenses will be deductible in 1989; only 10 percent in 1990; and none in 1991 (see Chapter 4 for full details). And this applies to most types of consumer loans, *including all the different types of loans discussed in this chapter, regardless of whether they're used to buy a car or finance an education.*

To appreciate what this means, take a look at Exhibit 8.1. It shows what $1,000 in consumer loan interest expense will be worth in different tax years and under different tax rates. Notice in 1989, for example, that even though the borrower paid $1,000 in interest expense, only $200 of it is tax deductible—that is, $1,000 × 20 percent. Then, depending on what tax bracket the borrower is in (*and assuming he itemizes deductions*), he'll save only $30 to $66 in taxes! Clearly, that's not a lot of tax savings for $1,000 worth of interest expense; and it only gets worse in 1990 and 1991.

The net effect of all this is that the borrower will have to carry a greater burden of the cost of consumer debt. This fact becomes most evident when you look at the effective after-tax cost of a loan (by *effective cost* here we mean the actual *out-of-pocket*

EXHIBIT 8.1

Consumer Loans and Income Taxes

At present (1989), you can deduct only a small portion of consumer interest expenses
from federal tax returns, and in a couple of years, you won't be able to deduct any of
it. Thus, the after-tax cost of borrowing is becoming more and more expensive.

	1989	1990	1991 and beyond
Deductability of consumer interest expense	20%	10%	0
Amount of $1,000 in interest expense that is deductible	$200	$100	0
Taxes saved under following tax brackets:			
15%	$ 30[a]	$ 15	0
28%	$ 56	$ 28	0
33%	$ 66	$ 33	0
After-tax cost of $1,000 in interest expense:			
15% tax bracket	$970	$985	$1,000
28% tax bracket	$944	$972	$1,000
33% tax bracket	$934	$967	$1,000
Effective (After-tax) cost of a 12% loan:			
15% tax bracket	11.6%	11.8%	12.0%
28% tax bracket	11.3%	11.7%	12.0%
33% tax bracket	11.2%	11.6%	12.0%

[a]Taxes saved equals amount deductible multiplied by borrower's tax bracket; for example, in
1989: $200 × .15 = $30.

(Assumptions: $1,000 in annual consumer loan interest expenses; borrower itemizes deductions;
and loans carry 12% rate of interest)

cost of borrowing). As you can see in the exhibit, the effective cost of credit—at all three tax rates—remains very close to the stated rate (of 12 percent); and by 1991, the effective and stated rates will be equal. Thus, by eliminating the tax subsidy, the government has made the cost of borrowing a lot higher than it used to be. Consequently, as a borrower you should take greater care when using consumer credit. The more expensive credit becomes, the less attractive it is.

Where Can You Get Consumer Loans?

Consumer loans can be obtained from a number of sources, including commercial banks, consumer finance companies, credit unions, savings and loan associations, sales finance companies, life insurance companies, possibly even friends and relatives. The selection of a lender often depends on both the rate of interest charged and the ease with which the loan can be negotiated. Exhibit 8.2 provides a summary of the characteristics of the major sources of consumer loans.

Commercial Banks. Because they offer various types of loans at attractive rates of interest, commercial banks are a popular source of consumer loans. One nice thing about commercial banks is that they typically charge lower rates than most other lenders, in large part because they take only the best credit risks and are able to obtain relatively inexpensive funds from their depositors. The demand for their loans is generally high, and they can be selective in making consumer loans. Commercial banks usually lend only to customers with good credit ratings who can readily demonstrate an ability to make repayment in accordance with the specified terms. They also give preference to loan applicants who are account holders. The fact that an applicant is a good customer of the bank greatly enhances his or her chances of being approved for the requested financing. Although banks prefer to make loans secured by some type of collateral, they also make unsecured loans to their better customers. The interest rate charged on a bank loan may be affected by the loan's size, terms, and whether it is secured by some type of collateral.

EXHIBIT 8.2

The Major Sources of Consumer Loans

Banks, finance companies, and other financial institutions provide a full range of consumer credit to their customers; these institutions follow a variety of lending policies and lend money at different rates of interest.

	Commercial Banks	Consumer Finance Companies
Types of Loan	▪ Single-payment loans ▪ Personal installment loans ▪ Passbook loans ▪ Check-credit plans ▪ Credit card loans ▪ Second mortgages	▪ Personal installment loans ▪ Second mortgages
Lending Policies	▪ Seek customers with established credit history ▪ Often require collateral or security ▪ Prefer to deal in large loans such as auto, home improvement, and modernization, with the exception of credit card and check-credit plans ▪ Determine repayment schedules according to purpose of loan ▪ Vary credit rates according to the type of credit, time period, customer's credit history, and security offered ▪ May require several days to process a new credit application	▪ Often lend to consumers without established credit history ▪ Often make unsecured loans ▪ Often vary rates according to size of loan balance ▪ Offer a variety of repayment schedules ▪ Make a higher percentage of small loans than other lenders ▪ Maximum loan size limited by law ▪ Process applications quickly, frequently same day as application is made
Costs	▪ Lower than some lenders because they: —Take fewer credit risks —Lend depositors' money, a relatively inexpensive source of funds —Deal primarily in large loans, which yield larger dollar income without raising administrative costs	▪ Higher than most because they: —Take greater risks —Must borrow and pay interest on money to lend —Deal frequently in small loans, which are costly to make and yield a small income
Services	▪ Offer several different types of consumer credit plans ▪ May offer financial counseling ▪ Handle credit transactions confidentially	▪ Provide credit promptly ▪ Make loans to pay off accumulated debts willingly ▪ Design repayment schedules to fit the borrower's income ▪ Usually offer financial counseling ▪ Handle credit transactions confidentially

Source: This information adapted from the booklet, *Managing Your Credit,* published by the Money Management Institute of Household Financial Services, Prospect Heights, Illinois, 1985.

Consumer Finance Companies. Sometimes called *small loan companies,* **consumer finance companies** make secured and unsecured, or signature, loans to qualified individuals. These companies do not accept deposits but obtain funds from their stockholders and through open mar-

ket borrowing. Because they do not have the inexpensive sources of funds that banks and other deposit-type institutions do, their interest rates are generally quite high. The actual rates charged by consumer finance companies are regulated by interest rate ceilings (or usury laws) set by the states

Credit Unions	Savings and Loan Associations	Life Insurance Companies
▪ Personal installment loans ▪ Share draft credit plans ▪ Credit card loans ▪ Second mortgages	▪ Personal installment loans ▪ Home improvement loans ▪ Education loans ▪ Savings account loans ▪ Second mortgages	▪ Single or partial payment loans
▪ Lend to members only ▪ Make unsecured loans ▪ May require collateral or cosigner for loans over a specified amount ▪ May require payroll deductions to pay off loan ▪ May submit large loan applications to a committee of members for approval ▪ Offer a variety of repayment schedules	▪ Will lend to all creditworthy individuals ▪ Often require collateral ▪ Loan rates vary depending on size of loan, length of payment, and security involved	▪ Lend on cash value of life insurance policy ▪ No date or penalty on repayment ▪ Deduct amount owed from value of policy benefit if death or other maturity occurs before repayment
▪ Lower than most because they: —Take fewer credit risks —Lend money deposited by members, which is less expensive than borrowed money —Often receive free office space and supplies from sponsoring organization —Are managed by members whose services in most cases are donated —Enjoy federal income tax exemptions	▪ Lower than some lenders because they: —Lend depositors' money, a relatively inexpensive source of funds —Secure most loans by savings accounts, real estate, or some other asset	▪ Lower than many because they: —Take no risk —Pay no collection costs —Secure loans by cash value of policy
▪ Design repayment schedules to fit borrower's income ▪ Generally provide credit life insurance without extra charge ▪ May offer financial counseling ▪ Handle credit transactions confidentially	▪ Often offer financial counseling ▪ Specialize in mortgages and other housing-related loans ▪ Handle credit transactions confidentially	▪ Permit repayment at any time ▪ Handle credit transactions confidentially

in which they operate. The maximum allowable interest rate may vary with the size of the loan, and the state regulatory authorities may also limit the length of the repayment period. Loans made by consumer finance companies typically are for $5,000 or less and are secured by some type of

consumer finance company

A firm that makes secured and unsecured personal loans to qualified individuals; also called a *small loan company.*

asset. Repayment is required on an installment basis, usually over a period of five years or less.

Consumer finance companies generally make small loans to high-risk borrowers. Of course, these loans are quite costly, but they may be the only alternative for people with poor credit ratings. Some people are attracted to consumer finance companies because of the ease with which they may obtain loans. Due to the high rates of interest charged, individuals should consider this source only after exhausting all others.

Credit Unions. Only members can obtain installment and single-payment loans from credit unions. Because they are nonprofit organizations with minimal operating costs, credit unions charge relatively low rates on their loans.

They make either unsecured or secured loans, depending on the size and type of loan being requested. The maximum allowable size of loans is often set by certain regulatory agencies. In addition, the directors of a credit union frequently set their own in-house loan limits. Generally speaking, membership in a credit union provides the most attractive borrowing opportunities available, since their interest rates and borrowing requirements usually are more favorable than other sources of consumer loans. An added convenience of a credit union loan is that loan payments can often be deducted directly from payroll checks.

Savings and Loan Associations. Savings and loan associations (as well as savings banks) primarily make mortgage loans. However, they are also permitted to make loans on such consumer durables as automobiles, televisions, refrigerators, and ranges. In addition, they can make certain types of home improvement and mobile-home loans, as well as some personal and educational loans using passbook savings as collateral. Among other things, financial deregulation has enabled S&Ls to enter the consumer loan market. Since 1982, federally chartered S&Ls have been allowed to invest up to 30 percent of their assets in consumer loans, and most experts fully expect them to become a more important force in the consumer loan field as they go after a bigger share of this market (particularly in the wake of the "S&L crisis"). As a rule, the rates of interest on consumer loans at S&Ls are fairly close to the rates charged by commercial banks,

though if anything, they tend to be a bit more expensive. Like their banking counterparts, the rates charged on specific loans will, in the final analysis, depend on such factors as the type and purpose of the loan, the duration and type of repayment, and the overall creditworthiness of the borrower.

An S&L is the only type of financial institution that is prohibited from making consumer loans. **Fantasy:** Financial deregulation has opened up the consumer loan market to S&Ls. Since they can allocate up to 30 percent of their assets to consumer loans, they are in fact an important source of such credit.

Sales Finance Companies. Businesses that sell more expensive items—such as automobiles, furniture, and appliances—often provide installment financing to purchasers of their products. Because dealers cannot afford to tie up their funds in installment contracts, they sell them to a **sales finance company** for cash. This procedure is often referred to as "selling paper," since merchants in effect sell their loans to a third party. When the sales finance company purchases these notes, customers are usually notified to make payments directly to it.

The largest sales finance organizations are the **captive finance companies** owned by manufacturers of big-ticket items—automobiles and appliances. General Motors Acceptance Corporation (GMAC) and General Electric Credit Corporation (GECC) are just two examples of captive finance companies that purchase the installment loans made by dealers of their products. Also, most commercial banks act as sales finance companies by buying paper from auto dealers and others businesses. The cost of financing through a sales finance company is generally a little higher than the rates charged by banks and S&Ls, particularly when you let the dealer do all the work in arranging the financing (dealers normally get a cut on the finance income, so it's obviously to their advantage to secure as *high* a rate of interest as possible). However, starting in late 1982, auto manufacturers began aggressively using interest rates on new-car loans as a marketing tool. They did this by dropping the rates of interest on car loans (*for selected models*) to levels that were well below the market—for example, in the spring of 1989, Ford and GM were offering 2 percent, 2-year financing on some of their cars, and Chrysler was making 2-year loans at *zero* interest. In this way the auto manufacturers are able to use these loan rates (along with rebates) to stimulate sales by keeping the cost of buying a new car down; clearly, cutting the cost of borrowing for a new car can result in big savings!

Life Insurance Companies. Life insurance policyholders often can obtain loans from their insurance companies. Certain types of policies not only provide death benefits but also have a savings function, in which case they can be used as collateral for loans. (Be careful with these loans, however, as they could involve a tax penalty if certain conditions are not met. A detailed discussion of life insurance is presented in Chapter 9.) Life insurance companies are required by law to make loans against the **cash values**—the amount of accumulated savings—of certain types of life insurance policies. The rate of interest on this type of loan is stated on the policy, and it used to be set as low as 5 or 6 percent. The newer policies, however, carry loan rates that aren't set until the loans are made; that usually means borrowing money at or near prevailing market rates. While you will be charged interest for as long as the policy loan is outstanding, these loans do not have repayment dates—in other words, you do not have to pay them back. The reason for this is when you take out a loan against the cash value of your life insurance policy, you are really borrowing your own money. Therefore, the amount of the loan outstanding, plus any accrued interest, will be deducted from the amount of coverage provided by the policy. The chief danger in life insurance loans is that they do not have a firm maturity date; consequently, borrowers may lack the motivation to repay them.

Friends and Relatives. Sometimes a close friend or relative will be willing to lend you money. In many cases, such loans are attractive because little or no interest is charged. The terms will, of course, vary depending on the financial needs of the borrower, but they should be specified in some type of loan agreement that states the costs, conditions, and maturity date of the loan as well as the obligations of both borrower and lender. Not only does a written loan agreement reduce opportunities for disagreement and unhappiness, it also protects both borrower and lender should either of them die or other unexpected events occur. Still, *given the potential for disagreement and conflict*

inherent in this type of arrangement, borrowing from friends or relatives is not advisable, and should be seriously considered only when there are no other viable alternatives, or perhaps if the terms of credit are so much better than those available from the more traditional sources. Indeed, as the accompanying *Money in Action* box suggests, a loan to or from a friend or family member is far more than a run-of-the-mill banking transaction: the interest is emotional, and the risks are the relationship itself!

Managing Your Credit

Borrowing money to make major acquisitions—and, in general, using consumer loans—is a sound and perfectly legitimate way to conduct your financial affairs. Meeting a major financial goal by buying on credit can be worked into your network of financial plans, while servicing the debt can be factored into your monthly cash budget. Doing it this way certainly is far superior to borrowing in a haphazard manner, giving little or no consideration to debt repayment. When borrowing is well thought out in advance and full consideration is given not only to the need for the asset or item in question but also to the repayment of the ensuing credit, sound credit management is the result. And sound credit management underlies effective personal financial planning.

Basically, you should address two questions when considering the use of a consumer loan: (1) Does making this acquisition fit into your financial plans? (2) Does the required debt service on the loan fit into your monthly cash budget? If the expenditure in question will seriously jeopardize

---

sales finance company
A firm that purchases notes drawn up by sellers of certain types of merchandise, typically big-ticket items.

captive finance company
A sales finance company that is owned by a manufacturer of big-ticket merchandise; GMAC is a captive finance company.

cash value (of life insurance)
An accumulation of savings in an insurance policy that can be used as a source of loan collateral.

MONEY IN ACTION

Lending Money to a Relative: How to Say 'No'; When to Say 'Yes'

Everyone has a story to tell about lending money to family members, but few want to be quoted. With good reason: Not many have endings where lender and borrower walk away hand-in-hand.

"I made every mistake possible when my daughter asked me for a $25,000 loan for a down payment on the home she wanted to buy," says an embarrassed 50-year-old Chicago woman. "It was 10 years since her father and I were divorced, but I was still guilt-ridden about the anguish it had caused her. My financial situation was simple. I had a $40,000-a-year job, a heavily mortgaged house and a $30,000 certificate of deposit. Without telling her of my financial position, I said 'yes'—and cashed in my CD."

The saga gets worse. The daughter added hot tubs, a greenhouse and a stereo system to the house—but didn't repay the loan. The mother resented it—and said something. The daughter became defensive. The relationship soured. It's a familiar story. Tangled in emotions,

people frequently say "yes" to a family loan when they want to say "no."

Saying "No"

Shy of real need—a debilitating illness, a sum to tide someone over during a few problem months, a life-threatening situation—there are good reasons to say "no" when Cousin Joe asks for a loan.

▪ *I can't afford it.* Some people find these four words impossible to mouth. They really want to help out, but can't. For these people, Linda Barbanel, a New York City psychotherapist who writes about money matters, suggests a three-step approach to saying "no."

"Repeat what it is that the borrower wants," she advises. "In case you've misunderstood, you allow Cousin Joe to clarify the situation. Then explain, in general terms, why you can't lend the money. Finally, and most important, suggest joint problem-solving. Perhaps you know people who are in a better position to finance Joe's new business. Maybe he can use the

spare desk in your den as a 'starter office.'" It's a way of providing support without dollars.

▪ *I think the borrower is irresponsible.* "Any time a person asks you for money, you have a right to know what the money is going to be used for and how it's going to be repaid," says Paul Westbrook, a certified financial planner in Watchung, N.J. "If a person is evasive on either score, I recommend saying 'no.'"

▪ *I don't like Joe.* Bank lending officers don't assess personalities, but a family lender has every right to. Financial dealings among family members are difficult enough when there's a good relationship built on trust.

▪ *I don't think it's a good deal.* The nouvelle cuisine restaurant Joe plans to open with a friend he met three months ago is miles out of town. Not only that, all Joe and his friend know about food is that they like to eat. Just because Joe is kin doesn't mean that someone has to finance a failure.

your financial plans and/or if the repayment of the loan is likely to place an undue strain on your cash flow, you should definitely reconsider the purchase! Perhaps it can be postponed, or you can liquidate some assets in order to come up with more down payment, or you may even have to alter

some other area of your financial plan in order to work the expenditure in. Whatever route you choose, the key point is to make sure that it will be fully compatible with your financial plans and cash budget *before* the loan is taken out and the money spent.

Saying "Yes"

But family *is* family. And more and more, family loans are the source of down payments on first homes, seed money for new businesses and financial first aid when there's a break in earnings. When handled properly, lending money to relatives can be a source of great personal pleasure.

When Cindy Ley, a young Minneapolis attorney, left her apartment for work one morning in July 1987, she found her car in two feet of water. It was ruined. "My insurance company gave me $1800 for it," she says. "I found a wonderful $5000 used car, but I was short $3200. Mom and Dad suggested I borrow the money from them." Cindy admits she was hesitant. "I didn't want to feel like a failure in the real world. I wanted to be financially independent. But they dispelled my fears."

Cindy has never missed a payment. ("I'd make this payment before any others," she says), though her parents aren't concerned. So what makes for a successful transaction? Here are some suggestions:

- *It's handled in businesslike fashion:*

1) It needn't be more than a one-page handwritten agreement, but the terms should be explicit and agreed upon by both parties.

2) Is interest being charged? If so, how much and when is it due—monthly, quarterly or yearly?

3) When is the loan to be repaid? Whenever the borrower can or at stated intervals? At the end of the loan period?

4) If the loan can't be paid off as agreed upon, what are the alternative solutions?

5) If the lender needs the money unexpectedly, what should the borrower be prepared to do?

6) If the lender dies, what happens to the outstanding loan? Is it terminated? Is it owed to the estate?

- *Both parties understand that this is a loan—not a gift.* If this is not clearly spelled out, the loan agreement can fade from the borrower's memory (though the lender rarely has the same amnesia).

- *The borrower is investing something of himself in the deal.* In Cindy Ley's case, it was her $1800 insurance money. But it doesn't have to be money. It can be time invested in making a new business work or improving a home. Whatever it is, it's important, so that the lender doesn't feel he or she is being taken advantage of.

- *The lender understands the downside if the loan can't be repaid.* When a family loan *can't* be repaid because a business fails or the borrower falls on hard times, chances are the lender will do nothing—no lien will be put on the borrower's home, no salary will be attached. A relative has to be able to accept that— both financially and emotionally.

Source: Adapted from Patricia Schiff Estess, "Should You Lend Money to a Relative? When to Say 'Yes' & How to Say 'No,'" *Parade Magazine,* July 24, 1988, pp. 4–5. Reprinted with permission from *Parade* and Patricia Schiff Estess.

Shopping for Loans. Once you have decided to use credit, it is equally important that you shop around and evaluate the various costs and terms available. Now that truth-in-lending laws require creditors to clearly state all finance charges, it may appear that the only thing you need do to make a sound credit decision is determine which source offers the lowest finance charge. This could not be further from the truth—for while the charge for credit is of obvious concern to most borrowers, there are other factors that should be considered when shopping for credit.

EXHIBIT 8.3

Tracking Your Consumer Debt

A worksheet like this allows you to keep track of your outstanding credit along with your monthly debt service requirements. Such information is a major component of sound credit management.

AN INVENTORY OF CONSUMER DEBT

Name _____ Date _____

Type of Consumer Debt		Current Monthly Payment[a]	Latest Balance Due
Auto loans	1.	$	$
	2.		
	3.		
Education loans	1.		
	2.		
Personal installment loans	1.		
	2.		
Home improvement loan			
Other installment loans	1.		
	2.		
Single-payment loans	1.		
	2.		
Credit cards (retail charge cards, bank cards, T&E cards, etc.)	1.		
	2.		
	3.		
	4.		
	5.		
	6.		
	7.		
Overdraft protection line			
Personal line of credit			
Home equity credit line			
Loan on life insurance			
Margin loan from broker			
Other loans	1.		
	2.		
	3.		
Totals		$	$

$$\text{Debt safety ratio} = \frac{\text{Total monthly payments}}{\text{Monthly take-home pay}} \times 100 = \frac{\$}{\$} \times 100 = \underline{\qquad}\%$$

[a] Leave the space blank if there is *no* monthly payment required on a loan (e.g., as with a single-payment or education loan).

Loan maturity. Try to make sure that the size and number of payments will fit comfortably into your spending and savings plans. As a rule, the cost of credit increases with the length of the repayment period. Thus, to lower your cost, you should consider shortening the loan maturity—but only to the point where doing so will not place an unnecessary strain on your cash flow. For while a shorter maturity may reduce the cost of the loan, it will also increase the size of the monthly loan payment. Indeed, finding a monthly loan payment that you will be comfortable with is a critical dimension of sound credit management. Fortunately, the personal computer provides an effective way of evaluating different loan configurations. Altering the loan maturity is just one way of coming up with an affordable monthly payment; with the aid of a personal computer, you can quickly run through all sorts of alternatives to find the one that will best fit your monthly budget.

Total cost of the transaction. When comparison shopping for credit, you should always look at both the total cost of the price of the item purchased *and* the price of the credit. Retailers often manipulate both sticker prices and interest rates, so you really will not know what kind of deal you are getting until you look at the total cost of the transaction. Along this line, comparing *monthly payments* is a good way to get a handle on total cost. It is a simple matter to compare total costs: Just add the amount put down on the purchase to the total of all the monthly loan payments; other things being equal, the one with the lowest total is the one you should pick.

Collateral. You should make sure that you know up front what collateral (if any) you will have to pledge on the loan and what you stand to lose in case you default on your payments. Actually, if it makes no difference to you and if it is not too inconvenient, using collateral makes sense, since it often results in lower finance charges—perhaps half a percentage point or so.

Other credit considerations. In addition to the above guidelines, other questions that you should address include the following: Can you choose a payment date that will be compatible with your spending patterns? Can you obtain credit promptly and conveniently? What are the charges for late payments, and are they reasonable? Will you receive a refund on credit charges if you prepay your loan? Taking the time to look around for the best credit deal will pay off not only in reducing the cost of such debt but also in keeping the burden of credit in line with your cash budget and financial plans. In the long run, you are the one who has the most to gain (or lose). Thus, you should see to it that the consumer debt you undertake does in fact have positive effects on your financial condition.

Keeping Track of Your Credit. In order to stay abreast of your financial condition, it is a good idea to periodically take inventory of the consumer debt you have outstanding. You should do this a minimum of once a year, and ideally every three or four months. To take inventory of what you owe, simply prepare a list of all your outstanding consumer debt. Include everything except your home mortgage—installment loans, single-payment loans, credit cards, revolving credit lines, overdraft protection lines, and home equity credit lines.

You might find a worksheet like the one in Exhibit 8.3 (on facing page) helpful in preparing a list of your debts. To use it, simply list the current monthly payment and the latest balance due for each type of consumer credit outstanding; then, total both columns to see how much you are paying each month and how large a debt load you have built up. Hopefully, when all the numbers have been totaled up, you will not be surprised to learn just how much you really do owe.

A way to quickly assess your debt position is to compute your *debt safety ratio* (we looked at this ratio in Chapter 7). You do this by dividing the total monthly payments (from the worksheet) by your monthly take-home pay. If 20 percent or more of your take-home pay is going to monthly credit payments, you are relying too heavily on credit; in contrast, if your debt safety ratio works out to 10 percent or less, you are in a strong credit position. Keeping track of your credit and holding the amount of outstanding debt to a reasonable level is the surest way to maintain your creditworthiness.

SINGLE-PAYMENT LOANS ▪

> The cost of a single-payment loan depends not only on the stated rate of interest, but also on the type of interest used to calculate finance charges. In addition to the cost of the loan, what other loan provisions—like the need for collateral, the maturity of the loan, and the existence of a prepayment penalty— would be important to you? Stop to think about this question before going on.

The single-payment loan differs from other loans in that it is repaid in full with a single payment on a given due date. The payment usually consists of principal and all interest charges. Sometimes, however, interim interest payments may have to be made (for example, every quarter), in which case the payment at maturity is made up of principal plus any unpaid interest. Single-payment loans can be secured or unsecured and can be taken out for just about any purpose, from buying a new car to paying for a vacation. They are most useful, however, when the funds needed for a given purchase or transaction are temporarily unavailable but expected to be forthcoming in the near future. By helping you cope with a temporary cash shortfall, these loans can serve as a form of interim financing until more permanent arrangements can be made. In contrast, some borrowers use single-payment loans on a *routine* basis simply because they like the freedom from making installment payments— indeed, since the respite from installment payments frees up their cash flow for other purposes, they have no intention of converting their single-payment loans to more "permanent" forms of financing.

Important Loan Features

The first thing you have to do when applying for either a single-payment or installment loan is submit a **loan application**, an example of which is shown in Exhibit 8.4. Basically, the loan application provides the lending institution with information about the purpose of the loan, whether it will be secured or unsecured, and the financial condition of the borrower. The loan officer uses this document, along with other information (such as a credit report from the local credit bureau), to determine whether or not you should be granted the loan. Once approved, you must consider the various features of the debt, the three most important of which are loan collateral, loan maturity, and loan repayment.

Loan Collateral. Most single-payment loans are secured by certain specified assets. For *collateral,* lenders accept only items that they feel will be readily marketable at a price sufficiently high to cover the principal portion of the loan—for example, an automobile, jewelry, or stocks and bonds. If a loan is obtained to purchase some personal asset, that asset may be used to secure it. In most cases, lenders do not take physical possession of the collateral but file a **lien**, which is a legal claim that permits them to liquidate collateral in order to satisfy the loan in the event of borrower default. The lien is filed in the county courthouse and is a matter of public record. If borrowers maintain possession or title to *movable* property—such as cars, TVs, and jewelry—the instrument that gives the lenders title to the property in the event of default is called a **chattel mortgage**. If lenders hold title to the collateral—or actually take possession of it, as in the case of stocks and bonds—the agreement giving them the right to sell these items in case of default is a **collateral note**.

Loan Maturity. As indicated earlier, the maturity, or term, on a single-payment loan usually extends for a period of one year or less and very rarely goes out to two years or longer. When you request a single-payment loan, you should be sure that its term is long enough to allow you to receive the money needed for repayment but not any longer than necessary; don't stretch the maturity out too far, since the dollar amount of the finance charges paid increases with time. Because the loan is paid off in a single payment, the lender must be assured that you will be able to repay it even if certain unexpected events occur in the future. The term of your single-payment loan therefore must be reconciled with your budget as well as your ability to pay. If the money you plan to use for repayment will be received periodically over the term of the loan, an installment type of loan may be more suitable.

Most single-payment loans are secured with some type of collateral and are usually relatively short term in duration (maturities of one year or less). **Fact:** Because these loans require only one payment at maturity, banks and other lenders generally keep them fairly short term and require some type of collateral.

Loan Repayment. The repayment of a single-payment loan is expected to take place on its maturity date. Occasionally the funds needed to repay this type of loan will be received prior to maturity. Depending on the lender, the borrower might be able to repay the loan early and thereby reduce the finance charges on it. Credit unions often permit early repayment of these loans with reduced finance charges. Commercial banks and other single-payment lenders, however, may not accept early repayments; or if they do, they will charge a **prepayment penalty** on them. This penalty normally amounts to a set percentage of the interest that would have been paid over the remaining life of the loan. The Truth in Lending Act requires lenders to disclose in the loan agreement whether or not, and in what amount, prepayment penalties are charged on a single-payment loan. A borrower should understand this information prior to signing a loan agreement.

Occasionally an individual will borrow money using a single-payment loan only to discover that he or she is short of money when the loan comes due—after all, making one big loan payment can cause a real strain on one's cash flow. Should this happen to you, don't just let the payment become past due; rather, inform the lender in advance so that a partial payment, loan extension, or some other arrangement can be made. Under such circumstances, the lender will often agree to a **loan rollover**, in which case the original loan is paid off by taking out another loan. The lender will usually require that all the interest and at least part of the principal be paid at the time of the rollover. Thus, if you originally borrowed $5,000 for 12 months, the bank might be willing to lend you, say, $3,000 for another 6 to 9 months as part of a loan rollover. In this case, you'll have to "pay down" $2,000 of the

original loan along with all interest due. However, you can expect the interest rate on a rollover loan to go up a bit; that is the price you pay for falling short on the first loan. Also, you should not expect to get more than one, or at the most two, loan rollovers—a bank's patience tends to grow somewhat short after a while!

Finance Charges and the Annual Percentage Rate

As indicated in Chapter 7, the Consumer Credit Protection Act, or Truth in Lending Act, requires lenders to disclose both the dollar amount of finance charges and the annual percentage rate (APR) of interest. A sample **loan disclosure statement** applicable for either a single-payment or in-

---

loan application
An application that provides a lender with information about the purpose of the requested loan, whether it will be secured or unsecured, and the applicant's financial condition.

lien
A legal claim that permits the lender, in the event of borrower default, to liquidate the items serving as collateral in order to satisfy the obligation.

chattel mortgage
A mortgage on personal property given as security for the payment of an obligation.

collateral note
A legal note that gives the lender the right to sell collateral in the event of the borrower's default on the obligation.

prepayment penalty
A penalty sometimes charged by a financial institution for advance payment of a loan.

loan rollover
The process of paying off a loan by taking out another, usually with the requirement that all interest and part of the principal on the original loan be paid at the time of rollover.

loan disclosure statement
A document that lenders are required to supply borrowers that states both the dollar amount of finance charges and the APR applicable to a loan.

EXHIBIT 8.4

A Bank Loan Application

The loan application contains information about the person(s) applying for the loan, including source(s) of income, current debt loan, even a short balance sheet.

THE Arizona BANK
Member FDIC
Equal Opportunity Lender and Employer M:F

APPLICATION FOR CREDIT

☐ READY RESERVACCOUNT $ _____ ($500 to $10,000)
☐ INSTALMENT LOAN FOR $ _____
PURPOSE _____

IMPORTANT NOTICE: Under Arizona law, property (including salary or wages) acquired by either husband or wife during marriage is the community property of both; property acquired before marriage or acquired after marriage by gift or inheritance and the income therefrom is the separate property of the spouse who acquired it.

Community Obligation: "This application, UNLESS OTHERWISE MARKED BELOW, is as an application for credit extended as a debt of the marital community, based upon the creditworthiness of that community." Supply all information requested on the application.

☐ Sole and Separate Obligation: This is an application for individual credit as a SOLE AND SEPARATE DEBT which will be evaluated without regard to the assets, income or creditworthiness of the applicant's spouse or the applicant's marital community. (The applicant should list only marital status, and no other information should be given regarding the spouse (if any) except name and address. Applicant should also list all debts for which he/she is obligated by signing a promise to pay and should also list all sole and separate assets and income.)

APPLICANT(S) INFORMATION

If there is a co-applicant and the co-applicant is not your spouse, the co-applicant is required to complete a separate application.

APPLICANT'S NAME	Last	First	Middle	AGE	BIRTHDATE	SOCIAL SECURITY NUMBER	HOME PHONE

PRESENT ADDRESS		CITY	STATE	ZIP	HOW LONG

FORMER ADDRESS		CITY	STATE	ZIP	HOW LONG

PRESENT EMPLOYER	NO. HRS WORKED PER WK	POSITION	GROSS INCOME $ MONTHLY	BUSINESS PHONE	HOW LONG

PREVIOUS EMPLOYER		POSITION	GROSS INCOME $ MONTHLY	BUSINESS PHONE	HOW LONG

☐ UNMARRIED	☐ MARRIED	☐ SEPARATED	SELF EMPLOYED ☐ YES ☐ NO	NUMBER OF DEPENDENTS	NO. YRS LIVED IN ARIZONA

SPOUSE OR CO-APPLICANT NAME (See "IMPORTANT NOTICE" above)	AGE	BIRTHDATE	SOCIAL SECURITY NO.	HOME PHONE

ADDRESS		CITY	STATE	ZIP	HOW LONG

EMPLOYER	POSITION	GROSS INCOME $ MONTHLY	BUSINESS PHONE	HOW LONG

Income from alimony, child support, or maintenance payments need not be revealed if you do not choose to disclose such income in applying for credit. As a creditor, we may inquire whether any income stated in an application is derived from such a source.

SOURCE OF OTHER INCOME	GROSS AMOUNT OF OTHER MONTHLY INCOME

NAME OF NEAREST RELATIVE OR FRIEND NOT LIVING WITH YOU	ADDRESS

BANK OR SAVINGS AND LOAN ASSOCIATION (NAME & BRANCH)	CHECKING ACCOUNT NO	SAVINGS ACCOUNT NO

☐ RENT ☐ OWN	MORTGAGEHOLDER OR LANDLORD	PURCHASE PRICE $	AMOUNT OWING $	MONTHLY PAYMENT OR RENT $

YEAR & MAKE OF AUTO	AUTO FINANCED THROUGH	DRIVERS LICENSE NO	AMOUNT OWING $	MONTHLY PAYMENT $

CREDIT REFERENCES AND DEBTS OUTSTANDING

(BANKS, FINANCE COMPANIES, CREDIT UNIONS, CREDIT CARDS AND OTHERS - EXCLUDING THOSE LISTED ABOVE)

NAME AND ADDRESS OF CREDITOR	ACCOUNT NUMBER	ORIGINAL AMOUNT	BALANCE OWING	MONTHLY PAYMENT
		$	$	$
		$	$	$
		$	$	$
		$	$	$
		$	$	$

HAVE YOU EVER HAD A REPOSSESSION? ☐ YES ☐ NO	HAVE YOU EVER FILED BANKRUPTCY? ☐ YES ☐ NO	IF YES WHERE?	YEAR

DO YOU HAVE LIFE INSURANCE? ☐ YES ☐ NO	AMOUNT $	NAME OF COMPANY

In submitting the foregoing application, I guarantee its accuracy with the intent that it be relied upon by the bank in extending credit or service to me. I warrant that I have no known obligations, direct or contingent, which have not been set forth hereon and that I have not knowingly withheld any material information of an adverse nature. I hereby authorize you to obtain such credit information and verification as you may require.

X _____ _____   X _____ _____
Applicant's Signature   Date   Spouse or Co-Applicant's Signature   Date

03003001 (Rev 3-84)   TUMBLE

Source: Courtesy of The Arizona Bank.

SHORT FORM STATEMENT

ASSETS		LIABILITIES	
Cash (on hand or in banks)	$ _____	Current Liabilities (short term loans due to pay off within one year.)	$ _____
Stocks & Bonds (Series E, etc.)	$ _____		$ _____
Loan Value Life Ins. (Face Amount $ _____)	$ _____	Loans on Life Insurance	$ _____
Furniture & Appliances (Present Value)	$ _____	Contracts & Loans on Furn. & Appliances	$ _____
Auto (Present Value)	$ _____	Contracts & Loans on Auto, Trailer, etc.	$ _____
Real Estate (Home, Estimated Value)	$ _____	Due on Home (Mortgage & Contracts)	$ _____
Real Estate (Other, Estimated Value)	$ _____	Due on Other Real Estate	$ _____
Other Assets (Describe)	$ _____	Other Loans, Notes or Contracts Owed	$ _____
		Other Liabilities (Describe)	$ _____
			$ _____
			$ _____
		TOTAL LIABILITIES	$ _____
		NET WORTH	$ _____
TOTAL ASSETS $ _____		**TOTAL** $ _____	

THIS FINANCIAL STATEMENT IS MADE WITH THE INTENT THAT THE BANK RELY THEREON IN EXTENDING CREDIT TO ME. I REPRESENT THAT THIS STATEMENT IS COMPLETE AND ACCURATE AND SETS FORTH ALL MY OBLIGATIONS. I AGREE TO GIVE THE BANK IMMEDIATE WRITTEN NOTICE OF ANY UNFAVORABLE CHANGE IN MY FINANCIAL CONDITION. ANY CONTINGENT LIABILITIES I HAVE ARE FULLY EXPLAINED ABOVE.

FINANCIAL STATEMENT AS OF _____ , 19 ____ SIGNATURE _____

FOR BANK USE

INSPECTION

YEAR/CYL.	MAKE	MODEL	SERIAL OR I.D. NUMBER	LICENSE NUMBER	ODOMETER READING

CONDITION - EXPLAIN (PAINT, BODY, GLASS, MOTOR, TIRES, UPHOLSTERY, ETC.)

☐ P/B ☐ P/S ☐ P/W ☐ A/T ☐ AIR ☐ OTHER

BOOK WHOLESALE	BOOK RETAIL	DEALER INVOICE	AUTO INSPECTED BY	DATE

COLLATERAL DESCRIPTION — LEGAL DESCRIPTION IF REAL ESTATE:

INSURANCE VERIFICATION

INSURANCE COMPANY

POLICY NUMBER | EXPIRATION DATE

POLICY COVERAGE | DATE VERIFIED

DESCRIPTION OF IMPROVEMENTS OR REPAIRS TO BE MADE:

INSURANCE AGENT

ADDRESS | TELEPHONE

ADDITIONAL INFORMATION

LOSS PAYABLE REQUESTED BY:

REMARKS

DETAILS OF LOAN

Cash Price of Purchase	$ _____
Down Payment	$ _____
Trade in Allowance	$ _____
Fees (Title, etc.)	$ _____
Insurance	$ _____
Balance to Finance	$ _____

CROSS SELLING

DID YOU ATTEMPT TO SELL OTHER BANK SERVICES, SUCH AS:
☐ Automatic Loan Payment
☐ DDA/Visa Banking Card
☐ Savings Account
☐ Safe Deposit Box

APPROVED	DECLINED	SIGNATURE OF LOAN OFFICER	DATE

EXHIBIT 8.5

A Loan Disclosure Statement

The loan disclosure statement informs the borrower of all charges (finance and other-wise) associated with the loan and the annual percentage rate (APR). In addition, it specifies the payment terms as well as the existence of any balloon payments.

DISCLOSURE STATEMENT OF LOAN

BORROWERS (NAMES AND ADDRESSES):

LOAN NO _____ DATE _____

LENDER: _____

(Mailing Address)

(City)   (State)   (Zip)

DISCLOSURES REQUIRED BY FEDERAL LAW:
(Supplementing Those Above Given and Those Given in Note and Security Agreement)

PAYMENT TERMS: Payable: _____ after date; or Payable in _____ equal monthly payments of $_____, com-mencing on _____, 19____, and on the same day of the month thereafter, plus an irregular payment of $_____, due on _____, 19____; (Delete pay-ment terms inapplicable.); together with a delin-quency or late charge not exceeding the lesser of $5.00 or 5% of each installment in default for 10 or more days. Further, if suit is instituted, upon borrowers' Default, to collect outstanding balance or otherwise to enforce Note and Security Agree-ment, borrowers are liable for lender's legal ex-penses not exceeding 15% of the unpaid balance at the time of suit.

BALLOON PAYMENT, if any, and conditions (if any) for refinancing same, if not paid when due: $_____

BASIC TERMS OF LOAN CONTRACT:
1. LOAN PROCEEDS: . . . . $_____
2. OTHER CHARGES: (TOTAL) . . . . $_____
   a. Premium, Credit Life: . . . . $_____
   b. Premium, Disability Ins.: . . . . $_____
   c. Premium, Physical Dam. Ins.: . . . . . $_____
   d. Title & Notary Fees: . . . . $_____
   e. Filing & Related Fees: . . . . $_____
   f. Other: _____ . . . . . $_____
3. LESS: Prepaid FINANCE CHARGE: . . . . . $_____
   Required Deposit Balance: . . . . $_____
   TOTAL PREPAID FINANCE CHARGE
   & REQUIRED DEPOSIT BALANCE: . . . . . . $_____
4. AMOUNT FINANCED (No. 1 + No. 2 minus No. 3): . $_____
5. FINANCE CHARGE: . . . . $_____
6. TOTAL OF PAYMENTS: . . . . $_____
7. ANNUAL PERCENTAGE RATE: . . . . _____%

---

stallment loan is given in Exhibit 8.5. Note that such a statement discloses not only interest costs, but also other fees and expenses that may be tacked on to the loan. Although disclosures like this allow you to compare the various borrowing alternatives, you still need to understand the methods used to com-pute finance charges, since similar loans with the same *stated* interest rates may have different fi-nance charges and APRs. The two basic procedures used to calculate the finance charges on single-payment loans are the *simple interest method* and the *discount method*.

Simple Interest Method. Interest is charged only on the *actual loan balance outstanding* in the **simple interest method**. This method is com-monly used on revolving credit lines by commer-cial banks, S&Ls, and credit unions. To see how it is applied to a single-payment loan, assume that you borrow $1,000 for two years at a 12 percent annual rate of interest. On a single-payment loan, the ac-tual loan balance outstanding for the two years will be $1,000, since no payments will be made until this period has elapsed. With simple interest, the finance charge, F_s, is obtained by multiplying the *principal* outstanding by the stated annual rate of interest and then multiplying this amount by the term of the loan:

$$F_s = P \times r \times t,$$

where

F_s = finance charge calculated using simple in-terest method
P = principal amount of loan
r = stated annual rate of interest
t = term of loan as stated in years (e.g., t would equal 0.5 for a 6-month loan, 1.25 for a 15-month loan, and 2.0 for a 2-year loan)

Substituting $1,000 for P, .12 for r, and 2 for t in the equation, we see that the finance charge, F_s, on this loan equals some $240 ($1,000 × .12 per year × 2 years). Since the size of the loan payment with this type of credit arrangement is found by add-

EXHIBIT 8.6

Finance Charges and APRs for a Single-Payment Loan ($1,000 Loan for 2 Years at 12% Interest)

Sometimes what you see is not what you get—such as when you borrow money through a discount loan and end up paying quite a bit more than the quoted rate.

Method	Stated Rate on Loan	Finance Charges	Approximate APR
Simple interest	12%	$240	12.0%
Discount	12	240	15.8

ing the finance charges to the principal amount of the loan, you would have to make a loan payment of $1,000 + $240 = $1,240 at maturity to retire this debt.

To calculate the true, or annual, percentage rate (APR) of interest on this loan, the average annual finance charge is divided by the average loan balance outstanding, as follows:

$$APR = \frac{\text{Average annual finance charge}}{\text{Average loan balance outstanding}}.$$

The figure for the average annual finance charge is found by dividing the total finance charge by the life of the loan (in years). In our example, the result is $120 ($240/2). Because the loan balance outstanding remains at $1,000 over the life of the loan, the average loan balance outstanding is $1,000. Dividing the $120 average annual finance charge by the $1,000 average loan balance outstanding, we obtain an APR of 12 percent. Thus, the APR and the stated rate of interest are equivalent: They both equal 12 percent. This is always the case when the simple interest method is used to calculate finance charges, *regardless of whether loans are single-payment or installment.*

Discount Method. With the **discount method**, the finance charges are calculated and then subtracted from the amount of the loan. The difference between the amount of the loan and the finance charge is then disbursed (paid) to the borrower—in other words, finance charges are paid in advance and represent a discount from the principal portion of the loan. The finance charge on a single-payment loan using the discount method, F_d, is calculated in exactly the same way as for a simple interest loan:

$$F_d = F_s = P \times r \times t.$$

Using the above method, the finance charge, F_d, on the $1,000/12 percent/two-year single-payment loan is, of course, the same $240 as we calculated earlier. However, in sharp contrast to simple interest loans, the loan payment with a discount loan is the original principal amount of the loan, P, since the finance charges on the loan are deducted from the loan proceeds. Thus, for the $1,000 loan above, the borrower will receive $760—which is found by subtracting the interest charges from the loan principal ($1,000 − $240)—and in two years will be required to pay back $1,000.

To find the APR on this discount loan, substitute the appropriate values into the APR equation. For this two-year loan, the average annual finance charge is $120 ($240/2). However, as explained above, since this is a discount loan, the borrower will receive only $760. Because this is a single-payment loan, and thus the average amount of money outstanding is also $760. When these figures are used in the APR equation we find the true rate for this 12 percent discount loan is more like 15.8 percent ($120/$760). Clearly, the discount method yields a much higher APR on single-payment loans than does the simple interest method. Exhibit 8.6

simple interest method
A method of computing finance charges in which interest is charged on the actual loan balance outstanding.

discount method
A method of calculating finance charges in which interest is computed, then subtracted from the principal, and the difference is disbursed to the borrower.

EXHIBIT 8.7

An Installment Purchase Contract

The installment purchase contract contains all the particulars of a given installment loan, including terms of payment, type and amount of credit insurance, financing arrangement, and other pertinent information.

RETAIL INSTALLMENT CONTRACT AND SECURITY AGREEMENT (Goods)

Date _____ , 19 _____

SELLER (CALLED "YOU")
NAME _____
ADDRESS _____
CITY _____ STATE _____ ZIP _____
SALESMAN _____

BUYER (CALLED "I")
NAME _____
NAME _____
ADDRESS _____
CITY _____ STATE _____ ZIP _____

ANNUAL PERCENTAGE RATE The cost of my credit as a yearly rate.	FINANCE CHARGE The dollar amount the credit will cost me.	Amount Financed The amount of credit provided to me or on my behalf.	Total of Payments The amount I will have paid after I have made all payments as scheduled.	Total Sale Price The total cost of my purchase on credit, including my downpayment of $_____
%	$	$	$	$

— Terms

My payment schedule will be:

Number of Payments	Amount of Payments	When Payments Are Due
		.19 _____ and same date of each following month.

— Security Agreement

Security: I gave you a security interest in the goods or property being purchased.
Late Charge: If I don't pay any payment in 10 days after it's due, I shall also pay 5% of that payment, but not over $5.00.
Prepayment: If I pay off early, I may be entitled to a refund of part of the finance charge.
See the contract document for any additional information about nonpayment, default, any required repayment in full before the scheduled date, and prepayment refunds.

— Late Charges

DESCRIPTION OF GOODS	MANUFACTURER	MODEL NO.	RETAIL NO.	CASH SALE PRICE
				$
				$

— Insurance

INSURANCE DISCLOSURE
NO INSURANCE IS REQUIRED FOR THIS SALE. I may buy any insurance from anyone I choose. Only if requested and for cost stated below, you or buyer of this contract will obtain insurance. Charges will be included in the Amount Financed. I understand this is the only insurance you offer and you (or buyer of this contract) expect to profit from its sale. I consent to this. The one Buyer signing this Insurance Disclosure will be insured when coverage begins, unless a different Buyer's name appears here:
_____
(WRITE "YES" OR "NO" AS DESIRED, DATE, AND SIGN. IF NONE DESIRED, SIGN BELOW.)
_____ Credit Life* .... $ _____
_____ Credit Disability* .... $ _____
_____ Property Insurance .... $ _____

DATE _____ SIGNATURE _____
NO INSURANCE DESIRED: _____
SIGNATURE _____

ITEMIZATION OF AMOUNT FINANCED
Sales Tax (if any) $_____
1. Cash Sale Price .... $_____
2. a. Cash Downpayment .... $_____
   b. Trade-in .... $_____
DESCRIPTION
   Total Downpayment (a+b) .... $_____
3. Unpaid Balance of Cash Sale Price (1-2) ...... $_____
4. Insurance (for term of credit)
   Credit Life .... $_____
   Credit Disability .... $_____
   Property .... $_____
   Total Insurance Charges .... $_____
5. Amount Financed (3+4) .... $_____
6. Finance Charge .... $_____
7. Total of Payments (5+6) .... $_____
8. Total Sale Price (1+4+6) .... $_____
9. Payable in _____ monthly payments of $_____ each beginning _____ and continuing same day of each month until fully paid.

— Financing

PROMISE TO PAY. Instead of the Cash Price, I promise to pay the Total Sale Price and I agree to pay you (or buyer of this contract) a Total of Payments in monthly payments in the amounts and on the dates stated above. I will pay at your business address, or other address given me. If more than one Buyer is named above, you may enforce this contract against all or any Buyers, but not in a combined amount greater than amount owed.

— Note

PREPAYMENT. If I fully prepay before the final due date, the amount I owe will be reduced by (a) unearned Finance Charges computed at the Annual Percentage Rate shown above, the unpaid balances of Amount Financed scheduled for the time after prepayment to maturity, (b) unearned credit insurance charges determined by the "Rule of 78ths", and (c) unearned property insurance charges determined by assuming an equal part is carried each month.

— Prepayment Provision

FAILURE TO PAY. If I don't pay on time, all my payments may become due at once, and without notifying me before bringing suit, you may sue me for the total amount I owe, less the same unearned Finance Charges I would receive if I fully prepaid. You may also repossess the goods described above.
SECURITY. You waive any security interest in my home that could result if the goods are installed.

— Acceleration Clause

NOTICE
ANY HOLDER OF THIS CONSUMER CREDIT CONTRACT IS SUBJECT TO ALL CLAIMS AND DEFENSES WHICH THE DEBTOR COULD ASSERT AGAINST THE SELLER OF GOODS OR SERVICES OBTAINED PURSUANT HERETO OR WITH THE PROCEEDS HEREOF. RECOVERY HEREUNDER BY THE DEBTOR SHALL NOT EXCEED AMOUNTS PAID BY THE DEBTOR HEREUNDER.
NOTICE TO THE BUYER: 1. Do not sign this agreement before you read it or if it contains any blank spaces. 2. You are entitled to an exact copy of this contract.

I HAVE READ AND RECEIVED A COMPLETED, READABLE, SIGNED COPY OF THIS CONTRACT.

SELLER: _____
By: _____

BUYER: _____
BUYER: _____

Source: This material taken from the booklet, *Managing Your Credit,* published by the Money Management Institute of Household Financial Services, Prospect Heights, Illinois, 1986, p. 22. Used with permission.

contrasts the results from both methods for the single-payment loan example discussed here.

Using the discount method to figure interest is one way of lowering the effective cost of a consumer loan. **Fantasy:** Because the interest is paid in advance on discount loans, the net effect is to substantially raise the cost of borrowing—in essence, a discount loan results in a true interest rate (APR) that is much higher than the stated rate.

INSTALLMENT LOANS ▪

Installment loans are paid off with a series of payments over time; these payments, along with the accompanying finance charges, can be figured using either simple interest or add-on interest. Does it really make much difference which procedure is used? Give some thought to this question before reading on.

Installment loans (ILs) differ from single-payment loans in that they allow the borrower to repay the debt in a series of installment payments (usually on a monthly basis) over the life of the loan. Installment loans are far more popular than single-payment loans—in fact, they rank as one of the most popular forms of consumer credit. Much of this popularity is, of course, due to the convenient way in which the loan repayment is set up; not surprisingly, most people find it easier on their checkbooks to make a series of small payments rather than one big one. In addition, ILs can be used to finance just about any type of big-ticket asset or expenditure imaginable—although new-car loans are the dominant type. ILs can be made as either secured or unsecured loans and have maturities ranging from as short as 6 months to as long as 7 to 10 years. (Technically, the home equity loans discussed in Chapter 7 are forms of installment credit.)

The Installment Purchase Contract

All of the information relevant to a transaction that's being financed on an installment loan basis is included in the **installment purchase contract**.

This agreement specifies the obligations of both the purchaser (borrower) and the lender. Although its form is likely to vary with the lender, it will probably contain four basic components: a sales contract, a security agreement, a note, and an insurance agreement. A sample installment purchase contract containing all four of these components is presented in Exhibit 8.7 (on facing page).

Security Agreement. The **security agreement** (or **security interest**) indicates whether or not the lender has control over the item being purchased. Although state laws determine whether or not the borrower retains legal title to the collateral, the lender files a lien on the collateral in order to make the security interest public. In either case, the lender retains legal control over the collateral. If default does occur, the lender can sell the collateral and use the proceeds to satisfy the unpaid loan balance and cover any costs incurred in this process. The lender must pay the borrower any excess funds obtained from the liquidation of the collateral. However, if the proceeds from liquidation are not sufficient to satisfy the loan, the borrower may or may not be liable for the unsatisfied portion of the debt depending on state law (in some states, the lender cannot turn to the borrower to make up the deficiency).

The Note. The formal promise on the part of the borrower to repay the lender as specified is spelled out in the **note**. It states all the legal obligations of

installment purchase contract
An agreement that specifies the obligations of both the purchaser (borrower) and seller (lender), issued when a purchase transaction is being financed on an installment basis.

security agreement (security interest)
In an installment purchase contract, a legal agreement that indicates whether or not the lender retains control over the item being purchased.

note
In an installment purchase contract, the formal promise on the part of the borrower to repay the lender in accordance with the terms specified in the agreement.

both borrower and lender and outlines all details concerning repayment, default, and disposition of collateral. The note is normally secured by the sales contract, or security agreement, which provides the lender with a security interest in the assets being acquired. It is the document that, when signed by both borrower and lender, legally binds the two parties to the items and conditions stated therein. Although many of the detailed provisions of the note in Exhibit 8.7 are on the reverse side of the contract (not shown), the entire document, once signed, is considered to be the note.

Credit Life Insurance. Sometimes, as a condition of receiving an installment loan, a borrower is required to buy **credit life insurance** and possibly **credit disability insurance**. Credit life (and disability) insurance is tied to a particular IL and basically provides insurance that the loan will be paid off if the borrower dies (or becomes disabled) before the loan matures. In essence, these policies insure the borrower for an amount sufficient to repay the outstanding loan balance. By requiring this coverage, the seller (or lender) is assured that if the borrower dies or becomes disabled the loan will be repaid. The seller's (or lender's) ability to dictate the terms of these insurance requirements is restricted by law in some states. If insurance is required as a condition of purchase, its cost must be added in to the finance charges and included as part of the APR. From the borrower's perspective, credit life and disability insurance is NOT a very good deal: *it's very costly and really does little more than provide lenders with a very lucrative source of income.* Not surprisingly, because it is so lucrative, some lenders aggressively push it on unsuspecting borrowers and, in some cases, even require it as a condition for granting a loan.

Special Features. In addition to the major points discussed above, installment purchase contracts often contain several other features that should be of interest to borrowers. These special features generally are contained in clauses to the sales contract and/or note, and pertain to additional collateral, default, repossession, and balloon payments.

Add-on clause. An **add-on clause** enables the lender to add assets that are acquired after the contract has been signed to the collateral on the loan. The lender need not release the security interest in any of these items until the entire loan has been paid off. In the past, this would have allowed lenders to repossess items of merchandise already purchased and paid for if the borrower defaulted on other items purchased under the agreement. The Consumer Credit Protection Act disallowed such practices. It is still advisable, however, to use separate purchase agreements for each item purchased rather than one agreement with an add-on clause.

Acceleration clause. The **acceleration clause** allows the lender to demand immediate repayment of the entire amount of the unpaid debt if the purchaser defaults on loan payments. Although this clause is always included in installment loans, the lender is likely to allow a late payment or levy a penalty instead of calling the loan by exercising the acceleration clause.

Recourse clauses. Most installment purchase contracts contain some type of provision that stipulates the type of action the lender can take in case of default; especially important here are provisions pertaining to wage assignment, garnishment, and repossession.

Some purchase agreements allow the lender to collect a portion of the purchaser's (borrower's) wages if he or she defaults on payments. By signing a purchase agreement with such a **wage assignment** clause, the purchaser agrees to these terms and gives the lender the right to collect part of his or her wages *without obtaining a court order.*

Even if an assignment clause is not enforceable (as is often the case) or not included in the agreement, a lender can still garnish a borrower's wages. **Garnishment** is a legal method of getting an employer to pay a portion of a borrower's wages to the lender. The borrower must, of course, be in default, and a court order must be issued enabling the employer to take such action. The *Federal Garnishment Law* specifically limits the amount of an employee's weekly wages that can be garnished to no more than the smaller of (1) 25 percent of take-home pay or (2) the amount by which weekly take-home pay exceeds 30 times the federal minimum *hourly* wage. The law also prohibits firms from firing employees as a result of their wages being garnished to repay a single debt. Many state laws have completely prohibited garnishing or have placed severe restrictions on this practice.

The act of seizing collateral when the borrower defaults on a loan is termed **repossession**. In many states, the ability of the lender to repossess collateral is limited (and may even require a court order), but in others, collateral can be repossessed without notice and even "stolen," in effect, from the borrower. Quite often there are detailed procedures that the lender must follow when selling repossessed items in order to satisfy unpaid debts. The repossessed item is usually sold—probably not very enthusiastically—by the merchant, and the amount due him or her, along with legal and other expenses in connection with the repossession, is taken from the sale proceeds. If this is not enough to cover the loan, the customer may or may not be liable for the remaining portion.

Balloon clause. Sometimes installment purchase agreements are set up in such a fashion that the final payment is considerably larger than all the others. The Truth in Lending Act requires that any **balloon payment**, which is defined as a payment more than twice the normal installment payment, be clearly identified as such. For example, if a loan required payments of $200 per month for 23 months followed by a final payment of $1,000 in the 24th month, the existence of the $1,000 balloon payment would have to be clearly disclosed. Because balloon clauses have been abused by some lenders and can place borrowers in an undesirable position, some states prohibit their use in loans. It is best not to enter into an agreement that includes such a clause, since balloon payments can cause real financial strain when they fall due. Only if you had adequate savings, or were expecting a known sum of money at some future date, could the use of a balloon payment be justified.

Finance Charges, Monthly Payments, and APR

Earlier in this chapter, the finance charges and annual percentage rates (APRs) on single-payment loans were discussed. The simple interest and discount methods of determining finance charges were described and illustrated for single-payment loans. In this section, we look at the use of simple and add-on interest to compute finance charges and monthly payments for installment loans (technically, discount interest can also be used with ILs, but because this is rare, we ignore it here). For

purposes of illustration, we will use a 12 percent, $1,000 installment loan that is to be paid off in 12 monthly installment payments. As in the earlier illustration for single-payment loans, interest is the only component of the finance charge; the presence of any other loan charges (such as credit life insurance, or title and notary fees) is ignored.

Using Simple Interest. When simple interest is used with ILs—and most major banks and S&Ls do use it on their installment loans—interest is charged only on the outstanding balance of the loan. Thus, as the loan principal declines with monthly payments, the amount of interest being charged decreases as well. Because finance charges change each month, the procedure used to find the

---

credit life (or disability) insurance
A type of life (or disability) insurance sold in conjunction with installment loans in which the coverage decreases at the same rate as the loan balance.

add-on clause
A clause that permits the lender to add certain assets to the loan's collateral that are acquired after the installment purchase contract has been signed and to keep its security interest in these items until the loan has been paid off in full.

acceleration clause
A clause in an installment loan contract that allows the lender to demand immediate repayment of the entire outstanding loan balance if the purchaser defaults on loan payments.

wage assignment
A type of recourse against borrower default in which the lender is allowed to collect a specified portion of the borrower's wages without obtaining a court order.

garnishment
Court-ordered payment of a portion of a defaulting borrower's wages to a lender.

repossession
The act of seizing collateral when the borrower defaults on an installment loan.

balloon payment
A final payment on an installment loan that is substantially larger than the normal installment payment.

EXHIBIT 8.8

A Table of Monthly Installment Loan Payments (to Repay a $1,000 Simple-Interest Loan)

A table like this can be used to find the monthly payments on a wide variety of simple interest installment loans; while it's set up in reference to a $1,000 loan, with a little modification, it can easily be used with any size loan (the principal can be more or less than $1,000).

Rate of Interest	Loan Maturity						
	6 Months	12 Months	18 months	24 Months	36 Months	48 months	60 Months
7½%	$170.33	$86.76	$58.92	$45.00	$31.11	$24.18	$20.05
8	170.58	86.99	59.15	45.23	31.34	24.42	20.28
8½	170.82	87.22	59.37	45.46	31.57	24 65	20.52
9	171.07	87.46	59.60	45.69	31.80	24.89	20.76
9½	171.32	87.69	59.83	45.92	32.04	25.13	21.01
10	171.56	87.92	60.06	46.15	32.27	25.37	21.25
10½	171.81	88.15	60.29	46.38	32.51	25.61	21.50
11	172.05	88.50	60.64	46.73	32.86	25.97	21.87
11½	173.30	88.62	60.76	46.85	32.98	26.09	22.00
12	172.55	88.85	60.99	47.08	33.22	26.34	22.25
12½	172.80	89.09	61.22	47.31	33.46	26.58	22.50
13	173.04	89.32	61.45	47.55	33.70	26.83	22.76
14	173.54	89.79	61.92	48.02	34.18	27.33	23.27
15	174.03	90.26	62.39	48.49	34.67	27.84	23.79
16	174.53	90.74	62.86	48.97	35.16	28.35	24.32
17	175.03	91.21	63.34	49.45	35.66	28.86	24.86
18	175.53	91.68	63.81	49.93	36.16	29.38	25.40

interest expense is mathematically very complex. Fortunately, this problem is avoided in practice, since the convention in the industry is to use *finance tables*. Essentially, these tables provide the *monthly payment* that would be required to retire an installment loan that carries a given simple rate of interest and has a given term to maturity. Because the tables have the interest charges built right into them, the monthly payments cover both principal and interest. Exhibit 8.8 provides an excerpt from such a table for a variety of interest rates and maturities.

The values in the table represent the monthly payments required to retire a $1,000 loan. Even though it's assumed you're borrowing $1,000, the table can be used with any size loan. For example, if you're looking at a $5,000 loan, just multiply the monthly loan payment from the table by 5—that is, $5,000/$1,000 = 5; or if you have, say, a $500 loan, multiply the loan payment by .5 ($500/$1,000 = .5). In many respects, this table is just like the mortgage loan payment schedule introduced in Chapter 6 (see Exhibit 6.6), except we use much shorter loan maturities here than we do with mortgages.

Here is how the table in Exhibit 8.8 is used. Suppose we want to find the monthly payment re-

quired on our $1,000, 12 percent, 12-month loan. Looking under the 12-month column and across from the 12 percent rate of interest, we find a value of $88.85; that is the monthly payment it will take to pay off the $1,000 loan in 12 months. When the monthly payments ($88.85) are multiplied by the term of the loan in months (12), the result will be total payments of $88.85 × 12 = $1,066.20. The difference between the total payments on the loan and the principal portion represents the *finance charges on the loan*—in this case, $1,066.20 − $1,000 = interest charges of $66.20.

Now, from each monthly payment, a certain portion goes to interest and the balance is used to reduce the principal. Because the principal balance declines with each payment, the amount that goes to interest *decreases* while the amount that goes to principal *increases*. Exhibit 8.9 illustrates this pattern. Note that since *monthly* payments are used with the loan, the interest column in Exhibit 8.9 is also based on a *monthly* rate of interest—that is, the annual rate is divided by 12 to obtain a monthly rate (12 percent per year/12 = 1 percent per month). This monthly rate is then applied to the outstanding loan balance to find the monthly interest charges in column 3. Because interest is

EXHIBIT 8.9

Monthly Payment Analysis for a Simple-Interest Installment Loan (Assumes a $1,000, 12%, 12-Month Loan)

Part of each monthly payment on an installment loan goes to interest and part to principal; as the loan is paid down over time, less and less of each payment goes to interest, and more and more goes to principal.

Month	Outstanding Loan Balance (1)	Monthly Payment (2)	Interest Charges [(1) × 0.01] (3)	Principal [(2) − (3)] (4)
1	$1,000.00	$ 88.85	$10.00	$ 78.85
2	921.15	88.85	9.21	79.64
3	841.51	88.85	8.42	80.43
4	761.08	88.85	7.61	81.24
5	679.84	88.85	6.80	82.05
6	597.79	88.85	5.98	82.87
7	514.92	88.85	5.15	83.70
8	431.22	88.85	4.31	84.54
9	346.68	88.85	3.47	85.38
10	261.30	88.85	2.61	86.24
11	175.06	88.85	1.75	87.10
12	87.96	88.85	0.89	87.96
Total		$1,066.20	$66.20	$1,000.00

Note: Column 1 values for months 2 through 12 are obtained by subtracting the principal payment shown in column 4 for the preceding month from the outstanding loan balance shown in column 1 for the preceding month.

charged only on the outstanding loan balance, the annual percentage rate (APR) on a simple interest IL will always equal the stated rate—in this case 12 percent. But as the accompanying *Issues in Money Management* box illustrates, there are other things to consider in ILs besides just the size of the monthly loan payments and the APR.

Add-on Method. A large number of installment loans are made using the **add-on method**, which results in a very costly form of credit. Add-on loans, in fact, rank as one of the most costly forms of consumer credit, with APRs that are often well above the rates charged on many credit cards. Unfortunately, the add-on procedure is still widely used, particularly among retail merchants, consumer finance companies, and sales finance companies; it is even used by some banks and S&Ls. With add-on interest, the finance charges are calculated using the *original* balance of the loan and then the finance charges are added to the original loan balance. Thus, the amount of finance charges on an add-on loan can be found by using the familiar simple interest formula:

$$F = P \times r \times t.$$

Given the $1,000 loan we have been using for illustrative purposes, the finance charges on a 12 percent, one-year add-on loan would be

$$F = \$1,000 \times .12 \times 1 = \$120.$$

Compared to the finance charges for the same loan on a simple interest basis ($66.20), the add-on loan is a lot more costly, a fact that will also show up in monthly payments and APR. Keep in mind that both of these loans would be quoted as "12 percent" loans; you may think you are getting a 12 percent loan, but looks can be deceiving—especially when you are dealing with add-on interest!

To find the monthly payments on an add-on loan, all you need to do is add the finance charge ($120) to the *original* principal amount of the loan ($1,000) and then divide this sum by the number of monthly payments to be made. In the case of our

---

add-on method

A method of calculating interest by computing finance charges on the original loan balance and then adding the interest to that balance.

ISSUES IN MONEY MANAGEMENT

The Hidden Perils of Long-term Car Loans

When Rebecca Schaffer went to buy a new car last year, she discovered she was "upside-down"—and she didn't like it one bit. Her old Mazda, which she wanted to trade in on a Mercury Tracer, wasn't worth the $1,200 she still owed on her five-year loan, a condition the auto industry calls being *upside-down*. Before she could swing the new deal, she had to borrow from her mother to pay off the Mazda loan. "I felt pretty robbed," Ms. Schaffer says.

She also should have felt pretty typical. More than half the car buyers at many dealerships find themselves in a similar bind, as consumers increasingly turn to longer-term loans. These contracts, for five or more years, mean lower

monthly payments—but they also can mean headaches at trade-in time.

"Actually, most car buyers who borrow are 'upside-down' as soon as they drive off the lot," says William E. Odom, chairman of Ford Motor Credit Co., the automaker's finance arm. But that didn't last long for the average owner back when car prices were lower and most loans lasted two or three years. In 1987, though, the average car buyer paid about $13,000 for a new car, up from $6,000 a decade ago. *And the higher prices have brought longer loans.* More than 70 percent of Ford Motor Credit and General Motors Acceptance Corp. contracts, for example, now extend to at least five years—but many

people don't want to keep the vehicles that long. They prefer to trade in for a new model every two or three years—and that's when the upside-down pinch hurts the most. The pain extends to the automakers, since upside-down shoppers have a harder time buying new models.

Suppose a buyer purchases a $14,000 car, borrowing $11,500 at an interest rate of 12.5 percent. Also assume the car loses 50 percent of its original purchase value over the first two years, and about 6 percent of its value each year after that. A three-year loan would result in monthly payments of $384; after 11 months, the buyer reaches "positive equity," meaning that the vehicle's trade-in value

---

$1,000 1-year loan, this results in monthly payments of $93.33, found as follows:

$$\text{Monthly payments} = \frac{\$1,000 + \$120}{12} = \frac{\$1,120}{12} = \$93.33.$$

As expected, these monthly payments are much higher than the ones with the simple interest loan ($88.85).

Because the actual rate of interest with an add-on loan is considerably higher than the stated rate, we must determine the loan's APR. The procedure for finding the mathematically precise APR is highly complex and far beyond the scope of this book. Fortunately, there are several ways to approximate the APR on an add-on loan, the most accurate of which is the so-called **N-ratio method**. The N-ratio

method actually results in an APR that is remarkably close to the precise figure. This method uses the following formula to find the approximate APR:

$$\text{Approximate APR} = \frac{M(95N + 9)F}{12N(N + 1)(4P + F)},$$

where

APR = annual percentage rate of interest
M = number of payments in a year
N = number of loan payments scheduled over life of loan
F = total finance charges
P = principal amount of loan

To see how this formula works, let's return to our $1,000, 12 percent, 1-year add-on loan. With this

exceeds the unpaid portion of the loan. The customer who finances the same amount for five years pays only $258 a month, but must wait 37 months to achieve positive equity. Stretch the loan out even farther—to six years—and you'll be upside-down for a whopping 51 months. That's a long time to wait for the market value of your vehicle to exceed the unpaid balance on the loan you took out to pay for the car!

Some owners who find they are upside-down grudgingly decide to keep the car, though that can compound their problem, as their aging car declines even further in value. Others wind up borrowing to pay off the old loan, sometimes folding the un-paid amount into the loan for the new vehicle. Consumers who want to cut the length of time they will be upside-down on a new purchase do have other choices, though some aren't much fun: Buy a less ex-pensive car or truck. Finance for a shorter period of time. Make a larger down payment. Switch to a lease contract with a term matching the length of time the car is likely to be kept. Unfortunately, "consumers have been conditioned [by advertise-ments promising] no money down, the lowest payment, the lowest everything," says Roy V. Smith, president of a Mel-bourne, Florida, car-finance consulting firm. "It's hard to convince them to take a pay-ment of $290 a month when they can have a payment of $230." Moreover, the finance managers at the dealerships themselves are often behind the push for longer-term contracts and smaller down payments, because their compensation is based, in part, on how much they can per-suade customers to finance. But as the consumer/borrower, its obviously in your best interest to resist the temptation of longer-term loans—just think of how hard it is to steer when you're upside-down!

Source: *Adapted from:* Melina Gren-ier Guiles, "Hidden Perils of Longer-Term Car Loans," *The Wall Street Jour-nal,* August 10, 1988, p.17. Reprinted by permission of *The Wall Street Jour-nal,* © Dow Jones & Company, Inc. 1988. All Rights Reserved Worldwide.

loan, $M = 12$, $N = 12$, $F = \$120$, and $P = \$1,000$. *The approximate APR in this case works out to be 21.4%:*

Approximate APR

$$= \frac{(12)[(95)(12) + 9](\$120)}{(12)(12)(12 + 1)[(4)(\$1,000) + \$120]}$$

$$= \frac{(12)(1149)(\$120)}{(12)(12)(13)(\$4,120)}$$

$$= \frac{\$1,654,560}{\$7,712,640} = 21.4\%.$$

As a matter of interest, the precise APR on this loan is 21.36 percent.

When viewed from an APR perspective, this 12 percent add-on loan turns out to be *very expensive,* as it has an actual rate of interest (21.4 percent) that is considerably higher than the quoted rate of 12 percent. This is because when add-on interest is applied to an installment loan, the interest included in each payment is charged on the initial principal even though the outstanding loan balance is re-duced as installment payments are made. A sum-mary of comparative finance charges and APRs for this example is presented in Exhibit 8.10.

N-ratio method

A formula used for estimating the annual per-centage rate (APR) on an add-on loan.

EXHIBIT 8.10

Comparative Finance Charges and APRs (Assumes a $1,000, 12%, 12-Month Installment Loan)

In sharp contrast to simple interest loans, the APR with add-on installment loans is usually *much higher* than the stated rate.

	Simple Interest	Add-on Interest
Stated rate on loan	12%	12%
Finance charges	$ 66.20	$ 120.00
Monthly payments	$ 88.25	$ 93.33
Total payments made	$1,066.20	$1,120.00
APR	12%	21.4%

Under the Truth in Lending Act, the exact APR (accurate to the nearest 0.25 percent) must be disclosed to borrowers. Note that not only interest, but also any other fees required to obtain a loan are considered part of the finance charges and should be included in the computation of the APR.

The Rule of 78s. One of the problems in using add-on interest is that it does not account for *monthly* interest charges when installment payments are made. To overcome this deficiency, the finance industry has developed the **Rule of 78s** (or **sum-of-the-digits method**), which is used to determine *monthly interest charges* on add-on ILs. In addition, the Rule of 78s is used to determine monthly premiums on credit life and disability insurance. The object of the Rule of 78s is to derive a monthly factor that can be applied to the loan's *total finance charges* so as to determine interest charges on a monthly basis.

To find the *monthly factors,* the first thing we do is add up all the digits for the number of payments to be made on the loan. For example, with a 12-month loan, we would add up the numbers from 1 to 12 (that is, $1 + 2 + 3 + 4 + \ldots + 10 + 11 + 12$); doing so would result in a total of 78. (Note that while the Rule of 78s gets its name from the sum of the 12 digits in a year, it can be applied to ILs with any maturity.) Instead of computing the sum of the number of payments in a loan—which can become quite a job with long-term loans—the following simple formula can be used:

Sum of the digits = (Number of payments ÷ 2) × (Number of payments + 1)

For example, to find the sum of the digits for a 12-month loan, we would have:

Sum of the digits = (12 ÷ 2) × (12 + 1)
= 6 × 13 = 78.

The sum of the digits provides the bottom half of the *monthly factor* (that is, its denominator); to complete the factor, we simply use the monthly digits of the loan in descending order. Thus, in our example the factor for the first month would be 12/78 (always use the actual *monthly* digits for a given loan, so that if you are working with a 2-year loan, the digit for the first month would be 24, for the second 23, and so on down to 1 for the last month). The logic behind this system of declining monthly factors is that the borrower has full (12/12) use of the principal in the first month of a 12-month loan, then, after the first payment is made, only 11/12 in the second month, and so forth. Given that the borrower has use of more money in the early stages of the IL, he or she should pay more in finance charges in the early months of the loan and progressively less with the passage of time. This is exactly what's accomplished with the monthly factors derived from the Rule of 78s.

Applying the monthly factors to the *total finance charges* on the loan results in the monthly interest charges. With our $1,000, 12 percent, one-year loan as an example, the interest charges for the first month would be (12/78) × $120 = .1538 × $120 = $18.46; for the second month (11/78) × $120 = .1410 × $120 = $16.92; and so on. Exhibit 8.11 shows how the monthly payments on our $1,000, 12 percent add-on loan are divided between prin-

EXHIBIT 8.11

Monthly Payment Analysis for an Add-on Installment Loan (Assumes a $1,000, 12%, 12-Month Loan)

The monthly interest charges on add-on loans are found by using the Rule of 78s.
Like simple interest loans, the monthly finance charge declines each month as the
outstanding loan balance goes down.

Month	Outstanding Loan Balance (1)	Monthly Payment (2)	Monthly Interest Factor (3)	Interest Charges[a] [(3) × $120] (4)	Principal [(2) − (4)] (5)
1	$1,000.00	$ 93.33	12/78	$ 18.46	$ 74.87
2	925.13	93.33	11/78	16.92	76.41
3	848.72	93.33	10/78	15.39	77.94
4	770.78	93.33	9/78	13.85	79.48
5	691.30	93.33	8/78	12.30	81.03
6	610.27	93.33	7/78	10.77	82.56
7	527.71	93.33	6/78	9.23	84.10
8	443.61	93.33	5/78	7.69	85.64
9	357.97	93.33	4/78	6.15	87.18
10	270.79	93.33	3/78	4.63	88.70
11	182.09	93.33	2/78	3.07	90.26
12	91.83	93.37	1/78	1.54	91.83
Total		$1,120.00		$120.00	$1,000.00

[a]To find monthly interest charges (col. 4), simply convert the monthly *interest factor* (from col. 3)
to a *decimal* value and then multiply by the total interest charges on the loan (in this case, $120).
For example, in the first month, 12 ÷ 78 = .1538; multiplying this value by $120, we have .1538 ×
$120 = $18.46.

cipal and interest, when interest charges are determined according to the Rule of 78s. Principal and interest behave with add-on credit just like the simple interest loan that we saw in Exhibit 8.9, to the extent that the amount that goes to interest decreases with each payment while the amount that goes to principal increases.

Actually most borrowers come in contact with the Rule of 78s only when they pay off an add-on loan prior to maturity. Under such circumstances, the lender is entitled to all *interest* earned to date, while the borrower needs to know how much *principal* is left unpaid on the loan—that is, how much he or she will have to come up with to pay off the loan. To see how this works, let us assume we want to pay off the $1,000, 12 percent, one-year loan after three months. Using the Rule of 78s, the lender would be entitled to 33/78 of the total finance charges—(12 + 11 + 10)/78; in dollar terms, this amounts to $50.77 [(33/78) × $120]. Because the lender is entitled to $50.77 in interest charges, the borrower should receive the rest of the add-on finance charges as a "refund." This is found by sub-

tracting the amount earned by the lender from the total finance charges on the loan; in this case, it amounts to $120.00 − $50.77 = $69.23. The **loan payoff** can now be found as follows:

Amount of loan, including add-on finance charges	$1,120.00
Less: Interest refunded to borrower	69.23
	$1,050.77
Less: Payments to date (3 × $93.33)	279.99
Loan payoff	$ 770.78

Thus, right after our third payment, we could pay the loan off with another payment of $770.78,

---

Rule of 78s (sum-of-the-digits method)
A procedure that is used to determine monthly interest charges on an add-on loan, and to determine the portion of total finance charges that the lender will receive when an add-on loan is paid off prior to its maturity.

loan payoff
The amount required to terminate a loan.

EXHIBIT 8.12

To Borrow or Not to Borrow

Using a worksheet like the one shown here, you can decide whether to buy on time or pay cash by comparing the after-tax cost of interest paid on a loan with the after-tax interest income lost by taking the money out of savings and using it to pay cash for the purchase.

BUY ON TIME OR PAY CASH

Cost of Borrowing

1. Total Loan Payments Made
   (monthly loan payments x term of the loan in months:
   $ _3/2.03_ per month x _36_ months) . . . . $ _11,233_

2. Less: Principal Amount of the Loan . . . . <$_9,000_>

3. Total Interest Paid Over Life of Loan (line 1 − line 2) . . . . $ _2,233_

4. Average Annual Interest Expense
   (total interest paid from Line 3 divided by term of the loan in years:
   $ _2,233_ ÷ _3_ years) . . . . $ _744_

5. Taxes Saved—note: ignore this step if you do not itemize deductions
   (annual interest paid (line 4) x amount deductible from taxes (20% in
   '89, 10% in '90, 0 in '91) x tax rate):

Year 1	$ _744_	x _20_ % x	_28_ % =	$ _42_
Year 2	$ _744_	x _10_ % x	_28_ % =	$ _21_
Year 3	$ _744_	x _0_ % x	_28_ % =	$ _0_
Year 4	$ _—_	x __ % x	__ % =	$
5 & beyond	$ _—_	x __ % x	__ % =	$

   Total Taxes Saved . . . . $ _63_

6. Total After-Tax Cost of Borrowing
   (Annual Interest Paid from Line 4 less Yearly Tax Savings from Line 5):

Year 1	$ _744_	− $ _42_	=	$ _702_
Year 2	$ _744_	− $ _21_	=	$ _723_
Year 3	$ _744_	− _0_	=	$ _744_
Year 4	$ _—_	− __	=	
5 & beyond	$ _—_	− __	=	

   Total After-Tax Cost of Borrowing . . . . $ _2,169_

Cost of Paying Cash

7. Annual Interest Earned on Savings
   (Annual rate of interest earned on savings x amount of loan:
   _7.5_ % x $_9,000_) . . . . $ _675_

8. Annual After-Tax Interest Earnings
   (Annual interest earned from Line 7) x (1 − tax rate) [e.g. 1 − 28% = 72%]
   $ _675_ x 1 − _28_ % . . . . $ _486_

9. Total After-Tax Interest Earnings
   (Line 8 x term of loan in years:
   $ _486_ x _3_ years) . . . . $ _1,458_

Net Cost of Borrowing
   (Line 6 − Line 9) . . . . $ _711_
   BASIC DECISION RULE: Pay Cash if Line 10 is positive;
   Borrow the money if Line 10 is negative.

Note: For simplicity, compounding is ignored in calculating both the cost of interest and interest earnings.

which is the amount of principal that we still owe on the loan.

The Rule of 78s is a regulation that grew out of the Consumer Credit Enhancement Act of 1978 and mandates how installment loans will be set up. **Fantasy:** The Rule of 78s is a procedure that is used to find the monthly finance charges on add-on loans.

Buy On Time or Pay Cash? Oftentimes, when you buy a big-ticket item, you have little choice but to take out a loan to finance the purchase—the acquisition (perhaps it's a new car) is just so expensive that you cannot afford to pay cash. And even if you do have the money, you may still be better off using something like an IL *if the cash purchase would end up severely depleting your liquid reserves.* But don't just automatically take out a loan. Rather, take the time to find out if, in fact, that's the best thing to do. Such a decision can easily be made by using a worksheet similar to the one in Exhibit 8.12 (on facing page). This worksheet basically considers the after-tax cost of a loan relative to the after-tax earnings generated from having your money in some type of short-term investment vehicle. A basic assumption here is that the consumer has an adequate level of liquid reserves, and that these reserves are being held in some type of savings account. (Obviously, if this is not the case, there's little reason to go through the exercise, since you have no choice but to borrow the money.) Essentially, it boils down to this: *If it costs more to borrow the money than you can earn in interest, then draw the money from your savings to pay cash for the purchase; if not, then consider taking out a loan.*

To see how this works, consider the following situation: You're thinking about buying a second car (a nice low-mileage used vehicle) and after the normal down payment, you still need to come up with $9,000. This balance can be taken care of in one of two ways: (1) you can take out a 36-month, 15 percent IL (according to the *Table of Monthly Loan Payments* on page 278, such an IL would have monthly payments of: $34.67 × 9 = *$312.03*); or (2) you can pay cash for the car by drawing the money from a money fund (the fund currently pays 7½ percent interest, and that's expected to hold for the foreseeable future). We can now use the worksheet to decide whether to buy on time or pay cash—the complete details of which are provided in Exhibit 8.12. In this case, we assume a 28 percent tax rate, and that the loan is being taken out in early 1989, so 20 percent of the interest expense is deductible in 1989, 10 percent in 1990, and nothing thereafter. Note in the exhibit that by borrowing the money, you'll pay over $2,200 in interest over the life of the loan (line 3), and since you can write off so little, you'll save only about $60 in taxes (line 5); thus, on an after-tax basis, you'll end up paying $2,169 in interest (line 6). Now, by leaving your money on deposit in the money fund, you'll gain only $1,458 in interest earnings, after taxes (see line 9). In essence, you'll be paying nearly $2,200 to save less than $1,500—which doesn't make much sense. It's far more cost effective in this case to pay cash for the car, for by doing so, you'll save over $700.

While such a figure provides a pretty convincing reason for avoiding a loan, there may be occasions where the actual dollar spread between the cost of borrowing and interest earned is very small, perhaps only $100, or less. This could occur, for example, if the amount being financed is relatively small—say, you want $1,500 or $2,000 for a ski trip to Colorado. Under these circumstances, and so long as the spread stays sufficiently small, you may decide it's still worthwhile to borrow the money in order to maintain a higher level of liquidity. Although this course of action is perfectly legitimate when very small spreads exist, it makes less and less sense as the gap starts to widen.

SUMMARY

▪ Single-payment and installment loans are formally negotiated consumer loan arrangements that are used mainly as a way to finance big-ticket items; most of these consumer loans are taken out as auto loans, loans for other durable goods, education loans, personal loans, and consolidation loans.

▪ Consumer loans can be obtained from a number of sources, including commercial banks (the biggest providers of such credit), consumer finance companies, credit unions, S&Ls, sales finance (and captive finance) companies, life insurance companies, and finally, as a last resort, there are your friends and relatives.

▪ When shopping for credit, it's in your best interest to seek loan maturities, monthly payments, and collateral considerations that are fully compatible to your financial plans and cash budgets.

▪ In a single-payment loan, the borrower is obligated to make just one principal payment (at the maturity of the loan), though he/she may be required to make one or more interim interest payments. Such loans are usually made for a period of one year or less, and normally are secured by some type of collateral; a major advantage of the single-payment loan is that it doesn't tie up the borrower's cash flow.

▪ In an installment loan, the borrower agrees to repay the loan through a series of equal installment payments (usually on a monthly basis) until the obligation is fully repaid; in this way, the borrower can come up with a loan-repayment schedule that fits neatly into his/her financial plans and cash budget. This highly popular form of consumer credit can be used to finance just about any type of big-ticket asset or expenditure.

▪ Most single-payment loans are made with either simple or discount interest, whereas most ILs are made with either simple or add-on interest. So long as simple interest is used, the actual finance charge will always correspond to the stated rate of interest; in contrast, when discount or add-on rates are used, the APR will always be more than the stated rate.

QUESTIONS AND PROBLEMS

1. Define and differentiate between a (a) single-payment loan and (b) installment loan.
2. List and briefly discuss the five major reasons for borrowing money through a consumer loan.
3. Lina Martinez is in the 28 percent tax bracket; during 1989 she paid $820 in interest on a consumer loan. How much of that interest expense is tax deductible, and how much will she be able to save in taxes because of this deduction?
   a. How much would this deduction be worth in tax savings if Lina were in the 15 percent tax bracket?
   b. Repeat the calculations assuming the year is 1991.
   c. Will the loss of this tax deduction affect the cost of consumer credit? Explain.
4. Compare the consumer lending activities of (a) consumer finance companies and (b) sales finance companies. Describe a captive finance company.
5. Discuss the role of (a) credit unions and (b) savings and loan associations in consumer lending. Point out any similarities or differences in their lending activities.
6. What two questions should be answered before taking out a consumer loan? Explain.
   a. One way to shop for credit is to compare the total cost of the transaction. Explain how this can be done.
   b. Assume you have been shopping for a new car and intend to finance it, in part, through an installment loan. The car you are looking for has a sticker price of $10,000. Big A Autos has offered to sell it to you for $2,500 down and a loan to finance the balance that will require 36 monthly payments of $253.12; Cars-Are-Us will sell you exactly the same vehicle for $3,000 down plus a 48-month loan for the balance, with monthly payments of $177.65. Which is the better deal? Explain.
7. Every three months, Keith Clark takes an inventory of the consumer debts he has outstanding. The latest tally showed the following: He still owed $4,000 on a home

improvement loan (monthly payments of $125); he was making $85 monthly payments on a personal loan that had a remaining balance of $750; he had a $2,000, secured single-payment loan that is due late next year; he had a $70,000 home mortgage on which he was making $820 monthly payments; he still owed $8,600 on a new-car loan (monthly payments = $205); he had a $960 balance on his Visa card (minimum payment = $40), a $70 balance on his Shell credit card (balance due in 30 days), and a $1,200 balance on a personal line of credit ($60 monthly payments). Use a worksheet like the one in Exhibit 8.3 to prepare an inventory of Keith's consumer debt. Find his debt safety ratio given that he has a take-home pay of $2,500 per month; would you consider this ratio good or bad? Explain.

8. Describe the two methods used to calculate the finance charges on a single-payment loan. As a borrower, which method would you prefer? Explain.

9. Indicate whether the following statements are true or false, and explain your response:
   a. The simple interest method is one in which interest is charged on the average loan balance outstanding.
   b. Under the discount method, the finance charge is calculated and then added to the total amount of the loan.
   c. Most unsecured single-payment loans are only for the highest-quality borrowers with proven credit reputations.
   d. The instrument giving the lender title to the property in the event of default is called a lien.
   e. A loan rollover is one way to pay off a single-payment loan.

10. Briefly describe and differentiate between a (a) chattel mortgage and (b) collateral note.

11. Find the finance charges on a 14 percent, 18-month single-payment loan when interest is computed using the simple interest method. Find the finance charges on the same loan when interest is computed using the discount method. Determine the APR in each case.

12. Bill Withers has to borrow $4,000. First State Bank will lend him the money for 12 months through a single-payment loan at 13½ percent discount; Home Savings and Loan will make him a $4,000 single-payment, 12-month loan at 15 percent simple. Where should Bill borrow the money? Explain.

13. Briefly describe an installment purchase contract, and define the four basic components such a contract is likely to contain.

14. Explain the purpose and describe the general content of the note that is ordinarily included as part of an installment purchase agreement.

15. Why is a borrower often required to purchase credit life and disability insurance as a condition for receiving an installment loan? Explain. Is this a good deal for the borrower?

16. Discuss each of the following features that may be included in an installment purchase agreement: (a) add-on clause, (b) acceleration clause, (c) wage assignment or garnishment, (d) repossession feature, and (e) balloon clause.

17. Define simple interest as it relates to an installment loan. Assuming that interest is the only finance charge, how much interest would be paid on a $500 installment loan to be repaid in six monthly installments of $87.02? If simple interest were charged at an annual rate of 15 percent on the outstanding balance, how much would the APR be on this loan? Explain.

18. Return to the opening paragraph of this chapter and take another look at the car loan that Chris Jenkins had to take out in order to buy his new car; recall that after his down payment, Chris still had to borrow some $12,000. Assuming Chris can obtain the money by taking out a 48-month installment loan at a simple interest rate of 12½ percent, answer the following questions:
   a. What will be the size of his monthly payments? (Use the loan payment table in Exhibit 8.8.)
   b. What will be the total amount of interest Chris pays in the first year of the loan? (Use a monthly-payment analysis procedure similar to the one in Exhibit 8.9.)
   c. How much interest will Chris pay over the full (48-month) life of the loan?
   d. What is the APR on this loan?

19. Stan Lee plans to borrow $5,000 and repay it in 36 monthly installments. This loan is being made at an annual add-on interest rate of 13 percent.

    a. Assuming that the only component of the finance charge is interest, calculate this charge.

    b. Use your finding in part a to calculate the monthly payment on the loan.

    c. Use the N-ratio method to estimate the APR on the loan.

20. What is the Rule of 78s? Ken Pitowski borrowed $4,000 to be repaid in 36 monthly installments; the loan was made at an add-on interest rate of 9 percent. Using the Rule of 78s, what is the amount the *lender* will receive if Ken repays the loan after six months? Determine the loan payoff at that time.

21. Under what conditions does it make more sense to pay cash for a big-ticket item than to borrow the money to finance the purchase? Are there ever times when borrowing the money is the best course of action?

    a. Consider the following situation: Sherman Jacobs wants to buy a home entertainment center; complete with a big-screen TV, VCR, and sound system, the unit would cost $4,500. Sherman has over $15,000 in a money fund, so he can easily afford to pay cash for the whole thing (the fund is currently paying 8 percent interest, and Sherman expects that yield to hold for the foreseeable future). To stimulate sales, the dealer is offering to finance the full cost of the unit with a 36-month installment loan at 9 percent, simple. Use a worksheet like the one in Exhibit 8.12 to determine whether Sherman should pay cash for this home entertainment center or buy it on time. (Note: assume Sherman is in the 28 percent tax bracket, and that the purchase will be made in early January 1989.) Briefly explain your answer.

CASE PROBLEMS

8.1 Financing Marilyn's Education

At age 19, Marilyn Bronson is in the middle of her second year of studies at a community college in San Diego. She has done well in her course work; majoring in prebusiness studies, she currently has a 3.75 grade-point average. Marilyn currently lives at home and works part-time as a filing clerk for a nearby electronics distributor. Her parents cannot afford to pay her tuition and college expenses—she is virtually on her own as far as college goes. Marilyn hopes to transfer to the University of Michigan next year. She has already been accepted and feels that she would get an excellent education there. After talking with her counselor, Marilyn feels that she will not be able to hold down a part-time job and still manage to complete her bachelor's degree program at Michigan in two years. Knowing that on her twenty-second birthday she will receive approximately $20,000 from a trust fund left her by her grandmother, Marilyn has decided to borrow against the trust fund in order to support herself during the next two years. She estimates that she

will need $10,000 to meet tuition, room and board, books and supplies, travel, personal expenditures, and so on during that period. Unable to qualify for any special loan programs, Marilyn has found two sources of single-payment loans, each requiring a security interest in the trust proceeds as collateral. The terms required by each potential lender are as follows:

    a. California State Bank will lend $13,513 at 13 percent discount interest. The loan principal would be due at the end of two years.

    b. National Bank of San Diego will lend $10,000 under a two-year note. The note would carry a 15 percent simple interest rate and would also be due in a single payment at the end of two years.

Questions

1. How much would Marilyn (a) receive in initial loan proceeds and (b) be required to repay at maturity under the California State Bank loan?

2. Compute (a) the finance charges and (b) the APR on the loan offered by California State Bank.

3. Compute (a) the finance charges and (b) the APR on the loan offered by the National Bank of San Diego. How big a loan payment would be due at the end of two years?

4. Compare your findings in Questions 2 and 3, and recommend one of the loans to Marilyn. Explain your recommendation.

5. What other recommendation might you offer Marilyn relative to the disposition of the loan proceeds?

◼ 8.2 Glen Gets His Camaro

Glen Watson, a 27-year-old bachelor living in Charlotte, North Carolina has been a high school teacher for the past five years. For the past two years, he has been thinking about buying a Chevrolet Camaro, but he has not been able to afford a brand-new one. Recently, however, a friend, John McKenzie, has offered to sell him his year-old, fully loaded Camaro Z-28. John wants $12,500 for his car, which has been driven only 8,000 miles and is in very good condition. Glen is eager to buy the car but has only $6,000 in his savings account at Chemical Bank. He expects to net $3,000 from the sale of his 1983 Chevrolet Vega, but this will still leave him about $3,500 short. He has two alternative for obtaining this sum:

a. Borrow $3,500 from the First National Bank of Charlotte at a fixed rate of 15 percent per annum simple interest. The loan would be repaid in equal monthly installments over a 3-year (36-month) period.

b. Obtain a $3,500 installment loan requiring 36 monthly payments from the Charlotte Teacher's Credit Union at a 7 percent stated rate of interest. The add-on method would be used to calculate the finance charges on this loan.

Questions

1. Using Exhibit 8.8, determine the required monthly payments if the loan is taken out at First National Bank of Charlotte.

2. Compute (a) the finance charges and (b) the APR on the loan offered by First National Bank of Charlotte.

3. Determine the size of the monthly payment required on the loan from the Charlotte Teacher's Credit Union.

4. Compute (a) the finance charges and (b) the APR on the loan offered by the Charlotte Teacher's Credit Union.

5. Compare the two loans and recommend one of them to Glen. Explain your recommendation.

FOR MORE INFORMATION

General Information Articles

Graham, Janis, "Credit for Couples," *Sylvia Porter's Personal Finance,* April 1986, p. 24.

Klein, Robert J., "Want Fair Treatment From Lenders? Know Your Rights," *Money,* December 1988, pp. 183–184.

McCormally, Kevin, "How to Find the Best Loans Now," *Changing Times,* February 1987, pp. 22–29.

————, "Best Ways to Pay For Your New Car," *Changing Times,* October 1988, pp. 93–96.

Morris, Betsy, "Eager to Lend: Banks and Thrifts Aggressively Pitch Personal Loans," *The Wall Street Journal,* September 9, 1987, p. 33.

Schurenberg, Eric, "Getting on Top of Your Debt," *Money,* April 1987, pp. 95–108.

Government Documents and Other Publications

The ABC's of Figuring Interest. Public Information Department; Federal Reserve Bank of Chicago; 230 S. LaSalle St.; Chicago, IL 60690.

The Arithmetic of Interest Rates. Consumer Information Center; P.O. Box 100; Pueblo, CO 81002.

Borrowers, Lenders, and Interest Rates. Public Services Department; Federal Reserve Bank of Richmond; P.O. Box 27622; Richmond, VA 23261.

Two Faces of Debt. Division of Consumer and Community Affairs; Board of Governors; Federal Reserve System; Washington, D.C. 20551.

1. What is Mark and Ana's debt safety ratio? Evaluate their ability to handle this debt.

2. Calculate the minimum monthly payments on each of Mark and Ana's credit cards using the data in the original case.

3. Calculate the finance charges on Mark and Ana's Visa and Master Card if monthly transactions are as follows:

VISA				MASTER CARD		
Date	**Transaction**	**Amount**		**Date**	**Transaction**	**Amount**
6/1	Beginning balance	$1,403		6/1	Beginning balance	$2,555
6/10	Purchase	51		6/5	Purchase	35
6/20	Payment	100		6/14	Purchase	104
				6/26	Payment	250

4. If all of Mark and Ana's credit cards were stolen, what would their maximum potential liability be according to federal legislation?

5. After paying off all of their revolving credit lines, Mark and Ana plan on keeping only one bank credit card. Compare and evaluate the terms on their Visa and Master Cards, given that all charges will be paid at the end of the billing cycle (i.e., they will not allow any charges to revolve). They expect their charges will produce an average daily balance of about $100 a month in a typical month. Recommend the card that would be least expensive for Mark and Ana under these conditions.

6. After moving into their new condominium, Mark and Ana suddenly realize that their old furniture looks pretty shabby. They feel that it would take about $2,500 to buy the furnishings they would like. Upon reviewing their latest balance sheet, they decide they do not want to sell any assets to pay for the furniture, so they investigate the possibility of borrowing $2,500 to buy the furniture. The following loans are available:

First Federal Savings	**Acme Furniture Company**
12% stated interest rate	10% stated interest rate
simple interest loan	add-on interest loan
24 monthly payments	24 monthly payments

   a. Compare the monthly payments, the total finance charges, and the APRs on the two loans. Which would you recommend as the best loan for Mark and Ana? Why?

   b. *(For students using the computer disk)* Run the amortization table for the above loan from First Federal Savings. How much interest would be paid in the first year of this loan? During the second year?

   c. Before Mark and Ana decide on either of these loans, they decide to take an inventory of their consumer debt. Complete this inventory for them using the information in the original case. Would you recommend their taking on more debt at this time?

PART IV

Managing Insurance Needs

CHAPTER 9

Insuring Your Life

Financial Facts or Fantasies

Are the following statements financial facts (true) or fantasies (false)?

- In a cafeteria-style benefits plan, it is the employee who decides what type of benefits coverage he or she will receive.
- The best way to figure out how much life insurance you need is to use a multiple of your earnings.
- Social security survivor's benefits should be factored into your life insurance plans if you have a dependent spouse and/or minor children.
- Term insurance provides nothing more than a stipulated amount of death benefits and, as a result, is considered the purest form of life insurance.
- Since most life insurance policies are pretty much the same, you need not concern yourself with differences in specific contract provisions.
- Selecting an insurance company is the first thing you should do when buying life insurance.

A key ingredient of every successful financial plan is adequate life insurance coverage. The overriding purpose of life insurance is to protect your family from financial loss in the event of your untimely death. In addition, some types of life insurance also possess attractive investment attributes. Place yourself in the following situation: Suppose that through careful financial planning and a lot of hard work, you have acquired a nice home, furnishings, and other assets, along with a comfortable standard of living for your family. Wouldn't you want to protect all this? Most people would, and they do so through various forms of life insurance. In essence, life insurance provides an umbrella for your financial plans. It not only protects that which you have already acquired (like providing funds to pay off the mortgage on your home) but also helps to assure the attainment of unfulfilled financial goals (such as the future education of your children). Being informed about life insurance is clearly just as important to financial planning as being well versed about taxes and investments. As with any other aspect of financial planning, you want to get as much from your insurance dollar as possible. In the case of life insurance, this means not only comparing costs but also buying the proper amount of insurance and picking the right type of policy.

This is the first of three chapters dealing with insurance. After studying life insurance in this chapter, we will look at health insurance in Chapter 10 and at property insurance in Chapter 11. Together these three forms of insurance make up the insurance planning function.

BASIC INSURANCE CONCEPTS

> Sound insurance planning rests on a basic understanding of your exposure to risk and how insurance can protect you against those risks. Before reading on, give some thought to the different ways that insurance could help protect you personally. Why is it important to have adequate life insurance, and what role should life insurance play in your financial plans?

Over a period of years, the difference between buying life insurance wisely and unwisely can easily add up to thousands of dollars in extra premiums and many times that amount in lost protection. Wide differences exist among the types of life insurance policies that are available, their costs, and the quality of the companies and the agents that sell them. This chapter shows how you can intelligently determine how much life insurance protection you and your family need. In addition, it explains the different types of life insurance policies available today. Although the diversity of market offerings may seem overwhelming, we will show that most policies, despite their different names, are essentially variations of several basic types.

Insurance Planning

For one reason or another, the financial goals that you've set for yourself may never be reached. A weak economy may result in your earning less income or in realizing a lower return on your investments than expected. Also, unless you plan carefully and with foresight, you may discover that you have embarked on a career than will produce a lower level of earnings than anticipated. Finally, events may occur that cause you to experience substantial financial losses. The fact is, fulfilling your financial goals depends not only on fortitude but also on fate! Everything you have acquired and planned for can all too easily slip away in the face of an unforeseen major emergency. But there are ways to safeguard against such risks—which is where *insurance* comes into the financial planning process, for the basic purpose of insurance is *to protect from loss the things that you have already acquired and to shield you from an interruption in your expected earnings.* Insurance, in short, lends a degree of certainty to your financial plans.

Auto and homeowners insurance, for example, reimburse you for damage or destruction to existing assets. Life insurance is meant to replace income that would have been earned had premature death not occurred. Disability insurance does the same should you become disabled, while hospitalization and medical insurance cover the additional expenses that arise from being sick or in an accident. Insurance planning involves anticipating the losses to which your assets and income could be exposed and considering how you can provide protection against such losses by weaving insurance into your financial plans. To do so, you will have to make decisions about life, health, and property insurance.

Employee Benefits—Your Coverage Begins at Work

If you hold a full-time job, chances are your employer is providing you with certain types of *fringe benefits.* Indeed, every major company in the country today (and many not-so-major ones) provides its employees with a variety of *employee benefits,* ranging from health and life insurance to pension plans. Evolving from the earliest benefit packages that provided little more than "final expense" life insurance, today's greatly expanded benefit plans are what most people rely upon for a large part of their financial security. Consider health insurance, for example. The vast majority of American families rely solely on company-sponsored *group plans* for their health and major medical insurance coverage. And much the same can be said about life insurance and pension plans: Other than social security, most families rely on their employee benefits for a big piece of their life insurance coverage and retirement needs.

Actually, the well-defined employee benefits packages of today cover a full spectrum of benefits, including:

- Health and life insurance
- Disability insurance
- Pension and profit-sharing plans
- Supplemental retirement programs, like 401(k) plans
- Dental and vision care
- Child-care and educational assistance programs
- Subsidized employee food services

Of course, not all companies provide such a complete menu of benefits; some are more generous than others. But even so, these benefits have taken on an increased importance as a form of compensation and presently account for roughly 30 percent of the average employee's total compensation package. Put another way, for every dollar received in wages and salaries, the average employee receives another 40 cents in fringe benefits. All or most of these benefits are paid in full by the employer, though it's not unusual for the employee to pay for at least part of the tab for group health insurance coverage on his/her family, supplemental life insurance, and participation in voluntary retirement programs.

Getting Your Benefits From a Cafeteria. Traditionally, most group benefit programs were set up in such a way that the employee had little, if any, direct input into the make-up of the fringe benefits package. The types of benefits included and the dollar amount of coverage provided were pretty much set by the company—for example, life insurance coverage was usually defined as a multiple of your annual salary, and medical benefits were the same for everyone. Such benefit packages are still the standard for many companies, but a rapidly growing number of employers today are offering *flexible-benefit,* or **cafeteria-style plans**, in which the employee selects the benefits most desirable to him or her. (Technically, cafeteria-style plans are nothing more than a variation of flexible-benefit programs—you're given just about the same choices with either approach, except that there are some additional tax advantages available with the

cafeteria-style plans.) The growing sentiment in the employee benefits field is that the traditional, rigid programs just are not appropriate with today's diverse group of employees. Financial security needs vary greatly with age, marital status, number of dependent children, level of income, and so forth. Enter the flexible-benefit or cafeteria-style programs in which the employer allocates a certain amount of money to each employee and then lets the employee "spend" that money by selecting the benefits that he or she wants the most. In effect, employees are provided with a "menu" of benefits (usually covering everything from child-care to retirement benefits) to pick and choose from until the allotted money is gone. These plans usually require a minimum amount of life and health insurance coverage, and there are a few limits set on the maximum amount of coverage you can obtain, but within these constraints, you're free to select the benefits that do you the most good. And in some plans, you can even take some of the benefits in the form of more take-home pay or extra vacation time! The accompanying *Smart Money* box provides further discussion about these plans, and offers a few suggestions that should help you get the most from them.

One final point: whether you're covered by a traditional rigid plan or a more flexible cafeteria-style program, it's a good idea to periodically assess the benefits package you have at work relative to your own individual/family needs, and if you discover a shortfall in coverage, then try to supplement it with your own personal policy. In short, make sure you have the coverage or protection you need, either from your company benefits package and/or your own supplemental coverage. Except perhaps for group medical coverage, *don't rely on your employer as the sole source of financial secur-*

---

cafeteria-style plans
A type of employee benefits plan wherein the *employee,* rather than the employer, picks the type of benefit coverage received from a menu covering everything from child-care to life and health insurance to retirement benefits. (These plans are similar in many respects to so-called flexible-benefit programs.)

S·M·A·R·T M·O·N·E·Y

Filling Your Tray with Cafeteria-Style Benefits

One decade after the first flexible benefits plan debuted in this country, the idea of letting employees choose their own benefits—from child care to health insurance to extra vacation time—is finally catching on. Once limited because of tax law uncertainties and because the plans made sense only for large companies, flexible—or cafeteria—benefits are now offered by more than 800 major companies, and this year (1989) that number is expected to jump by 25 percent.

"Benefits used to be designed for Ward Cleaver," says Wayne Page, who heads the human resources division of Transamerica Life Companies in Los Angeles. "He supported the family and June stayed home cooking for Wally and the Beav." No longer is that the case. Nancy Oroumieh, 35, has two children and works at Transamerica as a department manager. She used to worry that her benefits package didn't include enough life insurance or disability insurance, so when Transamerica introduced its own flex plan in 1986, she promptly upgraded both benefits. "Now I feel confident my family is covered," she says. Oroumieh can also take advantage of a benefits option that lets her set aside money each week, before taxes, to pay for child care.

Flexible benefits plans come in many shapes and sizes, but they typically give employees a number of credits they can use to "buy" benefits. Most plans, for instance, offer a choice among different levels of health and life insurance. Many plans have options to help pay for dependent care or eye and dental benefits, and some even allow employees to trade benefits for more take-home pay or vacation time.

If your company introduces a flex plan, you should keep these basics in mind:

- *Ask questions.* Unlike standard benefits packages of the past, flexible plans force employees to learn how benefits work and know which ones are right for them. Read those company handouts, and if you don't understand something, speak up.
- *Study the options.* If your spouse has a traditional benefits plan, it helps to coordinate your choices. And remember, if your current benefits suit you and you have the option of keeping them, there's no reason to change.
- *Consider tax consequences.* Flexible-benefit "spending accounts," which allow money to be set aside for dependent care before taxes, don't always make sense: Some people are better off spending their take-home pay and then taking a dependent-care tax deduction come April 15.
- *Make sure you're covered.* In times of fat mortgages and shrinking raises, extra cash in the paycheck can be tempting. But beware of swapping basic medical insurance for more pay or vacation.
- *Plan ahead.* By law you can adjust your coverage in cases of birth, death, marriage, divorce, etc. But if you require elective surgery or your child needs braces and you didn't choose the right coverage, you're out of luck until the next annual enrollment deadline.

Source: Adapted from Ray Alvarez-torres, "Flexible Benefits Can Stretch Your Coverage," *Savvy,* February 1989, p. 32.

ity. More often than not, especially when it comes to life insurance and retirement plans, you'll find that such coverage falls short of your total financial needs. Later in this chapter, and in a couple of others, we'll see how you can assess your life insurance, disability insurance, and pension programs to see if they meet your needs and if not, how to bring your coverage up to a desirable standard.

In a cafeteria-style benefits plan, it is the employee who decides what type of benefits coverage he or she will receive. **Fact:** In a flexible-benefit or cafeteria-style program, employees pick from a wide-ranging menu of company-sponsored fringe benefits, including health, life and disability insurance, pension plans, dental care, educational assistance programs, child care, and so forth. Working with this menu of benefits and a stipulated amount of money, an employee is free to put together a benefits package that best meets his or her needs.

Transferring the Risks

An insurance policy is a contract between you (the insured) and an insurance company (the insurer) under which the insurance company promises to pay for your losses according to the specified terms. From your perspective, *you are transferring the risk of loss to the insurance company.* The insurance company is willing to accept the risk because it hopes to make a profit by collecting premiums from a large number of insureds, investing the money, and paying out losses and expenses that are less than the premiums collected and investment earnings. The premiums you pay for insurance usually come out of your current income. Thus, the heart of the insurance decision is the comparison of the premiums you are willing (and able) to take from your current income relative to the need for, and the amount of, protection you will receive from the insurance that you buy. The decision is difficult, because you do not know for sure whether or not losses will occur but only that you might suffer losses from certain unforeseen events. The following discussion of risk, insurable exposures, and underwriting should help you to better understand the whole concept of insurance and the role that it can play in your financial planning; later in this chapter we'll also provide some discussion

of the factors to consider when making decisions about life insurance coverage.

The Concept of Risk

In insurance, *risk* is defined as uncertainty with respect to economic loss. Whenever you and your family have a financial interest in something—whether it be your life, health, home, car, boat, or job—you face risk. You face the chance that your budget will be upset and that your net worth will perhaps be drastically reduced. Because of the great effect that losses can have on your financial well-being, you must devise ways to deal with risk. Obviously it makes sense to take steps *before* a loss occurs, as is done in *risk avoidance* and *loss prevention.* However, when losses do occur, you will need an economical way of covering them, which is what you obtain from *risk assumption* and *insurance.*

Risk Avoidance. Perhaps the simplest way to deal with risk is to avoid the act that creates it. For example, people who are afraid they might lose everything they own because of a lawsuit resulting from an automobile accident could avoid driving. Many new college graduates avoid the risk of unstable or low earnings by refusing to accept a job that pays on a commission-only basis.

Although **risk avoidance** can be an effective way to handle some risks, such action is not without its costs. For instance, the people who avoid driving suffer considerable inconvenience, and the graduates who steer clear of sales positions may forfeit an opportunity for commission earnings well in excess of their guaranteed salaries. Risk avoidance is an attractive way to deal with risk only when the estimated cost of avoidance is less than the estimated cost of handling it in some other way.

Loss Prevention. In a broad sense, **loss prevention** can be defined as any activity that reduces

risk avoidance
Avoidance of an act that would create a risk.
loss prevention
Any activity that reduces the probability that a loss will occur.

the probability that a loss will occur (for example, driving within the speed limit), or lessens the severity of the loss should it occur (for example, wearing a safety belt and shoulder strap). Loss prevention should be an important part of the risk management program of every individual and family. In fact, insurance provides a reasonable means for handling risk only when people use effective loss prevention measures. For example, if everybody drove fast and recklessly, risk avoidance might be the only effective way to deal with the risk of an automobile accident because automobile insurance would be too expensive to buy.

Risk Assumption. With **risk assumption**, you choose to accept and bear the risk of loss. Risk assumption can be an effective way to handle many types of potentially small exposures to loss when insurance would be too expensive (for example, the risk of having your *Personal Financial Planning* text stolen). It is also a reasonable approach in the face of very large exposures that you cannot ordinarily prevent, or against which you cannot secure insurance (nuclear holocaust, for instance). Unfortunately, people often assume risks because they are unaware of various exposures to loss or think that their insurance offers adequate protection when in fact it does not. Therefore, one objective of these three chapters on insurance is to help you recognize the loss exposures that you will face and provide you with an understanding of when risk assumption is the preferred manner for handling certain risks.

Insurance. Insurance permits society to reduce financial risks and share losses. Risk or uncertainty can be reduced because insurers are able to combine the loss experiences of large numbers of people and, with certain actuarial data, estimate the chance of loss faced by the insured population. This prediction then allows each person to contribute a relatively small amount (the insurance premium) to an insurance company in exchange for a promise that he or she will be reimbursed for covered losses. Insured individuals gain because they are able to transfer their risk to the insurer. The insurance company, in turn, can realize a gain if the amount of insured losses has been accurately estimated.

Characteristics of an Insurable Exposure

Although insurance can be an ideal method for handling the risk of economic loss, not all risks are insurable. In order for the insurance mechanism to work well, certain criteria must be met. Several of the more important criteria are (1) there must be a large number of similar exposures to loss; (2) the potential loss must be fortuitous; (3) the cost of the insurance must be reasonably low; and (4) losses must be noncatastrophic.

Large Number of Exposures. Insurers need a large group of similar exposures because they base rate calculations on what may loosely be called "the law of averages." Unless the number is large enough to permit a good estimate of average expected losses, premiums cannot be accurately computed. If rates are set too low, the insurance company may not have enough funds to pay claims; if set too high, people may pay more than is necessary or desirable.

Fortuitous Loss. A **fortuitous loss** is one that happens by chance or accident; its timing and/or occurrence is for the most part unintentional and unexpected from the standpoint of the insured. If individual losses that were certain or intentional could be insured, insurance companies would be plagued by *adverse selection*—that is, the tendency for those who anticipate losses in the near future to seek insurance more often than the norm.

Reasonable Cost. The cost of an insurance premium should be reasonably low with respect to the potential loss that it covers. Thus, insurance should be used for protection only against large losses that are suffered by a very small percentage of those who buy a given coverage. A company cannot economically insure against small losses, because the expenses of selling and administering such policies could, when coupled with the claims that would be made, total as much as or more than the potential loss covered. Similarly, insurance cannot be economically offered for losses that occur too frequently, because the premiums would exceed the amount that most people are willing to pay.

An excellent example of the application of the reasonable-cost criterion is life insurance for persons over age 70. While insurance companies will issue a new policy to people in this age category, the relatively high probability of loss makes the premiums much larger than most people can afford. Life insurance, of course, is not the only place where high probability of loss can lead to very expensive insurance premiums. For example, in recent years, this phenomenon has played a significant role in increased automobile and professional liability insurance premiums. Insurance works best when in any given year only a relatively few people file claims. In this way, the total amount received in premiums (plus interest earnings) should exceed the total amount paid out for losses and administrative expenses.

Noncatastrophic Loss. The last criterion—**noncatastrophic loss**—means that insurers should not accept risks that have the potential for widespread catastrophe. Foremost for insurance companies is the need to protect their solvency. A company that goes bankrupt is no good to anyone. Thus, such catastrophic occurrences as war, nuclear explosion, and large-scale flooding generally cannot be adequately insured by private insurance companies.

Underwriting

In all types of insurance, the company must decide whom it can insure and then determine the applicable rates. This function is called **underwriting**. Through underwriting, insurance companies try to guard against adverse selection. Underwriters design rate-classification schedules so that people pay premiums commensurate with their chance of loss. The success of any insurance company is highly dependent on the quality of the work done here. If the underwriting standards are too high, people will be unjustly denied coverage, and insurance sales will drop. On the other hand, if standards are too low, many insureds will pay less than their fair share, and the insurance company's solvency could be jeopardized.

A basic problem facing underwriters is the choice of appropriate criteria to apply when they select and classify insureds. Since a perfect relationship does not exist between available criteria and loss experience, some people invariably believe that they are being charged more than they should be for their insurance. This situation is most apparent in underwriting automobile insurance. Many young male motorists who have never had an auto accident must pay two or three times the premium that a person age 35 would pay. Similarly, a car owner who has never had a claim but who lives in Manhattan could well pay a considerably higher premium than a small-town driver with a poor driving record.

In recognition of the difficulties experienced in selecting and classifying insured, some vocal consumer advocates have urged the removal of rate classifications and the application of the same rates to everyone. This idea, however, is not the solution to the problem. In fact, it would probably increase the number of complaints made about insurance, because even though a few hazard-prone people would receive large decreases in premiums, *many more would get rate increases*. Similarly, several states have moved toward eliminating age and sex as legal criteria for automobile underwriting decisions. Insurance companies have often opposed such actions because they do not know of any other criteria to use that would be as practical or accurate.

It should be obvious from this discussion that underwriting is a difficult task. It is perhaps an art as much as a science. Insurers are always trying to improve their underwriting capabilities in order to set rates that will provide adequate protection against insolvency and yet be reasonable for most policyholders. From your standpoint, though, you should recognize that insurance companies often use very different underwriting standards and rate-

---

risk assumption
The choice to bear or accept risk.

fortuitous loss
A loss that is for the most part unintentional and unexpected.

noncatastrophic loss
A loss that is not the result of a catastrophic occurrence, such as war, nuclear explosion, or large-scale flooding.

underwriting
With respect to insurance, the process of deciding who can be insured and determining the applicable rates.

classification systems. Therefore, you can usually save money by shopping around for a company that has underwriting practices more favorable to your specific characteristics and needs. For instance, some life insurers offer discounts to nonsmokers and to people in better-than-average health. A few companies even offer discounts to those in preferred low-risk occupations, such as professionals and business executives.

HOW MUCH LIFE INSURANCE IS RIGHT FOR YOU? ⊡

While there are several ways to determine the amount of life insurance that's right for you, probably the best is to base the decision on an assessment of your needs. Place yourself in the shoes of a married person with two young children: What kinds of financial needs and obligations would you want to cover with a life insurance policy? Take a moment to think about this question before reading on.

"Life insurance is sold, not bought" is an axiom in the life insurance business. As a rule, people just don't get as strong an urge to buy life insurance as they might to buy a house, car, or new television set. Far too many people simply wait until an agent contacts them and then reluctantly accept "being sold." A partial explanation for this tendency to wait is that life insurance is intangible; and even after you purchase it, you can't see, smell, touch, or taste its benefits. In addition, although most people (especially family breadwinners) recognize they should buy life insurance, many believe it can be delayed another month—or two or three. The need is felt, but it is neither obvious nor pressing. And perhaps as much an explanation as anything else is the fact that the purchase of a life insurance policy is associated with something unpleasant—namely, death. People don't like to talk about death, or the things closely associated with it, so they all too often put off taking care of their life insurance needs. That's unfortunate, because life insurance does have definite benefits to offer, the most im-

portant being all the things that a family will still be able to buy after a loss occurs—things they very likely could not otherwise buy.

The point is not to push you to go out and stock up on as much life insurance as you can get, but rather to find out whether or not you do, in fact, need life insurance. If you do, you should give its purchase a high priority. Deciding whether or not, and in what amount, you need life insurance is an important issue. In practice, there are three methods that can be used to compute an individual's need for life insurance: the human life value approach, the multiple earnings approach, and the needs approach. By far, most financial planners prefer the needs approach. Because the other two approaches are so widely used, however, they are discussed here in order to help you learn their shortcomings.

Human Life Value Approach

One of the oldest—and probably the most abstract—techniques for determining the amount of life insurance a person should have is the **human life value approach**. This approach attempts to convert the future earnings of an individual to a present value. This sum is then defined as that person's human life value. Specifically, this computation considers two factors: (1) the total amount of income that a person will earn from the present to retirement, minus related income taxes and personal maintenance expenses and (2) an appropriate interest rate at which these anticipated future net earnings can be discounted to a present value amount. For example, assume that a person aged 25 is expected to net $17,000 per year after taxes and personal maintenance expenses during the next 40 years; given a discount rate of 8 percent, the present value of those earnings work out to about $200,000. This amount would represent the human life value of the individual in our example.

The human life value concept may be useful in certain legal proceedings or by economists concerned with studying the human capital of a nation. However, it should not be used in computing the amount of life insurance you should buy, because it neglects both the financial obligations and the resources external to life insurance that are available to you.

EXHIBIT 9.1

A Multiple Earnings Table

Some insurance experts suggest that a table like the one below be used to estimate life insurance needs. To do so, first find the factor that corresponds to your age and level of income; then multiply this by your level of income. For example, if you are a married 30-year-old with two children and earn $30,000 a year, you will use a factor of 7.4 to find out how much insurance you need: $30,000 × 7.4 = $222,000.

Gross Annual Pay	Age of Insured					
	30	35	40	45	50	55
$ 7,500	5.3	6.2	7.3	8.5	7.9	5.6
9,000	5.1	6.0	7.0	8.1	7.8	5.5
12,000	5.0	5.8	6.7	7.9	7.6	5.4
15,000	4.9	5.7	6.7	7.9	7.4	5.3
20,000	4.9	6.5	7.4	8.1	7.3	5.2
30,000	7.4	8.2	8.4	8.3	7.2	5.1
40,000	8.4	8.7	8.6	8.2	6.9	4.9
60,000	9.0	8.9	8.4	7.8	6.5	4.6

Insurance Requirements in Addition to Social Security to Replace 75 Percent of Earnings after Taxes for a Family of Four

Source: *A Consumers' Guide to Buying Life Insurance* (Des Moines, Iowa: Bankers Life).

Multiple Earnings Approach

The **multiple earnings approach** gained its popularity on the basis of its simplicity rather than soundness. Using this technique, you calculate the amount of life insurance to buy by simply multiplying your gross annual earnings by some arbitrarily selected number. Multiples of 3, 5, or even 10 times earnings are frequently used to find the amount of life insurance coverage needed.

Exhibit 9.1 illustrates the type of multiples that would be used to estimate life insurance needs with the multiple earnings approach. Note that the multiples in the exhibit are based on replacing 75 percent of lost earnings for a married breadwinner with two children; they would, of course, change if you wanted to replace more or less than that amount. Given the desired replacement rate, the proper multiple to use is based on current gross annual income and the age of the insured. Thus, we can see from the exhibit that, according to this procedure, a married 35-year-old earning $40,000 a year should use a multiple of 8.7 times if he wants to replace 75 percent of this income. His *total life insurance coverage,* therefore, should amount to $40,000 × 8.7 = $348,000. Now, keep in mind this is *total* life insurance coverage, so from this amount, the individual should subtract the cover-

age already provided from group and/or personal policies, as well as any pension plan death benefits. For example, if the individual is covered at work by a group life insurance policy in the amount of $50,000, and if he's entitled to another $50,000 in death benefits from the company's pension plan, then his remaining life insurance needs are $248,000 (i.e., $348,000 − $50,000 − $50,000). According to the multiple earnings approach, that's the amount of additional life insurance this individual needs to buy to be "adequately" covered.

At best, this procedure should be used only to get a first, rough approximation of life insurance

human life value approach

A method of determining the amount of life insurance coverage needed, it attempts to convert the individual's future earnings into a present value as the way to quantify the economic value of a human life.

multiple earnings approach

A method of determining the amount of life insurance coverage needed in which gross annual earnings are multiplied by some largely arbitrarily selected number.

needs. While it is simple to use, it fails to fully recognize the financial obligations and resources of the individual—the same major shortcoming cited for the human life value approach.

Needs Approach

Most professional life insurance agents have abandoned the human life value and/or multiple earnings approach in favor of the **needs approach**. This method specifically considers the financial obligations that a person may have and the financial resources that are available, *in addition to life insurance*. Essentially, the needs approach involves three steps: (1) estimating the total economic resources needed; (2) determining all financial resources that would be available, including life insurance and pension plan death benefits already in force; and (3) subtracting the amount of resources available from the amount needed in order to determine the amount of *additional* life insurance required to provide for an individual's financial program.

The best way to figure out how much life insurance you need is to use a multiple of your earnings. **Fantasy:** While the multiple earnings approach is probably the simplest procedure, it suffers from a number of serious shortcomings. A better choice is the *needs approach.*

Economic Needs. The basic question asked in the needs approach is: What financial resources will the survivors need should the income producer die tomorrow? Although life insurance is often used in retirement planning, it primarily protects families from financial loss resulting from the death of an income producer. In this role, life insurance can provide money for the following financial needs: (1) family income, (2) additional expenses, (3) debt liquidation, (4) surviving spouse's income, (5) money for special requirements, such as the children's education, and (6) liquidity. For the well-heeled, the proceeds from a life insurance policy can also be used to pay estate taxes, thereby leaving intact all or most of the family estate. Such tax payments aside, let's look more closely at the six major financial needs of a typical family.

Family income. For most people with dependents, the principal financial need is to protect

their families' incomes. If they die, they want to make sure that their families' ability to live comfortably is not seriously impaired. Perhaps the best way to estimate the amount of monthly income necessary to sustain a family is to develop a budget covering all expenses that are likely to be incurred. As discussed in Chapter 3, major items in most family budgets are housing costs; utilities; food; automobile expenses; medical and dental needs; clothing; life, health, property, and liability insurance; property taxes; recreation and travel; and savings.

One important question that you must face in developing a post-death family budget is "What standard of living do I want my family to have?" Some feel a reduced level of consumption is in order; others want their families to maintain their present standard of living; and still others would like to leave their families with the level of consumption that would have been achieved had the providers continued to live and work.

One other point to keep in mind concerning family income is that many families today depend on two incomes. Emphasis traditionally has been placed on insuring the family against the income loss of the father. But working mothers can also die unexpectedly. Therefore, to the extent that a family (with either one or two incomes) depends on the woman's income to make ends meet, *that income should be counted as part of the family income need.* Equally important, because the death of a working mother can have devastating effects on the family structure as well as the family budget, *her life should also be adequately insured.* In keeping with the growing importance of women in the work force, life insurance sales on the lives of women have increased dramatically in recent years, as seen in Exhibit 9.2 Unfortunately, however, nearly three times as much life insurance is still being written on men than on women. That indicates that this need is not yet receiving the attention that it deserves—and thus family income is often inadequately protected.

Additional expenses. In most households, adult family members are responsible for performing many family and household services. These services perhaps are most evident with a homemaker and mother. She cooks, cleans, shops, looks after the children, and does whatever is necessary to keep the family happy and cared for. If she dies,

EXHIBIT 9.2

Relative Amount of Life Insurance Sold to Men and Women

Even in spite of the surge in two-income families, the vast majority of insurance is still sold on the lives of male wage earners. In 1986, there was nearly three times as much life insurance sold on men as on women.

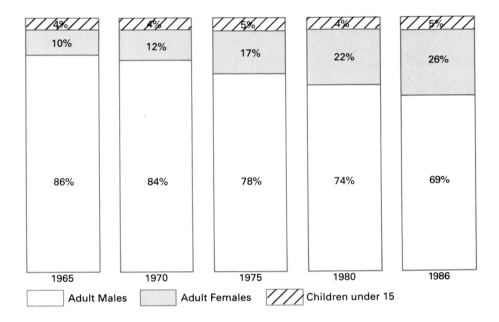

| | | Adult Males | | Adult Females | | Children under 15 |

Source: *Life Insurance Fact Book 1987* (Washington, D.C.: American Council of Life Insurance, 1987), p. 8.

many of these services will have to be paid out of the husband's income. Such additional expenses can stretch the budget to the breaking point and should be recognized as an important economic need.

Pay off debts. In the event of their deaths, most breadwinners prefer to leave their families relatively debt-free. Therefore, to accomplish this objective a person must determine the average amount due for outstanding bills. Included in this amount would be the balances on installment loans, credit cards, department store accounts, and other similar obligations, as well as estimated funeral expenses. In addition, some heads of household will want to leave enough money to pay off their home mortgages and will include this amount in their debt-liquidation estimates. The debt-liquidation component of financial needs can

be viewed as an estimate of the individual's average liabilities.

Surviving spouse's income. Once children are on their own, the monthly household expenses should decrease substantially. Nevertheless, the surviving spouse may need monthly support income for the remainder of his or her life. Therefore, the amount of income needed, as well as the duration of the survivor's life, needs to be estimated.

needs approach

A method of determining the amount of life insurance needed that considers the person's available financial resources (including life insurance), along with specific financial obligations.

EXHIBIT 9.3

Determining the Need for Life Insurance

A worksheet like this one can be used to determine your life insurance requirements according to the needs approach.

Insured's Name *Bill and Joan Benson*   Date *January, 1990*

A.	Family Income Needs				Totals
1.	Debt Liquidation:				
	a. House mortgage	$ *65,000*			
	b. Other loans	$ *5,000*			
	c. Total debt (a + b)				$ *70,000*
2.	Final expenses				$ *5,000*

3.	Annual income needs:	Period 1	Period 2	Period 3	
	a. Monthly living expenses	*2,600*	*2,000*	*1,800*	
	b. Less: Social security survivor's benefits	*1,700*	*0*	*1,000*	
	c. Less: Surviving spouse's income	*0*	*2,000*	*0*	
	d. Less: Other pension benefits and income	*0*	*0*	*500*	
	e. Net monthly income needed (a − b − c − d)	*900*	*0*	*300*	
	f. Net yearly income needed (12 × e)	*10,800*	*0*	*3,600*	
	g. Number of years in period	*12*	*18*	*22*	
	h. Funding needed each period (f × g)	$ *129,600*	$ *0*	$ *79,200*	
	i. Total living needs (add line h for each period)				$ *208,800*
4.	Spouse reeducation fund				$ *25,000*
5.	Children's opportunity fund				$ *50,000*
6.	Other needs				$ *0*
7.	TOTAL INCOME NEEDS (add right column)				$ *358,800*

B.	Financial Resources Available		
1.	Savings and investments	$ *50,000*	
2.	Group life insurance	$ *40,000*	
3.	Other life insurance	$ *0*	
4.	Other resources	$ *0*	
	TOTAL RESOURCES AVAILABLE (1 + 2 + 3 + 4)		$ *90,000*

C.	Additional Life Insurance Needed (A − B)	
	(Note: no additional insurance is needed if number is negative.)	$ *268,800*

Special financial needs. In addition to the economic needs that have been discussed, some families would like to have the resources available to meet certain special financial requirements, such as a college education fund for the children and/or surviving spouse, an emergency fund for unexpected financial burdens, or, as previously mentioned, a fund for paying off the mortgage.

Liquidity. Often we may have assets but no cash. Real estate investors, for example, are notorious for owning several million dollars' worth of properties but bouncing checks for $100. Similarly, many farmers are land rich and cash poor. People who keep a very high percentage of their wealth in illiquid assets often need life insurance to provide enough cash to avoid estate shrinkage. The life insurance proceeds keep the mortgages paid and assets maintained until they can be sold in an orderly fashion at their fair market value.

Available Resources. After estimating the amount of financial needs that a family must try to satisfy upon the death of an income provider, a list of all available resources for meeting those needs must be prepared. For most families, money from savings and social security survivor's benefits make up the largest non-life insurance financial resources. In addition, there are the proceeds from company-sponsored group life insurance policies and the death benefits payable from accumulated pension plans and profit-sharing programs. Another important source is income that can be earned by the surviving spouse or children. If the surviving spouse is skilled and readily employable, his or her earnings could be a family's largest available resource. Also, many families have real estate (in addition to their home), jewelry, stocks, bonds, and other assets that can be liquidated in order to obtain funds to meet financial needs. After a complete list of available resources is developed, some reasonable estimate of their value should be made. Although this step can be difficult due to the changing values of many of the assets, coming up with a set of reasonably accurate estimates is certainly within reach.

Needs Less Resources. The last step in determining the amount of life insurance required is to subtract the amount of available resources from the total needed to satisfy all of the family's financial objectives. If the amount of available resources exceeds the needs, no (additional) life insurance needs to be purchased. If, as in most families with children, the resources are less than the needs, that difference is the amount of life insurance necessary to provide the family with its desired standard of living.

Generally, insurance proceeds can be invested, until the money is actually needed, at a rate of return that exceeds taxes and inflation. This after-tax, after-inflation return may be 1 to 2 percent for reasonably conservative investments, and even higher for more risky investments.

By now you can see that insurance planning based on the needs concept can become quite complex. When a family uses a competent financial planner or life insurance agent who understands the process, the planning stage can proceed quite smoothly. Many major life insurance companies have computer programs set up to determine the life insurance requirements of families using the needs approach. Remember, though, that *life insurance needs are not static.* The amount and type of life insurance you need today probably will differ from the amount and type suitable for you five or ten years from now. Life insurance programs should be reviewed and adjusted (as necessary) at least every five years, or after major changes in the family have occurred (for example, the birth of a child or the purchase of a home).

An Illustration of the Needs Approach in Action

To illustrate how the needs approach can be used in insurance planning, consider the hypothetical case of Bill and Joan Benson. At the present time, the Bensons' primary desire is to have enough insurance on Bill's life to take care of Joan (age 35) and their two children (ages 6 and 8) should Bill die. Their priorities are to (1) leave the family debt free; (2) insure an income for Joan and their children until the youngest child is age 18; (3) provide funds for Joan to make the transition from homemaker to gainful employment; and (4) establish a fund that will permit the children to obtain college educations or begin careers. Because the Bensons know that insurance needs change, they believe a five-year planning horizon is appropriate. At the end of that period, the family's needs and resources

EXHIBIT 9.4

Approximate Monthly Social Security Survivor's Benefits

These benefits existed in 1988 and applied to the families of qualified wage earners who died in 1987; like other aspects of social security, the amount of monthly benefits depends in large part on the covered worker's level of income.

Worker's Age	Salary Level	Monthly Survivor's Benefits		
		One Child Only	Spouse and One Child or Two Children Only	Maximum Family Benefits
25	Low[a]	$334	$ 668	$ 717
	Medium[b]	613	1,226	1,432
	High[c]	786	1,572	1,834
35	Low	$331	$ 662	$ 706
	Medium	610	1,220	1,424
	High	758	1,516	1,769
45	Low	$331	$ 662	$ 705
	Medium	608	1,216	1,420
	High	692	1,384	1,616
55	Low	$330	$ 660	$ 703
	Medium	597	1,194	1,395
	High	653	1,306	1,524

[a]Low Salary Level = Annual income of $10,000.
[b]Medium Salary Level = Annual income of $25,000.
[c]High Salary Level = Annual income of $43,800 or more.

will be reevaluated to see if their life insurance program warrants modification. A worksheet like the one in Exhibit 9.3 (on page 306) will be used to calculate the life insurance needs of the Benson family.

Family Economic Needs. Since the Bensons use credit sparsely, their outstanding debts are limited to a mortgage (with a current balance of $65,000), an automobile loan ($4,000), and miscellaneous charge accounts ($1,000). The balances on these debts currently total $70,000. The mortgage is in its early years and will not be reduced significantly during the five-year planning period. Although the existing auto loan will be amortized, a new loan for a replacement vehicle will probably be necessary. Bill therefore believes that $70,000 will be adequate to meet their need for paying off debts. In addition, the Bensons would like to have $5,000 available to pay estate administration expenses, taxes, and funeral costs. (These items are listed on lines A.1 and A.2 of the worksheet in Exhibit 9.3.)

Bill and Joan have reviewed their budget and feel that the family's monthly living expenses would be $2,600 while the children were still living at home

(12 years). During the period after both children leave home and until Joan retires at age 65 (18 years), the Bensons estimate her monthly living expenses to be $2,000 in current dollars. After Joan's retirement, they anticipate her living expenses to fall to $1,800 a month. The life expectancy of a woman Joan's age is 87 years, so the Bensons calculate that Joan will spend about 22 years in retirement. Because Joan and the children would be eligible for **social security survivor's benefits**, they decide to factor such benefits into their estimate of family income needs. Basically, survivor's benefits are paid to the dependents of deceased workers and are included as part of the social insurance provisions of the social security system; such benefits are intended to provide basic (minimum) support to families faced with the loss of their principal wage earners. In addition to the elderly and disabled, the principal recipients of social security survivor's benefits include (1) unmarried children under age 18 (or 19 if still in high school), (2) nonworking spouses with children under age 16, and (3) surviving spouses age 60 and over.

Exhibit 9.4 lists some figures provided by the Social Security Administration showing *approxi-*

mate monthly social security benefits available in 1988 to the survivors of qualified wage earners. Note that the level of benefits depends on the wage earner's age at death, earnings history, and the number of survivors. While these benefits used to be notoriously difficult to predict, the Social Security Administration has recently introduced an easy-to-use computer-based estimation system that will provide a fairly accurate estimate of the benefits your *survivors* would be entitled to receive in the event of your death. Such benefit projections are included on a *Personal Earnings and Benefit Estimate Statement* that can be obtained by calling the Social Security toll-free number, 1–800–937–2000, and requesting a short application form to fill out and send back in. (This statement is discussed in more detail in Chapter 15, and an actual sample is reproduced in Exhibit 15.4.)

Bill Benson knew about this program and, several weeks ago, sent the application form in for a statement of his own, which he recently received in the mail. Looking under the "Survivor's" portion of "Estimated Benefits," he learned that, based on his age (35) and recent income (he's close to the "high" level of earnings), his family would receive benefits of around $1,700 a month. Note that the Bensons would be entitled to the *maximum family benefits,* which is paid to a surviving (nonworking) spouse with two or more minor children. However, when their youngest child reaches age 16, the benefits for Joan would cease, and as each child graduates from high school his benefits would also stop. Even so, since the worksheet we are using is an estimate, we will assume they receive $1,700 a month for the full 12 years. Knowing what they'd receive from social security, they subtracted that amount from their target income (of $2,600 a month) to arrive at a *net monthly income* (line 3.c on the worksheet); this is the amount of income they'll have to come up with from some source other than social security in order to preserve their present standard of living. This is the basic level of income they want to maintain until the children are grown—when the youngest child has reached 18 years of age, a period of 12 years from now. Thus, they estimate that it should take about $129,600 to provide the family with $10,800 a year for 12 years. (All of which is listed under the "Period 1" column of the worksheet.) Actually, given that money has a time value, it would take something *less* than the

$129,600 to provide the needed income, but this complication can be ignored so long as we also disregard future inflation, which in fact would add to the amount needed. In essence, since one element (inflation) will have at least a partially offsetting effect on the other (present value), we will ignore both of them in our calculations.

A similar procedure is used to estimate available income for Period 2, the years after the children leave home and until Joan retires; and then, the years after Joan retires, Period 3. Period 2 is called the "Widow's Gap," so named because it is a time during which the surviving spouse receives no Social Security benefits. However, Joan expects to work during this period, and as a result, feels she should be able to make a net monthly income of around $2,000 (in current dollars). After retirement, the Bensons estimate that Joan's living expenses should drop even more (to around $1,800 a month). Because Joan will have worked for nearly 20 years, they think it is reasonable to assume she will earn retirement benefits of her own; to be on the safe side, they estimate Joan's retirement benefits should amount to around $500 a month. In addition, once Joan reaches retirement age, she will once again be eligible for monthly Social Security benefits—which they estimate should amount to around $1,000 a month. Based on this information, Joan will be able to support herself during Period 2, but she will need a total of $79,200 to preserve her standard of living during retirement. (These calculations are summarized under columns marked Periods 2 and 3 in Exhibit 9.3.) Therefore, the Bensons' total income needs over Joan's lifetime (Periods 1 through 3) are $208,200, which is listed as the total income needs by 3i on the worksheet.

Although Joan is trained as a stockbroker, because she will not go to work until both children are raised, they are concerned that her previous education may be somewhat out of date. Thus, they

social security survivor's benefits
Benefits included in the social insurance provision of the social security system that are intended to provide basic support for families who have lost their principal wage earners.

would like to have enough money to allow Joan to return to college for several years. They believe $25,000 should be sufficient for this purpose. If Bill dies prior to his next life insurance review date (that is, in five years), the $25,000 can/will be invested and also provide a cushion against any major unforeseen economic setbacks for the family.

Finally, both Bill and Joan want to guarantee that their children will have the money necessary to take advantage of education or other opportunities that may be available to them when they reach age 18. To do this, they want to establish an opportunity fund of $50,000. This fund would also grow substantially before it was needed should Bill die during the five-year time horizon. The top part of the worksheet in Exhibit 9.3 summarizes the Bensons' economic needs. Note that they feel that the total amount necessary to meet their financial goals, should Bill die within the next five years, would be $358,800.

Social security survivor's benefits should be factored into your life insurance plans if you have a dependent spouse and/or minor children. **Fact:** Survivor's benefits are paid to the dependents of eligible deceased workers and can be a big factor in helping your family meet their annual income needs.

Available Financial Resources. Bill is employed as an assistant professor at a state university. Although the university has a retirement program, no preretirement survivor's benefits are available, other than social security. However, Bill is covered by an employer-sponsored group life insurance policy in the amount of one year's gross salary ($40,000). Also, the Bensons have roughly $50,000 socked away in a couple of mutual funds and a money market deposit account; these investments were obtained in part from an inheritance and from a $20,000 advance against Bill's textbook royalties.

Other potential resources, such as a promised gift of $20,000 from Joan's Aunt Sarah, a travel accident life insurance policy with a $10,000 face value, and assorted personal property, are ignored in the planning process because of uncertainty as to either their amount or their availability. For example, Aunt Sarah may decide to donate the money to charity, or Bill may die from a cause unrelated to his travel insurance. Overall, then, the resources that the Bensons can count on to help

achieve their economic objectives total $90,000, as summarized in the lower part (Section B) of Exhibit 9.3.

Additional Life Insurance Needed. As shown in the bottom line of Exhibit 9.3, the difference between the monies available and those that will be required is $268,800; this sum equals the amount of life insurance the Bensons will need to insure Bill's life and meet the family's desired standard of living. Often the amount of life insurance needed to fulfill a family's desired expenditures will exceed the family's willingness or ability to pay for it. Even after a careful search for the right type of policy at the best price, a family might decide they just cannot afford all of the insurance they would like. In these cases, a priority ranking of needs, coupled with a reassessment of available resources, is necessary. For example, in the preliminary plans a college education fund might have been included while consideration was not given to income from employment of the surviving spouse or children. The family could decide, however, to let the children work their way through college and have the surviving spouse seek employment. In this manner, ability and willingness to pay for life insurance can be adjusted to meet economic needs.

WHAT KIND OF POLICY IS RIGHT FOR YOU?

> Once you have determined how *much* insurance to buy, the next thing you must do is decide on the *kind* of life insurance that's best for you. What factors would you want to consider when deciding on the type of life insurance policy to buy? Would you look for a good investment, or the most life insurance coverage for the money? Stop to think about these questions before going on.

After you have determined the amount of life insurance necessary to meet your family's financial requirements, you must decide on the type of insurance contract that will best fit your needs. Generally speaking, most families can effectively satisfy their insurance needs through the use of one of the three basic types of life insurance: term life, whole life, or universal life insurance. Indeed, these three products account for 90 to 95 percent of all life insurance sales—with whole life being the biggest seller, closely followed by term policies, and universal life being a distant third. Now, there are, of course, other types of life insurance policies available to consumers, but as we'll see, most of these are simply modifications of these three types.

Term Insurance

Under the provisions of a **term life insurance** policy, the insurance company agrees to pay a stipulated amount if the insured dies during the policy period. The period of coverage is often five years, with premiums payable annually, semiannually, or quarterly. Many other periods of coverage and payment plans are available. Term insurance is the purest form of life insurance in that it provides a stipulated amount of life insurance (that is, death benefits) and nothing more; there are *no* investment or savings features associated with it. Term insurance can be an economical way to purchase life insurance, on a temporary basis, for protection against financial loss resulting from death, especially in the early years of family formation. A representative premium schedule for five-year renewable term insurance is illustrated in Exhibit 9.5 (on page 312).

Nearly all life insurance companies sell some form of term insurance. In addition, employer-sponsored group life insurance plans and companies that sell directly to the public through the mail or newspaper and magazine advertisements often offer term insurance at low rates. Unfortunately, in the past many families, because of either lack of knowledge or poor advice, did not properly incorporate term life insurance into their insurance programs. As consumers have become more knowledgeable, however, term life insurance sales have increased accordingly. Today, in fact, term policies account for about a third of all (group and individual) life insurance sales.

Term insurance provides nothing more than a stipulated amount of death benefits and, as a result, is considered the purest form of life insurance. **Fact:** Term insurance basically provides a given amount of life insurance (that is, death benefits) for a stipulated period of time and nothing more—no investment features or cash value.

Types of Term Insurance. The most common types of term insurance are straight term, renewable term, convertible term, and decreasing term. Term insurance features are not necessarily unique; for instance, a policy may be a straight term with both guaranteed renewable and convertible features.

Straight term. Policies written for a given number of years—for example, 1, 5, 10, or 20 years—are called **straight-term** (or **level-term**) **policies**. In such policies, the amount of life insurance coverage remains unchanged throughout the effective period of the policy. In contrast, the *annual premium* on a straight-term policy may increase each year, or every five years. In many cases, however, it will remain level throughout the policy period. Of course, a policy with a premium that increases each year will start off below the level premium amount, subsequently equal it, and finally exceed it.

Renewable term. A **renewable-term policy** allows the insured to renew his or her policy for another term of equal length, without having to show evidence of insurability. Renewal is at the option of the insured, but the premium will increase to offset the greater chance of death at older ages. Generally, term policies may be renewed each period until the insured attains age 65 or 70. If you

---

term life insurance
Insurance that provides only death benefits, for a specified period (typically five years), and does not provide for the accumulation of any cash values.

straight-term policy
A term insurance policy that is written for a given number of years and whose coverage remains unchanged throughout the effective term; also called level-term policy.

renewable-term policy
A type of term insurance policy that may be renewed, without evidence of insurability, for another term of equal length.

EXHIBIT 9.5

A Premium Schedule for Term Life Insurance (Premiums per $1,000 of Level Premium Term Insurance)

When you buy term insurance, you are basically buying a financial product that provides life insurance coverage and nothing more.

Age Nearest Birthday		Five-Year Renewable Term		
Male	**Female**	**Annual**	**Semiannual**	**Quarterly**
20	25	$ 2.37	$ 1.23	$ .64
21	26	2.40	1.25	.65
22	27	2.44	1.27	.66
23	28	2.50	1.30	.68
24	29	2.55	1.33	.69
25	30	2.58	1.34	.70
26	31	2.62	1.36	.71
27	32	2.67	1.39	.72
28	33	2.73	1.42	.74
29	34	2.78	1.45	.75
30	35	2.88	1.50	.78
31	36	2.97	1.54	.80
32	37	3.11	1.62	.84
33	38	3.27	1.70	.88
34	39	3.49	1.81	.94
35	40	3.73	1.94	1.01
36	41	3.99	2.07	1.08
37	42	4.28	2.23	1.16
38	43	4.59	2.39	1.24
39	44	4.93	2.56	1.33
40	45	5.30	2.76	1.43
41	46	5.69	2.96	1.54
42	47	6.12	3.18	1.65
43	48	6.59	3.43	1.78
44	49	7.08	3.68	1.91
45	50	7.74	4.02	2.09
46	51	8.47	4.40	2.29
47	52	9.25	4.81	2.50
48	53	10.13	5.27	2.74
49	54	11.10	5.77	3.00
50	55	12.16	6.32	3.28
51	56	13.34	6.94	3.60
52	57	14.69	7.64	3.97
53	58	16.14	8.39	4.36
54	59	17.76	9.24	4.80
55	60	18.76	9.76	5.07
56		19.55	10.17	5.28
57		20.56	10.69	5.55
58		22.52	11.71	6.08
59		24.66	12.82	6.66
60		27.03	14.06	7.30

Note: All policies shown are participating, which means that the company will pay policyholders a dividend at the end of each year. Of course, the amount of the dividend cannot be determined beforehand.

buy term insurance, it's a good idea to obtain a **guaranteed renewable provision** in your policy. Otherwise, if you become uninsurable due to accident or illness during the policy period, you will lose your chance to renew your protection. This valuable feature usually is available at a modest cost.

Convertible term. A **convertible-term policy** allows the insured to convert coverage to a whole life policy (discussed in the section below) without evidence of insurability. The convertibility feature serves as a guarantee to the insureds that (1) they will not lose their insurance protection at the end of the period and (2) upon conversion, they will have lifelong protection (as long as they pay their premiums, of course). The convertible-term policy can be useful to persons who need a large amount of death protection at a relatively low cost, but who also want to continue their insurance coverage throughout their entire lives. This way, term coverage can be purchased to provide for a large amount of immediate death protection, and then later, when the insured has more income (and saving for retirement and liquidity for estate taxes become the more dominant issues), it can be converted to whole life. The convertibility option is available with most term insurance contracts at a reasonable price.

You should note that many convertible-term policies place some limitation on when the conversion can take place. For example, a ten-year term policy may stipulate that the conversion has to be made before the end of the eighth year, or a term policy to age 65 may require conversion prior to age 61.

Decreasing term. Because the death rate increases for each year of life, the premiums on straight-term policies for each successive period of coverage will also increase. As an alternative to such a situation, many companies offer a term policy that *maintains a level premium* throughout all periods of coverage, while *the amount of protection decreases.* Such a policy is called a **decreasing-term policy**, since the amount of protection decreases over its life. Decreasing term can be used when the amount of needed coverage declines over time. For example, decreasing-term policies are popular with homeowners who want a level of life insurance coverage that will decline at about the same rate as the balances on their home mortgages. In addition, these policies are often purchased by families with young children as a way to ensure a sufficient level of family income while the kids are growing up. (As they grow older, the amount of coverage needed decreases until the last child becomes independent and the need expires.)

Advantages and Disadvantages of Term. Since term insurance offers an economical way to purchase a large amount of life insurance protection over a given (relatively short) period of time, it is particularly advantageous during the child-rearing years. And with the guaranteed renewable and convertible options, coverage can be continued throughout the insured's life, although, of course,

the cost continually grows due to the increased chance of death. Indeed, this characteristic of increasing cost is the main disadvantage of term insurance, and is a principal reason why people discontinue needed coverage.

Criticizing term insurance on the basis of increasing cost, however, is similar to finding fault with homeowner's insurance for not paying for a loss caused by an automobile accident. Clearly, the purpose of homeowner's insurance is not to provide automobile coverage, just as the purpose of a term policy is *not* to provide lifelong coverage. The objective of term insurance is to provide a large amount of protection for a limited period of time—something it accomplishes very well!

Whole Life Insurance

Few people ever outlive the need for some type of life insurance. Accordingly, **whole life insurance**, as the name implies, is designed to offer financial protection for the whole life of an individual. In addition to death protection, whole life insurance has a *savings* feature, called **cash value**, which

---

guaranteed renewable provision
A provision in a term insurance contract that guarantees the insured the right to renew the policy.

convertible-term policy
A term insurance policy that allows the insured the privilege of converting coverage into a whole life or endowment life policy without providing evidence of insurability.

decreasing-term policy
A term insurance policy in which the protection decreases over the policy's life.

whole life insurance
Life insurance that is designed to offer financial protection for the entire life of the insured; allows for the accumulation of cash values, along with providing stipulated death benefits.

cash value
The accumulated refundable value of an insurance policy that is based on insurance premiums paid and investment earnings; can be used as a source of loan collateral.

EXHIBIT 9.6

A Premium Schedule for Whole Life Insurance (Premiums per $1,000 of Insurance Coverage)

As with any life insurance product, the older you are, the more expensive it is to buy whole life. Also, whole life is more costly than term because you are getting an investment/savings account in addition to life insurance coverage.

Age Nearest Birthday		Straight Life			20-Pay Life			30-Pay Life		
Male	Female	Annual	Semiannual	Quarterly	Annual	Semiannual	Quarterly	Annual	Semiannual	Quarterly
20	25	$10.13	$ 5.27	$ 2.74	$16.44	$ 8.55	$ 4.44	$12.85	$ 6.68	$ 3.47
21	26	10.50	5.46	2.84	16.91	8.79	4.57	13.23	6.88	3.57
22	27	10.86	5.65	2.93	17.40	9.05	4.70	13.61	7.08	3.67
23	28	11.26	5.86	3.04	17.89	9.30	4.83	14.02	7.29	3.79
24	29	11.68	6.07	3.15	18.41	9.57	4.97	14.43	7.50	3.90
25	30	12.07	6.28	3.26	18.87	9.81	5.09	14.82	7.71	4.00
26	31	12.47	6.48	3.37	19.34	10.06	5.22	15.21	7.91	4.11
27	32	12.90	6.71	3.48	19.83	10.31	5.35	15.62	8.12	4.22
28	33	13.34	6.94	3.60	20.34	10.58	5.49	16.05	8.35	4.33
29	34	13.81	7.18	3.73	20.87	10.85	5.63	16.50	8.58	4.46
30	35	14.30	7.44	3.86	21.42	11.14	5.78	16.98	8.83	4.58
31	36	14.82	7.71	4.00	21.99	11.43	5.94	17.46	9.08	4.71
32	37	15.37	7.99	4.15	22.57	11.74	6.09	17.98	9.35	4.85
33	38	15.94	8.29	4.30	23.18	12.05	6.26	18.52	9.63	5.00
34	39	16.54	8.60	4.47	23.83	12.39	6.43	19.09	9.93	5.15
35	40	17.18	8.93	4.64	24.50	12.74	6.62	19.68	10.23	5.31
36	41	17.86	9.29	4.82	25.19	13.10	6.80	20.31	10.56	5.48
37	42	18.58	9.66	5.02	25.90	13.47	6.99	20.96	10.90	5.66
38	43	19.32	10.05	5.22	26.66	13.86	7.20	21.64	11.25	5.84
39	44	20.11	10.46	5.43	27.45	14.27	7.41	22.37	11.63	6.04
40	45	20.94	10.89	5.65	28.27	14.70	7.63	23.13	12.03	6.25
41	46	21.80	11.34	5.89	29.13	15.15	7.87	23.93	12.44	6.46
42	47	22.72	11.81	6.13	30.02	15.61	8.11	24.74	12.86	6.68
43	48	23.69	12.32	6.40	30.95	16.09	8.36	25.63	13.33	6.92
44	49	24.71	12.85	6.67	31.91	16.59	8.62	26.55	13.81	7.17
45	50	25.91	13.47	7.00	33.07	17.20	8.93	27.66	14.38	7.47
46	51	27.17	14.13	7.34	34.30	17.84	9.26	28.84	15.00	7.79
47	52	28.52	14.83	7.70	35.56	18.49	9.60	30.08	15.64	8.12
48	53	29.95	15.57	8.09	36.90	19.19	9.96	31.43	16.34	8.49
49	54	31.47	16.36	8.50	38.34	19.94	10.35	32.84	17.08	8.87
50	55	33.10	17.21	8.94	39.84	20.72	10.76	34.35	17.86	9.27
51	56	34.82	18.11	9.40	41.42	21.54	11.18	35.97	18.70	9.71
52	57	36.65	19.06	9.90	43.10	22.41	11.64	37.71	19.61	10.18
53	58	38.61	20.08	10.42	44.89	23.34	12.12	39.56	20.57	10.68
54	59	40.70	21.16	10.99	46.80	24.34	12.64	41.56	21.61	11.22
55	60	42.79	22.25	11.55	48.34	25.14	13.05	43.43	22.58	11.73
56	61	42.95	22.33	11.60	48.83	25.39	13.18	43.69	22.72	11.80
57	62	45.01	23.41	12.15	50.32	26.17	13.59	45.55	23.69	12.30
58	63	47.36	24.63	12.79	52.40	27.25	14.15	47.82	24.87	12.91
59	64	49.85	25.92	13.46	54.62	28.40	14.75	50.24	26.12	13.56
60	65	52.50	27.30	14.18	56.97	29.62	15.38	52.81	27.46	14.26

Note: All policies shown are participating.

results from the investment earnings on paid-in insurance premiums. Thus, whole life provides not only insurance coverage but also a modest return on your investment! The idea behind cash value is to provide the insurance buyer with a tangible return while he or she is also receiving insurance coverage—the savings rates on whole life policies are normally *fixed* and *guaranteed* to be more than a certain rate (say, 4 to 6 percent). Whole life is available through several different payment plans, including continuous-premium, limited-payment, and single-premium. All of these payment plans provide for accumulation of cash values.

Life insurance companies set aside assets (that is, they "accumulate reserves") to pay the claims expected from the policies they issue. As time goes by, the cash value of a policy—the amount of assets allocated for each person insured—increases to reflect the greater chance of death that comes with age. If policyholders decide to cancel their contracts prior to death, that portion of the assets set aside to provide payment for the death claim is available to them. This right to a cash value is termed the policyholder's **nonforfeiture right**. Policyholders, by terminating their insurance contracts, forfeit their rights to death benefits. Correspondingly, the company must forfeit its right to keep all of the monies paid by these policyholders for the future death benefit it is no longer required to pay.

Types of Whole Life Policies. Although a wide variety of whole life policies exist, only the major ones—continuous-premium, limited-payment, and single-premium—are described here. To get a feel for the cost of these policies, a sample premium schedule for several types of whole life policies is illustrated in Exhibit 9.6. By contrasting the premiums in this exhibit with those in Exhibit 9.5, you can readily see how much more expensive whole life is relative to term life. That is the price you pay for the savings/investment feature that comes with whole life.

Continuous-premium. Under a *continuous-premium whole life* policy, or *straight life,* as it's more commonly called, individuals pay a level premium each year until they die or exercise a nonforfeiture right. The earlier in life the coverage is purchased, the lower the annual premium. This concept is often used as a selling point by some life insurance agents to convince younger persons to buy now. Their argument is that the sooner you buy, the less you pay. What they mean by this is what you pay *annually* rather than the total payments over the life of the policy. Of course, the sooner people purchase whole life, the longer they have coverage in force, but (all other things being equal) the *more* they pay in total. While good reasons (such as securing needed protection, savings and insurability) do exist for many young persons

to buy whole life, it should seldom be purchased by anyone simply because the annual premium will be less than if it is purchased at a later date. Of the variety of whole life policies available, continuous-premium/straight life offers the greatest amount of permanent death protection and the least amount of savings per dollar of premium paid. Since the emphasis of whole life insurance for most families is *death protection* rather than savings, the continuous-premium policy is usually the wisest choice when filling a permanent life insurance need.

Limited-payment. The *limited-payment whole life* policy offers coverage for the entire life of the insured but schedules the payments to end after a certain period of time. For example, 20-pay life, 30-pay life, paid-up age 55, and paid-up age 65 are types of frequently sold limited pay whole life policies. Under the 20-pay and 30-pay life contracts, the policyholder is most often required to make 20 or 30 annual level premium payments, respectively. Under the premium schedule of paid-up at age 55, 65, or other stipulated-age policies, the policyholder makes premium payments until he or she attains the stated age. Of course, for any individual, the shorter the period of time over which premiums are payable, the larger the amount of the annual premium. Upon completion of the scheduled payments, the insurance remains in force at its face value for the remainder of the insured's life.

Some insurance companies emphasize the sale of limited-pay policies to the detriment of those who purchase them. In the sales presentation, considerable attention is focused on the "large" savings element that will develop and the fact that the policyholder is relieved of having to pay premiums for the entire life of the insured. However, this logic fails at two points. First, for most people, the primary purpose of whole life insurance is permanent protection against financial loss resulting from death—not the accumulation of savings. Second, even if people buy continuous-premium whole life

---

nonforfeiture right
A life insurance option that gives the policyholder the portion of those assets that had been set aside to provide payment for future death claims. This amount, or *cash value,* is given to the policyholder upon cancellation of the policy by the insured.

policies, they need pay the premium only as long as they wish to keep the policies in force for their full face value. Policyholders may stop payment of premiums at any time after some nonforfeiture value has been accumulated. Rather than take this benefit in cash, they can convert the policies to ones that are paid up for some amount less than the original face value of the policy. (This is discussed in subsequent sections.)

The preceding discussion is not intended to imply that limited-payment policies are not desirable; rather, the point is that if lifelong death protection is the primary aim of the life insurance policy, continuous-premium whole life should be purchased instead of a limited-payment policy. Since more continuous-premium whole life insurance can be purchased with the same number of dollars as limited-payment whole life, people who need whole life insurance are probably better off using continuous-premium life insurance so they can make the most of their insurance coverage. Once their insurance needs are reduced, they can convert the policy to a smaller amount of paid-up life insurance. On the other hand, if people have life insurance already in force that is sufficient to protect against income loss, they can use limited-payment policies as part of their savings or retirement plans.

Single-premium whole life. Continuous-premium and limited-payment whole life policies represent methods of acquiring life insurance on an installment basis. In contrast, a *single-premium whole life* policy is one that is purchased on a cash basis. You make one premium payment at the inception of the contract, and that buys life insurance coverage for the rest of your life. The single-premium policy has only limited usefulness in the life insurance programs of most families. However, because of its investment attributes, single-premium life insurance, or SPLI for short, does hold some appeal for those who are looking for a way to invest in a type of *tax-sheltered investment vehicle*. The fact is that today, even though SPLI is an insurance product, more often than not it's touted as an investment vehicle.

From an investment perspective, SPLI is attractive because, like any whole life insurance policy, it allows the holder to accumulate interest/investment earnings within the policy on a tax-deferred basis. It also provides some life-insurance coverage—usually just enough to qualify under IRS rules—but

this amounts to an added bonus. (Of course, the death benefits from an SPLI policy are treated like those from any other life insurance policy in that they pass tax-free to the beneficiaries.) Single-premium policies are purchased with a single payment made right up front, much like you would do when buying a stock, bond, or some other investment vehicle. Minimum premiums usually run around $5,000, though most buyers today put in much more. Once the purchase is made, investment earnings start to build up tax-free! If all this sounds to good to be true, it's because *there is a catch:* any cash withdrawals made before you reach age 59½ are subject to a 10 percent tax penalty.

Prior to the latest (1988) changes in the tax laws, you could "borrow" up to 90 percent of the value of your SPLI policy and not pay any taxes. Not any more! Indeed, about the only way you can borrow free of any tax trouble from a life insurance policy today is if you pay premiums over a period of at least seven years—which, of course, rules out all SPLI policies. (As we'll see in Chapter 15, these policies are treated for tax purposes just like annuities and individual retirement programs.)

There are two basic types of SPLI plans available:

- The single-premium *whole life* policy, which preserves the principal and usually guarantees the return for the first year or so. After that, the rates of return are changed periodically to reflect prevailing money market rates; however, rates normally cannot fall below a certain minimum level (usually, around 4 to 6 percent) as specified in the policy.
- The single-premium *variable life* policy, which lets you put your money in a number of investment choices, ranging from stocks and bonds to mutual funds and money market instruments. However, keep in mind that in such a policy, *your funds are at risk;* there's no minimum rate of return or preservation of principal assured. Substantial investment losses do occur, and these can result in big cuts in your insurance coverage, or even termination of your policy!

Despite the tempting sales pitches, most experts agree that this product is ill-suited for young, moderate-income families. For one thing, it's not a very effective form of life insurance, and for another, there are usually better ways to invest your money.

Advantages and Disadvantages of Whole Life.
The most noteworthy feature of whole life insurance is that premium payments contribute toward building an estate regardless of how long the insured lives. This feature results because the face value of the policy is paid upon death; or alternatively, the cash value may be withdrawn when the need for insurance protection has expired. A corresponding benefit of whole life (except single-premium) is that it permits individuals who need insurance for an entire lifetime to budget their premium payments over a relatively long period, thus eliminating the problems of unaffordability and uninsurability often encountered with term insurance in later years. Also, some people like whole life because the periodic payments force them to save regularly. And, of course, there's the favorable tax treatment afforded to accumulated earnings—which means that as your earnings build up on a tax-sheltered basis, the underlying cash value of the policy also increases at a much faster rate than it would otherwise. This feature applies to any whole life policy; and from an insurance perspective, it means not only a greater cash value, but more importantly, a greater amount of paid-up life insurance coverage.

The most frequently cited disadvantages of whole life insurance are that (1) it provides less death protection than term insurance, and (2) it provides lower yields than many other investment vehicles—the fact is that the returns on most whole life insurance policies are just not all that attractive. As with term insurance, the negative aspects of whole life arise from misuse of the policy. In other words, a whole life policy should not be used to fulfill the objective of obtaining maximum return on investment. However, if a person wishes to combine a given amount of death protection for the entire life of the insured (or until the policy is terminated) with a savings plan that provides a reasonable tax-sheltered rate of return, whole life insurance may be a wise purchase.

Universal Life Insurance

The stockbrokerage firm of E. F. Hutton, through its life insurance subsidiary, is generally credited with marketing the first universal life insurance policy in 1979. Today most life companies sell universal life insurance or similar policies. Basically,

universal life insurance combines term insurance, which provides the death benefits of the policy, with a tax-sheltered savings/investment account that pays interest at *competitive money market rates.* The acceptance of universal life is demonstrated most vividly by the fact that in 1988—less than ten years after it was introduced—universal life products accounted for about 30 percent of *individual* life policy sales (note: the rate is lower in relation to *total* insurance sales, since universal life is used in very few *group* life policies).

A Type of Whole Life Insurance. Universal life insurance is like whole life in that it provides both death protection and a savings element, or cash value. The special aspect of a universal life policy is that the death protection (or pure insurance) portion and the savings portion are identified separately in its price. This is referred to as *unbundling.* Traditionally, for whole life insurance, you would pay a premium that would purchase a stated face amount of coverage in a policy with a *fixed cash-value schedule.* Not so with universal life. Here's what happens: When you make a premium payment on a universal life policy, part of that premium is used to pay administrative fees and the remainder is put in the cash value, or savings portion of the policy, where it earns a certain rate of return—this rate of earnings varies with market yields, but is guaranteed to be more than some stipulated minimum rate (say, 4 percent). Then, each month, the price of one month's term insurance is withdrawn from the cash value to purchase the required death protection. So long as there's enough in the savings portion to buy death protection, the policy will stay in force. Should the cash value grow to an unusually large amount, then the amount of insurance coverage will be increased in order for the policy to retain its favorable tax treatment (tax laws require that the death benefits in a universal life policy *must always exceed the cash value).*

---

universal life insurance
A type of insurance contract that combines term insurance (death benefits) with a tax-deferred savings/investment account that pays competitive money market interest rates.

The clear separation of the protection and savings elements in the universal policy has raised the question of whether or not this type of insurance is in fact whole life insurance. This question is important, because the accumulation of cash values in whole life policies arises partly from interest credited to them. Under present tax laws, *this accumulation occurs income tax–free as long as the cash value does not exceed the total premiums paid to the insurer.* However, if a whole life policy is surrendered for its cash value, and that cash value exceeds the premiums paid, then *the gain* is taxed. Through an Internal Revenue Service ruling and federal legislation, universal life insurance policies enjoy the same favorable tax treatment as do other forms of whole life insurance—that is, death benefits are income tax–free and, prior to the death of the insured, amounts credited to the cash value, including investment earnings, accumulate on a tax-deferred basis.

Basic Structure.   Insurance companies sell a variety of policies under the heading of universal life. In spite of the different names, the basic structure of these policies is pretty much the same and can be described as follows. The premium you pay for the policy, which is called the *annual contribution* or *annual outlay,* is deposited in a fund, known as an *accumulation account.* The insurer credits interest to the account at a current rate and deducts from it the cost of the death benefits (and other expenses). The size of the deduction for the death protection depends on the amount of term insurance to be purchased and the age of the insured. The crediting of interest and the deductions for expenses and insurance coverage usually occur monthly.

Within the basic structure of a universal life insurance policy, there are two types of death protection. In the first type, a level death benefit is provided. As the cash value increases, the amount of pure insurance protection *decreases.* The second type provides a stated amount of insurance plus the accumulated cash value. Thus, the death benefit at any time varies with the rate of earnings on the savings plan and will increase along with the accumulated cash value.

The Flexibility Feature.   A characteristic of a universal life insurance policy that is important in your financial planning is its flexible nature. The annual premium you pay can be increased or decreased from year to year. This feature is based on the fact that the cost of the death protection *may be covered from either the annual premium or the accumulation account* (that is, cash value). Thus, as long as the accumulation account is adequate, you can choose to skip an annual premium and cover the cost of the death protection from the accumulation account. In addition, the death benefit can be increased or decreased, and you can change from the level benefit type of policy to the cash value plus a stated amount of insurance. Note, however, that evidence of insurability is usually required if the death benefit is to be increased.

Some Precautions.   One of the attractions of a universal life insurance policy is the promise of the cash value being credited with the "current" rate of interest. For example, the current rate of interest may be 10 percent as compared to a guaranteed minimum rate of 4 percent. Make it a point to find out just what current rate of interest is used to credit earnings to your accumulation account. A common rate is that of 90-day Treasury bills. Other rates, however, may be used. Another caution regarding universal life is that you may be attracted to the relatively low interest charge on loans that you take from your cash value. However, the cash value that is equal to the loan is usually then credited with only the *guaranteed interest rate* of 4 to 4½ percent.

You should also evaluate the charges or fees that the insurance company levies on its universal life policies. Ask the insurance agent about the front-end load or commission you'll have to pay on the first premium, the expense charge on each annual premium, investment expenses charged by the insurer in determining the "current" rate of return, and any other charges you may be assessed. Most states require that the insurance company issue an annual disclosure statement that spells out premiums paid, expenses and mortality costs, interest earned, and beginning and ending cash values.

Other Types of Life Insurance

In addition to term, whole, and universal life, several other types of life insurance policies are available, including variable life insurance, group life, credit life, mortgage life, industrial life insurance, special purpose policies, and deferred-premium life insurance. With the exception of group life insurance, the other types of contracts should either be avoided or used with extreme care.

Variable Life Insurance. A basic feature of *whole* life insurance is that it combines insurance coverage and a savings account into one package. *Universal* life extends this concept by being a bit more aggressive with the savings component, and thereby offering the potential for slightly higher returns and a quicker build-up of the cash value. *Variable life* goes even further, for it allows the policyholder to decide on how the money in the savings (cash value) component should be invested and as a result, offers the highest and most attractive level of investment returns—but unlike whole or universal life policies, no minimum return is guaranteed. In addition, as the name implies, the amount of insurance coverage provided will vary with the profits (and losses) being generated in the investment account. Thus, in **variable life insurance** policies, the amount of death benefits payable are, for the most part, related to the policies' investment returns.

A variable life policy, in short, combines insurance protection with the ability to spread your money over a variety of different investment accounts, all in one convenient, tax-favored package. The investment accounts are set up just like *mutual funds,* and most firms that offer variable life policies let you choose from a full menu of different types of funds, ranging from money market accounts and bond funds to aggressively managed stock funds. As a policyholder, you can specify that your money be placed into any one or more of the funds offered under the policy, and you can also freely move your money from one fund to another as market conditions dictate. Furthermore, like all life insurance products, variable policies offer attractive tax benefits: investment earnings can grow within the policy free of any current taxation; you can switch between funds with no tax consequences; and the policy's death benefit is passed on tax-free to your beneficiaries.

While all these features may sound great, it's important to keep in mind that if you want the benefits of higher investment returns, you must also be willing to assume the risks of reduced insurance coverage—bigger investment profits do, indeed, lead to more death benefits and an accelerated build-up in cash value, but investments can also end up losing money (sometimes in a big way), and that can lead to lower cash values and reduced insurance coverage (though it can never fall below the minimum death benefit stated in the policy). All of which means you should use extreme care when buying variable life insurance. More than anything else, variable life insurance is an *investment vehicle* wrapped in a life insurance policy (the life insurance coverage, in effect, is just a feature that's added on to meet the standards for favorable tax treatment). In this regard, it's certainly no coincidence that the vast majority of variable life insurance is purchased as *single-premium* policies. They're bought for their investment attributes, not their terrific insurance coverage. Look at the advertising literature that these companies put out—more often than not, you'll find that these products are being touted as one of the few remaining *tax-sheltered investment vehicles*. If that's not what you're looking for you may want to consider a variable life policy; but if it's *primary* life insurance coverage you're after, you'd be well advised to look somewhere else.

Group Life Insurance. Under **group life insurance**, one master policy is issued, and each eligible member of the group receives a certificate of insurance. Group life is nearly always term insurance, and the premium is based on the characteristics of the group as a whole, rather than related to any specific individual. Group life insurance is often provided by employers as a fringe benefit for their employees. However, just about any type of group (be it a labor union, professional association, or alumni organization) can secure a group life

---

variable life insurance
Life insurance in which the benefits payable to the insured are related to the returns being generated on the investments that support the policy's payment obligations.

group life insurance
A type of life insurance that provides a master policy for a group and a certificate of insurance for each eligible member.

policy, so long as the insurance is only incidental to the reason for the group.

Accounting for about 50 percent of all life insurance in force in the United States, group life insurance is one of the fastest-growing areas of insurance. Many group life policies now offer coverage for not only the group members but also their dependents. In addition, group life policies generally provide that if individual members leave the group, they may continue the coverage by converting their protection to individually issued whole life policies—and such conversion normally does not require evidence of insurability so long as it occurs within a specified period of time. Of course, after exercising the option to convert, these individuals assume all responsibility for the payment of premiums.

As noted earlier in the chapter, the availability of group coverage should be considered when developing a life insurance program. However, because of its potentially temporary nature and relatively low face amount (often equal to about one year's salary), it should fulfill only low-priority insurance needs. Only in rare cases should a family rely solely on group life insurance to fulfill its primary income-protection requirements.

Credit Life Insurance. Banks, finance companies, and other lenders generally sell **credit life insurance** in conjunction with installment loans. Usually credit life is a term policy with a face value that decreases at the same rate as the outstanding balance on the loan. Although liquidating debts upon the death of a family breadwinner is often desirable, the funds for this need should be fulfilled through an individual's term or whole life insurance program. Buying credit life insurance per se is one of the most expensive ways to buy life insurance and should be avoided. Further, contrary to popular belief, a lender cannot legally reject a loan just because the potential borrower chooses not to buy credit life insurance.

Mortgage Life Insurance. Mortgage life insurance is a form of credit life insurance that's designed to pay off the mortgage balance on a home in the event of the death of the borrower. As in the case of credit life, this need can usually be met less expensively by shopping the market for a suitable decreasing-term policy. Credit life

and mortgage life are relatively expensive, because lenders are often influenced by the amount of sales commission they receive in selecting the insurers with whom they place the coverage. Also, as might be expected, an insurer who pays high commissions is frequently one who charges a high premium.

Industrial Life Insurance. Industrial life insurance, now called **home service life**, is a type of whole life insurance that is issued in policies with small face amounts, often $1,000 or less. It is sold by agents who call on policyholders weekly or monthly to collect the premiums. The term *industrial* arose because when these policies first became popular, they were sold primarily to low-paid industrial wage earners. Because of high marketing costs, industrial life insurance costs a good deal more per $1,000 of coverage than regular whole life policies. Even so, some insurance authorities believe that industrial life insurance offers the only practical way to deliver coverage to low-income families. Industrial/home service life today accounts for a very small portion of the total amount of life insurance in force in the United States.

Special-Purpose Policies. Certain types of policies frequently combine some form of term and whole life insurance for coverage on one or more family members. These policies have often been developed by life insurers because of the highly competitive nature of the life insurance business. You should try to determine whether such a policy truly meets your needs or is primarily a marketing gimmick. Although many of the special-purpose policies are sold under various company trade names, general designations are as follows: family plan policies, family income policies, family maintenance policies, multiple protection plans (especially joint husband-wife policies), and jumping juveniles.

One appealing feature of certain "family plans" is that they offer the guaranteed insurability of children. For example, the policy might specify that when the children reach a certain age (say, 21 or 25), they can convert to a specified type of life insurance at a predetermined price regardless of their physical condition. Although special-purpose policies can fill some family needs, more than likely you'll find that these needs can be satisfied at less cost if you simply buy convertible-term or continuous-premium whole life as separate policies. There are a couple of exceptions, however—perhaps the most noteworthy being something called a *last survivor policy*. This is a specially designed life insurance policy that's set up to pay estate taxes on the death of the last surviving spouse, and as a rule, it's a less expensive way of preserving an estate than buying individual policies on each spouse.

Deferred-Premium Life Insurance. Several life insurance companies actively market their products to college students. These companies recognize, though, that most college students have little money to spend on life insurance. Their answer is to sign students up for **deferred-premium life insurance**, whereby a modest amount of life insurance is actually *purchased with an interest-bearing debt obligation* that is later paid off through a series of deferred-premium payments. Apart from the fact that many college students do not have enough significant financial responsibilities to need life insurance, these deferred-payment plans are generally undesirable because they place students in debt. Students who accept this type of payment plan generally are required to sign a legally binding installment loan contract. Although deferred-payment plans have some legitimate business and tax-planning uses, for the majority of college students their purchase is unwise.

ALTERNATIVE LIFE INSURANCE CONTRACT PROVISIONS

Because all life insurance contracts are not alike, it's a good idea to review the various provisions contained in your policy to make sure you're getting just what you want. For example, things like policy loans, dividend participation provisions, settlement options, and so forth, are spelled out in most life insurance policies. What features would you like to see in a life insurance policy? Give some thought to this question before reading on.

All life insurance contracts have various provisions that establish the rights and obligations of the policyholder and the insurance company. Standard or uniform life insurance policies do not exist, and the wording of policy provisions and features varies among companies and according to the state in which the policy is sold. Nevertheless, many elements are common to most life insurance contracts. They can be broken into two groups: (1) life insurance contract features and (2) other policy features. After we review these contract provisions, we'll take a look at the competitive features of life insurance and suggest some guidelines to follow when buying life insurance.

Life Insurance Contract Features

The key features found in most life insurance contracts are (1) the beneficiary clause, (2) settlement options, (3) policy loans, (4) payment of premiums, (5) nonforfeiture options, (6) policy reinstatement, and (7) change of policy.

Beneficiary Clause. All life insurance policies should have one or more beneficiaries. The **beneficiary** is the person or persons who will receive

credit life insurance
A type of life insurance sold in conjunction with installment loans; the coverage decreases at the same rate as the loan balance.

mortgage life insurance
An insurance policy on the borrower's life that names the lender as beneficiary, allowing for the mortgage balance to be automatically paid off in the event of the borrower's death.

industrial life insurance (home service life)
A type of whole life insurance that is issued in policies with relatively small face amounts (usually $1,000 or less); formerly was offered to low-paid industrial workers.

deferred-premium life insurance
Life insurance that allows for the deferral of premium payments.

beneficiary
In life insurance, a person who receives the death benefits of an insurance policy upon the insured's death.

the death benefits of the policy if the insured dies. Otherwise the money is paid to the estate of the deceased and is often subject to lengthy legal and other proceedings associated with estate settlement. In addition, when naming the beneficiary, the policyholder should make certain the identification is clear. For example, a man could buy a policy and simply designate the beneficiary as "my wife." However, if a subsequent divorce and remarriage were to occur, a controversy could arise as to which "wife" was entitled to the benefits. Similarly, if children are the intended beneficiaries, problems can arise when other children become part of the insured's family. For instance, if a man named "my children" as beneficiaries, would proceeds be payable only to his natural and legitimate children, or would his adopted, illegitimate, or stepchildren also share in the proceeds? As a precaution, a secondary beneficiary should also be named to reduce the possibility that the insurance proceeds would go to unintended persons via the estate. This could occur if the primary beneficiary were to die before or at the same time as the insured and a new primary beneficiary had not been designated.

In sum, make sure you have named both a primary and a secondary beneficiary in any life insurance policies you buy and that no mistake can be made in determining who the beneficiaries are. Note, too, that the person you name as a beneficiary can be changed at any time as long as you did not indicate an *irrevocable beneficiary* when you took out the policy. Thus, if your wishes change, all you need do is notify the insurance company—easy to do but also easy to forget. Therefore, when you write the premium check each year, verify that your policy's named beneficiary is also your desired beneficiary. (Similarly, you should update any prescribed settlement options—discussed next—with desired changes.)

Settlement Options. Insurance companies generally offer several ways of paying death proceeds from a life insurance policy. The decision as to how the funds will be allocated may be permanently established prior to the death of the insured, or the beneficiary may be allowed to select the desired **settlement option** when the policy matures. The most common settlement options besides lump-sum cash payment are (1) interest only, (2) pay-ments for a stated period, (3) payments of a stated amount, and (4) income for life.

Interest only. Under the interest-only settlement option, the policy proceeds are left on deposit with the insurance company for a designated period of time. In exchange, the insurer guarantees to make interest payments to the beneficiary during the time it holds the funds. In some cases, the beneficiary is not permitted to withdraw the proceeds, and upon his or her death the funds are paid to a secondary beneficiary. In other cases, the beneficiary may have the right to fully withdraw policy proceeds at any time. The interest-only option can be useful when there is no current need for the principal amount or when the principal sum is large enough to provide a satisfactory annual income (in the form of interest) to the beneficiary. Typically, however, the rate of interest paid by insurers will be less than that paid by other types of savings medium.

Payments for stated period. With the payments-for-a-stated-period option, the face amount of the policy, along with interest earned, is systematically liquidated over a selected number of years. For example, a beneficiary at age 55 may not be eligible for social security benefits until age 65 but may be in need of a monthly income for that ten-year period. Consequently, the option of receiving a monthly income for that duration may be more attractive than taking a lump sum. The amount of the periodic payment is determined by the face amount of the policy and the length of time over which the funds are to be distributed. For any given amount, the shorter the period is, the larger the monthly benefit.

Payments of stated amount. The payments-of-a-stated-amount option is similar to the preceding alternative in that it provides for a systematic liquidation of the policy proceeds. However, it enables you to set the size of the periodic benefit payments rather than the number of years over which income is to be received. Because payments will be made (in the stipulated amount) for as long as the money holds out, it follows that the greater the size of the periodic benefit payment, the quicker the money will run out. Payments of a stated amount offer more flexibility than payments for a stated period, because beneficiaries usually retain the right to change the amount of income as their needs dictate. Under the stated-period option, the term cannot be be modified, except that in some cases total withdrawal is permitted. In essence, the payment-for-a-stated-amount option can be used to accomplish the same objective as the stated-period option. All the beneficiaries need do is estimate the period of time over which they will want to receive payments and determine the amount that will be payable. Then they can select the stated-amount option to provide that amount of income. Should their needs change during the period, they can modify the terms of the settlement agreement.

Life income. Under the life-income option, the insurer guarantees a certain payment amount to the beneficiary for the remainder of his or her life. In contrast to the preceding options, payments under the life-income alternative are related to the age and sex of the beneficiary at the inception of the periodic benefits. The amounts are essentially a function of the face value of the policy, interest rate assumptions, and the life expectancy of the beneficiary. (Technically, mortality rates rather than life expectancy are used in these computations. A *mortality rate* designates the number of deaths per 1,000 that will occur at specified ages each year, whereas *life expectancy* is the mean number of years of life remaining at a given age.)

The life-income option may appeal to people who want to be certain that they will not outlive the income from the policy proceeds and subsequently have to depend on others for support. Under this option, a company usually will agree to guarantee payments for five or ten years to a secondary beneficiary should the original recipient die prior to the passage of that time period. This arrangement is sometimes referred to as a *guaranteed payment life income* option. Of course, if the guaranteed payment life income option is selected, the monthly benefit will be less than if the option providing for the life of the primary beneficiary only is chosen.

Policy Loans. An advance made by a life insurance company to a policyholder is called a **policy loan**. Such a loan is secured by the cash value of the life insurance policy. A provision in nearly all whole life policies grants this right (except, as noted earlier, recent tax code changes have effec-

tively eliminated these loans with *single-premium* whole or variable life policies). Although these do *not* have to be repaid, any balance plus interest on the loan remaining at the death of the insured is *subtracted from the proceeds of the policy.* The rate of interest charged on some of the older policies is customarily 5 to 8 percent per annum, and it is stated in the policy. However, in most new policies, the interest rate on policy loans is set not for the life of the policy but instead, the advances are obtained at prevailing market rates.

Policy loans should be taken out only in unusual circumstances because of the reduction of death proceeds that can occur. One long-time advocate of whole life insurance has decried policy loans as "stealing from your widow." Although not all would agree with this emotional assessment, life insurance is intended to provide basic financial protection for most families, and spending those proceeds prematurely is an unwise practice. On the other hand, because these loans are less expensive than borrowing from other financial institutions, they may appeal to certain persons who wish to keep their borrowing costs low and are not bothered by the accompanying loss of death proceeds if the loans are not repaid. A word of caution: *Be very careful with these loans, because unless certain conditions are met, the IRS may treat them as withdrawals, meaning they could be subject to tax penalties.* If you're in any way unsure, consult your insurance agent or a tax advisor.

Payment of Premiums. All life insurance contracts have a provision that specifies when premiums are due. With most insurers, the policyholder may elect to pay premiums on an annual, semi-

---

settlement option
A specified way of paying the death proceeds from a life insurance policy, such as lump-sum cash payment, payments for a stated period, payments of a stated amount, or income for life.

policy loan
An advance made by an insurer to a life insurance policyholder that is secured by the cash value of the policy.

EXHIBIT 9.7

Various Nonforfeiture Options (For a 21-year-old Male; Dollar Amount of Benefits for Each $1,000 of Insurance)

Even if the insured stops making premium payments on his whole life policy, he still has certain benefits that he owns in the form of a specified amount of cash value or paid-up (whole life or term) insurance coverage.

End of Policy Year	Cash or Loan Value	Paid-up Insurance	Extended Term Insurance	
			Years	Days
1	$ 0.00	$ 0	0	0
2	0.00	0	0	0
3	4.79	15	1	315
4	16.21	48	6	161
5	27.91	81	11	15
6	39.91	113	14	275
7	52.20	145	17	158
8	64.78	176	19	157
9	77.66	206	20	342
10	90.84	236	22	29
11	104.33	265	22	351
12	118.13	294	23	231
13	132.25	322	24	54
14	146.69	350	24	191
15	161.43	377	24	290
16	176.47	403	24	356
17	191.79	429	25	28
18	207.38	454	25	42
19	223.22	478	25	36
20	239.29	502	25	13
Age 60	563.42	806	17	26
Age 65	608.49	833	15	272

Source: *Principles of Insurance* by George E. Rejda. Copyright © 1989 Scott, Foresman and Company, p. 373, Reprinted by permission.

annual, or monthly basis. Some premium checks are mailed directly to the company; in other instances, a sales agent collects premiums from the policyholder. Another method of payment allows policyholders to pay premiums through an automatic deduction from their bank accounts. In the case of the death of a policyholder who has paid premiums more than one month in advance, many companies refund those premiums along with the policy death proceeds.

Nonforfeiture Options. As discussed earlier, a nonforfeiture option provides the policyholder with some benefits when a policy is terminated prior to its maturity. State laws require that all permanent whole life policies (and term contracts that extend coverage over a long period) contain a nonforfeiture provision. In addition to cash with-

drawal, companies ordinarily offer the following options to the policyholder: (1) a paid-up policy for a reduced amount or (2) a term policy for an extended period. Exhibit 9.7 shows a variety of these options for a $1,000 whole life policy issued to a male age 21.

Paid-up for reduced amount. Under the reduced-amount option, the policyholder receives a policy exactly like the one that was terminated except that it has a lower face value. In effect, the policyholder has purchased a new policy with his or her cash value at the single-premium rate. For example, you can see in Exhibit 9.7 that if this insured cancelled the policy after ten years, it would have a cash value of $90.84 per $1,000 of face amount. This $90.84 could also be used to buy $236 of paid-up whole life insurance. Under that option, the $90.84 cash value would continue to grow because of future interest earnings, even though the policyholder is relieved of any further premium payments. This option is useful when a person's income and need for death protection decline, while at the same time some coverage is still desired. Many elect this option on whole life policies when they reach age 60 or 65.

Extended term. Under an extended-term option, the accumulated cash value is used to purchase a term life policy for the same face value as the policy that has lapsed. The period of coverage is determined by the amount of term protection a single-premium payment (equal to the total cash value) will purchase at the present age of the insured. If the insured in Exhibit 9.7 (at the end of 10 years) chose the extended-term option instead of the paid-up insurance, he would receive $1,000 in coverage for a period of 22 years and 29 days. The extended-term option is usually the option that automatically goes into effect if the policyholder quits paying premiums and gives no instructions to the insurer.

Policy Reinstatement. While a policy is under the reduced paid-up option or the extended-term option, the policyholder may reinstate the original policy by paying all back premiums plus interest at a stated rate and providing evidence that he or she can pass a physical examination and meet any other insurability requirements. *Reinstatement* means that the original contractual relationship between the company and the policyholder is revived. Most often the policyholder must reinstate the policy within a specified period (three to five years) after the policy has lapsed. However, before exercising a reinstatement option, a policyholder should make some effort to determine whether buying a new policy (from the same or a different company) might be less costly.

Change of Policy. Many life insurance contracts contain a provision that permits the insured to switch from one policy form to another. For example, policyholders may decide that they would rather have paid-up age 65 policies as opposed to their current continuous-premium whole life policies. A change of policy provision would allow this change without penalty. When policyholders change from high- to lower-premium policies, they

may need to prove insurability. This requirement reduces the possibility of adverse selection against the company.

Since most life insurance policies are pretty much the same, you need not concern yourself with differences in specific contract provisions. **Fantasy:** All insurance policies are *not* the same. Thus, it is important to familiarize yourself with the provision of the contract, including the beneficiary clauses, the settlement options, and so forth.

Other Policy Features

In addition to the key contractual features described in the preceding section, some other policy features that you should be aware of are (1) the grace period, (2) a multiple indemnity clause, (3) a disability clause, (4) insurability options, (5) a suicide clause, (6) an incontestability clause, (7) a misstatement of age or sex clause, (8) exclusions, and (9) participation.

Grace Period. The *grace period* permits the policyholder to retain full death protection for a short period of time (usually 31 days) after a premium due date has been missed. In other words, you won't lose your insurance protection just because you're a little late in making the premium payment. If the insured dies during the grace period, the face amount of the policy less the scheduled premium is paid to the beneficiary.

Multiple Indemnity Clause. **Multiple** (most often double or triple) **indemnity clauses** double or triple the face amount of the policy if the insured dies as a result of an accident. This benefit is usually offered to the policyholder at a small additional cost. Many insurance authorities dismiss the use of a multiple indemnity benefit as irrational. This coverage should be ignored as a source of funds when programming insurance needs, since it provides no protection in the event of death due to illness.

---

multiple indemnity clause
A clause in a life insurance policy that typically doubles or triples the policy's face amount in the event of the insured's accidental death.

Disability Clause. A **disability clause** in a life insurance contract may contain a waiver-of-premium benefit alone or coupled with disability income. *A waiver-of-premium benefit* excuses the payment of premiums on the life insurance policy if the insured becomes totally and permanently disabled prior to age 60 (or sometimes age 65). Under the *disability income portion,* the insured not only receives a waiver of premium, but also receives a monthly income equal to $5 or $10 per $1,000 of policy face value. Some insurers will continue these payments for the life of the insured; others will terminate them at age 65. Disability riders that provide waiver-of-premium and disability income protection are relatively inexpensive and can be added to most whole life policies. They are generally not available with term policies.

Insurability Options. The policyholder who has an **insurability option** may purchase additional coverage at stipulated intervals without providing evidence of insurability. This option is frequently offered with the purchase of a whole life policy to buyers under age 40. The increases in coverage usually can be purchased every three, four, or five years in amounts equal to the amount of the original policy or $10,000, whichever is lower. This option should be quite attractive to individuals whose life insurance needs and ability to pay are expected to increase over a 5- to 15-year period.

Suicide Clause. Nearly all life insurance policies have a *suicide clause* that voids the contract if an insured commits suicide within a certain period after its inception. In these cases, the company simply returns the premiums that have been paid. If an insured takes his or her own life after this initial period has elapsed, the policy proceeds are paid without question.

Incontestability Clause. All life insurance policies contain an **incontestability clause**, which gives the insurance company one to two years to investigate all information provided by the insured in the application. If during that period a material false statement is discovered, the company can seek a recision of the contract. After the elapsed period, the insurer is prohibited from challenging the validity of the policy regardless of whether the insured has died or is still living.

Misstatement of Age or Sex Clause. Notwithstanding incontestability, the insurance company can adjust the payment made under a policy at any time if the insured misstated his or her age or sex in the application. For example, assume that a male age 35 applied for a life insurance policy by mail and stated that he was a female age 35. The incentive for making this misstatement was that for a given amount of coverage, females of the same age as males pay a lower premium because of lower mortality rates. If upon the insured's death ten years later the company discovered the error, it would award a sum equal to the amount of insurance that the premiums paid would have purchased had the insurer known the applicant was a male. Note that technically this is not a violation of the incontestability provision, because the policy has not been voided but simply modified to conform to the facts. However, some observers say that the misstatement of age and sex clause conflicts with the spirit of the incontestability rule and places an undesirable burden on the beneficiaries.

Exclusions. Although all private insurance policies exclude some types of losses, life policies offer very broad protection. In addition to the suicide clause, the only other common exclusions are aviation and war. In aviation exclusions, the primary types of losses not covered are those occurring when the insured is a relatively inexperienced private pilot or is flying in military aircraft. No restrictions apply to fare-paying passengers of commercial airlines. (Most life insurers accept without premium surcharge the pilots and crews of schedules airliners.) War exclusions often are inserted in policies in anticipation of or during periods of combat. They typically provide that should the insured die as a result of war, a return of premiums with interest will be made. War exclusions are intended to guard against adverse selection, which could materially disrupt the mortality experience of the company and consequently its solvency. When the potential insured has a hazardous occupation or hobby, the company will either exclude coverage for that activity or charge an additional premium to cover the added risk exposure. Seldom, if ever, would a company be able to modify the premium charged or coverage offered should the insured take up, say, Formula I racing or hang gliding after a policy has been issued.

Participating Policies. Many life insurance companies offer **participating policies**, which means that the policyholder is entitled to receive policy dividends that reflect the difference between the premiums that are charged and the amount of premium necessary to fund the actual mortality experience of the company. When the base premium schedule for participating policies is established, a company estimates what it believes its mortality and investment experience will be and then adds a generous margin of safety to these figures. The premiums charged the policyholder are based on these overly conservative estimates.

When company experience is more favorable than estimated, a return of the overcharge is made to policyholders in the form of **policy dividends**. These policy dividends may be received as cash payments (which, since they are viewed as a return of premium, are not subject to taxation), left with the company to earn interest, used to buy additional paid-up coverage, or applied toward the next premium payment. The dividend option selected is purely a matter of the individual policyholder's preference. Note that it is advantageous to use the dividends to buy paid-up options when more insurance coverage is desired, since these additions are available at their *net* rates, meaning they contain no load for sales expenses and consequently provide an economical way to increase coverage.

Competitive Features of Life Insurance

In addition to the elements that make up the insurance contract and other policy features, the following competitive features of life insurance require discussion: (1) protection from creditors, (2) medium for savings, and (3) tax benefits.

Protection from Creditors. When an insured dies, all assets and liabilities are totaled, and the heirs receive what is left after all legitimate claims against the estate have been satisfied. However, the purchase of life insurance can be structured so that death benefits will be paid to a named beneficiary rather than the deceased's estate; this way the cash proceeds do not become a part of the estate. Even if the insured had more liabilities than assets, the proceeds would not be used to liquidate them. Similarly, creditors who have successfully secured judgments against persons with substantial accu-

mulations of life insurance cash values often cannot levy any claim on those assets. State laws differ with respect to the rights of creditors to the death benefits or cash values of life insurance policies, but in nearly all cases, both can be better protected than such assets as stocks, bonds, mutual funds, and investment real estate.

Medium for Savings. In addition to protection from creditors, life insurance can be an attractive medium for savings for some people, particularly those who are looking for safety of principal. Many life insurance companies are more than 100 years old and have assets totaling into the billions of dollars. Even the banking industry encounters insolvencies more frequently than the life insurance industry. No major life insurance company has failed to meet its financial obligations in the last 50 years, or so. No other industry can match that record.

---

disability clause
A clause in a life insurance contract that may contain either a waiver of premium benefit or a waiver of premium coupled with disability income.

insurability option
An option in a life insurance contract that allows the policyholder the right to purchase additional coverage, at stipulated intervals, without having to provide evidence of insurability.

incontestability clause
A clause in a life insurance contract that gives the insurer one or two years to investigate all information provided on the insured's application and to rescind the contract if false statements are found within this period.

participating policy
A life insurance policy that pays dividends that reflect the difference between the premiums that are charged and the amount of premium necessary to fund the insurer's actual mortality experience.

policy dividends
Payments made to participating policyholders that represent a refund of overcharges which result from the insurance company's overestimation of its mortality experience.

ISSUES IN MONEY MANAGEMENT

How to Get the Life Insurance You Really Need

An informed consumer never relies solely on an insurance agent's advice when buying life insurance. Not that the agent is trying to mislead or gouge you, but such an important decision should not be placed totally in another's hands; you ought to know precisely what you're getting for your insurance dollar. To make the best decision for yourself and your family, keep the following points in mind: (1) buy it only if you need it; (2) get the right dollar amount; (3) pick the right type of policy; and (4) compare costs.

Buy It Only If You Need It

The only reason to buy life insurance is if someone depends on your salary or services. If you have children under 21, or you contribute substantially to your spouse's or parents' support, you probably need coverage. On the other hand, if you're married, have no children, and you and your spouse earn roughly equal salaries, neither of you is likely to need life insurance. Your savings plus other liquid assets may be enough to cover the increased living costs of the survivor. And odds are very high that you don't need coverage if you're single and have no financial responsibility for children or parents.

Get the Right Dollar Amount

You should have enough coverage to bridge the gap between what your family will need and the resources it will have after your death. On one side of the ledger, figure what costs your family will face: mortgage payments, other loans, college expenses, everyday living expenses, and so on. On the other side, consider your spouse's income, employer-provided life insurance, liquid assets, potential pension benefits, and so forth.

Even if you have fixed in your mind an estimate of how much you need, it's still easy to mistakenly buy too much or too little insurance.

Pick the Right Kind of Policy

For all practical purposes, there are four basic types of coverage commonly sold today. Once you understand the concepts behind these four types, you will realize that every policy you come across is a simple variation on the same theme.

- *Term Insurance* Best for you if all you want is inexpensive but solid life protection. It provides the most insurance for the lowest price and is the simplest, most straightforward type of policy sold.
- *Whole Life* Best for you if you have absolutely no risk tolerance or self-discipline when it comes to saving and investing.
- *Universal Life* Best for you if you'd like a combination insurance/savings plan and you're somewhat flexible and self-directed when it comes to money matters.
- *Variable Life* Best for you if you need a tax shelter and are an experienced, risk-tolerant investor.

The financial returns on the savings element in life insurance are often contrasted with investments in stocks, bonds, mutual funds, and real estate. Granted, most variable life/single-premium policies are more investment vehicles than they are life insurance products, and as such, they can legitimately be compared to other investment outlets. For other types of insurance, though, the comparison is inappropriate. Certainly, any time the purchase of life insurance is being considered primarily because of its tax-sheltered investment properties, that transaction should be evaluated relative to what you can earn (on an after-tax basis) from alternative investment vehicles. More often than not, you'll find that *better returns are available from alternative investments,* especially when you factor in load fees, steep surrender charges, and other expenses.

Even though there's been a lot of growth recently in variable life/single-premium policies, these products still account for only a small segment of

Compare Costs to Save

There are no two ways about it: it pays to shop around. For example, $100,000 of universal life may cost a healthy 35-year-old woman $650 in annual premiums at one company and over $1,000 at another. So after you pick the policy type that seems best tailored to your needs, compare rates and policy features.

If You Are Buying Whole or Variable Life, Compare:

- Death benefits and annual premium payments.
- Guaranteed cash-value growth or projected investment yields after one year, three years, five years, seven years, ten years, and so on. Don't look at just the long-term gain, even though you intend to keep the policy for 20 years: statistics show that one person out of four drops his or her coverage within two years of buying it.
- Loan rates.

- How the annual dividends (if any) offset the premium costs.
- Cost-index numbers supplied by the insurance company (the smaller the index number, the lower the cost). But be wary of relying too heavily on these figures. Although ostensibly developed to help consumers comparison shop, they can easily be manipulated to produce misleading results.

If You Are Buying Universal Life, Compare:

- Interest rates or projected investment returns: Are they competitive with prevailing market rates?
- Premium payments: How are they calculated, and what is the highest possible payment you may have to make to maintain your account?
- Cash surrender values: How much cash build-up can you reasonably expect after one year, three years, five years, and so forth?

- Loan rates (and how interest is credited to your cash value during a lending period).
- One-time or first-year fees.
- Recurring fees (insurers deduct a percentage of all premium payments each year to cover company expenses and profits).
- Insurance costs: How much are you billed for term insurance?

If You Are Buying Term, Compare:

- First-year premiums, as well as those charged in following years, since some companies offer low entry rates but relatively high renewal rates.
- Renewal provisions: How long will you be able to renew without proving insurability?

Source: Adapted from Janis Graham, "The Facts of Life (Insurance)," *Sylvia Porter's Personal Finance,* March 1986, 31–40.

life insurance sales. By far, the biggest share of life insurance is sold for the insurance protection it provides—without question, that's why most people buy whole or universal life policies. It's the death protection they're after, and the savings feature is just a pleasant by-product. It's not something to be overlooked, but it's not the principal reason for purchase. In both whole and universal life insurance, the approach to investing the cash-value part of the policy is very much toward the safe, conservative side where stability of income and preservation of capital are the primary concerns of the money managers. Under these conditions, it doesn't make any sense to compare the returns on these accounts to stocks, long-term bonds, and other forms of investing. More appropriately, the returns on whole and universal life insurance cash values should be compared to savings accounts, money funds, U.S. Treasury bills, and the like. When that's done, you're likely to find that the returns on these insurance products stack up very well: indeed, they compare favorably in providing returns ranging from 5 to 8 percent for recently issued policies, especially when you consider these are after-tax returns.

Tax Benefits. Life insurance proceeds, as a rule, are not subject to state or federal *income* taxes. Further, if certain requirements are met, policy proceeds can pass to named beneficiaries free of any *estate* taxes. Generally, though, to qualify for this estate tax exemption, the insureds must relinquish various "incidents of ownership" in their policies, including the right to change the beneficiary, to take the policy's cash surrender value, and to choose a settlement option. When the named beneficiary is a spouse, the sacrifice of these rights is unnecessary. In these cases, the life insurance proceeds typically can be excluded from estate taxes as part of the marital deduction.

An equally attractive benefit is that the *investment earnings* in whole, universal, and variable life products build up within the policy on a tax-deferred basis (this is called *inside build-up*). Such a feature means that the cash surrender value will build up much quicker than if you had to pay taxes annually on any investment earnings for the year.

Another tax advantage is that when cash values are withdrawn from an insurer, income taxes are payable only on the amount by which the cash value exceeds the total premiums that have been paid. In practice, this excess seldom results, because part of the premium that is paid is allocated to the death benefit cost incurred by the company during the time the policy is in force. Consequently, it does not become a part of the cash value of the policy. But, here again, *be very careful with cash withdrawals,* because in some cases, unless you're over age 59½, you may be hit with a good-sized tax penalty. The IRS rules governing cash withdrawals can get a bit complex (to say the least); and to make matters even worse, Congress has had a tendency lately to change things almost annually. The best course is to check with someone in the know (like a tax accountant) if you're in doubt.

Some Suggestions to Follow When Buying Life Insurance

Before buying life insurance, you should (1) estimate the amount of life insurance you need to cover you and your family's financial requirements, (2) consider the types of policies available to meet your needs, and (3) familiarize yourself with the various provisions that life insurance contracts typically include. With this understanding of life insurance in mind, you can then shop the market for the insurance protection best suited for you.

To help you in shopping, the following discussion reviews the needs concept and the types of policies you might want to consider; in addition, it explains several criteria you can use to select life insurance companies and agents that offer the kind of services you'd like.

Selecting an insurance company is the first thing you should do when buying life insurance. **Fantasy:** The first thing you should do is determine the *amount* of life insurance you need and then select the type of policy that is best for you. Only after you have taken these steps should you concern yourself with *where* you will buy the insurance.

Review Needs and Coverages. As discussed earlier, life insurance is used in a person's financial program to fill the gap between the resources that will be available after death and those that will be needed. In addition, some life insurance policies can be effectively used as a savings medium. For most young families on limited budgets, though, the need for a large amount of death protection greatly exceeds the need for a savings plan. If you fall into this category, guaranteed renewable and convertible-term insurance should account for the largest portion of your insurance protection. Most families also need some amount of permanent insurance and savings, which a continuous-premium whole life policy can satisfy. Limited-payment, variable life, and single-premium policies should be purchased only when the primary need is savings and not protection against financial loss resulting from death. Overall, then, parents of young children should give highest priority to term life insurance, some attention to continuous-premium whole (or universal) life, and little or no attention to limited-payment, variable, and/or single-premium policies. The accompanying *Issues in Money Management* box provides additional suggestions for getting the most from your insurance dollar.

Selecting a Company. The life insurance company should be selected before the agent is, since in the life insurance business many agents represent only one company. Consequently, before looking for an agent, you might want to develop useful criteria with which to screen out companies. Usually they can be evaluated on the basis of their financial stability, reputation in the community and nation, liberality of policy provisions, and whether they offer participating policies (if this feature is important to you). In addition, you should pay attention to the relative costs and fees of similar policies from competing companies. There is no question that there are substantial differences in policy costs from one insurance company to another. Also, in view of these cost differences, you should be sure that the policies you are comparing *are similar in terms of provisions and amounts.* In other words, you should not compare a $100,000 term policy from one company with a $150,000 universal policy from another. Instead, you should first decide how much and what kind of policy you want and then compare costs.

In shopping around, you might find that one company is preferable for your term protection and another for you whole life needs. Age and size of company are useful indicators of the financial stability of life insurance companies. Unless a good reason exists to do otherwise, you should probably limit your choice of companies to those that have been doing business for 25 years or more and have annual premium volume in excess of $50 million. Although these criteria will screen out a lot of smaller firms, there'll still be plenty of companies left from which to choose. Information on financial stability can be obtained from *Best's Reports,* which are available in most university and public libraries. To be on the safe side, look for companies with A or A+ ratings. (Note: You can obtain Best's ratings on any life insurance company simply by calling the American Council of Life Insurance at the following toll-free number: 1–800–423–8000.) Most important, always make sure the company is licensed to do business in your state.

Selecting an Agent. Your selection of a life insurance agent is important because you will be relying on him or her for guidance with respect to some very important financial decisions. Do not assume that just because agents are licensed they are competent and will serve your best interests. Consider an agent's formal and professional level of educational attainment. Does the agent have a college degree with a major in business or insurance? Does the agent have a *CLU (Chartered Life Underwriter)* designation? The CLU is awarded only to those who meet certain experience requirements and pass college-level examinations in such fields as life and health insurance, estate and pension planning, investments, and federal income tax law. In addition, observe how an agent reacts to your questions. Does he or she use fancy buzzwords and stock answers or instead listen attentively and, after a period of thought, logically answer your questions? These and other personal characteristics should be considered. In most instances, you should talk with several agents before making your decision and give yourself a chance to discuss the pros and cons of each agent with your spouse. Then, when you have decided, call and ask that agent to return for another visit.

When seeking a good life insurance agent, try to obtain recommendations from other professionals who work with agents. For example, bankers in trust departments, professional financial planners, and attorneys and accountants who are specialists in estate planning are typically good sources. In contrast, be a bit wary of selecting an agent simply because of the agent's aggressiveness in soliciting your patronage.

SUMMARY

- Adequate life insurance coverage is vital to sound personal financial planning, as it not only protects that which you have already acquired, but also helps to assure the attainment of unfulfilled financial goals.

- The whole notion of insurance is based on the concept of risk and the different methods of handling it: risk avoidance, loss prevention, risk assumption, and insurance (a cost-effective procedure that allows families to reduce financial risks by sharing losses).

■ There are basically three ways to determine the amount of life insurance that a family should have: the human life value approach, the multiple earnings approach, and the needs approach. Most experts agree that the *needs approach* is the best procedure, since it systematically considers such variables as family income, household expenses, debt liquidation, and liquidity needs, all of which are weighed against the amount of financial resources available to meet these needs.

■ The three basic types of life insurance policies are term life, whole life, and universal life; term life insurance basically provides a stipulated amount of death benefits, whereas whole life combines death benefits coverage with a modest savings program, and universal life packages term insurance with a tax-deferred investment account that pays competitive money market returns. Other types of life insurance include variable life (which is basically an extension of the universal life concept), group life, credit and mortgage life, industrial life, and deferred-premium life insurance.

■ Some important life insurance policy provisions that you should become familiar with are the beneficiary clause, settlement options, policy loans, payment of premiums, nonforfeiture options, policy reinstatement provisions, and insurability options.

■ To get as much coverage as possible from your insurance dollar, it is important that you not only compare costs, but also buy the proper amount of life insurance and pick the right type of insurance policy.

QUESTIONS AND PROBLEMS

1. Discuss the role that insurance plays in the financial planning process. Why is it important to have enough life insurance?

2. What does the term *employee benefits* mean, and who foots the bill for these benefits? What are *cafeteria-style plans,* and how do they differ from the normal employee benefits packages? Why is it important to assess your own individual needs relative to the benefits package you receive at work?

3. Define the terms (a) risk avoidance, (b) risk assumption, (c) loss prevention, (d) fortuitous loss, and (e) underwriting. Explain their interrelationships, if any.

4. Discuss the various ways of determining a person's life insurance needs.

5. Name and explain the most common economic needs that must be satisfied after the death of a family breadwinner.

6. What is term insurance? Describe some of the common types of term life insurance policies.

7. What are the advantages and disadvantages of term life insurance?

8. Explain how whole life insurance offers financial protection to an individual throughout his or her entire life.

9. Describe the different types of whole life policies. What are the advantages and disadvantages of whole life insurance?

10. Using the premium schedules provided in Exhibits 9.5 and 9.6, how much in *annual* premiums would a 25-year-old male have to pay for $150,000 in five-year renewable term versus the same amount of straight life? How much would a 25-year-old woman have to pay for the same coverage? Comment on your findings. Now, consider a 40-year-old male (or female): using annual premiums, how much straight life insurance coverage could he (or she) buy for $3,000 a year? How much term life coverage would that same amount buy? Comment on your findings.

11. What is universal life insurance? Explain how it differs from whole life and from variable life.

12. There are some life insurance contracts that should be avoided. Explain why (a) credit life insurance, (b) mortgage life insurance, (c) industrial or home service life insurance, and (d) deferred-premium life insurance fall into this category.

13. Explain the meaning of group insurance.

How is it different from term insurance? Explain what employees stand to gain from group insurance.

14. What is a beneficiary? What is a secondary beneficiary? Explain why it is essential to designate a beneficiary.

15. Explain the basic options that are available for the payment of life insurance proceeds upon a person's death.

16. Explain the following clauses often found in life insurance policies: (a) multiple indemnity clause, (b) disability clause, (c) suicide clause, and (d) incontestability clause.

17. Describe what is meant by a participating life insurance policy, and explain the role of policy dividends in these policies.

18. "Besides the regular policy features, some important competitive features are often found in life insurance policies." Discuss some of these features.

19. Briefly describe the steps one should take when shopping for and buying life insurance.

CASE PROBLEMS

9.1 The Parkers' Insurance Decision: Whole Life, Variable Life, or Term?

Charles and Judith Parker are a married couple in their late thirties. They have three children, ages 12, 10, and 4. Charles, who works as a product analyst for Ralston Purina, is considering the purchase of some life insurance (Charles is covered by a group policy at work, but based on some rough calculations, he feels he could use additional protection). David Dustimer, an insurance agent from Siegfried Insurance, has been trying to persuade Charles to buy a $15,000, 25-year limited-payment whole life policy. However, Charles is contemplating buying a variable life policy. To further complicate matters, Judith feels that they should buy term insurance, since it would be more suitable to the needs of their young family. In order to resolve the issue, Charles has decided to consult Zachary Lawrence, a childhood friend who is now a professor of finance and insurance at a nearby private university.

Questions

1. Explain to Charles the differences among (a) a whole life policy, (b) a variable life policy, and (c) a term policy.

2. What are the major advantages of each type of policy? What are the major disadvantages of each?

3. In what way(s) is a whole life policy superior to either a variable or term policy? In what way(s) is a variable life policy superior? How about term insurance?

4. Given the limited information in the case, which type of policy would you recommend for the Parkers? Defend/explain your recommendations.

9.2 The Sutters Want to Know When Enough is Enough

Dave and Karen Sutter are a two-income couple in their early thirties; they have two children, ages 6 and 3. Dave's monthly take-home pay is $1,800 and Karen's is $2,100. The Sutters feel that because they are a two-income family, they both should have adequate life insurance coverage. Accordingly, they are presently trying to decide how much life insurance *each one of them* should carry.

To begin with, they would like to set up an education fund for their children in the amount of $80,000 (this would guarantee that college funds would be there for both children, as it would provide $10,000 a year—in today's dollars—for four years for each child). Moreover, in the event of either's death, they want the surviving spouse to have the funds for paying off all outstanding debts, including the $110,000 mortgage on their house. They estimate that they have another $15,000 in consumer installment loans and credit cards. They also project that if either of them dies, the other probably will be left with about $10,000 in final estate and burial expenses.

As far as their annual income needs are concerned, Dave and Karen both feel very strongly that each should have enough insurance to replace their respective current income levels until the youngest child turns 18 (a period of 15 years). Though neither Dave nor Karen would be eligible for social security survivor's benefits, because they both intend to continue working, both children would qualify, in the amount of around $1,100 a month. The Sutters have amassed about $75,000 in investments, and they have a declining-term life policy *on each other* in the amount of $85,000, which would be used to partially pay off the mortgage. Further, Dave has a $60,000 group policy at work and Karen a $90,000 group policy.

Questions

1. Assuming that Dave's gross annual income is $30,000 and Karen's $40,000, use the multiple earnings factors in Exhibit 9.1 to find the amount of life insurance each should have if they wanted to replace 75 percent of their lost earnings. Use the age-35 column for Dave and the age-30 column for Karen.

2. Use a worksheet like the one in Exhibit 9.3 to find the additional insurance needed on both Dave's and Karen's lives. (*Note:* Because Dave and Karen hold secure, well-paying jobs, both agree they won't need any additional help once the kids are grown; each also agrees that he/she will have plenty of income from their social security and company pension benefits to take care of themselves in retirement. Thus, when preparing the work-sheet, assume "funding needs" of zero in periods 2 and 3.)

3. Is there a difference in your answers to Questions 1 and 2? If so, why? Which number do you think is more indicative of the Sutters' life insurance needs?

4. Using the amounts computed in Question 2 (employing the needs approach), what kind of life insurance policy would you recommend for Dave? For Karen? Briefly explain your answers.

FOR MORE INFORMATION

General Information Articles

Donlan, Thomas G., "Not Risk-Free: A Look at Life Insurance Tax Shelters," *Barron's,* January 25, 1988, p. 61.

Harris, Diane, "Life Insurance: Should Your Protection Double as an Investment?" *Money,* March 1987, pp. 140–148.

Kosnett, Jeff, "Best Buys in Life Insurance," *Changing Times,* April 1988, pp. 40–48.

_____, "Insurance You Can Live Without," *Changing Times,* November 1988, pp. 56–62.

McGrath, Anne, "Your Money and Your Life," *U.S. News & World Report,* November 10, 1986, p. 69.

Paré, Terence, "The New Game in Life Insurance," *Fortune,* March 27, 1989, pp. 140–144.

Government Documents and Other Publications

A Consumer's Guide to Life Insurance. American Council of Life Insurance, 1850 K Street, NW; Washington, DC 20006.

The Fundamentals of Employee Benefit Programs. Employee Benefit Research Institute, P.O. Box 4866, Hampden Station, Baltimore, MD 21211.

Principles of Insurance, 3rd ed., by George E. Rejda (Glenview, IL: Scott, Foresman & Co.; 1989).

Taking the Bite Out of Life Insurance. National Insurance Consumers Association, 121 N. Payne St.; Alexandria, VA 22314.

C H A P T E R 10

Insuring Your Health

Financial Facts or Fantasies

Are the following statements financial facts (true) or fantasies (false)?

- Health care insurance coverage should be viewed as an essential component of your personal financial plans.
- Hospital insurance is the most comprehensive type of medical insurance you can buy.
- Disability insurance is helpful only if you make a lot of money—and then only if you are out of work for along period of time (at least six months to a year).
- With health care insurance that covers the whole family, children may be included in the coverage up to age 24 as long as they are full-time students.
- The difference between a health maintenance organization (HMO) and a preferred provided organization (PPO) is that the HMO offers a wider range of choices of physicians, hospitals, and so forth.
- The cost of coverage and the quality of the agent and insurance company are two important variables to consider when shopping for health care insurance.

Probably the next best thing to good health is a good health care insurance plan. Should you ever suffer a serious illness or accident, you may discover that the road to recovery can be painful in more ways than one. In addition to the physical pain that sickness and injury can bring, there is also economic pain. The cost can easily run into the tens of thousands of dollars, because you must deal with not only hospitalization and medical expenses but also the *loss of income* while you are recovering and rehabilitating. Clearly, without adequate health insurance to pay expenses and disability insurance to replace lost income, a person's economic health can suffer long after he or she has recovered physically.

As a case in point, consider the case of Paul Murphy, who fell off a ladder while painting his house. An ambulance was called, and he was taken to the hospital, where he was examined, X-rayed, and assigned to a semi-private room. Results of the examination revealed that he had a broken leg and a badly sprained back. Treatment included setting the fracture and four days of traction for the back sprain, followed by four weeks of recuperation before Paul could return to work. In all, he spent five days in the hospital and incurred medical and hospitalization costs of over $3,500. In addition, because he could not work for four weeks, he lost $2,500 in pay. Expenses of this magnitude certainly would devastate most family budgets. Fortunately, people can

335

obtain protection from such medical and economic catastrophes through health care insurance. This chapter looks at health care insurance programs and their role in your personal financial plans.

THE NEED FOR HEALTH CARE INSURANCE COVERAGE

> Health care insurance coverage is an essential element of the personal financial planning process because of the umbrellas of protection it provides for your financial plans. What are your current health care coverage exposures and needs? Before reading on, take a few moments to list some of the potential health care needs and costs to which you are exposed.

Assume you have done everything possible to establish and implement fully operational personal financial plans. You have an effective budget, you keep track of expenditures, you have several ongoing investment and retirement plans, and so forth. Imagine what would happen to all of this if a member of your family or you became seriously ill. Without adequate health care insurance, all of your financial accomplishments and goals could be destroyed. Obviously, health care insurance coverage should be part of your financial plan. Think of it as not only a way to meet the costs of illness or injury, but more importantly, a vehicle for protecting your existing assets and financial plans.

Health care insurance coverage should be viewed as an essential component of your personal financial plans. **Fact:** Health care insurance not only helps you meet the costs of illness or injury, but it also protects your existing assets and financial plans.

The Early Days

Health insurance policies were first introduced around 1850. At that time the common coverage was the accident policy, which paid a small amount

for injuries sustained in specific types of accidents. As more health insurers began writing health coverages, the number of accident perils insured against increased. By 1900, individual accident policies were being written for nearly every type of accident. At about the same time, health insurers began issuing "sickness insurance policies," which offered protection for a small amount of income loss if the insured contracted any of several named diseases. In other words, comprehensive coverage was impossible to obtain, and "extensive" coverage could be achieved only by buying a basketful of policies, each one covering different types of accidents and illnesses.

In the 1930s the modern concept of broadly based health care insurance was born. At that time, Blue Cross began selling policies that provided families with coverage for hospital and surgical care. Although from the 1930s to the present great strides have been made in the provision of comprehensive health care plan coverages, amounts of reimbursement provided, and number of persons protected, no standardized all-risk policy has yet been adopted. Needed coverage is often obtained only through a collection of types of health insurance policies. Unfortunately, the heritage of the 1800s and early 1900s is still with us.

Multiple Coverage

Despite the extensiveness of various health coverages, many people are covered by more than one policy. Employer-sponsored group plans, social security, worker's compensation, automobile medical payments, veterans' benefits, and individually purchased coverages represent the most popular plans. Yet, even a combination of these programs seldom completely meets the needs of any one person or family. Instead, the result is usually multiple coverage for some risks and gaps in coverage for others.

An Industry in Change

The health care field is undergoing rapid changes today. One such change falls under the heading of *medical entrepreneurism,* which is based on the belief that there is "money to be made in health care." This new philosophy about medicine has led to new ways of delivering it. Only a few years ago, a consumer's basic choices were the doctor's office, a hospital, or a health maintenance organization (HMO). Today there is also a *neighborhood emergency center (NEC),* which handles minor emergencies on a walk-in, often 24-hour-a-day basis, an *ambulatory outpatient surgical center* (both usually less costly than comparable in-hospital treatment), an *individual practice association (IPA),* and a *preferred provider organization (PPO)* for hospital and medical services. These new ways of providing health care are discussed later in the chapter.

Another ongoing change is the rising cost of health care, particularly hospital room charges, and the percentage of personal expenditures devoted to it. Today more than 13 percent of all of our personal expenditures in the United States are made on health care, an increase from less than 11 percent in 1980. Also, the rate of increase substantially exceeds that of the consumer price index (CPI). And of the various costs that make up the medical care portion of the CPI, hospital charges lead the list of price increases. They have nearly doubled since 1980. Rates of $300 per day for a semiprivate room are not uncommon, and when we include ancillary hospital services costs, the average rises to between $500 and $600 per day. Physicians' fees, nurses' salaries, and other product and service costs essential to health care also have increased faster than the CPI, though not as fast as hospital charges.

Several major factors account for this phenomenon, chief among them probably being the aging U.S. population (which needs more health care), the government's medicare and medicaid programs, and the rapid growth in the broad base of private health plans. More than 87 out of every 100 noninstitutionalized Americans are now eligible for at least some cost reimbursement for losses resulting from illness or accident. In addition, major acquisitions of expensive new health care equipment and facilities by hospitals and clinics have pushed costs upward. A poor demand-and-supply distribution of health care facilities and services may be still another factor. Unfortunately, no immediate relief is foreseen. In light of these spiraling costs, the need for health financing plans and insurance is greater now than it has ever been.

Making Sense of It All

If we ranked consumer insurance programs on a complexity scale, life insurance would be at the "simple" end and health insurance at the opposite. In all but rare instances, life insurance pays regardless of the cause of loss. What's more, the loss itself is seldom arguable, and the amount of the loss is the face amount of the policy (or some multiple thereof). In addition, each life insurance policy you own will pay regardless of any other policies you have; there are no deductibles, waiting periods, participation clauses, or chances of cancellation; and differences in policy provisions among leading insurers are relatively slight. In contrast, each of these issues is pertinent to health insurance coverages. Because of these complicating factors, designing the best way to meet your health care needs requires a truly systematic approach. You need to learn what coverages are available, their various policy provisions, and from whom they can be obtained. Next, you need to inventory your needs and existing coverages. With that task completed, you then can shop the market for the right protection at the best price.

TYPES OF HEALTH CARE COVERAGE

> Today's consumer can choose from a wide variety of health care insurance products to obtain precisely the type of protection desired. Are you familiar with any particular types of health care policy coverages? Make a list of these coverages and relate them to your health care needs before reading on.

Although many of today's health insurance policies provide much broader coverages than those offered in the past, the wide variety in quality of policies makes caution imperative when shopping among them. By understanding the basic uses of the various types of policies—hospital, surgical expense, physician expense, major medical, comprehensive major medical, dental, long-term care, other special coverages, and disability income insurance—you can purchase more wisely.

Hospital Insurance

Hospital insurance policies offer reimbursement plans covering the costs of hospital room (semiprivate) and board and other expenses incidental to hospitalization. In the United States, more people are covered by some type of hospitalization insurance than any other kind of private health insurance. Basically, hospital insurance pays for a portion of (1) the per-day hospital room (semiprivate) and board charges, which typically include floor nursing and other routine services, and (2) ancillary expenses, such as use of an operating room, laboratory tests, X-ray examinations, and medicine received while hospitalized. Although a few hospital insurance policies will pay for an in-hospital private duty nurse, most will not. In some cases, the hospital plan will simply pay a flat daily amount for each day the insured remains in the hospital, regardless of the actual amount of charges levied. Numerous hospital plans now also offer reimbursement for some outpatient and out-of-hospital services, among which might be in-home rehabilitation or ambulatory center care, diagnostic and preventive treatment, and preadmission testing.

In most policies, hospital insurance is written to provide the daily benefit semiprivate room and board charges for up to a specified number of days, such as 90, 120, or 360. The maximum reimbursement for ancillary expenses, in contrast, may be a stated dollar amount or sometimes a multiple of the daily room rate. In the first instance, frequently found maximums are $1,000, $2,000, and $5,000, whereas in the second, the multiple might be 15 or 20. Thus, if the room and board rate were $250 per day, applying this multiple would result in an ancillary expense limit of either $3,750 or $5,000.

Surgical Expense Insurance

Surgical expense insurance provides coverage for the cost of surgery in or out of the hospital. Typically, a schedule of benefits is available that prescribes the amount the insurer is obligated to pay for listed surgical procedures (for instance, $300 for an appendectomy, $800 for removal of a kidney,

or $200 for a tonsillectomy). Sample surgical benefit payment schedules for selected procedures are shown in Exhibit 10.1. The three schedules ($1,200, $2,000, and $2,800) differ on the basis of the premiums charged for the policy. By paying a little more, the insured can receive benefits under a schedule providing higher maximum payments. Surgical expense coverage usually is quite extensive and will pay for almost any type of surgery that is required to maintain the health of the insured. In the event that a necessary surgical procedure is not named in the policy, the company will pay the amount listed for a comparable operation. The amounts shown in the schedule usually approximate the average fees charged in a specific geographic area. Reimbursement for the cost of anesthetics and their administration is provided in most surgical expense policies. These benefits may also be covered in an "additional benefits" provision of a hospital insurance policy. Specific surgical expense policies may also allow payment for the nonemergency treatment of tumors and other afflictions using X-rays or radium. Some policies in addition provide a limited diagnostic allowance for X-rays and lab fees. Surgical expense coverage is typically sold in conjunction with a hospital insurance policy either as an integral part of that policy or as a rider. A surgical schedule is also available as a rider to certain accident policies.

Second Surgical Opinions. Today it is well known that in spite of a physician's opinion, many types of recommended nonelective surgeries are either unnecessary or can be delayed. Therefore, it is good medical practice to obtain a **second surgical opinion** in these cases. Most surgical expense plans provide for full reimbursement of the cost of second surgical opinions. Indeed, some group health plans require second opinions on specific procedures, and in their absence may reduce the surgical benefits paid.

Physicians Expense Insurance

Physicians expense insurance, previously called *regular medical expense,* can cover the cost of such services as physician fees for nonsurgical care in a hospital, including consultation with a specialist. Also covered are X-rays and laboratory tests performed outside of a hospital. Home, clinic, or doc-

EXHIBIT 10.1

An Illustrative List of Benefit Payments from a Hospital/Surgical Expense Policy

The amount of coverage (benefits) you receive depends not only on the type of operation being performed but also on the amount of insurance coverage purchased—which is determined by the "schedule" you have selected.

Type of Operation	Maximum Payment		
	$1,200 Schedule	$2,000 Schedule	$2,800 Schedule
Appendectomy	$ 240.00	$ 300.00	$ 560.00
Brain tumor, suboccipital craniectomy	900.00	1,500.00	2,100.00
Breast tumor, removal (one breast involved)	90.00	150.00	210.00
Gall bladder, removal	360.00	600.00	840.00
Heart, replacement of aortic valve (open)	1,200.00	2,000.00	2,800.00
Hernia, repair of inguinal, femoral, or epigastric	210.00	350.00	490.00
Hip or knee dislocation, closed reduction	120.00	200.00	280.00
Hysterectomy			
Subtotal or supracervical	330.00	550.00	770.00
Total (uterus and cervix)	360.00	600.00	840.00
Kidney, removal	480.00	800.00	1,120.00
Knee joint, excision of cartilage	300.00	500.00	700.00
Lung, removal	600.00	1,000.00	1,400.00
Spinal fusion, with removal of disc	720.00	1,200.00	1,680.00
Suturing wound(s), not as a hospital inpatient, up to a total of 2 1/2 inches	12.00	20.00	28.00
Tonsils, or tonsils and adenoids, removal			
Under age 18	90.00	150.00	210.00
18 or over	120.00	200.00	280.00

Note: A more complete list of procedures and the related maximum payments is usually contained within the policy itself.

Source: A major life and health insurance company.

tor's office visits normally are not covered except through special provisions. These plans usually provide maximum amounts payable for services as listed in a schedule of allowances. Often the first few visits with the physician for any single cause will be excluded. This exclusion serves the same purpose as the deductible and waiting period features found in other types of insurance.

Major Medical Insurance

Major medical plans are those that provide benefits for nearly all types of medical expenses resulting from either illnesses or accidents. As the name implies, the amounts that can be collected under this coverage are relatively large. Lifetime limits of $25,000, $100,000, $1,000,000 or higher are common, while some policies have no limits at all. The trend in recent years has been toward the higher benefit levels. Today nearly all persons covered under group major medical have benefits of $100,000 or more available.

Major medical coverage was first offered in the early 1950s to supplement the basic coverages of hospital, surgical, and physicians expenses discussed earlier. This basic concept still applies today. Because the other three hospital and physicians expense coverages are available to meet the smaller health care costs, major medical is used to

second surgical opinion
A second opinion relative to the necessity and/or immediacy of a prescribed surgical procedure; most surgical expense plans provide full reimbursement of the cost of second opinions, and some require them as a condition for full surgical benefit payments.

major medical plan
An insurance plan designed to supplement the basic coverages of hospital, surgical, and physicians expenses; used to finance medical costs of a more catastrophic nature.

finance medical costs of a more catastrophic nature. Approximately three out of every four Americans are covered by some type of major medical health plan. The popularity of this insurance has grown more since inception than that of any other kind of health insurance in history. To give insureds an incentive to avoid unnecessary medical costs, major medical plans typically are written with provisions for deductibles, participation or coinsurance, and internal limits.

Deductibles. Because major medical plans are designed to supplement the basic hospital, surgical, and physicians expense policies, they frequently have a relatively large **deductible**, typically of $500 or $1,000. Most plans currently offer a calendar-year, all-inclusive deductible. In effect, this allows a person to accumulate the deductible from more than one incident of use. Some plans also include a *carryover provision* wherein any part of the deductible that occurs during the final three months of the year (October, November, and December) can be applied to the current year, and can also be included in the following calendar year's deductible. In a few plans, the deductible is on a per-accident or per-illness basis. Thus, if you were covered by a policy with a $1,000 deductible and suffered three separate accidents in the course of a year, each requiring $1,000 of medical expenses, you would not be eligible to collect any benefits from the major medical plan.

Participation (Coinsurance). Another feature of most major medical insurance policies is some type of **participation**, or **coinsurance**, **clause**. This provision stipulates that the company will pay some portion—say, 80 or 90 percent—of the amount of the covered loss in excess of the deductible rather than the entire amount. The purpose of requiring the insured to participate as "coinsurers" is to reduce the possibility that they will feign illness and to discourage them from incurring unnecessary medical expenses.

Because major medical limits now go up to $1 million or more, many plans have a **stop-loss provision** that places a cap on the amount of participation required. Otherwise, a $1 million medical bill could still leave the insured with, say, $200,000 of costs. Often such provisions limit the

insured's payment to less than $10,000, and sometimes as little as $2,000.

Internal Limits. Most major medical plans are written with internal limits. **Internal limits** place constraints on the amounts that will be paid for certain specified expenses, even if the overall policy limits are not exceeded by the claim. Charges that are commonly subject to internal limits are hospital room and board, surgical fees, mental and nervous conditions, and nursing services. Providing internal or inside limits is similar in purpose to participation, or coinsurance, clauses. The insurer wants to give the insured an incentive not to incur unreasonably high medical expenses and to control costs, thereby keeping premiums down. Therefore, if an insured elects a highly expensive physician or medical facility, he or she will be responsible for paying the portion of the charges that are above a "reasonable and customary" level or beyond a specified maximum amount. The example in the following section illustrates how deductibles, coinsurance, and internal limits constrain the amount a company is obligated to pay under a major medical plan.

Major Medical Policy: An Example. Assume that an insured person has coverage under a major medical insurance policy that specifies a $25,000 overall limit of protection, a $1,000 deductible, an 80 percent coinsurance clause, internal limits of $190 per day on hospital room and board, and $1,000 as the maximum payable surgical fee. Assume further that the insured was hospitalized for 14 days at $245 a day and required an operation that cost $900. Other covered medical expenses incurred with the illness totaled $1,800. Therefore, the medical expenses incurred by the insured amount to $6,130, the total of $3,430 for hospital room and board, plus $900 for the surgeon, plus $1,800 for the other medical expenses.

Because of the coinsurance clause in the policy, however, the maximum the company has to pay is 80 percent of the covered loss in excess of the deductible. In the absence of internal limits, the company would pay $4,104 (.80 × [$6,130 − $1,000]). The internal limits further restrict the payment. Even though 80 percent of the $245-per-diem hospital charge is $196, the most the company would have to pay is $190 per diem. Therefore, the insured becomes liable for $84 ($6 per day × 14 days). The internal limit on the surgery is not exceeded, since after considering coinsurance, the insurer will have to pay $720 (.80 × $900), which is below the $1,000 internal limit. The company's obligation is reduced to $4,020 ($4,104 − $84), while the insured must pay a total of $2,110 ($1,000 deductible + .20 [$6,130 − $1,000] coinsurance + $84 excess hospital charges). The lesson here is that although major medical insurance can offer very large amounts of reimbursement, you may still be left responsible for substantial payments.

Comprehensive Major Medical Insurance

A **comprehensive major medical insurance** plan combines the basic hospital, surgical, and physicians expense coverages with major medical protection to form a single policy. In contrast to an ordinary major medical plan, the deductible under a comprehensive major medical plan is relatively small, often $100 or less. Most of these plans also have a more favorable participation feature than major medical policies in that they may require no coinsurance on basic hospital expense claims. Comprehensive major medical insurance is frequently written under a group contract. However, some efforts have been made to make this type of coverage available on an individual basis.

Hospital insurance is the most comprehensive type of medical insurance you can buy. **Fantasy:** Major medical or comprehensive major medical provides the most complete coverage, whereas hospital insurance covers only the costs incurred while confined to a hospital.

Dental Insurance

Dental insurance covers necessary dental health care as well as some dental injuries sustained through accidents. (Accidental dental coverage to natural teeth is normally covered under standard surgical expense policies.) The coverage may provide for oral examinations, including X-rays, cleanings, fillings, extractions, inlays, bridgework, dentures, oral surgery, root canal therapy, and orthodontics. Of course, dental policies vary with respect to the number of these items included within the coverage. Some dental plans contain deductible and coinsurance provisions, and others have "first dollar protection"—they pay for all claims. Most present dental coverage is written through group insurance plans, although some companies do offer individual and family policies. However, since many types of dental insurance function more as budgeting techniques than as true insurance, premiums are often relatively large in light of the dollar amount of coverage obtained.

Long-Term Care Insurance

The aging population, together with the public's heightened awareness of the financially devastating consequences of catastrophic illnesses (such as Alzheimer's disease, heart disease, Huntington's disease, Parkinson's disease, and stroke),

deductible
The first amount not covered by an insurance policy, usually determined on a per-illness, per-accident, or on a calendar year basis.

participation (coinsurance) clause
A provision in many health insurance policies stipulating that the insurer will pay some portion—say, 80 or 90 percent—of the amount of the covered loss in excess of the deductible.

stop-loss provision
A cap in a major medical insurance policy that limits the insured's payment under the participation, or coinsurance, clause to a specified amount, such as $10,000.

internal limits
A feature commonly found in health insurance policies that places a constraint on the amount that will be paid for certain specified expenses regardless of whether the overall policy limits are exceeded by a given claim.

comprehensive major medical insurance
A health insurance plan that combines into a single policy basic hospital, surgical, and physicians expense coverages with major medical protection.

have stimulated the demand for **long-term care insurance**. Such policies, covering the cost of medical, personal, and social services provided at home, in a community program such as an adult day-care center, or in a nursing home, are now available for individual purchase from a growing number of insurers. They are often called *nursing home insurance*. Without such coverage, it doesn't take long for the estates of most people with a catastrophic illness requiring *custodial care*—help with activities such as getting out of bed, walking, eating, and bathing—to be destroyed. (Nursing home care, for example, in most parts of the country totals $25,000 or more per year.)

Because neither comprehensive major medical nor government health insurance programs cover most of these costs, long-term care insurance should be considered by those over 50 years of age—although the required annual premiums of around $1,000 (depending on age of insured and level of coverage) are a barrier to purchase for many. It is expected that in the future long-term care coverage may become available either as an employee benefit or more likely through a government program, possibly as an expansion of Medicare.

Other Special Insurance Coverages

An examination of every type of health insurance coverage available would fill a book twice the size of this one. However, the types of health insurance plans previously discussed are sufficient to meet the protection needs of most families and individuals. Other popularly available contracts often are simply frills and gimmicks. These plans may be classified as accident policies, sickness policies, and hospital income policies. Sound insurance programming seldom dictates the purchase of these types of policies. Nevertheless, large-scale marketing efforts by some insurers, coupled with public misunderstanding, has brought about their proliferation. Hopefully, the following discussion will help you guard against a potentially unwise purchase.

Accident policies are those that pay a specified sum to an insured who is injured in a certain type of accident. The most common types of accident policies are those relating to travel accidents. These

first became widespread with the growing railroad passenger traffic during the 1800s and today include private and for-hire automobiles and commercial aviation. These policies often are sold in conjunction with oil company and travel and entertainment credit cards. Their primary shortcoming is that the amount of the payment is not directly related to the amount of the loss. Also, as noted earlier, since only certain types of accidents are covered, it becomes impossible to structure a systematic insurance program using these coverages that will not have serious gaps in some places and duplicate coverage in others.

Sickness policies are similar in design and shortcomings to accident policies except that a named disease, as opposed to an accident, conditions the payment. Sickness policies may be written separately or in conjunction with accident policies. *Dread disease policies* are a popular version of sickness insurance. Today's renditions limit health care coverage to a specific type of disease or illness. Cancer policies appear to be the most common, with some organ transplant policies also being offered. Some states, such as New York, prohibit the sale of single dread disease policies; that is, such coverage can only be sold as part of other hospital, surgical, or accident policies.

Hospital income policies typically guarantee the insured a specified daily, weekly, or monthly amount as long as the insured remains hospitalized. However, they generally exclude illness that could result in extended hospitalization (for example, mental illness or those resulting from health conditions that existed at the time the policies were purchased). Several of these plans have been accused of returning in benefits only 10 to 20 cents of each $1 of premiums collected.

The basic problem with buying policies that cover only a certain type of accident, illness, or financial need is that major gaps in coverage will occur. Clearly, the financial loss can be just as great regardless of whether the insured falls down a flight of stairs or contracts cancer, lung disease, or heart disease. Most limited-peril policies should be used only to supplement a comprehensive insurance program if the coverage is not overlapping. Both dread disease and hospital income policies are frequently offered directly through television and newspaper advertisements.

EXHIBIT 10.2

Terms of Endowment

The cost of disability income insurance varies with the terms of payment as well as the length of deferral (waiting period).

Waiting Period	Term of Disability Benefits			
	1 Year	3 Years	5 Years	Age 65
7 Days	$30.88	$34.40	$37.30	$53.80
14 Days	24.40	29.10	32.00	47.90
30 Days	14.16	17.60	19.90	31.80
60 Days	9.70	12.75	15.00	26.20
90 Days	—	10.20	12.50	23.50
1 Year	—	—	10.90	19.50

Note: Premiums shown are annual charges per $100 per month of coverage for a 35-year-old male with a desk-type job.

Disability Income Insurance

While technically not a form of health insurance, disability income insurance is discussed here since the need for its coverage results from the potentially devastating financial consequences of a health-related disability. **Disability income insurance** is designed to provide families with weekly or monthly payments to replace income when the insured person is unable to work as a result of a covered illness, injury, or disease. Some companies also offer disability income protection for an unemployed spouse; in that case, the coverage helps pay for the services that the spouse would normally provide. These policies frequently include *waiting period* or *elimination period* provisions that are similar to the deductibles found in property insurance contracts. The purpose of both is to omit coverage for the frequent small loss, which is very expensive to administer. A family can save a substantial amount in premiums by purchasing a policy that has a relatively long waiting period.

Most individual disability income policies also include a *probationary period,* which is a time delay from the date of issuance of the policy until benefit privileges are activated. For example, a 10-day probationary period means the policy must be in force for 10 days before any benefits are available. No illness, injury, or disease that occurs during the probationary period is covered—even if it continues beyond the probationary period. The probationary period may run from 7 to 30 days—

with 10 days most common. The purpose of this feature is to keep costs down, thereby making these policies more affordable.

The maximum period for which disability payments are made normally ranges from 13 weeks to age 65. In some cases, a disability policy will state that payments will continue for a specified period if the disability occurred because of sickness (for example, 5 years) and another period if the disability resulted from accident (for example, to age 65). With most companies, the insured can trade off, say, an increase in the waiting period from 7 to 90 days for an increase in the duration of benefits from 5 years to age 65. In fact, as can be seen in Exhibit 10.2, the premium charged by this insur-

long-term care insurance
Insurance coverage available from a growing number of insurers to cover the cost of medical, personal, and social services provided at home, in a community program such as an adult day care center, or in a nursing home for those with catastrophic illnesses—such as Alzheimer's disease, heart disease, Huntington's disease, Parkinson's disease, and stroke—requiring long-term care.

disability income insurance
Insurance that replaces a portion of income when the insured person is unable to work as a result of a covered illness, injury, or disease.

ISSUES IN MONEY MANAGEMENT

Shopping for Long-Term Disability Insurance

Most Americans don't give much thought to what they'd do for income if a disabling illness or accident were to rob them of their livelihood. Yet at the age of 35, the chance of becoming seriously disabled for three months or more is nearly three times as great as the chance of dying. And at 50, the odds are nearly four times greater.

Income protection available through social security or your employer is often not the answer. Seven of every ten disability claims under social security are rejected because of the agency's strict eligibility standards. You won't collect a penny under social security disability insurance (SSDI) if you expect to be out of action less than a year and if you are able to do *any* significant work—not just what you do best or do in your present job. Nor will you qualify if you are over 31 and haven't worked at a covered job for at least five of the last ten years.

How do you close the gap? Check your employer's group coverage carefully, keeping in mind that only a fraction of

American workers are covered by a long-term plan at work. And even then, the definition of eligibility may be as rigid as social security's. As you figure how far benefits would go toward meeting your needs if you can't work, note that you'll pay taxes on benefits.

Picking A Private Plan

Your age, occupation, income level, and health will all have a bearing on the kind of protection you can get and its cost. Shopping around is crucial these days, because premiums are rising sharply and are likely to go even higher in the future.

Policies on white-collar employees will probably provide payments for life, but they are unlikely to cover your whole salary. You can probably cover two-thirds of a $50,000 income, but only half of a salary that reaches $300,000. A benefit of a private policy is that proceeds are not taxed as they would be in an employer's plan. Any policy under consideration should be checked for these key elements.

- **Future insurability.** Usually guaranteed, the provision means that you can boost coverage to match future pay raises so that protection will be more in line with your needs if you are disabled. In calculating the premium, which can go up only enough to cover the higher benefit, the insurer can't take into account advancing age or poor health.
- **Noncancellation clause.** As long as you pay the premiums, the insurer can't cancel the policy; nor can premiums rise unless you choose higher benefits. Most good policies have this clause.
- **Own occupation.** This clumsy phrase included in a policy means you can collect benefits if you cannot do your present job, even if your disability allows you to do other work. "Any occupation" coverage is cheaper, but earnings on the substitute job would reduce your benefits accordingly.
- **Residual rider.** Even prolonged disability may allow you to ease back into the job

ance company for a policy with a 1-year term and a 7-day waiting period is about the same as one charged for benefits payable to age 65 with a 30-day waiting period. Since the purpose of all insurance is to protect against a catastrophic loss rather than smaller losses that could be better handled

through budgeting or savings, accepting this type of trade-off usually makes sense. Because the prolonged disability of the family breadwinner can have a severely adverse impact on the family's finances (often more so than in the case of death), disability income insurance should be an integral

on a part-time basis. A residual rider in a disability policy raises premiums by 15 to 25 percent, but without it you would have to lose all of your salary—that is, not work at all—to collect any benefits.

▪ **Cost-of-living adjustment (COLA)**. A COLA protects against inflation by raising benefits by, say, 6 percent a year. But you'll pay an additional 20 to 25 percent for it.

Shaving Premiums

Premiums on individual disability policies range from several hundred dollars to as much as $2,000 or more a year; so you'll want to look for ways you can trim some of the fat.

▪ **Elimination period.** Usually 30 days, this is the span between the time income stops and benefits start building up. Stretch this to 60 days, and you can cut the premium by nearly 20 percent. Gamble that your resources will hold you for 90 days without regular income, and you can save even more.

▪ **High investible net worth.** Sources of cash other than your job—an IRA, for example—may allow you to shrink the portion of your income that you want to protect. Before age 59 1/2 you can use this resource without the 10 percent penalty if you can show that you will be disabled for the foreseeable future.

▪ **Social security rider.** This rider in effect lowers the company's liability by permitting it to pay you less because you're collecting from the government. Typically, the company can reduce its payment by the amount social security pays but guarantees that its payments will never drop below a specified level despite the amount of your social security payment.

The savings show up dramatically in a hypothetical case based on average premiums and benefits from four of the top ten companies in disability insurance, assembled from information supplied by Allan Hemp, senior marketing consul-

tant for the Principal Financial Group in Des Moines. Benefits of $2,700 monthly, or 72 percent of his $45,000 salary, could be made available to the 40-year-old executive in a top-of-the-line policy bought without regard to cost. Besides the income, the $2,294 high-option policy buys a 6 percent annual COLA, guaranteed future insurability, own-occupation coverage, a residual rider (as well as guaranteed renewability), a noncancellation feature and a 30-day elimination period.

Now rejigger the policy, adding a social security rider, substituting any-occupation coverage for own-occupation, stretching the elimination period to 90 days, and limiting benefits to age 65. The new premium: $1,174, which still guarantees the executive a $2,700 monthly income until age 65, when social security and a pension kick in.

Source: Adapted from "What If You Can't Work?" *Changing Times,* May 1988, p. 56.

part of its insurance program and financial plans. In fact, the lack of adequate long-term disability income insurance is the most common weakness in the health insurance programs of most families. The accompanying *Issues in Money Management* box provides some useful suggestions for choosing and lowering the premium costs of a private long-term disability income policy.

In rating most types of health insurance, underwriters normally consider an applicant's occupation, age, sex, and medical history. In addition, to avoid "encouraging" a disability, most insurers limit

EXHIBIT 10.3

Estimating Disability Insurance Needs

Using a worksheet like this makes the job of estimating disability benefit needs a lot easier.

DISABILITY BENEFIT NEEDS

Name(s) _____ Date _____

1. Estimate current monthly *take-home* pay $ _____
2. Estimate existing benefits: $ _____
   a. Social security benefits   _____
   b. Other government benefits   _____
   c. Company programs   _____
   d. Group disability policy benefits _____
3. Total existing disability benefits
   (2a + 2b + 2c + 2d) $ _____
4. Estimated monthly disability benefits
   needed ([1] − [3]) $ _____

---

the monthly payment amount to 60 to 70 percent of the insured's gross wages. Other sources of income such as that from investments and rental property are not normally considered, since these forms of income are not usually affected by a disability. Also, disability income policies often specify a shorter maximum period for illness-created disabilities as opposed to those caused by accident. The reasons are that (1) the determination of sickness is more subjective than that of injury and (2) there is a greater risk that the insured will pretend to be ill than pretend to have an accident.

Disability insurance is helpful only if you make a lot of money—and then only if you are out of work for a long period of time (at least six months to a year). **Fantasy:** Disability income insurance replaces some or all of the weekly earnings lost in case you are physically unable to work. The coverage usually begins after a short waiting period and is just as valuable—perhaps more so—to the low-income family as it is to those with high incomes.

Estimating Your Disability Insurance Needs.
The overriding purpose of disability insurance is to replace all (or most) of the income—that is, earnings—that would be lost in the event you became disabled and physically unable to hold a job. In essence, it should enable you to maintain a standard of living at or near the level you have presently achieved. To help decide how much disability insurance is right for you, you can use the worksheet in Exhibit 10.3 to estimate your monthly disability benefit needs (this is a procedure developed and recommended by the Consumer's Union of United States, publishers of *Consumer Reports*). Here is all you have to do:

1. Disability benefits are generally, but not always, tax-free, so you need replace only your take-home (after-tax) pay. (Note: Be sure to ascertain whether or not, and to what extent, your disability benefits are tax-free.) Estimate this roughly from your previous year's federal income tax return by subtracting the taxes paid, including social security taxes, from your gross earned income (salary only, since any dividend and interest income you now receive should continue). Divide this total by 12 to get your monthly take-home pay.

2. You may already have disability benefits from government or employer programs. Estimate them as follows:

   a. The local social security office may help you estimate your social security benefits, but don't count on it. An insurance agent can often help you make the estimate, since many insurance companies have a computer program that can easily calculate it. As of early 1988, the average social security disability benefit was around $1,100 a month for a wage earner with dependents. To be "disabled" under social security, however, you must be unable to do any job whatever. Benefits are payable only if your disability is expected to last at least a year (or to be fatal). Payments do not begin until you have been disabled for at least five months. The amount paid is a percentage of your previous monthly earnings, with some statistical adjustments. The percentage is higher for people with low earnings. Once you have received benefits for two years, you are eligible to have medical expenses covered by medicare.

b. Other government programs that provide certain disability benefits, if you qualify, include armed services disability benefits, Veterans Administration pension disability benefits, civil service disability benefits, the Federal Employees Compensation Act, and state workers' compensation systems. There are also special programs for railroad workers, longshoremen, and people with black-lung disease.

c. Ask your company benefits supervisor to help you calculate the company benefits. In a few states (including California, Hawaii, New Jersey, New York, and Rhode Island, plus the Commonwealth of Puerto Rico), employers must provide a certain minimum level of benefits. However, the state-mandated *minimums* tend to be small (up to a maximum of $145 per week in New York, for example), and benefits typically expire after 26 weeks in any 52-week period.

Ask first about sick pay or wage continuation plans (for all practical purposes, these are disability income insurance). Then ask about any plans formally designated as insurance. For each benefit your employer offers, check on the tax treatment. Some disability income benefits, if funded entirely by an employer, are fully or partially taxable.

d. Your company may have sponsored a group disability insurance plan. A private insurer provides the coverage, and you pay for it, often through a payroll deduction. A major advantage of a group plan is that it is usually considerably less expensive than individual coverage—sometimes half as much. In addition, enrollment requirements are usually less stringent than for individually purchased policies. A disadvantage is that if you change jobs, you may lose the coverage. The benefits from a group plan in which you pay the premiums are tax-free.

3. Add up the monthly disability benefits to which you are already entitled.

4. Subtract these from your current monthly take-home pay. The result will show the monthly disability benefits you will need in order to maintain your present after-tax income. Note that investment income and spousal income (if he or she is presently employed) are ignored, since it is assumed that this income will continue and is necessary to maintain your current standard of living. If your spouse is presently unemployed but would enter the work force in the event you ever became disabled, his or her estimated monthly income (take-home pay) could be subtracted from item 4 of Exhibit 10.3 to determine net monthly disability benefit needs.

WHAT ARE THE PROVISIONS OF YOUR POLICY?

> The two most important provisions in health care insurance plans pertain to payment terms and coverage arrangements. Do you understand these provisions in your health insurance policy? Before reading on, spend a few moments familiarizing yourself with them.

To compare the health insurance coverages offered by different insurers, you need to evaluate whether they contain liberal or restrictive provisions. Generally, these provisions can be divided into two classes: terms of payment and terms of coverage.

Terms of Payment

Five provisions govern how much your health care plan will pay: (1) deductibles, coinsurance, and waiting periods, (2) duration of benefits, (3) policy limits, (4) coordination of benefits, and (5) method of payment.

Deductibles, Coinsurance, and Waiting Periods. In order to reduce administrative costs and frequent small claims, nearly all types of health insurance policies include deductible, coinsurance, and/or waiting period clauses. On individual and family policies, the policyholder usually has a broad range of deductibles, coinsurance, and waiting periods from which to choose. Of course, all other things equal, the higher the deductible is, the greater the coinsurance, and the longer the waiting period, the lower the annual premium.

Duration of Benefits. Another item that you should evaluate in health insurance policies is the length of the benefit period. It is often limited to three years after the first charge is incurred. For disability coverage, it typically ranges from six months to life.

Policy Limits. Almost all private health insurance contracts place some limit on the benefit amounts they will pay, including lifetime maximums. Specific dollar amounts often are stipulated. In their absence, the payments are limited to an amount considered *reasonable and necessary.* "Reasonable" usually means that the prevailing charges are in line with those given for similar services in the same geographic area. Remember that many health policies specify maximum total amounts payable and have stated internal limits for certain types of expenses and services.

Coordination of Benefits. In contrast to most property and liability insurance coverages, which are discussed in Chapter 11, health insurance policies are not contracts of *indemnity.* This means that insureds can collect multiple payments for the same accident or illness unless a **coordination of benefits provision** (also called "nonduplication procedure") is included in their health insurance contracts. For example, many private health insurance policies have coordination of benefits provisions with medical benefits paid under worker's

compensation. In contrast, some companies widely advertise that their policies will pay claims regardless of how much other coverage the policyholder has. Of course, these latter types of insurance contracts are often more expensive per dollar of protection. From the standpoint of insurance planning, use of policies with coordination of benefits clauses can help you prevent coverage overlaps and, ideally, reduce your premiums.

Method of Payment. The financing method used to pay your covered medical expenses will be specified as (1) the indemnity approach, (2) the valued approach, or (3) the service approach. Under the **indemnity approach**, insurers reimburse insureds for either the actual amount of their covered losses or the stated policy maximum, whichever is lower. The policy maximum is a specified dollar amount such as those shown in Exhibit 10.1 for surgical expense payments. Under the **valued approach**, the amounts to be paid are specified in the policy and do not necessarily bear a direct relationship to costs incurred. Under the **service approach**, typically no monies pass to the insured—he or she is simply entitled to a specified level of medical and hospital care. As is pointed out later, Blue Cross/Blue Shield plans and HMOs are usually service-providing organizations. Among these methods of payment, your best protection comes from service plans, since you are guaranteed care rather than partial reimbursement. These plans, however, frequently have higher premiums.

Terms of Coverage

Some of the major terms of health insurance coverage derive from the following: (1) persons and places covered, (2) definition of accident, (3) change of occupation, (4) definition of disability, (5) house confinement, (6) cancellation, (7) renewal, (8) continuation of group coverage, (9) rehabilitation, (10) pre-existing conditions, (11) pregnancy and abortion, and (12) mental illness.

Persons and Places Covered. Some health insurance policies cover only the named insured, while others offer protection to all family members. Of those that offer family coverage, some terminate benefits payable on behalf of children at age 18 and others continue them to age 24 as long as the child remains in school or is single. *If you are in this age group, you or your parents should check to see if you are covered under your parents' policy.* If not, sometimes by paying an additional premium, you can add such coverage. (Note: If a child is over the age stipulated in the policy, and if the additional premium to add the child to the family policy has not been paid, that individual could be without any health care insurance. If anything should happen to him or her—no matter how severe—the parents and/or child may have to bear the full cost of the accident or illness.) Some policies protect you only while you are in the United States or Canada; others offer worldwide coverage but exclude certain named countries.

Definition of Accident.   Health policies that pay for losses caused by accident define an *accident* in one of two ways. The first, which applies in the majority of policies, is a liberal definition stipulating only that the result of a given action be accidental. This is called an **accidental injury clause**. Other health insurance policies contain an **accidental means clause** under which both the act and the injury must have been accidental. Consider the following example. After cleaning leaves out of the gutters on his house, Steve Urse purposely jumped to the ground from the roof and accidentally broke his leg in the process. Payment would be made under the policy with an accidental injury clause, but no payment would be available if an accidental means provision applied, since the cause of the injury (jumping from the roof) was not accidental.

Change of Occupation.   In underwriting disability income policies, insurance companies consider the hazards related to the insured's job and hobbies. Consequently, people who work in dangerous occupations or have a dangerous hobby (such as skydiving or stock car racing) must pay a higher premium than those with less accident-prone jobs or hobbies. In order to protect the insurance company, most disability income contracts explicitly state that a lower level of benefits will be paid if an insured person switches to a more hazardous occupation or begins a hazardous hobby during the policy period.

Definition of Disability.   In some disability income policies, people are defined as disabled if

they no longer have the capacity to undertake gainful employment. In fact, this is the definition used by the Social Security Administration to qualify a covered worker for disability payments. The practical enforcement of this provision, however, is often more liberal than might be expected from reading the policy. In contrast, more liberal policies classify insureds as disabled simply if they cannot pursue occupations for which they have been trained. Under some coverages, an insured person may be eligible for disability **dismemberment benefits** if he or she loses both arms or both legs, or in some other cases, one of each, sight in one

---

coordination of benefits provision
A provision (also called "nonduplication procedure") often included in health insurance contracts; it requires that benefit payments be coordinated in the event that the insured is eligible for benefits under more than one policy.

indemnity approach
A method of financing medical expenses in which the insured is reimbursed for either the actual amount of covered losses or the stated policy maximum, whichever is lower.

valued approach
A method of financing medical expenses in which the insured is paid amounts specified in the policy that may not be directly related to actual costs incurred.

service approach
A method of financing medical expenses that provides a specified level of medical and hospital care, typically with no money passing to the insured.

accidental injury clause
A clause in a health insurance policy that states that as long as the result of a given action is accidental, coverage will apply.

accidental means clause
A clause in a health insurance policy that requires both the action and the injury to have been accidental in order for coverage to apply.

dismemberment benefit
Eligibility for disability benefits under some coverages for loss of both arms or both legs, or in other cases, one of each, sight in one or both eyes, or sometimes a thumb and forefinger on the same hand.

or both eyes, or sometimes a thumb and forefinger on the same hand. In these instances, no employment test would be applied in order to determine the benefit eligibility of the insured.

House Confinement. Another requirement imposed by some disability income policies is that insureds must be confined to their homes in order to become eligible for benefits. Obviously, policies with this provision should be avoided.

Cancellation. Many health insurance policies are written to permit *cancellation* at any time at the option of the insurer. Some policies explicitly state this; others do not. To protect yourself against premature cancellation, you should buy policies that contain a provision that specifically states that the insurer will not cancel coverage as long as premiums are paid.

Renewal. Whereas cancellation pertains to termination of the contract during the policy period, *renewal* refers to the right of the insured to continue coverage upon expiration of the policy period. For maximum protection, you should find health coverage contracts that either provide for guaranteed renewal or are noncancellable to at least age 65.

Continuation of Group Coverage. At one time, people who lost their jobs or were temporarily laid off could lose their group health insurance coverage in addition to their salary. Because the lack of income and health coverage could place an employee and his family in a precarious position, in 1986 Congress passed the *Consolidated Omnibus Budget Reconciliation Act (COBRA)*. Under COBRA an employee who leaves the group voluntarily or involuntarily (except in the case of "gross misconduct") may elect to continue coverage for up to 18 months by paying premiums to his former employer on time (up to 102 percent of the company cost). All benefits previously available—except for disability income coverage—are retained, including hospital, surgical, major medical, dental, and vision coverages.

Similar continuation coverage is available for retirees and their families for up to 18 months or until they become Medicare eligible, whichever occurs first. The dependents of an employee may be covered for up to 36 months under COBRA under special circumstances such as divorce or death of the employee. If the employee worked in a firm of less than 20 employees (minimum COBRA requirements) or after COBRA requirements expire, most states provide for conversion of the group coverage to an individual policy without evidence of insurability. Premium charges and benefits of the converted policy would be determined at the time of conversion. However, the most important aspect of the conversion feature is that group coverage can be changed to individual coverage regardless of the current health of the insured. Clearly, it is important to understand your continuation rights under COBRA as well as the laws of the state in which you are employed.

With health care insurance that covers the whole family, children may be included in the coverage up to age 24 as long as they are full-time students. **Fact:** A child may be covered in a family insurance plan only so long as he or she is a full-time student under 24 years of age. Students 24 and older usually can be added to their parents' plans by paying an additional premium.

Rehabilitation Coverage. In the past, health insurance plans focused almost exclusively on reasonable and necessary medical expenses. If an illness or accident left an insured partially or totally disabled, no funds normally would be available to help the person retrain for employment and a more productive life. Now, though, many policies include expense reimbursement for counseling, occupational therapy, and even some educational or job training programs. With this **rehabilitation coverage**, the goal is not to medicate but to rehabilitate. This is a good feature to look for in disability income and major medical policies.

Preexisting Conditions. Most health insurance policies that are sold to individuals (as opposed to group/employer-sponsored plans) contain **preexisting condition clauses**. This means that the policy might exclude coverage for any physical or mental problems that you had at the time you bought it. In some policies, the exclusion is permanent; in others, it last only for the first year or two that the coverage is in force. Group insurance plans may also have preexisting condition clauses, but these tend to be less restrictive than those in individually written coverages.

Pregnancy and Abortion. Many individual and group health insurance plans include special clauses that pertain to medical expenses incurred through pregnancy or abortion. The most liberal of these policies pay for all related expenses, including sick-leave pay during the final months of pregnancy. Other, middle-of-the-road policies will pay for medical expenses that result from pregnancy or abortion complications but not for routine procedure expenses. In the most restrictive cases, no coverage for any costs of pregnancy or abortion is granted.

In recent years, the federal government and many states have passed laws that require certain employer-sponsored group health insurance programs to provide more liberal pregnancy and abortion reimbursement plans. Even in the absence of law, though, many employers are expanding their coverage for employees in this area. Because of adverse self-selection problems, individual health insurance will continue to restrict this policy feature.

Mental Illness. Mental illness and emotional disorders are perhaps America's most prevalent but least talked about health problems. The high-pressure "get ahead" lives that many people lead often give rise to drug and alcohol abuse, stress-related physical disability, and various forms of psychosis or neurosis. In addition, family problems, economic setbacks, and chemical imbalances within the body all can contribute to poor mental health. Yet, even though mental illness or emotional disorder at some time strikes one out of three families, many of those affected will not admit they need help.

Compounding this problem of denial is the fact that many health insurance coverages omit or offer reduced benefits for treatment of mental disorders. Both hospital insurance and major medical insurance often restrict the duration over which they will reimburse victims. For example, one widely marketed health insurance policy offers hospital benefits that continue to pay as long as you remain hospitalized—except for mental illness. Under this policy, payment for mental illness is restricted to one-half the normally provided payment amounts

and for a period not to exceed 30 days. Unfortunately, mental illness is the number one sickness requiring long-term hospital care.

As you can see from this discussion, coverage for mental illness is an important type of insurance protection. Therefore, make sure you check your policies to learn how liberal—or how restrictive—they are with respect to this feature.

WHO ARE THE PROVIDERS OF HEALTH CARE COVERAGE?

> Health care coverage is available from several government agencies, private carriers, and various types of organizations, such as HMOs. From which of these broad groups of providers do you receive health care coverage? Spend a few moments listing them and the coverages they provide before reading ahead.

There are five traditional sources of financial aid available for losses arising from illness or accidents: (1) social security, (2) worker's compensation, (3) group health insurance, (4) Blue Cross/Blue Shield, and (5) individual health coverage from insurance companies. In addition, health maintenance organizations and similar group providers can help individuals and families meet their health care needs—in fact, HMOs and the like represent the fastest-growing segment of the health care delivery industry.

rehabilitation coverage
Insurance that covers the expenses of counseling, occupational therapy, and even some education or job training for persons injured or disabled by illness or accident.

preexisting condition clause
A clause commonly included in most individual health insurance policies that permits permanent or temporary exclusion of coverage for any physical or mental problems that existed at the time the policy was purchased.

Social Security

Many people think of social security as merely a retirement system. It can, however, provide a considerable amount of coverage for losses arising from illness and accidents as well as disability. In fact, the official name for what is commonly referred to as social security is *old-age, survivor's, disability, and health insurance (OASDHI)*. Health benefits are provided under two separate programs: (1) medicare and (2) disability income. Although the medicaid program also provides medical benefits under social security, it is not discussed here since it is a public assistance program designed to provide benefits for those persons who are unable to pay for health care.

Medicare. **Medicare** is a health care plan that has two primary components: (1) basic hospital insurance and (2) supplementary medical insurance. Although medicare was primarily designed to help persons 65 and over meet their health care costs, it now also covers many persons under age 65 who are current recipients of monthly social security disability benefits.

Basic Hospital Insurance. Under the basic hospital insurance coverage of medicare (commonly called *Part A*), inpatient hospital services are included for 365 days per year after an annual deductible ($564 in 1989). Along with the coverage of hospital room and board, medicare hospital insurance contributes toward the payment of all services normally provided to inpatients, as well as covering stays for limited periods in post-hospital extended-care facilities such as nursing homes providing *skilled care.* (However, the most common type of nursing home care—*custodial care*—is not covered under medicare.) Some post-hospital health services, such as intermittent nursing care, therapy, rehabilitation, and home health aid, are also provided. Benefits offered under the basic hospital plan of medicare are subject to deductible provisions and time limits; coinsurance is required on skilled nursing home care. These amounts are revised each year to reflect changes in medical costs. The funds for medicare benefits come from the social security taxes paid by covered workers and their employees.

Supplementary Medical Insurance (SMI). The **supplementary medical insurance (SMI)** program under medicare (commonly called *Part B*) provides payment for the following items: (1) physicians' and surgeons' services that are provided either at home or in a health care facility; (2) home health service (visitations by a registered nurse); and (3) medical and health services such as X-rays, diagnostics, laboratory tests, rental of necessary durable medical equipment, prosthetic devices, and ambulance trips. Limited psychiatric care is also covered under this part of medicare.

In contrast to the basic hospital plan, this supplementary protection is a voluntary program. Financing is provided by charging premiums to those who participate. These premiums are then matched by funds from general tax revenues of the United States. Unlike private health insurance, SMI assesses no premium differential because of differences in enrollees' ages, health status, or sex. The coverage under SMI is open to nearly anyone age 65 or over as long as he or she is properly enrolled in the program and pays the required monthly premiums. (As a budgeting device, the SMI premium may be subtracted from the social security check the covered worker is receiving.) SMI is similar to many other types of health insurance in that payments are subjected to a deductible in excess of which the insured participates at the rate of 20 percent of costs incurred. However, SMI pays only 80 percent of the *approved charges,* not 80 percent of whatever amount is billed by the physician for the service. As a result, an insured may be covered for substantially less than 80 percent of the total bill. Beginning in 1989, the *Medicare Catastrophic Protection Act* requires Medicare recipients to pay an additional $4 monthly premium plus a surcharge of 15 percent of income taxes paid, if any, up to a maximum of $800 per year. (This amount will increase in the future.)

Disability Income under Social Security. The disability income benefits under social security can be important to families during child-rearing years as well as thereafter. Nearly all families in the United States are covered by social security. The only major exceptions are certain groups of state and local employees who before 1984 elected not to be covered (although they do have the option to voluntarily join) and most employees of the federal government hired before 1984 (who are enrolled in a special system). In order to be eligible for disability income benefits, a covered employee needs 20 quarters (5 years) of coverage out of the 40 quarters (10 years) immediately preceding the date of disability and must have suffered a total disability that has been in effect for at least 5 months and is expected to prevent employment for a minimum of 12 months. After becoming eligible for disability benefits, the worker and his or her family can receive benefits for the duration of the disability, even if it lasts for life. The amount of the monthly family benefit paid on behalf of the disabled worker, say, under age 35 often would range between 40 and 80 percent of his or her pre-disability monthly earnings. The exact percentage used decreases as a covered worker's average earnings increase.

Eligibility requirements for workers who become disabled before age 31 are more liberal. Benefits may be paid on behalf of young workers if they have coverage in one-half of the quarters elapsing in the period after they attained age 21 up to and including the quarter in which the disability occurred. A minimum of 6 quarters of coverage is required. Unmarried children 18 or under whose disabled, retired, or deceased parents are covered under social security can draw benefits under the parents' accounts without ever having worked themselves.

A very desirable feature of disability income, as well as the other cash benefit programs of social security, is that all payments are automatically adjusted periodically to reflect increases in the cost of living. No private insurance plan can make such a guarantee. Of course, the reason that social security can make this promise is that the financing mechanism is based on the assumption that taxes can always be raised, if needed, to fund the benefits. Another desirable feature of disability income under social security is that it can be paid during periods of rehabilitation even if the recipient may have some type of gainful employment.

Worker's Compensation Insurance

Worker's compensation insurance statutes have been enacted in every state in the union and by the federal government. These laws generally provide for compensation to workers for job-related illness or injuries. Although the worker's compensation legislation differs in each state, ben-

efits often include medical expenses, rehabilitation, disability income, and scheduled lump-sum amounts for death and certain injuries, such as dismemberment. Wide variations are found among the individual states in benefit amounts and payment periods.

In most instances, covered employees become eligible for worker's compensation benefits when they show that an illness or injury has occurred in the course of their employment. Payments are made without question of fault—employee or employer—except in certain cases in which the worker was intoxicated or acted outside the scope of his or her authority. The primary purpose of these laws is to lighten the burden of job-related illness or injury to the worker. The cost of worker's compensation plans in all states is borne directly by employers. However, the amount of premium charged is computed on a merit basis; employers who file the most claims pay the highest rates. Consequently, employers try to reduce accidents and injuries to help keep their premiums low. Employees are not required to make any direct premium payments for this coverage. Self-employed persons who are covered under the law must make contributions for themselves and their employees. The four basic areas of coverage provided by worker's compensation insurance are discussed in the following paragraphs.

---

medicare
A health plan administered by the federal government to help persons age 65 and over, and others receiving monthly social security disability benefits, meet their health care costs.

supplementary medical insurance (SMI)
A voluntary program under medicare (commonly called *Part B*) that provides payments for extra services, such as physicians' and surgeons' services, home health service, and X-ray and laboratory services, and requires payment of premiums by participants.

worker's compensation insurance
A type of medical and disability insurance, required by state and federal governments, paid for by employers and designed to compensate workers for job-related injuries, illnesses, and disabilities.

EXHIBIT 10.4

Health Insurance Benefits Paid by U.S. Insurance Companies (Millions of Dollars)

Insurance companies pay out billions of dollars annually in health care benefits, and most of that goes to people covered by group policies.

Year	Total Benefits	Group				Individual and Family Policies		
		Total	Medical Expenses	Dental Expense	Loss of Income	Total	Medical Expense	Loss of Income
1970	$ 9,089	$ 7,476	$ 6,043	$ 140	$ 1,293	$ 1,613	$ 1,090	$ 523
1971	9,498	8,018	6,541	175	1,301	1,480	1,006	474
1972	10,622	8,943	7,315	201	1,427	1,679	1,148	531
1973	11,863	9,764	7,924	262	1,578	2,099	1,462	637
1974	13,636	11,439	9,260	332	1,847	2,197	1,517	680
1975	16,470	14,191	11,607	599	1,985	2,279	1,557	722
1976	20,217	17,795	14,425	1,187	2,183	2,422	1,691	731
1977	22,113	19,479	15,683	1,452	2,344	2,634	1,869	765
1978	26,352	22,868	18,696	1,771	2,401	3,484	2,480	1,004
1979	31,692	27,934	22,159	2,185	3,590	3,758	2,644	1,114
1980	37,002	33,002	25,895	2,795	4,312	4,000	2,970	1,030
1981	41,622	37,691	30,057	3,474	4,160	3,931	2,935	996
1982	49,159	44,202	36,074	3,984	4,144	4,957	3,572	1,385
1983	51,665	46,890	39,853	4,372	3,869	4,775	3,751	1,024
1984	55,980	50,305	42,424	4,913	3,907	5,675	4,422	1,253
1985	59,962	53,669	44,340	5,292	4,037	6,293	4,696	1,597
1986	64,303	58,926	49,640	5,262	4,024	5,377	3,800	1,577

Source: Adapted from *Source Book of Health Insurance Data, 1988 Update* (Washington, D.C.: Public Relations Division of the Health Insurance Association of America, 1988), p. 10.

Medical and Rehabilitation Expenses. A basic objective of worker's compensation legislation is to help employees recover and reenter the work force as productive members of society. Thus, the laws provide for the payment of hospital, surgical, and other related expenses, including such prosthetic devices as artificial limbs, that may be required to aid in the worker's recovery. In addition, a number of jurisdictions provide compensation for retraining seriously injured victims for new employment.

Disability Income under Worker's Compensation. Disability income benefits are most often paid to covered workers suffering loss due to disease or injury. The amount paid represents a set percentage of their predisability earned wages up to some maximum amount. The duration of disability payments is as short as 50 weeks in some states and as long as a lifetime in others. The maximum weekly benefit payable is seldom more than one-and-half times the average weekly wage of workers within the state in which they are employed, and often much less.

Lump-Sum Payments. Worker's compensation legislation also provides for the payment of lump-sum amounts to employees who suffer dismemberment in work-related accidents or to their beneficiaries in the case of death. The lump-sum amounts payable for any specific type of loss are usually listed in a schedule of benefits that applies to all covered workers. These scheduled amounts vary considerably from state to state. In some states, payment for the loss of an arm exceeds the payment for death allowed by other states.

Second-Injury Funds. Second-injury funds are established by the states to operate in conjunction with worker's compensation statutes. Their purpose is to relieve employers of the additional worker's compensation premium burden they might incur if an already handicapped worker sustained further injury on the job. For example, an employer might be reluctant to hire a worker with one eye, because if that individual's other eye were lost, the injury would constitute total disablement under the law. In light of the merit-rating system

EXHIBIT 10.5

Health Insurance Premiums (Millions of Dollars)

The amount of money spent on health insurance premiums has risen dramatically in dollar terms and—more important—as a relative amount of disposable income.

Year	Private Health Insurance Companies	Blue Cross/ Blue Shield and Other Plans	Total Premiums (1)	Disposable Personal Income (2)	Ratio [(1) ÷ (2)] (3)
1970	$11,546	$ 8,439	$ 19,985	$ 715,600	2.79%
1971	12,777	10,058	22,835	776,800	2.94
1972	14,771	11,465	26,236	839,575	3.12
1973	16,104	12,908	29,012	949,775	3.05
1974	17,915	14,533	32,448	1,038,350	3.12
1975	20,795	17,611	36,967	1,142,775	3.23
1976	24,502	21,455	43,468	1,252,625	3.47
1977	28,676	25,333	50,449	1,379,325	3.66
1978	32,713	32,517	63,067	1,551,225	4.07
1979	37,941	37,625	73,930	1,729,275	4.28
1980	43,666	43,674	84,742	1,917,900	4.42
1981	48,998	50,460	95,136	2,127,600	4.47
1982	58,341	57,222	109,472	2,261,425	4.84
1983	63,190	63,188	119,876	2,428,100	4.94
1984	70,440	68,518	127,635	2,668,600	4.78
1985	75,169	78,199	139,525	2,841,100	4.91
1986	75,486	84,122	159,586	3,022,100	5.28

Source: Adapted from *Source Book of Health Insurance Data, 1988 Update*d (Washington, D.C.: Public Relations Division of the Health Insurance Association of America, 1988), p. 11.

used in worker's compensation, this would adversely affect the employer's premiums. Established to relieve employers of this burden, second-injury funds are financed in some jurisdictions from state tax revenues and in others from an assessment levied against worker's compensation insurers.

Group Health Insurance

Group health insurance consists of health care contracts that are written between a group (usually an employer, union, credit union, college or university, or other organization) and an insurance company. The coverages of each specific plan are subject to negotiation between the group and the insurer. All of the health care coverages that have been discussed, except disability income, are widely provided by group plans. Group insurance accounts for a large majority of all private health insurance benefits paid in the United States. As can be seen in Exhibit 10.4 (on facing page), of the $64 billion in health insurance *benefits paid* in 1986, nearly $59 billion was accounted for by group insurance. In addition to private insurance compa-

nies, Blue Cross/Blue Shield plans—prepaid medical expense plans discussed in the following section—provide health care coverage for groups. In fact, total benefits paid in 1986 by Blue Cross/ Blue Shield and a few other minor hospital-medical plans amounted to more than $77 billion.

Exhibit 10.5 shows how the *premium volume* for both private health insurers and Blue Cross/Blue Shield grew between 1970 and 1986 in relation to

second-injury funds
Funds established by states to relieve an employer of the additional worker's compensation premiums it would incur if an already handicapped worker sustained further injury on the job.

group health insurance
A type of health insurance consisting of contracts written between a group (employer, union, and so forth) and an insurance company; typically provides all types of coverage except disability income.

disposable personal income. In 1940 (not shown) only .42 percent of disposable personal income went for health care premiums, while by 1970 this figure had reached 2.79 percent. As of 1986, the figure had risen to 5.28 percent. The proportion of personal disposable income spent on health insurance is expected to continue to increase.

The chances are that if you go to work for an organization of more than just a few employees, you will be covered by some type of group health care plan. In many group plans, the employer pays the total premium for basic coverage on employees and their dependents. In others, employees must pay the portions of their premiums that provide protection for their families. Much of the rapid expansion of both benefits and persons covered under group plans has been a direct result of the collective bargaining process involving unions and employers. In recent years, many employee benefit plans have included, in addition to the coverages previously discussed, medical expenses for maternity (in or out of wedlock), abortion, alcoholism, mental and nervous disorders, and drug addiction.

Blue Cross/Blue Shield

In a technical sense, **Blue Cross/Blue Shield plans** are not insurance policies but rather can be viewed as nonprofit prepaid hospital expense plans. Blue Cross contracts with hospitals, who in exchange for a specified fee or payment agree to provide specified hospital services to members of groups protected by Blue Cross. Similarly, Blue Shield plans are nonprofit contracts providing for surgical and medical services. These plans serve as intermediaries between groups who want these services and physicians who contractually agree to provide them. Although technically Blue Cross/ Blue Shield organizations are nonprofit, they compete for business with private insurance companies (many of which are nonprofit mutual insurance companies) and attempt to retain a portion of their income to finance growth. However, if premium income is substantially larger than necessary to meet all expenses and surplus requirements, benefits are rendered to subscribers in the form of lower premiums and/or expanded coverage.

Currently, over 40 percent of the U.S. population is covered by some type of Blue Cross/Blue Shield protection. Blue Cross/Blue Shield organizations have been formed on a geographic basis and now

have more than 100 separate plans in operation. Because they are producer cooperatives, benefit payments are seldom made to the enrollee. Instead, direct payments to the participating hospitals and physicians are the norm. When Blue Cross/Blue Shield first began, premiums were based on a communitywide rating structure. No experience rating or rate adjustment was utilized. However, because of resulting adverse selection, the original rating system was dropped, and premiums are now calculated in much the same way as those for policies from insurance companies. From the standpoint of individuals, both Blue Cross/Blue Shield and group private insurers can provide good protection against medical expenses. However, since Blue Cross/Blue Shield are prepaid health service plans, they do not offer disability income programs.

Individual Health Coverages

All of the coverages discussed previously (including disability income) can be purchased in the open market as *individual health insurance.* Existing group plan coverage can also be converted to an individual plan when a person leaves the group. Since individual insurance policies provide protection directly to policyholders and/or their families, individuals can tailor the coverage to their needs. In contrast, an individual under a group plan is entitled only to the benefits that are available in the master group plan. And although the protection afforded under many group plans is excellent, most families still need to supplement this coverage with an individual health plan. This situation is especially true with respect to disability income insurance for upper-middle-income wage earners.

In contrast to group life insurance (which is not recommended as a basis for a life insurance plan— see Chapter 9), group health insurance can serve as the foundation on which a family builds its individual health insurance program.

Health Care Provider Groups

The health insurance programs discussed above are used in situations in which the person or organization from which you get the health care services is separate from the insurer. The insurer pays the provider or reimburses you for expenses. A growing trend in health care is a type of plan under which subscribers/users contract with and make monthly payments to the organization *that provides the health care service.* Insurance companies may not even be involved. Examples are health maintenance organizations (HMOs), individual practice associations (IPAs), and preferred provider organizations (PPOs).

Health Maintenance Organization. The original **health maintenance organization (HMO)** was started by Kaiser in Los Angeles in 1929. Today over 28 million people in the United States belong to more than 625 HMOs, which is nearly eight times as many members and nearly nineteen times as many plans as in the early 1970s. The traditional HMO is often referred to as a *group HMO,* because a group of doctors who are employed by the HMO provide the health care services from a central facility. These HMOs have developed primarily in larger cities. Usually the doctors and the hospital are in the same complex.

An HMO provides comprehensive health care services to its members. The plan includes outpatient care, such as minor surgery, doctors' office visits, and X-ray and laboratory services; hospital inpatient care; surgery; maternity care; mental health care; and prescriptions. As a member of an HMO, you pay a monthly fee that varies according to the number of persons in your family. Also, you may pay $2 to $7 each time you use an outpatient service or need a prescribed drug. However, there are no other charges to worry about—there are no doctors' fees, X-ray charges, or other expenses to HMO members who use the facilities for their health care needs.

The primary purpose of HMOs is to reduce the costs of health care, both by using resources more efficiently and by practicing "preventive medicine"—most HMOs provide physical exams and sponsor pro-health activities such as smoking clinics, exercise programs, and so on. The advantage to members is that they are not faced with exclusions, deductibles, or coinsurance. The primary disadvantage is that members are not always able to choose their physicians. Also, because group HMOs practice in central facilities, members should be sure to ask about the benefits provided if they should need care outside the geographic area of their HMOs.

Individual Practice Association. An **individual practice association (IPA)** is often considered to be little more than a variation of a standard HMO, because the financial and service arrangements are similar, with only the physical facility being different. As a member of an IPA, you prepay monthly and are entitled to a wide range of health care services. However, the services are not provided from a central facility. Physicians operate out of their own offices and from community hospitals that provide services to IPA members as well as others. IPAs appeal to people who would like some choice of physician. They also serve to extend the advantages of an HMO into less populated regions where central facilities are not feasible.

Preferred Provider Organization. A **preferred provider organization (PPO)** has characteristics of both an HMO and an insurance plan. It offers comprehensive health care services to its subscribers within a network of physicians and hospitals. In addition, it provides insurance coverage for medical services not provided by the PPO network. You typically would have access to a PPO only through your employer. Your employer would negotiate for services from designated physicians and hospitals at a discount of 10 to 20 percent from usual charges. You will benefit from the lower price

---

Blue Cross/Blue Shield plans
Nonprofit prepaid expense plans providing for hospital and surgical/medical services, rendered to plan participants by member hospitals and physicians, respectively.

health maintenance organization (HMO)
An organization consisting of hospitals, physicians, and other health care personnel who have joined together in a central facility to provide necessary health services to its subscribers.

individual practice association (IPA)
An organization similar to an HMO in financial and service arrangements but whose subscribers receive services from physicians operating out of their own offices and from community hospitals rather than from a central facility.

preferred provider organization (PPO)
A hybrid health care provider that combines the characteristics of an HMO with an insurance plan to provide comprehensive health care services to its subscribers within a network of physicians and hospitals.

MONEY IN ACTION

Health Insurance Coverage for the Transition from Student to Employee

One of the new responsibilities you're likely to face as you move from the campus to the workaday world is making sure you're protected against health care costs. The importance of this can't be overstated. In 1988 the rates for a semiprivate hospital room in this country averaged $250 a day, and that didn't include doctors' bills, medical tests, drugs, or anything else. Even a short stay can run up five-digit bills.

You may be in good shape— for a while, anyway—if your parents have high-benefit health insurance and you will be living with them. The typical insurance program includes grown children who remain in the household, but the coverage stops after a specified age, generally between 19 and 25. Check the policy to see where you stand.

If your family belongs to a prepaid health care plan—a health maintenance organization (HMO) or similar provider—find out whether you're included in the plan and what benefits you could count on.

You'll probably get health care benefits when you start your job. Most employers provide group insurance or membership in a prepayment plan. But if you're job hunting and have no family protection, consider a temporary or short-term policy. This would also fill the void if your new employer's coverage doesn't start immediately.

Temporary insurance is designed specifically for people who are leaving school, looking for work, or between jobs. The policies run for three, six, nine,

or twelve months. They are sold by Blue Cross and Blue Shield plans and several for-profit companies, including Aetna, Washington National (based in Evansville, Ill.) and Time Insurance (based in Milwaukee). Nationwide expects to be offering a new plan by June.

Rates are comparatively low because the policies are, as a rule, nonrenewable or renewable only once so as to limit the risk for issuers. There's a wide variety to choose from, however, so look at as many policies as you can. For example, Blue Cross and Blue Shield of Maryland has five separate plans. Prices range from $61.50 to $361 a quarter, depending on how much protection you get.

If you'll need coverage for a longer period, you could buy a regular individual policy, but

---

if you use those physicians and hospitals. The savings from the lower cost may be passed on to you by your employer in the form of additional benefits or a higher salary. An insurance company is often used in a PPO to negotiate with health care providers and handle health care expense payments.

The difference between a health maintenance organization (HMO) and a preferred provider organization (PPO) is that the HMO offers a wider range of choices of physicians, hospitals, and so forth. **Fantasy:** One of the drawbacks of an HMO is that you must be treated at its central facility and by its own doctors. In a PPO, on the other hand, you can choose your health care providers from a network of designated physicians and hospitals.

Other Sources of Health Care Coverage

Supplementing the traditional health payment plans are several other sources of funds or services. As discussed in Chapter 11, both homeowners and automobile insurance policies contain limited amounts of medical expense protection. Homeowners policies cover accidents that happen around the home to people who are visiting you (although not to members of the insured household). Automobile policies cover you if you are involved in an automobile accident regardless of whether you are in a car, on foot, or on a bicycle. Further, if someone negligently injures you, you have legal grounds on which to collect from that person or his or her liability insurer.

such policies are costly. Do you belong to or could you join an organization that sponsors group insurance for members? That would almost certainly be less expensive for you.

When you shop for a policy, start with Blue Cross and Blue Shield plans. They are non-profit, their rates are generally among the lowest, plus they may have a broader range of policies than other insurers. None of this is certain, however. The products vary from place to place.

When you consider job offers, get the full story about the company's health care program. Does it offer you a choice between a prepayment plan and group insurance? Under federal law, many employers are required to. A high-quality HMO could be a better bet, especially

if you have children, since it provides most health care requirements—physicians, hospitals, lab tests and more. Though you may have to pay part of the monthly premiums, an HMO is often more economical than insurance in the long run because of the broader protection.

Health insurance generally pays up to 80 percent of the bills. You pay the difference. There are two categories of coverage: *basic protection,* which pays for hospitalization and certain other costs, and *major medical,* which picks up where basic protection leaves off. Policies that combine the two are often referred to as *comprehensive.*

Opinions vary as to how much coverage is adequate. One study recommends, as

a minimum, basic protection that pays 80 percent of the cost of 15 days' hospitalization, including physicians' fees and lab tests.

A 1985 Department of Labor study of insurance contracts with large and medium-size companies found that the major medical limit—the lifetime total amount that each employee could receive—averaged $530,000. The limit in 22 percent of the contracts was $1 million; in 19 percent, $250,000; and in 15 percent, $500,000.

Source: Morton C. Paulson, "Health Insurance: Covering the Bills," *Changing Times,* February 1987, p. 60. Reprinted with permission from *Changing Times* Magazines, © 1987 Kiplinger Washington Editors, Inc. This reprint is not to be altered in any way, except with permission from *Changing Times.*

In addition to social security, various other government programs help pay for medical expenses. Medical care is provided for people who have served in the armed services and were honorably discharged and for military personnel and their dependents. Public health programs exist to treat communicable diseases, handicapped children, and mental health disorders. In total, federal, state, and local governments now spend well over $175 billion a year on health care expenses. When people—especially the elderly and low-income—suffer accident or illness, often a government program is available to help out.

A GUIDE TO BUYING HEALTH CARE INSURANCE

The best way to buy health care insurance is to match your insurance needs with the various types of coverage available. What types of coverage would best meet your current health care insurance needs? Before reading on, spend a few moments relating available forms of health care insurance to your needs.

EXHIBIT 10.6

A Checklist of Sources and Types of Coverage

Health care coverage can be obtained from a variety of providers, each offering various types of coverage.

Social Security

Disability income
Medicare (medical expenses)
Medicaid (medical expenses)

Worker's Compensation

Disability income
Medical expenses
Rehabilitation
Lump sum

Group Health Plans

Hospital expenses
Surgical expenses
Physicians expenses
Major medical
Comprehensive major medical
Pharmaceuticals
Chiropractic, optometry, etc.
Dental
Mental illness
Rehabilitation
Long-term care

Blue Cross/Blue Shield

Hospital expenses
Surgical expenses
Physicians expenses
Other expenses

Existing Individual Resources

Present individual coverages
Family dependency
Savings

Wage Continuation Plan (Employer)

Sick leave
Short-term disability
Long-term disability

Other Plans

Homeowner's medical expenses
Auto medical expenses
Negligence claim
Veterans' medical benefits
Indian health services
Public health clinics (e.g., communicable diseases, maternal and child health, migrant health expense.

We have now reached the point where we should address the matter of how to systematically plan your health care insurance purchases. In many ways, the approach here is similar to that proposed for life insurance programming in Chapter 9. The primary difference is that with health insurance you generally must consider a variety of both coverages and sources for your protection. In addition to the following general guidelines, the accompanying *Money in Action* box offers some specific health insurance planning suggestions that should prove useful in making the transition from student to employee.

You should list your potential areas of loss; determine what types of coverages and other resources are available to you; and, to spot gaps in your present protection, subtract your coverages and resources from the amount of your potential losses. Once you have identified gaps in protection,

you should structure a health care plan that is best for you.

Needs

Most people need protection against two types of losses that can result from accident or injury: (1) expenses for medical bills, rehabilitation counseling, training and education, and, in some cases—such as loss of a homemaker—replacement services and (2) loss of income due to time spent away from work. The amount needed to pay medical expenses cannot be easily estimated, but in cases of long-term, serious illnesses, medical bills and related expenses can run into the hundreds of thousands of dollars. Thus, you should probably figure you face potential hospital, surgical, pharmaceutical, and other charges of at least $250,000 and, with a protracted disability, as high as $1 mil-

EXHIBIT 10.7

A Checklist of Policy Features

Listed here are the principal features you should look for in a well-defined health care insurance program. If you do not have one or more of these, you should find out why.

Terms of Payment

Deductibles, coinsurance, and
     waiting periods:
    Per occurrence
    Per period
    Cap on participation
Duration of benefits
Policy limits:
    Internal limits
    Maximum payable
Coordination of benefits
Method of payment:
    Indemnity
    Valued approach
    Service approach
Second surgical opinion

Terms of Coverage

Persons covered
Places covered
Definition of accident:
    Accidental injury
    Accidental means
Change of occupation
Definition of disability:
    Gainful employment
    Reasonably trained
    Blindness or loss of limbs
House confinement
Insurer rights of cancellation
Insured renewal rights
Continuation (of group coverage)
Rehabilitation
Exclusions:
    Pre-existing conditions
    Pregnancy
    Abortion
    Named activities or illnesses
      (e.g., student pilot, drug
       abuse, or mental disorders)
    Cosmetic surgery

lion. In contrast, the income need is relatively easy to calculate; it is simply a percentage of your (or your spouse's) current monthly earnings—most people believe that 60 to 75 percent is sufficient.

Matching Needs and Resources

In the next step of your health insurance purchase planning, you should match your present resources against your needs. Exhibit 10.6 (on facing page) should help you perform this task. It sets forth a checklist for the sources and types of coverages you might already have. Among these resources you should rely most on social security, present group coverages, Blue Cross/Blue Shield, individual coverages, savings, and employer wage continuation plans. The remaining sources of recovery are less significant for planning purposes, since they typically restrict payments to specified types of illnesses or accidents.

After you have identified your present coverages, you should examine them to learn what terms of payments and coverage apply. Exhibit 10.7 can aid you in this analysis, as it summarizes the various policy features. By checking these features against your health care plan, you can evaluate the quality of your existing protection. For those areas in which you find gaps not provided for by your coverages, family dependency, or savings, you need to arrange ways in which to meet potential losses.

Preparing a Health Care Plan

Throughout this chapter, we have emphasized the need for good health insurance protection to cover the costs of illness or accident. However, a good health care plan encompasses much more than a means of financing medical expenses, replacement services, and lost income. It should also incorporate other means of risk reduction. Accordingly, recall from Chapter 9 that you can deal with risk in four ways: risk avoidance, loss prevention, risk assumption, and insurance. Although these four methods apply to all types of risks, each is especially useful in developing health care plans.

Risk Avoidance. Risk avoidance means avoiding the exposure that creates potential for loss. For example, people who do not stand on the backs of chairs to reach into high places never fall off chairs; people who do not take illegal drugs never have to worry about disability from overdose; people who refuse to ride on motorcycles avoid the risk of injury from this relatively dangerous means of transportation; and people who do not smoke in bed will never doze off and start a fire in their house. Looking for ways to avoid exposure to loss is a good starting point for a health care plan.

Loss Prevention.   For many instances of illness or accident, risk avoidance is not applicable. This is when you can turn to loss prevention.

Illness.   Steven Tiger, senior editor of *Hospital Physician,* has written, "The majority of [poor health] conditions treated by medical doctors are totally—and easily—preventable. The answer [to high health care costs] is to encourage a wellness-oriented lifestyle, with individuals recognizing and accepting responsibility for their own well-being." Mr. Tiger believes that instead of self-reliance, "we slavishly worship high tech medical marvels that cost more and more." These assertions are backed up by life and health insurance company data as well as public health statistics showing that smoking, alcohol and drug dependency, improper diet, inadequate sleep, and lack of regular, vigorous exercise contribute to more than 60 percent of all diagnosed illnesses. Heart disease, cancer, tuberculosis, and mental disorders all have been positively linked to these forms of self-abuse. In contrast, the odds are overwhelming that if you maintain a basic program for fitness, you will miss fewer days of work, spend less on medical bills, and live a healthier and happier life.

Accidents.   The National Safety Council reports that more than one-half of all automobile accidents could be prevented if motorists followed highway safety laws. Topping the list of violations is driving under the influence of alcohol and drugs (DUI). This unnecessary exposure to loss accounts for about half of all automobile fatalities; specifically, alcohol abuse is a leading cause of injury and death among college students and other young persons. (This toll on youth has prompted most states to raise the minimum legal drinking age.)

Further, accident data overwhelmingly document the loss prevention effectiveness of safety belts, shoulder straps, and child passenger seats. Smoke alarms, bathtub safety mats, and proper storage of chemicals, pesticides, cleaning fluids, and prescription drugs also pose easy and effective measures for reducing loss frequency and severity. In sum, regardless of whether you are at home, school, work, or play—or traveling in between—you should integrate accident prevention measures into your health care plans.

Risk Assumption.   The next essential step in preparing a health care plan involves considering the risks you are willing to retain. Some risks pose relatively small loss potential and therefore can be budgeted for. Of course, this is a primary reason to choose insurance coverages that include deductibles and waiting periods, as it is more economical to pay small losses from savings than to pay higher premiums to insure them. Similarly, although you are wise to buy policies with high limits, few people are willing to pay the premium for 100 percent reimbursement of all losses above the deductible. To increase insurance affordability, most assume part of the risk for large losses through participation or coinsurance, internal limits, and maximum aggregate limits. It is impossible to live in a world in which all of your risks are either avoided, prevented, or insured. Thus, before you buy health care coverages—or, for that matter, any type of insurance coverage—you should explicitly identify the types and amounts of risk that you are willing and able to bear.

Shopping for Health Insurance

We now return to the focus of this discussion. It is very important for you to recognize that a health care plan should incorporate methods of risk avoidance, loss prevention and risk assumption. However, our goal throughout this chapter has been to give you a systematic way to decide what health insurance (or other health care financing plan—Blue Cross/Blue Shield, PPO, and so on) you should buy. To proceed, then, through this step of shopping for health insurance, you need to consider two items: (1) costs of coverage and (2) quality of agent and company.

Costs of Coverage.   In some ways, shopping for health insurance is like shopping for a car. You would not simply compare, say, a major medical coverage from Blue Cross/Blue Shield to that of

Prudential any more than you would blindly choose between a Chevrolet and a Ford. In each instance you need to size up competitive offerings on a feature-for-feature basis (What size engines do the cars have? Does either have air conditioning, AM-FM stereo, radial tires, higher gas mileage, a longer warranty, or better styling?). Similarly, what provisions do available health insurance policies contain? What are their definitions of an accident? What exclusions apply? What persons and places are covered? What are the applicable deductibles, methods of payment, duration of benefits, and participation percentages? Big cost differences exist among health insurance coverages just as they do among different models of Chevrolets and Fords, but you can judge which is the best buy only after you have compared the costs of the coverages in relation to the features they offer.

Quality of Agent and Company. As with all types of insurance, you should buy your health care coverages from an agent who will listen to your needs and answer your questions with well thought out responses—not sales jargon and pressure—and from a company that is rated A or A+ for financial soundness by *Best's Reports*. Also, your health care insurer should be known to settle claims fairly and promptly. You should avoid companies with narrow and unusual legalistic claims practices. Friends with claims-settlement experience and the consumer division of your state's department of insurance regulation can help you learn about an insurer's record for service after a loss.

The cost of coverage and the quality of the agent and insurance company are two important variables to consider when shopping for health care insurance. **Fact:** Even with health care insurance, it pays to shop around to get the best value for your money. However, you should use a knowledgeable agent that understands your needs and choose a high-rated company with good claims-settlement experience.

SUMMARY

- Health care insurance coverage is essential because the potential amount of economic loss (from illness or injury) is so great; and the rapidly rising health care delivery costs of today make adequate coverage increasingly important.

- The types of health care coverage available include hospital insurance, surgical expense insurance, physicians' expense insurance (that covers the costs of nonsurgical procedures), and major medical policies (which cover catastrophic medical expenses; some health insurers offer comprehensive major medical policies that combine basic hospital, surgical, and physicians expense coverage with a major medical plan to provide a packaged health care protection policy), dental insurance, long-term care insurance (that covers out-of-hospital care for those with catastrophic illnesses), and disability income insurance (designed to replace wages lost due to illness or injury).

- The two most important provisions in health care insurance policies pertain to terms of payment and terms of coverage. Basically, five provisions govern how much your health care plan will pay: deductibles, coinsurance and waiting periods, duration of benefits, policy limits, coordination of benefits, and methods of payment. Likewise, terms of coverage are dependent on such variables as persons and places covered, type of accident, occupation, type of disability, house confinement, cancellation, renewal, continuation of group coverage, the presence of preexisting conditions, pregnancy and abortion, and mental illness, among other things.

- There are several important providers of health care coverage, including social security (which provides both medical insurance and long-term disability insurance), worker's compensation (for job-related injuries), group health insurance programs, Blue Cross/Blue Shield (with hospital coverage by Blue Cross, and surgical and medical coverage by Blue Shield), and individual health insurance policies (that provide protection directly to policyholders and/or their families).

- In addition to the traditional health care insurance programs, a rapidly growing trend is for individuals/families to obtain health care services directly from specific provider groups. Under these plans the subscribers/users contract with and make monthly payments to the organization that provides the health care services. The most prevalent examples of these groups are health maintenance organizations (HMOs), individual practice associations (IPAs), and preferred provider organizations (PPOs).

■ From a health care insurance perspective, most people need protection from two types of losses: (1) the cost of medical bills and other associated expenses and (2) loss of income due to time away from work. The best way to buy health care insurance is to match your insurance needs with the various types of coverages available; in this respect, when shopping for health care insurance, you should carefully consider the cost of coverage, as well as the quality of both the agent and the insurer.

QUESTIONS AND PROBLEMS

1. What factors have contributed to today's high costs of health care?

2. Differentiate between hospital and surgical expense insurance. What role do second surgical opinions play in surgical expense insurance decisions?

3. What is major medical coverage? What are the common features of a major medical policy? What is comprehensive major medical insurance?

4. Describe (a) physicians' expense insurance, (b) dental insurance, and (c) long-term care insurance.

5. What is disability income insurance? Explain the waiting period provisions found in such policies.

6. Briefly describe the following policy provisions affecting the amount paid by a health care plan: (a) deductibles, coinsurance, and waiting periods; (b) duration of benefits; (c) policy limits; (d) coordination of benefits; and (e) method of payment.

7. Define and differentiate between an accidental injury clause and an accidental means clause as they relate to the definition of an accident in a health insurance policy. Which is the more liberal definition?

8. Describe the restrictive and liberal definitions used to establish whether or not an insured is disabled. Why is term of coverage an important consideration in shopping for health care coverage?

9. Briefly describe the key provisions of the Consolidated Omnibus Budget Reconciliation Act (COBRA) as they relate to continuation of group coverage when an employee voluntarily or involuntarily leaves the group.

10. What is the formal name used for social security? Briefly describe the health care benefits provided under social security.

11. What is medicare? Explain the eligibility requirements and benefits provided by this plan.

12. What is the objective of worker's compensation insurance statutes? Explain (a) lump-sum payments and (b) second-injury funds as they relate to worker's compensation.

13. What is group health insurance? Differentiate between group health insurance and individual health insurance.

14. Discuss the basics of the Blue Cross/Blue Shield plans.

15. "Health maintenance organizations (HMOs) attempt to reduce the cost of health care to families and individuals through more efficient utilization of health care personnel and facilities, and by practicing preventive medicine." Explain basically how these organizations work. Contrast HMOs with IPAs and PPOs.

16. Describe the procedures used to evaluate an individual's current health insurance coverages.

17. Briefly discuss the procedures for (a) determining health insurance needs, (b) matching needs and resources, and (c) preparing a health care plan.

18. Describe the role played in the process of preparing a health care plan of (a) risk avoid-

ance, (b) loss prevention, and (c) risk assumption.

19. Describe the key considerations that must be

addressed when shopping for health insurance relative to (a) costs of coverage and (b)
quality of agent and insurance company.

CASE PROBLEMS

10.1 Evaluating John's Health Care Coverage

John Lannefeld was a self-employed window
washer earning approximately $400 per week. One
day, while cleaning windows on the eighth floor of
the First National Bank Building, he tripped and fell
from the scaffolding to the pavement below. He
sustained severe multiple injuries but miraculously
survived the accident. He was immediately rushed
to Mt. Sinai Hospital for surgery. He remained there
for 60 days of treatment, after which he was allowed
to go home for further recuperation. During his
hospital stay, he incurred the following expenses:
surgeon, $2,500; physician, $1,000; hospital bill,
room and board, $250 per day; nursing services,
$1,200; anesthetics, $300; wheelchair rental, $70;
ambulance, $60; and drugs, $350. John has a major
medical policy with LIC Corporation that has a
$3,000 deductible clause, an 80 percent coinsur-
ance clause, internal limits of $180 per day on hos-
pital room and board, and $1,500 as a maximum
surgical fee. The policy provides no disability income benefits.

Questions

1. Explain the policy provisions as they relate to
deductibles, coinsurance, and internal limits.

2. How much should John recover from the insurance company? How much must he pay out
of his pocket?

3. Would any other policies have offered John
additional protection? What about his inability
to work while recovering from his injury?

4. Based upon the information presented, how
would you assess John's health insurance coverage? Explain.

10.2 Benito and Teresa Get a Handle on Their Disability Needs

Benito Fernandez and his wife, Teresa, have been
married for two years and have a one-year-old son.

They live in Detroit, where Benito is a supervisor
for Ford Motor Company. He earns $2,200 per
month, of which he takes home $1,580. As an em-
ployee of Ford, he and his family are entitled to
receive the benefits provided by the company's
group health insurance policy. In addition to major
medical coverage, the policy provides a monthly
disability benefit amounting to 20 percent of the
employee's average monthly take-home pay for the
most recent 12 months prior to incurring the disability. (Note: Benito's average monthly take-home
pay for the most recent year is equal to his current
monthly take-home pay.) In the instance of complete disability, Benito would also be eligible for
social security payments of $700 per month.

Teresa is also employed. She earns $500 per
month after taxes working part-time at a nearby
grocery store. The store provides her with no benefits other than social security. In the event Benito
became disabled, Teresa would continue to work
at her part-time job. If she became disabled, social
security would provide monthly income of $300.
Benito and Teresa spend 90 percent of their combined take-home pay in order to meet their bills
and provide for a variety of necessary items. They
use the remaining 10 percent to fulfill their entertainment and savings goals.

Questions

1. How much, if any, additional disability income
insurance does Benito require in order to insure adequate protection against his becoming
completely disabled?

2. Does Teresa need any disability coverage?
Explain.

3. What specific recommendations with respect
to disability income insurance coverage would
you give Benito and Teresa in order to provide
adequate protection for themselves as well as
their child?

FOR MORE INFORMATION

General Information Articles

Goodwin, Phillip, "Health Insurance: What You Need, What You Get," *Changing Times,* April 1988, pp. 49–54.

Klein, Robert J., "The Right Way to Buy Disability Income Insurance," *Money,* August 1988, pp. 121–122.

Luciano, Lani, "HMO, Yes or No?" *Money,* July 1988, pp. 111–120.

Trunzo, Candace E., "Taking the Pulse of Your Health Plan," *Money,* October 1987, pp. 137–147.

"Who Can Afford a Nursing Home?" *Consumer Reports,* May 1988, pp. 300–311.

Zinn, Laura, "Thinking About an HMO? Give It a Thorough Checkup," *Business Week,* September 5, 1988, pp. 108–109.

Government Documents and Other Publications

The Consumer's Guide to Long-Term Care Insurance (Health Insurance Association of America); 1025 Connecticut Avenue, N.W.; Washington, DC 20036–3998.

Risk and Insurance, 6th ed., by James L. Athearn, S. Travis Pritchett, and Joan T. Schmit (St. Paul: West Publishing Company, 1989), Chaps. 8, 13, 14, 15.

What You Should Know About Disability Insurance (Health Insurance Association of America); 1025 Connecticut Avenue, N.W.; Washington, DC 20036–3998.

Your Insurance Dollar (Money Management Institute of Household Financial Services, 1987); 2700 Sanders Road; Prospect Heights, IL 60070.

C H A P T E R 11

Protecting Your Property

Financial Facts or Fantasies

Are the following statements financial facts (true) or fantasies (false)?

- Homeowners insurance provides protection not only on the home itself but also on most of its contents.
- If you rent an apartment, you don't need to worry about property insurance since your furniture and other personal belongings are already covered by the landlord's insurance policy.
- Uninsured motorists coverage is available as part of most automobile insurance policies.
- The type of car you drive has no bearing on how much you will have to pay for automobile insurance.
- As a rule, you must obtain an umbrella personal liability policy if you want liability coverage of $1 million or more.
- Filing a property or liability claim is quick and easy to do: Just call your agent, supply a few basic details, and look for your check in a few days.

Because you own assets, you are exposed to a variety of losses that could result in financial disaster. Suppose a severe storm destroyed your house. Could you afford to replace it? Most people could not. To protect yourself from this and similar types of property loss, you need *property insurance.* Also, every day you face the risk of negligence. For example, you might be distraught over a personal problem and unintentionally run a red light and seriously injure a pedestrian. Because the consequences of this and other potentially negligent acts can cause financial ruin, appropriate *liability insurance* is essential. Property and liability insurance should be as much a part of your personal financial plans as life and health insurance. Such coverage is needed to protect the assets you have already acquired and to ensure the achievement of your financial goals. In particular, property insurance is used to guard against catastrophic losses of real and personal property caused by perils such as fire, theft, vandalism, wind storms, and many other calamities. Liability insurance, in contrast, offers protection against the financial consequences that may arise from certain types of legal actions. Make no mistake about it: the threat of being hit with a costly lawsuit is real (particularly if you're financially secure), and it's something you should protect yourself against.

Although people spend a lot of money for insurance coverage, few really know what

EXHIBIT 11.1

A Partial Personal Property Inventory Form

Using a form like this will help you keep track of your personal property, including date of purchase and original cost. (Note: This part of the form covers only the living room, dining room, and/or family room.)

Living Room				Dining and/or Family Room			
Items	Model and Serial No.[a]	Original Cost	Year Purchased	Items	Model and Serial No.[a]	Original Cost	Year Purchased
Books (see page 12)				Buffet			
Bric-a-brac (Total estimate)				Cabinets			
Cabinet, contents				China closet			
Chairs				China (see page 11)			
Clocks				Chairs			
Curtains, drapes				Curtains, drapes			
Desk, desk sets				Glassware (see page 11)			
Fireplace accessories				Lamps			
Lamps				Linens			
Mirrors				Mirrors			
Musical instruments				Pictures, paintings (see page 12)			
Pictures, paintings (see page 12)				Rugs, carpeting			
Stereo, hi-fi				Silver (see page 11)			
Phonograph				Tables			
Radio				Electrical appliances			
Records							
Rugs, carpeting							
Sofas				Other articles			
Tables							
Television							
Other articles							
Total:				**Total:**			

[a] Law enforcement officers will often not release recovered items unless the owner can identify them by a serial number.
Source: *Insurance Record and Household Inventory,* Farmers Insurance Group, pp. 2–3. Reprinted by permission of Fire Insurance Exchange, a member company of the Farmers Insurance Group, Los Angeles.

they're getting for their premium dollars. Even worse, the vast majority of people are totally unaware of any gaps, overinsurance, and underinsurance that exist in their property and liability insurance programs. Since such inefficient and inadequate insurance programs are completely at odds with the objectives of personal financial planning, you should become familiar with the basics of property and liability insurance. *This chapter discusses the property and liability risks that most families face and explains the coverages available for dealing with them.*

SOME BASIC INSURANCE PRINCIPLES

> The effective use of property and liability insurance requires an understanding of the types of losses to which you are exposed and how to best cover them. Consider your present situation: What kinds of property losses are you exposed to at this point in your life? Do you think your exposure to loss will be any different in 10 or 15 years? Take a minute or two to think about these questions before reading on.

The basic principles of property and liability insurance pertain to types of exposure, criteria for an insurable exposure, the principle of indemnity, and coinsurance. Each of these is discussed in the following sections.

Types of Exposure

Most individuals face two basic types of exposure: physical loss of property and loss through liability.

Exposure to Property Loss. The vast majority of property insurance contracts define the property covered directly in the policy and name the perils (causes of loss) for which insurance proceeds will be available. Some property contracts do offer protection on a comprehensive basis, however, and limit coverage by excluding certain types of property and perils. These contracts impose two obli-

gations on the property owner: (1) developing a complete inventory of the property in need of insurance coverage and (2) identifying the perils against which protection is desired.

Property Inventory. Most people neither fully appreciate the value of all the property they own nor attempt to itemize their property for insurance purposes. Nevertheless, a *property inventory* should be prepared not only to help you select coverages but also to help you settle a claim if a loss occurs. All property insurance companies require you to show proof of loss when making a claim. Consequently, a prepared schedule of property with corresponding values can serve as evidence to satisfy the company.

Ordinarily, a family has a home, household furnishings, clothing and personal accessories, lawn and garden equipment, and motor vehicles (intended for road use), all of which need to be insured. Fortunately, the majority of homeowners and automobile package insurance policies provide coverage for these types of belongings. Many families also own such items as motorboats and trailers, various types of off-road vehicles, business property and inventories, jewelry, stamp or coin collections, furs, cash, musical instruments, important papers and documents, antiques, paintings, bonds and other securities, and items of special value, such as expensive cameras, golf clubs, electronic recording and playing equipment, or citizen-band radios. Coverage for these types of belongings often must be specially arranged with the insurer. In order to help policyholders prepare inventories, many property insurance companies have easy-to-complete personal property inventory forms available. A sample of a portion of such a form is shown in Exhibit 11.1 (on facing page). In addition, people can supplement inventory forms with photographs or videotapes of their belongings. For insurance purposes, a picture may truly be worth a thousand words.

Identifying Perils. Many people feel a false sense of security after buying insurance, because they believe that they are safeguarded for all contingencies. However, certain **perils** (defined as a

> **peril**
> A cause of loss.

cause of loss) cannot be reasonably insured against. For example, many homeowners or automobile insurance policies limit or exclude coverage for flood, earthquake, mud slides, mysterious disappearance, war, nuclear radiation, and wear and tear. In addition property insurance contracts routinely limit coverage on the basis of location of the property, time of loss, persons involved, and the types of hazards to which the property is exposed. These limitations are explained further in subsequent sections of this chapter.

Liability Exposures.   Every day you face the risk that you might negligently cause property damage or bodily injury to someone else. For example, when golfing you might become impatient and tee off before the people in front of you are clearly out of range. If your ball struck one of them and you were found legally liable for that injury, a judgment ranging into the thousands, or in some cases millions, of dollars could be levied against you. Of course, a debt that size could force many families into financial ruin and even bankruptcy. Many different liability exposures are encountered every day. Driving a car, entertaining guests at home, and being careless in performing professional duties are some of the more common liability risks. However, even if you were never negligent and always prudent, you still would run the risk that someone might think that you were the cause of a loss and therefore bring a costly lawsuit against you.

Fortunately, *liability insurance* coverage is available to protect against losses resulting from each of these risks, including the high legal fees required to defend yourself against suits that may or may not have merit. But before discussing the methods available for insuring against liability exposures, let us look at the ways in which legal liability arises, as well as the defenses available for defeating claims.

Liability Based On Negligence.   Legal definitions of negligence and liability have evolved over hundreds of years of court decisions and enactments of statutes, and these definitions are expected to continue to be modified as society's values change. In addition, specific rules of law vary not only over time but also in their interpretations depending on judges, juries, and locations throughout the country. Consequently, only a general overview of these concepts can be presented here.

A person is said to have performed a **negligent action** when his or her behavior has been inconsistent with the **reasonable person doctrine**. This doctrine holds that if a person fails to act in a reasonable manner—as would one with normal intelligence, perceptions, and experiences common to the community—that person is negligent. However, evidence that someone was negligent is only the first step in establishing liability. In addition, the defendant (the person accused of negligence) must be proven to have had a duty toward the plaintiff (the accuser) and to have caused the plaintiff a compensable loss as a result of a breach of that duty. Further, it must be shown that (physical or financial) injury to a person or damage to property actually occurred. If any of these elements is missing, the defendant is relieved from legal liability. The defendant can also escape payment by the successful use of one of several defenses.

Defenses to a Negligence Action.   The two most common defenses to a charge of negligence are assumption of risk and contributory negligence. Under the **assumption of risk defense**, the allegation is that some action of the plaintiff relieved the defendant of his or her duty to protect the plaintiff. For example, assume that Bill Putnam voiced his intent to try to cover a 15-mile stretch of highway in less than 10 minutes on his motorcycle. If Janice Morris asked to go with him on this daredevil ride, she may forgo any right to later collect from Bill should an accident occur due to his reckless behavior.

With a **contributory negligence defense**, the defendant maintains that the plaintiff contributed to his or her own loss by also acting in a negligent manner. This defense might be successful, for example, in a case in which motorist A failed to yield the right of way (a negligent act) and was struck by motorist B, who had the right of way but was speeding. If it could be shown that the accident would not have occurred had motorist B been in reasonable control of his or her vehicle, motorist B's claim against motorist A might be defeated. However, because of the potential harshness of the doctrine of contributory negligence, many states have enacted **comparative negligence statutes**. Under this legislation, an attempt is made to allocate the loss to each party in proportion to the degree to which each contributed to the accident.

Note that the preceding discussion relates to the legal elements necessary for the successful defense against damages based on a negligent act. In practice, though, juries often make awards on the basis of their sympathy for the plaintiff rather than from the facts pertaining to the case. This is especially apparent when the defendant has substantial ability to pay—or, as plaintiffs' lawyers say, "Look for defendants with deep pockets."

Criteria for an Insurable Exposure

As noted in Chapter 9, insurance can be an effective way to deal with risk only when the following conditions are met: (1) There are a large number of similar exposure units; (2) the loss covered is fortuitous, or accidental; (3) the cost is relatively low and measurable; and (4) losses are noncatastrophic. For certain types of property and liability exposures, such as medical malpractice, product liability, and automobile collision and liability, insurance is becoming less and less able to provide the necessary protection. This undesirable situation is developing because losses in these areas are increasing in both frequency and severity, thereby pushing premiums beyond the levels that many insured persons are willing or able to pay. In fact, over the last several years, property and liability insurers have lost billions of dollars through their underwriting activities. Therefore, unless these losses are reduced to tolerable levels, fewer and fewer types of risks will meet the criteria of an insurable exposure. While some people believe that letting the state or federal government establish insurance operations will solve the problem, such optimism is unjustified. Unless losses are reduced, premiums will continue to increase regardless of whether private companies or the government administers the program.

Principle of Indemnity

The **principle of indemnity** states that the insured may not be compensated by the insurance company in an amount exceeding the economic loss. Most property and liability insurance contracts are based on this principle. Recall from Chapters 9 and 10 that life and health insurance contracts, in contrast, are not specifically contracts of indemnity.

Four important concepts that are related to the principle of indemnity are found in property and liability insurance: (1) insurable interest, (2) actual cash value, (3) subrogation, and (4) other insurance.

Insurable Interest. The concept of **insurable interest** means that the individuals who insure property must stand to lose something if that property is subject to loss and that they cannot receive more in payment than their financial interest in the

---

negligent action
An action that is deemed inconsistent with the reasonable person doctrine.

reasonable person doctrine
A doctrine stating that if a person fails to act in a reasonable manner—as would someone with "normal" intelligence, perceptions, and experiences—he or she is guilty of negligence.

assumption of risk defense
A form of defense against a charge of negligence in which it is alleged that some action by the plaintiff relieved the defendant of his or her duty to protect the plaintiff.

contributory negligence defense
A form of defense against a negligence charge in which the defendant maintains that the plaintiff contributed to his or her own loss by personally acting in a negligent manner.

comparative negligence statutes
Laws existing in certain states under which losses to contesting parties in a lawsuit may be allocated to each party in proportion to the degree to which each contributed to the accident or loss in question.

principle of indemnity
An insurance principle stating that an insured may not be compensated by his or her insurer in an amount exceeding the amount of economic loss.

insurable interest
A concept stating that individuals who insure property must stand to lose something if that property is subject to loss and that they cannot receive more in compensation than the extent of their legal interest in the property.

property. For example, assume that John and Mary own equal shares in an apartment house that has a market value of $200,000 (excluding the value of the land, which is uninsurable). If the building is destroyed, the maximum the insurer will pay to each partner is $100,000, since that is the extent of either party's economic interest in the property. If these partners sell the property but forget to cancel their insurance policy, and the property is subsequently destroyed by fire, the insurance company will pay them nothing (since they have no interest in the property at the time of loss).

Ownership, however, is not the only way someone can develop an insurable interest in a property. For instance, an owner of a dry cleaning operation has a legal obligation to return the clothing received in the course of business. If a fire damages the clothing, the proprietor may be liable to customers for the value of the damaged clothing. Thus, the proprietor, although not the owner of the clothing, does have a legal obligation to maintain the clothing in good condition and may insure it in order to be protected against loss.

Actual Cash Value. The principle of indemnity also *limits the amount an insured may collect to the actual cash value of the property.* **Actual cash value** is defined as replacement cost less physical depreciation, although some insurers do guarantee replacement cost without taking depreciation into account—for example, most homeowners policies will settle building losses on a replacement basis if the proper type and amount of insurance is purchased. But since it is common practice in most other situations to deduct depreciation in order to obtain the actual cash value, only that is considered here. If an insured property is damaged, the insurer is obligated to pay no more than what the property would cost new today (its replacement cost) less depreciation from wear and tear. For example, assume that fire destroys two rooms of furniture that have a replacement cost of $5,000. The average age of the furnishings was six years, and they were estimated to have a useful life of ten years. Therefore, at the time of loss the items were subject to an assumed physical depreciation of 60 percent (6 years ÷ 10 years)—in this case, $3,000. Since the actual cash value is estimated at $2,000 ($5,000 replacement cost minus $3,000 depreciation), the maximum the insurer would have to pay is $2,000.

Note that the original cost of the property has no bearing on the settlement.

Subrogation. After an insurance company pays a claim, its **right of subrogation** allows it to request reimbursement from the person who caused the loss or from that person's insurance company. For example, assume that you are in an automobile accident in which the other party damages your car. You may collect from your insurer or the at-fault party's insurer but not from both (at least not for the same loss). If you receive payment from your insurance company, you must subrogate (transfer) to it your right to sue the other person. Clearly, to collect the full amount from both parties would leave you better off after the loss than before it. Such an action would violate the principle of indemnity. An important by-product of the subrogation clause is that it makes the party who caused the accident (or loss) ultimately responsible for paying the damages. In this way, the *insurance company* can go after the responsible party to collect its loss (the amount it paid out to you); and best of all, it's not your problem.

Other Insurance. Nearly all property and liability insurance contracts have an *other-insurance clause,* which also supports the concept of indemnity. This provision prohibits insured persons from insuring their property with two or more insurance companies and then collecting in full for a loss from all companies. The other-insurance clause normally states that if a person has more than one insurance policy on a property, each company is liable only for a pro rata amount of the loss based on its proportion of the total insurance covering the property. For example, assume that John and Mary in the earlier example purchased two policies of $200,000 each on their $200,000 building. If a total loss occurred, each company would pay 50 percent, because the ratio of the coverage purchased from each company to the total coverage on the property is one-half ($200,000/$400,000). Similarly, if each of *three* companies had issued a $200,000 policy, their individual shares would be one-third ($200,000/$600,000). Without this provision, insured persons could use duplicate property insurance policies to profit from their losses. In liability insurance policies, the other-insurance clause usually provides that if two (or more) policies cover the same exposure, only one of them will provide coverage until its limits are used up, after which the other will provide coverage above that amount up to no more than the amount of the allowable loss.

Coinsurance

Coinsurance, a provision commonly found in property insurance contracts, requires policyholders to buy insurance in an amount equal to a specified percentage of the value of their property. If the insureds comply with this requirement, they will be reimbursed for covered losses dollar for dollar up to the amount of the policy limits. Otherwise, payment will be based on a specified percentage of loss. For example, assume that John and Mary's fire policy on their $200,000 apartment building contained an 80 percent coinsurance clause. This means that the policy limits must equal or exceed 80 percent of the value of their building. Further assume that they had run short of money and decided to save by buying a single $120,000 policy instead of a minimum of $160,000 (80% × $200,000) as required by the coinsurance clause. If a loss of any amount occurred, the company would be obligated to pay only 75 percent ($120,000 ÷ $160,000) of it up to the amount of the policy limit. Thus, on damages of $40,000, the insurer would pay only $30,000 (75% × $40,000). Obviously, it is important that you closely evaluate the coinsurance clause of any property insurance policy in order to make sure that you will not have an unexpected additional burden in the event a loss does take place.

HOMEOWNERS INSURANCE

> Because your home is likely to be your biggest (and most expensive) possession, every effort should be taken to make sure that it's adequately insured. What kinds of protection should you look for when insuring a home? Would you want the same protection if you were renting rather than buying a home? Give some thought to these questions before going on.

Although homeowners insurance is often thought of as a single type of insurance policy, four different forms (HO-1, HO-2, HO-3, and HO-8) are actually available to homeowners, and two other forms (HO-4 and HO-6) are designed to meet the needs of renters and owners of condominiums (see Exhibit 11.2). An HO-4 policy offers essentially the same broad protection as an HO-2 policy, except that the coverage does not apply to the rented dwelling unit because tenants usually do not have a financial interest in the real property. All HO forms are divided into two sections. Section I applies to the dwelling, its contents, and accompanying structures; Section II deals with comprehensive coverage for personal liability and for medical payments to others. The forms differ in that the scope of coverage under Section I is least with an HO-1 policy and greatest with an HO-3 policy. HO-8 is a modified coverage policy for older homes. It is used by homeowners to insure houses that have market values well below their costs to rebuild. The coverage in Section II is the same for all forms.

In the following paragraphs, the important features of homeowners forms HO-2 and HO-3 are emphasized because these are the most frequently sold policies. The coverage offered under these forms is basically the same; the differences lie only in the number of perils against which protection applies.

Perils Covered

As mentioned previously, a peril is defined as a cause of loss. Some property and liability insurance agreements, called *comprehensive* policies, cover

actual cash value
A value assigned to an insured property that is determined by subtracting depreciation from replacement cost.

right of subrogation
The right of an insurer who has paid a claim to request reimbursement from the person who caused the loss or that person's insurer.

coinsurance
In property insurance, a provision that requires a policyholder to buy insurance in an amount equal to a specified percentage of the value of their property, including improvements.

EXHIBIT 11.2

A Guide to Homeowners Policies

The amount of insurance coverage you receive depends on the type of homeowners (HO) policy you select. Insurance coverage can also be obtained for those who live in *rental units* (HO-4) or who own units in a *condominium* (HO-6).

Coverage	HO-1 (Basic Form)	HO-2 (Broad Form)	HO-3 (Special Form)
	Section I Coverages		
A. Dwelling	$15,000 minimum	$15,000 minimum	$20,000 minimum
B. Other structures	10% of A	10% of A	10% of A
C. Personal property	50% of A	50% of A	50% of A
D. Loss of use	10% of A	20% of A	20% of A
Covered perils	Fire or lightning Windstorm or hail Explosion Riot or civil commotion Aircraft Vehicles Smoke Vandalism or malicious mischief Theft Breakage of glass or safety glazing material (limit of $100) Volcanic eruption	Fire or lightning Windstorm or hail Explosion Riot or civil commotion Aircraft Vehicles Smoke Vandalism or malicious mischief Theft Breakage of glass or safety glazing material Falling objects Weight of ice, snow, or sleet Accidental discharge or overflow of water or stream Sudden and accidental tearing, cracking, burning, or bulging of a steam, hot water, air conditioning, or automatic fire protective sprinkler system, or appliance for heating water Freezing Sudden and accidental damage for artificially generated electrical current Volcanic eruption	Dwelling and other structures covered against risks of direct physical loss to property except losses specifically excluded Personal property covered by same perils as HO-2 plus damage by glass or safety glazing material, which is part of a building, storm door, or storm window
	Section II Coverages (Minimums)		
E. Personal liability F. Medical payments to others	$100,000 $1,000 per person	$100,000 $1,000 per person	$100,000 $1,000 per person

all perils except those specifically excluded, while others name the perils covered individually. The latter type is called a **named peril policy**.

Section I Perils. The perils against which the home and its contents are insured are shown in Exhibit 11.2. The coverage on household belongings is the same for the HO-2 and HO-3 forms, but coverage on the house and other structures (for

example, a detached garage) is comprehensive under HO-3 and named peril in HO-2. Whether homeowners should buy an HO-2 or an HO-3 form depends primarily on the amount they are willing to spend to secure additional protection. In some states, the premium differential is small, making an HO-3 policy the better buy. In other states, the HO-2 form has a substantially lower premium. Also, the size of the premiums for the HO-2 and HO-3 poli-

EXHIBIT 11.2 (*Continued*)

HO-4 (Renters—Contents, Broad Form)	HO-6 (Condominimum Unit Owners)	HO-8 (Older House Form)
Section I Coverages		
Not applicable Not applicable $6,000 minimum 20% of C	$1,000 minimum Not applicable $6,000 minimum 40% of C	Same as HO-1, except losses are paid based on the amount required to repair or replace the property using common construction materials and methods.
Same perils as HO-2 for personal property	Same perils as HO-2 for personal property	Same perils as HO-1, except theft coverage applies only to losses on the residence premises up to a maximum of $1,000; certain other coverage restrictions also apply.
Section II Coverages (Minimums)		
$100,000	$100,000	$100,000
$1,000 per person	$1,000 per person	$1,000 per person

cies can differ substantially among insurance companies. Because of its more limited coverage, the purchase of an HO-1 is not recommended. (A special note on the HO-8 is presented later.)

Section II Perils. The peril insured against under Section II of the homeowners contract is the (alleged) negligence of an insured. As discussed earlier in this chapter, negligence is defined as fail-

ure to act in a reasonable manner. The coverage is called *comprehensive personal liability coverage,* because it offers protection against nearly any

named peril policy
An insurance policy that names the perils covered individually.

source of liability (major exclusions are noted later) resulting from negligence. It does not insure against other losses for which one may become liable, such as libel, slander, defamation of character, and contractual or intentional wrongdoings. For example, coverage would apply if you carelessly, but unintentionally, knocked someone down your stairs. If you purposely struck and injured another person, however, or harmed someone's reputation either orally or in writing, the homeowners liability coverage would not protect you. An additional feature of Section II is the limited amount of medical coverage of persons other than the homeowner's family in certain types of minor accidents on or off the insured's premises. The basic purpose of this coverage is to help homeowners meet their moral obligations and also to help deter possible lawsuits. The limited medical payment coverage pays irrespective of negligence or fault.

Property Covered

The homeowners policy offers property protection under Section I for the dwelling unit, accompanying structures, and the personal property of homeowners and their families. Coverage for certain types of losses also applies to lawns, trees, plants, and shrubs. However, structures on the premises used for business purposes (except incidentally) are excluded from coverage, as are animals (pets or otherwise) and motorized vehicles not used in the maintenance of the premises. This latter exclusion means there is no coverage for motorcycles, autos, golf carts, or snowmobiles (an exception is small boats). Further, business inventory (goods held by an insured who is a traveling salesperson or other goods held for sale) is not covered. Even though business inventory is excluded, business property (such as books, typewriters, working materials, and microcomputers) is covered, up to a maximum of $2,500, while it is on the insured premises.

Also, as we will see later in this chapter, there are *limits* to the types and amounts of coverages provided. As a result, your homeowners policy may offer less protection than is necessary for many expensive items of personal property. To meet this need, insurers have developed the **personal property floater (PPF) policy** to provide either

blanket or scheduled coverage of such items. Essentially a PPF policy extends protection to items that are otherwise slighted in a standard homeowners policy.

Homeowners insurance provides protection not only on the home itself but also on most of its contents. **Fact:** Homeowners insurance covers the home itself and most of the contents in the home, including furniture, stereos and TVs, and clothing. On the other hand, cars, motorcycles, golf carts, and so on usually are not covered under a homeowners policy.

Renters Insurance: Don't Move in Without It

If you live in an apartment (or some other type of rental unit), you should be aware that while the building you live in very likely is fully insured, your furnishings and other personal belongings are not. Rather, as a renter (or even as the owner of a condominium unit), you need a special type of HO policy in order to obtain insurance coverage on your possessions. Consider, for example, the predicament of Lois Weaver. She never got around to insuring her personal possessions in the apartment she rented in Denver. One wintry night, a water pipe ruptured, and escaping steam damaged her furniture, rugs, and other belongings. When the building owner refused to pay for the loss, Ms. Weaver hauled him into court—and lost. How could she have lost? Simple: *Unless a landlord can be proven negligent*— and this one wasn't—*he or she isn't responsible for a tenant's property.* The moral of this story is clear—once you've accumulated a good deal of personal belongings (from clothing and home furnishings to stereo equipment, VCRs, and TVs), you'd better make sure they are covered by insurance, even if you're only renting a place to live! Otherwise you risk the loss of everything you own. Apparently a lot of tenants don't realize that, as surveys show most of them are without insurance. And that's unfortunate, since insurance for tenants, or renters, is available everywhere at reasonable rates. It's simply a scaled-down version of homeowners insurance, wherein the contents of a house, apartment or cooperative unit are covered, but not the structure and grounds.

The policy is called Renters Form HO-4. For owners of condominium units, there's one called HO-6; it's similar but includes a minimum of $1,000 in protection for any building alterations, additions, and decorations paid for by the policyholder. Both the HO-4 and HO-6 include liability coverage. Like regular homeowners insurance, they protect you at home and away. For example, if somebody is injured and sues you, the policy would pay for damages up to a specified limit, generally $100,000, although some insurers go as high as $500,000. A tenant who doesn't want this protection could probably save some money by buying a personal property policy instead.

A standard renters policy covers furniture, carpets, appliances, clothing, and most other personal items for their cash value at the time of loss. The cost of renters insurance isn't high: Expect to pay $80 to $100 a year for about $8,000 in coverage, depending on where you live. For maximum protection, you can buy *replacement cost insurance* (discussed again later in this chapter), which pays the actual cost of replacing articles with comparable ones—though some policies limit the payout to four times the cash value. You'll pay more for this, naturally—perhaps as little as another 10 percent, or perhaps much more, depending on the insurer. Also, the standard tenants policy provides only limited coverage of such valuables as jewelry, furs and silverware. Coverage varies, although some insurers now pay up to $1,000 for the loss of watches, gems and furs, and up to $2,500 for silverware. For larger amounts, you need a separate policy or a supplement, called a *personal property floater,* as discussed earlier.

Renters insurance pays for losses caused by fire or lightning, windstorms, hail, theft, civil commotion, aircraft, vehicles, smoke, vandalism and malicious mischief, falling objects, building collapse, and the weight of ice and snow. Certain damages caused by water, steam, electricity, appliances, and frozen pipes are covered as well. If your residence can't be occupied because of damage from any of those perils, the insurance will pay for any increase in living expenses resulting from, say, staying at a hotel and eating in restaurants. The liability coverage pays for damages and legal costs arising from injuries or damage caused by you, a member of your family or a pet, on or off your premises.

If you rent an apartment, you don't need to worry about property insurance since your furniture and other personal belongings are already covered by the landlord's insurance policy. **Fantasy:** If you rent and do not have some sort of insurance coverage on your furniture and other personal property, your possessions are uninsured and could be lost! Your landlord is liable only if you can prove that your loss was due to his or her negligence.

Types of Losses Covered

A person can suffer three different types of property-related loss when misfortune occurs: (1) the direct loss of property, (2) an indirect loss that occurs due to the loss of damaged property, and (3) extra expenses resulting from direct and indirect losses. The homeowners insurance contract offers compensation for each of these types of loss.

Section I Coverage. When a house is damaged by an insured peril, the insurance company will pay reasonable living expenses that a family might incur while the home is being repaired. Also, in many instances the insurer will pay for damages caused by perils other than those mentioned in the policy if a named peril is determined to have been the underlying cause of the loss. Assume, for instance, that lightning (a covered peril) strikes a house while a family is away and knocks out all the power, which causes $400 of food in the freezer and refrigerator to spoil. The company will pay for the loss even though temperature change (the direct cause) is not mentioned in the policy.

Section II Coverage. In addition to paying successfully pursued liability claims against an insured, the homeowners policy includes coverage for (1) the cost of defending the insured, (2) any reasonable expenses incurred by an insured in helping the company's defense, and (3) the payment

> **personal property floater (PPF) policy**
> An insurance policy that provides coverage to expensive personal property not otherwise covered in a standard homeowners policy.

of court costs. Since these three types of costs apply even in cases in which the liability suit is without merit, coverage in these areas is an added benefit that can save you thousands of dollars in attorney fees.

Persons Covered

The homeowners policy covers the persons named in the policy and the members of their families who are residents of the household. A person can be a resident of the household even while temporarily living away from home. For example, college students who live at school part of the year and at home during vacations are normally regarded as household residents. The homeowners contract also extends limited coverage to guests of the insured for property losses that occur at the insured house if the insured wants such coverage to apply. If the insured does not choose to file a claim for the guest's property loss, the guest will be reimbursed only if he or she can prove negligence on the part of the homeowner. If the home is financed, coverage for loss to the house will also apply to the mortgage lender, provided that the lender is named in the insurance policy.

Locations Covered

While some insurance contracts have territorial exclusions, homeowners policies offer coverage worldwide. Consequently, an insured's personal property is *fully covered* regardless of whether it is loaned to the next-door neighbor or kept in a hotel room in Outer Mongolia. The only exception is property left at a second home, such as a beach house or resort condominium—in which case, coverage is reduced to 10 percent of the policy limit, except while the insured is actually residing there. Homeowners and their families have liability protection for their negligent acts wherever they occur. This liability protection, however, does not include negligent acts involving certain types of motorized vehicles (like large boats and aircraft), or arising in the course of employment or professional practice. It does include golf carts (when used for golfing purposes) and recreational vehicles such as snowmobiles and minibikes, provided they are used on the insured premises.

Limitation on Payment

The insurable interest, actual cash value, subrogation, and other insurance features that restrict the amount paid under a property and liability insurance contract have already been described. In addition to these features, replacement cost, policy limits, and deductibles can also influence the amount an insurance company will pay for a loss.

Replacement Cost. The amount necessary to repair, rebuild, or replace an asset at today's prices is the **replacement cost**. The homeowner's coverage on a house and the accompanying structures is based on replacement cost coverage. This means that the insurer will repair or replace damaged items without taking any deductions for depreciation. An illustration of a replacement cost calculation is given below for a 2,400-square-foot home with a two-car garage:

Dwelling: 2,400 sq. ft. at $62 per sq. ft.	$148,800
Extra features: built-in appliances, mahogany cabinets, 3 ceiling fans	8,600
Porches, patios: back screened and trellised patio	2,700
Two-car garage: 900 sq. ft. at $24 per sq. ft.	21,600
Other site improvements: driveway, storage, landscaping	4,700
Total replacement cost	$186,400

The $186,400 represents the amount of money it would take *today* to fully replace the home in question. Keep in mind, however, that *in order for homeowners to be eligible for reimbursement on a replacement-cost basis, they must keep their homes insured for at least 80 percent of the amount it would cost to build them today exclusive of the value of the land.* In periods of inflation, homeowners must either increase their coverage limits on the dwelling unit every year or take a chance on falling below the 80 percent requirement. If the 80 percent condition is not met, the maximum compensation allowable for total or partial losses may be determined on an actual cash value basis.

Contrary to popular opinion, actual cash value and replacement cost need not bear any relationship to a home's market value. Because replacement cost and actual cash value relate only to the physical structure and do not consider the influence of location, a home's market value can be in excess of its replacement cost or below its actual cash value. Also, even if a home is in an excellent state of repair, its market value may be lessened because of functional obsolescence within the structure. In fact, the HO-8 homeowners form was adopted in partial response to this problem. In many older neighborhoods, a 2,200-square-foot home might have a market value, excluding land, of, say, $60,000; the replacement cost, though, might total $160,000. Thus, to get good protection a homeowner would have to buy a policy with limits of $128,000 (.80 × $160,000). This is expensive to the homeowner and creates moral hazard to the insurer. With the HO-8, however, homeowners generally can get their property repaired in full up to the amount of their loss or up to the property's market value, whichever is less. This reduced limit saves the insureds premiums and reduces the risk that people will burn their houses down to make money on the insurance proceeds.

Although coverage on a house is often on a *replacement-cost basis,* standard coverage on the contents may be on an *actual cash value basis.* Therefore, depreciation is taken into account in calculating the amount of any payments made for losses to furniture, clothing, and other belongings. The depreciation amount is subtracted from the *current replacement cost* of the items—not from what may have been paid for the property several years ago. Thus, it is possible to collect more in insurance than the property's original price if the rate of inflation has exceeded the rate of depreciation.

Recently, many insurers have begun offering, for a slight increase in premium, replacement-cost coverage on contents. It seems likely that in the future the standard coverage on contents will become replacement cost rather than actual cash value. Because the additional premium required to buy replacement-cost coverage is generally small, you should seriously consider this option when buying homeowners insurance.

Policy Limits. In Section I of the homeowners policy, the amount of coverage on the dwelling unit (coverage A) establishes the amounts applicable to the accompanying structures (coverage B), the unscheduled personal property (coverage C), and the temporary living expenses (coverage D). Generally, the limits under coverages B, C, and D are 10, 50, and 10 to 20 percent, respectively, of the amount of coverage under A (see Exhibit 11.2). For example, if the house were insured for $50,000, the respective limits for coverages B, C, and D would be $5,000, $25,000, and $10,000 (10% × $50,000, 50% × $50,000, and 20% × $50,000, respectively). Each of these limits can be increased if insufficient to cover the exposure. Also, for a small reduction in premium, some companies will permit a homeowner to reduce coverage on unscheduled personal property to 40 percent of the amount on the dwelling unit.

Remember that homeowners policies usually specify internal limits for certain types of personal property as included under the coverage C category. These coverage limits are within the total dollar amount of coverage C, and they in no way act to increase that total. The limited dollar coverages for each reported loss are as follows:

From any covered peril:

1. $200 on money, bank notes, bullion, gold other than goldware, silver other than silverware, platinum, coins, and medals
2. $1,000 on securities, accounts, deeds, evidences of debt, letters of credit, notes other than bank notes, manuscripts, passports, tickets, and stamps
3. $1,000 on watercraft, including their trailers, furnishings, equipment, and outboard motors
4. $1,000 on trailers not used with watercraft
5. $1,000 on grave markers

From theft only:

6. $1,000 for loss by theft of jewelry, watches, furs, and precious and semiprecious stones
7. $2,000 for loss by theft of firearms
8. $2,500 for loss by theft of silverware, silver-plated ware, goldware, gold-plated ware, and pewterware; includes flatware, hollowware, tea sets, trays, and trophies made of or including silver, gold, or pewter

In Section II, the standard liability limit (coverage E) is $100,000, and the medical payments portion (coverage F) normally has a limit of $1,000 per person. Additional coverages included in Section II consist of claim expenses such as court costs and attorney fees, first aid and medical expenses, including ambulance costs, and damage to others' property of up to $500 per occurrence.

Although these limits are the ones most commonly sold, most homeowners need additional

---

replacement cost
The amount necessary to repair, rebuild, or replace an asset at today's prices.

protection, especially liability coverage. In these days of high damage awards by juries, a $100,000 liability limit may not be adequate—in fact, a greater amount is advisable for persons with higher incomes and net worths. The liability limit with most companies can be increased for only a nominal cost. For example, the annual premium difference between a $100,000 personal liability limit and a $300,000 limit is likely to be only $40 to $50!

Deductibles. Each of the preceding limits on recovery constrains the maximum amount payable under the policy. In contrast, *deductibles* place constraints on what a company must pay for small losses. Deductibles help reduce insurance premiums, because they do away with the frequent small loss claims that are proportionately more expensive to administer. The standard deductible in most states is $250 on the physical damage protection provided in Section I. However, deductible amounts of $500 or $1,000 are available on an optional basis. The premium savings on policies with larger deductibles are often significant. For example, in some states an increase in the deductible from $250 to $500 results in an annual premium savings of $40 to $75, depending on the amount of coverage purchased. Homeowners should check with their insurance agents to see whether it is feasible to increase the deductible. Deductibles do not apply to the liability and medical payments coverage, since insurers want to be notified of all claims, no matter how trivial. If companies did not set this procedure, they could in some cases be notified too late to properly investigate and prepare adequate defenses for resulting lawsuits.

Homeowner's Premiums

Perhaps it might be useful to bring together here previous comments concerning the premiums on homeowner's insurance policies. Generally speaking, a homeowners contract form is selected by an insured, and it usually provides physical damage coverage on the dwelling up to at least 80 percent of the cost to rebuild at today's prices. With the amount of coverage on the dwelling set, basic amounts of coverage apply to the other structures on the site, personal property, and loss of use. As you will recall, these other coverages are stated as a percentage of the amount of protection placed on

the dwelling unit. As a standard provision, each of these property damage coverages is subject to a $250 deductible. Also included in the homeowners policy are basic amounts of protection for liability losses ($100,000), medical payments to others ($1,000), and additional coverages, such as damage to property of others ($500). For this basic package of protection, an insurer will quote a premium.

As we have discussed, most people need to modify this basic package of coverages. Some will want to increase coverage on their homes to 100 percent of the replacement cost. Also, changing the contents protection from actual cash value to replacement cost and scheduling some items of expensive personal property may be desirable. Most insurance professionals also advise homeowners to increase their liability and medical payments limits. Each of these changes will result in an additional premium charge.

At the same time, you may want to try to *reduce* your total premium by increasing the amount of your deductible, as discussed earlier. Since it is better to budget rather than insure small losses, larger deductibles are becoming more popular. In sum, recognize that although the homeowners policy is good protection for some people, most homeowners (and tenants) will need to modify the basic coverages offered. Thus, when you compare premiums among insurers, make sure the premiums quoted reflect the same additions to and subtractions from the standard coverages, limits, and deductible.

AUTOMOBILE INSURANCE

Probably no asset involves more exposure to loss than the automobile. Stop for a moment to consider why it's so important to have adequate insurance coverage on your car. What are some of the different types of exposure to loss you face when you get behind the wheel of a car?

Another asset that provides major exposure to loss is the automobile. Damage to this asset as well as negligence in its use can result in significant loss.

EXHIBIT 11.3

Travel, Deaths, and Death Rates (1986)

This exhibit shows some grim statistics on motor vehicle accidents in the United States. Motor vehicle accidents result not only in death and injury but in tremendous economic loss as well, which explains why auto insurance premiums are so high.

Deaths	47,900
Disabling injuries	1,800,000
Cost	$ 57.8 billion
Motor vehicle mileage	1,861 billion
Death rate per 100 million vehicle miles	2.57
Registered vehicles in the United States	181,900,000
Licensed drivers in the United States	158,600,000

Accident Totals (Rounded)	Number of Accidents	Drivers (Vehicles) Involved
Fatal	42,300	59,500
Disabling injury	1,200,000	2,000,000
Property damage and nondisabling injury	16,500,000	33,000,000
Total	17,700,000	35,000,000

Source: *Accident Facts, 1987* (Chicago: National Safety Council, 1987), 45.

As can be seen from Exhibit 11.3, U.S. motor vehicle accidents accounted for nearly 48,000 deaths, 1.8 million disabling injuries, and economic loss of some $57.8 billion in 1986. In addition, indirect monetary losses to society result from police and legal costs, as well as from the lost productive capacity of capital and human resources. Fortunately, from the standpoint of the individual, a big part of these costs can be protected against through insurance.

The major features of automobile insurance are discussed in the next several sections of this chapter. In the first of these sections, the coverages of a typical private passenger automobile policy are discussed. However, about half the states now have legislatively provided for the modification of automobile insurance coverages through no-fault insurance. Therefore, following the section on the automobile policy is an explanation of how no-fault laws typically affect reimbursement for losses caused by automobile accidents. Next, auto insurance premiums and financial responsibility laws are discussed.

Insurance Coverages

For years, individuals and families insured their automobiles by purchasing a *family automobile policy (FAP)*. Many considered the legal terms and other language used in this policy to be too difficult for the typical insurance buyer to understand. As a result, in the late 1970s an "easy-to-read" automobile insurance policy was developed by insurers: The **personal auto policy (PAP)**. An example of the personal nature of this policy is that the named insured is referred to as "you" and "your" and the insurer as "we" and "our." The PAP is made up of six parts; the first four identify the coverages provided in the policy and are as follows:

- Part A: Liability coverage
- Part B: Medical payments coverage
- Part C: Uninsured motorists coverage
- Part D: Coverage for damage to your auto

You are almost sure to purchase liability, medical payments, and uninsured motorists protection. You

personal auto policy (PAP)

A comprehensive automobile insurance policy developed in the 1970s to be easily understood by the "typical" insurance purchaser (for example, personal pronouns are substituted for legal designations); replaced the family automobile policy (FAP).

may, however, choose not to buy protection against damage to your automobile if it is of relatively little value. If you have a loan against your car, you will probably be *required* to have physical damage coverage—part D—at least equal to the amount of the loan. Let's now take a closer look at the coverage provided by parts A through D.

Part A: Liability Coverage. As part of the liability provisions of PAP, the insurer agrees to (1) pay damages for bodily injury and property damage for which you become legally obligated to pay due to an automobile accident, and (2) settle or defend any claim or suit asking for such damages. This provision for legal defense is quite important. It can mean a savings of thousands of dollars, since even a person who is not at fault in an automobile accident may be compelled to prove his or her innocence in court. Note, though, that the coverage is for a defense in civil cases only. It provides no defense against any criminal charges that may be brought against the insured as a result of an accident (such as a drunk driver who's involved in an accident).

In addition to providing reimbursement for bodily and property damages, the automobile liability insurance policy stipulates that certain supplemental payments may be made. Examples of supplemental payments include expenses incurred by the insurance company in settling the claim, and other reasonable expenses incurred by the insured at the request of the insurance company (for instance, food and travel expenses). Supplemental payments can also take the form of reimbursement for premiums spent on appeal bonds, bonds to release attachments of the insured's property, and bail bonds required of an insured as a result of an accident. The amount of these supplemental payments is not restricted by the applicable policy limits. In other words, the insurance company does not reduce your policy limits by the amount that it costs to protect you in these ways.

Policy Limits. Although the insurance company provides both bodily injury and property damage liability insurance under part A, there is likely to be a single dollar limit up to which it will pay for damages from any one accident. Typical limits are $50,000, $100,000, $300,000, and $500,000. You should consider at least $300,000 of

coverage in today's legal liability environment. Damage awards are increasing, and the PAP policy provides that the insurer's duty to defend you *ends when the coverage limit has been exhausted;* it is very easy to "exhaust" $50,000 or $100,000.

Some insurers make so-called *split limits* of liability coverage available. For example, policy limits to protect individuals against claims made for **bodily injury liability losses** may be available in the following combinations: $10,000/$20,000; $25,000/$50,000; $50,000/$100,000; $100,000/$300,000; and $500,000/$1,000,000. The first amount in each combination is a limit per individual and the second a limit per accident. Thus, if you purchased the $50,000/$100,000 policy limits, the maximum amount any person negligently injured in an accident could receive from the insurance company would be $50,000. Further, the total amount that the insurer would pay to all injured victims in one accident normally would not exceed $100,000. If a jury awarded a claimant $80,000, the defendant whose insurance policy limits were $50,000/$100,000 could be required to pay $30,000 out of pocket ($80,000 award − $50,000 paid by insurance). For the defendant, this could mean loss of home, cars, bank accounts, and other assets. In many states, if the value of these assets is too little to satisfy a claim, the defendant's wages may be garnished (taken by the court and used to satisfy the outstanding debt).

The policy limits available to cover **property damage liability losses** are typically $10,000, $25,000, and $50,000. In contrast to bodily injury liability insurance limits, property damage policy limits are stated as a per-accident limit without specifying any limits applicable on a per-item or person basis.

Persons Insured. There are two basic sets of definitions in the PAP that determine the persons covered under the liability coverage: insured person and covered auto. Essentially, an *insured person* includes you (the named insured) and any family member, any person using a covered auto, and any person or organization that may be held responsible for your actions. The *named insured* is the person named in the declarations page of the policy. The spouse of the person named is considered to be a named insured if he or she resides in the same household. Family members are persons related by blood, marriage, or adoption who are residing in the same household. An unmarried college student living away from home usually would be considered a family member.

The named insured and family members have part A liability coverage regardless of the automobile they are driving. To have the liability coverage, however, other persons must be driving a covered auto and there must be reasonable belief that they are entitled to do so. *Covered autos* are the vehicles shown in the declarations page of your PAP, autos acquired during the policy period, any trailer owned, and any auto or trailer used as a temporary substitute while your auto or trailer is being repaired or serviced. An automobile that you lease for an extended time period can be included as a covered auto.

When a motorist who is involved in an automobile accident is covered under two or more liability insurance contracts, the coverage *on the automobile* is primary and the other coverages secondary. For example, if Dan Slegal, a named insured in his own right, were involved in an accident while driving Deeann Bauer's automobile (with permission), a claim settlement in excess of the limits of Deeann's liability policy would be necessary before Dan's liability insurance would apply. If Deeann's insurance had lapsed, Dan's policy would then offer primary protection (but it would apply to Dan only and not Deeann).

Part B: Medical Payments Coverage. *Medical payments coverage* provides for payment to a covered person of an amount no greater than the policy limits for all reasonable and necessary medical expenses incurred with three years after an automobile accident. It provides for reimbursement even if other sources of recovery, such as health or accident insurance, also make payment. In addition, in most states the insurer reimburses the insured for medical payments even if the insured proves that another person was negligent in the accident and receives compensation from that party's liability insurer.

As with liability and uninsured motorists insurance, a person need not be occupying an automobile when the accidental injury occurs in order to be eligible for benefits. Injuries sustained as a pedestrian or on a bicycle in a traffic accident are covered, too. (Motorcycle accidents normally are not covered.) This insurance also pays on an excess basis. For instance, if you are a passenger in a friend's automobile during an accident and suffer $8,000 in medical expenses, you can collect under your friend's medical payments insurance up to his or her policy limits. Further, you can collect (up to the amount of your policy limits) from your insurer the amount in excess of what the other medical payments provide. Of course, you may also collect from the liability insurance of another person involved in the accident if that person can be shown to have been at fault. In addition, you may be able to collect from your own health insurance protection.

Policy Limits. Medical payments insurance usually is available with per-person limits of $1,000, $2,000, $3,000, $5,000, and $10,000. Thus, an insurer conceivably could pay $60,000 or more in medical payments benefits for one accident involving a named insured and five passengers. Most families are advised to buy the $5,000 or $10,000 limit, because even if they have other adequate health insurance coverages available, they cannot be certain that their passengers are equally well protected. Having automobile medical payments insurance also reduces the probability that a passenger in your auto will sue you and attempt to collect under your liability insurance coverage (in those states that permit it).

Persons Insured. Coverage under an automobile medical payments insurance policy applies to the named insured and family members who are injured while occupying an automobile (whether owned by the named insured or not) or while struck by an automobile or trailer of any type. Also, it applies to any other person occupying a covered auto.

---

bodily injury liability losses
A clause in a PAP that protects individuals against losses from bodily injury; may specify coverage as a combination of per-individual and per-accident limits.

property damage liability losses
A provision in a PAP that covers damage to property on a per-accident basis.

Part C: Uninsured Motorists Coverage. **Uninsured motorists coverage** is available to meet the needs of "innocent" accident victims negligently injured by uninsured, underinsured, or hit-and-run motorists. Legislation requiring that uninsured motorists insurance be included in each liability insurance policy issued has been enacted in nearly all states. The insured is allowed, however, to reject this coverage in most of these states. In many states, a person may also collect if the negligent motorist's insurance company is insolvent. Under uninsured motorists insurance, an insured is legally entitled to collect an amount equal to the sum that could have been collected from the negligent motorist's liability insurance had such coverage been available, up to a maximum amount equal to the *uninsured motorists limit* stated in the policy.

Three points must be proven in order to receive payment through uninsured motorists insurance: (1) another motorist was at fault; (2) this motorist had no available insurance; and (3) damages were incurred. Property damage is not included in this coverage in most states. Therefore, under uninsured motorists coverage, you generally can collect only for losses arising from bodily injury. If the motorist and insurer cannot agree on the terms of the settlement of a claim under uninsured motorists coverage, the motorist can seek an attorney to negotiate the claim. If a mutually agreeable settlement still cannot be worked out, the insured has the right to have the case arbitrated by a neutral third party. In most cases, the accident victim and the insurer are then bound to accept the decision of the arbitrator. In addition to *uninsured* motorists, for a nominal premium you can also obtain protection for *underinsured* motorists—that is, for coverage when you're involved in an accident where the driver at fault has a liability limit much lower than you're entitled to. Under such coverage, your insurance company makes up the difference and then goes after the negligent driver for any deficiency.

Policy Limits. Uninsured motorists insurance is available at minimum cost (usually less than $10 per year). It often is sold with basic limits of $10,000 to $20,000, with additional amounts available for a small increase in the premium. At the least, uninsured motorists insurance should be purchased with the minimum limits available. The cost of this coverage is small relative to the amount of protection it provides.

Persons Insured. The named insured, family members, and any other person occupying a covered auto are covered by the uninsured motorists protection.

Uninsured motorists coverage is available as part of most automobile insurance policies. **Fact:** Such insurance is available under standard auto insurance policies and offers protection against uninsured, underinsured, or hit-and-run motorists.

Part D: Coverage for Physical Damage to an Auto. This part of the PAP provides coverage for damage to your auto. There are two basic types of coverage provided: collision and comprehensive (or "other than collision").

Collision Insurance. **Collision insurance** is first-party property damage coverage that pays for collision damage to an insured automobile regardless of fault. The amount of insurance payable is the actual cash value of the loss in excess of a stated deductible. Remember that actual cash value is defined as replacement cost less depreciation. Therefore, if a car is demolished, an insured will be paid an amount equal to the car's depreciated value minus any deductible.

Lenders often require the purchase of collision insurance on cars they finance. In some cases—especially when the auto dealer is handling the financing—the lender will attempt to sell this insurance. Generally, the purchase of automobile insurance from car dealers or finance companies *should be avoided.* This is not to imply that all insurance purchases through automobile dealers or finance companies are bad. Still, a full-time insurance agent is better trained to properly assess and meet a motorist's insurance needs. Moreover, it is likely that the collision provisions of your insurance policy fully protect you even in a *rental car.* Thus, as the accompanying *Smart Money* box notes, not only is rental car collision insurance expensive—it is probably also unnecessary!

Individuals who purchase collision insurance may select from one of several *deductibles* available—$50, $100, $250, or even $1,000. Significant premium savings often can be obtained by increasing the amount of the deductible. For example, one large automobile insurance company reports that a $50 deductible on a relatively new car can be purchased for an annual premium of $177, whereas the $100 deductible costs $150. Thus, a motorist who buys the $50 deductible is paying $27 for this additional $50 worth of protection.

Comprehensive Automobile Insurance. **Comprehensive automobile insurance** protects against loss to an insured automobile caused by any peril (with a few exceptions) *other than collision*. As one might imagine, this coverage offers broad protection and includes, but is not limited to, damage caused by fire, theft, glass breakage, falling objects, malicious mischief, vandalism, riot, and earthquake. Contrary to popular belief, theft of personal property kept or left in the insured automobile normally is not covered under the automobile insurance policy. (It may, however, be covered under the off-premises coverage of the homeowners policy if the auto was locked at the time the theft occurred.) The maximum compensation provided under this coverage is the actual cash value of the automobile.

Automobile No-Fault Insurance

The purchase of automobile insurance has been widespread. Nevertheless, over the years many accident victims have received inadequate compensation for their losses. Critics of this undercompensation have complained that the existing first-party medical payments portion of the PAP is too low. Further, in order to collect from the automobile policy liability coverage, an injured victim must prove that another motorist was at fault (that is, negligent) in the accident. In addition, even in those cases in which fault is proved, the liability limits of, say, $10,000 or $20,000 may still be too small to provide full reimbursement for a seriously injured victim. Medical costs, lost wages, and funds spent for replacement services have accounted for the bulk of the economic losses that remain undercompensated. And in contrast, these critics maintain the liability system pays too much for pain and suffering (called *general damages*), especially for minor injuries.

An early critic of the auto liability insurance system has alleged that automobile insurance companies have been selling the wrong product (auto liability insurance) because today the public is more concerned with the compensation of all accident victims rather than just those who can prove another was at fault for the accident. As a consequence, a major reform movement began during the mid-1960s to push adoption of automobile no-fault insurance.

The concept of **automobile no-fault insurance** is based on the belief that the liability system should be replaced by a system that reimburses without regard to negligence. The principle is, "My insurance policy should pay the cost of my injuries, and your insurance policy should pay the cost of yours," regardless of who is at fault in an accident. Under the concept of *pure* no-fault insurance, the driver, passengers, and injured pedestrians are reimbursed by the insurer of the car for economic losses stemming from bodily injury. The insurer thus does not have to provide coverage for claims made for losses caused to other motorists. Each insured party is compensated by his or her own company, regardless of which party caused the accident. In return, legal remedies and payments for pain and suffering are restricted.

Unfortunately, the advocates of no-fault forgot that liability insurance was never intended to serve as the primary system for compensating injured

---

uninsured motorists coverage
Automobile insurance that is designed to meet the needs of innocent accident victims who are involved in an accident in which an uninsured or underinsured motorist is at fault.

collision insurance
Automobile insurance that pays for collision damage to an insured automobile regardless of who was at fault.

comprehensive automobile insurance
Coverage that provides protection against loss to an insured automobile caused by any peril other than collision.

automobile no-fault insurance
A concept of automobile insurance that favors reimbursement without regard to negligence.

S·M·A·R·T   M·O·N·E·Y

A Crash Course on Car Rental Insurance

Picture this: You're in the airport. You've been waiting in line for half an hour to pick up your rental car. You get up to the counter, acutely aware of the impatient customers behind you. The person behind the counter hands you a pen and says, "Sign here, then initial here, here and here." Chances are you're not going to take time to decipher the voluminous fine print on the back of the car-rental agreement. So you walk away loaded with rental-car insurance that you may or may not need—*and that may even be worthless.* The only thing you're sure of is that the car you'd reserved for $29.95 a day now costs closer to $45.

Rental-car companies are infamous for offering these price-boosting "insurance options." The one that's come under fiercest attack is the so-called *collision damage waiver,* in which you pay the car-rental company to waive its right to hold you responsible for damages. Every state legislature is currently considering legislation regulating or banning the waiver; in Illinois, a bill banning the waiver is awaiting the governor's signature. The National Association of Insurance Commissioners has endorsed a ban, and the National Association of Attorneys General is considering the issue.

"[The collision damage waiver is] a trap for the unwary," says Tony Schrader, director of the market conduct division for the Texas State Board of Insurance. "It's something consumers can pay a lot for and not get much." That's the problem with most rental-car insurance, experts say. Either consumers already have the insurance and simply don't know it, or they can get the same insurance free simply by using the right credit card.

For example, personal accident insurance (PAI), which costs from $2 to $5 a day, pays for any injuries the driver suffers during the time he or she is renting the car (whether or not the injuries are incurred while in the car) and for injuries suffered by passengers while in the car. PAI, in other words, is nothing more than supplemental health insurance. If you already have a health policy, paying for personal accident coverage can be a waste. Personal effects coverage, which costs between $1 and $3 a day, protects you if your rental car is burglarized; the policy pays the cost of replacing possessions. But while the coverage is cheap, deductibles of up top $500 may render it useless. Moreover, most homeowners-insurance policies—and numerous travel-insurance policies—cover the loss of possessions while away from home.

And then there is the controversial collision damage waiver,

parties. Its sole purpose is to protect the assets of the insured, not to pay losses per se. This same concept applies to all liability insurance. The coverages of medical payments, collision, and comprehensive insurance discussed earlier do serve this compensation purpose to a certain extent. In addition, families can and should purchase widely available life, health, and disability income protection, which will protect them not only for losses resulting from automobile accidents but also for nearly all other types of economic losses resulting from accident or illness. In fact, the numerous cries that automobile no-fault insurance is needed so that people can be compensated for their losses incurred in automobile accidents have probably had a harmful effect, since they have detracted from public understanding of the need for full life and health insurance programming. After all, there is no reason to be more concerned about the person who is injured in an automobile accident than for

which can cost anywhere from $7.95 to $12.95 a day—in some cases nearly doubling the price of renting the car. Companies are making a bundle off these waivers, according to David Cohen, a Massachusetts state representative. He calculates that at Boston's Logan Airport alone, Avis grosses $2 million a year from the collision damage waiver. Where do the profits come from? That rate of around $10 a day adds up—a car that's rented almost every day for a year will bring in well over $3,000. The likelihood of damage is so small that the largest rental-car companies don't insure individual cars; they simply put the proceeds from the collision damage waiver in their coffers and hope you'll return the car undamaged. What's more, for the majority of consumers, the waiver is unnecessary, since 55 to 60 percent of all conventional auto policies already cover the policyholder for

damages incurred while driving a rental car. As Cohen puts it, "They are making me pay for something I don't need, and they're using high-pressure tactics. They really have the consumer over the barrel."

Demetria Mudar, an Avis spokeswoman, disagrees. "Whenever we get the opportunity, we encourage people to check their policies," she says. "We don't want to encourage people to buy something they don't need." But what if you don't have auto insurance? Must you pay the collision damage waiver? No, not since a number of *credit-card companies* (such as American Express and Diner's Club) have stepped in to fill the gap, offering free collision coverage *if you pay for a rental car using their card.*

If you are intent on beating the collision damage waiver, though, beware of certain risks. First, if you decide to rely on your personal policy, make sure

you find out what the deductible is and whether there are exclusions—for example, whether the policy covers trips outside U.S. borders. If you plan to charge your rental car on a credit card that offers free collision protection, remember that most programs only provide so-called secondary coverage. Translation: The card companies will pay only the amount not covered by your own auto policy. That means that if you have an accident in your rental car, you will have to file a claim with your own insurance company. As a result, that relaxing vacation may cause your premiums—not to mention your blood pressure—to shoot up.

Source: Adapted from Eric N. Berg, "Crash Course: Read Before You Sign on the Dotted Line," *Savvy*, October 1988, 73–74

the homeowner who sustains injury while repairing his or her house. Nevertheless, because some valid arguments have been put forth by proponents of no-fault insurance, about half of the states have legislated for a modification of the coverages offered by the family automobile policy. *No state has yet adopted a pure no-fault insurance plan,* though.

Basically, the various state laws governing no-fault insurance can be differentiated according to

whether or not (1) no-fault and liability insurance is compulsory and/or (2) there are any restrictions on lawsuits. The laws of the separate states vary substantially as to both the amount of no-fault benefits provided and the degree to which the restrictions for legal actions apply. For example, the Virginia statute places no limits on the right to sue for damages for pain and suffering, and requires only that automobile insurers make available modest amounts of medical expense, funeral expense,

EXHIBIT 11.4

Comparative Auto Insurance Premiums

Average auto insurance rates vary all over the map; while the national average is about $490 a year, the annual rate in the most expensive state (Massachusetts) is better than *two and one-half times* the cost for the same coverage in the least expensive state (Iowa). You might want to check this list to see where your state stands in the cost of auto insurance.

Rank	State	Average Premium	Rank	State	Average Premium
49	Alabama	$306.73	38	Montana	405.22
7	Alaska	588.88	43	Nebraska	348.27
4	Arizona	601.96	5	Nevada	600.04
21	Arkansas	494.29	18	New Hampshire	508.85
3	California	623.44	2	New Jersey	634.84
28	Colorado	434.97	33	New Mexico	415.57
15	Connecticut	519.93	8	New York	583.69
12	Delaware	536.96	36	North Carolina	408.42
9	District of Columbia	579.82	48	North Dakota	328.23
29	Florida	433.91	42	Ohio	350.84
20	Georgia	501.14	39	Oklahoma	370.28
13	Hawaii	530.13	27	Oregon	435.09
44	Idaho	345.66	10	Pennsylvania	568.97
25	Illinois	439.46	11	Rhode Island	549.00
32	Indiana	423.13	16	South Carolina	514.93
51	Iowa	255.61	50	South Dakota	295.08
40	Kansas	369.14	47	Tennessee	328.38
34	Kentucky	409.43	22	Texas	474.33
14	Louisiana	529.68	30	Utah	431.01
41	Maine	364.59	37	Vermont	405.36
6	Maryland	597.08	26	Virginia	436.20
1	Massachusetts	655.72	31	Washington	430.20
17	Michigan	509.28	19	West Virginia	506.81
24	Minnesota	456.48	35	Wisconsin	409.29
46	Mississippi	331.16	45	Wyoming	345.02
23	Missouri	460.88			

Source: *USA Today*, February 1, 1989.

and wage replacement coverage. At the other extreme is the Michigan law, which eliminates legal action for bodily injury claims for pain and suffering except when the accident victim is killed or incurs serious bodily dysfunction or disfigurement. Michigan is also the only state that restricts the victim's legal recovery of property damage caused by someone else's negligence. For its no-fault benefits, Michigan requires the insured to buy coverage that provides reimbursement for unlimited medical and hospital expenses. In addition, it covers rehabilitation, lost wages, replacement services, and funeral expenses. In contrast to Michigan, most states provide from $2,000 to $10,000 in first-party benefits (often called *personal injury protection*) and restrict legal recovery for pain and suffering to cases in which medical or economic losses exceed some threshold level, such as $500 or $1,000. In all states, recovery based on negligence is permitted for ec-

onomic loss in excess of the amount payable by no-fault insurance.

Overall, most of the no-fault laws that have been passed fell short of accomplishing the two objectives fundamental to no-fault insurance—that is, elimination of liability as a basis for recovery, and provision of adequate compensation for all accident victims. Further, the no-fault concept gained its largest public support because its advocates promised that it would contribute to lower insurance premiums. As might be expected, based on the laws now on the books, that has not always been achieved. In those states with substantive laws, though, some efficiencies have been gained. Still, because only a few states have required first-party benefits of substantial size, most seriously injured accident victims will continue to turn to the liability system or their life and health insurance coverages for large amounts of compensation.

Automobile Insurance Premiums

What you pay for car insurance depends on many things, including where you live, what kind of car you drive, what kind of coverage you have, the amount of your deductibles, and so forth. One thing is sure, the size of the typical car insurance premium is anything but uniform. The fact is, average auto insurance premiums—for basically the same coverage—vary all over the map. Exhibit 11.4, which lists average insurance premiums for the 50 states and District of Columbia, shows a range from $255 (in Iowa) to $655 (in Massachusetts). And, remember, this is for comparable coverage. If you're fortunate enough to live in one of the low-premium states (say one of the bottom 20), you're probably *relatively* satisfied with the cost of your car insurance; on the other hand, if you're in one of the more expensive states (like New Jersey, California, Arizona, or Pennsylvania), you may well be feeling the pinch of these high and, in many cases, rapidly increasing auto insurance rates. Indeed, residents in many of the high-premium states have begun to rally against these rates and are demanding—through their state legislators and/or the ballot box—a return to what they see as more reasonable premiums. This matter is a highly emotional one, because it hits the pocketbooks of so many consumers, and it very likely is an issue that's going to be with us for some time to come. The insurance companies on one side arguing why the rates are necessary and justified; consumers on the other side arguing that the rates are too high and they're going up too fast.

With this perspective in mind, let's look now at how auto insurance premiums are set. Basically, the starting point for determining them in nearly all states is the *rating territory*. Since more accidents occur in some geographic areas than others, higher rates are applied in those where claims are greatest. Even an insured who is the pillar of the community and has a perfect driving record will be charged the rates in effect for the territory in which he or she resides regardless of how high they might be. The location in which an automobile is principally garaged usually determines the applicable rating territory. Because insurance rates are influenced by local accident rates and the average cost of resulting claims paid under the various coverages in the area—reflecting auto repair costs, hospital and medical expenses, jury awards, thefts, and vandalism in the locale—where you live can make a big difference in how much you pay for auto insurance. Accordingly, Herbert Dennenburg, former insurance commissioner of Pennsylvania, stated that he had found a magic formula for reducing auto insurance premiums: "I moved from Philadelphia [a high-rate area] to Harrisburg [a low-rate area]."

Among the other factors that influence automobile insurance rates are (1) the amount of use the automobile receives, (2) the personal characteristics of the drivers, (3) the type of automobile, (4) the insured's driving record, and (5) applicable discounts. Note that while these have been and presently are the determining factors for rates in all but a few states, several jurisdictions prohibit the use of rating territories, age, and/or sex factors. The belief has been that these factors unfairly discriminate against the urban, the young, and the male.

Use of the Automobile. If an insured has a non-business automobile that is not customarily driven to work—or if an automobile is driven fewer than three miles one way to work—it probably will be classified as a pleasure car. This is a favorable rating for the use classification. A motorist who drives more than 3 but fewer than 15 miles to work will pay a slightly higher premium. If an auto is driven more than 15 miles each way to work, an even higher premium will be charged. Generally, higher premiums are charged for automobiles driven for business purposes than for those that qualify for other classifications, and a farm-use designation qualifies for the lowest rates.

Personal Characteristics of Drivers. Such items as the age, sex, and marital status of the insured affect the premium that is assessed for automobile insurance. As many young people and their parents already know, the rates applicable to youthful motorists can be relatively high. Generally, unmarried females age 24 or under and unmarried males age 29 or under are placed in higher-rate categories than individuals who are older. Married males under age 25 also fall into a relatively high-rate category. Females over age 24 and married females of any age are exempt from the youthful operator classification and thus need not pay the higher premiums. Insurance companies believe that such premium differentials based on age are justified because of the great number of accidents that involve youthful operators. For example, drivers in the 20 to 24 age group made up 10.9 percent of the driving population in 1986 but were involved in 18.3 percent of all automobile accidents and 19.3 percent of those accidents in which a fatality occurred.

Type of Automobile.   Automobiles may be classified as standard performance, intermediate performance, high performance, sports, and rear engine. In some states, even four-door cars are rated differently than two-door models of the same make. As might be expected, if an automobile is not classified as standard performance, higher rates are usually charged. Automobiles that have high horsepower-to-weight ratios and more than three forward gears on the floor frequently are classified in higher-rate categories. Thus, if you are thinking of buying, say, a Corvette or a Trans Am, you'd better be prepared to handle some pretty hefty insurance rates.

The type of car you drive has no bearing on how much you will have to pay for automobile insurance. **Fantasy:** The type of car you drive is one of the major determinants of auto insurance premiums. You can expect to pay a lot more for insurance on a sporty model than on a more "sedate" one.

Driving Record.   The driving records of the insured and those who live with them play an important part in the determination of premiums. Both traffic violation convictions and traffic accidents are normally considered in assessing driving records. The more severe types of traffic convictions are for driving under the influence of alcohol or drugs (DUI), leaving the scene of an accident, homicide or assault arising out of the operation of a motor vehicle, and driving with a revoked or suspended driver's license. In addition—on a less severe basis—any conviction for a traffic violation that results in the accumulation of points under a state point system may result in higher insurance premiums. Included in this category are such violations as speeding, running a red light, failure to yield the right of way, and illegal passing. Typically, points under a state system are assigned only for moving traffic violations. Therefore, convictions for offenses such as parking violations, improper regis-

tration, lack of an operator's license, and lack of a valid safety sticker usually do not result in increased insurance premiums. In most states, a *premium surcharge* is made for traffic offenses and accidents that are determined to be the fault of the insured. Under these plans, designated points are charged against the insured. The first point may eliminate the safe driving discount, with each additional point resulting in a certain dollar surcharge being added to the monthly premium. The idea behind surcharge plans is that motorists will exercise safer driving practices to avoid the expense of a surcharge.

Sometimes traffic violations do not directly enter into the premium computations but instead influence whether a motorist will be offered a regular policy or placed in an **automobile insurance plan** (formerly called an *assigned-risk plan*). These plans have been organized in many states to provide automobile insurance to drivers who are refused coverage when they have sought it in a normal manner. Motorists who are placed in an automobile insurance plan generally have less coverage and pay higher premiums. Even with the high premiums, however, insurers lost $2.3 billion on this type of business in a recent five-year period.

Driving Down the Cost of Car Insurance. One of the best ways to drive down the cost of car insurance is to take advantage of *discounts;* and, indeed, most auto insurers today offer a variety of them. Taken together, such discounts can knock 5 to 50 percent off your annual premium. A summary of some of the discounts given by the top auto insurance companies is provided in Exhibit 11.5. Some give overall *safe-driving* discounts, and others give youthful operators lower rates if they have had *driver's training.* Youthful drivers may also receive *good student* discounts for maintaining a B average or by being on the dean's list at their school. Such student discounts, by the way, apply to both high school and college students. Nearly all insurance companies provide discounts to families with two or more automobiles, if each car is insured by the same company. Most insurers also offer discounts to owners who install *air-bags* or *anti-theft devices* in their cars. Likewise, *nonsmoker and nondrinker* discounts are offered by a number of insurers. There are even some companies that specialize in insuring certain portions of the general population. For example, certain insurers accept only persons who are educators or executives and others only government employees. While not offering discounts in the normal sense, these companies frequently do have lower premiums because, through more selective underwriting, they are able to reduce losses and operating expenses.

Clearly, it's to your advantage to look for and use as many of these discounts as you can. Another very effective way to drive down the cost of car insurance is to **raise your deductibles** (as discussed earlier in this chapter). This often overlooked tactic can have a dramatic effect on the amount of insurance premium you pay. For example, the difference between a $100 deductible and a $500 deductible may be as much as 30 percent on comprehensive coverage and 25 percent on collision insurance; request a $1,000 deductible and you may save as much as 45 to 50 percent on both comprehensive and collision insurance.

Financial Responsibility Laws

The annual losses from automobile accidents in the United States run into billions of dollars. For this reason, **financial responsibility laws** have been enacted in most states, whereby motorists are required to buy automobile liability insurance. As their name implies, financial responsibility laws attempt to force motorists to be financially responsible for the damages they cause as a result of automobile accidents. A summary of the financial responsibility requirements in each of the 50 states and the District of Columbia is given in Exhibit 11.6 (page 394). As pointed out earlier, many states are now forcing insurance companies to develop policies that conform with no-fault insurance statutes. Federal legislation with respect to financial responsibility as well as no-fault insurance may soon be forthcoming as well.

Two basic types of laws compel motorists to assume financial responsibility. The first is one in which all automobile owners in a given state are required to show evidence that they have liability insurance coverage prior to obtaining registration for their motor vehicles. Until 1971 only three states had these compulsory liability insurance requirements. Today about half of the states require

motorists to show evidence of insurance coverage before they will sell them license plates.

Under the second type of financial responsibility legislation, motorists do not have to show evidence of their insurance coverage until after they are involved in an accident. If they then fail to demonstrate compliance with the law, their registrations and/or driver's licenses are suspended. This law has been criticized on the grounds that it allows negligent motorists to have one "free" accident. Even though the motorists who are not financially responsible lose their driving privileges, the losses to their victims may remain uncompensated.

OTHER PROPERTY AND LIABILITY INSURANCE

> Besides homeowners and automobile insurance, there are several other types of property insurance policies that you should be aware of. For example, you can increase your personal liability coverage with a personal liability umbrella policy, you can insure certain types of recreational vehicles, and you can even get repair insurance when you buy a car. Do you think there'll ever be a time when you'll find it necessary to use such policies? Take a minute to think about this question before reading on.

While homeowners and automobile insurance policies represent the basic protection needed by most families, there are still other insurance contracts

automobile insurance plan
An arrangement that provides automobile insurance to drivers who have been refused coverage under normal procedures; formerly called an *assigned risk plan*.

financial responsibility laws
Laws that attempt to force motorists to be financially responsible for the damages they become legally obligated to pay as a result of automobile accidents.

EXHIBIT 11.5

A Guide to Discounts at the Top Ten Auto Insurance Companies

There are over a dozen different types of discounts offered by the major auto insurance companies. However, as seen in this guide, the amount of discount given will vary by company.

Insurance Company	Driver Training	Good Student	Good Driving Record	Student Away at School	Car Pools	Antitheft Devices
State Farm	10% where available	5–25%	5–10%	Covered under parents' rate	10–15%	5–10% where available
Allstate	Not offered	Not offered	10–15%	30–35%	Not offered	Up to 20%
Farmers Insurance	10% where available	25% in all states 20% in Oregon Not available in Michigan	20% in all states. Not available in Michigan	Up to 50%	Not offered	5–15% Illinois only
Nationwide	10% where available	5–25%	No discount, but higher rates for bad driving record	Up to 40%	Credit for lower weekly mileage	5–10% where available
Aetna Life & Casualty	4–7%	12–15%	Not offered	Not offered	10%	5%
Liberty Mutual	10%	15–20%	No discount, but have a feature in policy	Not offered	10%	10–15%
United Services	Up to 10%	Up to 25%	5%	Up to 25%	Not offered	Up to 15%
Travelers	15%	Up to 25%	20%	Up to 50%	15%	5–20%
United States Fidelity & Guaranty	10–15%	15–18%	15%	35%	15%	Active device 5%, passive device 15%
Geico	10%	7–25% Virginia only	3–20%	20–50%	Credit for lower weekly mileage	5–15% New York/ New Hampshire only

Source: Reprinted from "Driving a Bargain in Auto Insurance" by Katharine L. Ramsdeu, *Sylvia Porter's Personal Finance,* August 1985, 58–59. Copyright 1985 by The Sylvia Porter's Personal Finance Magazine Company. Reprinted by courtesy of *Sylvia Porter's Personal Finance Magazine,* and may not be reproduced without written permission of the Publisher.

that some people may find appropriate. Among those discussed here are the personal property floater policy, umbrella personal liability policy, mobile-home insurance, boat insurance, recreational vehicle insurance, automobile repair insurance, earthquake insurance, flood insurance, professional liability insurance, and group plans.

Personal Property Floater (PPF) Policy

This policy provides comprehensive coverage on a blanket basis for virtually all of the insured's personal property. It is designed for persons who desire the maximum protection available. In fact, the personal property coverage of this form of insur-

Passive Restraints	Senior Citizens	Professional: Farmer, Government Employee, Etc.	Defensive Driving	Multicar Discount	Low-Mileage Discount	Other
Not offered	5–10%	Farmers, 10%	5% where available	10%	Less than 7,500/year, 10%	—
Airbags only—30%	10–15%	Farmers, 10%	Not offered	10%	Not offered	Economy car, 15%
Not offered	10% (North Dakota, Arkansas, Illinois) 5% (Michigan)	Farmers, 20%	Only in connection with senior citizen discount	10–20%	5–15% with special rate classification applications	After 2 years, nonsmoker, 15–20% (not available in Michigan)
30% off medical and no-fault for airbags only	10%	Farmers, 10–25%	5–10% where available	Up to 15%	Less than 8,000/year, 10% where available	—
30% off medical and personal liability where available	10–20%	Not offered	5–10% where available	20%	Not offered	More cars than drivers, 10%
20% off liability, 30% off no-fault	Not offered	Farmers, 25%	5–10%	20%	Less than 7,500/year, 15%	—
30% on some coverages	5%	Not offered	Up to 10%	Up to 20%	15%	—
15–30% off medical or no-fault	5–15%	Not offered	5–10%	15–20%	Less than 7,500/year, 10%	—
30% on medical or no-fault	10%	Farmers, 10%	13% for 36 months after course completion	20%	Not offered	—
30% on medical or personal injury protection	Up to 18%	Not offered	10%	5–27%	13%	—

ance is the same as that found on HO-3 form contracts with special endorsements attached. Because floater coverage is on an all-risk basis, the only property or perils not covered are those listed in the exclusions. Most notably these exclusions are for wear and tear, damage from insects or vermin, nuclear energy, and gradual deterioration.

A personal property floater policy offers protection on a blanket basis supplemental to coverage under a homeowners policy. In addition, many types of scheduled personal property floaters are available to supplement coverage under a homeowners contract. These coverages are especially useful for the types of property that may not receive

EXHIBIT 11.6

Financial Responsibilty Requirements by State

Most states have financial responsibility laws that require motorists involved in auto accidents to furnish proof of financial accountability up to certain minimum dollar limits.

State	Liability Limits[a]	State	Liability Limits[a]
Alabama	20/40/10/or 50	Montana	25/50/5
Alaska	50/100/25 or 125	Nebraska	25/50/25
Arizona	15/30/10	Nevada	15/30/10
Arkansas	25/50/15	New Hampshire	25/50/25
California	15/30/5	New Jersey	15/30/5
Colorado	25/50/15	New Mexico	25/50/10
Connecticut	20/40/10	New York	10/20/5[b]
Delaware	15/30/10 or 40	North Carolina	25/50/10
District of Columbia	10/20/5	North Dakota	25/50/25
Florida	10/20/5	Ohio	12.5/25/7.5
Georgia	15/30/10	Oklahoma	10/20/10
Hawaii	25/unlimited/10	Oregon	25/50/25
Idaho	25/50/15	Pennsylvania	15/30/5
Illinois	15/30/10	Rhode Island	25/50/10
Indiana	25/50/10	South Carolina	15/30/5
Iowa	20/40/15	South Dakota	25/50/25
Kansas	25/50/10	Tennessee	20/40/10 or 50
Kentucky	10/20/5 or 25	Texas	20/14/15
Louisiana	10/20/10	Utah	20/40/10 or 30
Maine	20/40/10	Vermont	20/40/10
Maryland	20/40/10	Virginia	25/50/10
Massachusetts	10/20/5	Washington	25/50/10
Michigan	20/40/10	West Virginia	20/40/10
Minnesota	30/60/10	Wisconsin	25/50/10
Mississippi	10/20/5	Wyoming	25/50/20
Missouri	25/50/10		

[a] The laws of all states express the requirement in terms of *split limits*. For example, if the chart shows "25/50/10," the law requires that the policy provide at least $25,000 for bodily injury to each person, $50,000 for all bodily injury, and $10,000 for property damage, each accident.

The insurance laws of some states also state the requirement in terms of a *combined single limit*. For example, if the chart shows "15/30/10 or 40," the law provides that a policy with a combined single limit of at least $40,000 will also satisfy the requirement. A combined single limit of $40,000 means that the insurance will pay up to $40,000 for all bodily injury and property damage arising out of each accident.

[b] 50/100 for wrongful death.

Source: George E. Rejda, *Principles of Insurance,* 3d ed. (Glenview, Ill.: Scott, Foresman, 1989), p. 220.

adequate protection under the homeowners policy because of limits on amounts payable and perils insured. Coverage under a scheduled personal property floater is extensive and is a good way to guard against loss of or damage to expensive belongings. Some of the more popular policies apply to furs, jewelry, photographic equipment, silverware, fine art and antiques, musical instruments, and stamp and coin collections.

Umbrella Personal Liability Policy

Persons with relatively high levels of income and assets may find the **umbrella personal liability policy** useful. It provides excess liability coverage for both homeowners and automobile insurance as well as coverage in some areas not provided for in either of these policies. These policies are often sold with limits of $1 million or more. In addition, some include excess coverage for a family's major medical insurance.

Because upper-income individuals are often viewed as good targets for liability claims, umbrella personal liability protection can be a desirable coverage. In addition, the premiums are usually quite reasonable for the broad coverage afforded ($100 to $300 a year for as much as $1 million in coverage). While the protection is written on a comprehensive basis, it does contain a number of exclusions of which purchasers should be aware.

As a rule, you must obtain an umbrella personal liability policy if you want liability coverage of $1 million or more. **Fact:** Such policies provide added liability protection for both homeowners and automobile insurance (simultaneously). They are intended primarily for upper-income families, who are often viewed as prime targets for large liability claims.

Mobile-Home Insurance

Several hundred thousand mobile homes are sold each year, and several million now serve as homes for young couples, transients (such as those whose jobs involve a number of moves from one place to another), and retirees. Because of this widespread use, insurers offer special package insurance policies for mobile-home owners just as they do for owners of single-family residences. Coverage on mobile homes may be written to offer protection on a blanket basis against the same perils that are covered on an HO-2 form. In addition, personal property and personal liability coverage is included. Although the coverage offered for mobile-home owners is similar to that available for more permanent structures, rates per $100 of protection are typically higher for mobile homes because they present a greater chance of wind and fire loss. Total losses on mobile homes occur much more frequently than they do for either wood or brick houses.

Boat Insurance

Most people underinsure their boats. This situation exists partly because homeowners policies offer limited protection for boat owners, which misleads many into a false sense of security. However, the fact is, only boats less than 26 feet in length (or some other stipulated maximum) or those with motors under 25 horsepower are typically afforded liability coverage under a homeowners policy. Moreover, the physical damage coverage is usually limited to only a few perils, and in most cases reimbursement cannot exceed $1,000. Consequently, for all but small fishing or sailboats, the coverage provided by the homeowners policy is insufficient. Fortunately, this problem is easily remedied through

either a boat and motor endorsement of the homeowners policy, or a specially designed boat-owner's policy. These endorsements or policies typically contain liability, physical damage and theft, and medical payments coverage. The liability and medical payments protection is similar to that offered in an automobile policy.

The physical damage and theft coverage under boat policies can be either limited or comprehensive, excluding only a few perils such as nuclear explosion, warfare, and government actions. Perils commonly insured against are fire and lightning, collision, overturning of a transporting land conveyance, windstorms, and theft. Other contingencies that can be covered include damage resulting from submersion, vandalism, a motor falling overboard, and burglary from a closed and locked garage or boathouse. Because the physical damage and theft provisions of boat policies are not highly standardized, you should not assume that coverage exists for any given type of loss. Make certain that your insurance agent explains which coverage applies and which losses are not covered.

Recreational Vehicle Insurance

Although a consistent definition of the term "recreational vehicle" does not exist, the following vehicles generally fall within this classification: all-terrain vehicles, antique automobiles, dune buggies, go-carts, minibikes, trail motorcycles, camping vehicles (both motorized and trailer type), snowmobiles, and customized vans. Complete coverage generally is available for these vehicles, including bodily injury and property damage liability, medical payments, physical damage, and theft. You may have to shop around for the policy that best fits your needs, since not all insurance companies write coverage for recreational vehicles. Among those that do, more restrictions are likely to apply than on, say, a personal automobile policy. Rates

---

umbrella personal liability policy
An insurance policy that provides excess liability coverage for both homeowners and automobile insurance as well as coverage in some areas not provided for in either of those policies.

will also vary substantially depending on the age of the driver, how the vehicle is used, and the location of the policy owner. As with insuring a boat, when insuring a recreational vehicle you need to discuss with a property insurance agent how best to insure your recreational vehicle, giving particular attention to who and what are covered and where and when they are covered.

Many types of recreational vehicles—including motorcycles and mopeds—can be insured under the personal auto policy through a *Miscellaneous Type Vehicle Endorsement*. With this endorsement, insureds get the same protection for their recreational vehicles that they do for their private passenger automobiles.

Automobile Repair Insurance

Most automobile dealers today offer plans under which a person buying an automobile can pay an additional fee to warrant the repairs resulting from certain mechanical problems. These plans, however, aren't really a form of insurance, but rather an arrangement whereby a fee is paid up front in exchange for future contracted services.

Earthquake Insurance

Although most people think of California when earthquakes are mentioned, areas in every other state are also subject to this type of loss. At the present time, very few homeowners buy this coverage even though the premiums are relatively inexpensive. Surprisingly, the vast majority of Californians were without earthquake coverage when the major San Fernando Valley quake occurred in 1971.

Flood Insurance

Before 1969 flood was regarded by most private insurers as an uninsurable peril because the risk could not be spread among enough people who were not located in flood-prone areas. But in 1969, the federal government established a subsidized flood insurance program in cooperation with pri-

vate insurance agents, who can now sell this low-cost coverage to homeowners and tenants *living in communities that have been designated as part of the federal flood program*. In addition, the flood insurance program is encouraging communities to initiate land-use controls in order to reduce future flood losses.

Professional Liability Insurance

Lawsuits against medical doctors for malpractice have increased substantially in recent years—in fact, liability claims against nearly all types of professionals, including lawyers, architects, financial planners, and engineers, are also rising rapidly. Professional liability insurance is available to these individuals, but because of the increasing number of claims, rates are skyrocketing, while stricter underwriting standards are being imposed by insurers.

Group Plans

As a benefit to members of some groups (labor unions, credit unions, fraternal organizations, and various other organizations), group property and liability plans are being introduced. Unlike life and health insurance agreements, these plans are not true group plans because they do not issue a single master policy to the group. Instead, they are arrangements for mass marketing homeowners and automobile policies, and the policies are individually sold and issued. The primary benefit of group plans is that the lower marketing expense of the insurance company is passed along to the group members in the form of lower premiums.

Some groups also have **group legal insurance**. These plans are fee-for-services agreements into which the group enters with a given law firm on behalf of its members. The plans typically cover only basic legal matters such as divorce, writing of wills, small claims settlement, and landlord-tenant problems. In some cases, the group member is entitled to lower charges on other legal services provided by the participating firm.

BUYING INSURANCE AND SETTLING CLAIMS

Buying property and liability insurance requires a decision on what kinds of protection you need. What factors would you consider in making this decision? How about when it comes to filing a claim with an insurance company—do you know what's involved in such a process and how to go about filing a claim? Take some time to think about these questions before going on.

When preparing to buy property and liability insurance, you should first develop an inventory of exposures to loss and arrange them from highest to lowest priority. Losses that lend themselves to insurance protection are those that seldom occur but have the potential for being substantial—for example, damage to a home and its contents or liability arising out of a negligence claim. Less important, but nevertheless desirable, is insurance to cover losses that could be disruptive to the financial plans of a family even though they would not result in insolvency. Such risks include physical damage to automobiles, boats, and other personal property of moderate value. Lowest priority should be given to insuring exposures that can easily be covered by savings or from current income. *Low-dollar deductibles, for instance, usually serve only to increase premiums.* Likewise, personal property of minor value, such as an old auto (one that is not a collectible), normally does not merit coverage. In addition to inventorying exposures and deciding on appropriate coverage and deductibles, you should exercise care in selecting both the property insurance agent and the insurer. Also, a knowledge of the procedures involved in settling property and liability claims can help you obtain maximum benefits from policies when claims do arise.

Property and Liability Insurance Agents

Most property insurance agents can be classified as either captive or independent. A **captive agent** is one who represents only one insurance company and is more or less an employee of that company. Allstate, Nationwide, and State Farm are major insurance companies that market through captive agents. **Independent agents**, in contrast, typically represent between two and ten different insurance companies. These agents may place your coverage with any of the companies with which they have an agency relationship as long as you meet the underwriting standards of that company. Names of companies that may be familiar to you that operate through independent agents include Aetna, Hartford, and Travelers. It is difficult to generalize with respect to the superiority of agents. In some cases an independent agent will provide the best combination of low-cost insurance and good service, while in others the captive agent might be the better choice. Because of wide differences in premiums charged and services rendered, it usually does pay to shop around.

Property insurance agents should be willing to take the time to go over your total property and liability insurance exposures with you. As you should now know, there is much more to the purchase of property insurance than simply signing a homeowners and an automobile insurance application. Decisions must be made about types of property and uses, perils to be covered, limits, deductibles, and floater policies, as well as other items that have been discussed throughout this

group legal insurance
A type of insurance plan consisting of a fee-for-service agreement between a group and a law firm; typically covers only such basic legal matters as divorce, wills, and small claims settlement.

captive agent
An insurance agent who represents only the company that employs him or her.

independent agent
An insurance agent who may place coverage with any company with which he or she has an agency relationship as long as the insured meets that company's underwriting standards.

chapter. An agent should be willing to talk with clients about these items. In the property insurance industry, agents who meet various experiential and education requirements, including passing a series of written examinations, qualify for the **Chartered Property and Casualty Underwriter (CPCU)** designation. Agents who have been awarded CPCUs have proven knowledge and experience in their field.

Property and Liability Insurance Companies

Although the selection of an agent is probably the most important step in the purchase of property and liability insurance, you should also ask some questions about the company, including its financial soundness, claims-settlement practices, and the geographic extent of its operations (this could be important if you are involved in an accident 1,000 miles from home). The agent should be a good source of information about the technical aspects of a company's operations, whereas friends and acquaintances often can provide insight into its claims-settlement policy.

Settling Property and Liability Claims

Generally speaking, insurance companies settle claims promptly and fairly, especially for life and health insurance coverages. In settling property and liability claims, though, some chance for claimant-insurer disagreement does exist. The following discussion reviews the claims-settlement process and the people who participate in it. First, however, let's consider what you should do immediately following an accident.

First Steps Following an Accident. After an accident, the names and addresses of all witnesses, drivers, occupants, and injured parties, along with the license numbers of the automobiles involved, should be recorded. Law enforcement officers as well as your insurance agent should be immediately notified of the accident. You should never admit liability at the scene of an accident or discuss it with anyone other than the police and your insurer. Remember: Prior the determination of who, if anyone, is legally liable for an accident, the requisites of liability must be established. Also, the

duties of the police are to assess the probability of a law violation and maintain order at the scene of an accident—not to make judgments with respect to liability.

Steps in Claims Settlement. If you're involved in an accident, one of the first things you're going to have to decide is whether or not you even want to file a claim. If it's a minor "fender bender," you may be better off paying for the damages out of your own pocket—particularly if you have a relatively high deductible (of $500 to $1,000). Be careful, however, if there's another party involved—and *never* follow this procedure if there's any kind of bodily injury to any of the parties! Even if you don't file a claim, let your agent know that you've been involved in an accident and discuss the incident with him or her. As the accompanying *Issues in Money Management* box points out, deciding on whether or not to file a claim is not as easy as it sounds—there are a number of factors that have to be considered.

Should you opt to file a claim, it'll probably involve the following steps. First, you must give notice to the company that a loss (or potential for loss) has occurred. Timely notice is extremely important because it leads to the second step, which is the investigation of the claim. To properly investigate a claim, insurance company personnel may have to talk to witnesses or law enforcement officers, gather physical evidence to determine whether the claimed loss is covered by the policy, and check to make sure that the date of the loss falls within the policy period. If you delay filing your claim, you hinder the insurer's ability to check the facts. *All policies specify the time period within which you must give notice.* Failure to report can result in your loss of the right to collect.

Third, you must prove your loss. This step usually requires you to give a sworn statement. When applicable, you must also show medical bills, an inventory and certified value of lost property (for example, a written inventory, photographs, and purchase receipts), an employer statement of lost wages, and, if possible, physical evidence of damage (X-rays if you claim a back injury; a broken window or pried door if you claim a break-in and theft at your house). After you have submitted proof of loss, the insurer either (1) pays you the amount you asked for; (2) offers you a lesser amount; or

(3) denies that the company has legal responsibility under the terms of your policy. In the case of a disputed amount—when you are a named insured or covered family member—most policies provide for claim arbitration. You hire a third party, the company hires a third party, and these two arbitrators together select one more person. When any two of the three arbitrators reach agreement, their decision binds you and the company to their solution.

When a company denies responsibility, you do not get the right of arbitration. In such an instance, the company is saying the loss does not fall under the policy coverage. You must then either forget the claim or bring in an attorney or, perhaps, a public adjustor (discussed next).

Filing a property or liability claim is quick and easy to do: Just call your agent, supply a few basic details, and look for your check in a few days. **Fantasy:** Filing a property or liability claim is often a detailed and time-consuming process wherein you must prove your loss. The insurance company can offer you an amount less than the loss you claim or deny your claim altogether.

Claims Adjustment. Usually the first person to call when you need to file a claim is your insurance agent. If your loss is relatively minor, the agent can quickly process it. If it is more complex, your company will probably assign a claims adjustor to the case.

Adjustors. The **claims adjustor** works either for the insurance company, as an independent adjustor, or for an adjustment bureau. In any case, the adjustor is primarily looking out for the interests of the company—which might very well be to keep you, its customer, satisfied. However, many claimants think insurance companies have more money than they know what to do with and are out to collect all that is possible. Thus, the adjustor walks a fine line: He or she must diligently question and

investigate, while at the same time offering service to minimize settlement delays and financial hardship. To help your own interest, you should cooperate with the adjustor and answer inquiries honestly—while keeping in mind that the company writes the adjustor's paycheck.

Public Adjustors and Attorneys. To this point, we have been referring primarily to the claims that you collect from your own insurance company. In accidents in which a question of fault arises, you may have to file a claim against a negligent party's insurer. In these instances, the insurer will still use an adjustor, but this person will be looking out for the insurer's (and its policyholders') economic interests without the problem of keeping you satisfied. If you are not happy with the offered settlement, you might have to hire an attorney to negotiate the claim for you. Because the attorney will have a better understanding of the law and the legal provisions of your policy than you do, hiring one greatly improves your chances of collecting an amount you're entitled to. Keep in mind that for their services, attorneys will often charge 25 to 50 percent of any amount they get for you (the exact amount of the fee is negotiable). Many times, though, the use of a costly attorney is worthwhile if you are not being treated fairly by the insurance company's adjustor.

Chartered Property and Casualty Underwriter (CPCU)

An agent who has met various experiential and educational requirements and passed a series of written examinations in the fields of property and liability insurance.

claims adjustor

An insurance specialist, employed by an insurance company, an adjustment bureau, or self-employed, who investigates claims.

ISSUES IN MONEY MANAGEMENT

To File a Claim, or Not to File a Claim—That Is the Question

Last winter, Gene Robbins was driving just 15 mph, hit an ice patch, and skidded into a tree. His insurer paid the bill: $650, minus a $200 deductible. A few months later, Gene's teenage son backed the same car into a neighbor's empty parked car, denting the door. Again, the insurer paid: $800 net. Then Gene received his new insurance bill—with a 30-percent hike in premiums.

That 30-percent rate rise was a blow, especially since Gene's insurance already cost a bundle, with a teenage driver in the house. Would he have been better off not making the claims, paying out of his own pocket instead? That's not an uncommon question, but the answer isn't necessarily clear.

On the one hand, too many claims in too short a time or for too much money *can boost your premiums considerably and may jeopardize your cover-*

age. On the other hand, not filing might risk serious financial liability later on. Most experts advise that you not take any chances where there's potential liability for serious damage to someone else's property or any damage to a person. But what about the gray areas, such as Gene experienced? He wasn't driving recklessly when he skidded. No one was in the car Gene's son hit, and repair costs were moderate. What would your best move be in a similar situation? The following information can help you make an informed decision. If you have any doubts, check with an attorney as well.

How the insurers figure it

Most insurers work under a concept of "chargeable" accidents, though definitions vary somewhat among companies and states. State Farm, for example, considers an accident

chargeable when the company must pay at least $400 to $600, depending on locale. Exceptions include when your legally parked car is hit, or the other driver gets a moving violation and you don't. Whatever their definition of chargeable, all insurers get nervous when you file more than one claim in a short period—two claims in three years, or three in five, for example.

How much will premiums rise?

Some companies apply simple formulas: for example, an extra 10 percent on your premium for your first accident with a chargeable claim, an additional 20 percent for a second chargeable claim within three years, up to 50 percent more for a third claim. Other companies forgive a first accident if you've been a customer for several years, but premiums could take

SUMMARY

Property and liability insurance protects against the loss of real and personal property that can occur from various types of perils. In addition, such insurance protects against loss from lawsuits based on negligence.

- Most homeowners insurance contracts are divided into two major sections. Section I covers the dwelling unit, accompanying structures, and the personal property of the insured. Section II pertains mainly to comprehensive coverage for

personal liability and medical payments.

- Except for the house and garage, which are covered on a replacement basis, homeowners insurance normally provides for the payment of *all losses on an actual cash value basis,* subject to applicable deductibles and policy limits. However, for an additional premium, you usually can obtain replacement-cost coverage on personal belongings.
- Automobile insurance policies usually contain

a big leap—at least 40 percent, and as much as 100 percent— for a second incident within three years or some other specified period.

Can they drop your policy?

Companies aren't eager to cancel insurance policies, as long as you can pay ever-higher premiums. Even if you are among the few who are cut, the general rule is that *someone* will insure you, presuming you have a driver's license. The hitch: Your claim record could get you turned down at a new company, or at least cost higher rates. Ultimately, you may have to go to the "assigned risk" pool or a similar plan, often at double the regular cost.

Your agent is key

Get her or him to explain how your present insurer defines chargeable accidents and how much rates will rise under what circumstances. How long do rate hikes stay in force? What happens if the company finds you have avoided making claims? (Some insurers will cancel.) If you don't like your insurer's rules, shop around with the same questions in hand. You may find a better deal. *Also find out whether your agent is willing after an accident to help you figure whether filing a claim or paying the bill yourself will cost less.*

If you're tempted to settle on your own, whatever your reason, follow the precautions in the section below.

What if You Don't File?

Insurers stress that today's minor accident may turn into next year's personal injury lawsuit. If you don't file a timely claim, they say, you may jeopardize your coverage. Still, it can be tempting not to file under certain circumstances. If so:

- *Always* report to your agent any accident involving another person or someone else's property. Hopefully, the agent will help you decide the smart course to take (see above).
- Try to get a formal release (drawn up by an attorney and witnessed) from the other party, if any, indicating that he or she will not sue. If you pay anything, be sure to get a release saying "paid in full." This isn't guaranteed protection, but it may help.
- If you don't intend to make small claims, *take a large deductible on your policy.* You'll save money.

Source: Adapted from Margaret Daly, "Car Insurance—Is It Ever Smart *Not* to File a Claim?" *Better Homes and Gardens,* September 1987, pp. 91, 93.

---

provisions that protect the insured from loss due to personal liability, uninsured motorists, medical payments, collision (property damage to the vehicle), and comprehensive coverage (which applies to nearly any other type of noncollision damage your car might suffer, such as theft or vandalism).

- In addition to the major forms of homeowners and automobile insurance, a variety of property and liability coverages is available, including personal property floater policies, umbrella personal liability policies, mobile-home insurance, boat insurance, recreational vehicle insurance, auto-

mobile repair insurance, earthquake insurance, flood insurance, and professional liability insurance.

- Before buying property and liability coverage, you should evaluate your exposure to loss and determine the coverage needed. You should also carefully select both the insurance agent(s) and the insurance company in order to obtain appropriate coverage at a reasonable price and— equally important—make sure that your agent and company have reputations for fair claims-settlement practices.

QUESTIONS AND PROBLEMS

1. Briefly explain the fundamental concepts related to property and liability insurance.

2. Explain the principle of indemnity. Are there any limits imposed on the amount an insured may collect under this principle?

3. Patricia Murphree's luxurious home in the suburb of Broken Arrow, Oklahoma, was recently gutted in a fire. Her living and dining rooms were completely destroyed, and the damaged personal property had a replacement price of $27,000. The average age of the damaged personal property was 5 years, and its useful life was estimated to be 15 years. What is the maximum amount the insurance company would pay Patricia, assuming it reimburses on an actual cash value basis?

4. Explain the right of subrogation. How does this feature help lower insurance costs?

5. Describe how the coinsurance feature works. Assume that Clayton Barrow had a property insurance policy of $100,000 on his home. Would a 90 percent coinsurance clause be better than an 80 percent clause in such a policy? Give reasons to support your answer.

6. What are the perils against which most properties are insured under various types of homeowners policies?

7. What types of property are covered under a homeowners policy? Are the following included in the coverage: (a) an African parrot, (b) a motorbike, (c) Avon cosmetics held for sale, and (d) Tupperware for home use?

8. Describe (a) types of losses, (b) persons, (c) locations, and (d) periods that are covered under a homeowners policy.

9. Describe replacement cost coverage, and compare this coverage to actual cash value. Which is preferable?

10. What are deductibles? Do they apply to either liability or medical payments coverage under the homeowners policy?

11. Briefly explain the major coverages available under the personal auto policy (PAP). Which persons are insured under (a) uninsured motorists coverage and (b) automobile medical payments insurance?

12. Explain the nature of (a) automobile collision insurance and (b) automobile comprehensive insurance.

13. Define auto no-fault insurance, and discuss its pros and cons.

14. Describe the important factors that influence the availability and cost of auto insurance.

15. Discuss the role of financial responsibility laws, and describe the two basic types of laws currently employed.

16. Briefly describe the following property and liability insurance coverages: (a) personal property floater (PPF) policies, (b) umbrella personal liability policies, (c) mobile-home insurance, (d) boat insurance, (e) earthquake insurance, and (f) flood insurance.

17. What guidelines should be used to distinguish between exposure to high-priority and low-priority risk when buying property and liability insurance?

18. Differentiate between captive and independent insurance agents. What characteristics should you look for when choosing both an insurance agent and an insurance company for purposes of buying property and/or liability insurance?

19. Briefly describe the key aspects of the claims settlement process, explaining what to do after an accident, the steps in claim settlement, and the role and types of claims adjustors.

CASE PROBLEMS

11.1 The Salvatis' Homeowners Insurance Decision

Phil and Anita Salvati, ages 30 and 28, respectively, were recently married in Chicago. Phil is an electrical engineer with Geophysical Century, an oil exploration company. Anita has a master's degree in special education and teaches at a local junior high school. After living in an apartment for six months, the Salvatis have negotiated the purchase of a new home in a rapidly growing Chicago suburb. Republic Savings and Loan Association has approved their loan request for $108,000, which represents 90 percent of the $120,000 purchase price. Prior to closing the loan, the Salvatis must obtain homeowners insurance for the home. The Salvatis currently have an HO-4 renter's insurance policy, which they purchased from Phil's tennis partner, Kelly Duvall, who is an agent with Kramer's Insurance Company. In order to learn about the types of available homeowners insurance, Phil has discussed their situation with Kelly, who has offered a variety of homeowners policies for Phil's and Anita's consideration. He has recommended that the Salvatis purchase an HO-3 policy, since it would provide them with comprehensive coverage.

Questions

1. What forms of homeowners insurance are available? Which forms should the Salvatis consider?
2. What are the perils against which the home and its contents should be insured?
3. Discuss the types of loss protection provided by the homeowners policies under consideration.
4. What advice would you give the Salvatis regarding Kelly's suggestion? What coverage should they buy?

11.2   Auto Insurance for the Turners

Marjorie and Rodney Turner, of Phoenix, Arizona, are a couple in their late 20s. Rodney is a loan officer at the Frontier National Bank of Arizona, and Marjorie is the merchandising manager at a major department store. At present the Turners own one car, but they have decided to use Rodney's Christmas bonus as a down payment on a second car. One Saturday afternoon in late December, they visited Chuck Thomas's Auto Mall, where they purchased a new, fully equipped Pontiac for $13,500. In order to obtain insurance on the car, Rodney called his agent, Jane Cunningham, who represents Farmers Insurance Company. He explained his auto insurance needs, and Jane said she would investigate the various options for him. Three days later, Rodney and Jane got together to look over the alternative coverages. Jane offered several proposals, including various combinations of the following coverages: (a) basic automobile liability insurance, (b) uninsured motorists coverage, (c) automobile medical payments insurance, (d) automobile collision insurance, and (e) comprehensive automobile insurance.

Questions

1. Describe the key features of these insurance coverages.
2. Are there any limitations on these coverages? Explain.
3. Indicate the persons who would be protected under each of these coverages.
4. What kind of insurance coverages would you recommend the Turners purchase? Explain your recommendation.

FOR MORE INFORMATION

General Information Articles

Goldschmidt, Ellen, "To Claim, or Not to Claim . . .," *Sylvia Porter's Personal Finance,* March 1987, pp. 87–92.

Henry, Ed, "10 Ways to Cut the Cost of Car Insurance," *Changing Times,* July 1988, pp. 47–54.

Lynch, Richard A., "How to Save $500 a Year on Insurance . . .," *Money,* September 1986, pp. 85–92.

McGrath, Anne, "The Right Way to Cut Insurance Costs," *U.S. News & World Report,* September 1, 1986, pp. 53–54.

Paulson, Morton C., "Car Insurance: Picking the Policy," *Changing Times,* February 1987, p. 62.

————, "Car Insurance: Cut the Cost of Your Coverage," *Changing Times,* May 1987, pp. 59–62.

————, "Making Sure Your Insurance Pays," *Changing Times,* October 1988, pp. 111–116.

Porter, Hal and Suzan Richmond, "Home Insurance: Protecting Almost Everything You Own," *Changing Times,* June 1988, pp. 26–33.

Wiener, Leonard, "Will Your Car Insurance Vanish?" *U.S. News & World Report,* January 9, 1989, p. 62.

Government Documents & Other Publications

Buyer's Guide to Insurance: What the Companies Won't Tell You. National Insurance Consumers Organization; 121 N. Payne St.; Alexandria, VA 22314.

1. Use the needs approached to calculate the amount of additional insurance needed on Mark's life. Assume that Mark would like Ana to receive enough money from his life insurance to pay off all of the consumer debt (but not the home mortgage). He would also like to provide an extra $20,000 to add to their emergency fund and $3,000 to cover final expenses. They estimate that Ana's monthly living expenses would be approximately $2,500 while she is working and $1,800 after she retires. Ana's monthly income while working is estimated to be $2,448 and $0 after retirement. Investment income should be about $50 a month for the rest of her life. She should also receive about $1,200 a month from social security once she retires. Assuming Ana retires at age 65, she has 41 years of work and about 20 years of retirement to look forward to (given the average life expectancy of a woman her age). Mark and Ana currently have about $9,000 in assets that could be used for Ana's support in addition to the group life policy Mark has through his employer.

2. Use the needs approach to calculate the amount of additional insurance needed on Ana's life. Use the same assumptions as above except that Ana would also like her life insurance proceeds to provide $5,000 for Mark to return to college for his MBA. In addition, Mark's monthly income while working will be only $2,042, but during retirement he will receive $800 a month from his employer pension plan in addition to $1,200 a month from social security. Assuming he retires at age 65, he will be working 40 more years and be retired 18 years. In addition to their savings, Ana has a group life policy through her employer to supplement Mark's needs.

3. Evaluate the group term life policies Mark and Ana currently have. Should they keep these policies and/or buy additional life insurance coverage? If so, how much, and what type? Using the examples in this text, calculate the approximate cost of the recommended policies.

4. Recommend appropriate beneficiary and settlement options for Mark and Ana's policies.

5. Calculate Mark's disability income needs. Assume that he does not want to rely on social security or other government programs and that no company programs are available. He has 30 days of paid sick leave accumulated. How much disability coverage does he need? What length of waiting period and duration of benefits would you recommend? Using the examples in this text, calculate the approximate cost of this coverage.

6. Calculate Ana's disability income needs. Use the same assumptions about government and company benefits as in Question 5. Ana has 15 days of paid sick leave accumulated. Disability benefits from her current disability policy would be tax-free, since she pays the premiums on the policy. Does Ana need additional coverage? If so, how much? What terms would you recommend? Approximately how much would it cost?

7. Evaluate Mark's group major medical policy in terms of maximum limit, deductible, participation, etc. What is the maximum dollar amount of covered expenses Mark would have to pay per year (assuming the insurance benefits remain below the maximum limit)? Is this an acceptable policy for Mark, considering his health and financial conditions?

8. Evaluate Ana's group HMO coverage. What are the potential out-of-pocket costs under this coverage? Is this an acceptable policy for Ana, considering her health and financial conditions?

9. Would you recommend that Ana be covered under Mark's policy or vice versa? Why? If so, how much would it cost?

10. Evaluate Mark and Ana's homeowners insurance needs. Do they need homeowners insurance? If so, why, and what HO form is appropriate for them? How much coverage do you recommend for their personal property, personal liability, etc.? Approximately how much will the recommended coverage cost?

11. Evaluate Mark and Ana's auto insurance policy. Is their coverage adequate for their insurance needs? Recommend any needed changes. Approximately how much would the recommended changes cost?

12. Do Mark and Ana need any other types of insurance coverage? If so, what types and why? About how much will the additional insurance cost?

13. Revise Mark and Ana's budget to reflect the change in expenditures caused by all of your insurance recommendations.

WILLIAMS *Insurance Needs*

PART  V

Managing Investments

CHAPTER 12

Investing in Stocks and Bonds

Financial Facts or Fantasies

Are the following statements financial facts (true) or fantasies (false)?

- You would have to save $2,500 a year in order to end up with a $25,000 nest egg in ten years.
- A good investment is one that offers a positive rate of return.
- Income stocks have relatively high dividend yields and, as such, appeal to individuals who seek a high level of current income.
- Putting your money into stocks that offer dividend reinvestment plans is a great way of building up your investment capital.
- When interest rates go down, bond prices also go down because such securities become less valuable.
- Convertible bonds are so named because they can be exchanged for a set number of shares of common stock.

Have you ever stopped to think about all the different ways you could invest your money? In addition to savings and short-term investment vehicles, you could choose common and preferred stocks, bonds, convertible securities, limited partnerships and annuities, mutual funds, real estate, commodities, financial futures, and puts and calls. Some of these vehicles are highly conservative and easy to understand; others are very speculative and subject investors to considerable risk. With such an extensive menu to choose from, it's easy to understand why a basic knowledge of these securities is so important. In most cases, the cornerstone of a successful long-term investment program is not luck but *know-how!* The knowledgeable and informed investor understands the world of investing and knows how and when to use the various investment vehicles and strategies to his or her advantage. While knowledge alone will not guarantee success in the uncertain world of investing, it certainly will help you avoid unnecessary exposure to loss. Moreover, a basic understanding of investments is important from a financial planning perspective because *investing is the vehicle through which we reach many of our financial goals.* Alan and Barbara Tracey, for example, regularly invest money as a way to build up a fund for their daughter's college education. In addition, they invest a sizable amount each year as part of their retirement plans and also put away money toward the funds that Barbara feels she will need in the next five to eight years to set up her own law practice. For now, the Traceys confine most of their investing to blue-chip stocks, high-grade bonds, and a few highly regarded mutual funds. However, as they learn more about investing, they intend to be a little more aggressive with their capital.

THE OBJECTIVES AND REWARDS OF INVESTING ▪

> Getting the most from your investment capital requires not only a clear understanding of your investment objectives, but also a familiarity with the concepts of risk and return. Assume you've just inherited some money and have decided to invest a big chunk of it (say, $40,000). What kind of investment characteristics would you look for when deciding where to put your money? Are dividends and current income important to you? How about capital appreciation? What kind of risk would you be willing to tolerate? These are important questions for an investor—stop to think about them before reading on.

People invest their money for all sorts of reasons. Some do it as a way to accumulate the down payment on a new home; others do it as a way to supplement their income; still others invest in order to build up a nest egg for retirement. Actually, the term "investment" means different things to different people. Millions of people *invest* regularly in such securities as stocks, bonds, and mutual funds; others *speculate* in commodities or options. **Investing** is generally considered to take more of a long-term perspective and is viewed as the process of purchasing securities in which stability of value and level of returns are somewhat predictable. **Speculating**, on the other hand, is viewed as a short-term activity that involves the buying and selling of securities in which future value and expected returns are highly uncertain. Obviously,

speculation is considered far more risky than investing.

At first, you will probably keep your investment funds in some form of savings vehicle (as described in Chapter 5). Once you have *sufficient savings*—for emergency and other purposes—you can begin to put funds into various forms of investments. However, before embarking on a full-scale investment program, it's also important to have adequate *insurance coverage* in order to provide protection against the unexpected (we discussed different kinds of insurance in Chapters 9, 10, and 11). For our purposes here, we will assume that you are adequately insured and that the cost of insurance coverage is built into your family's monthly cash budget. Ample insurance and liquidity (cash and savings) with which to meet life's emergencies are two *investment prerequisites* that are absolutely essential for the development of a successful investment program. Once these two conditions are met, you are ready to start investing.

But How Do I Get Started?

Contrary to what you may believe, there is really nothing mystical about the topic of investments—in fact, it is quite easy to get started in investing. The terminology may indeed seem baffling at times and some of the procedures and techniques quite complicated. But don't let that mislead you into thinking there is not room for the small, individual investor. Nothing could be farther from the truth! As we will see in this and the next two chapters, there is a wide array of investment vehicles from which to choose. Further, opening an investment account is no more difficult than opening a checking account.

How, then, do you get started? To begin with, you need some money—not a lot; perhaps $500 to $1,000 will do, though $3,000 to $5,000 would be even better (remember, this is *investment capital* we're talking about here—money you've accumulated above and beyond any basic emergency savings). In addition to money, you need knowledge and know-how. You should never invest in something you are not sure about—that is the quickest way to lose your money. Learn as much as you can about the market, different types of securities, and various trading strategies. This course you're taking on personal finance is a good start, but you may want to do more. You can become a *regular* reader of publications such as *Money, Changing Times, The Wall Street Journal, Barron's* and *Forbes* (these and other sources of information are reviewed in Chapter 13). Keep up-to-date on developments in the market; start following the stock market, interest rates and developments in the bond market.

We strongly suggest that, after you have learned a few things about stocks and bonds, you set up a portfolio of securities on paper and make *paper trades* in and out of your portfolio for six months to a year in order to get a feel for what it is like to make (and lose) money in the market. Start out with an imaginary sum of, say, $10,000 (as long as you are going to dream, you might as well make it worthwhile). Then keep track of the stocks and bonds you hold, record the number of shares bought and sold, dividends received, and so on. Throughout this exercise, be sure to use actual prices (as obtained from *The Wall Street Journal* or your local newspaper) and keep it as realistic as possible. If you are going to make mistakes in the market, you are much better off doing so on paper. Also, if your parents, relatives, and/or friends have done a lot of investing, talk to them! Find out what they have to say about investing, pick up some pointers, and possibly even learn from their mistakes. Eventually you will gain a familiarity with the market and become comfortable with the way things are done there. When that happens, you will be ready to take the plunge.

At this point, you need a way to invest—more specifically, you need a broker and some investment vehicle in which to invest. As we will see in the next chapter, the stockbroker is the party through whom you will be buying and selling stocks, bonds, and other securities. If your relatives or friends have a broker they like and trust, have them introduce you to him or her. Alternatively, visit several of the brokerage firms in your community; talk to one of their brokers about your available investment funds and your investment objectives.

As a beginning investor with limited funds, it is probably best to confine your investment activity to the basics. Stick to stocks, bonds, and mutual funds. Avoid getting fancy, and certainly *don't* try to make a killing each and every time you invest—that will only lead to frustration, disappointment, and, very possibly, heavy losses. Instead, go for "relatively" high returns; for example, those that comfortably exceed what you can get from a savings account. Further, *be patient!* Don't expect the price of the stock to double overnight, and don't panic when things fail to work out as expected in the short run (after all, security prices do occasionally go down). Finally, remember that you do not need spectacular returns in order to make a lot of money in the market. Instead, be *consistent* and let the concept of compound interest work for you: Do that and you'll find that just $2,000 a year invested at the fairly conservative rate of 10 percent will grow to well over $100,000 in 20 years! While the type of security in which you invest is a highly personal decision, you might want to give serious consideration to some sort of mutual fund as your first investment (see Chapter 14). Mutual funds provide professional management and diversification that small-time individual investors can rarely obtain on their own.

The Role of Investing in Personal Financial Planning

Buy a car, build a house, enjoy a comfortable retirement—these are goals that we would all like to attain some day and are, in many cases, the centerpieces of well-developed financial plans. As a rule, a financial goal such as building a house is not something we pay for out of our cash reserves; the cost (even the down payment) is simply too great to allow for that. Instead, we must accumulate the funds over time, which is where investment planning and the act of investing enter into the personal financial planning process. By investing our money, we are letting it work for us.

---

investing
The process of placing money in some medium such as stocks or bonds in the expectation of receiving some future benefit.

speculating
A form of investing in which future value and expected returns are highly uncertain.

It all starts with an objective—a particular financial goal that we would like to achieve in a certain period of time. Take the case of the Zacharys. Shortly after the birth of their first child, they decided to start building a college education fund. After performing some rough calculations, they concluded they'd need to accumulate about $40,000 over the next 18 years in order to have the money for their daughter's education. Simply by setting that objective, the Zacharys created a well-defined, specific financial goal. The *purpose* is to meet the education needs of their child, and the *amount* of money involved is $40,000 in 18 years. But how do they reach their goal? The first thing they must decide is where the money will come from. While part of it will come from the return (profit) on their investments, they still have to come up with the *investment capital*.

Coming Up with the Capital. So far, the Zacharys know how much money they want to accumulate, and how long they have to accumulate it. The only other thing they need to determine at this point is the *rate of return* they feel they can earn on their money. Having taken a financial planning course in college, the Zacharys know that the amount of money they'll have to put into their investment program depends in large part on *how much they can earn from their investments*—the higher their rate of return, the less they'll have to put up. Let's say they feel comfortable using a 9 percent rate of return. That's a fairly conservative number, and they're reasonably certain they can reach that level of return, on average, over the long haul. It's important to use some care in coming up with a projected rate of return. Don't saddle yourself with an unreasonably high rate, since that will simply reduce the chance of reaching your targeted financial goal. Probably the best way of arriving at a reasonable projection is to look at what the market has done over the past three to five years, and then use the average return performance over that period as your estimate—or, if you want to be a bit more conservative, knock a point or two off the market's return.

There are two ways of finding the amount of capital needed to reach a targeted sum of money:

(1) you can make a lump-sum investment right up front and let that amount grow over time; or (2) you can set up a systematic savings plan and put away a certain amount of money each year. The worksheet in Exhibit 12.1 is designed to help you find the amount of investment capital you'll need to reach a given financial goal. It employs the *compound value* concept discussed in Chapter 3, and is based on a given financial target (line 1), and a projected average rate of return on your investments (line 2). Note that you can use the worksheet to find either a required lump-sum investment (part A), or an amount that will have to be put away each year in a savings plan (part B). For our purposes here, we'll assume the Zacharys have $4,000 to start with (this comes mostly from gifts their daughter received from her grandparents). Since they know they'll need a lot more than that to reach their target, the Zacharys decide to use part B of the worksheet to find out how much they'll have to save annually.

The first thing to do is find the future value of the $4,000 initial investment—the question here is: how much will that initial lump-sum investment grow to? Using the compound value concept and the appropriate "future value factor" (from Appendix A), we see, in line 7, that this deposit will grow to some $18,880. So, that's nearly $19 thousand of our targeted $40 thousand that we already have covered. Thus, by subtracting the terminal value of the initial investment (line 7) from our target (line 1), we come up with the amount that must be generated from some sort of annual savings plan—see line 8. (*Note:* if you were starting from scratch, you'd enter a zero in line 5, and the amount in line 8 would be equal to the amount in line 1.) Again, using the appropriate future value factor (this time from Appendix B), we find the Zacharys will have to save $511 a year in order to reach their target of $40,000 in 18 years. That is, the $511 a year will accumulate to $21,120, which when added to the $18,880 that the initial $4,000 will grow to, equals the targeted $40,000. (By the way, they can also reach their target by making a lump-sum investment right up front of $8,475—try working out part A of the worksheet on your own, and see if you can come up with that number.)

EXHIBIT 12.1
Finding the Amount of Investment Capital

A worksheet like this one can be used to find out how much money you're going to come up with in order to reach a given financial goal; note that this worksheet is based on the same future value concept we first introduced in Chapter 3.

DETERMINING AMOUNT OF INVESTMENT CAPITAL	
Financial goal: *To accumulate $40,000 in 18 years for the purpose of meeting the cost of daughter's college education.*	
1. Targeted Financial Goal (see Note 1)	$ *40,000*
2. Projected Average Return on Investments	*9.0 %*
A. Finding a Lump Sum Investment:	

3. Future Value Factor, from Appendix A
  ▪ based on _____ years to target date and a projected average
   return on investment of _____	

4. Required Lump Sum Investment ▪ line 1 ÷ line 3	$
B. Making a Series of Investments Over Time:	
5. Amount of Initial Investment, if any (see Note 2)	$ *4,000*

6. Future Value Factor, from Appendix A
  ▪ based on *18* years to target date and a projected
   average return on investment of *9 %*
	4.72

7. Terminal Value of Initial Investment ▪ line 5 × line 6	$ *18,880*
8. Balance to Come From Savings Plan ▪ line 1 − line 7	$ *21,120*

9. Future Value Annuity Factor, from Appendix B
  ▪ based on *18* years to target date and a projected
   average return on investment of *9%*
	41.3

10. Series of Annual Investments Required Over Time ▪ line 8 ÷ line 9	$ *511*

Note 1: The "targeted financial goal" is the amount of money you want to accumulate by some target date in the future.

Note 2: If you're starting from scratch—i.e., there is no initial investment—enter a zero in line 5, skip lines 6 and 7, and then use the total targeted financial goal (from line 1) as the amount to be funded from a savings plan; now proceed with the rest of the worksheet.

You would have to save $2,500 a year in order to end up with a $25,000 nest egg in ten years. **Fantasy:** Simply dividing your financial target ($25,000) by the length of time you have to get there (ten years) fails to take into account the fact that your money can earn a positive rate of return over time. Indeed, the amount you'll have to save each year depends on the rate of return you can earn on your money: the more you can earn, the less you'll have to put up each year.

An Investment Plan Provides Direction.

Now that the Zacharys know how much they have to save each year, their next step is to decide how they will save it. Probably the best thing to do in this regard is to follow some type of *systematic routine*—for example, building a set amount of savings each month or quarter into the household budget. But whatever procedure is followed, keep in mind that all we are doing here is accumulating the required investment capital. That money still has to be put to work in some kind of investment program, and that's where an investment plan comes into the picture. Basically, an **investment plan** is nothing more than a simple, preferably written, statement that explains how the accumulated investment capital will be invested for the purpose of reaching the targeted goal. In the example we've been using, the Zacharys' savings plan set a 9 percent rate of return as a target they felt they could achieve. Now they have to come up with a way of obtaining that 9 percent return on their money—meaning they have to specify, in general terms at least, the kinds of investment vehicles they intend to use. When completed, an investment plan is a way of translating an abstract investment target (in this case, a 9 percent return) into a specific investment program.

What Are Your Investment Objectives?

Some people buy securities for the protection they provide from taxes (that's what tax shelters are all about). Others want to have money put aside for that proverbial rainy day or, perhaps, to build up a nice retirement nest egg. Your goals tend to set the tone for your investment program, and they play a major role in determining how conservative (or aggressive) you're likely to be in making investment decisions. In a very real way, they provide a purpose for your investments. Given that you have

adequate savings and insurance to cover any emergencies, the most frequent investment objectives are to (1) enhance current income, (2) save for a major purchase, (3) accumulate funds for retirement, and (4) seek to shelter income from taxes.

Current Income. The idea here is to put your money into investments that will enable you to supplement your income. In other words, it's for people who want to live off their investment income. A secure source of high current income, from dividends or interest, is the principal concern of such investors. Retired people, for example, often choose investments offering high current income— at low risk. Another common reason for seeking supplemental income is that a family member requires extended costly medical care. Even after insurance, such recurring costs can heavily burden a family budget without this vital income supplement.

Major Expenditures. People often put money aside, sometimes for years, in order to save up enough to make just one major expenditure, the most common ones being:

- Save up for the down payment on a home
- Have the money for a child's college education
- Pay for an expensive (perhaps once-in-a-lifetime) vacation
- Build up some capital for going into business
- Pay for most or all of the purchase of a very special, expensive item
- Accumulate funds for retirement (discussed in the following section)

Whatever your goal, the idea is to set your sights on something and then go about building your capital with that objective in mind. It sure makes the act of investing more pleasurable. Once you have a handle on how much money you're going to need to attain one of these goals (following a procedure/ worksheet like the one illustrated in Exhibit 12.1), you can specify the types of investment vehicles you intend to use. For example, you might follow a low-risk approach by making a single lump-sum investment in a bond that matures in the year in which you need the funds; or you could follow a more risky investment plan that calls for investing a set amount of money over time in something like a growth-oriented mutual fund (where there is little or no assurance of what the terminal value of the investment will be). Of course, for some purposes—such as the down payment on a home or a child's education—you will probably want to accept a lot less risk than for others, as the attainment of these goals should not be jeopardized by the types of investment vehicles you choose to employ.

Retirement. Accumulating funds for retirement is *the single most important reason for investing.* Too often, though, retirement planning occupies only a small amount of our time, since we tend to rely very heavily on employers and social security for our retirement needs. As many people learn too late in life, this can be a serious mistake. A much better approach is to review the amounts of income you can *realistically* expect to receive from social security and your employee pension plan, and then decide based on your retirement goals, *whether or not they will be adequate to meet your needs.* You'll probably find that you'll have to supplement them through personal investing. Obviously, the earlier in life you make this assessment, the greater your opportunity to accumulate the needed funds. (Retirement plans are discussed in Chapter 15.)

Shelter from Taxes. As Chapter 4 explained, federal income tax law does not treat all sources of income equally. For example, if you own real estate—either directly or through some pooling arrangement—you *may* be able to take depreciation deductions against certain other sources of income, thereby reducing the amount of your final taxable income. This tax write-off feature can make real estate an attractive investment vehicle *for some investors,* even though its pre-tax rate of return may not appear very high. The goal of sheltering income from taxes was made considerably more difficult with the Tax Reform Act of 1986; even so, such a goal for some investors still goes hand in hand with the goals of saving for a major outlay or for retirement. Clearly, if you can avoid paying taxes on the income from an investment, you will, all other things considered, have more funds available for reinvestment during the period.

Different Ways to Invest

Once you have established your investment objectives, you can choose from a variety of investment vehicles with which to fulfill them. The various types of investment vehicles are briefly described in the following paragraphs; each will be more fully examined later in this chapter and in Chapters 13 and 14.

Common Stock. *Common stock* is basically a form of *equity*—as an investment, it represents an ownership interest in a corporation. Each share of stock symbolizes a fractional ownership position in a firm; for example, one share of common stock in a corporation that has 10,000 shares outstanding would denote a 1/10,000 ownership interest in the firm. The return on a share of stock comes from either dividends and/or appreciation in share price. A typical share of common stock, the ownership of which is evidenced by a **stock certificate**, is shown in Exhibit 12.2.

Bonds. In contrast to stocks, *bonds* are *liabilities*—they're IOUs of the issuer; the bondholder actually loans money to the issuer. Governments and corporations issue bonds that pay a stated return, called *interest.* When an individual invests in a bond, he or she receives a known interest return, typically paid every six months, plus the return of the principal (face) value of the bond at maturity. For example, if you purchased a $1,000 bond that paid 10 percent interest in semiannual installments, you could expect to receive $50 every six months (that is, 10% × $1,000 × .5 years) and at maturity recover the $1,000 face value of the bond. Of course, a bond can be bought or sold prior to maturity at a price that differs from its face value since bond prices, like common stock prices, do fluctuate in the marketplace.

Preferreds and Convertibles. These are forms of hybrid securities in that each has the character-

---

investment plan
A statement, preferably written, that specifies how investment capital will be invested for the purpose of achieving a specified goal.

stock certificate
A document serving as evidence that the shareholder owns shares of the stock and is entitled to all rights and privileges of ownership.

EXHIBIT 12.2

A Share of Common Stock

This stock certificate is evidence that the shareholder owns shares of the stock and is entitled to all rights and privileges of ownership.

Source: Courtesy of NCR Corporation, Dayton, OH.

istics of both stocks and bonds; in essence, they are a cross between the two. *Preferred securities* are issued as stock and, as such, represent an equity position in a corporation. Unlike common stock, however, preferreds have a stated (fixed) dividend rate, payment of which is given preference over dividends to holders of common stock. Like bonds, preferred stocks are usually purchased for the current income (dividends) they pay. A *convertible security* is a special type of fixed-income obligation (bond or preferred stock) that carries a conversion feature permitting the investor to convert it into a specified number of shares of common stock. Convertible bonds, therefore, provide the fixed-income benefits of a bond (interest) while offering the price appreciation (capital gains) potential of common stock.

Mutual Funds. A company that invests in a diversified portfolio of securities is called a *mutual fund*. A mutual fund sells shares to investors, who then become part-owners of the fund's securities portfolio. Most mutual funds issue and repurchase shares at a price reflecting the proportionate value of the portfolio at the time the transaction is made.

Real Estate. Investments in *real estate* can take many forms, ranging from raw land speculation to limited-partnership shares in commercial property. The return on real estate can come from rents, capital gains, and certain tax benefits. Unfortunately, estimating both risk and return in a real estate venture can be difficult and usually requires expert advice, particularly with respect to income tax implications.

Commodities, Financial Futures, and Options. *Commodities* and *financial futures* are contracts to buy/sell such things as agricultural products and other raw materials, or certain types of financial instruments, at a given price, at some future date. Because they do not pay interest or dividends, their return depends solely on the change in the price of the underlying commodity or financial instrument. These are very risky investments, because losses can be far greater than the amount invested. Like futures, *options* give the holder the right to buy or sell common stocks (and other financial instruments) at a set price over a specified period of time. Again, to earn a positive return one must correctly anticipate future price movements in the underlying financial asset. In contrast to futures contracts, the price paid for an option is the maximum amount that can be lost; however, options have very short maturities, and consistent losses can quickly exhaust one's investment capital.

Precious Metals and Collectibles. *Precious metals* and *collectibles* are specialized investments that are sometimes associated with hobbies. While price appreciation for many of these assets has come pretty easily in the past, there is no assurance that it will continue in the future. Before investing in them, one should consider their future salability. Resale markets are very often hard to find, and/or sales agents receive large commissions.

The Risks of Investing

In selecting investments, you should also consider the possible risks or uncertainties associated with them. The basic types of investment risk are business risk, financial risk, market risk, purchasing power risk, interest rate risk, liquidity risk, and event risk. Obviously, other things being equal, you'd like to reduce your exposure to these risks as much as possible.

Business Risk. When you invest in a company, you may have to face up to the possibility that the issuing firm will fail, due either to economic or industry factors or, as is more often the case, to poor decisions on the part of management. In a general sense, this is **business risk** and it may be thought of as the degree of uncertainty surrounding the firm's earnings and subsequent ability to meet principal, interest, and dividend payments on time. Companies that are subject to high degrees of business risk generally experience wide fluctuations in sales, have widely erratic earnings, and can, in fact, end the year with substantial operating losses.

Financial Risk. **Financial risk** relates to the amount of debt used to finance the firm. Look to the company's balance sheet to get a handle on a firm's financial risk. As a rule, companies that have little or no long-term debt are fairly low in financial risk. This is particularly so if a company has a healthy earnings picture as well. The problem with debt financing is that it creates principal and interest obligations that have to be met regardless of how much profit the company is generating. As with business risk, financial risk can lead to failure (as in the case of bankruptcy), or a rate of return that is sharply below your expectations.

Market Risk. **Market risk** results from the behavior of investors in the securities markets. The fact is, prices of stocks and bonds will sometimes change even though business and financial risks, and other intrinsic factors, stay about the same. Such changes have little to do with the securities themselves but instead are due to changes in political, economic, and social conditions, and/or in investor tastes and preferences. Although it is diffi-

business risk
The degree of uncertainty associated with the firm's earnings and consequent ability to pay interest and dividends.

financial risk
A type of investment risk associated with the mix of debt and equity financing used by the issuing firm.

market risk
A type of investment risk associated with factors such as changes in political, economic, and social conditions and in investor tastes and preferences that may cause the market price of a security to change.

cult to estimate this type of risk, investors can evaluate past price movements in order to get a feel for the extent to which a given security is exposed to it.

Purchasing Power Risk. Possible changes in price levels within the economy also result in risk. In periods of rising prices (inflation), the purchasing power of the dollar declines. This means that a smaller quantity of goods or services can be purchased with a given number of dollars. In periods of declining price levels, the purchasing power of the dollar increases. An awareness of **purchasing power risk** and changes in purchasing power allows investors to select investments that are best suited for a given price level environment. In general, investments whose values move with prices are most profitable during periods of price rise.

Interest Rate Risk. **Fixed-income securities**, which include preferred stocks and bonds, offer purchasers a fixed periodic return and, as such, are most affected by **interest rate risk**. As interest rates change, the prices of these securities fluctuate, decreasing with increasing interest rates and increasing with decreasing interest rates. For example, the prices of fixed-income securities drop when interest rates increase in order to provide purchasers with a rate of return that is competitive with those available from other, similar securities. Changes in interest rates are the result of fluctuations in the supply of and/or demand for money. These fluctuations are caused by various economic actions of the government or the interactions of business firms, consumers, and financial institutions.

Liquidity Risk. The risk of not being able to liquidate an investment conveniently and at a reasonable price is called **liquidity risk**. The liquidity of a given investment vehicle is important because it provides the investor with a safety valve just in case he/she ever has to get out, for one reason or another. In general, investment vehicles traded in *thin markets,* in which supply and demand are small, tend to be less liquid than those traded in *broad markets.* However, to be liquid, an investment must be easily salable at a reasonable price. One can generally enhance the liquidity of an investment merely by cutting its price. For example, a security recently purchased for $1,000 would not be viewed as highly liquid if it could be sold only at a significantly reduced price, such as $500. Vehicles such as mutual funds, or the stocks and bonds of major companies listed on the New York Stock Exchange, are generally highly liquid; others, such as an isolated parcel of raw land in rural Georgia, are not.

Event Risk. More than just a buzz word used by the financial media, **event risk** is real, and it can have a direct and dramatic impact on investment return. Basically, it occurs when something substantial happens to a company and that event, in itself, has a sudden impact on the company's financial condition. Event risk goes beyond business and financial risk, and it doesn't necessarily mean the company or market is doing poorly. Instead, it involves an event that is largely (or totally) unexpected, and which has a significant and usually immediate effect on the underlying value of an investment. Two good examples of event risk are *corporate takeovers* and so-called *leveraged buyouts.* Either one of these events usually involves the use of enormous amounts of debt-financing; and as a result, they present a genuine risk for conservative bond investors. Consider, for example, the celebrated buyout of RJR Nabisco. Here was a situation where the debt that was piled on in the buyout transformed investment-grade bonds into junk overnight. Granted, this buyout had a positive effect on stock prices, but for bondholders, the impact was devastating, as the market value of RJR bonds plunged nearly 20 percent in just two days! Event risk can take many forms, though, fortunately, its impact tends to be confined in most cases, to certain companies, securities, or segments of the market.

The Returns from Investing

Any investment vehicle—be it a share of stock, a bond, a piece of real estate, or a stock option—has just two basic sources of return: *current income* and/or *capital gains*. Some investments offer only one source of return (for example, options provide only capital gains), but most offer both income and capital gains, which together make up what is called the *total return* from an investment. Of course, where both elements of return are present, the relative importance of each will vary among investments. Whereas current income is more important with bonds, capital gains probably makes up a larger portion of total return in the case of common stocks. Further, in practice taxes should also be considered in the investment decision, since *taxes determine how much of the current income and capital gains one gets to keep!* As a rule, it is a good idea to use after-tax cash flows or after-tax returns when evaluating investment vehicles.

Current Income.   Income, such as dividends on stock, interest from bonds, and rents from real estate, is often a primary motive for investing. People who invest to obtain income look for investment vehicles that will provide regular and predictable patterns of income. Preferred stocks and bonds, which are expected to pay known amounts at specified times (quarterly or semiannually, for example), are usually good income investments.

Capital Gains.   The other type of return available from investments is capital appreciation (or growth), which is reflected in an increase in the market value of the investment vehicle. Capital gains occur when you're able to sell a security for more than you paid for it, or when your security holdings go up in value. Investments that provide greater growth potential through capital appreciation normally have lower levels of current income, since the firm achieves its growth by reinvesting its earnings instead of paying dividends out to the owners. Many common stocks, for example, are acquired for their capital gains potential.

Interest-On-Interest: An Important Element of Return For The Investor

Question: When does an 8 percent investment end up yielding only 5 percent? Answer: Probably more often than you think! Of course, it can happen when investment performance fails to live up to expectations. But it can also happen even when everything goes right. For example, say an investor buys an 8 percent U.S. Treasury bond and holds it to maturity, a period of 20 years. Each year the bondholder receives $80 in interest, and at maturity, the $1,000 in principal is repaid. There is no loss in capital, no default; everything is paid right on time. Yet this sure-fire investment ends up yielding only 5 percent. Why? Because the investor failed to reinvest

the profits. By not plowing back all the investment earnings, the bondholder failed to earn any *interest-on-interest*.

Consider, for example, the graph on page 420. It shows the elements of return for our 8 percent, 20-year bond; observe that since the bond was originally bought at par ($1,000), you start off with an 8 percent investment. Where you end up depends on what you do with the profits from this investment; that is, whereas current income and capital gains make up the profits from an investment, interest-on-interest is a measure of what you do with those profits! If you don't reinvest the interest income, you'll end up on the 5 percent line.

To move to the 8 percent line, you have to earn interest-on-interest from your investments. Specifically, since you started out with an 8 percent investment, that's the rate of return you have to earn when reinvesting your income. The rate of return you start with, in effect, is the required, or minimum, reinvestment rate. Put your investment profits to work at this rate and you'll earn the rate of return you set out to; fail to do so and your return will decline accordingly. And keep in mind that

purchasing power risk
A type of risk resulting from possible changes in price levels that can have a significant effect on investment returns.

fixed-income securities
Securities such as preferred stocks and bonds that offer purchasers fixed periodic returns.

interest rate risk
A type of risk resulting from changing market interest rates that mainly affects fixed-income securities.

liquidity risk
A type of risk associated with the inability to liquidate an investment conveniently and at a reasonable price.

event risk
The risk that some major, unexpected event will occur, leading to a sudden, substantial change in the financial condition of a firm; for example, a company could go through a leveraged buy-out, or the money manager of a highly successful mutual fund could quit.

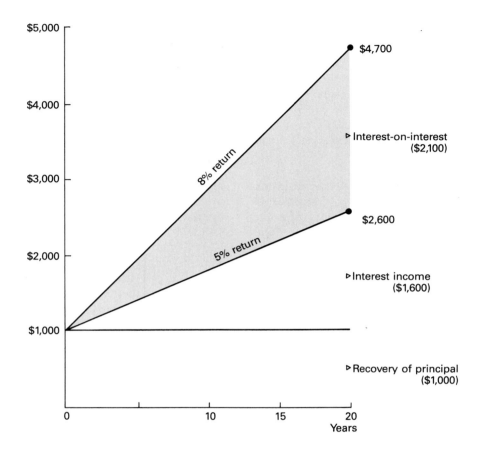

even though we used a bond in our illustration, this same principle applies to any type of investment vehicle. It's just as relevant to common stocks, mutual funds, or T-bills as it is to long-term bond instruments. This notion of earning interest-on-interest is what the market refers to as a *fully compounded rate of return*. It's an important concept because you can't start reaping the full potential from your investments until you start earning a fully compounded return on your money.

So long as periodic investment income is involved, the reinvestment of that income and interest-on-interest are matters you're going to have to deal with. In fact, *interest-on-interest is a particularly important element of return for investment programs that involve a lot of current income.* This is so because, in contrast to capital gains, current income has to be reinvested by the individual investor. (With capital gains, the investment vehicle itself is doing the reinvesting, all automatically.) It follows, therefore, that if your investment program

tends to lean toward income-oriented securities, then interest-on-interest—and the continued reinvestment of income—will play an important role in defining the amount of investment success you have.

The Risk-Return Trade-off

The amount of risk associated with a given investment vehicle is directly related to its expected return. This is a *universal* rule of investing and means that if you want a higher level of return from your investment, you will probably have to accept a greater exposure to risk. Thus, investors should *expect* to be compensated for taking higher levels of risk by earning higher rates of return. Since most people are believed to be risk averse—they dislike taking risks—some incentive to taking risks must be offered. If a low-risk investment offered the same return as a high-risk one, investors would naturally opt for the former—or, put another way,

EXHIBIT 12.3

The Risk-Return Relationship

In the field of investments, there generally is a direct relationship between risk and return: The more risk you face, the greater should be the return you expect to generate from the investment.

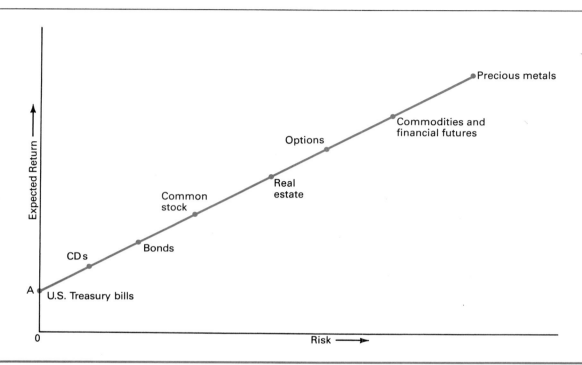

investors would choose the highest return available for a given level of risk.

The direct relationship between risk and return is shown in Exhibit 12.3, which generalizes the risk-return trade-off for some popular investment vehicles. Note that it is possible to receive a positive return for zero risk, such as at point A; this is sometimes referred to as the **risk-free rate of return**, which is often measured by the return on a short-term government security, such as a 90-day Treasury bill.

What Makes a Good Investment?

In keeping with the above risk-return discussion, it follows that the value of any investment depends on the amount of return it is expected to provide the investor relative to the amount of perceived risk involved. This basic rule applies to any type of in-

vestment vehicle, be it stocks, bonds, convertibles, options, real estate, or commodities. In this respect, they should all be treated the same.

Future Return. In the field of investments, the only return that matters is *the expected future return*. Except to the extent that they can help you get a handle on future income, past returns are of little value to investors—after all, it is not what the security did last year that matters, but what it is expected to do next year.

> **risk-free rate of return**
> The rate of return on short-term government securities, such as Treasury bills, that have no default risk or maturity premiums.

Earlier, we defined returns as being made up of current income and capital gains. Thus, to get an idea of the future return on an investment, we must formulate expectations of its future current income and future capital appreciation. To illustrate, assume you are thinking of buying some stock in Rose Colored Glasses, Inc. (RCG). By reviewing several financial reports, you have come up with an estimate of the future dividends and price behavior of RCG as follows:

Expected average annual dividends, 19X1 − 19X3	$ 2.15 a share
Expected market price of the stock, 19X3	$75.00 a share

Since the stock is now selling for $60 a share, the difference ($75 − $60) represents the amount of *capital gains* you can expect to receive over the next three years—in this case, $15 a share. Thus, you have estimates of the stock's future *income stream*; what you need now is a way to measure future *return*.

Approximate Yield

Finding the exact rate of return of this (or any) investment involves a highly complex mathematical procedure. However, you can obtain a close estimation of return by computing the investment's *approximate yield*. This measure is widely used by seasoned investors and results in a rate of return (yield) that is remarkably close to the exact figure; and it is relatively easy to use. Best of all, this barometer of return considers not only current income and capital gains, but interest-on-interest as well. As such, *approximate yield provides a measure of the fully compounded rate of return* from an investment and is the preferred way to measure return performance.

The method of finding the approximate yield on an investment is shown in Equation 12.1. If you briefly study the formula, you will see that it is really not as formidable as it may at first appear. All it does is relate (1) average current income and (2) average capital gains to the (3) average amount of the investment.

To illustrate, let's use the Rose Colored Glasses example again. Given the average annual dividends (*CI*) of $2.15, current stock price (*CP*) of $60, future stock price (*FP*) of $75, and an investment period (*N*) of 3 years (you expect to hold the stock through 19X3), you can now use Equation 12.1 to find the expected approximate yield of this investment:

Equation 12.1

$$\text{Approximate yield} = \frac{\text{Average annual current income} + \left[\dfrac{\text{Future price of investment} - \text{Current price of investment}}{\text{Number of years in investment period}}\right]}{\left[\dfrac{\text{Current price of investment} + \text{Future price of investment}}{2}\right]}$$

$$= \frac{CI + \left[\dfrac{FP - CP}{N}\right]}{\left[\dfrac{CP + FP}{2}\right]}$$

where
CI = *average* annual current income (amount you expect to receive annually from dividends, interest, or rent)
FP = expected future price of investment
CP = current price of investment
N = investment period (length of time, in years, that you expect to hold investment)

$$\text{Approximate yield} = \frac{\$2.15 + \left[\dfrac{\$75 - \$60}{3}\right]}{\left[\dfrac{\$60 + \$75}{2}\right]}$$

$$= \frac{\$2.15 + \left[\dfrac{\$15}{3}\right]}{\left[\dfrac{\$135}{2}\right]}$$

$$= \frac{\$2.15 + \$5.00}{\$67.50} = \frac{\$7.15}{\$67.50}$$

$$= 10.6\%.$$

In this case, if your forecasts of annual dividends and capital gains hold up, an investment in Rose Colored Glasses should provide a return of around 10.6 percent per year.

Whether or not you should consider RCG a good investment depends on how this level of expected return stacks up to the amount of risk you must assume. Suppose you have decided that the stock is moderately risky. To determine whether the rate of return on this investment will be satisfactory, you can compare it to some benchmark. One of the best is the rate of return you can expect from a *risk-free* security such as a *U.S. Treasury bill*. The idea is that the return on a *risky* security should be greater than that available on a *risk-free* security (the concept underlying the graph in Exhibit 12.3). If, for example, U.S. T-bills are yielding, say, 7 percent, then you'd probably want to receive something like 12 to 15 percent for a moderately risky security like RCG. In essence, the 12 to 15 percent is your **desired rate of return**—it is the minimum rate of return you feel you should receive in compensation for the amount of risk you must assume. *An investment should be considered acceptable only if it's expected to generate a rate of return that meets (or exceeds) your desired rate of return*. In the case of RCG, the stock should be considered a poor investment since it fails to provide the minimum or desired rate of return. In short, because of the risks involved with the stock, the amount of expected return falls short of the amount you deserve.

A good investment is one that offers a positive rate of return. **Fantasy:** A good investment is one that offers an expected return that equals or exceeds the investor's desired rate of return, which is defined relative to the amount of risk imbedded in the investment. Thus, what might be a good return in one case may be totally inadequate in another.

INVESTING IN COMMON STOCK

Remember that money you inherited and decided to invest? Let's say you want to use part of it to buy some common stocks—a popular form of investing that offers attractive returns from both price appreciation and the receipt of dividends. What kinds of stocks (for example, blue-chips, growth stock, etc.) would you be most interested in, and how would you decide what price to pay for them? Give some thought to these questions before reading on.

Common stocks appeal to investors for a variety of reasons. To some, investing in stocks is a way to hit it big if the issue shoots up in price; to others, it is the level of current income they offer. In fact, given the size and diversity of the stock market, it is safe to say that no matter what the investment objective, there are common stocks available to fit the bill. Not surprisingly, common stocks are a popular form of investing, used by literally millions of individuals and a variety of financial institutions.

The basic investment attribute of a share of common stock is that it enables the investor to participate in the profits of the firm, which is how it derives its value. Every shareholder is, in effect, a part-owner of the firm and, as such, is entitled to a piece of its profit. However, this claim on income is not without its limitations, for common stock-

desired rate of return
The minimum rate of return that an investor feels should be earned in compensation for the amount of risk assumed.

EXHIBIT 12.4

The Stock Market in 1987

A not-so-funny thing happened in the stock market in October of 1987. The stock market "crashed"; it experienced a "major correction"; it went though a "melt down." No matter how you describe it, the events in October certainly weren't very pleasant! The incredible bull market that had begun some five years earlier was over. It was now the bears' turn to have the run of Wall Street.

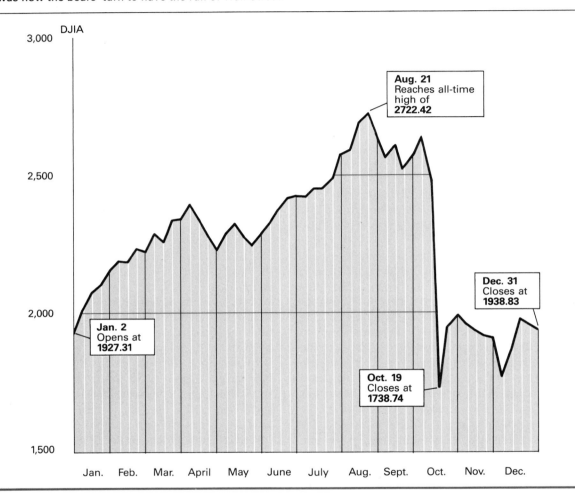

holders are really the **residual owners** of the company, meaning they are entitled to dividend income and a prorated share of the company's earnings only after all the other obligations of the firm have been met. Equally important, as residual owners, *holders of common stock have no guarantee that they will ever receive any return on their investment.*

Common Stock As A Form of Investment

The stock market can perform beautifully, or it can behave "like a dog." A good example of the latter occurred in 1987. As Exhibit 12.4 illustrates, stock prices shot up in the first part of the year, only to experience a terrible market crash on October 19th, when stock prices, as measured by the Dow Jones Industrial Average, fell over 500 points on volume of over 600 million shares. October 19, 1987 was not just another bad day in the market—it was history! As far as the market was concerned, it was like no other day on record and hopefully, it's a situation that won't reoccur any too soon. To give you a feel for what that day was like on Wall Street, take a look at the accompanying *Issues In Money Management* Box as it traces the events of that fateful day.

Fortunately, the October 19ths of this world are the rare exception rather than the rule. And as a result, the stock market is not all risk and wild price volatility. There are also some pretty attractive rewards. Consider the fact that even though the last quarter of 1987 was a wild and woolly one, the market still ended the year on the plus side—if only up by a meager 2 percent. In a similar fashion, if you look at the five-plus years from August 1982 through December 1987, you'll find the market went up over 150 percent; and that's *after* factoring in the impact of the October crash. Obviously, it's this kind of performance that explains the appeal of common stocks.

Issuers of Common Stock. Shares of common stock can be issued by any corporation in any line of business. Although all corporations have stockholders, not all have publicly traded shares. The stocks of interest to us in this book are the so-called *publicly traded issues*—the shares that are readily available to the general public and that are bought and sold in the open market. Just about every facet of American industry is represented in the stock market. You can buy shares in public utilities, airlines, mining concerns, manufacturing firms, and retail organizations, or in financial institutions like banks and insurance companies. The number of shares issued by a firm depends on its size and financial needs; though once issued, a share of common stock has no maturity date and thus remains outstanding indefinitely.

Aside from the initial sale of common stock when a corporation is formed, subsequent sales of additional shares may be made through a procedure known as a *public offering*. Here the corporation, working with its underwriter, simply offers the investing public a certain number of shares of its stock at a certain price. The new shares are then commingled with the outstanding shares (since

they are all the same class of stock), and the net result is an increase in the number of shares outstanding.

Common stock may also be issued through *rights offerings*. These are used when a firm with a new issue of common stock must, under state law, let the current stockholders purchase new shares in proportion to their existing share ownership; this right is known as a *preemptive right*. In order to efficiently carry out the rights offering, the firm issues *rights*—negotiable instruments allowing the holder to purchase a certain number of shares of the new issue at a specified price—to each shareholder. These rights normally must be exercised within a few weeks. Because the *exercise price* at which the new shares can be purchased is usually below the prevailing market price, *rights have value and may be sold in the stock market.*

Companies can also use *warrants* to issue additional shares of common stock. Basically, a warrant gives an investor the right to purchase shares of stock at a certain price over some specified period of time. The purchase price of the stock as specified by a warrant is usually higher than the stock's market price at the time of issue. Therefore, warrants become valuable only after the market price of the stock has risen above the purchase price stipulated on the warrants. For instance, suppose a warrant allows the holder to purchase two shares of stock at $30 per share. As long as the warrant is outstanding, this company's stock can be purchased (with the warrant) at $30 a share *no matter how high the market price of the stock goes.* If the current market price of the stock is $45 per share, the warrant will be valuable since the market price of the stock will exceed the $30 price stipulated on the warrant; in effect, even though the current market price of the stock is $45 per share, a warrant holder can still buy the stock at *$30* a share! Warrants, therefore, do have value and, as such, are actively traded

residual owners
Shareholders who are entitled to dividend income and shares of the company's profits only after all of the firm's other obligations have been met.

ISSUES IN MONEY MANAGEMENT

Meltdown Monday: The Day the Market Crashed

Starting in August 1982, the stock market took off on a five-year ascent that eventually turned into a flight of fancy. The value of shares on the New York Stock Exchange nearly tripled, from $1.1 trillion to $2.8 trillion. One of every three adult Americans climbed aboard for the ride, directly participating in the market. Millions of others had a stake in its fortunes through pension funds, IRA accounts, insurance policies, savings programs. Then came "Meltdown Monday." It would change both the mood and shape of our financial markets and force major shifts in U.S. economic policy. Even if we managed to avert a crippling recession, many experts claimed that neither our money markets nor our country would ever be quite the same again. Here's what happened:

Friday, October 16, 1987. "When you go home tonight," advises John Gavin, an official of a Wall Street firm, "walk close to the buildings"—referring, of course, to falling bodies. As trading approaches the closing bell, a trader in stock-index options on the American Stock Exchange shrieks, "It's the end of the world!"

Not quite. But the Dow Jones Industrial Average closes down a record 108.35 points to 2246.74, on record volume of 338.5 million shares. What began some two months ago as a tame decline in stock prices has degenerated into a terrifying rout. The value of New York Stock Exchange common stock has slumped about $220 billion over the week—more than eight percent.

8 p.m. At Harry's bar, a Wall Street watering hole, hordes of yuppie brokers and traders are pre-occupied with getting dates for the evening. "They've never seen a sick market before," says an over-the-counter stock trader. "They think it's going back up a hundred points on Monday." But Robert L. Pelz, Jr., 33, a grain broker in Leawood, Kan., goes home Friday night and says to his wife, "I think the world as you and I know it has changed." A New York real-estate attorney notes: "I've got a nine-month-old daughter and I'm buying a house. A volatile stock market is no place for me." He had planted much of his savings in stocks. Worried, on this day he has begun to sell.

There were 44.1 million individuals in the stock market at the beginning of 1987—and a record 50.7 million at the end of August. Now, in October, the number has shrunk to 45.1 million. Investors have been growing gloomier because of signs that inflation is advancing, interest rates are edging higher and the dollar is weakening. Two leading banks have increased their prime lending rate, jolting some investors. Foreign investors are worried by the worsening U.S. trade deficit. A frenzied sell-off the week before by small and large investors as well as arbitragers—professionals who hedge their trading by buying in one market and selling in another—has cracked the market's foundations.

The snowballing has begun.

Sunday, October 18, 1987. At a party in Dallas, Richard W. Fisher, who manages about $200 million for a group of wealthy investors, finds his suspicions confirmed. After dinner, one of the guests goes to a phone to check on markets in Asia. She returns and says they are tumbling. The guest is Margaret Thatcher, the British prime minister, and the dinner is at the Dallas home of her son, Mark.

Monday, October 19, 1987. Troubling news: an Iranian oil platform in the Persian Gulf has been bombed by U.S. warships. John Phelan, chairman of the New York Stock Exchange, arrives at work expecting a tough day. He will be startled by what actually happens.

9 a.m. In the 34th-floor trading room of the Donaldson, Lufkin & Jenrette (DLJ) brokerage firm on Wall Street, corporate officials, deluged by sell orders, know a difficult day is ahead. The firm's brokers are perspiring at their telephone consoles, staring at banks of blinking buttons. Dudley Eppel, a managing director, delivers a grim pep talk: "Well, here we go. Let's keep our cool and maybe we'll all get through this thing alive. Let's go get 'em!"

9:30 a.m. Right from the opening bell, a tidal wave of sell orders swamps the exchange. The ticker shows that IBM might trade as low as $125, down ten points from Friday. But actual trading can't take place unless some buyers show up, and there aren't any. At the bell, the Dow is off 200 points. "We're going underwater!" shouts DLJ trader John Sesko as he pops candies into his dry mouth. "Fifty-five thousand Pepsi's to sell!" barks one trader. "Sixty thousand GM to sell!" yells another. Long before lunchtime, a trader shouts, "Hamburgers to go in six figures!" He wants to peddle 100,000 shares of McDonald's.

10 a.m. The men who run Wall Street's leading brokerage houses pour into the exchange. Phelan wants to assess firsthand how they are handling the strains. He has spoken to David S. Ruder, chairman of the Securities and Exchange Commission, and decided they have to "tough it out." Even a brief closing might give the impression that the system is falling apart.

"Everybody in the world is watching," he says. "You have to prove the system is holding together."

10:30 a.m. The Dow has sunk 93 points, to 2153.55. In Los Angeles, where it is 7:30 a.m., physician Richard Weiss listens to radio reports as he drives to work. He pulls off the freeway and phones his broker to sell his entire portfolio. The broker ticks off plummeting quotes: "There's Disney going 56, 55, 54. We're making history here!" Says Weiss: "Yes, but we're doing it with my money!" He loses $100,000.

Investors crowd the sidewalk outside a Fidelity Investments office on the corner of Park Avenue and 51st Street in New York, watching the stock postings in horrified fascination. A young, well-dressed woman says simply, "The sky is falling." Small investors are becoming increasingly nervous. Robert C. McCollum, an elementary-school principal in Galena Park, Texas, says, "For someone on my salary to lose $10,000 or $15,000 in a few days, you know it hurts. I'd jump out of the window, but it's a first-story window and I'd only skin my knee."

10:40 a.m. The SEC's Ruder arrives at the Mayflower Hotel in Washington to deliver a speech before a conference of the American Stock Exchange. But during a break, the room

empties out into the lobby, where people huddle around a Quotron machine for market data. Some race back and forth to a bank of pay phones to call their offices. The market has plunged more than 200 points when one person bursts from the phones shouting, "The buy programs have kicked in!" The computer-assisted trading rooms of the major firms have started issuing orders to buy stock. The market starts to improve.

11:30 a.m. Ruder emerges from his speech and is engulfed by reporters. He is asked what actions could be taken against a market collapse, and he lists several, including one calling for a brief trading halt. When the statement reaches financial markets, it is interpreted to mean that such a halt is in the works. Far from calming the markets, it further roils them, and the SEC chief spends the day trying to clarify his remarks.

Noon. The Dow is at 2103. Lines of people form in the NYSE's visitors' gallery. One young woman wonders if the plunging market means she will never be a mother. "Even in good times, men are scared of getting married," she says. Brokers across the United States keep phones pressed to both ears. "This is going to make '29

(continued)

ISSUES IN MONEY MANAGEMENT

(Continued)

look like a kiddie party," shouts a trader on the Los Angeles floor of the Pacific Stock Exchange.

1 p.m. A number of small investors conclude it is too late to bail out. "I'm scared to death, but I'm going to leave it there," says Jerry Nasello, a salesman at Global Imports, Inc., an Atlanta BMW dealership, who says he is "about 90 percent" invested in the market.

2 p.m. The Dow Jones average crashes through the 2000 barrier, down about 250 points from Friday's close. Volume sweeps past 400 million shares, a record, with two hours still remaining.

The exchange witnesses its first insolvency. A small firm called H.B. Shaine & Co. in Grand Rapids, Mich., is sucked under. According to a New York Stock Exchange press release, this firm has fallen below minimum financial requirements

and reports that it can no longer do business as a member firm. Within days, five more firms will be declared insolvent.

A mob gathers outside the New York Stock Exchange, clogging the sidewalk and spilling out to Broad Street. The heart of the financial district has become a combination carnival and tent revival, replete with gaping bystanders, hawkers, pickpockets, prophets, hymn-singing religious groups, and comedians. "The end is near!" yells a wraithlike man with a drooping mustache. "It's all over for the yuppies!"

Needing money for a new truck, a forestry consultant in Marietta, Ga., sells the mutual funds in which he has invested most of his savings. Their value is down about 30 percent. Never again, he says, will he put money in a mutual fund.

2:44 p.m. The ticker tape is two hours late. Nobody knows

where the market is, but it doesn't matter. People are selling at any price. Del Barrows, a Johnson, Vt., clothing manufacturer is a conservative investor who has always favored blue-chip stocks. Even so, Barrows's portfolio loses 25 to 30 percent of its value. "Every day seems to erase more of my gains," he laments.

3:40 p.m. White House Chief of Staff Howard Baker has been on the telephone with Wall Street to get market reports. Twenty minutes before the close of trading, he gives President Reagan a status report. But prices are tumbling too rapidly for anyone to keep track. A couple who own a photo-reproduction business in New York City say they have three-quarters of their assets in the stock market. "We've lost more than $200,000," the wife observes. But they have made a decision to hold fast. "We're praying a

---

in the securities markets. When warrants are exercised, a corporation issues new shares. of common stock.

The Par Value of a Share of Stock

A stated value that used to be placed on stock certificates, **par value** was intended to represent not the value of a stock, but the minimum price at which it could be sold without causing the shareholder to assume any liability for the firm's actions. Par value is no longer important; despite its name,

it does not reflect value. Many stocks issued today are in fact no-par stocks, which should attest to the insignificance of par value. Occasionally stocks do sell for less than their par value, although in most instances they sell above par.

Basic Tax Considerations

Common stocks provide income in the form of dividends, usually paid quarterly, and/or capital gains, which occur when the price of the stock appreciates. As indicated in Chapter 4, from a tax

lot," she adds, "but it's not working." In the final half-hour, the average falls another 130 points.

4 p.m. The New York Stock Exchange closes. But there is no sense of relief, because harried traders and clerks now have to face the damage. Many stand around and just stare at each other. For the first time, people use the word "crash." The Dow Jones Industrial Average has plunged 508 points, or an incredible 22.6 percent, to close at 1738.74. The eventual paper loss will total some $560 *billion,* a sum roughly equal to the gross national product of France. Volume on the New York exchange reached 604.8 million shares, nearly doubling the all-time record. Brokers can find only one word to describe the rout, a word long out of fashion: panic.

The drop far exceeds the 12.8-percent decline on Oc-tober 28, 1929, one of the first—and worst—days of the stock-market crash that marked the beginning of the Great Depression. The decline today and last week totals 743.47 points, or 30 percent. By comparison, the total drop on October 28 and October 29, 1929, was 68.90 points, or 23.1 percent.

4:30 p.m. From Maine to California, the news causes consumers to reassess their plans. In Atlanta a secretary at an engineering firm and her husband decide to put off buying a new car: "We figure people will be desperate to sell cars, furniture, houses. If we wait awhile, maybe we can get a better price." In Berwyn, Pa., a real-estate agent and her husband drop plans to buy a second home as an investment. "This shake-up convinces us that we have to be more liquid," she explains.

Although the turmoil on Wall Street has been the focus of intense national and international attention, plenty of Americans don't see it as a crisis. Some even see a certain justice in the market's collapse, especially in the farm and rust belts, where thousands of people have suffered through bankruptcies and factory closings. Donald Sutter, a farmer in Pleasantville, Iowa, thinks it was "good the way those rich people were getting hit just as us poor guys have been." But as he watches grain, hog and cattle prices follow stocks down, he becomes concerned. And on Wall Street that night, Harry's bar is as packed and boisterous as ever. The pizza is still free, but a bartender jokes that credit cards are no longer accepted.

Source: Adapted from "Meltdown Monday—The Day the Market Crashed," *Reader's Digest,* February 1988, pp. 86–92.

perspective, it makes no difference how the investment income was earned; *it's all taxed at the same rate!* That is, the tax liability on a dollar of dividends is basically the same as the tax liability on a dollar of capital gains. And it makes no difference how long you have held the stock—for ten days or ten years—the tax rate is still the same. Of course, there is no tax liability on any capital gains until the stock is actually sold (*paper gains*—i.e., any price appreciation that occurs on stock that you still own—accumulate tax-free). Taxes are due on any dividends and/or capital gains in the year in which the dividends are received and/or the stock is actually sold. Thus, if you received, say, $125 in dividends in 1989, you would have to include that income on your 1989 tax return.

---

par value
The stated value placed on stock certificates to reflect the minimum price at which the stock could be sold without causing the shareholder to assume any liability for the firm's actions, carries no significance in the market today.

Here is how it all works: Assume, for example, that you just sold 100 shares of common stock for $30 per share. Also assume that the stock was originally purchased two years ago for $20 per share and that during the current year you received $1.25 per share in cash dividends from it. For tax purposes, you would have a capital gain of $1,000 ([$30/share − $20/share] × 100 shares) and $125 in dividend income ($1.25/share × 100 shares). Thus, you would have a total of $1,125 in investment income, and if you were in the 28 percent tax bracket, you would have to pay taxes of $315 (i.e., $1,125 × .28) on this income. Whatever you are left with would represent your after-tax income—in this case, it would be $1,125 − $315 = $810.

The Voting Rights of Common Stockholders

The holders of common stock normally receive *voting rights,* which means that for each share of stock held, they receive one vote. In certain instances, common stock may be designated as nonvoting at the time of its issue, but this is the exception rather than the rule. Although different voting systems exist, the small stockholders need not concern themselves with them since, regardless of the system used, the chance that they will be able to affect corporate control with their votes is quite slim. Corporations have annual stockholders' meetings at which time new directors are elected and special issues are voted on. Since most small stockholders are unable to attend these meetings, they can use a proxy to assign their votes to another person, who will vote their stock for them. A **proxy** is merely a written statement assigning voting rights to another person.

Types of Dividends

Corporations pay dividends to their common stockholders in the form of cash and/or additional stock. *Cash dividends* are the most common. Since firms can pay dividends from earnings accumulated from previous periods, stockholders may receive dividends *even in periods when the firm shows a loss.* Cash dividends are normally distributed on a quarterly basis in an amount determined by the firm's directors. For example, if the directors declared a quarterly cash dividend of 50 cents a share, and you owned 200 shares of stock, you would receive a check for $100.

A popular way of assessing the amount of dividends received is to measure the stock's dividend yield. Basically, **dividend yield** is a measure of common stock dividends on a relative (percent), rather than absolute (dollar), basis—that is, the dollar amount of dividends received is related to the market price of the stock. As such, dividend yield is an indication of the rate of current income earned on the investment dollar. It is computed as follows:

$$\text{Dividend yield} = \frac{\text{Annual dividends received per share}}{\text{Market price per share of stock}}.$$

Thus, a company that annually pays $2 per share in dividends and whose stock is trading at $50 will have a dividend yield of 4 percent ($2/$50 = .04).

Occasionally the directors may declare a stock dividend as a supplement to or in place of cash dividends. **Stock dividends** represent new shares of stock issued to existing stockholders. Although they often satisfy the needs of some investors, stock dividends really have no value, since they represent the receipt of something already owned. For example, when a firm declares a 10 percent stock dividend, each shareholder receives one-tenth of a share of stock for each share owned—in other words, a stockholder with 100 shares of stock will receive 10 new shares. Since all stockholders receive a 10 percent increase in the *number* of shares they own, their proportion of ownership in the firm remains unchanged. Moreover, the total market value of the shares owned is the same after the stock dividend as before; the reason being that a stock dividend will usually result in a drop in share price. Therefore, in our example, a drop in price will bring the total market value of 110 shares (after the stock dividend) to about the same as the total market value of the 100 shares that existed before the dividend. Clearly, under such circumstances, the investor's right back where he started from: he's received nothing of value. The shareholder who's received a stock dividend can, of course, sell the new shares in order to cash out the dividend. But then the value of the stocks owned by that shareholder will be reduced—granted, he'll then own the same number of shares as before the stock dividend, but they'll be worth less.

Some Key Measures of Performance

Professional money managers and seasoned investors tend to use a variety of financial ratios and measures when making investment decisions, particularly when common stock is involved. They look at such things as dividend yield (mentioned earlier), book value, return on equity, earnings per share, and price/earning multiples to get a feel for the investment merits of a particular stock. In short, they use these and other ratios to help them decide whether or not to invest in a particular stock. Fortunately, most of the widely followed ratios can be found in published reports (like *S&P Stock Reports* or *Value Line*), so you don't have to compute them yourself. Even so, if you're thinking about buying, or already have a position in common stock, there are a few measures of performance you'll want to keep track of.

Book Value. The amount of stockholders' equity in a firm is measured by **book value**. This is an accounting measure that is determined by subtracting the firm's liabilities and preferred stocks from the value of its assets. Book value indicates the amount of stockholder funds used to finance the firm. For example, assume Rose Colored Glasses (RCG) had assets of $5 million, liabilities of $2 million, and preferred stock valued at $1 million. The book value of the firm's common stock would be $2 million ($5 million − $2 million − 1 million). If the book value is divided by the number of shares outstanding, the result is *book value per share*. If RCG had 100,000 shares of common stock outstanding, its book value per share would be $20 ($2,000,000/100,000 shares). Because of the positive impact it can have on the growth of the firm, you'd like to see book value per share steadily increasing over time; also, look for stocks whose market prices are comfortably above their book values.

Net Profit Margin As a yardstick of profitability, the **net profit margin** is one of the most widely followed measures of corporate performance. Basically, this ratio relates net profits of the firm to its sales, providing an indication of how well the company is controlling its cost structure. The higher the net profit margin, the more money the company earns. Look for a relatively stable—or even better, an increasing—net profit margin.

Return on Equity Another very important and widely followed measure, **return on equity** (or ROE, for short) reflects the overall profitability of the firm. It captures, in a single ratio, the amount of success the firm is having in managing its assets, operations, and capital structure. Return on equity is important because it has a direct and significant impact on the profits, growth, and dividends of the firm. The better the ROE, the better the financial condition and competitive position of the firm are. Look for a stable or increasing ROE, and watch out for a falling ROE, as it could spell trouble.

---

proxy
A written statement used to assign a stockholder's voting rights to another person, typically one of the existing directors.

dividend yield
The percentage return provided by the dividends paid on common stock; calculated by dividing the cash dividends paid during the year by the stock's market price.

stock dividends
New shares of stock distributed to existing stockholders as a supplement to or substitute for cash dividends.

book value
The amount of stockholders' equity in a firm; determined by subtracting the company's liabilities and preferred stock value from the value of its assets.

net profit margin
A key measure of corporate profitability that relates the net profits of a firm to its sales; it shows the rate of return the company is earning on its sales.

return on equity (ROE)
ROE captures the overall profitability of the firm, as it provides a measure of the returns to stockholders; is important because of its impact on the growth, profits, and dividends of the firm.

Earnings per Share. With stocks, the firm's annual earnings are usually measured and reported in terms of **earnings per share (EPS)**. Basically, EPS translates total corporate profits into profits on a per-share basis and provides a convenient measure of the amount of earnings available to stockholders. Earnings per share is found by using the following simple formula:

$$EPS = \frac{\text{Net profit} - \text{Preferred dividends paid}}{\begin{array}{c}\text{Number of shares} \\ \text{of common stock} \\ \text{outstanding}\end{array}}.$$

For example, if RCG reported a net profit of $350,000, paid $100,000 in dividends to preferred stockholders, and had 100,000 shares of common outstanding, it would have an EPS of $2.50 [($350,000 − $100,000)/100,000]. Note that preferred dividends are *subtracted* from profits since they have to be paid before any monies can be made available to common stockholders. The magnitude of earnings per share is considered important by most stockholders because it represents the amount that the firm has earned on behalf of each outstanding share of common stock. Here, too, look for a steady rate of growth in EPS.

Price/Earnings Ratio. When the prevailing market price per share is divided by the annual earnings per share, the result is the **price/earnings (P/E) ratio**, which is viewed as an indication of investor confidence and expectations. The higher the price/earnings multiple, the more confidence investors are presumed to have in a given security. In the case of RCG, whose shares are currently selling for $30, the price/earnings ratio is 12 ($30 per share/$2.50 per share). This means that RCG stock is selling for 12 times earnings. P/E ratios are important to investors because they provide a feel for the general expectations of the firm. They reveal how aggressively the stock is being priced in the market. Watch out for real high P/Es, since that could indicate the stock is being overpriced (and thus might be headed for a big drop in price). P/E ratios are not static, but tend to move with the market: when the market's soft, a stock's P/E will be low, and when things heat up in the market, so will the stock's P/E.

Beta. A stock's **beta** is an indication of its *price volatility;* it shows how responsive the stock is to the market. In recent years, the use of betas to measure the *market risk* of common stock has become a widely accepted practice, and as a result, published betas are now available from most brokerage firms and investment services. The beta for a given stock is determined by a statistical technique that relates the stock's historical returns to the market. The market (as measured by something like the S&P index of 500 stocks) is used as a benchmark of performance, and it always has a beta of 1.0. From there, everything is relative: low-beta stocks—those with betas of less than 1.0—have low price volatility (they're relatively price-stable), while high-beta stocks—those with betas of more than 1.0—are considered to be highly volatile. In short, the higher a stock's beta, the more risky it is considered to be. Stock betas can be either *positive* or *negative,* though the vast majority are positive, meaning that the stocks move in the same general direction as the market (that is, if the market is going up, so does the price of the stock).

Actually, beta is an *index* of price performance and is interpreted as a percentage response to the market. Thus, if RCG has a beta of, say, 0.8, it will rise (or fall) only 80 percent as fast as the market—if the market goes up by 10 percent, RCG will go up only 8 percent (10 percent × .8). In contrast, if the stock had a beta of 1.8, it would go up or down 1.8 times as fast—the price of the stock would rise higher and fall lower than the market. Clearly, if you're looking for a relatively conservative investment, you should stick with low-beta stocks; on the other hand, if it's capital gains and price volatility you're after, then go with high-beta securities.

Putting a Value on Stock

No matter what kind of investor you are or what your investment objectives happen to be, sooner or later you will have to face one of the most difficult questions in the field of investments: *How much are you willing to pay for the stock?* In order to answer this question, you have to put a value on the stock. Measures such as book value, earnings per share, P/E multiples, and betas are a part of the *fundamental analysis* used to determine the underlying value of a share of stock. Basically, the notion of fundamental analysis is that the value of a stock depends on its expected stream of future earnings. Once you have a handle on the expected stream of future earnings, you can use that information to find the *approximate yield* of an investment (from Equation 12.1). If the expected yield from the investment exceeds your desired or minimum rate of return, you should make the investment—in effect, you should be willing to pay the current or prevailing market price. Put another way, with fundamental analysis you are trying to determine whether or not you should pay the current or prevailing market price of the stock. If the expected yield is less than your desired rate of return, you should not buy the stock (at its current market price), since it is currently "overpriced" and, as such, will not allow you to earn your desired rate of return. While stock valuation and fundamental analysis can become a bit tedious, the process can be made a lot easier if you have access to a personal computer, as the accompanying *Smart Money* box explains.

Types of Common Stock

Common stocks are often classified on the basis of their dividends or their rate of growth in EPS. Among the more popular types of common stock are blue-chip, growth, income, speculative, cyclical, and defensive stocks.

Blue-Chip Stock. Those stocks known to provide a stable and safe return are called **blue-chip stocks**. They are issued by the most stable and strongest companies (such as IBM, GE, Merck, and Bristol-Meyers) and provide uninterrupted streams of dividends and strong long-term growth prospects. Their proven records of earnings and dividends make them attractive investments when stable and reasonably predictable returns are desired. Due to the high levels of investor confidence and the higher than average predictability associated with them, blue-chips normally sell at relatively high P/E ratios and have betas near 1.0 (indeed, these stocks often have betas of less than 1.0, and seldom do they go over 1.1 or 1.15).

Growth Stocks. Stocks that have experienced, and are expected to continue experiencing, consistently high rates of growth in operations and earnings are known as **growth stocks**. A good growth stock might exhibit a *sustained* rate of

growth in earnings of 15 to 20 percent (or more) over a period during which common stocks are averaging only 5 to 6 percent. MCI, Abbott Labs, Stone Container, Raychem, and Kelly Services are all prime examples of growth stocks. These stocks normally pay little or nothing in dividends, since the firm's rapid growth potential requires that its earnings be retained and reinvested. The high growth expectations for these stocks usually cause them to sell at relatively high P/E ratios, and they typically have betas in excess of 1.0. Because of their potential for dramatic price appreciation, they appeal mostly to investors who are seeking capital gains rather than dividend income.

Income Stocks versus Speculative Stocks. Stocks whose appeal is based primarily on the dividends they pay out are known as **income stocks**.

---

earnings per share (EPS)
The return earned on behalf of each share of common stock during a certain time period; calculated by dividing all earnings remaining after paying preferred dividends by the number of common shares outstanding.

price/earnings (P/E) ratio
A measure of investors' presumed confidence in and expectations for a given security; calculated by dividing the prevailing market price per share by the annual earnings per share.

beta
An index of the price volatility imbedded in a share of common stock; provides a reflection of how the price of a share of stock responds to market forces.

blue-chip stock
A stock that is known to provide a safe and stable return; generally issued by companies that are expected to provide an uninterrupted stream of dividends and have good long-term growth prospects.

growth stock
A stock whose earnings and market price have increased over time at a rate that is well above-average level.

income stock
A stock whose chief appeal is the dividends it pays out; typically offers dividend payments that can be expected to increase over time.

S·M·A·R·T   M·O·N·E·Y

Computer-Based Investment Analysis

At a recent investment seminar, a top analyst from a major brokerage firm was asked what he considered to be the single most important factor in finding undervalued stocks. When he responded "a computer," the audience expressed surprise. But, as he explained: "It is virtually impossible to screen through the thousands of actively traded stocks without the aid of the computer. With access to a database of financial information and a computer, you can quickly sift the wheat from the chaff and identify those opportunities that best meet your investment objectives." For years, professional investors have relied on computers to sift through financial records in search of stocks that are undervalued from a fundamental-analysis perspective—that is, focusing on such factors as a company's sales, cash, current assets, and profits rather than its stock price and volume trends. Now, with the advent of personal computers and stock-screening programs, individual investors have the same capability.

Stock-screening programs allow you to extract, from the thousands of stocks traded, a short, specific list of stocks that meet your predefined investment criteria. For example, you might want to identify small, relatively obscure stocks priced between $4 and $10 per share that have a price/earnings (P/E) ratio of less than 10. Or you might prefer to locate relatively large, established companies that distribute generous dividends. Once you specify your investment criteria, these programs will search through a financial database and identify the stocks that meet your requirements. Three of the most popular programs are provided by companies that have long been recognized as leading suppliers of financial information. They are Value/Screen Plus from Value Line Inc., Stockpak II from Standard & Poor's Corp., and Dow Jones Market Microscope from Dow Jones & Co.

Value/Screen Plus

(Value Line Inc., 711 Third Ave., New York, NY 10017; 800/654–0508; $211–$396 a year, depending on frequency of updates; designed for IBM PCs, IBM

compatibles, and Apple Macintosh.) Value/Screen Plus is a combination stock-screening program and fundamental-analysis service that's based on information obtained from Value Line. The service provides updated information on 37 key investment measures for each of the over 1,600 stocks in the database. Users can screen stocks on up to 25 different criteria simultaneously. Once you specify the variables, the program will quickly list the stocks that satisfy your requirements; for example, you can easily screen for stocks that have betas of less than 1.0, ROEs in excess of 15 percent, P/E ratios below 12, and a 5-year growth in earnings of more than 20 percent. With this program, in a matter of minutes, you can generate a manageable list of stocks for further analysis.

Stockpak II

(Standard & Poor's Corp., 25 Broadway, New York, NY 10004; 800/852–5200; $275 a year for a database of 1,500 widely held stocks on the New York Stock

They have a fairly stable stream of earnings, a large portion of which is distributed in the form of dividends. Income shares have relatively high dividend yields and, as such, are ideally suited for individuals who are seeking a relatively safe and high level of current income from their investment capital. An added (and often overlooked) feature of these stocks is that, unlike bonds and preferred stock,

Exchange, American Stock Exchange and over-the-counter market; $275 a year for all NYSE stocks; $275 a year for all Amex stocks; $520 a year for all OTC stocks; designed for the Apple II series and IBM PC or compatibles.) This is a fundamental-analysis software package consisting of a program diskette and one or more database diskettes depending on your subscription choice. Like Value/Screen Plus, you receive diskettes (updated monthly or bimonthly) that contain the latest information. Stockpak II allows you to look up more than 100 items of information about 4,500 companies, graphically compare and analyze information on groups of companies and perform simple or complex screens to find certain types of companies. The information available for each company includes five years of information on annual sales and earnings and data on stock prices, dividends, net income, book value per share, cash, assets, debt, and a variety of ratios. In less than 30 seconds, you can search for stocks with combined attributes

(such as large companies with stable earnings and low P/E ratios, or companies with low prices and high betas) to find those issues meeting your criteria.

Dow Jones Market Microscope

(Dow Jones & Co., P.O. Box 300, Princeton, NJ 08540; 800/257–5114; $349; for IBM PC or compatibles.) This program operates differently than Value/Screen and Stockpak II. Rather than receiving a diskette periodically in the mail, you get the fundamental information required for stock screening via telephone hookup with Dow Jones News Retrieval, a leading information service. Market Microscope is a fundamental-analysis program; with it, you can automatically collect and store fundamental data on more than 4,300 companies and 180 industries. Using a screening routine, you can choose up to 68 financial indicators to select industry groups that meet your predefined requirements. Similar screening routines can then be used to choose individual

companies within the selected industries.

While the above list pertains to common stock investments, similar programs are available for investors interested in bonds and other types of investment vehicles. Examples of some popular bond-analysis software packages include the following: *Bond Manager* ($80—available from Analytical Service Associates; 21 Hollis Rd., Lynn, MA 01904); *Bondcalc* ($125—available from Investment Software of Dallas; Box 38064; Dallas, TX 75238); *Bond$mart* ($335—available from MicroTempo, Inc.; 122 B N. Bedford St.; Arlington, VA 22201); and *BondWare* ($450—available from Davidge Data Systems Corp.; 12 White Street; New York, NY 10013). These programs perform a variety of complicated yield calculations and analytical functions.

Source: Adapted from Thomas A. Meyers, "Computerline: Fundamental Analysis Software," *Personal Investor,* November 1985, 73–74.

holders of income stock can expect *the amount of dividends paid to increase over time*. Examples of income stock would include Central & South West

Utilities, Texas Utilities, Bank of N.Y., and Brooklyn Union Gas. Because of their low risk, these stocks commonly have betas of less than 1.0.

Rather than basing their investment decisions on a proven record of earnings, purchasers of **speculative stocks** gamble that some new information, discovery, or production technique will favorably affect the growth of the firm and inflate the price of its stock. For example, a company whose stock is considered speculative may have recently discovered a new drug or located a valuable resource such as oil. The value of speculative stocks and their P/E ratios tend to fluctuate widely as additional information with respect to the firm's future is received. The betas for speculative stocks are nearly always well in excess of 1.0. Investors in speculative stocks should be prepared to experience losses as well as gains, since *these are high-risk securities.* They include the likes of Intel, Home Depot, Lotus Development, and Shoney's.

Income stocks have relatively high dividend yields and, as such, appeal to individuals who seek a high level of current income. **Fact:** Income shares are those having a long and sustained record of regularly paying a much higher than average level of dividends; because of this, they are highly sought after by investors who are seeking a safe and steady source of current income.

Cyclical Stocks or Defensive Stocks. Stocks whose price movements tend to follow the business cycle are called **cyclical stocks**. This means that when the economy is in an expansionary stage (recovery or inflation), the prices of cyclical stocks increase, and during a contractionary stage (recession or depression), they decline. Most cyclical stocks are found in the basic industries—automobiles, steel, and lumber, for example; these are industries sensitive to changes in economic activity. Investors try to purchase cyclical stocks just prior to an expansionary phase and sell just before the contraction occurs. Since they tend to move with the market, these stocks always have positive betas. Dow Chemical, Alcoa, Phelps Dodge, and Worthington Industries are examples of cyclical stocks.

The prices and returns from **defensive stocks**, unlike those of cyclical stocks, are expected to remain stable during periods of contraction in business activity. For this reason, they are often called *countercyclical.* The shares of consumer goods companies, certain public utilities, and gold mining companies are good examples of defensive stocks. Because they are basically income stocks, their earnings and dividends hold the market price up during periods of economic decline. Betas on these stocks are quite low and occasionally even negative. Philip Morris, Bandag, Clorox, and Humana are all examples of defensive stocks.

Investing in Common

The first step in investing is to know where to put your money; the second is to know when to make your moves. The first question is fairly straightforward, as it basically involves matching your risk and return objectives with the available investment vehicles. As noted earlier, *a stock (or any investment vehicle for that matter) should be considered a viable investment candidate only so long as it promises to generate a sufficiently attractive rate of return* and, in particular, one that fully compensates you for any risks you have to take. Thus, if you're considering the purchase of a stock, you should expect to earn more than what you can get from T-bills or high-grade corporate bonds. The reason: stocks are riskier than bills or bonds, so you *deserve more return.* Indeed, if you can't get enough return from the security to offset the risk, then you shouldn't invest in the stock!

Once you find a stock that you think will give you the kind of return you're looking for, you're ready to deal with the matter of timing your investment. So long as the prospects for the market and the economy are positive, the time may be right to invest in stocks. On the other hand, there are a couple of conditions when investing in stocks just doesn't make any sense at all. In particular, *don't* invest in stocks if:

▪ You feel *very strongly* that the market is headed down in the short run. If you're absolutely certain the market's in for a big fall (or will continue to fall, if it's already doing so), then wait until the market drops, and buy the stock when it's cheaper.

▪ You feel uncomfortable with the general tone of the market—it lacks direction, or there's way too much price volatility to suit you. This became a problem prior to and after the October crash, when program trading started taking over the market. The result was a stock market that behaved more like a commodities market, with an intolerable amount of price volatility. When this happens, fundamentals go out the window, and the market simply becomes too risky. Do what the pros do, and wait it out on the sidelines.

Why Invest in Stocks?   There are three basic reasons for investing in common stock: ① to use the stock as a warehouse of value, ② to accumulate capital, and/or ③ to provide a source of income. Storage of value is important to all investors, since nobody likes to lose money. However, some investors are more concerned about it than others and therefore put safety of principal first in their stock selection process. These investors are more quality-conscious and tend to gravitate toward blue-chips and other nonspeculative shares. Accumulation of capital generally is an important goal to individuals with long-term investment horizons. These investors use the capital gains and/or dividends that stocks provide to build up their wealth. Some use growth stocks for such purposes; others do it with income shares; still others use a little of both. Finally, some people use stocks as a source of income; to them, a dependable flow of dividends is essential. High-yield, good-quality income shares are usually their preferred investment vehicle.

Advantages and Disadvantages of Stock Ownership.   Ownership of common stock has both advantages and disadvantages. Its advantages are threefold. First, the potential returns, in the form of both dividend income and price appreciation, can be quite attractive. The return performance of common stocks over the recent past, as well as over extended periods of time, has been very good. Second, many stocks are actively traded (there are literally thousands of such actively traded stocks) and as such they are a highly liquid form of investment—they can be quickly bought and sold. Finally, they don't involve any direct management (or unusual management problems) and market/company information is usually widely published and easily available.

Risk, the problem of timing purchases and sales, and the uncertainty of dividends are all disadvantages of common stock ownership. Although potential common stock returns may be high, the risk and uncertainty associated with the actual receipt of that return will also be great. Even though careful selection of stocks may somewhat reduce risk, the risk-return trade-off cannot be completely eliminated. In other words, high returns on common stock are not guaranteed; they may or may not occur depending on numerous economic, industry, and company factors. The timing of purchases and sales is closely related to risk. Many investors purchase a stock, hold it for a period of time during which the price drops, and then sell it below the original purchase price—that is, at a loss. The proper strategy, of course, is to buy stocks low and sell high, but the problem of predicting price movements make it difficult to implement such a plan.

Be Sure to Plow Back Your Earnings.   Unless you're living off the income, the basic investment objective with stocks is the same as it is with any other security: to earn an attractive, fully compounded rate of return. This requires regular reinvestment of dividend income. There is no better way to accomplish such reinvestment than through a **dividend reinvestment plan (DRP)**. The basic investment philosophy at work here is that if the

---

speculative stock
Stock that is purchased in the hope that its price per share will increase.

cyclical stock
Stock whose price movements tend to parallel the existing business cycle.

defensive stock
Stock that tends to exhibit price movements that are contrary to the downward movements of the business cycle; often called *countercyclical stock*.

dividend reinvestment plan (DRP)
A program offered by over 1,000 major corporations whereby stockholders can choose to take their dividends in the form of more shares of the company's stock, rather than cash; it provides a relatively painless way of earning a fully compounded rate of return.

EXHIBIT 12.5

Cash or Reinvested Dividends

Participating in a dividend reinvestment plan is a simple, yet highly effective way of building up capital over time. Over the long haul, it can prove to be a great way of earning a fully compounded rate of return on your money.

Situation: Buy 100 shares of stock at $25 a share (total investment $2,500); stock currently pays $1 a share in annual dividends. Price of the stock increases at 8% per year; dividends grow at 5% per year.

Investment Period	Number of Shares Held	Market Value of Stock Holdings	Total Cash Dividends Received
Take Dividends In Cash			
5 years	100	$ 3,672	$ 552
10 years	100	5,397	1,258
15 years	100	7,930	2,158
20 years	100	11,652	3,307
Participate in Dividend Reinvestment Plan			
5 years	115.59	$ 4,245	$0
10 years	135.66	7,322	0
15 years	155.92	12,364	0
20 years	176.00	20,508	0

company is good enough to invest in, it's good enough to reinvest in. In a dividend reinvestment plan, shareholders can sign up to have their cash dividends automatically reinvested in additional shares' of the company's common stock—in essence, it's like taking your cash dividends in the form of more shares of common stock. The idea is to put your money to work by building up your investment in the stock. Such an approach can have a tremendous impact on your investment position over time, as seen in Exhibit 12.5.

Today, over 1,000 companies (including most major corporations) have DRPs in existence, and each one provides investors with a convenient and inexpensive way to accumulate capital. Stocks in most DRPs are acquired free of any brokerage commissions, and some plans even sell stocks to their DRP investors at below-market prices—often at discounts of 3 percent to 5 percent. In addition, most plans credit fractional shares to the investor's account. Shareholders can join these plans simply by sending in a completed authorization form to the company. Once you are in the plan, your number of shares held will begin to accumulate with each dividend date.

Putting your money into stocks that offer dividend reinvestment plans is a great way of building up your investment capital. **Fact:** In a dividend reinvestment plan, you receive *additional shares of stock,* rather than cash every time the company pays a dividend. It's a great way to reap the benefits of compounding and watch your money grow over time.

INVESTING IN BONDS ▪

Bonds are fixed-income securities issued by corporations and various types of governments that provide investors with a high, secure, and regular source of current income. Stop for a moment and give some thought to how you might be able to use bonds in your own investment program. Do you think you'd want to use them if you were an aggressive investor interested mostly in capital gains? Also, consider the question of what causes bond prices to change.

Bonds represent a form of *debt capital,* meaning that they are borrowed funds. Bonds are often referred to as *fixed-income securities* because the debt service obligations of the issuer are fixed—that is, the issuing organization agrees to pay a *fixed amount of interest periodically to the bondholder and to repay a fixed amount of principal* at or before maturity. Bonds normally have face values of $1,000 or $5,000, and maturities of 10 to 30 years.

Why Invest in Bonds?

Like any type of investment vehicle, bonds provide investors with two kinds of income: (1) They provide a generous amount of current income, and (2) they can often be used to generate substantial amounts of capital gains. The current income, of course, is derived from the interest payments received over the life of the issue. Capital gains, in contrast, are earned whenever market interest rates fall. A basic trading rule in the bond market is that interest rates and bond prices move in opposite directions: When interest rates rise, bond prices fall; and when they drop, bond prices rise. Thus, it is possible to buy bonds at one price and, if interest rate conditions are right, to sell them some time later at a higher price. Of course, it is also possible to incur a capital loss should market rates move against the investor. Taken together, the current income and capital gains earned from bonds can lead to attractive and highly competitive investor yields.

In addition to being high-yielding securities, bonds are a versatile investment outlet. They can be used conservatively by those who seek high current income, or aggressively by those who actively go after capital gains. Bonds have long been considered an excellent way of getting high current income, but only since the advent of high and volatile interest rates have they also become recognized as excellent trading vehicles—that is, as a way to earn fat returns from capital gains. Investors found that the number of profitable trading opportunities increased substantially as wider and more frequent swings in interest rates began to occur.

Finally, bond issues, being of generally high quality, can be used for the preservation and long-term accumulation of capital. Many individuals, regularly and over the long haul, commit all or most of their investment funds to bonds because of this attribute.

Basic Issue Characteristics

A bond is a negotiable, long-term debt instrument that carries certain obligations on the part of the issuer. Unlike the holders of common stock, bondholders have no ownership or equity position in the issuing firm or organization. This is so because bonds are debt, and bondholders, in a roundabout way, are only lending money to the issuer.

As a rule, bonds pay interest every six months. The amount of interest paid is a function of the **coupon**, which defines the annual interest that will be paid by the issuer to the bondholder. For instance, a $1,000 bond with an 8 percent coupon would pay $80 in interest every year—generally in the form of two $40 semiannual payments. The principal amount of a bond, also known as *par value,* specifies the amount of capital that must be repaid at maturity—thus, there is $1,000 of principal in a $1,000 bond. To facilitate the marketing of bonds, issues are broken down into standard principal amounts known as *denominations;* for instance, corporate bonds are usually issued in minimum denominations of $1,000. Of course, debt securities regularly trade at market prices that differ from their principal (or par) values. This occurs whenever an issue's coupon differs from the prevailing market rate of interest; in essence, the price of an issue will change until its yield is compatible with prevailing market yields. Such behavior explains why a 7 percent issue will carry a market price of only $825 when the market yield is 9 percent; the drop in price is necessary to raise the yield on this bond from 7 to 9 percent. Issues with market values lower than par are known as *discount bonds* and carry coupons that are less than those on new issues. In contrast, issues with market values in excess of par are called *premium bonds* and have coupons greater than those currently being offered on new issues.

Types of Issues. A single issuer may have many different bonds outstanding at a given point in time. In addition to their coupons and maturities, bonds

---

coupon

That feature on a bond that defines the annual interest income that the issuer will pay the bondholder.

EXHIBIT 12.6

An Announcement of a New Corporate Bond Issue

This unsecured bond was issued by Alltel Corp. in 1989 and will not mature until the year 2009. Each year the company will pay more than $15.5 million in interest and, over the full 20-year life of the bond, more than $300 million in interest will be paid.

This advertisement is neither an offer to sell nor a solicitation of offers to buy any of these securities. The offering is made only by the Prospectus and the related Prospectus Supplement.

April 10, 1989

$150,000,000

CORPORATION

10⅜% Debentures due April 1, 2009

Price 99.368%

Plus accrued interest, if any, from the date of issuance.

Copies of the Prospectus and the related Prospectus Supplement may be obtained in any State in which this announcement is circulated only from such of the undersigned as may legally offer these securities in such State.

Stephens Inc.

Merrill Lynch Capital Markets

Nomura Securities International, Inc.

Source: *The Wall Street Journal*, April 10, 1989.

can be differentiated from one another by the type of collateral behind them. Issues can be either junior or senior. *Senior bonds* are *secured* obligations, since they are backed by a legal claim on some specific property of the issuer that acts as *collateral* for the bonds. Such issues would include **mortgage bonds**, which are secured by real estate, and **equipment trust certificates**, which are backed by equipment and are popular with railroads and airlines. *Junior bonds,* on the other hand, are backed only with a promise by the issuer to pay interest and principal on a timely basis. There are several classes of *unsecured* bonds, the most popular of which is known as a **debenture**. Exhibit 12.6 shows the announcement of a debenture bond that was issued in 1989. Note that even though there was no collateral backing up the obligation, Alltel Corporation was able to issue $150 million worth of these 20-year bonds.

Sinking Fund. Another provision important to investors is the **sinking fund**, which specifies the annual repayment schedule that will be used to pay off the issue and indicates how much principal will be retired each year. Sinking fund requirements generally begin one to five years after the date of issue and continue annually thereafter until all or most of the issue has been paid off. Any amount not repaid by maturity (which might equal 10 to 25 percent of the issue) is then retired with a single balloon payment.

Call Feature. Every bond has a **call feature**, which stipulates the conditions under which the bond can be retired prior to its maturity date. As a rule, a bond cannot be called until it has been outstanding for five years or more. Call features are used most often to replace an issue with one that carries a lower coupon; in this way, the issuer benefits by being able to realize a reduction in annual interest cost. In an attempt to compensate investors who have their bonds called out from under them, a *call premium* (usually equal to about one year's interest) is tacked on to the par value of the bond and paid to investors, along with the issue's par value, at the time the bond is called. For example, if a company decides to call its 12 percent bonds some 15 years before they mature, it might have to pay $1,120 (a call premium of one year's interest— $120—would be added to the par value of $1,000) for every $1,000 bond outstanding.

While this might sound like a good deal, it's really not. Indeed, the only party that really benefits from a bond refunding is the issuer. The bondholder loses a source of high current income—for example, the investor may have a 12 percent bond called away at a time when the best you can do in the market is maybe 8 or 9 percent (which is exactly what happened in 1985 and 1986). To avoid this, stick with bonds that are either *non-callable,* or that have long *call-deferment periods,* meaning they can't be called for refunding (or any other purpose) until the call-deferment period ends.

Registered or Bearer Bonds. Regardless of the type of collateral or kind of issue, a bond may be registered, or many of the older issues could be in bearer form. **Registered bonds** are issued to specific owners and the names of all bondholders formally registered with the issuer, who keeps a running account of ownership and automatically pays interest to the owners by check. In contrast, holders of **bearer bonds** are considered to be the owners, as the issuing organization keeps no record of ownership; they receive interest by "clipping coupons" and sending them in for payment. Bearer bonds once were the most prevalent type of issue but are destined to become a thing of the past, as Congress has mandated that, effective July 1983, all bonds must be issued as *registered* securities.

The Bond Market

Today's bond market offers issues to meet just about any type of investment objective and to suit virtually any type of investor, no matter how conservative or aggressive. As a matter of convenience,

---

mortgage bond
A bond secured by real estate.

equipment trust certificate
A bond secured by certain types of transportation equipment, like railroad cars and airplanes.

debenture
An unsecured bond that is issued on the general credit of the firm.

sinking fund
A provision in a bond issue that specifies the annual repayment schedule that will be used to pay it off and the amount of principal that will be retired each year.

call feature
A feature often included in bond or preferred stock issues that allows the issuer to retire the security during some specified time period at a predetermined price.

registered bond
A bond that automatically pays interest to the owner, who is formally registered as such with the issuer.

bearer bond
A bond whose owner is not formally registered with the issuer and who receives interest not automatically but by redeeming coupons.

the bond market is usually divided into four segments, according to type of issuer: Treasury, agency, municipal, and corporate.

Treasury Bonds. **Treasury bonds** (sometimes called *Treasuries* or *governments*) are a dominant force in the bond market and, if not the most popular, certainly are the best known. The U.S. Treasury issues bonds, notes, and other types of debt securities (such as the Treasury bills discussed in Chapter 5) as a means of meeting the ever increasing needs of the federal government. All Treasury obligations are of the highest quality (backed by the full faith and credit of the U.S. government), a feature that, along with their liquidity, makes them extremely popular with individual and institutional investors. Treasury notes carry maturities of 2 to 10 years, whereas Treasury bonds have maturities as long as 25 years or more. Except for a few of the older issues, Treasury bonds and notes come in minimum denominations of $1,000 (though shorter notes often are available with $5,000 minimum denominations); both bonds and notes are issued in registered form. Interest income is subject to normal federal income tax, but is exempt from state and local taxes.

Agency Bonds. **Agency bonds** are a rapidly growing segment of the U.S. bond market. Though issued by political subdivisions of the U.S. government, *these securities are not obligations of the U.S. Treasury.* They customarily provide yields comfortably above the market rates for Treasuries and therefore offer investors a way to increase returns with little or no real difference in risk. Some of the more actively traded and widely quoted agency issues include the Tennessee Valley Authority, the U.S. Postal Service, the Government National Mortgage Association (or "Ginnie Maes," as they are more commonly known), the Federal Land Bank, the Private Export Funding Corp., the Student Loan Marketing Association, and the Federal Home Loan Bank. Although these issues are not the direct obligations of the U.S. government, a number of them actually do carry government guarantees and thus effectively represent the full faith and credit of the U.S. Treasury. Moreover, some have unusual interest-payment provisions (interest is paid monthly in

a few instances and yearly in one case), and many are exempt from state and local taxes.

Municipal Bonds. **Municipal bonds** are the issues of states, counties, cities, and other political subdivisions, such as school districts and water and sewer districts. They are unlike other bonds in that their interest income is usually free from federal income tax (which is why these issues are known as *tax-free bonds*). Any capital gains that might be earned from municipals, however, is subject to the usual federal taxes. The tax-free yield is probably the most important feature of municipal bonds and is certainly a major reason why individuals invest in them. Exhibit 12.7 shows what a taxable bond (like a corporate or Treasury issue) would have to yield in order to equal the take-home yield of a tax-free municipal bond. It demonstrates how the attractiveness of municipal yields varies with an investor's income level; clearly, the higher the individual's tax bracket, the more attractive municipal bonds become.

As a rule, the yields on municipal bonds are substantially lower than the returns available from fully taxable issues. Thus, unless the tax effect is sufficient to raise the yield on a municipal to a figure that equals or surpasses taxable rates, it obviously doesn't make sense to buy municipal bonds. You can determine the return a fully taxable bond would have to provide in order to match the after-tax return on a lower-yielding tax-free issue by computing what is known as a municipal's *fully taxable equivalent yield:*

$$\begin{array}{c} \text{Fully taxable} \\ \text{equivalent yield} \end{array} = \frac{\begin{array}{c} \text{Yield of} \\ \text{Municipal bond} \end{array}}{1 - \text{Tax rate}}$$

For example, if a certain municipal bond offered a yield of 6 percent, an individual in the 33 percent tax bracket would have to find a fully taxable bond with a yield of nearly 9 percent in order to reap the same after-tax return: that is, $6\% \div (1 - .33) = 6\% \div .67 = 8.95\%$.

Municipal bonds are generally issued as **serial obligations**, meaning that the issue is broken into a series of smaller bonds, each with its own maturity date and coupon rate. Thus, instead of the bond having just one maturity date 20 years from now, it

EXHIBIT 12.7

Table of Taxable Equivalent Yields

Tax-exempt securities generally yield less than fully taxable obligations, and because of that, you have to be in a sufficiently high tax bracket (28 percent or more) to make up for the yield shortfall.

Tax Bracket	To Match a Tax-Free Yield of:							
	5%	6%	7%	8%	9%	10%	12%	14%
	You must earn this yield on a taxable investment:							
15%	5.88	7.06	8.24	9.41	10.59	11.76	14.12	16.47
28	6.94	8.33	9.72	11.11	12.50	13.89	16.67	19.44
33	7.46	8.95	10.45	11.94	13.43	14.92	17.91	20.90

will have a series of, say, 20 maturity dates over the 20-year time frame. The serial feature of municipal bonds is illustrated in Exhibit 12.8, which contains the announcement of a recently issued municipal bond. Because there is such a diversity of municipal bonds available, investors must also be careful to assess their quality in order to ensure that the issuer will not default. Although it may not seem that municipal issuers would default on either interest or principal payments, it does occur! Investors should be especially cautious when investing in **revenue bonds**, which are municipal bonds that are serviced from the income generated from specific income-producing projects, such as toll roads. Unlike issuers of so-called **general obligation bonds**—which are backed by the full faith and credit of the municipality—the issuer of a revenue bond is obligated to pay principal and interest *only if a sufficient level of revenue* is generated. General obligation municipal bonds, however, are required to be serviced in a prompt and timely fashion regardless of the level of tax income generated by the municipality.

Caution should be used when buying municipal bonds because *some of these issues are tax-exempt and others are not.* One effect of the far-reaching 1986 Tax Reform Act was to change the status of municipal bonds used to finance nonessential projects, so that their interest income is no longer exempt from federal taxes. Such bonds are known as *taxable munies,* and they offer yields that are considerably higher than normal tax-exempt securities.

Buy one of these issues and you'll end up holding a bond whose interest income is fully taxable by the IRS.

Treasury bond
A federal government obligation that has a maturity of more than ten years and pays interest semiannually; also call a *government.*

agency bond
An obligation of a political subdivision of the U.S. government; typically provides yields above the market rates for Treasury bonds.

municipal bond
A bond issued by state and local governments for the purpose of financing certain projects; interest income is usually exempt from federal taxes.

serial obligation
An issue, usually a municipal bond, that is broken down into a series of smaller bonds, each with its own maturity date and coupon rate.

revenue bond
A municipal bond that is serviced from the income generated from a specific project.

general obligation bond
A municipal bond that is backed by the full faith and credit of the issuing municipality rather than by the revenue generated from a given project.

EXHIBIT 12.8

A Municipal Serial Bond Issue

Like many municipal issues, this bond was sold as a serial obligation. Observe that it has a series of 24 maturity dates running from 1990 to 2013, each with its own coupon rate. Note, for example, that $2.725 million of the issue matures in 1998 and carries a coupon "rate" of 7.0 percent; another $2.945 million matures in 1999 and carries a 7.10 percent coupon; and so forth through the year 2013, when the last issue is retired.

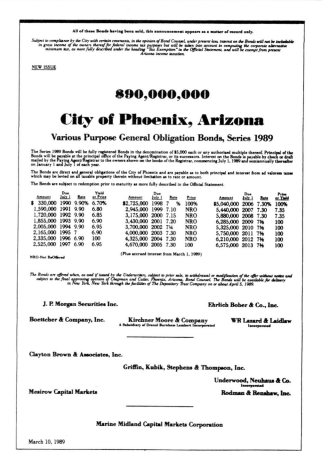

Corporate Bonds. The major nongovernmental issuers of bonds are corporations. The market for **corporate bonds** is customarily subdivided into several segments, which include *industrials* (the most diverse of the groups); *public utilities* (the dominant group in terms of volume of new issues); *rail and transportation bonds*; and *financial issues* (banks, finance companies, and so forth).

The corporate bond market offers not only a full spectrum of bond qualities but also the widest range of issue types. There are *first mortgage bonds, convertible bonds* (discussed in the next section), *debentures, subordinated debentures,* and *income bonds.* Interest on corporate bonds is paid semiannually, and sinking funds are very common. The bonds usually come in $1,000 denominations and are issued on a term basis with a single maturity date. Maturities usually range from 25 to 40 years. Nearly all carry call provisions that prohibit prepayment of the issue during the first 5 to 10 years. Corporate issues are popular with individuals because of their relatively high yields.

The Special Appeal of Zero Coupon Bonds and Junk Bonds. In addition to the standard bond vehicles described above, investors can also choose from a growing number of *specialty issues*—bonds that, for the most part, have unusual coupon or repayment provisions. Specialty issues are often among the more popular types of bonds on Wall Street. In fact, two of the hottest issues today are securities that are out-of-the-ordinary in one way or another; one is the zero coupon bond and the other is something known as a junk bond. As the name implies, **zero coupon bonds** have no coupons. Rather, they are sold at a deep discount from their par values and then increase in value over time at a compound rate of return, so that at maturity they are worth much more than their initial investment. Other things being equal, the cheaper the bond, the greater the return one can earn (for example, whereas a 10 percent bond might sell for $239, an issue with a 15 percent yield will cost only $123). Because they have no coupons, these bonds pay nothing to the investor until they mature. In this sense, zero coupon bonds are like the Series EE savings bonds that we examined in Chapter 5. Strange as it might seem, this is the main attraction of zero coupon bonds. Since there are no interest payments, investors need not worry about reinvesting coupon income twice a year; instead, the fully compounded rate of return on a zero coupon bond is virtually guaranteed at the rate that existed when the issue was sold. For example, in early 1989 good-grade zero coupon bonds with 20-year maturities were available at yields of around 11 percent; thus, for just $124 investors could buy a bond that could be worth 8 times that amount, or $1,000, when it matures in 20 years. Best of all, they would be *locking in* an 11 percent compound rate of return on their investment capital for the full 20-year life of the issue.

Because of their unusual tax exposure (even though the bonds do no pay regular yearly interest, the IRS treats the annually accrued interest as taxable income), zeros should be used only in tax-sheltered investments, such as individual retirement accounts (IRAs), or be held by minor children who are likely to be taxed at low rates, if at all. Zeros are issued by corporations, municipalities, federal agencies, and the U.S. Treasury. In addition, many of the major brokerage houses package U.S. Treasury securities as zeros and sell them to the investing public in the form of investment trusts marketed under such names as *TIGRS, CATS,* and *LIONS.*

Another type of specialty issue that appeals to a large segment of the investment public is the **junk bond**, or *high-yield bond,* as it's also called. Essentially, these are highly speculative securities—issued primarily by corporations and by a growing number of municipalities—that have received low ratings from bond-rating agencies like Moody's and Standard & Poor's. Despite their derogatory name, such bonds are booming in popularity in large part because of the very high returns they offer; in early 1989, for example, returns of 16 percent or more were not unusual. However, *such returns are available only because of the very high risk involved.* Traditionally, the term has been applied to the issues of *troubled companies,* securities that might have been highly rated when first issued, only to slide to low ratings through corporate mismanagement, heavy competition, or other factors. In the past few years, however, most of the junk bonds have originated not with troubled companies, but rather with a growing number of companies that use enormous amounts of this form of debt to finance corporate takeovers and leveraged buyouts.

---

corporate bond
A bond issued by a corporation; categories include industrials, public utilities, railroad and transportation bonds, and financial issues.

zero coupon bond
A bond that pays no annual interest but sells at a deep discount below par.

junk bond
Also known as *high-yield* bonds, these are highly speculative securities that have received low ratings from Moody's or Standard & Poor's; the low ratings mean that the issuers could have difficulty meeting interest and principal payments as they come due.

EXHIBIT 12.9

Moody's and Standard & Poor's Bond Ratings

Agencies like Moody's and Standard & Poor's rate corporate and municipal bonds; the ratings provide an indication of the bonds' investment quality (particularly with respect to an issue's default risk exposure).

BOND RATINGS[a]		
Moody's	**S&P**	**Description**
Aaa	AAA	*Prime-Quality Investment Bonds*—This is the highest rating assigned, denoting extremely strong capacity to pay.
Aa A	AA A	*High-Grade Investment Bonds*—These are also considered very safe bonds, though they're not quite as safe as Aaa/AAA issues; double-A-rated bonds (Aa/AA) are safer (have less risk of default) than single-A-rated issues.
Baa	BBB	*Medium-Grade Investment Bonds*—These are the lowest of the investment-grade issues; they're felt to lack certain protective elements against adverse economic conditions.
Ba B	BB B	*Junk Bonds*—With little protection against default, these are viewed as highly speculative securities.
Caa Ca C	CCC CC C D	*Poor-Quality Bonds*—These are either in default or very close to it.

[a]Some ratings may be modified to show relative standing within a major rating category; for example, Moody's uses numerical modifiers (1, 2, 3), whereas S&P uses plus (+) or minus (−) signs.

Even though these firms, known as *fallen angels,* may not be considered troubled in the normal sense of the word, investors should keep in mind that these issues are still low-rated debt that carry with them a *high risk of default!* Junk bonds should be used only by investors who are thoroughly familiar with their risk and, equally important, who are comfortable with it. And even then, most experts agree that the best way to invest in junk bonds is through a diversified portfolio of these securities—as in a *junk bond mutual fund.*

Bond Ratings

Bond ratings are like grades: A letter grade assigned to a bond issue designates its investment quality. Ratings are widely used and are an important part of the municipal and corporate bond markets. The two largest and best known rating agencies are Moody's and Standard & Poor's. Every time a large, new issue comes to the market, it is analyzed by a staff of professional bond analysts to determine its default risk exposure and investment quality. The financial records of the issuing organization are thoroughly worked over and its future prospects assessed. The result of all this is the assignment of a bond rating at the time of issue that indicates the ability of the issuing organization to service its debt promptly. Exhibit 12.9 lists the various ratings assigned to bonds by each of the two major services. Except for slight variations in designations (Aaa versus AAA, for example), the meaning and interpretation are basically the same. Older, outstanding issues also are regularly reviewed to insure that their assigned ratings are still valid. Most issues will carry a single rating to maturity, but it is not uncommon for some to undergo revision. Finally, although it may appear that the firm is receiving the rating, it is actually the individual issue that is being rated. As a result, a firm can have different ratings assigned to its issues; the senior securities, for example, might carry one rating and the junior issues another, lower one. Most bond investors pay careful attention to ratings, since they can affect comparative market yields—specifically, the higher the rating, the lower the yield of an obligation, other things being equal. Thus, whereas an A-rated bond might offer a 10 percent yield, a comparable AAA issue would probably yield something like 9½ to 9¾ percent.

Bond Prices and Yields

The price of a bond is a function of its coupon, maturity, and movement of market interest rates. When interest rates go down, bond prices go up, and vice versa. The extent to which bond prices move in a given direction, however, depends on the magnitude of interest rate movements, for the greater the moves in interest rates, the greater the swings in bond prices. But there's more, for bond prices will also vary according to the coupon and maturity of the issue—that is, bonds with *lower coupons* and/or *longer maturities* will respond more vigorously to changes in market rates and undergo *greater price swings.* It should be obvious, therefore, that if interest rates are moving *up,* the investor should seek high coupon bonds with short maturities, since this will cause minimal price variation and act to preserve as much capital as possible. In contrast, if rates are heading *down,* that's the time to be in long-term bonds—if you're a speculator looking for a lot of capital gains, then go with long-term, *low coupon* bonds, whereas if you're trying to lock in a high level of coupon (interest) income, then stick with long-term, *high coupon* bonds that offer plenty of call protection (which you can get from issues that are non-callable or have extended call-deferment periods). In order to fully appreciate bond prices, however, you've got to understand the concept of bond yields and the effects of interest rates on prices.

When interest rates go down, bond prices also go down because such securities become less valuable. **Fantasy:** Bond prices and interest rates move in the *opposite* direction; as a result, when interest rates go down, bond prices go up.

Current Yield and Yield to Maturity. The *yield* on a bond is the rate of return that you would earn if you held the bond for a stated period of time. The two most commonly cited bond yields are current yield and yield to maturity. **Current yield** reflects the amount of annual interest income the bond provides relative to its current market price. The formula for current yield is

$$\text{Current yield} = \frac{\text{Annual interest income}}{\text{Market price of bond}}$$

As you can see, the current yield on a bond is basically the same as the dividend yield on a stock. Assume, for example, that a 9 percent bond with a $1,000 face value is currently selling for $910. Since annual interest income would equal $90 (.09 × $1,000) and the current market price of the bond is $910, its current yield would be 9.89 percent ($90/$910). This yield, which is commonly quoted in the financial press, would be of interest to investors seeking current income; other things being equal, the higher the current yield, the more attractive a bond would be to such an investor.

The annual rate of return that a bondholder would receive *if he or she held the issue to its maturity* is captured in the bond's **yield to maturity**. This measure captures two types of return; the annual interest income and the recovery of the principal value of the bond at maturity. If a bond is purchased at its face value, its yield to maturity will equal the coupon, or stated, rate of interest. If it is purchased at a discount, its yield to maturity will be greater than the coupon rate because the investor will receive, in addition to annual interest income, the full face value of the bond even though he or she paid something less than par—in effect, the investor will earn some capital gains on the investment. Of course, if the bond is purchased at a premium, the opposite will be true: The

---

current yield
The amount of current income a bond provides relative to its current market price.

yield to maturity
The annual rate of return that a bondholder purchasing a bond today would earn if he or she held it to maturity.

yield to maturity on the issue will be less than its coupon rate since the transaction will involve a capital loss—that is, the investor will pay more for the bond than he or she will get back at maturity.

You can find the yield to maturity of a bond by using the *approximate yield* formula introduced earlier in this chapter. In particular, by setting the future price (FP) of the investment equal to the bond's face value ($1,000), you can use the following version of the approximate yield equation to find the *approximate yield to maturity of a bond:*

$$\text{Approximate Yield to Maturity} = \frac{CI + \left[\dfrac{\$1,000 - CP}{N}\right]}{\left[\dfrac{CP + \$1,000}{2}\right]}$$

As you will recall, *CI* equals annual current income (or annual interest income, in the case of a bond), *CP* stands for current price (of the bond), and *N* is the investment period (the number of years to maturity). Assume, for example, that you are contemplating the purchase of a $1,000, 9 percent bond with 15 years remaining to maturity, and that the bond currently trades at a price of $910. Given *CI* = $90, *CP* = $910, and *N* = 15 years, the approximate yield to maturity on this bond will be

$$\begin{aligned}\text{Approximate Yield to Maturity} &= \frac{\$90 + \left[\dfrac{\$1,000 - \$910}{15}\right]}{\left[\dfrac{\$910 + \$1,000}{2}\right]}\\[2em]&= \frac{\$90 + \left[\dfrac{\$90}{15}\right]}{\left[\dfrac{\$1,910}{2}\right]} = 10.05\%.\end{aligned}$$

This is above both the 9 percent stated rate and the 9.89 percent current yield, since the bond is purchased at a discount from its face value. (Note that had the bond been selling at $1,090, it would have had a current yield of 8.26 percent and an approx-

imate yield to maturity of 8.04 percent—both below the 9 percent coupon rate; such behavior would be due to the fact that the bond was selling at a premium price.)

Yield to maturity measures are used by investors to assess the underlying attractiveness of a bond investment. The higher the yield to maturity, the more attractive the investment, other things being equal. *If a bond provided a yield to maturity that equaled or exceeded an investor's desired rate of return, it would be considered a worthwhile investment candidate,* as it would promise a yield that would adequately compensate the investor for the level of risk involved.

Effects of Interest Rates on Bond Prices. Interest rate fluctuations directly affect the prices at which bonds sell. If market interest rates increase, bond prices will decrease in order to provide investors with competitive yields. In contrast, if market rates decline, bond prices will increase in order to adjust the yield to a level that will be competitive with the prevailing rate of interest. If you purchase a bond with the intention of holding it to maturity, changes in market rates will not affect the actual return you receive; in other words, you will get the expected yield as long as you hold the bond to maturity. This is because, so long as the bond doesn't default, *the price of a debt security will always move towards its par value,* no matter what happens to interest rates. However, if you have to sell a bond prior to maturity, the effects of changing interest rates can be significant. For example, if you bought a 10 percent, 20-year bond at par ($1,000) and had to sell it after, say, five years, when market interest rates had risen to 13 percent, you would be able to sell the bond at only $800 —that is, you would take a $200 loss on your investment, all because interest rates went up! Further, *such price behavior would apply even to the highest-grade investment vehicles, from triple-A rated corporate bonds and U.S. Treasury bonds.* Such price behavior actually is the result of *interest rate risk,* since it is the change in market interest rates that leads to decreases in bond price. Of course, interest rates can also go down, in which case an investor would realize a capital gain if he or she sold the bonds prior to maturity.

PREFERREDS AND CONVERTIBLES

While stocks and bonds are the most basic of investment vehicles, there are some securities (like preferred stocks and convertible bonds) that combine the features of both equity and debt issues. Can you think of some ways that preferred stocks are like common stocks? In what ways are they like bonds? How about convertibles: in what way are they like bonds? Like stocks? Think about these questions before going on.

Preferred stocks and convertible securities are corporate issues that hold a position senior to common stock. Although preferreds are actually a form of equity ownership, they, along with convertibles, are considered to be fixed-income securities because their level of current income is fixed. Convertible securities, initially issued as bonds or preferred stocks, are subsequently convertible into shares of the issuing firm's common stock. Preferred stocks, in contrast, are issued and remain as equity. They derive their name in part from the preferential claim on income they command—that is, all preferred dividends must be paid before any payments can be made to holders of common stock.

Preferred Stocks

Preferred stocks carry a fixed dividend that is paid quarterly and stated either in dollar terms or as a percent of par (or stated) value. They are considered *hybrid securities* because they possess features of both common stocks and corporate bonds. They are like common stocks in that they pay dividends, *which may be passed* when corporate earnings fall below certain levels. Moreover, preferreds represent equity ownership and are issued without stated maturity dates. They are, however, also like bonds in that they provide investors with a prior claim on income and assets, and the level of current income is usually fixed for the life of the issue. Most important, because these securities usually trade on the basis of the yield they offer to investors, they

are viewed in the marketplace as fixed-income obligations and, as a result, are treated much like bonds.

Preferred Stock Features. Preferred stocks possess features that not only distinguish them from other types of securities, but also help to differentiate one preferred from another. For example, the amount of dividends that a stock pays is a common way of describing an issue of preferred stock—thus, a company could have a "three dollar" preferred stock outstanding (meaning the issue pays $3 per share in annual dividends) and another issue of preferred that pays $4.75 a share in yearly dividends. These are two separate issues and they would trade at two different prices. A number of preferred stocks are issued with call features, which means they can be retired if the issuing company decides to do so, and some even have sinking fund provisions, indicating how they will be paid off over time (sinking fund preferreds, in effect, have implied maturity dates). In addition to these features, there are two other provisions that preferred stock investors should be aware of: (1) the cumulative-dividends provision, and (2) the dividend-participation feature.

Cumulative versus Noncumulative. Most preferred stock is **cumulative**, which means that any dividends passed by the directors in previous periods must be paid prior to distributing any dividends to common stockholders. For example, assume a firm has outstanding a *$4 preferred stock* (which means the stated dividend is $4 per year, or $1 per quarter) and that the last two quarterly dividends have been passed. Before any dividends can be paid to the common stockholders, the preferred stockholders must be paid the $2 of past dividends *plus the current quarterly dividend of $1.* Had the preferred stock been *noncumulative,* only the current $1 dividend would have had to be paid prior to distributing any earnings to the common stockholders.

> **cumulative (preferred stock)**
> A preferred stock feature requiring that any passed dividends must be paid prior to distributing any dividends to common stockholders.

Participating versus Nonparticipating.
As a rule, preferred stocks are issued as *nonparticipating,* which means that the preferred stockholders receive only the stated amount of dividends. Occasionally, a **participating** preferred stock is issued. Such an issue allows the preferred stockholders to share in the distribution of additional dividends once the common stockholders have received a specified dividend. An example might be a preferred stock in which the preferred stockholders participate equally with the common stockholders on a per share basis once the latter have received a specified per share dividend. Participating preferred stock is normally issued when a firm is unable to obtain needed financing using more conventional types of securities.

Investing in Preferreds. Most individuals invest in preferred stocks because of the high current income they provide in the form of annual dividends. Moreover, such dividend income is highly predictable even though it lacks legal backing and can be passed. It is not surprising, therefore, that dividend yield is viewed by many investors as the key ingredient in determining the return behavior and investment appeal of most preferred stocks. *Dividend yield*—which is found by dividing annual dividend income by the market price of the stock—is a reflection of an issue's current yield and, as such, is used to assess preferred stock investment opportunities. Other things being equal, the higher the dividend yield is, the more attractive the investment vehicle. For example, suppose a certain preferred stock pays a dividend of $2 per year and is currently priced at $20; this preferred would have a dividend yield of $2/$20 = 10%. Whether or not a 10 percent return from this preferred stock makes for a good investment depends on (1) the amount of risk exposure involved and (2) the kinds of returns you can generate elsewhere—in other words, if you can earn better than 10 percent on other similarly risky investments then do it!

Once you invest in a preferred, you should keep your eyes on market interest rates, since preferred stock prices are closely related to prevailing market rates; after all, you are investing in a *fixed-income* security whose value is determined chiefly by dividend yield. When the general level of interest rates moves up, the yields on preferreds rise and their prices decline accordingly; in contrast, when rates drift down, the yields on preferreds decrease and their prices rise. Thus, like that of any fixed-income security, the price behavior of most good-grade preferred stocks is inversely related to market interest rates.

Convertible Securities

Convertible issues, more popularly known as simply *convertibles,* represent still another type of fixed-income security. Although they possess the features and performance characteristics of both fixed-income and equity securities, *convertibles should be viewed primarily as a form of equity.* Most investors commit their capital to such obligations not because of their attractive yields, but because of the potential price performance that the stock side of the issue offers. In short, convertible securities are popular with individual investors because of the *equity kicker* they provide. Not surprisingly, whenever the stock market is strong, convertibles tend to be strong, and vice versa. Convertible bonds and convertible preferreds are equally linked to the firm's equity position and are therefore usually considered interchangeable for investment purposes. Except for a few peculiarities, such as the fact that preferreds pay dividends rather than interest and do so on a quarterly rather than semiannual basis, convertible bonds and convertible preferreds are evaluated similarly. The following discussion on convertible bonds, therefore, applies to convertible preferreds as well.

Issue Features. A convertible bond basically is issued as a *debenture* (that is, unsecured debt), but it carries the provision that, within a stipulated time period, *it may be converted into a certain number of shares of the issuing company's common stock.* Generally, the investor merely trades in the convertible bond for a stipulated number of shares of common stock. Exhibit 12.10 provides the details of a recently issued convertible bond. Note that this obligation originally came out as a 9% debenture bond but in time, each $1,000 bond can be exchanged for (converted into) Western Digital stock at $14.45 per share. Thus, *regardless of what happens to the market price of the stock,* the convertible

EXHIBIT 12.10

A Newly Issued Convertible Bond

Investors who hold this Western Digital bond can convert it, anytime prior to maturity, into the company's common stock at a stated price of $14.45 per share, and in so doing, receive 69.2 shares of stock in exchange for each $1,000 convertible bond they hold. Prior to conversion, the bondholders will receive annual interest income of $90.00 for each bond.

This announcement is neither an offer to sell nor a solicitation of offers to buy any of these securities. The offering is made only by the Prospectus.

NEW ISSUE   May 11, 1989

$60,000,000

WESTERN DIGITAL

C O R P O R A T I O N

9% Convertible Subordinated Debentures Due 2014

The Debentures are convertible at any time prior to maturity, unless previously redeemed, into shares of Common Stock of the Company at a conversion price of $14.45 per share, subject to adjustment under certain conditions.

Price 100%

plus accrued interest, if any, from May 17, 1989

Copies of the Prospectus may be obtained in any State in which this announcement is circulated only from such of the undersigned as may legally offer these securities in such State. These securities are redeemable prior to maturity as set forth in the Prospectus.

The First Boston Corporation

Needham & Company, Inc.

Dillon, Read & Co. Inc.

Source: *The Wall Street Journal,* May 11, 1989.

bond investor can redeem each $1,000 bond for 69.2 shares of stock: $1,000/$14.45 = 69.2. If at the time of conversion the stocks were trading in the market at $25 a share, then the investor would have just converted a $1,000 bond into $1,730 worth of stocks (69.2 × $25).

participating (preferred stock)
A preferred stock provision that allows the holder to share in the distribution of additional dividends once common stockholders have received their specified dividends.

The key element of any convertible issue is its **conversion privilege**, which stipulates the conditions and specific nature of the conversion feature. First, it states exactly when the debenture can be converted. Generally, there will be an initial waiting period of six months to perhaps two years after the date of issue, during which time the debenture cannot be converted. The *conversion period* then begins, after which the issue can be converted at any time. Technically it is the *bondholder* who has the right to convert the bond into the common stock, but more commonly the issuing firm will initiate the conversion by calling the issue. From the investor's point of view, the most important item of information is the **conversion ratio**, which specifies the number of shares of common stock that the bond can be converted into. For example, a $1,000 convertible bond might stipulate a conversion ratio of 20, meaning that you can "cash in" one convertible bond for 20 shares of the company's stock.

Convertible bonds are so named because they can be exchanged for a set number of shares of common stock. **Fact:** Convertible securities carry the provision that they may, within a stipulated time period, be converted into a certain number of shares of the issuing company's common stock.

Conversion Value. Given the significance of the price behavior of the underlying common stock to the value of a convertible security, one of the most important measures to a convertible bond investor is conversion value. In essence, **conversion value** is an indication of what a convertible issue would trade for *if it were priced to sell on the basis of its stock value.* Conversion value is easy to find: Simply multiply the conversion ratio of the issue by the current market price of the underlying common stock. For example, a convertible that carried a conversion ratio of 20 would have a conversion value of $1,200 if the firm's stock traded at a current market price of $60 per share (20 × $60 = $1,200). Unfortunately, convertible issues seldom trade precisely at their conversion values; rather, they invariably trade at **conversion premiums**, which means that the convertibles are priced in the market at more than their conversion values. For example, a convertible that traded at $1,400 and had a conversion value equal to $1,200 would have a conversion premium of $200 ($1,400 − $1,200 = $200).

Investment Merits. Convertible securities appeal to investors who want the price potential of a common stock along with the downside risk protection of a corporate bond. This two-sided feature is critical with convertibles and is virtually impossible to match with straight common or straight debt. As a rule, whenever a convertible trades near or above its par value ($1,000), it will exhibit price behavior that closely matches that of the underlying common stock: If the stock goes up in price, so will the convertible, and vice versa. In fact, the price change of the convertible will *exceed* that of the common, because of the presence of a conversion ratio. For example, if a convertible carries a ratio of, say, 20, then for every point the common stock goes up (or down) in price, the price of the convertible will move in the *same direction by a mul-*

---

conversion privilege
The provision in a convertible issue that stipulates the conditions of the conversion feature, such as the conversion period and conversion ratio.

conversion ratio
A ratio that specifies the number of shares of common stock into which a convertible bond can be converted.

conversion value
A measure of what a convertible issue would trade for it it were priced to sell on the basis of its stock value; found by multiplying the conversion ratio by the current market price of the underlying common stock.

conversion premium
The difference between a convertible security's market price and its conversion value.

tiple of 20. Because of the obvious importance of the underlying common stock, investors should carefully consider this element before investing in convertibles. If the future prospects of a stock are promising, the convertible could turn out to be a good investment.

A final feature of convertible bonds is that the current income from their interest payments normally exceeds the income from the dividends that would be received from a comparable investment in the underlying common stock. For example, a

$1,000 convertible with an 8 percent coupon would yield $80 per year to the holder; if the convertible carried a conversion ratio of 20, and each share of stock paid $2.50 in dividends, an investment in 20 shares of the firm's stock would provide only $50 in per year dividend income. Thus, with convertibles it is possible to reap the advantages of common stock (in the form of potential upward price appreciation) and still generate improved current income.

SUMMARY

- Investing plays an important part in personal financial planning, as it is the vehicle by which your financial goals can be reached. Your investment activities should be based on a sound investment plan that is linked to an ongoing savings plan.
- Most people invest their money in order to enhance their current income, accumulate funds for a major expenditure, save for retirement, and/or shelter some of their income from taxes. These objectives can be achieved most effectively when you confine your investment activities to investment vehicles that are expected to provide satisfactory rates of return—that is, rates of return that provide adequate compensation for risk and that meet or exceed desired rates of return.
- While investing offers returns in the form of current income and/or capital gains, it also involves risk; the basic types of investment risk are business risk, financial risk, market risk, purchasing power risk, interest rate risk, liquidity risk, and event risk—all of which combine to affect the level of return from an investment.
- Common stocks are a popular form of investing that can be used to meet just about any investment objective—investors can choose from blue-

chip stocks, growth stocks, income stocks, speculative stocks, even cyclical or defensive stocks. Regardless of the type, the value of such stocks is based on measures like net profit margin, ROE, earnings per share, price/earnings (P/E) ratio, beta, and approximate yield.

- Bonds are another popular form of investing; such securities are basically the publicly issued debt of corporations and various levels of government (from the U.S. Treasury and various agencies of the U.S. government to state and local—municipal—governments). Known as fixed-income securities, such obligations can be used to generate either current income or capital gains (as when market interest rates go down).
- Preferred stocks and convertible bonds combine the features of both equity and debt securities, and are also widely used by individual investors. Preferred stocks are like common stocks to the extent that they pay dividends, but they are also like bonds in that they provide investors with a fixed claim on assets and a fixed level of income; in contrast, convertible bonds are issued as debt securities but they carry a provision that allows their holders to convert the bonds into shares of common stock.

QUESTIONS AND PROBLEMS

1. Briefly discuss the relationship between investing and personal financial planning. Do these two activities complement each other?

2. Identify the four major investment objectives. Why are investment objectives important?

3. Describe the various types of risk to which investors are exposed. What is meant by the risk-return trade-off? What is the risk-free rate of return?

4. Beth Kaminski is a young career woman who's presently employed as the managing editor of a well-known financial journal. While she thoroughly enjoys her job and the people she works with, what she would really like to do is open a bookstore of her own. In particular, she would like to open her store in about eight years, and she figures she'd need about $50,000 in capital to do so. Suppose she thinks she can make about 8 percent on her money, use a worksheet like the one in Exhibit 12.1 to find the following:

   a. How much would she have to invest today, in one lump sum, to end up with $50,000 in eight years?

   b. If she's starting from scratch, how much would she have to put away annually to accumulate the needed capital in eight years?

   c. How about if she already has $12,000 socked away; how much would she have to put away annually to accumulate the required capital in eight years?

   d. Given Beth now has a handle on how much she has to save, briefly explain how she would use an *investment plan* to help her reach her objective.

5. What makes for a good investment? Use the approximate yield formula (Equation 12.1) to rank the following investments according to their expected returns:

   a. Buy a stock for $45 a share, hold it for three years, and sell it for $75 a share (the stock pays annual dividends of $3 a share).

   b. Buy a security for $25, hold it for two years, and sell it for $60 (current income on this security is zero).

   c. Buy a one-year, 12 percent note for $950 (assume the note has a $1,000 par value and that it will be held to its maturity).

6. What are rights? How do they differ from warrants?

7. Define and briefly discuss each of the following common stock measurements: (a) book value, (b) ROE, (c) earnings per share (EPS), (d) price/earnings (P/E) ratio, and (e) beta.

8. Selected financial information about Engulf and Devour, Inc. is as follows:

Total assets	$20,000,000
Total liabilities	$ 8,000,000
Total preferred stock	$ 3,000,000
Total annual preferred stock dividends	$ 240,000
Net profits after tax	$ 2,500,000
Number of shares of common stock outstanding	500,000 shares
Current market price of common stock	$50.00 per share
Annual common stock dividends	$2.50 a share

Using the above information, compute the following:

   a. The stock's dividend yield
   b. Book value per share
   c. Earnings per share
   d. P/E ratio

9. Briefly discuss some of the different types of common stock. Which type(s) would be most appealing to you, and why?

10. Under what conditions would a stock be considered a viable investment candidate? What are dividend reinvestment plans, and how do they fit into a stock investment program?

11. What is the difference between a secured bond and an unsecured bond? Give a few examples of each. Briefly describe the following bond features: (a) sinking funds, (b) call features, and (c) registration.

12. Identify and briefly discuss the four major classes of bond issuer.

13. Are junk bonds and zero coupon bonds the same? Explain. What are the basic tax features of a tax-exempt municipal bond? Are there such things as *taxable* municipal bonds? Explain.

14. Illustrate why an investor in a high tax bracket would prefer municipal bonds to other investment vehicles.

15. Explain the system of bond ratings used by Moody's and Standard & Poor's.

16. What effects do current market interest rates have on the price behavior of outstanding bonds?

▪ **17.** Describe and differentiate between a bond's (a) current yield and (b) yield to maturity. Why are these yield measures important to the bond investor? Explain. Find the approximate yield to maturity of a 20-year, 13 percent, $1,000 par value bond that is trading at a price of $850.

18. What is preferred stock? Distinguish between (a) cumulative and noncumulative preferred stock and (b) participating and nonparticipating preferred stock.

19. What is a convertible bond? Why do investors buy convertible securities?

20. Describe the "conversion privilege" of a convertible security. Explain how the market price of the underlying common stock affects the market price of the convertible bond.

21. Find the conversion value of an issue that carries a conversion ratio of 24, given that the market price of the underlying common stock is $55 a share. Would there be any conversion premium if the convertible bond had a market price of $1,500? If so, how much?

22. Using the resources available at your campus or public library, work the following problems. (Note: Show your work for all your calculations.)

a. Select any two *common stocks,* and determine the dividend yield, earnings per share, and P/E ratio for each.

b. Select any two *bonds,* and determine the current yield and approximate yield to maturity of each.

c. Select any two *preferred* stocks, and determine the current yield of each.

d. Select any two *convertible debentures,* and determine the conversion ratio, conversion value, and conversion premium for each.

CASE PROBLEMS

12.1 Developing an Investment Plan for the Potters

Ellen and Steve Potter are the working parents of two school-age children. Ellen takes home $22,000 a year as a high school English teacher; Steve brings home another $18,000 from his job as an executive assistant. The Potters live rather modestly in a suburban home. Their monthly expenditures, including mortgage and car payments, amount to $1,900. Over ten years of marriage, they have managed to save about $10,000, all of which is held in a money market deposit account at their bank. Their only other source of protection comes from a $40,000 life insurance policy on Steve.

Steve is anxious to invest some of the family savings in the stock market. He is not deterred by the contrary advice of a financial planner friend who has told him to wait until their savings have increased to at least $15,000. He argues that the time

has come to begin planning for their children's education.

Questions
1. Would you recommend that the Potters start investing some of their money in various types of securities now, or would you agree with the financial planner? Explain your position.

2. Prepare an investment plan for the Potters, taking into consideration (a) the risks involved in stock or bond investments, (b) the relative returns expected from different types of stocks and bonds, and (c) the risk-return trade-off from the securities chosen.

12.2 Jill Decides to Try Her Hand at Investing

Jill Karras is a 26-year-old management trainee at a large chemical company. She is single and has no plans for marriage. Her annual salary is $34,000 (placing her in the 28 percent tax bracket), and her monthly expenditures come to approximately $1,500. During the past year or so, Jill has managed to save around $8,000, and she expects to continue to save at least that amount each year for the foreseeable future. Her company pays the premium on her $35,000 life insurance policy. Since Jill's entire education was financed by scholarships, she was able to save the money from summer and part-time jobs she held as a student. Altogether, she has a nest egg of nearly $18,000, out of which she would like to invest about $15,000. She will keep the remaining $3,000 in a money market account that pays 7.5 percent interest; she will use this money only in the event of an emergency. Although Jill can afford to take more risks than someone with family obli-

gations, she does not wish to be a speculator; rather, she simply wants to earn an attractive return on her investments.

Questions

1. What options are open to Jill?
2. What chances does she have of earning a satisfactory return on her investments if she invests her $15,000 in (a) blue-chip stocks, (b) growth stocks, (c) speculative stocks, (d) corporate bonds, or (e) municipal bonds?
3. Discuss the factors you would consider when analyzing these alternative investment vehicles.
4. What recommendation would you make to Jill with respect to her available investment alternatives? Explain.

FOR MORE INFORMATION

General Information Articles

Frailey, Fred W., "How to Tell How You're Doing," *Changing Times,* January 1988, pp. 37–42.

Kehrer, Daniel M., "Make Your Dividends Pay Again and Again," *Changing Times,* November 1988, pp. 73–77.

Kosnett, Jeff, "Taking the Plunge: How to Start Investing," *Changing Times,* April 1987, pp. 22–28.

Myers, David W., "The Ups and Downs of Bond Investing," *Personal Investor,* September 1987, pp. 72–75.

Rock, Andrea, "Zero-Coupon Bonds: Lovely for Savers, Lively for Speculators," *Money,* September 1988, pp. 151–154.

Government Documents & Other Publications

How the Bond Market Works. Standard & Poor's Corp.; 25 Broadway; New York, NY 10004.

How to Invest. Standard & Poor's Corp.; 25 Broadway; New York, NY 10004.

An Investor's Guide to Tax Exempt Securities. Public Securities Association; 40 Broad Street, 12th floor; New York, NY 10004.

Investors Information Kit. New York Stock Exchange; Publications Division; 11 Wall Street; New York, NY 10005.

What Every Investor Should Know. U.S. Securities & Exchange Commission; Publications Section; 450 5th St., NW; Washington, D.C. 20549.

13

Making Securities Investments

Financial Facts or Fantasies

Are the following statements financial facts (true) or fantasies (false)?

- Stocks listed on the New York Stock Exchange are traded in the over-the-counter market.
- Bo Derek and James Bond are names given to certain types of Treasury securities.
- If you lose a lot of money because of a lousy investment recommended by your broker, you can recover all or most of your loss by filing a claim with the Securities Investor Protection Corporation.
- An investor would short sell a stock if he or she expects its price to go down.
- Because they are so biased, you should pay little attention to annual stockholders' reports.
- Coming up with a sound asset allocation plan is likely to have more of an impact on long-term return than the specific securities you hold in your portfolio.

Amy Rosen started investing in the stock market during her junior year in college. It all started when her grandmother left her $25,000. After careful deliberation, Amy decided to invest $15,000 of her inheritance and to spend the rest on herself and her education. Though she knew almost nothing about the market, she started dabbling in stocks and mutual funds and, in a relatively short period of time, had invested all of her $15,000. Now would come the fun part: She could sit back and watch her money grow. Much to her dismay, however, she watched her investments steadily go down in price! Finally, after Amy had lost nearly $6,000, she decided to sell out and put what was left of her investment capital into something safer—at least until she learned more about securities and the markets. If nothing else, the experience taught Amy a valuable albeit costly lesson: that is, *it takes more than money to be a successful investor.* In order to carry out a successful investment program, you must understand the institutions, mechanisms, and procedures involved in making security transactions. We looked at some investment fundamentals, particularly with regard to stocks and bonds, in the preceding chapter. In this chapter, we will examine the different securities markets, sources of investment information, and ways to manage investment holdings. The overriding theme of this chapter is that *there is no substitute for being an informed investor!*

SECURITIES MARKETS

> Stocks, bonds, and other securities are traded in a highly efficient market network that includes both organized exchanges and over-the-counter (OTC) markets. Would it really make any difference to you, as an investor, if a security is traded on an organized exchange or in the OTC market? How does trading on an exchange differ from that in the OTC market? Take a few moments before reading on to think about these questions.

The term **securities markets** is generally used to describe the place where stocks, bonds, and other financial instruments are traded. The securities markets can be broken into two parts: the capital markets and the money markets. The *capital market* is where long-term securities (those with maturities greater than one year) are traded, while the *money market* is the marketplace for short-term low-risk credit instruments with maturities of one year or less, like U.S. Treasury bills, commercial paper, negotiable certificates of deposit, etc. Both types of markets provide a vital mechanism for bringing the buyers and sellers of securities together. Some of the more popular money market securities were discussed in Chapter 5, where we looked at short-term investment vehicles. This chapter considers the capital markets.

Primary or Secondary Markets

The securities markets can also be divided into primary and secondary segments. The *primary market* is the market where new securities are sold to the public—where one party to the transaction is always the issuer. The *secondary market,* in contrast, is where old (outstanding) securities are bought and sold—here the securities are "traded" between investors. A security is sold in the primary market just once: when it is originally issued by the corporation. Subsequent transactions, wherein securities are sold by one investor to another, take place in the secondary market. As a rule, when people speak of the securities markets, they're referring to the secondary market, since that's where the vast majority of security transactions take place.

Primary Markets. When a corporation sells a new issue, several financial institutions participate in the transaction. To begin with, the corporation will probably use an *investment banking firm,* which specializes in *underwriting* (selling) new security issues. The investment banker will give the corporation advice on pricing and other aspects of the issue and either will sell the new security itself or arrange for a *selling group* to do so. The selling group is normally made up of a large number of stockbrokerage firms, each of which accepts the responsibility for selling a certain portion of the new issue. On very large issues, the originating investment banker will bring in other underwriting firms as partners and form an *underwriting syndicate* in an attempt to spread the risks associated with underwriting and selling the new securities. In such cases, each underwriter forms a selling group that is responsible for selling its portion of the new issue. Exhibit 13.1 depicts this selling process for a new security issue.

A potential investor in a new issue must be provided with a **prospectus**, which is a document describing the firm and the issue. Certain federal agencies have the responsibility of insuring that all information included within a prospectus is an accurate representation of the facts. Sometimes investors have trouble purchasing new security issues because all shares allocated to the stockbrokers have been sold—often prior to the official sale date. Also, if the new shares are sold using *rights* or *warrants* (discussed in Chapter 12), the ability to purchase the new securities will be somewhat restricted, since only the holders of these rights or warrants can buy the stock.

Secondary Markets. The secondary markets permit investors to execute transactions between themselves—it's the marketplace where an investor can easily sell his or her holdings to someone else. Included among the secondary markets are the various *securities exchanges,* in which the buyers and sellers of securities are brought together. In addition, there is the **over-the-counter (OTC) market**, which is made up of a nationwide network of brokers and dealers who execute transactions in securities that are not listed on one of the ex-

EXHIBIT 13.1
The Participants in the Issuance of a New Corporate Security
There are many parties that come into play when a corporation decides to sell its securities to the investing public. This is also the *only* time the issuer is a party to the transaction and, as such, directly benefits from the sale.

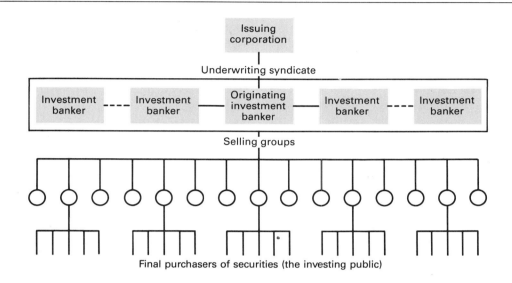

Final purchasers of securities (the investing public)

changes. The **organized securities exchanges** typically handle transactions in the securities of larger, better known companies, and the over-the-counter market handles mostly the smaller, lesser known firms. The organized exchanges are well-structured institutions that bring together the market forces of supply and demand; the over-the-counter market is basically a mass telecommunications network linking buyers and sellers. Since most transactions of small investors are made in the secondary market, we will focus on it throughout this chapter.

Organized Securities Exchanges

The forces of market supply and demand are brought together in organized securities exchanges. So-called **listed securities** are traded on organized exchanges and account for about two-thirds of all shares traded in the stock market. All trading is carried out in one place (such as the New York Stock Exchange on Wall Street) and under a broad set of rules by persons who are *members* of the exchange. Members are said to "own a seat" on

the exchange, a privilege that is obtained by meeting certain financial requirements. Only the secur-

securities markets
The marketplace in which stocks, bonds, and other financial instruments are traded.

prospectus
A document made available to prospective security purchasers that describes the firm and a new security issue.

over-the-counter (OTC) market
The market in which securities not listed on one of the organized exchanges are traded, usually those of smaller, lesser known firms.

organized securities exchanges
Exchanges where various types of securities are traded by (exchange) members for their own accounts and the accounts of their customers.

listed security
A security that has met the prerequisites for, and thus is traded on, one of the organized securities exchanges.

ities of companies that have met certain listing requirements are traded on the exchange, and those firms must comply with established regulations to ensure that they will not make financial or legal misrepresentations to their stockholders. Firms must not only comply with the rules of the specific exchange but also fulfill certain requirements established by the Securities and Exchange Commission (discussed later).

New York Stock Exchange. *The New York Stock Exchange (NYSE)* is the largest and most prestigious organized securities exchange in the country. Known as "the big board," there are over 70 *billion* shares of stock listed on it that, at year-end 1988, had a market value of over *$24 trillion*. Membership on the NYSE is limited to 1,366 seats. During this century, the cost of a seat has ranged from $17,000 (in 1942) to over $1 million (in 1987). Most seats are owned by brokerage firms, the largest of which—Merrill Lynch, Pierce, Fenner and Smith, Inc.—owns more than 20.

The NYSE has the most stringent listing requirements of all the organized exchanges. For example, in order to be listed, a firm must have at least 2,000 stockholders, each owning 100 shares or more. It must also have a minimum of 1.1 million shares of publicly held stock outstanding; have demonstrated pre-tax earning power of $2.5 million at the time of listing and of $2 million for each of the preceding two years; have $18 million in market value of publicly held shares; and must pay a listing fee. Firms that fail to continue to meet listing requirements can be *delisted*. Nearly 1,700 firms accounting for over 2,200 different stocks and over 3,100 different bonds are currently listed on the NYSE. Some of the NYSE's largest companies, in terms of number of shareholders and total market value are listed in Exhibit 13.2.

American Stock Exchange. The *American Stock Exchange (AMEX)* is the second largest organized stock exchange in terms of the number of listed companies; when it comes to the dollar volume of trading, however, the AMEX is actually smaller than a couple of *regional* exchanges (the Midwest and Pacific). Its organization and procedures are similar to those of the NYSE, though its membership costs and listing requirements are not as stringent. There are approximately 650 seats on the AMEX and over 1,100 listed stocks. The AMEX handles only about 5 percent of the total annual share volume on *organized* security exchanges. In contrast, the NYSE handles around 85 percent of all common shares traded on organized exchanges, so the AMEX is nowhere near the New York exchange in terms of size or stature. Further, whereas the NYSE is home for most of the biggest and best-known companies in the world, firms traded on the AMEX are much smaller and, with few exceptions, would hardly qualify as "household names."

Regional Stock Exchanges. In addition to the NYSE and AMEX, there are 13 **regional exchanges**. The number of securities listed on each is typically in the range of 100 to 500 companies. As a group they handle perhaps 10 percent of all shares traded on organized exchanges. The 13 regional exchanges are as follows:

> Boston Stock Exchange
> Cincinnati Stock Exchange
> Colorado Stock Exchange
> Detroit Stock Exchange
> Honolulu Stock Exchange
> Intermountain Stock Exchange
> Midwest Stock Exchange
> Pacific Stock Exchange
> Philadelphia Stock Exchange
> Pittsburgh Stock Exchange
> Richmond Stock Exchange
> Spokane Stock Exchange
> Wheeling Stock Exchange

Of these, the Midwest, Pacific, Philadelphia, Boston, and Cincinnati exchanges are the dominant ones.

These 13 exchanges deal primarily in securities with local and regional appeal. Most are modeled after the NYSE, but their membership and listing requirements are considerably more lenient. Regional exchanges will often list securities that are also listed on the NYSE or AMEX in order to enhance their trading activity.

The Over-the-Counter Market

Unlike an organized exchange, the over-the-counter (OTC) market is not a specific institution but, instead, exists as an intangible relationship between the buyers and sellers of securities. Securities traded in this market are sometimes called **unlisted securities**. It is the fastest-growing segment of the stock market and today trades close to *30,000* issues. The market is linked together by a

EXHIBIT 13.2

Some NYSE Leaders (1988)

The companies listed here, like others on the NYSE, are some of the largest corporations in the world in terms of both number of shareholders and market value. It's interesting to note that while there are some 1,700 firms on the NYSE, the 25 companies listed here (in the right-hand column) account for almost 25 percent of the total market value of all stocks traded on the NYSE!

NYSE Companies with Largest Number of Common Stockholders

Company	Stockholders
American Tel. & Tel.	2,782,000
General Motors	1,854,000
BellSouth Corp.	1,578,000
Bell Atlantic	1,335,000
US WEST	1,250,000
NYNEX Corp.	1,249,000
Southwestern Bell	1,246,000
American Information Tech.	1,206,000
Pacific Telesis Group	1,109,000
International Business Machines	788,000
Exxon Corporation	733,000
General Electric	506,000
GTE Corporation	441,000
Occidental Petroleum	355,000
Bell Canada Enterprises	332,000
Sears, Roebuck	320,000
Pacific Gas & Electric	298,000
Philadelphia Electric	293,000
Southern Company	287,000
Ford Motor	268,000
American Electric Power	264,000
Mobil Corp.	261,000
Commonwealth Edison	253,000
Texaco Inc.	219,000
Detroit Edison	218,000

NYSE Stocks with Greatest Market Values (Dollars in Millions)

Stock	Market Value
Exxon Corporation	$81,123
Int'l Business Machines	68,348
General Electric Co.	40,189
American Tel. & Tel. Co.	28,052
Merck & Co., Inc.	26,306
Ford Motor Co.	23,837
General Motors Corp.	23,455
Philip Morris Cos., Inc.	23,183
Bellsouth Corporation	20,116
DuPont de Nemours E.I. & Co.	19,561
Amoco Corporation	18,971
Dow Chemical Co.	18,925
Mobil Corporation	18,465
Wal-Mart Stores, Inc.	18,140
Eastman Kodak Co.	16,913
Atlantic Richfield Co.	16,852
Chevron Corp	16,592
Johnson and Johnson	16,475
Minnesota MNG & MFG Co.	15,193
GTE Corp.	15,162
Coca-Cola Co.	14,924
Sears Roebuck Co.	14,609
Bell Atlantic	14,381
American Information Tech.	13,808
Proctor & Gamble Co.	13,583

Source: New York Stock Exchange, 1989.

mass telecommunications network. Unlike those in the organized securities exchanges, the trades in the OTC market represent *direct* transactions between investors and securities dealers—that is, the investors buy from and sell to the securities dealers, whereas on the listed securities exchanges the broker acts as a middleman between buyers and sellers. All municipal bonds, along with most governments and corporate bonds, as well as a numerical majority of common stocks are traded in the OTC market. This market has *no listing requirements:* All unlisted securities are traded here. Dealers make markets in certain securities by offering to either buy or sell them at stated prices.

A part of the OTC market is linked through the *National Association of Securities Dealers Automated Quotation System (NASDAQ),* which provides up-to-date quotes and bid/ask prices on

several thousand securities. (The **bid** and the **ask prices** represent, respectively, the highest price offered to purchase a given security and the lowest

regional exchanges
Organized securities exchanges (other than the NYSE and AMEX) that deal primarily in securities having a local or regional appeal.

unlisted security
A security that is traded in the over-the-counter market; such a trade is made directly between the investor and the security dealer.

bid price
The price at which one can sell a security.

ask price
The price at which one can purchase a security.

price at which the security is offered for sale. In effect, an investor pays the ask price when *buying* securities and receives the bid price when *selling* them.)

There are over 5,100 different issues traded in the NASDAQ portion of the OTC market, and of these, nearly 3,000 are part of the so-called *national market system (NMS)*. The national market system is reserved for the biggest and most actively traded stocks; and, in general, for those stocks that have a *national following*. These securities are widely quoted, and the trades are executed about as efficiently here as they are on the floor of the NYSE. A number of large and well-known firms are found on the NASDAQ National Market System, including companies like Apple Computers, Intel, MCI, Liz Claiborne, Lotus, Citizens Utilities, and Nordstroms, as well as many big banks and insurance companies. Generally speaking, the big-name stocks traded on the NASDAQ/NMS receive about as much national visibility and are about as liquid as those traded on the NYSE. Indeed, because of this, *NASDAQ is now the second biggest market in the U.S.,* in terms of dollar volume of trading, and the third largest in the world! The situation is considerably different, however, for OTC stocks that are not part of NASDAQ—which is the case for the vast majority of the firms traded in the OTC market. These include the very small firms that may not even have much of a regional following, let alone a national constituency. These stocks are *thinly traded,* meaning there's not much of a market for them, and they often lack any measurable degree of liquidity. They are not the easiest things to buy and sell, since buyers and sellers of these securities must find each other through the *market makers,* scattered around the country, who specialize in making markets in these securities.

Stocks listed on the New York Stock Exchange are traded in the over-the-counter market. **Fantasy:** Stocks not listed on organized exchanges are traded in the over-the-counter (OTC) market; listed securities are traded on stock exchanges, which are not part of the OTC market.

Regulating the Securities Markets

The **Securities and Exchange Commission (SEC)** is an agency of the federal government and was established to enforce the Securities Exchange Acts of 1933 and 1934. These acts were aimed at regulating not only securities exchanges and securities markets, but also the disclosure of information on both new and outstanding securities. In addition to SEC regulations, most states have laws regarding the sale of securities within their borders. These so-called *blue sky laws* protect investors by preventing firms from attempting to sell nothing but "blue sky." The exchanges themselves also perform a self-regulatory function through their governing bodies.

The OTC market is regulated by the **National Association of Securities Dealers (NASD)**, which is made up of all brokers and dealers who participate in the OTC market. The NASD is a self-regulatory organization that polices the activities of brokers and dealers in order to insure that its standards are upheld. The SEC supervises the activities of NASD, thus providing investors with further protection from fraudulent activities.

Bull Market or Bear?

The general condition of the market is termed *bullish* or *bearish,* depending on whether security prices are rising or falling over extended periods of time. Changing market conditions generally stem from changing investor attitudes, changes in economic activity, and certain governmental actions aimed at stimulating or slowing down the economy. Prices go *up* in **bull markets**; these favorable markets are normally associated with investor optimism, economic recovery, and governmental stimulus. In contrast, prices go *down* in **bear markets**, which are normally associated with investor pessimism and economic slowdown. These terms are used to describe conditions in the bond and other securities markets as well as the stock market. For example, the bond market is considered bullish when interest rates fall, causing bond prices to rise; on the other hand, a bear market in bonds exists when bond prices fall (which occurs when rates rise). As a rule, investors are able to earn attractive rates of return during bull markets and only low (or negative) returns during bear markets. Market conditions are difficult to predict and usually cannot be identified until after they exist.

Over the past 50 or so years, the behavior of the stock market has been generally bullish, reflecting the growth and prosperity of the economy. As Exhibit 13.3 (on page 464) shows, there have been five major bull markets since World War II, the longest of which lasted *97 months*—from June 1949 to July 1957. The most notorious of the five was surely the latest one, which started in August of 1982 and peaked out in August of 1987. This is the one that's associated with the big market crash of October 19, 1987, when in a *single day,* the market, as measured by the Dow Jones Industrial Average, dropped by a whopping 508 points! Actually, the market had started dropping in late August and by mid-October had already fallen some 400 points. Then came "Black Monday," when the market experienced its biggest and hardest crash in history, not only in absolute numerical terms (508 points), but also in percentage and dollar terms: in one day, the market fell nearly 23 percent and lost roughly half a *trillion* dollars in value.

MAKING TRANSACTIONS IN THE SECURITIES MARKETS

> Individual investors use the services of stockbrokers to buy and sell securities in the marketplace. Stop for a moment to consider the different kinds of services offered by brokers. How great do you suppose the difference would be in the services and cost of a discount broker as opposed to a full-service broker?

In many respects, dealing in the securities markets almost seems like you are operating in another world—one with all kinds of unusual orders and strange-sounding transactions. Actually, making securities transactions is relatively simple once you understand a few of the basics—in fact, you will probably find it is no more difficult than using a checking account! Indeed, while making money in the market isn't all that easy, making transactions is.

Stockbrokers

Stockbrokers, or **account executives**, as they're also called, purchase and sell securities for their customers. Although deeply ingrained in our language, the term "stockbroker" is really somewhat of a misnomer, as such an individual assists you in the purchase and sale of not only stocks but also bonds, convertibles, mutual funds, options, and many other types of securities. Brokers must be licensed by the exchanges on which they place orders and must abide by the strict ethical guidelines of the exchanges and the SEC. They work for brokerage firms and in essence are there to execute the orders placed. The largest stockbrokerage firm, Merrill Lynch, Pierce, Fenner and Smith, Inc., has brokerage offices in most major U.S. cities. Orders from these offices are transmitted by brokers to the main office of Merrill Lynch and then to the floor of one of the stock exchanges, or to the OTC market, where they are executed. Confirmation that the order has been executed is transmitted back to the original broker and then to the customer. This process is carried out in a matter of minutes with the use of sophisticated telecommunications networks. Although the procedure for executing orders on organized exchanges differs a bit from that

Securities and Exchange Commission (SEC)
An agency of the federal government that regulates the disclosure of information about securities and generally oversees the operation of the securities exchanges and markets.

National Association of Securities Dealers (NASD)
An agency made up of brokers and dealers in over-the-counter securities that regulates the operations of the OTC market.

bull market
A condition of the market normally associated with investor optimism, economic recovery, and government stimulus; characterized by generally rising securities prices.

bear market
A condition of the market typically associated with investor pessimism, economic slowdown, and government control; characterized by generally falling securities prices.

stockbroker (account executive)
An individual who buys and sells securities on behalf of clients and provides them with investment advice and information.

EXHIBIT 13.3

The Five Biggest Bull Markets Since World War II (as Measured by Changes in the DJIA)

The prices of most stocks will go up in a bull market. Thus, it is hard to lose money—though not impossible, since not all stocks will appreciate in value during such markets.

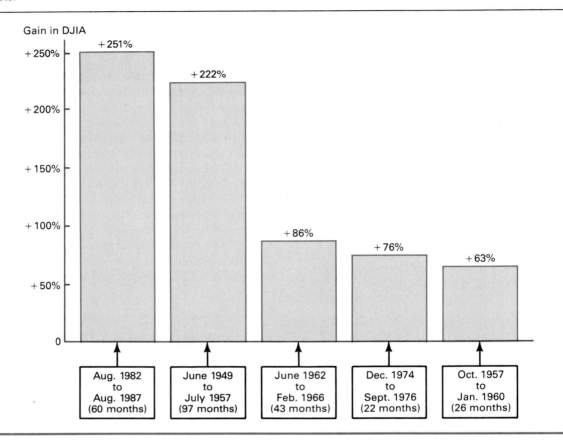

in the OTC market, you as an investor would never know the difference, since you would place your order with the broker in exactly the same fashion.

Selecting a Broker. It is important to select a broker *who understands your investment objectives and can effectively assist you in pursuing them.* If you choose a broker whose own disposition toward investing is similar to yours, you should be able to avoid conflict and establish a solid working relationship. It is probably best to ask friends or business associates to recommend stockbrokers. It is not important—and often even inadvisable—to know your stockbroker personally since most, if not all, of your transactions/orders will probably be

placed by phone. In addition, a strict business relationship eliminates the possibility of social concerns interfering with the achievement of your investment objectives. This does not mean, of course, that your broker's sole interest should be commissions. Indeed, a broker should be far more than just a salesperson; for a good broker is someone who's more interested in your investments than in commissions. Should you find you're dealing with someone who's always trying to get you to trade your stocks, or who's pushing new investments on you, then by all means, dump that broker and find a new one!

One of the problems you must contend with when dealing with a broker is that of properly in-

EXHIBIT 13.4

Interpreting "Broker Babble"

Sometimes the slang of Wall Street has hidden meanings. Certainly it behooves you to become better prepared so as to avoid being beleaguered by broker babble.

Alligator spread. Any options transaction in which commissions eat up all potential profit.

Baby bond. A bond sold in denominations of less than $1,000.

Blue-chip performer. This meaningless expression, the Wall Street equivalent of "nice," is used to encourage investors to buy the stock of a company that may or may not have the solid record of a true blue chip.

Bo Dereks. Treasury bonds maturing in the year 2010; also known as Tens.

To cut a melon. To declare a large stock dividend.

Going naked. Selling an option without owning the underlying security.

Indication of interest. Asking a customer for an indication of interest gets a broker's foot in the door. If you decide not to buy a recommended stock, the broker can pressure you through guilt: "Oh, but you asked me to reserve this for you!"

James Bond. A Treasury security due in 2007, hence bearing the same code name as agent 007.

"Let me give you an investment strategy analysis." A broker's way of saying: "Let me talk you into buying something."

Lift your shorts. Commodity jargon for: "Prices are going up, so cover yourself by closing out your short positions." (A short position is a pledge to deliver the underlying commodity at a set price on a future date.)

Promises a greater than average return. Code for: "You could lose your shirt." High potential return is the flip side of high risk.

Shallow river running deep. A stock whose price has moved greatly in response to an unsubstantiated rumor.

Technical correction or technical rally. Translation: "The market just reversed direction and I don't have the vaguest clue why."

"This seems to run contrary to your financial objectives." A broker's way of criticizing a customer's investment idea. Hidden meaning: "You'll never make any money on this."

Transfer your assets. Used most often when an investor has acquired a loser on the broker's recommendation, the expression means: "Cut your losses."

"You're not going to marry this, just take it to the motel." A way of encouraging a reluctant customer to buy a risky stock.

Source: Patricia Dreyfus, "Mastering Broker Babble," *Money*, June 1984, 78.

---

terpreting some of the jargon he or she may use. Every occupation, it seems, develops its own "jargonese," and certainly the brokerage business is no exception! Buzzwords and nicknames speed transactions while giving insiders warm feelings of belonging to an elite fellowship. Euphemisms often make unpalatable situations seem sweeter and exert subtle pressures. Understanding the lingo of Wall Street will spare beginning investors a lot of confusion and may even save them some money that would otherwise be lost in the fog. The abridged dictionary of "brokerisms" in Exhibit 13.4 hopefully will help you avoid being taken in by "broker babble."

Bo Derek and James Bond are names given to certain types of Treasury securities. **Fact:** As described in Exhibit 13.4, Bo Derek is the nickname given to Treasury bonds that mature in 2010, and James Bonds are Treasury securities that mature in 2007.

Brokerage Services. In addition to carrying out purchase and sale transactions for commission,

stockbrokers offer their clients a variety of other services. Selecting a good brokerage firm is just as important as choosing a good broker, since not all brokerage firms provide the same services. Try to select a broker with whom you can work and who is affiliated with a firm that provides the types of services you are looking for. Many brokerage firms, for example, provide a wide array of free information, ranging from stock and bond guides to research reports on specific securities or industries. Some have a research staff that periodically issues analyses of economic, market, industry, or company behavior and events, and relates them to its recommendations for buying or selling certain securities. As a client of a large brokerage firm, you can expect to receive monthly bulletins discussing market activity and possibly even a recommended investment list. You also will receive a statement describing all of your transactions for the month, commission charges, interest charges, dividends and interest received, and your account balance.

Most brokerage offices have some type of electronic equipment that provides up-to-the-minute stock price quotations and world news. Stock price information can be obtained either from the quotation board (a large screen that electronically displays all NYSE and AMEX security transactions within minutes of their occurrence) or by keying into the telequote system, which relies on a computer terminal to provide a capsulized description of most securities and their prices. World news, which can significantly affect the stock market, is obtained from a news wire service subscribed to by the brokerage office. Most offices also have a reference library available for use by the firm's clients.

Another valuable service offered by most major brokerage firms is the automatic investment of surplus cash left in a customer's account into one of the firm's money funds, thereby allowing the customer to earn a reasonable rate of return on temporarily idle funds. Brokerage houses will also hold your securities for you, as protection against their loss; the securities kept in this way are said to be held in *street name*. As a client, you are protected against the loss of securities or cash held by your broker by the **Securities Investor Protection Corporation (SIPC)**, an agency of the federal government that insures each customer's account against the financial failure of the brokerage firm. SIPC insurance covers each account for up to $500,000 (of which up to $100,000 may be in cash balances held by the firm). Note, however, that SIPC insurance does not guarantee that the dollar value of the securities will be recovered. It only insures that *the securities themselves will be returned*.

SIPC provides protection in case your brokerage firm fails. But what happens if your broker gives you bad advice, and as a result, you lose a lot of money on an investment? SIPC won't help you, as it's not intended to insure you against bad investment advice. Instead, if you have a dispute with your broker, the first thing you should do is discuss the situation with the managing officer at the branch where you do your business. If that doesn't do any good, then write or talk to the firm's compliance officer, and contact the securities office in your home state. If you still don't get any satisfaction, you may have to take the case to **arbitration**, a process whereby you and your broker present the two sides to the argument before an arbitration panel, which then makes a decision about how the

case shall be resolved. If it's *binding* arbitration, and it usually is, you have no choice but to accept the decision—you cannot go to court to appeal your case. To make matters worse, many brokerage firms require you to resolve disputes by going to binding arbitration. Thus, before you open an account, check the brokerage agreement to see if it contains a binding arbitration clause.

Now, binding arbitration wouldn't be so bad if the track record were more evenly balanced. But the fact is that the decisions handed down in the past have been heavily stacked in favor of the brokers. Fortunately, that may change as the SEC has recently handed down changes aimed at reforming the arbitration process. Even so, the best way to avoid such a mess is to use care when selecting a broker in the first place, and then carefully evaluate the advice he or she offers.

If you lose a lot of money because of a lousy investment recommended by your broker, you can recover all or most of your loss by filing a claim with the Securities Investor Protection Corporation. **Fantasy:** SIPC insurance applies only if you happen to be dealing with a *brokerage firm* that goes out of business; if the brokerage firm fails, you are protected against the loss of securities or cash held by the broker, but that has nothing to do with getting bad advice from a broker (SIPC does not cover such situations).

Odd or Round Lots. Security transactions can be made in either odd or round lots. An **odd lot** consists of fewer than 100 shares of a security, while a **round lot** represents a 100-share unit or multiples thereof. The sale of 400 shares of stock would be considered a round-lot transaction, but the purchase of 75 shares would be an odd-lot transaction; trading 250 shares of stock would involve two round lots and an odd lot. Because the purchase or sale of odd lots requires additional processing and the assistance of a specialist (an *odd-lot dealer*), an added fee—known as an *odd-lot differential*—is tacked on to the normal commission charge, driving up the costs of these small trades. Indeed, the relatively high cost of an odd-lot trade is why it's best to deal in round lots whenever possible.

Brokerage Fees. Brokerage firms receive commissions for executing purchase and sale transac-

EXHIBIT 13.5

Broker Commissions on Common Stock Transactions

The amount of broker commissions paid on a common stock transaction obviously will vary with the market value of the transaction. You will pay a commission when you buy stocks and again when you sell them.

Value of Transaction	Fees for an Odd or Round Lot	Surcharge
Up to $800	$8.43 + 2.7% of the value of the transaction	
$800 to $2,500	$16.85 + 1.7% of the value of the transaction	+3.15¢/share
$2,500 to $5,000	$29.50 + 1.3% of the value of the transaction	+3.15¢/share

Source: A major stockbrokerage firm.

tions on behalf of their clients. Brokerage commissions are said to be *negotiated,* which means that they are not fixed. In practice, however, most firms have *established* fee schedules that they apply to small transactions (on larger, institutional trades, negotiation of commissions actually does take place). Although these fees are not really negotiated, they do differ from one brokerage firm to another; thus, it pays to shop around.

The suggested fee schedule used by one large brokerage firm to set commissions on *common stock* transactions is given in Exhibit 13.5. Although this schedule does not specifically levy a premium on odd-lot transactions, the fixed-cost fee component does tend to raise their per share cost. (In addition to the fees shown in the schedule, some brokerage firms charge a differential of 12.5 cents per share on odd-lot transactions.) If the fee schedule in Exhibit 13.5 were used to calculate brokerage fees on the purchase of 80 shares of XYZ stock at $30 per share, the total value of the transaction would be $2,400 (80 shares × $30/share) and the brokerage fee would therefore be $16.85 + 1.7% ($2,400) + $.0315 (80 shares) = $16.85 + $40.80 + $2.52 = $60.17; that amounts to about 2½ percent of the value of the transaction. A common rule of thumb is that brokerage fees on a round lot of common stock will amount to approximately 2 to 3 percent of the transaction value.

Brokerage commissions on bond transactions differ from those on stock transactions. Brokerage firms typically charge a minimum fee of $25 to $30,

regardless of the number of bonds involved. For multiple bond transactions, the brokerage cost per $1,000 corporate bond typically amounts to around $10 (which is decidedly lower than that on a stock transaction). The commission schedules for other securities, such as mutual funds and options, differ from those used with stocks and bonds (we will look at some of these in the next chapter).

The magnitude of brokerage commissions obviously is an important consideration when making security transactions, since these fees tend to raise the overall cost of purchasing securities and lower the overall proceeds from their sale.

Securities Investor Protection Corporation (SIPC)
An agency of the federal government that insures brokerage customers' accounts.

arbitration
A procedure that's used to settle disputes between a brokerage firm and its clients; both sides of the "story" are presented to a board of arbitration, which makes a final and binding decision on the matter.

odd lot
A quantity of fewer than 100 shares of a stock.

round lot
A quantity of 100 shares of stock, or multiples thereof

Discount Brokers

Security transactions can also be made at **discount brokers**, many of which are now affiliated with major banks. Discount brokers tend to have low overhead operations and offer little or nothing in the way of customer services. Transactions are initiated by calling a toll-free number and placing the desired buy or sell order. The brokerage firm then executes the order at the best possible price and confirms the details of the transaction by mail. In order to discourage small orders, most discounters charge a minimum transaction fee ranging between $18 and $35. Depending on the size of the transaction, *discount brokers can save investors from 30 to 80 percent of the commissions charged by full-service brokers.* The investor who does not need the research and advisory help available from full-service brokers may find discount brokers especially attractive. Listed below are some major discount and full-service brokerage houses:

- ▪ Discount Brokers

    Brown & Company
    Charles Schwab
    Fidelity Brokerage Services
    Muriel Siebert & Company
    Quick & Reilly
    Rose & Company

- ▪ Full Service Brokers

    Dean Witter
    Kidder, Peabody
    Merrill Lynch
    Paine Webber
    Prudential-Bache-Thomson
    Shearson Lehman Hutton

Types of Orders

Investors may choose among several different kinds of orders when making purchase or sale transactions. The type of order chosen normally depends on the investor's goals and expectations with respect to the given transaction. The three basic types of orders are the market order, limit order, and stop-loss order.

Market Order.   An order to buy or sell a security at the best price available at the time it is placed is a **market order**. These orders are executed through a process that attempts to allow *buy orders* to be filled at the lowest price and *sell orders* at the highest, thereby providing the best possible deal to both purchasers and sellers of a security. Because of the speed with which market orders are transacted, the investor can be sure that the price at which the order is completed will be very close to the market price that existed at the time it was placed.

Limit Order.   An order to buy at a specified price (or lower), or sell at (or above) a specified price is known as a **limit order**. When a limit order is placed, the broker transmits it to a *specialist* dealing in the given security on the floor of the exchange. The specialist makes a notation in his or her "book" indicating the limit order and limit price. The order is executed as soon as the specified market price is in effect and all other such orders with precedence have been satisfied. The order can be placed to remain in effect until a certain date or until cancelled; such an instruction is called a **good 'til cancelled (GTC) order**. For example, assume that you place a limit order to buy 100 shares of a stock at a price of 20, even though the stock is currently selling at 20½. Once the specialist has cleared all similar orders received before yours, and the market price of the stock is still at $20 or less, he or she will execute the order. Although a limit order can be quite effective, it can also cost you money! If, for instance, you wish to buy at 20 or less and the stock price moves from its current $20.50 to $32 while you are waiting, your limit order will have caused you to forgo an opportunity to make a profit of $11.50 ($32.00 − $20.50) per share. Had you placed a market order, this profit would have been yours.

Stop-Loss Order.   An order to sell a stock when the market price reaches or drops below a specified level is a **stop-loss**, or **stop order**. Used to protect the investor against rapid declines in stock prices, the stop order is placed on the specialist's book and activated when the stop price is reached. At that point, the stop order becomes a *market order* to sell. This means that the stock is offered for sale at the prevailing market price, which could be *less* than the price at which the order was initiated by the stop. For example, imagine that you own 100 shares of DEF, which is currently selling for $25. Because of the high uncertainty associated with the price movements of the stock, you decide to place a stop order at $21. If the stock price drops to $21, the specialist will sell all your DEF stock at the best price then available, which may be $18 or $19 a share. If the market price increases, nothing will have been lost by placing the order.

Margin Trades: Buying Securities on Credit

It is possible to borrow some of the money needed to purchase securities. *Buying on margin,* as it is called, is a common practice that allows investors to use borrowed money to make security transactions. Margin trading is closely regulated and is carried out under strict *margin requirements* set by the Federal Reserve Board. These requirements specify the amount of *equity* an investor must put up when buying stocks, bonds, and other securities. The most recent requirement was 50 percent for common stock, which means that at least 50 percent of each dollar invested must be the investor's own; the remaining 50 percent may be borrowed. For example, with a 50 percent margin requirement, you could purchase $5,000 worth of stock by putting up only $2,500 of your own money and borrowing the remaining $2,500. Other securities besides stocks can be margined, and these have their own margin requirements; Treasury bonds, for example, can be purchased with a margin of as low as 10 percent.

In order to make **margin purchases**, you must open a *margin account* and have a minimum of $2,000 in cash (or *equity* in securities) on deposit with your broker. Once you have met the necessary requirements, the brokerage firm will loan you the needed funds (at competitive interest rates) and retain the securities purchased as collateral. You can also obtain loans for purchasing securities from your commercial bank, but the Fed's margin requirements will still apply even though they may be a bit more difficult to enforce. To see how margin trading works, assume that the margin requirement is 50 percent; also suppose that your brokerage firm charges 14 percent interest on margin loans (brokerage firms usually set the rate on margin loans at 1 to 3 points above prime, or at the prime rate for large accounts). If you want to purchase a round lot (100 shares) of LMN, which is currently selling for $50 per share, you can either make the purchase entirely with your own money or borrow a portion of the purchase price. The cost of the transaction will be $5,000 ($50/share × 100

shares). If you margin, you will have to put up only $2,500 of your own money (50 percent × $5,000); you can then borrow the $2,500 balance. Exhibit 13.6 compares the rates of return you would receive with and without the 50 percent margin. This is done for two cases: (1) a $10 per share increase in the stock price, to $60 per share, and (2) a $10 per share decrease in the stock price, to $40 per share. It is assumed the stock will be held for one year and all broker commissions are ignored.

As indicated in Exhibit 13.6, the use of margin allows you to increase the return on your investment when stock prices increase. Indeed, one of the major attributes of margin trading is that it allows you to *magnify your returns*—that is, you can use margin to reduce your equity in an investment and thereby magnify the returns from invested capital when stock prices go up. The return on your investment when the stock price increases from $50 a share to $60 a share is 20 percent without margin and 26 percent with margin. However, when the stock price declines from $50 to $40 per share, the return on your investment will be a negative 20 percent without margin and a whopping 54 percent loss with margin. Clearly, the use of

---

discount broker
A broker with low overhead who charges low commissions and offers little or no services to investors.

market order
An order to buy or sell a security at the best price available at the time it is placed.

limit order
An order to either buy a security at a specified or lower price or to sell a security at or above a specified price.

good 'til cancelled (GTC) order
A limit order placed with instructions that it remain in effect indefinitely or until cancelled.

stop-loss (stop) order
An order to sell a stock when the market price reaches or drops below a specified level.

margin purchase
The purchase of securities with borrowed funds, the allowable amount of which is limited by the broker and/or the Federal Reserve Board.

EXHIBIT 13.6

The Impact of Margin Trading on Investment Returns

The rate of return that an individual earns on his or her investment is affected by the amount of margin being used; unfortunately, while margin trading can magnify returns, it can also magnify losses.

Transaction	Without Margin	With Margin
The Initial Investment		
Amount invested	$5,000	$2,500
Amount borrowed	0	2,500
Total purchase (100 shares @ $50)	$5,000	$5,000
Price *Increases:* Sell Stock for $60/Share One Year Later		
Gross proceeds (100 shares @ $60)	$6,000	$6,000
Less: Interest @ 14% of borrowing	0	350
Net proceeds	$6,000	$5,650
Less: Total investment	5,000	5,000
Net profit (loss)	$1,000	$650
Return on your investment (profit ÷ amount invested)	$\frac{\$1,000}{\$5,000} = 20\%$	$\frac{\$650}{\$2,500} = 26\%$
Price *Decreases:* Sell Stock for $40/Share One Year Later		
Gross proceeds (100 shares @ $40)	$4,000	$4,000
Less: Interest @ 14% of borrowing	0	350
Net proceeds	$4,000	$3,650
Less: Total investment	5,000	5,000
Net profit (loss)	($1,000)	($1,650)
Return on yor investment (profit ÷ amount invested)	$\frac{(\$1,000)}{\$5,000} = (20\%)$	$\frac{(\$1,350)}{\$2,500} = (54\%)$

margin magnifies losses as well as profits! If the price of the stock in our example continues to drop, you will eventually reach the point at which your equity in the investment will be so low that the brokerage house will require you to either provide more collateral or liquidate the investment. The risks inherent in buying on margin make it imperative that you thoroughly acquaint yourself with the risk-return trade-offs involved *before* using the margin in your investment program.

Short Sales: The Practice of Selling Borrowed Securities

Most security transactions are *long transactions;* they are made in anticipation of increasing security prices in order to profit by buying low and selling high. A **short sale** transaction, in contrast, is made in anticipation of a decline in the price of a security. Although not as common as long transactions, the short sale is often used by the more sophisticated investor to profit during a period of declining prices. When used by individual investors, most short sales are made with common stocks. When an investor sells a security short, the broker borrows the security and then sells it on behalf of the short seller's account. The borrowed shares must, of course, be replaced in the future. If the investor can repurchase the shares at a lower price, a profit will result. In effect, the objective of a short sale is to take advantage of a drop in price by first selling high and then buying low (which, of course, is nothing more than the old "buy low, sell high" adage in reverse).

Because the shares sold are *borrowed shares,* numerous rules and regulations govern the short sale process. One, for example, permits stocks to be sold short only when the last change in the market price of the stock has been upward. Another safeguard is the requirement that all proceeds from the short sale of the borrowed securities be held by the brokerage firm—the short seller never sees any of this money! In addition, the short seller must deposit with the broker a certain amount of money (equivalent to the prevailing initial margin requirement) when the transaction is executed—so even a short-sale transaction involves an investment of capital.

A short-sale transaction can be illustrated with a simple example (and one that ignores brokerage fees). Assume that Patrick O'Sullivan wishes to sell short 100 shares of ABC at $52.50 per share. After Pat has met the necessary requirements, his broker borrows the shares and sells them, obtaining proceeds of $5,250 (100 shares × $52.50/share). If the stock price goes down as Pat expects, he will be able to repurchase the shares at the lower price. Now suppose the price drops to $40 per share, and he repurchases the 100 shares. Pat will make a profit, since he will have been able to replace the shares for $4,000 (100 shares × $40/share), which is below the $5,250 received when he sold the stock. His profit will be $1,250 ($5,250 − $4,000). If, on the other hand, the stock price rose to, say, $60 per share, and Pat repurchased the stocks at that price, he would sustain a loss of $750 ($52.50 − $60.00 = −$750.00). Because of the high risk involved in short sales, you should thoroughly familiarize yourself with this technique and all its pitfalls *before* attempting to short sell any security.

An investor would short sell a stock if he or she expects its price to go down. **Fact:** Short sales are made in anticipation of a drop in the price of a security; an investor makes money on a short sale when prices decline.

BECOMING AN INFORMED INVESTOR

Basing investment decisions on sound information lies at the very heart of most successful investment programs. What do you think it takes to become an informed investor? What kinds of information do you think you should have, and where would you look for such information? Stop to think about these questions before reading on.

Face it: some people are more knowledgeable about investing than others. As a result, they may use certain investment vehicles or tactics that are not even in the vocabulary of others. Investor know-how, in short, defines the playing field. It helps determine how well you'll meet the investment objective you've set for yourself. Being knowledgeable about investments is important since one of the key elements in successful investing is *knowing how to achieve decent rates of return without taking on unnecessary risks.*

There's no substitute for being informed when it comes to making investment decisions. While it can't guarantee success, it can help you avoid unnecessary losses—like the ones that happen all too often when people put their money into investment vehicles they don't fully understand. Such results aren't too surprising, since these investors violate the first rule of investing, which is: *Never start an investment program, or buy an investment vehicle, unless you're thoroughly familiar with what you're getting into.* Indeed, before making any major investment decision, you should thoroughly investigate the security and its merits. Formulate some basic expectations about its future performance, and gain an understanding of the sources of risk and return. This need not involve fancy, time-consuming security analysis but can usually be done simply by *regularly* reading the popular financial press and occasionally referring to one of the other basic sources of investment information. There are four basic types of investment information that you should try to stay abreast of:

- *Economic developments and current events*—to help you evaluate the underlying investment environment.
- *Alternative investment vehicles*—to keep you abreast of market developments.
- *Current interest rates and price quotations*—to enable you to monitor your investments and

short sale
A transaction that involves selling borrowed securities with the expectation that they can be replaced at a lower price at some future date; generally made in anticipation of a decline in the securities' price.

also stay alert for developing investment opportunities.

■ *Personal investment strategies*—to help you hone your skills and stay alert for new techniques as they develop.

In the final analysis, the payoff of such an informed approach to investing is both an improved chance of gain and a reduced chance of loss. While there are many sources of investment information, you, as a beginning investor, should concentrate on the more common ones, such as annual stockholders' reports, the financial press, brokerage reports, advisory services, and investment advisors.

Annual Stockholders' Reports

Every publicly traded corporation is required to provide its stockholders and other interested parties with **annual stockholders' reports**. These documents provide a wealth of information about companies, including balance sheets, income statements, and summarized statements for several prior years. (The balance sheets and income statements for business firms are similar in form to the personal financial statements examined in Chapter 2.) Annual reports usually describe the firm's business activities, recent developments, and future plans and outlook. Financial ratios describing past performance may also be included, among other relevant statistics. In fact, as the *Money In Action* box explains, a great deal of insight into the company's past, present, and future operations can be gained from the stockholders' report. These reports are sent to all stockholders; other interested parties can obtain them for free directly from the companies, through a brokerage firm, or at a large library.

Because they are so biased, you should pay little attention to annual stockholders' reports. **Fantasy:** While they do tend to accentuate the positive, annual stockholders' reports are nonetheless an excellent source of information and are widely used by *informed* investors to obtain financial information about specific companies.

The Financial Press

The most common source of financial news is the local newspaper. The newspapers in most larger cities often devote several pages to business and financial information and, of course, big-city papers, like the *New York Times* and the *Los Angeles Times,* provide investors with an abundance of financial information. Other, more specific sources of financial news include *The Wall Street Journal, Barron's, Investor's Daily,* and the "Money" section of *USA Today.* These are all national publications that include articles on the behavior of the economy, the market, various industries, and individual companies. The most comprehensive and up-to-date coverage of financial news is provided Monday through Friday by *The Wall Street Journal. Barron's* concentrates on the week's activities as they relate to the financial markets and individual security prices. Other excellent sources of investment information include magazine-type publications such as *Money, Forbes, Fortune, Personal Investor, Changing Times, Business Week, U.S. News and World Report,* and *Financial World.*

Economic Data. Summaries and analyses of economic events can be found in all of the above sources. Economic data include news items related to government actions and their effects on the economy, political and international events as they pertain to the economy, and statistics related to price levels, interest rates, the federal budget, and taxes.

Market Data. Usually presented in the form of averages, or indexes, *market data* describe the general behavior of the securities markets. The averages and indexes are based on the price movements of a select group of securities over an extended period of time. They are used to capture the overall performance of the market as a whole. You would follow one or more of these measures *to get a feel for how the market is doing over time* and, perhaps, to get an indication of what lies ahead. The absolute level of the index at a given point in time (or on a given day) is far less important than *what's been happening to that index over a given period of time.* The most frequently cited market measures are those calculated by Dow Jones, Standard & Poor's, the New York Stock Exchange, the American Stock Exchange, and the OTC market. These measures are all intended to keep track of the behavior in the stock market, particularly stocks on the NYSE (the Dow, S&P, and NYSE averages all follow stocks on the big board). In addition, there are several averages and indexes that follow the action in other markets, including the bond, commodities, and options markets and even the markets for mutual funds, real estate, and collectibles. However, because all these other averages and indexes are not followed nearly as much as those of stocks, we will concentrate primarily on stock market performance measures.

Dow Jones Averages. The granddaddy of them all and the most widely followed measure of stock market performance is the **Dow Jones Industrial Average (DJIA)**. Actually, the Dow Jones averages, which began in 1896, are made up of four parts: (1) an industrial average based on 30 stocks; (2) a transportation average based on 20 stocks; (3) a utility average based on 15 stocks; and (4) a composite average based on all 65 industrial, transportation, and utility stocks. The makeup of the 30 stocks in the DJIA does change a bit over time as companies go private, are acquired by other firms, or become less of a force in the marketplace; for example, in the past few years, American Can, Inco, and Owens-Illinois were dropped from the DJIA and replaced with Boeing, Coca-Cola, and Primerica. The stocks are all picked from the NYSE, and while they are intended to represent a cross-section of companies, there is a strong bias toward blue-chips, which is one of the major criticisms of the Dow Jones Industrial Average. Critics also claim that an average made up of only 30 blue-chip stocks—out of a total of some 2,200 issues—is hardly representative of the market. However, the facts show that as a rule, the behavior of the DJIA closely reflects that of other stock market measures. Exhibit 13.7 (on pae 476) lists the 30 stocks in the DJIA, along with some important dates in its life.

Standard & Poor's Indexes. The **Standard & Poor's (S&P) indexes** are similar to the Dow Jones averages to the extent that they both are used to capture the overall performance of the market. However, there are some important differences in the two measures. For one thing, the S&P uses a lot more stocks: the popular S&P 500 composite index is based on 500 different stocks, whereas the DJIA uses only 30 stocks. What's more, the S&P index is made up of all large NYSE stocks, as well as some major AMEX and OTC stocks, so there's not only more issues in the S&P sample, but also a greater breadth of representation. And finally, there are

some technical differences in the mathematical procedures used to compute the two measures: the Dow Jones is an *average,* while the S&P is an *index*. In spite of these technical differences, however, the two measures are still used in much the same manner.

There are five basic indexes: (1) an industrial index based on 400 stocks; (2) a transportation index of 20 stocks; (3) a public utility index of 40 stocks; (4) a financial index of 40 stocks; and (5) a composite index for all 500 of the stocks used in the first four indexes. The S&P 500, like the DJIA, is widely followed by the financial media, and is reported not only in publications like *The Wall Street Journal* and *Barron's,* but also in most of the major newspapers and other market outlets. The S&P has a much lower value than the DJIA—for example, in December 1988, the Dow stood at about 2,100 while the S&P index of 500 stocks was around 270. Now this does not mean that the S&P consists of less valuable stocks; rather, the disparity is due solely to the different methods used to compute the measures.

The NYSE, AMEX, and OTC Indexes. The three most widely followed exchange-based indexes are those of the New York Stock Exchange (NYSE), the American Stock Exchange (AMEX), and, for the OTC market. The **NYSE index** includes about 1,600 of the stocks listed on the "big board." In addition to the composite index, the NYSE pub-

---

annual stockholders' report
A report made available to stockholders and other interested parties that includes a variety of financial and descriptive information about a firm's operations during the past year.

Dow Jones Industrial Average (DJIA)
The most widely followed measure of stock market performance; consists of 30 blue-chip stocks listed on the NYSE.

Standard & Poor's (S&P) indexes
Indexes compiled by Standard & Poor's Corporation; similar to the DJIA but employ different computational methods and consist of far more stocks.

NYSE index
An index of the performance of all stocks listed on the New York Stock Exchange.

MONEY IN ACTION

"There's More to an Annual Report Than Meets the Eye"

On balance, the 1986 annual report of HRE Properties, a real estate investment trust, was upbeat. "Our retail properties generally performed well," it said. Expansion of a regional mall "should produce substantial income increases." Tax reform "will be a positive force." Furthermore, chances are good that "we will see opportunities to increase income."

But a careful reader would have found reason for concern. The year had been difficult for the real estate industry, the report noted, "and many markets will be no better in 1987." Office vacancies were higher than ever. HRE's president said he thought the trust was "very well positioned for the longer term"—a statement that seemed to raise questions about the short term. More disturbing: Net income had been slipping.

As it turned out, the slippage continued in 1987, and HRE cut its dividend by 15.7%. The price of the stock fell proportionately. What does this tell you? That any annual report should be read with care. A dash of skepticism is in order, too. Although they're usually accurate, these presentations always accentuate the positive. Bad news is likely to be downplayed or obscured by majestic prose and flashy graphics.

Yet an annual report should never be ignored. "It's a good way to get a feel for the company, its history and prospects," says John Markese, research director for the American Association of Individual Investors. From there you can go on to sources that are likely to be more revealing and objective, such as *Value Line Investment Survey,* Standard & Poor's, Moody's and reports of securities analysts.

Here are the most important points to check in any annual report:
- Look first at the section headed *highlights* or *selected financial data.* It's usually in the front and includes such key information as revenues, net income, assets, earnings per share of common stock, and dividends for the last two years. You'll quickly get a sense of how things have been going. Usually, earnings per share have the greatest impact on a stock's price and are the most closely watched figures. A leveling or drop in earnings or in any of the other numbers could be a danger sign, though not neces-

---

lishes indexes for industrials, utilities, transportation, and finance subgroups.

The **AMEX index** reflects share prices on the American Stock Exchange. Made up of all stocks on the AMEX, it is set up in such a way that it directly captures the actual percentage change in share prices. For example, if the price change in AMEX stocks from one day to the next were +3 percent, the AMEX index would likewise increase by 3 percent over the previous day's value. Like the NYSE indexes, the AMEX index is often cited in the financial news.

Activity in the OTC market is captured by the **NASDAQ indexes**, which are calculated like the S&P and NYSE indexes. The most comprehensive of the NASDAQ indexes is the OTC composite index, which is calculated using more than 4,700 stocks traded on the NASDAQ system. The other five NASDAQ indexes are the industrial, insurance, bank, National Market composite, and National Market industrial. Although their degrees of responsiveness may vary, these averages do tend to move in the same general direction over time. Because the *NASDAQ OTC composite index* is highly reflective of the price behavior of the smaller, more speculative stocks, it tends to be closely followed by investors and speculators interested in the small-stock segment of the market.

sarily sufficient cause for dumping the stock. Its current price will in most cases reflect any significant change that has occurred.

■ Go next to the *chief executive's message.* Unless the company is obviously in traction, this review and forecast is likely to glow with optimism. In General Motors' 1986 report, Chairman Roger Smith allowed that during "one of the automobile industry's most competitive years ever, we achieved record sales and revenues . . . and emerged . . . with strong . . . cash flow capabilities." Strong capabilities? Cash reserves had diminished sharply; but to find that out, you had to read the financial tables. Lesson: Don't be awed by rhetoric. Watch out for euphemisms. A bad year might be described as a "period

of adjustment," a drop in earnings as a "slowing of growth."

■ Check on the year's operations in the section called *management discussion and analysis* or something similar. Details about sales, earnings, debt, inventories, new plants or plant closings, the book value of the stock, pending litigation and taxes will be found here. Be wary of vagueness or emphasis on projected achievements.

■ Look next at the financial statements. The *income statement, balance sheet* and *footnotes* may cause your eyes to glaze, but even here you may find clues to the company's health. Are sales improving? Are costs up or down? Has there been a change in the cash position? A significant increase in inventories of new products could mean sales are slowing,

and a price drop could diminish income. Any serious shrinkage in net working capital could be a bad enough omen to warrant selling the stock.

■ Go now to the *auditor's report.* This is a statement from independent accountants who examined the figures, and it usually consists of two brief, perfunctory paragraphs when everything appears in order. If there is more, and you see terms such as "except for" or "subject to," the auditors may have spotted problems. Look for an explanation elsewhere in the report.

Source: Adapted from Morton C. Paulson. " 'Tis the Season for Annual Reports, and There's More to See Than Meets the Eye," *Changing Times,* December 1988, p. 16.

Industry Data. Local newspapers, *The Wall Street Journal, Barron's,* and various financial publications regularly contain articles and data about different industries. For example, Standard & Poor's *Industry Surveys* provides detailed descriptions and statistics for all the major industries; on a smaller scale, *Business Week* and other magazines regularly include indexes of industry performance and price levels. Other industry-related data can be obtained from industry trade associations, one example of which is the American Petroleum Institute.

Company Data. Articles about the performance and new developments of companies are included in local newspapers, *The Wall Street Journal,*

AMEX index

An index of the performance of all stocks listed on the American Stock Exchange.

NASDAQ index

An index, supplied by the National Association of Securities Dealers Automated Quotation, that tracks the performance of stocks traded in the OTC market.

EXHIBIT 13.7

The Dow Jones Industrial Average

The DJIA is made up of 30 of the bluest of blue-chip stocks and has been closely followed by investors for the past 90 years or so.

The 30 Stocks in the DJIA:

Allied Signal	Exxon	Philip Morris
Aluminum Co	General Electric	Primerica
Amer Express	General Motors	Procter & Gamb
Amer T&T	Goodyear	Sears Roebuck
Boeing	IBM	Texaco
Bethlehem Steel	Inter Paper	Union Carbide
Chevron	McDonalds	United Technologies
Coca-Cola	Merck	USX Corp.
DuPont	Minnesota M&M	Westinghouse El
Eastman Kodak	Navistar Inter	Woolworth

Some Important Dates for the Dow:

May 26, 1896	The Dow Jones Industrial Average makes its debut; originally made up of just 12 stocks.
January 12, 1906	Closes above 100 for the first time.
October 28, 1929	The infamous "1929 crash"; Dow drops 38.33 points in one day.
October 29, 1929	The Dow drops another 30.57 points—in just *two* days, the market value of stocks drops an incredible 25 percent; these two days are considered as the start of the Great Depression.
March 12, 1956	Closes above 500 for the first time.
January 18, 1966	Reaches 1000 during the day but closes at 994.20.
November 14, 1972	Closes above 1000 for the first time.
December 6, 1974	Closes at 577.60 to end the worst bear market since the 1930s.
April 27, 1981	Closes at eight-year high of 1024.0.
August 12, 1982	Closes at 776.92, as the market bottoms out and the Great Bull Market of 1982–1987 is born.
December 31, 1982	Closes at 1046.54; DJIA rises 35% in the first 3½ months of the bull market.
December 31, 1985	Closes at 1546.67; in a little over 3 years, the market has nearly doubled in value.
December 31, 1986	Closes at 1895.95; the market's up another 23% for the year.
August 25,1987	Closes at 2722.42 (an all time high); in the first 8 months of the year, the market rises 44%—this marks the peak of the 1982–1987 bull market; in 5 years, the DJIA has gone up almost 2,000 points (250%).
October 19, 1987	The market crashes; the DJIA closes at 1738.74, for a record one day drop of 508 points (23%).
October 21, 1987	Closes at 2027.85, as the market goes up nearly 290 points in the two days following the crash.
December 31, 1987	Closes *the year* at 1938.83, up 2% for the year, even after the crash.
December 31, 1988	Closes at 2168.57, up a very respectable 12% for the year; this marks the first time the market has ended the year above 2000.
April 27, 1989	Market moves to a post-crash high of 2433.10, which totally wipes out the loss of October 19th, with about 200 points to spare.

Barron's, and most investment magazines. The prices of the securities of all listed companies and the most active over-the-counter stocks are quoted daily in *The Wall Street Journal, Investor's Daily,* and *USA Today* and weekly in *Barron's.* Many daily newspapers also contain stock price quotations, though in the smaller ones the listing may be selective; in some cases, only stocks of local interest might be included.

Stock Quotes. To see how price quotations work and what they mean, consider the quotes that appear daily (M-F) in *The Wall Street Journal.* As we'll see, the quotations give not only the most recent prices of each stock, but a great deal of additional information as well. A portion of the NYSE stock quotations from *The Wall Street Journal* is presented in Exhibit 13.8. Let's use the Walt Disney quotations for purposes of illustration. These

EXHIBIT 13.8

Listed Stock Quotes

Common and preferred stocks are listed together and, except for a couple of minor differences, basically follow the same price quotation system.

		52 Weeks Hi	52 Weeks Lo	Stock	Sym	Div	Yld %	PE	Vol 100s	Hi	Lo	Close	Net Chg	
		28	24⅛	DiaShamRM	pf	2.00	7.2	...	110	28	27¾	27¾	− ¼	
		8⅜	4	DianaCp	DNA		...	...	10	5	4⅞	7⅞	− ⅛	
		48	34	Diebold	DBD	1.40	3.4	15	409	41⅛	40½	40⅞	+ ⅛	
		38	16½	DigitalComm	DCA		...	13	1355	25	23⅞	24½	− ½	
		127⅜	86⅜	DigitalEqp	DEC		...	12	17032	111¾	109½	111⅝	+3	
		21¼	12	DimeSvgNY	DME	.60	4.8	5	1425	12⅞	12¼	12⅜	− ⅜	
Disney common →	↑	71⅞	54	Disney	DIS	.40	.6	19	7936	72½	71¾	72	+ ½	← Common stock quote
		29⅝	23½	DivrsEngies	DEI	1.52	6.3	11	219	24	23¾	24	...	
		6⅛	3½	DivrsInd	DMC		...	...	37	6⅛	6	6⅛	...	
		47¼	40⅞	DominRes	D	3.20	7.5	9	502	42⅝	42⅜	42½	...	
		13⅝	9⅝	Domtar	DTC	.50	...	...	1828	13½	13⅜	13½	+ ⅛	
	s	25¾	17¾	Donaldson	DCI	.38	1.8	11	48	20⅞	20⅝	20¾	+ ⅛	
		38¾	30⅝	Donelley	DNY	.78	2.1	15	1559	36⅞	36¼	36⅞	+ ¼	
	s	36⅝	26⅝	Dover	DOV	.68	2.3	13	637	29⅝	29⅛	29½	+ ⅛	
		93	76¾	DowChem	DOW	2.80	3.0	8	9083	02½	91⅝	92½	+1	
		36½	27¾	DowJones	DJ	.72	2.3	13	1488	31½	30¾	31¼	+ ⅜	
		19⅝	13¼	DowneySL	DSL	.40	2.3	10	34	17⅝	17⅜	17⅝	+ ¼	
		17⅜	11⅝	Dravo	DRV		...	29	784	17	16⅞	17	+ ⅛	
		35⅝	24⅜	DresserInd	DI	.80	2.6	14	1372	30⅞	30½	30½	...	
		10½	5	Dresher	DSR	.16	2.8	11	143	5¾	5½	5⅝	− ⅜	
		30½	24¼	Dreyfus	DRY	.52	1.9	12	636	28½	27¾	28	− ⅜	
		10½	9⅜	DreyfusMuni	LEO	.78a	7.5	...	246	10½	10⅜	10⅜	...	
	n	12	10⅜	DreyfStrGvFd	SDI	1.20	10.9	...	107	11	10⅞	11	+ ⅛	
	↑	96⅜	77⅜	DuPont	DD	3.80	3.9	11	13495	98½	95½	98½	+2⅛	
DuPont preferred →		57	49¾	DuPont pf		4.50	8.9	...	14	50¾	50¾	50¾	− ¼	← Preferred stock quote
	x	9⅜	7¾	DuffPhelps	DNP	.72a	8.6	...	x2558	8½	8¼	8⅜	− ⅛	
		49	42¼	DukePwr	DUK	2.96	6.4	9	447	46⅝	46¼	46⅜	+ ⅛	
		97½	88	DukePwr pf		8.70	9.5	...	z100	92	92	92	+ ½	
		90½	82	DukePwr pf		8.20	9.4	...	z7540	88	87¼	87¼	+ ¼	
		99	89½	DukePwr pfM		8.84	9.4	...	z1240	94	94	94	...	
	n	6½	5⅜	DukeRltyInv	DRE	.68e	11.6	...	88	6⅛	5⅞	5⅞	− ⅛	
		57½	45⅞	DunBradst	DNB	1.74	3.3	20	7661	53⅝	52⅜	52½	− ½	
		18⅞	12½	DuqLght	DQU	1.28	7.1	9	324	18¼	18⅛	18⅛	− ⅛	
		23	19¾	DuqLght pfA		2.10	9.8	...	z1000	21¾	21½	21½	− ⅜	
		20½	18¼	DuqLght pf		2.00	10.3	...	z210	19½	19½	19½	...	
		22	19½	DuqLght pfG		2.10	10.2	...	z1150	20¾	20½	20½	− ¼	
		23	19⅜	DuqLght pfK		2.10	10.1	...	7	20¾	20¾	20¾	...	
		24	21⅝	DuqLght pr		2.31	10.3	...	z100	22½	22½	22½	...	
		23⅞	16⅞	DynaAmer	DYA	.20	.9	12	7	23⅜	23¼	23¼	...	

Source: *The Wall Street Journal*, January 26, 1989.

quotes were published on Thursday, January 26, 1989, and are for trading activity that occurred on Wednesday, January 25, 1989. A glance at the quotations shows that stock prices are quoted in eighths of a dollar, with the fractions reduced to their lowest common denominator (2/8, 4/8, and 6/8 are expressed as 1/4, 1/2, and 3/4, respectively). The first two columns, labeled "Hi" and "Lo," contain the highest and lowest price at which the stock sold during the preceding 52 weeks; Disney, for example, traded between 54 and 71⅞ during the 52-week period ending January 25, 1989. By the way, note the arrow pointing up (↑) in the margin: It means the stock just set a new high for the year. Listed to the right of the company's name is its *stock symbol* (Disney goes by the three-letter initial "DIS"); these stock symbols are the abbreviations used on the *market tapes* seen in brokerage offices and on the FNN and CNN channels to identify specific companies. The figure listed right after the stock symbol is the cash dividend expected to be paid on each share during the year; this is followed by the dividend yield. (Note: Since Disney is expected to pay a cash dividend of 40 cents a share, its dividend yield is 0.6 percent, which is found by dividing $0.40 by the closing price of $72.) The next entry is the P/E ratio, which is the current market price divided by the per share earnings for the most recent 12-month period. Since it is believed to reflect investor expectations concerning the firm's future prospects, the P/E ratio is closely followed by investors as part of the stock-valuation process. Disney's P/E ratio was 19.

The daily volume follows the P/E ratio. Here, the sales numbers are listed in round lots (of 100 shares); thus the figure 7936 for Disney means that there were 793,600 shares of Disney stock traded on January 25. The next entries, in the "Hi," "Lo," and "Close" columns, contain the highest, lowest, and last (closing) price, respectively, at which the stock sold on the day in question. Disney closed up ½ on January 25, which means that it had closed at 71½ the day before.

The same quotation system is used for AMEX and NASDAQ *National Market* stocks. However, a slightly different procedure is used with OTC securities that are not part of the National Market System—that is, for many OTC stocks, only the bid and ask prices are included in the quotes. In particular, the *highest* bid price for the day is listed along with the *lowest* ask price. (Recall that the bid price is what you can *sell* a stock for and the ask price is what you must pay to *buy* the security.)

Preferred stocks are also listed with the common stock quotes. To find a preferred stock, just look for the letters "pf" or "pr" right after the company's name, as shown for the DuPont preferred in Exhibit 13.8. While a company may have any number of preferred issues outstanding (look at Duke Power and Duquesne Lighting), a quote will appear in the paper only if the stock actually traded on the day in question. Thus, whereas DuPont has two preferred issues outstanding, only one of them, *the $4.50 perferreds,* traded on January 25th. This particular preferred stock pays $4.50 a year in dividends and based on the closing price for the day (50¾), it is currently yielding 8.9 percent. Normally, it's the *annual dividend* that separates one preferred stock from another—for example, look at the three Duke Power issues. As for the rest of the quotation, you'll notice that preferred quotes are about the same as common stock quotes, except that the P/E ratios are left blank because they are irrelevant in the case of preferred stocks.

Bond Quotes. Exhibit 13.9 contains examples of some NYSE bond quotes; these quotes were also for trades that occurred on January 25, 1989. To understand the system used with listed bonds, look at the Alabama Power (AlaP) issue. The column of numbers immediately following the company name gives the coupon and the year in which the bond matures; the "8¾07" means that this particular bond carries an 8¾ percent annual coupon and will mature sometime in the year 2007. Such information is important, since it lets investors differentiate among the various bonds issued by the same corporation; notice that there were 7 different Alabama Power bonds listed on the day of this quote. The next column, labeled "Cur Yld," provides the *current yield* being offered by the issue at its *current market price*. Current yield is found by dividing the bond's annual coupon (here, 8.75) by the issue's closing price (90½, or 90.50), which in this case amounts to 9.7 percent. The "Vol" column represents the number of bonds traded; there were 64 Alabama Power bonds traded on this day. Price information is contained in the last two columns. Unlike stocks, instead of high, low, and closing prices, bond quotes usually show just the closing price, along with the net change in the closing price from the day before. *All bonds are quoted as a percent of par,* meaning that a quote of 85 translates into a price of 85 percent of the bond's par value. Since corporate bonds typically have par values of $1,000, a bond quote of 85 means that the price is really $850 (85% × $1,000). Corporate bonds are also traded in fractions of ⅛, but each fraction is worth 1.25 *dollars.* Thus, Alabama Power's closing price for the day was $905, found by multiplying the quoted price by $1,000: that is, 90½ = 90.5% × $1,000 = $905.

Convertibles are also listed along with other corporate bonds. They are easy to find: Just look for the letters "cv" in the current yield column, such as in the case of the American Medical (AmMed) 8¼ of 08 convertible in Exhibit 13.9. Except for the "cv" in the current yield column, all other aspects of the quote are exactly like that for any other listed bond. Also listed in Exhibit 13.9 are some zero coupon bonds issued by Allied Chemical Corporation (AlldC). Such bonds have the letters "zr" in place of their coupons; for example, with the Allied bonds, the "zr09" means the issue is a zero coupon bond that matures in 2009.

In addition to corporate bonds, Treasury and agency bond prices are also reported in *The Wall Street Journal* and other major publications. The quotes for these bonds are only slightly different

EXHIBIT 13.9

Listed Corporate Bond Quotes

Bond prices are always quoted as a *percent of par*. Since par for corporate bonds is normally $1,000, each point in a bond quote is worth $10 (and each ⅛ of a point is worth $1.25). Thus, a quote of 89¼ is *not* $89.25, but $892.50 ($1,000 × .8925); likewise, a quote of 115 translates into $1,150 ($1,000 × 1.15).

Bonds	Cur Yld	Vol	Close	Net Chg.
Advst 9s08	cv	50	83	+ ½
AlaP 9s2000	9.5	20	95	+ ⅞
AlaP 8⅞s03	9.6	9	92¼	+ ¼
AlaP 8¾07	9.7	64	90½	...
AlaP 9¼07	9.7	10	95	+ ⅜
AlaP 9½08	9.9	1	96⅛	+ ⅛
AlaP 9⅝08	9.8	42	98¼	+1
AlaP 12⅝10	12.0	12	105¼	...
AlskH 12⅞93	12.4	5	103½	−5
AlldC zr92	...	8	70⅞	+1
AlldC zr2000	...	8	33⅝	+ ⅝
AlldC zr91	...	85	79	...
AlldC zr01	...	5	30¼	+ ⅛
AlldC zr09	...	115	13⅞	...
Alcoa 6s92	6.6	5	91¼	− ⅜
Alcoa 9s95	9.2	15	97¾	...
AMAX 14¼90	13.6	55	105	...
AMAX 14½94	12.4	50	117¼	+ ⅝
AForP 5s30	9.2	5	54½	+2½
ACeM 6¾91	cv	2	20	...
AExC 14¾92	14.4	20	102⅜	− ½
AmMed 8¼08	cv	29	73¾	+ ⅝
AmMed 11¾99	11.7	30	100½	...
ATT 3⅞s90	4.1	103	94½	...
ATT 5⅝95	6.8	4	82⅛	+ ⅜
ATT 6s00	7.8	20	76½	...
ATT 8¾00	9.3	551	94¼	− ¼
ATT 7s01	8.4	56	82⅞	+1⅛
ATT 7⅛03	8.8	62	81⅛	− ⅜
ATT 8.80s05	9.3	64	94¼	+ ¼
ATT 8⅝s07	9.3	40	92⅜	+ ½
ATT 8⅝26	9.6	101	90	+ ⅛
Amoco 9.2s04	9.4	5	97⅞	+ ⅜
Amoco 8⅜05	9.2	55	90¾	+ ½
Amoco 7⅞07	9.2	5	85¾	+ ¼
Amoco 8⅝16	9.5	1	91	...
AmocoCda 7⅜13	7.5	113	98½	− ¼
Andarko 5¾12	cv	5	95½	− ½
Arml 13½94	12.7	25	106¼	+ ⅛
Arml 8½01	10.6	10	80½	+ ½

Alabama Power → Corporate bond quote (points to AlaP 8¾07 row)

Allied Chemical Corporation → Zero coupon bond quote (points to AlldC zr09 row)

American Medical → Convertible bond quote (points to AmMed 8¼08 row)

Source: *The Wall Street Journal*, January 26, 1989.

than those for corporates. These issues are also quoted as a percent of par, and the quote also specifies the coupon rates and maturity dates.

Brokerage Reports

Another important source of investor information is the reports produced by the research staffs of major (full-service) brokerage firms. These reports cover a wide variety of topics, from economic and market analyses to industry and company reports, news of special situations, and reports on interest rates and the bond market. Reports on certain industries or securities prepared by the house's back-office research staff may be issued on a scheduled basis and often contain lists of securities within certain industries classified as to the type of investment return they provide and the type of market behavior they are expected to exhibit. Also, brokerage houses often will issue lists of securities classified as either "buy" or "sell" depending on the research staff's analysis of their anticipated market behavior. Occasionally brokerage houses issue extensive analyses of specific securities, along with recommendations as to the type of investment returns expected and whether to buy or sell.

Advisory Services

A number of subscription advisory services provide information and recommendations on various industries and specific securities. The services normally cost from $50 to several hundred dollars a year. Although these costs may be tax deductible, only the most active investors will find them worthwhile, since you can usually review such materials at your broker's office and, in fact, your broker may even provide you with relevant portions. Many university as well as public libraries also have these services available for reference use. Probably the best known financial services are those provided by Standard & Poor's Corporation, Moody's Investors Service, and Value Line Investment Survey. Each of these companies offers an array of subscription services. Both Standard & Poor's and Moody's publish manuals containing historical facts and financial data on thousands of corporations; these are broken down into industry groups. On a monthly basis, Standard & Poor's publishes a stock guide and a bond guide, each of which summarizes the financial conditions of a few thousand issues; Moody's also publishes stock and bond guides.

Separate reports on specific companies are another valuable type of subscription service. An example of one such stock report is given in Exhibit 13.10. This report, prepared by Standard & Poor's, presents a concise summary of a company's financial history, current finances, and future prospects; a similar type of report, with even more emphasis given to the security's investment merits and future prospects, is also available from *Value Line.* Recommended lists of securities, broken down into groups on the basis of investment objectives, constitute still another type of service. In addition to these popular subscription services numerous *investment letters,* which periodically advise subscribers on the purchase and sale of securities, are available. Through subscription chart books, investors may also obtain graphs showing stock prices and volume over a period of time.

Investment Advisors

Successful investors often establish themselves as professional investment advisors. In this capacity, they attempt to develop investment plans consistent with the financial objectives of their clients. They may operate their own business, or be associated with large firms that employ research staffs and often publish various subscription materials. Many of the better known investment advisors limit their business to a select group of wealthy individuals who have similar investment objectives, while others accept clients with diverse goals. Professional advisors generally do not accept clients with investment assets of less than $50,000, and the more "elite" ones are likely to require considerably larger holdings. Annual fees for advisory services, which may involve the complete management of the client's money, are likely to range from 0.25 to 2 or 3 percent of assets under management.

There are several different ways you can obtain the services of a professional money manager: (1) you can hire an *independent investment advisor* (but they're usually pretty expensive and prefer to deal with well-heeled clients); (2) you can go to the *trust department of a major bank* (many offer their investment services to the general public at very reasonable costs, and you don't have to die or have a trust account to obtain such services—instead, all you have to do is enter into a simple *agency agreement*); (3) if you deal with a full-service brokerage firm, you can check with your broker to see if they offer fee-based *wrap accounts* (in these portfolio management accounts, your brokerage firm takes over the full-time management of your investments, in return for a flat annual fee—but watch out, that annual fee can get pretty hefty); or (4) you might consider the services of a *financial planner* (preferably one who has a strong track record in the field of *investments*). If you're thinking of using a professional money manager, the best thing to do is shop around—look at the kind of returns they've been able to generate (in good markets and bad), and don't overlook the matter of cost—find out right up front how much you'll have to pay and what the fee is based on. Equally important, find out if the advisor has a specialty and if so, make sure it's compatible with your investment objectives; for example, don't go to a financial planner that specializes in high-risk limited partnerships if you're not interested in that kind of investment.

The PC as a Source of Investment Information

Any discussion of investment information would be incomplete without mentioning the personal computer. There is no question that one of the greatest technological revolutions taking place in the market today is the widespread introduction of the personal computer to the investment decision-making

EXHIBIT 13.10

An S&P Stock Report

An S&P report like this one provides a wealth of information about the operating results and financial condition of the company and is an invaluable source of information to investors.

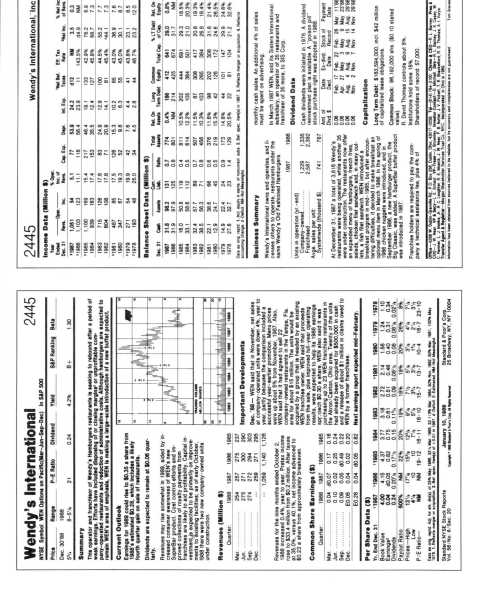

Source: Standard & Poor's Corporation.

process. This is occurring not only with professional investors and money management firms but also with individual investors. As we saw in the *Smart Money* box in Chapter 12, a variety of software is now available for helping the individual investor analyze and evaluate the investment merits of stocks and bonds; in essence, such software provides assistance in the security selection process. In addition, the personal computer can also be used to manage and keep track of *whole portfolios* of securities.

Another significant development has been the introduction of computerized *databases* that literally convert your home computer to an on-line library of investment information. Through these database programs, you can get immediate access to a vast array of historic and up-to-the-minute information on thousands of companies and securities. All sorts of financial information and financial ratios are available, along with equally extensive data on the market performance of stocks, bonds, and other securities—from yields and price/earnings multiples to market prices. For example, if you are thinking about buying a stock, you can have displayed on your computer screen recent news stories about the company, its current financial statements, estimates of its future earnings, and even its current and past stock price and volume data. These computerized databases in effect provide everything from quarterly corporate earnings reports to the latest stock prices. You can even *trade securities* with these services, by placing orders in your computer. And the store never closes: You can access the data and/or place orders 24 hours a day, any day of the week (in fact, it is usually cheaper to use the service at night and on weekends and holidays). All you need is a PC that is equipped with a *modem,* which enables computers to communicate with one another over phone lines. To subscribe to one of these services, you must pay a modest, one-time hook-up fee and then a monthly fee based on your usage of the service.

To get an idea of how these computerized databases work, let us look at one of the biggest: *CompuServe* (5000 Arlington Centre Blvd., Columbus, OH 43220). *CompuServe* is easy to learn, and requests are filled almost instantaneously. The service functions as a conduit to other resources and, as a result, makes available to subscribers such databases as Value Line and Standard & Poor's (each of which provides extensive financial and market information on a multitude of com-

panies and securities), earnings projections for several thousand companies from the Institutional Brokers' Estimate System, detailed financial statements filed with the Securities and Exchange Commission (SEC) by over 10,000 companies, and more. As a subscriber, you have immediate access to any and all of this information—just indicate what you want to see, and it will show up almost instantaneously on your home computer screen. Subscribers can also trade stocks, bonds, and options electronically through a hook-up with a major New York-based discount brokerage firm. Other popular computer-based investor information services include *Dow Jones News/Retrieval* (P.O. Box 300, Princeton, NJ 08540); *The Source* (1616 Anderson Rd., McLean, VA 22102); and *Trade* Plus* (480 California Ave., Palo Alto, CA 94306). Prices for these databases vary and may include a nominal ($30–$40) registration, or start-up, fee and possibly even a minimum monthly service charge. All four of the services noted here have a usage, or connect, fee every time you access the service. (Such fees are charged by the minute or by the hour.)

MANAGING YOUR INVESTMENT HOLDINGS

Developing a portfolio of security holdings is an important part of investing because a portfolio enables you to diversify your holdings. Why do you suppose diversification is such an important attribute? How would you go about building a portfolio of securities? Give some thought to these questions before going on.

Actually, buying and selling securities is not difficult; the hard part is finding securities that will provide the kind of return you're looking for. Like most individual investors, in time you too will be buying, selling, and/or trading securities with ease. Eventually your investment holdings will increase to the point where you are managing a whole portfolio of securities. In essence, a **portfolio** is a collection of investment vehicles assembled to meet a common investment goal. For instance, Bill Hansen's investment portfolio is made up of 20 shares of IBM, 100 shares of Chrysler, and 3 Georgia-Pacific convertible bonds. But a portfolio is far more than a collection of investments! For a portfolio breathes life into your investment program; *it's an investment philosophy that provides guidelines for carrying out your investment program.* A portfolio, in effect, combines your personal and financial traits with your investment objectives to give some structure to your investments.

Seasoned investors often devote a good deal of their attention to constructing diversified portfolios of securities. Such portfolios consist of stocks and bonds selected not only for their returns but also for their combined risk-return behavior. The notion of **diversification** is that combining securities with dissimilar risk-return characteristics will result in a portfolio of reduced risk and more predictable levels of return. In recent years, investment researchers have shown that you can achieve a measurable reduction in risk simply by diversifying your investment holdings. For the small investor with a moderate amount of money to invest, this means that *investing in a number of securities rather than a single one should be beneficial.* The payoff from diversification comes in the form of reduced risk without a significant impact on return. For example, Joan Rainer, who has $25,000 invested in Stock A, might find that by selling two-thirds of her holdings and using the proceeds to buy equal amounts of Stocks B and C, she will continue to earn the same level of return—say, 10 percent—while greatly decreasing the associated risk. Professional money managers emphasize the point that investors should not put all their eggs in one basket but instead should hold portfolios that are diversified across a broad segment of businesses. The accompanying *Smart Money* box provides further insights about the attributes and investment merits of diversification.

Building a Portfolio of Securities

Developing a portfolio of investment holdings is predicated on the assumption that diversification is a desirable investment attribute that leads to improved return and/or reduced risk. Again, as emphasized earlier, holding a variety of investments is far more desirable than concentrating all your investments in a single security or industry (for example, a portfolio made up of nothing but auto stocks such as GM, Ford, and Chrysler would be a poorly balanced one). Of course, when you first start investing, you will not be able to do

much if any, diversifying because of insufficient money. However, as you build up your investment capital, your opportunities (and need) for diversification will increase dramatically. By the time you have $5,000 to $10,000 to invest, you should start to diversify your holdings. In order to formulate an effective portfolio strategy, you should carefully consider your personal and financial situation and your investment objectives.

Investor Characteristics. An investor's personal financial condition and family situation are important inputs when determining a portfolio approach to investing. The following items are vital determinants:

- Level and stability of income
- Family factors
- Investment horizon
- Net worth
- Investor's experience and age
- Investor's disposition toward risk

These are the variables that set the tone for your investments. They determine the kinds of investments you should consider and how long you can tie up your money. In order for your portfolio to work, it must be tailored to meet your personal financial needs. Your income, family responsibilities, relative financial security, experience, and age all enter into the delicate equation that yields a sound portfolio strategy. For example, a married investor with young children probably will not be seeking high-risk investments until some measure of financial security has been provided for the family. Once that investor has ample savings and insurance protection for the family, he or she may be ready to undertake more risky ventures. On the other hand, a single investor with no family responsibilities would probably be better able to handle risk than one who has such concerns. Simply stated,

> **portfolio**
> A collection of securities assembled for the purpose of meeting common investment goals.
>
> **diversification**
> The process of choosing securities having dissimilar risk-return characteristics in order to create a portfolio that will provide an acceptable level of return and an acceptable exposure to risk.

"Diversification: Your Key to Sound Investing"

Whether you're a saver or an investor, a stock plunger, a bond buyer or a real-estate fanatic, you are probably committing the cardinal sin of prudent investing. You are putting too much of your money on one type of investment. We know too little, and markets change too quickly, for this approach to work. One moment you're up, the next moment you're down, and ten years later you're back where you started.

"Diversification" used to mean "buy a wide selection of stocks, or buy a mutual fund that does it for you." Now it means "own a variety of investments that respond to differing economic circumstances." You need short-term bonds for inflation and long-term bonds for deflation. Stocks for growth and money market funds for safety and liquidity.

During the October (1987) stock market crash, the bond market rallied. That saved the assets of balanced investors who had split their money between stocks and bonds. Only those who focused on stocks alone went away bare.

"Diversification" has another use. It matches your investments to the specific things you are going to have to pay for in your life in order to ensure that the money you need will always be there. For example, you are missing the boat if you invest for retirement—20 years away—entirely in bank CDs. Over that length of time stocks should do better than anything else.

To get the most from your diversification plan, it's important to carefully consider your investment horizon—to avoid potentially serious problems down the road, you ought to know going in how long you can keep your money tied up. For example, for money that you'll need within two years, you want investments (1) whose price doesn't change (or changes only slightly); (2) that give you easy access to the funds, without penalty; and (3) that pay a reasonable income while keeping your principal safe. Good choices are money market funds, short-term CDs, and short-term bonds.

For money you'll need in three to five years, you should still stick with things that keep your principal reasonably safe. Good choices are three- to five-year bonds, bank CDs that give you the right to raise your interest rate if the general level of interest rates rise, and high-dividend stocks (although any stock is vulnerable to a market decline).

For long-term money, you'll want growth investment that can outpace inflation. But you must give yourself time to let your strategy work. The longer you can leave your money invested, the less you need to worry about short-term concerns, and the more you can focus on earning a high return. Stocks, real estate, gold and longer-term bonds can all satisfy long-term objectives. Some of each is better than betting all of your money on just one.

The purpose of diversification is to preserve the savings you have worked so hard to amass, have money on tap when you need it, and still earn a decent return in any kind of market. This can be done even with a small amount of money. For once you have a good idea of what types of investments would be best for you, your investment decisions will be easier to make and much more productive in the long run.

Source: Adapted from Jane Bryant Quinn. "Diversification: Your Key to Sound Investing," *Phoenix Gazette,* June 27, 1988, A–8.

an *investor's risk exposure should not exceed his or her ability to bear risk.*

The size and certainty of an investor's employment income has a great bearing on portfolio strategy. An investor with a secure job is more likely to embark on a risk-oriented investment program than one with a less secure position. Income taxes bear on the investment decision as well. The higher an investor's income, the more important the tax ramifications of an investment program become. For example, municipal bonds normally yield about one-third less in annual interest than corporate bonds because the interest income of municipal bonds is tax-free. On an after-tax basis, however, municipal bonds may provide a superior return if an investor is in the 28 or 33 percent tax bracket.

An individual's investment experience also influences the appropriateness of the investment strategy. Normally, investors gradually assume levels of higher investment risk over time. It is best to "get one's feet wet" in the investment market by slipping into it gradually rather than leaping in head first. Investors who make risky initial investments very often suffer heavy losses, damaging the long-run potential of the entire investment program. A cautiously developed investment program will likely provide more favorable long-run results than an impulsive, risky one. Finally, investors should carefully consider risk. High-risk investments not only have high return potential but also a high risk of loss. Remember: By going for the home run (via a high-risk, high-return investment), the odds of striking out are much higher than by going for a base hit (a more conservative investment posture).

Investor Objectives.   Once an investor has developed a personal financial profile, the next question is: "What do I want from my portfolio?" This seems like an easy question to answer. We would all like to double our money every year by making low-risk investments. However, the realities of the highly competitive investment environment make this outcome unlikely, so the question must be answered more realistically. There generally is a trade-off between earning a high current income from an investment portfolio and obtaining significant capital appreciation from it. An investor must choose one or the other; it is difficult to have both. The price of having high appreciation potential in the portfolio is low current income potential. One must balance the certainty of high current income and limited price appreciation with the uncertainty of high future price appreciation.

The investor's needs may determine which avenue to choose. For instance, a retired investor whose income depends on his or her portfolio will probably choose a lower-risk, current income-oriented approach out of the need for financial survival. In contrast, a high-income, financially secure investor (a doctor, for instance) may be much more willing to take on risky investments in the hope of improving net worth. Likewise, a young investor with a secure job may be less concerned about current income and more able to bear risk. This type of investor will likely be more capital gains-oriented and may choose speculative investments. As an investor approaches age 60, the desired level of income likely rises as retirement approaches. The aging investor will be less willing to bear risk and want to keep what he or she has, because these investments will soon be needed as a source of retirement income.

Asset Allocation and Portfolio Management. A portfolio must be built around the individual's needs, which depend on income, family responsibilities, financial resources, age, retirement plans, and ability to bear risk. These needs shape one's financial goals. But to create a portfolio that is geared to those goals, you need to develop an **asset allocation** scheme. Basically, all that asset allocation involves is a decision on how to divide your portfolio among different types of securities. For example, what portion of your portfolio is going to be devoted to short-term securities, longer bonds and/or bond funds, and common stocks and/or equity funds? In asset allocation, emphasis is placed on *preservation of capital*. The idea is to position your assets in such a way that you can protect your portfolio from potential negative developments in the market, while still taking advantage of potential positive developments. This is one of the most overlooked yet most important aspects of investing. Indeed, there's overwhelming evidence that, over the long run, the total return on a portfolio is influenced more by its asset allocation plan than by specific security selections.

Asset allocation deals in broad categories and *does not tell you which individual securities to buy or sell*. It might look something like this:

---

asset allocation
A plan for dividing a portfolio among different classes of securities in order to preserve capital by protecting the portfolio against negative market development.

Type of Investment	Asset Mix
Short-term securities	35%
Longer bonds (7- to 10-year maturities)	40
Equity funds	25
Total portfolio	100%

As you can see, all you're really doing here is deciding how to cut up the pie. You still have to decide which particular securities to invest in. Once you've decided that you want to put, say, 35 percent of your money into short-term securities your next step is to select those specific securities. Security selection and portfolio management are recurring activities that become an almost routine part of your investment program. You receive an interest or dividend check, and you have to find a place to put it; you add new capital to your investment program, or one of the Treasury notes you're holding matures, and you have to decide what to do with the money. These events occur with considerable regularity, so you're likely to be faced with a series of little (and sometimes not so little) investment decisions over time. This, in short, is portfolio management: the initial construction and ongoing administration of a collection of securities and investments.

Portfolio management involves the buying, selling, and holding of various securities for the purpose of meeting a set of predetermined investment needs and objectives. To give you an idea of portfolio management in action, Exhibit 13.11 provides examples of four different portfolios, each developed with a particular financial situation in mind. Note in each case that the asset allocation schemes and portfolio structures change with the different financial objectives. The first one is the *newlywed couple;* in their late twenties, they earn $45,000 and spend just about every cent. They have managed to put away some money, however, and are quickly beginning to appreciate the need to develop a savings habit. Next there is the *two-income couple;* in their early forties, they earn $84,000 a year and are concerned about college costs for their children, ages 17 and 12. Next is the *divorced mother;* she is 34, has custody of her children, ages 7 and 4, and receives $28,000 a year in salary and child support. Finally, we have the *older couple;* in their mid-fifties, they are planning for retirement in ten years, when the husband will retire from his $70,000-a-year job.

Coming up with a sound asset allocation plan is likely to have more of an impact on long-term return than the specific securities you hold in your portfolio. **Fact:** Studies have shown that, over the long run, the total return on a portfolio is influenced more by its asset allocation plan—that is, its mix of assets—than by specific security selections.

Keeping Track of Your Investments

Keeping track of investment holdings is essential to a well-managed securities portfolio. Just as you need investment objectives to provide direction to your portfolio, so you need to *monitor* it by keeping informed of what your investment holdings consist of, how they have performed over time, and whether or not they have lived up to expectations. Sometimes investments fail to perform the way you thought they would: Their return may be well below what you would like, or perhaps you may even have suffered a loss. In either case, it may be time to *sell* the investment(s) and put the money elsewhere. A monitoring system for keeping track of your investments should allow you to identify such securities in your portfolio. In addition, it should enable you to stay on top of the holdings that are performing to your satisfaction. Knowing when to sell and when to hold can make a significant impact on the amount of return you will be able to generate from your investments—certainly it will help you keep your money fully invested.

Exhibit 13.12 (on page 488) provides a simple worksheet that you can use to keep an inventory of your investment holdings. All types of investments can be included on the worksheet—from stocks, bonds, and mutual funds to real estate and savings accounts. To see how it works, consider the investment portfolio that has been built up over the last ten years or so by John and Mary Maffeo, a two-income couple in their late thirties. As the figures in Exhibit 13.12 reveal, John and Mary hold common and preferred stock in four companies, three bond issues, two mutual funds, some real estate, and two savings accounts. In addition to the type and description of the investment vehicles, the worksheet contains the dates the investments were made (the purchase date is needed for tax pur-

EXHIBIT 13.11

Four Model Portfolios

The type of portfolio you put together will depend on your financial and family situation as well as on your investment objectives. Clearly, what is right for one family may be totally inappropriate for another.

Family Situation	Portfolio
Newlywed couple:	70% in common stocks, with three quarters in mutual funds aiming for maximum capital gains and the rest in growth funds 30% in a money market fund or other short-term money market securities
Two-income couple:	50% in common stocks, with three quarters of that in blue-chips or growth mutual funds and the remainder in more aggressive issues or mutual funds aiming for maximum capital gains 40% in discount Treasury notes whose maturities correspond with the bills for college tuition 10% in money market funds or other short-term money market securities
Divorced mother:	50% in money market funds or other short-term money market securities 50% in growth and income mutual funds
Older couple:	60% in blue-chip common stocks or growth mutual funds 30% in municipal bonds or short- and intermediate-term discount bonds that will mature as they start to need the money to live on 10% in CDs and/or money market funds

poses), the original amount of the investment, the amount of annual income currently being earned from it, and its latest market value.

Such a report would list all the investments John and Mary held as of December 1988, regardless of when they were purchased. In contrast, any securities/investments sold during the year (1988) would not be included. A report like this should be prepared at least once a year, and preferably every quarter. When completed, it will provide a quick overview of your investment holdings and enable you to easily identify securities that are performing well and those that are not. Such information is invaluable in effectively managing an investment portfolio, as it lets you know where you stand at a given point in time. Note that the Maffeos earn over $4,300 a year from their investments and that—thanks, in large part, to their investment in real estate—their holdings have grown from $73,000 to over $200,000! In fact, they have only one security that is not doing too well: Emery Air Freight. All the rest are quite profitable.

SUMMARY

- Stocks, bonds, and other long-term securities are traded in the capital markets; listed securities are traded on organized exchanges, like the New York and American stock exchanges, as well as more than a dozen smaller regional exchanges. In contrast, the over-the-counter (OTC) market handles the thousands of unlisted securities.
- Whether your broker is with a full-service or discount brokerage firm, he or she is the one who provides you with access to the securities market—in essence, brokers buy and sell securities for their customers. Investors can buy or sell securities in odd or round lots by simply placing one of several different kinds of orders with their brokers. The three basic types of orders are the market order, limit order, and stop-loss order.
- When you buy a security, you can pay cash for it or you can buy it on margin, where part of the cost of the security is paid with borrowed money. The objective of a margin transaction is to obtain magnified returns. It is also possible for an investor to make money when the price of a security

EXHIBIT 13.12

A Worksheet for Keeping Tabs on Your Investment Holdings

A worksheet like this one will enable you to keep track of your investment holdings and identify investments that are not performing up to expectations.

AN INVENTORY OF INVESTMENT HOLDINGS

Name(s): _John & Mary Maffeo_   Date: _December 1988_

Type of Investment	Description of Investment Vehicle	Date Purchased	Amount of Investment (Quote—$Amount)	Amount of Annual Income from Dividends, Interest, Etc.	Latest Market Value (Quote—$Amount)	Comments/ Planned Actions
Common stock	200 shares—Chrysler Corp.	6/8/84	18¾—$3,750	$450	25¼—$11,365	450 shs.
Common stock	300 shares—Emery Air Frt.	7/2/84	12¼—$3,675	0	4½—$1,350	Sell now?
Common stock	400 shares—Apple Computer	9/4/81	6¼—$2,500	$320	36¾—$29,400	800 shs.
Preferred stock	150 shares—AT&T p.03.64	5/20/78	24¼—$3,638	$546	48½—$7,275	
Corporate bond	$5,000—Pacific Telephone 11.35-90	8/19/79	75½—$3,775	$568	103—$5,150	
Corporate bond	$7,000—Texaco 5¾-97	2/27/77	39¼—$2,748	$402	74½—$5,215	
Treasury bond	$6,000—US Treasury 8⅝-93	9/1/80	62—$3,720	$518	99—$5,940	
Mutual fund	300 shares—Fidelity Magellan (growth)	6/16/76	9—$2,700	$78	47½—$14,250	
Mutual fund	200 shares—Fidelity high-yield (bond)	1/17/79	6½—$1,300	$260	12¼—$2,450	
Real estate	Four-plex at 1802 N. 75 Ave.	9/16/78	$140,000—$28,000	N/A	(est.)$250,000—$138,000	Time to sell?
Savings	1-year/7% CD at First National Bank	6/10/88	N/A—$10,000	$700	N/A—$10,000	
Savings	Money Fund at Paine Webber	3/13/83	N/A—$7,200	$540	N/A—$7,200	
	TOTALS		$73,006	$4,382	$237,595	

Instructions: List number of shares of *preferred stock* purchased as part of the description of securities held; then put the price paid *per share* under the "Quote" column and total amount invested (number of shares × price per share) under the "$ Amount" column. Enter the principal (par) value of all *bonds* held in place of number of shares: "$ Amount" column for bonds = principal value of bonds purchased × quote (for example, $5,000 × .755 = $3,775). List *mutual funds* as you did for stock. For *real estate*, enter total market value of property under "Quote" column and amount actually invested (down payment and closing costs) under "$ Amount." Ignore the "Quote" column for *savings* vehicles. For "Amount of Income" column, list *total* amount received from dividends, interest, and so on (for example, dividends per share × number of shares held). Under "Latest Market Value," enter market price as of the date of this report (for instance, in December 1988, Emory Air Freight was trading at 4½). The latest market value for *real estate* is entered as an *estimate* of what the property would likely sell for (under "Quote") and the *estimated* amount of equity the investor has in the property (under "$ Amount").

drops. This can be done by short selling *borrowed* securities and then repurchasing them after they have dropped in price.

▪ Becoming an informed investor is essential to developing a sound investment program. Vital information about specific companies and industries, the securities markets, the economy, and different investment vehicles and strategies can be obtained from sources such as annual stockholders' reports, brokerage and advisory service reports, and the financial press. In addition, the personal computer is rapidly becoming a popular source of investment information.

▪ Information about daily market performance can be obtained from various averages and indexes, such as the Dow Jones Industrial Average, the Standard & Poor's Indexes, and the NYSE, AMEX, and OTC (or NASDAQ) Indexes. These averages

and indexes not only measure performance in the overall market, they also provide standards of performance for specific types of stocks such as transportation issues, banks, insurance companies, and public utilities.

▪ Developing a well-diversified portfolio of investment holdings enables an investor not only to achieve given investment objectives, but also to enjoy reduced exposure to risk and a more predictable level of return. A vital ingredient to developing such a portfolio is that full consideration be given to the investor's level and stability of income, family factors, financial condition, experience and age, and disposition toward risk; designing an asset allocation scheme that's based on these personal needs and objectives is also an important part of portfolio management.

QUESTIONS AND PROBLEMS

1. Explain what is meant by the securities markets. Briefly describe the various markets. How does a primary market differ from a secondary market? What is the difference between the money market and the capital market? Give some examples of the types of securities found in the money market; in the capital market.

2. What are organized securities exchanges? What is the difference between the New York Stock Exchange and the American Stock Exchange? What are regional exchanges, and what role do they play?

3. Describe the operations of the over-the-counter market; compare and contrast it with organized securities exchanges.

4. Explain the difference between a bull market and a bear market. How would you characterize the current state of the stock market; are we in a bull market or a bear market?

5. What is a stockbroker? Why does the selection of a broker play such an important role in the purchase of securities?

6. "Stockbrokers not only execute buy and sell orders for their clients but they also offer a variety of additional services." Explain what some of these services are.

7. Barbara Moses has just purchased two different stocks: Her first transaction was 100 shares of Xerox Corporation at $49.50 per share, and the second was 60 shares of Prime Computers at $15 per share. For each transaction, calculate the amount of brokerage commissions Barbara will have to pay, and express them as a percentage of the total purchase cost of each stock. Use the brokerage fee schedule in Exhibit 13.5.

8. Describe the role that discount brokers play in carrying out security transactions. To whom are their services especially appealing? Explain.

9. Name and describe three basic types of orders. Assume Cecile Higgins places an order to buy 100 shares of Kodak; explain how the order will be processed if it is a market order. Would it have made any difference if it had been a limit order? Explain.

10. What are margin requirements? Helen Emerson wants to buy 300 shares of PepsiCo, which is currently selling in the market for $45 a share. Rather than liquidate all her savings, she decides to borrow through her broker. Assume the margin requirement on common stock is currently 50 percent and the

brokerage firm charges 12 percent interest on margin loans. What would be the interest cost on the transaction if Helen sold the stocks at the end of one year? If the stock rises to $60 a share by the end of the year, show the kind of profit (in dollars) and return (in percentages) that Helen would earn if she makes the investment with 50 percent margin; contrast this to what she would make if she uses no margin.

11. Which of the following would offer the best return on investment? Assume you buy $5,000 in stock in all three cases; also, *ignore* interest costs in all your calculations.
    a. Buy a stock at $80 without margin, and sell it at $120 one year later.
    b. Buy a stock at $32 with 50 percent margin, and sell it one year later at $41.
    c. Buy a stock at $50 with 75 percent margin, and sell it in one year at $65.

12. What is a short sale? Explain the logic behind it. How much profit (if any) would Don Summers make if he short sold 300 shares of stock at $75 a share and the price of the stock suddenly tumbled to $60?

13. Briefly describe the SIPC, and note the kind of protection it provides to investors. Is SIPC protection of any help if you should fall victim to bad advice? Explain. What can you do if you lose money as a result of bad advice from a broker?

14. Identify and briefly discuss the four basic types of information that you, as an investor, should try to stay abreast of. Describe some of the major sources of investment information; briefly note how you can use your PC as a source of investor information.

15. What role do market averages and indexes play in the investment process? Using something like *The Wall Street Journal* or *Barron's,* find the latest values for each of the following market averages and indexes, and indicate how each has performed over the past six months:
    a. DJIA
    b. Dow Jones Utilities
    c. S&P 500
    d. NYSE Composite index
    e. AMEX index
    f. NASDAQ Composite OTC index

16. Using the stock quotations in Exhibit 13.8, find the 52-week high and low for Dow Chemical. How much does the stock pay annually in dividends, and what is its latest dividend yield? How many shares of Dow Chemical changed hands (were traded), what was the closing price, and at what P/E ratio was the stock trading? According to the information in Exhibit 13.8, which of the Duke Power preferred stocks has the best dividend yield?

17. Using the bond quotes in Exhibit 13.9, how much would you have to pay for the following bonds? (Assume all the bonds have $1,000 par values.)
    a. A 7 percent AT&T bond that matures in 2001.
    b. An 8¾ percent AT&T bond that matures in 2000.
    c. A zero coupon Allied Chemical bond that matures in 2001.
    How much annual interest income will you receive from each of these bonds, and which bond offers the highest current yield? Which has the lowest current yield?

18. Explain why it might be preferable for a person to invest in a portfolio of securities rather than in a single security. Be sure to mention risk and return in your response.

19. Briefly describe the concept of asset allocation and note how it works. Give an example of an asset allocation scheme. Discuss the role that asset allocation plays in the management of a portfolio.

20. What, if anything, is there to be gained from keeping track of your investment holdings?

21. Using the S&P report in Exhibit 13.10, find the following information as it pertains to Wendy's:
    a. Amount of revenues (that is, sales) the company generated in 1987.
    b. Latest annual dividends per share and dividend yield.
    c. Earnings (profit) projections for 1989.
    d. Number of common shares outstanding.

e. Book value per share and earnings per share in 1987.

f. Where the stock is traded.

g. Amount of long-term debt the company has.

h. Given its beta, to approximately what price would this stock jump if the market went up by 15 percent over the next 12 months? (Assume the stock is currently priced at 8½.)

CASE PROBLEMS

13.1 The Gordons' Problem: What to Do with All That Money?

A couple in their early thirties, Allen and Sandra Gordon recently inherited $90,000 from one of their relatives. Allen earns a comfortable income as a sales manager for Smith and Johnson, Inc., and Sandra does equally well as an attorney with a major law firm. Since they have no children and do not need the money, they have decided to invest all of their inheritance in stocks, bonds, and perhaps even some money market instruments. However, they are not very familiar with the market, nor do they know how to go about selecting a broker. As a result, they turn to you for help.

Questions

1. In what markets and on what exchanges do you think most of the Gordons' transactions should take place?

2. What characteristics should the Gordons look for in a stockbroker? Take into consideration brokerage services and brokerage fees.

3. Construct an investment portfolio that you feel would be right for the Gordons; invest the full $90,000. Put *actual* stocks, bonds, preferreds, and/or convertible securities in the portfolio; also, if you like, you may put up to *one-third* of the money into short-term securities like CDs, Treasury bills, money funds, or MMDAs. Select any securities you want, so long as you feel they would be suitable for the Gordons. (Hint: you might want to refer back to Chapters 5 and 12 for some ideas.) Make sure the portfolio consists of *six or more different securities;* use the latest issue of *The Wall Street Journal* to determine the market prices of the securities you select. Show the amount invested in each security, along with the amount of current in-come (from dividends and/or interest) that will be generated from the investments. Briefly explain why you selected the particular securities for the Gordons' portfolio.

13.2 Steve Takes Stock of His Securities

Steve Harrington is 32 years old, single, and works as a research chemist for a major pharmaceutical firm. He is well paid and over time has built up a sizable portfolio of investments. He considers himself an aggressive investor and, because he has no dependents to worry about, likes to invest in high-risk–high-return securities. His records show the following:

1. In 1987 he bought 100 shares of *Delta Air Lines* a NYSE stock) at $50 a share; the stock paid a dividend of $1.10 in 1987.

2. In 1986 he bought 250 shares of *WD-40 Co.* (an OTC stock quoted on the NASDAQ National Market System) at $28 a share; at the time, the stock was paying annual dividends of $1.04 a share.

3. In 1987, Steve bought 400 shares of *Tonka* toys at $22½ (Tonka is on the NYSE); in 1987 the stock paid annual dividends of 6 cents a share.

4. In early 1988 he bought 200 shares of *Phelps Dodge* (an NYSE stock) at $48 a share; the stock was expected to pay a dividend of 60 cents a share in 1988.

5. Also in early 1988, Steve bought 300 shares of *Intel* (another OTC-NASDAQ) stock quoted on the National Market System) at $29 a share; as of early 1988 this stock had never paid a dividend.

6. He has $8,000 in an 8 percent money market mutual fund.

Every three months or so, Steve prepares a complete, up-to-date inventory of his investment holdings.

Questions

1. Use a form like the one in Exhibit 13.12 to prepare a complete inventory of Steve's investment holdings (Note: Look in the latest issue of *The Wall Street Journal* to find the most recent market value of the five *stocks* in Steve's portfolio.)

2. What is your overall assessment of Steve's investment portfolio? Does it appear that his personal net worth is improving as a result of his investments?

3. Based on the worksheet you prepared in Question 1, do you see any securities that you think Steve should consider selling?

FOR MORE INFORMATION

General Information Articles

Egan, Jack, "Somewhere, Over the Counter," *U.S. News & World Report,* February 29, 1988, p. 72.

Fromson, Brett Duval, "A Low-Risk Path to Profits," *Fortune/1989 Investor's Guide,* pp. 14–22.

Hager, Bruce, "Where to Get Great Investment Advice for Free," *Money,* September 1987, pp. 131–138.

Hedberg, Augustin, "Diversification: The Proven Way to Cut Risk and Protect Profits," *Money,* September 1988, pp. 62–72.

Morgenson, Gretchen, "The Perils of Margin Investing," *Money,* February 1986, pp. 141–146.

Schiffres, Manuel, "When Your Broker Fouls Up," *Changing Times,* January 1988, pp. 65–68.

Wiener, Daniel P., "How to Pick a Broker," *U.S. News & World Report,* June 6, 1988, pp. 68–75.

Government Documents & Other Publications

How SIPC Protects You. Securities Investors Protection Corp.; 805 Fifteenth St., N.W.—Suite 800; Washington, D.C. 20005.

How to Proceed with the Arbitration of a Small Claim. U.S. Securities & Exchange Commission; Publications Dept.; 450 - 5th Street, N.W.; Washington, D.C. 20549.

How to Read a Financial Report. Merrill Lynch, Pierce, Fenner & Smith, Inc.; 111 - 19th Street, N.W.; Washington, D.C. 20036.

CHAPTER 14

Buying Mutual Funds, Real Estate, and Other Investments

Sound investment planning involves finding investment vehicles that have risk-return characteristics which are consistent with your established financial objectives. In order to fully appreciate your available investment opportunities, you must complement your understanding of the basics of stocks and bonds with a knowledge of the functions and characteristics of other investment vehicles, including mutual funds, real estate, commodities, financial futures, and options. Each of these investment outlets offers risk-return opportunities that you may not be able to obtain from stocks and bonds. The investor who is interested in receiving the benefits of professional portfolio management but does not have funds sufficient to purchase a diversified portfolio of securities may find mutual fund shares attractive. Sometimes real estate is purchased as an investment; although there may be some similarities between housing and investment purchases of real estate, persons interested in real estate investments must justify them not on the basis of need but on strict economic grounds. Still other investors who are willing to take higher risks in expectation of higher return may find commodities, financial futures, or options attractive.

Financial Facts or Fantasies

Are the following statements financial facts (true) or fantasies (false)?

- When a mutual fund is open-ended, it means there's no limit to how high the price of its stock can go.
- Phone switching is a service that enables you to move your money from one fund to another, so long as you stay within the same family of funds.
- In many types of real estate investments, appreciation in the value of the property has more of an impact on return than annual rental income.
- A REIT (real estate investment trust) is a popular form of limited partnership that enables individuals to directly invest in income-producing property.
- Commodities trading is popular with individual investors because it is so affordable, and with all the safeguards, it's relatively hard to lose a lot of money.
- The two basic types of options are puts and calls. Puts give you the right to sell something, and calls give you the right to buy.

INVESTING IN MUTUAL FUNDS ▪

> Mutual funds are a very popular form of investing—they offer an attractive level of return from a professionally managed, widely diversified portfolio of securities, as well as a variety of investor services. Today there are more than 2,700 different mutual funds available—enough to meet just about any investment need you can think of. Stop for a moment to think about the different types of mutual funds that are available to investors. What kind of fund (or funds) would you be most interested in? What types of investor services would you look for in a mutual fund?

Mutual funds are popular because they offer not only a variety of interesting investment opportunities, but also a wide array of services that many investors find appealing. They are an easy and convenient way to invest, and are especially suited to beginning investors and those with limited funds. A mutual fund is basically a financial services organization that receives money from its shareholders and then invests those funds for them in a diversified portfolio of securities. As such, an investment in a mutual fund represents an ownership position in a professionally managed *portfolio of securities;* when you buy shares in a mutual fund you become a part-owner of that portfolio. This concept underlies the whole mutual fund structure and is depicted in Exhibit 14.1.

The Mutual Fund Concept

The first mutual fund in this country was started in Boston in 1924; by 1940, there were 68 funds with $488 million in assets and nearly 300,000 shareholder accounts. That was only the beginning, however, as the growth in funds really took off in the late 1970s. Indeed, by 1989, assets under management had grown to over three-quarters of a trillion dollars, as 50 million investors held shares in over 2,700 publicly traded mutual funds. The fact is, we've reached the point where there are more mutual funds today than there are stocks on the NYSE!

Mutual fund investors come from all walks of life and all income levels. And they share one common view: they've decided, for one reason or another, to turn the problems of security selection and portfolio management over to professional money managers. In essence, a mutual fund is a company that combines the investment funds of many people with similar investment goals and invests them for these people in a wide variety of securities. The individual investor receives shares of stock in the mutual fund and thus is able to enjoy much wider investment diversity than could otherwise be achieved. As the securities held by the fund move up and down in price, the market value of the mutual fund shares moves accordingly. When dividend and interest payments are received by the fund, they are passed on to the mutual fund shareholders and distributed on the basis of prorated ownership. When a security held by the fund is sold for a profit, this too is passed on to fund shareholders. The whole mutual fund idea rests on the concept of pooled diversification and works in much the same way as insurance: individuals pooling their resources for the collective benefit of all contributors.

Open-End versus Closed-End

Questions of which stock or bond to select, when to buy, and when to sell have plagued investors for about as long as there have been organized securities markets. Such concerns lie at the very heart of the mutual fund concept and, in large part, are behind the growth in funds. A lot of people lack the time, the know-how, or the commitment to manage their own securities. As a result, they turn to others. And more often than not, that means mutual funds. But as many investors quickly learn, not all mutual funds are alike. Not only do they offer different types of services, they also differ in structure. Essentially, funds can be organized either as *open-end companies,* which can sell an unlimited number of ownership shares, or as *closed-end companies,* which can issue only a limited number.

Open-End Investment Companies. The term *mutual fund* is commonly used to denote an open-end investment company. Such organizations are the dominant type of investment company and account for over 90 percent of assets under manage-

EXHIBIT 14.1

The Basic Mutual Fund Structure

A mutual fund brings together the funds from numerous investors and uses this pool to acquire a diversified portfolio of stocks, bonds, and other securities.

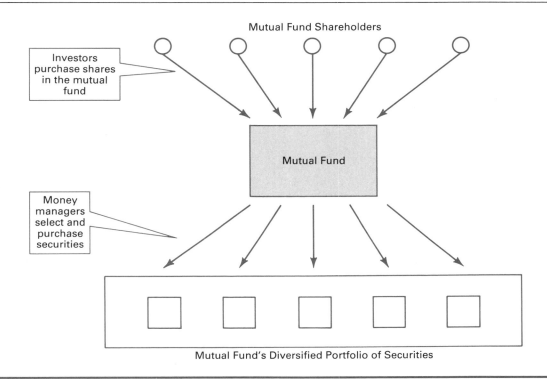

Mutual Fund Shareholders

Investors purchase shares in the mutual fund

Mutual Fund

Money managers select and purchase securities

Mutual Fund's Diversified Portfolio of Securities

---

ment. In an **open-end investment company**, investors actually buy their shares from, and sell them back to, the mutual fund itself. When they buy shares in the fund, the fund issues new shares of stock and fills the purchase order with them. There is no limit on the number of shares the fund can issue; the only restraint in the actual number issued is investor demand. Further, all open-end mutual funds stand behind their shares and buy them back when investors decide to sell, Thus, there is never any trading among individuals.

When a mutual fund is open-ended, it means there is no limit to how high the price of its stock can go. **Fantasy:** In an open-end mutual fund there is no limit to the *number* of shares the fund can issue, but the price of the shares depends on how well the fund invests its money.

Both buy and sell transactions in a mutual fund are carried out at prices based on the current value of all the securities held in the fund's portfolio. This is known as the fund's **net asset value (NAV)**; it represents the value of a share of stock in a particular mutual fund. NAV is found by taking the total

open-end investment company
A company that can issue an unlimited number of shares which it buys and sells at a price based on the current value of the securities it owns; also called a *mutual fund.*

net asset value (NAV)
The price at which a mutual fund will buy back its own shares; NAV represents the current market value of all the securities the fund owns.

market value of all securities held by the fund, subtracting any liabilities, and dividing the result by the number of shares outstanding. For example, if on a given day the market value of all the securities held by the XYZ mutual fund equaled some $10 million, and if XYZ on that day had 500,000 shares outstanding, the fund's net asset value per share would amount to $20 ($10,000,000/500,000 = $20).

This figure would then be used to derive the price at which the fund shares could be bought and sold.

The NAV is included in the mutual fund price quotation system and indicates the price at which an investor can *sell* shares. Consider, for example, *The Wall Street Journal* mutual fund quotations as shown below:

	NAV	Offer Price	NAV Chg.
Fidelity Selects:			
SIAir r	10.16	10.37	+.04
SIAGI r	15.34	15.65	−.04
SIAut r	12.05	12.30	+.05
SIBio r	10.55	10.77	+.06
SIBrd r	14.16	14.45	+.10
SIBrk r	8.07	8.23	+.07
SICap r	10.33	10.54	+.10
SIChe r	22.85	23.32	+.12
SICmp r	10.90	11.12	+.11
SIDef r	11.57	11.81	+.02
SIElec r	6.84	6.98	+.07
SIEng r	13.20	13.47	+.03
SIEnS r	7.94	8.10	−.01
SIFnS r	27.36	27.92	+.12
FiduCap	15.30	NL	+.08
Financial Prog:			
Dynam	6.70	NL	−.01
FSB Gv	6.97	NL	−.01
FSP Eg	9.81	NL	−.05
FSP Eu	9.36	NL	+.03
FSP Fn	7.67	NL	+.03
FSP U	8.63	NL	+.01
FinTx	14.64	NL	. . .
Gold	5.29	NL	−.01
HISci	14.91	NL	+.01
HiYld	7.93	NL	. . .
Indust	3.68	NL	+.02
Incom	8.17	NL	+.02
Leisr	12.50	NL	+.04
Pacif	13.47	NL	−.02
Select	6.45	NL	. . .
Tech	10.58	NL	+.04
FstEag r	11.77	11.77	+.01
Flex Funds:			
Bond p	18.24	18.24	
Grth p	9.79	NL	+.01
IncGr p	18.78	NL	+.02
Muirf p	5.15	NL	. . .
RetGr p	9.84	NL	. . .
Fortress Invst:			
GISI r	9.15	9.24	−.02
HiQal t	12.48	12.61	+.02
HY Mu t	10.10	10.20	+.01
TP US r	9.95	10.05	−.04
44 WlEq	4.51	4.56	+.04
44Wall r	2.47	2.47	+.02
Founders Group:			
BlueC p	6.52	NL	+.02
Frntr p	14.14	NL	+.15
Gwth p	7.87	NL	+.04
Inco p	7.06	NL	. . .

Fidelity Select—Computers → SICmp r ←— A load fund with a redemption fee (r)

Financial Prog. High Yield Fund → HiYld ←— A true no-load fund

Flex Fund–Growth → Grth p ←— A no-load fund that charges a 12(b)-1 fee (p)

Fortress Investment's High-Quality Fund → HiQal t ←— A fund with a little of everything: a front load, back load, and 12(b)-1 fee (t)

Source: *The Wall Street Journal,* January 26, 1989.

The first price column is labeled "NAV." For example, Fidelity Select–Computers has an NAV of $10.90 and an offer price of $11.12; that means the investor can *buy* shares in the fund at an offer price of $11.12 a share or *sell* them at the NAV price of $10.90. The "NAV Chg." column shows the change in the price of the fund; in the case of Fidelity Select–Computers, the NAV went up 11 cents from the day before.

Closed-End Investment Companies. While the term *mutual fund* is supposed to be used only with open-end funds, it is, as a practical matter, regularly used with closed-end investment companies as well. Basically, **closed-end investment companies** operate with a fixed number of shares outstanding and do not regularly issue new ones. In effect, they have a capital structure like any corporation, except that the corporation's business happens to be that of investing in marketable securities. Closed-end company shares are actively traded in the secondary market, just like any other common stock. Most are traded on the New York Stock Exchange, several are on the American Exchange, and a few are traded in the OTC market. Some of the largest closed-end investment companies include Adams Express, ASA Ltd., General American Investors, Korea Fund, and Niagara Share Corporation, all of which are actively traded on the NYSE.

The share prices of closed-end companies are determined not only by their net asset values but also by general supply and demand conditions in the stock market. As a result, closed-end companies generally trade at a discount or premium to NAV. For example, a fund with a net asset value of $10 per share would be selling at a *discount* of $1 if it were trading at $9 and at a *premium* of $1 if it were quoted at a price of $11. Share price discounts can become quite large at times—for example, it is not unusual for discounts to amount to as much as 25 to 30 percent of net asset value. In contrast, price premiums occur less often and seldom exceed 10 to 15 percent.

Some Important Cost Considerations

When you buy or sell shares in a closed-end investment company, you pay a commission just as you would with any other listed or OTC common stock transaction. This is not so with open-end funds, however. In particular, the cost of investing in an open-end mutual fund depends on the types of fees and load charges that a fund levies on its investors.

Load Funds. Most open-end mutual funds are so-called **load funds**, since they charge a commission when the shares are purchased. Load charges can be fairly substantial, often ranging from 7 to 8½ percent of the *purchase* price of the shares. Normally there is no charge when you sell your shares. It is easy to find the amount of the load charge: It is part of the price quotation system and is found by taking the difference between the fund's offer price and its NAV. For example, refer back to the quote for the Fidelity Select–Computer fund. The difference between its offer price ($11.12) and NAV ($10.90) represents its load charge of 22 cents a share and is the commission you would pay for each share of Fidelity Select–Computers you bought.

Compared to what it costs to buy and sell common stock, the costs of many load funds are pretty steep, even after taking into account the fact that you normally pay no commission on the sale of most funds! Since 1975, the *maximum* load charge has been set at 8½ percent of the purchase price. However, most mutual funds offer quantity discounts to investors who buy in large blocks (usually 1,000 or more shares). In addition a growing number of so-called **low-load funds** like Fidelity Se-

---

closed-end investment company

An investment company that issues a fixed number of shares, which are themselves listed and traded on an organized securities exchange or in the OTC market.

load fund

A mutual fund on which a transaction cost (associated with the purchase of shares) is levied.

low-load fund

A mutual fund in which commissions charged on purchases of shares range between only 1 and 3 percent of the purchase price.

lect–Computers charge commissions of only 1 to 3 percent; on the other hand, there's also an increasing number of **back-end load funds**, which charge a commission—or a so-called *redemption fee*—when you *sell* your shares.

No-Load Funds. Some open-end investment companies charge no commission when you buy their funds; these are known as **no-load funds**. It is easy to spot no-loads: Just look for the letters "N.L." under the "Offer Price" column in mutual fund price quotes. For example, the Financial Program funds shown in our illustrative quotes (above) are no-load funds. This means that the Financial Program High-Yield Fund, for example, can be bought and sold at its NAV price of $7.93 a share. Actually, there are relatively few pure no-loads left today, charging nothing to buy, sell, or hold their funds! For example, there's nothing to prevent a so-called no-load fund from charging a back-end load when you sell your fund shares; and there are a lot of no-loads that charge something called a 12(b)-1 fee for as long as you hold your shares.

12(b)-1 Fees. Also known as *hidden loads,* **12(b)-1 fees** have been allowed by the SEC since 1980, and were originally designed to help no-load funds cover their distribution and marketing expenses. Not surprisingly, their popularity spread rapidly among fund distributors, so that they are now used by around 40 percent of all open-end mutual funds. The fees are assessed annually and can amount to as much as 1¼ percent of assets under management. In good markets and bad, they're paid, right off the top. And that can take its toll. Consider, for instance, $10,000 in a fund that charges a 1¼ percent 12(b)-1 fee. That translates into an annual charge of $125, which means $125 a year *less* for you!

Management Fees. The **management fee** is the cost you incur to hire the professional money managers to run the fund's portfolio of investments. These fees are also assessed annually and usually run from about ½ percent to 2 percent of assets under management. All funds—whether they're load or no-load, open- or closed-end—have these fees; and like 12(b)-1 fees, they bear watching, since high management fees will take their toll on performance. As a rule, the size of the manage-ment fee is totally unrelated to the performance of the fund—you'll pay the same amount whether it's been a winning year or a real loser.

Keeping Track of Fund Fees and Loads. Critics of the mutual fund industry have come down hard on the proliferation of fund fees and charges. Indeed, some would argue that all the different kinds of charges and fees are really meant to do one thing: confuse the investor. The fact is, a lot of funds were going to great lengths to make themselves look like something they weren't—they lower a cost here, but tack on a fee there and hide a charge somewhere else. These funds all follow the letter of the law in that they do indeed fully disclose all their expenses and fees. Trouble was, the funds were able to neatly hide all but the most conspicuous of their charges in a bunch of legalese. Fortunately, all this is beginning to change as steps are being taken to bring fund fees and loads out into the open.

For one thing, these charges are more fully reported by the financial press. You don't have to look any farther than the mutual fund quotations found in *The Wall Street Journal* and most other major papers. For example, refer back to the quotations on page 496; notice the use of the letters "r," "p," and "t." If you see an "r" behind a fund's name, it means the fund charges some type of *redemption fee* when you sell your shares (this is the case, for example, with Fidelity Select–Computers); use of a "p," in contrast, means the fund levies a *12(b)-1 charge* (which you'll have to pay if you invest in Flex Fund–Growth); finally, a "t" will appear with funds that charge both redemption fees and 12(b)-1 fees (notice that's what you get with Fortress Investment's High-Quality Fund). If you look closely at the quotation, you'll see that Fortress High-Quality not only levies redemption and 12(b)-1 fees, *it also has a front-end load*—as indicated by the difference in its NAV and offer price. The point is: Don't be surprised to find *load* funds that also charge redemption and/or 12(b)-1 fees, and the same goes for no-load funds. The quotations, of course, only tell you what kinds of fees are charged by the funds; they don't tell you how much is charged. To get the specifics on the amount charged, you'll have to turn to the fund itself.

All (open-end) mutual funds are required by the SEC to fully disclose all their expenses in a stan-

EXHIBIT 14.2

Mutual Fund Expense Disclosure Table

Mutual funds are now required by the SEC to make full disclosure of load charges, redemption fees, and annual expenses in a three-part table like the one shown here; and the table must be conspicuously placed in the front part of the prospectus, not hidden somewhere in the back.

Expenses and Cost of Investing in the Fund

The following information is provided in order to assist investors in understanding the transaction costs and annual expenses associated with investing in the Fund.

A. Shareholder Transaction Costs:

Sales Load on Purchases	2%
Sales Load on Reinvested Dividends	None
Redemption Fees or Deferred Sales Charges.	None
Exchange (or Conversion) Fees	None

B. Annual Fund Operating Expenses:
(as a percentage of average net assets)

Management Fees	0.40%
12(b)-1 Fees	None
Other Expenses (estimated).	0.32%

C. Example of Fund Expenses Over Time:

You would pay the following total expenses over time on a $1,000 investment, assuming a 5% annual return, and a complete redemption of the investment at the end of each indicated time period:

1-year	3-years	5-years	10-years
$27	$43	$59	$108

Source: The prospectus of a major mutual fund.

dardized, easy-to-understand format. Every fund prospectus must contain, right up front, a fairly detailed *fee table;* much like the one illustrated in Exhibit 14.2. Notice that this table has three parts. The first section specifies all *shareholder transaction expenses.* In effect, this tells you what it's going to cost to buy and sell shares in the mutual fund. The next section lists all the *annual operating expenses* of the fund. Showing these expenses as a percentage of average net assets, the fund must break out management fees, those elusive 12(b)-1 fees, and any other expenses. The third section provides a complete rundown of the *total cost over time* of buying, selling, and owning the fund. This part of the table contains both transaction and operating expenses, and it shows what the total costs would be over hypothetical 1-, 3-, 5-, and 10-year holding periods. To assure consistency and comparability, the funds have to follow a rigid set of guidelines when constructing the illustrative costs.

It's obviously in your best interest to pay close attention to the fee table whenever you're consid-ering an investment in a mutual fund. Other things being equal, look for low initial charges as well as low expense ratios over time. As a rule, the longer you intend to hold a fund, the more willing you

---

back-end load fund

A commission charged for redeeming mutual fund shares.

no-load fund

A mutual fund on which no transaction fees are charged.

12(b)-1 fee

A type of fee that's charged annually and which is supposed to be used to offset the promotion and selling expenses of a mutual fund; known as a *hidden load* because it's often used by funds as an indirect way of charging commissions.

management fee

A fee paid to the professionals who administer a mutual fund's portfolio.

should be to trade a higher load charge for lower annual management and 12(b)-1 fees. That will help keep your total holding period costs down. In the final analysis, keep in mind that costs are only one element in the decision. Another very important variable is *performance.* There may be times when higher costs are justified; there may be other times when they're not. Following are two guidelines you might want to follow:

- Consider a *more expensive* fund if it has a better performance record (and offers more return potential) than a less expensive fund—it's all a matter of whether you'd rather own a costly performer or a low-cost dog!
- If there's little or no difference in performance records or return potential, go with the *less expensive* fund. In this case, lower expenses will make a difference in comparative returns.

Buying and Selling Funds

Buying and selling shares of *closed-end investment companies* is no different from buying shares of common stock. The transactions are executed on listed exchanges or in the OTC market through brokers or dealers who handle the orders in the usual way. They are subject to the normal transaction costs; and because they are treated like any other listed or OTC stock, their shares can even be margined or sold short. The situation is considerably different, however, with *open-end funds.* There are several ways of acquiring such shares, depending on whether the fund is load or no-load. However, the fund, regardless of type, should provide you with a recent prospectus that explains its operations and other pertinent financial matters. The prospectuses received from many mutual funds today are not as extensive as they used to be, so you should be careful when using such information for investment purposes. Even so, as the accompanying *Money in Action* box suggests, these prospectuses should be required reading for anybody who's thinking about investing in a mutual fund.

In the case of load funds, investors buy the stocks from a broker or through salespeople employed by the funds—not surprisingly, these funds usually carry the full 8½ percent load charge, or something very close to it. Most brokerage firms are authorized to sell shares in a variety of load funds, and

this is the easiest and most convenient way of buying funds for investors who have established brokerage accounts. Sometimes, however, the fund may not be sold through brokerage houses, in which case the investor would deal directly with its commissioned salespeople—individuals who are employed by the mutual fund for the sole purpose of selling its shares. If you happen to be interested in a no-load, or perhaps even a low-load fund, you're pretty much on your own. You'll have to write or call the mutual fund directly in order to obtain information. You will then receive an order form and instructions on how to buy shares; no salesperson will ever call on you. To complete the transaction, you simply mail your check, along with the completed order form, to the mutual fund or its designated agent.

Selling shares in a fund is also a do-it-yourself affair, whether the fund is load or no-load. Because brokers and salespeople usually don't make anything on fund *sales,* they have little motivation to execute sell orders. As a result, you may find you'll have to redeem your fund shares by directly notifying the mutual fund (by mail) of your intention to sell. The fund then buys the shares back and mails you a check. But before you go through all this, check to see if the fund offers *phone switching.* This service is available from most investment companies, and it enables you to simply pick up the phone to move money from one fund to another—the only constraint is that the funds must be managed by the same investment company. Most companies charge little or nothing for these shifts, although funds that offer free exchange privileges often place a limit on the number of times you can switch each year. (We'll discuss this service in more detail later in the chapter when we cover *conversion privileges.*)

Types of Funds

Some mutual funds specialize in stocks and others in bonds; some funds have maximum capital gains as their investment objective, and some seek high income. Some funds thus will appeal to speculators and others primarily to income-oriented investors. Every fund has a particular investment objective, some of the more common ones being capital appreciation, income, tax-exempt income, preservation of investment capital, or a combination thereof. Disclosure of a fund's investment objective is required by the SEC, and each fund is expected to do its best to conform to its stated investment policy and objective. Categorizing funds according to their investment policies and objectives is widely practiced in the mutual fund industry, as it tends to reflect similarities not only in how the funds manage their money, but also in their risk and return characteristics. Some of the more popular types of mutual funds include growth, maximum capital gains, equity-income, balanced, growth-and-income, bond, money market, and sector funds. Exhibit 14.3 (on pages 504–505) lists some top-performing funds from each of these eight categories.

Growth Funds. The objective of a *growth fund* is simple: capital appreciation. Long-term growth and capital gains are the primary goals of such funds, and as a result they invest principally in common stocks that have above-average growth potential. Because of the uncertain nature of their investment income, growth funds are believed to involve a fair amount of risk exposure. They are usually viewed as long-term investment vehicles that are most suitable for the more aggressive investor who wants to build capital and has little interest in current income.

Maximum Capital Gains Funds. These are so-called *performance* (or *go-go) funds* that tend to increase in popularity when the markets heat up. They are highly speculative funds that seek large profits from capital gains; in many respects, they are really an extension of the growth fund concept. Many are fairly small with portfolios consisting mainly of high-flying common stocks. Performance funds often buy stocks of small, unseasoned companies, stocks with relatively high price/earnings multiples, and stocks whose prices are highly volatile. Some maximum capital gains funds go so far as to use leverage in their portfolios (that is, they buy stocks on margin by borrowing part of the purchase price). All this is designed, of course, to yield big returns. However, maximum capital gains funds are also highly speculative and are perhaps the most volatile of all the fund types. When the markets are good, these funds do well; when the markets are bad, they typically experience substantial losses.

Equity-Income Funds. *Equity-income funds* emphasize current income, which they provide by investing primarily in high-yielding common stocks. Capital preservation is also a goal of these funds, and so is some amount of capital gains, although capital appreciation is not their primary objective. They invest heavily in high-grade common stocks, some convertible securities and preferred stocks, and occasionally even some investment-quality bonds. They like securities that generate hefty dividend yields, but also consider potential price appreciation over the longer haul. In general, because of their emphasis on dividends and current income, these funds tend to hold higher-quality securities that are subject to less price volatility than the market as a whole. They're generally viewed as a fairly low-risk way of investing in stocks.

Balanced Funds. *Balanced funds* are so named because they tend to hold a balanced portfolio of both stocks and bonds, and they do so for the purpose of generating a well-balanced return of both current income and long-term capital gains. In many respects, they're a lot like equity-income funds, except that balanced funds usually put much more into fixed-income securities; generally they keep at least 25 percent to 50 percent of their portfolios in bonds, and sometimes more. The bonds are used principally to provide current income, and stocks are selected mainly for their long-term growth potential. The funds can, of course, shift the emphasis in their security holdings one way or the other. Clearly, the more the fund leans toward fixed-income securities, the more income-oriented it will be. For the most part, balanced funds tend to confine their investing to high-grade securities. As such, they're usually considered to be a relatively safe form of investing, one where you can earn a competitive rate of return without having to endure a lot of price volatility.

Growth-and-Income Funds. Like balanced funds, *growth-and-income funds* also seek a balanced return made up of both current income and long-term capital gains, but they place a greater emphasis on growth of capital. Moreover, unlike balanced funds, growth and income funds put most of their money into equities—indeed, it's not unusual for these funds to have 80 percent to 90 per-

MONEY IN ACTION

"What to Look for in a Mutual Fund Prospectus"

The Securities and Exchange Commission requires that a mutual fund's prospectus be in your hands before the fund can accept your investment. That might seem like a cruel joke, because the typical prospectus is about as readable as the Rosetta Stone. Yet if you don't plow through this document, you lay yourself open to nasty surprises later.

Investors often complain that a lot of funds go to great lengths to camouflage important information in the prospectus. Usually it's because prospectuses are written by lawyers, whose prose can be opaque. Fortunately, more sponsors are seeing benefits in sharper writing. T. Rowe Price has shifted its prospectus-writing largely to marketing people and has

attorneys review the legal points. More good news: Funds must now include a table of all fees near the front of the prospectus, followed by a hypothetical total of all fees over several years, assuming the fund earns a 5% return. This feature should end disjointed disclosure of costs.

To help you get the most out of a mutual fund prospectus, here's a guided tour through this document:

Investment objective.

Certain words and phrases appear regularly. Bond funds all seem to aim for "highest level of current income" that's "consistent with preservation of capital." Stock funds tell their top and secondary priorities: capital

growth, dividend income, a combination of the two and, possibly, a narrow strategy, such as hunting for "special situations" or "undervalued stocks." Strategies may or may not be well-defined. If they are, the prospectus is telling you about the riskiness of the fund. For example, Fidelity Special Situations explains, "We expect to be fully invested in stocks under most market conditions." So don't cry that its manager should have been in Treasury bills if stocks crash again. The Franklin Short-Intermediate U.S. Government Securities Fund says it will maintain an average portfolio maturity of two to five years. That tells you that Franklin's investments will be subject to less price volatility than an "intermediate" fund empow-

cent of their capital in common stocks. They tend to confine most of their investing to high-quality issues, so you can expect to find a lot of growth-oriented blue-chip stocks in their portfolios, along with a fair amount of high-quality income stocks. One of the big appeals of these funds is the fairly substantial returns many of them have been able to generate over the long haul. But then, these funds do involve a fair amount of risk, if for no other reason than the emphasis they place on stocks and capital gains. Consequently, growth-and-income funds are most suitable for those investors who can tolerate their risk and price volatility.

Bond Funds. As their name implies, *bond funds* invest exclusively in various kinds and grades of bonds. Income is their primary investment objective, although they do not ignore capital gains. There are two important advantages to buying shares in bond funds rather than investing directly in bonds: First, bond funds generally are more liquid; second, they offer diversification. They are usually considered to be fairly conservative investment vehicles, but they are not totally without risk, since the prices of bonds held in their portfolios will fluctuate with changing interest rates. Though many of the funds are basically conservative, a growing number are becoming increasingly aggressive—in

ered to stretch to perhaps 12 years' maturity.

Past performance.

Established funds include five years of results—if they are that old—in a table of *per-share income and capital changes.* These condensed financial statements reveal such facts as the ratio of expenses to average net assets (over 1% is high, unless it's an international or sector fund) and the portfolio turnover rate (100% means the manager trades every stock in the portfolio every year). Many, but by no means all, prospectuses compare the fund's results to the S&P 500 or another recognized index. Total return—the measurement of price gains or losses plus dividend and interest income—is still a voluntary

feature in a prospectus. But you can estimate total return from the prospectus by taking the latest year-end share price, adding back all capital gains and dividends paid during the previous year and taking the percentage change from the previous year's ending price.

Management.

Funds don't have to tell the name and qualifications of the portfolio manager, though IDS even goes so far as to run color photos of its managers. Sometimes a fund will go out of its way to mention a resident celebrity. Dreyfus Capital Value, which performed extraordinarily well in 1987, ballyhoos in its prospectus the fund's adviser, Stanley Salvigson.

Miscellaneous.

The back pages of the prospectus are the guts that describe such services as exchange privilege between funds in the family or signing up to a systemic withdrawal plan. If you're unfamiliar with these services, call shareholder services with questions. Ask the fund about anything you can't easily find in the prospectus. If enough investors tie up the phones to ask about what should be explained clearly in the prospectus, funds are apt to do a better job of writing them.

Source: Adapted from Jeff Kosnett, "What to Look for—and Look Out for—as You Read a Mutual Fund Prospectus," *Changing Times,* May 1988, p. 18.

fact, much of the growth that bond funds have experienced recently can be attributed to this new investment attitude. No matter what your tastes, you'll find there's a full menu of bond funds available, including:

- *Government bond funds,* which invest in U.S. Treasury and agency securities.
- *Mortgage-backed bond funds,* which put their money mostly into various types of mortgage-backed securities of the U.S. government (like GNMA issues).
- *High grade corporate bond funds,* which invest chiefly in investment-grade securities rated triple-B or better.

- *High yield corporate bond funds,* which are risky investments that buy *junk bonds* for the yields they offer.
- *Municipal bond funds,* which invest in tax-exempt securities, and which are suitable for investors looking for tax-free income. Like their corporate counterparts, municipals can also come out as either high-grade or high-yield funds.
- *Intermediate-term bond funds,* which invest in bonds with maturities of 7 to 10 years, or less, and offer not only attractive yields but relatively low price volatility as well.

EXHIBIT 14.3

A Partial Menu of Mutual Funds

With well over 2,000 mutual funds in existence, today's investor has a wide array to securities to choose from. Indeed, it's no exaggeration to say that there are funds available today to meet just about any investment objective imaginable.

	Load (L) or No-Load (N) Fund	5-Year Performance (1984 –'88 Return[a])
Growth Funds		
Fidelity Magellan	L	17.5%
Linder Fund	N	15.0
Loomis-Sayles Cap. Dev.	N	14.8
Merrill Lynch Phoenix	L	17.6
Nicholas Fund	N	13.3
Phoenix Growth Series	L	15.6
Maximum Capital Gains Funds		
Dreyfus Leverage Fund	L	13.9%
Omega Fund	L	12.8
Oppenheimer Time Fund	L	12.2
Phoenix Stock Fund	L	13.2
Putnam Voyager	L	14.0
Value Line Leveraged Growth	N	9.3
Equity-Income Funds		
Decatur Fund I	L	16.0%
Fidelity Equity-Income	L	14.3
Financial Industrial Income	N	14.7
Lindner Dividend	N	14.2
SAFECO Income	N	14.2
Stratton Monthly Dividend	N	13.0
Balanced Funds		
Fidelity Puritan	L	14.9%
Franklin Income	L	12.6
Income Fund of Amer.	L	14.3
Mass. Financial Tot. Return	L	14.2
Wellesley Income	N	14.4
Wellington Fund	N	14.9
Growth-and-Income Funds		
American Leaders	L	14.7%
Evergreen Total Return	N	13.6

[a]Five-year performance figures are fully compounded returns (like those obtained from the approximate yield formula) and assume reinvestment of all dividends and capital gains distributions; these are average annual returns, and they cover the period from January 1984 through December 1988, except as noted with sector funds.
Source: Compiled from information found in *Donoghue's Mutual Fund Almanac*, 1989.

Money Market Mutual Funds. From the introduction of the very first *money fund* in 1972, the concept of investing in a portfolio of short-term money market instruments caught on like wildfire. There actually are several different kinds of money market mutual funds. **General-purpose money funds** essentially invest in any and all different types of money market investment vehicles, from Treasury bills to corporate commercial paper and bank certificates of deposit. They invest their money wherever they can find attractive short-term

returns. The vast majority of money funds are of this type. The **tax-exempt money fund** limits its investments to tax-exempt municipal securities with very short (30- to 90-day) maturities. Since their income is free from federal income tax, they appeal predominantly to investors in high tax brackets. **Government securities money funds** were established as a way of meeting investors' concern for safety. In essence, these funds eliminate any risk of default by confining their investment to Treasury bills and other short-term securities of the

EXHIBIT 14.3

	Load (L) or No-Load (N) Fund	5-Year Performance (1984–'88 Return[a])
Growth-and-Income Funds		
Investment Co. of America	L	15.7%
Merrill Lynch Capital	L	15.5
Mutual Qualified Income	N	18.8
Strong Total Return	L	15.3
Bond Funds		
Kemper U.S. Gov. Secs.	L	11.8%
Vanguard Fxd. Inc. Secs.-GNMAs	N	11.3
Kemper Income & Capt. Preserv'n	L	12.3
Pioneer Bond Fund	L	10.5
SAFECO Muni Bonds	N	12.8
SteinRoe Managed Munies	N	13.6
Money Funds		
General Purpose:		
Kemper Money Market Fund	N	7.9%
Transamerica Cash Reserves	N	7.8
Vanguard MM Reserves-Prime	N	7.9
Government Only:		
Cardinal Gov. Secs. Trust	N	7.6
Fidelity U.S. Govt. Reserves	N	7.4
Pru-Bache Money Mkt. Assets	N	7.7
Tax-Exempt:		
Calvert Tax-free Reserves	N	5.2
Dreyfus Tax-exempt Mon. Mkt.	N	4.8
T. Rowe Price Tax-exempt Mon. Fd	N	5.0
Sector Funds		
Century Shares Trust	N	14.1% (5 yrs)
Criterion Technology	L	23.3 (3 yrs)
Fidelity Select-Retailing	L	13.6 (3 yrs)
Freedom Regional Banks	N	15.9 (3 yrs)
Pru-Bach Utility Fund	N	22.4 (5 yrs)
Vanguard Special-Health Care	N	22.6 (4 yrs)

Source: Compiled from information found in *Donoghue's Mutual Fund Almanac*, 1989.

U.S. government or its agencies (such as the Federal National Mortgage Association).

Money funds are highly liquid vehicles and are very low in risk, since they are virtually immune to

general-purpose money fund
A money market mutual fund that invests in virtually any type of short-term investment vehicle, so long as it offers an attractive rate of return.

tax-exempt money fund
A money market mutual fund that limits investments to tax-exempt municipal securities with short maturities.

government securities money fund
A money market mutual fund that limits its investments to short-term securities of the U.S. government and its agencies, thus eliminating any default risk.

capital loss. However, the interest income they produce tends to follow interest rate conditions, and as such, the returns to shareholders are subject to the ups and downs of market interest rates. (Money funds are discussed more fully in Chapter 5, along with other short-term investment vehicles.)

Sector Funds. One of the newer products on Wall Street is the so-called *sector fund*—a mutual fund that restricts its investments to a particular sector of the market. In effect, these funds concentrate their investment holdings in the one or more industries that make up the targeted sector. For example, a *health care* sector fund would confine its investments to those industries that make up this segment of the market: drug companies, hospital management firms, medical suppliers, and biotech concerns. Its portfolio would then consist of promising growth stocks from these industries. The underlying investment objective of sector funds is *capital gains.* In many respects, they are similar to growth funds and thus should be considered speculative in nature.

The idea behind the sector fund concept is that the really attractive returns come from small segments of the market. Thus, rather than diversifying the portfolio across wide segments of the market, you should put your money where the action is. This notion may warrant consideration by the more aggressive investor who is willing to take on the added risks that often accompany these funds. Among the more popular sector funds are those that concentrate their investments in the so-called "glamour" industries: aerospace and defense, energy, financial services, gold, leisure and entertainment, natural resources, electronics, chemicals, computers, telecommunications, utilities, and health care.

Why Invest in Mutual Funds?

Mutual funds can be used by individual investors in a variety of ways. For instance, performance funds can serve as vehicles for capital appreciation, whereas bond funds may be used to provide current income. Regardless of the kind of income a fund provides, individuals tend to use these investment vehicles for one or more of the following reasons: (1) to achieve diversification in their investment holdings; (2) to obtain the services of

professional money managers; (3) to generate an attractive rate of return on their investment capital; and (4) for the convenience they offer.

Diversification. The primary motive for investing in mutual funds is the *ability to diversify* and diminish risk by indirectly investing in a number of different types of securities and/or companies. If you have only $500 to $1,000 to invest, you obviously will not achieve much diversification on your own. However, if you invest that money in a mutual fund, you will end up owning part of a diversified portfolio made up of perhaps 100 or more securities.

Professional Management. Another major appeal of a mutual fund is the professional management it offers. Of course, management is paid a fee from the fund's earnings, but the contributions of a full-time expert manager should be well worth the cost. These pros know where to look for return, and how to avoid unnecessary risk; their decisions should result in better returns than the average investor can achieve.

Financial Returns. While professional managers *may* be able to achieve returns that are better than what small investors can generate, the relatively high purchase fees, coupled with the management and operating costs, tend to reduce the returns actually earned on mutual fund investments. However, the mutual fund industry has not attracted millions of investors because of the substandard returns they generate! Quite the contrary: over the long haul, mutual funds have been able to provide relatively attractive returns. Look at Exhibit 14.4. It shows the average return performance on a variety of different types of mutual funds and is indicative of the kind of return investors were able to achieve during the five years from 1983 through 1988. With such return potential, it's easy to see why investors are so anxious to put their money into mutual funds—in many cases, it's probably safe to say that these returns are better than what investors could have done on their own.

Convenience. The fact that mutual fund shares can be purchased through a variety of sources is still another reason for their appeal. Mutual funds make it easy to invest, and most do not require a

EXHIBIT 14.4

The Comparative Performance of Mutual Funds (for the Ten-year period, September 1978 through September 1988)

The type of fund you invest in has a lot to do with the kind of return you can expect. For example, had you put $10,000 in a typical equity-income fund in 1978, that investment would have grown to $32,583 in 1988; in contrast, if you had invested that same amount of money in a balanced fund, it would have been worth some $26,245 in 1988.

Type of Fund	Total Return (%)
International funds	335.53
Equity-income funds	325.83
Capital appreciation funds	301.47
Growth & income funds	292.54
Growth funds	289.21
Convertible securities funds	266.74
Balanced funds	262.45
Income funds	218.28
Public utility funds	185.69
Bond funds	163.98

[a]Assumes reinvestment of all dividends and capital gains distributions.
Source: Lipper Analytical Services, Inc.; and *Barron's,* November 7, 1988, p. 83.

great deal of capital to get started. They are relatively easy to acquire, they handle all the paperwork and recordkeeping, their prices are widely quoted, and it is usually possible to deal in fractional shares. Opening a mutual fund account is nearly as easy as opening a checking account: Just fill in a few blank spaces, send in the minimum amount of money, and you will be in business!

Services Offered by Mutual Funds

Many people are drawn to mutual funds because of their attractive returns. However, there are other reasons to invest in them, including their automatic reinvestment plans, regular income programs, conversion privileges, and retirement plans. These are all examples of *mutual fund services* that many investors consider valuable—and, in fact, are sometimes the primary reasons for buying these funds.

Automatic Reinvestment Plans. Earning a fully compounded rate of return is a very important part of investing, and that's exactly what you get with an automatic reinvestment plan. This is one of the real draws of mutual funds, and it's a service offered by virtually every open-ended fund. A lot like the dividend reinvestment plans we looked at with stocks, the **automatic reinvestment plans** of mutual funds enable you to keep all your capital fully employed. Through this service, dividend and/or capital gains income is *automatically used to buy additional shares in the fund*. Keep in mind, however, that even though you reinvest your dividends and capital gains, the IRS still treats them as cash receipts and taxes them in the year in which they are paid. The funds deal in fractional shares,

---

automatic reinvestment plan

A plan frequently offered by mutual funds that allows share owners to elect to have dividends and capital gains distributions reinvested in additional fund shares.

and these purchases are often commission-free. The important point it that by plowing back your earnings, you can generate substantially more earnings over the long haul than would be otherwise possible.

Regular Income. While automatic reinvestment plans are great for the long-term investor, how about the investor who's looking for a steady stream of income? Once again, mutual funds have a service to meet this kind of need. It's called a **systematic withdrawal plan**, and it's offered by most open-ended funds. Once enrolled in one of these plans, you'll automatically receive a predetermined amount of money every month or quarter.

To participate, shareholders are usually required to have a minimum investment of $5,000 to $10,000, and the size of the withdrawal must usually be $50 or more per month. Depending on how well the fund has done and the specified amount of the withdrawals, income derived from it may actually be greater than the withdrawals, thus allowing the investor to not only receive regular income but also enjoy an automatic accumulation of *additional* shares in the plan. On the other hand, if the fund has not performed well, the withdrawals could eventually deplete the original investment of funds.

Conversion Privileges. Sometimes investors find it necessary to switch out of one fund and into another; for example, their investment objectives may change, or the investment environment itself may have changed. **Conversion** (or **exchange**) **privileges** meet the needs of these investors in a convenient and economical manner. Investment companies that offer a number of different funds to the investing public—these are known as *fund families*—usually provide conversion privileges that enable shareholders to easily move from one fund to another; and as we saw earlier, this is usually done by phone (as in *phone switching*). The only limitation is that the investor must confine the switches within the same *family* of funds. For example, an investor can switch from a Dreyfus growth fund to a Dreyfus money fund, or to its income fund, or to any other fund managed by Dreyfus. With some fund families, the alternatives open to investors seem almost without limit; indeed, some of the larger families offer 20 or 30

funds (or more). One investment company (Fidelity) has over 100 different funds in its family, as it provides everything from high-performance stock funds to bond funds, tax-exempt funds, a couple dozen sector funds, and half a dozen money funds.

Most fund families, especially the bigger ones, offer investors a full range of investment products, as they all try to provide one-stop mutual fund shopping. Whether you want an equity fund, a bond fund, or a money fund, these fund families have something for you. There are more than a hundred fund families in operation today, every one of which has some type of conversion privilege. Twenty of the largest of these fund families are listed in Exhibit 14.5; note that, together, these 20 families offer nearly 650 different mutual funds to the investing public. Conversion privileges are attractive because they permit investors to manage their holdings more aggressively by allowing them to move in and out of funds as the investment environment changes. Unfortunately, there is one major drawback: even though you never see the cash, the exchange of shares from one fund to another is regarded, for tax purposes, as a sale transaction followed by a subsequent purchase of a new security. As a result, if any capital gains exist at the time of the exchange, the investor is liable for the taxes on that profit.

Phone switching is a service that enables you to move your money from one fund to another, so long as you stay within the same family of funds. **Fact:** Phone switching is a type of conversion (or exchange) privilege that allows you to simply pick up the phone to call in an order to sell one fund and buy another, with the only condition being that you confine your switches to the same family of funds.

Retirement Plans. As a result of government legislation, self-employed individuals are permitted to divert a portion of their pre-tax income into self-directed *retirement plans*. And all working Americans, whether they are self-employed or not, are allowed to establish individual retirement accounts—note that IRAs can still be set up by anyone who is gainfully employed, although, as noted in Chapter 4, the tax deductibility of IRA *contributions* is limited to certain individuals. Today all mutual funds provide a special service that allows individuals to quickly and easily set up tax-deferred retire-

EXHIBIT 14.5

All in the Family

Here's a list of 20 of the largest fund families, each one of which offers investors a full range of stock, bond, and money funds; these companies do everything they can to keep your money in the family.

Fund Families	Number of Stock, Bond Funds	Number of Money Funds	Total Number of Funds
American Capital Marketing	17	1	18
Colonial Investment Services	23	1	24
Dean Witter Reynolds	19	7	26
Dreyfus Service Corp.	24	7	31
Federated Securities Corp.	17	3	20
Fidelity Distributors Corp.	96	8	104
Franklin Distributors	27	4	31
IDS Financial Services	25	3	28
Kemper Financial Services	13	5	18
Keystone Distributors	18	1	19
Mass. Financial Services	26	2	28
Merrill Lynch Funds	51	8	59
Oppenheimer Fund Mgmt	20	1	21
T. Rowe Price Assocs.	21	3	24
Prudential-Bache	35	7	42
Putnam Financial Services	33	1	34
Shearson Lehman Hutton	30	9	39
Stein Roe & Farnham	13	3	16
Vanguard Group	44	5	49
Waddell & Reed (United Fds)	15	1	16

ment programs as either IRA or Keogh accounts. The funds set up the plans and handle all the administrative details in such a way that the shareholder can take full advantage of available tax savings.

Getting a Handle on Mutual Fund Performance

If you were to believe all the sales literature, you'd think there was no way you could go wrong by investing in mutual funds. Just put your money into one of these funds and let the good times roll! Unfortunately, the hard facts of life are that when it comes to investing, performance is never guaranteed. And that applies just as much to mutual funds as it does to any other form of investing. Perhaps even more so, because with mutual funds, the single variable that drives a fund's market price and return behavior is the performance of the fund's portfolio of securities.

Measuring Fund Performance. If you're thinking about investing in a mutual fund, one of the first things you should do is make sure the fund's *investment objectives* match your own. In addition,

carefully check out the fund's *load charges* and other fees; and if a certain kind of *service* is important to you, then make sure the funds you're looking at offer it. Remember, though, while each of these characteristics is important in the mutual fund selection process, the most essential is still *investment performance*.

Basically, any mutual fund (or closed-end investment company) has three potential sources of return: ① dividend income, ② capital gains distribution, and ③ change in the fund's price. Dividend income is the amount derived from the dividend and interest income earned on the security holdings of the mutual fund. When the fund

---

systematic withdrawal plan

A plan offered by mutual funds that allows shareholders to be paid specified amounts each period.

conversion (exchange) privileges

A feature offered by many investment companies that allows investors to switch from one mutual fund to another within a specified family of funds.

receives dividends or interest payments, it passes these on to shareholders in the form of dividend payments. The fund accumulates all the current income it has received for the period and then pays it out on a prorated basis. Capital gains distributions work on the same principle, except that they are derived from the capital gains actually earned by the fund. This capital gain distribution applies only to *realized* capital gains—that is, the case in which the securities holdings were actually sold and the capital gains actually earned. *Unrealized* capital gains (or paper profits) are what make up the third and final element in a mutual fund's return, for when the fund's holdings go up or down in price, its net asset value moves accordingly.

A simple but effective way of measuring performance is to describe mutual fund returns in terms of the three major sources of return noted above: dividends earned, capital gains distributions received, and change in share price. These payoffs can be converted to a convenient return figure by using the standard *approximate yield* formula that was introduced in Chapter 12. The calculations necessary for finding such a return measure can be shown with a simple illustration. We will use data from a hypothetical no-load mutual fund that paid dividends of 50 cents and capital gains distributions of 25 cents per share over the course of the year. In addition, we will assume that at the beginning of the year the fund had a per share price of $9.50 that rose to $10.50 by the end of the year. This data is put into the familiar approximate yield formula in Equation 14.1 (on page 511). Using this measure, we see that the hypothetical mutual fund provided an annual rate of return of 17.5 percent. This measure is simple to calculate, yet it captures all the important elements of mutual fund return.

What About Future Performance? There's no question that approximate yield is a handy measure of return. Unfortunately, looking at past performance is one thing, but how about the future? Ideally, we want to evaluate the same three elements of return for the future as we did for the past. The trouble is, when it comes to the future performance of a mutual fund, it's extremely difficult—if not impossible—to get a handle on what the future holds as far as dividends, capital gains, and NAV are concerned. The reason: a mutual fund's future investment performance is directly linked to the future

makeup of its securities portfolio—which is something that is next to impossible to predict. It's not like evaluating the expected performance of a share of stock, where you're keying in on one company. With mutual funds, investment performance depends on the behavior of many different stocks and bonds.

So, where do you look for insight into the future? Most market observers suggest you do two things. First, give careful consideration to the *future direction of the market as a whole*. This is important because the behavior of a well-diversified mutual fund tends to reflect the general tone of the market. Thus, if the feeling is that the market is going to be generally drifting up, that should bode well for the investment performance of mutual funds.

Second, take a good hard look at the past performance of the mutual fund itself, as that's a good way to get an indication of how successful the fund's investment managers have been. In essence, the success of a mutual fund rests in large part *on the investment skills of the fund managers*. So, when investing in a mutual fund, look for consistently good performance, in up as well as down markets, over extended periods of time (five to seven years, or more). Although past success is certainly no guarantee of future performance, a strong team of money managers can have a significant bearing on the level of fund returns. Put another way, when you buy a mutual fund, you're buying a formula (investment policy + money management team) that has worked in the past, in the expectation that it will work again in the future.

Where to Look for Information About Mutual Funds

Given the importance of a fund's past performance, where can you find the kind of information you're looking for? A good place to start is with the mutual fund itself. Not too long ago, you would have been putting your financial health in considerable jeopardy if you'd followed such a course of action. But with some recent changes instituted by the SEC, that's no longer so. Along with their load charges and management fees, mutual funds must now report historical return behavior in a standardized format. The funds are *not* required to report such information, but if they do cite performance in their promotional material, they must follow a stan-

Equation 14.1

$$\text{Approximate yield} = \frac{\text{Dividends and capital gains distributions} + \left[\dfrac{\text{Ending price} - \text{Beginning price}}{\text{1-year time period}}\right]}{\left[\dfrac{\text{Ending price} + \text{Beginning price}}{2}\right]}$$

$$= \frac{(\$.50 + \$.25) + \left[\dfrac{\$10.50 - \$9.50}{1}\right]}{\left[\dfrac{\$10.50 + \$9.50}{2}\right]}$$

$$= \frac{\$.75 + \$1.00}{\$10.00} = \frac{\$\ 1.75}{\$10.00} = 17.5\%.$$

dardized, full-disclosure manner of presentation. In particular, the funds must disclose the average annual return for the preceding one-, five-, and ten-year periods. The returns must include not only dividends and capital gains distributions, but also any increases or decreases in NAV. In other words, these are fully compounded, total-return figures, similar to the ones you'd obtain from the approximate yield measure.

In addition, publications like *Barron's, Forbes,* and *Donoghue's Mutual Funds Almanac* provide a wealth of operating and performance information in a convenient and easy-to-read format. What's more, publications like *Money* and *Changing Times* regularly list the top-performing funds. There are also services available that provide background information and assessments for a wide variety of funds. Some of the best in this category include Morningstar's *Mutual Fund Values* (an excerpt from which is shown in Exhibit 14.6) and Wiesenberger's *Investment Companies.* From these sources, you can obtain information on such things as investment objectives, load charges and annual expense rates, portfolio analyses, services offered, historical statistics, and reviews of past performance. And, of course, as in so many other areas of investing, you can use your personal computer to evaluate the past and current performance of mutual funds. A full menu of reasonably priced mutual fund software is available, two of the more popular

ones being the *Business Week Mutual Fund Scoreboard* and *Forbes Mutual Fund Evaluator.*

INVESTING IN REAL ESTATE

Investors seeking attractive profit opportunities often turn to real estate. They may speculate in raw land, buy income-producing properties, invest in limited partnerships, or purchase REITs. Which of these vehicles would you use if you wanted to invest in real estate? What kind of return would you want to earn from your investment, and what do you suppose would be the most important source of return: rents or appreciation in value? Take a few minutes before reading on to think about these questions.

Generally speaking, investing in real estate during most of the 1970s was quite lucrative! Real estate, it seemed, was one of the few investment vehicles that consistently outperformed the rate of inflation. While inflation was running at 10 to 15 percent a year, a lot of real estate investments were yielding rates of return of 15 to 20 percent, or more. You just couldn't go wrong—*everybody* was making big money in real estate, and according to all the self-proclaimed "experts," there was no end in sight.

EXHIBIT 14.6

Mutual Fund Information

Investors who want in-depth information about the operating characteristics, investment holdings, and market performance of mutual funds can usually find what they're looking for in publications like Morningstar's *Mutual Fund Values* (shown here) or Weisenberger's *Investment Companies.*

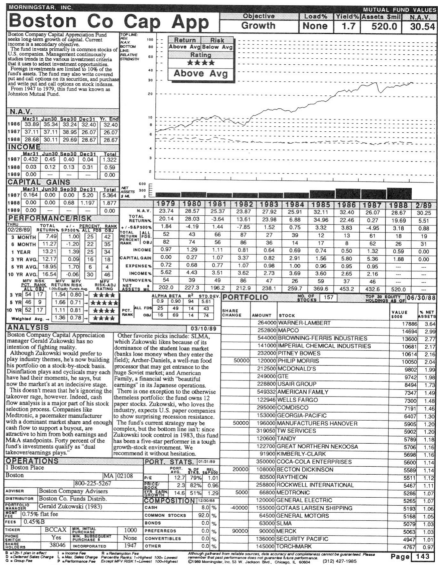

REPRINTED BY PERMISSION. MORNINGSTAR, INC. 53 W. JACKSON BLVD., CHICAGO, IL 60604, (312) 427-1985

Source: Morningstar, Inc., *Mutual Fund Values,* 1988.

Unfortunately, the "experts" were wrong, for when inflation dropped to more normal levels, the big real estate boom died—at least in most parts of the country. Granted, there are still some areas where the real estate market is strong, but the record is spotty: in a lot of markets, prices remain "soft," and even some of those areas that were red-hot a couple of years ago are now flat as a pancake. Of course, this doesn't mean that real estate prices are in a nosedive. Far from it: *prices in most regions are still going up, but at a much slower pace.* And so long as inflation remains in check, you can probably expect more of the same from most real estate investments.

Some Basic Considerations

Investing in real estate takes time and should always be based on a careful analysis of the facts. As with any investment, look at the future cash flow you expect to realize from the property, and compare it to the returns obtainable from alternative investment vehicles (like stocks, bonds, mutual funds, and so on). Obviously, don't put your money in real estate if you think you can earn more in some other type of equally risky investment. Current income and capital gains are important sources of return to real estate investors, but measuring such returns involves more than just counting rent receipts. Taxes, cash flow, and the use of leverage are all important in real estate investments. The following material provides a brief description of the basic factors that affect the value of real estate investments, including cash flow and taxes, appreciation in value, risk versus return, and the use of leverage.

Cash Flow and Taxes.   The investor's *cash flow,* or annual after-tax earnings, depends not only on the particular piece of property, but also on depreciation and taxes. Certain types of real estate result in large depreciation write-offs that tend to lower the taxable income of certain (*qualified*) investors. Since real estate in general tends to deteriorate over time, **depreciation** provides the property owner with an allowance for this decline in value. Depreciation is basically a bookkeeping entry that is considered an expense for tax purposes even though it involves no outflow of cash. Thus, depreciation can result in lower taxes and, therefore, its existence is viewed as a *tax shelter.* But there's a

catch: Depreciation can be used only up to a certain amount and only by investors who meet certain income qualifications.

First of all, keep in mind that real estate is considered a *passive* investment, no matter how actively involved you are in managing the property. As such, the amount of expenses (*including depreciation*) that can be written off is generally limited to the amount of income generated by this and any other passive investments of the taxpayer/investor. Thus, if you owned some apartments that generated rental income of, say, $25,000 a year, and (in the absence of any other passive investments) if you had mortgage interest and other operating expenses (like property taxes and minor repairs) of, say, $20,000 annually, you may be able to write off no more than $5,000 in depreciation ($25,000 in income − $20,000 in other expenses). However, if your *adjusted gross income* is less than $100,000 a year, you may be able to write off even more depreciation—specifically, as much as $25,000 in losses on *rented real estate* can be used each year to offset the ordinary income of people who "actively participate" in the rental activity of the buildings *and* whose adjusted gross income is less than $100,000 (this provision is phased out at $150,000).

In our example above, if you had, say, $90,000 in adjusted gross income and if there were $15,000 in depreciation expense, then $5,000 of it could be written off against the remaining $5,000 in net rental income, and the other $10,000 could be charged directly against your ordinary income, thereby reducing your taxable income and taxes! Because of its effects on taxes, depreciation is considered an important part of investing in real estate. Since depreciation and taxes are so important in measuring cash flow, an individual investor should employ a tax expert to evaluate proposed real estate investments.

Appreciation in Value.   Some types of real estate—especially raw land—have experienced significant growth in value, particularly during certain

> **depreciation**
> In real estate investment, a way of writing off the cost of the investment; it is meant to reflect the decline in the value of real estate property.

periods like 1975 to 1980. Other types, such as apartments and duplexes, have also appreciated in value. An investment evaluation of a proposed piece of real estate, therefore, should include not only the recurring cash flows from the property (like rents), but also expected changes in property values (i.e., price appreciation). In many cases, such appreciation has a much bigger impact on rate of return than the net annual cash flow from the property! Thus, if the market price of the real estate is expected to increase by $100,000, that price appreciation should be treated as capital gains and included as part of the return from the investment.

In many types of real estate investments, appreciation in the value of the property has more of an impact on return than annual rental income. **Fact:** Like most forms of investing, the biggest bang for your buck usually comes from capital gains; you'll find that's the way the really big money is made, and real estate is certainly no exception to that rule.

Risk versus Return.   If you can earn 6 percent on some type of savings deposit, any money you invest in real estate should promise a considerably higher potential return. For the 6 percent return you receive on your savings is certain, whereas the returns on a real estate investment are subject to considerable risk. The anticipated level of return on the investment, as well as the stability (or certainty) of those periodic returns, are important in evaluating proposed real estate investments. The risk and return characteristics of such investments should always be judged in light of those available from other investment vehicles.

Use of Leverage.   One attraction of investing in real estate is the high degree of financial leverage it permits. Basically, **leverage** involves the use of borrowed money to magnify returns. Because real estate is a tangible item, investors are able to borrow as much as 75 to 90 percent of its cost. As a result, if the total return on the investment is greater than the cost of borrowing, the net profit on a leveraged investment will be *proportionately greater* than one that does not use leverage. For example, imagine that you're considering a real estate investment that costs $100,000—like the one in Exhibit 14.7. Now let's further assume that you can purchase the property in one of two ways: you can either pay cash for it, or you can put up $10,000

of your own money and borrow the remaining $90,000 at, say, 10 percent annual interest. If the property earns $13,000 per year after all expenses, including property taxes and depreciation, *but before the deduction of interest and income taxes,* the leveraged investment, as shown in Exhibit 14.7, will provide a much better rate of return: indeed, note that in the no-leverage case, your return on investment will be 9.36 percent, but in the leverage case, you stand to make a return of 28.80 percent.

Because a portion of the leveraged investment is made with borrowed money, the return on investment in Exhibit 14.7 reflects *only your investment in the property*—that is, the amount of money that *you* put up to buy it. Thus, even though the leveraged investment will have provided less earnings after taxes, it will also have had a lower investment, the net result being a higher return on investment. In essence, if you leverage your investment, you will get a bigger bang from your investment dollars! Note from this example, however, that when no borrowing is used, there is no risk of default; but in the leverage case, minimum earnings (before interest and taxes) of $9,000 are necessary to avoid default. The risk that comes with leverage therefore must be considered along with the potential benefits—indeed, many people have been driven into bankruptcy as a result of having used too much leverage.

Speculating in Raw Land

Investing in real estate can take numerous forms. One approach that's popular with many individual investors is to *speculate in raw land.* In this approach, which is usually very risky, investors seek to generate high rates of return by investing in property that they hope will undergo dramatic increases in value. The key to such speculation is to isolate areas of potential population growth and/or real estate demand (ideally, before everyone else does) and purchase property in these areas in the hope that the expectations for their development will be realized. Undeveloped acreage with no utilities or improvements is often purchased by land speculators either to hold for future development or to merely sell at a higher price at some later date. Speculation in raw land often occurs near an area in which some type of new development is anticipated. Both residential and commercial devel-

EXHIBIT 14.7

The Use of Leverage in Real Estate Investments

Although earnings after taxes are less with the leveraged investment, the return on investment is considerably higher because the investor puts a lot less of his or her own money into the deal.

	No Leverage		Leverage
Owner investment	$100,000		$ 10,000
Borrowed money	0		90,000
Total investment	$100,000		$100,000
Earnings before interest and income taxes[a]	$ 13,000		$ 13,000
Less: Interest	0	(0.10)($90,000) =	9,000
Earnings before taxes	$ 13,000		$ 4,000
Less: Income taxes (assumed 28% rate)	3,640		1,120
Earnings after taxes	$ 9,360		$ 2,880

$$\text{Return on investment} = \frac{\text{Earnings after taxes}}{\text{Amount of owner investment}} \quad \frac{\$9,360}{\$100,000} = 9.36\% \qquad \frac{\$2,280}{\$10,000} = 28.80\%$$

[a]All expenses, including property taxes and depreciation, are assumed to have already been deducted from earnings.

opments tend to increase the value of nearby property. Raw land speculation, because of the high degree of uncertainty involved, should be reserved for real estate investors who recognize and can accept the inherent risks.

Investing in Income Property

Income property is a relatively common type of real estate investment that can provide both attractive returns and *tax shelters* for many investors. The real estate purchased is leased to tenants in order to generate income in the form of rent receipts. Although the primary purpose in investing in income property is to produce an attractive annual cash flow, certain types of strategically located income properties also offer substantial opportunities for appreciation in value. The two basic types of income property are residential property and commercial property.

Residential Property. Apartments, duplexes, and rental houses are all examples of *residential property* that provide income. This type of income property is available in a variety of sizes, prices, and types ranging from multi-family apartment complexes to single-family rental homes. First-time investors in real estate usually choose investments of this type. Aside from purchase and financing cost

considerations, the major factors influencing the profitability of these investments are the occupancy rates—the percentage of available space rented over the year—and maintenance and management costs.

Commercial Property. Office buildings, stores, strip shopping centers, and warehouses are examples of the variety of investments included in the category of *commercial property*. The risks and returns on commercial property depend more on business conditions and location than do those for residential property. The value of commercial property—especially retail businesses—is enhanced by a location in a high-traffic area. Due to the need for professional management and the magnitude of the expenses involved, investment in commercial types of income property is generally the domain of more seasoned real estate investors.

leverage
The use of borrowed money to magnify returns.

income property
Real estate purchased to be leased to tenants in order to generate income in the form of rent receipts.

Investing in Real Estate through Limited Partnerships

Limited partnerships are professionally managed *syndicates* that invest in, among other things, various types of real estate. The managers assume the role of *general partner,* which means that their liability is unlimited, while the other investors are *limited partners,* meaning they are legally liable for only the amount of their initial investment. Most limited partnerships require a minimum investment of between $2,500 and $10,000. You can invest in limited partnerships directly through ads in financial newspapers, through stockbrokers or financial planners, or with the assistance of a commercial real estate broker.

Types of Syndicates.   There are two basic kinds of real estate limited partnerships: single property and blind pool syndicates. The **single property syndicate** is established to raise money to purchase a specific piece (or pieces) of property. For example, 50 units of a partnership could be sold at $7,500 each to buy a piece of property for $1 million. (Note: A **unit** in a limited partnership is like a share of stock in a company and represents an ownership position in the partnership.) In this case, a total of $375,000 (50 units × $7,500) would come from the partners and the remaining $625,000 would be borrowed. The **blind pool syndicate**, on the other hand, is formed by a syndicator—often well known—in order to raise a given amount of money to be invested at his or her discretion, though the general partner often has some or all of the properties already picked out. The blind pool syndicator takes a specified percentage of all income generated as a management fee. Large real estate brokerage firms commonly arrange these types of syndicates.

Returns and Risks.   Prior to the 1986 Tax Reform Act, much of the appeal of real estate limited partnerships came from the tax-sheltered income that these investments provided. That is no longer the case. Instead, like other forms of real estate, these limited partnerships are considered to be *passive* investments; as such, the amount of write-offs that can be taken on these investments is limited to the amount of income they generate (see Chapter 4). This means that the write-offs from

these investments cannot be used to shelter ordinary income from taxes. While limited partnerships may have lost some of their appeal, they still remain a popular way to invest in real estate, especially for those with limited investment capital. The big difference is that rather than emphasizing the tax-sheltered nature of their income, many of the real estate limited partnerships of today are less leveraged (some use no debt at all), and are structured to provide attractive current incomes (from rents, etc.) and/or capital gains. An example of this new breed of investment vehicle is the *triple-net limited partnership,* which is discussed in the *Issues in Money Management* box. The bottom line is that these partnerships, like many others, are now being promoted on the basis of their underlying investment merits and not on the basis of some artificial tax motive. Certainly, for an investor with as little as $1,000 or $5,000 to invest, a carefully selected limited partnership may be a sensible way to invest in real estate.

Real Estate Investment Trusts

The **real estate investment trust (REIT)** is a type of closed-end investment company that invests money in mortgages and various types of real estate investments. A REIT is like a mutual fund in that it sells shares of stock to the investing public and uses the proceeds, along with borrowed funds, to invest in a portfolio of real estate investments. The investor, therefore, owns a part of the real estate portfolio held by the real estate investment trust. There are three basic types of REITs: those that invest in *properties,* such as shopping centers, hotels, apartments, and office buildings (the so-called *property,* or *equity,* REITs); mortgage REITs—those that invest in mortgages; and *hybrid* REITs, which invest in both properties and mortgages. REITs must abide by the Real Estate Investment Trust Act of 1960, which established requirements for forming a REIT, as well as rules and procedures for making investments and distributing income. Since they are required to pay out nearly all of their earnings to the owners, they do quite a bit of borrowing to obtain funds for their investments.

A number of insurance companies, mortgage bankers, commercial banks, and real estate investment companies have formed REITs, many of which are traded on the major securities exchanges. Like mutual funds, the income earned by a REIT is not taxed, but the income distributed to the owners is designated and taxed as ordinary income. Although the poor performance of REITs during the 1973 to 1975 recession caused them to fall into disfavor among investors, subsequent restructuring of their portfolios has rekindled a good deal of interest in this form of investing.

Indeed, in 1989, there were over 150 such investment companies. Some of the better known and more actively traded REITs include Federal Realty, Pennsylvania REIT, First Union Realty, Lomas and Nettleton Mortgage Investors, ICM Property, and Mortgage Growth Investors. Your stockbroker should be able to give you advice with respect to REITs and help you select those that will be consistent with your investment objectives.

A REIT (real estate investment trust) is a popular form of limited partnership that enables individuals to directly invest in income-producing property. **Fantasy:** A REIT is a type of closed-end investment company (it's like a mutual fund) that issues stocks and invests the proceeds in mortgages and various kinds of real estate properties.

OTHER INVESTMENT VEHICLES

In addition to, or instead of, the more traditional forms of investing, some individuals prefer to put their money into the more esoteric world of commodities, financial futures, options, and precious metals, all of which are highly specialized investment vehicles that subject investors to considerable exposure to risk. Why do you suppose someone would want to put their money into things like commodities and options? Do you think investor know-how is all that important when investing in these things—or is it all a matter of luck? Stop to give some thought to these questions before reading on.

In addition to the more traditional investment outlets, like stocks, bonds, mutual funds, and real estate, a variety of other investment vehicles are available. Although they may be less commonly used by the small investor (due to their relatively high risk and/or lack of liquidity), a very basic understanding of some of the more popular alternatives should prove useful in developing your portfolio. Accordingly, we will now direct our attention to commodities, financial futures, options, precious metals, and collectibles.

Commodities

Commodities markets provide a mechanism through which producers of certain goods and products can protect themselves against potential future price declines. Suppliers of commodities, such as cattle, coffee, silver, soybeans, and wheat, who believe that the prices of their products are likely to drop might sell contracts to deliver specified quantities of the commodity at some future date. The buyers of these contracts protect themselves against price increases and guarantee themselves the future availability of needed raw materials at known prices. Once these contracts are created, *they can be actively traded.* The need (and

limited partnership
A type of syndicate in which the managers' (general partners') liability is unlimited and the investors' (limited partners') liability is restricted to the amount of their initial investment; used with real estate investments.

single property syndicate
A syndicate established to raise money to purchase a specific piece of real estate.

unit
Represents a share of ownership in a limited partnership deal.

blind pool syndicate
A syndicate formed by a well-known syndicator in order to raise a given amount of money for investment in real estate at the syndicator's discretion.

real estate investment trust (REIT)
A business that accumulates money for investment in real estate ventures by selling shares to investors; like a mutual fund, except REITs confine their investments to real estate and/or mortgages.

ISSUES IN MONEY MANAGEMENT

"Hold the Risks: Triple-Net Partnerships Offer Built-in Safety"

You may think that risk goes with limited partnerships as fleas go with dogs. But if you pick carefully, one breed of real estate partnership offers the safety of blue-chip stocks plus the generous income of bonds. Called *triple-net lease deals,* these partnerships buy buildings used by fast-food, day care, auto parts, and other chains and franchisees that don't want to tie up their money in ownership or have mortgage debt on their balance sheets. The partnerships collect rents and pass it along to investors.

They are known as triple net because the rents are net of three costs—insurance, upkeep, and property taxes—borne by the tenants. Many partnerships also reduce their risk by requiring that rent payments be guaranteed, at least for a portion of the lease. Should a Sizzler restaurant fizzle, for example, the chain or an insurance company keeps up the payments for a while.

Limited partners hope, of course, that the tenant's busi-

ness will be a barn-burner. By putting up a minimum—usually $5,000—they stand to receive distributions of about 8% to 10% of their investment annually, even after a portion is deducted for front-end and other fees. The partnerships pay cash for the properties, so distributions tend to be fatter in the early years than those paid by leveraged partnerships, which must siphon off a hefty portion of the rent to pay mortgage interest. Also, since the owners can deduct depreciation, 20% to 25% of the income is sheltered from income taxes. When the partnership liquidates, typically in 20 years, the property is sold, and the limited partner receives his principal plus a share of any capital appreciation.

Unlike bondholders, however, investors need not content themselves with a fixed payment while they await the hoped-for bonanza. Instead, many of these partnerships have leases entitling them to higher rents as revenues from the en-

terprises grow. Steven Bleier, president of Diversified Financial Management of White Plains, New York, a company that analyzes partnerships, urges investors to make sure theirs has such a "sales override." Says Bleier: "You want an income stream that keeps up with inflation." The partnerships listed in the table on the next page all have this provision:

Sounds good? The growing number of investors buying into triple-net partnerships think so. This doesn't mean there aren't some mutts out there. You don't want a partnership invested in shaky stores on third-rate strip malls, even if the prospective yield is dazzling. "There's a trade-off between income and security," says Bleier. "A high yield means more risk."

Thomas Fendrich, a managing director of Standard & Poor's partnership research service, prefers partnerships that own diversified properties, since they are better hedged in case one of the businesses comes on hard times. He also looks over

desire) to trade commodities contracts, not surprisingly, led to the creation of the commodities market. You need not be a producer or user of a commodity in order to buy or sell these contracts; instead, you, as an individual investor, can buy and sell commodities contracts as millions of others do. Generally speaking, commodities contracts are traded by individuals who want to *make money*

with commodities by speculating on their price swings. However, investing in commodities involves a considerable amount of speculation and an enormous amount of risk. The payoffs from speculating in commodities can be spectacular; but so can the losses! *These are specialized investment vehicles that require specialized investor skills.*

the pedigree of the sponsor, or general partner. "Rent insurance only covers lost payments for a while," Fendrich says. So if the restaurant folds, "you need a strong sponsor who will quickly get new tenants." One partnership he ranks highly is *Insured Income Properties 1988*, offered by Franchise Finance Corp.: "It's got a strong sponsor with a good history of handling defaults, and has strong income flows." Tenants include every major fast-food chain except McDonald's.

Robert A. Stanger & Co., a firm in Shrewsbury, New Jersey, that evaluates partnerships, gives its highest AAA+ rating to *RPS Growth & Income Fund*, which rents to Arby's, Taco Bell, and Avis Lube establishments. Rated AAA for safety and reasonable front-end loads are *Brauvin High Yield Fund II*, which rents to the Ponderosa Steak House and Taco Bell chains, and *DiVall Insured Income Properties II*, whose tenants include Denny's family restaurants and 7-Eleven. Bleier's favorite is *RIC*

Partnership Sponsor	Size of Offering in Millions	Properties
Insured Income Properties 1988 Franchise Finance Corp. of America; Phoenix	$100	Fast-food franchises
RIC 24/25 Realty Income Corp.; Burbank, Calif.	$100	Fast-food franchises, day care centers, auto parts stores
DiVall Insured Income Properties II DiVall Real Estate; Madison, Wis.	$25	Family restaurants, fast-food franchises, convenience stores
Brauvin High Yield Fund II Brauvin Realty; Chicago	$25	Fast-food franchises, convenience stores, auto service centers
RPS Growth & Income Fund ASB Enterprises; Carlsbad, Calif.	$20	Fast-food franchises, automotive repair, motel chains

24/25, which collects rent from Children's World centers and Schuck's Auto Supply outlets.

Source: Adapted from Ellen Schultz, "The Built-in Safety of Triple-Net Partnerships," *Fortune*, December 5, 1988, p. 24.

Because commodities contracts deal with the future delivery of a product, they are also known as *futures contracts*. Today there is an active market for futures contracts—in fact, such trading activity in many ways rivals that of the stock market. It is nearly as easy to buy and sell commodities as it is stocks and bonds, since all commodities trading is conducted on organized exchanges. The following is a list of major commodity exchanges:

- Chicago Board of Trade
- Chicago Mercantile Exchange
- Chicago Rice and Cotton Exchange
- Commodities Exchange of New York
- Kansas City Board of Trade

▪ Mid-America Commodities Exchange
▪ Minneapolis Grain Exchange
▪ New York Coffee, Sugar and Cocoa Exchange
▪ New York Cotton Exchange
▪ New York Mercantile Exchange
▪ Winnipeg Commodity Exchange (Canadian)

Each exchange deals in a variety of futures contracts, although some are more limited in their activities than others. Another exchange—the New York Futures Exchange—deals only in financial futures contracts, an investment vehicle that we will review later in this chapter.

Futures Contracts. A **futures contract** is a commitment to deliver a certain amount of a particular item at some specified future date. The seller of the contract agrees to make the specified future delivery, and the buyer agrees to accept it. Each exchange establishes its own contract specifications, which include not only the quantity and quality of the item but the delivery procedure and delivery month as well. For example, the Chicago Board of Trade specifies that each of its soybean contracts involve 5,000 bushels of USDA grade No. 2 yellow soybeans; delivery months include January, March, May, July, August, September, and November. The *delivery month* on a futures contract specifies when the commodity or item must be delivered and thus defines the life of the contract. The maximum life of a futures contract is about one year or less, although some have longer lives.

Exhibit 14.8 lists a number of popular commodities, along with the size of their respective contracts; here we can see that investing in the futures market involves large quantities of the underlying commodity. Note, however, that while the value of a single contract is normally quite large, the amount of investor capital required to deal in these vehicles is actually very small—often no more than a few thousand dollars—since all trading in this market is done on a *margin* basis.

Trading Commodities. Like common stocks and other traditional investment vehicles, futures contracts are bought and sold through local brokerage offices. Except for setting up a special commodities trading account, there is really no difference between trading futures and dealing in stocks or bonds. The same types of orders are used, and the use of margin is a standard way of trading futures. Any individual can buy or sell any contract, with any delivery month, at any time, so long as it is currently being traded on one of the exchanges. All trades are subject to normal transaction costs, which include **round-trip commissions** of about $50 to $80 for each contract traded (a round-trip commission includes the commission costs on both the buying and selling ends of the transaction). One significant aspect of commodity futures is the very low margin requirements placed on transactions. Persons with commodities trading accounts are required to put up only 5 to 10 percent of the value of a futures contract at the time of the transaction. If the price of the commodity declines over the holding period, the brokerage firm may require the customer to put up additional money as collateral on the contract. The use of low margin on commodities transactions enhances returns on investments *but also noticeably increases the risks involved.*

To better appreciate the impact of low margins on commodity trading, consider the following example from the silver market. Assume it is January and you purchase a silver contract for delivery in May at a price of, say, $13.50 per troy ounce (there are 5,000 troy ounces in 1 silver contract). If the price of silver increases to, say, $16.50 per troy ounce on or before the maturity date of the contract (May), you will make a profit of $3.00 per ounce, or a total of $15,000 on the contract ($3 per troy ounce × 5,000 troy ounces)—all from one contract and all from a mere $3 change in the price of the underlying commodity. But there is more good news: You will have been able to earn this profit with a relatively small amount of investment capital, because commodities are traded on margin. For example, assume the margin deposit on silver is $7,000 per contract; thus, rather than pay full market value for the contract ($13.50 per troy ounce × 5,000 troy ounces = $67,500), you would have had to put up only about one-tenth that amount in your own money. In effect, for $7,000 you would have been able to purchase one silver contract with a market value of $67,500! Given the $15,000 profit, you would have made a return on invested capital of a whopping 214 percent ($15,000 ÷ $7,000). Keep in mind, however,

EXHIBIT 14.8

Futures Contract Specifications—Selected Commodities

The size and market value of most commodities contracts are quite large. Thus, investors are subject to wide variations in prices—for example, if the price of coffee goes up (or down) by just 25 cents a pound, the value of one coffee futures contract will go up (or down) by a whopping $9,375 (that is, 37,500 × .25)!

Commodity	Size of Contract	Price System	Recent Market Value of a Single Contract[a]
Corn	5,000 bushels	Cents/bushel	$13,475
Oats	5,000 bushels	Cents/bushel	10,612
Soybeans	5,000 bushels	Cents/bushel	39,275
Wheat	5,000 bushels	Cents/bushel	21,500
Live cattle	40,000 pounds	Cents/pound	28,240
Pork bellies	40,000 pounds	Cents/pound	16,800
Cocoa	10 metric tons	Dollars/ton	14,560
Coffee	37,500 pounds	Cents/pound	47,250
Cotton	50,000 pounds	Cents/pound	29,000
Orange juice	15,000 pounds	Cents/pound	24,750
Copper	25,000 pounds	Cents/pound	39,000
Heating oil	42,000 gallons	Dollars/gallon	20,160
Unleaded gasoline	42,000 gallons	Dollars/gallon	18,480
Lumber	150,000 board feet	Dollars/1,000 board feet	26,610

[a]Contract values are representative of those that existed in January 1989. The market value of a contract is found by multiplying the size of the contract by its price system.

that had the price of silver declined by the same amount, you would have lost a lot of money. Although trading commodity futures can provide high potential returns, the risks are also very great.

Commodities Are Not for Everyone. Most individual investors use commodities for *speculation* as a way of going after the high rates of return that they offer. These vehicles can play an important role in a portfolio so long as the investor understands the risk involved and is well versed in the principles and mechanics of commodities trading. The quickest way to lose money in commodities is to jump in without knowing what you are doing. Because there is a lot of price volatility in commodities, and because commodities trading is done on a very low margin, the potential for loss is enormous. Only a portion of an individual's investment capital should be committed to commodities; the specific amount will, of course, be a function of the investor's aversion to risk and the amount of resources he or she has. An investor must be prepared mentally and should be in a position financially to absorb losses, perhaps a number of them.

Commodities trading is popular with individual investors because it is so affordable, and with all the safeguards, it's relatively hard to lose a lot of money. **Fantasy:** The low margin requirements may make commodities affordable to many investors, but it is *very easy* to lose money in the commodities market—and in a *big* way! It is certainly no place for inexperienced investors.

Financial Futures

In addition to commodities, futures contracts are also available on a wide variety of financial instruments. Known as *financial futures*, these contracts

---

futures contract

A contract providing for the delivery of a specified quantity of some commodity or financial instrument at some specified future date; there is an active secondary market for these products.

round-trip commission

A commission on a futures contract that covers both the buying and selling ends of the transaction.

EXHIBIT 14.9

Financial Futures Contract Specs

Financial futures are simply commodities contracts written on a wide assortment of financial assets, including everything from foreign currencies to various debt securities and the stock market. As with most commodities, the size and market value of financial futures contracts can be quite large.

Financial Instrument	Size of Contract	Recent Market Value of a Single Contract[a]
British pound	62,500 pounds	$114,925
Canadian dollar	$100,000 Canadian	83,460
Japanese yen	12,500,000 yen	103,587
Eurodollar	$1,000,000	908,100
U.S. Treasury bond	$100,000	89,220
U.S. Treasury bills	$1,000,000	921,100
S&P 500 Stock Index	$500 × index	140,350
NYSE Composite Stock Index	$500 × index	78,825
Value Line Stock Index	$500 × index	122,050
Major Market Index	$250 × index	106,550

[a]Contract market values are representative of those that existed in January 1989.

cover everything from foreign currencies to Treasury bonds and the stock market. Exhibit 14.9 lists some of the more actively traded financial futures. Note that financial futures, as a rule, are even bigger than commodities contracts; many have market values that approximate or exceed $100,000 and a few approach $1 million! Financial futures are simply an extension of the commodities concept. They are traded in the same market; their prices behave much like those of commodities; and they have the same low margin requirements. Although financial futures did not come into existence until the early 1970s, they enjoy an active market today—in fact, a number of them equal or exceed the trading volume of many of the old-line commodities contracts. For investors who regularly deal in bonds and other forms of fixed-income securities, they offer still another way of speculating on the behavior of interest rates. In addition, they offer a convenient way to speculate in the stock market or in the highly specialized, and often very profitable, foreign currency markets.

From the perspective of the individual investor, probably the most popular type of financial futures are the stock index contracts. **Stock index futures**—like the S&P 500 Stock Index or the Value Line Stock Index—can be used for purposes of speculating in the stock market. If you think the market is going up, you *buy* stock index futures; if you think it is headed down, you *sell* stock index futures. The key to success is the ability to *correctly predict the future course of the market*. Speculating in this way would prove profitable so long as the investor's expectations about the market actually materialize.

Options: Puts and Calls on Stocks and Other Financial Instruments

An *option* is a type of contract that gives an individual the right to either buy or sell a specific security or some other financial instrument. By far, the most popular form of option with individual investors is the *stock option*. Options are also available on stock market indexes (such as the S&P 500 Index), various debt instruments, foreign currencies, commodities, and financial futures. For a variety of reasons, however, these options simply have not caught on with many individual investors; accordingly, we will confine our discussion here to stock options.

Stock Options. A **stock option** is basically a negotiable instrument that gives the holder the right to buy or sell 100 shares of common stock in a given company at a specified price for a designated period of time. The price specified in the option is called the **striking price**; it is the price at which the holder of the option can buy or sell the stock, *regardless of what the stock itself is priced at in the market*. The period of time over which the option can be used is defined by its **expiration**

date (at which time the option, if not used, will be totally worthless). Thus, if you held a six-month option on Chrysler Corporation, that option would give you the right to, say, buy 100 shares of Chrysler common stock at a striking price of, say, $40 per share at any time over the next six months. Thus, no matter what happens to the market price of Chrysler stock, you can buy 100 shares of it at $40 per share for the next six months. If the price moves up, you stand to make money; if it does not, you will be out the cost of the option. Stock options have relatively short lives—most are written with expiration dates of eight months or less, meaning that the price of the underlying stock must move within the corresponding life of the option in order for the option holder to make money on the transaction.

Stock options can be bought and sold just like any other security. Today there exists a large and very active market for listed options. Nearly all the trading in options takes place on five listed options exchanges, the largest (and oldest) of which is the **Chicago Board Options Exchange (CBOE)**. In addition, stock options are traded on the AMEX, the NYSE, the Philadelphia Stock Exchange, and the Pacific Stock Exchange. There are over 600 stock options listed on these exchanges, most of which are on big NYSE stocks. There are also options on several dozen OTC stocks, such as Apple Computer, Intel, Liz Claiborne, and MCI. Exhibit 14.10 provides a short list of some popular and widely traded listed stock options.

Puts and Calls. So far we have discussed options that give the holder the right to either buy or sell stock or some other financial asset. Technically, an option to sell something is a put, and an option to buy is a call. More specifically, a **put** enables the option holder to sell the underlying security at a specified price over a set period of time; a **call**, in contrast, gives the holder the right to buy the securities at a stated price within a certain time period. Puts and calls possess value because they allow the option holder to participate in the price behavior of the underlying financial asset; they also provide attractive leverage opportunities, because they carry prices that are low relative to the market price of the underlying stock.

To illustrate, consider a call that gives the holder the right to buy 100 shares of a $50 stock at a price of, say, $45 a share. The stock would be priced at $50, but (in the absence of any price premium) the call would trade at an effective price of only $5 a share (which is the difference between the market price of the common and the price at which it can be purchased as specified on the call). However, since a single stock option always involves 100 shares of stock, the actual market price of the $5 call would be $5 × 100 shares = $500. Thus, if the price of the underlying stock went up $10 a share, the value of the stock option would go up 100 times that amount, or $1,000!

Puts and calls are unique because instead of being issued by the corporations that issue the underlying stocks, they are *created by investors*. The process works as follows. Suppose an individual wants to sell the right to buy 100 shares of common stock. The individual would *write* a call; the individual (or institution) writing the option is known as

---

stock index futures
Futures that allow for speculation in the performance of the whole stock market.

stock option
A negotiable instrument that gives the holder the right to buy or sell 100 shares of a particular common stock at a specified price for a designated time period.

striking price
The price at which the holder of a stock option can buy or sell the stock, regardless of the stock's market price.

expiration date
The period of time over which a stock option can be used.

Chicago Board Options Exchange (CBOE)
The dominant exchange on which listed stock options are traded.

put
An option to sell a specified financial asset on or before a given future date for a stated striking price.

call
An option to buy a specified financial asset on or before a given future date for a stated striking price.

EXHIBIT 14.10

Selected Stock Options

There are over 600 stock options listed on the various options exchanges. These options are written on large, well-known stocks that enjoy an active market.

Apple Computers	Digital Equipment	Merck
AT&T	Disney	Merrill Lynch
Atlantic Richfield	Eastman Kodak	Microsoft
Avon	Exxon	Motorola
Bank of America	Ford	Sony
Baxter Labs	GM	Smithkline-Beckman
Boeing	IBM	Sperry
CBS	Lotus	Unisys
Chrysler	McDonald's	Wall Mart
Coca Cola	MCA	Xerox

the **option maker** or **writer**. The option maker is entitled to receive the price paid for the put or call, less modest commissions and other transaction costs. The put or call option is now a full-fledged financial asset and trades in the open market much like any other security.

Puts and calls are both written and purchased through brokers and dealers and thus can be actively bought and sold in the secondary market. The writer stands behind the option at all times, regardless of how many times the security has been traded or who the current owners are; it is the writer who must buy (or deliver) the stocks according to the terms of the option.

The two basic types of options are puts and calls. Puts give you the right to sell something, and calls give you the right to buy. **Fact:** A put gives the holder the right to *sell* a specified amount of a particular stock, or some other financial asset, at a given price for a designated period of time. A call, in contrast, lets the holder *buy* a certain stock, or financial asset, at a stated price for a certain period of time.

How puts and calls work. Using the buyer's point of view, let us now briefly examine how puts and calls work and how they derive their value. To understand the mechanics of puts and calls, it is best to look at their profit-making potential. For example, consider a stock currently priced at $50 a share; assume we can buy a call on the stock for $500 that would enable us to purchase 100 shares of the stock at a fixed price of $50 each. A rise in the price of the underlying common stock is what we are hoping for. What is the profit from this transaction if the price of the stock in fact moves up to,

say, $75 by the expiration date on the call? The answer is that we will earn $25 ($75 − $50) on each of the 100 shares of stock in the call, or a total gross profit of some $2,500—and all from a $500 investment! This is because we own an option (a call) on the stocks, and as such, we can buy 100 shares of stock—from the option writer—at $50 each and immediately turn around and sell them in the market for $75 a share. We could make the same profit by investing directly in the common stock, but because we would have to invest $5,000 (100 shares × $50 per share), our rate of return would be much lower.

We can work out a similar situation for puts. Assume that for the same $50 stock we can pay $500 to buy a put, which gives us the right to sell 100 shares of stock at $50 each. Now we want the price of the stock to drop so that we can use the put as a way to make money. Assume our expectations are correct and the price of the stock drops to $25 a share. Again we can realize a profit of $25 for each of the 100 shares in the put. We can do this by going to the market and buying 100 shares of the stock at a price of $25 a share, and immediately turning around and selling them to the writer of the put at a price of $50 per share.

Fortunately, put and call investors do not have to exercise these options and make simultaneous buy and sell transactions in order to receive their profits, *since options do have value and can be traded in the secondary market.* The value of both puts and calls is directly linked to the market price of the underlying stock. The value of calls, therefore, increases as the market price of the underlying security rises, whereas the value of puts increases as the stock price declines. Thus, investors can get their money out of an option by selling it in the open market just as they would any other security.

Investing in Options. While there are several ways of investing in options, *buying puts and calls for speculation* is probably the simplest technique and the most popular with individual investors. Basically, it is just like buying stock (buy low and sell high) and, in fact, represents an alternative to investing in stock. For example, if an investor feels the market price of a particular stock is going to move up, one way of capturing that price appreciation is to buy a call on it. In contrast, if the investor feels the stock is about to drop in price, a put could convert the price decline into a profitable situation. In essence, investors buy options rather than stock whenever the options are likely to yield greater returns. The principle here, of course, is to get the largest return from one's investment dollar— something that can often be done with puts and calls because of the desirable leverage they offer.

To illustrate the essentials of speculating with options, consider a situation in which we have found a stock that we feel will move up in price over the next six months. What we would like to find out at this point is: What would happen if we buy a call on this stock rather than investing directly in the firm's common? To find out, let's see what the numbers show.

Assume the price of the stock is now $49, and we anticipate that within six months it will rise to about $65. Thus, if our expectations are correct, it should go up by $16 a share and, in so doing, generate a 33 percent rate of return over the six-month period ($16/$49 = .33). However, there are also some listed options available on this stock, and we want to see how they would do. We will use a six-month call with a $45 striking price as the basis for discussion. In this case, if the stock does indeed move to $65 a share before the option's expiration date, the call itself will be worth $2,000—that is, its value will be equal to the current market price of the underlying stock less the striking price stated on the call, or $65 − $45 = $20 × 100 shares in the call = $2,000. Given that the call could have been purchased for around $400 (the stock's market price of $49 less the striking price of $45 = $4 × 100 shares in the call), we would earn an incredible 400 percent rate of return in just six months!

(Again, the rate of return is found by dividing the profit from the investment—$2,000 − $400 = $1,600—by the amount invested—$400; thus, $1,600/$400 = 400%.)

Note in this example that the profit would be the same for both investments: Buying 100 shares of stock would result in $1,600 in profits, and so would the purchase of 1 call. Why, then, the big difference in the rate of return? The answer is simple: It takes $4,900 to buy 100 shares of the stock but only $400 to buy 1 call! This is the concept of leverage at work; with a call, we are able to capture all (or most) of the price appreciation of the underlying stock for a fraction of the cost. The result is a bigger bang from our investment dollar and a much higher rate of return. *There is also less risk on the down side,* since the most we can lose is the cost of the call. If the price of the stock failed to live up to our expectations and instead *dropped* to, say, $40 a share, we would lose $900 if we owned the stock, versus only $400 if we owned the call. Such performance explains why speculating with options is so popular with individual investors. Clearly, it does not take a lot of money to speculate in the market with options, and the payoffs can be substantial.

Making Options Transactions. Your broker can easily make transactions for you in any of the options listed on the CBOE, AMEX, or other options exchanges. The brokerage fees on the purchase or sale of options may differ slightly depending on the exchange on which they are traded or the options dealer through which the transaction is made. As a rule, the fees are similar to those charged on transactions in other listed securities. Information and price data on options can also be obtained from your stockbroker. Price quotations on listed options appear daily in *The Wall Street Journal;* an example and an explanation of how to read stock option quotations is provided in Exhibit 14.11.

Trading in options is not recommended for the beginning investor because of their highly special-

option maker (writer)
An individual or institution that writes (creates) a put or call option.

EXHIBIT 14.11

How to Read Put and Call Quotes

Note the effect that the expiration date has on the options. Options that mature in later months characteristically are more expensive than those with near-term expiration dates, because they have more time to move above or below the striking price.

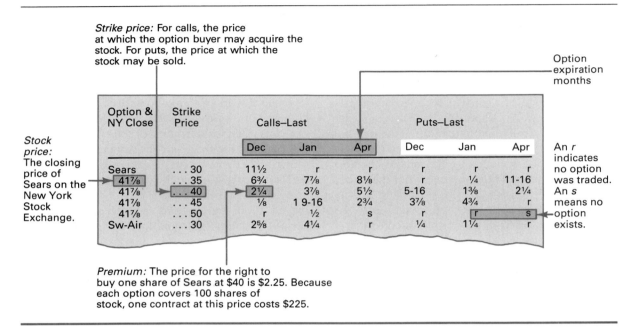

Strike price: For calls, the price at which the option buyer may acquire the stock. For puts, the price at which the stock may be sold.

Option expiration months

Stock price: The closing price of Sears on the New York Stock Exchange.

An *r* indicates no option was traded. An *s* means no option exists.

Premium: The price for the right to buy one share of Sears at $40 is $2.25. Because each option covers 100 shares of stock, one contract at this price costs $225.

ized nature. Also, although high potential returns exist, the probability of achieving them is quite low. In most situations, exercising the option doesn't make any sense; it winds up expiring as a worthless piece of paper—which results in a 100 percent loss on the investment in the option. Before attempting to trade in options, you should consult your broker or, better yet, talk to an experienced investor. Above all, you should be fully aware of the risk associated with options trading: They sound a lot safer than they really are!

Precious Metals and Gemstones

In addition to financial assets, such as stocks, bonds, and mutual funds, some people like to invest in precious metals, gemstones, and other so-called *hard assets*. During periods of high inflation, many of these investments tend to perform very nicely. Unfortunately, when inflation drops off—as it has since the early 1980s—they do not perform very well at all, as the demand for them drops off dra-

matically. The most popular forms of *precious metals* and *gemstones* include gold, silver, and diamonds. Although ownership of such minerals can be obtained in a variety of ways, the basic return from these investments comes in the form of growth in value—in other words, one attempts to "buy low and sell high." Because future prices tend to be affected by inflation as well as the changing supply of these minerals, such investments tend to be fairly risky. A slowdown in inflation or a sizable discovery of new sources of a given mineral can unfavorably affect its market price. On the other hand, increasing inflation and continued scarcity can favorably influence the return. Another factor that tends to affect the market value—and therefore the return—of precious metals and gemstones is the international political environment. In normal times, these investments are not especially popular, while in times of turmoil their demand tends to rise due to their tangible nature.

As a result of their somewhat speculative behavior, investments in precious metals and gemstones are not for everyone. Before making such an investment, you should assess its risk exposure/return potential, and its role in your investment plans.

Collectibles

Collectibles include a broad range of items that are found desirable for any number of reasons, such as beauty, scarcity, and age. Probably most significant is their ability to provide a hedge against inflation—the major factor accounting for the rapid growth in their popularity as investments during recent years. Some of the items commonly included in this market are stamps, coins, antiques, art, books, autographs, and antique cars. These forms of collecting often provide a great deal of pleasure and satisfaction as well as attractive potential returns.

The investment returns from collectibles come in the form of appreciation in value. While certain psychic income may be realized in the form of aesthetic pleasure, the financial return, if any, is realized only when the item is sold. The acquisition of collectibles commonly results from an individual's personal interests, yet on a strictly financial basis items that have a good market and are likely to appreciate in value are the ones to collect. If an item under consideration is expensive, its value and authenticity should be confirmed by an expert prior to purchase (there are many unscrupulous dealers in collectible items). After purchase, one should make certain to store collectibles in a safe place and adequately insure them against all relevant perils (see Chapter 11).

SUMMARY

- Mutual fund shares represent an ownership position in a managed portfolio of securities; since the late 1970s, mutual funds have enjoyed considerable growth in amount of assets under management, as many investors who lacked the time, know-how, or commitment to manage their own portfolios turned to mutual funds as as an investment outlet.

- By investing in one or more of the many types of mutual funds, shareholders benefit from a level of diversification and investment performance they might otherwise find difficult to achieve; moreover, they can establish a sound investment program with a limited amount of capital and obtain a variety of investor services not available elsewhere.

- Real estate has appeal as an investment vehicle due to its attractive cash flow attributes, possible tax benefits, and the general tendency for property to appreciate in value; most real estate transactions involve the use of leverage, which adds risk to the investment but often makes for much higher returns. Investing in real estate can take many forms, including speculating in raw land, buying income-producing residential or commercial property, or investing in limited partnerships or REITs.

- Commodities and financial futures are contracts that call for the future delivery of a given product or financial asset; such futures contracts are actively traded, and can be bought and sold just like common stocks. These are highly specialized investment vehicles that involve tremendous exposure to loss—the futures contracts control large amounts of the underlying commodity or financial instruments and, as a result, can undergo *very* wide price swings.

- An option provides the investor with the right to buy (a call) or sell (a put) a specified financial asset at a specified price for a specified period of time; while options are available on stock market indexes, various debt instruments, foreign currencies, commodities, and financial futures, the most popular type of option with individuals is the *stock option*. There are listed stock options actively traded on over 600 companies, each giving investors the right to buy or sell 100 shares of common stock in one of these 600 companies.

- Precious metals (gold and silver), gemstones (diamonds and rubies), and collectible items (stamps, coins, and antique cars) can be acquired for investment purposes; such investments not only provide potentially attractive returns, in the form of price appreciation, they also provide pleasure and satisfaction to the investor.

QUESTIONS AND PROBLEMS

1. Define and discuss investment companies. Distinguish between open-end and closed-end types. Which is more popular?

2. What is a mutual fund? Discuss what is meant by the load charge on a mutual fund. Distinguish between a normal load fund and a back-end load fund. What are 12(b)-1 fees? How can you tell what kind of fees and charges a fund has?

3. Look at the mutual fund quotes on page 496. How much would you have to pay to buy Fidelity Select–Financial Services (SIFnS)? How much would you receive if you wanted to sell it? How much would you pay if you wanted to buy shares in the Fiduciary Capital (Fidu Cap) fund? What front-end load charges would you pay with each of these funds? Which of the funds listed in these quotes (on page 496) levy 12(b)-1 fees; which ones have some sort of redemption fees; which ones are true no-loads?

4. How are mutual funds classified? Briefly describe four different types of mutual funds. How do the objectives of various mutual funds differ?

5. What's the difference between an equity-income fund and a growth-and-income fund? Which is likely to be subject to a greater amount of share price volatility: a high-yield bond fund or an intermediate-term bond fund? Explain.

6. What are the most common reasons for purchasing mutual funds? Is financial return important to mutual fund investors? Explain.

7. Describe several types of services offered by mutual funds. How do automatic reinvestment plans work? What is phone switching, and why would investors want to use this type of service?

8. What are fund families? What advantages do these families offer investors? Are there any disadvantages? Using something like *The Wall Street Journal,* or perhaps your local newspaper, find a couple examples of fund families; list some of the mutual funds they offer.

9. Using a source of information like *Barron's, Forbes,* or *Money,* select four mutual funds— (a) a growth fund, (b) a balanced fund, (c) a sector fund, and (d) a high-yield corporate bond fund—that you feel would make good investments. Briefly explain why you selected the funds.

10. About a year ago, Dave Kidwell bought some shares in the Hi-Flyer Mutual Fund. He bought the stock at $24.50 a share, and it now trades at $26.00. Last year the fund paid dividends of 40 cents a share and had capital gains distributions of $1.83 a share. Using the approximate yield formula (Equation 14.1), what rate of return did Dave earn on his investment? Would he have made a 20 percent rate of return if the stock had risen to $30 a share?

11. Define and briefly discuss the role of each of the following in evaluating a proposed real estate investment: (a) cash flow and taxes, (b) appreciation in value, and (c) the use of leverage.

12. How and why is leverage used in real estate? What effect, if any, does leverage have on an investment's rate of return?

13. Describe, compare, and contrast some of the more popular forms of real estate investing.

14. Briefly distinguish between (a) a real estate limited partnership, and (b) a real estate investment trust (REIT). Briefly note the different types of real estate limited partnerships; do the same for REITs.

15. Patti Arneson is thinking about investing in some residential income property; it can be purchased for $200,000. Patti can either pay cash for the property or put up $50,000 of her own money and borrow $150,000 at 9½ percent interest. The property is expected to generate $30,000 a year after all expenses but *before* interest and income taxes. Assume that Patti is in the 28 percent tax bracket. Calculate her return on investment assuming that she (a) borrows $150,000 as proposed, and (b) pays the full $200,000 from her own funds.

16. Briefly define, compare, and contrast commodity futures and financial futures. Why are specialized investor skills so important when investing in commodities and financial futures? What role does the size of the futures contracts play in the profit or loss exposure

of commodities and financial futures investors?

17. Using the contract specifications in Exhibit 14.8, describe how much profit or loss you would make in the following transactions:

   a. You buy a wheat contract at $2.26 a bushel and sell it at $3.10 a bushel.

   b. The price of soybeans goes up 90 cents a bushel, and you own four soybean contracts.

   c. You recently purchased a coffee contract, and the price drops 27½ cents a pound.

   d. You sell two heating oil contracts at $1.10 a gallon, and the price of heating oil drops to 78 cents a gallon.

   e. You hold a lumber contract, and the price of lumber just jumped $2.25 per 1,000 board feet.

18. Mike Jefferson bought three cotton futures contracts when cotton was trading for 68½ cents a pound. Cotton has since risen to 90 cents a pound, and Mike decides to sell his three contracts. What return on investment will Mike make given that he purchased each contract with a margin deposit of only $5,000?

19. What are options? What is a put option? How does a put differ from a call? Briefly explain how an investor could make money by buying puts on a stock; by buying calls on a stock.

20. Judy Rothman recently bought a six-month call on a stock with a $65 striking price; she paid $300 for the call. How much profit, and what rate of return, would Judy make if the price of the underlying stock went to $80 a share by the call's expiration date? What would happen to Judy's profits if the stock stayed at $65? How about if the price of the stock dropped to $50 a share?

21. Not long ago, Frank Stevic bought a 3-month *put* on a stock—he did this because he thought the stock in question (Roller Aerobics, Inc.) was overpriced and due to take a big fall. The put carried a striking price of $35, and he paid $250 for the option. How much profit, and what rate of return, will Frank make if the price of the underlying stock does, in fact, fall from $35 a share to $22.75 by the expiration date on the put? What will happen to Frank's profits if he's wrong, and the stock continues to go up—to, say, $50 a share?

22. Briefly discuss the popularity of precious metal investments, and explain their basic risk-return characteristics.

23. What are collectibles? Briefly describe their risk-return characteristics, as well as any other benefits they might offer an investor.

CASE PROBLEMS

14.1 Dave's Dilemma: Common Stocks or Mutual Funds?

Dave Brubaker has worked in the management services division of Ace Consultants for the past five years. He currently earns an annual salary of about $45,000. At 33, he is still a bachelor and has accumulated about $25,000 in savings over the past few years. He keeps his savings in a money market account at CitiBank Savings and Loan, where it earns about 6.5 percent interest. Dave is contemplating withdrawing $15,000 from this account and investing it in common stock. He believes that such an investment will probably earn more than 6.5 percent. Marlene Anson, a close friend, suggests that he invest in mutual fund shares. Dave has approached you, his broker, for advice.

Questions

1. Explain to Dave the key reasons for purchasing mutual fund shares.

2. What special fund features might help Dave achieve his investment objectives?

3. What type(s) of mutual fund(s) would you recommend to Dave?

4. What recommendations would you make with respect to Dave's dilemma about whether to go into stocks or mutual funds? Explain.

14.2 Jane Decides to Dabble in Options

Jane Normington, a systems analyst for Butler Products, is interested in buying 100 shares of Xerox. The stock is selling at $52 a share, but because Xerox will soon receive certain large orders from abroad, Jane expects the stock price to increase to $60 per share. If Jane buys the stock at $52 and sells it one year later at $60, she stands to make a profit of $800, or a 15.4 percent gain (ignoring any dividends). Jane recently read an article about options in a magazine published by a brokerage firm and, as a result, has decided to purchase a call option on Xerox rather than buy the stock itself. She pays $300 for the call, which allows her to buy 100 shares of Xerox at $50 per share any time during the next 90 days.

Questions

1. How high must the price of Xerox stock rise in order for Jane to break even on the option transaction?

2. If the price of Xerox rises to $60 per share before the expiration date on the call, what will Jane's net profit be from the option transaction?

3. Based on comparative profits figures, would Jane have been better off by investing directly in the stock? What about in terms of comparative return on investment figures? Explain.

FOR MORE INFORMATION

General Information Articles

Boroson, Warren, "Real Estate for the Small Investor," *Sylvia Porter's Personal Finance,* November 1988, pp. 54–57.

Meyer, Marsha, "The Right and Wrong Ways to Buy Gold," *Money,* August 1987, pp. 47–54.

Rachlin, Jill, "Racing the Market with Options," *U.S. News & World Report,* September 21, 1987, pp. 75–76.

Schurenberg, Eric, "Selling a Fund: When to Take the Money and Run," *Money,* November 1986, pp. 237–240.

Serwer, Andrew Evan, "Picking a Limited Partnership," *Fortune 1989 Investor's Guide,* pp. 145–150.

Walbert, Laura, "How to Pick a Mutual Fund," *Forbes,* September 7, 1987, pp. 162–164.

Government Documents & Other Publications

The ABC's of Option Trading. Education Service Bureau; Dow Jones & Co.; Box 300; Princeton, NJ 08540.

The Basic Facts About Commodity Futures Trading. Commodity Futures Trading Commission; Office of Communication and Education; 2033 K Street, N.W.; Washington, D.C. 20581.

The Investment Company Institute's Guide to Mutual Funds. Investment Company Institute; 1600 M Street, N.W.; Washington, D.C. 20036.

REIT Fact Book. National Association of REIT's; 1101 – 17th Street, N.W., Suite #700; Washington, D.C. 20036.

1. Using the asset values on Mark and Ana's latest balance sheet (after they buy the condo) and the interest rates given in the case, calculate how much annual interest income they should receive in 1990 from

    - their checking account
    - their money market account
    - their $1,000 1-year certificate of deposit
    - their $500 1-year certificate of deposit

2. Prepare an inventory of Mark and Ana's savings and investment holdings as of March 1, 1990. Assume that the market value of the Fidelity Mutual Fund has not changed substantially from its value on January 1, 1990, and that the dividends and capital gains distributions from this investment will be the same as in 1989.

3. Approximately how much will Mark and Ana's total annual income from dividends, capital gains distributions, and interest be in 1990? Why will it probably be less than in 1989?

4. What is the current dividend yield on the Fidelity Puritan mutual fund investment?

5. Mark and Ana purchased their Fidelity Puritan shares in December, 1988. What was the approximate yield on this investment from December 1988 to December 1989? Compare the yield on this stock mutual fund to the yield on Mark and Ana's less risky investments. Did the fund provide an adequate yield for the risk taken over that one-year period?

6. Track the net asset value (NAV) of Fidelity Puritan over a two-week period. The needed information can be found in *The Wall Street Journal* and in many daily newspapers.

7. From looking at the mutual fund listings, can you tell whether Fidelity Puritan Fund charges a front-end load? If so, what percent?

8. In March 1990, Mark and Ana sold their Apple stock for $37.75 a share and their General Motors stock for $85.50 a share, paying broker's commissions of $205. Of this amount, $96 was for selling the Apple stock and the rest for selling the General Motors stock. Calculate the before-tax capital gain (loss) on the

    - Apple stock investment
    - General Motors stock investment

9. Given their marginal tax bracket, approximately how much of their capital gain would be paid in federal income taxes in 1990? Or in the case of a net loss, approximately how much would their capital loss save them in federal income taxes in 1990?

10. Mark and Ana's certificates of deposit will mature in June 1990, and they are trying to decide how to reinvest $1,500 plus interest. They are considering two different stock investments (described on page 532). What is the current dividend yield on each of these investments? What would the approximate total yield be on each given the following assumptions? They plan to keep the investment five years.

	Blue-Chip Stock	Aggressive Growth Stock
Current market value	$35.50	$22.25
Current dividend income	1.90	.20
Average annual dividend income	2.00	.25
Market value in five years	45.00	50.00

11. Mark and Ana are also considering investing this $1,500 plus interest in two corporate bonds that are currently selling at discount of $787.50 each. The bonds have a face value of $1,000, mature in five years, and have an A rating from Moody's. They pay annual interest of $50 each. What is the current yield on this bond investment? Calculate the yield-to-maturity on these bonds.

12. An acquaintance of Mark and Ana thought that they should invest in the aggressive growth stock on margin. Would you recommend this strategy for Mark and Ana? Why or why not?

13. What type of savings/investment vehicle would you recommend for Mark and Ana—the blue-chip stock, the aggressive growth stock, the corporate bond, or something else? Remember their goals and their tolerance for risk when making the recommendation. Justify your recommendation.

PART VI

Retirement and Estate Planning

C H A P T E R 15

Meeting Retirement Goals

Financial Facts or Fantasies

Are the following statements financial facts (true) or fantasies (false)?

- The first step in retirement planning is to set your retirement goals.
- In order to receive maximum social security retirement benefits, a worker must retire before his or her 65th birthday.
- Social security retirement benefits should be sufficient to provide retired workers and their spouses with a comfortable standard of living.
- Since an annuity is only as good as the insurance company that stands behind it, you should check the company's financial rating before buying an annuity.
- Because participation in a company's basic pension plan is mandatory, you're entitled to immediate vesting of all contributions.
- Your contributions to an IRA account may or may not be tax deductible, depending in part on your level of income.

Do you know your life expectancy? Well, if you're like most college students, and are in your late teens or early twenties, it is very likely that you have another 50 or 60 years to live. While such a prospect can indeed be viewed with delight, it should also bring into focus the need for careful retirement planning. After all, you will not be working all of those 50 or 60 years; you will probably work for only about 40 years—and perhaps less—before you retire. If this scenario holds true, you will spend 10 to 20 years in retirement. The challenge, of course, is to do it in style—and that is where retirement planning comes into play! Rudy and Maria Ramirez appreciate the importance of retirement planning. In their mid-thirties, they both work: He's a construction superintendent and she's an elementary school principal. Several years ago, they set up a retirement program that they feel will enable them to retire in comfort by the time they are in their late fifties. The Ramirezes strongly believe that if they want to enjoy a comfortable retirement, they must do something about it now. And they're right! The biggest mistake people make in retirement planning is that *they wait too long to start doing something about it.* It is understandable that when you are young, it is difficult to get excited about an event that will not take place for another 35 to 40 years. But don't wait too long! For the longer you wait, the harder it will be to reach the kind of retirement income you'd like.

AN OVERVIEW OF RETIREMENT PLANNING ■

> Retirement planning is a key element in the financial planning process; to be effective, however, it should begin relatively early in life and involve a strategy of systematically accumulating retirement funds. Stop for a moment and think about how you intend to plan for retirement. At what age do you want to retire? What size nest egg do you want at retirement, and how do you intend to reach that goal?

Like budgets, taxes, and investments, retirement planning is vital to your financial well-being and should be viewed as a critical link in your personal financial plans. Yet it's difficult for most people under the age of 35 to develop a well-defined set of plans for retirement. The reason is that there are just too many years to go to retirement and thus too many uncertainties that have to be dealt with. Uncertainty about inflation, social security, family size, the type of pension to which you will be entitled, and the amount of assets you will have accumulated by the time you are ready to retire all make accurate forecasting extremely difficult. However, contrary to what some people may think, it is just this kind of uncertainty that makes retirement planning so important! To cope with uncertainty, you must plan for a variety of outcomes; and you need to monitor and modify your plans as your hopes, abilities, and personal finances change.

Role of Retirement Planning in Personal Financial Planning

The financial planning process would be incomplete without *retirement planning*. Certainly there is no financial goal more important than achieving a comfortable standard of living in retirement. In many respects, retirement planning captures the very essence of financial planning: It is forward looking (perhaps more so than any other function of financial planning), has an impact on both current and future standard of living, and, if successful, can be highly rewarding and make a significant contribution to net worth. Because of the power of compound interest, it is really *never too early to start doing something about retirement planning.* For example, if you start putting $2,000 a year away when you're 35, it will grow to $482,000 by the time you are 65, when invested at a 12 percent rate of return. Not a bad deal, considering your total out-of-pocket investment over this 30-year period would amount to only $60,000. But look at what you end up with if you start this investment program 10 years earlier, at age 25: That same $2,000 a year will grow to more than *$1.5 million* by the time you're 65. Think of it—for another $20,000 ($2,000 a year for an extra 10 years), you can more than triple the terminal value of your investment! Of course, its not the extra $20,000 that's tripling your money; rather, it's *compound interest* that's doing all the work. The message is clear: *Because of compound interest, the sooner you start a retirement plan, the better off you're going to be.* Practically speaking, it is probably best to start thinking seriously about retirement when in your late twenties or early thirties, and *after* you have addressed career planning and early family formation matters.

The first step in retirement planning is to set *retirement goals* for yourself; take some time to define the things you want to do in retirement, the standard of living you hope to maintain, the level of income you would like to receive, and any special retirement goals you may have (like buying a retirement home in Arizona, or taking an around-the-world cruise). Such goals are important in giving direction to your retirement planning. Of course, like all goals, they are subject to change over time as the situations/conditions in your life change. Once you know what you want out of retirement, the next step is to establish the *size of the nest egg* you're going to have to build in order to achieve your retirement goals. In essence, how much money will you need to retire the way you would like?

The final step is to formulate an *investment program* that will enable you to build up your required nest egg. This usually involves creating some type of systematic savings plan (putting away a certain amount each year) and identifying the types of investment vehicles that will best meet your retirement needs. This phase of your retirement program is closely related to two other aspects of financial planning—investment and tax planning. Investments and investment planning (see Chapters 12 through 14) are the vehicles through which retirement funds are built up. They comprise the active, ongoing part of retirement planning in which you manage and invest the funds you have set aside for retirement. It is no coincidence that a major portion of most individual investor portfolios is devoted to building up a pool of funds that can be used in retirement; instead, this is consistent with the vital role that retirement plays in financial planning. Taxes and tax planning (see Chapter 4) are also important, since one of the major objectives of sound retirement planning is to legitimately shield as much income as possible from taxes and, in so doing, maximize the accumulation of retirement funds.

The first step in retirement planning is to set your retirement goals. **Fact:** In order to provide direction to your retirement plans, you should begin by defining your goals: the things you want to do in retirement, the standard of living you want to maintain, and the level of income you would like.

Retirement Goals

People have all sorts of retirement goals. Playing more golf, fishing, traveling, or pursuing a favorite hobby are just a few examples. To have the income to realize these goals, people should consider the age at which they will retire and what their financial position is likely to be at that time.

Age at Retirement. Estimating when you are likely to retire is important, because it lets you know how much time you have to save for retirement. Many workers used to elect to retire at age 60, or even 55, several years ago. But the last couple of years have seen a trend toward later retirement. Some people now remain in the work force until age 70 or longer. If you think that a *shorter* working career is for you, then you must take the steps to put more money aside each year for retirement than others who plan to work for as long as they are physically and mentally capable.

Financial Position and Goals. Your financial position at retirement depends not only on your retirement plans but—perhaps even more so—on your choice of career and life style. Remember that the quality of your life and life style goals must be chosen on the basis of projected income and expenditures. Devoting some income toward retirement is essential to economic security in old age. You must be careful not to satisfy low-priority, short-run desires at the expense of high-priority, long-run objectives.

Estimating Income Needs

Retirement planning would be much simpler if we lived in a static economy. Unfortunately (or perhaps fortunately), we don't and as a result, both your personal budget and the general economy are subject to considerable change over time, making accurate forecasting of retirement needs difficult at best. Even so, it is a *necessary task,* and one that you can handle in one of two ways. One strategy is to plan for retirement in a *series of short runs*. A good way to do this is to state your retirement income objectives as a percentage of your present earnings. For example, if you desire a retirement income equal to 80 percent of your final take-home pay, you can determine the amount necessary to fund this need. Then, every three to five years, you can revise and update your plan.

Alternatively, you can follow a *long-term* approach in which you actually formulate the level of income you would like to receive in retirement, along with the amount of funds you must amass in order to achieve the desired standard of living. Rather than addressing the problem in a series of short-run plans, this approach goes 20 or 30 years into the future—to the time when you will retire—in order to determine how much saving and investing you must do today to achieve your long-run retirement goals. Of course, if conditions and/or expectations change dramatically, it may be necessary to make corresponding alterations to your long-run retirement goals and strategies.

Determining Future Retirement Needs. To illustrate how future retirement needs and income requirements can be formulated, let us consider the case of Jack and Lois Winters. In their mid-thirties, they have two children and an annual income of about $60,000 before taxes. Jack and Lois have given some thought to retirement but now believe that even though it is still some 30 years away, they should give some serious thought to their situation to see if they will be able to pursue a retirement life style that appeals to them. Exhibit 15.1 contains a worksheet that provides the basic steps to follow in determining retirement needs; this exhibit shows how the Winters have used the worksheet to estimate their retirement income and determine the amount of investment assets they must accumulate to meet their retirement objectives.

Jack and Lois began their calculations by determining what their *household expenditures* will likely be in retirement. They have made their estimate on the basis of being able to maintain a "comfortable" standard of living—one that will not be extravagant yet will allow them to do the things they would like in retirement. A simple yet highly effective way to derive an estimate of expected household expenditures is to base it on the current level of such expenses. Assume the Winterses' annual household expenditures (excluding savings) currently run about $42,000 a year—this information can be readily obtained by referring to their most recent income and expenditures statement. Making some obvious adjustments for the different lifestyle they will have in retirement—their children will no longer be living at home, their home will be paid for, and so on—the Winters estimate that they will be able to achieve the standard of living they'd like in retirement at an annual level of household expenditures equal to about 70 percent of the current amount. Thus, *in terms of today's dollars,* their estimated household expenditures in retirement will be $42,000 × .70 = *$29,400.* (This process is summarized in steps A through D in Exhibit 15.1.)

Estimating Retirement Income. The next question is: Where will they get the money to meet their projected household expenses of $29,400 a year? They have addressed this problem by estimating what their *income* will be in retirement— again *in terms of today's dollars.* Their two basic sources of retirement income are social security and employer-sponsored pension plans. Based on today's retirement tables, they estimate that they will receive about $13,000 a year from social secur-

ity (as we'll see later in this chapter, you can now receive an estimate directly from the Social Security Administration of what your future social security benefits are likely to be when you retire) and another $9,000 from their employer pension plans, for a total projected income of *$22,000.* When this is compared to their projected household expenditures, it is clear that the Winters will be facing an annual shortfall of $7,400 (see steps E through I in Exhibit 15.1). This is the amount of retirement income that they must come up with; otherwise, they will have to reduce the standard of living they hope to enjoy in retirement.

At this point, we need to introduce the *inflation factor* to our projections in order to put the annual shortfall of $7,400 in terms of retirement dollars. Here we make the assumption that both income and expenditures will undergo the same average rate of inflation, causing the shortfall to grow by that rate over time. In essence, 30 years from now, the annual shortfall is going to amount to a lot more than $7,400. How large it will grow to will, of course, be a function of what happens to inflation. Let us assume that the Winters think inflation, on average, over the next 30 years will amount to 5 percent. Using the compound value table from Appendix A, we find that the *inflation factor* for 5 percent and 30 years is 4.32; multiplying this inflation factor by the annual shortfall of $7,400 gives the Winters an idea of what that figure will be by the time they retire: $7,400 × 4.32 = *$31,970,* or nearly $32,000 a year (see steps J to L in Exhibit 15.1). Thus, based on their projections, the shortfall will amount to $32,000 a year when they retire 30 years from now. This is the amount they will have to come up with through their own supplemental retirement program.

Funding the Shortfall. The final two steps in this estimation process are (1) to determine *how big the retirement nest egg must be* in order to cover the projected annual income shortfall and (2) to determine *how much to save each year* in order to accumulate the required amount by the time the Winters retire. To find out how much money they are going to have to accumulate by retirement, they must estimate the rate of return they think they will be able to earn on their investments *after* they retire. This will tell them how big their nest egg will have to be by retirement in order to eliminate the

EXHIBIT 15.1
Estimating Future Retirement Needs

This worksheet will help you define your income requirements in retirement, the size
of your retirement nest egg, and the amount that you must save annually to achieve
your given retirement goals.

PROJECTING RETIREMENT INCOME AND INVESTMENT NEEDS

Name(s) *Jack & Lois Winters*   Date *June, 1990*

I. Estimated Household Expenditures in Retirement:

A. Approximate number of years to retirement *30*
B. *Current* level of annual household
   expenditures, excluding savings .... $ *42,000*
C. Estimated household expenses in retirement *as a
   percent* of current expenses *70%*
D. Estimated annual household expenditures
   in retirement (B × C) .... $ *29,400*

II. Estimated Income in Retirement:

E. Social security, annual income .... $ *13,000*
F. Company/employer pension plans,
   annual amounts .... $ *9,000*
G. Other sources, annual amounts .... $ *0*
H. Total annual income (E + F + G) .... $ *22,000*

I. Additional required income, or *annual shortfall* (D − H) .... $ *7,400*

III. Inflation Factor:

J. Expected average annual rate of inflation
   over the period to retirement *5%*
K. Inflation factor (in Appendix A):
   Based on *30* years to retirement (A) and an expected
   average annual rate of inflation (J) of *5%* *4.322*
L. Size of inflation-adjusted
   annual shortfall (I × K) .... $ *32,000*

IV. Funding the Shortfall:

M. Anticipated return on assets held
   after retirement *10%*
N. Amount of retirement funds required — size of nest egg (L ÷ M) .... $ *320,000*

O. Expected rate of return on
   investments *prior* to retirement *12%*

P. Compound interest factor (in Appendix B):
   Based on *30* years to retirement (A) and an expected
   rate of return on investments of *12%* (O) *241*
Q. Annual savings required to fund
   retirement nest egg (N ÷ P) .... $ *1,328*

Note: Parts I and II are prepared in terms of current (today's) dollars.

expected annual shortfall of $32,000. Let us assume this rate of return is estimated at 10 percent, in which case the Winters must accumulate *$320,000* by retirement. This figure is found by *capitalizing* the estimated shortfall of $32,000 at a 10 percent rate of return: $32,000 ÷ .10 = $320,000 (see steps M and N). Given a 10 percent rate of return, such a nest egg will yield $32,000 a year: $320,000 × .10 = $32,000. And so long as the capital ($320,000) remains untouched, it will generate the same amount of annual income for as long as the Winters live and can eventually become a part of their estate.

Now that the Winters know how big their nest egg has to be, the final question is: How are they going to accumulate such an amount by the time they retire? For most people, that means setting up a *systematic savings plan,* and putting away a certain amount *each* year. To find out how much must be saved each year to achieve a targeted sum in the future, we can use the table of annuity factors in Appendix B. The appropriate interest factor is a function of the rate of return one can (or expects to) generate and the length of the investment period. In the Winterses' case, there are 30 years to go until retirement, meaning the length of their investment period is 30 years. If they feel they will be able to earn an average rate of return of 12 percent on their investments over this 30-year period, they will want to use a 12 percent, 30-year interest factor; from Appendix B, we see that this equals 241. Because the Winters must accumulate $320,000 by the time they retire, *the amount that they will have to save each year* (over the next 30 years) can be found by *dividing* the amount they need to accumulate by the appropriate interest factor, that is, $320,000 ÷ 241 = *$1,328* (see steps O to Q in Exhibit 15.1).

The Winters now know what they must do to achieve the kind of retirement they want: Put away nearly $1,350 a year and invest it at an average annual rate of 12 percent over the next 30 years. If they can do that, they will have their $320,000 retirement nest egg in 30 years. How they actually invest their money so as to achieve the desired 12 percent rate of return will, of course, be a function of the investment strategy they adopt. They will have to decide which investment vehicles and strategies to use in building up their pool of retirement funds. All the worksheet tells us is how much money we will need, not how we will get there; it is at this point that investment management enters the picture.

The procedure outlined here admittedly is a bit simplified and does take a few shortcuts, but considering the amount of uncertainty imbedded in the long-range projections being made, it does provide a viable estimate of retirement income and investment needs. The procedure certainly is far superior to the alternative of doing nothing! One important simplifying assumption in the procedure, though, is that it ignores the income that can be derived from the *sale of a house*. The sale of a house not only offers some special tax features for older people (see Chapter 4) but can generate a substantial amount of cash flow as well. Certainly, if inflation does occur in the future (and it will!), it will very likely drive up home prices right along with the cost of everything else. A lot of people sell their homes around the time they retire and either move into smaller houses (often in Sun Belt retirement communities) or decide to rent in order to avoid all the problems of homeownership. Of course, the cash flow from the sale of a house can have a substantial effect on the size of the retirement nest egg. However, rather than trying to factor it into the forecast of retirement income and needs, we suggest that you *recognize* the existence of this cash flow source in your retirement planning, and consider it as a cushion against all the uncertainty inherent in retirement planning projections.

Computer-Based Retirement Planning

Most of the fully integrated financial planning software packages contain retirement planning programs that will perform the same basic forecasting functions as those in Exhibit 15.1. In essence, you respond to a few key questions about expected inflation, desired rate of return on investments, and current levels of income and expenditures, and the computer will determine the size of any income shortfall, the amount of retirement funds that must be accumulated over time, and different ways to achieve the desired retirement nest egg. An example of one such program is *Capital Accumulation Analysis* by Micro Planning Systems (of Burlingame,

EXHIBIT 15.2

Sources of Income for Retired Workers (in Percentages of Those Receiving Income from Source)

Nearly all retired workers (and/or their spouses) derive at least part of their income from social security benefits; in contrast, only about half of the retired population receive income from employer-sponsored pension plans.

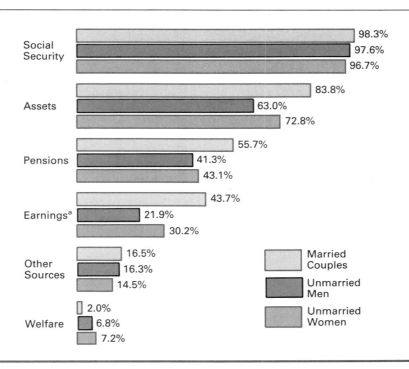

California); it is available for use on IBM PCs and compatible machines. One of the attractive features of these programs is that they allow you to easily run through a series of "what if" exercises. By just punching a few buttons, you can change one or more of the key variables to see their impact on the size of your retirement nest egg and the amount of money you must put away annually. For example, you can find out *what* would happen *if* you failed to achieve the desired rate of return on your investments. In addition to this important retirement planning function, such software will often have routines that allow you to keep track of various retirement accounts. In this way, you can readily see how your performance is stacking up to your retirement goals—whether you are ahead of schedule and, if not, what you can do to get back on track. Thus, modern, computer-based retirement planning assists you not only in establishing retire-

ment goals and plans, but also in keeping track of your progress toward those objectives.

Sources of Retirement Income

As Exhibit 15.2 reveals, the three principal sources of income for retired people are social security, assets (income-producing types such as savings, stocks, and bonds), and pension plans. Just about every retired worker receives social security income, about 65 to 85 percent obtain at least some of their income from savings and/or investment assets, and, surprisingly, only about half (40 to 55 percent) receive benefits from some type of employer-provided pension plan. However, keep in mind these are *sources* of retirement income and not dollar amounts. The *amount* of income retired individuals receive will, of course, vary from amounts that are barely above the poverty line to six-figure incomes. The amount received in retirement depends on a number of variables, the most important of which is the level of preretirement earnings. Obviously, the more individuals make before they retire, the more they will receive in social security benefits and from company-sponsored pension plans—and, very likely, the greater the amount of income-producing assets they will hold. In this chapter, we will examine social security and various types of pension plans and retirement programs. In addition, we will look briefly at an investment vehicle that is designed especially for retirement income: the *annuity*.

SOCIAL SECURITY

Social security is an important source of income for retired people; however, if it's the *only* source, the retiree is likely to find that his or her standard of living will be considerably less than what had been hoped for. Do you think social security will be around when you're ready to retire, and assuming it is, how much do you think you'll receive in monthly benefits? How important will these social security benefits be to you—that is, what portion of your total retirement income do you suspect they will constitute? Take a few minutes before reading on to consider these questions.

The Social Security Act of 1935 was a piece of landmark legislation. Not only did it create a basic retirement program for working Americans at all income levels, it also established a number of other social programs, all of which are administered under the auspices of the *Old Age, Survivor's, Disability, and Health Insurance (OASDHI) program.* Some of the other services include supplementary security income (SSI), unemployment insurance, public assistance, welfare services, and provision for black lung benefits. This chapter gives primary attention to the old age and survivor's portion of the act, since it has a direct bearing on retirement planning. The disability and health benefits of social security are discussed in Chapter 10.

Basic Concepts

To fully appreciate the underlying merits of social security as a retirement program, you need to understand (1) its financing, (2) its solvency, and (3) its investment attributes.

Financing. The cash benefits provided by social security are derived from the payroll taxes (FICA) paid by covered employees and their employers. As pointed out in Chapter 4, the tax rate in 1989 was 15.02 percent, of which one half, or 7.51 percent, was paid by the employee and the other half by the employer. Self-employed persons are also covered by social security. In 1989 they paid a slightly lower *total* rate (of 13.02 percent), but because there are no employers to share the burden, self-employed people have to pay the full amount themselves. Regardless of whether the individual is an employee or self-employed, the indicated tax rate applies to a maximum *wage base,* which increases each year with the average wage inflation rate. For 1989, social security taxes were paid on the first $48,000 of wages earned, or self-employed income. Thus, the maximum social security tax for an *employee* in 1989 was $3,605 ($48,000 × 7.51 percent) and for the *self-employed,* it was $6,250 ($48,000 × 13.02 percent).

For years, social security operated on a *pay-as-you-go* approach, collecting roughly enough in payroll taxes each year to cover benefit payments to retirees. But because of some growing problems with this system, Congress passed legislation in the late 1970s and early 1980s that moved social security away from a current funding approach and in the direction of a pension fund, in which resources to at least partially finance future benefits are accumulated well in advance. Because of these changes, the social security system is now running *fairly substantial annual surpluses,* as it's taking in more than it pays out—for example, in 1988 this surplus amounted to nearly $50 billion, and it's growing every year! These surpluses are channeled into social security trust funds, and they're starting to accumulate so fast that by the year 2000—in roughly ten years—it's estimated that there'll be a staggering $1.4 trillion in these trust funds. What this all means is that the current payroll tax system is now collecting enough to not only meet the benefit payments of today's retirees, but also to put money aside for the next generation of retired workers.

Solvency. A lot of people fear that social security will run out of money by the time they are ready to collect their benefits. That's highly unlikely, since surpluses are expected to continue for the next 40 years or so. However, there are some dark clouds lurking on the horizon of this otherwise bright picture. The surpluses won't last forever, and by the year 2050, trillions of dollars in social security reserves will disappear altogether unless steps are taken to replenish them. This is because a larger percentage of our population will be elderly in future years than has been the case in the past. For example, as shown in Exhibit 15.3, the percentage of persons age 65 or over is expected to increase to 18.4 percent by the year 2030, up from just 5.4 percent in 1930 and 11.3 percent in 1980. This trend means that *retirement benefits will be mushrooming at the very same time that proportionately fewer people will be available in the work force to support those collecting social security.* For example, whereas in 1955 there were seven workers supporting each person on social security, it is estimated that by the year 2000 there will be only *two workers* for each social security beneficiary.

While Congress has long been aware of the existence of this problem, it took action only recently by beginning to slowly raise the retirement age from 65 to 67. As the current legislation stands, by the year 2027 a person will have to wait until age 67 in order to collect full social security benefits. At the same time, the penalty for early retirement (age 62) is being increased substantially. Whereas today an individual can retire at age 62 and collect 80 percent of the full benefits, in the future that person will collect only *70 percent* of the full benefits upon early retirement. This revised penalty structure will be fully phased in by the year 2027.

Investment Attributes. If you are like most people, you probably wonder what social security holds for you. First, you might ask "Will there be any money left when I get to retirement age?" As discussed here, the probability that social security will have funds to pay out is as close to 100 percent as any future economic plan can be—at least for the next 40 or 50 years. As a second concern, you might wonder, "What kind of investment return will

I get on my contributions? Wouldn't I be better off to invest the money myself?" This type of question can be answered in terms of (1) social security as an investment and (2) expected rates of return under social security.

To begin with, social security should not be viewed as an investment. It is properly viewed as a social insurance system: an insurance system that insures covered workers and their families against poverty resulting from retirement, death, disability, or health problems. If you die or become disabled at age 30 and have a spouse and two small children, your family could be eligible for monthly social security payments that would total more than $150,000—even if, up to that point, you had paid less than $10,000 in taxes. Similarly, you might retire and live for another 15, 20, or even 30 years. It makes no difference to social security. You will continue to draw benefits even though they will greatly exceed the amounts you paid into the system. On the other hand, you might contribute social security taxes for 40 years and then die (without dependents) the day you retire—and not collect a penny. An insurance system works only when some participants collect less than they pay in—otherwise no one could collect more. This principle holds regardless of whether we are talking about private life insurance, homeowners insurance, automobile insurance, or the retirement, life insurance, and disability coverages offered by social security.

Many critics have complained that the investment yields on social security could easily be exceeded through comparable investments in stocks, bonds, or real estate. Even if this claim were true, it would be irrelevant. The fact is that after allowing for all of the cash and noncash (for example, medicare) benefits of social security, the relatively safe nature of the benefits, and a moderate premium for the risk reduction features of the program, *the expected value of most workers' benefits far exceeds the expected value of their tax payments into the system.*

Who Is Covered?

Recent legislation enacted by Congress extended the coverage of social security to just about all gainfully employed workers. There are now only two major classes of employees exempt from *mandatory* participation in the social security system: (1) federal *civilian* employees who were hired before

EXHIBIT 15.3

The Growing Importance of the Senior Citizen

As the population grows older, the demands and pressures on the integrity of the social security system will increase accordingly.

Year	Percent of Population 65 and Over	Year	Percent of Population 65 and Over
1930	5.4	1990	12.1
1940	6.8	2000	12.1
1950	8.2	2010	12.6
1960	9.1	2020	15.5
1970	9.7	2030	18.4
1975	10.3	2040	18.1
1980	11.3	2050	17.1

Note: The projected values (that is, 1990 and beyond) are based upon the population projections for the central assumptions in the 1977 long-range cost estimates from the *1977 Annual Report of the Board of Trustees of the Federal Old-Age and Survivors Insurance and Disability Trust Funds.*
Source: Adapted from Robert M. Ball, *Social Security* (New York: Columbia University Press, 1978), 66, and *Information Please Almanac* (New York: A & W Publishers, Inc., 1983), 766.

1984 and are covered under the Civil Service Retirement System; and (2) employees of state and local governments that have chosen not to be covered (nearly 70 percent of all state and local government employees are covered, through voluntary participation, by social security). In addition, certain marginal employment positions, such as newspaper deliverypersons under age 18 and full-time college students working in fraternity and sorority houses, are also exempt. But by far, the largest number of workers in these excluded classifications are employees of state and local governments. These groups are not forced to participate because the federal government is not empowered to impose a tax on state and local governments.

When Are You Eligible for Benefits?

Social security payments are not paid automatically to eligible individuals (or their dependents). An application for benefits must be filed with the Social Security Administration, which then determines the applicant's eligibility for benefits based on whether he or she had enough quarters (three-month periods) of participation in the social security system. In order to qualify for retirement benefits, nearly all workers today must be employed in a job covered by social security for at least 40 quarters, or ten years. These quarters need not be consecutive. Once this 40-quarter requirement is met, the worker becomes fully insured and remains eli-

gible for retirement payments even if he or she never works again in covered employment. Note, however, that when yearly covered wages are computed, zeros are inserted for years in which no social security taxes were paid—which substantially reduces the size of future monthly benefit payments.

A spouse and/or dependent children of a deceased worker are also eligible for monthly benefits if the worker was fully insured at the time of death or, in some special cases, if certain other requirements are met. Workers may be considered fully insured if they had six quarters of coverage during the three-year period preceding the date of death.

Social Security Retirement Benefits

Basic social security benefits that are important to retired people and their dependents include (1) old-age benefits and (2) survivor's benefits. Both of these programs provide extended benefits to covered workers and/or their spouses; the major provisions of each of these programs is briefly described in the material that follows.

Old-Age Benefits. Workers who are fully covered (that is, who have worked the required 40 quarters under social security) may receive old-age benefits for life once they reach the age of 65. However, as stated above, the normal retirement age will gradually be increased starting in the year 2000, until it reaches age 67 in the year 2027. In addition, workers may elect to retire early—at age 62—in which case they will receive *reduced benefits*. Currently, a 62-year-old retiree will receive 80 percent of the full benefits; this amount is scheduled to gradually decline, however, so that by the year 2027, the benefits at age 62 will equal only 70 percent of the full amount. If the retiree has a spouse 65 or older, the spouse may be entitled to benefits equal to one-half of the amount received by the retired worker. The spouse may also elect early receipt of reduced benefits at age 62.

In the case of two-income families both the husband and wife may be eligible for full social security benefits. When they retire, they can choose to receive their benefits in one of two ways: (1) They can each take the full benefits to which each is entitled from his or her account, or (2) they can take the husband and wife benefits of the higher-paid spouse. If each takes his or her own full share, there are no spousal benefits; if they take the husband and wife benefits of the higher-paid spouse, they effectively receive 1.5 shares. Obviously, the two-income couple should select the option that provides the greatest amount of benefits (the amount of social security benefits will be described later).

In order to receive maximum social security retirement benefits, a worker must retire before his or her 65th birthday. **Fantasy:** To qualify for maximum benefits, a worker must be 65 *or older* AND have career earnings (prior to retirement) that were equal to or greater than the maximum social security tax base.

Survivor's Benefits. If a covered worker dies, the spouse can receive survivor's benefits from social security. These benefits include a small lump-sum payment of several hundred dollars, followed by monthly benefit checks. The lump-sum amount is paid automatically upon application. In order to be eligible for monthly payments, the widowed spouse generally must be at least age 60, or have a dependent and unmarried child of the deceased worker in his or her care. If the children of a deceased worker reach age 16 before the spouse reaches age 60, the monthly benefits cease and do not resume until the spouse turns 60. This period of time during which survivor's benefits are not paid is called the *widow's gap*.

How Much Are Monthly Social Security Benefits?

The amount of social security benefits to which an eligible person is entitled is set by law and defined according to a fairly complex formula. Up until recently, it was next to impossible to say with any degree of accuracy what your future benefits might be. All that changed in 1988, however, when the Social Security Administration introduced a computerized benefits estimation service. Under this program, you provide the Social Security Administration with some basic information about yourself and in return, it provides you with something called a *Personal Earnings and Benefit Estimate Statement.* To get one of your own, simply call their toll-free number (1–800–937–2000). You'll then receive a short questionnaire asking for a few basic facts, including your name, social security number, date of birth, previous and current year's earnings, and the age at which you plan to retire. About four to six weeks after you mail the form, you'll receive a personalized statement just like the one shown in Exhibit 15.4. This report lists the year-by-year social security earnings you've been credited with, and shows (in today's dollars) what benefits you can expect under three scenarios: (1) if you retire at age 62 and receive 80 percent of the full benefit (or less, depending on your age); (2) the full benefit at age 65 to 67 (depending on year of birth); and (3) the 33 percent larger benefit available if you continue working until age 70. The statement also estimates what your children and surviving spouse would get if you die, and how much you'd receive monthly if you were disabled. This statement is a valuable financial planning tool and is something that every working American should obtain—also, it's a good idea to get an updated report every five to ten years.

Using information provided by social security, we can describe the *current level of benefits* (for someone who retired in 1988), and at least get an idea of what *future retirement benefits* might look like (for workers in several age classes). This is done in Exhibit 15.5. The benefits schedule *as of 1988* is shown in the top half of the exhibit. The figures show monthly benefits for a retired worker, a retired worker and (nonworking) spouse, and a two-income couple for low, medium, and high career income levels (a *high* income worker is one whose

EXHIBIT 15.4

Personal Earnings and Benefit Estimate Statement

The Social Security Administration keeps a lifetime record of your earnings; and when you apply for benefits, it checks your earnings record to see if you've worked long enough to qualify, and then it determines the amount of your monthly benefits. The statement shown on this and the facing page, prepared by the Social Security Administration, is intended to provide an estimate of what one's future benefits are likely to be.

Facts About Your Social Security

The Facts You Gave Us

Your Name . . . . I. M. Somebody

Your Social Security Number 000-00-0000

Your Date of Birth . . . . Feb. 32, 1942

1987 Earnings . . . . Over $43,800

1988 Earnings . . . . Over $45,000

Your Estimated Future Average Yearly Earnings . . . . Over $45,000

The Age You Plan To Retire 65

We used these facts and the information already on our records to prepare this statement for you. When we estimated your benefits, we included any 1987 and 1988 earnings you told us about. We also included any future estimated earnings up to the age you told us you plan to retire.

If you did not estimate your future earnings, we did not project any future earnings for you.

Your Social Security Earnings

The chart below shows the earnings on your Social Security record. It also estimates the amount of Social Security taxes you paid each year to finance benefits under Social Security and Medicare. We show earnings only up to the maximum amount of yearly earnings covered by Social Security. These maximum amounts are also shown on the chart. The chart may not include some or all of your earnings from last year because they may not have been posted to your record yet.

Years	Maximum Yearly Earnings Subject To Social Security Tax	Your Social Security Taxed Earnings	Estimated Social Security Taxes You Paid
1937-1950	$ 3,000	$ 0	$ 0
1951	3,600	0	0
1952	3,600	0	0
1953	3,600	0	0
1954	3,600	0	0
1955	4,200	0	0
1956	4,200	18	0
1957	4,200	369	8
1958	4,200	45	1
1959	4,800	1,645	41
1960	4,800	889	26
1961	4,800	259	7
1962	4,800	566	17
1963	4,800	1,840	66
1964	4,800	4,800	174
1965	4,800	4,800	174
1966	6,600	6,600	277
1967	6,600	6,600	290
1968	7,800	0	0
1969	7,800	0	0
1970	7,800	7,053	338
1971	7,800	7,800	405
1972	9,000	9,000	468
1973	10,800	10,800	631
1974	13,200	13,200	772
1975	14,100	14,100	824
1976	15,300	15,300	895
1977	16,500	16,500	965
1978	17,700	17,700	1,070
1979	22,900	22,900	1,403
1980	25,900	25,900	1,587
1981	29,700	29,700	1,975
1982	32,400	32,400	2,170
1983	35,700	35,700	2,391

Years	Maximum Yearly Earnings Subject To Social Security Tax	Your Social Security Taxed Earnings	Estimated Social Security Taxes You Paid
1984	37,800	37,800	2,532
1985	39,600	39,600	2,791
1986	42,000	42,000	3,003
1987	43,800	43,800	3,131
1988	45,000	0	0
1989		0	0

Your Social Security Credits

To qualify for benefits, you need credit for a certain amount of work covered by Social Security. The number of credits you need will vary with the type of benefit. **Under current law, you do not need more than 40 credits to be fully insured for any benefit.** (See "How You Earn Social Security Credits" on the reverse side.)

Our review of your earnings, including any 1987 and 1988 earnings you told us about, shows that you now have **at least 40 Social Security credits.**

Estimated Benefits

Retirement

You must have 40 Social Security credits to be fully insured for retirement benefits. Assuming that you meet all the requirements, here are estimates of your retirement benefits based on your past and any projected earnings. The estimates are in today's dollars, but adjusted to account for average wage growth in the national economy.

If you retire at 62, your monthly benefit in today's dollars will be about $892

The earliest age at which you can receive an unreduced retirement benefit is 65 **and 4 months.** We call this your full retirement age. If you work until that age and then retire, your monthly benefit in today's dollars will be about $1,115

If you continue to work and wait until you are 70 to receive benefits, your monthly benefit in today's dollars will be about $1,535

Survivors

If you have a family, you must have 27 Social Security credits for certain family members to receive benefits if you were to die this year. They may also qualify if you earn 6 credits in the 3 years before your death. The number of credits a person needs to be insured for survivors benefits increases each year until age 62, up to a maximum of 40 credits.
Here is an estimate of the benefits your family could receive if you had enough credits to be insured, they qualified for benefits, and you died this year:

Your child could receive a monthly benefit of about . . . . $ 675

If your child and your surviving spouse who is caring for your child both qualify, they could each receive a monthly benefit of about . . . . $ 675

When your surviving spouse reaches full retirement age, he or she could receive a monthly benefit of about . . . . $ 905

The total amount that we could pay your family each month is about $1,585

We may also be able to pay your surviving spouse or children a one-time death benefit of . . . . . . $ 255

Disability

Right now, you must have 27 Social Security credits to be insured for disability benefits. And, **20 of these** credits had to be earned in the **10 year period immediately before you became disabled.** If you are blind or received disability benefits in the past, you may need fewer credits. The number of credits a person needs to be insured for disability benefits increases each year until age 62, up to a maximum of 40 credits.

If you were disabled, had enough credits, and met the other requirements for disability benefits, here is an estimate of the benefits you could receive right now:

Your monthly benefit would be about . . . . $ 890

You and your eligible family members could receive up to a monthly total of about $1,335

If You Have Questions

If you have any questions about this statement, please read the information on the reverse side. If you still have questions, please call **1–800–937–7005.**

EXHIBIT 15.5

Selected Monthly Social Security Retirement Benefits

The social security benefits listed here are initial, *first-year benefits.* As time passes, the beneficiary will receive correspondingly higher benefits as the cost of living goes up. For example, the maximum benefit payable to someone who retired in 1980 was $572 a month; by 1988, those benefits had grown to well over $800 a month.

	Career Earnings Level		
I. Latest Benefits (1988)	**Low**	**Medium**	**High**
Retired worker, age 65	$425	$768	$838
Retired worker, age 62	340	614	670
Family benefits:			
Retired worker and spouse, both 65	$637	$1,152	$1,257
Retired worker and spouse, both 62	490	890	970
Two-income couple:[a]			
Both retire at 65	$850	$1,536	$1,676
Both retire at 62	680	1,228	1,340

		Career Earnings Level		
II. Estimated Future Benefits[b]	**Worker's Age in 1988**	**Low**	**Medium**	**High**
Retired Worker	25	$ 618	$1,129	$1,471
	35	572	1,045	1,358
	45	523	958	1,201
	55	475	862	1,003
Retired Worker and Spouse	25	$ 927	$1,693	$2,206
	35	858	1,567	2,037
	45	784	1,437	1,801
	55	712	1,293	1,504
Two-Income Couple[a]	25	$1,236	$2,258	$2,942
	35	1,144	2,090	2,716
	45	1,046	1,916	2,402
	55	950	1,724	2,006

[a]*Both* in the same career income category and *both* eligible for normal benefits at their career income levels.
[b]Future benefits assume retirement at normal age (65 to 67); thus, these are estimated full benefits for the indicated career income levels.
Source: *Social Security: How It Works For You.* Social Security Administration, SSA Publication No. 05–10006, August 1988.

annual earnings equaled or exceeded the maximum social security tax base). Estimated *future* benefits for workers with low, medium, and high career income levels are shown in the lower part of the exhibit for the same three classes of retired worker. Bear in mind that the figures listed in the exhibit represent amounts that the beneficiaries will receive in the *first year* of their retirement. Those amounts will, of course, be adjusted upward each year with subsequent increases in the cost of living.

Retired social security recipients (age 65 to 69) will have their benefit payments *reduced* if they earn an annual income (in 1988) in excess of $8,400; this same (1988) earnings limitation was $6,120 for retirees between age 62 and 65. (Note that these earnings limitations rise annually with wage inflation.) The applicable rule generally states that for each $2 earned in excess of the stipulated thresholds, the beneficiary loses $1 in benefits. However, the earnings limitation ceases at age 70; thus, anyone 70 or older will receive full social security benefits regardless of how much they earn. In contrast, *unearned income such as interest, dividends, and rent may be of an unlimited amount without a corresponding benefits reduction.* The fact that benefits are subject to reduction with earned income, but not with unearned income, is one of the most criticized features of social security.

Taxes on Benefits.   No longer are social security benefits a source of tax-free income. Not since 1984, anyway, when Congress passed legislation to tax up to half the benefits paid to "upper-income beneficiaries." Specifically, as the law presently stands, *social security retirement benefits are subject to federal income taxes if* the beneficiary's annual income exceeds one of the following base amounts: $25,000 for a single taxpayer, $32,000 for married taxpayers filing jointly, or zero for married taxpayers filing separately. In determining the amount of income that must be counted, the taxpayer starts with his or her *adjusted gross income* as defined by the present tax law (see Chapter 4) and then adds all nontaxable interest income (such as income from municipal bonds) plus one-half of the social security benefits received. If the resulting amount exceeds one of the qualifying bases (above), the retiree must pay federal income taxes on *up to half* of the amount of social security benefits received—and then only the amount *in excess of the base* is subject to tax.

Social Security and Retirement Planning

No one can accurately predict the amount of social security benefits that will be paid 30 or 40 years from now. For retirement planning purposes, however, it seems reasonable to expect social security to provide the average retired wage earner who is married with about 40 to 60 percent of the wages that he or she was earning in the year before retirement. This, of course, assumes that the retiree has had a full career working in covered employment. Social security should therefore be viewed as *a foundation for your retirement income.* By itself, *it is insufficient to allow a worker and spouse to maintain their preretirement standard of living.* For people who earn in excess of the wage base, a lower percentage of total preretirement wages will be replaced by social security. Consequently, both average and upper-middle-income families must plan to supplement their social security retirement benefits with income from other sources. Two popular sources are annuities, and pensions and retirement programs. These topics are discussed in the next two sections.

Social security retirement benefits should be sufficient to provide retired workers and their spouses with a comfortable standard of living. **Fantasy:** Social security is intended to be only a foundation for retirement income; by itself, it will likely permit retirees only a small fraction of their preretirement standard of living.

ANNUITIES

An annuity is a type of investment vehicle that systematically pays out benefits, usually over an extended period of time. They're widely used as a supplemental source of income by people in retirement. When you buy an annuity, you're essentially making a long-term commitment with your money; accordingly, it's important to consider the kind of return you'll get on your investment. You can choose a *fixed-rate* annuity, where your returns are closely linked to yields in the money market, or a *variable-rate* annuity, which allows you to aggressively play the stock and bond markets. What kind of annuity would you find most attractive? What would you see as the advantages and disadvantages of each type? Give some thought to these questions before reading on.

In spite of some well-publicized difficulties in the industry (most noteworthy, perhaps, was the collapse of Baldwin-United in the early 1980s), the number of annuity contracts in force with U.S. life insurance companies has grown tremendously in the past 20 years. This growth has resulted primarily from the greater public awareness of annuities, brought about by the increased marketing efforts of life insurance companies. In addition, the surge in retirement programs has contributed to the growth of annuities and so have the tax laws, which treat annuities as tax-sheltered investment vehicles—indeed, the demand for these products has been greatly heightened in recent years as changes in the tax laws have made annuities one of the few tax shelters left to investors. Stripped down, annuities represent little more than an agreement to make contributions now (or in installments) in return for a series of payments later—for a fixed number of years, or for life.

The Annuity Principle

An annuity is actually just the opposite of life insurance. As we pointed out in Chapter 9, life insurance is the systematic accumulation of an estate for protection against financial loss resulting from premature death. In contrast, an **annuity** is the systematic liquidation of an estate in such a way that it provides protection against the economic difficulties that could result from outliving personal financial resources. The period during which premiums are paid for the purchase of an annuity is called the **accumulation period**; correspondingly, the period during which annuity payments are made is called the **distribution period**.

Under a pure life annuity contract, a life insurance company will guarantee regular monthly payments to an individual for as long as he or she lives. These benefits are composed of three parts: principal, interest, and survivorship benefits. The *principal* consists of the premium amounts paid in by the *annuitant* (person buying the annuity) during the accumulation period. *Interest* is the amount earned on these funds between the time they are paid and distributed. The interest earnings on an annuity accrue (that is, accumulate) tax-free. The portion of the principal and interest that has not been returned to the annuitant prior to death is the **survivorship benefit**. These funds are available to those members of the annuity group who survive in each subsequent period. By using mortality tables and estimated investment returns, life insurance companies can calculate for a group of annuitants of a given age the amount of monthly payment they can guarantee to each individual without prematurely depleting the total amounts that have accumulated. Consequently, the risk of outliving one's income is eliminated.

Classification of Annuities

Annuities may be classified according to several key characteristics, including the way the premiums are paid, the disposition of proceeds, inception date of benefits, and the method used in calculating benefits. Exhibit 15.6 presents a chart of this classification system.

Single Premium or Installments. There are two ways to pay the premiums when you purchase an annuity contract: you can make a large single (lump-sum) payment right up front or pay the premium in installments. The **single-premium annuity contract** usually requires a minimum investment of anywhere from $2,500 to $10,000, with $5,000 the most common figure. These annuities have become very popular recently, primarily because of the attractive tax features they offer investors. Also, they are often purchased just before retirement as a way of creating a future stream of income. Sometimes the cash value of a life insurance policy will be used at retirement to acquire a single-premium annuity. This is a highly effective use of a life insurance policy: You get the insurance coverage when you need it the most (while you're raising and educating your family) and then a regular stream of income when you can probably use it the most (after you've retired).

While the majority of *group* annuity policies are funded with single premiums, many *individuals* still buy annuities by paying for them in installments. In these so-called **installment-premium annuity contracts**, the set payments, starting as low as $100, are made at regular intervals (monthly, quarterly, annually) over an extended period of time. Sometimes, these annuities are set up with a fairly large initial payment (of perhaps several thousand dollars), followed by a series of much smaller installment payments (of, say, $250 a quarter). There are even plans that combine the features of both single-premium and installment-premium annuities. Known as *flexible plans,* they start out with a sizable initial investment, very much like single-premium annuities, except that the investor can put more money in later, *as desired.* In this type of contract, which is commonly found with variable annuities, the individual is under no obligation to make future set payments at set intervals.

Installment-premium annuity contracts also carry an important *life insurance provision,* which stipulates that if an annuitant dies before the distribution period begins, the annuitant's beneficiaries will receive the market value of the contract or the amount invested, whichever is greater (note that single-premium annuities contain similar life insurance provisions, so long as the payout of benefits is deferred to some future date). In addition, the annuitant can terminate an installment-premium contract at any time and withdraw the cash value (though this would involve a *substantial tax penalty* if withdrawal occurs before age 59½), or simply stop paying the periodic installments and take a paid-up annuity for a reduced amount. One potential advantage of purchasing an installment-type annuity early is that the scheduled benefits are based on mortality rates in effect when the contract is purchased. Even if the mortality rate improves, as it normally does with the passage of time, the annuitant will not be required to pay the higher premium stipulated in contracts issued later on.

Disposition of Proceeds. All annuities revolve around the basic *pay-now, receive-later* concept. As such, they allow individuals to prepare for future cash needs, like planning for retirement, while obtaining significant tax benefits. When it comes to the distribution of an annuity, you can either take a lump-sum payment, or, as is more often the case, you can *annuitize* the distribution by systematically parceling out the money into regular payments over a defined, or open-ended, period of time. Since most people choose to annuitize their proceeds (which is *conceptually* the way an annuity should be used), let's look at the options that are the most widely followed in the distribution of an annuity—these include the life annuity with no refund, the guaranteed minimum annuity, the annuity certain, and the temporary life annuity.

Life annuity with no refund (straight life). Under the **life annuity with no refund (straight life)** option, the annuitant receives a specified amount of income for life, regardless of whether the period over which income is distributed turns out to be 1 year or 50 years. *No refunds or payments are made to the estate or family when the annuitant dies.* This disposition procedure entitles the annuitant to the largest monthly payments of any of the distribution methods. These larger payments result because when the annuitant dies, the issuer (a life insurance company) does not have

to distribute the principal, if any, to the annuitant's heirs.

Only a minority of individuals select the life annuity with no refund. Most people who purchase annuities are opposed to sacrificing the large unused portion of their capital should they die relatively soon after retirement. However, this option often is used under group annuity contracts.

Guaranteed-minimum annuity. The **guaranteed-minimum annuity** was developed to help overcome the emotional and economic objections to the straight life annuity. The two basic types of this annuity are the (1) life annuity, period certain, and (2) refund annuity. With each of these options, the annuitant designates a beneficiary who

---

annuity
An investment product sold by life insurance companies that provides a series of payments over time.

accumulation period
The period during which premiums are paid for the purchase of an annuity.

distribution period
The period during which annuity payments are made to an annuitant.

survivorship benefit
On an annuity, the portion of premiums and interest that has not been returned to the annuitant prior to his or her death.

single-premium annuity contract
An annuity contract that is purchased with a lump-sum payment.

installment-premium annuity contract
An annuity contract that is purchased through periodic payments made during the annuitant's working life.

life annuity with no refund (straight life)
An option under which an annuitant receives a specified amount of income for life regardless of the length of the distribution period; in turn, no payments or refunds are made to the person's family or estate upon his or her death.

guaranteed-minimum annuity
An annuity that provides a guaranteed minimum distribution of benefits.

EXHIBIT 15.6

Different Types of Annuity Contracts

The different types of annuity contracts vary according to how you pay for the annuity, how the proceeds will be disbursed, how earnings accrue, and when you will receive the benefits.

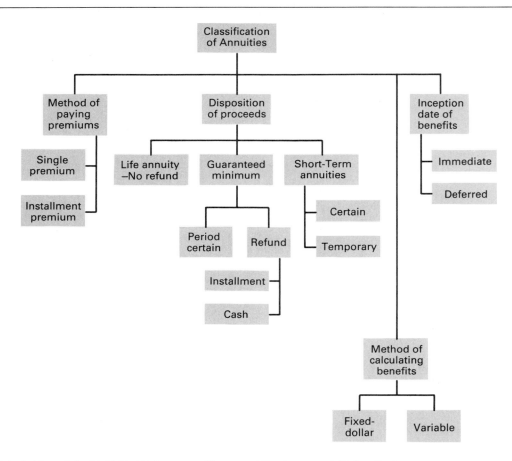

Source: Adapted from Robert I. Mehr, *Life Insurance: Theory and Practice,* rev. ed. (Dallas: Business Publications, 1977).

also may become eligible for benefits. Under the **life annuity, period certain**, the annuitant is guaranteed a stated amount of monthly income for life. In addition, the insurance company agrees to pay the stipulated monthly benefits for at least a minimum number of years (five or ten, for example) regardless of whether the annuitant survives. Thus, if the annuitant dies soon after the distribution begins, his (or her) beneficiaries will receive the monthly benefits for the balance of the "period

certain." A **refund annuity** provides that upon the death of the annuitant, monthly payments will be made to the designated beneficiary *until the total purchase price of the annuity has been refunded.* In place of the monthly payments, the refund may be taken in cash if so specified in the contract.

Annuity certain. A specified amount of monthly income for a specified number of years without consideration of any life contingency is provided by the **annuity certain**. For example, if an annuitant selected a ten-year annuity certain, payments would continue for ten years after that individual retired, regardless of whether he or she lived two or twenty more years. The annuity certain can fill a need for monthly income that will expire after a certain length of time. For example, a widow age 52 could choose a ten-year annuity certain contract to fill the need for income until she reaches age 62, when she plans to apply for social security benefits.

Temporary life annuity. Although similar to the annuity certain, the **temporary life annuity** continues benefits for the specified period only if the annuitant survives. If the above widow had chosen a ten-year temporary life annuity but died at age 60, no further payments would be made under the contract. Since the temporary life annuity provides no survivorship benefit, it provides a larger monthly income than the annuity certain. The insurer selling the temporary life annuity may not have to pay the benefits over the stated period, while the insurer selling the annuity certain must. Therefore, unless the widow had a beneficiary who needed extra income, she would be wise to select the temporary life annuity instead of the annuity certain. In actuality, annuitants purchase temporary life annuity contracts only infrequently for the same basic reason that they avoid straight life annuities—they do not want a major portion of the purchase price of their annuities to be wasted should they die shortly after payments begin.

Immediate versus Deferred Annuity. An annuitant often has the choice of receiving monthly benefits immediately upon buying an annuity or of deferring receipt for a number of years. Logically, the first type is called an immediate annuity and the latter a deferred annuity. An **immediate annuity**, purchased with a single premium, is most often used in conjunction with the cash value or death proceeds of a life insurance policy to create a stream of cash receipts needed for retirement or to support a widow and/or dependent children. A **deferred annuity**, in contrast, can be bought with either a single payment (the more popular kind) or through an installment plan. This contract is quite flexible and can be issued with numerous options to the annuitant for both paying the premiums and receiving the proceeds. Most annuities

purchased under group contracts are immediate annuities, whereas those purchased by individuals are usually of the *deferred* type. In fact, because of their attractive tax features, a lot of people buy deferred annuities—and especially single-premium deferred annuities—more as a tax-sheltered *investment vehicle* than anything else.

Fixed versus Variable Annuity. When you put your money into an annuity, the premium is invested on your behalf by the insurance company, much like a mutual fund invests the money you put into it. From the time you pay the annuity premium until it is paid back to you as a lump sum or as an annuitized monthly benefit, you'll be earning a rate of return on your investment. How that rate of re-

---

life annuity, period-certain
A type of guaranteed-minimum annuity in which the annuitant is guaranteed a stated amount of monthly income for life and the insurer agrees to pay that amount for a minimum number of years regardless of whether or not the annuitant survives.

refund annuity
A type of guaranteed-minimum annuity that provides that upon the annuitant's death, monthly payments will be made to the designated beneficiary until the total purchase price of the annuity has been refunded.

annuity certain
An annuity that provides a specified amount of monthly income for a stated number of years without consideration of any life contingency.

temporary life annuity
An annuity in which benefits continue for a specified period, only for as long as the annuitant survives.

immediate annuity
An annuity, in which the annuitant begins receiving monthly benefits immediately; usually purchased with a single premium.

deferred annuity
An annuity in which benefit payments are deferred for a certain number of years; purchased with either a lump-sum payment or in installments.

turn is figured determines whether you own a fixed or variable annuity. In a **fixed-rate annuity**, the insurance company safeguards your principal and agrees to pay a guaranteed minimum rate of interest over the life of the contract. These are conservative, very low-risk annuity products that essentially promise to return *the original investment plus interest* when the money is paid out to the annuitant (and/or any designated beneficiaries). As a result, once a distribution, or payout, schedule has been selected, the annuitant knows right up front what the (minimum) monthly benefit will be, as that's guaranteed by the annuity contract. These *interest-earning annuities,* as they're also called, are ideally suited for the cautious investor, but as discussed in the *Smart Money* box, they should nevertheless be purchased with care.

Imagine an investment vehicle that lets you move between stocks, bonds, and money funds, and at the same time, accumulate profits tax-free. That, in a nutshell, is a variable annuity. With a **variable annuity** contract, the amount that's ultimately paid out to the annuitant varies with the investment results obtained by the insurance company—*nothing* is guaranteed, not even the principal! When you buy a variable annuity, you decide where you want your money invested, based on your investment objectives and tolerance for risk: you can usually choose from stocks, bonds, money market securities, or some combination thereof. Insurance companies typically offer five or six stock and bond funds, as well as money market investments for short-term safety; some companies even offer a relatively exotic fleet of alternatives, ranging from zero coupon bonds to real estate and foreign securities. As an annuity holder, you can stay put with a single investment for the long haul, or, as with most variable annuities, you can aggressively play the market by switching from one fund to another. Variable annuities became very popular and were experiencing rapid growth until the October 1987 market crash, when a lot of investors learned the hard way that the returns on these policies can also go DOWN—and sometimes, in a very big way.

Because the payoff from a variable annuity depends to such an extent on the fate of the markets, the annuitants take a chance that their monthly income will be less than anticipated. Of course, most people who participate in variable annuity plans fully expect to be able to outperform fixed annui-

ties. But that doesn't always happen, as we saw in the 1970s when a sluggish stock market led to variable annuity payments that were well below the amounts paid on corresponding fixed-rate plans. Annuitants, however, do have some control over this type of risk exposure, since they can choose to go with high- or low-risk investment vehicles and in so doing, influence the certainty of return. In effect, if you go with an annuity that stresses high-risk securities, you should expect a good deal of uncertainty in return—the potential for high return might be there, but so is the chance for loss. If you're uncomfortable with that, then stick to annuities that offer safer investment choices (like zero coupon bonds or Treasury securities). Also, although there's nothing to prohibit you from staying with market-sensitive variable annuities during both the accumulation and distribution periods, in most cases you can convert to a fixed annuity at distribution. What you do, in effect, is use the cash value in your variable annuity to buy a paid-up fixed annuity. In this way, you use a *variable annuity during the accumulation period* to build up your capital as much as possible, and then switch to a *fixed annuity for the distribution period* to obtain a certain, well-defined stream of future income.

Sources and Costs of Annuities

Annuities are administered by life insurance companies, and for that reason, it should come as no surprise that they're also the leading sellers of these financial products. In addition, annuities can also be purchased from stock brokers, mutual fund organizations, and financial planners. When you buy an annuity, the cost will vary considerably with the age of the annuitant at issue, the age of the annuitant when payments begin, the method used to distribute benefits, the number of lives covered, and the sex of the annuitant. Exhibit 15.7 presents the lump-sum costs of several leading companies for two types of immediate annuities. Note the substantial differences that exist among the companies' premiums. These differences confirm the need to shop around before making an annuity purchase. Note, too, that in every category the cost to females is higher than the cost to males. This is due to the lower mortality rates among women. The differences in mortality rates for males and females can

EXHIBIT 15.7

Lump-Sum Costs Necessary for Funding Payments of $100 a Month

Annuity costs vary not only by the type of annuity and the sex and age of the beneficiary but also by the company selling the contract. Clearly, it pays to shop around: What it would cost a 65-year-old male to buy $100 a month through a 10-year certain contract from Company 1 would cost almost 20% more if the same type of contract were bought from Company 3.

	Life Annuity with No Refund				Life—10 Years Certain			
	Male		Female		Male		Female	
Company	65	75	65	75	65	75	65	75
1	$10,430	$7,420	$11,560	$8,640	$11,220	$ 9,370	$12,090	$10,020
2	11,300	8,350	12,444	9,230	11,980	9,930	12,820	10,350
3	12,410	8,680	13,870	9,840	13,320	10,850	14,390	11,410

Source: Compiled from *Best's Flitcraft Compend,* 95th ed.

be seen in Exhibit 15.8. Mortality differences notwithstanding, legislation is pending that would exclude sex as a criterion for annuity rate making.

The Investment and Income Properties of Annuities

One of the major attributes of annuities is that they are a source of income that cannot be outlived. While individuals might create a similar arrangement by simply living off the interest or dividends from their investments, they would find it difficult to engage in the systematic liquidation of their principal in a manner that would be timed to closely (or exactly) coincide with their death. Also viewed very positively is the fact that the income earned in an annuity is allowed to accumulate tax-free; thus, it provides a form of *tax-sheltered investment!* Actually, the income from an annuity is *tax-deferred,* meaning that taxes on the earnings will have to be paid when the annuity is liquidated.

While shelter from taxes is an attractive investment attribute, there is a hitch! You may be faced with a big tax penalty if you close out or withdraw money from an annuity before its time. Specifically, the IRS treats annuity withdrawals like withdrawals from an individual retirement account, meaning that except in cases of serious illness, *anybody who takes money out before reaching age 59½ will incur a 10 percent tax penalty.* Thus, if you're under 59½ and in the 28 percent tax bracket, you'll end up paying a 38 percent tax rate on any funds withdrawn from an annuity. (The IRS views withdrawals

entirely as taxable income until the account balance falls to the amount of original paid in principal—after which any further withdrawals would be tax-free.) Short of some type of serious illness, about the only way to tap your account penalty-free before you're 59½ is to *annuitize.* Unfortunately, the annuity payments must be spread out over your estimated remaining life span, which means the size of each monthly payment could end up being pretty small. Because of this threat of a tax penalty, the purchase of an annuity should always be considered as a type of long-term investment. Assume it's a part of your retirement program (that's the way the IRS looks at it) and that you're getting in for the long haul, because it's not that easy to get out before you turn 59½.

From an investment perspective, the returns generated from an annuity can prove disappointing. For example, as we discussed before, the returns on *variable annuities* are tied to returns in the

fixed-rate annuity
An annuity in which the insurance company safeguards your principal and agrees to pay a guaranteed rate of interest on your money; in addition, the (minimum) monthly benefit is set by the contract.

variable annuity
An annuity in which the monthly income provided by the policy varies according to the actual investment experience of the insurer.

"Fixed Annuities Have Their Rewards—But Be Careful!"

Investors hungering for safety and high yields are pouring record sums into single-premium, interest-earning annuities. The insurance contracts have several enticing features: current (1988) interest rates as high as 9.5%, no tax until money is withdrawn and very little risk. But financial advisers urge caution. Steep penalties on some withdrawals make annuities strictly a long-term savings vehicle. And high initial rates can drop unexpectedly.

"If you are looking for a long-term investment, it is a very good option," says Daniel R. Fleming, a Vienna, Va., financial adviser. But he and other financial advisers say, "It's not something you go into lightly."

Unlike "variable" annuities, which incorporate riskier stock and bond investments and don't guarantee an investor's principal, interest-earning annuities promise to pay back the original investment plus interest when the money is withdrawn.

There's a big penalty, however, for taking money out too soon. The federal government imposes a 10% penalty tax on most money withdrawn before the investor reaches age 59½. Accumulated gains are subject to ordinary income tax, as well, when they are withdrawn.

That is the same treatment that applies to individual retirement accounts for people who aren't permitted to take a tax deduction on IRA contributions. But while IRA contributions are limited to $2,000 a year, there is no limit on annuity purchases. Indeed most single-premium annuities, or those purchased with a single lump sum, require a minimum investment of $5,000, or more.

Most annuities also impose contract surrender charges that typically start at 7% of the account balance and are then gradually phased out over time. These provisions effectively lock in investors for several years. Another pitfall is that this hand-

cuff enables some insurers to pay disappointing rates after an initial high-rate honeymoon. Most insurers guarantee minimum interest rates of only 3% to 6% a year. "The big problem (with annuities) is getting caught in a product that you won't be happy with later on," says Glenn Daily, insurance product analyst with Seidman Financial Services, the financial planning unit of accountants BDO Seidman in New York.

Interest rates on annuities generally move up and down with rates in the financial markets—*but at the insurer's discretion*. And at any given time, some investors may be paid more than others in the same annuity. Consider *Federal Kemper Life Assurance Co.*, which is paying an initial 9.5% on a contract with an unusual permanent surrender charge of 6%. In recent years, the rates paid on older dollars invested in that annuity have frequently been two percentage points or more

money and capital markets, but even so, they are still no better than what you can get from other investment vehicles—and oftentimes, they're considerably less. But keep in mind that the returns from an annuity are tax-sheltered so that makes those lower returns look more attractive. And as far as *fixed-rate annuities* are concerned, while many of them advertise vary high rates of return, a close look at the fine print usually reveals that such rates

are guaranteed only for the first one to five years, after which time the rates drop to something closer to money market yields—or less. True, there are minimum guaranteed rates that the annuities have to stand behind, but these are usually much lower than prevailing market rates, so they're not much help. Investors generally have little choice but to accept the going rate or surrender the policy. Surrender can be painful, however, not only because

below the new-money rate. Now, for instance, the Kemper Corp. unit is paying only 7% on money invested between 1979 and 1984. The company pays higher rates and takes smaller profits on newly invested sums because "we feel we have to do it to put the business on," says Federal Kemper Vice President James Bickler. Averaging the first-year and later rates to investors, he says, "they will receive a fair return" over time.

Still, the extraordinary nature of Federal Kemper's first-year rate may not be clear to all buyers, says Mr. Daily. "I would not put my money in it," he says. "I don't like the fact that they lure me in in the first year and then drop the rate after that." To avoid disappointment, annuity buyers can ask insurance agents or other sellers for the rates a particular company has paid on both new and old money over the past five years. Past performance is the best guide a prospective purchaser can have.

Investors can also look for annuities that make it easier to get out if future results prove uncompetitive. For example, such insurers as *North American Co. for Life & Health Insurance* in Chicago prohibit surrenders during the period for which the rate is guaranteed and then provide a set period for penalty-free surrenders. Money can be moved to another company's annuity without incurring tax. Other annuities include a "bailout" provision that allows holders to take their funds without penalty if the rate falls below a specified level. Opting for that protection can mean a lower initial rate, however.

Both Mr. Daily and James H. Hunt, a director of the National Insurance Consumer Organization, also suggest investors consider buying from *USAA,* an insurer that sells directly to consumers by mail and phone. In part because the company doesn't have the usual sales

commissions to pay, its surrender charge is only 4% and $25 initially, dropping to just $25 after three years. Unlike some other companies, USAA's current rate of 9.1% on old money is slightly *higher* than its new-money rate. The company says that's only fair. Many older annuities were purchased when overall interest rates were higher, so they were invested at higher yields than are available today.

Unlike a bond, *the principal of an annuity won't decline if interest rates rise in the future.* But the security of the annuity balance depends on the issuing insurer. So most financial advisers suggest buyers stick to insurers whose financial strength is rated A+ or A by A.M. Best Co.

Source: Karen Slater. "Annuities Offer Rewards But Require Investor Caution," *The Wall Street Journal,* October 26, 1988, pp. C1, C16. Reprinted by permission of *The Wall Street Journal,* © Dow Jones & Company, Inc. 1988. All Rights Reserved Worldwide.

of IRS penalties, but also because of the hefty *surrender fees* that are found on many of these contracts (these fees often amount to 5 to 10 percent of the account balance in the first year and then gradually decline to zero over a seven- to ten-year period).

It's possible to get around a surrender fee if the annuity has a *bailout* clause. Such a provision allows you to withdraw your money, free of any surrender fees, if the rate of return on the annuity falls below a certain level (say, a point or so below the initial rate). But you have to act fairly quickly, since the bailout provision may only exist for a limited period of time. Of course, even if you exercise a bailout provision, you may still have to face a tax penalty for early withdrawal—unless you transfer the funds to another annuity through what is known as a *1035 exchange.*

EXHIBIT 15.8

Life Expectancies of American Men and Women (Latest Available Statistics, 1985)

Life expectancy measures the number of years a person has left to live—for example, on average, a 20-year-old has a little over 56 years remaining. Note, however, that life expectancy varies by age, sex, and race.

| | | Expectation of Life in Years | | | |
| | | White | | All Other | |
Age	Total Persons	Male	Female	Male	Female
0	74.7	71.9	78.7	67.2	75.0
1	74.5	71.6	78.4	67.4	75.1
2	73.6	70.7	77.4	66.5	74.1
3	72.6	69.7	76.5	65.5	73.2
4	71.7	68.7	75.5	64.6	72.2
5	70.7	67.8	74.5	63.6	71.2
6	69.7	66.8	73.5	62.6	70.3
7	68.7	65.8	72.5	61.7	69.3
8	67.7	64.8	71.5	60.7	68.3
9	66.8	63.8	70.6	59.7	67.3
10	65.8	62.9	69.6	58.7	66.3
11	64.8	61.9	68.6	57.7	65.4
12	63.8	60.9	67.6	56.8	64.4
13	62.8	59.9	66.6	55.8	63.4
14	61.8	58.9	65.6	54.8	62.4
15	60.9	58.0	64.6	53.8	61.4
16	59.9	57.0	63.7	52.9	60.4
17	58.9	56.1	62.7	51.9	59.5
18	58.0	55.1	61.7	51.0	58.5
19	57.0	54.2	60.7	50.1	57.5
20	56.1	53.3	59.8	49.1	56.5
21	55.1	52.3	58.8	48.2	55.6
22	54.2	51.4	57.8	47.3	54.6
23	53.3	50.5	56.9	46.4	53.7
24	52.3	49.6	55.9	45.5	52.7
25	51.4	48.7	54.9	44.6	51.7
26	50.4	47.7	53.9	43.7	50.8
27	49.5	46.8	53.0	42.8	49.8
28	48.5	45.9	52.0	42.0	48.9
29	47.6	44.9	51.0	41.1	47.9
30	46.7	44.0	50.1	40.2	47.0
31	45.7	43.1	49.1	39.3	46.0
32	44.8	42.2	48.1	38.4	45.1
33	43.8	41.2	47.1	37.6	44.2
34	42.9	40.3	46.2	36.7	43.2
35	42.0	39.4	45.2	35.8	42.3
36	41.0	38.4	44.3	35.0	41.4
37	40.1	37.5	43.3	34.1	40.4
38	39.2	36.6	42.3	33.3	39.5
39	38.2	35.7	41.4	32.4	38.6
40	37.3	34.7	40.4	31.6	37.7
41	36.4	33.8	39.5	30.8	36.8
42	35.5	32.9	38.5	30.0	35.9

Source: *The 1989 Information Please Almanac* (New York: Houghton Mifflin, 1985), 795–796.

One final point, if you're seriously considering buying an annuity, make sure you carefully read the contract and see what the guaranteed rates are, how long the initial rate applies, and if a bailout provision exists. Just as important, since *the annuity is only as good as the insurance company that stands behind it,* check to see how the company is rated in *Best's Insurance Reports.* These ratings are much like those found in the bond market and are meant to reflect the financial strength of the firm. Letter grades (ranging from A+ down to C) are assigned on the principle that the stronger the company, the lower the risk of loss—accordingly, if security is important to you, stick with insurers that carry A+ or A ratings. And if you're considering a *variable annuity,* go over it much the same way as you

		Expectation of Life in Years			
	Total Persons	**White**		**All Other**	
Age		**Male**	**Female**	**Male**	**Female**
43	34.5	32.0	37.6	29.1	35.0
44	33.6	31.1	36.5	28.3	34.1
45	32.7	30.2	35.7	27.5	33.2
46	31.8	29.3	34.8	26.7	32.3
47	31.0	28.4	33.9	26.0	31.5
48	30.1	27.6	32.9	25.2	30.6
49	29.2	26.7	32.0	24.4	29.8
50	28.3	25.8	31.1	23.7	28.9
51	27.5	25.0	30.2	22.9	28.1
52	26.6	24.2	29.4	22.2	27.3
53	25.8	23.3	28.5	21.5	26.4
54	25.0	22.5	27.6	20.8	25.6
55	24.2	21.7	26.7	20.1	24.9
56	23.4	21.0	25.9	19.4	24.1
57	22.6	20.2	25.0	18.8	23.3
58	21.8	19.5	24.2	18.1	22.6
59	21.1	18.7	23.4	17.5	21.8
60	20.3	18.0	22.6	16.9	21.1
61	19.6	17.3	21.8	16.3	20.4
62	18.8	16.6	21.0	15.7	19.7
63	18.1	15.9	20.2	15.1	19.0
64	17.4	15.3	19.4	14.6	18.3
65	16.7	14.6	18.7	14.0	17.6
66	16.1	14.0	17.9	13.5	17.0
67	15.4	13.3	17.2	13.0	16.3
68	14.7	12.7	16.4	12.4	15.7
69	14.1	12.1	15.7	11.9	15.0
70	13.5	11.6	15.0	11.4	14.4
71	12.9	11.0	14.3	10.9	13.8
72	12.3	10.5	13.6	10.5	13.2
73	11.7	9.9	13.0	10.0	12.6
74	11.1	9.4	12.3	9.6	12.1
75	10.6	9.0	11.7	9.2	11.5
76	10.1	8.5	11.1	8.8	11.0
77	9.5	8.0	10.5	8.3	10.4
78	9.0	7.6	9.9	7.9	9.9
79	8.5	7.2	9.3	7.5	9.4
80	8.1	6.8	8.7	7.2	8.9
81	7.6	6.4	8.2	6.8	8.4
82	7.2	6.0	7.7	6.5	8.0
83	6.7	5.7	7.2	6.2	7.6
84	6.4	5.4	6.8	6.0	7.3
85	6.0	5.1	6.4	5.9	7.0

would a traditional mutual fund: look for superior past performance, proven management talents, moderate expenses, and the availability of attractive investment alternatives that you can switch in and out of.

Since an annuity is only as good as the insurance company that stands behind it, you should check the company's financial rating before buying an annuity. **Fact:** Because it's a life insurance company that guarantees the payout of the policy during the period of distribution, it's a good idea to see how the company's financial strength is rated in *Best's Insurance Reports*—and if you're looking for maximum protection, stick with companies that are A + or A rated.

PENSION PLANS AND RETIREMENT PROGRAMS

There are two basic types of retirement programs: employer-sponsored and self-directed—together, these programs can provide the funds needed for an active and comfortable retirement. If you're covered by a company-sponsored pension plan, why would you need to open a self-directed retirement program? Try to answer this question before going on.

Accompanying the expansion of the social security system and the increase in annuity sales has been the growth of employer-sponsored pension and retirement plans. In 1940, when the social security program was in its infancy, fewer than 25 percent of the work force had the benefit of an employer-sponsored plan. Today, approximately 50 percent of all wage and salaried workers in the United States are covered by some type of employer-sponsored retirement or profit-sharing plan.

What's Behind the Growth?

Although there are many reasons for the widespread development of pension and retirement plans, three stand out the most. Basically, pension plans have been developed by employers to (1) attract and retain quality employees, (2) meet the demands of collective bargaining, and (3) provide benefits to owners and key managers of firms. Many employers stress the advantages of their retirement plans in attracting and keeping valuable employees. In fact, a lot of companies have more or less been forced to implement retirement plans to counteract the effects of other employers competing for the same workers. Of course, few of these firms would go so far as to say that a good retirement plan encourages workers to put forth more effort. Nevertheless, evidence indicates that the lack of a good plan can serve as a job deterrent to prospective employees and may increase labor turnover, especially for employees age 40 and older.

In 1948 the National Labor Relations Board (NLRB) ruled that pensions and other types of insurance are legitimate subjects for collective bargaining. Since that time, many employers have established new pension plans or liberalized the provisions of existing ones to meet or anticipate union demands. Qualified pension plans (discussed later) allow firms to deduct for tax purposes their contributions to employee retirement programs. These contributions are not included in employees' taxable income. As a result, many firms, especially smaller ones, have established pension or retirement plans to help owners and key managers accrue retirement funds on a tax-deferred basis. Eventually, of course, when the funds are paid out as benefits, the employees will have to pay taxes on this income.

Government red tape, however, has slowed things down a bit. In particular, the **Employee Retirement Income Security Act** (sometimes referred to as **ERISA** or the *Pension Reform Act*) of 1974, established to protect employees participating in private employer retirement plans, has actually led to a reduction in the number of new retirement plans started among smaller firms. More liberal rules with respect to individual retirement accounts (IRAs) have also diminished the advantages of small employer-sponsored pension plans.

Effects of Growth. The overall growth of employer-sponsored retirement plans is important in two major areas. First, payments made under these plans represent a needed source of income to millions of retired workers and their dependents. For example, more than 16 million retirees received over $75 billion in benefits from private and public pension plans in 1989—and this *excluded* social security retirement benefits. Of course, as more of these pension plans mature, both the number of persons and dollar payments involved can be expected to increase substantially.

The second major effect of growth in these pension plans is the related spread of their influence on the behavior of U.S. capital (security) markets. Assets of all pension and retirement programs (excluding social security) in the United States now total well over *$2 trillion.* The largest portion of this money is invested in corporate and government bonds as well as common stocks. In fact, pension and retirement funds as a group are now the largest institutional owners of corporate bonds and stocks. In addition, pension fund money is becoming more widely available for commercial and investment real estate, as well as for providing mortgages to other investors.

Employer-Sponsored Programs: Basic Plans

Employers can sponsor two types of retirement programs—*basic plans,* in which employees automatically participate after a certain period of employment, and *supplemental plans,* which are mostly voluntary programs that enable employees to increase the amount of funds being set aside for retirement. We will look first at some of the key characteristics of basic plans. Apart from financing, there are certain features of employer-sponsored pension plans that you should become familiar with, including participation requirements, contributory obligations, benefit rights, retirement age, and methods of computing benefits.

Participation Requirements.   In many pension plans, employees must meet certain criteria before they become eligible for participation. Most common are requirements relating to years of service, minimum age, level of earnings, and employment classification. Years of service and/or minimum-age requirements are often incorporated into retirement plans in the belief that a much greater labor turnover rate applies to both newly hired and younger employees. Therefore, to reduce the administrative costs of these plans, employees in these categories are excluded from participation. Pension plans that limit enrollment to employees who earn in excess of a given salary amount generally are designed to integrate with social security. Recall that social security replaces a much higher percentage of lost earnings for workers who receive relatively low pay, but employees who earn higher salaries need a supplemental plan to prevent a material reduction in income at retirement.

What's Your Contribution? Whether or not you, as an employee, have to make any payments toward your own pension depends on the type of plan you're in. If you belong to a **noncontributory pension plan**, the employer pays the total cost of the benefits—you don't have to pay a thing. Under a **contributory pension plan**, the cost is shared by both the employer and the employee.

While most corporate pension plans today are noncontributory, a growing number of them are rapidly switching to the contributory type. In addition, nearly all plans for employees of federal, state, and local government require a contribution from the employee. In contributory plans, the employee's share of the costs is frequently between 3 and 10 percent of annual wages and is typically paid through a payroll deduction. Probably the most common arrangement is for the employer to match the employee's contribution such that the employee puts up half the annual contribution and the employer puts up the other half. When employees who have participated in a contributory retirement plan terminate employment prior to retirement, they are legally entitled to some benefit based on the amount of their own contributions. Usually this benefit is a cash lump sum, but in some cases it can be taken as a monthly payment at retirement. Whether departing employees receive any benefit from the *employer's* contributions depends on the plan's benefit rights.

Vested Interest: A Right to the Benefits.   Not everyone who participates in a pension plan will earn the right to receive retirement benefits. Pension plans impose criteria that must be met before the employee can obtain a nonforfeitable right to a pension. When nonforfeitable rights are secured by employees, they are said to be **vested rights**. Prior

---

Employee Retirement Income Security Act (ERISA)
A law passed in 1974 to ensure that workers eligible for pensions would actually receive such benefits; also permits uncovered workers to establish individual tax-sheltered retirement plans. Also known as the *Pension Reform Act.*

noncontributory pension plan
A pension plan in which the employer pays the total cost of the benefits.

contributory pension plan
A pension plan in which the employee bears a portion of the cost of the benefits.

vested rights
Employees' nonforfeitable rights to receive benefits in a pension plan based on their own and their employer's contributions.

to 1974, employers often required workers to be employed for 25 years or more before vesting would occur. An employee who left before completing this specified period of employment would lose all of the employer-sponsored pension benefits previously earned. Because of the high mobility of labor and capital, many workers at retirement faced the prospect of no pension. One of the principal purposes of the Pension Reform Act of 1974 (ERISA) was to eliminate this unfair practice (which indirectly contributed to the social problem of low incomes among the aged). ERISA required covered employers to grant employees vested rights after no more than 10 years of employment (when there was no partial vesting prior to 10 years of service), or alternatively, 15 years, where partial vesting began after five years.

While ERISA was certainly a step in the right direction, even better vesting requirements came in 1986 with the passage of the Tax Reform Act. A provision of that act accelerated the vesting period so that, as it now stands, *full vesting* rights are required after only five to seven years of employment. More specifically, companies must now choose between two vesting schedules. One, the so-called *cliff* vesting, requires full vesting after no more than five years of service—but you obtain no vesting privileges until then. It's sort of a "zero-one" proposition: there are no vesting privileges at all for the first five years, and then all of a sudden you're fully vested. Once vested, you're entitled to everything that's been paid in so far (your contributions plus your employer's) and everything that will be contributed in the future. Under the alternative procedure, the so-called *graded* schedule, vesting takes place gradually over the first seven years of employment. At the minimum, after three years you would have a nonforfeitable right to at least 20 percent of the benefits, with an additional 20 percent each year thereafter until you're 100 percent vested after seven years. Note, however, that these are minimum standards, and there's nothing to prohibit employers from granting more favorable vesting terms.

To illustrate the vesting process, assume that a medium-sized firm offers a plan in which full vesting of benefits occurs after five years. The plan is contributory, with employees paying 3 percent of their salaries and the employer paying an amount equal to 6 percent of the salaries. Under this plan,

employees cannot withdraw the contributions made by the employer until they reach retirement. The plan provides annual benefits in the amount of $11 per year of service for each $100 of an employee's final monthly earnings—the amount earned during the final month in the employ of the firm. Therefore, an employee who worked a minimum of five years for the firm would be eligible for a retirement benefit from that company even if he or she left the company at, say, age 30. However, because of inflation, the value of the benefit for a worker who left the firm long before retirement age would be very small.

Two cases, one for a career employee and one for the minimum-years-of-service employee, might help to clarify this concept. A career employee with 40 years of service and final monthly earnings of $4,200 would be entitled to an annual pension of $18,480 (40 years × $11 × $4,200/$100).

In sharp contrast, the benefits at retirement would be considerably smaller for an employee who, earning the same $4,200 monthly, worked for only five years before leaving the firm at, say, age 35. In this case, the employee would receive only $2,310 annually (5 years × $11 × $4,200/$100) when he or she retires at the company's normal retirement age of 65. However, the amount of inflation that would occur over the 30 years before reaching the standard retirement age would seriously diminish the purchasing power of the $2,310. Consequently, the employee might be better off simply withdrawing his or her own contributions (which always vest immediately) and terminating participation in the plan at the same time he or she leaves the employer. Any worker who left the firm prior to accumulating five years of service would be entitled only to a return of his or her own contributions to the plan (plus nominal investment earnings).

Because participation in a company's basic pension plan is mandatory, you're entitled to immediate vesting of all contributions. **Fantasy:** While your employer may offer immediate vesting, that's usually not the case. By law, you're entitled to full vesting rights within a maximum of five to seven years, depending on whether the company is using cliff or graded vesting procedures.

Retirement Age. Nearly all retirement plans specify when an eligible employee is entitled to benefits—in most cases, at age 65. Often pension plans also provide an early retirement age. In these cases, employees may begin receiving benefits prior to the normal retirement age, but the amounts paid out will also be less than normal. Many retirement plans for public employees also give workers the option of retiring after a stated number of years of service (say, 30 or 35) at full benefits, regardless of their age at the time. In the past, the trend in pension plans was toward earlier permissible retirement ages. However, now that many have begun to argue in favor of increasing the age for mandatory retirement, it is expected that there'll be little motivation to further reduce the normal retirement age.

Defined Contributions or Defined Benefits. The method used to compute benefits at retirement is spelled out in detail in every retirement plan. The two most commonly used methods are the defined contribution plan and the defined benefits plan. A **defined contribution plan** is one that specifies the amount of contribution that the employer and employee must make. At retirement, the worker is awarded whatever level of monthly benefits those contributions will purchase. While factors such as age, income level, and the amount of contributions made to the plan have a great deal to do with the amount of monthly benefits received at retirement, probably no variable is more important than the level of *investment performance* generated on the contributed funds. A defined contribution plan, in effect, is like a variable annuity: nothing is promised at retirement except the returns that the fund managers have been able to obtain. The only thing that's defined is the amount of contribution that the employee and/or employer have to make (generally stated as a percent of the employee's income); the benefits at retirement depend totally on investment results. Of course, there's a certain standard of care that's followed by the investment managers, so there is some protection provided to the plan participants (indeed, most of the investing is confined to high-quality investment vehicles). But even so, that still leaves a lot of room for variability in returns. There'll be a big difference in retirement benefits for someone who's in a fund that's earned 6 percent versus someone else who's in a fund that's earned 9 percent.

Under a **defined benefits plan**, the formula for computing benefits, not contributions, is stipulated in the plan provisions. These benefits are paid out regardless of how well (or poorly) the retirement funds are invested. If investment performance falls short, the employer has to make up the difference to come up with the benefits agreed to in the plan. This type of plan allows employees to determine before retirement how much their monthly retirement income will be. Often the number of years of service and amount of earnings are prime factors in the formula. For example, a worker might be paid 2½ percent of his or her final three-year average annual salary for each year of service. Thus, the *annual* benefit to an employee whose final three-year average annual salary was $65,000 and who was with the company for 20 years would be $32,500 (2½% × $65,000 × 20 years). Other types of defined benefits plans may simply pay benefits based on (1) a consideration of earnings excluding years of service, (2) a consideration of years of service excluding earnings, or (3) a flat amount with no consideration given to either earnings or years of service. Many defined benefits plans also increase retirement benefits periodically to help retirees keep up with the cost of living. In periods of high inflation, these increases are essential to maintain retirees' standards of living.

Regardless of the method used to calculate benefit amounts, the employee's basic concern should be with the percent of final take-home pay that the plan is likely to produce at retirement. A pension is usually thought to be good if, when combined with social security, it will result in a monthly income of 70 to 80 percent of preretirement net earnings. To reach this goal, however, today's employee

defined contribution plan
A pension plan that specifies the amount of contributions that both employer and employee must make; it makes no promises concerning the size of the benefits at retirement.

defined benefits plan
A pension plan in which the formula for computing benefits is stipulated in its provisions, thus allowing the employee to determine prior to retirement how much his or her retirement income will be.

must take some of the responsibility, because there's a growing trend for *companies to switch from defined benefits plans to defined contributions programs.* Companies don't like the idea of being faced with undefined future pension liabilities—after all, the pension/retirement payments that don't come from investment earnings have to be made from company earnings, and that means lower profits. So a lot of firms are avoiding these problems by gradually changing over to defined contributions plans. And in cases where the firms are sticking with their defined benefits plans, the benefits are often so meager that they don't come close to the desired 70 to 80 percent income target. (Some of the defined contributions plans don't either.) In either case *the employee is being forced to assume more responsibility for assuring the desired level of post-retirement income.* The logic from the company's perspective is that if obtaining a comfortable standard of living in retirement is a worthwhile objective, the employee should be willing to help achieve it. That might mean participating in a company-sponsored supplemental retirement plan and/or possibly even setting up your own self-directed program (we'll look at both supplemental and self-directed plans later).

Funding Procedures. Pension plans must provide for the financing of benefits that will be paid out to retired workers. An **unfunded pension plan** allows the employer to make payments to retirees from current income. One expert has called unfunded pensions "owe as you go" plans. This name really is appropriate, since employers accumulate liabilities throughout the working careers of their employees but do not necessarily put any assets aside to offset them. In the past, only a small minority of employees have been covered under unfunded pension plans; and they have received a good deal of unfavorable publicity as being too risky for employees. Consequently, the Employee Retirement Income Security Act sets forth minimum funding standards for pension plans.

Funded pension plans are those that formally establish charges against current income to allow for the pension liabilities as they accrue. The amount of liability that arises under the plan each year is determined by actuarial computations. (An *actuary* is an expert in calculating risks and pre-

miums for insurance.) These computations take into account such factors as mortality rates among workers and retirees, actual and potential investment earnings, labor turnover, normal and early retirement ages, and salary levels. In order for a funded plan to be "actuarially sound," the assumptions concerning the foregoing factors must be realistic. In addition, the method of funding must be sound. Few persons advocate placing pension fund assets in speculative investments such as land development projects or commodity futures. On the other hand, many persons support the now common practice of investing a large percentage of the fund assets in common stocks, corporate bonds and convertible securities, mortgages, and income-producing real estate.

Funding of pension plans represents an attempt to minimize the risk that benefits will not be available to an eligible employee upon retirement. Nonetheless, the unfunded plan of a large, solvent government unit or corporate employer sometimes can offer a better guarantee of payment than the funded plan of a financially weak firm. This may be particularly true when the primary objective of the actuarial assumptions of a funded system shifts from certainty of future payment to minimization of the employer's annual contributions to the plan. Requirements under the Employee Retirement Income Security Act attempt to control the lack of adequate funding in funded plans by requiring that *reasonable actuarial estimates* be used when calculating employer contributions.

Qualified Pension Plans. The Internal Revenue Code permits a corporate employer making contributions to a **qualified pension plan** to deduct from taxable income its contributions to the plan. As a result, the employees on whose behalf the contributions are made do not have to include these payments as part of their taxable income until the benefits are actually received. Further, in contributory plans, *the employee can also shelter his or her contribution from taxes.* In other words, such contributions are not counted as part of taxable income in the year in which they are made, but instead act to reduce the amount of taxable income reported to the IRS, and therefore lead to lower taxes for the employee. Still another tax advantage of these plans is that any and all investment income is allowed to accumulate tax-free; as a result, investment capital can build up quicker. Yet, in spite of all these tax benefits, a lot of firms still believe that the costs of regulation exceed any benefits that might result and therefore choose to forgo the procedures required for having a plan qualified. Probably the biggest disadvantage of nonqualified pension plans from the employee's perspective is that any contributions made to *contributory* plans are fully taxable and as such, are treated just like any other type of income.

Employer-Sponsored Programs: Supplemental Plans

In addition to basic retirement programs, many employers offer supplemental plans. These plans are often *voluntary* and enable employees to not only increase the amount of funds being held for retirement but also enjoy the attractive tax benefits that accompany some of these plans. Essentially, there are three types of supplemental plans: profit-sharing, thrift and savings, and salary reduction plans.

Profit-Sharing Plans. Profit-sharing plans permit employees to participate in the earnings of their employer. A **profit-sharing plan** may be qualified under the IRS and become eligible for essentially the same tax treatment as other types of pension plans. An argument in support of the use of profit-sharing plans is that they encourage employees to work harder because the employees benefit when the firm prospers. Whether these types of plans accomplish this goal is debatable. One advantage of profit-sharing plans from the firm's viewpoint, however, is that they do not impose any specific levels of contribution or benefits on the part of the employer. When profits are low, the employer is liable for a proportionately smaller contribution to the plan; when profits are high, the firm pays proportionately more, and the employees benefit.

In order to provide reasonable returns, many employers establish minimum and maximum amounts to be paid as contributions to profit-sharing plans, regardless of how low or high corporate earnings are. Contributions from profit-sharing plans can be invested in life insurance annuity contracts, stocks and bonds, or, in many cases, securities issued by the employing firm.

Employees who opt to purchase the firm's securities may benefit twice. When profits are good, larger contributions are made to the profit-sharing plan *plus* the price of the shares already owned is likely to increase. A number of big-time, major firms offer voluntary profit-sharing plans that invest heavily in their own stock. It's not unusual in many of these cases for long-term career employees to accumulate several hundred thousand dollars worth of the company's stocks. And we're not talking about highly paid corporate executives here; rather, these are just average employees who had the discipline to consistently divert a portion of their salary to the company's profit-sharing plan.

Thrift and Savings Plans. **Thrift and savings plans** were established to supplement pension and other insurance fringe benefits. Most plans require the employer to make contributions to the savings plan in an amount equal to a set proportion of the amount contributed by the employee. For example, an employer might match an employee's contributions at the rate of 50 cents on the dollar up to, say, 6 percent of salary. An employee making $20,000 a year could pay $1,200 into the plan annually, and

---

unfunded pension plan
A pension plan in which the employer must make payments to retirees from current income, because the plan itself has insufficient assets to cover existing liabilities.

funded pension plan
A pension plan that formally establishes charges against current income to allow for pension liabilities as they accrue in order to minimize the risk that benefits will be unavailable to an eligible employee upon retirement.

qualified pension plan
A pension plan that meets specified criteria established by the Internal Revenue Code.

profit-sharing plan
An arrangement in which the employees of a firm participate in the company's earnings.

thrift and savings plan
A plan established by an employer to supplement pension and other fringe benefits, in which the firm makes contributions in an amount equal to a set proportion of the employee's contribution.

the employer would add another $600. These contributions are then deposited with a trustee, who invests the money in various types of securities, including stocks and bonds of the employing firm. With IRS-qualified thrift and savings plans, the employer's contributions and earnings on the savings are not included in the *employee's* taxable income until he or she withdraws these sums. Unfortunately, this attractive tax feature does not extend to the employee's contributions, and as a result, any money put into one of these savings plans is still considered to be part of the employee's taxable income—subject to regular income taxes.

Thrift and savings plans usually have more liberal vesting and withdrawal privileges than pension and retirement programs. Often the employee's right to the contributions of the employer becomes nonforfeitable immediately upon payment, and the total savings in the plan can be withdrawn by giving proper notice. Those employees who terminate participation in such a plan, however, are frequently prohibited from rejoining it for a specified period, such as one year. An employee who has the option should seriously consider participation in a thrift plan, since the returns are usually pretty favorable—especially when you factor in the added kicker provided by the *employer's* contributions.

Salary Reduction Plans. Another type of supplemental retirement program—and certainly the most popular as judged by employee response—is the **salary reduction plan**, or the so-called **401(k) plan** as it's more popularly known. While our discussion here will center on 401(k) plans, similar programs are available for employees of public, nonprofit organizations; known as 403(b) plans, they offer many of the same features and tax shelter provisions as 401(k) plans.

A 401(k) plan basically gives the employee the option to divert a portion of his or her salary to a company-sponsored, tax-sheltered savings account. In this way, the earnings diverted to the savings plan accumulate tax free. Taxes must be paid eventually, but not until the employee starts drawing down the account at retirement, presumably when in a lower tax bracket. In 1989 an individual employee could put as much as $7,627 (depending on his/her salary) into a tax-deferred 401(k) plan—the annual dollar cap increases yearly, as it's indexed to the rate of inflation. (The contribution limits for a

403(b) plans are currently set at a maximum of $9,500 a year, and that amount won't be indexed to inflation until 401(k) contributions attain parity with these plans.) Of course, in order for you to participate in one of these plans, the company you work for must offer it. Fortunately, the vast majority of medium- to large-sized firms have done just that!

To see how such tax-deferred plans work, consider an individual who earned, say, $45,000 in 1989 and would like to contribute the maximum allowable—$7,627—to the 401(k) plan where she works. Doing so would reduce her taxable income to $37,373 and, assuming she's in the 28 percent tax bracket, lower her federal tax bill by some $2,136 (i.e., $7,627 $\times$ .28). Such tax savings will offset a good portion of her contribution to the 401(k) savings plan—specifically, it will fund about 28 percent of her contribution. In effect, she will add $7,627 to her retirement program with only $5,491 of her own money; the rest will come from the IRS via a reduced tax bill! Further, all the *earnings* on her savings account will accumulate tax-free as well.

These plans are generally viewed as highly attractive *tax shelters* that offer not only substantial tax savings but also a way to save for retirement. As a rule, so long as you can afford to put the money aside, you should seriously consider joining a 401(k)/403(b) plan if offered at your place of employment. This is especially true today because the restrictions placed on IRA's by the Tax Reform Act of 1986 mean these plans may be the only avenue you have for setting up a supplemental tax-sheltered retirement program. But there's more: A special attraction of 401(k) plans is that the firms offering them can sweeten the pot by matching all or a part of the employee's contributions. Presently, about 85 percent of the companies that offer 401(k) plans have some type of matching contributions program, often putting up 50 cents (or more) for every dollar contributed by the employee. Such matching plans provide both tax and savings incentives to individuals and clearly enhance the appeal of 401(k) plans.

Evaluating Employer-Sponsored Pension Plans

When you participate in a company-sponsored pension plan, you're entitled to certain benefits in return for meeting certain conditions of membership—which may or may not include making contributions to the plan. Whether your participation is limited to the firm's basic plan or includes one or more of the supplemental programs, *it's vital that you take the time to acquaint yourself with the various benefits and provisions* of these retirement plans. And be sure to familiarize yourself not only with the basic plans (even though participation is mandatory, you ought to know what you're getting for your money), but also with any (voluntary) supplemental plans that you may be eligible to join.

So, how should you evaluate these plans? Most experts agree that while there are many aspects that go into a typical company-sponsored pension plan (some of which are a bit complex and difficult to evaluate), you can get a pretty good handle on essential plan provisions and retirement benefits by taking a close look at these features:

- *Eligibility requirements*—precisely what they are, and if you're not already in the plan, when will you be able to participate?
- *Defined benefits* or *contributions*—which are defined? If it's the benefits, exactly what formula is used to define them? Pay particular attention to how social security benefits are treated in the formula. If it's a defined contributions program, do you have any control over how the money is invested? If so, what are your options?
- *Vesting procedures*—does the company use a cliff or graded procedure, and precisely when do you become fully vested?
- *Contributory or noncontributory*—if the plan is contributory, how much comes from you and how much from the company; and what is the total of this contribution, as a percent of your salary? If it is noncontributory, what is the company's contribution, as a percent of your salary.
- *Retirement age*—what is the normal retirement age, and what provisions are there for *early retirement?* What happens if you leave the company before retirement? Are the pension benefits *portable*—i.e., can you take them with you if you change jobs?
- *Voluntary supplemental programs*—how much of your salary can you put into one or more of these plans, and what, if anything, is *matched* by the company? Remember, these are like defined contributions plans, so there's nothing guaranteed as far as benefits are concerned.

Indeed, as the *Money In Action* box notes, when it comes to defined contributions plans, it's important to find out just who's managing your money—you may be surprised to find out its *Y-O-U.*

Getting answers to these questions will help you determine where you stand and what, if any, improvements need to be made in your retirement plans. As part of this evaluation process, you should try to work up, as best you can, *a rough estimation of what your benefits are likely to be at retirement*—you're going to have to make some projections about future income levels, investment returns, etc., but it's an exercise well worth taking (before you start cranking out the numbers, however, check with the people who handle employee benefits at your place of work: they'll often give you the help you need). Then, using a procedure similar to what we did with the worksheet in Exhibit 15.1, you can estimate what portion of your retirement needs will be met from your company's basic pension plan. If there's a shortfall—*and there likely will be one*—it will indicate the extent to which you need to participate in some type of company-sponsored supplemental program, such as a 401(k) plan, or (alternatively) how much you're going to have to rely on your own savings and investments to come up with the kind of standard of living you're looking for in retirement. Such insights will enable you to more effectively dovetail the investment characteristics and retirement benefits of any company-sponsored retirement plans you're entitled to with the savings and investing that you do on your own.

Self-Directed Retirement Programs

In addition to participating in company-sponsored retirement programs, individuals can also set up their own tax-sheltered retirement plans. There are

> **salary reduction,** or **401(k), plan**
> An agreement under which a portion of a covered employee's pay is withheld and invested in an annuity or other qualified form of investment; the taxes on both the contributions and the account earnings are deferred until the funds are withdrawn.

MONEY IN ACTION

"Who's Managing the Money in Your Plan?"

Millions of Americans are trusting their retirement money to inexperienced and confused investment managers—themselves. With more and more companies offering so-called defined contribution plans, workers are calling more of the shots about their retirement investments. And with those decisions go the risk, so investment mistakes made by workers in the new plans come straight out of their pension nest eggs, rather than being made up by companies.

In a defined contribution plan, an employer regularly contributes money to an employee's retirement account, but doesn't promise the size of the payout the employee will get on retirement. Defined contribution plans linked to profit-sharing, stock bonuses and other savings schemes have been around since the 1940s, but they've gotten a big boost in the past decade from expanded tax breaks that shelter contributions and investment earnings until a worker retires or changes jobs.

A major attraction of many plans is that companies will match half or more of worker contributions to the plan, producing automatic returns of 50% or better on the worker's contribution. But while employees often like the sense of control they get in defined contribution programs, serving as your own money manager is earthshaking to those people who haven't had the responsibility in the past. Furthermore, says financial consultant Jonathan Pond: "Some people are getting hurt along the way that wouldn't have gotten hurt with professionals" managing their retirement accounts.

Fastest Growing Benefit

So-called defined benefit plans, under which companies shoulder all the investment risk in promising to make specific payouts, still cover more workers and contain more assets. But defined contribution plans have become the fastest growing employee benefit, usually as a supplement to existing defined benefit pension plans.

Supplemental retirement income has become the focus of greater attention as people increasingly will spend as much time in retirement as they spend working. "Social Security was never meant to be the sole provider of your retirement income, and pension plans were never meant to be the sole provider," says Majorie Neville of pension consulting firm TPF&C. "There has to be a third leg, and that's personal saving."

With so much at stake, many participants in defined contribution plans just run for cover. Far and away the most popular investment choice in defined contribution plans are low-risk, fixed-rate guaranteed investment contracts offered by insurance companies. "Employees do not understand all their alternatives, so they do the safe thing," says Steven G. Vernon of pension consultants Wyatt Co. "They're afraid of the stock market, and they're not aware that over the longer term, the stock market gives them a better rate of return."

For participants, tax benefits

two basic types of self-directed retirement programs available: *Keogh plans,* which are for self-employed individuals, and *individual retirement accounts (IRAs),* which can be set up by just about anybody.

Keogh Plans. **Keogh plans** go back to 1962, when they were introduced as part of the Self-

Employed Individuals Retirement Act (HR-10), or simply the Keogh Act. Keogh plans allow self-employed individuals to establish tax-deferred retirement plans for themselves and their employees. Like contributions to 401(k) plans, payments to Keogh accounts may be taken as deductions from taxable income. As a result, they reduce the tax bills of self-employed individuals. The maxi-

and other provisions of individual company plans vary widely, so before you can take advantage of your plan, you need to know its features. Some 89% of defined contribution plans allow tax-deferred employee contributions (dubbed 401(k) plans) according to a Bankers Trust Co. survey.

In other plans, only the company contribution gets a tax shelter, although employees sometimes can make after-tax contributions on which gains accumulate tax-free. Some companies provide no matching funds; others contribute $1.50 for each $1 contributed by workers. A handful of companies place no restrictions on where plan assets are invested, while a few others offer no choice on investments, limiting them to company stock, for example. But together, the tax deferral and matching features can add up to produce handsome results: A worker making the 1988 maximum contribution of $7,313 a year with a 50% employer match and earning an annual 9% return would take only 25 years to reach $1 million with a tax-deferred retirement or savings plan.

So, faced with a number of investment decisions, what should an employee with a defined contribution plan do?

Diversify, Diversify, Diversify

Not putting all your eggs in one basket is becoming easier—or more complex, some say—because of the rapid growth in the number of investment options being offered under defined contribution plans. A 1977 Bankers Trust survey of plans found 15% offered more than three investment choices; a decade later, 41% of plans had more than three choices, and the number continues to rise. A typical investment menu would include stock, bond and money market mutual funds, a "balanced" fund combining stocks and bonds or perhaps different stock investment styles, and a fixed-rate guaranteed investment contract. Stock index funds, which mimic moves of the Standard & Poor's 500 index, were unheard of in defined contribution plans 10 years ago, but now are increasingly common.

A very basic diversification formula for allocating assets involves dividing investments into thirds—with equal amounts going to stocks, long-term bonds and short-term funds, including guaranteed investment contracts and money market funds. Investors willing to spend time on economic homework might make a bigger bet on either stocks or bonds. A 60–40 split in favor of stocks would pay off in a rising economy, and the opposite mix should do better in a declining economy. Whatever investment mix you decide on, force yourself to stick with those choices for at least a couple of years, preferably longer. Don't get caught in the trap of trying to time the market—that truly is a losing proposition. No matter what you do, don't forget: It's your money!

Source: James A. White. "Are You Your Own Pension Manager?" *The Wall Street Journal,* January 16, 1989, C1, p. 13. Reprinted by permission of *The Wall Street Journal,* © Dow Jones & Company, Inc. 1989. All Rights Reserved Worldwide.

mum contribution to this tax-deferred retirement plan is $30,000 per year or 20 percent of earned income, whichever is less.

Any individual who is self-employed, either full- or part-time, is eligible to set up a Keogh account. Not only can self-employed businesspeople or professionals use Keoghs; they can also be used by individuals who hold full-time jobs and "moon-

> **Keogh plan**
> An account to which self-employed persons may make payments, up to the lesser of $30,000 or 20 percent of earned income per year, that may be taken as deductions from taxable income; the earnings on such accounts also accrue on a tax-deferred basis.

light" on a part-time basis—for example, the engineer who has a small consulting business on the side or the accountant who does tax returns in the evenings and on weekends. If the engineer, for example, earns $10,000 a year from his part-time consulting business, he can contribute 20 percent of that income ($2,000) to his Keogh account and, in so doing, reduce both his taxable income and the amount he pays in taxes. Further, he is still eligible to receive full retirement benefits from his full-time job, as well as having his own IRA (though, as we'll see below, contributions to his IRA probably will not qualify for tax shelter). The only catch to Keogh accounts is that the individual must be self-employed—that is, the income must be derived from the net earnings (after all expenses except taxes and retirement contributions) of a self-employed business.

Keogh accounts can be opened at banks, insurance companies, brokerage houses, mutual funds, and other financial institutions. Annual contributions must be made at the time the respective tax return is filed or by April 15th of the following calendar year (for example, you have until April 15, 1990, to make the contribution to your Keogh for 1989). While a designated financial institution acts as custodian of all the funds held in a Keogh account, *the actual investments held in the account are under the complete direction of the individual contributor.* Unlike 401(k) plans, these are self-directed retirement programs and, as such, the *individual* decides which investments to buy and sell (subject to a few basic restrictions).

The income earned from the investments must be plowed back to the account and it, too, accrues tax free. All Keogh contributions and investment earnings must remain in the account until the individual turns 59½, unless he or she becomes seriously ill or disabled. However, the individual is *not required* to start withdrawing the funds at age 59½; the funds can stay in the account (and continue to earn tax-free income) until the individual is 70½, at which time he or she has ten years to clean out the account. In fact, so long as the self-employment income continues, an individual can continue to make tax-deferred contributions to a Keogh account until reaching the maximum age of 70½. Of course, once he or she starts withdrawing funds from a Keogh account (upon or after turning 59½), all such withdrawals are treated as ordinary income and subject to the payment of normal income taxes. Thus, the taxes on all contributions to and earnings from a Keogh account will eventually have to be paid, a characteristic of any tax-*deferred* (as opposed to tax-*free*) program. (*Note:* A program that's similar in many respects to the Keogh account is something called a *Simplified Employee Pension Plan*—or SEP-IRA for short. It's aimed at small-business owners, particularly those with *no employees,* who want a plan that is simple to set up and administer. SEP-IRA's *can be used in place of Keoghs* and while they are simpler to administer and have the same dollar annual contribution cap ($30,000), their contribution rate is less generous: you can put in only 15 percent of earned income for a SEP-IRA, versus 20 percent for a Keogh.)

Individual Retirement Accounts (IRAs) Some people mistakenly believe that an IRA is a specialized type of investment. It is not. Actually, an **individual retirement account (IRA)** is virtually the same as any other investment account you open with a bank, savings and loan, credit union, stockbroker, mutual fund, or insurance company. The form you complete designates the account as an IRA and makes the institution its trustee. That is all there is to it.

Basically, any gainfully employed individual can have an IRA account, though the *annual contributions* of only certain individuals qualify as tax deductions. Specifically, in order to be able to use your annual IRA contributions as a tax deduction, one of the following two conditions has to be met: (1) neither you nor your spouse (if filing a joint return) can be covered by a company-sponsored pension plan, or (2) your adjusted gross income has to be less than $40,000 (for married couples) or $25,000 (for singles). Translated, this means your IRA contributions would fully qualify as a tax deduction if you were covered by a company-sponsored pension plan but your adjusted gross income fell below the specified amounts (of $40,000 for joint filers or $25,000 for singles), *or if* you (or your spouse) weren't covered by a company-sponsored pension plan, no matter how much your adjusted gross income was. (Note that the income ceilings are phased out, so that people with adjusted gross incomes of $40,000 to $50,000 (or $25,000 to $35,000) who are covered by employer pension plans, are still entitled to prorated *partial deductions.*) The annual contribution limits are $2,000 for an individual and $2,250 for an individual and nonworking spouse. If both spouses work, each can contribute up to $2,000 to his or her own IRA. If the contributions qualify as tax deductions (as per the two conditions noted above), then the amount of the IRA contributions can be shown on the tax return as a deduction from taxable income—which, of course, will also reduce the amount of taxes that have to be paid. And understand that even if you don't qualify for a tax deduction, *you can still contribute up to the maximum of $2,000 a year to an IRA account;* the only difference (and it's a big one) is that these nondeductible contributions will have to be made with after-tax income.

As with Keoghs and 401(k) programs, the taxes on all the *earnings* from an IRA account are deferred until you start drawing down the funds, and this provision applies regardless of your income or whether you're already covered by a pension plan at your place of employment! You can deposit as much or as little as you want (up to the ceilings), and there are no percentage of income limitations; if your earned income is only, say, $1,800, you can contribute all of it to your IRA.

IRAs are like Keogh plans in that they are both *self-directed accounts*—meaning you are free, within limits, to make whatever investment decisions you want. Actually, as with any investment, an individual can be conservative or aggressive in choosing securities for an IRA (or Keogh), though the nature of these retirement programs generally favors a more conservative approach. In fact, conventional wisdom favors funding your IRA (and Keogh) with *income-producing assets;* this would also suggest that if you are looking for capital gains, it is best to do so *outside* your retirement account. The reasons are twofold: (1) growth-oriented securities are by nature *more risky,* and (2) you *cannot write off losses* from the sale of securities held in an IRA (or Keogh) account. This does not mean it would be altogether inappropriate to place a good-quality growth stock or mutual fund in a Keogh or IRA—in fact, many advisors contend that growth investments should always have a place in your retirement account due to their often impressive performance: Such investments may pay off handsomely, since they can appreciate totally free of taxes. In the end, of course, *it is how much you*

have in your retirement account that matters rather than how your earnings were made along the way. Also, regardless of what type of investment vehicle you use, keep in mind that once the money's been placed into an IRA, it's meant to stay there for the long haul. For like most tax-sheltered retirement programs, there are severe restrictions on when you can withdraw the funds from an IRA. Specifically, except in the case of serious illness, any funds withdrawn from an IRA prior to age 59½ are subject to a penalty, on top of the regular tax paid on the withdrawal.

Prior to the Tax Reform Act of 1986, IRAs had become immensely popular. By 1985 over 40 million Americans held IRAs, with an estimated worth of nearly $250 billion! The tax overhaul bill, however, sharply curtailed the tax-shelter feature of IRAs, and as a result, these accounts lost a lot of their appeal. Contributions plunged as most people who no longer qualified for tax-sheltered contributions simply quit putting their money into IRAs. And those who continued to make contributions even though they were nondeductible got hit with horrendous recordkeeping requirements and an IRS tax form that is second to none in complexity. In particular, anyone who contributes money that is not tax deductible must now file a *Form 8606* (for "Nondeductible IRA Contributions") with his or her federal tax returns. It's pretty clear that Congress wants to sharply curtail the use of IRAs; and if tax statutes don't do the job, then a bunch of mostly unnecessary red tape will! This is all very unfortunate, since most retirement experts agree that the original IRA concept was a great one.

So, should you contribute to an IRA or not? Obviously, if you qualify for *fully deductible* contributions (as per the two provisions as spelled out above) you should seriously consider making the maximum payments allowable. You do not need to

---

individual retirement account (IRA)
A retirement plan, open to any working American, to which a person may contribute a specified amount each year (up to $2,000 in the case of an individual taxpayer); while annual contributions to IRAs may or may not be tax deductible, the earnings for all IRAs do accrue on a tax-deferred basis.

worry about onerous recordkeeping requirements or filing a Form 8606 with your taxes. For these individuals, the IRA continues to be an excellent vehicle for sheltering some of their income from taxes. But if your contributions don't qualify for full deductability, the prevailing sentiment seems to be to avoid nondeductible IRAs; for not only do you have a number of substantial hurdles to overcome, but some equally attractive alternatives are available for sheltering your income. As a starter, find out if the company you work for has a 401(k)—or 403(b)—plan in existence and if so, use it. Or you might want to consider parking your money in a *tax-sheltered annuity*. It offers basically the same advantages as a nondeductible IRA, with the added kicker that there's no limit as to how much you can put in each year (remember, you can only put $2,000 a year into an IRA).

Your contributions to an IRA account may or may not be tax deductible, depending in part on your level of income. **Fact:** Whether or not your IRA contributions are fully deductible depends to a large extent on your adjusted gross income—specifically, the contributions are considered *fully* deductible if your adjusted gross income is less than $40,000, for joint returns ($25,000 for individual returns); if your income is more than this, your IRA contributions would be fully deductible only if you're not already covered by a company-sponsored pension plan.

Government Influence on Pension Plans

The two major areas of government influence on pension plans are the Internal Revenue Code (IRC) requirements for plan qualification and the rules and regulations established by the Employee Retirement Income Security Act of 1974 (ERISA). The major stipulations of the IRC were discussed earlier in the chapter. At this point, we will look at the most important features of ERISA. As the name implies, the act's primary objective is to increase the probability that employees who are covered by a retirement plan throughout their working careers will in fact receive benefits upon retirement. ERISA covers nearly all pension and retirement plans created by private employers engaged in interstate commerce. It does not cover plans sponsored by government, charitable organizations, or firms exclusively involved in intrastate commerce. The law regulates only plans that are in existence. It does not require firms to begin a retirement plan for their employees, nor does it prohibit them from discontinuing an existing plan (as many have done to avoid the myriad ERISA rules and regulations). Similarly, ERISA does not force companies to pay any minimum amounts to employees, other than those specified in the plans.

ERISA basically prescribes minimum standards with which covered plans must comply. These standards apply to plan provisions, funding, and administration. Among the major items treated are vesting, eligibility for participation, definition of service, minimum funding requirements, disclosure to participants, and employer fiduciary responsibility. Another important provision establishes the **Pension Benefit Guarantee Corporation (PBGC)**. The purpose of this organization is to guarantee eligible workers that certain benefits will be payable to them even if their employer's plan has insufficient assets to fulfill its commitments. The funding for the PBGC comes from charges that are levied against all employers regulated by ERISA. In essence, the PBGC provides plan termination insurance to covered employees. Although the implementation of ERISA has not been problem-free, most observers agree that this law is a good start in insuring that employees who have earned pensions will receive them.

SUMMARY

- Retirement planning plays a vital role in the personal financial planning process and for many people is its centerpiece. It employs many of the same basic principles and concepts of effective financial planning, including the establishment of financial goals and strategies, the use of savings and investment plans, and the use of certain insurance products, like annuities.
- Rather than address retirement planning in a series of short-run (three- to five-year) plans, the

long-term approach goes 20 to 30 years into the future to determine how much saving and investing you must do today to achieve the retirement goals you've set for tomorrow. To implement a long-term retirement plan, certain steps should be followed, including determining future retirement needs, estimating retirement income from known sources (like social security and company pension plans), finding the amount of the estimated funding shortfall, determining how big the retirement nest egg has to be to cover the income shortfall, and finally, deciding on how much to save and invest each year in order to build up the desired nest egg.

- Social security is the basic foundation of the retirement programs of most families; except for a few exempt classes (of mostly government employees), almost all gainfully employed workers are covered by social security. Upon retirement (at age 62 to 65), covered workers are entitled to certain monthly benefits, as determined mainly by the employee's earning history and age at retirement.

- Annuities are also an important source of income to retired people; basically, an annuity is an investment vehicle that provides for the systematic *liquidation (payout)* of all invested capital, and earnings, over an extended period of time. A wide variety of annuities exists, including single-payment and installment-premium, fixed and variable, immediate and deferred, life, and guaranteed-minimum.

- Private and government employer pension and retirement plans provide a third—and often vital—source of retirement income: Such plans can often spell the difference between enjoying a comfortable standard of living in retirement or a bare subsistence. In addition to *basic* retirement programs, in which all employees participate after a certain period of employment, there are also several forms of *supplemental* employer-sponsored retirement plans including profit-sharing plans, thrift and savings plans, and perhaps the most popular of all, salary reduction plans (the so-called 401k plans).

- In addition to company-sponsored retirement programs, individuals can also set up their own self-directed tax-sheltered retirement plans; it is through such plans that most individuals can build up the nest egg they will need to meet the retirement objectives they have set for themselves. The two basic types of self-directed retirement programs are Keogh plans, which are for self-employed individuals, and IRAs, which can be set up by any salary or wage earner.

QUESTIONS AND PROBLEMS

1. Discuss the relationship of retirement planning to financial planning; does investment and/or tax planning have a role in retirement planning? Identify and briefly discuss each of the steps in the retirement planning process.

▪ **2.** Al and Linda Chung would like to retire while they are still relatively young—in about 20 years. Both have promising careers, and both make good money. As a result, they are willing to put aside whatever is necessary to achieve a very comfortable lifestyle in retirement. Their current level of household expenditures (excluding savings) is around $60,000 a year, and they expect to spend even more in retirement; they think they'll need about 125 percent of that amount (note: 125 percent equals a multiplier factor of 1.25). They estimate that their social security benefits will amount to $15,000 a year in today's dollars and that they will receive another $25,000 annually from their company pension plans. They feel that future inflation will amount to about 3 percent a year; in addition,

---

Pension Benefit Guarantee Corporation (PBGC)

An organization established under ERISA that guarantees to eligible workers payability of certain pension benefits regardless of the employer's ability to fulfill its commitments.

they think they will be able to earn about 10 percent on their investments prior to retirement and about 8 percent afterward. Use a worksheet like the one in Exhibit 15.1 to find out how big their investment nest egg will have to be and how much they will have to save annually in order to accumulate such an amount within the next 20 years.

3. What benefits are provided under the Social Security Act? Describe the basic operations of the social security system.

4. Many critics of the social security program feel that participants are getting a substandard investment return on their money. Discuss why you agree or disagree with this point of view.

5. Are all employed and self-employed persons covered under the social security program? Explain.

6. Discuss the old-age and survivor's benefits provided to retirees and their dependents under the social security program.

7. Use Exhibit 15.5 to determine the amount of social security retirement benefits that Elwood Cheeseater would receive annually if he had a high level of career earnings, is age 62, and has a dependent wife. If Elwood also receives another $47,500 a year from a company pension and some tax-exempt bonds that he holds, will he be liable for any tax on his social security income? Explain.

8. Does social security coverage relieve you of the need to do some retirement planning on your own? Explain. What is a *Personal Earnings and Benefit Estimate Statement,* and how would such a statement help you in your retirement planning?

9. What is an annuity? Briefly explain how an annuity works, and also how it differs from a life insurance policy?

10. Differentiate between a single-premium annuity and an installment-premium annuity.

11. Briefly explain the four procedures that are most widely used in the distribution of annuity proceeds. Which one results in the highest monthly payment?

12. Describe and differentiate among (a) an immediate annuity, (b) a deferred annuity, (c) a straight life annuity, and (d) a refund annuity.

13. What is a fixed-rate annuity, and how does it differ from a variable annuity? Does the type of contract (whether it's fixed or variable) have any bearing on the amount of money you'll receive at the time of distribution? Explain. Which type of contract would probably be most suitable for someone who wants a minimum amount of risk exposure? What's the purpose of a *bailout provision* in a fixed-rate annuity?

14. Explain how the purchase of a variable annuity is much like an investment in a mutual fund. Do you, as a buyer, have any control over the amount of investment risk to which you're exposed in a variable annuity contract? Explain.

15. Briefly explain why annuities are a type of tax-sheltered investment; is there anything you have to give up in order to obtain this tax-favored treatment (*Hint:* age 59½)?
   a. Why is it important to check the financial ratings of an insurance company when buying an annuity?
   b. Why is it important to look at past performance when considering the purchase of a variable annuity?

16. Which basic features of employer-sponsored pension plans should you be familiar with? Explain.

17. Discuss the distinguishing features of (a) funded, (b) qualified, (c) defined benefit, and (d) contributory pension plans. Under which procedure will you become *fully vested* the quickest: cliff or graded vesting? Explain.

18. What is the difference between a profit-sharing plan and a salary reduction, or 401(k), plan? Are these basic or supplemental plans?

19. Why is it important to evaluate the pension plan(s) offered by your employer? What do you stand to gain by becoming familiar with your employer's pension plan provisions and retirement benefits? Identify and briefly discuss at least six different plan provisions that you feel would be important in such an evaluation.

20. Briefly describe the tax provisions of 401(k) plans and IRAs. Would you describe these plans as tax-deferred or tax-free programs? Explain.

21. Describe and differentiate between Keogh plans and individual retirement accounts (IRAs).

22. Describe ERISA, and discuss its influence on pension plans.

CASE PROBLEMS

15.1 Evaluating Kerry Cooper's Retirement Benefits

Kerry Cooper, age 55, works as the general manager for a large department store chain headquartered in Dallas. Although Kerry has been with the company for 25 years and does not wish to retire in the immediate future, it is the company's policy that workers retire at age 65. The company has a defined benefit plan that pays a retired employee 2.5 percent of the last 12 months' salary annually for each year of service completed. Kerry will also be eligible for social security and medicare. He has already paid off the mortgage on his $240,000 home and has no other debts. His two children are married and do not depend on him for any financial assistance. Upon retirement, he plans to go on a long vacation abroad, play golf, and fish. He does not anticipate any financial problems. However, his wife, Olivia, is concerned that with his reduced income, they will not be able to retain their maid, attend social gatherings, and make regular visits to the country club. In short, she is afraid that in view of the benefits Kerry is to receive and the rising rate of inflation, they will not be able to maintain their current standard of living once Kerry retires.

Questions

1. If Kerry's average salary in his last year of service with the company is $108,000, how much per year will the defined benefit plan pay him?

2. Assume Kerry's average yearly earnings have always equaled or exceeded the maximum social security tax base. Using Exhibit 15.5, determine the annual social security payments he would be entitled to receive. (Assume Olivia has never held a job outside the home.)

3. Do you believe that given the quality of life the Coopers desire, the above amounts (company pension and social security) will be sufficient? How would you view Olivia's concerns?

4. Express Kerry's total annual retirement benefits from the company and social security as a percentage of his annual preretirement salary of $108,000. Comment on this percentage, and make appropriate recommendations to Kerry.

5. Based on the information provided, evaluate the effectiveness of Kerry's retirement planning.

15.2 Comparing Pension Plan Features: Which Plan Is Best?

Mary Carpenter and Ellen Shoemaker are neighbors in Kansas City. Mary works as a systems engineer for United Foods Corporation, Topeka Foods Division, while Ellen works as an executive assistant for U.S. Steel and Castings. Both are married, have two children, and are well paid. Before Mary and Ellen joined their respective companies, there had been some employee unrest and strikes. To counteract these problems, their firms had developed job enrichment and employee motivation programs. Of particular interest are the portions of these programs that deal with pensions and retirement.

Topeka Foods has a contributory plan under which 5 percent of the employees' annual wages is deducted to meet the cost of the benefits. An amount equal to the employee contribution is also contributed by the company. The plan uses a seven-year graded vesting procedure; it has a normal retirement age of 60 for all employees and the benefits at retirement are paid according to a defined contribution plan.

Although U.S. Steel and Castings has a minimum retirement age of 60, it provides for an extension period of five to six years before compulsory retirement. Employees (full-time, hourly, or salaried) also must meet participation requirements. Further, in contrast to the Topeka plan, the U.S. Steel and Castings program has a noncontributory feature. Annual retirement benefits are computed according to the following formula: 1 percent of the employee's final annual salary for each year of service with the company is paid upon retirement. The plan vests immediately.

Questions

1. Discuss the basic features of the retirement plans offered by Topeka Foods and U.S. Steel and Castings.
2. Which plan do you think is more desirable considering the basic features, retirement age, and benefit computations explained?
3. Explain how you would use each of these plans in developing your own retirement program.
4. What role, if any, could the purchase of annuities play in these retirement programs? Discuss the pros and cons of using annuities as a part of retirement planning.

FOR MORE INFORMATION

General Information Articles

Albright, Philip, "Is a Nondeductible IRA for You?" *Sylvia Porter's Personal Finance,* March 1988, pp. 57–58.

Marsa, Linda, "401(k) Plans: Even Better Than IRAs," *Sylvia Porter's Personal Finance,* June 1987, pp. 91–93.

Schiffres, Manuel, "Social Security: Should You Count on It?" *Changing Times,* October 1988, pp. 71–76.

Updegrave, Walter L., "Annuities: How to Cut Through the Flimflam," *Money,* April 1988, pp. 129–136.

Wiles, Russ, "Annuities: Income Streamers," *Personal Investor,* March 1988, pp. 82–87.

Willis, Clint, "Retiring Soonest with the Mostest," *Money,* November 1988, pp. 78–87.

Government Documents & Other Publications

Are You Planning on Living the Rest of Your Life? U.S. Government Printing Office; Superintendent of Documents; Washington, D.C. 20402.

Securing Your Retirement Dollars. American Council of Life Insurance; 1850 K Street, NW; Washington, D.C. 20006.

What You Should Know About Your Pension Plan. Labor-Management Services Administration; Pension & Welfare Benefit Programs; U.S. Department of Labor; 200 Constitution Avenue, NW; Washington, D.C. 20216.

Your Social Security. Consumer Information Center; General Services Administration; Washington, D.C. 20405.

1. One of Mark's and Ana's long-term goals is to retire in 35 years when Mark is 60. Their current living expenses are approximately $55,000, but they feel they would be able to live during retirement on about 80 percent of their current living expenses. While future income is difficult to estimate, Mark and Ana expect to receive approximately $1,700 a month from social security and about $700 a month from Mark's company pension plan. The company Ana is employed by does not offer a corporate pension plan. Calculate Mark's and Ana's retirement income and investment needs assuming an average rate of inflation of 5 percent, an 8 percent return on investments after retirement, and a 10 percent return on investments prior to retirement.

2. Mark and Ana are uncertain about their ability to invest so much a year for retirement out of their current budget. Calculate their retirement income and investment needs if they decided to retire in 40, rather than 35, years. In this case, they would expect to receive $1,850 a month from social security and $800 a month from Mark's pension plan.

3. As part of Mark's and Ana's restated goals (presented at the end of Part One), they indicated that they wanted to each contribute $1,000 a year to their respective 401(k) retirement accounts. After looking at their retirement needs and reviewing the 401(k) arrangements for each of their employers, recommend an investment strategy for their retirement funds. You might also want to consider an IRA versus the 401(k) accounts.

4. Refer to Mark's and Ana's most recent budget. Can they afford your recommendation? If yes, revise their budget, if needed, to reflect any changes in expenditures resulting from this investment strategy.

CHAPTER 16

Preserving Your Estate

Financial Facts or Fantasies

Are the following statements financial facts (true) or fantasies (false)?

- Estate planning is one of the key elements of personal financial planning.
- The wealthy are the only ones who have to worry about making out wills.
- Due to recent changes in the law, a person no longer has to be mentally competent in order to draw up a valid will.
- Once a will is drawn up, it is a relatively simple matter to make minor changes to it.
- In order for a living trust to be legally enforceable, it must be irrevocable.
- There are no federal estate taxes on estates of up to $600,000.

Like it or not, no one lives forever! Although this thought may depress you, its reality certainly warrants your attention. For if you do not give some consideration to the ultimate disposal of your accumulated wealth, chances are that only a part of your estate will be left for your heirs and beneficiaries—the rest will go (often unnecessarily) to taxes and various administrative costs. The importance of developing plans and taking action during your lifetime to ensure that your wealth will be accumulated, preserved, and, upon your death, distributed in the desired fashion cannot be underestimated. This process, which is called *estate planning*, requires knowledge of wills, trusts, and taxes. An understanding of these components and their interrelationships should make it possible for you to minimize the estate shrinkage that will occur after your death while still achieving your lifetime personal financial goals. Also, keep in mind that not only wealthy people but also individuals of modest or moderate means need to plan their estates. Estate planning can be defined as a goal-oriented activity that uses tax-minimization tools and techniques to provide the greatest possible financial security for an individual and his or her heirs or beneficiaries.

PRINCIPLES OF ESTATE PLANNING

> The overriding objective of estate planning is to ensure the orderly transfer of as much of one's estate as possible to heirs and/or designated beneficiaries. Do you need estate planning? How about your parents? Before reading on, spend a few moments assessing the importance of estate planning by you and by your parents.

Estate planning is one of the key elements of personal financial planning. It is closely related to both insurance and retirement planning. Certainly the most important reason for buying life insurance is to provide for your family in the event of your premature death. Likewise, one of the principal challenges of effective retirement planning is to achieve a comfortable standard of living in retirement while at the same time *preserving* as much of your accumulated wealth as possible. This not only reduces the chances of you (or your spouse) outliving your financial resources but also leaves money for your estate that can be passed on to your heirs and designated beneficiaries. Another aspect of financial planning that is important to estate planning is *taxes*. As with other parts of financial planning, one of the major objectives of estate planning is to eliminate or minimize tax exposure. Doing so, of course, will increase the amount of your estate that ultimately will be passed on to your heirs and beneficiaries.

Estate planning is very goal-oriented. The goals that usually motivate people to engage in estate planning include securing enough capital to meet college education costs and other special needs; insuring financial security for family members in the event of the death of the head of household; taking care of oneself and one's family during a long-term disability; and providing for a comfortable retirement.

Planning occurs in every estate. Some planning is controlled by the estate owner and/or his or her professional counselors. Other planning—uncontrolled by the estate owner—is done by the federal and state governments. This *uncontrolled planning* occurs when the estate owner forfeits the right to arrange for the disposition of assets and the minimization of tax and other estate settlement costs. Individuals who wish to plan their estates must systematically uncover problems in a number of important areas and provide solutions for them. Exhibit 16.1 itemizes the major types of problems along with their associated causes or indicators. These problems can be minimized or eliminated by maximizing the after-tax return on personal and business investments while minimizing the forces of estate impairment, such as taxes and administrative costs. Techniques for accomplishing this objective are discussed in later sections.

Estate planning is one of the key elements of personal financial planning. **Fact:** One of the principal objectives of financial planning is to be able to transfer as much accumulated wealth to your heirs and designated beneficiaries as possible—a goal that is made easier through effective estate planning.

Who Needs Estate Planning?

Estate planning is indicated when there is a need for either "people planning" or *"asset planning."*

People Planning. *People planning* means anticipating the psychological and financial needs of those people and organizations you love and providing enough income or capital or both to ensure a continuation of their way of life. People planning also means keeping Mother's cameo brooch in the family and out of the pawnshop or preserving the business that Granddad started in the early 1900s. People planning is especially important to those individuals with (1) children who are minors, (2) children who are exceptionally artistic or intellectually gifted, (3) children or other dependents who are emotionally, mentally, or physically handicapped, and (4) spouses who cannot or do not want to handle money, securities, or a business.

Minor children cannot legally handle large sums of money or deal directly with real estate or securities. Custodial accounts, guardianships, or trusts are necessary for providing administration, security, financial advice, and the legal capacity to act on behalf of minors. Few children are exceptionally artistic or intellectually gifted, but those who are often need—or should have—special (and often expensive) schooling, travel opportunities, or

EXHIBIT 16.1

Potential Estate Planning Problems and Major Causes or Indicators

A number of problems can arise during the settlement of an estate that could have been prevented through careful estate planning. The first step toward prevention of problems is an awareness and understanding of their major causes or indicators.

Problem	Major Cause or Indicator
▪ Excessive transfer costs	Taxes and estate administrative expenses higher than necessary.
▪ Lack of liquidity	Insufficient cash. Not enough assets that are quickly and inexpensively convertible to cash within a short period of time to meet tax demands and other costs.
▪ Improper disposition of assets	Beneficiaries receive the wrong asset or the proper asset in the wrong manner or at the wrong time.
▪ Inadequate income at retirement	Capital insufficient or not readily convertible to income-producing status.
▪ Inadequate income, if disabled	High medical costs, capital insufficient or not readily convertible to income-producing status, difficulty in reducing living standards.
▪ Inadequate income for family at estate owner's death	Any of the above causes.
▪ Insufficient capital	Excessive taxes, inflation, improper investment planning.
▪ Special problems	A family member with a serious illness or physical or emotional problem, children of a prior marriage, beneficiaries who have extraordinary medical or financial needs, business problems, or opportunities.

equipment. Emotionally, mentally, or physically handicapped children (and other relatives) may need nursing, medical, or psychiatric care. Clearly, outright gifts of money or property to those who cannot care for themselves are foolishly inappropriate. These individuals may need more (or less) than other children. An individual who gives all of his or her children equal shares may not be giving them equitable shares.

How many of us have handled hundreds of thousands of dollars? Think of the burden we place on others when we expect a spouse who cannot—or does not want to—handle such large sums of money or securities to do so with what may be his or her only assets. The bottom line of "people planning" is that one engages in the process for only one reason: because one cares. Sometimes "spend it" is the best planning under the circumstances.

Asset Planning. From the standpoint of wealth alone, estate planning is essential for anyone—single, widowed, married, or divorced—with an estate exceeding $600,000. When a closely held business is involved, estate planning is essential in order to stabilize and maximize the asset- and income-producing value, both during the owner's lifetime and at the owner's death or disability. Likewise, es-

tate planning is essential to avoid the special problems that occur when an estate owner holds title to property in more than one state, such as incurring attorneys' fees in each state or being taxed on the same assets by more than one state.

Why Does an Estate Break Up?

Quite often, when people die, their estates die with them—not because they have done anything wrong but because they have not done *anything*. There are numerous forces that, if unchecked, tend to shrink an estate, reduce the usefulness of its assets, and frustrate the objectives of the person who built it. These include death-related costs, inflation, improper management, lack of liquidity, incorrect use of vehicles of transfer, and disabilities.

Death-Related Costs. Last-illness and funeral expenses are good examples of **first-level death-related costs**. Most people also die with some cur-

> **first-level death-related costs**
> Death-related costs that include last-illness and funeral expenses, unpaid debts, and unpaid income and property taxes.

rent bills unpaid and long-term obligations, such as mortgages, business loans, and installment contracts, outstanding. Unpaid income taxes as well as property taxes also constitute debts often payable by the deceased's estate. **Second-level death-related costs** consist of the fees of attorneys, appraisers, and accountants and probate expenses—so-called administrative costs, federal estate taxes, and state death taxes (some states have both inheritance and estate taxes).

Inflation. Death-related costs are only the tip of the estate-impairment iceberg. Less obvious but often more damaging is the profound effect of inflation. Failure to continuously reappraise and rearrange an estate plan so as to counter the effects of inflation can impair the ability of assets—liquid, real and personal property, or investments—to provide steady and adequate levels of financial security.

Improper Management. Business assets, as well as some commercial real estate properties, require continuous attention; often the estate beneficiaries are unable or unwilling to provide this needed care. The failure to note a change in consumer preferences or product or equipment obsolescence may result in a rapid decline in the value of a decedent's business or of various types of assets included within the estate.

Lack of Liquidity. Insufficient cash to cover death costs and other estate obligations has always been a major factor in estate impairment. Forced sacrifice sales of assets with substantial income-producing power usually result in a disproportionately large loss of assets and family income. Further, such sales—of the choicest parcel of farmland or a business that has been in the family for generations, for instance—often have undesirable psychological effects on the heirs. The outcome can be a devastating financial and emotional blow.

Incorrect Use of Vehicles of Transfer. It would be criminally negligent to put a high-powered car in the hands of a child. Yet assets are often put into the hands of beneficiaries who are unwilling or unable to handle them. Because of improper usage of vehicles of transfer, property often passes to unintended beneficiaries or to the proper beneficiaries in an improper manner or at an incorrect time. For example, spendthrift spouses or minors may be left large sums of money outright in the form of life insurance, through joint ownership of a savings account, or as the beneficiaries of an employee fringe benefit plan.

Disabilities. A prolonged and expensive disability of a family wage earner is often called a *living death*. Loss of income due to disability is frequently coupled with a massive financial drain caused by the illness itself. The financial situation is further complicated by inadequate management of currently owned assets. This not only threatens the family's financial security but also diminishes the value of the estate at an incredible speed.

What Is Your Estate?

Your *estate* is your property—whatever you own. Your **probate estate** consists of the real and personal property that you own in your own name that can be transferred according to the terms of a will at death or under *intestate* laws if you have no valid will. A distinction must be made between the probate estate (a property law concept that essentially encompasses assets passing by will) and the gross estate (a tax law term that may encompass a considerably larger amount of property). Your **gross estate** includes all the property subject to federal estate tax at your death, both probate and nonprobate. Life insurance, jointly held property with rights of survivorship, and property passing under certain employee benefit plans are common examples of nonprobate assets that might be subject to federal (and perhaps state) estate taxes.

In addition, you may have property that is not probate property and will not be part of your estate for federal estate tax purposes yet will pass to your family and form part of their financial security program. There are two types of such assets. One is *properly arranged* life insurance. For instance, your adult daughter could purchase, pay the premiums for, and be the beneficiary of a policy on your life. At your death, the proceeds would not be included as part of your estate. The other type of financial asset that falls into this category is social security. Payments to a surviving spouse and minor children generally are neither probate assets nor subject to any federal (or state) estate taxes. Because of the freedom from administrative costs and taxes, this category of assets provides unique and substantial estate planning opportunities.

The Estate Planning Process

The estate planning process consists of a number of important steps. First, comprehensive and accurate data on all aspects of the family must be gathered. Exhibit 16.2 summarizes the types of factual data required by professionals in order to prepare detailed estate plans. Next, the data gathered must be categorized into general problem areas, and estate transfer costs must be estimated. With this information, the estate plan is then formulated and preparations made for its implementation. The objective of estate plans, of course, is to maximize the usefulness of people's assets during their lives and to achieve their personal objectives after their death. The final steps in the estate planning process involve testing and implementing the proposed plan.

Once the plan has been implemented, it is important to keep in mind that it is good only for as long as it fits the needs, desires, and circumstances of the parties involved. As these elements change, the estate plan must also be modified. Marriage or remarriage, divorce, the birth of a child, a change of job or location, and substantial changes in income, health, or living standards are the types of events that indicate a need for a review. Even if none of these occur, a review of life insurance needs should automatically be scheduled at least once every two years and a full estate audit made at least once every three to five years (or whenever there has been a major change in the federal or state death tax laws). Because of the general complexity of the laws relating to estate transfer, the assistance of estate planners, life insurance professionals (CLUs), chartered financial consultants (ChFCs), certified financial planners (CFPs), accountants, and attorneys is often necessary in the planning and evaluation process. Due to the com-

plexity and individual nature of estate planning, more specific guidelines are not included in this chapter.

WILLS

A will is a legal document that specifies the details of how an individual wishes to dispose of his or her estate. Have you prepared a will? Spend a few moments listing reasons why you have or have not yet prepared a will before reading ahead.

A *will* is a written legal expression or declaration of a person's wishes as to how his or her property is to be disposed upon his or her death. The importance of a valid will can be illustrated in light of what happens when a person dies without one.

Absence of a Valid Will: Intestacy

Intestacy describes the situation that exists when a person dies without a valid will. Some intestacy laws "draw the will the decedent failed to make" to

second-level death-related costs
Administrative death-related costs such as attorneys', appraisers', and accountants' fees, probate expenses, federal estate taxes, and state death taxes.

probate estate
The real and personal property owned by a person that can be transferred at death according to the terms of a will or under intestate laws in the absence of a valid will.

gross estate
All property—both probate and nonprobate—subject to federal estate taxes at a person's death.

intestacy
The condition that exists when a person dies without a valid will.

EXHIBIT 16.2

Factual Data Required in Estate Planning

The first step in developing an effective estate plan is to gather comprehensive and accurate data on all aspects of the family. The types of factual data required by professionals are listed below.

Personal data:
Names, addresses, phone numbers, family consultants
Family birthdates, occupations, health problems, support needs
Citizenship, marital status, marital agreements, wills, trusts, custodianships, trust beneficiary, gifts or inheritances, social security numbers, education, and military service.

Property (except life insurance or business):
Classification, title, indebtedness, basis, date and manner of acquisition, value of marketable securities, and location

Life insurance

Health insurance:
Medical expense insurance
Disability income

Business interest:
Name, address, ownership
Valuation factors; desired survivorship control; name, address, and phone number of business attorney and accountant

Employee census data

Employee benefits

Family income:
Income of client, spouse, dependent children, income tax information

Family finances:
Budget information, investment preferences
Ranking of economic objectives, capital needs, other objectives

Income and capital needs:
Retirement: Age, required amount, potential sources
Disability: Required amount, sources
Death: Expected sources of income

Liabilities:
Classification of liabilities, creditors, amounts, whether insured or secured

Factors affecting plan:
Gift propensity, charitable inclinations, emotional maturity of children, basic desires for estate distribution

Authorization for information:
Life insurance

Receipt for documents:
Personal and business

Observations from interview

Source: Copyright © 1988 by The American College, Bryn Mawr, Pa. Reprinted from Confidential Personal and Financial Data form, *Advanced Estate Planning Course.* All rights reserved.

determine the disposition of the probate property of persons who have died intestate. These statutes enumerate certain preferred classes of survivors. Generally, the decedent's spouse is favored, followed by the children and then other descendants. If the spouse and children or other descendants, such as grandchildren or great-grandchildren, survive, they will divide the estate, and other relatives or charitable organizations will receive nothing. If

no spouse, children, or other descendants survive, the deceased's parents, brothers, and sisters will receive a share of the estate.

The disposition of a typical intestate estate can be illustrated with a simple example. Assume an individual died with no valid will. That individual's separately owned property would be distributed as shown in Exhibit 16.3 after deduction of debts, taxes, and state family exemptions. If the deceased

EXHIBIT 16.3

Distribution of a Typical Intestate Estate

If an individual dies intestate—without a valid will—the estate will be distributed according to preestablished state statutes or guidelines.

Decedent Dies Leaving	Distribution	
Spouse and children or their descendants.	Spouse receives one third	Children receive two-thirds divided equally
Spouse and one child or child's descendants	Spouse receives one half	Child receives one-half
Spouse but no children or their descendants, and decedent's mother or father survives	Spouse receives $10,000 plus one half of balance	Father and mother or surviving parent (if one is already deceased) receive one-half of balance
Spouse but no children or their descendants, and no parent survives	Spouse receives $10,000 plus one half of balance	Brothers and sisters receive one half of balance divided equally
Spouse but no children or their descendants, and no parent, brother, sister, niece, nephew, grandparent, uncle, or aunt survives	Spouse receives all	
Child or children but no spouse		Child or children receive all divided equally
No spouse and no children or their descendants, and decedent's mother or father survives		Mother and father receive all
No spouse and no children or their descendants, and no parent of the decedent survives		Brothers and sisters receive all divided equally

Source: Courtesy of Stephan R. Leimberg, Esq., Bryn Mawr, Pa.

left no wife or husband, child or descendant, parent, brother or sister or descendant, grandparent, or uncle or aunt or their children, the state normally would take all of the property. Had the deceased even in this situation had a will, the property could have been directed to some nonrelated individual or to a charity. Aside from having lost control of the disposition of property to individuals or charities, the person who died intestate has also forfeited the privileges of naming a personal representative to guide the disposition of the estate, naming a guardian for persons and property, and specifying which beneficiaries would bear certain tax burdens. In addition, with a valid will the amount of estate shrinkage can be minimized through the use of certain deductions and exclusions that may not be available when a person dies intestate. The importance of a valid will—regardless of the size of an estate—

must not be overlooked in the personal financial planning process.

Preparation of the Will

A will can be defined as a written document that allows a person, called a **testator**, to determine the disposition of property at his or her death. A key characteristic of a will is that it can be changed or revoked at any time prior to the testator's (will owner's) death. Upon the death of the testator, it becomes operative and applies to the situation that

testator

A person whose will directs the disposition of property at his or her death.

exists at that time. Will preparation, or drafting, varies with respect to difficulty and cost depending on individual circumstances. In some cases a two-page will costing $100 may be adequate, while in others a complex document costing $1,500 or more may be necessary. A will must not only effectively accomplish the objectives specified for distribution of assets but also take into consideration income, gift, and estate tax laws. Often a knowledge of the corporate, trust, real estate, and securities laws is required as well. Note that a will, important as it is, is useless and perhaps even dangerous if it does not consider and coordinate assets passing outside its limits.

Information Requirements. A properly prepared will should (1) provide a plan for distributing the testator's assets in accordance with his or her wishes, the beneficiaries' needs, and federal and state dispositive and tax laws; (2) consider the changes in family circumstances that might occur after its execution; and (3) be unambiguous and complete in describing the testator's desires. By following these general guidelines, the testator generally can develop a satisfactory will.

Use of an Attorney. *Will drafting, no matter how modest the size of the estate, should not be attempted by a layperson.* The complexity and interrelationships of tax, property, domestic relations, and other laws make the homemade will a frivolous if not dangerous document. Nowhere is the old adage, "He who has self for attorney has fool for client," more true, and nothing is more expensive in the long run than the do-it-yourself will—except, perhaps, the do-it-yourself heart transplant!

Common Features of the Will

Although there is no absolute format that must be followed in will preparation, most wills contain eight distinct parts: (1) introductory clause, (2) direction of payments, (3) dispositive provisions, (4) appointment clause, (5) tax clause, (6) common disaster clause, (7) execution and attestation clause, and (8) witness clause. Generalized examples of each of these clauses are briefly illustrated and described as follows. *These must be tailored to individual needs and circumstances by an attor-*

ney familiar with the testator's own statutory requirements.

The wealthy are the only ones who have to worry about making out wills. **Fantasy:** Nothing could be further from the truth! While the wealthy may have more motivation to do so, anyone who has accumulated an estate—no matter how small—should have a will drawn up that sets out how the estate is to be distributed to heirs and/or beneficiaries.

Introductory Clause. An introductory clause, or preamble, would normally take the following form:

> I, _____, of the city of _____, state of _____, do, hereby make my last will and revoke all wills and codicils made prior to this will.

The declaration of residence that is included here helps to determine the county that will have legal jurisdiction and be considered the testator's domicile for tax purposes. The portion of the clause related to revocation nullifies old and forgotten wills and *codicils*—legally binding modifications of an existing will.

Direction of Payments. The clause related to directing the estate with respect to certain payments of expenses is typically formulated along the following lines:

> I direct payment out of my estate of all just debts and the expenses of my last illness and funeral.

In many states, the rights of creditors are protected by law and such a clause is largely useless. However, the will of a married woman should contain a direction to pay debts and expenses. Otherwise, in a number of states the burden of funeral and medical expenses will lie primarily on her husband.

Dispositive Provisions. Three examples of dispositive clauses follow:

> I give and bequeath to my wife, Sally Fabian, all my jewelry, automobiles, books, and photography equipment, as well as all other articles of personal and household use.
>
> I give to the Chicago Historical Society the sum of $100,000.

All the rest, residue, and remainder of my estate, real and personal, wherever located, I give in equal one-half shares to my children, Charlee and Lara, their heirs and assigns forever.

The first type of clause disposes of personal effects. A testator should make a detailed and specific list of intimate personal property and carefully identify each item. The second type of clause, called a **pecuniary legacy**, passes money to a specified party. The correct title of a charity should be ascertained by direct and discreet inquiry. Note that the popular name is seldom the correct or full legal name. The third clause describes the distribution of residual assets after specific gifts have been made. The share of a person who dies before the testator will normally pass to the other residual heirs unless provision is made to the contrary. Of course, this result varies from state to state.

Appointment Clause. Examples of appointment clauses, which are typically included to appoint executors (the decedent's personal representatives), guardians, and trustees, as well as their successors, follow:

I hereby nominate, constitute, and appoint as Executor of this last Will and Testament my beloved husband Elrod Wilmeyer and my brother, Charles S. Warren III. In the event any persons named herein predecease me, or for any cause shall cease or fail to act, then I nominate, constitute, and appoint as Executor of my said will in the place and stead of any or one of said persons named herein, the Farmers and Merchants Bank of Omaha, Nebraska.

I appoint my brother, Eugene Smith, guardian of the person and property of my son, Farnsworth, during his minority.

The first clause is used to appoint executors and alternates, whose responsibility it is to administer the estate of the deceased (the importance of naming an executor and alternate is highlighted in a subsequent section of this chapter). The second clause is used to appoint a guardian. In many states, the surviving parent of an unmarried minor child can appoint a guardian of the person and property of the child. Often, the surviving parent is not allowed to become sole guardian of the property of a minor child.

Tax Clause. An example of a tax clause follows:

I direct that there shall be paid out of my residuary estate (from that portion which does not qualify for the marital deduction) all estate, inheritance, and similar taxes imposed by a government in respect to property includable in my estate for tax purposes, whether the property passes under this will or otherwise.

In the absence of a specified provision in the will, so-called **apportionment statutes** of the testator's state will allocate the burden of taxes among the beneficiaries. The result may be an inappropriate and unintended reduction of certain beneficiaries' shares or adverse income tax effects.

Common Disaster Clause. A sample of the type of clause often included within the will to protect against a common disaster or simultaneous death follows:

If my wife and I shall die under such circumstances that there is not sufficient evidence to determine the order of our deaths, then it shall be presumed that she survived me. My estate shall be administered and distributed in all respects in accordance with such assumption.

The assumption that the spouse survives is used mainly to permit the marital deduction, which offers a tax advantage. Other types of clauses are similarly designed to avoid double probate of the same assets—duplication of administrative and probate costs. One such clause requires that the survivor live for, say, 30 days in order to be a beneficiary under the will.

---

pecuniary legacy
A type of clause in a will that passes money to a designated party.

apportionment statutes
State laws that allocate the burden of taxes among the beneficiaries of a will in the absence of a specific provision for apportionment therein.

Execution and Attestation Clause. An example of the execution and attestation clause follows:

> In witness whereof, I have affixed my signature to this, my last will and testament, which consists of _____ pages, to each of which I have initialed, this _____ day of _____, One Thousand Nine Hundred and Ninety (1990).
>
> _____(Seal)

Every will should be in writing and signed by the testator at its end as a precaution against fraud; many attorneys suggest initialing each page after the last line and including a signature in the left-hand margin. Each page should, of course, be numbered.

Witness Clause. The final clause, which helps to affirm that the will in question is really that of the deceased, is similar to the following:

> Signed, sealed, and published by John S. Bragg, the testator, as his last will, in the presence of us, who, at his request, and in the presence of each other, all being present at the same time, have written our names as witnesses.

It is wise to use at least three witnesses and have them sign in the presence of one another. Their addresses should be noted on the will. If the testator is unable to sign his or her name for any reason, most states allow the testator to make a mark and to have another person (properly witnessed) sign for him or her.

Requirements of a Valid Will

To be valid, a will must be the product of a person with a sound mind; there must have been no *undue influence* (influence that would remove the testator's freedom of choice); the will itself must have been properly executed; and its execution must be free from fraud.

Mental Capacity. In order to be judged mentally competent, testators must have (1) a full and intelligent knowledge of the act in which they are involved, (2) an understanding of the property they possess, (3) a knowledge of the dispositions they want to make of it, and (4) an appreciation of the objects they desire to be the recipients of their bounty. Generally, such capacity is presumed; clear and convincing proof of mental incapacity is required to set aside a will, and the burden of proof is on the contestant.

Due to recent changes in the law, a person no longer has to be mentally competent in order to draw up a valid will. **Fantasy:** A person still must be mentally competent in order to draw up (or have drawn up) a legally enforceable will.

Freedom of Choice. A will is considered invalid if it can be shown that the testator was subject to the undue influence of another person at the time the will was made and executed. Threats, misrepresentations, inordinate flattery, or some physical or mental coercion employed to destroy the testator's freedom of choice are all types of undue influence.

Proper Execution. To be considered properly executed, a will must meet the requirements of the state's wills act or its equivalent. It must also be demonstrable that it is in fact the will of the testator. Most states have statutes that spell out (1) who may make a will—generally any person of sound mind, age 18 or older (age 21 in some states); (2) the form and execution a will must have—most states require a will to be in writing and signed by the testator at the logical end, preferably in black ink; and (3) requirements for witnesses. (Since no state requires more than three witnesses, this is the number that should sign as witnesses in the presence of the testator and one another. If at all possible, somebody other than a beneficiary should sign as a witness, since in a few states this could result in the disinheritance of that beneficiary. Many states have now provided for a *self-proving* will. For example, in Pennsylvania, if a testator's signing of the will is witnessed by two individuals who sign in the presence of each other and of a notary, those witnesses do not have to appear at the probate of the will. This saves time, money, and often a great deal of inconvenience to the executor.) The accompanying *Money in Action* box describes the benefits of videotaping the signing of a will in order to fend off any challenges that could arise in the future.

Changing or Revoking the Will: Codicils

A will is inoperative until the testator's death and therefore can be changed at any time until then. Wills should be revised periodically for many reasons. Modification is generally in order if there is a significant change in the testator's (or the beneficiaries') health or financial circumstances; if births, deaths, marriages, or divorces have altered the operative circumstances; or if substantial changes in the tax law have occurred. An existing will can be either changed or revoked, although in certain states a so-called *right of election* (explained later) exists.

Changing the Will.   In order to change an existing will, a **codicil**, which is a simple and convenient legal means of modifying an existing will, is drawn up. It is used when the will needs only minor modifications and is often a single-page document that reaffirms all the existing provisions in the will except the one to be changed. The codicil should be executed in accordance with the same formalities as a will and should be typed, signed, and witnessed in the same manner. Where substantial changes are required, a new will is usually preferable to a codicil. In addition, if a gift in the original will is removed, it may be best to draw a new will and destroy the old even if substantial changes are not required. This may help to avoid offending the omitted beneficiary. Sometimes, however, the prior will should not be destroyed even after the new will has been made and signed. If the new will fails for some reason (because of the testator's mental incapacity, for example), the prior will may qualify. Also, a prior will could help to prove a "continuity of testamentary purpose"—in other words, that the latest will (which may have provided a substantial gift to charity) was not an afterthought or the result of an unduly influenced mind.

Revoking the Will.   A will may be revoked either by the testator or automatically by the law. A testator can revoke a will by (1) making a later will that expressly revokes prior wills; (2) making a codicil that expressly revokes any wills; (3) making a later will that is inconsistent with a former will; and (4) physically mutilating, burning, tearing, or defacing the will with the intention of revoking it. The law automatically revokes or modifies a will under certain circumstances, which vary from state to state but generally revolve around (1) divorce, (2) marriage, (3) birth or adoption, and (4) murder. In many states, if a testator becomes divorced after making a will, all provisions in the will relating to the spouse become ineffective. If a testator marries after making a will, the spouse receives that portion of the estate that would have been received had the testator died without a valid will—unless the will gives the spouse a larger share. If a testator did not provide for a child born or adopted after the will was made (unless it appears that such lack of provision was intentional), the child receives that share of the estate not passing to the testator's spouse that would have been given to him or her had the deceased not had a will. Finally, almost all states have some type of *slayer's statute* forbidding a person who participates in a willful and unlawful murder from acquiring property as the result of the deed.

Once a will is drawn up, it is relatively simple to make minor changes to it. **Fact:** As long as the changes are minor, a simple and convenient way of legally modifying an existing will is a *codicil,* which is a short, legal document that specifies the changes.

Right of Election.   Many states provide still another way to change a will: through the **right of election** the survivor has the right to "take against the will"—to take a specified portion of the probate estate regardless of what the will provides. Most states give this right only to surviving spouses, while at least one state extends a similar right to the testator's children. One state, for example, allows a surviving spouse to take at least that share that would have been allowed had the deceased died without a valid will. This right is generally

---

codicil
A simple and convenient way of legally modifying an existing will without revoking it.

right of election
The right of a surviving spouse to take a specified portion of the probate estate regardless of what the will provides.

MONEY IN ACTION

Videotaping the Signing of Your Will

A videotape of the signing of your written will may be just what's needed to fend off would-be challengers. The procedure varies by state, but it does not usually involve (as popular legend has it) reading one's will into a camera to be played back before spellbound heirs. Explains Miami probate attorney Clay Craig: "A person can be pretty far around the bend and still retain the ability to read out loud." But if your will-signing ceremony also includes a discussion with your lawyer of the reasons for your bequests or of current affairs or hobbies, any slighted heirs can hardly claim that the document was the spawn of undue influence or unsound mind. Furthermore, by recording the signing and witnessing of the will, you preserve proof that proper legal procedures were carried out, thus eliminating a common ground for challenging a will.

Before putting on your best TV smile, though, ask yourself whether your will is really likely to prompt a fight. Prime candidates for estate battles are people who have been married more than once, have children from more than one marriage, disinherit expectant heirs, or make unusual bequests. "If you've been married only once and you're leaving half your estate to your wife and half to your kids, you probably won't be challenged," says Craig. "But if you're cutting out relatives and leaving it all to your housekeeper, watch out." Remember also that a video may not deter relatives who are determined to squabble. Auto magnate Henry Ford II left a videotaped letter explaining his paper will when he died in December 1987. But after one of the trustees of the estate also died, Ford's family battled for months over the trustee's successor and other issues.

Still, if you think your will may one day face a challenge, and you decide videotaping is the best defense, you may be asked to leave your camcorder home. Many attorneys insist on bringing in a legal videographer, a precaution that can add $200 to $700 to your legal bill. Of course, the cost may be worth it. A professional knows what and when to shoot so you can be sure your will is properly authenticated. And a professional can provide an affidavit attesting that the tape is accurate and hasn't been edited.

Lawyers and wills aside, there is no reason why you can't use your own camcorder to deliver a personal message to friends and family. A tape containing final words of affection and wisdom can help soothe grieving relatives while serving as a kind of video portrait for future generations.

Or it could serve as a video mallet over the head, if the not-yet-deceased has a mean streak. A woman in California left a seating chart with her lawyer along with her video will so she could turn to face each hopeful heir as she spoke. Then she went around the group, enumerating her reasons for rewarding or disinheriting them. A man in a New York City suburb was subtler. To make sure he was taken care of in his old age, he showered his family with expressions of undying love in a maudlin postmortem message—which he made sure they saw long before his demise. In his will, none of them got a cent.

Source: Excerpted from Charles E. Cohen, "Okay, Videotaping Buffs, Let's Get Real!", *Money*, January 1989, pp. 117–124. Used with permission.

forfeited by a spouse who deserted the testator or participated in the testator's willful and unlawful murder.

Safeguarding the Will

In most cases, the original of the will should be kept in a safe-deposit box together with deeds, contracts, and other valuable papers. (Although some authorities and many attorneys recommend leaving the original of a will with the attorney who drafted it, this may make make it awkward for the executor to choose his or her own attorney, a right that most states give the executor regardless of who drew the will or what the will states about who should be the estate's counsel. Further, it discourages the estate owner from changing the will or engaging a new attorney even if he or she moves out of the state in which the will was drawn.)

Exhibit 16.4 contains an executor's checklist of documents and information that should be kept in a safe-deposit box. If each spouse has a separate safe-deposit box, the couple may want to keep their wills in each other's boxes. Some states provide for *lodging* of the will, a mechanism for filing and safekeeping it in the office of the probate court (also called *orphan's* or *surrogate's court*). In those states, this procedure satisfies the need to safeguard the will.

Letter of Last Instructions

People frequently have thoughts they want to convey and instructions they wish to have carried out that cannot properly be included in their wills. These suggestions or recommendations should be included in a **letter of last instructions** in the form of an informal memorandum separate from the will. (Note: No bequests in this letter of last instructions should be made, since such documents have no legal standing.) Usually it is best to make several copies of the letter and keep one at home and the others in the hands of the estate's executor or an attorney or accountant to be mailed or delivered to beneficiaries at the appropriate time.

A letter of last instructions might provide directions with respect to (1) location of the will and other documents; (2) funeral and burial instructions (often a will is not opened until after the funeral); (3) suggestions or recommendations as to

the continuation, sale, or liquidation of a business (it is easier to freely suggest a course of action in such a letter than it is in a will); (4) personal matters that the testator might prefer not to be made public in the will, such as statements that might sound unkind or inconsiderate but would prove of great value to the executor (for example, comments about a spendthrift spouse or a reckless son); (5) legal and accounting services (executors are free, however, to choose their own counsel—not even testators can bind them in that selection); and (6) an explanation of the actions taken in the will, which may help avoid litigation (for instance, "I left only $1,000 to my son, Ramon, because . . ." or "I made no provisions for my oldest daughter, Melissa, because . . .").

Administration of an Estate

When people die, they usually own property and owe debts. Often they will have claims (accounts receivable) against other persons. A process of liquidation called a **probate process**, similar to that which occurs when a corporation is dissolved, must take place. In this process, money owed is collected, creditors (including the tax authorities) are satisfied, and what remains is distributed to the appropriate individuals and organizations. A local court generally supervises the probate process through a person designated as an **executor** in the decedent's will, or if the decedent died intestate (without a valid will), through a court-appointed administrator.

---

letter of last instructions
An informal memorandum separate from the will and containing suggestions or recommendations for carrying out its provisions.

probate process
The process of liquidation that occurs when a person dies, consisting of collecting and/or paying the deceased's debts and distributing the remaining assets to the designated individuals and organizations.

executor
The administrator of an estate designated in the decedent's will, or if the decedent died intestate, through a court-appointed administrator.

EXHIBIT 16.4
An Executor's Checklist of Items to Keep in a Safe-Deposit Box

This checklist itemizes the various documents and information that the executor will need to effectively carry out the terms of the will. These items should be kept in a safe-deposit box.

EXECUTOR'S CHECKLIST

Name (Testator) _____ Date _____

_____ 1. Birth Certificates	_____ 7. Bonds, Stocks, and Securities
_____ 2. Marriage Certificates (Including Any Prior Marriages)	_____ 8. Real Estate Deeds
	_____ 9. Business (Buy-Sell) Agreements
_____ 3. Your Will (and Spouse's Will) and Trust Agreements	_____ 10. Automobile Titles and Insurance Policies
_____ 4. Listing of Life Insurance Policies or Certificates	_____ 11. Property Insurance Policies
	_____ 12. Letter of Last Instructions
_____ 5. Your Social Security Numbers	_____ 13. Additional Documents
_____ 6. Military Discharge Papers	

List numbers of all checking and savings accounts including bank addresses and location of safe deposit boxes:

_____ _____ _____

_____ _____ _____

List name, address, and phone number of property and life insurance agent:

_____ _____ _____

_____ _____ _____

List name, address, and phone number of accountant:

_____ _____ _____

List name, address, and phone number of (current or past) employer. State date when you retired if applicable. Include employee benefits booklets:

_____ _____ _____

_____ _____ _____

List all debts owed to and owed by you:

_____ _____ _____

_____ _____ _____

List the names, addresses, telephone numbers, and birth dates of your children and other beneficiaries (including charitable beneficiaries):

_____ _____ _____

_____ _____ _____

_____ _____ _____

Source: Stephen R. Leimberg, Herbert Levy, Stephen N. Kandell, Morey S. Rosenbloom, and Ralph Gano Miller, *The Tools and Techniques of Estate Planning*, 7th ed. (Cincinnati: National Underwriter Company, 1989). Reprinted by permission of the publisher.

An executor or administrator, who is sometimes also referred to as the decedent's personal representative, must collect the assets of the decedent, pay debts or provide for the payment of debts that are not currently due, and distribute any remaining assets to the persons entitled to them by will or by the intestate law of the appropriate state. Estate administration is important for many reasons. One is that bank accounts and other contracts could not be collected without such a formal process because there would be no one who legally could bring suit or be entitled to give a release of liability. Another is that title to real estate could not be made marketable because there would be no insurance against the existence of a creditor with claims against the property. Due to the importance of the estate administration process, executors should be selected who are not only familiar with the testator's affairs but also exhibit good administrative skills.

What about Joint Ownership?

Many people take title to property jointly either through a joint tenancy or as tenants by the entirety. (There is a third common form called **tenancy in common**. This means that each tenant owns an interest that can be left to whomever he or she desires rather than to the other joint tenant. Likewise, a tenancy in common can be sold or given away without the consent of the other joint tenant.) These two forms of joint ownership have the following characteristics:

1. The interest of a decedent passes directly to the surviving joint tenant (that is, to the other joint owner) by operation of the law and is free from the claims of the decedent's creditors, heirs, or personal representatives.
2. A **joint tenancy with right of survivorship** may consist of any number of persons regardless of whether they are related by blood or marriage. A **tenancy by the entirety**, on the other hand, can exist only between husband and wife.
3. In the case of joint tenancy, each joint tenant can unilaterally sever the tenancy. This is not the case with a tenancy by the entirety, which can be severed only by mutual agreement or terminated by divorce or conveyance by both

spouses to a third party. In some states a tenancy by the entirety can exist only with respect to real property, while others do not recognize such tenancies at all.

The advantage of joint tenancy, the more common form of joint ownership, is that it offers a sense of family security, quick and easy transfer to the spouse at death, exemption of jointly owned property from the claims of the deceased's creditors, and avoidance of delays and publicity in the estate-settlement process. The key disadvantage of joint tenancy is that the jointly owned property cannot be controlled by a will and therefore does not permit the first joint owner to die to control the property's disposition and management upon his or her death. Another disadvantage is that higher potential tax costs are often incurred in both the creation and the severance of a joint tenancy. For example, a father who purchases and pays for property and places it in his own and his daughter's name is making a gift to her. Upon the termination of the tenancy, if the daughter receives the entire proceeds (for example, upon the sale of a jointly owned home), the father is making a second gift to her. In both situations, he will have gratuitously transferred an interest to her that she did not have before. Fortunately, since federal gift tax law does not tax most interspousal transfers, the problem will not arise on a federal level between a married

---

tenancy in common
Title to property under which each tenant who owns an interest is free to dispose of that interest without the consent of other tenants.

joint tenancy with right of survivorship
A type of ownership by two or more parties who share equal rights in and control of the property, with the survivor(s) continuing to hold all such rights on the death of one or more of the tenants. Each joint tenant can unilaterally sever the tenancy.

tenancy by the entirety
A form of ownership by husband and wife recognized in certain states in which the rights of the deceased spouse automatically pass to the survivor. Tenancy can be severed only by mutual agreement or divorce.

couple (although many states do tax such unintentional gifts). Because most people believe the advantage of joint ownership of major assets, such as a home or automobile, far outweigh the potential disadvantages, it is commonly utilized by married couples.

TRUSTS

> A trust is a legal document that facilitates the transfer of property, and/or the income from that property, to another party or parties. Why do you think trusts are frequently employed in the estate planning process? Before reading ahead, spend a few moments speculating as to the potential estate planning benefits of trusts.

A *trust* is a relationship created when one party, the **grantor** (also called the *settler* or *creator*) transfers property to a second party, the **trustee**, for the benefit of third parties, the **beneficiaries**, who may or may not include the grantor. The property placed in the trust is called *trust principal* or *res* (pronounced "race"). The trustee holds the legal title to the property in the trust and must use the property and any income it produces solely for the benefit of trust beneficiaries. The trust generally is created by a written document. The grantor spells out the substantive provisions (such as how the property in the trust is to be allocated and how income is to be distributed), as well as certain administrative provisions. A trust may be *living* (created during the grantor's life) or *testamentary* (created in a will). It may be *revocable* or *irrevocable*. Property placed into a revocable trust can be regained and the terms of the trust altered or amended. Property placed into an irrevocable trust cannot be recovered by the grantor during its term. The establishment of trusts is generally for those with substantial means; however, we will briefly describe the features of trusts as they relate to estate planning.

Purposes of Trusts

Trusts are designed for any number of reasons. The most common motives are to (1) attain income and estate tax savings and (2) manage and conserve property.

Income and Estate Tax Savings. Under certain circumstances, the burden of paying taxes on the income produced by securities, real estate, and other investments can be shifted from a high-bracket taxpayer to a trust itself or to its beneficiary, both of whom are typically subject to lower income tax rates than the grantor. However, the Tax Reform Act of 1986 severely limits the ability of a person to shift income in this manner. Specifically, with certain types of trusts, the beneficiary must be over 14 years of age; otherwise the income from the trust will be taxed at the same rate as the person setting up the trust. In addition to possible income tax benefits, impressive *estate tax* savings are also possible, because the appreciation in property placed into such a trust can be entirely removed from the grantor's estate and possibly benefit several generations of family members without incurring adverse federal estate tax consequences.

Management and Conservation of Property. Minors, spendthrifts, and mental incompetents need asset management for obvious reasons. However, busy executives and others who cannot or do not want to take the countless hours necessary to learn to handle large sums of money and other property often utilize trusts to relieve themselves of those burdens. The trustee assumes the responsibility for managing and conserving the property on behalf of the beneficiaries. The use of independent trustees is frequently employed by members of Congress and presidents to avoid potential conflicts of interest regarding investments. In some cases, management by the trustee is held in reserve in case a healthy and vigorous individual is unexpectedly incapacitated and becomes unable or unwilling to manage his or her assets.

Selecting a Trustee

Five qualities are essential in a trustee. He or she must (1) possess sound business knowledge and judgment, (2) have an intimate knowledge of the beneficiary's needs and financial situation, (3) be skilled in investment and trust management, (4) be available to beneficiaries (specifically, this means the trustee should be young enough to survive the trust term), and (5) be able to make decisions impartially. A corporate trustee, such as a trust company or bank that has been authorized to perform trust duties, may seem best able to meet these requirements. A corporate trustee is likely to have investment experience and will not impose the problems created by death, disability, or absence. Unlike a family member, a corporate trustee can be relied on to be impartial and obedient to the directions of the trust instrument. Such objectivity has added value if there are several beneficiaries. On the other hand, a corporate trustee may charge high fees or be overly conservative in investments, impersonal, or lacking in the familiarity with and understanding of family problems and needs. Often a compromise is suggested: the appointment of one (or more) individual(s) and a corporate trustee as co-trustees.

Common Types and Characteristics of Trusts

Although there are various types of trusts, the most common are the living trust, the testamentary trust, and the life insurance trust and pour-over will.

Living Trust. A **living** or **inter vivos trust** is one created during the grantor's lifetime. It can be either revocable or irrevocable and can last for a limited period or continue long after the grantor's death.

Revocable living trust. The grantor reserves the right to revoke the trust and regain the trust property in a **revocable living trust**. For federal income tax purposes, grantors of these trusts are treated as owners of the property in the trust—in other words, just as if they held the property in their own names. Therefore, they are taxed on any income produced by the trust. Three basic advantages of revocable living trusts are often cited. The first is that management continuity and income flow are assured even after the death of the grantor.

No probate is necessary, since the trust continues to operate after the death of the grantor just as it did while he or she was alive. A second advantage is that the burdens of investment decisions and management responsibility are assumed by the trustee. A good example of this can be found in the case of individuals who want to control investment decisions and management policy as long as they are alive and healthy but who set up a trust to provide backup help in case they become unable or unwilling to continue managing their assets. This type of living trust is, appropriately, called a **step-up trust**, because the trustee steps up to take the grantor's place in decision making and day-to-day management. A final advantage of the revocable living trust is that its terms and the amount of assets placed into it do not become public knowledge. Unlike with the probate process, the public has no right to know the terms or conditions of a revocable living trust. Disadvantages of such trusts include the fees charged by the trustee for manage-

grantor
A party (first party) in a trust relationship who transfers property to a second party for the benefit of third parties, who may or may not include the first party.

trustee
An organization or individual hired by the grantor to manage and conserve her or his property for the benefit of the beneficiaries.

beneficiary
An individual who receives benefits—income or property—from a trust or from the estate of a decedent.

living (inter vivos) trust
A trust created during the grantor's lifetime.

revocable living trust
A trust in which the grantor reserves the right to revoke it and regain the trust property.

step-up trust
A type of living trust in which the trustee "steps up" to take the grantor's place in decision making and day-to-day management of the trust when the grantor becomes unable or unwilling to continue managing his or her assets.

ment of the property placed into the trust as well as the legal fees charged for drafting the trust instruments.

Irrevocable living trust. Grantors who establish an **irrevocable living trust** relinquish title to the property they place in it as well as the right to revoke or terminate it. Such trusts have all the advantages of revocable trusts as well as the potential for reducing taxes. Disadvantages of such a trust relate to the fees charged by trustees for management of assets placed in it, the gift taxes on assets put into it, the grantor's complete loss of the trust property and any income it may produce, and the grantor's forfeiture of the right to alter the terms of the trust as circumstances change.

In order for a living trust to be legally enforceable, it must be irrevocable. **Fantasy:** A legally enforceable living trust, which is created and exists during the lifetime of the person(s) setting it up, may be either revocable (giving the grantor the right to revoke the trust) or irrevocable (beyond the reach of the grantor).

Testamentary Trust. A trust created by a deceased's will is called a **testamentary trust**. Such a trust comes into existence only after the will is probated. No tax savings are realized by the grantor with this type of trust, since there is no divestiture of property until his or her death.

Life Insurance Trust and Pour-Over Will. A will can be written so that it "pours over" certain assets into a previously established **life insurance trust**. This type of trust can be revocable or irrevocable and is created during the grantor's lifetime. The trust is named beneficiary of the grantor's insurance policies and may be *funded* (contain income-producing assets) or *unfunded*. Generally, a **pour-over will** contains a provision passing the estate—after debts, expenses, taxes, and specific bequests—to the specified trust. The trust contains provisions as to how those assets (together with insurance proceeds payable to it) will be administered and distributed. Such an arrangement provides for easily coordinated and well-administered management of estate assets.

GIFT TAXES

Sometimes, even when you *give money away,* you may end up having to pay taxes on at least part of the gift. Why do you think a tax may be levied on gifts you make? Try to answer this question before reading ahead.

Federal tax law provides for a tax on certain gifts made during one's lifetime (the **gift tax**) as well as on "deathtime" gifts (the **estate tax**). Both lifetime and deathtime gifts are considered cumulatively and are subjected to the integrated progressive tax rate schedule given in Exhibit 16.5. The tax on gifts is imposed on the right to transfer property and is measured by the value of the property transferred. The *donor* is primarily liable for the tax; a gift tax return must be filed by the donor and is due when his or her income tax return is filed. The graduated table of rates in Exhibit 16.5 is used for *both* gift and estate tax purposes and is known as the **unified rate schedule**. These rates are applied to all taxable gifts after a number of adjustments and computations have been made.

Transfers Subject to Gift Tax

Almost all property can be the subject of a transfer on which the gift tax must be paid. There is no tax on services that one person performs for another, nor is the rent-free use of property a taxable transfer. A tax may be payable on cash gifts, gifts of personal or real property, and both direct and indirect gifts. For example, if a father makes the mortgage payments on his adult son's home, the payment is an indirect gift from father to son. In fact, almost any shifting of financial advantage in which the recipient does not provide consideration in money or money's worth may be considered a gift. Gifts are generally defined with reference to the *consideration* received; in other words, a transfer for less than adequate and full consideration in money or money's worth is viewed as a partial gift. Where some consideration is received by the transferor, the measure of the gift is found by subtracting the consideration received from the value of the property transferred. For example, suppose your father gave you a summer home having a market value of $75,000 in exchange for $10,000. The $65,000 excess of the value received over the consideration paid would be treated as a gift. Of course, if you gave no consideration for the property, its market value ($75,000) would represent the amount of the gift.

When Is a Gift Made?

The question of when a gift is made is important, because it determines (1) when the gift must be reported and the gift tax, if any, paid and (2) the date at which the value of the gift is measured. Usually a gift is considered to be made when the donor relinquishes dominion and control over the property or property interest transferred. For example, if a husband places cash in a bank account held jointly with his wife, no gift is made until the wife makes a withdrawal. Until that time, the husband can completely recover the entire amount placed in the account. Similarly, when parents place property into a revocable trust for their children, no gift occurs, since they have not relinquished control over the assets placed in it. However, if they later make the trust irrevocable and thereby relinquish their right to revoke the gift, the transfer will be considered a completed gift. A transfer is not subject to gift taxes until the donor gives up (1) the power to take or reclaim the property and (2) the right to alter the time or manner of enjoyment of the gift by the recipient.

Determining the Amount of a Taxable Gift

All that is transferred by an individual is not necessarily subject to a gift tax. Annual exclusions, gift splitting, charitable deductions, and marital deductions are all means of reducing the total amount for tax purposes.

Annual Exclusions. Almost all gifts are subject to the gift tax, but for reasons of administrative convenience, certain transfers, or gift equivalents, are not counted. The gift tax law eliminates from the computation of taxable gifts transfers by a donor of amounts up to $10,000 to each of any number of donees. For example, a person could give gifts of $10,000 each to 30 donees for a total of $300,000 without paying any gift tax. Further, the ability to give tax-free gifts of $10,000 per donee regenerates *annually*. This **annual exclusion** is available only for gifts of a present interest in property—gifts that the donee has the immediate and unrestricted right to use, possess, or enjoy upon receipt. If the donee has to wait to use, possess, or enjoy a gift or if his or her use, possession, or legal right to enjoyment is conditioned in any substantive way, it is then a gift of a future interest in property,

---

irrevocable living trust
A trust in which the grantor relinquishes the title to the property placed in it as well as the right to revoke or terminate it during his or her lifetime.

testamentary trust
A trust created in a decedent's will.

life insurance trust and pour-over will
A provision in a will that provides for estate assets—after debts, expenses, taxes, and specific bequests—to be "poured over" into a previously established life insurance trust, which is the named beneficiary of the grantor's insurance policies.

gift tax
A tax levied by federal and/or state governments on the value of certain types of gifts made during the giver's lifetime.

estate tax
A tax levied by federal and/or state governments on the value of certain types of gifts (or an estate) made upon the giver's death.

unified rate schedule
A graduated table of rates applied to all taxable gifts after a number of adjustments and computations; used for both federal gift and estate tax purposes.

annual exclusion
An amount up to $10,000 annually to each donee that is eliminated from the computation of a donor's taxable gift transfers.

EXHIBIT 16.5

Unified Rate Schedule for Federal Gift and Estate Taxes[a]

The schedule below defines the amount of federal gift and estate taxes that would have to be paid with gifts/estates of different sizes. Actually, estates of $600,000 or less pay no federal tax, although anything over that amount is currently taxed at 37 to 55 percent.

Amount with Respect to Which the Tentative Tax is to Be Computed	Tentative Tax
Not over $10,000	18% of such amount
Over $10,000 but not over $20,000	$1,800 plus 20% of the excess of such amount over $10,000
Over $20,000 but not over $40,000	$3,800 plus 22% of the excess of such amount over $20,000
Over $40,000 but not over $60,000	$8,200 plus 24% of the excess of such amount over $40,000
Over $60,000 but not over $80,000	$13,000 plus 26% of the excess of such amount over $60,000
Over $80,000 but not over $100,000	$18,200 plus 28% of the excess of such amount over $80,000
Over $100,000 but not over $150,000	$23,800 plus 30% of the excess of such amount over $100,000
Over $150,000 but not over $250,000	$38,800 plus 32% of the excess of such amount over $150,000
Over $250,000 but not over $500,000	$70,800 plus 34% of the excess of such amount over $250,000
Over $500,000 but not over $750,000	$155,800 plus 37% of the excess of such amount over $500,000
Over $750,000 but not over $1,000,000	$248,300 plus 39% of the excess of such amount over $750,000
Over $1,000,000 but not over $1,250,000	$345,800 plus 41% of the excess of such amount over $1,000,000
Over $1,250,000 but not over $1,500,000	$448,300 plus 43% of the excess of such amount over $1,250,000
Over $1,500,000 but not over $2,000,000	$555,800 plus 45% of the excess of such amount over $1,500,000
Over $2,000,000 but not over $2,500,000	$780,800 plus 49% of the excess of such amount over $2,000,000
Over $2,500,000 but not over $3,000,000	$1,025,800 plus 53% of the excess of such amount over $2,500,000
Over $3,000,000	$1,290,800 plus 55% of the excess of such amount over $3,000,000

[a]In the case of decedents' dying and gifts made in 1993 and later, the following substitution should be made to the above schedule:
Over $2,500,000 $1,025,800 plus 50% of the excess of such amount over $2,500,000
Source: Copyright © 1988 by The American College. Reprinted from *Advanced Estate Planning Course*. All rights reserved.

and, therefore, the donor will not be allowed the $10,000 annual exclusion.

Gift Splitting.   **Gift splitting** is permitted in order to equate the tax treatment of married taxpayers domiciled in common-law states with the tax treatment of married taxpayers domiciled in community-property states. When a spouse earns a dollar in a community-property state, such as California or Texas, half of that dollar is deemed to be owned by the other spouse immediately and auto-

matically. If a gift is made of that dollar, each spouse is considered to have given 50 cents. Similarly, in common-law states, such as Colorado, New York, and Pennsylvania, federal law provides that a married donor, with the consent of his or her spouse, can elect to treat gifts as if they were made one-half by each spouse. Because of this gift-splitting option, if a wife transfers $20,000 to her son and the required consent is given by her husband, for tax computation purposes her gift will be viewed as $10,000 and her husband will be considered to have given the other $10,000. Because of the split, the total amount will be entirely gift tax–free, since a $10,000 annual exclusion is allowed to each spouse. The wife could give $20,000 to any number of donees and, by splitting the gift with her husband, avoid the tax on the entire gift. This tax reduction technique is available even if one spouse makes all the gifts and the other spouse gives nothing. Gift splitting is allowed, however, only for gifts from married couples to third parties.

Charitable Deductions. There is no limit on the amount that can be given gift tax–free to a qualified charity (one to which deductible gifts can be made for income tax purposes). Therefore, people could give their entire estates to charity and receive gift tax deductions for the total amount. There would be no federal gift taxes regardless of the type or amount of assets transferred.

Marital Deductions. Federal law permits an unlimited deduction for gift tax purposes for property given by one spouse to another. An individual conceivably could give the entire estate to his or her spouse during their lifetimes without gift tax cost.

Reasons for Making Lifetime Gifts

There are several tax-oriented reasons why estate planners recommend gift giving.

Gift Exclusion. A single individual can give any number of donees up to $10,000 each year entirely gift tax–free. There are no tax costs to either the donee or the donor for making the transfer. If the donor is married and the donor's spouse consents, the gift tax–free limit will be increased to $20,000 even if the entire gift is made from the donor's assets.

Gift Tax Exclusion. Regardless of the size of a gift—and even if it is made less than three years before the donor's death—it typically will not be treated as part of the donor's gross estate. However, the taxable portion of the gift will have an effect on the estate tax return. The taxable portion of lifetime gifts (technically called an *adjusted taxable gift*) pushes up the rate at which the donor's estate will be taxed. Fortunately, to the extent to which cash or other property qualifies for the annual exclusion, it is not taxable and therefore is both gift and

estate tax–free in all respects. The estate tax savings from this type of exclusion can be significant.

Appreciation in Value. One of the most important reasons for making a lifetime gift is that the appreciation on the gift from the time it is made will not be included in the donor's estate unless the gift is, for some reason, includable in the estate. For instance, it would be if the donor retained the right to receive all the dividends for life, in which case the entire value of the gift as of the date of the decedent's death would be brought back into the estate. If Larry gives his son Steve a taxable gift of $10,000, and it grows to $60,000 by the date of Larry's death five years later, only the $10,000 taxable value of the stock at the time of the gift will enter into the tax computation of Larry's estate (as an adjusted taxable gift).

Payment Limit. Because of the credit that can be used to offset otherwise taxable gifts, gift taxes do not have to be paid on gifts totaling $600,000 or less. Of course, once this credit is taken, it cannot be used to offset the taxes generated by future lifetime (or deathtime) gifts.

Impact of Marital Deduction. Because of the gift tax marital deduction, it is possible to give a spouse an unlimited amount of money or other property entirely gift tax–free.

ESTATE TAXES AND PLANNING ▪

Estate taxes may be payable when property is transferred at time of death, so one of the goals of effective estate planning is to minimize the amount of estate taxes paid. Are you aware of any strategies frequently used to plan for estate tax minimization? If so, spend a few moments listing them before reading on.

gift splitting
A method of reducing gift taxes whereby a gift given by one spouse, with the consent of his or her spouse, can be treated as if each had made one-half of it.

The federal estate tax is levied on the transfer of property at death. The tax is measured by the value of the property that the deceased transfers (or is deemed to transfer) to others. The parenthetical phrase "deemed to transfer" is important, because the estate tax applies to not only transfers that a deceased actually makes at death but also certain transfers made during the person's lifetime. In other words, to thwart tax-avoidance schemes, the estate tax is imposed on certain lifetime gifts that in essence are the same as dispositions of property made at death. For example, if Max gives his son Eric a $1 million policy on Max's life the day before Max's death, the tax law treats the gift as if it were actually made at Max's death. The $1 million is therefore subject to the federal estate tax. This section discusses key facts related to estate taxes and the estate planning process.

Computation of the Federal Estate Tax

There are five stages to computing federal estate taxes. The first involves determining the *gross estate,* the total of all property in which the decedent had an interest and that is required to be included in the estate. Second, the *adjusted gross estate* is determined by subtracting from the gross estate any allowable funeral and administrative expenses, debts, certain taxes, and losses incurred during administration. Third, the *taxable estate* is calculated by subtracting any allowable marital deduction or charitable deduction from the adjusted gross estate.

The computation of the *estate tax payable before credits* is the fourth stage. After determining the value of the taxable estate, any "adjusted taxable gifts"—which include certain taxable lifetime transfers not included in the deceased's gross estate— are added to the taxable estate. The unified rate schedule—the same one applicable to gift taxes that was shown in Exhibit 16.5—is then applied to determine a tentative estate tax. After this tentative tax is found, any gift taxes the decedent paid on certain gifts are subtracted. The result is the estate tax payable before reduction by any available credits.

The final stage involves the determination of the *net federal estate tax payable.* Certain credits are allowed against the estate tax payable, which result in a dollar-for-dollar reduction of the tax: (1) unified tax credit, (2) state death tax credit, (3) credit for tax on prior transfers, and (4) credit for foreign death taxes. After reducing the estate tax payable for any eligible credits, the net federal estate tax is payable by the decedent's executor, generally within nine months of the decedent's death. The worksheet in Exhibit 16.6 can be used to estimate federal estate taxes. The exhibit depicts the computations for a hypothetical situation involving the death in 1989 of a widow who left a gross estate of $1,500,000. This worksheet is useful in following the flow of dollars from the gross estate to the net federal estate tax payable. In 1981 the federal estate tax code was liberalized in a number of ways. Most notably, the maximum tax rate on estates was dropped from 70 to 55 percent and is slated to drop to 50 percent in 1993. In addition, the law liberalized the **unified tax credit** (the amount one may bequeath tax free). That means that there are *no federal taxes* to pay on estates up to $600,000. Thus, if someone died in 1989 and had taxable estate of $1 million, only $400,000 would be subject to federal estate tax; the other $600,000 would pass on to the heirs tax free.

The worksheet in Exhibit 16.6 factors this exemption into the calculation on line 9a. The value shown on that line ($192,800) is the amount of tax that would be due on the first $600,000 of the estate. It is shown as a *credit* and thus reduces the amount of federal estate taxes due. The value shown on line 9a will, of course, be the same for all estates: $192,800. Obviously, if line 9a is equal to or greater than line 8, the estate will owe no federal taxes.

State Death Taxes

More individuals are subject to state *death taxes* than are liable for federal estate taxes. This is because (1) federal laws permit certain deductions, such as the marital deduction, that many state laws do not and (2) the amount of property exempted from tax under federal law is larger than that exempted by the laws of most states. The three basic types of state death tax are the state inheritance tax, state estate tax, and credit estate tax.

Inheritance Tax. An **inheritance tax**, which is the most common type of state death tax, is a tax on the right to receive a decedent's property. The amount of the tax depends on the value of the

EXHIBIT 16.6

A Worksheet for Computing Net Federal Estate Taxes Payable

This worksheet is useful in determining net federal estate taxes payable. Note that taxes are payable at the marginal tax rate applicable to the total taxable estate (line 5), which is the amount that exists before the tax-free exemption is factored in.

		COMPUTING NET FEDERAL ESTATE TAXES PAYABLE		
Name	Mary Widow		Date	1989
Line	Computation	Item	Amount	Total Amount
1		*Gross estate*		$1,500,000
	Subtract sum of:	(a) Funeral expenses	$ 5,000	
		(b) Administrative expenses	30,000	
		(c) Debts	20,000	
		(d) Taxes	5,000	
		(e) Losses	—	
2	Result:	*Adjusted gross estate*		$1,440,000
	Subtract sum of:	(a) Marital deduction	—	
		(b) Charitable deduction	—	
3	Result:	*Taxable estate*		$1,440,000
4	Add:	*Adjusted taxable gifts*		$ 0
5	Result:	*Tentative tax base*		$1,440,000
6	Compute:	*Tentative estate tax*[a]	$530,000	
7	Subtract:	Gift taxes payable on post-1976 gifts	—	
8	Result:	*Estate tax payable before credits*		$ 530,000
9	Subtract sum of:	(a) Unified tax credit	$192,800	
		(b) State death tax credit[b]	60,560	
		(c) Credit for tax on prior transfers	—	
		(d) Credit for foreign death taxes	—	$ 253,360
10	Result:	*Net federal estate tax payable*		$ 276,640

[a]This value was calculated using the unified rate schedule presented in Exhibit 16.5 as follows: $448,300 + ($1,440,000 − $1,250,000) × .43 = $448,300 + ($190,000) × .43 = $448,300 + $81,700 = $530,000.
[b]Line 9(b) was determined from Exhibit 16.7 in the same fashion as line 6.
Source: Stephan R. Leimberg, Herbert Levy, Stephen N. Kandell, Morey S. Rosenbloom, and Ralph Gano Miller, *The Tools and Techniques of Estate Planning,* 7th ed. (Cincinnati: National Underwriter Company, 1989). Reprinted by permission of the publisher.

property received and the relationship of the beneficiary to the deceased. In most states, beneficiaries are divided into categories. The lowest rates and largest exemptions are allocated to lineal descendants—that is, those beneficiaries most closely related to the deceased. For example, in Pennsylvania, property left to a child of the deceased is taxed at 6 percent, while the same property left to a cousin is subject to a 15 percent rate. Real property held jointly with rights of survivorship by

unified tax credit
The first $600,000 of an estate that can pass to the deceased's heirs free of federal estate taxes.

inheritance tax
A state death tax on the right to receive a decedent's property; the amount is based on the value of the property received and the beneficiary's relationship to the deceased.

spouses is exempt from state death taxes, while the same property held jointly with rights of survivorship by siblings is subject to a 15 percent tax.

Estate Tax. A *state estate tax*, like the federal estate tax, is imposed on the deceased's right to transfer property and is measured by the value of the property transferred. Some states impose both an inheritance and an estate tax.

There are no federal estate taxes on estates of up to $600,000. Fact: Such estates pass to their heirs and/or beneficiaries free from federal estate taxes; thus, only larger estates are subject to these taxes.

Credit Estate Tax. The **credit**, or **gap, estate tax** is designed to bridge the gap between the state's inheritance and estate taxes and the maximum state death tax credit allowed against the federal estate tax (see line 9b of the form for computing the net federal estate tax payable in Exhibit 16.6). The credit tax is best illustrated by a simple example. If a deceased's taxable estate for federal estate tax purposes is $500,000, a credit of up to $10,000 against the federal tax is allowed for taxes paid to the state as death taxes. (See Exhibit 16.7, which gives federal estate tax credits for state death taxes, for determination of this credit.) The amount of any state death taxes paid may be subtracted from the federal tax, provided, however, that the maximum to be subtracted not exceed the maximum shown in the exhibit. If the state's inheritance tax amounts to only $8,000, an additional tax—a $2,000 credit estate tax—is imposed such that the total state death tax is increased to $10,000, the maximum amount of credit allowed by the federal government for state death taxes.

Other Factors Affecting Amount of State Death Tax. Other factors that affect the amount of state death tax include (1) state exemptions and deductions, (2) multiple state taxation, and (3) tax rates.

Exemptions and deductions. Not all property is subject to taxation. Generally, states exempt property transferred to the United States, to the state itself, and to certain charitable organizations. A few states exempt property passing to a surviving spouse. Other states either totally or partially exempt life insurance proceeds unless payable to or

for the benefit of the estate or its creditors. Most states allow deductions for administrative costs, debts, funeral and last illness expenses, and certain property taxes that are unpaid at the deceased's death.

Multiple taxation. Many individuals have summer and winter homes or land and other property in states other than where they live. Although most estates are taxed by only one state, in certain situations an estate or its beneficiaries may be liable for the taxes of more than one state. The right of a state to impose a death tax depends on the type of property involved. The general treatment of the major types of property is as follows:

- *Real estate.* Land and permanent buildings can be taxed only by the state in which the property is located.
- *Tangible personal property.* Cars, boats, and household goods can be taxed only in the state in which they are situated. A boat, for example, is taxed where it is permanently docked. It registry and location for insurance purposes are examined in order to determine its legal location.
- *Intangible personal property.* Securities such as stocks, bonds, notes, and mortgages may, in the absence of interstate agreements, be taxed by several states. Generally, intangible personal property is taxed only by the state of the deceased's domicile. Unfortunately, if a deceased has residences in more than one state or does not clearly establish his or her state of domicile, two or more states can impose death taxes on the same intangible personal property.

Tax rates. The rates at which transfers or receipts of property are taxed vary widely from state to state. Some states have graduated rates similar to the federal tax, while others, such as Pennsylvania, have flat rates that do not grow with the size of the estate. If fact, because the impact of state death taxes can be so significant, many individuals go "domicile shopping" at retirement to find a state with favorable rates, exemptions, and deductions.

Tools and Techniques of Estate Planning

The federal and state tax laws described in the preceding paragraphs provide both problems and opportunities for the estate planner. Estate shrinkage can be minimized and financial security maximized

EXHIBIT 16.7

Federal Estate Tax Credit for State Death Taxes

Credit is given on federal estate tax returns for state estate taxes paid up to certain maximum amounts as specified in the table below.

Taxable Estate	Maximum Tax Credit
Not over $150,000	8/10ths of 1% of the amount by which the taxable estate exceeds $100,000
Over $150,000 but not over $200,000	$400 plus 1.6% of the excess over $150,000
Over $200,000 but not over $300,000	$1,200 plus 2.4% of the excess over $200,000
Over $300,000 but not over $500,000	$3,600 plus 3.2% of the excess over $300,000
Over $500,000 but not over $700,000	$10,000 plus 4% of the excess over $500,000
Over $700,000 but not over $900,000	$18,000 plus 4.8% of the excess over $700,000
Over $900,000 but not over $1,100,000	$27,600 plus 5.6% of the excess over $900,000
Over $1,100,000 but not over $1,600,000	$38,800 plus 6.4% of the excess over $1,100,000
Over $1,600,000 but not over $2,100,000	$70,800 plus 7.2% of the excess over $1,600,000
Over $2,100,000 but not over $2,600,000	$106,800 plus 8% of the excess over $2,100,000
Over $2,600,000 but not over $3,100,000	$146,800 plus 8.8% of the excess over $2,600,000
Over $3,100,000 but not over $3,600,000	$190,800 plus 9.6% of the excess over $3,100,000
Over $3,600,000 but not over $4,100,000	$238,800 plus 10.4% of the excess over $3,600,000
Over $4,100,000 but not over $5,100,000	$290,800 plus 11.2% of the excess over $4,100,000
Over $5,100,000 but not over $6,100,000	$402,800 plus 12% of the excess over $5,100,000
Over $6,100,000 but not over $7,100,000	$522,800 plus 12.8% of the excess over $6,100,000
Over $7,100,000 but not over $8,100,000	$650,800 plus 13.6% of the excess over $7,100,000
Over $8,100,000 but not over $9,100,000	$786,800 plus 14.4% of the excess over $8,100,000
Over $9,100,000 but not over $10,100,000	$930,800 plus 15.2% of the excess over $9,100,000
Over $10,100,000	$1,082,800 plus 16% of the excess over $10,100,000

Source: Copyright © 1988 by The American College. Reprinted from *Advanced Estate Planning Course*. All rights reserved.

by judicious use of certain tax-oriented arrangements and maneuvers. It is important to recognize that, as pointed out in the accompanying *Smart Money* box, in addition to preparing your estate plan, you should discuss and possibly advise your parents relative to their estate plans. Techniques of estate planning can be summarized by the "four Ds": divide, deduct, defer, and discount.

Dividing. Each time a new tax-paying entity can be created, income taxes will be saved and estate accumulation stimulated. Some of the more popular techniques are:

1. *Giving income-producing property to children, either outright or in trust.* Since each child can receive a specified amount of unearned income each year, some income tax savings may be realized each year even by persons who are not in high tax brackets.
2. *Establishing a corporation.* Incorporation may permit individuals in high tax brackets, such as

doctors or other professionals, to save taxes by accumulating income in a manner subject to relatively lower income tax rates.

3. *Fully qualifying for the federal estate tax marital deduction.* This marital deduction allows an individual to pass—estate tax–free—unlimited amounts to a spouse. It also helps obtain the full advantage from the surviving spouse's unified credit. (Properly qualifying in some estates may mean something less than fully qualifying. In other words, there are circumstances in which an advisor may properly recommend passing a lower amount of property than the

---

credit (gap) estate tax

A tax designed to bridge the gap between a state's inheritance and estate taxes and the maximum state death tax credit allowed against the federal estate tax.

S·M·A·R·T M·O·N·E·Y

Discussing Estate Plans with Your Parents

Mark Edinberg, director of the Center for the Study of Aging of the University of Bridgeport in Connecticut, offers a multi-step formula for handling the inheritance discussion—its acronym is PRISSTOW.

"The 'P' stands for **purpose**," he explains. "You have to determine why you're bringing up the subject, and then tell your parents your reasons once the discussion begins." Ask yourself, are you merely curious, or do you want to make sure they have a will and have done some financial planning? Are you concerned about whether they have enough money to take care of themselves as they get older? Is there time pressure for the discussion, such as an upcoming hospital stay? Finally, are you really thinking of yourself rather than them? Is your main desire to find out how much money you will receive?

The other steps:

"R"—What is the **response**
likely to be? Children generally know how their parents deal with sensitive topics. Are they likely to react matter-of-factly or emotionally? If the latter, some of the suggestions offered under the heading "Time and Place for Discussions" in this box may help.

"I" is for **information**. Edinberg suggests children have at least a modest understanding of wills and trusts before the discussion begins. They also should know the names and phone numbers of estate attorneys, financial planners, and accountants that they may recommend.

The next two letters stand for **steps** and **strategy**. Think about who should be present for the discussion. In addition to all the immediate family, should there be other family, such as spouses of the children? Most experts believe spouses should take part, inasmuch as openness is preferable to se-
crecy and suspicion. Any inheritance, however, probably should go directly to the child, not jointly to the child and his or her spouse.

"The reality, unfortunately, is that divorce is very common, even among couples who've been married for years," says James Podell, executive editor of the American Journal of Family Law and an attorney in Milwaukee. "Parents should take the possible divorce of children into consideration to avoid costly litigation for their heirs later on."

Next, Edinberg says, **timing** should be considered. "The discussion may require three one-hour sessions over the course of a month. Since feelings need time and privacy to unfold, don't plan the meetings to coincide with emotionally demanding family events, such as holiday celebrations, weddings, or big parties."

"O" represents **outcome**—a

---

maximum marital deduction amount, that is, an individual's entire estate.)

Deducting. Any dollar that is deductible from taxable income (or from a deceased's gross estate) is more useful to the taxpayer than a nondeductible dollar. The higher the income (or estate tax bracket), the greater the value that results from the privilege of deductibility. Some of the retirement plans discussed in Chapter 15 that enable an individual to obtain deductions for money set aside for retirement include (1) qualified pension plans, (2)
Keogh plans, (3) individual retirement accounts (IRAs), (4) SEP/IRAs, (5) qualified profit-sharing plans, and (6) salary reduction plans.

Deferring. Progressive tax rates (rates that increase as the income or size of the estate increases) penalize taxpayers whose maximum earnings (or estates) reach high peaks. This hinders the job of gaining and retaining financial security. There are devices, however, that help minimize the total tax burden by spreading income over more than one tax year or deferring the tax to a later period so

"to do" list that might include drawing a new will, amending an old one, or talking to an accountant about tax planning.

Finally, the "W" represents **what** you would like to say and what you can live with saying.

"Talking about inheritance and your parents' death is very difficult," says Edinberg, author of *Talking With Your Aging Parents*. "But everyone has a bottom line: the core of what you must say so you don't punish yourself later on and, at the same time, don't damage your current relationship with your parents. You might be tempted to say, 'Dad, how can anyone *not* have a will?' But you probably can live with saying, 'Dad, your not having a will bothers me. It could cause a lot of trouble after you're not here to look after things.'"

Time and Place for Discussions

Marc Hankin, a lawyer and estate planner in Beverley Hills, Calif., says a good time to begin this type of discussion is when the grown children do their own wills and estate planning. "Parents can become a lot more comfortable discussing their finances and plans if 'everyone's' doing it," he says. For example, children can include parents in *their* wills and tell parents of their arrangements. Most parents would be touched by this generosity and may feel less reticent about discussing their own financial plans.

Upon a parent's recovery from an illness is another appropriate juncture, Hankin notes, because at that time there is a greater realization of mortality.

Finally, the death of an elderly relative may prompt discussion. Learning of the deceased's planning—or lack of it—can induce the living to act responsibly.

The place where inheritance is discussed can be as important as timing. The parents' home is a good choice, as it is their "turf" and thus gives them a psychological advantage. Some parents, however, may prefer to have the discussion at their attorney's office, with the attorney present to act as umpire or referee should they feel impartial advice is needed.

Another choice might be a lower-stress locale, such as a hotel where the family is spending a vacation. Or even a long-distance car ride might provide the solitude and intimacy needed to encourage discussion.

Source: Excerpted from "Talking to Your Parents About . . . Inheritance," by Allen Evans, copyright © 1988 by Sylvia Porter's Personal Finance Magazine Company. Reprinted by permission of the publisher and may not be reproduced without written permission.

---

that the taxpayer can invest the tax money for a longer period of time. Examples follow:

1. Nonqualified deferred-compensation plans for selected individuals in corporate businesses, as well as private contractors.
2. The making of installment sales instead of cash sales so that the taxable gain can be spread over several years.
3. Private annuities, which are arrangements whereby one person transfers property to another, usually younger family member. This recipient promises in return to pay an annuity to the original owner for as long as he or she lives. The income tax attributable to such an annuity can thereby be spread over a number of years.
4. Qualified pension and profit-sharing plans that allow tax deferral on the income and gains from investments.
5. Government Series EE bonds, since their earnings can be treated as taxable income at maturity rather than yearly as earned.

6. Stocks that yield low dividends but provide high price appreciation as a result of investing retained earnings in profitable projects.

7. Life insurance policies in which lifetime growth is not taxed and death values are income tax–free. If the insured survives, earnings inherent in policy values become taxable only as received; thus, the tax on any gain can be deferred over a lifetime.

8. Depreciable real estate that yields high write-offs in years when the estate owner is earning high levels of taxable *passive* income.

9. Installment payment of federal estate taxes applicable to a business interest. Payments can be spread over as many as 14 years with only the interest being paid on the unpaid tax during the first 4 years.

Discounting. Even after everything has been done to accumulate an estate and reduce the income and estate tax burdens on it, there may still be a tax payable. But there are two instruments that make it possible to, in effect, pay estate taxes at a discount: flower bonds and a special type of life insurance policy.

Flower bonds, although no longer issued by the federal government, can be acquired by anyone—even the terminally ill—in the secondary market with the assistance of a stockbroker. They are redeemed by the government at par in payment of the federal estate tax; therefore, whenever they can be purchased at a price below their par value,

the result is a "discount" in the estate taxes. Such savings are reduced, however, by inclusion of the bond at par in the gross estate of the deceased.

Life insurance, one of the primary tools of estate planners, can be purchased by a person other than the insured or the insured's spouse, or by a trust, for an annual premium of from 3 to 6 percent of the face (death) value of the policy. If proper arrangements are made, the proceeds of such insurance will pass to the decedent's beneficiaries free of income tax, estate tax, inheritance tax, and probate costs. Such proceeds may be used to pay death taxes, debts, and other probate and administrative costs. Life insurance proceeds can also be used to pay family expenses, special needs (such as college costs), mortgage balances, and other major expenditures. What's more, life insurance acts as an attractive form of loan collateral in the case of whole life and endowment policies. As pointed out in Chapters 8 and 9, some lending institutions and other creditors require borrowers to obtain life insurance in an amount sufficient to repay them in the event borrowers die prior to fully repaying their loans.

---

flower bonds
Outstanding government bonds that can be redeemed at par to pay federal estate taxes; when these bonds can be purchased at a price below par, they provide an opportunity to, in effect, pay estate taxes at a discount.

SUMMARY

■ Estate planning involves the accumulation, preservation, and distribution of an estate in a manner that will most effectively achieve an estate owner's personal goals. The four major steps to estate planning are (1) gathering data, (2) identifying possible problems, (3) formulating a plan and preparing for its implementation, and (4) testing and implementing the plan (subject to periodic reviews and revisions, as necessary).

■ Important privileges are forfeited when a person dies without a valid will, including the right to decide how property will be distributed at death, along with the opportunity to select who will administer the estate and who will bear the burden

of estate taxes and administrative expenses. The will should provide a clear and unambiguous expression of the testator's wishes, be flexible enough to encompass possible changes in family circumstances, and give proper regard to minimizing federal and state estate taxes.

■ A will is valid only if properly executed by a person of sound mind. Once drawn up, wills *can be changed* by codicil or *fully revoked* by a later will. The executor, who is often named in the will, is responsible for collecting the decedent's assets, paying his or her debts and taxes, and distributing any remaining assets to the beneficiaries in a prescribed fashion.

▪ The trust relationship arises when one party, the grantor, transfers property to a second party, the trustee, for the benefit of a third party, the beneficiary. While there are a variety of different types of trusts, each is designed primarily to accomplish one or more of three purposes: to save income and estate taxes, to provide asset management, and/or to conserve property.

▪ Federal estate taxes are essentially a levy on the transfer of assets at death. They are unified (coordinated) with the gift tax—which imposes a graduated tax on the transfer of property during one's lifetime—so that the rates and credits are the same for both. Once federal estate taxes are computed, certain credits are allowed, and the resulting amount is generally payable in full within nine months of the decedent's death.

▪ The "four Ds" of estate planning—divide, deduct, defer, and discount—are found, to one extent or another, in most well-defined estate plans. *Dividing* involves the creation of new tax entities; *deducting* includes any type of retirement benefit that provides financial security with before-tax dollars; *deferring* gives an individual the use of money that would otherwise have been paid in taxes; and *discounting* involves paying expenses with "discounted" dollars.

QUESTIONS AND PROBLEMS

1. Discuss the importance and goals of estate planning. Explain why estates often break up. Distinguish between the probate estate and the gross estate.

2. Briefly describe the steps involved in the estate planning process.

3. What is a will? Why is it important? Describe the consequences of dying intestate.

4. Describe the basic clauses that are normally included as part of a will.

5. Indicate any requirements that exist with respect to who may make a valid will.

6. How can changes in the provisions of a will be made legally? In what two ways can a will be revoked?

7. Indicate what is meant by each of the following: (a) intestacy, (b) codicil, (c) right of election, (d) lodging of the will, and (e) letter of last instructions.

8. What is meant by the probate process? Who is an executor, and what role does the executor play in estate settlement?

9. Define and differentiate between joint tenancy with right of survivorship and tenancy by the entirety. Discuss the advantages and disadvantages of joint ownership.

10. Describe the basic trust arrangement, and discuss purposes for which trusts are typically established. What essential qualities should a trustee possess?

11. Explain what is meant by each of the following? (a) grantor, (b) trustee, (c) beneficiary, (d) testamentary trust, and (e) life insurance trust and pour-over will.

12. What is a living (inter vivos) trust? Distinguish between a revocable living trust and an irrevocable living trust.

13. Answer and/or describe the following as they relate to federal gift taxes: (a) what is a gift? (b) when is a gift made? (c) annual exclusion, (d) gift splitting, (e) charitable deduction, (f) marital deduction, (g) application of the tax rate, and (h) payment of the gift tax.

14. Discuss the reasons estate planners cite for making lifetime gifts. How and in what ways might gift giving help reduce estate shrinkage?

15. Explain the following as they relate to federal and/or state estate taxes: (a) general nature of the estate tax, (b) computation of the federal estate tax, (c) state inheritance tax, (d) state estate tax, (e) credit estate tax, (f) amount of exemptions and deductions, (g) multiple estate taxation, and (h) rates of state estate taxation.

16. The tools and techniques of estate planning can be summarized by the "four Ds"—divide, deduct, defer, and discount. Describe and discuss each of the four Ds and their associated strategies.

CASE PROBLEMS

16.1 A Long Overdue Will for Kris

Kris Pappadopolus, a Greek national, migrated to the United States during the early 1950s. A man of many talents and deep foresight, he has during his stay in the United States built a large fleet of ocean-going oil tankers. Now a wealthy man in his 60s, he resides in Palm Springs, Florida, with his second wife, Veronica, age 35. He has two sons, who are both high school seniors. For quite a while, Kris has considered preparing a will in order to ensure that his estate will be aptly distributed if some unforeseen tragedy or natural cause takes his life. A survey of his estate—all legally owned by him—reveals the following:

Ranch in Amarillo, Texas	$ 500,000
Condominium in San Francisco	200,000
House in Palm Springs	600,000
Franchise in ice cream stores	2,500,000
Stock in Seven Seas International	5,000,000
Shares in Fourth National Bank	1,000,000
Corporate bonds	3,000,000
Other asset	200,000
Total assets	$13,000,000

In addition to $1 million for their education and welfare, he would like to leave each of his sons 20 percent of this estate. He wishes to leave 40 percent of the estate for his wife. The rest of the estate is to be divided among relatives, friends, and charitable institutions. He has scheduled an appointment for drafting his will with his attorney and close friend, Leonard Wiseman. Kris would like to appoint Leonard and his cousin, Plato Jones, as coexecutors of his estate. If one of them predeceases Kris, he would like his bank, Fourth National Bank, to act as coexecutor.

Questions

1. Does Kris really need a will? Explain why or why not? What would happen to his estate if he were to die without a will?
2. Explain to Kris the common features that need to be incorporated into a will.
3. What are the options available to Kris if he decides to change or revoke the will at a later date?
4. Give Kris appropriate advice for drawing up a will that will carry out his wishes.
5. What duties will Leonard Wiseman and Plato Jones have to perform as coexecutors of Kris's estate?

■ 16.2 Estate Taxes on Philip Colburn's Estate

Philip Colburn, of Arlington Heights, Delaware, was 65 and in good health in 1982. He and his wife, Delores, who predeceased him, had been married for 35 years. They had an adult son who had been made sole beneficiary of their estate. When Philip retired as chairman of the Vilanto Corporation in 1982, his net worth (estate) was valued at $1 million. The value had increased 20 percent by 1989. When Philip died in 1989, he had no debts. Funeral costs amounted to $10,000, and the cost of administering the estate was $50,000. Miscellaneous debts totaled $10,000. These items were the only applicable deductions from his gross estate. Philip left $75,000 of his estate to his alma mater. Four years prior to his death, he had made adjusted taxable gifts (taxable gifts not included in his gross estate) of $160,000. No gift taxes were paid or payable on any of his post-1976 gifts. A state death tax credit was also available to the estate. Assume that current estate tax laws permit an unlimited marital deduction when applicable. Using a worksheet like the one in Exhibit 16.6 as a guide to the calculations, answer each of the following questions.

Questions

1. Compute the value of Philip's gross estate at the time of his death.
2. Determine the value of his adjusted gross estate.
3. Determine the taxable estate at Philip's death.
4. Calculate (a) the tentative tax base, (b) the tentative estate tax (using Exhibit 16.5), and (c) the estate tax payable before credits.
5. Determine the value of the net federal estate tax payable on Philip's estate.
6. Comment on the estate shrinkage experienced on his estate. What might have been done to reduce this shrinkage? Explain.

FOR MORE INFORMATION

General Information Articles

"Estate Planning: Take Care of Your Heirs," *Changing Times,* September 1988, pp. 32–38.

"Gifts That Give Back," *Changing Times,* June 1986, pp. 81–86.

Hutton, Cynthia, "Keeping It in the Family," *Fortune 1988 Investor's Guide,* pp. 111–124.

McGrath, Anne, "Smart Ways to Plan Your Estate," *U.S. News & World Report,* June 1, 1986, pp. 46–47.

Schurenberg, Eric, "A Short Course in Estate Planning," *Money,* October 1987, pp. 74–82.

Wiles, Russ, "Heir-Tight Estates," *Personal Investor,* September 1988, pp. 54–59.

Government Documents & Other Publications

Estate Planning: A Guide for Advisors and their Clients by D. Larry Crumbley and Edward E. Milam (Homewood, IL: Dow Jones-Irwin, 1986).

The Financial Planner's Guide to Estate Planning, 2nd edition by Paul J. Lochray (Englewood Cliffs, NJ: Prentice-Hall, 1989).

Introduction to Estate Planning, 2nd edition by Chris J. Prestopino (Homewood, IL: Irwin, 1989).

The Tools and Techniques of Estate Planning, 7th edition by Stephan R. Leimberg, Stephen W. Kandell, Herbert L. Levy, Ralph Gano Miller, and Morey S. Rosenbloom (Cincinnati, OH: National Underwriter, 1989).

Mark and Ana own their new condo jointly with right of survivorship (community property in community property states). Assume all other property is owned jointly unless stated differently in the original case.

1. Identify and evaluate the assets that would be included in Mark's gross estate. Would his estate be subject to federal estate taxes? If yes, what steps should be taken to reduce estate taxes?

2. Which of Mark's assets would be probate and which would be nonprobate assets?

3. Identify and evaluate the assets that would be included in Ana's gross estate. Would her estate be subject to federal estate taxes? If yes, what steps should be taken to reduce estate taxes?

4. Which of Ana's assets would be probate and which would be nonprobate assets?

5. Given the Williams' estate planning needs, should Mark and Ana have wills written? If yes, what should be included in these wills?

WILLIAMS *Estate*

APPENDIX A

Table of Future Value Factors

Instructions: To use this table, find the future value factor that corresponds to both a given time period (year) and an interest rate. To illustrate, if you want the future value factor for 6 years and 10 percent, move across from year 6 and down from 10 percent to the point at which these two rows intersect: 1.772. Other illustrations: For 3 years and 15 percent, the proper future value factor is 1.521; for 30 years and 8 percent, it is 10.062.

Interest Rate

Year	3%	5%	6%	8%	9%	10%	12%	15%	20%	25%	30%
1	1.030	1.050	1.060	1.080	1.090	1.100	1.120	1.150	1.120	1.250	1.300
2	1.060	1.102	1.120	1.166	1.190	1.210	1.254	1.322	1.440	1.562	1.690
3	1.090	1.158	1.190	1.260	1.290	1.331	1.405	1.521	1.728	1.953	2.197
4	1.130	1.216	1.260	1.360	1.410	1.464	1.574	1.749	2.074	2.441	2.856
5	1.160	1.276	1.340	1.469	1.540	1.611	1.762	2.011	2.488	3.052	3.713
6	1.190	1.340	1.420	1.587	1.670	1.772	1.974	2.313	2.986	3.815	4.827
8	1.260	1.477	1.590	1.851	1.990	2.144	2.476	3.059	4.300	5.960	8.157
10	1.340	1.629	1.790	2.159	2.360	2.594	3.106	4.046	6.192	9.313	13.786
12	1.420	1.796	2.010	2.518	2.810	3.138	3.896	5.350	8.916	14.552	23.298
15	1.560	2.079	2.390	3.172	3.640	4.177	5.474	8.137	15.407	28.422	51.185
20	1.810	2.653	3.210	4.661	5.600	6.727	9.646	16.366	38.337	86.736	190.047
25	2.090	3.386	4.290	6.848	8.620	10.834	17.000	32.918	95.395	264.698	705.627
30	2.420	4.322	5.740	10.062	13.260	17.449	29.960	66.210	237.373	807.793	2619.936
35	2.810	5.516	7.690	14.785	20.410	28.102	52.799	133.172	590.657	2465.189	9727.598
40	3.260	7.040	10.280	21.724	31.410	45.258	93.049	267.856	1469.740	7523.156	36117.754

Note: All factors to nearest 1/1000 as shown to agree with Chapters 3 and 5 of text.

APPENDIX B

Table of Annuity Factors

Instructions: To use this table, find the annuity factor that corresponds to both a given time period (year) and an interest rate. To illustrate, if you want the annuity factor for 6 years and 10 percent, move across from year 6 and down from 10 percent to the point at which these two rows intersect: 7.716. Other illustrations: For 3 years and 15 percent, the proper annuity factor is 3.472; for 30 years and 8 percent, it is 113.282.

Interest Rate

Year	3%	5%	6%	8%	9%	10%	12%	15%	20%	25%	30%
1	1.000	1.000	1.000	1.000	1.000	1.000	1.000	1.000	1.000	1.000	1.000
2	2.030	2.050	2.060	2.080	2.090	2.100	2.120	2.150	2.200	2.250	2.300
3	3.090	3.152	3.180	3.246	3.270	3.310	3.374	3.472	3.640	3.813	3.990
4	4.180	4.310	4.380	4.506	4.570	4.641	4.779	7.993	5.368	5.766	6.187
5	5.310	5.526	5.630	5.867	5.980	6.105	6.353	6.742	7.442	8.207	9.043
6	6.460	6.802	6.970	7.336	7.520	7.716	8.115	8.754	9.930	11.259	12.756
8	8.890	9.549	9.890	10.637	11.030	11.436	12.300	13.727	16.499	19.842	23.858
10	11.460	12.578	13.180	14.487	15.190	15.937	17.549	20.304	25.959	33.253	42.619
12	14.190	15.917	16.870	18.977	20.140	21.384	24.133	29.001	39.580	54.208	74.326
15	18.600	21.578	23.270	27.152	29.360	31.772	37.280	47.580	72.035	109.687	167.285
20	26.870	33.066	36.780	45.762	51.160	57.274	72.052	102.443	186.687	342.945	630.157
25	36.460	47.726	54.860	73.105	84.700	98.346	133.333	212.790	471.976	1054.791	2348.765
30	47.570	66.438	79.060	113.282	136.300	164.491	241.330	434.738	1181.865	3227.172	8729.805
35	60.460	90.318	111.430	172.314	215.700	271.018	431.658	881.152	2948.294	9856.746	32422.090
40	75.400	120.797	154.760	259.052	337.870	442.580	767.080	1779.048	7343.715	30088.621	120389.375

Note: All factors to nearest 1/1000 as shown to agree with Chapters 3 and 5 of text.

INDEX

FINANCIAL PLANNING ON THE PERSONAL COMPUTER (FP/PC) SOFTWARE PACKAGE

FP/PC is an easy-to-use, menu-driven financial planning software package designed to run on IBM PCs and PC-compatible microcomputers.

You can obtain a copy from your instructor and will need the following equipment to use it:

- an IBM PC or close compatible with at least 384K of RAM memory
- DOS Version 2.1 or higher
- dual 5¼ drives, a single 3½ drive or one hard disk drive and one floppy disk drive
- a printer is strongly recommended to get the most benefit from FP/PC, but is not required

The FP/PC Main Menu allows you to choose routines to assist with personal financial planning tasks in 10 key areas:

1. **Personal Financial Statements**

   - personal balance sheet
   - personal income and expenditures sheet
   - personal financial ratios

2. **Monthly Cash Budgets**

   - income estimates
   - expenditure estimates
   - monthly cash budget summary

3. **Finding Future Value**

   - future value of a single cash flow
   - rate required to accumulate a given future value from a single cash flow
   - future value of an annuity
   - rate required to accumulate a given future value with a given annuity payment
   - yearly savings required to accumulate a given future sum of money

4. **Dealing with Taxes**

   - preparing Form 1040 tax returns
   - preparing Form 1040EZ tax returns
   - estimating estate taxes

5. **Balancing the Checkbook**

   - reconciling a checking account

6. **Purchasing a Home**

   - home affordability analysis
   - mortgage payment analysis
   - refinancing a mortgage
   - the decision to buy or rent a house

7. **Issues in Consumer Finance**

   - analysis of single payment loans
   - analysis of installment loans
   - buy on time or pay cash
   - the decision to lease or buy a car

8. **Life Insurance**

   - life insurance needs analysis

9. **Investment Analysis**

   - setting investment goals
   - measuring investment returns
   - assessing the investment performance of a stock

10. **Retirement Planning**

    - setting future retirement needs

Each screen contains a reference to corresponding pages in the text. Even if you have never used a personal computer, you will quickly learn to employ FP/PC in your course of study and for your own personal financial planning.

Personal Financial
Planning
Fifth Edition